THE BUILDINGS OF SCOTLAND

FOUNDING EDITORS: NIKOLAUS PEVSNER
AND COLIN MCWILLIAM

ARGYLL AND BUTE

FRANK ARNEIL WALKER

ARGYLL and BUTE
Showing areas covered by text maps
Towns underlined have street plans in the text

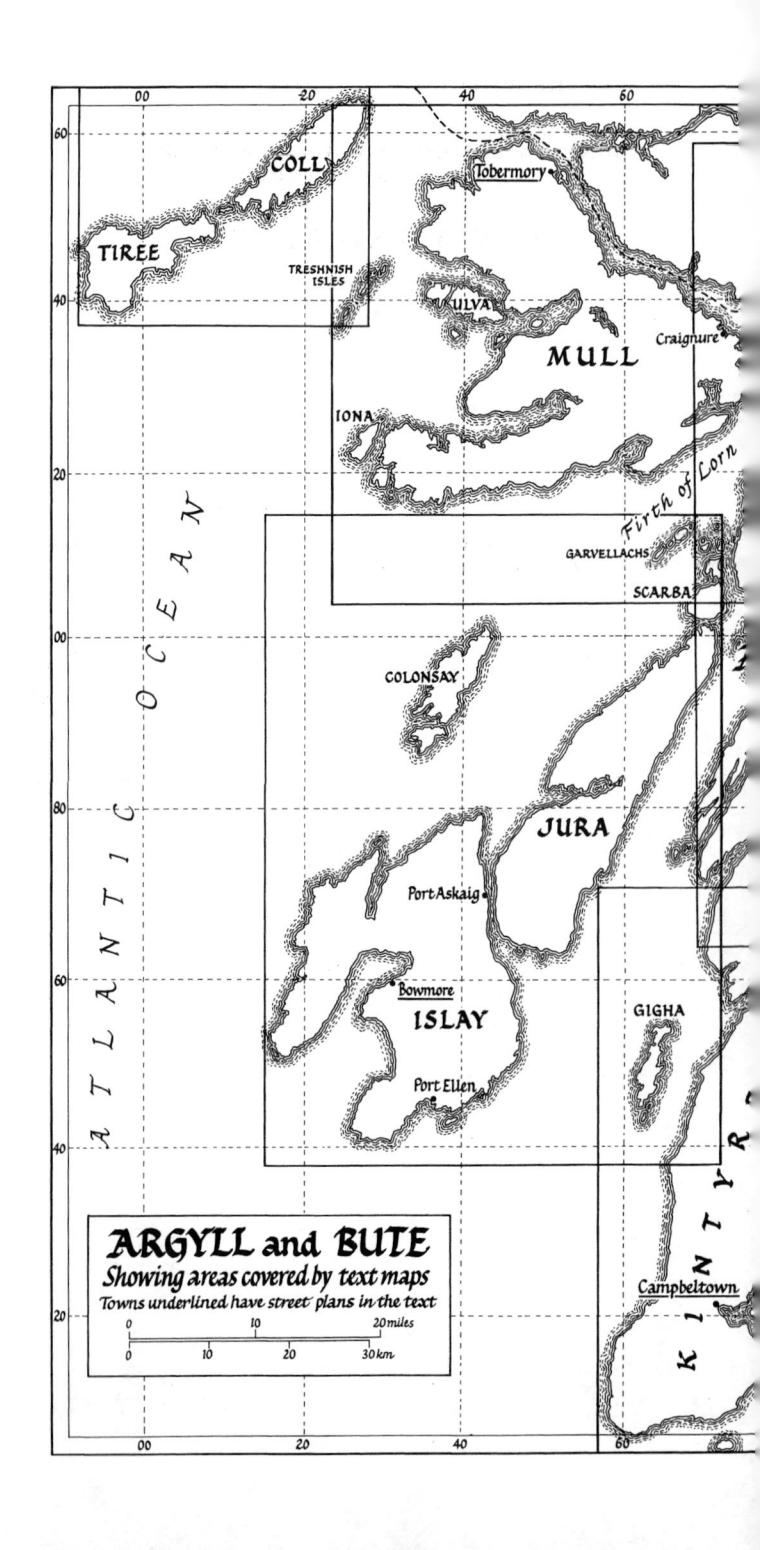

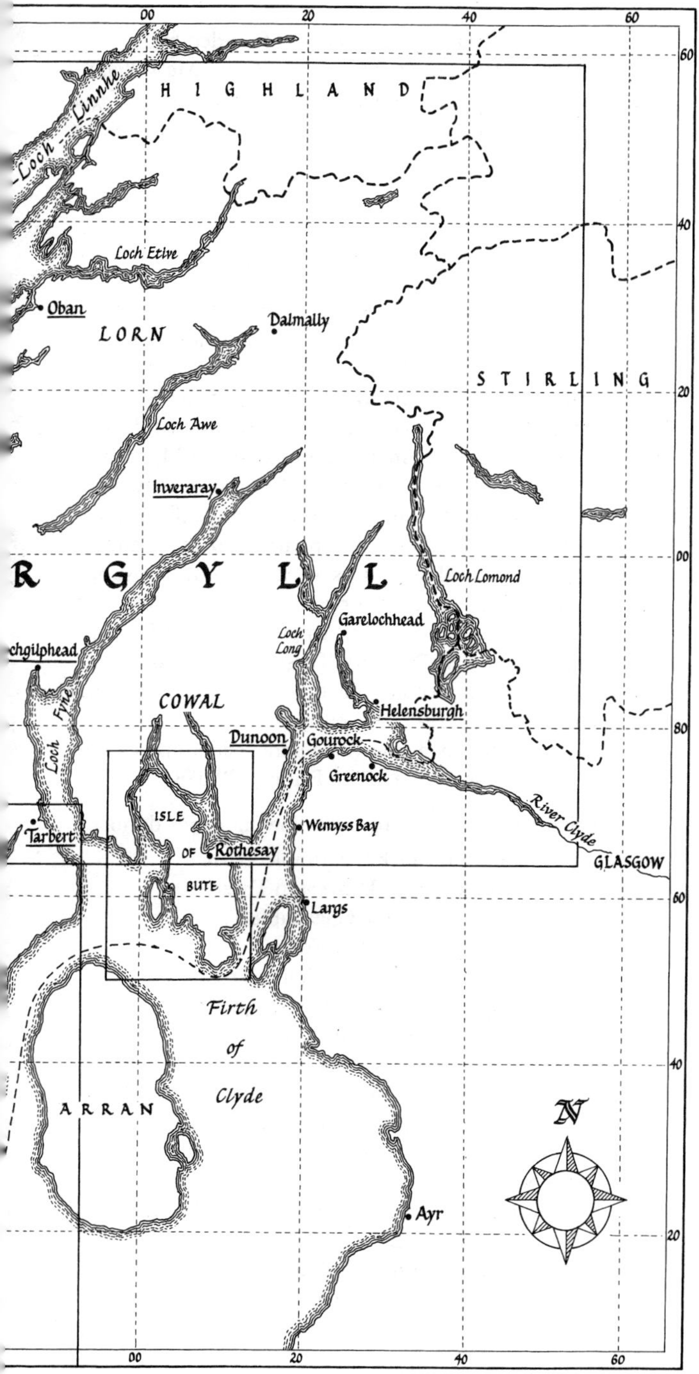
HIGHLAND
Loch Linnhe
Loch Etive
Oban
LORN
Dalmally
STIRLING
Loch Awe
Inveraray
ARGYLL
Loch Lomond
Garelochhead
Loch Long
chgilphead
Loch Fyne
COWAL
Helensburgh
Dunoon
Gourock
Greenock
ISLE OF BUTE
Rothesay
Wemyss Bay
River Clyde
GLASGOW
Tarbert
Largs
Firth of Clyde
ARRAN
Ayr
N
00
20
40
60

PEVSNER ARCHITECTURAL GUIDES

The Buildings of Scotland was founded by
Sir Nikolaus Pevsner (1902 83) and Colin McWilliam
(1928–1989) as a companion series to *The Buildings of England*.
Between 1979 and 2001 it was published by Penguin Books.

THE BUILDINGS OF SCOTLAND TRUST

The Buildings of Scotland Trust is a charitable trust, founded in 1991, which manages and finances the research programme needed to sustain *The Buildings of Scotland* series. The trust is sponsored by Historic Scotland (on behalf of the Secretary of State for Scotland), the National Trust for Scotland, and the Royal Commission on the Ancient and Historical Monuments of Scotland. The Buildings of Scotland Trust is grateful for and wishes to acknowledge the support of the many individuals, charitable trusts and foundations, companies and local authorities who have given financial help to its work. Without that support it would not be possible to look forward to the completion of the research programme for the series. In particular the Trust wishes to record its thanks to the National Trust for Scotland, which carried the financial responsibility for this work over a considerable period before the new trust was set up.

The Trustees wish to acknowledge the generous support of H.M. The Queen and H.R.H. The Prince of Wales.

Special thanks are due to the following major donors
Aberbrothock Charitable Trust,
Binks Trust, Dulverton Trust,
Esmée Fairbairn Charitable Trust,
Marc Fitch Fund,
Gordon Fraser Charitable Trust,
A.S. and Miss M.I. Henderson Trust,
Historic Scotland, Imlay Foundation,
Leverhulme Trust, MacRobert Trusts,
Merchants House of Glasgow,
Nancie Massey Charitable Trust,
National Trust for Scotland, Pilgrim Trust,
Radcliffe Trust, Joseph Rank Benevolent Trust,
Royal Bank of Scotland plc, Russell Trust,
Scottish Tourist Board,
Colin McWilliam Memorial Fund,
James Wood Bequest Fund

Argyll and Bute

BY

FRANK ARNEIL WALKER

WITH CONTRIBUTIONS FROM

FIONA SINCLAIR

THE BUILDINGS OF SCOTLAND

YALE UNIVERSITY PRESS
NEW HAVEN AND LONDON

YALE UNIVERSITY PRESS
NEW HAVEN AND LONDON
302 Temple Street, New Haven CT 06511
47 Bedford Square, London WC1 3DP
www.pevsner.co.uk
www.lookingatbuildings.org
www.yalebooks.co.uk
www.yalebooks.com
for
THE BUILDINGS OF SCOTLAND TRUST

Published by Penguin Books 2000
First published, with corrections, by Yale University Press 2005
2 4 6 8 10 9 7 5 3 1

ISBN 0 300 09670 4

Copyright © Frank Arneil Walker and Fiona Sinclair, 2000

Printed in China
through World Print
Set in Monotype Plantin

All rights reserved.
This book may not be reproduced
in whole or in part, in any form (beyond that
copying permitted by Sections 107 and 108 of the
U.S. Copyright Law and except by reviewers
for the public press), without written
permission from the publishers

TO MY MOTHER AND FATHER

CONTENTS

LIST OF TEXT FIGURES AND MAPS	x
ACKNOWLEDGEMENTS FOR THE PLATES	xii
HOW TO USE THIS BOOK	xiii
FOREWORD	xv
PRELUDE	1
INTRODUCTION	**5**
GEOLOGY BY JUDITH LAWSON	5
PREHISTORIC AND EARLY HISTORIC ARGYLL AND BUTE BY J. N. GRAHAM RITCHIE	16
ARGYLL AND BUTE: MONUMENTS OF THE EARLY CHRISTIAN PERIOD BY IAN FISHER	23
MEDIEVAL CHURCHES AND MONUMENTS	27
POST-REFORMATION CHURCHES	32
MAUSOLEA AND MONUMENTS	42
CASTLES AND TOWER-HOUSES	48
COUNTRY HOUSES	53
ROADS, RAILWAYS, CANALS, HARBOURS AND LIGHTHOUSES	67
BURGH AND VILLAGE BUILDINGS	77
RURAL BUILDINGS	91
INDUSTRIAL BUILDINGS	94
ARGYLL: THE MAINLAND	**99**
ARGYLL: THE ISLES	**499**
BUTE	**603**
GLOSSARY	631
INDEX OF ARTISTS	659
INDEX OF PLACES	671

LIST OF TEXT FIGURES AND MAPS

Iona, St John's Cross, St Martin's Cross (RCAHMS)	27
Tiree, Dwelling House (RCAHMS)	92
Ardchattan Priory (after RCAHMS)	108
Ardkinglas House. Principal floor plan (after R. S. Lorimer, 1906. Plan in NMRS)	116
Ardlamont House. Plan of ground floor (after RCAHMS)	118
Ardmaddy Castle. Plans of ground floor (incorporating late fifteenth century tower) and first floor of 1737 (after RCAHMS)	121
Auchindrain Township. Plan of north-east portion of the township (after RCAHMS)	134
Barbreck House. First-floor plan and elevation (RCAHMS)	136
Barcaldine Castle. Ground- and first-floor plans (RCAHMS)	139
Cardross, St Peter's College. Plan (after Gillespie, Kidd & Coia)	170
Carnasserie Castle. Ground- and first-floor plans (RCAHMS)	175
Castle Sween. Plan (after RCAHMS)	185
Cour House. Plan of the ground floor (after the *Architectural Review*)	200
Dunstaffnage Castle. Plan (after RCAHMS)	238
Duntrune Castle. Plan (after RCAHMS)	243
Garbhallt, Old Castle Lachlan. Ground-floor plan (after RCAHMS)	254
Helensburgh, The Hill House	293
Innis Chonnell Castle. Plan (after RCAHMS)	301
Inveraray Parish Church. Ground-floor plan (RCAHMS)	306
Inveraray Court House. Plan (RCAHMS)	309
Inveraray Castle. Principal floor plan (RCAHMS)	316
Kerrera, Gylen Castle. Plan of tower-house and outer bailey (RCAHMS)	330
Kilchurn Castle. Plan (after RCAHMS)	339
Lochawe, St Conan's Kirk	370
Lochgair, Asknish House. South elevation, ground- and first-floor plans (RCAHMS)	377
Lochgoilhead and Kilmorich Parish Church. Plan (after RCAHMS)	386
Oban, Cathedral Church of St John the Divine. Plan provided by The Very Reverend Allan Maclean	403

LISTS OF TEXT FIGURES AND MAPS

Port Appin, Airds House. Plan and elevation (RCAHMS)	428
Skipness Castle. Plan (after RCAHMS)	458
Strachur House. Plan (after RCAHMS)	468
Taynuilt, Bonawe Ironworks. Plan and section of the furnace (RCAHMS)	485
Iona, Iona Abbey. Development plans (RCAHMS)	510
Iona, Iona Abbey. Capitals of south choir arcade (RCAHMS)	515
Iona, Iona Nunnery. Plan (after RCAHMS)	522
Islay, Bowmore, Kilarrow Parish Church	531
Mull, Duart Castle. Ground-floor plan and section	571
Oronsay, Oronsay Priory. Plan (after RCAHMS)	590

MAPS

Argyll and Bute, showing areas covered by text maps	ii–iii
Geology of the region	6
Argyll	100–1
Kintyre	102
Islay, Jura, Colonsay, Scarba, Garvellachs	500
Tiree and Coll; Mull, Ulva, Iona	501
Isle of Bute	604

TOWN PLANS

Campbeltown	152
Dunoon	227
Inverary	304
Lochgilphead	380
Oban	400
Tarbert	474
Islay, Bowmore	534
Mull, Tobermory	585
Bute, Rothesay	623

ACKNOWLEDGEMENTS FOR THE PLATES

We are grateful to the following for permission to reproduce photographs:

Photographs are copyright of the Royal Commission on the Ancient and Historical Monuments of Scotland, with the exception of the following:

Gillespie, Kidd & Coia: 45
Martin Charles: 103
National Trust for Scotland: 104
Buteshire Natural History Society: 115
Alan Forbes and Reiach & Hall: 123
Fiona Sinclair: 134

The plates are indexed in the indexes of artists and places, and references to them are given by numbers in the margin of the text.

HOW TO USE THIS BOOK

Arrangement of the gazetteer

The area of Scotland covered in this voume is that which comes under the administration of Argyll & Bute Council as designated by the Local Government (Scotland) Act of 1994. This is a large stretch of the country's western seaboard but it does not embrace the whole of historic Argyllshire; local government changes in 1975 already removed the parishes of Ardnamurchan, Morvern, Ardgour and parts of northern Lorn to the Lochaber District of what was at that time Highland Region. On the other hand, the 1994 Act added that part of historic Dunbartonshire lying between Loch Lomond and Loch Long to the new Argyll & Bute Council. The map on pp. ii–iii shows the boundaries of the area covered.

The gazetteer has been arranged in three sections. The first is devoted to mainland Argyll and includes all smaller islands close to the mainland; these islands (listed here south to north, but alphabetically in the text) are Sanda, Cara, Gigha, Shuna (Luing), Torsa, Seil, Kerrera, Lismore and Shuna (Appin). The second section deals with the outer islands: Islay, Jura, Scarba, the Garvellach Isles, Colonsay, Oronsay, Mull, Ulva, Iona, the Treshnish Isles, Tiree and Coll. The third part of the Gazetteer covers Bute, which is treated separately in deference to its historic administrative distinction from Argyllshire. Maps are placed at the beginning of each of these three sections on pp. 100–2, 501–2, 604.

Map references

The numbers printed in italic type in the margin against the placenames in the gazetteer indicate the position of the place in question on the maps, which are divided into sections by the 10-kilometre reference lines of the National Grid. The reference given here omits the two initial letters (formerly numbers), which in a full grid reference refer to the 100-kilometre squares into which the country is divided. The first two numbers indicate the western boundary, and the last two the southern boundary, of the 10-kilometre square in which the place is situated. For example, Garelochhead, reference 2080, will be found in the 10-kilometre square bounded by grid lines 20 (on the west) and 40, and 80 (on the south) and 00; Tobermory, reference 4040, in the square bounded by grid lines 40 (on the west) and 60, and 40 (on the south) and 60.

Access to buildings

Many of the buildings described in this book are in public places, and in some obvious cases their interiors (at least the public sections of them) can be seen without formality. But it must be emphasized that the mention of buildings or lands does not imply any right of public access to them, or the existence of any arrangements for visiting them.

Some churches are open within regular hours, and it is usually possible to see the interiors of others by arrangement with the minister, priest or church officer. Particulars of admission to Ancient Monuments and other buildings in the care of the Scottish Ministers (free to the Friends of Historic Scotland) are available from Historic Scotland, Longmore House, Salisbury Place, Edinburgh EH9 1SH. Details of access to properties of the National Trust for Scotland are available from the Trust's head office at 28 Charlotte Square, Edinburgh, EH2 4ET. Admission is free to members, on whose subscriptions and donations the Trust's work depends. Scotland's Churches Scheme, Dunedin, Holehouse Road, Eaglesham, Glasgow G76 0JF, publishes an annual directory of churches open to visitors.

Local Tourist Offices can advise the visitor on what properties in each area are open to the public and will usually give helpful directions as to how to get to them. It is worth remembering that many of the roads on the mainland and on the islands, though they may be classified A or B, are in fact often narrow, single-track carriageways with passing-places. On such routes courtesy is expected and customary.

FOREWORD

It is now almost exactly half a century since Sir Nikolaus Pevsner published the first volume of The Buildings of England *series. Since then the Pevsner/Penguin project has expanded to embrace the architecture of Ireland, Scotland and Wales. Colin McWilliam undertook the task of editing* The Buildings of Scotland *series which began with his own* Lothian *volume, published in 1978. In 1984 he was co-author of* Edinburgh, *collaborating with John Gifford and David Walker, and in 1988 wrote the introduction to John Gifford's* Fife. *A year later, Colin McWilliam died suddenly. Since then his scholarship, his enviable facility in writing about buildings and townscape with an engaging fluency and perceptive wit, his friendship, and his endearing diffidence are much missed. But the venture has not foundered.* Glasgow, *written by Elizabeth Williamson, Anne Riches and Malcolm Higgs, appeared in 1990. During the last decade two more volumes,* Highland and Islands, *1992, and* Dumfries and Galloway, *1996, both the work of the indefatigable John Gifford, have been published. The process is slow, a consequence in some degree of the research needed to support an enterprise which, from its beginnings in what Colin McWilliam described as 'the knowledge and judgement of one man and his personal view', seems to have grown remorselessly, increasingly juggling what aspires to be a more and more definitive record with the critical and idiosyncratic comment of a handful of individual authors. For my own part, I have at times struggled to keep on track. Fitting time for travel, study and writing into an otherwise busy academic life, which at the outset entailed the administrative burden of running a university department, has not always been easy. But once achieved, it was always a pleasure, whether in fact or in creative reverie, to take the ferry over to Bute or cross the Rest and Be Thankful to Loch Fyne. Moreover, like other authors in the series, I have been relieved of some of the chores of research by the massive amount of work done by John Gifford and his assistants who, in search of every morsel of information, have trawled through the architectural journals and building periodicals of the c19 and c20 and have pored over manuscript sources, estate papers and ecclesiastical archives in the National Library of Scotland, the Scottish Record Office and the National Monuments Record of Scotland (NMRS) at the Royal Commission on the Ancient and Historical Monuments of Scotland (RCAHMS). None of this work could have been done without the financial support of The Buildings of Scotland Trust. The volumes of loose-leaf notes produced have been invaluable.*

Besides these notes, ranged in broad-backed binders along the top shelves in my study, my most frequent recourse has been to the inventories published by the Royal Commission on Argyll, *especially Vol. 1*

(1971), Vol. 2 (1974), Vol. 3 (1980), Vol. 4 (1982), Vol. 5 (1984) and Vol. 7 (1992). For several years these treasures have been piled on the floor below my desk, their pages increasingly limp with the usage of regular reference. For archaeology and architecture, everything from the standing stones of prehistory to the buildings of the early C19, they are indispensable. So thorough is their research that it seems it can no longer be afforded and a programme that began in the first decade of the C20 has had to be abandoned in the last with little more than half of Scotland covered. At a time when the country is recovering its Parliament and much of its cultural self-respect, it is nothing short of a national disgrace that parsimony should blight such a necessary task of scholarship.

Exhaustive as they are, the RCAHMS inventories have little to say about the C19 and nothing on the C20. There is, however, much information on these more recent periods in the Lists of Buildings of Special Architectural or Historic Interest prepared by Historic Scotland, particularly the more recently revised and expanded lists which greatly augment the data contained in the original documentation compiled by the Scottish Development Department. The Statistical Accounts of Scotland *(the First appearing in the 1790s; the Second in the 1830s and '40s; and the Third from the 1950s) frequently prove valuable. Victorian gazetteers always have something to offer, especially the six volumes of the* Ordnance Gazetteer of Scotland *(1882–5), edited by Francis H. Groome. It is impossible to do without the five volumes of* The Castellated and Domestic Architecture of Scotland *(1887–92) or the three of* The Ecclesiastical Architecture of Scotland *(1896–7), both by David MacGibbon and Thomas Ross. From time to time and place to place, Stewart Cruden's* The Scottish Castle *(1960), John R. Hume's* The Industrial Archaeology of Scotland *(2 vols., 1976–7), and Allan MacLean's* Telford's Highland Churches *(1989) have all been helpful. I have also made intermittent use of* The Historic Architecture of Scotland *(1966) by John G. Dunbar and the more recent* A History of Scottish Architecture *(1996) by Miles Glendenning, Ranald MacInnes and Aonghus MacKechnie. As may be imagined, many other publications have been consulted: general histories, local histories, biographical works, building studies, guides, etc. It would be tedious to attempt to list all these here, but I must mention a few. At one extreme, the monumental achievement of Ian G. Lindsay and Mary Cosh,* Inveraray and the Dukes of Argyll *(1973); suitably scholarly in its response to the family motto* Ne Obliviscaris*, wonderfully readable and essential to any writer on Argyll. At the other, useful in a more diffuse, fragmentary way, the many editions of* The Kist*, the magazine of the Natural History and Antiquarian Society of Mid-Argyll. I should also add that the introductory essay on communications could not have been written without reference to* New Ways through the Glens *(1962) by A. R. B. Haldane,* The Military Roads in Scotland *(1976) by William Taylor,* The Golden Years of the Clyde Steamers *(1969) by A. J. S. Paterson, and J. Thomas's books on* The West Highland Railway *(1965) and* The Callander and Oban Railway *(1966). The archaeological material collected in the Royal Commission's Inventories, including volume 6 (1988), is conveniently brought together in* The Archaeology of Argyll*, edited by Graham Ritchie in 1997. An extract from Volume 6 covering the monuments in Kilmartin was published by the Commission in 1999.*

Many individuals have given me the benefit of their knowledge and opinion. Foremost among these have been Murdo MacDonald, Archivist at Lochgilphead, and Michael C. Davis, Librarian at Sandbank. Not only did they generously read and comment upon sections of my text, correcting mistakes and filling in blanks, but they have repeatedly volunteered information and suggestions which pointed me in many fruitful directions. I must thank Simon Green and Diane Watters at the National Monuments record and Simon Montgomery and Debbie Mays at Historic Scotland. Time and again Malcolm Allan turned up gems in the Rare Books section of the Andersonian Library at the University of Strathclyde. Alan Buchan of the Scottish Historic Organs Trust provided data on a subject of which I knew nothing. With Charles McKean, Professor of Architectural History at the University of Dundee, I discussed a number of issues; this was always stimulating – though, faced with some of his more challenging interpretations, I confess to having played safe and have clung to the conventional wisdom of the RCAHMS Inventories. Countless architects have been kind enough to answer my inquiries, many providing dates, drawings and photographs. As it is impossible to mention all of them, I hope they will accept this simple but sincere acknowledgement of thanks. I am, however, particularly grateful to David Anderson, Shauna Cameron, William G. Cowie, Philip Flockart, Stephen Hunter, Diana Maclaurin, Bill Murdoch, David Page, Brian Park, John Renshaw, Fiona Sinclair, Donald Wilson and John Wilson. Besides architects, many ministers, priests, session clerks, local historians and residents have opened doors, answered letters and generally taken trouble on my behalf. Again I cannot name them here but express my grateful thanks.

It would, of course, be impossible to complete a book like this without the indulgence of those individuals whose properties feature in the pages that follow. Behind the rhododendrons, at the end of a sometimes intimidatingly long drive, I almost always found a friendly reception, not only polite interest but a willingness to show me around, some unexpected snippet of information about the building's story, sometimes even coffee in the kitchen. I hope that, in return, I have been tolerably accurate in my descriptions and have been able to capture something of the flavour of each place visited.

Travelling costs have been subsidized by The Buildings of Scotland Trust, which raises funds from public and private sources to support the completion of the series. I am extremely grateful to the Trust for this assistance. At a more personal level I have enjoyed the hospitality and help of many friends in Argyll and Bute; among them are Peter and Moira MacGillivray (Islay), Douglas and Allison Fairbairn (Coll), Elaine Campbell and Graeme Bartrup (Bute), Bill and Caroline Murdoch (Whitehouse), Gordon and Efric MacNeil (Campbeltown).

At different times and in differing ways several people have contributed to the production of this book. I thank my co-authors, Judith Lawson, Graham Ritchie and Ian Fisher, for their introductory chapters, and I am especially grateful to Fiona Sinclair who wrote the entries for Colgrain, Craigendoran, Helensburgh, Rhu, Shandon, Kilcreggan, Craigrownie and Cove. Building plans and town plans were drawn by Alan Fagan, maps by Reg and Marjorie Piggott. Ellen Thomson and Barbara Macdonald were ever willing to help with typing and printing.

At Penguin, valuable assistance was provided by Sue Machin, Mark Handsley and Barbara Phelan, and by Georgina Widdrington who designed the text. The inset was designed by Lesley Straw. The index was prepared by Judith Wardman. Acknowledgement for the illustrative plates is made elsewhere, but I must particularly thank Anne Dick for the splendid cover photographs, which were specially taken. The collation of photographs was begun by Susan Rose-Smith but continued and completed by Graham Ritchie, who also co-ordinated the inclusion of plans, maps and map references; his thoroughness and organizational skill were vital. To John Dunbar I am deeply indebted, not only for reading my text but for helpful suggestions and amendments made with graceful erudition. Above all, I thank my editors at Penguin, Elizabeth Williamson and Bridget Cherry. Both were long-suffering with my delays and admirably scrupulous in their attention to form and content, their stringency tempered by a willingness to pencil the occasional 'I like that' in the margin. How encouraging that was when the task seemed without end.

The format of this volume remains largely similar to that of those which have preceded it in the series. The inclusion of archaeological monuments in the gazetteer has had to be selective. Almost all churches and public buildings are described. In towns and villages the Descriptions will make mention of these and all other significant buildings, many of which may, in fact, be of modest architectural quality but critically located in the townscape. The more important rural buildings such as castles and country houses have individual entries. Although it has not been possible to visit a few of the more remote places such as the Garvellach Islands, Treshnish Islands, Scarba, etc., I have taken the view that nothing should be included without some measure of description. It is inevitable that mistakes and omissions will have been made. No amount of cross-checking, textual emendation or editing will eliminate error. Flawed assumptions may have been made, important sources overlooked. The writing of this book has stretched over several years, long enough for demolition and new-build to impair the accuracy of the gazetteer. But this is what makes the game worth playing; new facts emerge, new interpretations intrigue. For the moment, however, all errors are mine.

Finally, I thank my family. My son, Davor, and daughter, Dara, who in visits and telephone calls would ask how the book was progressing, have always seemed able to sustain the belief that completion was within my capability. Twenty years ago, in the preface to my doctoral dissertation, I mentioned the 'loving disinterest' with which my wife, Jasna, nurtured my writing. This was no careless oxymoron but a most precise choice of words. It is still true, and I love her for it.

PRELUDE

Travelling in Argyll is very much an up-and-down affair. Up one side of a long sea-loch and then down the other. Up hill, down dale. The road from Loch Long to Loch Fyne is perhaps the most dramatic among many such routes, certainly the best known. Beginning below The Cobbler, it climbs from Ardgartan up through Glen Croe to Loch Restil. There, a narrow tracks diverts south-west, winding down to Hell's Glen and Lochgoilhead, while the main road continues north before swinging west into Glen Kinglas and on to Loch Fyne and Inveraray. The summit, beside the loch that lies in the saddle between the two glens, is known as the 'Rest and Be Thankful'. The height is not spectacular, about 250m. above sea level; nor is the ascent more than moderately demanding. But looking down from the modern road into the deep valley below, the old military track which served travellers until the realignment of the A83 in the C20 can be seen snaking up the steep end of the valley, and it is easy to understand what prompted such a name.

Seventy years ago my father drove that difficult road, pushing his small second-hand Austin Seven to the limit. Behind him, stacked across the back seat, were rolls of cloth, material for farmers' suits and farmers' wives' skirts. Beside him sat his brother; both joiners, thrown out of work by the Depression, they had given up their tools and were trying to make a living carrying cloth to the more remote farms and crofts of Argyll. Back on Bute was another brother, a draper in Rothesay. For a time, this modest enterprise worked, but the war came and my father returned to his trade in the Clyde shipyards. Years later he would occasionally recall those days: the wild Argyll landscape; the tramp from the road across heather and field to the farms; the welcome and the hospitality, soup, herring and potatoes eaten from the same plate. I listened, more out of filial politeness than interest. I was an architecture student, captivated by thoughts of Paris, Venice and Prague, indifferent to my own country. I travelled to Europe. Argyll, even Bute, remained a world away.

Perhaps it is necessary to travel in order to put the near-at-hand into proper perspective. Stay-at-home provincial smugness should be avoided at all costs. Yet the more discovered, the more recovered; sooner or later the obligation mounts to find a place for proximate pleasures. And now, later rather than sooner, I find myself regretting my disdain for my father's memories and my failure to learn and write more about the buildings on my west-coast doorstep. This book may perhaps make some amends.

What fills the eye in Argyll is not, of course, architecture but landscape. It is a landscape for ever appearing and disappearing, up on the misted summits or down in the skittish reflections of dark lochs. Hills rise to crags and fall in screes. Hills, bent with the rounded shoulders of glacial age, roll across the skyline from glen to glen. The slopes are bare or forested with fir or fern. Everything is green beyond summer dreaming, russet or burnt sienna in autumn, swirled in the amorphous white of winter. Everywhere there is water. Sea and sea-loch tremble in mother-of-pearl blushes as the sun sinks over a wide western horizon. Around the islands, a turquoise sea edged with rock-girt moorings and long deserted sweeps of dune-backed sandy shore.

The buildings are secondary. Set between sea and sky, some seem almost part of the natural scene. Hill forts, duns and brochs, scarcely visible, all but sucked back into the earth. On Islay, Mull and Tiree, turf-wrapped chapels barely emerge from meadow or machair. On the mainland and the islands, ruinous castles crumble down into the rock that bore them: Achadun, Ascog, Cairnburgh, Dunivaig, Sween, Tarbert. At Finlaggan, architecture has become archaeology, the reversionary process almost complete, fusing stone, timber, earth, water and peat into a topographical puzzle; once the power-house of the MacDonald Lords of the Isles, it is now a place brought low, ambiguous, bleak. Yet the corruption of time is never complete. The stones resist. In Kilmartin Glen, the stones still stand; circles, henges and linear cemeteries millennia old. The high crosses of Iona, Keills, Kildalton and Kilmory Knap, most of them wounded, some miraculously intact, are no less impressive markers of unflagging faith and intransigent art. They, too, address eternity. Ruinous on remote hillsides, worn medieval chapels retain this same religious assertion, none more mysterious and evocative than St Blane's Chapel in a hidden dell near the south end of Bute. Worship continues within the restored walls of the Abbey on Iona and in the choir of the C14 cathedral of St Moluag on Lismore. Great castles of enclosure confirm the grip of temporal power: Duart, Dunstaffnage, Kilchurn, Rothesay, Skipness. Many tower-houses survive: some battered but erect, like Achallader and Gylen; others, more robust, their masonry shell remarkably intact, like Carrick and Moy; still others, Barcaldine, Dunderave, Kilberry, Saddell and Stalker, given new life. All stand tall. All have a presence, a thrawn determination to look into the face of nature and survive. Even Finlaggan, levelled to deception, is a place still.

This, perhaps, is the clue to all that is best in the architecture of Argyll and Bute. It is, after all, a county of Atlantic winds and rain. Buildings are built to stand against the elements. They may be raised with the materials to hand: stone, lime and slate shipped up the loch or carried over the hills, timber cut from the woods, turf from the land. But, *pace* Ruskin, this is not 'all that is required'. These buildings are conceived with a 'sense of elevation, or proud, free stature'. They want to be independent of nature. It is this intent that transcends or translates the pragmatic. It is this that persists when local conventions and resources have in some way been superseded, when what we call the 'traditional' gives way to what we call the 'modern'. The 'sense of elevation' that the

Swedish historian Eric Forssman had in mind was strictly Palladian (he was describing La Malcontenta on the Brenta Canal) but, though the flat marshlands of the Veneto bear no similarity to the ups and downs of the loch-riven landscape of Argyll, the idea that architecture strives to be free, to raise itself above rock and moss, is far from being an out-of-context irrelevance. Airds House, Barbreck House and Strachur House do, indeed, have a similar if less sophisticated classical composure to the elevational elegance found in the Villa Foscari. But this is not the point. It is the abstraction of the façade that matters. A proud verticality, a prismatic simplicity, an abrupt junction with the ground; some or all of these qualities characterize the architecture described in this book. Overall there is a deliberate, even brutal, detachment of stone from soil: architecture confronts nature.

This defiance presents itself in countless lonely farms, in the black-and-white homes of Balemartine and Mannal on Tiree, in a single, single-sided, single-storey street in Arinagour, Coll, in humble lime-washed rubble cottages scattered around Taynuilt, in slate-workers' rows at Easdale, in local authority housing from the 1930s in Arrochar, Garelochhead and Rhu, and, most recently, in a white residential ridge raised behind the South Pier at Oban. The same spirit invests foursquare, four-towered Inveraray Castle and the extravagant red Gothic box of Mount Stuart on Bute. It stares out from the small harled churches of Bowmore and Dalmally, one cylindrical, the other octagonal, both towered. It establishes urban scale and colour in the white-walled streets of Inveraray, wonderfully stark in Arkland and Relief Land, only to challenge this with tall tenements, red in Rothesay, polychromatic in Campbeltown. In bourgeois Helensburgh, it takes to task the comfortable residents of half-timbered, tile-hung Tudor villas in the hard Scots morality of The Hill House.

I think about all this on a seat perched above the rocks that fall into the narrow bay of Portnahaven. Here, on the Rinns of Islay, I am at the edge. Out there, through the spumey gap of Caolas nan Gall, the Atlantic crashes against Europe, pounding the first ragged fringes of Argyll and churning up the racing currents that run from Frenchman's Rocks to Orsay. Nature is fierce here. The sea cuts deep treacherous clefts into the coast. The wind screams. Fogs fall like night. Against this onslaught, only the familiar white-walled streets of gable-to-gable houses, stepping up each side of the creek. They look tired, and no wonder. Not relaxed and picturesque as in sheltered Port Charlotte, not neatly regimented like the streets in Bowmore, Lochgilphead or Inveraray, not pastel-painted and picture-postcard-prim like Tobermory. But they face the worst here, and they still stand. Up the hill, the Telford church, still in Sunday use; halfway down, the post office shop; at the water's edge, the pub. This is a place, a place that gives architecture its most fundamental meaning.

Argyll and Bute has many such places. This book tries to see them more clearly. My father knew some. I think of him, traveller too.

Kilmacolm
July 1999

INTRODUCTION

GEOLOGY

BY JUDITH LAWSON

The area of Scotland covered by this volume includes some of the most spectacular, dramatic and varied scenery in the British Isles. A major change in the geology occurs at the Highland Boundary Fault (fig. 1), often called the Highland Line, crossing Scotland from Stonehaven in the E to Loch Lomond, Helensburgh, Bute and Campbeltown in the W. To the N is the high ground of the Caledonian mountain range, deeply dissected by valleys which, in the W, have been drowned by the sea to give the islands and sea lochs of the complex coastline. To the S of the Highland Line is greatly contrasting scenery with a broad area of low rolling country covered with pasture and woods, while further S again rise the rocky volcanic hills of the Kilpatrick Hills and Campsie Fells.

Scenery and Geology

To the N of the Highland Boundary Fault there are peaks rising to over 3000 ft (912m.) with soaring rocky summits, looking down on deep broad valleys. The prevailing W winds bring high rainfall to the W and much snow on the hills in winter, where conditions can be extreme. Near the coast, however, the influence of the sea results in a climate which is exceptionally mild and where rare and tender rhododendrons can be cultivated in the majestic gardens at Arduaine, Crarae or Benmore. Originally, pine or mixed oak woodlands would have covered the lower slopes, while the higher land was clothed in peat and heather. Man has greatly modified the original vegetation by cutting or coppicing the old oak woods for charcoal, clearing the land for grazing and, in the twentieth century, planting vast areas with conifers. Different farming methods have also left their mark with the clearances of the crofting communities, based on cattle, for the open tracts favoured by the sheep farmers. After the depopulation of the Highlands and Islands in the C19 there has been some recent movement of people back to the Highland areas, but this is still a relatively underpopulated part of the British Isles, with few towns and villages.

The highest mountains were well described by Scott as 'Caledonia! stern and wild ... land of brown heath and shaggy wood, land of the mountain and the flood'. The mountains E of Loch Etive epitomize the scenery of the Highlands. Ben Starav and Ben Cruachan,

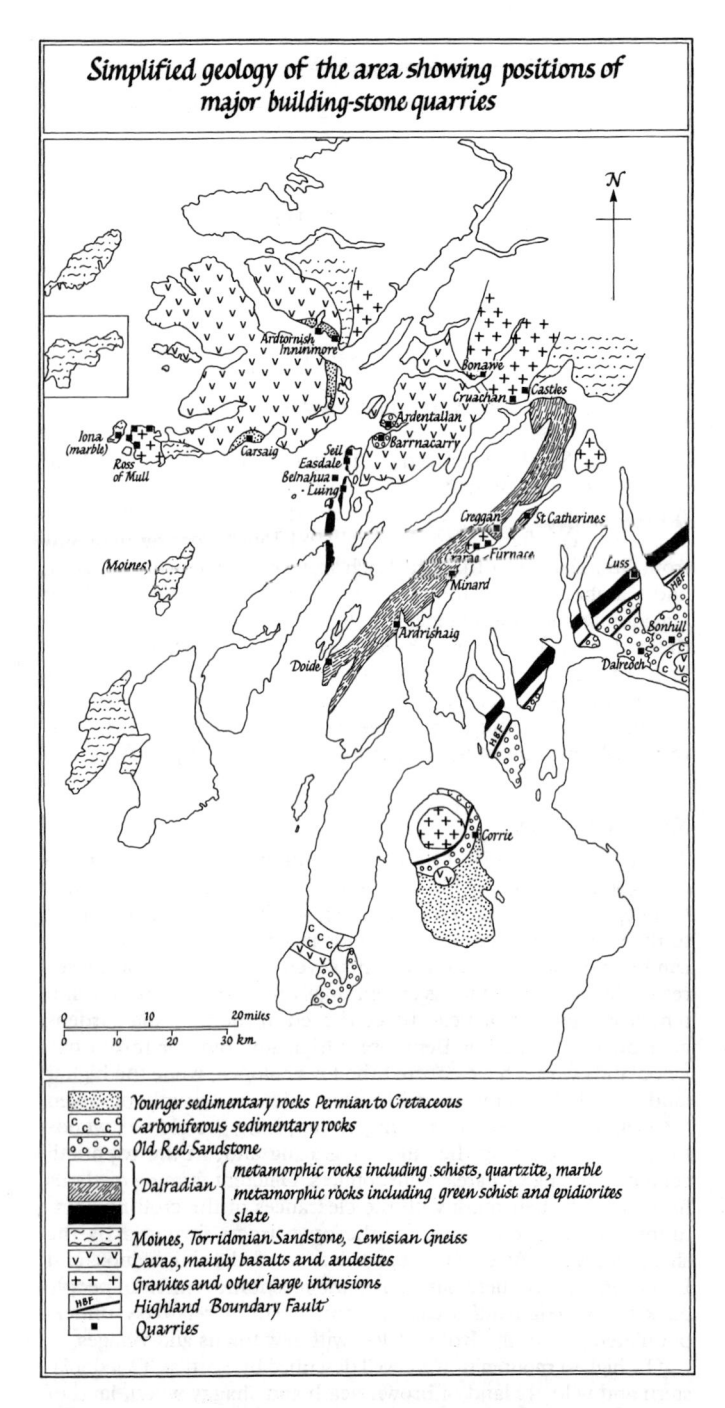

FIGURE 1. Map of the area covered by this volume, with simplified geology and positions of quarries.

with their rocky, sharp-edged tops and steep, scree-covered slopes, tower over the waters of the loch. The peaks are often white in winter and even on a summer's day it is possible to find patches of snow. Further E are Ben Lui, Ben More, Ben Lomond, Stobinian and many more high peaks. Deep lochs may occupy the valley floors. Loch Lomond, the largest freshwater loch in Britain, with its surface only a few metres above sea level, plunges down to about 200m below sea level. Below Ben Cruachan is Loch Awe. The view of the mountain with Kilchurn Castle reflected in the loch is often photographed and painted, particularly when Highland cattle graze in the foreground: for many, this represents the 'typical' Highland scene. The typically U-shaped valleys may be smooth or covered in the hummocks of glacial debris left by the melting of the last ice, and have always been vital arteries for the transport of people, animals and goods. Roads, railways and villages are largely confined to the valley floors. Villages such as Dalmally and Loch Awe exist primarily as service areas on the main routes through the hills.

To the W the mountains are not so high and many valleys have been eroded below sea level and subsequently drowned by the sea. There are hundreds of islands, some inhabited but most uninhabited, and a long indented coastline. As the roads wind round the coasts the views are continually changing: there can be no lovelier sight than the interplay between the sea, islands and tree-clad rocky coast, particularly on a sunny day.

A marked change in the scenery occurs S of the Highland Boundary Fault. The lower ground, generally less than 300m., would also have been extensively wooded at one time but has long been used for mainly pastoral farming. To the S, the area is dominated by the flat-topped, rocky Kilpatrick Hills and Campsie Fells. Rising to over 500m., the high ground is used as rough grazing or has been planted with conifers.

The scenery, land use, and the materials used in the buildings of Argyll are enormously influenced by its long and complicated geological history. Almost all types of rock are found here and have an important control on the scenery. The last major geological event, the Pleistocene Ice Age, in the last few tens of thousands of years, has also had a very marked effect on the final moulding of the countryside.

The fault-line scarp of the Highland Boundary Fault marks the boundary separating the more resistant rocks of the Highlands to the N from sediments to the S. The main framework of the Highlands is formed of metamorphic rocks of Precambrian age, from approximately 800 to 600 million years old, divided into the Moine and Dalradian Supergroups (fig. 1, fig. 2). Of sedimentary and igneous origin, these rocks have been altered by heat and pressure from shales, sandstones and limestones to slate, schists, marbles and quartzites and from basaltic lavas and intrusions to 'green beds' – green schists and epidiorites. In general the degree of metamorphism is less in the W so that the original character of the sediments or lavas can still be seen, for example, on Jura. The original sediments of the Precambrian rocks were deposited in the sea at the edges of a large ocean, called Iapetus, which separated older continental areas in the NW of Scotland from those in England and Wales. The ocean shrank in size as the two continents moved together until they finally collided and the rocks were metamorphosed, folded and faulted, and intruded by massive granites, in the Caledonian mountain-building episode. By the end of this time, about 400 million years ago, the Highlands probably looked something like the Himalayas of today. The trend of the metamorphic rocks is from NE to SW. Some bands, particularly the quartzites, are resistant to erosion and form lines of hills, for example, the Paps of Jura. The softer rocks have been preferentially eroded and form the valleys which in the W have been drowned by the sea. This gives the marked NE–SW pattern of the coastline and valleys. The granites give some of the highest ground of the area, as in the Cruachan massif. The W margin of the Iapetus Ocean and the Caledonian mountains is represented by small areas of ancient, highly metamorphosed gneisses which outcrop on Coll and Tiree, Iona and Islay. An immense amount of erosion has occurred since then so that only the lowest part of that mountain chain still exists.

After the Caledonian mountains and the Highland Boundary Fault were formed, products of the erosion of the high ground were deposited by rivers as sands and gravels. To the S of the Highland Boundary Fault these sandstones and conglomerates of the Old Red Sandstone are relatively soft rocks which outcrop extensively from southern Loch Lomond to Bute and Campbeltown in the W. They are often strongly coloured brown or red. Coarse conglomerates are also common around Oban. While the sediments were being deposited there was andesitic volcanic activity in the Lorn area around Oban. Later, in the Carboniferous period, volcanoes were active in the Central Lowlands, with outpourings of basaltic lavas forming the Kilpatrick Hills and Campsie Fells. Finally, Carboniferous sediments, including shales, sandstones and coal, were deposited.

Evidence of more recent geological activity is found in Mull. After some relatively thin sediments including sandstones were deposited in the Mesozoic, there was again extensive volcanic activity some 65 million years ago at the beginning of the Tertiary era. There are basaltic lavas and intrusions associated with a large volcano, now mostly eroded, on Mull. Characteristic rocks, such as the well-jointed basalt lavas, can be seen in Fingal's Cave on Staffa and on Mull itself.

Since this time Scotland has been a land surface with rivers eroding deep valleys. In the last few tens of thousands of years the Pleistocene Ice Sheet covered virtually the whole of Scotland and modified the river valleys into the deep, wide U-shaped valleys with steep sides and the sharp craggy ridges and peaks of the mountains so characteristic of the Highlands. As the ice melted, moraine was dumped on the lower ground and many valleys are covered with small hummocks of poorly sorted drift. Such ground can be well seen in the upper Aray valley. The ice stretched far to the W and, after the ice melted, the rise in sea level resulted in the flooding of the valleys to give the fiord coastline. Re-adjustments of the land since the ice melted have resulted in the raised beaches which are found round most of the coasts: there is a prominent one at about 9m. above sea level, and rather less well-preserved ones at higher levels. Such higher raised beaches are well seen on the W coast of the island of Jura.

Building Materials

For the purpose of describing the building materials, the area can be divided into two: the W and N with its long coastline and low hills, and a S and E, more landlocked area. The building materials used in these areas reflect their varied geology and topography. There are very few clays suitable for brick-making so this is not a traditional building material in the area. The dominant building material, apart from timber, was stone, and this would have been collected or quarried locally for use since early times. For larger buildings stone was brought from further afield. In the C16 to C19, relatively few quarries, those with easy access to water transport, became important and supplied stone widely throughout the area. The advent of rail transport at the end of the C19 allowed new sources of stone to be used: Correnie granite, from Aberdeenshire, used in Argyll Mansions, Oban, would almost certainly have been transported by this means. The positions and horizons of the most important quarries are shown in fig. 1. A stone much favoured by sculptors was quarried for many centuries at Doide on Loch Sween.

The north and west, south of the Highland Boundary Fault

In the W area, from prehistoric times until the advent of mass-produced materials such as breeze blocks, 'small' buildings, the houses and byres, would have been of turf, timber, wattle and daub with heather-thatched roofs and with only a limited use of stone for fireplaces and, later, chimneys. In many houses low stone walls were also common. Any stone used would have been gathered very locally from beaches, rivers or the deposits of glacial drift. Such boulders, having survived natural transport over long distances by ice or water, were often of very durable material but were usually rounded and therefore difficult to build into neat walls. Thus most croft walls were of random rubble of boulders broken to shape only roughly, with the wide joints filled with numerous pinnings. The walls were often harled. The stone found in these walls can be of virtually any rock type, which may have been transported a considerable distance from its source. Another important use of stone was in the making of querns and millstones, and many settlements had their own millstone quarries.

Larger, medieval fortifications or ecclesiastical buildings were built of stone, which was needed in great volume. The builders of these larger structures had greater resources in terms of labour and access to materials. Even here the main part of the walls was almost universally built using local stone, usually as rubble roughly brought to courses. There is, therefore, a variety of stone to be seen in these walls. Some use a rock which is common locally, for example basalt rubble in Pennygown Church on Mull (p. 582), mica schist in Skipness Castle (p. 457), granite in many of Iona's buildings, or pink and white quartzite in Kilmory Knap Chapel (p. 354). The walls were usually harled but are now often exposed. These structures needed larger openings: doorways, arches and windows. The relatively small amount of stone for these dressing stones needed to be cut to shape and to be of larger or longer size and was often transported considerable distances from relatively few, but large and long-lived quarries. Carnasserie Castle (p. 174) is a good example which shows how stone was used. It sits on a ridge of coarse Crinan Grit which rises above an alluvial valley, with glacial deposits to the W and N. The lower, light-coloured part of the walls is largely made up of the local grit, either quarried near by or collected from the glacial debris. Much of it is large rounded boulders. The dressing stones are 'greenstones', darker metamorphic rocks, probably quarried a few miles to the S. The darker, upper walls are also of a similar greenstone, but in less regular sizes – possibly the rubble left after the dressing stones had been cut.

In most cases water was the vital transport link: the long sea and freshwater lochs which dissect the area mean that no part of Argyllshire is further than about 25km. from water. The castles and many of the churches were also near the coasts or on islands, and all the main medieval quarries were also situated near the sea (fig. 1). Some of these quarries are of great antiquity and, where suitable good-quality rock occurred, it was widely 'exported' both within the area and further afield. A quarrying method that was often used involved the use of wooden wedges which were inserted into cracks or holes when dry and allowed to swell as the tide rose. This method was used at Carsaig, on Mull, and in some of the slate quarries.

The oldest rocks, which outcrop on Coll, Tiree, Iona and Islay, include the Lewisian Gneiss which is hard to work and has a tendency to split and so is used only locally near its source. It can be seen in the walls of the parish church on Coll. Torridonian Sandstone outcrops on Iona and was used in part of the Abbey.

The regionally metamorphosed rocks of the Dalradian are not generally suitable for building stone as most tend to break too easily along their cleavage. However, the green schists of the Ardrishaig Phyllites have been used extensively. In medieval times the quarries at Doide on Loch Sween supplied stone slabs of the green, chlorite–albite schist for numerous crosses and tombstones and it was also used in building for pinnings and lintels, as at Castle Sween (p. 184). This outcrop has vertical joints which allow the rock to be split into slabs a few centimetres thick. It was easily carved and was the preferred stone for this purpose for many centuries. Further N along the outcrop a somewhat similar chlorite schist occurs in the Loch Fyne area. It was quarried between Brainport Bay and Minard, at Creggan Quarry, S of Inveraray, and at St Catherine's Quarry, where it was known locally as potstone, on the E side of the Loch Fyne. Stone from Creggan Quarry was used in the lower walls of Inveraray Castle and the quarry at St Catherine's was opened specially for the construction of the upper part of the Castle and other estate buildings such as Cherry Park Farm and several bridges. It was also used in Inveraray town. Somewhat similar greenish black epidiorites have also been quarried at Lochgilphead and Ardrishaig.

Marble is found in small outcrops but its use has been confined to such features as altars and fireplaces. Pink marble was produced on Tiree and a red-and-white one at Caddleton Quarry, Ardmaddy, which was worked only from 1745 to 1751. Local marble from the estate was also used on a very small scale in Inveraray Castle. The most well-known rock of this type was quarried on Iona. The green-and-white stone was often used for altars, fireplaces and memorial monuments and can be seen on Iona and, for example, in the retable of the altar in St John's Cathedral in Oban.

Within the group of sedimentary rocks sandstone was commonly used for dressing stones in rubble walls and there are several quarries which were active over a long period. The horizons of the more important sandstones are shown in fig. 3. Sandstone is a very variable material and is not necessarily a durable stone. In some cases it has weathered more than the local rubblestone walls, for example in Pennygown Chapel, Mull (p. 582). The oldest, geologically, from the Precambrian, is the reddish brown Torridonian Sandstone used locally on Iona. A coarse greenish or purple sandstone of Lower Old Red Sandstone age was quarried over many centuries at Ardentallan on Loch Feochan. The quarry was partly on the foreshore and is now largely flooded. The stone can be seen in the old Parish Church at Kilmore (p. 351), s of Oban, and Gylen Castle (p. 329) on Kerrera. The Free High Church in Oban (p. 406) is a prominent building constructed in 1846 from the green sandstone. A similiar rock at Barrnacarry Bay on the other side of Loch Feochan was also used, for example in the coach house at Ardmaddy Castle (p. 120). Younger, coarse, white and yellow Carboniferous sandstone was quarried in the C18 and C19 at Inninmore Bay, in Morvern, but was mainly used for millstones and gravestones. A small outcrop of coarse sandstone of similar age near the old Bridge of Awe was used for dressings at Fraoch Eilean Castle (p. 250) and later at Kilchurn Castle (p. 338) on Loch Awe. Rocks of the New Red Sandstone occur widely, though in small, isolated outcrops, and have often been used. Such red sandstones were quarried on the Isle of Arran, at Corrie, and on the w coast at Machrie Bay and were used, for example, in Skipness Castle and later in Oban. A buff-coloured Triassic sandstone was quarried from the C13 to the C19 between Inninmore Bay and Ardtornish in Morvern. This was used in both Aros (p. 566) and Duart Castles (p. 570) on the Isle of Mull. Higher in the succession is the sandstone quarried at Carsaig Bay. This is a greenish or buff, fine-grained sandstone of Lower Jurassic age which was widely used, particularly on Iona, but also in many other buildings on the mainland. It can be seen in the C13 part of Ardchattan Priory (p. 107) and in Mull in several buildings around Loch Buie. Younger sandstones were sometimes used but are not very common. Cretaceous sandstones occur very locally. A green, glauconitic sandstone, possibly from SE Mull, was used in Pennygown Church, where it has not weathered well. Other local sediments are little used in Argyllshire. The limestone of Lismore is found in rubble walls on the island but does not appear to have been used as a major building material. The quarries on that island were primarily for the production of lime.

In the C19 sandstone was imported from the Central Belt of Scotland and used in the construction of C19 mansion houses and as dressing stone in the characteristic granite houses of Oban. Cream sandstone from Dullatur was used in Ardkinglas House (p. 114) and Giffnock stone, from the S side of Glasgow, is known to have been used in Oban's Parish Church (p. 407). Another import was the bright red Permian sandstone from the St Bees region of Cumbria used in the Bonawe Iron Works, presumably brought in by the owners of the works, who were from that region. It can also be seen in part of St John's Cathedral in Oban. A very unusual stone, for Scotland, was used in the high altar and Lady Chapel of St Columba's R.C. Cathedral, Oban. This is a green and grey limestone with sections of fossil belemnites from Hornton on the borders of Warwickshire and Oxfordshire.

Igneous rocks are also used in building. The basalt lavas which occur so widely on Mull and the andesites of Lorn, while strong and durable, are not easy to cut into shape and are therefore mainly used in rubble walls. Such basalt rubble can be seen in Aros Castle on Mull, and the bridge to Seil Island is of local andesite lava. Dolerite dykes may also be used to a limited extent. One such dyke was quarried at Inverlochy, near Dalmally, and the dolerite can be seen in some houses in that village.

The more acid, that is granitic, igneous rocks are also strong and durable and can often be obtained in large blocks. Granite is tough to cut into shape but, perhaps because the finished surface with its large crystals of quartz, feldspar, mica or hornblende has an attractive colour and texture, it has been used locally and exported and has also been imported from other parts of Scotland.

S of Inveraray is an outcrop of a microgranite with white crystals of feldspar set in a fine-grained, pink matrix. Enormous quantities of this stone were quarried, at Crarae and Furnace, mostly for road setts. It was used locally as a building stone in Inveraray, for example in the Bell Tower, in parts of the parish church and in the sea wall. There is still an aggregate-producing quarry at Furnace. Granite and quartz diorite quarries operated on the E side of Ben Cruachan, just W of Castles Farm. The Cruachan granite is a grey, medium-coarse-grained hornblende – biotite granite. The long, green-black crystals of hornblende and the black, shiny biotite are very conspicuous. It was extensively used in Oban, for example in the older part of the Columba Hotel and in the interior walls of St Columba's Cathedral. Granites can also be well seen in St Conan's Church, Lochawe. The dark, rather more basic quartz diorite, also quarried to the E of Ben Cruachan, was used in the abutments of Connel Bridge. At the edge of the Ben Cruachan granite, on the shore of Loch Etive at Bonawe, there is a small area of finer-grained, black-and-white speckled granite. This was mainly used for road setts and is still a working quarry, producing aggregates.

The most well-known and widely exported granite occurs on the Ross of Mull. This is a coarse-grained red granite quarried at several localities, all close to the coast and with their own jetties. It was used locally in buildings on Iona from medieval times, but it was also widely used in lighthouses (e.g. Skerryvore) and for docks and bridges all over Britain. There is a possibility that in the future Tormore Quarry may re-open for the supply of facing stone. Granites were imported from the E of Scotland when Oban expanded in the C19. St Columba's Cathedral is largely built of the pink Peterhead granite, while the pillars and dressing stones of Argyll Mansions are from Correnie, in Aberdeenshire.

The main roofing material for smaller buildings until quite recently was heather thatch. Slates were used only for larger buildings. The Easdale Slates of Middle Dalradian age outcrop widely in the slate islands of Easdale, Seil, Luing and Belnahua. The working was at first on a small scale, with slate being provided for Castle Stalker in 1631 and Ardmaddy Castle in 1676. In the middle of the C18 the industry expanded until hundreds of men were employed and millions of slates exported, by sea, each year. The slate is intensely black with golden cubes of iron pyrite, although this unfortunately may weather to a rusty colour. It was of reasonable quality and could be split into fairly thin sheets. Many of the quarries were below sea level and were flooded in the great storm of 1881. The industry began to decline from that date, although the last quarry, at Balvicar, did not close until the 1960s. The somewhat older but rather similar Ballachulish slate was also widely used in the area. Further S, in an outcrop parallel with the Highland Boundary Fault, is another, younger, slate horizon. Large quarries operated at Luss, on Loch Lomond, where the slate was transported by water, and at Aberfoyle, where a mineral line connected with the railhead at Aberfoyle. The slates here do not contain large crystals of pyrites and may be grey, green or red in colour. They were widely used in the towns and cities of the Midland Valley.

The only other rock used as roofing in this area is a flagstone of Moine age from the Ross of Mull which was quarried for use on Iona. This rock does split into sheets, but these are thicker than can be produced from slates and are thus too heavy for most roofing purposes.

South of the Highland Boundary Fault

To the S of the Highland Boundary Fault, sandstones have long been the preferred building stone. They occur at many horizons in the Old Red Sandstone and the Carboniferous, and large quarries have been extensively developed at some levels (figs. 1 & 3). Old Red Sandstone sediments underlie the broad area of low-lying ground, S of Loch Lomond to Helensburgh, Bute and Campbeltown. The Hill House, in Helensburgh, has walls of local stone although these are harled. A pink sandstone was quarried at Bonhill and at Dalreoch. Many of the sandstones are of excellent quality. They vary in colour from chocolate brown through red, pink and buff to cream. Some are streaked or blotched in colour. There are some coarser sediments in the Old Red Sandstone and these may be used locally but are not generally preferred for building because the pebbles may drop out.

Carboniferous sediments are found further S, and sediments of similar age are also found in Bute and near Campbeltown. Most of the older buildings on the Isle of Bute, including Rothesay Castle, were constructed of sandstones from the Old Red Sandstone or Carboniferous, quarried locally. In Victorian times, when rail transport became available, many quarries in the Central Belt, with their good-quality cream or buff sandstones, expanded their production and many of the Victorian country- and town-houses throughout the area and beyond were built of this 'imported' stone.

FIGURE 2. Geological succession of rocks in Argyll and Bute

Youngest rocks at top of table	* more important building stone
Tertiary	extensive basaltic lava flows in Inner Hebrides numerous small intrusions of dolerite
Cretaceous – Jurassic	buff/cream sandstones*, shales, thin limestones
Trias – Permian	red sandstones*
Carboniferous	white/ yellow/pink sandstones* shales, coals Basaltic lavas
Old Red Sandstone	brown, reddish, buff sandstones* some conglomerates Andesitic and basaltic lavas
Dalradian	slates*, phyllites, mica schists, marble, quartzites green schists*, epidiorites*
Moine	granulites and gneisses
Torridonian	reddish brown sandstones
Lewisian	gneisses
Granite intrusions of more than one age*	

FIGURE 3. Sandstones used as building stone in Argyll and Bute

Cretaceous	SE Mull green, glauconitic C13	Pennygown Church, Mull
Jurassic	Carsaig, Mull buff, greenish C12–C19	Ardchattan Priory
Triassic	Ardtornish, Morvern buff C13–C19	Aros and Duart Castles, Mull
Permian	Corrie, Arran St Bees, Cumbria red C18–C19	Argyll Mansions, Oban Bonawe Iron Works
Carboniferous	Inninmore, Morvern white/yellow C18–C19	Ardtornish Castle
	Bridge of Awe white/pink C13	Kilchurn Castle
	Giffnock cream C18–C19	Oban Parish Church
Old Red Sandstone	Dalreoch red/pink C18–C19	The Hill House, Helensburgh
Torridonian	Iona reddish brown C12	Iona Abbey (part)

PREHISTORIC AND EARLY HISTORIC ARGYLL AND BUTE

BY J.N. GRAHAM RITCHIE

The discovery of the archaeology of Argyll and Bute owes much to the indefatigable sense of exploration of c18 and c19 antiquarian travellers. The parish ministers in the preparation of the entries for the *Statistical Accounts* (1791–9) and the *New Statistical Account* (1845) had recorded, to varying degrees, the most visible antiquities and the traditions associated with them. Thus by the time that the first Ordnance Survey maps were being surveyed on the ground a remarkable amount of information about the location and traditions of the forts, duns, cairns and standing stones could be incorporated. Nor was the area neglected as the new science of archaeological prospecting and excavation gained acceptance. Canon William Greenwell's excavations in Kilmartin in 1864 may have left many questions unanswered, but they were promptly reported in the *Proceedings of the Society of Antiquaries of Scotland* and helped to alert antiquarians to the richness of the area. The Society's own campaigns of excavation in 1904-5 and 1929 examined several fortifications and burial cairns. The techniques of the day meant that the disentangling of phases in stone-built structures, still a difficult and time-consuming operation, could not be adequately addressed. Nevertheless an impressive array of artefacts was added to the national collections. The extensive sheets of decorated rock surfaces, particularly cup-and-ring markings, had been well known from the time of Sir James Young Simpson's publication in 1868. Prehistoric antiquities in Argyll and Bute have been listed on several occasions, in guidebooks prepared by local societies and, for Argyll, in the *Inventories* of the Royal Commission on the Ancient and Historical Monuments of Scotland. Thus, as with 'Buildings of Scotland, *Highland and Islands*', this volume is selective in the inclusion of archaeological sites in order to maintain the focus on the *Buildings of* . . . rather than on the *Archaeology of* Argyll and Bute.

The first people began to make their way into Argyll and Bute from before 7000 B.C., by which time the inhospitable conditions of late glacial times were being replaced by warmer weather and by a range of vegetation and fauna that could provide food and shelter for the groups of hunters, fishermen and foragers. Such a way of life, known as MESOLITHIC, made use of the resources of the land and sea and depended on an intimate knowledge of the seasonal bounties of Nature's larder. It did not involve more than the simplest habitation sites or the use of caves. This way of life continued until the introduction of a knowledge of farming practice, some three thousand years later. The discovery of scatters of small flint tools, or microliths, shows the presence of groups of hunters and foragers in many parts of Argyll and Bute, notably round Campbeltown Bay, on Islay, Jura and Bute. Bone artefacts and animal remains do not survive in normal conditions, but excavations at two exceptional groups of sites, caves round Oban Bay and mounds of shell on Oronsay, have greatly expanded our information about the economy of this period. Formerly the material from Oban and Oronsay was seen as so different from the microlithic artefacts of other areas that it was accorded separate status as the *Obanian Culture*: bone and antler tools, including 'mattocks', barbed points, pins and boring implements. Special types of stone tools and pitted pebbles, perhaps hammer- or anvil-stones, have been discovered. Current assessment, however, is that the excavations revealed distinctive aspects of a broader way of life and that either differential patterns of preservation, or the residue of seasonal activities at certain times of year, or both, have resulted in the distinct artefact assemblage. On Oronsay examination of the fish-remains (predominantly of saithe or coalfish) in the middens has shown that different sites were used for fish processing at different times of the year. Settlement evidence has been limited to the discovery of stake holes that may indicate the erection of temporary shelters around a central hearth. Pits for storage (including hazelnutshells) have been found on Colonsay. The archaeological information about mesolithic activity in Argyll and Bute may be fragmentary, but it indicates well-adapted groups making the best use of the natural resources around them and a knowledge of transport by water, although the types of vessels are not known. Ethnographic parallels for the social organization even of such scattered groups show that there may have been greater complexity than may be apparent from the surviving artefacts.

At about 4000 B.C. the knowledge of agriculture and stock-rearing became widespread in Argyll and Bute and the economic basis changed radically to one described as NEOLITHIC. The archaeological evidence is more extensive than in the preceding Mesolithic Period, for there are not only recognizable monuments but also chance discoveries of stone axes, the essential tool for clearing trees and scrub for fields and for shaping timber for building purposes. The distribution of CHAMBERED CAIRNS designed to receive the dead of such farming groups is an important indicator of the spread of the new way of life. Such cairns are comparatively common in coastal Kintyre, southern Islay, western Bute, Kilmartin, along Loch Fyne and Loch Awe. There are more isolated examples at the southern end of Loch Lomond and around Oban; and a single cairn has been identified in eastern Mull. The major architectural feature of such monuments is the slab-built chamber set within a large cairn, but accessible from the outside, of the type known as *Clyde Cairns*. The chamber comprised a number of compartments, the side slabs of which overlapped one another, with lower slabs set crosswise to increase support. The height of the chamber might be increased with the use of drystone walling, before a roof of large slabs was engineered into place. Many cairns appear to have been built in stages, either with additional compartments added to a simple structure, and the cairn enlarged, or with several (originally separate) chambers incorporated within one cairn, as at Glenvoiden, on Bute. In some cases, as at Nether Largie South, Kilmartin, the chamber is clearly a unitary structure, with the four compartments constructed of massive overlapping slabs and drystone walling. At many cairns an impressive façade of upright slabs flanked the entrance, with the tallest stones on either side of the entrance and the others diminishing in size towards the tips of the façade. The burial chambers were clearly used over a long period of time, and it is likely that earlier burials were swept to one side or cleared out altogether to make way for later interments. Only a small number of chambered cairns has been excavated with the care that would now be demanded, but several types of artefacts are commonly found with the burials, including round-based vessels sometimes decorated with impressions and incisions (the fine assemblages from Beacharra, Kintyre, and Glenvoiden, Bute, are on display in the Campbeltown Museum and the Bute Museum, Rothesay, respectively). Several flint artefacts have also been recovered.

Chambered cairns were in some cases remodelled in later times with the insertion of secondary burials in cists (slab-built coffins) and the cairn perhaps enlarged in area. This can most clearly be seen at Nether Largie South.

The cairns at Achnacree and Achnacreebeag, North Connel, belong to a distinct category of monument known as *Passage Graves*, more common in the Hebrides than in Argyll and Bute. The chamber of the former is now hidden, but the short passage and small oval chamber of the latter can still be seen. This is a monument of two distinct periods as a simple chamber of large boulders was surrounded by a circular cairn; the passage grave was set into the SE side of the cairn, which was then increased in size.

Chambered cairns would certainly require a degree of communal effort on the part of small farming groups, but other forms of ceremonial sites that involved considerable engineering skill were also built. It is likely that many of the single STANDING STONES and linear arrangements of standing stones also belong to the Neolithic Period. The reasons behind the setting up of such impressive monoliths can only be guessed at, but there is a sense of the creation of a landscape designed to provide a backdrop for ritual events associated with death or seasonal ceremonial. The visitor will see many more chambered cairns and standing stones marked on the OS maps than can be included here. The ritual landscape is helpfully explained in the displays at Kilmartin House.

Similarly no attempt has been made to describe the many groups of rock-carvings, known as CUPMARKINGS or CUP-AND-RING MARKINGS, but rather to concentrate on the more architectural aspects of prehistory. However, the dramatic rocksheets at Achnabreck, Kilmichael Glassary, and Cairnbaan are such integral parts of the prehistoric ritual landscapes of Mid Argyll that they must surely be included. Pecked into the smooth natural rock surfaces are small cupmarks, often surrounded by concentric rings creating extensive patterns made up of many separate motifs. In some examples a linear groove or gutter runs from the central cup to the outer ring. The repertoire is more restricted than the rock art of Brittany for example, but the effect (particularly in the late afternoon sun) is very striking. Other motifs include spirals, peltae and stars. Decoration of this type occurs not only on natural rock surfaces but also on standing stones, and a cup and a cup-and-ring marking has been found on a structural slab in a chambered cairn at Ardmarnock, in Cowal. Many interpretations have been offered for cupmarks and cup-and-ring markings, including celestial symbolism, but their significance is not known.

Several of the complex settings of standing stones, particularly in Kilmartin, are also decorated with cupmarks and cup-and-ring markings, notably Ballymeanoch and Nether Largie. The settings are linear arrangements of monoliths, with their flatter faces on the same axis as at Ballymeanoch or Dervaig on Mull. Standing stones are also found in close association with round cairns, as at Kintraw. There are very few STONE CIRCLES in Argyll and Bute and they have a very scattered distribution: two at Hough, Tiree, although all but one stone have been toppled; a fine circle at Lochbuie, Mull; Cultoon, Islay; Kilchattan, Bute; Strontoiller, near Oban; and Temple Wood in Kilmartin. Extensive excavation at Temple Wood has shown a sequence of building development that is unparalleled in Argyll. The earliest feature was a ring of upright timbers for which there is a radiocarbon date that suggests that it was set up early in the fourth millennium B.C. This appears to have been superseded by a free-standing ring of uprights, two of which bear pecked decoration (a double oval and a double spiral); several small cairns containing cists were later added and the upright stones were linked by walling; cairn material was piled up outside the central area, and latterly this too was filled in to create a circular mass of cairn material. This sequence of ritual activity over a long period gives an impression of how such a monument may change in function over time.

By the later third millennium B.C. communal burial in chambered cairns was no longer practised and individual interment in a stone-lined cist or coffin became the norm. Some cists were covered by round cairns of stones, and such cairns are a familiar part of the Argyll landscape dating from the BRONZE AGE. Many other burial cists were not marked in any way, and these are discovered only in the course of ploughing or land development. Round cairns are sometimes dramatically situated on a hilltop, others form cemetery groups, while yet others occur singly, indicating perhaps a single burial of an important individual. In some cases later burials were inserted into an existing cairn. The cairns of the Kilmartin area are among the most interesting to visit because several display unusual features in the construction of the burial cists that they covered, and these are displayed in ways that can still be seen today. A number of the slabs which were used to form such cists were decorated in distinctive ways, and representations of bronze axeheads can be seen at Nether Largie North and Ri Cruin, both in the Kilmartin Valley. The construction of a stone coffin has parallels with joinery construction, but it is only in Argyll that this influence is reflected in stone, with several examples having a groove pecked out of the side slabs to receive the end slabs, rather in the manner of tongued-and-grooved woodwork. Ri Cruin is one example. Discovered at Badden, to the N of Lochgilphead, one of the finest side slabs decorated with lozenge ornament and with two distinct grooves is now on display in Glasgow Art Gallery and Museum. Such sophisticated use of woodworking techniques is a reminder of the importance of timber in domestic construction, even if traces are scant, while the ornamentation in stone may imply that there was also elaborate interior decoration in materials such as timber or woven fabrics. Only a very few settlements of Neolithic and Bronze Age date have been identified in the past, but a greater understanding of the types of structure and their associated fields is now growing as a result of excavation.

The Bronze Age monuments of Argyll and Bute are important landmarks in the landscape for residents and visitors alike, but the range of artefacts, pottery, bronzework, necklaces in jet, ornaments in gold, speaks of contact over wide areas and of a complex society that the monuments alone cannot suggest. The major displays of such objects may be found in the Museum of Scotland, Edinburgh.

By the middle of the first millennium B.C. the nature of the archaeological evidence changes from one in which ritual and burial monuments predominate to one in which defensive structures in stone are the most numerous, and the term IRON AGE becomes appropriate. The Ordnance Survey sheets contain many mentions of FORTS, BROCHS and DUNS, and among the unresolved questions relating to the archaeology of Argyll and Bute are the details of classification and chronology of the drystone defensive structures of later first millennium B.C. and early first millennium A.D. date. The position is not helped by the fact that so few of these structures have been excavated in the past or that those excavations that were undertaken almost a hundred years ago were less than satisfactory. The small number of sites examined in more recent times, although indicating individual sequences or chronological pointers, has not provided the ready template for the area as a whole. The classification may be clear at certain monuments: *brochs* are circular drystone walled constructions with a median gallery within the wall either from ground level or from first-floor level, and a distinct ledge or scarcement on the inside to help support internal timber arrangements, sometimes with external defences; *duns* are small circular or less regular structures (their shape often dictated by the rock stack on which they were built), also sometimes with external defences; *forts* are larger defensive works, enclosing a sufficient area for several houses as well as the cattle of the local community. Most brochs are found in N Scotland, Orkney, Shetland and the Hebrides, and only a very few are located in Argyll; Dun Mor Vaul, Tiree, and Tirefour, Lismore, are, however, well-preserved examples. A date of C I B.C.–A.D. C I is proposed for their construction, but it is likely that all such drystone-walled buildings were used over long periods in differing guises. The small number of radiocarbon dates and the unsatisfactory evidence from the few forts that have been excavated combine to suggest that some have an origin in the later first millennium B.C. In a number of cases the stone wall-construction was strengthened by the use of timbers set within the wall to help add to the stability. The employment of this technique is not a chronological indicator, for it has been used at several periods of drystone construction.

When such a timber-laced wall catches fire, either accidentally or as a result of enemy action (during attack or as a deliberate slighting), the beams may burn with such intensity that the wall-core fuses into masses of vitrified stone. Such masses of vitrified material may be found at the entrance, as this area was for reasons of defence particularly strengthened with cross-timbers; but often the masses of fused stone may be seen all round the perimeter. In some cases the fire was of such intensity that whole sections of the burning walls seem to have rolled downhill, as at Carradale, in Kintyre. One of the most characteristic forts is that on the ridge at Dunagoil, on Bute; other forts on elongated ridges include Dun mac Sniachan, Benderloch, Lorn, and Dun Skeig, Kintyre. The latter site is one of the few where a structural sequence can be inferred; the rather fugitive remains of the ridge-top fort are overlain by two later fortifications, one at each end of the ridge. A small timber-laced structure at the SW end, now heavily vitrified, appears to be earlier than a well-preserved drystone dun at the NE end, for lumps of vitrified material have been incorporated into the building core. In this case at least the dun appears to be late in the sequence.

The classification of the small defensive drystone structures of Argyll and Bute has undergone careful scrutiny in recent years. The initial rationale behind the distinction between forts and duns was made on size; the latter were thought of as circular, sub-circular or oval on plan not exceeding about 375sq. m., though the rock stack on which a dun might be built might well dictate its ground plan. The size was what might be expected for a prehistoric house, and indeed duns were no more than stoutly defended houses in a local style that made much use of drystone walling. A distinction might be made between those duns that might readily be roofed (dun-houses) and those that were rather larger and more probably contained an internal structure as well as open areas (dun-enclosures). More recently it has been suggested that the majority of the structures of the W coast should be seen as part of a wide tradition of Atlantic Round Houses, embracing brochs, duns and other Hebridean forms. This approach is useful in that it stresses that classification should not be seen as a straitjacket and that many sites, particularly unexcavated field monuments, will be difficult to classify. In the present volume the classification of the various *Inventory* volumes has been followed, as these will normally be mirrored on the appropriate Ordnance Survey maps, but the problems of nomenclature are fully recognized.

The dating of this broad building tradition is also the subject of discussion. The discovery of artefacts of C1–2 A.D. date certainly suggests that some belong to this span, though the possibility that the objects are not related to the construction phases has to be borne in mind. Some objects are of Roman origin and are reminders that, although Argyll and Bute were never occupied by Roman military authority, the Firth of Clyde was a Roman seaway with naval access to the W end of the Antonine Wall in C2 A.D. as well as to a series of coastal forts. The names of the various tribes are recorded by classical geographers, and there is every reason to think that regular trade took place. The circumnavigation of Scotland by Agricola's fleet in A.D. 83 may have brought the W islands of Argyll into contact with Roman authority. Objects dating from the middle of the first millennium A.D. have also been recovered and these have been used to infer a later date. Given the disparate nature of the sites, there is every reason to accept the earlier origin for some duns, doubtless with later reoccupation, and a mid-first-millennium origin for others, within a political framework that will be outlined below. Most forts and duns are on private land and care should be exercised in obtaining permission to visit them. Some are on the lines of Forestry Commission trails and may be visited if forestry working allows.

The middle of the first millennium A.D. saw Argyll and Bute move gradually from prehistory into history, albeit very tentatively. The movement of people from Ireland into Argyll had probably been underway for some time before the traditional transfer (under Fergus Mor, son of Erc) of the capital of the kingdom of Dál Riata from Dunseverick, on the Antrim coast, to Scotland. A monastery was founded by Columba on Iona in A.D. 563 and the important archaeological remains of the Early Christian Period in Argyll and Bute are the subject of the next section. The secular evidence results from excavations at Dunadd, near Kilmartin, and Dunollie, on the outskirts of Oban. Although no structural remains can now be seen at Dunollie, careful excavation revealed that the summit of a prominent rock stack had been the seat of a local chieftain in C7–9 A.D., for fine metal-working appropriate to a centre of authority was being undertaken. Excavations on Dunadd have shown that, although there was intermittent activity on the site between C1 and C6 A.D., the major structural elements belong to the C7, and the major work as it is seen today belongs to C8–C9 A.D. The entrance is through a natural gully and the interior was doubtless filled with the timber halls and workshops of an important leader. The fort has particular interest because of the series of rock carvings including a boar, an ogham inscription and the pecked hollow of a footprint (there is also a less certain second print). The ogham alphabet consists of groups of one to five strokes placed in various positions relative to a median stem-line. Dunadd has been interpreted as the place of royal inauguration by the kings of Dál Riata. The Dunadd inscription appears to be written in the Irish language. Dunadd is mentioned in two early sources. A siege at 'Dun Att' is recorded in the Annals of Ulster for A.D. 683, and in A.D. 736 the same Annals record that 'Aengus son of Fergus, king of the Picts, laid waste the kingdom of Dal Riata and seized Dun At'. With such tentative entries the history of Argyll and Bute begins.

VIKING activity in Argyll is recorded in the Annals of Innisfallen for the year A.D. 795 with the devastation of Iona, and from that time the islands of the S Inner Hebrides were on the major sea-route between the Norse spheres of influence in Orkney, Shetland and the Western Isles and Ireland. In subsequent centuries settlement followed, although no confirmed habitation sites have so far been found in Argyll itself. Place-names illustrate the importance of the Norse in identifying parts of the landscape with distinctive linguistic elements like *dalr* (dale) that are present in many parts of Argyll today, but particularly those where Norse influence was likely to have been strongest, including Islay, Jura, Mull and Kintyre. Another element of naming relates more specifically to farms, and names that incorporate *bolstaðr* are found in Coll, Tiree, Mull, Islay and Jura. Norse graves are a clear indication of settlement, however, and on Colonsay, Oronsay, and Islay burials with distinctive Norse artefacts mostly of later C9 and C10 date have been discovered; the objects are now in the Museum of Scotland, Edinburgh. The graves are of warriors, as indicated by their swords, and of women with more domestic equipment; the most distinctive burials are those from Ballinaby, Islay, and Kiloran Bay, Colonsay, where in 1882 the burial of a man was discovered in a stone setting, accompanied by an iron sword and other weapons, a balance and decorated weights, and cross-marked slabs; outside the setting lay the skeleton of a horse. Boat rivets found over the burial enclosure suggest that it may originally have been covered by an upturned boat. The sand hills of the islands may yet reveal the settlements to which such burials relate.

ARGYLL AND BUTE: MONUMENTS OF THE EARLY CHRISTIAN PERIOD

BY IAN FISHER

The settlers in the Irish colony of Dál Riata (Argyll) were probably Christian already in the early C6. The religion was consolidated by the monasteries of Iona, founded in 563 by Colum Cille or Columba (†597), Lismore founded by Moluag (†592), and Kingarth in Bute, associated with Blaan. As in many Irish sites, the most prominent remains at each of these monasteries are of the *vallum* or enclosing rampart. At Iona this apppears to have reached a maximum area of about 8ha. as the monastery developed, and includes impressive standing earthworks and buried ditches whose excavation has produced a range of C7 timber artefacts. At Lismore an oval enclosure is partially defined by field boundaries, and at Kingarth a stone wall, rebuilt in the 1890s, curves out from a cliff-face to enclose a two-level churchyard. Historical evidence shows that early churches and monastic buildings were mainly of timber, 'in the Irish style', and remains of circular and rectangular buildings, constructed in post-holes or with sill-beams, have been excavated at Iona. The grouping of major crosses W of the medieval abbey church suggests that the liturgical focus, including the principal early church, was in that area, and a small stone chapel of Irish type, rebuilt in the 1960s, may mark the original site of Columba's burial. Excavations at Iona and Kingarth have produced evidence of metal- and other craft-working, while Lismore preserves a notable relic, the *bachuil* or crozier of its founder saint, in the custody of its hereditary family of keepers at Bachuil House.

Abbot Adomnán's *Life of Columba* of about 690 shows that Iona had subsidiary monasteries on Tiree and other islands, and the search for an isolated hermitage or *dìseart*, a 'desert place in the ocean', was an important element in Columban monasticism. Oval enclosures from sites of this nature remain at Kenvara on Tiree, at the N end of Kerrera, at Kilbride on the E shore of Loch Fyne, and on Nave Island (Islay). The monastic site on the rocky island of Eileach an Naoimh (Garvellach Islands), associated in local tradition with St Brendan 'the Navigator', rises in a series of terraces from the landing-place to a circular inner enclosure. Overlooking the site is 'Eithne's Grave', a small circular grave-enclosure with a marker bearing a simple cross of early type, and near the shore there is a drystone double beehive cell resembling examples in w Ireland. The crosses carved on the walls of caves in Mull, Knapdale and Kintyre may have originated with their use by hermits, added to by later pilgrims.

While archaeological evidence confirms the picture of a hierarchy of monasteries given by Adomnán, the pattern of lay worship and burial is less clear. The wide distribution of place-names beginning in 'Kil-' (Gaelic *Cill*, 'church' or 'burial-ground') suggests considerable provision by about 800, and many of these sites preserve early sculpture. The excavation of small chapels at St Ronan's Church, Iona, and at St Ninian's Point, Bute, has shown that both overlay earlier burials. Remains of other small drystone or clay-mortared chapels are found throughout Argyll, most commonly on Islay, and they may represent the provision made by individual farmers or estate-owners for itinerant clerics. The closest parallels are found in the Isle of Man, where the distribution of *keills* or chapels is thought to relate to Norse land-ownership, and their date within the Early Christian period remains uncertain. The veneration for holy wells, which originated in pre-Christian times, was widespread, and many were associated with saints. Most of these now appear as natural springs, but a cross-slab stands beside a fine slab-lined well at Kilmory Oib, Knapdale.

The most widespread evidence of Christian activity is stone-carving, which ranges from simple cross-incised pillars or slabs, resembling those found at hermit sites and small monasteries in w Ireland, to some of the largest and most elaborate high crosses in the British Isles. Such monuments could serve not only as personal memorials but as the focus of prayer and preaching, for even if a chapel existed it might be too small to house the congregation. The thin ringless cross at Kilnave (Islay), with its fine panels of spiral ornament, may have marked a centre of worship in an area of domestic settlement, served from an offshore monastic site on Nave Island. Crosses might also mark monastic or churchyard entrances or areas of sanctuary, and processional or pilgrimage routes. About 350 examples survive at 110 sites in Argyll and Bute, with a mainly coastal distribution. Over one hundred of these carvings are on Iona, and there is a remarkable concentration in the Knapdale area, with about thirty at the burial-ground of Cladh a'Bhile, Ellary, and smaller groups at Kilmory Knap and Keills. In contrast, the area of Lorn to the N, with very similar topography, preserves carvings at only five sites, and most of these are of late character. A varied group from the offshore island of

Inchmarnock, now in Bute Museum, may be of monastic origin, but the few early stones recorded at the nearby monastery of Kingarth have been lost. Simple crosses also extend as far E as Luss on the shore of Loch Lomond and Kilmahew near Cardross, although this area belonged to the British kingdom of Strathclyde.

Many of these carvings bear incised linear crosses, plain or with forked or barred terminals, and outline crosses are also numerous. Both forms were often ornamented with hollows in the armpits, and later outline crosses have rings copied from high crosses, while features such as pointed bases might be inspired by early timber crosses of the type mentioned by Adomnán and Bede. One Iona graveslab bears a ringed cross with a circular base, perhaps inspired by the 'cross fixed in a millstone' that marked a site where Columba had rested, shortly before his death. A frequent feature, seen especially at Cladh a'Bhile, is the multiplication of crosses, for example the placing of several incised crosslets in the angles or on the arms of an outline cross. Many of the cross-forms were inspired by types familiar in the E Mediterranean world, or in Gaul. These included the six-pointed marigold, of which a fine example ornaments a pillar at Cladh a'Bhile, and equal-armed crosses formed by intersecting arcs. An attractive gravemarker of this type at Iona bears a loop converting the cross into the Chi-Rho (the first two Greek letters of the name 'Christ'), a favourite Christian symbol since the time of Constantine. This stone commemorates Echoid but there are few other inscriptions, even at the highly literate monastery of Iona, and they take the form of simple requests for prayers for individuals identified only by Christian name. Many of the monuments at Iona are marked by a simplicity continuing the ascetic tradition of the founder, Columba, whose grave was marked by the rounded boulder that he had used as a pillow. The dating of these carvings is notoriously difficult, for simple forms might be copied over a long period, but most of them probably date between C7 and C9, with the outline crosses continuing rather later. Simple cruciform stones, found as gravemarkers at remote hermitages from Skellig Michael (Co. Kerry) to North Rona, also occur at Iona. The most elaborate of the type, from Riasg Buidhe on Colonsay, has the face of Christ in the top arm and a fish-like body, which refers to another familiar Early Christian symbol.

The only significant carvings without crosses are the small group of stones bearing inscriptions in the Irish ogham alphabet, composed of groups of strokes of varying number and angle. The much-weathered pillar at Kilchattan (Gigha), which appears to be of the form 'X son of Y', and a small stone reading 'CRONAN', from a burial at Poltalloch, resemble early Irish inscriptions in using an angle of the stone as the base-line. The largely illegible ogham on a rock-surface in the great hill-fort of Dunadd is associated with a sunken footprint and an incised boar of Pictish type, and may have played a part in the inauguration of kings of Dál Riata. A short ogham inscription, probably a single personal name, appears with an incomplete Roman alphabet on a recently discovered stone at Lochgoilhead.

By the C8 Iona was the head of a powerful group of monasteries in Scotland and Ireland, with links to Pictland and Northumbria. Artistic connections with all of these areas are seen in the early stone crosses of the monastery, as well as in the Book of Kells, the most elaborate of Irish manuscripts, which was probably also produced on Iona in the second half of the C8. The Irish tradition of timber crosses, attested at Iona in Columba's time, is perpetuated in the mortice-and-tenon joints of St Oran's and St John's Crosses. The same technique was used to add ring-segments to the latter, perhaps repairing an early fall and thus creating the first ringed cross. Its arms, with an immense span of 2.2m., were double-curved like those of the narrower Northumbrian crosses, and it may have been inspired by them, but its ornamental language was purely Celtic, with intricate interlace and spiralwork. A favourite motif which links the crosses at Iona and that at Kildalton (Islay), despite their varying proportions, was the cruciform grouping of bosses surrounded by undulating serpents, some with fierce dragon-heads. This motif is also found in the Book of Kells and in metal-work of the period, and it seems that the carvers of Iona, with no native tradition to draw on, were creating an ornamental repertoire from the monastic arts of illumination and church treasures. This experimental character is also seen in the geology of the crosses, which extends from the unsatisfactory Mull mica-schist of St Oran's Cross to the chlorite-schist and epidiorite, imported from the distant Loch Sween area, of St John's and St Martin's Crosses. Their figure sculpture was entirely biblical in character, emphasizing familiar Early Christian examples of God's salvation, with the Virgin and Child appearing three times and Daniel and Abraham's sacrifice of Isaac each twice. St Martin's Cross, the one Iona cross that still stands in its original position, shows all three of these scenes, as well as musicians who may include David as harper. The fine cross at Kildalton adds to the theme of sacrifice with Cain's murder of Abel, and surrounding the cross-head are four high-relief lions, perhaps symbolizing Christ as the Lion of Judah. The latest of the Iona group of crosses is at Keills (Knapdale), an important ferry-point from Islay and Jura, where the stubby ringless head displays Daniel with several agile lions, and a winged figure which may combine references to St Michael and the eagle symbol of St John.

Iona was repeatedly attacked by Norse raiders in the early C9, and the headship of the Columban family of monasteries, along with the tradition of sculpture, was finally transferred to Kells (Co. Meath), but the community survived. The damaged St Matthew's Cross has an Adam and Eve scene that is almost identical with one at Kells. The C10 also saw a vogue for cross-slabs, perhaps inspired by those of E Scotland. An earlier example, beside a holy well at Kilmory Oib (Knapdale), shows a cross surrounded by birds in the Mediterranean tradition, and there are notable slabs at Ardchattan (Lorn), including musicians, and Kilfinan (Cowal) with fierce dragon-and-boss ornament. The Norse settlers in the Western Isles themselves became Christian, and an Iona graveslab combines an Irish interlaced cross with the runic inscription 'Kali

Iona, St John's Cross; Iona, St Martin's Cross

son of Ölvir laid this stone over his brother Fugl', while a slab from Dòid Mhàiri (Islay), now in the Museum of Scotland, bears florid foliage in the Scandinavian Ringerike style. At Kingarth there are numerous round-headed gravemarkers, almost unknown elsewhere in Scotland, but with Anglo-Saxon parallels and probably of the CII. Other carvings at that site and at Rothesay have connections with the Scandinavian-influenced art of Govan and other sites in Strathclyde, including armed riders. Also of Anglo-Scandinavian inspiration is the unique 'hogback' monument at Luss, which was altered in the C12 with ornament in the Romanesque style.

MEDIEVAL CHURCHES AND MONUMENTS

For centuries Iona, the islands and the Argyll mainland maintained their close links with Ireland. In the long run, however, the Celtic church, lacking hierarchical structure and without territorial organization, failed to establish itself. Despite extending its influence N and E into Pictland and Northumbria, by the beginning of the C8 it was already in retreat before Rome. By the middle of the C9, Norse raids and settlement along the fringes of the W coast from the Hebrides to the Isle of Man and Anglesey had made contact with Ireland difficult and dangerous. Dalriada in Scotland, its religious and secular links with Ireland in jeopardy, now allied itself with the Picts under Kenneth MacAlpin, a step which not only marked the beginning of the unification of modern Scotland but also helped to ensure the spiritual dominance of the Roman church. As Strathclyde and Lothian were brought under the Scottish crown, Norse settlement intensified along the W seaboard. While Roman religious polity was gradually extended, Celtic Christianity struggled. By the C10, however, the Norsemen themselves had become Christian and in 980 the Norse king of Dublin made a pilgrimage to Iona. By c. 1100, Norse power extended over the W isles and parts of the Argyll mainland, including the peninsula of Kintyre.

Half a century later an army raised in Argyll under Somerled took back Kintyre and the recapture of the W isles began. By 1156, Mull, Islay and the other islands S of Ardnamurchan had been taken from the Norsemen. Somerled himself was of Celtic-Norse descent and, like his brother-in-law Godfrey, king of Man, seems to have ruled subject to the competing overlordship of the kings of Norway and Scotland. An attempt to gain the Scottish crown failed and in 1164 Somerled was defeated by Malcolm IV and killed at Renfrew. Sovereignty in the W remained in doubt and it was not until 1263 when the Norsemen were finally crushed at Largs that the Hebrides were fully ceded to Scotland. Even then, and for centuries to come, descendants of Somerled maintained a more or less unchallenged authority along the Atlantic seaboard: the Clan Dougall in Mull and Lorn, the MacDonald Lords of the Isles (whose title *Dominus Insularum* was granted by David II in 1354) in Islay, Kintyre and Morvern. Meanwhile, increasingly integrated with the feudal nature of the unified Scottish state, the Roman church extended its authority too. A diocese of Argyll came into existence in the 1180s, though it was not formally recognized by the Pope until the middle of the C13. Later still, c. 1380, a Scottish diocese of the Isles was designated, though the original diocese of the Isles, or Sodor, which had been subject to the archbishop in Trondheim, Norway, went back to the C12.

Somerled's successes revitalized Christianity's roots in the W. At Saddell in Kintyre, Cistercians from Mellifont, County Armagh, established an abbey, possibly as early as 1160. Little survives, but the arrangement was evidently conventional; a cruciform church some 40m. in length with claustral buildings to the S. On Iona, the small mortuary chapel of St Oran was built and an Augustinian nunnery founded before the end of the C12. Though no more than a gabled oblong, the restored chapel has a W doorway splendidly carved with Romanesque ornament. The nunnery, ruinous but relatively well preserved, comprises a nave-and-aisle church with cloister ranges again conventionally placed S. By the early years of the C13, despite fierce protests from Derry, the Benedictines were building an abbey on Iona to replace the original Columban monastery. The abbey church, which has been subject to construction and reconstruction over several centuries, is cruciform in plan with an aisleless nave and a choir flanked by sacristy and s aisle. Twin chapel recesses in the E wall of the N transept survive from the early C13 (a feature recurring, if barely detectable, in the now much-reduced Valliscaulian* priory founded by Duncan MacDougall, Lord of Lorn, at Ardchattan on Loch Etive in 1230 or 1231). The abbey's conventual buildings lie on the N side of the church, an unusual arrangement though not unique, for a similar plan was later developed at the Augustinian priory established on Oronsay some time during the second quarter of the C14 by John I, Lord of the Isles.

Stylistic comparison suggests that in each of their foundations Somerled and his son Reginald may have engaged Irish masons. The jurisdiction and practices of the Irish clergy might be a thing of the past but in matters of construction and craftsmanship the old links lingered on. The placing of clearstorey windows above the columns of the nave arcade, the use of external angle shafts and stepping stringcourses, the particular character of the decorative carving of capitals and arches; all these were drawn from contemporary Irish work. Nor was this persistent architectural affinity limited to these relatively grander monastic buildings. From Iona and Saddell the influence of Irish Romanesque spread into Argyll, permeating a programme of local church building and reconstruction stimulated by a gradual tightening in parochial administration.

Across Argyll the weathered remains of simple stone-built chapels dating from these days are to be found in abundance. All are oblong in plan. Most are reduced to overgrown footings or low vestigial rubble walling, but many still survive as roofless ruins standing to wall height or as part of the fabric of a later church built on the same site. Of the latter, the tiny St Columba's Shrine, originally freestanding but incorporated into the W front of Iona Abbey in the C15, is exceptional both for its dimensions, little more than 2m. wide by 3m. long, and for its early date, possibly C9 or C10. In general, widths vary between 4m. and 5.5m. and rarely reach 6m. Many C12 and C13 chapels approximate to a double-square in plan: Keills, Kilmory Knap, Gigha and St Oran and St Ronan on Iona are in this respect typical. But lengths vary, with a few examples, such as the C13 Dunstaffnage Chapel and the slightly later Kilbrannan Chapel at Skipness, exceeding 20m. The Church of St Moluag, Lismore, established as the cathedral church of the Argyll diocese in the early C14, reached 40m. overall, with an internal nave and choir width of 7.2m. Though these relatively larger buildings tended to be more developed in architectural detail and ornament, certain features recur whatever the length. Coupled lights in the E gable, small symmetrically opposed N and S windows flanking the altar

*The Valliscaulians were a C13 French order whose practices were modelled on the Cistercians. They established only three priories in Britain, all in Scotland, at Ardchattan, Beauly and Pluscarden. Each Valliscaulian community was limited to twenty, including lay-brothers.

area, a doorway in the N wall; all or some of these appear in C13 chapels at Dunstaffnage, Eilean Mór, Faslane, Kilbride (Rhudil) and Kilmory Knap, as well as in the contemporary parish churches of Killean (Kintyre), Kilmarie on Loch Craignish, Kildalton on Islay and Inch Kenneth off Mull. But since these same features are also to be found in later medieval examples, their presence can be considered no more reliable a guide to dating than the use of round-headed or pointed arches, whose incidence seems similarly unrelated to any clear chronological pattern.

The unicameral rectangular plan is ubiquitous. Masonry recesses occasionally indicate the existence of a timber screen separating nave from chancel, for example at Southend and Skipness in Kintyre, Kilchattan on Luing, Kilvickeon on Mull, and at Dunstaffnage, but there is almost no evidence of any architectural development of this idea. A two-chamber church did exist at Kilmun, the only collegiate endowment in Argyll, but all trace of this C15 building save its W tower (also unique in Argyll) disappeared in C19 changes. On Bute, however, hidden in a hollow in the hills at the S end of the island, is the roofless C12 church of St Blane, nave and slightly narrower chancel (part C13) clearly divided one from the other by a high rubble gable. A communicating round-arched opening carved with chevron moulding underlines the Romanesque character of this unique and disturbingly atmospheric rural chapel.

Of medieval church furnishings there is almost no evidence. Some altar bases remain and at Oronsay Priory there is a late C15 *mensa*, extremely plain but housing an aumbry recess. At Inishail on Loch Awe, a horizontal slab carved with a crucifixion scene and several armed figures is believed to be an early C16 altar frontal. Late medieval stone fonts with basins cut in circular or hexagonal blocks survive at Caibeal Mheamhair on Mull and Kilchiaran, Islay; another is rehoused at All Saints Church, Inveraray.

Astonishingly, perhaps, the most outstanding religious MONU-MENTS in Argyll are among those that survive from the earliest Christian period. The three great high crosses of Iona dedicated to SS Oran, John and Martin are magnificent examples of the art and craftsmanship of the Celtic church in the late C8. Though undoubtedly linked to a sculptural type common in Ireland and Northern Britain, these freestanding Iona crosses may represent an experimental group whose pelleted bosses, serpent swirls and spiral ornament appear to have been derived as much from Hiberno-Saxon metalwork and jewellery techniques as from the sinuously beautiful Pictish motifs of the Book of Kells. The ringed cross-head, fortuitously introduced in the repair of St John's Cross and repeated in St Martin's, reappears as a majestic halo to the monolithic Kildalton Cross, Islay, C8. Closely related though ringless are the Kilnave Cross, also on Islay, C8, and the Keills Cross, Loch na Cille, early C9. The fragmentary St Matthew's Cross, Iona, late C9 or early C10, was evidently also ring-headed, but it is clear from this and various other broken remnants that artistic aspiration had become less ambitious. The freestanding cross nevertheless persisted as a public religious monument until the C16. Many later examples are disc-headed: among them, two late

C14 crosses at Kilchoman, Islay, and MacLean's Cross, Iona, the Oronsay Cross, and the MacMillan Cross, Kilmory Knap, all carved in the last quarter of the C15. Two late C14 crosses, at Campbeltown and Inveraray, have acquired a role more public than religious, becoming elements in the local townscape.

GRAVEMARKERS. Around eighty funerary stones and fragments, dating variously from the C6 to the C11, are in care on Iona. Almost all bear the mark of the cross: incised, sunken or in relief, plain or ringed. Nearly thirty cross-marked stones from the C7 and C8 are gathered in the burial-ground at Cladh a' Bhile, Ellary, Loch Caolisport. Most are upright slabs, including one pillar-stone, early C8, carved with a marigold cross. The finest of its kind in W Scotland, its hexafoil motif is anticipated on a rock-face on Eilean Mór, Loch Sween, which may have been carved as early as the C6 or C7. The concentrations of Early Christian stones on Iona and at Ellary are outstanding, but others are found sporadically in Mid Argyll and on Mull, Tiree and Islay. They are rare in Kintyre and Lorn; at Ardchattan Priory a richly carved cross-decorated upright, C10(?), later trimmed to form a coffin lid, was probably brought to Loch Etive from elsewhere.

Medieval tapered slabs are much more plentiful and broadly dispersed. But again the main collections are to be found in Mid Argyll, at Keills, Kilberry, Kilmarie, Kilmartin, Kilmichael Glassary and Kilmory Knap. Iona, Islay and Oronsay are also well endowed. Tapered slabs of C13 and C14 date are found on Iona but these examples, similar to some found in lowland Scotland, seem to have been superseded by a more distinctly West Highland range of stones. The production of these later, more ubiquitous, decorative gravemarkers, which began in the C14 and lasted until the Reformation, involved five different schools of carvers: Iona, Loch Sween, Loch Awe, Kintyre and Oronsay. While each had its own style, motifs such as the claymore, floral scrolls, bird and animal forms, inset figures, interlacing and knots repeatedly occur. Some slabs bear craft tools, others a galley rigged with furled or full sail. The effigies of priests or military figures may be carved in low or high relief; examples at Kilmory Knap and Kilmartin, C14–C15, and on Iona and Oronsay, C14–C16, are particularly sculptural or decorative in detail. Two full-length figures of C15 ecclesiastics rest opposite each other in the presbytery of Iona Abbey; one, of Abbot John MacKinnon, lies on a base slab inscribed on the edges and carried at the corners on lion pedestals. At Kilmun in Cowal, the almost fully three-dimensional C15 effigies of Sir Duncan Campbell of Lochawe and his wife are of exceptional quality. Originally housed in the medieval church (*see* above), they now lie in the Argyll Mausoleum built at the end of the C18. Two shallow tomb-recesses in the ruinous but recently re-roofed Chapel of St Mary, Rothesay, once the C16 chancel of the town's parish church, contain effigies, probably C16, but these are much weathered and cannot compare with the figures at Kilmun. The cusped arch tomb-recess introduced into St Oran's Chapel, Iona, in the C15 contains no funerary sculpture. A simpler recess set under a semicircular arch in the parish church at Lochgoilhead survives from the chancel of the late medieval church; it too is empty but incorporates two tomb-chest slabs, each carved with an arcade and decorated with rosettes, quatrefoils, shears, etc. Such survivors, whether cover-slabs or sides, are not common. A few, carved with swords, arcading and undulating plants, are to be found at Kilmarie, Kilmartin and Kilmichael Glassary; all are early c16. A tomb-chest lid at Ardchattan Priory, on which six figures stand in canopied Gothic niches, three upon three, carries an inscription recalling the priors Duncan and Dugall MacDougall and the date of the latter's death, 1502.

POST-REFORMATION CHURCHES

The gradual penetration of reformed religion into Argyll and the islands brought an end to monastic life, Roman practices died out or were suppressed and a new, less hieratic form of church polity and worship was introduced. The preaching of the word now acquired as significant a role as the dispensation of the sacraments, a development which had both liturgical and architectural consequences. Change, however, proved more pragmatic than iconoclastic. The few monastic houses were secularized, though not violently abused. Determined destruction was rare but indifference and neglect common. Iona, Oronsay and Saddell (already moribund by the end of the c15) fell into decay and ruin. At Ardchattan the conventual buildings became a dwelling-house. But many existing churches were adapted for Presbyterian use, their chancel furnishings stripped and the focus of worship moved to a pulpit raised against the s wall.

Early reports of repairs to the fabric of these rearranged buildings are plentiful. But few new churches were built. In a century when the Stuart monarchy's persistent attempts to maintain the rule of bishops met with equally intransigent resistance and religious controversy repeatedly led to civil war, this is scarcely surprising. Reformed religion was itself divided and the resolution of theological and liturgical conflict for long remained in doubt. Certainly the Presbyterian cause was by no means immediately dominant nor unchallenged on the islands. Catholicism was never wholly supplanted in the Hebrides and, in the 1620s and '30s, Irish Franciscans made temporary missionary headway in the Ross of Mull and on Oronsay, where their presence may account for the survival of the priory's medieval altar. Given royal support, Episcopalianism established a foothold. The choir of Iona Abbey itself was briefly conscripted in the 1630s, walled off from the ruinous nave and transepts as the cathedral church of the diocese of the Isles revived by Charles I. In Kintyre, in 1642, the Presbyterians built a Gaelic Church in the recently founded plantation town of Lochhead (Campbeltown), though only a dated skewputt survives. Elsewhere on mainland Argyll there was some private patronage; by 1650 family burial-aisles had been added to

POST-REFORMATION CHURCHES

the medieval churches at Lochgoilhead and Kilfinan and to the choir
at Ardchattan Priory, all of which were in parochial use. That at
Kilfinan, which later accommodated a laird's loft at the upper level
of the added N wing, transformed the medieval oblong into a T-plan.
Thus, in line with a pattern already exemplified elsewhere in the
country, builders could have recourse to two simple plan types: the
rectangle and the T, each arranged symmetrically around a centrally
placed pulpit with galleries in the wings. When the religious turmoil
of the c17 had subsided, these were the models adopted.

The earliest surviving T-plan kirk is the Old Lowland Church,
Campbeltown, of 1706. Its original form has, however, been lost
in later 'restoration'. Much more exemplary is the former
Kingarth Parish Church, Mount Stuart, Bute, built in 1727,
perhaps by *Alexander McGill*. Despite its adaptation at the beginning of the c20 as a Roman Catholic mortuary chapel for the
Marquess of Bute, its external appearance is unmistakably that of
an c18 Presbyterian kirk: hip-roofed symmetry to the front, laird's
loft in the T at the rear. The arrangement proved persistent, though
not inflexible. It recurred on the island of Seil at Kilbrandon and
Kilchattan Church, Cuan, in 1735, and at Kilmodan Parish
Church, Clachan of Glendaruel, in 1783, where, between two tall
round-arched windows, the symmetry of the main s elevation is
enhanced by a pedimented centre carrying a birdcage bellcote.
This classical façade is repeated at Castlehill Church, Campbeltown,
1778, Tayinloan, 1787, Strachur, 1789 (originally hipped-roofed
but gabled in a 1902 restoration), and Colonsay, 1801, in all of
which the pedimented centre becomes the gable of a frontal T-leg
or wing. Echoes are still discernible in *Thomas Burns*'s Gothic
Revival church of 1841 at Kilmun.

Examples of the simple rectangular plan are more common if
generally less architecturally engaging. Kilninian, Mull, 1755, is
among the earliest extant: a harled preaching box with a bellcote
over the w gable. Kilchrenan, 1771, Southend, 1773, and Jura,
1777, follow suit, varying the treatment of the symmetrical s
elevation, the first classically balanced with round-headed openings flanking a unique central forestair. The High Kirk in Rothesay,
1796 (later extended and recast internally), and the winsomely
austere parish church of Kilberry, 1821, are also oblong but
piended. So, too, are the churches at Kilmichael of Inverlussa,
1820, and Ardfern, 1826, each fronted by the bellcote-carrying
pedimented centrepiece more familiar from the T-plan type.

There are, of course, exceptions to these two models. Some are
splendid, and none more so than the round church of 1767 built
at Bowmore, Islay. Sophisticated in form yet conventional in
material, a slated cone on a white-harled drum, it sits at the head
of the town's main street, its civic presence further dramatized by
a squat tolbooth-like N tower. There is nothing to equal the exquisite
simplicity of this conceit. Two later churches, Glenorchy at Dalmally,
1811, and Kilmorich, Cairndow, 1816, are octagonal in plan with
frontal towers but, Gothic in detail, lacking the Islay church's
calm, almost vernacular dignity. Nor does either location carry
the same urban charge as Bowmore. In Campbeltown, however,

where the wide pedimented façades of the Lowlanders' Castlehill Church of 1778 and the Highlanders' Church of 1803 sit in axial alignment with the Old and New Quays, town and kirk are again united. At Inveraray, the Gaelic- and English-speaking congregations were combined, housed back-to-back in *Robert Mylne*'s double church of 1795. It, too, is locked into the townscape, a temple to Janus, identical pedimented façades looking N and S down Main Street.

The last church to be sited as an urban *point-de-vue* was the parish church erected at the N end of Lochgilphead's Argyll Street in 1828. Replaced by *John Honeyman*'s Early English gable and belfry steeple in 1884, the original church was one of several, more or less identical, 'Parliamentary' churches commissioned and paid for under the provisions of An Act for Building Additional Places of Worship in the Highlands and Islands of Scotland. The Act, which was passed in 1823 and amended a year later, envisaged the construction of up to forty new churches in the poorer rural areas of the country. In the event forty-three sites were agreed for forty-one manses and thirty-two churches, seven of which were built in 1828 in the area covered by this volume. To co-ordinate and oversee the work, the Commissioners appointed the engineer *Thomas Telford*. He in turn engaged three 'surveyors' to supervise contracts in what were termed the Northern, Middle and Southern Districts. The last of these areas, which covered Argyll and the southern islands, became the responsibility of *William Thomson*, who had already been involved in the construction of the Crinan Canal. It was Thomson, described in surviving papers as both 'architect' and 'civil engineer', who produced designs which, subject to Telford's revisions in 1825, became the model for all the 'Parliamentary' churches and manses subsequently built. His proposals followed the by-now-standard T-plan or oblong arrangement. As usual, worship was focused on the pulpit, placed at the centre of the S wall, with the possibility of galleries across the three (or two) gables. Tall Tudor-arched windows provided generous light. Two of these, framing the pulpit in the middle zone of the S wall, were themselves flanked by doorways giving dual access to small lobbies from which staircases rose against the gables to the galleries. Tipping the symmetry of this principal elevation, the obligatory birdcage bellcote perched on the W gable. The skyline church at Portnahaven, Islay, is characteristic; a harled and slated T, it still preserves its internal galleries. The churches at Ulva, Kinlochspelve on Mull and The Oa on Islay are all T-plans. Only Ulva maintains intermittent worship; the others are abandoned ruins. Iona, built in coursed Ross of Mull granite without the N 'aisle', has been recast internally. Tobermory, like Lochgilphead, has gone.

Plain as they are, these 'Parliamentary' churches capture the intimate community of Presbyterian worship: a congregation gathered around pulpit and table; a preacher tied by axial symmetry and heritable patronage to the laird sitting in the gallery opposite. In effect, they draw to a standardized conclusion the developments of the preceding century. And this is true, too, in architectural terms. A mild parochial classicism no longer evident in pedimented façade or round-arched openings but still present in the centralized plan and the detailing of furnishings and panelled galleries; a tentative Gothic appearing in the four-centred arches of windows and doors. Both stylistic streams had washed across the C18 and, though the current of classical fashion flowed strong, the stirring of medieval allusion and revival had never been far below the surface. At Kingarth Parish Church, Bute (*see above*), hefty Y-tracery had appeared in the late 1720s; pointed-arch windows are preferred at Southend, 1773, Bunessan, Mull, 1804, Inverchaolin, 1812 (demolished 1911), and Cairndow, 1816 (*see above*); at Strathlachlan, Garbhallt, 1792, there is a Gothick gable; at Glenorchy, Dalmally, 1811 (*see above*) and on Islay at Kilchoman, 1825, buttressed towers. But it is only at Dunoon that the Revival is finally triunphant in the parish church of 1816 by *James Gillespie Graham*. A buttressed four-bay rectangle with a square E entrance tower, its liturgical linearity superseded the customary centralized plan, a development that consigned the local Presbyterian tradition to history as completely as its imported language of Perpendicular Gothic did the same in matters of stylistic fashion. *front cover*

A decade later, as the Parliamentary Commissioners accepted the Thomson/Telford design, the Greenock architect *James Dempster* was adapting Graham's Gothic model for the parish church at Cardross, 1826 (reduced 1954). Ten years later he did the same at St Colmac, Bute. In 1834 *Joseph Gordon Davies* of London replaced the late C18 kirk at Kilmartin with a pretentious little church in Perpendicular style which combined crowstep-gabled nave and aisles with a battlemented w tower. By the 1840s this new approach had become the norm; Gothic, whether Early English, Decorated or Perpendicular, or simply a naïve addiction to the pointed arch, was in vogue. With the long axis of the oblong plan now the axis of worship and the need for galleries undiminished, churches became wider. The church built in 1836 for the parish of Ardchattan on Loch Etive is a good example of this change. Though far from assured in its handling of Gothic forms, its internal arrangement is typical of many later, larger churches: a dominant pulpit centred on the gable gripped magnet-like between the arms of a U-shaped gallery. *29, 30*

Gothic's 'changefulness' did, however, admit many possibilities. It was, as Ruskin wrote at the height of the Revival, 'undefined in its slope of roof, height of shaft, breadth of arch, or disposition of ground plan'. Plans, though consistently linear in orientation, might be rectangular, transeptal, even cruciform. Of the last, the West Church in Helensburgh, 1853, by the *Hays* of Liverpool, and St Oran, Connel, 1881, designed by the Oban architect *David Mackintosh* in emulation of Iona Abbey, are notable. St Mackessog at Luss, 1875, is cruciform in miniature. Occasionally, as at *David Cousin's* St Modan, Rosneath, 1852, a simple nave-and-chancel solution would be adopted, though this was much more favoured by the Episcopalians. If not confined to the rear of the church, galleries might be U-shaped or accommodated in the transepts. Towers or steeples could be centred on the entrance gable, as at Arrochar, 1847, Rhu, 1851, and Ardrishaig, 1860, or, later and more frequently, placed to the side so that light could be gained from a traceried or wheel window. The high crown spire at Tarbert, 1885, by *McKissack & Rowan* takes spectacular advantage of this asymmetrical setting, though the church itself is something of a disappointment. At the West Church, Helensburgh (*see above*), the tower, a broached spire, sits back in the re-entrant between nave and transept.

Not all architects abandoned the round arch. In Rothesay, *Charles Wilson* hid the gable of his West Parish Church, 1845, with a Norman blockhouse-portal from which soars a high pinnacled spire, becoming progressively more Gothic with height. A year later he was designing a square, somewhat Italianate tower in Helensburgh, all that remains today of his Old Parish Church. Like Wilson's work, the parish churches at Tarbert (*see above*) and Oban, 1893, are both Gothic in disposition but have round-arched windows. A more thorough-going Romanesque appears in the 1880s in the eccentric, eclectic little church of St Conan on Loch Awe, contrived over half a century by the amateur architect, *Walter Campbell*, and his family. Endearing and idiosyncratic, St Conan lacks repose. In the work of *Peter MacGregor Chalmers*, however, that tranquil spiritual quality of Romanesque is attained. St Kieran, near Port Charlotte on Islay, 1897, and Strone (St Columba) Church, 1907, are not large and perhaps suffer from an unnecessary complexity of form. But the small, round-towered church of Kilmore, Dervaig, Mull, 1904 is wonderfully simple and exquisitely sited. Equally well judged in form, material and setting is his Parish Church at Kirn, 1906, with its pyramid-roofed campanile seen and heard across the Firth.

After the First World War the Church of Scotland built few new churches. In 1923, Romanesque was still the choice for the rugged little kirk on Gigha by *J. Jeffrey Waddell*. Not until mid-century could a break with the past be contemplated, and then only a conservative Scandinavian Modernism proved acceptable. Nevertheless, for all its half-heartedness in style and scale, there is still a breezy optimism in *Leslie Grahame MacDougall*'s Christ's Church, built on the Esplanade at Oban, 1954.

The FREE CHURCH Disruption from the Church of Scotland in 1843 had a considerable impact in Argyll and the islands. Ministers who 'came out' and the congregations who came with them immediately set about building new churches. These Free kirks were often small and indistinguishable from their predecessors; Kilchoman at Port Charlotte on Islay, 1843 (now the Museum of Islay Life), and Lochfyneside, Minard, 1847, are plain skew-gabled oblongs with little more than an apex bellcote to denote their function. Lochgilphead, 1843, is no more than a Gothic box. Others, however, had architectural distinction. Already under construction at the time of the Disruption, *David Hamilton*'s church at Ascog, Bute, 1843, was small, too, but classically dignified by a blind Venetian window in one gable and an Italianate belfry tower at the other. Also on Bute, Trinity Church, Rothesay, 1843, by the Aberdeen architect *Archibald Simpson*, was a still grander affair; severe symmetrical Gothic with a streetfront steeple making its unequivocal mark in the centre of town. In Oban, *David Cousin* drew on Puginian Gothic for his hillside-sited Free High Church of 1846; behind an Early English gable-and-belfry front, it housed a congregation seated in traditional Presbyterian T-plan orientation.

The Free Church undertook a second building programme in the 1860s and '70s. This produced a number of large churches, all Gothic and all designed by Glasgow architects. Most developed the Oban model of frontal gable and asymmetrically placed steeple. At Park Church, Helensburgh, 1863, by *John Honeyman*, the steeple spire is broached. At Lochend, Campbeltown, 1868 (demolished 1985), by *Campbell Douglas & Stevenson*, and the much-gabled St John's, Dunoon, 1876, by *Robert Bryden*, it is tall and elegantly French following Glasgow fashion. At Cardross, 1871, again by *Honeyman*, a stone pyramid tops the belfry tower. *Boucher & Cousland*'s 1867 façade for Lorne Street Church, Campbeltown (originally the Gaelic Free Church), is the exception: in place of a steeple, elongated finialled buttresses and apex bellcote; instead of soft grey stone, violent polychromy. New churches in more modest Gothic style were also built in the smaller towns and rural communities. Tighnabruaich, Jura, Bellanoch and Ardrishaig were all completed before 1870. At Tobermory, Mull, 1877, the gable-and-belfry formula returns. A generation or so later, following the creation of the United Free Church in 1900, a third, much less ambitious phase of building began. Gothic continued to be favoured but there is little to remark. Perhaps *Alexander Cullen*'s church at Tarbert, 1908, deserves mention for its mild Arts and Crafts flavour, the U. F. church at Rothesay, 1911, for its astylar oddity. Ledaig U. F. Church at Benderloch, 1911, by *Hippolyte Blanc* retains some Gothic grace despite being converted to a dwelling.

NONCONFORMISTS were active in Argyll from the early years of the C19. Stimulated by the efforts of the Baptist Itinerant Society and the Baptist Home Missionary Society for Scotland, congregations were formed at Bellanoch (1805), Oban (1818), Colonsay (1821) and at Bowmore on Islay (1830). In 1815 a simple piend-roofed preaching hall was built at Lochgilphead. Now gabled and considerably altered, it still survives on the town's main street. In 1847 the Baptists took over the 1836 Independent Chapel at Ardbeg on Bute, later Gothicizing it. By mid-century they were well established on the islands and especially strong on Tiree, where two small chapels, built with atavistic simplicity at Baugh and Balemartine in 1856, still stand. But emigration to Canada weakened these congregations. Churches were later erected on the mainland at Helensburgh, 1886, and Oban, 1903, but these were realized in unprepossessing Gothic. In marked contrast, as if to identify its distinct brand of Nonconformism, the Oban Congregational Church of 1880 is confidently classical, a pedimented and pilastered temple, rare in Argyll's C19 religious architecture.

With a liturgy more akin to medieval practice, EPISCOPALIAN worship tended to favour a particular architectural response. But until the influence of the Oxford Movement began to make itself felt, this had not been prescriptive. The characteristic nave-and-chancel arrangement is not in evidence in Argyll until the middle of the C19, by which time the church, which had suffered for its Jacobite sympathies in the C18, was enjoying a spiritual revival. Only one Episcopalian building, Holy Cross at Portnacroish in Appin, is of an earlier date. It was consecrated in 1815 and, in its original oblong form with galleries W and E and the altar placed at the centre of the S wall, was indistinguishable from a Presbyterian kirk. But a generation later three Gothic churches were erected, each with nave and chancel clearly articulated in plan and section. The first was Holy Trinity, Dunoon, 1847, by the Edinburgh architect *John Henderson*. Three years later came Christ Church, Lochgilphead, where Henderson's 'correct' orthodoxy was preferred to a proposal by *William Butterfield*. An English architect, *Thomas Cundy* of London, was, however, commissioned to design St Columba Chapel, 1852, the private estate church of the Malcolms of Poltalloch. He, too, adopted the nave and-chancel plan, adding porch, vestry and memorial chapel. While all three buildings share formal affinities, Cundy's Gothic is the most controlled and convincing, an austere Early English container for its rich furnishings. No later churches match this cool reserve, least of all the Cathedral of St John the Divine in Oban. Begun as a parish church in 1863, St John's grew through a protracted century-long process of enlargement and alteration in which frustrated optimism was forced to repeated compromises which not only precluded any coherence of style but stretched the 'changefulness' of Gothic to quite unprecedented ends. Still unfinished, ill at ease inside and out, it is the most provocative of buildings.

In 1863, following the death of John Henderson, the young *Robert Rowand Anderson* undertook the first of a series of ecclesiastical commissions which quickly made him the darling of the Episcopalian establishment in Scotland. In the space of only three years he designed six churches, all Gothic. The sixth, St Michael and All Angels, begun in 1867, was in Helensburgh; French rather than English in character, it has a high nave with lean-to aisles and is scrupulously detailed. The interior, which Anderson enriched with a colourfully tiled chancel, is lavishly endowed with furnishings and stained glass. But few congregations were as prosperous as Victorian Helensburgh, and for those churches built in the last quarter of the C19 a more modest Gothic with minimal ornament inside and out sufficed. This was true of *Alexander Ross*'s St Columba at Gruline, Mull, 1874, and of All Saints, Inveraray, 1886, by *Wardrop & Anderson*, a plain affair in Early English style. At the diminutive church of St James, Ardbrecknish, Port Sonachan, 1891, where nave and chancel are again given their separate expression, the same stylistic conservatism prevails.

ROMAN CATHOLIC revival began slowly in the early years of the C19. The establishment of a small seminary on Lismore in 1803 was a sign of renewed activity, but the college was short-lived and the chapel at Kilcheran no more than a residential conversion. Numbers were small and few churches were commissioned. St

Kieran, Campbeltown, 1849, gable-fronted Gothic built to replace an earlier church of 1809, is a lone survivor. This paucity makes the outburst of private Catholic piety and plenty that marked the end of the century at Mount Stuart on Bute all the more astonishing and exuberant. The Bute family chapel, which in 1896 *Robert Rowand Anderson* began to add to the vast mansion-house he had already been working on for some twenty years or so, is no intimate retreat but a lofty Gothic church appropriately palatial in scale. Rising above its cruciform plan is an octagonal spire-carrying lantern from which light pours down into an interior opulent to the verge of ostentation. Nothing could be more removed from the tiny St Sophia Chapel of 1912 which *W. Hunter McNab* raised at Glendaruel, though it, too, is cruciform and served originally as a private place of worship.

Several substantial churches were built by Catholic parishes in the C20. St Joseph, Helensburgh, 1911, designed by *Charles J. Menart* in Free Style Gothic, has a long nave-and-aisles plan with gabled transepts; altogether different from the grand Il Gesù-derived St Aloysius Church which the architect had just completed in Glasgow. Also long, but Byzantine in concept, is *Reginald Fairlie*'s St Andrew's, Rothesay, 1923, which has a severity of form and detail owing as much perhaps to post-war austerity as to stylistic preference. But by far the greatest achievment is *Giles Gilbert Scott*'s St Columba Cathedral in Oban, where building began in 1932. Cut in pink Peterhead granite, ruthlessly plain lancets and buttresses punch vertical rhythms against the horizontality of nave and aisles, a contrast especially effective when seen rippling in the elongated reflections of a tall seafront tower. It is an austere building, but this is a matter of calculated judgement, an aesthetic restraint consistently maintained over the prolonged construction period both in the exterior and in the granite gloom of the interior. But better still was to come, for in 1953, the same year that the Cathedral was completed, the Glasgow firm of *Gillespie, Kidd & Coia* was engaged to design St Peter's College at Cardross, a seminary planned to accommodate around one hundred novice priests. The building was revolutionary and sacramental. It broke completely with the past, drawing instead on the poetic language of Modernist form, revealed in the religious architecture of Le Corbusier. Churches at Garelochhead, 1964, and Rosneath, 1967, neither by Gillespie, Kidd & Coia, also try hard to be Modern but seem almost banal by comparison. Further compromised by shabbiness, their fate is, nevertheless, no more than a matter of local regret. What has happened at Cardross is a catastrophe. Weakened by spiritual drought, abandoned in 1979, and stigmatized by neglect, the seminary sinks into despair, a rotting reproach to Scottish architecture and Scottish religion.

The FURNISHINGS of Presbyterian churches built before the middle of the C19 were few and simple: a pulpit placed centrally on the S wall, hard wooden pews, panelled galleries, perhaps a laird's loft. Some original layouts can still be seen, for example at Southend, Clachan of Glendaruel, Tayinloan, Lochgoilhead, Ardfern, Portnahaven and Ardchattan, though it is doubtful if any is without some alteration or replacement. The plain panelled pulpits at Southend (semicircular) and Clachan of Glendaruel (octagonal) may be c18; that brought to Lochgoilhead (half-octagonal) from Kiltearn, Ross & Cromarty, probably dates from the 1790s. The surviving original pulpit at Kingarth Church (*see* above) is hexagonal and supports a high, similarly shaped sounding-board with a dentilled cornice. This classical design appears to have been popular in the early c19 and was adopted for Telford's Parliamentary churches. A fine two-tier example stands idle at Ulva; another, formerly at Iona, is now in the Highland Folk Museum at Kingussie. Those at Ardfern, 1826, and Ardchattan, 1836, are still in use; both are octagonal and two-tier, the latter elegantly canopied on a slender back support. Ardchattan is also remarkable as it retains its bench pews and is the only church which preserves the long central communion table once customary in Presbyterian worship. On the other hand, its crude Gothic shell, orientated towards a pulpit placed against the gable, and its U-shaped gallery are distinctly c19 developments. Earlier galleries are, of course, common and a number of laird's lofts survive, though none is executed with that sophistication of design or craftsmanship often found in other, more prosperous parts of Scotland. The earliest, in the 1633 Lamont Aisle at Kilfinan, was formed in the late c17, reconstructed in 1759, but closed off from the church in c19 changes. At Kingarth Church on Bute (*see* above) and Killean Church, Tayinloan, c18 lofts sit in the stem of the T-plan. At Kilmodan Church, Clachan of Glendaruel, 1783, a different branch of the Campbell family was accommodated in each arm of the T. The early c19 Drimsynie Loft at Lochgoilhead curves in a shallow bow in the w aisle. At Kilmorich Church, Cairndow, 1816, the Ardkinglass Loft opens from the tower as a canted bay balcony, while at Kilmartin, 1834, the Malcolms of Poltalloch sat in a w gallery which also linked back into the church's tower.

Both Kilmorich and Kilmartin are, like Ardchattan, Gothic and adopt the more medieval linear plan. This was not the case at the Free High Church in Oban where, in 1846, behind the lancets of a gabled w façade, the pulpit remained centred on the s wall. But at Oban the pulpit, installed in 1861, is itself Gothic. Indeed, it was not long before Presbyterian churches began to treat both the pulpit and the gable against which it was now placed as a symmetrical Gothic stage-set before which the ritual of preaching and sacrament could be performed. Pulpits were raised high between flanking flights of stairs and when, later in the c19, music began to play a role in the service, the need to co-ordinate pulpit, communion table, elders' seats, choir stalls, and organ pipes afforded the opportunity for imaginative compositions busy with timber arcading and tracery. St John's, Dunoon, built for the Free Church in 1876, is the outstanding example; the interior created at Trinity, Rothesay, in the early years of the c20, also worthy of note.

The ecclesiological influence of the Gothic Revival is most evident in the churches of the Episcopalians and Roman Catholics. Chancels are busy with the accoutrements of worship: altars, reredos panels, sedilia and piscina, etc. They are also colourful with varying combinations of sandstones, marbles, brick, and tiles on walls and floors. There are tiled sanctuaries in the Episcopal churches at Dunoon, 1847, Lochgilphead, 1850, Helensburgh, 1861, and Inveraray, 1886; the dominant colour is terra cotta, but creams, blacks and blues are also used. At St Columba, Poltalloch, 1852, the brick-red Minton floor tiles in the chancel are patterned with quatrefoils and crosses, the blue panels of the ceiling bright with stars. Altars are often of stone. At Dunoon, the altar sits on a base of polychromatic Minton tiles edged with alabaster. In the Cathedral of St John the Divine in Oban, the high altar, installed in 1910, is of pink stone with marble inlays and retable. Towering behind it is a magnificent reredos in gilded and stained oak by *James Chalmers* incorporating paintings and sculpture under a cusp-fringed Gothic canopy. *Robert Rowand Anderson* combines alabaster and mosaic in the reredos at St Michael and All Angels, Helensburgh, 1872. But there is nothing in Argyll, or far beyond, to compare with the interior of *Anderson*'s chapel for the Butes at Mount Stuart. White Carrara marble everywhere, a pavement of spectacularly patterned Cosmati work, a 'Baroque-Gothic' organ screen traceried with whorls of grape-laden vines, an altar of bronze with silver-gilt figures of Scottish saints. The Marquess of Bute had been just as generous and lavish furnishing the Pro-Cathedral which the Roman Catholics built at Oban in 1886. But when this unusual building (a large cruciform church clad in corrugated iron) was finally replaced by *Giles Gilbert Scott*'s St Columba Cathedral, no latter-day Maecenas appeared. Tastes had, in any case, changed. Though a few pieces were retained from the so-called 'tin cathedral', Scott's furnishings are in the main more severe, and effectively so.

By the end of the century the Presbyterians had begun to assimilate some aspects of the Episcopalian layout. Many existing seating arrangements were recast, the axis of worship swung through ninety degrees. Chancels appeared. Choir stalls became more common. Pulpits were moved from the centre to the side. In the 1890s, at St Modan, Rosneath, which, rather unusually, had been built to a nave-and-chancel plan, the chancel was refurbished with polychromatic paving, delicate Gothic wall panelling, and an intricately carved communion table, gilded and painted. Comparable changes took place at Kilmun, 1898–9, where *Peter MacGregor Chalmers* revised the interior to create a sanctuary in Perpendicular style. At Kirn, 1906–7, his furnishings are Romanesque. A few years later, the same architect designed a wide communion table of Iona marble, carved with a Gothic arcade carrying fretted tracery; in effect an altar for the island's medieval Abbey.

STAINED GLASS begins to play a part in the embellishment of interiors in the second half of the C19. St Modan, Rosneath, retains its three-light chancel window of 1861, repositioned in the N transept. Its naïve crucified Christ marks it as the earliest installation in a church richly provided over more than a century with the work of *Clayton & Bell*, *Stephen Adam & Son*, *Douglas Strachan* and *Gordon Webster*. Another excellent collection is at St Michael and All Angels (Episcopal), Helensburgh, where, in a variety of windows from the 1870s, '80s and '90s, *Clayton & Bell* and *Adam* are again well represented, along with *Charles Kempe* whose Mary Magdalene washing the feet of Christ, 1882, is outstanding. The glowing colours of *Douglas Strachan*'s work are less readily accessible but well worth the journey. At Inverchaolain, 1921, a War Memorial St Michael; in the remote little church of Kilbrandon and Kilchattan on Seil, 1937, some wonderfully warm evocations of Christ's life, death and glory; at Iona Abbey, 1939, three saints high in the N clearstorey. *Gordon Webster* has many windows, his gaunt, high-cheekboned figures easily identified against metallic greys, blues and purples. Good examples are at St John's, Dunoon, along the Cowal shore at Kirn, and at St Oran, Connel.

Unified schemes are rare. At Kilmun, following his gift of a small Children's Window in 1895, *Stephen Adam* designed five more windows, 1899–1909, for the refurbished church. The last of these, completed in the year before his death, depicts a blue-robed Dorcas against a wonderfully muted background of olive-green. *Henry Holiday*'s Nativity lancets, 1904, in Lochgilphead Parish Church, are finely co-ordinated and full of incident, while in nearby St Margaret (R.C.) a series of mainly Scottish saints, by *John Hardman Studios*, 1958, fills the windows of nave and sanctuary.

Among individual windows of quality are *Louis Davis*'s light-filled centenary memorial window to the Revd John McLeod Campbell, installed at Rhu and Shandon Church, 1925; the Four Seasons by *Roland Mitton*, 1983, at St Oran, Connel; and, in the same church, *Christian Shaw*'s little harvest scene throbbing with palpable heat. Delicate and naïve: the dream visions painted by *Sarah Campbell* on two W lancets in the Cathedral of St John the Divine (Episcopal), Oban, in 1990. Drawn over a hundred years before but no less touching, the childlike flower motifs that fill the background of four Pre-Raphaelite virtues in the tiny church at Ford.

MAUSOLEA AND MONUMENTS

Well before the end of the C16 the Reformers had placed a proscription on burials being carried out inside church buildings. One of the last interments to be sanctioned within the church was that of Donald MacDuffie, Prior at Oronsay, who died in 1555, some years before the new strictures began to be imposed. Until the late C19 his graveslab lay in a round-arched tomb-recess in a small chapel that had been added to the S side of the Priory Church in the late C15. The chapel became known as the MacDuffie Aisle – a sign of things to come, since familial ascription and funerary association were soon repeated in a number of very similar post-Reformation burial-aisles. These were permitted by Presbyterian practice, subject to the proviso that they be entered from the churchyard and not from the church itself, though before the end of the C16 the Campbells of Ardkinglas had built a burial-aisle erected against the E end of the parish church at Lochgoilhead which seems to have been entered from the church through a doorway at the centre of the E gable. This small opening, blocked in the C19, is incorporated into the large Ardkinglas Monument, 53 c. 1590, a symmetrical composition of unscholarly classical elements tiered and scrolled around an inscribed panel topped with a steeply sloped pediment. The doorway is evidently intended as an impressive portal to the chamber beyond. At Ardchattan Priory the Campbells of Ardchattan built a family burial-aisle against the SE end of the choir, recording the date of construction, 1614, on the keystone of the round-arched S entrance. Six years after that, the Campbells of Lochnell added their aisle (rebuilt and enlarged, 1713) between the N transept and the sacristy, while later still, probably in the second half of the C17, the Campbells of Inverawe appear to have adapted the sacristy for similar purposes. All of these are roofless and ruinous, but at Kilfinan the Lamont Aisle of 1633 survives, forming a T with the oblong plan of the medieval church. Above the burial chamber, which remains sealed from the church as it always was, a laird's loft was created, but in the C19 this too was walled off from public worship. At Kilbrannan Chapel, Skipness, the Campbells had two open burial enclosures built against the S wall of the church, probably around the middle of the C18. They contain two fine mural monuments framed by pedimented Tuscan aedicules, one of which advances as a sheltering portico. A small rectangular plot which abuts the S front of Kilchrenan Church contains a C19 tablet commemorating the Campbells of Sonachan; its low walls were built in 1779 but were constructed on footings substantial enough to have supported the walls of an earlier burial-aisle. At Kilbride, the 1786 burial-aisle of the MacDougalls, identified by an armorial panel in the W gable, stands roofless close to the old Parish Church. Later in the C18, or perhaps early in the C19, the MacNeills of Colonsay began to use part of the E range of the conventual buildings at Oronsay for family burials. Shortly after 1850 they added an open burial-aisle to the E with a pointed-arch at the centre of the E gable.

Such walled enclosures, never intended to be roofed, are common. Often square in plan, most were not attached to the church building but stood apart, marking a family burial plot in the kirkyard or in a detached graveyard. The lapidarium at Kilmartin is a converted burial-enclosure with some dressed masonry which may be of C17 date and a built-in graveslab with a relief inscription that suggests that this was the resting-place of Neil Campbell, Bishop of Argyll until 1608. At Kilmalieu near Inveraray, the small stone-walled enclosure of the Campbells of Stonefield contains the tomb of James Campbell †1731, marked by a mural aedicule monument whose fluted Ionic pilasters bear a pedimented entablature with angel-flanked arms in the tympanum. At Kilberry, the heavily quoined walls of the Campbell Mausoleum carry bevelled coping stones of schist and, above the W doorway, dated 1733, a segmental pediment carved with a seaman's quadrant. On the W wall, commemorating the privateer Captain Dugald Campbell, is a mural monument with fluted pilasters, trumpeting angels, an armorial panel and a shaped pediment mantling an urn. In the Killevin burial-ground near Minard there is a rectangular enclosure with a blocked doorway dated 1727, empty wall recesses and a memorial inscription to the Campbells of Knockbuy and Kilberry. Similar recesses occur in the walls of a square burial-enclosure raised on the N shore of Loch Ederline, near Ford, in the same year, presumably by the Campbells of Ederline. The small square enclosure on the edge of the kirkyard at Clachan of Glendaruel, now the lapidarium, is believed to have served in the C18 as the mausoleum of the Campbells of Auchenbreck; ball finials from the wallhead lie by the doorway. In the graveyard at Kilnaish, between Tarbert and Kilberry, ball finials are still in position, marking the corners and gatepiers of another, almost square, C18 burial-enclosure. Pedestals surmount the angles of the walled plot at Dùn an Oir, Glendaruel, though the ornamental urns they originally carried have fallen; there are a few C18 mural tablets to the Campbells of Glendaruel, but the walls themselves may not have been constructed until the early 1800s. Enclosures built during the C19 were generally smaller, and by the beginning of the Victorian period it was not just the local lairds who were building walled enclosures to house their dead but any family who could afford to do so. Early C19 examples occur at Cardross, Kilfinan, Strachur and elsewhere. By this time, too, there were alternatives to the classical language of pedestal, pilaster and pediment.

Gothic burial structures appear towards the end of the C18. At Kilneuair on the SE shore of Loch Awe, near Ford, there is a roofless rubble enclosure with a symmetrical S front of three steeply pointed-arched openings, all blocked. Strange decorative carving (chevron, herringbone, rosette, etc.) is applied to the jambs and sills and to projecting quoins. The date of erection is conjectural but may be pre-1800. Nor is it known for whom this mysterious structure was built nor whether it was originally roofed. Certainly, the early evidence of Gothic Revival funerary architecture in Argyll is generally linked with enclosed mausolea. The late C18 Fletcher Mausoleum at Dunans, Glendaruel, is, in effect, a Gothic burial chapel, its traceried E gable and armorial interior a delight to discover, hidden in the wooded slopes above the Ruel River. At Inverneill, on the other hand, the small Campbell Mausoleum of 1802 could be described as astylar vernacular, were it not for a moulded pointed-arch recess in the W gable. The Maquarie Mausoleum at Gruline, Mull, *c.* 1825, though buttressed and gabled, is grimmer still and barely Gothic. At Keils on Jura, *William Burn*'s Mausoleum, 1838, built for the island's Campbells, is a gabled, barrel-vaulted cell with a stone-slabbed roof; medieval in character, if not quite pointed Gothic. But on Coll, at Ardnish, where the MacLeans were content to erect an open enclosure, *c.* 1835, there is a surprisingly ambitious tripartite façade of pointed arches with moulded surrounds flanked by high angle buttressing.

Strangely, the honouring of death and memory seems not to have occasioned any Grecian *gravitas* in Argyll. There are no Neoclassical mausolea; no temples and no tempietti. On the contrary, a certain provincial naïveté prevails, whether the preferred idiom is trabeated or arcuated. Indeed, it is unscholarly inventiveness which often produces memorable results, not least in the untutored conjunction of classical and medieval elements. At Rothesay, for example, the Bute Mausoleum in the graveyard of the High Kirk is quite aggressively eclectic, a red sandstone cell, probably late C18, with busily pedimented gables, Gothick tracery and six dumpy Neoclassical obelisks on the eaves skyline. The Argyll Mausoleum at Kilmun, though calmer, is similarly confused in its stylistic allegiance. Begun by *James Lowrie* in 1795 as a burial-aisle added on the N side of the choir of the old Parish Church, the mausoleum is square in plan and has a three-bay N façade of ashlar divided by Corinthian pilasters carrying a crude entablature, in effect a parapet, behind which rose a slated pyramid roof. In the early 1890s, however, a hooded, pointed-arch doorway with deeply moulded surround was inserted at the centre of the N front and Gothic windows with flat Y-tracery added in the flanking bays. A hemispherical dome replaced the original roof, and the mixture was further compounded with a Romanesque interior. It is a measure of the C19's pliant historicism that only a year or two before (and only a few yards away) the Douglas of Glenfinnart Mausoleum had been built as a classical octagon (more strictly, a chamfered square), while only a few years later, at Kilfinan, the Rankin enclosure could still flirt with neo-Grèc.

Of the many monuments placed on the walls of churches, burial enclosures and mausolea, the earliest is the Macfarlane Stone at Luss. Dated 1612 and carved with the symbols of mortality, it is set into the outer face of the N wall of the village church of 1875. On the W side of the sacristy at Ardchattan Priory, a small square panel, carved with a mantled shield and the motto SPERANS, bears the date 1682. Throughout the C18 memorial inscriptions were frequently framed by classical aedicules carrying pediments and armorial achievements. Good examples survive in Kintyre: the McEachern Monument, *c*. 1715, in the cemetery at Kilkerran; those in the Campbell burial-enclosure at Skipness (*see above*); and, in the churchyard at Saddell Abbey, the temple-front wall of *c*. 1784 dedicated to the Campbells of Saddell. Commemorative classicism continued to be adopted in the C19. Several scions of the Campbell of Duntrune and Malcolm of Poltalloch families are remembered in Kilmartin Church, their memorial panels plain marble tablets or sarcophagus gables sparingly ornamented with flaming urns, anthemion finials and armorial achievements. In the round church at Bowmore, Islay, the white marble monument to Walter Campbell of Shawfield and Islay, erected in 1819, is surmounted by a toga-clad figure carved in relief against a flat obelisk. It is not until the middle of the century that Gothic wall monuments appear. Though not plentiful, there are a few dating from the 1860s in the interior of St Modan, Rosneath, and two Gothic gable tombs from the same decade raised against the boundary wall in Dunoon Cemetery.

The earliest post-Reformation gravemarkers are recumbent slabs, essentially a continuation of medieval burial practice. By about 1650 headstones and table-tombs were being introduced. Good examples of C17 gravemarkers occur at Ardchattan (where a single tapered slab from the second half of the C16 survives), Kilmartin, Kilmun and particularly at Kilmalieu near Inveraray. At Inch Kenneth, a full-length effigy carved in high relief on a sandstone slab has, despite its seeming medievalism, been dated to the early C17. A recumbent slab at Clachan, Kintyre, commemorates Maurice Darroch †1638, pastor at Kilcalmonell. In the Cladh Odhráin burial-ground at Kirkapoll, Tiree, the table-tomb of Farquhar Fraser, Dean of the Isles, carries the date 1680. Table-tombs and burial slabs from the C18 are relatively common and widely distributed. There is, however, an unusual concentration of recumbent slabs at Old Kilarrow graveyard, Islay. Headstones are also more abundant in the C18 and many can be found enlivened not only by the emblems of mortality and immortality but by a fascinating variety of trade insignia. Graveyards at Kilmun and in Kintyre at Kilchousland, Kilkerran and Killean are especially rich in this respect, with carpenters, coopers, cordiners, farmers, gardeners, mariners, millers, shoemakers and tailors all in evidence. In Kintyre, too, the incidence of C18 headstones depicting four-horse plough teams is particularly marked; there are examples at Clachan, Glenbarr, Skipness and Kilchousland. The Rhind headstone at Strachur, a round-headed slab of Easdale slate erected in 1825, bears mason's dividers and compasses, with a wealth of additional symbols scattered round a crude pilaster-framed inscription. A small headstone at Kilchoman, Islay, dated 1845, shows a lighthouse in relief; it carries the name of the assistant keeper of the Rinns of Islay light. This is a remote and unique example, for the depiction of vocational symbols had already died out by the early years of the C19. The table-tomb and aedicule headstone were more persistent, but by 1850 these too are no longer in fashion. They survive, often in more elaborated forms, but alongside an expanded range of options offered by firms of monumental sculptors whose works stand ranked in regimented rows in enlarged churchyards and municipal cemeteries. Such gravemarkers vary from unadorned stelae bearing little more than a biblical verse and a simple record of death to more romantically inspired monuments such as broken columns, draped urns, sarcophagi, obelisks, Gothic kiosks, etc. Towards the end of the century Celtic crosses appear. They remain popular and provide a much-endorsed model for War Memorials. Imaginative departures from these standards crop up from time to time in the C20. The irregularly shaped Coats headstone at Inverchaolain, carved to depict a yacht in sail, is an endearingly personalized example. But the old patterns occasionally persist: at Ormsaray, the Lithgows are remembered in a finely cut mid-C20 sandstone table-tomb.

Many of these forms had, of course, a long association with funerary sculpture. What was new was the increasing democratization of death. The column, which at Mount Stuart had reached epic proportions in the high pillar dedicated to the mother of George III and been brought to Bute some time before 1800, memorializes many less socially elevated throughout the C19. Classically intact, broken or fallen, it is a common choice, though rarely elaborated to the barley-sugar complexities of the Davidson Monument in Faslane Cemetery, c. 1920. The sarcophagus, sculpted in black marble for the monument in Bowmore's round church to Lady Ellinor Campbell †1832, proves just as acceptable as a model for the tomb of Rothesay's provost, James Duncan, in the 1870s. The obelisk is particularly popular. It makes an early appearance in the McDowall Monument at Kilkerran, Campbeltown, c. 1795, a splayed ashlar shaft sitting on a heavily corniced plinth, which has a robust, almost Piranesian, presence in the kirkyard. At Kilchrenan, the base of the McIntyre Monument, c. 1815, frames a white marble inscription, the shaft a much squatter affair capped by a pedimented finial. In 1840, *Mossman*'s Gow Monument at Kilmartin improved the proportions by elongating the shaft, and by mid century the simple elegance of obelisk and plinth had been established as the model not only for countless graveyard tombs but also for a number of larger, more public, commemorative monuments. Frequently, these grander granite obelisks thrust through the skyline on hilltop sites: the monument to Lord Colonsay above Scalasaig, 1879, the Hutcheson Monument on Kerrera, 1883, and the Campbell Monument at Bridgend on Islay, 1887 (rebuilt 1911), are all good examples. The American Monument dramatically poised above the Atlantic on The Oa, Islay, 1918, which is constructed in rubble masonry and not at all Neoclassical in character, the War Memorial at Campbeltown, 1923, and the Monument to Neil Munro N of Inveraray, 1935, can all be regarded as rugged variations on this obelisk theme. Other public monuments exploit different themes. The Lamont Memorial in Dunoon, 1906, is a dolmen; the Coronation Monument at Lochbuie on Mull, 1902, a pyramid of rubble; *John T. Rochead*'s McIntyre Monument above Dalmally, 1859, a hilltop henge.

Memorial architecture may communicate through the drama of its setting, through the associational content of its forms or through the applied emblematic attributes of heraldry or vocation. It may well be true, as Geoffrey Scott wrote in 1914 in *The Architecture of Humanism*, that certain forms have 'a sensuous value apart from anything we *know* about them', but it is all but impossible to escape the literary gloss in the graveyard. Tombs tell tales. And LETTERING is a critical attribute of all funerary design. Along with the heraldic clues read from armorial carving it is a vital factor in the attribution of early graveslabs, table-tombs and headstones. But it has an aesthetic charge too. The elegant mural memorials already mentioned at Kilmartin amd Bowmore are particularly enhanced by beautifully cut lettering, and it is this attention to the graphic content of the memorial message that distinguishes several otherwise plain tablets carrying long inscriptions. Among these are the McIntyre Memorial, c. 1815, set into the inner face of the s wall of the parish church at Kilchrenan, and two round-headed panels in the w wall of the graveyard at Toberonochy, Luing, c. 1830. Also in the same wall at Toberonochy, a sandstone panel to the Glasgow merchant David Campbell †1818, aberrant but delightful, cut not with Trajan strictness but turbulent with the free-flowing curves of penmanship.

CASTLES AND TOWER-HOUSES

57 The oldest castellar construction in Argyll is Castle Sween. Begun towards the end of the C12, it has some claim to be the oldest existing castle in Scotland. A number of northern strongholds are known to have been established by the Norsemen at this time but they are all much smaller in size. Cubbie Roo's Castle on the Orkney island of Wyre, for example, may be older, perhaps *c.* 1150, and the promontory castles of Old Wick and Forse in Caithness are also thought to be C12. It is possible, too, that Dunivaig Castle on Lagavulin Bay, Islay, may be contemporary and Norse in origin, but, in terms of physical remains, there is little if anything surviving to substantiate such an early date. Castle Sween, on the other hand, built by Suibhne, an Irish forebear of the MacSween family who were lairds of Knapdale until the later C13, is a larger structure than the original summit fortress at Dunivaig. Raised above the rocky E shore of Loch Sween, its massive rubble walls, strengthened by buttressing at the corners and mid-points, are without any openings other than a round-headed arched S entrance and a mutilated sea-gate on the W. The C12 quadrilateral plan, which might be a rectangle or parallelogram but is neither one nor the other, encloses an inner court, 21.5m. by 16.5m. at its widest extent. But 'the impression of an open courtyard is', as Stewart Cruden has pointed out, 'illusory' since much of this inner space was evidently given over to various ranges of building, constructed first in timber and later in stone. Cruden's view that Castle Sween is 'a keep', comparable to Castle Rushen on the Isle of Man, is unconvincing. That such a precedent should be cited is, nevertheless, intriguing since Rushen was largely built in the third quarter of the C12 by the Norse rulers of Man. But Norse or not in its affinities, Castle Sween must be regarded as the earliest castle of enclosure on mainland Scotland.

Such CASTLES OF ENCLOSURE are well represented in Argyll 64 and Bute. At Rothesay, where the moated castle now sits in the middle of town, the walls date from the early years of the C13. If not raised as a royal fortress, it quickly became one and played a vital role in the conflict with the Norse and later in the pacification of the Western Isles. The *enceinte* is circular, with four circular towers added around the curtain before the end of the C13. This plan appears nowhere else in Argyll and Bute; indeed it is unique in Scotland. There are, however, several rectangular castles of enclosure, all dating from the C13. The minimal masonry remains at Dunoon, possibly dating from the second quarter of the C13, suggest such a layout, though the surviving evidence for this inference is scant. Scarcely less eroded, if less problematical, are the contemporary traces of the inner bailey at Tarbert. In contrast to Dunoon and Tarbert, both of which may, like Rothesay, have been built by the Crown, the early C13 walls of the island castle of Innis Chonnell, the stronghold of the Campbells of Loch Awe until their move to Inveraray in the C15, are not only impressive in bulk but sufficiently intact in their configuration to permit reliable interpretation. The plan is almost square, 25m. by 22m., with buttresses surviving at the mid-point of the SE wall and at the E angle. Nor are these simple but distinctive structural features the only similarities with Castle Sween. Openings in the curtain-wall are few and small; a single lintelled doorway (a C15 reconstruction of the original C13 entrance) penetrates the centre of the NE wall; in the inner 'court', from which a mural stair rises to the wallhead, ranges of accommodation survive which, though substantially the result of C15 building, also incorporate earlier work. At the castle of the bishops of Argyll at Achadun on Lismore, the ruinous late C13 walls, picturesquely silhouetted on their hilltop site, reveal considerably less. Like Innis Chonnell, the plan is square, *c*. 26m. by 26m., with evidence of an inner range of building along one side. Duart Castle, less than 8km. SW of Achadun across the Firth of Lorn, commands the entry to the Sound of Mull. Though transformed and dramatized by subsequent building, it began in the C13 as a castle of enclosure, raised by the MacDougall lords of Lorn on another roughly square plan, *c*. 25m. by 25m. Dunstaffnage Castle, however, is the castle of enclosure *par excellence*. It, too, is a MacDougall fortress, built opposite Duart on the E shore of the Firth of Lorn. Gaunt, massive and much less elaborated by later works, it seems to have assimilated many of the contemporary trends in the fortified architecture of the western seaboard. The plan is quadrilateral, but might be read as a misshapen square deformed to suit the rocky base below the great curtain-walls, completed *c*. 1250. Again ranges of accommodation are built against the inner sides of the curtain and, though these are all of later date, they may replace early timber structures. But what characterizes Dunstaffnage most, adding to its elevated massiveness, are the rounded angles of the *enceinte*. Three of these are circular towers, an arrangement perhaps not unrelated to that on Bute but which here results in the towers being pressed into the corners of the plan, in contrast to the attached cogwheel relationship at Rothesay.

Almost all of these C13 castles of enclosure are situated close to the sea. Water, of course, provided the most convenient means of transport, but a safe haven was critical and many sites already had a history of fortified settlement. Regional strategic considerations clearly governed the choice of location for Duart and Dunstaffnage, which face each other on opposite shores of the Firth of Lorn seaway. Rothesay provides good anchorage, protected from the prevailing SW winds. Castle Sween stands guard over the approach to a series of calm sheltered inlets further up Loch Sween. Innis Chonnell is effectively a fortified island close to the SE shore of Loch Awe. On the other hand, at Dun Ara, a craggy summit on the Mishnish shore of NE Mull, and at Cairnburgh Castle on the Treshnish Isles and Dun Chonnaill Castle on the Garvellachs, both important outposts on the sea-routes between Lorn and the southern Hebrides, the few surviving fortification walls seem simply to have reinforced the irregular natural defence lines of rock and shore.

Wood-framed construction, used for the domestic ranges which lay behind the masonry enclosures of these larger castles built by the Crown or nobility, must also have been adopted by lesser landowners for their much less ambitious dwellings. No such structure has survived but there are a few so-called 'HALL-HOUSES', the masonry equivalent of the fortified timber manor-house. At Finlaggan on Islay, where Eilean Mór was encircled by timber defence-work and many of the the buildings must have been of timber construction, there is evidence of a stone-built hall on the Council Isle, probably C13. In Kintyre, the C13 walls of a three-storey oblong building have been incorporated into the castle of enclosure constructed at Skipness at the turn of the C13 and C14. The hall itself, presumably on the first floor, and the accommodation housed on the uppermost floor were originally lit by a number of windows, all of which had round-headed inner arches. Skipness is not a naturally defensible site but, of four other hall-houses which survive in ruin from the C13 or early C14, three are strongly located on a promontory summit and one is on an island. All are more or less rectangular in plan. Fincharn Castle on the SE shore of Loch Awe and Castle Coeffin on Lismore are relatively small with an internal span of 5m. or 6m. Aros Castle on the Sound of Mull and Fraoch Eilean at the N end of Loch Awe are somewhat larger with clear widths of 8m. and 9m. necessitating the introduction of an axial beam supported on posts at mid-span. On an island in Loch Avich, the fragmentary remains of Caisteal na Nighinn Ruaidhe (Castle of the red-haired Maiden) may constitute vestiges of another hall-house, but the evidence is meagre and inconclusive.

Although their incidence is most marked in the C13 and early C14, castles of enclosure and hall-houses are not entirely confined to this period. Old Castle Lachlan, Garbhallt, for example, has a plan remarkably like that of Castle Sween, though rather smaller: a deformed rectangle with two internal parallel ranges divided by a narrow yard. But the enclosure is early C15, the inner walls built late in the same century. Constructed a hundred years later, *c.* 1600, the E range at Toward Castle, a single-storey building comprising chamber, hall and kitchen, is described by the RCAHMS Inventory (1992) as a 'late form' of hall-house. Nevertheless, these are exceptions, for by the end of the C14 the dominant castellar type was the tower-house.

Stone-built TOWER-HOUSES make their appearance in two ways. Some were constructed as adjuncts to existing masonry enclosures, for example at Castle Sween and Duart; no doubt they provided safer and more permanent residential accommodation than the timber buildings which crowded the inner yard. At Castle Sween, construction was staged: first, a small NW tower, now much degraded; later, *c.* 1300, the addition of a cylindrical garderobe tower which still bursts dramatically out of the rocky shore; later still, during the C15, a second rectangular block, the MacMillan Tower, added to the N. At Duart, a more substantial late C14 tower, oblong in plan with walls almost 4m. thick, rose from the cliff-face against the NW side of the castle curtain. But the tower-house also emerged as an independent structure. Already, before the end of the C14, the Campbells of Loch Awe had built Carrick Castle, a gabled tower of three storeys perched on a rocky islet close to the W shore of Loch Goil. The plan is a longish rectangle recalling the hall-house formula and its floors may, like Aros and Fraoch Eilean (*see above*), have relied on beam-and-post construction rather than vaulting, though the presence of springing stones does indicate a clear but unrealized intention to vault. There are straight-flight mural stairs and deep square reveals to the principal windows, several of which have pointed arches. Carrick may be early but, excessively elongated in plan and lacking vaulting, it is not typical. By the middle of the C15, however, several oblong towers with vaulted basement storeys had been built or were under construction. Craignish is one but is otherwise so altered by later interference and accretion as to be unrecognizable as a genuine tower-house. In Cowal, the ruined Lamont castles of Ascog, near Millhouse, and Toward, both destroyed during the Argyll rebellion in the late C17, were also vaulted below first-floor level; at Toward, however, instead of the customary longitudinal arrangement there are two transversal vaults over the ground-floor chambers. Ascog's plan is almost identical in dimension to the mid-C15 Campbell castles of Kilchurn and Inveraray. At Kilchurn, which was further elaborated into a courtyard barracks in the C17, the tower is still relatively well preserved, standing four storeys to a ruinous wallhead and garret gable. Inveraray, demolished in the estate improvements of the C18, was closely comparable in plan and elevation. The marked similarities of these three castles suggest that by *c*. 1460 a standard model had evolved for the oblong tower-house.

Some smaller towers are square in plan. The coastal castles of Moy on Mull and Breacachadh on Coll, both built by scions of the powerful MacLean of Duart family in the second quarter of the C15, are of this type. Each has an irregular barmkin appended to the SE side of the tower (now all but invisible at Moy). At Moy, there are superimposed barrel-vaults in opposed alignment over the chambers at ground- and first-floor levels; an unusual arrangement but perhaps one not unrelated to the absence of flues on the lower levels where the smoke from open fires was dissipated through mural vents. Dunollie at Oban preserves the orthodox single vault over the cellar. Here, on a high promontory site overlooking Kerrera and the narrow channel entry to Oban Bay, the square, four-storey tower, built by the MacDougall lords of Lorn, *c*. 1450, sits obliquely on the NE corner of a courtyard, also square. Hidden in ivy, the fragmentary masonry curtain rises abruptly off the cliff edge. The location is both spectacular and strategic, with a long history of occupation going back to the C7 fortress of the Dalriada kings.

Oblong tower-houses continued to be built throughout the C16. Following the forfeiture of MacDonald lands in Kintyre in 1493, the Crown authorized an extensive programme of building in the peninsula. James IV erected a new castle at Kilkerran in 1494 and in the same year had work begun on a tower at Tarbert. Operations continued at Tarbert well into the C16 under the authority of the Campbell Earls of Argyll. At Saddell and Skipness, where the same family were charged with guardianship, new towers were also raised in the early 1500s. Further N, the Stewarts of Appin, who were strong supporters of the monarchy in its efforts to control the Western Isles, built the spectacularly sited Castle Stalker. Completed some time during the second quarter of the C16, Stalker is still, despite much later alteration and restoration, the archetypally romantic tower-house. Very different is Carnasserie Castle in Kilmartin Glen, 1565–72, built by John Carswell, who held the lands of Carnasserie under grant from the Earl of Argyll and who, by the late 1560s, had risen from being rector at Kilmartin to a powerful position in the reformed church in Argyll with substantial revenues to draw on. This roofless but large and remarkably well-preserved castle is best described as a hall-tower. The in-line combination of a four-storey tower with a three-storey hall-house is unusual, but the continuity of masonry and the consistency of architectural detail make it clear that the structure belongs to a single building period. Carswell did not lack resources; enough, in fact, to attract masons from Stirling, whose decorative work left the castle with some fine examples of early Scottish Renaissance ornament.

Such aggrandized treatment of the tower-house plan is exceptional but, by the end of the C16, an increasing attention to comfort and convenience is evident. In several towers the more flexible L-plan was adopted. The wonderfully picturesque Gylen Castle impaled on a promontory on Kerrera, though exceptionally small, is surprisingly sophisticated in form and detail. Completed in 1582, its single-chamber tower is no more than *c*. 6m. square but has a SW jamb, also square, in which a turnpike stair climbs through four floors. This conventional arrangement, which had also been adopted at Carnasserie, is not common in Argyll. It may have existed at Kames Castle on Bute and at Inveraray, where the old castle (*see* above) was converted to an L-plan at the end of the C16, but in a number of towers constructed between 1590 and 1610 it is absent. At Dunderave, which carries a 1598 datestone among several ornamental details stylistically comparable to those at Gylen, the turnpike stair is housed instead in a square block tucked into the E re-entrant of the L-plan. Similar arrangements survive at Duntrune, where the tower-house of *c*. 1600 replaced an earlier, simpler structure in the S angle of a late medieval polygonal barmkin, and at Barcaldine, which was completed by 1609. Clearly, such solutions, which not only afforded good vertical circulation but could give greater privacy to those chambers planned in the jamb, found greater favour than the earlier alternative formula. Yet the more developed Z-plan seems disregarded in Argyll. Only Kilmartin Castle, a three-storey gabled hall-house built in the last quarter of the C16, might, by virtue of two full-height cylindrical towers located at opposite corners of the plan, qualify for such a classification. Even at this late date, earlier and more austere models could prevail. The castle built by John Stewart of Appin on the island of Shuna, probably in the 1590s, is little more than an oblong tower-house box. While Shuna is essentially domestic in character, the much-reduced island refuges in Loch an Sgoltaire,

Colonsay, and Loch Gorm, Islay, both of which were occupied and strengthened by Sir James MacDonald during his rebellion of 1614–16, were heavily fortified by bastion-buttressed walls.

COUNTRY HOUSES

The religious differences of the C17 left much of Scotland exhausted by warfare. Argyll, though peripheral, was fiercely partisan. Divisions between Episcopalian and Presbyterian, overflowing into a civil war that engulfed the country in the struggle between Monarchy and Commonwealth, were compounded in conflicts between the principal landowning families. Issues of land, religion and power became inextricably confused. MacDonalds and MacLeans declared for the royalist cause. Campbells took the opposite side. In 1644, the Marquis of Montrose's army, supported by MacDonald forces, was at Inveraray; town and castle were attacked on three separate occasions. The response was as punitive as it was fast. In 1647, a Covenanting army under David Leslie swept through Kintyre, Islay, Mull and Lorn with devastating effect; the castles at Dunaverty, Dunivaig and Gylen were never to recover. The Restoration brought peace, but the reintroduction of the 'Jacobean episcopacy' and the attempt to restore the rights of patronage in the nomination of parish ministers provoked renewed conflict. A period of religious repression precipitated emigration. Many Lowland Scots, particularly the Covenanters of SW Scotland, who had been treated brutally, crossed the Atlantic, but some settled in Kintyre in the small plantation town of Campbeltown established by the 7th Earl of Argyll earlier in the century and now, in 1667, made a burgh of barony. In April 1685 the 9th Earl of Argyll landed at Campbeltown, mustered an army and, in an alliance with the Duke of Monmouth, moved N in rebellion against James VII and II. Once again the whole region was in turmoil, though the revolt was put down within the year. After a brief forfeiture, the Argyll lands were restored to the 10th Earl in 1689.

FORTIFIED BUILDING continued through these unsettled times. A few new castles were constructed, for example on Colonsay and Islay (*see* above), but many more were repaired and reinforced. Some were permanently reduced to ruins. Of residential building there is little beyond the remains of two- and three-storey gabled dwellings constructed within the walls at Fraoch Eilean, Duart, Breacachadh and Dunstaffnage. Islay House, near Bridgend on Islay, begun in 1677, adopted the castellar L-plan, though the thickness of its three-storey-high walls (no more than a metre) raises doubts about just how fortified it may have been. A late C17 kitchen wing, certainly domestic in character, survives at Lochnell House; but nothing is known of the house (or castle) which this originally served. As late as 1690, continuing unrest in Lorn and further N led to the building of several four-storey barracks ranges at Kilchurn Castle, transforming it into a major regional fortress.

Not until the early years of the C18 did conditions become stable enough to permit the building of those residences that may properly be termed country houses. In 1722, on Colonsay, the McNeills constructed perhaps the first CLASSICAL MANSION-HOUSE in Argyll. No more than a harled two-storey-and-attic box with a piended roof, Colonsay House was later elaborated by extensive C19 additions wholly Palladian in their low quadrant wings and Venetian windows. It is an appropriate enhancement, for the three-bay symmetry of the original already alluded, albeit remotely, to this distant provenance. Appin House, Portnacroish, also of the early C18, did the same. Five bays wide, perhaps with a pediment before its attic floor was converted to a full third storey *c.* 1770, it was demolished in the mid 1960s. Limecraigs House in Campbeltown, constructed for Elizabeth Tollemache, widow of the 1st Duke of Argyll, is also five bays with a piended roof; it may be earlier than Colonsay but is much the worse for later alteration and encroachment. Much grander, Lochnell House, 1737–9, is three-storeyed and piended, the three central bays of the main NE front dignified by round arched windows at first-floor level and an urn-capped pediment raised above the eaves. Later C19 castellated accretions unbalance and undermine this originally symmetrical façade. But at Airds House, Port Appin, 1738–9, the tripartite organization of the five-bay façade is unimpaired. Calmer, if a little duller, but 'mindfull' (*sic*) (as the Campbell of Airds motto carved in the pediment tympanum below the family arms adjures) of Palladian precedent: the central block embraces a forecourt with quadrant links to flanking pavilions fronted by pedimented gables. Ardmaddy Castle can justify its more military designation on the basis, material as much as metaphorical, that its ground-floor storey is, in fact, the vaulted basement of a late C15 tower-house. This robust undercroft is, however, invisible, absorbed in a pretty little harled block of 1737, two storeys high, with a pedimented balcony-portico tucked intimately into the heart of a symmetrical U-plan.

This appearance of dilute Palladian ideas is at first largely localized. Indeed, prior to 1750, only one other house in Argyll can be compared with these architectural events in Lorn, and then not so much in terms of stylistic sophistication as simply size. At Islay House (*see above*), the late C17 L-plan was extended into a U in 1731, the long nine-bay SW elevation carefully contrived to achieve an approximately symmetrical arrangement in which a regularized three-bay centre sat between broad twin-chimneyed gables. But the result here, despite the vertical proportions of the three central windows at ground- and first-floor levels, seems more a matter of formal tidiness, a kind of involuntary vernacular classicism, rather than any applied fashion derived from the pages of *Vitruvius Britannicus*. Nevertheless, when stair-towers were added on the outer sides of each arm of the U, *c.* 1760, the landings were lit by superimposed, Palladian three-light windows.

It might be expected that the new fashion in country-house building would find favour at Inveraray, the seat of the Campbell Dukes of Argyll, by far the richest and most powerful lairds in

Argyll. And, indeed, since the 1660s when the 9th Earl first envisaged improvements, successive dukes had contemplated the reconstruction or replacement of their medieval tower-house home. The more peaceful conditions of the C18 intensified such considerations and several proposals were obtained before it was decided to proceed with a CASTELLATED GOTHIC design for a new mansion from the English architect *Roger Morris*. Morris had begun in Palladian mode but, finding the 3rd Duke favourably disposed to the romantic castellar attributes of earlier proposals from *Sir John Vanbrugh* and *Dugal Campbell*, had assimilated this more medieval cast of thought, producing a final scheme in 1744 that was in effect a Gothick fort. But only 'in effect', for the new castle was indefensible, set in open policies, its gardens and woodlands planned for pleasure and, in the upper reaches of the estate, progressively developed for productive farming. Morris's design is strongly symmetrical and preserves a certain elevational hierarchy in its fenestration, both aspects of classical composition, but the restrained elegance of the Palladian Revival then raging in the S is eschewed. Or, rather, it is confined to some of the building's interiors and to a few of the estate's ancillary structures, particularly the bridges, completed later in the century. But the castle's crenellated parapets, round corner towers, pointed-arch windows and its peripheral fosse all seem to proclaim the significance of Inveraray's context in place and time, if only in a rhetoric assumed for its symbolic connotation rather than its archaeological accuracy. Perhaps architect and patron found this castellar approach more suited to the wild Lochfyneside landscape; perhaps the Duke felt such allusion to the traditional forms of the past befitted his family's status as the premier landowner in the shire. At any rate, Inveraray was exceptional. One of the earliest and most influential buildings of the Gothic Revival in Britain, it was certainly the main architectural event in C18 Argyll. Yet its local influence was delayed. Meanwhile it was left to junior branches of the ubiquitous Campbell clan to introduce Palladian models to Mid Argyll.

Not far SW of Inveraray is Minard Castle. The designation 'castle' is again fanciful, the style again Castellated Gothic, though this time a matter of C19 pretension (*see* below). Hidden within is a three-bay box, square in plan, the small Palladian house built by Archibald Campbell of Knockbuy, *c.* 1775. A few years later and 5km. SW along the Loch Fyne shore, Campbell's kinsman and neighbour, the sheriff-depute of Argyll, Robert Campbell, raised Asknish House. It has escaped Victorian change: a three-storey, piend-roofed, classical mansion-house with tall pilaster strips defining a tripartite façade, no pediment, but a central Palladian window lighting the first-floor Drawing Room. This last feature also occurs on the five-bay SW front of Strachur House, begun in the 1780s by General John Campbell. At Strachur, however, the frontispiece of this principal façade is pedimented while the equivalent central zone on the garden front projects as a bow. Somewhat unexpectedly, this drum-like element is capped by a castellated coronet parapet. The feature is repeated as a crenellated eaves to flanking wings added to the gables later in the C18, and it recurs at nearby New Castle Lachlan, a three-bay classical house of *c.* 1790, later extensively baronialized. Strachur has some fine estate buildings: a rather grand Court of Offices, a rude but well-proportioned arched gateway in whitewashed rubble, and an ornamental bridge conceived with such aesthetic aplomb as to suggest hands across the water from Inveraray. But the outstanding Palladian mansion in Mid Argyll is Barbreck House. Built by General John Campbell in 1790, everything is orthodox but supremely elegant. A five-bay front with the three central bays advancing under an armorial pediment; blind arcades l. and r. widening the façade to low wings with pedimented gables; urns on the eaves: the composition is simple yet the heights and spacing of the elevational elements are perfectly judged. But there is something else, something more than the subtle, regulating lines of geometry. Landscape gives Barbreck a special presence. Calm, erect and perfectly poised in flat open country at the head of Loch Craignish, it seems to dream of the Veneto.

Palladian pretension lingered on in Mid Argyll. Not 2km. NE of Barbreck, Turnalt House, *c.* 1800, a two-storey-and-attic block linked to lower flanking pavilions, reflects the composition of its larger neighbour. But the design differs in detail and resolution. At the centre, the arch of a tall, first-floor Venetian window opens the pediment above, the same motif repeated with blind side-lights below steeper gable pediments in the wings. Turnalt lacks the assurance and composure of Barbreck but it is not short on ambition. Seldom, however, do later smaller properties assume such cultural aspiration. Carse House, Kilberry, designed first in 1816 but not built until 1828, has a projecting centrepiece like Turnalt but no pediment. On the other hand, at Glenshellish House, late 1820s, where the façade is still flat, the pediment is inelegantly steep like those on Turnalt's wings. In the main, the demands of proper Palladian fashion, inevitably more expensive, remained the preserve of the richer estate owners.

Elsewhere in Argyll classical houses are less remarkable. Nothing of note is to be found in Kintyre. In the islands, New Breacachadh was begun, *c.* 1750, as a three-bay, three-storey house with quadrant walls and pavilion wings but was later raised a storey and castellated. Lochbuie House on Mull, 1793, follows the five-bay model with a pedimented centrepiece and flanking wings; in contrast to Barbreck, the house itself is gabled, the wings piended. Foley House on Bute, late C18, is three-bay, but pedimented on the façade *and* the gables. On the W shore of Loch Lomond, Rossdhu House, built by the Colquhouns of Luss, 1772–4, is formulaic five-bay, but greatly enhanced some fifty years later by the addition of side wings, balustraded eaves and a pedimented portico. Keppoch House, Ardmore, 1820, reaches three storeys with superimposed tripartite windows below a central pediment. At Ardlamont House in Cowal, the gabled wings date in part from the C18 but the rather dull core of the house, again five-bay, is a reconstruction of 1819–20. Ardmarnock House, *c.* 1826, has more grace: a two-storey-and-attic house, compact and cubic, with a piended roof and Ionic porch. Despite Baronial encroachment and later neglect, it manages to preserve something of its original detached dignity.

Throughout the C18 the lesser lairds of Argyll had built their houses in downmarket emulation of the classical models adopted by their feudal superiors. Lower down the social ladder, the tacksmen, who held land in lease, subletting it to tenants, did the same. Manses, too, were austere followers of fashion. Three- and five-bay symmetry proved popular according to need and resources. But beyond this ordering of the plan and elevation, there is little architectural or ornamental elaboration. What emerges is the archetypal two-storey house, harled and gabled, common in the countryside and villages of rural Scotland for two hundred years and more. Crinan House, *c.* 1710, is an early example; later alteration has destroyed its original symmetry but it retains its precautionary domestic solidity with small window openings tight below the eaves. Old Kilmun House, early C18, is more ambitious with a pedimented doorpiece set off-centre as a result of the unusual six-bay plan. Glenure in Glen Creran, Erray House on Mull, and Taynish House near Tayvallich were all completed by 1750 following the five-bay model. Bonawe House, mid C18, built for the partner-manager of the ironworks at Taynuilt, adds a third storey. Grishipoll House on Coll, Island House on Tiree, and Upper Sonachan House at Port Sonachan are also mid C18 but smaller; the first is ruinous, the second much altered, the last distinguished by coupled ground-floor windows and small gabled wings. These patterns are continued into the early decades of the C19, becoming more pervasive and, occasionally, acquiring more decorative detail. Ardpatrick House on West Loch Tarbert and Stewart Hall, Bute, both dating from the 1760s, share rusticated quoins and jambs, the latter vigorously modelled with a pedimented Palladian centrepiece. Pediments were, however, a much less frequent feature of the smaller house. In Lorn the three-bay gabled simplicity seen at Achlian near Cladich, Ardlarach on Luing, Degnish, w of Melfort, and the Manor House, Oban, all probably 1780s, is more characteristic of the later C18 period; in Mid Argyll, Claonairigh near Auchindrain; on the islands, the remorselessly plain Old Gruline House at Salen, Mull. Country manses, generally stiff and erect, maintain the same severe reserve: among them, those at Ardchattan Point, 1773, Kilmartin, 1789, Muasdale, 1803, Dalmally, 1804, Inverchaolain, 1807, Kilfinan, 1808, Gigha, 1816, Kilmichael of Inverlussa, 1817, and Kilbrandon House on Seil, 1827. The manses at Dalmally and Inverlussa have a central gablet rising from the eaves; at Kilmore, 1828, and Ardfern, 1834, this has become a pediment. Such temptations are eschewed in those manses built to serve the Parliamentary kirks of 1828, the stark three-bay front of the two-storey version denied even a central entrance door.

By *c.* 1830, tacksmen's dwellings, farms and manses were all following the classic tripartite formula. Moreover, besides this rural vernacular, the classical language of architecture had acquired an urban dialect. Streetscapes appeared in various aggregations of symmetrical three-bay house units. Suburban villas displayed the same simple syntax, accented perhaps by a pilastered doorpiece or porch. Much of this has gone, but in the smaller towns and villages, like Rothesay, Inveraray, Lochgilphead, Tarbert, Tobermory and Bowmore, a pervasive demotic classicism survives. By contrast, many country houses had abandoned the grammar of column and cornice. By the 1820s, Gothic was in vogue.

It is surprising that the GOTHIC REVIVAL style, precociously introduced at Inveraray before the middle of the C18, should have found few immediate imitators. Even within the estate, most buildings, other than the Castle, were classical after a fashion. *Roger Morris*'s design for a battlemented 'Gothic temple', 1745, and *John Adam*'s proposal to erect a mock medieval ruin on the summit of Dùn na Cuaiche, *c.* 1750, remained on paper. The Physick Well, also by Adam, *c.* 1755, designed as a short spire rising from a crenellated base with pointed-arch openings, was built but demolished within twenty years. Morris's Tower on Dùn na Cuaiche, 1747–8, and the Old Schoolhouse in Glen Aray, 1781, now ruinous, were no more than tentatively medieval in character. On the other hand, the Castle itself, with its pointed-arch windows, corner towers and crenellated parapets, must have been specially potent and known across the county. And yet, apart from a Gothick folly at Barbreck, for more than half a century Inveraray remains unique. Further proposals to enhance the estate with castellar gateways and buttressed towers were prepared by *Alexander Nasmyth*, *c.* 1801. But these too were not built. Nasmyth was, however, engaged by Lord Lorne, later the 6th Duke of Argyll, to design the Home Farm at the Campbell estate at Rosneath, 1803. But at Rosneath, Castellated Gothic remained farmyard fancy; the new castle, built 1803–6 to the designs of *Joseph Bonomi*, was wholly Neoclassical in style.

Meanwhile, in 1802, 'the first gothick house in the Highlands since Inveraray' (McKean, 1998) had been begun by *James Gillespie Graham* at Achnacarry in Lochaber. Still symmetrical and tripartite in organization, the design is castellated (though not crenellated) with quatrefoil-pierced parapets between bartizans. Ten years later Gillespie Graham was working in Lorn. Designs of 1812 for Gallanach near Oban, delineating a small asymmetrical mansion, turreted and crenellated, are almost certainly his. The house remained unbuilt, the commission going instead to *William Burn*, who wrapped a balanced classical plan in a castellated casing with corner towers and hooded Tudor-arched windows, 1814–17. Nor were Graham's proposals for Barcaldine House, 1813–14, realized, though his Court of Offices was built; and when, in 1816, the nearby Campbells of Lochnell decided to extend their mansion-house, it was *Archibald Elliot* who added a four-storey wing which, though not especially Gothic, was boldly castellated with a half octagon tower at one end and a corner drum at the other. In Kintyre Graham was more successful. The MacAlister houses of Torrisdale Castle and Glenbarr, under construction *c.* 1815, remain conventionally tripartite in plan, but are thoroughly gothicized. Both have castellated parapets and hooded traceried fenestration; and both have Gothic interiors. At Glenbarr, crocketed finials and buttresses add an ecclesiastical flavour. Calgary House on Mull, completed by 1823, must surely also be Graham's, and it is difficult not to be persuaded that the Gothic interventions at Kinlochlaich, Appin, *c.* 1820, are from the same hand.

In 1816 Gillespie Graham's ecclesiastical Gothic found appropriate expression in the Parish Church at Dunoon. Residential commissions, however, eluded him. Here, on the Cowal coast, where the influences of Lowland Scotland were most keenly felt, country house building was the prerogative of a new kind of client. Borne on a tide of commercial prosperity washing across the Firth from Glasgow and W Central Scotland, a handful of successful merchants acquired land in Argyll. Palladian manners might still prevail in the older estates, for example at Ardlamont and Ardmarnock (*see* above), but new money needed new forms. Castellated Gothic had already appeared in nearby Dunbartonshire, where *Robert Lugar* introduced a freer, more picturesque interpretation of medieval forms at Tullichewan Castle, 1808, and Balloch Castle, 1809. Now the same style reached the Cowal shore. In 1816 James Hunter employed the Glasgow architect *David Hamilton* to gothicize Orchard Park, a small late C18 mansion at Ardnadam just N of the eponymously named Hunter's Quay. It became Hafton House. The new N and E elevations are Tudor Gothic in character, with tall castellated octagonal buttress-turrets dividing each façade into three bays generously lit by hooded mullion-and-transom windows. In 1820–1, Kirkman Findlay, a wealthy Glasgow merchant, built Castle Toward. His architect, Hamilton again, produced a more castellar design, crenellated and turreted like Graham's work but romantically asymmetric in composition like Lugar's. This was quickly followed by Castle House, Dunoon, 1822, for James Ewing, Lord Provost of Glasgow. Hamilton repeats his Toward idiom, though the building is tighter and smaller: more marine villa than castle. Ten years later, the Campbell landowners of the Ballimore estate at Otter Ferry had embraced the new style and Hamilton was at work on Ballimore House.

Castellated Tudor Gothic was popular with the new lairds. What had been begun in Cowal was soon carried on elsewhere, and sometimes in much grander style. Relatively modest Campbell houses at Kilmory on Loch Gilp and Minard on Loch Fyne (*see* above) were swallowed up in vast building programmes undertaken by the new owners of the estates, Sir John Orde and H. W. Askew. Both 'castles' are impressive residential fortresses, the first by the London architect *Joseph Gordon Davis*, 1828–36, the second by *John T. Rochead* of Glasgow, 1842–8: ugly and agglomerative, they are designed with undeniable bravura. No doubt battlemented towers and vaulted halls afforded some symbolic reassurance to a *parvenu* gentry whose wealth had no historic relationship with the land but had accrued from trade or industry. Perhaps, however, as much as these allusive qualities, it was the less constraining syntax of the castellated style, its ability to accommodate itself to more sophisticated standards of comfort, convenience and domestic comportment, that recommended it. The symmetrical layout of the C18 could no longer cope with the complexities of circulation and social separation implicit in the daily regime of Victorian country-house living; a freer, more flexible plan was needed.

In these respects, the eclectic language of the JACOBETHAN REVIVAL proved no less attractive. Its principal exponent, *William Burn*, built a number of rambling, multi-gabled houses in Argyll. Ardanaiseig House near Kilchrenan, 1833–4, Finnart House, c. 1835, and Ardarroch House, 1838, both at Finnart, are his. The three-storey wing added to Craignish Castle, 1837, much reduced and traduced by later meddling, is also probably by Burn. At Ardmaddy Castle, 1837–9, *James Gillespie Graham* recast a late C18, two-storey wing, introducing shaped gables, balustraded bay and oriel windows and a finialled octagonal stair turret, though none of this was built until 1862. *Charles Wilson* dabbled in the style at Ardchattan, 1847–55. But by far the greatest achievement of Jacobean fashion in Argyll was Burn's Poltalloch House, 1849–53. Roofless since 1957, it survives in romantic but reproachful isolation. The shell is impressive. Designed from the architect's London office, the mansion might have been intended for some Home Counties parkland setting: spread out behind balustraded terraces, its wide ashlar façades gridded with mullion-and-transom windows below balustraded eaves and strapwork-crested gables, Poltalloch is English in everything but name. Yet the Malcolms, who commissioned the house, were a long-established indigenous family. Old money, too, could be seduced by fashion.

The Englishness of Poltalloch's Jacobean is exceptional. The incorporation of recognizably Scottish features was, understandably, more common. Burn himself had already used crowstepped gables at Ardanaiseig. His rival, *William Henry Playfair*, went further. At Stonefield Castle, 1836–40, he added corbelled bartizans, both cylindrical and square, to the mixture. Jacobean elements are still present but, whereas Poltalloch is horizontal, expansive and relaxed in disposition, Stonefield is vertical and busily compressed. This is the beginning of the BARONIAL REVIVAL. Playfair continued in the same vein at Islay House, 1841–5, where he was responsible for the addition of various service buildings. But at Kilberry, in *Thomas Brown*'s small Baronial mansion of 1844, all traces of Jacobean have been expunged. It is not clear to what extent Brown's work absorbed vestiges of an earlier tower-house, but its L-plan form, with bartizaned gables and a cone-topped turnpike in the re-entrant, bears some similarity to the Baronial model mansion which his assistant *David Cousin* had drawn for Loudon's *Encyclopaedia of Cottage, Farm and Villa Architecture* in 1833. Brown's Baronial was modest, almost vernacular, too reserved for the aspirations of most Victorian patronage. Nevertheless, Baronial fired the romantic imagination, its up-front Scottishness and uncodified compositional flexibility alike attractive to patron and designer. By the late 1850s it had become the preferred style for country-house commissions. Stimulated and informed by the publication of *Robert Billings*'s *The Baronial and Ecclesiastical Antiquities of Scotland*, which appeared in four volumes between 1845 and 1852, almost every major architect in the country was able to deconstruct the castellar precedents of C16 and C17 Scotland, permutating old forms in new ways matched to the residential needs of the C19.

William Burn had backed the Billings publication to the tune of £1000, a considerable investment which must have been related to the perceived market. But it was Burn's assistant, later partner, *David Bryce*, also a subscriber, who became the master of Baronial design. Of his vast *œuvre* of country houses carried out in the style, only three are to be found in Argyll. Carradale House, 1844, retains a Jacobean flavour, but is lugged with bartizans and incorporates the characteristic canted gable end. Torosay Castle on Mull, 1856–8, is mature Bryce, a vigorously plastic mass of stone and slate raised above terraced lawns. Ellary House, 1870, has less to offer. Besides Bryce, other leading architectural practices in Edinburgh and Glasgow were active in the field. *Peddie & Kinnear* completed Glengorm Castle on Mull, 1858–60; double-height bartizans flank a crowstepped gable as at Torosay, but a high square entrance tower adds a castellar element suited to a harsher site, bleak and exposed above the rocky N coast of the island. Later, in 1873, the same firm extended Kilberry Castle, the new accommodation imperceptibly fused with Brown's work of thirty years before. In 1849, the Glasgow architect *Charles Wilson* built Shandon House overlooking Gare Loch: a wonderfully agitated *tour de force*, restless with Baronial knowledge and invention. The following year, in quieter Scots mood, he was altering Inverawe House near Taynuilt. But in 1862, again declamatory, he began to transform Benmore House in Glen Eck, N of Dunoon. His four-storey tower at Benmore, which was probably designed in collaboration with *David Thomson*, is full of confidence, a robust collage of almost every Baronial trick. Blairvadach, built at Shandon in the early 1850s, is as ambitious and eclectic as Wilson's work near by but much less discerning; it is as if the architect, *John T. Rochead*, had not yet digested Billings. Knockderry Castle, spectacularly sited on the cliffs at Cove, is more successful. Towered and gabled with corbelled canted oriels reminiscent of Huntly, it was begun by *John Honeyman*(?) in 1855 and completed forty years later by *William Leiper*. Also on Loch Long, Cove Castle, 1867, is better still: a Victorian tower-house by *James Sellars*, in every sense more composed. In the ten years between 1864 and 1873, *John Burnet* built four Baronial houses. Auchendennan House, 1864–7, and Arden House, 1867–8; palatial, towered and turreted neighbours erected at the S end of Loch Lomond, one for a tobacco baron, the other for a Lord Provost of Glasgow. Now abandoned, Kildalton Castle on Islay, 1867, is more domestic in scale though still towered. Killean House, Tayinloan, on the other hand, where the Burnet practice, *père et fils*, were continuously involved from the first designs of 1873 until the completion of the S service wing in 1907, has a bulbous sculptural grandeur about it, no doubt suitably blandiloquent for its shipping magnate proprietor. *John Honeyman*'s Baronial has fared badly. His Skipness House of 1878–81, substantially a four-storey tower-house with chimneyed gables and corbelled angle turrets, was destroyed by fire in 1969. Achamore

House on Gigha, 1882–4, suffered a similar fate in 1896 and, although rebuilt, has entirely lost its high, spiky, Baronial core. In 1884, the Edinburgh-based architect *Hippolyte Blanc* designed Eriska House, now the Isle of Eriska Hotel, around just such a central tower in an unusually polychromatic concoction of canted bays, gables and dormers.

Baronial dominated country-house design throughout the second half of the C19. But there were significant exceptions to the rule. Two architects, *Alexander Thomson* in Glasgow and *Robert Rowand Anderson* in Edinburgh, were responsible for buildings which, though wholly different in scale and style, are alike in their rejection of this national obsession. It is true that Thomson is customarily accredited with the design of Craigrownie Castle at Cove, c. 1854, but this attribution is by no means secure; its Baronial Tudor forms are certainly not typical. Craig Ailey at Cove, 1850, and Tor House at Rothesay, 1855, are much more characteristic, classical in Thomson's uniquely eclectic way, each with an Italianate belvedere tower raised in the re-entrant of the plan. By contrast, Seymour Lodge, also in Cove, 1850, is steeply roofed and Gothic, a *cottage orné* model for countless later gabled villas. If Thomson's own villas are too small to be validly classed as country houses, then Anderson's Mount Stuart on Bute, begun in 1879 for the 3rd Marquess of Bute, is large enough to be deemed a palace. It is a Gothic palace. Astonishing not only in its size but in the lavishness of its materials and detailing and in its realization of what Charles Eastlake had called 'Gothic architecture under modern conditions', Mount Stuart was, nevertheless, conceived as a residence. Not surprisingly, it remains without parallel or progeny. The project engaged Anderson for more than three decades, but not to the exclusion of other commissions and interests. Before the end of the century he was promoting the National Art Survey, incorporating Scots Renaissance forms into his work, and contemplating the possibility of a national style.

By the 1890s full-blown Baronial was on the wane. In an interlude of Anglophile enthusiasm, red tiles, red brick (usually reinterpreted as red sandstone) and half-timbering became fashionable, notably in Helensburgh and along the Gare Loch shore. *William Leiper*, who could be Baronial too, is the master of this softer, southern style. Besides several large villas in leafy upper Helensburgh, Ganavan House near Oban, 1888, Tighnabruaich House, 1895, and Ardchoille, Clynder, 1900–2, show him in full command of a language first enunciated by Norman Shaw and widely cultivated in the Arts and Crafts movement. But the social success of English manners, especially marked around the turn of the century in middle-class suburban settings, failed to frustrate the search for Scottishness. New Castle Lachlan, Garbhallt, was baronialized as late as 1903. Far to the s in the Mull of Kintyre, *Rennison & Scott* built Carskiey House, 1904–9, in a Scottish idiom which, if dull, hinted that vernacular roots might be as relevant as castellar. In Helensburgh, *Charles Rennie Mackintosh* confronted bourgeois prejudice with The Hill House, 1902–3, a grey-harled combination of Baronial and vernacular forms deployed 'under modern conditions'.

The addiction to Scottishness persisted into the C20, at least until the First World War. In a changing social climate, opportunities to design country houses diminished abruptly. *Robert Lorimer*, however, secured a succession of commissions in Argyll. In the mid 1890s he rebuilt David Bryce's Ellary House after a disastrous fire. At the same time, Stronachullin Lodge near Inverneill was completed in a quieter, less stridently Scots style. Ten years later, in 1906, he began work on a house for Sir Andrew Noble, the new owner of the Ardkinglas estate which spread from Loch Fyne E to Loch Long. Ardkinglas House, 1906–8, is one of Lorimer's finest houses. It is unmistakably Scottish. It lacks the hard edge of Bryce's Baronial, is without overt revivalist reference, and has none of the formal daring of Mackintosh. Yet it seems to sustain tradition. Across Loch Fyne at Dunderave, 1911–12, this is even more the case; in part because Dunderave is largely the restoration of a late C16 tower-house, but only in part, for there is the spell of genius here, a subtlety in Lorimer's touch that seems miraculously imbued with the enduring spirit of the place. Other domestic work at Ichrachan House, *c.* 1908(?), and Inverawe House, 1913–14, both near Taynuilt, is pedestrian by comparison. Dunderave is the last great country house in Argyll.

Or perhaps the last but one. In 1921 the English architect *Oliver Hill* spent two weeks living in a cottage on the E coast of Kintyre. Here, on a beautiful site falling across grassy slopes to the rocky shore, he designed Cour, 1921–2, a house that catches the breath. Hill captures and creates a palpable enchantment. Cour is lonely, strange, idiosyncratic yet contextual. The vast roof of Purbeck slates is cornered with bellcast domes, reminiscent of Lorimer's at Ardkinglas and Dunderave but swollen and tipped with an almost sexual provocation. Below, buttressed walls of random whin masonry fall across casement grids to paved terraces laid into the tumbling landscape. This is Arts and Crafts in castle country, Lutyens cast in rawer, rougher mould. Now weathered, wet and worn, Cour survives rapt in melancholy.

The remainder of the C20 produced few country houses of quality. In the mid 1950s, *Leslie Grahame MacDougall* rebuilt Ulva House in an effete classical manner typical for the time. His Melfort House of 1962–4, equally symmetrical, has a hint of Cape Dutch about it. Neither anachronism nor nostalgia compromises Tigh-na-Uisge, Kilchrenan, 1961, a bold boxy icon of '60s Modernism in Scotland by *Morris & Steedman*. Houses at Easdale, 1987–92, and Ardbrecknish, 1990–1, by *Julian Wickham* and *Donald Wilson* are best described as singular. Making the most of an exceptional site, the roofs of Rossdarroch, 1997–8, by *Coleman & Ballantine*, sail up from the shore of Loch Lomond s of Tarbet.

The outstanding INTERIORS of the C18 are those at Inveraray Castle. Behind Morris's precocious Gothic Revival walls are rooms of exquisite classical refinement. On the more public NE side of the house, formed in 1771 from what was originally the Gallery, both the State Dining Room and Tapestry Drawing Room are the creation of *Robert Mylne* a decade or so later, the delicate plasterwork of their panelled walls and ceilings a lavish but light confectionery of arabesques, sprays, swags and wreaths. In the former, mirrors, grisailles and gilding add to the decorative scheme; in the latter, the walls are hung with seven specially commissioned Beauvais tapestries, *Pastorales à Draperies Bleues*. Apart from the supernumerary display of weaponry in the Armoury Hall, the remaining apartments at this principal floor level are generally as *John Adam* intended in the 1750s. These are classical, too, with 'genteel Ornaments of Stucco' and fine marble chimneypieces, rooms altogether more temperate in their elegance. A more marked reserve characterizes the late C18 friezes, cornices and ceilings at Asknish House, Barbreck House and Strachur House. Vestiges of earlier C18 interiors (some pine panelling and roll-and-hollow moulded fireplaces) survive in Lorn at Ardmaddy Castle, Appin House near Portnacroish, and Glenure, Glen Creran.

While, paradoxically, there is only the slightest flirtation with medievalism in the interiors at Inveraray, the fashion for Gothic is later widely in evidence. In Kintyre, there are plaster rib vaults, Perp-panelled doors and shutters, and four-centred arched chimneypieces at Glenbarr Abbey and Torrisdale Castle, both the work of *James Gillespie Graham*, c. 1815. In Cowal, *David Hamilton*'s Tudor Gothic at Hafton House, Ardnadam, 1816, has ribbed and traceried ceilings; over the stairwell, added c. 1840 by his son *James Hamilton*, is a circular lantern ribbed and bossed in the ceiling below and dome above. The early 1820s interiors at Castle House, Dunoon, and Castle Toward, Toward, by *David Hamilton*, retain some similar features. At Minard Castle, the entrance hall, staircase and principal public rooms, by *John T. Rochead*, 1842–8, are grander, not Puginian perhaps but confident and convincing enough; Gothic with a Victorian swagger, part ecclesiastical, part Baronial. The culmination of this medievalizing rhetoric is Mount Stuart, *Robert Rowand Anderson*'s shamelessly ostentatious palace (to describe it as a country house seems absurdly euphemistic) carried out for the 3rd Marquess of Bute through the last two decades of the C19. In the consistency of its Gothic, in the scale of its central arcaded hall and the apartments which surround it, and in its staggering wealth of material and craft, Mount Stuart is without peer: in all Scotland this is the Revival's grandest interior.

Mount Stuart is a magnificent anachronism, but an anachronism none the less. It is not just that its Gothic forms are half a millennium old; in any case, however historicist its design, the house contained some of the most up-to-date domestic technology. Nor is it that by 1900 the Revival had long since sacrificed its polemical integrity; the moral crusade might be over but the aesthetic delight remained. The irony was that the Butes should build with such splendour in an age of rapidly declining aristocratic fortunes (though they were, exceptionally, as much industrial capitalists as landed lairds), at a time when significant residential patronage was increasingly coming from the middle classes, at a moment, indeed, when the villa was already in vogue and the country house decidedly *de trop* and all but *passé*. By the turn of the century, High Victorian Gothic had given ground to a simpler, more intimate, more vernacular medievalism. Architecturally enfranchised by this enthusiasm for a humbler tradition of building, well-to-do suburban society sought to create for itself a domestic world which, while still emblematic, was above all convenient and comfortable. The houses built in Helensburgh, around the Gare Loch, along the Cowal shore, at Craigmore in Rothesay, and on Low and High Askomill, Campbeltown (all of which, with good steamer and rail connections, were within commuting distance of Glasgow), were certainly not without regional allegiance, whether English or Scottish; red tiling, half-timbering, turreting and crowstepping were much in evidence. But this was largely an external attribute. Most interiors reflected a common desire for a congenial, even snug, environment contrived with Arts and Crafts care, a kind of inglenook *Gemütlichkeit*. *William Leiper*'s Brantwoode, 1895, and Longcroft, 1901, by *A. N. Paterson*, both in Helensburgh, one Shavian in derivation, the other more Scottish, are among the best examples.

There were, however, two important exceptions to this trend, each distinctly Scottish. At Ardkinglas House, 1906–8, *Robert S. Lorimer* embraced the stylistic language and social pretension of the past. Behind Baronial walls is a Scots Renaissance interior of timber-panelling and heavily moulded plaster ceilings. In his conversion of Dunderave Castle, 1911–12, the same retrospective stylistic provenance prevails, though the tower-house *mis-en-scène* is necessarily much less formally organized. At The Hill House, Helensburgh, 1902–3, *Charles Rennie Mackintosh* assimilated tradition to bourgeois need, elevating both into a realm of aesthetic experience that has little to do with craft or comfort. Behind harled, quasi-Baronial walls is an interior without precedent or parallel, an almost mystical domestic world in which 'delicacy and austerity' are combined and, as Hermann Muthesius wrote at the time, 'refined to a degree which the lives of even the artistically educated are still a long way from matching'. That distance remains.

Settings of PARKLAND and WOODLAND surround several of the larger country houses. Inveraray is the outstanding example. The landscaping of the estate, which was probably begun in earnest in the late C16, has created a world of wood and meadow spreading N from Loch Fyne up the Aray valley. In the C17 long avenues of beech and lime were laid out. Tree planting continued in the C18, a deerpark was created, the lower course of the river straightened and gardens devised with diagonal and serpentine paths. In the C19, the gardens close to the new Castle were redesigned, leaving the present rectilineal arrangement to the SW. At Mount Stuart on Bute, where planning and planting began in the early C18, there is comparable grandeur. Thick woodland, traversed by long walks, lines the island coast except immediately to the E of the house where the Firth can be viewed across gently sloping lawns. At Ballimore, Otter Ferry, the prospect to Loch Fyne is also channelled between banks of trees. Ardanaiseig House looks to Loch Awe in similar fashion. Calculated in subtler ways, the interplay of water, grass and trees in the C18 park at Rossdhu, Loch Lomond, none the worse for its late C20 transformation into an international golf course, is exquisitely picturesque.

Many of the GARDENS which beautified and supplied the country houses of the C18 and C19 have fallen into decay. Walled gardens are numerous; almost all are untended and overgrown, but that at Ardmaddy Castle, dating from the first half of the C18, survives. Low walls and lawns designed by *W.A. Nesfield*, *c.* 1846, still shape the platformed setting of a roofless Poltalloch House, though the parterres have gone. Torosay Castle on Mull preserves the terraced garden attributed to *Robert Lorimer*, 1897–1906, its tiered lawns spilling s over balustraded banks towards Duart Bay. *Thomas Mawson*'s pools and rock garden at Mount Stuart, 1896–1901, are still cared for, but at Ballimore all is in disarray, the formality of flower-bed and paths no longer precise, the romantic walks he contrived through the wooded glen of a winding burn swallowed up in wilderness. At Strachur, where the park was stocked with trees and shrubs in the 1770s, a new formal garden was created early in the C20. At Benmore House, the C19 walled garden has become a formal garden planted with rare conifers; set on the axis of the central avenue is Puck's Hut, a summer-house pavilion designed by *Lorimer* in 1928 and moved here forty years later. Woodland gardens, resplendent in spring with the variegated blossoms of exotic rhododendrons and azaleas brought to Scotland by Victorian and C20 collectors, are to be found at Achamore House on Gigha, Stonefield Castle, Benmore, Crarae near Minard, and at Arduaine, where the garden merits an admiration which the original house, now Loch Melfort Hotel, cannot command. There are arboretums at Ardkinglas, Benmore and Glenfeochan House, Kilmore; ferneries at Benmore and Ascog Hall on Bute. At The Hill House, Helensburgh, the garden designed by *Charles Rennie Mackintosh* has been carefully re-created.

STABLES courts provided the service accommodation needed to support country-house living. Most were sited some distance apart but presented a public face echoing, in lower key, the architectural order of the main house. This façade is usually symmetrical with a central gateway or pend above which might be a gable or pediment, perhaps incorporating a doocot, as at Ardlamont House, early C19, or a bellcote, as at Ballimore House, Otter Ferry, *c.* 1832. The Court of Offices at Cherry Park, Inveraray Castle, based on plans prepared by *John Adam*, 1759, and *William Mylne*, 1772, is a particularly ordered design, square in plan with raised corner pavilions lit by Venetian windows. Other classical courts of note are at Strachur (*see* above), late C18, Hayfield near Kilchrenan, early C19, and Barbreck House, *c.* 1790, where, although the service ranges themselves have little or no architectural merit, their axial arrangement immediately behind the main house is a unique example of a single integrated conception for the estate buildings. Other examples reflecting the stylistic fashions of the C19 include the Gothick offices at Hafton House, *c.* 1800, of which only the E façade survives; those at Castle Toward, 1820–1, in Castellated Gothic; the asymmetrical, vaguely Jacobean ranges at Ardmaddy Castle by *James Gillespie Graham*, 1837–9; and *David Thomson*'s Baronial court at Benmore, 1874.

LODGES generally mirror the same stylistic reflections found in stables and other ancillary buildings. Grandest of all is the s Lodge at Rossdhu House, early C19, its high arched gateway and flanking pavilions a dramatic, intimidating entry to the estate. In marked contrast is the late C18 s Cromalt Lodge, a doll's house posted on the A83, s of Inveraray. On Bute, the lodges on the Mount Stuart estate have no stylistic affinity with the great house itself. Those at the Kerrycroy entry to the policies are early C19 Tudor Gothic, one at least by *William Burn*, while Scoulag Lodge, 1896–8, is harled Scots by *Robert Weir Schulz*.

ROADS, RAILWAYS, CANALS, HARBOURS AND LIGHTHOUSES

Nowhere in Argyll is far from the sea. Long sea-lochs run deep into the heart of the county. The two great peninsulas of Cowal and Knapdale–Kintyre, lying between Loch Long, Loch Fyne and the Sound of Jura, are themselves fjord-fringed. From earliest times the sea provided the most convenient routes, carrying people and trade to the islands and to those mainland settlements which had naturally favoured sheltered coastal sites to the bleaker moorland and mountain between. Christianity came by sea. Materials to construct Argyll's castles, churches, country houses and towns had to be transported by sea. Bills of lading tell the story of the building of Inveraray Castle: stone from nearby Creggans and St Catherines, bricks from Glasgow, Gourock, Ayr and Campbeltown, slates from Easdale, glass from Newcastle, timber from Scandinavia; everything arrived by ship. More recently, from the late C19 until the Second World War, countless working-class families on holiday from Glasgow and the industrial Lowlands flooded 'doon the watter', filling the many steamers which plied across the Firth of Clyde to the resorts on Bute and the Cowal coast. The steamers have gone (all but one) but ferry links on the Firth and to the outer islands remain as important as they have always been. Only in the late C20 have road communications and, to some extent, air transport provided serious alternatives.

No proper ROADS existed in Argyll before the C18. Until then a few rough tracks clung to loch or sea shores or wound their way over the saddles that separated the glens. Travel was difficult and slow. Change came as a result of military strategy. Following the Jacobite rebellion of 1715, the government in London became convinced that communications in the Highlands needed urgent and extensive improvement. In 1725 Major-General George Wade began a programme of military road building conceived as part of a wider policy of pacification. His achievements, which were concentrated in Perthshire and Inverness-shire, set a course which would lead to the opening up of some of the more remote regions of what was then known as North Britain. They could not, however, immediately remove the festering sense of alienation in the Highlands and Islands, and in 1745 a second Jacobite uprising broke out. By this time Wade had gone, promoted to general in 1739, the role of road-builder, though not that of military command, taken over by *William Caulfield*, Wade's Inspector of Roads since 1732. Even before the '45, Caulfield had made a start on the road from Dumbarton to Inveraray.

After the Duke of Cumberland's forces had defeated the last shreds of Prince Charles's army at Culloden, the government intensified its control in the Highlands. Jacobite estates were forfeited, hereditary jurisdictions abolished, the strictures of earlier Disarming Acts were further tightened, the kilt and bagpipes proscribed. Regiments, now garrisoned in the N forts, provided the labour force put to the continued task of road building. In 1746, work on the Inveraray road resumed under Caulfield's direction. Between 1747 and 1749 the most difficult sections of the route through Glen Croe and Glen Kinglass were completed. Stretches of this old road, its waterside track along the valley floors and the slow sinuous climb up to the 'Rest and be Thankful', are still to be seen, sighted from the higher line of the A83, constructed in the 1930s. Butter Bridge, *c.* 1751, which crosses the Kinglass Water where the road turns sharply to the W, survives in good condition, stranded by the line of the modern road. But Caulfield's costs had mounted and progress was slow. Doubts began to be expressed about the wisdom of the undertaking. A report of 1749 recorded that the road was 'of no other use to the County but for the Ease of a certain great man', a scarcely veiled reference to the staunchly Hanoverian Duke of Argyll who, then beginning the wholesale transformation of his estate, had brought pressure to bear on the military authorities to improve communications with Lowland Scotland. Inveraray was finally reached in 1751, no fewer than nine bridges, including *Roger Morris*'s Garron Bridge of 1747–9 (closed to vehicular traffic in 1980), having been built on the route from Ardkinglass around the head of Loch Fyne.

Caulfield next envisaged a road N from Inveraray to Loch Awe. There roads would branch E to Tyndrum, where connections could be made with the military road N through Glen Orchy and Glencoe to Fort William, and W to Dalmally, Taynuilt and Oban. Work began on the Glen Aray stretch, and in 1751 the link W from Dalmally to Bonawe at Loch Etive was under construction. By 1754 this road along the N side of Loch Awe through the narrow Pass of Brander was complete, though the continuation W to Connel and Oban was not improved until the completion of the river crossing at Bridge of Awe in 1779. In 1761 the way E to Tyndrum was opened. By 1760 a further stretch of road along the W shore of Loch Lomond from Tarbet N to Ardlui and on through Glen Falloch to Crianlarich had linked the Dumbarton–Inveraray route with the military road from Stirling to Tyndrum and Fort William. Caulfield's routes were well judged for, apart from a short stretch of road NE of Cladich where the old road leaves the Loch Awe shore to take a shorter, more direct route to Dalmally and a second diversion to the drier N side of Strath Orchy through Stronmilchan, the modern lines of the A82, A83, A85 and A819 follow the military roads closely.

ROADS, RAILWAYS, CANALS, HARBOURS 69

The Commissioners of Supply, those local landowners who, since the C17, had acted as the agency of local administration, were also involved in upgrading the county's roads and bridges. Using statute labour (Commissioners could require local tenants to give six days' work per year) or, more frequently, military gangs, they were not only responsible for repair and maintenance but could also direct the constructon of new metalled roads and bridges. In 1737 the two-arch crossing of the River Add at Bridgend, near Kilmichael Glassary, was built. The track from Inveraray to Lochgilphead and on to Oban was realigned and improved in the 1760s. In the 1770s, the narrow coastal road s from Lochgilphead by Inverneill to Tarbert, still today a stretch subject to landslip, was completed. Beyond Tarbert, the road down the w coast of Kintyre had by 1776 been established as the main route s to Campbeltown.

Raw material for the making of the new roads was easily obtained; indeed, there were criticisms that some routes seemed more related to the ready availablility of stone and gravel rather than to topographical convenience. Bottomed with broken stones, surfaced with gravel and provided with drainage channels to prevent their being washed away by the frequent rains, the new roads were an immense improvement on previous lines of communication in the Highlands. Nevertheless, without any binding agent such as tar, this construction was vulnerable to heavy and prolonged rain, and regular maintenance was necessary if the roads were not to fall into disrepair. Reports to the Treasury in the 1780s and 1790s repeatedly evaluated the need for repair and reconstruction against cost. In 1799, one such report warned with patronizing superiority that 'If the government stop maintaining these roads the Highlanders will in a few years relapse into their former ignorance or desert their country.' Increasingly perturbed, as much perhaps by the threat to military recruitment which depopulation posed as by any cultural concern, the government turned to *Thomas Telford* for professional advice on what should be done about the Highland roads. His surveys, carried out in 1802 and 1803, argued strongly that the maintenance of proper communications in the N could lead to prosperity and help halt emigration. Telford was already familiar with the challenge through his work as Surveyor for the British Fisheries Society, which had been founded in 1786 to establish fishing stations on the w coast. For a time it looked as if herring fishing, coupled with the sudden boom in the kelp industry, could absorb at least some of the families leaving the glens as a result of the combined effect of over-population, intolerable rents, insecurity of tenure, and the widespread introduction of sheep farming. Although this proved to be a false dawn, the necessity for good communications to serve these new coastal industries did serve to underline the recommendations of Telford's report. In 1803 an Act was passed which brought into existence the Commissioners for Highland Roads and Bridges. At the same time a second Commission was set up to superintend the building of the Caledonian Canal through the Great Glen, connecting Loch Linnhe (and what was then N Argyll) with Inverness and the Moray Firth.

Applications for new roads were now made to the Parliamentary Commissioners who, approving a submission, would provide half of the cost of construction. Specifications were higher than those used by Caulfield, for the new 'Parliamentary' roads were designed for cart and coach traffic. In Argyll, early proposals aimed to improve the links available to the fishing industry. From Loch Fyne, where there were as many as 500 boats, new roads were planned across Hell's Glen to Loch Goil, s through Glendaruel to Colintraive where there was a ferry link to Bute, and down Loch Eck to Ardentinny on Loch Long. The 'Memorial respecting the Glendaruel Road', lodged in application in 1804 by the landowners through whose estates the route passed, was careful to argue that since 'the counties of Argyll, and of the island of Bute, are much connected in the trade of fishing, and are still more connected in civil and military policy, the circuit courts for both being held twice in the year at Inverary [sic]', the proposed link would be advantageous both from a local and a national point of view. All three routes were agreed and by 1812 the opening up of Cowal was well under way.

A proposal of 1806 for a road crossing the Muir of Leckan from Auchindrain to Ford was begun but later abandoned. This route had long been used by the drovers who annually brought their cattle across country to the great trysts at Crieff and Falkirk and, with the boom in the beef trade occasioned by the Napoleonic Wars, was only one of many for which upgrading was sought. Successful applications resulted in a new Parliamentary road from Portnahaven to Bridgend on Islay, beyond which the track to Port Askaig and the crossing to Jura seems to have been considered adequate. On Jura, the construction of the single E coast road from Faolin to Lagg, where cattle from Islay and Colonsay crossed to Keills in Knapdale, entailed the building of the three-arch bridge over the Corran River, near Leargybreck, and the slipway and pier at Lagg, both designed by *David Wilson* of Lochgilphead and built 1809–10. On Mull, c. 1790, the Duke of Argyll had financed the building of a road and two bridges linking Aros with Loch Don, where cattle were ferried to the mainland from Grass Point. His request for a second road connecting Bunessan in the w with Loch Don met, however, with protracted delay.

In 1814 Parliament passed an Act requiring the Commissioners to ensure that the roads and bridges they had built were kept in good repair. Provision was also made for the counties to pass responsibility for the upkeep of all military roads within their boundaries to the Commission, three-quarters of the cost of all repairs, after a first year met at public expense, to be paid by the county. Argyll took advantage of this option, handing over the Inveraray to Loch Long, Inveraray to Tyndrum and Tyndrum to Ballachulish stretches. Costs generally were high but reports on expenditure showed that the Argyll military roads were in particularly poor condition and had incurred nearly three times the repair cost per mile expended on the Commission's own approved roads. Work on these roads was, meanwhile, coming to an end. It was announced that no further applications for grant support for new roads and bridges would be entertained and by 1821 all construction had ceased. The Commission continued to carry out repairs and remained in existence until 1863. Its final report concluded that, by fostering better communications in the N counties, it had left the Highlands 'with wealthy proprietors, a profitable agriculture, a thriving population, and active industry'. Such a confident assessment was hardly justified; an increased tax-yield was one thing, social disruption and deprivation another. The new road system opened up large areas of the country which had hitherto been all but inaccessible; in doing so, it inevitably helped to accelerate the disintegration of Highland culture.

RAILWAYS, too, opened up the county. Prospectuses issued in 1845 already envisaged routes through Argyll linking the Central Lowlands to Oban, then still a very small but burgeoning burgh with good steamer connections to the islands (*see* below) and a growing reputation as a fashionable resort. Both the Scottish Western Railway and the Scottish South Midland Junction Railway put forward proposals but failed to find the necessary financial support. In the same year, the Scottish Central Railway's plan to link Stirling with Callander and the Trossachs met with a more favourable response, and in 1846 the Dunblane, Doune & Callander Railway was being promoted. It took twelve more years before the line was opened; even so, this was a vital first stage in the journey to Oban. In 1865 the Callander & Oban Railway Act was passed, the planned route W now part of the Caledonian Railway's wider network. By 1873 the track had been laid as far as Tyndrum; in 1877 Dalmally was reached. The engineer *John Strain* now began to survey the narrow route round the N end of Loch Awe and through the Pass of Brander to Taynuilt, Connel and Oban. Work began at both ends of this final stretch in 1878, and two years later the line was open. The entry into Oban itself proved a problem: not only was the topography hilly and difficult but there was a statutory inhibition on any interference with those coastal streets (Argyll Square and George Street) closest to the S Pier targeted by the railway company. In the event, the line held to the E side of Glen Cruitten, almost by-passing the town before swinging N to approach a new Railway Quay and Station constructed in deep water in front of Shore Street.

Within a decade of the railway reaching Oban, a second Argyll line, the West Highland Railway, a subsidiary of the North British Railway, was under construction. This time the journey began at the North British Railway's pier at Craigendoran on the Clyde, which had been completed, just E of the company's terminal at Helensburgh, in 1883. From here the route passed through Helensburgh, where a new 'high' station was built, on to the Gare Loch, then N by Loch Long to Arrochar where it crossed to Tarbet on Loch Lomond. Thereafter it continued N above the shoreside road into Glen Falloch. At Crianlarich it turned W, running through Strath Fillan in parallel with the Callander & Oban Railway, before heading N again at Tyndrum through Glen Orchy and across the Rannoch Moor to Glen Spean and, ultimately, Fort William. This W Highland line, simultaneously built to the design of Glasgow engineers *Formans & McCall* from construction camps at Craigendoran, Arrochar, Inveruglas, Crianlarich and the Loch Linnhe shore, was opened in 1894. Two years later, a branch S from Fort William to Ballachulish was approved and though this proposal was dropped the connection to the Ballachulish slate quarries was made from the S in 1903 when the Callander & Oban Railway crossed Lochs Etive and Creran into Appin.

The meeting of the West Highland Railway with the earlier Callander & Oban line at Crianlarich confirmed the importance of this rather unremarkable village as a transport junction. In 1931 the first through-train from Glasgow to Oban running on the W Highland line as far as Crianlarich established the route which has survived all C20 reductions in track mileage. On the other hand, in 1965 the rail connection between Dunblane and Tyndrum was closed, eliminating any direct rail link from Edinburgh and Stirling to Argyll and the W Highlands. Services between Connel and Ballachulish ceased in 1966. The only track to be laid in the C20 was a short branch line to the 'secret port' at Faslane, completed during the Second World War in 1941.

Towards the end of the C19 several unsuccessful attempts were made to extend the rail network in Argyll. The Ardrishaig & Lochawe Railway was mooted in 1870 with a view to linking the Crinan Canal (*see* below) with Dalmally. It came to nothing. In 1895 surveys were undertaken for a line from Dalmally to Inveraray and from Inveraray round the head of Loch Fyne through Glen Croe to Loch Long and Arrochar. At the same time the town council of Campbeltown considered financing a connection N to Dalmally. In 1896 the Callander & Oban Railway revived interest in the route S from Dalmally through Glen Aray to Loch Fyne, going so far as to propose a 335m.-long tunnel through the Inveraray estate policies in an effort to overcome the Duke of Argyll's objections. The West Highland Railway meanwhile obtained approval to lay track from Arrochar to St Catherines on the E shore of Loch Fyne, where a ferry would transfer passengers to Inveraray. Suggestions were made that this line might even continue S to Dunoon. But none of these proposals was realized.

The spectacular landscape through which the Argyll railway lines pass poses many problems for engineers. VIADUCTS are necessary to cross rivers or negotiate valleys without loss of gradient. The standard solution is a lattice-girder structure spanning between masonry piers. Most of these viaducts occur on the stretch of the line which lies in Stirling District. W of Tyndrum, however, there is a seven-span structure at the Lochy Crossing, while three spans are enough to carry the line over the Falls of Cruachan at Loch Awe. At Inveruglas on Loch Lomond, Craigenarden Viaduct, by *Formans & McCall*, 1891, takes the track high above the lochside road, its eight stone-faced concrete arches, each spanning 11m., carried on masonry piers.

BRIDGES are still more frequent. On the W Highland line alone there are more than 100 structures of one or two spans. A single lattice-girder bridge spanning between castellated piers, completed in 1880, takes the Callander & Oban Railway across the River Awe. The most dramatic crossings are, however, on that railway's now defunct branch-line to Ballachulish. Work on the Connel Bridge over the Loch Etive narrows, designed by Sir *John Wolfe Barry* on the cantilever principle adopted for the Forth Rail Bridge in 1890, began in 1898. Three-arch masonry viaducts form the approaches on both sides, with a span of 160m. between the centres of the cantilever frames. Trains crossed in 1903; road traffic in 1909, hauled by the 'Connel Bus'. From 1913 vehicles have crossed under their own power and, unlike the trains, continue to do so. Further N at Loch Creran, Creagan Bridge, designed by Barry with *John Formans*, is more orthodox: two lattice-girder spans of 46m. between castellated rock-faced ashlar piers. It was completed in 1903, but has been out of use since 1966.

Many of the W Highland line's RAILWAY STATIONS have gone. In 1964 those at Craigendoran, Rhu, Shandon and Whistlefield were closed. Others have decayed in 'unmanned' neglect. Garelochhead, Arrochar & Tarbet and Bridge of Orchy survive, tarnished examples of the standard Swiss-chalet solution adopted. Built to a design that was probably supplied by Glasgow architect *James Miller*, these low, wide-eaved, timber-and-brick structures sit on island platforms reached by subway. Light and jaunty in character, often open to wonderful views, they are imbued with a 'picturesqueness foreign to the prevailing dinginess of most of our country railway buildings' (so averred the obituary to the engineer *Charles Formans* in 1901). Other stations are without such charm. Oban, once a grand lattice-girdered shed fronted by offices and clock-tower, 1879–80, is reduced to brick-box triviality. Dalmally, crowstepped red sandstone, 1877, is disappointingly dreich. The North British terminal at Helensburgh, 1899, has some dignity with four platforms, a glazed roof and a Renaissance façade to the street.

CRINAN CANAL. The importance of the sea in the context of the general trend to improve communications was, as might be expected, well appreciated in Argyll. As early as 1771, more than thirty years before the Commission empowered to build the Caledonian Canal was set up, proposals had been put forward for a canal to be cut from Loch Gilp on Loch Fyne to Loch Crinan at the head of the Sound of Jura. Such an undertaking, it was argued, would 'be attended with the happiest effects to the poor mariner ... when navigation round the Maoil of Ceanntire is so difficult and dangerous' (Fraser, 1792). The Crinan link (14.5km. long when finally completed) was not the only one to be canvassed, for a shorter crossing of the Knapdale–Kintyre peninsula existed further S at Tarbert where the isthmus separating E Loch Tarbert from W Loch Tarbert was less than 2km. *James Watt* surveyed both routes for the Commissioners of Forfeited Estates. But, despite the difference in distance and the fact that the Norsemen had in 1098 dragged one of their ships across the narrower neck of land at Tarbert in order to designate Kintyre an island, a feat which seemed to give symbolic support to the idea of a canal, the more southerly transit failed to find backers. Following more surveys and designs carried out by the engineer

John Rennie, work on the Crinan Canal was begun in 1794. Seven years later the new waterway was opened, though construction was not completed for a further eight years. Even then there were problems, which brought *Thomas Telford* to Crinan on several occasions between 1813 and 1817. But, though plagued by continuing financial and technical troubles, the Canal was in operation. Avoiding the long and sometimes hazardous trip around Kintyre, small craft, particularly fishing smacks, sailed out directly into Hebridean waters, the flow of traffic increasing greatly after the opening of the Caledonian Canal in 1822. By this time, too, steamboats were crossing the Clyde to the Cowal shore.

Countless slips and jetties testify to the importance of sea communications in Argyll. Besides linking the mainland with the islands, the sea penetrates deep into the land mass of the county. Long but relatively narrow sea-lochs, far from inhibiting travel, frequently afford the easiest and most direct routes for moving people and goods from place to place. Ferry crossings provide an obvious alternative to long coastal journeys for both man and beast. There are records of regular crossings on the Holy Loch and on Loch Awe in the c15. Similar evidence of ferries at Inveraray on Loch Fyne, 1591, and Dunoon on the Clyde, 1617, no doubt confirms connections that had long existed.

1   There are many natural HARBOURS, the best occurring on the more protected E shores. Campbeltown, Tarbert, Rothesay and Tobermory all have the advantage of sheltered deep-water bays. Rubble quays were constructed at Campbeltown in 1722 and 1754 and at nearby Dalintober in 1767. In order to deal with the inflow of material needed in the building of the new town and castle, *John Adam* designed a jetty at Inveraray, 1759–62, though by 1771 it was in ruins. Work on the building of piers at Rothesay dragged on through most of the second half of the c18. The creation of the British Fisheries Society in 1786 led to the foundation of Tobermory on Mull, where by 1788 the Society's agent *James Maxwell* was directing the construction of the harbour breastwork. By 1790 a Customs House had been built to a design by *Robert Mylne*. Improvements in ferry connections, carried out by the Commissioners for Highland Roads & Bridges, were undertaken on Jura at Feolin and Lagg, where the drovers' quays were reconstructed, 1809–10, and across the Sound of Jura on the mainland at Keills where repairs were effected, 1805–7, and a new slipway built, 1817–20. The Commissioners also built piers at Craighouse on Jura, 1812–14, following a plan by the surveyor *John Sinclair*, and at Tobermory, 1814, and St Catherines on Loch Fyne, 1818–20, both under the direction of *Thomas Telford*. At the same time, 1817, Telford improved the pier facilities at Ardrishaig at the Loch Fyne entrance to the Crinan Canal.

It was, however, the advent of steam navigation that gave the greatest boost to sea travel and commerce, occasioning a sudden boom in pier-building, especially on the Firth of Clyde. In 1812 Henry Bell established the first commercially successful steamboat service between Helensburgh and Glasgow. Within a few years paddle steamers were crossing the Firth. A pier was constructed at

Helensburgh in 1816 and lengthened in 1822. The E Cowal shore, benefiting from its proximity to Gourock, Greenock and Glasgow, developed quickly. Piers appeared at Kirn, 1823, Kilmun, 1827, Hunter's Quay, 1828, and Dunoon, 1835. On Bute, also within easy reach of Renfrewshire and Ayrshire, Rothesay again reconstructed its harbour, 1822–4. At Tarbert, a new quay capable of taking steamers was built in 1825. At Campbeltown, the first steamer had tied up as early as 1815, the precursor of services which linked the town closely with Glasgow. By this time, too, steamers had reached Oban; here, the S Pier was constructed c. 1814 and the N Pier probably not much later. Lying in the lee of Kerrera, Oban Bay provided an anchorage unequalled on the exposed W shore of the long Knapdale–Kintyre peninsula and the town soon became the main departure-point for the islands.

Throughout the C19 steamer traffic increased. The railways improved trade links further and greatly increased the number of passengers. Dunoon, Rothesay, Campbeltown and Oban were particularly favoured, the quality and extent of their Victorian expansion made possible by the convenience and contacts brought by an integrated transport system which the C20 has only succeeded in destroying. By the 1880s there were around forty steamers on the Clyde with as many as half that number of vessels sailing to the islands. Until 1866, a horse-drawn track-boat negotiated the Crinan Canal link, conveying passengers between the two fleets. Thereafter, until 1929, a specially designed paddle-steamer, 'a sort of floating tram', made the transit. Meanwhile, piers were erected at almost every conceivable spot as first the private steamer companies and later the railway companies vied with one another for custom. There were steamers on the Gare Loch, on Loch Long, Loch Goil, the Holy Loch, at Innellan and Toward, around the Kyles of Bute, on Loch Fyne and on the E coast of Kintyre. There were steamers, too, on inland waters, on Loch Awe and Loch Lomond. On the islands not all the quays built were capable of taking steamers, and passengers and cargo often had to be taken ashore by ferry. The breakwater pier, dock and workers' housing constructed at Hynish, Tiree, 1836–43, to facilitate the building and servicing of the Skerryvore lighthouse (*see* below), is a remarkably fine example of harbour engineering, still in good repair. Smaller jetties, some dating from the late C18, served the quarries on Mull and Easdale, and the ironworks at Bonawe, near Taynuilt, while these were productive. Several of those at the coastal distilleries of Islay continue in use.

The C20 has seen a huge reduction in the number and frequency of sea connections, especially in the Clyde estuary and lochs and especially since the Second World War. The ending of passenger services to Campbeltown in 1940 was a significant moment, returning the town to a state of relative isolation from which it has scarcely recovered. Dunoon, Hunter's Quay and Rothesay preserve regular car-ferry links but not the annual inundation of holiday-makers they once enjoyed, nor the prosperity that went with it. A few other piers are intermittently used but the majority stand idle, neglected and dangerous or have rotted into the sea.

No original pierhead buildings remain: at Rothesay, the clock-tower-topped pavilion erected in 1992 has almost enough maritime *esprit* to compensate for the loss of its Baronial predecessor of the 1880s, while the half-timbered waiting-rooms and offices built at Dunoon at the very end of the C19 have been colourfully restored. Extensive improvements were carried out on many of the island piers in the 1960s. Two decades later, roll-on roll-off provisions were made at Oban, Kennacraig on W Loch Tarbert, Craignure on Mull, Port Ellen and Port Askaig on Islay, and at Scalasaig on Colonsay, Arinagour on Coll and Gott Bay on Tiree where the scale of the concrete structures necessary seems inordinately large. Vaster still are the naval bases at Faslane and Coulport, engineered into the coastal landscapes of the Gare Loch and Loch Long.

The first LIGHTHOUSE to be erected in Argyll and one of the earliest in Scotland was the Mull of Kintyre light of 1788. Sited on the rocky heights at the S end of the long peninsula separating the calmer inner waters of the Firth of Clyde from the open sea to the W, it was one of four lighthouses built under a statute of 1786 by the Commissioners for Northern Lighthouses. Adequately elevated by nature, its circular tower of harled rubble, designed by *Thomas Smith*, was not tall but it carried the first reflector lantern ever installed. In 1797 Smith was succeeded by his stepson, *Robert Stevenson*, as the Commissioners' principal engineer. It was he who designed the Rinns of Islay Lighthouse on Orsay Island, a short distance off-shore from Portnahaven and Port Wemyss. Built, 1824–5, by the contractor who would be responsible for the construction of Telford's Parliamentary kirk in Portnahaven a few years later, it rises over 45m. above high-water level. At the base of the tower, symmetrically disposed, are the flat-roofed keepers' houses. These appear again at the Eilean Musdile light which Stevenson designed for the SW tip of Lismore in 1833. Rising just over 31m. above high-water mark, this tower has a parapet walk ringed by a lattice railing and a cast-iron superstructure for the light room with intriguing decorative detail. Most spectacular of all the Argyll lighthouses is Skerryvore, constructed over a period of five years from 1838 to 1842, on a dangerous Atlantic reef, 20km. WSW of Tiree. Designed by *Alan Stevenson*, Robert's son, the granite tower soars to 42m. in a slow hyperbolic curve. Ruvaal Lighthouse at the N end of the Sound of Islay, 1857–9, by Alan's brothers *David & Thomas Stevenson*, is less ambitious; built in limewashed brick, it is 36m. high to the lantern.

While the concern of the Northern Lighthouse Commissioners was with safety on the high seas, others provided lights for inshore waters. A proposal by *Alexander Nasmyth*, *c.* 1800, for a monumental Gothick lighthouse on the pier at Inveraray came to nothing. In 1812, the Cumbrae Lighthouse Trust built the lighthouse at Toward Point on the Clyde at the S end of Cowal. Twenty years later, a light was erected on the E shore of the Mull of Oa, Islay, to mark the difficult entry into Port Ellen harbour. Appropriately, this unusual L-plan structure was raised as a memorial to Lady Ellinor Campbell, after whom the town was named.

BURGH AND VILLAGE BUILDINGS

In medieval Scotland the right to enjoy the king's protection and to trade freely at home and abroad was confined to the royal burghs. The majority of these lay on the E side of the country, particularly in the Lothians and Fife. Prior to 1600 only two such communities had been created in Argyll and Bute: Tarbert in 1327 and Rothesay in 1401. Significantly, both had excellent natural harbours guarded by royal castles but neither could have amounted to more than a few rude dwellings clustered close to the local castle. In 1597 the Scottish Parliament passed an Act authorizing 'that there be erected and builded three burghs', one on Lewis, another in Lochaber and the third in Kintyre, all proposed as bases in the pacification of the Highlands and intended to become royal burghs in due course. In 1607 Crown lands in Kintyre were feued to the 7th Earl of Argyll, subject to his agreeing to establish the proposed new town. Little was accomplished at first, but gradually the plantation burgh of Campbeltown, populated largely with Lowland immigrants from Ayrshire and Renfrewshire, grew to be the principal settlement on the Kintyre peninsula. In 1700 it, too, became a royal burgh. Meanwhile, in 1648, the seat of Campbell power in Argyll, Inveraray, had attained similar status.

Burghs of barony, which could hold weekly markets and annual fairs but were dependent for their more limited rights on the local landowner, were no more plentiful. Kilmun, 1490, and Melfort, 1688, fell into this category, but both remained villages; the burgh of Laggan in the Kildalton parish of Islay, founded in 1614, vanished without trace. The late designation of Helensburgh, 1802, and Oban, 1811 (reasserted in a charter of 1820), indicates how delayed the development of the county's larger towns was and suggests how much such development depended on improvements in communications by road, sea and rail (*see* 'Roads, Railways, Canals, Harbours and Lighthouses' above).

Planning

The built pattern of streets and houses which evolved in the older settlements, the solids and voids of urban form, might best be described as natural or organic. Originally no more than castle-toun clusters, from the C18 Tarbert and Rothesay stretched themselves out around their harbours. In each case, at the centre of this built-up arc, a road leaves town for the S, passing the parish church *en route*. Campbeltown held at first to the SW end of Campbeltown Loch, rounding the Loch Head to connect with Dalintober only in the early years of the C19. This linkage is indicated on an 1801 plan of the town prepared by *George Langlands* which also shows the beginnings of a more calculated, planned expansion. Following the precedent set by the placing of Castlehill Church at the head of Main Street in 1778, two new buildings, the School House and the Highland Parish Church, are deliberately sited as *points-de-vue* at the ends of St John Street and New Quay Street. These new streets run in parallel to the shore and are crossed at right angles by a third, Argyll Street. Not all of this was realized, but the predilection for a new geometrical order is unmistakable.

By virtue of its topography, the town of Tobermory on Mull, founded by the British Fisheries Society in 1787, is able to exemplify both the natural and the geometrical approaches to planning. A crescent of houses wraps itself around the harbour under the natural escarpment which defines the picturesque bay; above, on gently sloping ground, the upper town is based on a simple grid plan prepared by the Society's agent, *James Maxwell*. Contemporary efforts to establish other fishing communities at Crinan and at Creich on the Ross of Mull did not succeed. At Bunessan, also on the Ross of Mull, a village did develop, though it is little more than a haphazard scatter of houses at the head of Loch na Làthaich. The unimaginatively named hamlet of Newton on the E shore of Loch Fyne survives as a row of fishers' cottages with a few isolated rubble stores. On the opposite side of the loch, N of Furnace, is Kenmore, another former fishing village, now sadly degraded; designed by the surveyor *William Douglas* in 1771 (one of many ameliorative measures implemented on the estate of the 5th Duke of Argyll), it amounts to no more than two rows of single-storey cottages facing each other across a green. A single cottage row was built at Bonawe Ironworks, *c.* 1755, but, although more workers' housing was constructed later, there was no attempt at co-ordination on the ground. Proposals for planned villages at Craleckan Farm, Furnace, and at Auchindrain were drawn by *George Langlands* in 1789 but remained on paper. The plan envisaged at Auchindrain, where cottages were arranged around three sides of a square, was later echoed in Easdale, one of several slate quarriers' villages probably built in the first years of the C19. At the others, Balvicar, Cullipool, Ellanbeich and Toberonochy, even simpler layouts of cottage rows were adopted. A solitary row sufficed for the lime-workers' hamlet of Port Ramsay on Lismore. At Kerrycroy on Bute, cottages built, *c.* 1803, for the estate workers of Mount Stuart are arranged symmetrically in a crescent plan around a village green.

On Islay, the consistent endeavours of the Campbell superiors to improve agricultural production, encourage fishing and develop lead mining provided the stimulus for the building of a varied series of villages. Bowmore, founded in 1768 as the administrative centre of the island, follows a regular plan, gridded from a central street linking church and pier. Port Ellen, Port Charlotte and Portnahaven, on the other hand, all of which were under way in the third decade of the C19, adjust their geometries to the natural setting. Port Wemyss, *c.* 1830, is enigmatically disciplined to a plan based on the letter D. All are characterized by the austere order of simple gable-to-gable housing which, though it has escaped neither insensitive nor sentimental impairment, gives to the island that necessary sense of the distinction between the urban and the rural regrettably increasingly rare in the Hebrides.

The model for this crisp combination of urban geometry and severe, white-walled buildings is, of course, Inveraray, built through the second half of the C18 to a plan first conceived in 1744 but successively modified by *William Adam*, *John Adam* and *Robert Mylne*. Bowmore's circular church may owe something to a comparable proposal from John Adam for Inveraray, the Duke of Argyll's new town on Loch Fyne, but the layout of the Islay town, though gridded, lacks the inner orthogonal focus of Inveraray and its deliberate, even scenographic, integration with the lochside landscape. Moreover, the bi-axial plan of Inveraray is complemented by a more ambitious architecture. Its rigorous elegance varies from the sophisticated classicism of the Parish Church and Court House façades which close the axes of the two principal streets to the stark beauty of Relief Land and Arkland facing each other across s Main Street. Inveraray's influence is none the less evident if muted at Bowmore and, later, at Lochgilphead, which began to develop in 1811. Here, once again, is a simple network of a few gridded streets, at the centre of which is the axis of Argyll Street running from Colchester Square in the s, begun in 1824, to the Parliamentary Church of 1828 which originally terminated the view N.

2, 73

The grids at Inveraray, Bowmore and Lochgilphead are markedly axial but otherwise little developed. The grid which emerged at Helensburgh lacks such clear inflexion; it is, however, a great deal more extensive. Founded by the Colquhouns of Luss, who hoped to encourage settlement by bonnet-makers and weavers, Helensburgh covers an area of gently sloping ground on the N shore of the Clyde estuary W of Cardross. A plan of the town, drawn up in 1803 by *Peter Fleming*, following an earlier feuing plan prepared by Luss Estates' surveyor, *Charles Ross*, shows an open-ended regular grid similar to that then under development in the Blythswood New Town of Glasgow. A year later, James Denholm was describing 'a modern village, well built, and rapidly increasing in size and population. It is much frequented during the summer season, by the citizens of Glasgow and their families, for the purpose of bathing, and enjoying the free air of the country.' Aspirations to foster the textile industry remained unfulfilled but the town prospered as a resort, benefiting greatly first from steamer traffic and later from the railway, which arrived in mid-century. Close to the shore, the grid filled up with continuous street-front buildings of two and three storeys, while uphill, set back in leafy seclusion off streets 'planted, boulevard-fashion, with small trees' (Groome, 1883), were the villas of those industrialists, merchants and professional men who daily commuted by train to Glasgow.

The emergence of Oban as the principal port on the W seaboard got under way at the start of the C19. The boost to communications and commerce given by steam navigation was crucial. And this received further impetus when, much later, the Callander & Oban Railway finally reached the S Pier. But urban growth did not develop along geometrical lines. Unlike Helensburgh, there was no single coherent plan, for the ownership of town land lay in the hands of more than one feudal superior. More critically, the topography round Oban Bay is decidedly up-and-down: hill and glen tumble abruptly to the sea. Naïve rectilineal patterns make no sense. Yet development in the first years of the C19 did establish a simple grid at the heart of the town. Running N–S along the sea front, George Street is paralleled by Tweeddale Street to the E and crossed W–E by Stafford Street. A few other short streets also join George Street at right angles, but their extent is limited by the sea to the W and the sudden steep rise in the land to the E. Apart from the rough parallelism of Shore Street and Albany Street lying on flattish ground SW of the Black Lynn Burn behind the Railway Quay, Oban's subsequent C19 and C20 expansion has resulted in a plan contorted by the limiting possibilities of the landscape. Roads run with the shore or curve and climb, contour-conscious.

In Dunoon and Rothesay the terrain is less spectacularly Highland than in Oban but here, too, similar irregular patterns emerged. Clustered on high ground around Castle Hill, Dunoon had medieval beginnings. Never large, by the end of the C18 the village amounted to no more than a handful of dwellings, its long-established importance as a ferry crossing-point temporarily eclipsed by the building of the military road to Inveraray. Then came the steamboat. In 1822, the Lord Provost of Glasgow, James Ewing, built Castle House. Dunoon now became a popular summer resort. On the hill behind Castle House and the parish church, the old village began to extend its irregular network of streets. Below, running in a straight line NW from the pier, Argyll Street emerged as the town's principal thoroughfare. Round the W and E Bays, marine villas marched with the shore in a concatenation of residential development which, in 1868, united Dunoon, Kirn and Hunter's Quay as a single police burgh. By then, Dunoon had begun to develop an upper town. Royal Crescent and Victoria Road are formal in their layout but compromised by a certain unconsummated grandeur. They lead into a suburban grid-iron plan bounded on the W by the long line of Alexander Street.

The expansion of Rothesay, stimulated first by fishing and cotton production before the coming of the steamers transformed the town into the most popular 'watering place' on the Clyde, followed similar lines. A knot of narrow streets gathered around the moated castle, a single straight main street, Montague Street (later somewhat overshadowed by the reclamation of coastal land W of the pier and the creation of Victoria Street), and the long littoral spread of residential development out to Ardbeg and Craigmore. Whatever formality exists in the layout of Rothesay's streets is linear, following shore or contour; there are no axes, crescents or grids. But there is The Serpentine, a whimsical road twisting and turning uphill from Castle Street on a unique waveband plan.

Public Buildings

In several towns burgh status is most publicly signalled by the TOLBOOTH or town house, a building erected to house the meetings of the council and court, deal with the financial administration of tolls or taxes, and incarcerate local wrongdoers. In Inveraray *John Adam*'s Town House, 1754–7, takes the form of a Palladian mansion arcaded along Front Street. At Bowmore on Islay, the court met in the upper room of the Old Town Hall, a plain, late

BURGH AND VILLAGE BUILDINGS

C18, two-storey house on Main Street. Gibbsian details give Campbeltown's Town House, 1758–60, a robust urban quality especially evident in the impact made by its octagonal streetfront belfry steeple of 1778. But grimmer norms prevail at Rothesay, where the Town Hall and County Buildings by *James Dempster*, 1832–4, are battlemented and towered with all the implacable dourness of a Saharan fort.

During the C19 most COURT HOUSES, with their attached prison accommodation, were separated from the business of day-to-day administration carried on in the Town Halls. Criticism of the provision made for jail cells in the Town House at Inveraray led to the building of a new Court House and Jail, 1816–20, designed by *James Gillespie Graham* and set within lochside bastions at the SE end of the town's cross-axial plan. The main façade is splendidly classical, with a civic presence not more dignified but certainly more architecturally sophisticated than the residential reserve of its predecessor. Acts of Parliament in 1819 and 1839 laid down directions for the financing of these buildings, but it was the Sheriff Court Houses (Scotland) Act of 1860 which gave a major, country-wide impetus to the increase and improvement of accommodation provided for the dispensation of civil and criminal justice. In Tobermory, *Peddie & Kinnear* built the new Court House, 1861–2, in what was for them a remarkably dull version of a Baronial style fast becoming fashionable, not least for those buildings associated with Scots law. Other court houses in Argyll, however, seem unaware of this fashion. For Campbeltown, in a building of 1869–71 that might almost be mistaken for a Victorian Gothic villa were it not for its modestly institutional symmetry, *David Cousin* was content with crowstepped gables for national allusion. Oban's Court House came later, 1886–8, by which time Baronial was on the wane; *Ross & Mackintosh* preferred a rich Italianate symmetry. Later still at Dunoon, *John McKissack* won the competition for a new Court House, 1899–1900, with a design which was polychromatic and eclectic, but much less academic. POLICE STATIONS have none of the pretension of court buildings. Oban's is accommodated in a two-storey terrace on Albany Street. The harled Arts and Crafts Baronial of *A. N. Paterson's* station for Helensburgh, part of his 1906 extensions to the Municipal Buildings (*see* below), is, so to say, more arresting, but gentle rather than aggressive. At Rosneath, 1937, the mood is gentler still: village vernacular by *Joseph Weekes*, then County Architect of Dunbartonshire. Dunoon's more recent station, 1975–7, is respectably clean-cut but lacks the Scots charm of its 1870 predecessor across Argyll Road.

In some of the larger communities, new TOWN HALLS were required to house public meetings and municipal offices. For Dunoon's Burgh Buildings, 1873–4, *Robert Bryden* contrived a Baronial-Gothic pile. In Helensburgh, too, Baronial was considered appropriate, though *John Honeyman's* Municipal Buildings of 1878, turreted and crowstepped at the corner of Sinclair Street and E Princes Street, are more scholarly and fluent than the bulky aberrations at Dunoon. A decade later the Victoria Halls, built further up Sinclair Street with a symmetrical façade by the Kilmarnock architects *J. & R. S. Ingram*, are still stiffly Baronial. And in 1906, when *A. N. Paterson* added a Fire Station and Police Station to Honeyman's corner (*see* above), the Scots theme was continued, but in softer, more relaxed mood. In Rothesay, the Duncan Halls, 1876–9, could accommodate 1,350 people. The halls themselves have gone but the building which hid them from E Princes Street, a classical *palazzo*, cool below but with a busy French Renaissance roof above, preserves seafront dignity. At Oban, the Municipal Buildings of 1897–8 are Italianate like the Court House across the road: seven-bay symmetry by *Alexander Shairp*, agitated with Mannerist inventiveness. Such stylistic formality was hardly suited to the more intimate scale of VILLAGE HALLS, numerous examples of which can be found dating from the twenty years or so that bridge the turn of the century. Nor did Baronial bombast fit the bill. Not that aspiration was dulled: in Cardross, *Honeyman & Keppie*'s Geilston Halls, 1889–90, are Tudor Gothic, almost ecclesiastical, while the Burgh Hall and Reading Room in Cove, 1893–5, is grandly (a little too grandly, perhaps) Scots Renaissance. The solution found at Rhu seems much more appropriate: a freer, almost vernacular interpretation of the Scots tradition fused with the evident influence of the English Arts and Crafts movement, surely the work of *A. N. Paterson*. English materials and detailing dominate in the Halls at Slockavullin, 1897, Lochgoilhead, 1898, and Kilmun, 1910. The same is true at Port Ellen on Islay, where the red-tiled roofs of the Ramsay Hall by Edinburgh architects *Sydney Mitchell & Wilson*, 1901–2, splash an alien blot on the edge of the black-and-white town. By 1910 Anglophile fashion has passed. In the Masonic Lodge at Lochgilphead, 1909, and Ardrishaig's Public Hall built a year or two later, both by the idiosyncratic local architect *William Todd*, there are unsure but unmistakable signs of Art Nouveau.

In common with the rest of the country, Argyll and Bute benefited from the Reformers' zeal for universal education. By the C18, small rural SCHOOL BUILDINGS would have been widespread, though physical evidence is scant. The Old Schoolhouse in Glen Aray is a ruinous shell. Designed as a two-storey harled cube, classroom below, schoolhouse above, it was built at Argyll Estate's expense in 1781. Pointed arches and quatrefoil recesses defer to the fashion for Gothick. In Benderloch, Ledaig School also housed the dominie above the classroom, this time in a piend-roofed, three-bay box with a splayed front. Built in the early C19, it is now wholly in residential use. In the burghs, the one-room school at the head of Bishop Street, Rothesay, 1798, is probably the oldest survivor. By the middle of the C19, schools had grown larger, perhaps two or three classrooms arranged in a T- or L-plan. All were simple gabled structures, often with a bellcote on the roof, as at Kilfinichen on Mull, 1804 (1828), or Port Charlotte on Islay, 1830 (now the Village Hall). Most were without decorative elaboration, vernacular and domestic in character. At Kingarth on Bute, for example, where the master lived above his pupils, the Old Schoolhouse of *c.* 1835 is indeed a house, retaining its turnpike stair at the rear. Some, however, flirt with Gothic. No surprise perhaps that this temptation should entice ecclesiastical support: the Episcopal School at Slockavullin by *Joseph Gordon Davies*, 1835 (now Kilmartin Primary School), and the former Free Church Schools at Inveraray, 1848, and Kilcreggan, 1859 (now Cove & Kilcreggan Community Centre), all succumb to some degree. But the school most thoroughly thirled to the Gothic Revival was Rothesay Academy, 1869–70, another Free Church investment in sound education. Designed by *John Russell Thomson* with an ornamental tower and enough medieval allusion to invoke the sanctity of collegiate learning, it passed to the Burgh School Board in 1873. In the 1950s it was demolished, leaving two cusped arches to its successor (*see* below).

In 1872 the Education Act established School Boards and laid down standards for school buildings. As a result, in the decade that followed the Act, many new schools were commissioned. Most are in rural situations and differ little from their mid-Victorian predecessors: gabled classroom blocks with an occasional hint of Gothic, asymmetrical in layout where they incorporated a schoolhouse. Architects were engaged: *Robert A. Bryden* was responsible for schools at Strone, Innellan and Toward; *James Maitland Wardrop* for those at Kilmichael Glassary and Lochgair; *William Railton* built at Bowmore and Portnahaven on Islay (and perhaps also at Bridgend and Bruichladdich); on Mull, *Robert Rowand Anderson* dashed off a design used at Pennyghael. Towards the end of the century more commissions began to go to local architects. But architectural opportunities were lost. Lochgilphead, Kirn, Rothesay and Inveraray reiterated the familiar single-storey, gabled formula, only with more classrooms. Of the larger schools built before the First World War in Dunoon, Oban, Tarbert and Helensburgh, only one, *A. N. Paterson*'s Clyde Street School in Helensburgh, 1903, can claim distinction. Scots Revival in style, the building is forcefully articulated towards the street in a symmetrical composition accented by two bellcast-roofed towers that hit the skyline like oversize condiment twins. After this, c20 schools disappoint, not so much by their austerity of form as by a tawdriness of detail. Rothesay Academy, 1956–9, by *Harvey & Scott*, is at least daring, rashly so perhaps, but the tiered classroom blocks of the 1960s and '70s at Lochgilphead High, Campbeltown Grammar and Dunoon Grammar are simply dull. Sandbank Primary School, 1976, by *Thomas Smith, Gibb & Pate*, is a rare success: respectable boxed geometry. It marks a turning point for, with the creation of Strathclyde Regional Council in 1975, there are signs of improvement. Monopitch roofs appear, modish indeed but scaled to their context at Ardrishaig, Carradale, Taynuilt and Benderloch. At Bowmore, Islay, extensions to Islay High School, 1985–7, exhibit a long-overdue responsiveness to the *genius loci*, closing the axis of School Street with a rooftop belfry shaped to echo the pagoda-like ventilators on the skyline of the neighbouring distillery.

Until the late c20 there has been little to remark in the county's HOSPITALS. Poorhouses built at Lochgilphead, Oban and Campbeltown between 1859 and 1862, the last by *John Honeyman*, have been adapted and extended over the years to provide health accommodation. So, too, has *David Cousin*'s bleak and costive Asylum for the Insane at Lochgilphead, 1862–4. In the 1890s, Cottage Hospitals were built at Helensburgh, Dunoon, Rothesay, Campbeltown and Oban. Of these, *William Leiper*'s Victoria Infirmary at Helensburgh, two-storey, bell-capped bays at the centre with lower ward wings, is best. General Hospitals came much later. Dunoon General, 1957–8, is an anonymous curtain-walled slab, typical for its time; it might be an office block or a school. But on the edge of Oban *Reiach & Hall* have designed the Lorn & Islands District General Hospital, 1992–5, in a long low spread at once so humane in scale and so clinically crisp and white that it seems to guarantee the health and efficiency adumbrated a lifetime earlier in the first high hopes of Modernism.

Many POST OFFICES in rural areas and on the islands are simply rooms or shops conscripted from residential property. In Appin, for example, a piend-roofed rubble house, probably late C18, serves. In Inveraray, the Post Office is a shop in Arkland, *Robert Mylne*'s tenement of 1774–5. The same architect's much-altered Custom House of 1789–90 does the job in Tobermory. In Lochgilphead, the Post Office occupies part of the 1841 classical range on the E side of Colchester Square. Larger Government-built offices date from the last years of the C19. They are generally rather ambitious in conception and expensively detailed in good masonry. Helensburgh's palazzo Post Office, 1893, by *H. M. Office of Works* under *W. W. Robertson*, has a domed corner; Rothesay's, probably from the same office, 1895–7, is Netherlandish Renaissance with a scrolled gable façade; Oban's, by the *Office of Works* under *W. T. Oldrieve*, 1908–10, is asymmetrical C17 Scots. For Dunoon, 1901–2, *John Breingan* designed a much calmer affair with wide, round-arched, classical windows. In 1911, Oldrieve successfully merged a Telephone Exchange with the Helensburgh Office, but the prison-like Exchange constructed at Oban in 1938 strikes terror into the townscape.

LIBRARIES. Rothesay's is accommodated in an undistinguished 1960s building on Stuart Street opposite the Castle. Just as unprepossessing, Oban's is housed in the Corran Halls, a building of similar date and equally indifferent to its context. But at Campbeltown the Library and Museum of 1897–9, by *J. J. Burnet*, is outstanding. Built on a corner site, the building's polychromatic masonry, suavely assembled in Scots Renaissance style, conceals a richly carved interior and a suitably contemplative inner garden. A century on, the interpretative centre has supplanted the museum. Tarbert's Heritage Centre is not much more than a timber shed, albeit pleasantly sited. Equally well landscaped, the Loch Lomond Visitor Centre at Luss, by *Dallmann & Johnstone*, 1993–4, raises the shed to architectural distinction.

Commercial Buildings

Almost all combine retail or office accommodation with residential. The John Square group of four, high, single-storey shops on

George Street, Oban, 1865, is (or was) an elegant exception. In most cases, shops are designed integrally with the dwellings above. In the late C18 and for most of the C19 this occurred in a two-storey or two-storey-and-attic streetscape. Lochgilphead keeps this scale well, preserving particularly good shopfronts on the E side of Colchester Square, 1841, and at Nos. 10–11 Argyll Street, mid C19. Rothesay's Gallowgate is similar but badly mauled. In Dunoon, the NE side of Argyll Street is in part still two storeys high: original ashlar-fronted flats above, but much-butchered shops below. At No. 67, however, there is a good gushet shopfront of 1858. Here, the scale is already three storeys, anticipating the tenement-topped shops of later Victorian and Edwardian townscape. For this, Oban and Helensburgh are best. Looking out over the bay at Oban, Argyll Mansions, 1905–7, by *Leiper & McNab* is without peer, a *tour de force* in red sandstone with canted oriels and chimneys soaring above a pillared shopfront still largely intact. In 1911, Leiper's partner, *William Hunter McNab*, who probably played the major role at Oban, produced a somewhat less ebullient design, still busy with bays, gables and chimneys, for Nos. 8–12 W Princes Street, Helensburgh. Regrettably, the simple lines of his shopfronts have been lost. Still to be found, a handful of other, mostly Edwardian, examples of tenements carefully designed to absorb shops below; but few have avoided retail abuse. From the 1930s, some degraded vestiges of Woolworths' Art Deco remain in Helensburgh and Rothesay. From the 1980s, there are *Alan Berry*'s shops and flats on Colquhoun Square, Helensburgh, healing the space but somehow without architectural muscle.

BANKS, too, often operate from shops. In smaller communities, they may be entirely domestic in character, as is the Bank of Scotland's harled cottage on Church Square, Inveraray. But, here and there, some do make a more substantial investment in the street scene. In Helensburgh, for example, the classical Union Bank (now the Bank of Scotland), 1861, probably by *John Burnet*, plays its part in ensuring the spatial security of Colquhoun Square. In Tobermory, Mull, the Baronial irregularities in the small Clydesdale Bank of 1880 help swing the sea-front street wall E round the harbour. By contrast, in the demonstratively detailed little TSB Bank at the entrance to Montague Street, Rothesay, 1979, the architects, *Roxby, Park & Baird*, seem caught indecisively between the vernacular and the urban.

As the shores and hills of Argyll became increasingly accessible to the industrial labour force of Central Scotland, many towns and villages re-created themselves as holiday resorts. Sea-bathing, boating and yachting, hill-walking and mountain-climbing were all popular pursuits. But there was a demand for indoor entertainment too. Among several CINEMAS built, The Picture House in Campbeltown by *Albert V. Gardner*, 1912–13, is a precious survivor; endearingly quirky in design, it is, astonishingly, still in operation. By contrast, the La Scala in Helensburgh by *Neil C. Duff*, 1913, and *Alexander Cattanach*'s Ritz and Regal façades in Rothesay, 1937–8, are consigned to neglect. No theatres were constructed, but sea-front CONCERT HALLS made a marked impact along the promenades. At Rothesay, the domed Winter Garden, 1923–4, is an architectural asset of priceless value. Lightweight and light-hearted, its ironwork construction delights, from Art Nouveau arabesques to a spectacular roof structure of radiating ribs. No less exceptional for its confident Modernism is Rothesay Pavilion by *James Carrick*, 1936–8, perhaps the closest Scottish architecture came to the International Style. Post-war efforts, no longer *avant-garde*, display second-generation hubris. In Dunoon, opposite the pier, the garish glazed bulk of *Ninian Johnston*'s Queen's Hall, 1955–8, replaces an earlier, more frivolous seaside pavilion of 1903–5. With shops below, its balconied auditorium and terraced cafés fill the scene: big and blowzy but, ironically, short on kiss-me-quick kitsch. In Oban, the Corran Halls, 1963–5, make another over-vigorous intrusion.

HOTELS have a long lineage in Argyll. On the old droving routes and later along the military roads, inns were built to provide simple room and board for the traveller. Located originally as staging posts or at ferry crossings, many have survived, *mutatis mutandis*, to serve the modern tourist. The Great Inn at Inveraray by *John Adam*, built 1751–5, is, as its name declares, the grandest example. Among many, the hotels at Cairndow, Colonsay, Dalmally, Inveroran, St Catherines and Taynuilt all contain C18 cores, as do the former ferry inns at Ardentinny, Clachan on Seil, Craighouse on Jura, North Connel, Port Askaig on Islay, and Port Sonachan and Taychreggan on Loch Awe. Such coaching inns improved in the early C19. The Ardencaple Hotel at Rhu, a three-storey, three-bay block with pedimented flanking pavilions, has a classical dignity worthy of Inveraray. In Inveraray itself, a fine three-storey house on North Main Street became the George Hotel. The Argyll Hotel in Lochgilphead is similarly embedded in the streetscape, as are the Argyll and Oban Hotels in Oban, though the last is enhanced by a symmetrical gable front with a central Doric doorpiece. Beyond Oban, on the islands, the Mishnish Hotel in Tobermory and the Harbour Inn in Bowmore fit easily into the village vernacular.

Victorian tourism, fired by the enthusiasms of romantic travellers that included the Wordsworths, Mendelssohn and the Queen herself (who described Oban as 'one of the finest spots we have seen'), required more salubrious accommodation and, by the 1860s, while many older inns, responsive to new demands, had grown larger and more comfortable, the first hotels catering for leisure and pleasure rather than for the merely peremptory needs of the traveller had been built, mostly with a polite classical reserve already familiar in the urban terraces and tenements of Glasgow. In Oban, the wide symmetrical front of *Charles Wilson*'s Great Western Hotel, 1863–5, swept round the newly created Corran Esplanade with cool assurance. Rothesay, keen to establish itself as the major resort on the Clyde, reclaimed land from the sea W of the pier, building the Victoria Hotel at the heart of the new esplanade parade. In Dunoon, the Argyll Hotel had been begun, 1837, though it was not yet towered.

While tourism boomed, architectural fashions were changing. Most of the families who poured off the steamers for their annual week or fortnight's escape from the shipyards, mines and foundries of Central Scotland took rooms, with or without 'attendance', or lodged in one of the many small boarding-houses crowded along the shores of Cowal and Bute. For those holidaymakers or travellers who wanted, and could afford, better there was plenty of choice. Hotels became bigger and more stylistically adventurous. Nowhere is this more evident than in Oban, where the arrival of the railway in 1880 prompted a surge of building activity which soon transformed the harbour bay fron two-storeyed calm to a heterogeneous riot of residential establishments competing for the custom of tourists *en route* to the Highlands and Islands. *Ross & Mackintosh*'s high-rise Royal Hotel in Argyll Square, 1880, remained classical; the Station Hotel (now the Caledonian), 1880–1, assumed Jacobean gables; the Queen's, 1891, was Queen Anne; the King's Arms, 1888, and the Marine (now the Regent), 1890, Baronial; the Columba, at first given a French tower and much ornamental ironwork by *J. Fraser Sim*, 1885, was later enlarged like a red sandstone tenement with tall chimney stacks and bell-capped corner bays, 1902. This intensity and variety was unmatched. But the boom was widespread. On the N shore of Loch Awe, a vast railway hotel was built in Baronial style, 1880–1, its co-promoter, the Earl of Breadalbane, ensuring that the Callander & Oban Railway Company provided a pier on the loch. On Mull, on the hill above Tobermory pier, the Western Isles Hotel, 1882–3, dominated the skyline with its dour bulk. Far to the s, in Campbeltown, the long-established White Hart Hotel managed to contain its protracted enlargement, 1897–1907, in black-and-white vernacular. At Machrihanish, the lure of the links led to the building of *Sydney Mitchell & Wilson*'s golf hotel with its view from half-timbered bays out across fairways and dunes. Much more English, but not half-timbered, is the E wing of the Ferry Inn at Rosneath which *Edwin Lutyens* added 1896–7. At the head of Loch Long, on the other hand, the white walls and crowstepped gables of the Arrochar Hotel, by *A. N. Paterson*, 1911, are unequivocally Scots. White walls with an International Style evocation are the touchstone of a few, between-the-wars hotels: the Regent in Oban, McColl's Hotel at Dunoon, and the Moderne ruin of *J. Austen Laird*'s Keil Hotel stranded at Southend.

Most larger hotels have found survival difficult in the late C20. The fate of the castellated Queen's Hotel in Helensburgh which began in the early C19 as a coaching inn and is now flatted is not untypical. But many country houses, otherwise doomed to decay as private residences, have found new life as upmarket hotels. Ardanaiseig House near Kilchrenan, 1833–4, Stonefield Castle, 1836–40, and Eriska House, 1884, are good examples. Rossdhu House, 1772–4, has been saved as the exclusive residential Clubhouse of Loch Lomond Golf Club. Conversely, *T. L. Watson*'s Hunter's Quay headquarters of the Royal Northern (later Royal Clyde) Yacht Club, 1888–9, a multi-gabled mansion striped with Tudor timbering, has become the Royal Marine Hotel.

Domestic Building

The nature of HOUSING in Scottish towns and villages prior to the C18 is very much a matter of conjecture. There are few surviving buildings, particularly in the W of the country. Documentary evidence suggests most houses were constructed in timber, some 'framed with stone and timber', and only a few, those of the richer burghers, built entirely of stone. In the larger burghs, flatted buildings several storeys high crushed together along the town's main street. Generally, however, houses were low structures, though even at two storeys they could be flatted with forestair access to the upper level. Roofs were cruck-framed, covered in turf and heather or thatch. In Argyll and Bute only one C17 dwelling remains and this, as might be expected, is exceptional, a three-storey house not flatted but built as a single residence, the town-house of the powerful Bute family (now Bute Estates Office) in Rothesay. It juts its harled crowstepped gable into the High Street, bearing the date 1681 on the skew. Elsewhere in Scotland such residences were built by the landed aristocracy in the larger burghs; in Argyll, where no settlement attained any size or serious economic status before the C18, the Bute town-house is a rarity.

When, however, the town of Inveraray was constructed in the middle of the C18, the town-house reappears. Now it is built not for the local laird but for his estate administrator (the Chamberlain's House on Front Street, 1750) or for the town's provost (Silvercraig's House, N Main Street, 1773–80) or for a prosperous local merchant or tradesman (MacPherson's House, N Main Street, 1756). Now the architectural language is different: a severe harled classicism relieved only by stone quoins and margins. Moreover, this symmetrical two- and three-storey town-house is not the only model proposed for urban living. In S Main Street, Relief Land, 1775–6, and Arkland, 1774–5, both designed by *Robert Mylne*, are essentially harled tenements, three storeys high with separate dwellings at each floor level.

The gable-to-gable aggregation of symmetrical houses forming the two principal streets at Inveraray sets an architectural pattern followed, often in simpler, cruder fashion, in the late C18 and early C19 in other towns and villages. Unadorned classical houses, sometimes no more than single-storey cottages but usually two storeys high and three bays wide, perhaps with a pilastered door-piece, formed streets and terraces. This plain but consistent town-scape can be seen in the Islay towns (*see* above), around Tobermory harbour on Mull, in Tarbert and in Lochgilphead. In the larger towns much of this early development has been superseded by second- and third-generation building, most notably on George Street, Oban (*see* above). There are, however, some early C19 survivors. Cawdor Place, Oban, is a continuous close-packed run with a single ruggedly Doric porch. On Kirk Street, Campbeltown, the detail is a little finer, the houses detached. Argyle Place in Rothesay is similar, if poorer; a terraced stretch of Mount Pleasant Road better. In the same town, Bishop Street retains a few late C18 cottages, but for how long? Argyle Terrace has a row of rather later cottages with dormered attics and a few forestairs. Battery

Place is a terrace mix of early and mid-C19 classical houses. In Dunoon, on Argyll Street, Kirk Street and, to an increasingly smaller extent, George Street, there is more of the same. Workers' rows survive at John Street, Rothesay, 1805, and Pensioners' Row, Campbeltown, also early C19; these only slightly better appointed than those in the slate-quarrying villages of Lorn (*see* above). Occasionally there are individual town-houses of quality. Springfield House in Dalintober, Campbeltown, *c.* 1815, is a sea-captain's mansion with tripartite windows, a flying stair, and an urn-topped, columned doorway. Tripartite windows and columned doorpieces are repeated in two houses on Castle Street, Rothesay. But early tenements are rare. The best are in Campbeltown: MacLean Place, one of a group on Main Street, and Fleming's Land on Castlehill.

By the second half of the C19, TENEMENTS are being built almost everywhere. There are examples in such unlikely places as Tarbert, Lochgilphead, Port Bannatyne and Kilchattan Bay on Bute, Cardross, even a single three-storey block now shorn of its Baronial bartizans in the dead-end village of Carrick Castle on Loch Goil. But, of course, it is in the towns that this essentially urban building type is most evident and, by the turn of the century, most remarkable. Some of the best are again in Campbeltown, polychromatic and inventive, built by Glasgow architects and as good as anything in that city: the Baronial Craigdhu Mansions, 1896–7, by *J.J. Burnet*, Royal Avenue Mansions, 1900, by *Frank Burnet & Boston*, and Barochan Place, 1907, by *T.L. Watson*. In Oban, *Leiper & McNab*'s Argyll Mansions are outstanding (*see* above). A rather softer style blending harling and sandstone appears in Helensburgh. Arts and Crafts by *Robert Wemyss* in John Street, 1896, and W Princes Street, 1896; McNab again, also in W Princes Street, 1911 (*see* above). Kirn has a handful of good examples; among them, Argyll Terrace, late C19, a long street of bay windows repeating with mechanical discipline. But, for such rigours, Rothesay is difficult to beat. Mansefield Place, *c.* 1900, has the same marching display of bay windows. Lady Mary Mansions, *c.* 1905, and Bute Mansions, 1906, both on E Princes Street, reach five bay-windowed storeys; urban housing at its astringent best. More modelled, more decorative and more glazed, Glenfaulds on Mount Stuart Road, *c.* 1880, is perhaps the quintessential promenade tenement.

Some attempts were made to continue the tenement idea in the inter-war years of the C20. The courtyard blocks at Alma Place, Helensburgh, 1936, by *Stewart & Paterson*, deserve better. But the successes of this period are undoubtedly the LOCAL AUTHORITY HOUSING schemes prepared under the direction of Dunbarton County Architect, *Joseph Weekes*, and completed in the late 1930s at Arrochar, Garelochhead, Rhu and Rosneath. Designed in a low-scale Scots vernacular style, these intimate groupings are contextual, inventive and wholly unpretentious. Also Scots, the houses at Parliament Place, Campbeltown, by *James Thomson & Sons*; heavy-handed by comparison. Not until 1963, when *Ian Lindsay & Partners* built a harled terrace of local authority houses on Union Street, Lochgilphead, did anything approach the clear perception of Weekes, and then, wisely, by virtue of reserve rather than daring. Apart from some quiet housing by *Baxter, Clark & Paul* at Arrochar, 1975–9, and the white snake of flats daringly drawn along the skyline above the S Pier at Oban by *Andrew Merrylees Associates*, 1993–6, recent developments have succumbed to brown brick bathos.

Each town has its VILLAS. Grouped on a hillside or along the shore, they are the merchant and professional classes' compromise between the enviable but unattainable seclusion of country-house living and the possible but, to many, less than desirable limitations of the urban flat or terrace. Early C19 examples, mostly downmarket variants of the three-bay, late-Georgian country house, can still be seen on Low Askomill Walk, Campbeltown, and along the Holy Loch shore at Kilmun. They are the basis of a type which, given bay windows, better stone and more decorative detail (often a matter of ironwork frippery), was repeated throughout the century. A more architecturally imaginative development of classical themes is evident in the coastal villas of *Alexander Thomson* at Cove, Helensburgh and Rothesay, built between 1850 and 1855. Thomson's tendency to gather the house around a tightly embraced tower, his shallow-pitched roofs and pilaster-mullioned bows and bays, and his distinctive Greek detailing, all left their mark. There are individual villas at Blairmore, Lochgoilhead and Campbeltown which clearly pay their dues. On Bute, along Rothesay's Craigmore shore, not far from Thomson's Tor House of 1855, *James Duncan* built a series of derivative villas and terraces, 1875–85. On Crichton Road his fretted bargeboarding and overhanging eaves add a rustic, Swiss Cottage flavour to the mix. Of this particular Victorian fashion there is little. *James Boucher*'s own Swiss villa at Coulport, *c.* 1860, has been demolished but the Chalet Hotel at Tighnabruaich, a private house of 1857 known originally as 'Swiss Cottage', survives. So, too, does The Lodge, Lochgoilhead, begun 1863–4, probably by Boucher, and extended in 1874 by *William Leiper* with no loss of alpine fun.

Leiper's contribution to domestic architecture is considerable, not least because of his ability to perform well in a range of different styles. Cairndhu in Helensburgh, 1871, is French Renaissance, more château than villa. In the same town, Dalmore, 1873, is Baronial. But it was Leiper's red-tiled, half-timbered Englishness which became a suburban winner towards the end of the century. Toughened by tall chimneys and red sandstone walls, it appears repeatedly: Ganavan House, Oban, 1888, Tighnabruaich House, 1895, and Brantwoode, Helensburgh, 1895, are good examples. He was particularly active in Helensburgh, where the proximity of Glasgow ensured a rich commuting clientele for his Shaw-derived, Arts and Crafts houses. The language was popular enough to be shared by a handful of other architects working in the town, notably *T. L. Watson*, *Robert Wemyss* and *A. N. Paterson*. In distant Campbeltown and Machrihanish, *H. E. Clifford*'s houses were just as English in allusion, smaller and more intimately Tudor. Meanwhile, Paterson moved on, adopting a simpler Scottish style at Longcroft, 1901, and Moorgate, 1903, both in Helensburgh; harled walls, curvilinear gables and the occasional classical embellishment. In the White House by *M. H. Baillie Scott*, 1899, the walls have a flatter, whiter simplicity, not without a hint of Voysey. Then, finally, consummation: The Hill House, 1902–3, by *Charles Rennie Mackintosh*, a Scottish villa with Arts and Crafts attitude, a marriage that would be celebrated all across Europe.

But not much in Scotland. Certainly not much in Argyll. A few flat-roofed box houses from the 1930s in Helensburgh and Dunoon, scarred by alteration or neglect, are all there is by way of progeny. In its regionalist grasp of Modernism the local authority housing of *Joseph Weekes* (*see* above) was far ahead of any private inter-war house developments. Sad, too, the paucity of the second half of the C20. Lack of money, perhaps. More likely, lack of confidence.

RURAL BUILDINGS

Until the reorganization of estates was begun in the third quarter of the C18, agriculture was conducted very largely along lines which ensured no more than the most primitive self-sufficiency. 'Joint-farm' settlements, known as townships, were small, usually no more than half a dozen tenant households working the land in linear rig cultivation with common grazings and peat lands around the settlement. They were numerous and widely dispersed (in 1693, a hearth-tax schedule recorded almost 500 in Mid Argyll and Cowal) and, although from *c.* 1750 numbers were progressively reduced by the amalgamation of holdings which improvements in cultivation and stock-rearing demanded, many townships were still viable well into the C19. Finally, however, as enclosure continued and sheep-farming was introduced, these, too, were eliminated. Here and there, occupation persisted; Auchindrain, for example, remained in multiple tenancy until 1935, the last inhabitant leaving as late as 1963.

Auchindrain is exceptional, too, in other respects. It is considerably larger than the average 'joint-farm' settlement and it is much better preserved. While most townships are now no more than ruined rubble walls or turf-covered footings on a bleak hillside, Auchindrain has survived, its byre-dwellings, barns and yards reincarnated as a Museum of Country Life. The buildings are rubble-built, rectangular in plan, with a common overall width of *c.* 6m. As in all early rural building, the masonry is drystone or laid with clay mortar in the joints. Roofs are cruck-framed and gabled, though there is some evidence for piend-ends also. All this is typical of township building. But C19 and C20 alterations, which include the introduction of fireplaces and chimney stacks, the widening of some window openings and the adoption of corrugated iron instead of thatch, modify the original character. A more accurate view of the planning and construction of these rudimentary dwellings, described even in 1798 as 'low, narrow, dark, damp and cold', has to be inferred from other more ruinous, deserted settlements. Kintyre examples show a linear arrangement

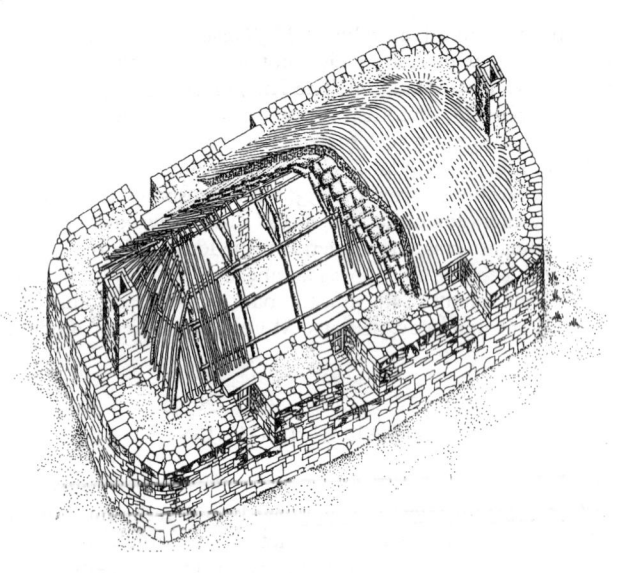

Tiree, dwelling house

of byre-dwelling, barn and outbuildings. At Drumgarve, Peninver, the combination of byre, dwelling, store and water-mill reaches nearly 34m.; at Keremenach Farm, Carskiey, an early C19 aggregation of room and kitchen, dairy, byre and barn, with stables added later, is almost as long. The remnants of a more dispersed township still stand at Balmavicar, N of the Mull of Kintyre Lighthouse, where a community was established at least as early as the second quarter of the C17; here, too, the linear plan is evident, though less extended. In Mid Argyll, at Achnaba near Port Ann, successive additions resulted in two 35m.-long steadings. At Tockmal on The Oa peninsula of Islay, where a settlement existed from the early C15, a single remodelled range of early C19 date reaches 40m. In many cases it is clear that the separation between the family and its animals was no more than a light partition, if it existed at all. Thatched cruck roofs survive at Keils on Jura. More frequently, evidence of roof structure is limited to the survival of cruck slots, for example at Arichonan township near Tayvallich (where stone thatch-pegs are preserved on a gable), Strontoiller in Lorn, Lurabus on The Oa, Islay, and on the Garvellachs. Those found in ruinous buildings within Loch Gorm Castle, Saligo, on Islay, which may date from the early C17, are among the earliest known in Scotland. On Islay, too, along the course of the Margadale River to the W of Bunnahabhain, there are the remains of an extended shieling, a particularly good example of the small stone-and-turf shelters associated with transhumance practices. Across the county there are many such ruinous hut structures on higher summer grazing lands linked to the townships.

Argyll is by no means the most agriculturally rewarding of Scottish counties. Nevertheless, from the middle of the C18 it began to feel the impact of improved procedures in cultivation and stock-rearing. Intent on improving estate production through enclosure, the 5th Duke of Argyll swept away the old townships in Glen Aray and Glen Shira. While the new castle and new town of Inveraray took shape, new farming methods refashioned the estate along the river valley to the N. A large walled garden, hot-houses, coach-houses, stables, labourers' cottages and a dairy court were built. Around Maltland 78 Square vast, well-ventilated hay barns were constructed with slatted floors so that corn could be dried and stored. On the Duke's cattle ranch in Glen Shira, another astonishing piece of agricultural architecture was proposed and, though only half of *Robert Mylne*'s circular Court of Offices with its barns and cowshed rings was built, 1787–90, Maam Steading marked the landscape with the new order of rational husbandry. Dorothy Wordsworth found the Maltland barns 'broad, out-spreading, fantastic and unintelligible buildings'. Perhaps this 'unintelligible' judgement is itself understandable as a measure of the changing times, for the rustic peasantry and their picturesque but dismally dank cottages were fast disappearing; farming had become commercial.

The pattern set at Inveraray was echoed elsewhere in Argyll, though nowhere were improvements on the same scale as those initiated by the 5th Duke. Towards the end of the C18 country houses acquired modernized home farms and steadings; among many were Barbreck, Craignish, Strachur and Rosneath, all Campbell estates. In the last decade of the C18 the Malcolms of Poltalloch began reclaiming land from the peat mosses S of Kilmartin, and in 1798 they commissioned the building of an experimental farm at Barsloisnach. Designed by architect *George Steuart* on a courtyard plan roughly 40m. square, it was fronted on the S by a two-storey, three-bay house. A water-driven threshing-machine, probably the first in Argyll, was provided. The model was adopted by the Malcolms who, between 1800 and 1850, built a number of such standard estate farms of which Nether Largie, Slockavullin, c. 1840, is a good example. Elsewhere, similar developments occurred as smallholdings and township settlements were amalgamated, the new tenant farmers often obliged both to enclose the land with stone dykes and to build a sound, slate-roofed farmhouse. The solution was everywhere the same: a two-storey, three-bay block, usually gabled but occasionally piended, often with flanking single-storey wings, sometimes with a courtyard behind, the walls of whitewashed rubble or harled; in effect, that classically derived model already evident in the lesser lairds' houses, tacksmen's dwellings and manses of the C18 (*see* above). At Dunbeg in Lorn, Dunstaffnage Mains is archetypal; in Cowal, Bealachandrain Farm: both probably date from around 1800. In Kintyre, where arable farming was better developed, there are good examples at Blasthill, early C19, and Machribeg, near Southend, 1843, and at W Trodigal Farm, Machrihanish, also early C19. On the islands, the stark symmetry of Rossal Farm, seen on the road to Pennyghael on Mull, is lonely and lovely. Kilchiaran 135 Steading on Islay, c. 1826, has an unexpected formality, the D-plan geometry of its cattle court reminiscent of Maam. Surprising, too, the extensive ranges of Kilchattan Farm, Toberonochy, on Luing, 1853–5. There is an octagonal horse-gang at Machrins Farm, Colonsay. Another, larger and circular, at Kilmory Castle, is ruinous and overgrown.

Water-mills were an essential element in any rural community. Evidence survives in a few ruinous townships, for example in Kintyre at Drumgarve and at Balmavicar where the lower chamber of a 'horizontal' clack-mill can be seen. Such early, horizontally mounted paddle-wheels are rare. The later meal-mills all have the more efficient vertically mounted wheels. Those on Gigha, Jura, Lismore, Tiree, Ulva and Islay, at Ballygrant, are in ruin, but the mills at Kiloran, Colonsay, and Acha on Coll have been converted to dwellings. On the mainland, mills are generally larger structures, as at Carloonan on the Inveraray Estate, late C18. Rhudil Mill, also probably late C18, is now a three-storey house. Early C19 L-plan mills at Kilfinan and Tangy, Kilchenzie, are also now in residential use, the latter preserving its overshot wheel and machinery. Machrimore Mill at Southend, 1843, remains a ruin.

It would be unforgivably disdainful not to draw attention to some of the humblest of rural buildings, those simple rubble cottages built to house estate workers, farm labourers or crofters. The white-harled houses at Arinagour, Coll, are a good example: window–door–window, built on exposed rubble footings, some roofs slated, some of corrugated iron. They run in line, gable-to-gable. Detached dwellings are, however, more typical, like those scattered around Taynuilt at Brochroy, Kirkton and Ichrachan. And sometimes, in their naïve directness, individual cottages attain an almost transcendental architectural quality, simple, blindingly pure and beautiful. Achnacroish Cottage at Balvicar on Seil, and Dairy Cottage at Kilninver are imbued with this rude elegance.

137 Croft-houses on Tiree are at once comparably rugged and attractive. Some are white, gabled cottages, thatched, slated or roofed (and sometimes walled) in corrugated iron. Some have black upper storeys: bitumen-tarred timber tents set up on the older rubble wallheads. Of the island's traditional double-skin, drystone dwellings, fewer and fewer survive. At Sandaig, three low buildings (house, byre and barn in township line) face the Atlantic winds, their deep, sand-packed, rubble walls, roughly trussed roofs and roped-down thatch and turfs carefully restored by the Hebridean Trust.

INDUSTRIAL BUILDINGS

Farming and fishing have always sustained life in Argyll and Bute, though for centuries at little more than subsistence level. Agricultural improvements, introduced principally but not only at the Inveraray and Poltalloch estates, stimulated the local economy in the late C18 and early C19, while a contemporary boom in the herring industry coupled with the activities of the the British Fisheries Society did the same. These developments left a built legacy: the former in farm-houses, barns and mills and in the ubiquitous drystone dykes traced across hill and valley, the latter in improved harbours and roads and, indeed, in the picturesque planted town of Tobermory. Pastoral and, to a lesser extent, arable farming remain important today and, although the herring have largely gone, floating fish-farms are now a frequent sight on almost every W coast loch and the refrigerated lorry, packed with shellfish for the Continental market, no less familiar.

Arable farming has had one significant industrial spin-off. Since the late C18 the growing of barley has been closely linked to the commercial production of whisky. DISTILLERIES were numerous in the C19. Of the forty-two which were once crowded into Campbeltown, however, only one remains in production. A single distillery is active in Oban, at Tobermory on Mull and another on Jura at Craighouse. But it is on Islay that the distinctive pagoda-roofed kilns and roadside malt barns are most frequently seen. There are eight plants on the island. At Bunnahabhainn, a shoreside 'street' of late Victorian warehouses is surprisingly urban, gaunt and industrial; at Caol Ila, the Still House, reconstructed in the 1970s, is fully glazed to the Sound of Islay. Along the S shore of the island, the white-walled distilleries of Ardbeg, Lagavulin and Laphroaig lie more easily in the rural landscape. In Bowmore, where the distillery is embedded in the town, the familiar pagoda skyline reappears in a belfry roof-ventilator over the local school.

A few TEXTILE MILLS survive. Almost all are ruinous or converted to other uses. Factory Land, Inveraray, originally a large upper workroom with eight workers' houses below, was established by the 5th Duke of Argyll as a spinning factory in 1774. It was soon, however, in residential use, for in 1777 operations were transferred to Clunary (Claonairigh) on the Douglas Water near Auchindrain. This more ambitious factory, built 1777–8 but now in ruins, comprised a number of buildings including a fulling-mill, dye-house, combing shop, a weaving house and several cottages. It continued making cloth and, later, carpets until 1809. On Bute, where cotton production began in 1779, the textile industry has fared better. Commercial activity continues in Rothesay in a long, classically pedimented, two-storey mill built in the early years of the C19. On Islay there are ruins of a carding mill, late C18(?), near Bridgend, while at the nearby Redhouses Mill, 1883, some of the oldest machinery of its kind in Britain is still in operation.

Stone QUARRYING has left its mark widely. Evidence of this ancient industry, so fundamental to the shaping of the built environment, can even be found on Iona in the marble quarry at Rubha na Carraig Géire. It seems likely that the now lost *mensa* of the high altar of the medieval Abbey came from this source. Here, close to the S shore of the island, cutting-frame machinery has been incongruously rusting since its abandonment at the time of the First World War, while above the gully workings there are remnants of a small drystone structure, probably built in the 1790s by the Iona Marble Company, another of the 5th Duke of Argyll's enterprising, if short-lived, economic ventures. The detritus of extensive slate quarrying, probably begun in medieval times but intensely developed in the C19 and early C20, on Seil (Easdale) and Luing is an unmistakable feature of the local landscape, as it is on the smaller, less accessible island of Belnahua, 2km. w of Cullipool. The burning of limestone, quarried at several locations but most commercially on Lismore, yielded lime for agriculture and building. Lime-kilns from the early C19 can be seen on the island at An Sàilean, Port Kilcheran and Port Ramsay. Earlier examples, dating from the last decade of the C18, exist on the tidal island of Danna near Keills at the mouth of Loch Sween and on Island Macaskin, Loch Craignish, the latter constructed by the improving Malcolms of Poltalloch. Associated with many of these quarrying activities are rude rows of workers' dwellings (*see* 'Burgh and Village Buildings' above).

Lead MINING, prosecuted on Islay from medieval times until the second half of the C19, has left few built remains. At Mulreesh, not far from Finlaggan, there is a ruinous engine-house as well as abandoned shafts and spoil heaps. Until the middle of the C19, coal was mined in the Mull of Kintyre at Drumlemble; some traces of the canal, almost 5km. long, cut to carry the coal to Campbeltown, are still to be found. The smelting of bog iron-ore, long widespread in Argyll in small open bowl-furnaces, became a serious commercial proposition in the C18. Augmenting local supplies with ore imported from Lancashire, large charcoal-burning BLAST-FURNACES were set up at Glen Kinglass, 1725, Bonawe Ironworks at Taynuilt, 1752, and Craleckan Ironworks at Furnace on Loch Fyne, 1754. Although the remains of the Glen Kinglass works (where production ceased *c.* 1738) are ruinous and difficult to reach, the surviving buildings at Bonawe (active until 1876) and Furnace (closed 1812) are generally well preserved and readily accessible. The Lorn Furnace at Bonawe is particularly impressive with its rubble-built blast-furnace of 1753, reconstructed in the second quarter of the C19, and large charcoal and ore sheds from the C18 substantially intact. Workers' housing was again an important concomitant element in several of these developments (*see* 'Burgh and Village Buildings' above).

The coincidence of water for power and timber for charcoal-making, so necessary for undertaking iron-smelting, also favoured the foundation of GUNPOWDER WORKS. In the ten years between 1835 and 1845 manufacturing began at Melfort, Clachaig, Millhouse and Furnace. A variety of small buildings associated with the process survive; most are constructed in brick, the majority degraded and overgrown, but some stone-built structures at Melfort have been converted as part of a holiday village.

There has been little industrial development in the C20 other than that associated with leisure and tourism. Disastrously aborted, the attempt made in the 1970s to construct concrete platforms for the oil exploration industry has left a 'ghost town' at Portavadie, haunted by the spectre of false economic hopes. Meanwhile, the extensive naval establishment at Faslane survives as a major employer, a sinister city with an explosive nuclear potential infinitely more dangerous than the gunpowder factories of the C19. But power of a different kind, benign and beneficial, its environmental impact considerable but decidedly more visually coherent than the serried sheds and offices of the naval base on the Gare Loch shore, has been released from the landscape itself. For some three decades DAMS and POWER STATIONS have been engineered into the hills of Argyll. At Loch Sloy above Inveruglas, the dam was designed by *James Williamson* in 1936 and begun by the North of Scotland Hydro-Electric Board immediately after the Second World War as the first concrete dam in Scotland to be constructed with round-arch buttressing. More recent is Williamson's Cruachan project on Loch Awe, 1959–65, with its immense Machine Hall cavern tunnelled a kilometre deep within the mountain.

ARGYLL: THE MAINLAND

ACHAFOLLA 7410

Barely a place, though its central location on Luing seems appropriate for mill, school and church.

KILCHATTAN CHURCH. Built 1936 as a parish mission church, it is now the only place of worship on the island. Harled gabled hall. A small granite ringed cross sits on the apex of the s gable. – Carved wooden LECTERN, gifted by Latvian ship-owners, grateful for the efforts made by islanders to save one of their vessels which had foundered in a storm, 1938.

LUING PRIMARY SCHOOL. Dated 1877. Symmetrical, with classroom gables at each end of W front. Whin rubble with hammered and chamfered sandstone dressings.

MILL. L-plan rubble mill, derelict and crudely roofed in corrugated iron. Large opening at ground level in s gable with rubble voussoirs but partly infilled. Dormered E door at upper level. On the N gable is the outshot iron wheel, 4.87m. in dia., with three flat and three rod spokes on each side and six bracing spokes crossing from one side to the other. Though long used as a cowshed, the mill retains its gearing mechanism and two pairs of millstones supported on heavy timber framing. Two more millstones lie on the hillside nearby.

DUN (An Caisteal), Leccamore, 850m. ENE of Primary School. Well-preserved oval dun, 19.8m. by 12.8m., enclosed by a drystone wall never less than 4m. thick. Entrances at SW and NE: the former checked with draw-bar slots on both sides of the opening; the latter, less well defined, but with a passage developing at the centre of the SE side and on the NW an oval guard-chamber formed in the thickness of the wall. The walls of this chamber are corbelled inwards and a flight of steps rises W to the wallhead. Several stretches of facing masonry intact.

ACHAHOISH 7875

A hamlet marking the junction of two single-track roads at the head of Loch Caolisport.

SOUTH KNAPDALE PARISH CHURCH, on the N bank of Achahoish Burn. A thinly harled gabled box, built 1775 for South Knapdale parish at the same time as the church at Inverneill. The church was at first conventionally focused on the short axis of the oblong and entered at the centre of the SE

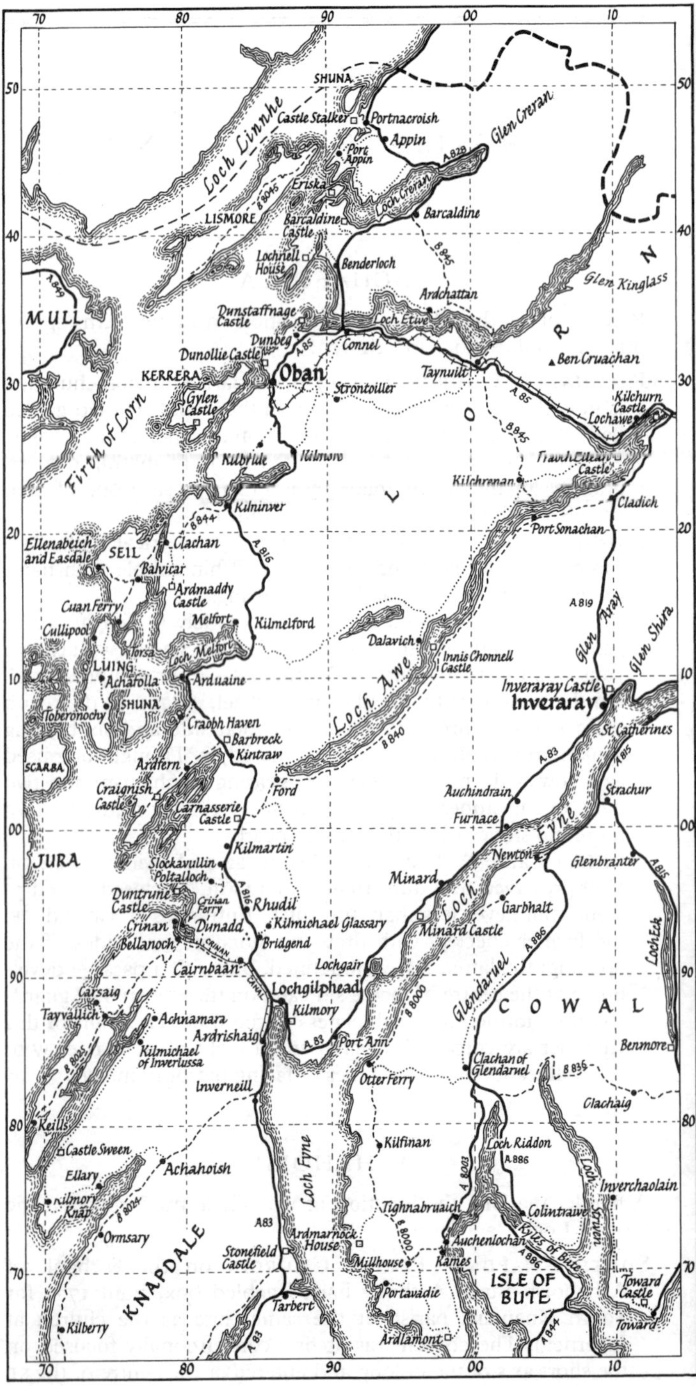

SHUNA
Castle Stalker
Portnacroish
Appin
Glen Creran
Port Appin
A 828
Loch Linnhe
Eriska
Loch Creran
B 8045
LISMORE
Barcaldine Castle
Barcaldine
Lochnell House
Benderloch
B 845
Glen Kinglass
Ardchattan
MULL
A 849
Dunstaffnage Castle
Loch Etive
Dunbeg
A 85
Connel
Dunollie Castle
Taynuilt
Ben Cruachan
KERRERA
Oban
Strontoiller
Kilchurn Castle
Lochawe
Gylen Castle
Firth of Lorn
Kilbride
Kilmore
Kilchrenan
Cladich
Kilninver
B 844
Port Sonachan
Ellenabeich and Easdale
Clachan
SEIL
A 816
Balvicar
Ardmaddy Castle
A 819
Glen Aray
Cuan Ferry
Cullipool
Melfort
Kilmelford
Dalavich
Innis Chonnell Castle
Glen Shira
Torsa
Loch Melfort
LUING
Achafolla
Arduaine
Loch Awe
Inveraray Castle
Inveraray
SHUNA
Toberonochy
Craobh Haven
St Catherines
Barbreck
B 840
Kintraw
A 815
SCARBA
Ardfern
Ford
A 83
Craignish Castle
Auchindrain
Strachur
Carnasserie Castle
Furnace
JURA
Kilmartin
Fyne
Slockavullin
Newton
Glenbranter
Poltalloch
Minard
Duntrune Castle
Crinan Ferry
Rhudil
Loch
Garbhalt
Crinan
Dunadd
Kilmichael Glassary
Minard Castle
Bellanoch
Bridgend
Loch Eck
A 886
Crinan Canal
Cairnbaan
Lochgair
Glendaruel
Carsaig
Lochgilphead
B 8000
COWAL
Tayvallich
Achnamara
Kilmory
Ardrishaig
A 83
Port Ann
Benmore
Kilmichael of Inverlussa
Clachan of Glendaruel
B 836
B 8025
Otter Ferry
Inverneill
Glachaig
Keills
Kilfinan
Castle Sween
Loch Riddon
A 886
Achahoish
Loch Fyne
A 8003
Ellary
Inverchaolain
Kilmory Knap
B 8024
Tighnabruaich
Colintraive
Loch Striven
Ormsary
A 83
B 8000
Kyles of Bute
KNAPDALE
Ardmarnock House
Auchenlochan
Stonefield Castle
Millhouse
Kames
A 886
ISLE OF BUTE
Toward Castle
Portavadie
Tarbert
A 844
Toward
Kilberry
A 83
Ardlamont

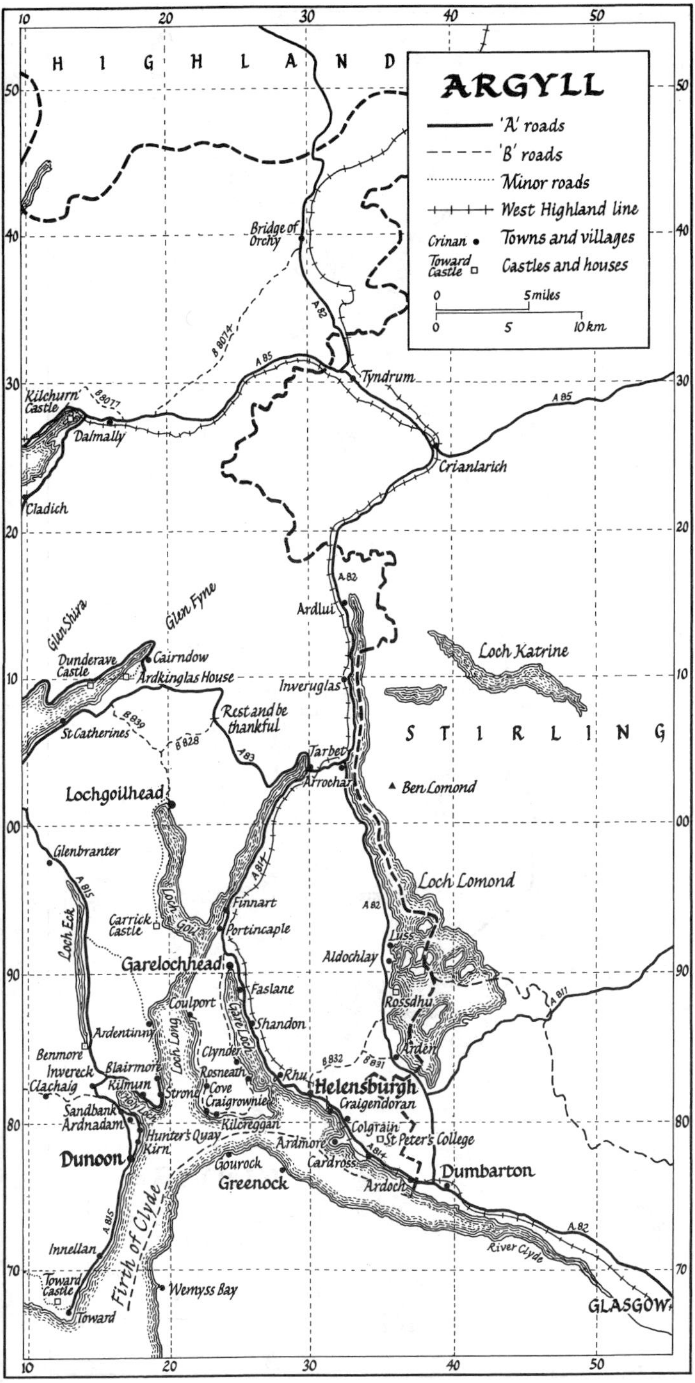
ARGYLL
'A' roads
'B' roads
Minor roads
West Highland line
Crinan
Towns and villages
Toward Castle
Castles and houses
0
5 miles
0
5
10 km
H I G H L A N D
S T I R L I N G
Bridge of Orchy
Tyndrum
Kilchurn Castle
Dalmally
Cladich
Crianlarich
A 85
A 82
B 8074
B 8077
Glen Shira
Glen Fyne
Dunderave Castle
Cairndow
Ardkinglas House
St Catherines
Rest and be thankful
B 839
B 828
A 83
Ardlui
Inveruglas
Loch Katrine
Tarbet
Arrochar
Ben Lomond
Lochgoilhead
Glenbranter
A 815
Loch Eck
Loch Goil
Carrick Castle
Finnart
Portincaple
A 814
Loch Lomond
Garelochhead
Faslane
Luss
Aldochlay
Rossdhu
A 811
Coulport
Loch Long
Gare Loch
Shandon
Arden
Ardentinny
Benmore
Inverеck
Clachaig
Blairmore
Kilmun
Holy Loch
Strone
Clynder
Rosneath
Cove
Craigrownie
Rhu
B 832
B 831
Helensburgh
Craigendoran
Sandbank
Ardnadam
Hunter's Quay
Kirn
Kilcreggan
Colgrain
St Peter's College
Ardmore
Cardross
Dunoon
Gourock
Greenock
Ardoch
Dumbarton
Firth of Clyde
River Clyde
Innellan
Toward Castle
Toward
Wemyss Bay
GLASGOW
10
20
30
40
50
00
70
80
90

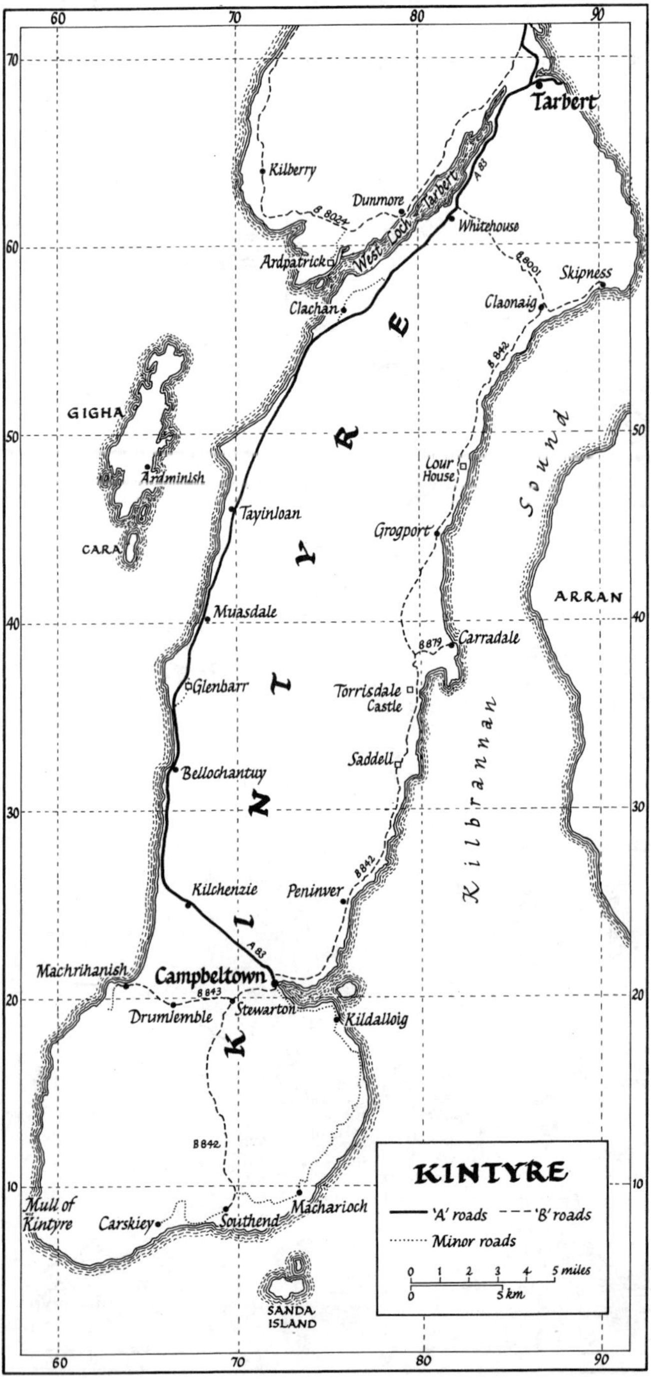
KINTYRE
'A' roads
'B' roads
Minor roads
0 1 2 3 4 5 miles
0 5 km
Tarbert
Kilberry
Dunmore
West Loch Tarbert
Whitehouse
Ardpatrick
Skipness
Claonaig
Clachan
GIGHA
Ardminish
CARA
Lour House
Tayinloan
Grogport
Sound
ARRAN
Muasdale
Carradale
Glenbarr
Torrisdale Castle
Saddell
Kilbrannan
Bellochantuy
Kilchenzie
Peninver
Machrihanish
Campbeltown
Drumlemble
Stewarton
Kildalloig
Mull of Kintyre
Carskiey
Southend
Macharioch
SANDA ISLAND
KINTYRE
A 83
B 8024
B 8001
B 842
B 879
B 843

wall. Above the door is a window with its lintel at the same height as two tall multi-paned, double-hung sashes l. and r. High level windows at each end of the NW wall appear to have anticipated the provision of galleries. In the mid C19 a battlemented belfry tower, rising through one coped offset, was constructed on the NE gable. As this provided a new access it became possible to block the original entrance and recast the interior towards the SW. A single gallery, supported on two cast-iron columns, is reached by a stone stair in the tower's lower stage. Porch and vestry/session house added to the SW gable. The interior, renovated 1928, is plastered, with a timber-lined ceiling panelled in three boarded squares at collar-tie level. The central aisle is paved with rough flagstones. – Furnishings undistinguished save for an ancient FONT basin said to come from St Columba's Cave (*see* below) and now supported on a modern carved stone base.

ST COLUMBA'S CHAPEL, Cove, close to the N shore of Loch Caolisport, 4.5km. WSW of Achahoish. Double-square plan, 5.2m. in internal width. Blasted by the elements, a single gable and some pieces of bouldered rubble walling survive. C13 dating is based on a single surviving door base moulding in the S wall. The roughly paved E end has a rectangular slab centrally placed. A few metres N are two CAVES, the larger to the E evidently adapted for religious purposes: a primitive altar, two weathered carvings of crosses and an oval water basin can be found. Traditionally claimed to antedate St Columba's arrival on Iona.

BURIAL GROUND, at Lochead on the N bank of Allt Cinn-locha, 650m. NW of South Knapdale Church. An oval enclosure containing recumbent SLABS and HEADSTONES of C18 date, some with mantling on rounded pediment tops. One stone, much weathered, depicts a two-masted craft with furled sail. There are also two schist FRAGMENTS, Early Christian, one probably the base for a wooden cross.

LOCHEAD HOUSE (Ceannloch House). A mid-C18 house altered and extended by *Robert S. Lorimer*, 1901. Three side-by-side gables face SW down Loch Caolisport. Located centrally in the three-bay, middle gable is a doorpiece with cornice and, below the apex, a circular window. Ambitious in spread but lacking in architectural sophistication. A WALLED GARDEN tails E; quadrant walls and GATEPIERS with ball finials are similarly rudimentary.

STANDING STONE, 20m. SW of Burial Ground at Lochead. A flat-topped stone 2.05m. high.

ACHNAMARA

7786

A hamlet of Forestry Commission timber houses 5.7km. SSW of Bellanoch.

CLAPPER BRIDGE, SW of village 50m. W of road. Built by the Laird of Oib Graham, *c.* 1684, at the order of Knapdale Parish

Kirk Session, in retribution 'for delinquency'. The only remaining flag bridge in Mid Argyll. It comprises two large flat tapered pieces of local schist, 100mm. thick and 4.03m. and 3.1m. long respectively. These rest on square flags and span from rubble abutments at the banks to a rock ridge at the centre of the burn. Each slab is holed where it rests on the central pier, possibly as an aid to manoeuvrability.

ACHNAMARA HOUSE, at the N end of the village on an elevated wooded site. Built *c.* 1855, for John Wingfield Malcolm, heir to the Poltalloch Estate (q.v.). Later extensions, by *Alexander Ross* (?). Numerous hipped eaves dormers, square and canted bays. Ruinous stable block to the N. Now an Outdoor Centre.

SEAFIELD FARM AND STEADINGS, 700m. N of Achnamara. Mid C19. Three-bay gabled rubble farm with short single-storey wings l. and r. Central gabled projection, entered at side, containing stair. Outbuildings to the N.

ALDOCHLAY

A few dwellings S of Luss.

DESCRIPTION. Single-storey cottages, early C19, erected for estate workers. BANDRY COTTAGES, three-in-a-row built in coursed rubble with low-gabled ashlar porches projecting slightly. On a wooded promontory knoll, ROSS ARDEN HOUSE is harled and gabled, its pointed-arch windows and central door all with Gothic astragals. ROSE COTTAGE has a rustic Gothic porch and a horseshoe-arched triple window in its projecting gable; its neighbour, BRAESIDE, round-arched lights in twos and threes. In the coupled windows of SOUTH ALDOCHLAY, more Gothic glazing.

APPIN

A village strung out along Strath Appin, halfway between Loch Creran and Loch Laich. A number of early rubble cottages survive, several radically converted.

APPIN PARISH CHURCH. Unpretentious four-bay Gothic design by *Donald Macintyre* in square-snecked granite with red sandstone dressings. Dated 1889. The buttressed NE porch has a moulded pointed-arch doorway with Gothic capitals and shafts. Plain geometrical tracery in the w gable. Almost classical birdcage belfry with pyramid top. Inside, five splendid king-post trusses, arch-braced down to corbel stones, carry a diagonally boarded roof. – Central PULPIT with a gabled Gothic back panel bearing the Church of Scotland's motto, NEC TAMEN CONSUMEBATUR, and the date 1889 in a roundel above four blind lancets.

OLD PARISH CHURCH, on the E side of the A828 close to Kinlochlaich House. Roofless rubble ruin. The internal arrangement of the original oblong church, built 1749, is unclear. A segmental arched S door, with a dated keystone, may have provided access to a central pulpit, and there is evidence that at least one doorway existed on the N. A forestair survives on the E gable, one of two which led to end galleries. In the late C18 a N aisle was added to create a T-plan; only the W and part of the N walls remain but these vestiges are enough to indicate a N entrance door and, in the NW re-entrant angle, a forestair rising to a third gallery. – In a recess later created on the outside of the W gable is a HEADSTONE brought from the Stewart of Appin grave at Culloden. It commemorates those clan members who fell there in 1746 with the inscription CLAN / STEWART / OF APPIN. – A RECUMBENT SLAB, C16 or C17, with crude carvings of a small cross, a plaited knot and a claymore, lies close to the E end of the church.

APPIN POST OFFICE, Tynribbie. Two-storey, piended dwelling with slated roof and chimneyed gables. Abutting the S gable is a low cottage, formerly a byre, and, next to that, another single-storey house; both have corrugated metal roofs. All three are of limewashed rubble and are late C18 or early C19.

APPIN SCHOOLHOUSE. Granite with droved sandstone dressings; *c.* 1880. One-and-a-half-storey schoolmaster's house with a gabled classroom block attached on the E.

GLENSTOCKDALE, 2.1km. NNE of Kinlochlaich House. A ruinous, three-bay laird's house, *c.* 1800, rubble-built and formerly harled. An elongated NW window opening on the NW end of the NE gable indicates that the staircase was, somewhat unusually, located at the N corner. Derelict since the end of the C19.

KINLOCHLAICH HOUSE (Lochend). When advertised for sale by public roup in 1822, this intriguing house was described by the *Edinburgh Evening Courant* as being 'in the Gothic style ... with a complete set of offices every way sufficient for the accommodation of a respectable family establishment'. These Gothic qualities were recent, acquired *c.* 1820, when John Campbell of Lochend decided to aggrandize his unpretentious, three-bay C18 house. This two-storey, gable-ended block became the kitchen wing of a taller Georgian Gothic mansion added to its NW gable. Sandstone was introduced for moulded details but the walls were harled throughout, a finish which does something to unify the grouping but cannot quite overcome changes in scale nor make good a lack of stylistic affinity between new and old.

A high, gabled entrance block, flanked by diagonal buttresses topped by obelisk finials, faces SW alongside the older house. At its centre, the principal doorway sits below a hooded round-arch with intersecting Gothic astragals in the semicircular fanlight. Attached NW of this is a piended, two-storey-and-basement wing of public rooms and bedrooms, given two crenellated corner turrets. Two larger windows are set within hood-moulded pointed arches, but most are in lintelled openings, their sashes thoroughly Gothicized. The interior, too, has a medieval cast: doors and shutters are panelled with cusped arcading and a plastered rib-vault appears over the new vestibule.

The drawing-room ceiling, however, has a more classical, radial centre-piece. The architect is unknown, though it is difficult to resist the speculation that the hand of *James Gillespie Graham* may have been directly or indirectly at work.

To the NE, across a yard at the rear, another two-storey, three-bay house with single-storey piended wings, early C19(?). A WALLED GARDEN lies N.

ROSEBANK. Former Free Church, gable-ended with SW porch, 1846. Converted to house, c. 1958. Short porched extension added to SE gable. Windows have segmental lintels; those to SW widened. Schist sills at rear.

STANDING STONE, 150m. NNE of Inverfolla. Fallen stone, 3.8m. long, lying S of A828.

ARDCHATTAN

A coastal strip facing S across Loch Etive between North Connel and Glen Salach. Despite its fertile lochside location on the sea route into the heart of Lorn and the auspicious foundation of a priory in the C13, it has remained a quiet rural backwater.

ARDCHATTAN CHURCH, 2.8km. WNW of Ardchattan Priory. Built 1836 at Achnaba by *John Thom* of Oban, in a crowstepped Gothic style, somewhat excessively castigated by the 1844 *Statistical Account* as being 'without any pretensions to elegance'. Pointed-arch lattice windows, bifurcated and transomed, are perhaps too liberally disposed across the principal SW front, but the louvred, domed and pinnacled octagonal belfry, though uneasily scalloped off the gable apex, has an erect elegance. The plan is symmetrical, entered on the SW gable. Tight vestibule with newel wall stairs rising l. and r. to the gallery; corridors lead to vestry and retiring rooms housed in two-storeyed, gabled NW and SE wings. The well-lit interior is austerely symmetrical, preserving its long central communion table, bench pews and two axial PULPITS, for minister and precentor, each approached by railed double stairs. Both pulpits are octagonal, panelled with blind Gothic arcading, and spring from swept pedestals. The higher pulpit is capped by a sounding board carried high on a single rear shaft to float ahead of the triple-light NE gable window, cleverly inverting the concave sweep of the supports. – FONT bracketed to pulpit; basin inscribed 'Ardchattan Church 1836'. – To l. of the pulpits, an elliptical memorial TABLET to Ensign John Peter Fraser †1848; to r., an idiosyncratic fretwork PANEL cut with the text of the Lord's Prayer. – Horizontally-panelled horseshoe GALLERY supported on seven cast-iron cluster shaft columns.

CHURCH, Baile Mhaodain, 400m. NW of Ardchattan Priory. Much overgrown ruinous rubble oblong, 19.2m. by 8.4m. overall. Dedicated to St Modan or St Baedan, it may date from the C15 or C16. In the E gable, built on a broader splayed rubble plinth, two aumbries and a small central window with splayed ingoes and a single lintel stone. Remaining walls stand c. 3m.

Probable s entrance now blocked. In 1678 the local presbytery found 'nothing but old walles'. Abandoned burial ground. 50m. NE is the lintelled well-mouth and trough of TOBAR MHAODAIN.

CHURCH OF THE HOLY SPIRIT (Episcopal), Bonawe, 3.4km. E of Ardchattan Priory. Built 1886. Gabled granite rubble: part church, part house. – Stone pedestal FONT and ancient stoup. – BELL from the Glen Line ship *Glenroy*, presented 1971.

OLD PARISH CHURCH, 45m. E of Ardchattan Manse. Little more than the lower courses of the S wall, *c.* 1.5m. high, remains of a building constructed 1731–2 to serve a congregation which until then had worshipped at Baile Mhaodain or at Ardchattan Priory. The church, built by *James Duff*, a Dunblane mason, seems to have plundered the Priory for freestone – 'appropriately enough', says the *New Statistical Account* of 1844, with now questionable conviction. The plan was rectangular with the pulpit at the centre of the S wall.

ARDCHATTAN POINT. Three-bay, two-storey, former manse, built 1773–4 in a sylvan lochside setting immediately W of the now-ruinous Parish Church (q.v.). Additional offices, described as 'commodious' by the *New Statistical Account*, augmented the accommodation in 1814. In 1820 stables were built by *John McIntyre*, wright. None of this impairs the simplicity and purity of the S front. A C20 hipped-roofed porch is less respectful. Despite this, and though it no longer functions as a manse, the house has relinquished little of its austere, almost religious beauty.

ACHNABA, 500m. N of Ardchattan Church. Single-storey laird's house, early C18, now a byre, on the N side of a U-plan court. W and E ranges, late C18, the former adapted as a dwelling house.

CAIRNS, Achnaba. Five cairns all within 500m. N and NW of Ardchattan Church. Most are denuded, but one, 15.3m. in diameter, preserves an arc of kerb stones on the W; it is located on the N edge of the track to Achnaba Farm.

CRUCK-FRAMED BUILDING, Cadderlie, 10km. E around the NW shore of Loch Etive. Late C18 or early C19. Harled granite rubble walls on a bouldered base enclose an area 22.5m. by 5.3m. overall which is subdivided equally into byre and dwelling, each five bays long, marked by scarf-jointed cruck-couples, sawn-off below the wallhead. The byre is roofless. The dwelling originally had opposed doorways N and S but was remodelled to face S, mid C19.

ARDCHATTAN PRIORY

on the N shore of Loch Etive, 6km. E of North Connel

9734

Valliscaulian Order conventual buildings and church founded *c.* 1230 by Duncan MacDougall, Lord of Lorn, on the N shore of Loch Etive. Some C13 work survives but the precise configuration of early development has been obscured by later accretion and alteration.

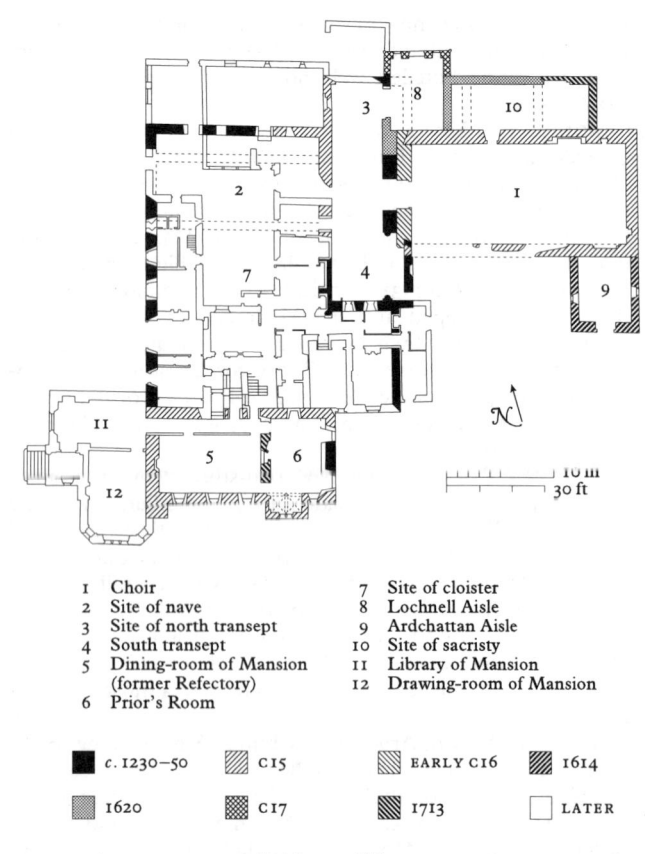

Ardchattan Priory

1	Choir	7	Site of cloister
2	Site of nave	8	Lochnell Aisle
3	Site of north transept	9	Ardchattan Aisle
4	South transept	10	Site of sacristy
5	Dining-room of Mansion (former Refectory)	11	Library of Mansion
6	Prior's Room	12	Drawing-room of Mansion

Key: c. 1230–50 · C15 · EARLY C16 · 1614 · 1620 · C17 · 1713 · LATER

Masonry is granite rubble, dressed with a grey-green sandstone probably from Carsaig on Mull but later with a buff Morvern stone. The church, of c. 1236, appears to have comprised nave, N aisle, N and S transepts with double chapels to the E in the Romanesque manner, and a small choir. The conventual buildings lay S, the cloister surrounded by W cloister walk, S refectory and E dormitory range. Of these, only the S transept and vestiges of the nave and crossing can be seen, while stretches of walling on the W and E of the monastic accommodation have been absorbed by later work. Extensive construction in the C15 and early C16 repaired the N transept, crossing and nave, remodelled the refectory range and produced a choir larger in size than the existing nave. These changes survive, at least in part. In 1602 the priory was secularized. By 1620, Alexander Campbell, hitherto its commendator, had converted the refectory range to serve as his own residence, while the choir and transepts were adapted for reformed worship. The Ardchattan Aisle, SE of the choir, and the Lochnell Aisle, NW of the choir, were also built (q.v.). By the C18, a new parish church (*see* above) having been built in 1731–2, the priory church was being quarried – 'destroyed by the possessor for the sake of the stones, much to the regret of the inhabitants' (Batten, 1877). The house, which continued to be occupied, was repaired in 1815 and around the middle of the century it was reshaped and extended as Ardchattan House (*see* below) by *Charles Wilson*.

The CHURCH. Expansion across the cloister site and N beyond the nave has all but obliterated evidence of the architectural character of the original church. A late medieval round-headed arched opening, mutilated and blocked, survives in the N wall of the nave, which Wilson utilized as a convenient division in his extensive outbuildings. In the transept ruins, another blocked window, the more northerly of the two E windows lighting the s transept chapels, can still be seen, as can the moulded N and S responds and central column base of the arcade to these chapels. Separating crossing from nave is a C15 pulpitum. Its central doorway, though not intact, preserves a semicircular arch of undulating profile springing from moulded capitals on multiple shafts. Opposite, opening E into the choir through a double thickness of C13 and early C16 walling, a barrel-vaulted passage: the earlier w arch, robbed of its dressings, exposes rubble voussoirs; E arch face wrought with roll-and-hollow moulding. N transept N wall, C18 or C19; in the W wall, a tall round-arched window, C15, with splayed ingoes, missing nook shafts and a continuous surround of dog-tooth ornament; in the E, no evidence of the C13 double chapel but a twice-chamfered, early C17, round-headed archway giving access to the Lochnell Aisle. Here the choir walls meet the crossing at a height of 8.2m. but reduce along the N, and on the E and S stand less than 2m. A splayed plinth and a moulded sill(?) stringcourse exist but window arrangements are impossible to determine. Springing from ground level at the E end of the S wall, a hood-moulded arch of doubled roll-and-hollow section defines a semicircular recess within which are three further recesses, each framed by a pointed arch. In the central arch, a piscina; on each side, a credence: probably pre-C19 insertions. At the E end of the N choir wall is a tomb chest recess and in the middle a doorway, with moulded w jamb. This led originally to the sacristy, now superseded by burial-aisle walling.

There are three walled burial plots appended to the choir. In what was originally the sacristy, C17 and C18 walling defines an area probably consecrated for the Campbells of Inverawe. At the SE, the ARDCHATTAN AISLE, with round-arched S doorway and lintelled W and E windows grooved for glazing. Door keystone dated 1614 and monogrammed ACKM for Alexander Campbell of Ardchattan and his wife Katherine MacDonald. At the NW, entered from both N and W, the LOCHNELL AISLE, which dates from 1620. The N door is square-headed, symmetrically flanked by two similarly lintelled openings, and surmounted by an inscribed panel and empty recess. The inscription records the C17 builder, Alexander Campbell, 3rd Laird of Lochnell, and the 1713 rebuilding by his kinsman, Alexander Campbell, the 6th Laird.

MONUMENTS. In the Lochnell Aisle is a decorated Early Christian SLAB. Though trimmed, presumably for re-use, its carved face clearly depicts a wheel-cross and is intricately incised with interlace and fret patterning, some Norse in style; flanking animal and figure ornament includes clerics playing a harp and pipes. – A large TABLE-TOMB, c. 1715, commemorates Alexander Campbell, 6th Laird of Lochnell, and his wife; heraldic devices and trumpeting angels in bold relief. – A number of architectural FRAGMENTS, C13–C16, are in the S conservatory of Ardchattan House. Amongst these, two pieces from the head of a disc-headed CROSS, its shaft showing a galley and two animals and bearing an inscription which records the date of its erection, 1500, stands in the choir. – Also in the choir, several tomb SLABS, c. 1500–60, and, built against the N wall, a tomb-chest with a tapered SLAB lid, Iona school, early C16, in which two superimposed groups of three figures in Gothic niches are surrounded by a dog-tooth border and an inscription memorializing the priors Duncan and Dugall MacDougall and their families. – Post-Reformation tombs located in different places in the Priory include a recumbent SLAB in the choir, its inscription and armorial elements carved with a naïve freedom and dated 1695.

The CONVENTUAL BUILDINGS: ARDCHATTAN HOUSE. Since the early C17, when the conventual buildings of Ardchattan Priory (q.v.) were adapted as a dwelling, the house has evolved as a strange but enchanting mixture of ecclesiastical and domestic forms. At first, residential arrangements were confined to the C15 refectory and, while certain internal changes occurred during the C18 and early C19, it was not until the mid C19 that the house was expanded by the Glasgow architect, *Charles Wilson*, between 1847 and 1855. Wilson's approach was in muted Jacobean style. From the N side of the refectory, he built extensive outbuildings which enclosed a service courtyard and spread beyond the Priory nave. He also revised the interior of the commendator's house, adding new staircases and a short W wing with a library and drawing room. On the S front, the pointed-arch heads of three blocked refectory windows are evident. The projecting gabled bay to the r., lit by a two-light pointed window which is medieval but has been repaired, contains the C15 refectory pulpit (*see* below). To the l., the canted bay of the drawing room, corbelled to a gabled first floor, is entirely C19, as its coursed masonry makes clear. In the re-entrant is a smaller projection which may once have contained a spiral stair connecting the refectory with an undercroft; now fronted by a flat-arched glazed loggia.

Inside, the PULPIT is the outstanding feature. This 'most unexpected little room' (Cruden, 1986), brought back to life by the restoration carried out by *Ian G. Lindsay & Partners* in 1960, opens through a pointed-arch arcade to what was the E end of the refectory and is now the so-called Prior's Room. It is a compartment or recess of two bays, each roofed by a ribbed quadripartite vault; one bay doubtless contained the lectern while the other gave access from the refectory. The arcade pier is a cluster of filleted columns which, having no capital, make an infelicitous transition into the mouldings of the two pointed arches. A bold hood-moulding of pointed trefoil shape on the W wall of the pulpit recess may not be in its original position. In the Prior's Room, separated from the dining room by a chimneyed cross-wall of 1713, C18 wood panelling survives. The utilization of the refectory roof space for additional accommodation, begun in post-Reformation conversion, was continued by Wilson; E attic timbers are probably those of C15 scissor-braced trusses.

ARDEN

Two large houses, a ruined castle and some farms 4km. NW of Balloch.

AUCHENDENNAN, 1.5km. SE of the roundabout. Bravura Baronial by *John Burnet*, 1864–7. Built for tobacco baron George Martin but from 1945 adapted, with amazingly little impairment, as a Youth Hostel. A vast conceit imbued with the belief that a Scotsman's home, too, is his castle; here, combined in massive but far from unadorned bulk, is that 'Scottish delight in sheer height' and 'in the fantastical' which Nikolaus Pevsner identified in his 1955 Reith Lectures. Towers abound, imploded into the mansion's square-snecked solidity: square at the NW, half-round and conically roofed on the W; square again for the S stair; round in the SE. A splendid stone-columned conservatory, in need of repair, pushes N then W. At the SW entrance, a colossal, round-arched porte-cochère, crusty with Mannerist detail; added by *Alexander N. Paterson*, 1902–3. Around forecourt and garden is a low balustraded wall regularly crested with pyramidal stone blocks. A pool, formed at the centre of the forecourt, 1888, retains its dolphin-buttressed base but not its bronze eagle (mysteriously removed, *c.* 1973).

The house is entered from the S through an oak-lined VESTIBULE, 1902–3, panelled with cusped-arch recesses and strapwork. Mosaic floor. Stone fireplace, grandly Gothic with carved figures and the first of several mottoes of cloying Victorian sentimentality: WELCOME . EVER . SMILES . FAREWELL . GOES . OUT . SIGHING. To the r., an oak staircase, carved with rinceau-like balustrading, rises to a landing at the centre of the S wall before returning to a galleried, top-lit HALL elongated S–N at the heart of the plan. This magnificently finished interior space is stunning. Decorative plasterwork in high relief features vine and grape motifs on huge coves below the second-floor balconies while draped female figures lure the eyes higher to more high-relief plasterwork, added 1902–3, round a rooflight-well crossed by arch-braced trusses with fretted spandrels. The floor is parquet. On the E wall, in a canted bay inglenook, a stone fireplace with a roll-moulded, shouldered arch and a decorative plaster panel above. Only the dado panelling, now falsely grained, disappoints. Opening off the hall at this *piano nobile* level are the principal public rooms. The Dining Room looks E to the loch. Heavily panelled plaster ceiling. Wide green marble fireplace incorporated in panelled N wall framed by fluted pilasters and Ionic columns; shallow niches with decorative marquetry inlays. w wall designed to serve as a sideboard: three arched bays with sunburst motifs under a Mannerist entablature carried on caryatid consoles and pilasters. In the Conference Room, a coved Jacobean ceiling with plaster pendants and a strapwork frieze enlivened by mermen and mermaids. Massive chimneypiece carved with Mannerist figures and decorative pilaster margins, shell niches, a cusp-edged mantel frame and a fireplace of striped grey marble. Windows have painted glass panels in the upper lights depicting the virtues. Across the hall, at the sw corner of the plan, is what is now the TV Room. Plain ceiling with egg-and-dart cornice. Chimneypiece pilasters decorated with floral ornament; mantel inlays of mother-of-pearl, rose motifs on the brass fire canopy. Art Nouveau stained glass: bluebirds and roses. At the centre of the s wall the staircase continues its rise, flights and landings arranged in square zones around a newel post cluster of four banded columns with Corinthian capitals from which four round arches spring between saucer domes. Hostel bedrooms occupy the upper floors.

Arden House. By *John Burnet*, 1867–8. Two and three storeys of square-snecked sandstone aggregating canted bays, bartizans, gables, turrets and a high, square, NE tower in a vigorous Victorian Scots concoction. Massive SW porte-cochère; round arches carried on short, thick, grey granite columns. Appropriately grand for the Lord Provost of Glasgow, Burnet's Baronialism is here none the less muted, even staid, by comparison with nearby Auchendennan (*see* above). Now flatted. Lean-to buildings in the walled garden converted to dwellings. Contemporary stables, ruinous in 1994, with polychromatic brickwork to the yard. Four octagonal, gabled Gothic gatepiers stand on the A82, at the end of the disused s drive.

Bannachra Castle, 1.7km. w of the roundabout. Erected by the Colquhouns at the start of the C16 but destroyed a century later by the Macgregors. Evidently rectangular in plan; parts of the s and E walls stand but all cornerstones and dressings have been pillaged. A few surviving windows, some with shotholes below the sills.

Fruin Bridge. Built 1931; now isolated by realignment of the A82. Three segmental-arches, with labelled voussoirs and keystones, spanning between cutwaters. Rough-faced sandstone with ashlar parapets. Inset tablet, from previous bridge, records the name of Sir Charles Preston, Bart, Inspector General of the Military Road, 1796.

ARDENTINNY 1887

Delightfully rural village on the w shore of Loch Long at a spot as beautiful as it was once functional, for here the drovers and their cattle crossed to Coulport *en route* s.

ARDENTINNY CHURCH. Built 1838–9. A simple oblong kirk with three tall lintelled windows each side. Gable front with gabled porch; both roughcast with thin sandstone quoins and lugged skews. Arched bellcote corbelled at apex. Stark interior with flat ceiling at low collar height. The preacher's sounding board, frugally decorated with finials and billet ornament, projects from a timber wall panel.

ARDENTINNY CENTRE. By *Renfrew County Council*, 1972–3. T-plan outdoor centre, the main flat-roofed block of classrooms and residential accommodation a two-to-three-storey run of horizontal glazing and stained timber boarding regularly interrupted by small, square, balconied bays. Profiled metal cladding adds a scarlet splash.

Former ARDENTINNY PRIMARY SCHOOL. By *Steele & Balfour*; opened 1892. Rubble classroom block with two mullion-and-transom windows below twinned gables. Crowstepped schoolhouse l. has cut-down turret over hooded doorway. Disused.

ARDENTINNY HOTEL. The three-bay, two-storey core of the inn is probably C18; gable-ended wings, set back l. and r., are later. Squat flat-roofed roadside porch at centre w front. Opposite are two parallel single-storey rubble outbuildings surviving from an early C19(?) farm.

COTTAGES, beside the church. A white-painted, single-storey row of early C19 dwellings. GLENCAIRN, closest to the church, splays in plan to finish the row with a piended half-octagon end; it was built, *c.* 1842, as the village school.

FERRY COTTAGES, immediately N of hotel. Early C19. Skew-gabled rubble row with a single pediment gablet surviving over the s doorway. Minute round-arch in N gable holding a religious figurine. Beside the slip, a short distance N, is a one-room rubble cottage of similar date also thought to have been linked with the former ferry to Coulport.

GLENFINART HOUSE, 900m. NNW. Remains of a plain Georgian mansion, reconstructed and enlarged in Tudor Gothic fashion, *c.* 1840; extended 1895–6. Incongruous in its caravan park setting, only a four-storey, ashlar tower survives in embarrassed limbo. It has hooded lintelled windows and is heavily battlemented; on the SE front, a castellated arched porch projects. The rest of the house, a dullish two-storey affair with some strapwork ornament, stretched NE until destroyed by fire in 1968.

ARDFERN 8004

A linear village on the sheltered NW coast of upper Loch Craignish, popular with yachtsmen.

CRAIGNISH PARISH CHURCH. Symmetrical hipped-roofed box of harled rubble with sandstone margins, built 1826–7 by *David McDougall*, 'architect in Craignish', to replace an earlier church of 1740, itself a successor to one of 1698. A pedimented centre carrying a block belfry projects slightly from the principal N front. All windows round-headed with intersecting astragals; those at the N end of side walls, where internal stone stairs rise to galleries, are blind. Low hipped-roofed vestry added behind pulpit on the S. The central entrance is now blocked and access is gained through the W staircase door. The plastered and painted interior has a flat ceiling. Panel-fronted galleries on three sides supported on five timber columns on timber socles. Columns have slight entasis and bulbous capitals, and preserve old light bracket rings. – Two-tier panelled PULPIT, in the centre of the S wall, with a narrow panelled back rising to an octagonal canopy swept above to a boss finial. – Later communion table and lectern in cusped and fretted oak. – White marble mural TABLET commemorates Colin Campbell of Jura †1848. – In the forecourt, aligned with the N–S axis of the church, is Ardfern's WAR MEMORIAL, *c.* 1920, a grey granite Celtic cross and rough block base set on a spreading cairn of stones.

ARDFERN HOUSE, opposite church up a drive. Former manse, erected 1833–4. By *David McDougall*. Harled rubble with droved ashlar margins. The SE front repeats the three-bay piended formula of the church with narrowed pedimented centre, this time capped by a roll-moulded chimney stack. Entrance door with moulded architraves and neat cornice.

THE GALLEY OF LORNE. Three-bay rubble inn with timber gabled dormers, *c.* 1800, much altered and extended.

CRAIGNISH PRIMARY SCHOOL. Gabled C19 Gothic in snecked rubble with sandstone dressings and moulded skewputts. Central porch with steep gable front; in it an inscription records 'A gift of Mr. and Mrs. Gascoigne of Craignish Castle to this Parish 1861'. Triple cusped lancets in the gables; the hooded SE windows have lost their original sashes.

THE SQUARE, Eileann Righ. Two-storey and single-storey rubble dwellings around courtyard. Mid C19(?); renovated 1934.

ARDKINGLAS HOUSE
600m. SW of Kilmorich Church, Cairndow

The earlier of two houses built by *Robert S. Lorimer* at the head of Loch Fyne. Constructed on the SE shore in only twenty-one months, 1906–8, Ardkinglas is essentially new; unlike its neighbour across the loch, Dunderave (q.v.), its Scottishness persuasively contrived, fabricated rather than restored. The estate, which stretches across country from Loch Fyne to Loch Long, has an intriguing architectural history from the time it came into Campbell hands at the end of the C14. A castle, 'of unascertained date' (Groome, 1882), stood perhaps 150m. S of the site of Lorimer's house; a squarish enclosure with three circular corner towers and a projecting SW gatehouse. It survived until the 1790s, though only as a ruin. Indeed, throughout the C18, successive proposals for a new residence had been entertained by the Campbells. Some time before his death in 1729, *Colen Campbell* produced drawings for a house based on Palladio's Villa Emo. In 1773 *Robert Adam* suggested a three-storey, three-bay mansion with short flanking wings, plain in design but for a fine tripartite doorpiece with sunburst fanlight. A few years later, *c.* 1780, another proposal envisaged a symmetrical castellated house with a bow-fronted projection not unlike nearby Strachur House (q.v.). Then came a number of ideas from *James Playfair*, including one for a 'marine pavilion', again classical, with advanced end bays and a high central drum raised over the staircase. In the end, the house built for Sir Alexander Campbell, *c.* 1795, was decidedly dull: still classical, the three central bays of its seven-bay façade were pedimented; 'new, large and convenient' was the far from effusive judgement of Thomas Garnett in 1798. Located some 120m. SE of the present house, it lasted little more than a generation, being destroyed by a fire in 1831. Once again, a variety of rebuilding proposals was canvassed. Drawings by *William Burn*, 1831, show a characteristically rambling Tudor-Jacobean house, while a perspective of 1832 signed by *A. M. Binning* prefers castellated Baronial. In fact, all that seems to have happened was the rehabilitation of the former stables block as 'Old Ardkinglas House', *c.* 1840. Not until the first years of the C20 would Sir Andrew Noble, who had purchased the estate in 1905, contemplate a new Ardkinglas.

Lorimer's concept is romantic and Scottish. His house is an assemblage of gabled forms, differing in height, irregular in plan, constantly varied in perspective. Picking up 'the rhythms of its setting', the design has, as Hussey observed in 1931, the 'undulating, weather-worn character of a group of hills, where ranges and peaks overtop one another'. Nature as model, in a fecund and fundamentally anti-Platonic way: this is romantic architecture. And, like the landscape, the elements of building are recognizably Scottish: crowstepped gables, ogee roofs, idiosyncratically pedimented eaves dormers, tall chimneystacks. Overall, binding concept and context, the golden-green hues of granite quarried locally. No matter that harling had been intended, this pervasive rubble, offset by dressings of Dullator sandstone, produces that soft-rough texture so characteristic of much of Lorimer's work.

EXTERIOR. A drive approaches the house in a slow curve from the S. The SE front is two storeys high, gable-ended, with a continuous ridge emphasizing the horizontal. A crowstepped gable pushes forward l. of centre, the entrance porch it contains marked by a round-arched opening. To the r., at first floor, three strangely pedimented eaves dormers. Behind this frontal block, the house rises a further storey, while diagonally N the corbelled caphouse and elongated bartizan of the watchtower can be seen, higher still. Advancing r. to give some sense of enclosure to the forecourt are the low buildings and wall

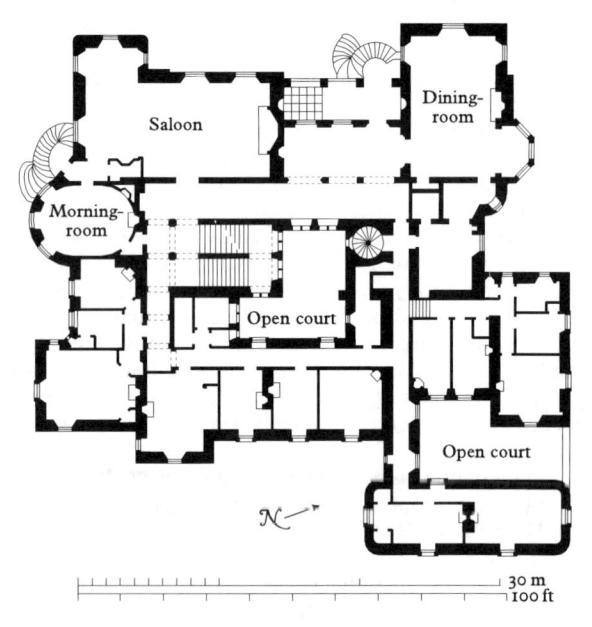

Ardkinglas House

of the service wing which terminates in a single-storey pavilion, the deer larder, charmingly capped by an ogee pyramid roof.

A second bell roof, similar in profile but circular in plan, marks the centre of the SW façade. It sits over a three-storey drum half embedded in the mass of the building and subtly thickened on a corbelcourse at first-floor lintel height. Three pedimented dormers cut through the eaves. To the r., a dormered two-storey link connects with the asymmetrical gable of the entrance block. To the l., the house rises higher, another asymmetrical gable stepping up from the bell roof of the drum. From a first-floor doorway, skewed across the re-entrant formed with the drum, a railed stair winds down on a curved rubble base to the pleasance. At first floor, two tall windows light what is evidently the *piano nobile*.

Three more tall windows appear round the corner on the NW elevation, the first in a one-bay, three-storey-high, gabled projection, the others aligned with two second-floor windows that break through the eaves into elaborate dormerheads. All five light the Saloon, giving this principal public room splendid views of Loch Fyne. To the l. of the Saloon the façade recesses slightly with a corresponding drop in height. Below three more eaves dormers is a loggia of round arches set on square piers, an open but sheltered spot from which to enjoy the prospect of loch, mountain and sky. Here, again, in the re-entrant formed by the crowstepped gable which terminates the elevation, a railed stair twists down to the garden.

Despite the formal complexity of the exterior, Lorimer's INTERIOR is compact and clear. At the centre of the plan is a rectangular zone around the perimeter of which circulation routes pass, opening up in the S to the Lower Hall and in the W to the main staircase; pointing towards the E is an open L-plan court, and tucked in the N corner a turnpike stair which climbs to the watch-tower. The Lower Hall, entered from the Porch, leads to the main staircase which is screened by a line of stone piers. Straight flights rise and return between parallel walls, the half-landing lit from the court by tall mullioned windows. Opposite the main stair is the Study, 'Sir Andrew's Room', an oval interior created behind the bow-fronted projection at the centre of the SW elevation. Beyond the stair, a door opens into a small seating area, the Smoking Room, from which a few steps lead down r. into the Billiard Room. Stores, kitchens and servants' quarters fill the remainder of the ground floor on the N and E.

On the upper level, bedrooms are disposed along the SE range; their ceilings vary (flat, segmental and combed) but all have decorative plasterwork with natural motif designs by *Thomas Beattie* and *Sam Wilson*. Opposite the stair is the Morning Room, which repeats the elliptical interior of the Study below, and r., taking up half of the NW range, the Saloon. This is the largest room in the house, a double square, and the most grandly appointed. Its plaster ceiling is heavily moulded with strong floral ornament around the margins, a deep rose at each end of the room and a flat central panel, rectangular with semicircular ends, in which *Roger Fry* has painted a chariot and rearing horses. Walls timber-lined with fielded panels. Door with moulded architraves set in a Baroque aedicule of fluted Ionic pilasters and elaborately carved broken pediment. On the NE wall, an immense granite chimneypiece, its deep, five-ton lintel 'carried' on provocatively thin decorative pilasters; by *Scott Morton & Co.*, following Lorimer's instructions. Back to back with this, warming the Upper Hall, another fireplace, less wide between Mannerist tapered pilasters but with a vigorous armorial panel in high relief filling the space between mantel and ceiling. Doors open from the Hall to the Loggia and to the Dining Room which, located at the N corner of the house, has views on three sides. Ranged along a corridor running SE are Pantry, Servery and more accommodation for servants.

150m. ENE of the house, a D-plan WALLED GARDEN, entered through a NE arched gateway, survives from the early C19. There is a fine ARBORETUM in the valley of the Kinglas Water where a rubble BRIDGE of late C18 date spans the gorge. Landscaping nearer the house is all Lorimer's. The approach from the S is neither abrupt nor direct but slow enough in its curve to ensure the clustered forms of the design exert their full romantic impact. Close to the SW side of the house there is a pleasance with pool, fountain, planted borders and yew hedges. On the NW the levels have been carefully controlled so that the architecture acquires an added elevational dignity from a long terrace, regularly balustraded and buttressed above banked lawns falling to the loch.

ARDLAMONT

Estate at the S end of the Cowal peninsula lying between Loch Fyne and the Kyles of Bute.

KILBRIDE CHURCH, at Kilbride Farm. A gable-ended, Gothic box with tall, four-centred arch windows. Built as a chapel of ease, 1839. Harled except for the gabled W front which has a central pointed-arch entrance with splayed ingoes set below a rectangular hood-moulding. Moulded skews step once in mid-rise. At the apex, heavily corbelled, a castellated birdcage bellcote. Plain interior. The church, now abandoned, sits on a gentle slope in a walled graveyard. Round GATEPIERS, reducing in diameter above a sandstone ring, are capped with nippled, domed stones.

ARDLAMONT HOUSE, 2.3km. NNE of Ardlamont Point. A five-bay, piended mansion, a little too wide and rectilineal in its proportions to be elegant, but dignified and well groomed. The house, which rises two storeys above a partly sunk basement, was built for the Lamont family by *Thomas Napier*, mason in Rothesay, in 1819–20, and replaces or, more probably, reworks an older structure, the wings of which survive. Napier's main block bulks large; N and S façades fill the gap between two gable-

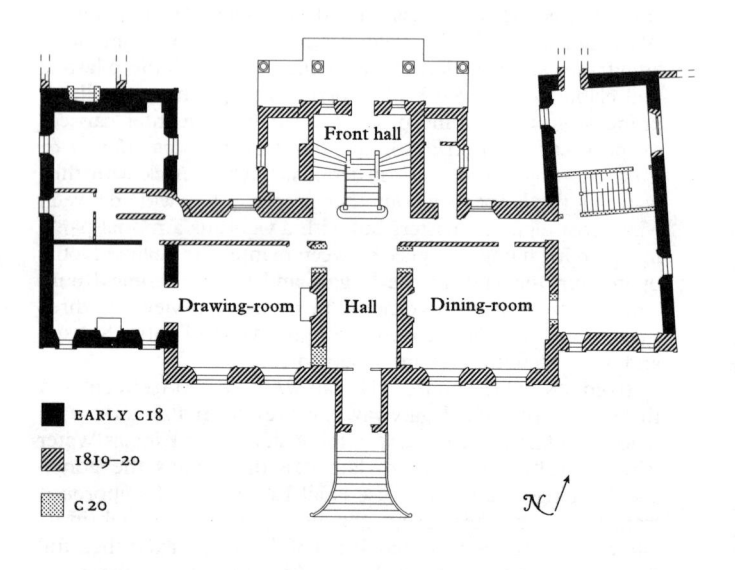

Ardlamont House. Plan of ground floor

ended, early C18, transverse wings, dominating their lower, domestic scale with seigneurial symmetry. This hauteur is, however, comparatively recent for, until a major restoration programme in 1970 re-created their original skewed and chimneyed gables, these wings had been crenellated screens elevated as part of the early C19 aggrandizement.

The S FRONT, which advances slightly from the flanking gables, is cement-rendered with ashlar margins, angle-pilasters, eaves cornice and a blocking course which rises in three shallow steps towards the centre, all painted. The flatness of the broad façade is relieved by a flat-roofed porch stolidly framed with coupled pilasters. From this a stone stair railed with plain iron balustrading spills down on to the lawn. Above the doorway, the central window at first-floor level has been given narrow blind side-lights. But none of this (not the stepped blocking course, not the quasi-tripartite window, not the porch itself) seems an adequate response to the assertive proportions of the tall ground-floor windows, almost 3m. in height; there is a lingering sense of bathos at the heart of this principal façade. Paradoxically, the N FRONT, decidedly the rear in the early C19 design, is less disappointing. Translated in 1970 into the entrance front by a reversal in plan orientation, it succeeds where the S fails. Its hipped-roofed stair-tower, already projecting centrally from the main body of the plan, acquired the added emphasis of a single-storey portico of four widely spaced Roman Doric columns to announce this as the new architectural approach. Above the portico's lean-to roof, which wraps around small, late C19, single-storey extensions symmetrically added in the re-entrants of the stair tower, three windows in almost Venetian relationship light the upper flights of the staircase, the tall round-arch opening at the centre axially echoed in a new doorway below.

INTERIOR. The N entrance into the stair tower opens directly on to a half-landing lobby. On each side of a narrow central flight descending to the basement, wider, shorter flights rise to the main hall. This disturbing duality in approach is dispelled on the ground floor where the original pattern of circulation asserts itself unequivocally. At the heart of the plan, where the projecting N stair tower meets the main block, the broad first flight of the STAIRCASE rises N from the centre of the hall to return l. and r. in imperial manner to the upper floor; at the far end of the hall, concealed by a glazed timber screen, is the S porch from which the approach to the stair would originally have been made; and, at right-angles to this N–S axis, running W and E along the N side of the house, corridors lead to the C18 wings. On each side of the hall is a single large room. To the W, the DRAWING ROOM, now entered through a doorway repositioned from the S to the N end of the hall wall in 1970, there is a pine chimneypiece, late C18 in character and particularly refined in detail with urns, swags and scrolled foliage. In the DINING ROOM to the E, a late C19 marble chimneypiece with bolection mouldings, on the W wall between two doors with reeded architraves;

the s conceals a cupboard, the N is contemporary with that to the Drawing Room immediately opposite across the hall. There is a plaster centrepiece with rosette and swags in the ceiling, perhaps original, and an elliptically-headed recess in the E wall. Foliated brackets and cornices in the hall and corridors and the plasterwork of the upper hall date from alterations in the 1890s. The first-floor apartments and those in the older transverse wings have been much re-modelled, though a sandstone fireplace surround and a dentilled cornice in one room in the W wing are probably C18.

In the WALLED GARDEN, an early C18 obelisk SUNDIAL, 1.74m. high. The shaft, comprised of four panels hollowed out with circle, heart and chevron motifs, is of red sandstone, the faceted octagon and obelisk top of grey. On the N face of the shaft two armorial shields have been coupled above the incised initials D L / M S for Duncan Lamont of Lamont and Margaret Stewart who married in 1684. A late C20 metal orrery sits on the obelisk.

COURT OF OFFICES. Early C19. Rubble-built with sandstone dressings. A pretty s-facing roadside range, symmetrical with piended, two-storey end pavilions and a gabled centrepiece through which, under a segmental archway, access is gained to a courtyard enclosed on the W and E by two-storey wings and on the N by a single-storey range roofed with corrugated iron. Above the entry arch, two tiers of doocot entries intervene below a steep concave-sided pediment-gable with rolled skewputts and a central oculus. Round-arched windows in the end pavilions and similar doorways in the linking ranges have intersecting Gothick glazing bars above impost height.

CORRA FARM, 700m. W of Ardlamont House. Roofless rubble shell with some Gothic detail and a wide s gable dated 1842. The screeded brick frames of square window bays, added later, survive. Ruined byres and outbuildings.

ARDLUI

A halt at the N end of Loch Lomond before road and rail enter Glen Falloch.

ARDLUI CHURCH. By *Burnet, Son & Campbell*, 1895. Roughcast mission hall with overhanging eaves, three-light cusped windows and a battered buttress rising against the E gable into an open bellcote in line with the ridge.

ARDMADDY CASTLE
6.9km. SW of Kilninver

A house of two stylistic phases (one Palladian, the other Jacobethan) concealing a third, less evident, core of medieval origin. In 1737 what was left of the late C15 tower-house built by the MacDougalls of Rarey was transformed by Colin Campbell,

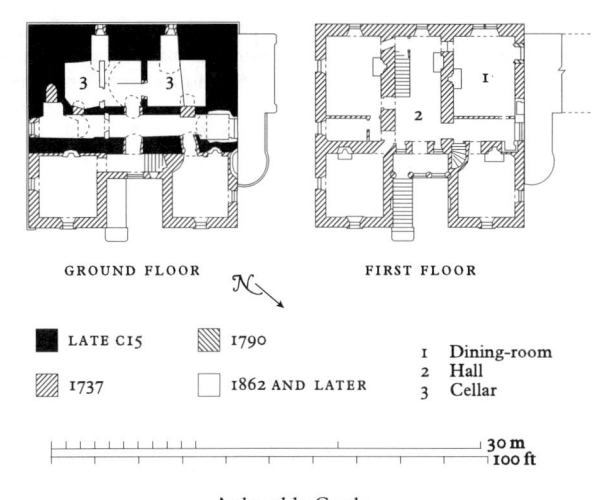

Ardmaddy Castle.
Plans of ground floor and first floor

chamberlain of the Breadalbane estate in Argyll, into a mansion of modest size but elegant pretension. From the thick-walled rectangular ground-floor storey of the tower, aligned SE–NW, two single-room wings projected NE on each side of a central recess. On this U-plan base a new first floor was constructed, the twin-jamb arrangement reminiscent of Borthwick Castle but smaller and, of course, wholly different in architectural character. For set back at the centre at first-floor level is a three-bay, columned and pedimented, Ionic portico which, despite its being reached by a forestair rising off-centre against the NW wall of the SE wing, plays its part in a design formula thoroughly Palladian in provenance. There is, admittedly, a certain cramped containment and modesty of scale in all of this but the building benefits splendidly from its elevated situation. But for the pitch of the piended roofs and the nature of the windows in the projecting wings (the larger round-arched with Gibbsian surrounds, the lower squarish with lugged and moulded architraves), the balanced tripartite composition of this principal NE front might just as easily have been applied to some minor mansion in the Veneto. Macaulay, indeed, specifically identifies the influence of Palladio's Villa Emo. The other elevations are decidedly plain. In the SE wall two small, medieval openings survive with C18 windows giving light to barrel-vaulted cellars within; above, three single-light openings were originally symmetrically related to each other and to the two openings below, but the widening of the NW window, 1924, unbalanced the intended arrangement. On the NW wall, most of which has been overlaid by later additions, is a monogrammed stone panel dated 1671, presumably a relic of some earlier alterations or extensions. All walls are harled with sandstone dressings, some of which, like the eaves cornice, are finely moulded.

In 1790–1 a separate wing was erected to the NW, connected to the house by an archway carrying a link passage. Plans to rebuild and extend on this side of the house were prepared by *James Gillespie Graham* in 1837 but nothing was done, and it was not until 1862 that the 2nd Marquess of Breadalbane consulted *David Bryce* with a view to realizing these proposals. Bryce's role in the subsequent programme of alterations and extensions is not wholly clear, and the matter is further complicated by the recorded involvement of *Robert Baldie*, but he seems to have respected Gillespie Graham's intentions fairly closely. Hingeing two storeys of new accommodation on a conically capped turnpike stair bedded into the wall of the old house, he pushed out an ashlar, twice-gabled wing to the NW, returning it through ninety degrees on the tall pivot of an octagonal W turret to create a second open-ended courtyard on the NE. Although the eaves line and roof pitch of the C18 house were more or less preserved and the high coped plinth on the older SW and SE walls continued, the stylistic idiom of the new work was far from classical. The gables on the SW façade were curvilinear; against each, beneath diamond balustrading, a broad canted bay; one corbelled at first floor from a central buttress, the other rising through two storeys. Chimneystacks were high, decorated with barley-sugar and chevron motifs. Jacobethan was the only possible description. But no longer. Most of these mid-Victorian additions have been demolished, leaving only the high W stair turret, with its diamond-patterned parapet and eight weather-vaned pinnacles, dramatically isolated. The 1790 link survives, but is now carried only one bay NW beyond its bridging arch in a smooth but misleading continuation of the wall and roof planes of the earlier C18 work. Some late C19 accommodation lies NE of the W turret; though physically disconnected, it succeeds in marking the N corner of the castle group. Despite repeated alteration and disruption, the buildings still have a powerful if disaggregated presence on their raised site, particularly on the NE where terrace and lawns look down on the long prospect of the WALLED GARDEN.

A few original interior features remain at first-floor level in the principal rooms in the C18 part of the house. These include timber panelling to walls and doors, a number of fireplaces with moulded surrounds of locally quarried marble, and stone flagging in the stair-hall which takes up the central third of the plan and is entered directly from the balustraded NE portico.

Below the castle, lying a short distance NW, is the COURT OF OFFICES, 1837–9, by *James Gillespie Graham*. Three irregular roughcast ranges, with a parapeted, three-storey, square tower at the W corner, group around a yard open to the NE. In a gable projecting into this yard are two four-centred archways to the coach-house, while a similar opening at the centre of the SW front is blocked. Crowsteps, quoins, plinths and dressings to the ingoes and shouldered lintels of the windows are all heavily detailed. Unlike the castle itself, the overall impression is disappointingly graceless. More rugged, yet far removed from this coarseness, is the rubble BRIDGE, mid C18, which crosses the Allt Dallermaig at the end of the garden, 240m. NE of the castle. The span of its segmental arch, 4.4m., is unremarkable but the six harled rubble pylons, a truncated cone set between flat-topped obelisks marking each, lend the structure a primitively Neoclassical charm. It is, however, a Gothick conceit which seems to have guided the design of the BOAT-HOUSE screen, 1790, fronting an opening cut into the cliff face of Ardmaddy Bay, about 1km. S of the castle.

ARDMARNOCK

9172

An estate on the E shore of Loch Fyne lying W of the Kilfinan–Millhouse road.

ARDMARNOCK HOUSE, 6.5km. SSW of Kilfinan. A neat, three-bay, late-Georgian box, raised on a sub-basement and hipped-roofed. Derelict in 1998. Built for John MacIver, c. 1826, when a number of farms were amalgamated to form the estate. The principal or W façade and the flanking N and S walls have been rendered and incised to simulate ashlar; dressings are of white sandstone. There is an ashlar base-course and a parallel horizontal band at ground-floor level. Quoining is broad to the basement but narrower above. Basement window margins are plain but those to the upper two floors have moulded architraves, the taller ground-floor openings surmounted by cornices. There is no pediment, only a simple projecting eaves cornice with a low parapet and a short central blocking piece on the main façade. At the centre of this W front, a stone stairway flanked by cast-iron balustrades rises to a portico of freestanding fluted Ionic columns carrying a heavy entablature.

The plan is conventional with a narrow, somewhat deep, central hall set between two flue-bearing walls. This hall has three distinct parts: first, a stone-flagged lobby; then, through a glazed screen which has a full-width elliptical fanlight, an inner hall from which the two principal rooms are entered l. and r.; and, finally, beyond a second elliptical arch springing from Ionic responds, the double-height space of the stair hall. Cornices add distinctive definition to each part: dentilled in the lobby, modillions and quatrefoils in the inner hall, and, in the upper hall over the curving geometrical stair, egg-and-dart. Decorative plasterwork also enriches the large SW ground-floor room: cornice with anthemion and Greek key motifs. White marble chimneypiece incorporates freestanding female terms bearing an allegorical lintel flanked by female masks among acanthus scrolls. The dining room behind this room has an egg-and-dart cornice and a chimneypiece of white-and-grey marble. At first-floor level, the depth of the plan originally permitted bedrooms front and back on both sides of the upper hall, with a central dressing room and closet serving each front bedroom. This arrangement survives on the S but has been altered at the NE corner by the addition of a NE wing, c. 1880, to provide guest bedrooms and improve the kitchen facilities until then accommodated in the basement. In cavalier Victorian manner, undeterred by the prevailing classical order, this extension presents a Baronial display of crowstepping and crenellation along its W front. Fortunately it does not encroach on the tall round-arched window lighting the house's main staircase at the centre of the E wall. At the entrance to the estate, a piend-roofed rubble LODGE, painted white.

CHAMBERED CAIRN, 150m. S. Two compartments orientated NNE–SSW, set within cairn material of now indeterminate extent. The outer chamber is open to the NNE and is separated from the inner by a septal stone somewhat lower than the side- and end-slabs; unusually, this stone has a cupmarking on one side and a cup-and-ring marking on the other.

DUN, Caisteal Aoidhe, 2km. S. Island dun connected to the E shore of Loch Fyne by a shingle spit. There are two walled areas, the larger and more complete measuring 11m. in dia. within a rubble curtilage *c.* 3m. thick. The site and the evidence of vitrification are described by the RCAHMS Inventory (1988) as 'spectacular'.

STANDING STONES, Inveryne, 800m. SW of Inveryne Farm. Linear group of three stones aligned NE–SW. Maximum height just over 1m.

ARDMORE

A one-hill peninsula pushing W into the Firth of Clyde between Cardross and Craigendoran. A nature reserve.

ARDMORE HOUSE. 1806. Five-bay, two-storey T-plan incorporating an earlier house, part of the fabric of which may date from the C17. Painted stucco, but short on Regency delicacy. A crenellated tower, gripped at the centre of the S front, rises an extra storey; coupled pilasters carrying a plain entablature frame the bowed entrance, the proportions echoed in the tripartite window at first floor and in the Diocletian window above. This same arrangement (ground-floor tripartite under Diocletian window) is repeated in the outer bays of the S façade and at the centre and wings of the N elevation. Single-storey STABLES, early C19(?); part of the piended N range extended over the courtyard on cast-iron piers. N of the house, the ruinous red sandstone OBSERVATORY, early C19, a telescope tower with a central spiral stair which rose to the viewing room. Adding to the picturesque scene, clinging to a cliff-top W of the house, is another circular building of uncertain date and function, a harled STORE, roofed, like a horse-mill, with a slated cone. Aligned below this, at the foot of the cliff, a D-plan TOWER, C16 or C17; gunloops and arrowslit lights suggest defensive intention.

KEPPOCH HOUSE, NE off the A814, 500m. NNW of the Ardmore road. 1820. A tall, abstemiously Classical but dignified white stucco mansion; three storeys on a raised basement. The wide three-bay SW front has a strong eaves cornice rising to a pediment at the centre above superimposed tripartite windows. Paired porch columns carry a projecting entablature with a bowed entrance screen in etched glass below (a late C19 addition). Late C18 panelling in the Dining Room removed in 1904 from St Anne's Church, Belfast. The D-plan WALLED GARDEN, early C19, lies SE; at the NW entrance, an 1816 datestone. SUNDIAL, early C19.

LYLESTON HOUSE, NE off the A814, 300m. NNW of the Ardmore road. 1798. Symmetrical two-storey farmhouse. Central SW door framed by pilasters and cornice. Tudor extension, late C19, forms L-plan to r. with parapeted porch in re-entrant.

ARDNADAM 1780

Residential fringe around the S shore of Holy Loch from Sandbank to Lazaretto Point. Before its later C19 development as one of a number of watering places along the Cowal shore, Ardnadam was chosen as the site of a quarantine station or lazaretto (1806) 'to receive infected goods of every description' (*NSA*, 1845). The stores built were demolished *c.* 1855. From 1961 until 1992 the Holy Loch was an American naval base servicing Polaris submarines. Some of the scars inflicted by this infection remain.

ARDNADAM PIER. Built 1858. The eponymous tidal shore, more mudflat than sandbank, produced a pier some 60m. long. Closed 1940 but called into service again when the Holy Loch became a US base in 1961.

HAFTON HOUSE, 650m. SE of Lazaretto Point. Late C18 house known as Orchard Park transformed into Tudor Gothic mansion by *David Hamilton*, 1816, for James Hunter. The principal two-storeyed E and N façades of harl-pointed rubble with sandstone dressings are each strongly divided into three bays by turreted octagonal buttresses rising like chimneys above parapet height. In the outer bays these parapets are crenellated, while at the centre the turrets are linked by flat-topped arcading. The three-light, mullion-and-transom E front windows are all hooded with flat label mouldings, except the central ground-floor canted bay. The N entrance front is similar, though asymmetrical, with another canted bay ground floor r. At its centre, concealing the crenellated porch of 1816, is a battlemented and turreted porte-cochère of three four-centred arches added *c.* 1840. This and further alterations carried out at the time were probably also by Hamilton, for the 'modern Gothic' style is maintained. A two-bay wing, recessed from the main N front and a little lower in height, was added W, returning three bays N. On the W and S sides, where the C18 house had survived, the service accommodation was revised and raised to three storeys while more crenellated additions were made to house a new S room and a spacious double staircase. A square tower with heavily corbelled battlemented parapet provides the obligatory picturesque skyline. SE conservatory of five arcuated bays, appropriately turreted at the angles; internal cast-iron columns with foliated capitals.

From the rib-vaulted porch to the rich arch-patterned ornament over the staircase, the interior is consistently Gothic. The

Green Room, r. from the hall, has a ribbed plaster ceiling with traceried star at the centre. To the l., in the NE room, another ribbed ceiling with bosses and a central roundel set over a trefoil frieze. Yet another in the SE room which is entered through double doors carved with Perp tracery. In the NW Billiard Room, a white marble Gothick chimneypiece. Moulded four-centred archways, with engaged shafts in the jambs, lead into and from the staircase hall at ground- and first-floor levels. Above the stair, decorative ribbed plasterwork again, curving up to a circular lantern surmounted by a shallow ribbed dome.

Terraced lawns extend S and E. A baluster SUNDIAL records the gratitude of Alexander Stewart, 'builder, Dunoon', to his patron, the younger James Hunter, who commissioned the alterations and extensions of *c.* 1840. Much of the estate N and W has been given over to holiday chalets. On higher ground, 120m. NW of the house, is the Gothick COURT OF OFFICES, *c.* 1800. The E façade survives. Over its main segmental archway (there are three others) is a large lancet with doocot entries set between blind dumb-bell slits, the whole within a pinnacled gable. Single-storey links connect l. and r. to gabled wings with blind quatrefoils. Iron FOOTBRIDGE, 100m. S of the house; three segmentally arched cast-iron beams, ornamented on the outer faces. LODGES, mid C19, on A815 and A885.

WAR MEMORIAL; unmissable landmark at Lazaretto Point. Built *c.* 1920. A stubby Baronial pencil of schist rubble and sandstone dressings rising from a rubble-paved octagonal base. Pedimented panel bears the names of the fallen.

DESCRIPTION

Around the pier the picture is bleak. Nor is the coastal parade of villas altogether attractive. Some oddities catch the eye. Front and back, ARDENGROVE, *c.* 1870, has parabola-like timber arches, gridded in the spandrels. From FIRPARK, *c.* 1860, a cantilevered five-light oriel bow looks NW up Holy Loch. Between the two, elevated above the coastal road, is what seems to be a deserted walled garden; it is all that remains of the quarantine station of 1807, all, that is, but a conically capped lookout TOWER, now derelict. Round the point, the former Customs House survives as GLEN COTTAGE, early C19, trim and ship-shape with bellcast eaves and flyover stair. Uphill on Fir Brae is THE CROMLECH, *c.* 1870, a broad symmetrical villa with gabled Gothic dormers, wide eaves and double-height segmental bays linked by balcony and veranda.

ARDOCH

A few houses by the A814 immediately W of Dumbarton.

ARDOCH. Built by Robert Cunninghame Graham of Gartmore who inherited Ardoch estate after his return from Jamaica in 1770. More cottage than mansion, the original house, *c.* 1780, was a symmetrical, single-storey, stucco dwelling with splayed, piend-roofed wings. This plantation model, which has been described as 'Georgian Colonial', was later altered, mid C19, when a two-stage central tower with a low pyramid roof and tall weather-vane finial was inserted at the centre of the plan. A round arch defines the SW entrance doorway under a tripartite window. Behind the house is a WALLED GARDEN, late C18 and early C19.

ARDOCHMORE BARN, N of Ardoch Farm. Early C18. Rectangular rubble barn with red sandstone dressings which include cornice and crowstepped gables. Ventilation slits. Built as the offices of Old Ardoch House, superseded by a second Ardoch (*see* above) and now demolished.

CATS CASTLE. 1888. Bull-faced Baronial; battered base, bartizans and battlements but lacking Bryce's exuberance. The heavily textured gabled walls are disappointingly flat, though a tall, somewhat overwindowed tower, complete with bartizan turret, does project boldly at the SW corner. Cat carvings explain the name.

ARDPATRICK

Headland clachan at Achadh-Chaorann at the mouth of West Loch Tarbert.

ARDPATRICK HOUSE, 800m. SSW of three cottages at Achadh-Chaorann. A street-length harled parade of two-storeyed domestic buildings faces E to the Loch. At its centre, a five-bay laird's house built 1769–76 by *John* and *Thomas Menelaws*, masons in Greenock, for Angus MacAlister of Loup, its simple integrity compromised by later additions and alterations. In 1798 Ardpatrick came into the possession of Walter Campbell of Shawfield and Islay whose descendants owned the property until the early 1920s.

The original house is gabled with rolled skewputts, has rusticated quoins and is entered at the centre of the main five-bay E front through a Gibbsian doorpiece regrettably hidden by a C19 gabled porch. Three-light windows were created *c.* 1923 by demolishing the walling between the original ground-floor openings l. and r. of the E entrance; a grievous assault. The more fortunate W elevation, which advances slightly at the centre under an open pediment, was opened at the half-landing of the central stair in the late C19 or early C20 on to a balustraded terrace. From this a narrow flight of steps, also balustraded, descends to the garden. The lower two-storey N wing, which continues the line of the E front, comprises a central three-bay stretch, probably late C18. It was flanked by gables added about a century later; the S one raised from an original single-storey link. The S wing, more radically revised and extended in muted Baronial style by *John Honeyman*, 1864–5, is dominated by a crowstepped gable with a corniced canted bay at ground level. Linked on the SW is the WALLED GARDEN and, beyond, the

HOME FARM offices. At the entrance to the grounds from the NE, rusticated GATEPIERS with ball finials.

The main feature of the interior is a central, scale-and-platt stone stair which preserves its original timber handrail. In the entrance lobby, two segmental-arched openings springing from Ionic pilasters are 1920s changes. An C18 chimneypiece survives in the link to the s wing.

FORT, Cnoc Breac, 1km. NW of Ardpatrick. Walled ridge. Entrance gaps on W and E.

STANDING STONE, Achadh-Chaorann. Leaning stone, 2.1m. high, with cupmarkings.

ARDRISHAIG

Linear village on the W shore of Loch Gilp. By the mid C19, following the protracted construction of the Crinan Canal and the 'fostering care and interest' of the local McNeill family, it developed into a small town, the 'entrepôt of the canal, the port of Lochgilphead, and the centre of an extensive herring fishery'. Today Groome's 1882 description rings hollow, for the fishing has long since ceased and the canal, despite the rebuilding of its sealock in the early 1930s, carries neither commercial nor passenger traffic. Seasonal activity survives: in summer, harbour and basin fill with yachts heading out towards Loch Fyne or waiting to move up through the locks to Crinan.

CHURCHES

Former ARDRISHAIG FREE CHURCH, Kilduskland Road. 1869. Gabled front with bellcote and three-light traceried arch. Converted to church hall, c. 1945, but later brutalized as garage.

ARDRISHAIG PARISH CHURCH, immediately SW of harbour bridge. Gothic tower-fronted nave with low semi-octagonal transepts. Built 1860; much altered and transepts added, 1904. Roughcast with sandstone dressings. Some Dec tracery. The square, diagonally buttressed tower at first rose only to ridge height but was later broached into an ashlar octagonal stage with clock faces, castellated (as are the parapets to the curved porches below and the transepts behind) and finished in a short sharp spire with louvred arrow-head lucarnes. – STAINED GLASS; plain, Edwardian Art Nouveau patterning in all windows.

FREE CHURCH HALL, Chalmers Street. Mid C19. Four-bay nave with lancets in gables. The sole survivor of 1970s shoreside demolitions.

PUBLIC BUILDINGS

ARDRISHAIG PRIMARY SCHOOL, Upper Glenfyne Park. By *Strathclyde Regional Council*, 1985–6. Split monopitch cross-section produces metal-decked cheese-wedge roof sweeping down over six glazed bays.

Former BOARD SCHOOL, St Clair Road. Mid C19. Symmetrical piended block, with forestair entrances and façade gables l. and r. Converted to four houses by *Broad & Hughes*, 1994.

CANAL OFFICE, Pier Head. Mid C19. Gabled, three-bay, two-storey rubble with ashlar dressings, now painted. Bipartite windows l. and r. of the corniced doorway.

CHALMERS MONUMENT, opposite the Royal Hotel. By *D. & A. Davidson*, Inverness. Roman Doric marble column on stepped marble plinth. Erected 1912 in memory of Revd James Chalmers, missionary, who died at the hands of New Guinea natives in 1901.

HARBOUR. Although *Thomas Telford* made improvements to Ardrishaig's old pier which allowed the first steamer to call in 1817, it was not until 1837 that the long curving rubble breakwater was constructed to the s to protect the approach to both pier and canal. Intermittent rebuilding culminated in major repair works in 1930s. Original SWING-BRIDGE by engineer, *L. John Groves*, 1890.

PIERHEAD BUILDING. 1891. Long single-storey, painted rubble block with piended roof. Small windowed gable rise on W and E asymmetrically placed. Above, on main roof ridge, is a small box tower with pyramid roof and metal weather vane. Centred below were three pends providing access and egress for steamer passengers.

PUBLIC HALL, Chalmers Street. By local architect *William Todd*, c. 1912. Gabled E front with shallow canted bay at first floor; pyramid-roofed stair tower on s. Art Nouveau flavour in domed, wide-eaved ridge ventilator. All-over roughcasting.

WAR MEMORIAL. Erected c. 1920. Grey granite Celtic cross on stepped base.

DESCRIPTION

Most of Ardrishaig lies N of the Harbour, attenuated between canal bank and lochside, a single-street strip of land stretching some 2km. almost as far as Lochgilphead. Until the 1970s, when virtually all its seaward-side shops and flats were demolished, CHALMERS STREET gave the town centre a feeling of largely two-storeyed linear containment. Now it is a one-sided place, exposed in more senses than one, for the quality of remaining or replacement building on the W side of the street fails to sustain its original architectural respectability. N of this dreary main street promenade, on Glenburn Road, the white-walled GREY GULL INN (former Royal Hotel), 1841, brightens things up. Perhaps by *William Burn*. Its tall front and the wide-lugged gables of its façade seem less Jacobean than overgrown vernacular Scots. More in tune with this idiom are the adjacent STABLES and COACH-HOUSE, c. 1800, which now form a tidy residential enclave, with four cart-entry arches fully glazed to an open U-plan court. Further N villas begin to appear on the lochside. Best is the gabled SEACLIFF HOUSE, mid C19, standing two storeys high at right angles to the road with single-storey wings W and E. Rude classical doorway set between bipartite windows l. and r.

Coachman's House at rear of same date. On West Bank Road beyond the site of the former Glenfyne Distillery, levelled *c.* 1990, is GLENDARROCH, mid C19, a single-storeyed skew-gabled cottage looking to the canal through hood-moulded French windows and an extended timber-framed veranda running N.

To the S of the Harbour and across the Canal Bridge, past the Parish Church (*see* above), CLIFF HOUSE, a two-storey-and-attic, black-and-white-gabled inn of *c.* 1850, and a terrace of three-storey, balconied local authority housing, another chain of villas begins to develop. OAKBANK is open eaved, with a bargeboarded gable l. and canted bay r. ARGYLE COTTAGE (*sic*), 1856, is lower and decidedly cottagey with bays l. and r. Both are built in green rubble with ochre sandstone dressings and both have arcuated sashes in the upper lights. ACHNASGIACH, late C19, is much more city-suburban: a big ashlar mansion with eaves on consoles. Good cast-iron gates. Back to rubble, but plain piended provincial Georgian at ATTICHUAN, *c.* 1840. ALLT NA-CRAIG, late C19, similar to Oakbank in material and manner but grander. ARDFINAIG, late C19, converted to an Eventide Home, has five attic gablets and a fine wooden porch with ball finials. Then FASCADALE, *c.* 1863, in best suburbanized Bryce-derived (or *Bryce*-devised?) Baronial: paired canted bays twice corbelled back to gables. Finally, TIGH AN RUADHA, late C19, Shavian gables hidden on a rocky outcrop among the rhododendrons.

ARDUAINE

Luxuriant woods and rhododendrons falling S across sheltered slopes on the headland separating Asknish Bay from the mouth of Loch Melfort. Founded in 1903 (woodland garden, 1922) and much developed from 1971. The gardens, gifted to the National Trust for Scotland, were opened in 1992.

ARDUAINE LODGE, close to the entrance to Arduaine Gardens but separate. By *Sue Thornley*, 1987–9. Elongated, one-and-a-half-storey, hillside house with canted corner windows.

GARDENER'S HOUSE, hidden in the woods high in Arduaine Gardens. By *Page and Park*, 1992–3. A long, one-and-a-half-storey, gabled dwelling of calculated white simplicity. Roughcast with an eaves frieze of cement render. Exquisitely judged update of laird's house vernacular.

LOCH MELFORT HOTEL. Built between 1897 and 1905 as Arduaine House. A large but unremarkable gabled house with remarkable prospects over the loch. Converted to hotel, 1964.

ARROCHAR

Village at the head of Loch Long, strung along the E shore.

ARROCHAR PARISH CHURCH. By *William Spence*. Built 1845–7 to replace the kirk of 1733, of which some harled rubble walling, incorporating a blocked doorway with dated lintel set between porthole openings, survives in the graveyard s. Four-bay hall, roughcast with ashlar dressings, lit by lancets and fronted by a square entrance tower at the centre of the battlemented NW gable. Gable and tower have diagonal buttresses. Hefty Gothic pinnacles erupt from the tower and outer buttresses. A pointed-arch doorway with roll-mould surround leads to a plain interior. Beams divide the flat plastered ceiling into six bays, each panelled as a double saltire. At the centre of the SE wall, a full octagon PULPIT with pointed-arch panels and a tall narrow back crowned by a cantilevered cusp-arched octagonal canopy. Winding stairs l. and r. have open rails with swept handrails. – Small pipe ORGAN with Gothic cresting; perhaps by Robert Mirrlees, c. 1860(?). – Memorial STAINED GLASS in Y-tracery lancets. In the W corner, stiffly geometrical floral repeats, late C19, from St MacKessog's, Luss (q.v.) 1954. N: Christ's baptism and entry into Jerusalem, colourful if overdrawn, c. 1933. E: a palely rendered mailed warrior and Christ with the chalice; by *J. Ballantine* of *A. Ballantine & Son*, 1911. S: a robed cleric and Christ the Good Shepherd, blues l., reds r.; by *David Gauld*, c. 1933. Flanking the pulpit, scenes outside the empty tomb; by *Stephen Adam & Son*, 1902.

SS PETER AND PAUL (R.C.) CHURCH. By *Gillespie, Kidd & Coia*, 1953. Utilitarian, with no intimation of the imaginative church architecture which the work of Le Corbusier would soon inspire in this award-winning firm. Desperately seeking some dignity, a random rubble portal wall, holed for a belfry, rises above eaves height.

ARROCHAR & TARBET STATION. *See* Tarbet.

PIER. Erected 1850. Of the original structure, only the timber-framed hammer-head and a few ironwork beams remain. Closed 1977.

DESCRIPTION

Filling the lochside gushet at the junction of the A83 and A814, the Scotstyle ARROCHAR HOTEL, 1911, by *Alexander N. Paterson*; white roughcast with ashlar crowstepping, skews and dormer heads. Engulfing enlargement by *Lane, Bremner & Garnett*, 1970. To the N, ASHFIELD, a late C19 cottage villa with a bold eaves cornice and a pilastered doorway set between consoled windows, and GLENLOIN, early C19, classical symmetry with an Ionic doorpiece and a square-plan ICEHOUSE adjacent N. S along the shore, at the rear of the bargeboarded COBBLER HOTEL, late C19, part of the fabric of INVERIACH HOUSE, 1697, survives with rolled skewputts of the C18. The U-plan STEADINGS, dated 1774–6, now residential, retain ball finials on gable pedestals. MANSEFIELD, late C19, has decoratively looped bargeboards and a small ogee pediment over the entrance door. Best of all is the former manse, now THE VILLAGE INN, 1837, a still-Georgian, skew-gabled mansion; three-bay, black-and-white symmetry with a pilastered doorway. Uphill, behind the church (*see* above), the harled walls and varied slated planes of KIRKFIELD PLACE, 1938, display the vernacular inventiveness of Dumbarton architect *Joseph Weekes*. In sympathy, if not quite so imaginative, more local authority housing on CHURCH ROAD by *Baxter, Clark & Paul*, 1975–9. In a different idiom, the half-timbered Tudor of BENREOCH, late C19. Compact, the mansarded mass of ADMIRALTY COTTAGES, 1939. Finally comes ARDMAY HOUSE, 1853, much enlivened by *Alexander N. Paterson*'s additions of gabled porch and conically-roofed S tower. In the hall is a two-manual organ, built *c.* 1940, by *R. Gardner* from the parts of two *William Hill & Son* instruments.

AUCHENLOCHAN

With its pier now derelict and ruinous and little more than a line of sea-side houses merging imperceptibly with Tighnabruaich to the N, the village's early independent existence is elusive.

Former HIGH CHURCH, uphill where the A8003 begins its dip into the village. Late C19. Scarred and crudely extended, it serves as the assembly hall for the adjacent school (*see* below). – STAINED GLASS retained in the sharply Decorated window that fills the SE gable and in a single cusp-arched NE window; the latter by *William Meikle & Sons*, *c.* 1905, personifies red-robed Charity.

PIER. Iron pier, built *c.* 1878–9. In use until 1948 but now only a few timber posts survive. Unprepossessing pierhead building, gabled to the road, hipped on the E, now a petrol station.

TIGHNABRUAICH PRIMARY SCHOOL, adjacent to the church. Gabled E-plan, 1874–5, probably by *James Boucher*. Extension to porch gable and addition of hipped-roofed Hall, roughcast with eaves-line glazing, by *Argyll & Bute Council*, 1997–8.

DESCRIPTION

Pier and hotel are located where the high road from the N drops to the shore. There is no enclosure, only a convergence of routes and a change in scale. The ROYAL HOTEL, *c.* 1865, extended S, *c.* 1900, stands three rubble storeys high with a chimneyed gablet at its centre. Giving shelter across the ground-floor front, a three-bay, ironwork veranda canopy, splendidly filigreed in the spandrels. A similar response to sea-side views may account for the two floors of timber-framed bays and linking balcony that front the neighbouring draper's SHOP, 1886. Certainly the prospect of Bute and the Kyles explains Auchenlochan's short parade of gable-fronted, shoreside villas. S of the pier are ARDVAAR, *c.* 1880, with fretted bargeboards and DUNSYRE, *c.* 1880, invisibly extended S with due respect to its roof lines, dormers and tripartite windows. To the N, NODFA, *c.* 1870, more dormers and an arcuated entrance balcony linking square bays; ALLT MOR, *c.* 1870, arched lintels and more decorative bargeboarding; and some plainer villas, 1880s, similarly gabled and bayed.

AUCHINDRAIN 0303

Characteristic West Highland township now preserved as a Museum of Country Life. A variety of farm buildings straggle along the valley beside the A83 between Inveraray and Furnace. A number of ruinous shielings are dispersed along the valley of the Douglas Water.

AUCHINDRAIN TOWNSHIP, 9km. SW of Inveraray. A scattered grouping of single-storey byre-dwellings and associated barns, cart-sheds, stables, etc., which remained in multiple-tenancy until 1935 and was still worked by a single tenant until 1963. Auchindrain then became a Museum of Country Life and, from 1975, a Visitor Centre. Most of the buildings date from the 1770–1840 period, but their irregular layout contrasts strongly with the improved estate planning of that time. It is, however, less haphazard than it seems, for a contingent response to sun, wind and rain determines the disposition of windows, doors and winnowing passages and the interrelationship of house and barn. In 1789 the Argyll Estate proposed field enclosure and a planned village of twelve detached houses arranged around an open court, but no such development took place.

All units are oblong rubble structures *c.* 6m. in overall width. Byre-dwellings accommodated men and beasts in a linear sequence of room, closet, kitchen and byre. Many alterations have occurred over the last two centuries, including the removal of open hearths, introduction of stone cross-walls with fireplaces, and the addition of attic floors, but most of the buildings remain cruck-roofed. A few have been re-thatched, while in most rust-coloured corrugated iron has replaced the original material. Gables prevail, though evidence of end crucks indicates that byres and smaller units were often piended.

BRENCHOILLE BRIDGE, 1.4km. SSW, just W of A83. Late C18 two-span structure over Leacann Water, a down-sized rubble version of Robert Mylne's 1773 bridge across the Aray (q.v.). E and W segmental arches of slab voussoirs span 4.6m. and 4.3m. to a central pier with triangular cutwaters N and S. Central circular recesses on both sides.

CLAONAIRIGH, 3.4km. NE. Archetypal three-bay, two-storey, gable-ended house with lower piended wings; probably late C18. No skews, no quoins, no margins: ascetic vernacular virtue. To the N, by Douglas Water, is a ruined MILL and W, the rubble shells of weavers' cottages. This is all that remains of the carpet and woollen industry established at 'Clunary' in 1776 by the 5th Duke of Argyll. A 'factory house', fulling-mill, dye-house, comb-shop, press house, weaving house, store and 'writing-room' were built, 1777–8, by masons *John Moodie* and *Robert Alexander*. Over a hundred were employed, but the enterprise foundered and by 1809 production had ceased.

Auchindrain Township. Plan of north-east portion of the township

KILLEAN, 2.4km. NE. Three-bay 'improved farmhouse', *c.* 1770, with later splay-gabled addition to SW. Steading buildings converted to holiday accommodation.

OLD BRIDGE OF DOUGLAS, 70m. N of Claonairigh. Early C18 rubble bridge over Douglas Water. 9m. span in a semicircular arch of slab voussoirs. Inconveniently narrow (2.1m.), it was superseded in 1771 by a broader crossing to the W which survived until the 1980s when it was demolished and the present bridge constructed.

CHAMBERED CAIRNS, Achnagoul. In a field, 300m. NE of Achnagoul Farm, a 34m.-long mound aligned roughly N–S. Main chamber at N end faces uphill: two compartments, one of which is roofed. A second cairn lies 190m. N. It too has a two-compartment chamber, at NE, and shows evidence of a concave forecourt.

BALVICAR 7616

Slate quarrying village port on the E coast of Seil. Four rows of two-room WORKERS' COTTAGES, rubble-built in the early C19 in parallel or right-angled relationship, struggle to maintain some spatial discipline in post-industrial disorder. Two recent four-in-a-row groups, KILBRANDON COTTAGES, 1993–4, by *Douglas Guest Associates*, contribute their help. So, too, a row of five houses with neat porches by *Kinghorn Mee*, 1991–2, at Cnoc Beag. Slate rubble QUAY, late C18 or early C19, still in use. A single small piend-roofed, rubble STORE, early C19(?) survives.

KILBRANDON OLD PARISH CHURCH, in burial enclosure 400m. SSW. All that remains of the medieval church is a short stand of rubble walling, barely 1m. high, in which a segmentally arched recess covers the recumbent grave SLAB of John McLauchlane, 'preacher of the gospel in Nether Lorn and Melfort', †1685. – Adjacent in the upper area of the graveyard are three carved SLABS, C14–C15, and a fourth, Loch Awe school, *c.* 1500. – Apart from the McLauchlane tomb, which displays a heraldic shield and the symbols of mortality in high relief, there are a few TABLE-TOMBS of C18 date and a cast-iron tombstone commemorating Duncan McCorkindale †1857, aged six years and three months.

ACHA, 800m. SSW. A rude rubble cottage, probably early C19, its ruggedness somewhat muted by renovation.

ACHNACROISH COTTAGE, 600m. SSW on W side of B8003. Early C19. Another primitive rubble cottage that seems to grow out of the rocky ground. White atavistic vernacular.

BARBRECK 8306

Estate stretching NE from the Lochgilphead–Oban road up the valley of the Barbreck River.

BARBRECK HOUSE, 800m. NE of Ardfern junction on A816. This classical mansion, one of the finest of its period in Argyll, stands erect and correct in the flat valley of the Barbreck River with a clear prospect across meadowland 1.4km. SW to the headwaters of Loch Craignish. It was built in 1790 for Major-General John Campbell whose family acquired the estate after the first Campbells of Barbreck had lost it through forfeiture in 1732.

The house, which faces sw, originally followed a T-plan arrangement, although the stem of the T containing the stairs has been somewhat obscured by later additions at the rear. It stands three storeys high with attic accommodation in its hipped roof. The principal sw front, Palladian in organization, has a pedimented centrepiece of three bays given added *gravitas* by wide, slightly recessed single bays on each side. Proprietorial pretension is further stressed by the breadth of the façade. To l. and r. are screen walls of three blind round-headed arches, their height coinciding with the stringcourse marking the floor level of the *piano nobile* of the main block. They connect the house to pedimented pavilion wings; in all, a spread of 50m. Possessing

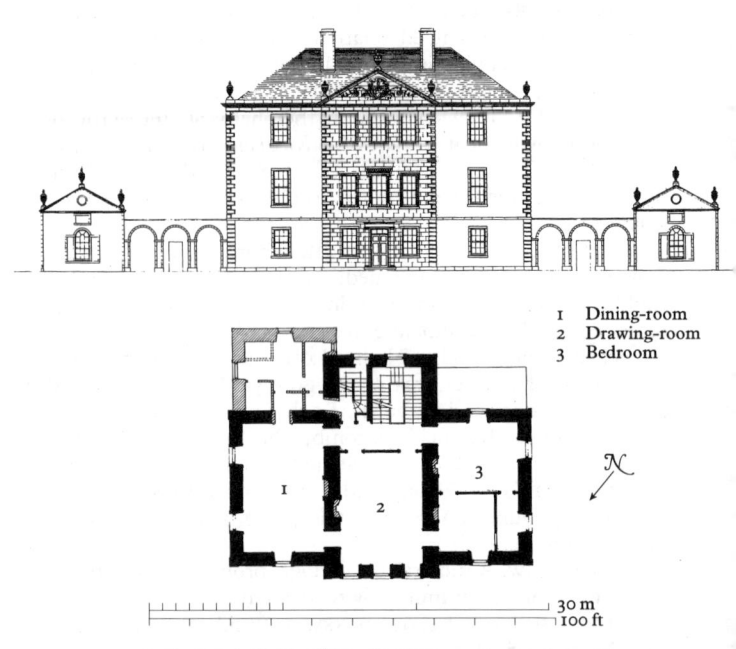

Barbreck House. First-floor plan and elevation

neither portico nor rising stair, the frontispiece relies on the repeated elevational emphases given to its central axis to establish domain over the level landscape laid out before it. It is built in grey sandstone ashlar to distinguish it from the ochre render and brown-painted dressings elsewhere. Urns accent the skyline, while in the pediment are the mantled arms of the landowner and the date 1790. At second-floor level, a single window is flanked by blind frames; on the first floor, the middle window of three architraved lights has shouldered surrounds, a fluted frieze and a dentilled cornice; and, at ground level, there is a plain but prominent central entrance doorway with pilasters and entablature. This symmetry reverberates in the pedimented wings, where again there are, or were, urns and, below, one over the other, a blind circular panel in the pediment, an uninscribed recessed rectangular panel and a Venetian window, the two side lights of which are blank. At the rear, symmetry has been compromised by unequal and ungainly C19 extensions in the N and E re-entrants. A stone TABLET in the pediment over the staircase wing commemorates MAJOR GENERAL JOHN CAMPBELL / OF BARBRECK / AND JANET COLQUHOUN HIS SPOUSE / 1790. Estate outbuildings, which surround a service courtyard behind the house, return in strict U-plan balance to stop short of the NW and SE pavilions.

The tripartite division of the main façade coincides with the structural compartmentalization of the plan; the side walls of the NE staircase projection continue through the house carrying flues from all rooms. Despite this arrangement, the plan is not wholly symmetrical. Two stairs provide contiguous vertical circulation: a public open-well stair of cantilevered stone treads with moulded soffits occupies some two-thirds of the NE projection and a solid newel scale-and-platt service stair fills the remainder of the space alongside. But while this imbalance necessitates an inflection to the r. in order to reach the first flight of the main stair from the ground-floor hall, it also ensures that arrival at each of the upper levels coincides with the central axis of the composition. To the r. of the ground-floor hall are two public rooms; to the l., a central corridor opens to the kitchen and service quarters.

At the centre of the first floor is the DRAWING ROOM. A low panelled dado runs between symmetrically positioned doors and windows with original brass furniture. Window shutter-handles retain decorative escutcheons depicting a series of differing urn designs in coloured enamel. The plaster frieze also incorporates urns with garlanding while the ceiling displays a design of circular and floral motifs. White marble chimneypiece with fluted pilasters. The DINING ROOM, which occupies the full width of the NW bay, is also Neoclassical in character. On the ceiling, two trophies of arms set in circular garlands. The chimneypiece is identical to that in the drawing room but of grey marble. A bedroom, ante-room and closet take up the SE bay. Five bedrooms are arranged around the staircase hall on the second floor, the central room separated from the hall by a curved wall. The two-storeyed NW wing, originally servants' quarters, has been adapted as a garage and workshop. The SE wing, altered in the C19, contains a two-storeyed cottage.

The extensive enclosure of single-storey late C18 OUTBUILDINGS which surround the courtyard behind is rubble-built. It accommodated a coach-house and stables on the SE, and byre, stables, cart shed and hen-house in the long NE range. Internal divisions in the NW range have been removed. Here and there paving and cobbling survive. A Gothick FOLLY, little more than a wall of three pointed-arch bays, stands 500m. NE of the house, its purpose merely to screen a lean-to farm building now destroyed. Built of random rubble with dressed sandstone facings, and surmounted by a corbelled battlemented parapet. All three arches are blind but with smaller, similar, pointed-arch openings in each. To the NW of the house is the WALLED GARDEN. E of the garden is a pyramid-roofed MAUSOLEUM, rubble-built on a square plan, in which are two white marble TABLETS inscribed in memory of Barbreck's laird, Major-General John Campbell †1794, and a later Campbell widow, Isabella †1861.

On the S drive to Barbreck, 200m. SE of the house, is a rubble BRIDGE across the Barbreck River. Built c. 1770, it spans 15m. in a single arch with a low flood arch to NW.

BARBRECK'S WELL, 450m. N of Ardfern crossroads. 1714. Inscribed red sandstone marker, probably erected by Archibald Campbell of Barbreck, laird of the estate from 1691 until 1732. Shaped like a gabled headstone with a circular head, halo-ed or bewigged, cut in relief on the SE face. Recovered from Kilkerran, Campbeltown, and re-erected here in 1910. Inscriptions fill both faces and edges.

TURNALT HOUSE, 1.9km. NE of Barbreck House. Like Barbreck, a classical mansion-house with flanking pavilions. Built c. 1800, probably by Captain Archibald Campbell, brother to the heir of Barbreck estate, its emulation is marked but restrained. The house is of only three bays and two storeys (admittedly with more generous attic space in a more steeply hipped roof) and the overall spread of the plan only 33m. A pedimented centre-piece projects slightly from the main SW façade. On the first floor, a Venetian window pushes its arch into the tympanum. Below, a piended porch added early in the C19. Single windows l. and r. of the Venetian one are echoed in the wider centre lights of tripartite windows at ground floor. Recessed single-storey links, each lit by a small squarish window, connect piended pavilions which, as at Barbreck, have Venetian windows with blind side lights. The plan is simple: at ground level, two principal rooms separated by a rebuilt staircase hall. Abandoned, 1985. C19 steading to NE.

KILBRIDE FARM, 750m. NW of Turnalt. A low gabled house of harled rubble, possibly C17. Implacably solid with minimal openings. A stone panel set above a door in the SE wall bears a mirrored AC monogram and the date 1746, perhaps recording the raising of the wallhead. Even so, first-floor lintels coincide with a low eaves line and skylights are needed for the upper storey. NE section of the block, early C19. The steading running SE at right angles is also C19.

CAIRN, Sluggan, 300m. SW of Turnalt. Conspicuous cairn, 23m. in dia., with some kerb stones on W.

STANDING STONES, Barbreck. Group close to Barbreck House on ENE comprising two adjacent stones, 1.5m. and 2.5m. high, and 23m. E a cluster of five other stones, only one of which exceeds 2m. in height.

STANDING STONE, Sluggan, c. 150m. SSE of Sluggan Cairn. Stone, 2.5m. high, with pointed top.

BARCALDINE

A scattered settlement strung out along the A828 on the s shore of Loch Creran between Barcaldine Castle in the w and the hamlet of Barcaldine in the E.

Former RHUGARBH FREE CHURCH. Built 1844–5. A five-bay, gabled granite nave fronted by a square castellated tower with angle buttressing. Now a dwelling.

BARCALDINE CASTLE. Archetypal L-plan tower-house, 'ane greit hows in Benderloch in Lorne of four hows heicht' (*The Black Book of Taymouth*, 1855), situated 2.2km. N of Benderloch village and 500m. from the s shore of Loch Creran. The castle, which comprises a principal rectangular block orientated roughly W–E, a SW jamb, and a cylindrical re-entrant staircase tower, was built 1601–9 by Sir Duncan Campbell, 7th Laird of Glenorchy, whose armorial shield and initials SDC appear in relief in a schist panel over the entrance doorway at the foot of the stair tower. By 1698, however, it was described as a 'ruineous place' and, although repair work was carried out early in the C18, by 1724 the family had transferred to the newly constructed Barcaldine House (*see* below). In 1842 the estate was sold but it returned to Campbell hands in 1896 and in the following year

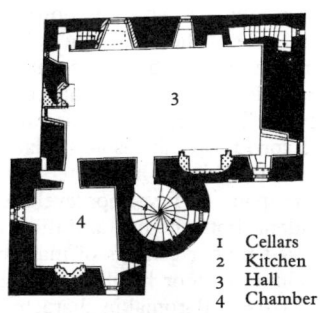

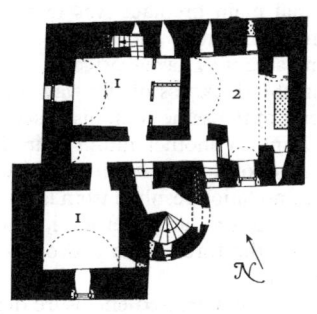

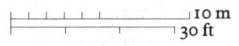

1 Cellars
2 Kitchen
3 Hall
4 Chamber

Barcaldine Castle. Ground- and first-floor plans

restoration of the castle began. Directed by *Alexander Buttar*, this entailed re-roofing, re-flooring and extensive internal refurbishment and lasted until 1911.

The walls are harled with, here and there, some dressings of schist or sandstone. At the NW, SE and SW corners, large angle-rounds carried on four courses of corbelling and roofed with slated conical caps only slightly smaller in diameter than that over the stair tower. The upper parts of all these date from the turn-of-the-century restorations when the castle's three, chimneyed, crowstepped gables, each of which interpenetrates with one of the corner turrets, were stabilized and repaired. Wall openings are original with the exception of two S ground-floor windows, widened in the early C20, and one at first floor at the W end of the N wall, apparently an early C18 enlargement. An inventory of 1621 indicates that several windows were originally half-glazed with shutters over the lower half; yett-like grilles were also provided, though most of those now in position are later replacements. The pedimented timber dormers, three to the N and one on the W roof of the wing, belong to the 1897–1911 period.

The entrance doorway, on the E side of the stair drum, has sandstone jambs and lintel with rounded arrises. Above the lintel is an oblong fanlight protected by a grille. Behind the modern door, the surviving upper part of the original yett. From the turnpike stair lobby, three steps down lead to a vaulted corridor on the S side of the main block. From this, access is gained ahead and l. to the NW and SW cellars, both vaulted, and r. to the kitchen which, across the E wall, retains the segmental arch of its fireplace. The kitchen, too, is vaulted but, since the intrusion of the corridor produces an L-plan, its ceiling is distinguished by the roughly groined intersection of two barrel vaults of differing spans. At first-floor level the effect of restoration work is evident: both the hall and the chamber in the SW wing have exposed timber ceilings of main beams and joists, pitch pine panelling to door height and late Victorian stone chimneypieces, coarsely Baronial in character. The largest fireplace, positioned towards the E end of the S wall of the hall, where the original main fireplace was located, is particularly crude in design. From the W end of the N wall, where a small pantry or serving area may have existed in the early C17, a stair descends within the thickness of the wall to the cellar below, while at the E end of the same wall, disguised by the panelling, a secret door opens to another mural stair rising to the floor above. Here, at second-floor level, improved bedroom and bathroom accommodation resulted from late C19 and early C20 restoration work. So, too, at garret level, where new dormers provided light and the three gable bedrooms each step down into an angle-turret.

The castle stands in a grassed enclosure defined by modern rubble walling. Cylindrical rubble GATEPIERS with flat circular coping stones and large ball finials mark entrances from the road on the E and S. In the grounds is a pillar SUNDIAL, C18, its copper face inscribed HORA FUGIT 1720.

BARCALDINE HOUSE. Quitting Barcaldine Castle (*see above*) in the early years of the C18, the Campbells built their new house 6km. to the E. This was extended in 1733 but appears to have been superseded *c.* 1759 by a three-storey, hipped-roofed mansion, now identifiable as the W end of the ungainly, compacted succession of alterations and extensions which accumulated over the next two centuries. Of the early C19, the canted bay added at the E end of the principal S façade and the full-height bow extension projecting on the N. Proposals which would have recast the house in fortified or ecclesiastical guise were prepared by *James Gillespie Graham* in 1813–14 and 1821 but were not realized, although the court of offices on the E, later much altered, was built to his design in 1815, during extensive alterations undertaken by the Oban mason, *John Drummond*. Jacobethan library wing, 1831, added to the SE end of the original house. N of this, a low, gable-ended bedroom wing of 1838, filling the gap on the W side of the office court. Finally, of the beginning of the C20, compounding this inelegant complexity, the three-storey, parapeted block containing the present main entrance and staircase, squeezed into the re-entrant corner between the 1838 wing and the earlier bow.

No C18 INTERIORS survive. Early C19 Adamesque plasterwork in the drawing room, at ground level at the W end of the mid-C18 house, has putti in medallions on the walls. A timber chimneypiece, framing a beaded marble surround to a cast-iron grate, has flanking Ionic columns which carry a high entablature above a mirror. A simpler, dark marble chimneypiece with fluted jambs and lintel meeting at rosettes frames another cast-iron fire in the first-floor dining room. In the library, the ceiling is coved and panelled above a rich cornice; in the pilastered white marble chimneypiece more classical allusion in the association of Venus and Cupid.

DALINTOBER FARM, 500m. E of Barcaldine Castle. Farm and byres refurbished as dwelling by *Kinghorn Mee*, 1993–4.

FERLOCHAN OLD SCHOOLHOUSE, opposite the junction with the minor road leading to Barcaldine Castle. Early C19, single-storey, rubble cottage. Its length originally accommodated the schoolmaster's two-roomed dwelling and the classroom. Oval plan chimney stacks. Now wholly residential.

FERRY HOUSE, South Shian, 1.7km. N of Barcaldine Castle. Three-bay, two-storey house, gable-ended but without skews; formerly an inn, but probably not the first ferry building on the site. Built *c.* 1840 in harled rubble. Single-storey S wing at rear and detached outbuildings, which retain cruck stumps, are a decade earlier. Rubble SLIPWAY, probably early C19.

CAIRN and STANDING STONE, Achacha, 1.8km WSW. An oval kerb-cairn with almost the complete circuit of granite erratic kerb-stones. Impressive standing stone, 2.5m. high, is situated 89m. E.

CAIRNS, Castle Farm, 400m. SE of Barcaldine Castle. Three small cairns in approximate linear relationship NE–SW. The SW cairn, 9.8m. in dia., is surrounded by a low stone bank, both occupying an artificial circular platform; an arrangement described as 'one of the most unusual in Lorn' (RCAHMS Inventory, 1975). A standing stone, 2.1m. high, which in the C18 stood nearby, has been re-erected 120m. E.

BELLANOCH

7992

Berthing basin on the Crinan Canal (q.v.). The settlement lies between Cairnbaan and Crinan at the junction with the road to Tayvallich and Loch Sween.

BELLANOCH CHURCH, on the hill above the village off the B8025. Former Free Church, built 1868–9. Basic Gothic with a porch. N gable belfry with weather vane. – STAINED GLASS in small S gable lancets: Nativity to l., Christ in Majesty to r.

ISLANDADD BRIDGE, carrying B8025 NNE across Crinan Canal. Designed by *John Gardner*, engineer, 1851. Cast-iron girders supported on masonry piers. Five spans. Arcaded cast-iron railings simple and remarkably elegant.

SCHOOL and SCHOOLHOUSE. Mid C19. Vicarage-like with bargeboarded gables and asymmetrically placed buttressed chimney on façade. Two- and three-light pointed-arch windows in sandstone under rubble relieving arches. Low pointed-arch entrance to r. under bossed hood moulding.

SHELTER, Barnluasgan, 1km. SW. 1997. Three-bay, cruck-framed structure in green oak for Argyll Green Woodworkers Association. Designed by *Stephen Hunter* and constructed using traditional techniques. Larch shingled roof.

DESCRIPTION. A few houses strung along the curves of the canal-side road. The oldest are early C19, like SMITHY HOUSE, a narrow, three-bay front in painted rubble. DOLPHINS HOUSE and DROVERS HOUSE stand gable-to-gable, roughcast, with a turnpike stair at the rear. Across the road from Islandadd Bridge, another three-bay cottage, BRIDGE HOUSE, with a quaint small window over the entrance and a long eaves skylight. And even here, a late C19 tenement, BRAEFACE, three storeys with broad gable stacks.

DUN, Druim an Dùin, 2.1km. SW of Bellanoch above a sharp bend in B8025. Oval dun on the ridge edge, with walls varying from 1m. to 5.2m. thick. Clearly defined entrance on the S where the walls stand to twelve courses and incorporate the narrow guard chamber. Secondary N entrance later blocked.

BELLOCHANTUY

6632

Coastal hamlet much diminished by the loss of its 1825 kirk, demolished in the 1970s for road realignment.

DRUMORE, at N edge of village. Former two-storey-and-attic gabled inn, built 1808. Asymmetrical three-bay front. Converted to dwelling, 1967.

OLD BRIDGES, Putechantuy, 400m. E of A83. Two rubble

bridges of single segmental span crossing the Allt na Dunaich. Lower bridge, c18; upper, mid c19.

PUTECHAN LODGE HOTEL, 700m. s of village. 1980s' conversion, cleverly absorbing earlier house. Wide, fully glazed veranda front faces the sea beneath a slated roof with inset balconies to bargeboarded bedroom dormers. Fluid open plan; austere sophisticated interiors. Rear courtyard in U-plan lee of linked bedroom wings.

DUN, Dùn Fhinn, on E side of A83, 300m. w of Killocraw Farm. Sub-rectangular in plan at summit of sheer rock stack. Internal dimensions, 13.4m. by 5.8m. Rebated entrance on narrow NW flank.

BENDERLOCH

Main road village 4km. N of Connel Bridge.

ST MODAN'S CHURCH. By *G. Woulfe Brenan*, 1904–5. Small and consistently Norman: round-arched windows, conically roofed s apse, and a N porch doorway with scalloped capitals on colonnettes. Even the unusual pencil belfry, clasped in the re-entrant angle formed by the short nave and its single w transept, might claim some grander Romanesque forebears. Inside, springing from low corbel stones, arch-braced trusses carry purlins, spars and cross boarding. Spars are carried down from the wallhead to a heavy plaster cornice. Tiled sanctuary floor. – Heptagonal PULPIT of pitch pine; panels quartered with arch and quatrefoil motifs. – STAINED GLASS. Sanctuary, three windows depict Christ the Good Shepherd flanked by Beatitude angels, by '*Meyer* of Munich', 1906. – S transept, a painterly representation of an angel with St Paul(?), memorializing Alexander Campbell Fraser (1819–1914), Professor of Logic and Metaphysics at Edinburgh University, with the quotation, 'Now we see through / a glass darkly, but / then face to face.' – The transept gable has two tall, late Victorian windows commemorating the professor's father, Revd Hugh Fraser, also by *Meyer*(?), 1906. – In the undistinguished Campbell Memorial Hall behind the church is a circular portrait window, 1899, dedicated to the memory of the Gaelic poet, John Campbell †1897, described as 'bard and postman and gardener to Oban and its vicinity' (Blackie). Moved from an earlier hall, built 1898–9, about 1 km. S, now adapted as CAMPBELL HALL COTTAGE but maintaining a spurious ecclesiastical allusion in its five red-brick-rimmed lancet windows.

Former LEDAIG U. F. CHURCH. By *Hippolyte J. Blanc*, 1911–12. A gabled nave and chancel with an octagonal NE vestry and low, square-towered SE porch. Built in oblique-snecked granite and red sandstone in a free late Decorated idiom. Adapted as a dwelling by *Lake Falconer*, 1938–9, when the red-tiled, 24m.-high spire was demolished, the sanctuary converted to a dining room, the vestry to a kitchen and hipped dormers were introduced to light the new bedroom floor. Double-height, square s bay also added then.

Ford Spence Court. Sheltered housing by *Argyll & Bute District Council*, 1990–1. A neat unpretentious grouping, domestic in scale and rural in character. Roughcast with smooth margins.

Ledaig Old Schoolhouse, 1.2km. s of St Modan's Church. Thinly harled, two-storey, early C19 block with single-storey N and s wings. The symmetrical three-bay plan is splayed to form a semi-hexagonal w front. E staircase projection is an addition. Piended roofs. Tall chimneystacks on the side walls. Originally the entire ground floor served as a classroom while the upper level, reached by a forestair at the rear, provided accommodation for the schoolmaster. Now wholly adapted as a dwelling.

Letterwalton House. Late C19(?) house in square-snecked granite, sited high above the road to catch a view of Mull. Canted bays; gabled sandstone porch with Campbell coat of arms.

Lochnell Primary School. Standard, double monopitch school by *Strathclyde Regional Council*, 1991–2. Heavy boarded fascias and gables. Classroom windows have stepping sills and astragal grids.

CHAMBERED CAIRN, Achnacree, 600m. sw of Achnacreemore Farm. Stone and boulder cairn, c. 24m. in dia., rising to 3.4m. on the s. The SE entrance is marked by four stones, two of which are the portal stones. Passage and three-compartment chamber now inaccessible.

CHAMBERED CAIRN, 275m. w of Achnacreebeag Farm. Two burial chambers indicate a staged development: the earlier chamber towards the NW comprises five uprights with a flat capstone; the later SE passage-grave retains two capstones.

FORTS and DUN, Dún Mac Sniachan, on a steep coastal ridge w of Benderloch village. A site once known as Beregonium, a mistaken echo of Rerigonium in Ptolemy's *Geography*, and alternatively associated with Ossian's Selma; in neither case with any convincing justification. The earlier elongated fort, not at all easy to see, stretches 245m. along the ridge in turf-covered stony debris, sections of which have been vitrified. The later fort is smaller and lies at the sw end of the ridge within the earlier fortified circuit; it is heavily vitrified. The dun, which is located at the lower NE end of the ridge, may represent the final phase of fortification of the ridge.

STANDING STONE, at the s end of Benderloch village, 250m. w of A828. 2.1m.-high stone aligned NW–SE.

BENMORE HOUSE
2.1km. NNW of the road junction at the head of Holy Loch

Baronial mansion located close to the confluence of the rivers Eachaig and Massan. Completed during the third quarter of the C19, Benmore lies at the heart of a beautifully wooded estate which, since the first conifer plantings in 1820, has grown to become a national centre for forestry, arboriculture and exotic shrubs. The house is set on a raised terrace between lawns and conifers, the result of successive building phases difficult to disentangle. In

September 1848 the *Glasgow Courier* advertised the sale of the mansion of Benmore, describing it as 'modern and in excellent repair ... capable of accommodating a large and genteel family'. It was bought by James Lamont, scion of a local dynasty, who returned from his estates in Trinidad in 1849 and, finding his purchase to be in fact 'very much decayed', immediately 'employed an architect, Mr Baird, of Glasgow' (perhaps *John Baird II*) to replace the old mansion. The extent of this new house, completed in 1851, is unclear. Most probably it is the three-bay, entrance block in the middle of the present S FRONT; an uneasy, Gothic-and-Baronial façade with three crowstep gablets carried on a continuous corbel course and a strange double-height open portico at the centre. In 1862 the estate was acquired by an American, Piers Patrick, for whom *Charles Wilson* built a tall, four-storey, square tower, linking this to a lower wing at the NW angle of the Lamont house. The tower, dated 1862, is vigorously Baronial with stepping stringcourses, roll-moulded jambs, crowstep gables on all four faces, a high conical roof over the circular stair at the SE angle and reverberating bartizans at the three other corners. Wilson also added a long conservatory to the E gable of the 1851 house and appears to have suggested a classical revision to the main S portico, though the latter was not carried out and the former was later superseded by a new E wing (*see* below).

In 1870 the estate again changed hands, and again the new owner, the sugar refiner James Duncan, enlarged the house. Kitchen and service accommodation, dated 1874 and monogrammed JD, were added in matching Baronial around a courtyard on the N by *David Thomson*. A sugar factory and a picture gallery (high walled and castellated to the E of the house) were built, though these have gone. Some time later, perhaps after the estate had been bought in 1889 by Henry J.Younger, the present E wing, terminating in the hipped-roofed billiard room, was constructed. In 1929 Benmore was adapted for use by the Forestry Commission and in 1965 it became an Outdoor Recreational Centre, which necessitated the building of the harled emergency staircase tower, fortunately hidden behind the NW corner of Wilson's 1862 tower.

Seventy years of institutional use have not quite vanquished the former grandeur of the INTERIOR. In the Drawing Room, r. of the hall, a panelled plaster ceiling and a bulging Baroque fireplace in white marble with brass grate and coloured marble cheeks. Further E, the Library has a heavy, beam-and-joist ceiling, dado panelling and tall bookcases framed by Ionic columns, all in oak. Massive oak chimneypiece; in the overmantel, carved between fluted Ionic columns which support a broken pediment, the Christian virtues FIDES SPES CARITAS. Pitch pine replaces oak in the Billiard Room at the E end of the ground floor, not only for the dado and ceiling but in the arcaded panelling and recesses of a wide ingle-neuk.

FORMAL GARDEN, 800m. N of Benmore House. Originally the estate's walled garden; from 1870, bounded W by an immense conservatory, demolished 1968, and E by Water Garden glasshouses, demolished 1930. Since 1965 it has been planted with a wide range of conifer species. At the W end of a central avenue of flagstones laid across the lawns, PUCK'S HUT by *Sir Robert S. Lorimer*, 1928. It is exquisitely placed. No more than an octagonal shelter, but a perfect piece of garden architecture, both precise and playful. A cedar-shingled, bell-shaped roof commands the axis yet charms the eye in every chance view glimpsed through the trees. At the apex, Puck, a wooden finial carved by *Phyllis M. Bone*. Moved here in 1968 from its original location, Puck's Glen on the E side of Strath Eachaig, the shelter commemorates the Regius Keeper of the Royal Botanic Garden in Edinburgh, Sir Isaac Bayley Balfour, whose foresight helped establish the Younger Botanic Garden at Benmore in the 1920s. – Halfway down the flagstone walk, an armillary SUNDIAL, 1978, in which the rough metal crescent of the Milky Way embraces a number of global rings, one carrying the signs of the Zodiac. – FOUNTAIN, of German provenance, 1875.

BENMORE STEADING, on the NW edge of the Formal Garden. Built 1874, probably by *David Thomson*. Baronial coach-houses, stables and stores with crowstep gables and dormered lofts. From the W, a high roll-moulded round archway, set within an asymmetrically turreted gable, leads through a pend into the courtyard. The yard is cobbled and slopes down gently to the open E end. At the NE corner, a three-storey house with cylindrical stair tower: crowstep gables with white clock faces, 1875, over doocot entries. Painstakingly rescued from decay by the *Property Services Agency Architects* and *James Taylor Partnership*, 1990–1; 'an astonishing restoration achievement' (Scottish Civic Trust, 1991).

Also in the estate: a round-gabled, rubble FERNERY, 1874, originally with its own heating plant; the WRIGHT MEMORIAL SHELTER, 1990, by *Robin Lorimer*, respectably classical with a whimsical piece of ridge carving in affectionate deference to the architect's grandfather; and, close to the Glen Massan road, between pedimented white marble piers, concentrically-scrolled GOLDEN GATES, wrought with the initials JD at their circled centres. The gates were commissioned by James Duncan for the Paris Exhibition of 1871 where they were premiated, and were brought to the estate in 1873. – Baronial SOUTH LODGE, eaves and gables on continuous corbel course like the core of the main house; by *Baird*(?), who was employed by John Lamont in 1849 'to build an entrance lodge'. – Tall wrought-iron GATES and PIERS with quadrant railings define the forecourt, 1874.

BERNICE, 6.9km. N on the W shore of Loch Eck. Mid C18. Isolated, white and archetypally solid; the perfect three-bay house, simple and symmetrical as a child's drawing. High piended roof with lower pitched roofs linked to chimneyed gables.

BLAIRMORE

1982

A string of C19 hillside and seaside villas stretched out along the W shore of Loch Long N of Strone Point.

BLAIRMORE PIER. Timber T-plan pier built 1855, much improved 1873, and in use for a century after that. At the roadside N, abandoned in melancholy fairy-tale disintegration, the former TICKET OFFICE, a rubble cottage with a gable-end wooden screen of holed and arched panels in chamfered frames.

DESCRIPTION

Opposite the pier are the only non-residential buildings: a six-bay ashlar block of shops with flats above and a single-storey hall with keystoned round-arch windows and door. To the N, a series of once grand villas and mansions, mid and late C19, look across the loch to Cove. Behind a long balustraded wall, lawns roll up to BLAIRMORE HOUSE, a tall ashlar pile coarsely endowed with a tower, a concavely canted NE corner and a plethora of hefty consoles along the eaves. APPIN LODGE and OTTERBURN are both gable-fronted Gothic, the former with ring-drip fretted bargeboards and quatrefoil balustrades over canted bays l. and r. CREGGANDARROCH, 1863, by *John Gordon*, vast and classical in a gawkily additive way, manages to combine an Italianate tower, a two-storey five-light bow and an octagonal corbelled corner on its hillside perch. The composition is uneasy but the elements and detail, down to the stepped, now lamp-less gatepiers, are not without echoes of Alexander 'Greek' Thomson. DUART TOWER defies stylistic attribution; a big, black-and-white concoction of gables and bays. Then come a number of smaller houses, several varying a gabled Gothic theme. SANDRINGHAM and MOSSKNOWE have more decorative fretted bargeboards. BLAIR ATHOL and THE BANNACHRA have arched windows and dormers and traceried balustrading over ground-floor canted bays. But CLADAIGH is unique: a symmetrical cottage with a two-storey, hipped-roofed, open-framed front in bracketed timber, veranda below, balcony above.

To the S of the pier the line of villas runs imperceptibly into Strone. LEE BANK sits well back, a plain, two-bay rubble house with tall segmental-arch windows; altogether self-effacing and respectable were it not for the attention-grabbing archway of quartzite rocks placed, grotto-like, at the roadside (a sentimentally romantic embellishment also favoured by DUNCREGGAN LODGE). On the hillside, FAIRYKNOWE, 1832, by Charles Wilson, spreads itself confidently under ring-drip bargeboards, with strapwork and quatrefoil balustrading cresting windows and bays. Then more modest Gothic villas, several with that two-light, diamond-canted bay that appears so often along the Cowal shore.

BRIDGE OF ORCHY

Rail stop village on the Glasgow–Fort William line. More recently, a walkers' stop on the West Highland Way.

ACHALLADER CASTLE, 5.2km. NNE. Small ruined tower-house on the bleak edge of Rannoch Moor. Built by Sir Duncan

Campbell of Glenorchy in the last years of the C16 but destroyed in a Jacobite attack of 1689. The one-room-and-stair plan rose through four storeys, the topmost being a garret floor with corbelled angle rounds NW and SE. Its shell survives on the N and E only. The E wall preserves the base of the SE round, part of its crowstepped gable, and is swollen on a shallow corbelled curve from above first-floor level to accommodate a few last remaining treads of the NE turnpike stair. The entrance, at the first floor, was at the E end of the S wall where part of its moulded jamb indicates that it was checked for a timber door and yett. The cellar space at ground level, which was not vaulted, may have been reached by a stair descending from the NE end of the hall above. Some small lintelled windows; several pistol-holes.

AUCH BRIDGE, Allt Chonoghlais, 5km. SSE. C18 rubble bridge reduced on the E. Segmental arch span of 11.7m.

BRIDGE, 400m. W of Inveroran Hotel crossing the Allt Tolaghan. Random rubble segmental-arch bridge. Late C18.

BRIDGE OF ORCHY. Hump-backed rubble bridge with segmental-arch span of 18.9m., built *c.* 1751 during the construction of the military road between Tyndrum and Kinlochleven. Engineer, Major *Edward Caulfield*. Parapets follow curving approaches before being nipped in plan at the crossing. C20 refacing.

BRIDGE OF ORCHY HOTEL. 1954 roughcast rebuild after the earlier hotel had burnt down. The hipped-roofed roadside block turns through the NE corner octagon to a three-storey N wing. Gutters carried across roughcast eaves dormers. Shallow NW bow window.

CLASHGOUR BOTHY. Corrugated hut built by *Speirs & Co.*, 1915; 'rare surviving example of a Side School' (MacDonald, 1998). Now used by mountaineers.

FOREST LODGE, 1km. NNW of Inveroran Hotel. One-and-a-half-storey C19 house with high gables and high polygonal chimneys. Decorative bargeboards.

INVERORAN HOTEL, 3km. NW of Bridge of Orchy. The three-bay house may date from 'Circa 1708', as the sign claims, for Inveroran was once an important stop on the drovers' routes; but the peaked eaves dormers and gabled W wing are later, the latter probably by *Robert Baldie*, 1855.

RAILWAY STATION. Attributed to *James Miller* but perhaps by *Robert Wemyss*. Opened by the West Highland Railway, 1894. Elongated central platform pavilion with canted bays to offices and waiting room. Timber-framed structure above brick base tiled with fish-scale shingles. Bellcast hip roof provides wide eaves shelter.

VICTORIA BRIDGE, Linne nam Beathach, 800m. NNW of Inveroran Hotel. Late C19 rubble bridge of two segmental arches with dressed cutwaters.

WAY IN BUNKHOUSE. Adventurous vernacular. Two floors of walkers' overnight accommodation tucked into a smart slate-roofed shed by *Stephen & Maxwell*, 1987. Low oversailing eaves designed to coincide with the stained timber bridge which crosses a bouldered sheugh to enter at the half landing. Lateral walls obliquely cut back in section below the eaves line.

BRIDGEND
8592

Former cattle-fair hamlet at the crossing of the River Add N of Lochgilphead. Scarred by C20 housing, the village retains some rehabilitated rubble cottages.

ACHNASHELLOCH FARM, 800m. SSW of Bridgend Bridge. Two-storey, three-bay gabled house, C19. Single-storey wings linked l. and r. are gabled. Rough hood-mouldings to ground-floor windows.

BRIDGE. A rubble bridge, 45m. long, crossing the River Add in two 10m. segmental arches and one of 6.1m. span to S; buttressed with triangular cutwaters. Parapet walls continue some distance N across the flood plain where an arched culvert penetrates the structure. Above the southernmost main arch, the inscription BUILT / BY THE SHIRE / 1737 cut in a stone panel. Repeatedly repaired in the C18 and later. Now bypassed by the A816.

THE HORSESHOE INN. Late C18(?). Two-storey, three-bay, painted rubble. Short single-storey wings attached to the gables have gabled eaves dormers. Rough hood-mouldings as Achnashelloch.

STANDING STONES, Dunamuck, 600m. W of Horseshoe Inn on l. bank of River Add. Three groups of three (one fallen), two and two (fallen) stones respectively. The highest stands to 4m.

CAIRNBAAN
8390

Linear hamlet marching with the N bank of the Crinan Canal.

CAIRNBAAN HOTEL. Solid early C19 staging-post inn serving the Canal and the Oban road. The gable-ended, three-bay ashlar front has cornices at eaves and over the ground-floor windows and former door. A slightly lower, recessed two-storey wing to w is hipped-roofed: was this added almost immediately or did an intended E wing fail to materialize? Later C20 expansion is less deferential. A flat-roofed restaurant, 1964, by *Frank Burnet, Bell & Partners*, spreads E clumsily. To the W, a balconied annexe with an Alpine flavour benefits from its detachment.

COTTAGES, on N bank of Canal. Built *c.* 1876 to house workers in the local slate quarries. Two ten-dwelling terraces with ten gabled eaves dormers front and back. White roughcast on concrete walls.

CAIRN, Cairn Bàn, 120m. SE of Cairnbaan Hotel. An indistinct eminence on a rocky site. Cist, aligned E–W, with capstone.

FORT, Dùn na Maraig, 450m. NNW of Achnabreck. Clifftop fort defined by a 3m.-wide tumbled drystone wall. The WSW entrance, reached by a steep approach, is marked by isolated boulders; 'an unusual and not readily explicable feature' (RCAHMS, 1988). N of Achnabreck Farm can be found the finest prehistoric cup-and-ring carvings in Scotland.

CAIRNDOW

A linear hamlet strung out along the right bank of the Kinglas Water as it flows N into Loch Fyne. A little more than the 'few inconsiderable houses' William Gilpin found in 1776, but not much more. At the N end of the village, three pleasantly Scottish, roughcast houses by *Ian G. Lindsay*, *c.* 1950; at the S, the grass-banked enclave of KILMORICH, a varied grouping of white cottages with hipped dormers rising off the eaves; by *John Boys*, early 1990s.

KILMORICH CHURCH, 100m. N of the entrance to Ardkinglas estate (q.v.). Erected 1816 to replace the kirk of *c.* 1700 which had stood a little to the N. The church, constructed by *Andrew McKindley*, builder at Colgrain, Dunbartonshire, lies W–E and is approached up a short, roughly flagged path from the road to the W. There is a superficial flavour of Commissioners' Gothic, but the architectural massing is strong. Three forms are clearly articulated in line: a square entrance tower, broader than might be expected for its height; a pyramid-roofed octagon (the church itself); and, appended axially at the rear in the late C19, a gabled vestry. White harled walls and slated roofs stress the solid geometry, an effect further emphasized by angle quoins and dressings in buff stone. At the top of the tower, a balustrade of quatrefoils and four tall finials. Coupled pointed-arch windows have intersecting glazing-bars, their Gothic impact reduced by square-headed frames. A stone panel set in the W face of the tower is dated AD MDCCCXVI and carries the initials DP.DN.JC.

The interior, with plastered walls and a boarded dado and ceiling, is painted. It is a late C19 remodelling. Pews run obliquely l. and r. from a central aisle. – The semi-octagonal PULPIT, 1902, axially placed on the E wall, is carved with pointed-arched panels surmounted by a frieze of quatrefoils. Matching sounding board above with six moulded drops. – Opposite the pulpit, reached by a stone stair in the tower, is the Ardkinglas pew, the original LAIRD'S LOFT. Its canted gallery front, with plain and reeded panels and a finely dentilled cornice, projects into the church, supported on two keeled quatrefoil timber columns. An open-grate fireplace survives in the N wall of the tower behind gallery seating. – In the entrance porch, a much reduced circular stone FONT, late C15 or early C16, incised with linear arcading; within an arch, the outline of a rigged ship with furled sail has been cut. – FRAGMENT from the head of a ringed CROSS, C12 or C13. – Tapered SLAB, C16(?), carved entirely with fretting and geometrical ornament. Both pieces appear to have been brought to Kilmorich from the burial ground associated with the medieval church at Clachan (q.v.) at the head of Loch Fyne.

BUTTER BRIDGE, Glen Kinglas, 5km. E of Cairndow and 2.2km. N of the Rest and Be Thankful. Built on the military road from Dumbarton to Inveraray, *c.* 1751. Hump-backed rubble structure of one segmental-arch span.

CAIRNDOW INN. C18 staging post, two-storey, three-bay, with skew-gables. The inn is longer than that 'single house by the side of the loch' which accommodated the Wordsworths, the inn has been much extended, particularly to the N. The original building is now decidedly overporched, the new overdormered.

OLD SMIDDY. Low, all but symmetrical house with deep dipping piends and swept eaves dormers. Mid C19.

STRONE HOUSE, S end of the village. Built *c.* 1930, reputedly(?) from plans prepared by *Sir Robert S. Lorimer*. The flat, unarticulated rubble front, seven bays wide with a central entrance, sits under a high hipped roof bracketed where the eaves overhang at the corners. End walls modelled with canted bays.

CAMPBELTOWN

Despite the magnificent natural harbour of Campbeltown Loch, sheltered from the Firth by Davaar Island and The Doirlinn sandbank, the town itself is a relatively recent foundation. Until the C17 the loch-head village of Ceanloch-Kilkerran remained no more than a clachan, its remoteness more significant than any advantage of picturesque aspect or protective anchorage. But in 1609 an Act of Parliament empowered Archibald the Grim, 7th Earl of Argyll, for long the Government's agent in pacifying the rebellious West Highlands, to 'plant a burgh, to be inhabited by Lowland men and trafficking burgesses, within the bounds of Kintyre'. The village was renamed Campbeltoune or Lochhead, feus were granted to incomers from Bute and the Cumbraes, and Argyll began to raise the 'castle or fortalice of Keanloch-Kilcheran', the so-called House of Lochhead, on a site known today as Castlehill.

By 1636 estate records were listing some thirty householders, of whom under half had been settled in the new town. Around midcentury, and again after the Restoration, more intensive policies of Plantation by the Marquess of Argyll resulted in an influx of Covenanting Lowland lairds from Renfrewshire and Ayrshire. Though the lands which they obtained in South Kintyre were not granted in feu but as tacks or leases, this new community evidently stimulated development both in the countryside and in Campbeltown itself. Herring and salmon fishing prospered, weaving was introduced, coal-mining and salt-making were under way. In 1667 the town became a burgh of barony and in 1700 a royal burgh. Just over a quarter of a century later, after an abortive start, the Town Council began work on the Old Quay. Completion was delayed until 1765, by which time not only was a New Quay under way to form 'an enclosed basin or harbour for the preservation and safety of ships loading and unloading', but the Laird of Saddell had constructed his own jetty at Dalintober.

It was a small place. A single street, today's Main Street, stretched downhill from the Argyll castle past the medieval Cross, which served to mark the marketplace in front of the Tolbooth, to the Old Quay. To the NW there may have been a few lanes and

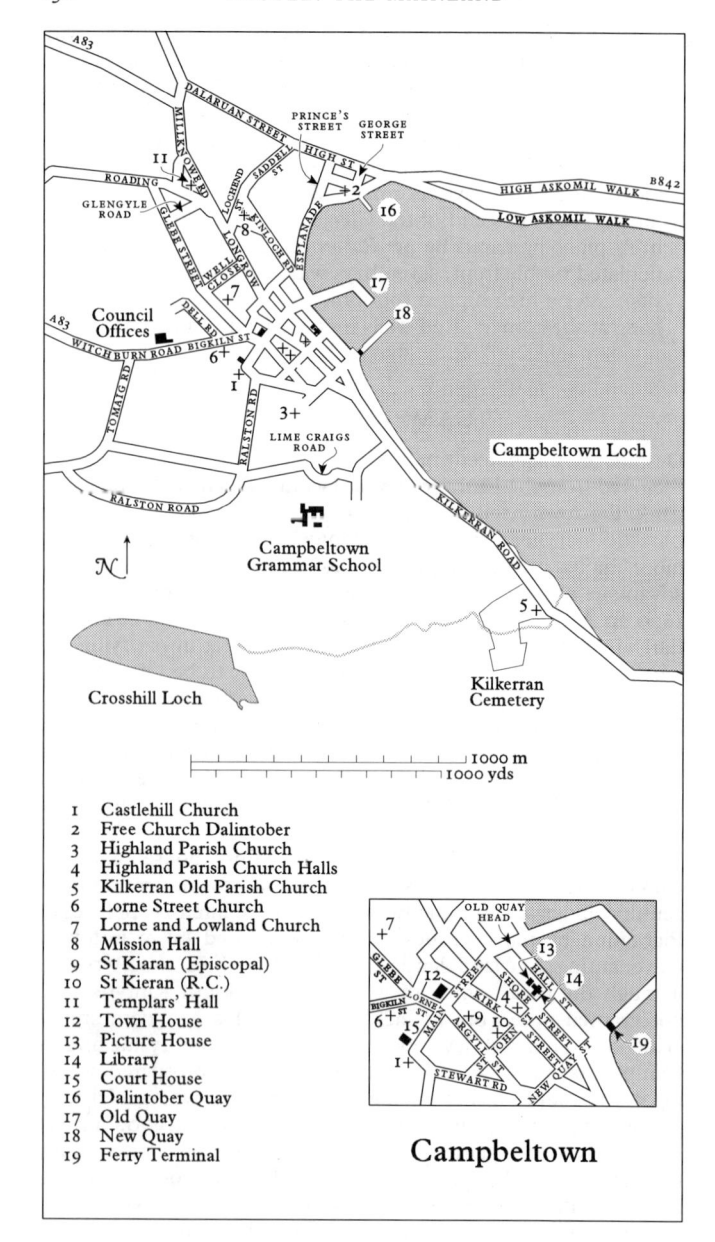

1   Castlehill Church
2   Free Church Dalintober
3   Highland Parish Church
4   Highland Parish Church Halls
5   Kilkerran Old Parish Church
6   Lorne Street Church
7   Lorne and Lowland Church
8   Mission Hall
9   St Kiaran (Episcopal)
10 St Kieran (R.C.)
11 Templars' Hall
12 Town House
13 Picture House
14 Library
15 Court House
16 Dalintober Quay
17 Old Quay
18 New Quay
19 Ferry Terminal

Campbeltown

houses but here, for the moment, the Campbeltown Water burn inhibited growth. Opposite the Cross, however, Kirk Street ran out parallel to Shore Street towards the SE, passing the Lowlanders' Church of 1654 to reach the cruciform Parish Church that had been built on open ground by the lochside in 1643.

Throughout the C18 this unexceptional pattern of economic and physical development was maintained, but by the 1790s the *Statistical Account* commented that unless some new manufacture were introduced the town 'must always remain poor'. For a few more decades the herring boats sailed out of Campbeltown Loch; mining, too, continued, benefiting from the cutting of a canal from the 'coal heughs' at Drumlemble in 1783; but it was whisky which became the dominant industry. Private stills had always existed in the town, but changes in the application of duty around 1814–15 made large-scale whisky production potentially profitable. No fewer than 34 distilleries appeared during the C19. Fortunes varied, but until 1920 there were usually at least 20 firms in business in the 'spiritual town' at any one time.

Economic growth was matched by developments in physical layout. A Plan of Campbeltown, inset into a map of Argyllshire prepared by *George Langlands & Son* in 1801, shows expansion to the NW along Long Row and around the head of the Loch towards the small but regularly planned village suburb of Dalintober, while to the SE the straight spine of Argyll Street is emerging. Renewal, too, was in train: *Pigot's Directory* of 1823 reported that 'In the principal street of the town a great improvement is being proceeded with, in the erection of several good buildings intended for shops and dwelling houses'. Both the spread and the density of development are confirmed by the Parliamentary Plan of 1832, by which time the burgh boundaries had extended to embrace both sides of the Loch. Gradually, Victorian building gave substance and containment to those lines of growth already determined at the start of the century. As the tenements and distilleries of Campbeltown and Dalintober began to merge in the W, a string of generously landscaped mansions and villas appeared along the N and S shores of the Loch. Finally, in 1876, with the transformation of the Mussel Ebb embankment at the head of the Loch into Kinloch Park, the shape of the modern town was complete.

For a time, regular steamer connections ensured commercial contact with West-Central Scotland. Business links with Glasgow were strong and it was Glasgow architects who gave Campbeltown some of its finest buildings. Since the 1920s, however, the community has been in decline. Nonetheless, unlike its distant neighbours to the N, Tarbert and Lochgilphead, the town still possesses an architectural quality and a distinctly urban intensity which its latter-day remoteness might not perhaps suggest.

CHURCHES

Former CASTLEHILL CHURCH, Main Street. Abandoning their earlier church in Kirk Street in the 1770s, those English-speaking worshippers who remained loyal to the Established

Church built Castlehill, 1778–80, on a site at the top of the town aligned with the Old Quay. Architect, *George Haswell*, and contractor, *John Brown*, both from Inveraray, constructed a five-bay-wide galleried rectangle. Harled rubble masonry with painted margins and quoins. On the NE entrance front, three central bays advance slightly under a pediment supporting urns and a tall elegant bellcote obliquely set on its square plinth. Interior recast to accommodate choir, 1868; in 1883, a rear wing extension produced a T-plan with three galleries. Closed 1971; flatted and renamed Castlehill Mansions in 1986–7. The façade is unimpaired, elevated, it seems, in supervisory detachment above the architectural *mêlée* of Main Street.

This raised location, so topographically significant in the burgh's townscape, was formerly occupied by the Castle or House of Lochhead (Ceanloch) which the Earl of Argyll erected *c.* 1610. Sometimes erroneously described as an ancient stronghold of the Macdonalds, this castle was probably the first structure to be built in the new Plantation burgh of Lochhead or Campbeltown. It was demolished towards the end of the C17.

FREE CHURCH, George Street, Dalintober. Following a dispute, 1900, over ownership of Lorne Street Church (q.v.), the 'continuing' congregation built this red sandstone snecked rubble gabled nave to the design of *Ronald Carsewell* of Lochgilphead, 1911–12. Plain bellcote; three round-arched windows in gable; tall square-headed windows to nave; S portal Gothic flavour.

HIGHLAND PARISH CHURCH, New Quay Street. Erected 1803–8 to house the town's Highland, i.e. Gaelic-speaking, worshippers. Obliged to quit their original cruciform Gaelic Church of 1642 for better accommodation and, no doubt, not to be outdone by the Lowlanders' *point-de-vue* setting of Castlehill Church, the Highlanders moved uphill from Kirk Street to an axial alignment with the New Quay. *George Dempster* of Greenock was the architect, *Robert Watt* of Glasgow the contractor. Pavilion-roofed five-bay mansion-house front made wider by lateral stair towers, equal in height but separately piended. Generous round-arched windows unify harled rubble walls. The classical calm is disrupted by a pinnacled ashlar belfry. Struck by lightning in 1830, the tower was rebuilt to a design by *John Baird* of Glasgow in 1833, later demolished and finally rebuilt in 1884–5. It may compromise the pedimented façade behind but is splendidly responsive to the townscape challenge of street and skyline.

Airy interior from 1884: flat ceiling with large circular ventilator grille; semi-octagonal gallery, with central projection opposite pulpit, supported on cast-iron and wood columns; original straight-backed PEWS. – Reformed austerity lost by 1954–5 refurbishment. – ORGAN, 1954, by *Harrison & Harrison*. In the porch, a marble BUST of Dr Norman MacLeod; minister from 1808 until 1825, he was known as *Caraid nan Gaidheal* ('friend of the Gaels') both for his work as a Gaelic scholar and for his strenuous efforts to relieve the famines of the 1830s and 1840s.

HIGHLAND PARISH CHURCH HALLS, Kirk Street. Built 1706, in a 'partly Gothic' probably T-plan manner, as the first church of Campbeltown's largely immigrant English-speaking population, on the site of the C17 'Thatched House' where they had worshipped hitherto. By *c.* 1770 this Lowlanders' Church had fallen into disrepair and by 1780 had been superseded by Castlehill Church (q.v.). In 1904 the Kirk Street building was reshaped by *H.E. Clifford* to serve as halls for the Highland Church. Three tall arched bifurcated windows in red sandstone rubble wall to street; that to the l. inserted in conversion. The Kirk Street eaves rise to Clifford's parapeted and gabled terminations. St John Street corner like a squat tower house. Unusual elliptical oculi, introduced perhaps to echo segmental arches of windows and doors.

Exposed rubble interior over crenellated boarded dado. Hammerbeam trusses on stone corbels. – In the Halls is a carved SKEWPUTT, dated 1642, and BELL, dated 1638, both relics from the Old Gaelic Church which stood at the SE end of Kirk Street and served the burgh's Highland congregation until *c.* 1770. – Brass TABLET, 1905, in memory of Elizabeth Tollemache †1735, 'Duchess of Argyll, daughter of Duchess of Lauderdale and mother of John, Duke of Argyll and Greenwich'.

KILCHOUSLAND OLD PARISH CHURCH, 3.8km. N from Campbeltown Pier on the Carradale road. Roofless rubble ruin of a reconstructed C16 church. W gable and S and N walls are still entire, the last incorporating masonry from an earlier C12 chapel. In the churchyard are several C18 HEADSTONES bearing the symbols of mortality, vocational imagery, trades insignia, etc., including one to Mary Robison †1759, remarkably similar to the McMillan grave at Cladh nam Paitean (*see* Glenbarr).

KILKERRAN OLD PARISH CHURCH and CEMETERY. Nothing remains of the C13 church dedicated to St Ciaran. The vast graveyard, entered through Gothic GATEPIERS, early C19, is planted with palms, yews, rhododendron and fuchsia. – In the older burial ground, now deemed dangerous, the RCAHMS Inventory records an Early Christian TOMBSTONE(?), with low relief wheel cross, some fragments of carved CROSSES and tapered SLABS, Kintyre School C14–C15, and numerous recumbent SLABS and HEADSTONES of C17 and C18 date bearing interesting inscriptions and images. – The MCDOWALL MONUMENT is an ashlar obelisk set obliquely on a heavily coped base with a central round-arched entrance; framed panels in two obelisk faces carry no inscription, but the monument is said to be raised in honour of the founder of the Campbeltown Coal Canal, Charles McDowall of Crichen †1791. – Several early C19 HEADSTONES with swan-neck pediments, their inscriptions combining Roman, Gothic, italic and penmanship scripts. – Numerous WALL MONUMENTS, mainly C19, with pilasters, pediments and inset panels; some randomly sited, some grouped in a series of stepping plots. – Tall neo-Grèc OBELISK to Jean Macalister Hall †1879. – MONUMENT to the family of Donald Mackay, shipbuilder, †1899: a dumpy cylinder incised with Grecian ornament and topped by an anchor; by *J. & G. Mossman* of Glasgow. – Nearby is a grander, three-bay, Grecian MONUMENT with a bold anthemion frieze and block pediment; to Jessie Eliza Weir †1908. – A low stone panel framed by block pilasters and pediment marks the grave of architect Henry Edward Clifford †1932 and his wife. – Raised on the hillside to the s is a War Memorial stone CROSS, inlaid with a bronze sword, *c*. 1950; below, a parade of 55 identical HEADSTONES, the simple graves of as many servicemen.

LORNE AND LOWLAND CHURCH, Longrow. *John Burnet*'s aggressively steepled church, 1869–72, for the United Presbyterians replaced the Longrow Relief Church, 1767, which stood a little NE of the present site. Flawed with formal conflicts: T-plan gables barely contain the convex swell of the church's amphitheatre seating, a tall top-heavy belfry crashes down through the pediment of the entrance façade, while the tower's 'open-ribbed lantern dome', despite its Gothic crown-spire affinities, rests on a classical obelisk-cornered plinth. Not Burnet's best. Did a desire to outreach the town's other spires and distillery stacks provoke this ill-proportioned hubris?

Through arcaded screens l. and r. of the vestibule, dog-leg stairs lead to a U-plan gallery supported by cast-iron columns. Decorative balcony panelling incorporates twin clocks. Plaster ceiling with dentilled cornice and decorative central dome with elliptical mouldings. – At the centre of the NW wall, a corbelled panelled PULPIT, 1895, approached by perron stair with strapwork balustrading; pedimented aedicule above. – Integrated ORGAN CASE with flanking panels surmounted by open segmental pediments. *Brindley & Foster* ORGAN, 1895. STAINED GLASS, partly hidden by the organ case: five lights with the four evangelists flanking St Paul, by *W. & J. J. Kier*, 1872. – Wall SUNDIAL from the Relief Kirk of 1767; by *John Jamieson*, 1780.

Former LORNE STREET CHURCH, Lorne Street. Originally the Gaelic Free Church. By *James Boucher* of *Boucher & Cousland*, Glasgow, 1867–8. Powerfully polychromatic Gothic, perhaps based on a design by E. W. Pugin for St Francis's, Gorton, Manchester, 1866–72. Banded stone to jambs, quoins and buttresses, the latter rising to tall pinnacles on gable front flanks. Full-width triple arched and gabled entrance; two plate-traceried windows above separated by a false buttress corbelled to carry the steepled bellcote obliquely set at its apex. Five-bay nave lit by banded lancets. Cast-iron columns support a U-plan gallery with stop-chamfered panelling and continue to a plaster vaulted ceiling. Gallery alterations, 1890, by *Charles Martin*; renovation, 1968. Ground floor cleared. Hall at rear by *H. E. Clifford*, 1889. Closed 1990, since 1995 the church has served as a Heritage Centre.

MISSION HALL, Kinloch Road, Lochend. By *H. E. Clifford*, 1887–8. Gable-ended hall and offices built for joint use by the Castlehill and Highland congregations in freely composed Gothic. Low belfry tower over pyramid roof incorporated the old bell from the Highland Church. Campbeltown polychromy.

ST KIARAN'S (Episcopal), Argyll Street. In 1849 *William Butterfield*, a 'Mr Niblett of Gloucester' and *James Wylson*, Glasgow, produced designs for a church, but none was favoured. A design by *H.E. Clifford*, 1885, proposing a tower, was abandoned, but his gates and adjacent RECTORY, 1885–6, were built. In 1891 the present plain Gothic church by *Ronald Walker* of Stirling was erected. Hooded triple lancet in the street gable. Curved king-post trusses support the roof. – PULPIT and REREDOS, which has a pediment over curved canopy, by Canon *C. T. Wakeham*. – Octagonal FONT, 1893, on columned support. – ORGAN by *J. Brook & Co.*, 1891.

ST KIERAN'S (R.C.), St John Street. Gothic chapel, 1849–50, replacing earlier building of 1809. Street gable with three plain traceried windows divided by pinnacled buttresses. Ogee-hooded entrance arch. Interior with false ceiling, *c.* 1960. – Memorial PLAQUE to James Cattenach †1836, believed to be the priest responsible for the building of an earlier church in 1809. – Adjacent ashlar Chapel House, gabled front with stepped hood-moulded door, dated 1880.

TEMPLARS' HALL, Millknowe Road. By local builder *James Wylie*. Dated 1871. Disused. Lancet Gothic with crowstepped nave gable and porch.

PUBLIC BUILDINGS

ARGYLL & BUTE COUNCIL OFFICES, Witchburn Road/Dell Road. Two-storey gabled mansion with attic bay dormers; built 1871–2 to plans prepared by local joiner, *Charles Martin*. Robust Roman Doric columned porch with block pediment.

ARGYLL & BUTE COUNCIL OFFICES, Witchburn Road. Former Poorhouse, 1859–61, by *John Honeyman*, with Witchburn Hospital at rear. Altered and extended, retaining a symmetrical front of three domestic gables connected by recessed single-storey links. Glazed corridors later successfully applied along links. Central porch entry approached axially across a garden from a gabled round-arch PORTAL in the roadside wall.

CAMPBELTOWN GRAMMAR SCHOOL, Hutcheon Road. Two- and four-storey flat-roofed blocks, 1965–8, by *Argyll County Council*. Dull curtain walling in duller grey brick.

CHRISTIAN INSTITUTE, Old Quay Head. 1885–7. *H. E. Clifford* decidedly ill at ease. A tall symmetrical façade confronts the Royal Hotel across the roundabout at Old Quay Head. The superimposition of hunched pedimented entrance, elongated tripartite window and distillery-like tower defies stylistic description. On Hall Street, four high round-arched windows light a first-floor hall. Here was the terminus of the narrow-gauge railway that ran between Campbeltown and Machrihanish from 1876 until 1933.

CIVIL DEFENCE TRAINING CENTRE, Bolgam Street. Part may date from the C18. Remodelled as Court House and Gaol, 1852–3, and used as such until 1868. First-floor hall lit by three round-arched windows. The central entrance in the symmetrical street façade leads through a close to a tiny inner yard: ahead, eaves-dormered domestic; to the l., stairs rise to a gabled doorway to the Court. Court-room with heavy cornice and open timber roof of A-frame trusses on timber corbels. Columned chimneypiece in N wall. Panelled dados and shutters; moulded architraves to doors and windows.

COMMUNITY EDUCATION CENTRE & AREA OFFICE, Stewart Road. Former Grammar School, C19, incorporates extensive additions by *H. E. Clifford*, 1899–1900. Asymmetrical grouping of varied classroom forms includes a Palladian windowed gable and a small square balustraded tower.

Former COTTAGE HOSPITAL, Witchburn Road. *J. J. Burnet*, 1894–6. Symmetrical front with gables, shallow canted bays, and five round top dormers. Roughcast with ashlar dressings. N wing by *H. E. Clifford*. Later alterations have robbed the building of its original Arts and Crafts character. Disused.

CROSS, Old Quay Head. Splendidly carved disc-headed cross, Iona school, c. 1380, 3.3m. high on a modern stepped base. Cut from Loch Sween schist, with the largest disc-head known (0.81m. dia.). Although some images have been removed from the front face, the carving is still extensive. In the head and lower sections, intertwining foliage incorporating various saints and animals. In the middle zone, two trefoil-headed niches and a ten-line Latin inscription in raised Lombardic capitals. This last indicates that the cross commemorates 'sir Ivor MacEachern, sometime parson of [?] Kilkivan, and of his son, sir Andrew, parson of Kilchoman, who caused it to be made'. The reverse face is filled with interlaced vegetation with a mermaid, sea-monster and other animals worked into the design at the extremities. The cross probably first stood at Kilkivan, near Machrihanish, being moved to Campbeltown in the early C17 to serve as the market cross. Until World War II it stood in Main Street in front of the Town House (q.v.).

DALINTOBER INFANTS' SCHOOL, Dalaruan Street, Dalintober. *H. E. Clifford*, 1899. Symmetrical classroom block in red sandstone with wide curvilinear gable at centre.

FERRY TERMINAL, New Quay. By *John Wilson Associates*, 1995–7. Scrupulously simple with dry-dash walls and slated roofs. Symmetrical gabled front. Elegant segmental-arch canopy roof carried on tubular-steel structure cable-stayed from four mast-columns; by engineers *Montgomery-Smith & Partners* with *Scott, Wilson, Kirkpatrick & Co.* (see Piers below).

MASONIC HALL, St John Street. By *H. E. Clifford*, 1912. Roughcast gabled Hall with open eaves and bargeboards; segmentally arched windows have red sandstone roll mould dressings.

PICTURE HOUSE, Hall Street. No longer prim but still determinedly pert and promenade-pretty; a priceless survivor. Designed by *Albert V. Gardner*, 1912–13, and renovated by him, 1934–5, its importance as one of the earliest surviving cinemas can scarcely be overstated. Bowed front, glazed at ground and first floor, sits in a broad recess between white pilastered brick book-ends. Elliptical oculi and decorative green ceramic tiles

l. and r. Oversailing inverted saucer roof with elliptical conning tower cupola. Gabled café annexe to r. Cinema interior remodelled 1988, but projection room and exotically stylized 'boxes' preserve their original form.

PIERS. Begun in 1722 at the instigation of Elizabeth Talmash (Tollemache), Duchess to the 1st Duke of Argyll, the OLD QUAY was not completed until 1765. Meanwhile construction on the NEW QUAY, promoted by the 2nd Duke, had started in 1754. A third, DALINTOBER QUAY, was built *c.* 1756. Later, the harbour created between Old and New Quays was improved when extension and rebuilding were carried out by engineers *Storry & Smith*, Glasgow, *c.* 1870. In 1898 the Old Quay was further extended. Almost a century later, 1997, the New Quay was adapted as a roll-on roll-off terminal.

PUBLIC LIBRARY AND MUSEUM, St John Street/Hall Street. Dated 1897–9, and bearing a carved reminder that it was 'gifted to the town by James Macalister Hall Esq. of Tangy and Killean'. A masterly exemplification of *J.J. Burnet*'s Scots Renaissance idiom. Campbeltown polychromy: square snecked ochre rubble with contrasting dressings in polished red sandstone. A vigorously Mannerist entrance leads into a foyer crowned with an ogee-domed lantern. To the l. is the Library, with three mullion- and-transom canted bays to St John Street, and, beyond, the roof-lit Museum. To the r., an octagonal Reading Room marks the street corner, and ahead, completing the L-plan composition along Hall Street, is a two-storey wing carved with five monogrammed blocks and four double panels illustrating those trades and activities important in the town's history – coal-mining, fishing, boat-building, flax, learning, distilling and cooperage, building. Accessible from the foyer, through a door over which are the carved names of Pericles, Leo X, and Francis I, is a long Loggia covered by the sweep of the Library roof but open to a sheltered inner garden. Librarian's house, with bartizan and eaves dormer, returns from the Museum into Shore Street.

110

Burnet's handsome interior is intact. Magnificent timber panelling, furnishings, chimneypieces and decorative plasterwork. Open crossed-truss roof carrying lantern over foyer. In the Museum, a segmental barrel-vaulted ceiling with glazed central cupola. – Memorial TABLET to the painter William McTaggart (1834–1910).

ST KIERAN'S SCHOOL, Kirk Street. Two-storey symmetrical gabled school with central façade gable over high three-light window. Built 1890–4, disused from 1970, from 1981 it has served as Parish Hall. Adjoining is single-storey St Kieran's League of the Cross and Young Men's Hall, 1900.

SHERIFF COURT HOUSE, Castlehill. Two-storey, crowstep gabled, French Gothic, 1869–71, by *David Cousin*; s wing added 1903. Almost domestic but for high upper floor and higher central tower. The three-stage tower rises above a pointed-arch entrance to a machicolated belfry and steep lampshade roof. Tripartite windows to the ground floor and, above, pushing through the eaves, tall two-light mullion-and-transom windows surmounted by gables. Rough-faced coursed rubble and equally rough dressings impart an almost Baronial ruggedness. Pink and ochre, their polychromy was reversed in later Campbeltown practice. Interior refurbished after 1989 fire.

TOWN HOUSE, Main Street/Cross Street. By *John Douglas*. Erected 1758–60 to replace the town's 'venerable and dilapidated' Tolbooth. Civic dignity and architectural aspiration are mutually enhanced by an octagonal steeple projecting into Main Street like a municipal lighthouse. In stuccoed rubble walls, hefty Gibbsian keystones, imposts, architraves and quoins mark openings and margins. Steeple and gabled hall are unified by a plain stringcourse which links the imposts of all ground-floor windows and doors and by a common cornice at eaves level. Above the latter, the steeple, freed from its lower abutment at the centre of the Hall, rises in two stages, diminishing in plan, to reach a stone spire. This built design, which the Inveraray mason-architect *John Brown* raised in 1778 to take the place of its timber forerunner, was a much reduced version of one of several proposals prepared at the time.

In 1865–6 *Campbell Douglas* reorganized the Town House internally while, to the SW, a single bay addition containing a scale-and-platt stair continued the roof slope, eaves cornice and tall round-arched first-floor window form of the original block. A pedimented dormer and columned Roman Doric porch provided new accents. Coat-of-arms sculpted by *William Mossman*. The porch in the tower, main vestibule and stair hall have a grey and white marble dado; dentilled cornice and coved ceiling with a glazed cupola over the stair. Panelled walls in the Council Chamber, by *James Thomson & Sons*, Airdrie, *c.* 1934; doors also panelled, with lugged architraves and keystone cornices. In the Hall, some panelled doors with consoled cornices survive. The wider central opening, now with modern doors, retains its segmental pediment on consoles, the foliage and shield in the tympanum carved by *James Steel*. The segmental vault of the plaster ceiling is ribbed and panelled.

The town BELL, hung behind louvred archways at the base of four of the eight faces of the spire, is dated 1779. – Steeple CLOCK, of similar date, is the work of *John Townsend* of Greenock. – Cast-iron Provost's LAMP STANDARDS with decorative fluted shafts.

WAR MEMORIAL, Esplanade. Built 1923. Tall, chunky 'obelisk' on battered buttressed base in massive olive masonry; won in competition by *A. N. Paterson*. Rugged stone cross looks out to sea from an arched recess, its axis bisecting the Loch between Davaar Island and the mainland. World War II commemorative panels crudely added to plinth buttresses.

INDUSTRIAL BUILDINGS

GLEN SCOTIA DISTILLERY, High Street, Dalintober. Three-storey-and-attic plain roughcast block; eleven window bays long with two gabled hoist dormers through the eaves. Built 1832 but completely reconstructed 1897.

Former GLENGYLE DISTILLERY, Glengyle Road. Early C19. Three-storey, white-painted rubble range.

JAEGER FACTORY & FACTORY SHOP, The Roading. 1980s. Buff and orange banded brick may be a reference to Campbeltown's older sandstone polychromy. Eaves glazing strip steps down to shop window corner.

LOCHEND EXCISE DUTY FREE WAREHOUSE, Lochend Street. Symmetrical, four-storey, six-bay, square-snecked sandstone block with a central pend, *c.* 1890. Segmentally lintelled windows diminish in height with each storey rise. Roofless shell.

SPRINGBANK DISTILLERY, Glebe Street/Well Close. Built 1828. Last surviving working distillery in the town (42 are known to have been in production at some time or another). Three-storey polychromatic buildings grouped round courtyard.

DESCRIPTION

TARBERT ROAD forms the approach from the N. It passes DRUMORE HOUSE, *c.* 1820, altered *c.* 1875, a large but plain piended mansion with columned porch, and leads into MILLKNOWE ROAD. Parallel ranges of workers' housing l. and r. make an interesting comparison. On the NE are two two-storey terraces, Nos. 90–100 and 110–120, 1951, flat harled façades punctuated by coupled entrances set, cave-like, behind semicircular arches. Opposite, Nos. 83–103, older: flatted artisans' row by *Robert Weir & Son*, 1878; a long symmetrical block, roughcast with ashlar dressings, penetrated by pends and rising to three storeys and gabled dormers at its centre. LONGROW continues south, relentlessly straight. No. 124 turns a neat convex corner into Lochend Street. Two- and three-storey tenements, early C19, form an urban corridor, tarnished but coherent. A gap in the street wall leads SW into a bare forecourt dominated by the bulky tower of Lorne & Lowland Church (*see* Churches, above). Aberrant but vigorous, the CLYDESDALE BANK, late C19, offers downmarket Ruskinian Gothic. Suddenly the clarity of Longrow disintegrates as its deliberately planned line meets a denser older pattern of streets at the centre of town. Oblique junctions and tight corners produce some attractively curved variants on familiar classical themes, especially where Nos. 5–7 and No. 9, both three-storey, early C19 tenements, link Union Street with Burnside Street, the latter aptly named to recall the margin of the C17 town. UNION STREET and CROSS STREET contribute more late C18/early C19 atmosphere, the COMMERCIAL INN claiming a 1774 date. MAFEKING PLACE, *c.* 1905, stands tall across the street, four storeys of polychromatic sandstone with mansard attic dormers; a three-light corner canted bay, five-light under an ogee-slated dome in the attic, looks ambitiously up to Main Street. With the removal of Wide Close in 1908–9, LONGROW SOUTH leads into the centre of town, Nos. 1–21 and 2–24 creating a three-storey channel of polychromatic shops and tenement flats. Designed by *T. L. Watson* in 1908 but not completed until 1915. Opposing sides of the street are similar but not identical: shallow canted bays separated by narrow aedicule strips which mark the mutual gables; tall transomed entries to white glazed brick closes leading to drying-greens on the shop roofs. Corner emphases, one gabled, one domed, give some sense of civic entry.

MAIN STREET bustles but cannot escape the monitorial gaze from Castlehill (*see* Churches, above). Set apart behind its railings in elevated *point-de-vue* detachment, the stern classical front of the former Church stares back, watching burgh life all the way down to the Old Quay. On the NW side is the Sheriff Court (*see* Public Buildings, above). Then come DRUMFIN HOUSE and its semi-detached reflection; two similar houses with projecting pedimented bays each end, built *c.* 1845 as Free Church manses; one for the English-speaking Lochend Kirk, by *Campbell Douglas and Stevenson*, 1868, (dem. 1985), the other for the now disused Gaelic-speaking Lorne Street Church (*see* Churches, above). At No. 64, in red Locharbriggs sandstone, THE CLUB, 1896–8, by *H. E. Clifford* turns into Lorne Street, corbelling a corner octagon from ground-floor sill height to second-floor dentilled eaves, its shallow ogee-profile roof nudged by a lozenge-shaped chimneystack on Main Street. Nos. 58–62, 1813: a three-bay, three-storey tenement with piended dormers and original astragals at second floor. A panel inset in the central chimney bears the date and motto, MANU FORTE ('With a strong hand'). Next, the gabled ashlar front of ARGYLL ARMS HOTEL, by *James Weir*, *c.* 1900, two linked canted oriels at first floor jutting forward on plain cyma recta consoles, and, at the junction with Cross Street, the white steepled civic accent of the Town House (*see* Public Buildings, above). Thereafter, with the exception of some polychromatic flourish at the entrance of Longrow South (*see* above), Main Street maintains a three-storey scale of plain Georgian tenements, late C18 or early C19. Nos. 50–52 and Nos. 2–4 CROSS STREET, late C18, form an L-plan, clasping a turnpike stair at the rear. Perhaps a little later in date, the wide, solidly symmetrical tenement range at Nos. 16–20 may well be part of that 'great improvement' reported in Pigot's Directory in 1823. On the corner of Bolgam Street is MACLEAN PLACE, also early C19, a roughcast, U-plan tenement of vernacular classical dignity.

Opposite the Sheriff Court, on the SE side of the street is the ROYAL BANK, late C19, a lopsided ashlar mansion with hefty unfluted Greek Doric columns in the porch. Castlehill continues with FLEMING'S LAND, three storeys, built in the early C19 for one of Nelson's officers, Captain John Fleming, RN, of Glencreggan, and recast by *T. L. Watson* in 1909: a seven-bay quoined tenement with a central pend, two consoled street doorways and two turnpike stairs at the rear. Then, the black and white WHITE HART HOTEL, an older property greatly altered and extended over a ten-year period, 1897–1907; tall, with a dormered mansard. Corbelled above a skewed corner entrance, a bay-windowed octagon rises to a slated ogee dome. Perhaps by *Sydney Mitchell*, then at work on Machrihanish Hotel (q.v.). A broad chimneystack gable, now without its original white hart sculpture, returns into Argyll Street with an echo of the ogee dome and canted bays tiered into the attic. In Argyll Street, more corbelled canted bays plus gables, aedicules and dormers in BAROCHAN PLACE, a magnificent polychromatic tenement by *T. L. Watson*, dated 1907; twenty-eight bays long yet rippling with invention. Most of the rest of Main Street is late-Victorian or Edwardian three-storey scale. But Nos. 31–35 are earlier, low-ceilinged and starkly plain, dwarfed alongside the elongated bays, steeply faceted dormer roofs and ironwork cresting of Nos. 9–17. Beyond Shore Street, where Main Street opens out to the Loch, WOOLWORTH'S scars Campbeltown where it hurts most.

Here, indeed, at OLD QUAY HEAD, nothing quite succeeds. The ROYAL HOTEL, 1907, more polychromatic sandstone, reinstated after war damage in 1941; its original architect, *James M. Monro*. It sports another ogee dome on another corbelled corner bow, but faces up to the Loch with little conviction. The pierhead is simply dull. Across the street, the Christian Institute (*see* Public Buildings, above) is big but brutal. Even the venerable Campbeltown Cross (*see* Monuments, above) located in front of Town House until World War II, has been marooned here in a roundabout.

Four more or less parallel streets extend the town SE from Main Street. HALL STREET, a short but somehow incongruous stretch of dual carriageway alongside the red sandstone sea wall of *c.* 1900, has shops and flats at ROYAL AVENUE MANSIONS by *Frank Burnet & Boston*: more tenement polychromy, dated 1900, with a third-floor attic storey full of gables and eaves dormers. Then come The Picture House and the splendid Public Library (*see* Public Buildings, above), appropriate partners in promenade pretension. SHORE STREET, once home to the town's fishermen, now belies its name; a few early C19 remnants. KIRK STREET preserves an early C19 series of three-bay, two-storey, Georgian town houses. THE MANSE, by *David Hamilton*, 1835, is plain but enhanced by flanking walls and a columned porch. At the end of the terrace, No. 70 has a similar doorpiece, to the l. of which a two-storey, tripartite bay, mid C19, seems deliberately placed to catch the view down New Quay Street. Similar small mansions appear in ARGYLL STREET (*see* above) at Nos. 27–29 and BAROCHAN HOUSE, No. 31, which is oddly distinguished by four bays over three.

At New Quay Street, overlooking a pleasant leafy square, a massy irregular tenement by *J. J. Burnet*, 1896–7, assimilates a variety of flats known collectively as CRAIGDHU MANSIONS. Familiar local materials, squared ochre sandstone rubble with contrasting red dressings; but the idiom is Baronial, the composition appropriately, and brilliantly, asymmetric. Overawed by all this, the restored L-plan range of cottages at PENSIONERS' ROW, early C19, win respect with quiet order, rehabilitated 1994–5; dormered single-storey to the street, rear open stair and deck access to first floor now replaced by stair towers.

KILKERRAN ROAD now runs SE along the wooded shore. Nos. 2–4 retain the plain early C19 character of Kirk Street (*see* above) but *John Burnet*'s ARDSHIEL, late C19, with its consoled tripartites and cornicing, initiates grander things. Simple elegance at COURT HILL, a three-bay, pavilion-roofed mansion and coachhouse; STRONVAAR, five-bay, recesses at the centre to a Venetian window and columned porch; NORTH PARK, wide canted bays to ground floor: all are early C19. A century older, LIMECRAIGS sits uphill 'embosomed in trees'. Probably built for Elizabeth Tollemache, 1st Duchess of Argyll. A drawing of 1757 prepared by *Alexander Rowatt* shows a piend-roofed two-storey house, five bays wide but only one room deep, raised above a forecourt flanked by single-storey offices; evidently the house's central gabled projection, porch, W and rear extensions are all later. Flatted in the 1970s. Back on the lochside road by Quarry Green, REDHOLME, 1896, by *H. E. Clifford*, is an asymmetric implosion of upmarket suburban bungalow and Tudor mansion. The interior retains a galleried stair-hall, timber panelling, a Jacobean chimneypiece with green glazed tiling and inglenook leaded glass by *Oscar Paterson*. SOUTH PARK, 1824–5, reverts to simple three-bay Georgian form with dissimilar flanking wings. EAST CLIFF, 1825, with its balustraded bowed bays, veranda wing and conservatory, has an almost Regency chic; in fact, the result of an 1896 rebuild by *Clifford*. And at the Children's Playground, suitably whimsical, is the LIFEBOAT HOUSE, 1898, an Arts and Crafts gabled structure in polychromatic snecked sandstone by RNLI engineer *W. T. Douglas*, battered and buttressed in Voysey manner, with a trapezoidal boat door.

DALINTOBER, on the other side of the Loch, is something of an urban backwater, retaining its separate character. A gridded suburb, neither village nor town. HIGH STREET keeps some early C19 housing, especially on the N. Architecturally outstanding is SPRINGFIELD HOUSE, *c.* 1815, a two-storey-and-attic skew-gabled mansion, the principal or upper floor of which is reached by a splendid flying stair. Columned porch, tripartite windows with column mullions and three parapet urns add ornamental richness. Commissioned by Thomas Lacy, the captain of a Revenue Cutter, one of a number of such residences built by Campbeltown's seafaring sons at the time. It looks down to Dalintober Quay and out to the Loch. First-floor tripartite windows reappear at SANDBANK, *c.* 1820, on North Shore Street close to the pier. On the S side of HIGH STREET, on PRINCES STREET, JOHN STREET and a little to the west at PARLIAMENT PLACE, some robust local authority housing, 1936–9; all by *James Thomson & Sons* of Airdrie; decidedly, if heavy-handedly, Scottish in aspiration.

Climbing E out of Dalintober, HIGH ASKOMIL WALK is the beginning of the coastal route N to Peninver, Saddell and East Kintyre. A succession of large houses overlooks the Loch from the N side of the road. AIRDALUINN, late C19, has five-light bows through both storeys, their conic caps incorporated into a pavilion roof crested with ridge ironwork. Altogether simpler,

ARDGOWAN, *c.* 1840, is crisp gabled Georgian. But the polychromatic spread of ROTHMAR, 1897–8, a shipbuilder's villa by *J.J. Burnet*, is impressively shaped and detailed with classical sophistication, not least in the 'cloistral veranda' entrance on the N and in the engaged Ionic columns and entablature of a tall single-storey bow pushing out S. In 1937, *Burnet, Tait & Lorne* extended the house, adding a garage. AUCHINLEE, *c.* 1883, now a Church of Scotland Eventide Home, is big and bulbous with a ponderous tower over the porch and voluminous double-height bow. But none of this vulgarity of size afflicts BELLGROVE, *c.* 1820, sitting calm and reserved above its flying stair, flanked by laundry and stable pavilions with due Palladian propriety.

LOW ASKOMIL WALK follows the water's edge. Nos. 1–3, *c.* 1870, terraced with attractive bargeboards and consoled tunnel hoods over the entrances. Set high in luxuriant gardens are five three-bay mansions, all early C19: SPRINGBANK HOUSE is gabled but FAIRVIEW, LILYBANK and ROCKBANK are piended, the last distinguished by pedimented tripartite windows with pilaster jambs and mullions; then ROSEMOUNT, 1810, similar in scale but even more elevated, wrapped in a magnificent rubble wall that falls castle-like to the road below. HAWTHORNE, late C19, extended 1896, is Italianate with fretted bargeboards; BELMOUNT, also late C19, is Baronial; BEACH HILL, early C19, almost Gothic; while EAGLE PARK, a white-walled bulging plan under red-tiled roofs round a central curvilinear wallhead, might be South African. CRAIGARD, 1882, has stilted round arches, a two-storey bow window and a tall tower which hint at the influence of Alexander 'Greek' Thomson, but this is by the ubiquitous *H.E. Clifford*. ASKOMEL END, 1948, by *Gillespie, Kidd & Coia*, employs a pavilion roof and strictly symmetrical mullioned glazing to hold its own in this C19 company. Finally, in a sheltering grove of trees, comes SEASIDE, 1831; in the raised parapet over its pilastered doorpiece the motto MANU FORTE and the carving of a hand clasping a sword.

CASTLE, Island Muller, 600m. NE of Kilchousland Church. C13 or C14. Barely discernible rubble remains of a small oblong tower-house. Approach is along a 90m. causeway from the shore.

CASTLE, opposite Kilkerran Churchyard by lochside. One stretch of rubble wall, 6m. long by 6m. high, is all that is left of James IV's late C15 'novum castrum de Kilkerane'.

STANDING STONE, Balegreggan, 400m. N of W end of Campbeltown Loch. Leaning stone which, if vertical, would reach 4m. Cup-marks on S face.

CARA

Small island off the south end of Gigha. Now uninhabited.

CARA CHAPEL. A roofless ruin, built in the C15(?), retaining some of its N wall and W and E gables. Oblong plan, *c.* 9m. by 5m., rubble-built with dressings of red sandstone. The N door, still arched at the end of the C18, preserves a draw-bar slot.

A vertical recess on the inner face of the N wall may have housed a cruck frame.

CARA HOUSE. Derelict tacksman's house. A dour, lonely dwelling. Built *c.* 1733. Original five-bay front now asymmetrical as a result of later blockings.

CARDROSS

Dormitory village between Dumbarton and Helensburgh.

ST MAHEW'S CHURCH (R.C.), Darleith Road, 650m. N of Geilston Halls. Formerly known as Kilmahew or Kirkton Chapel. C15 in origin, it was used as a chapel of ease and school in the C17. Abandoned 1846. Now substantially the reconstruction of *Ian Lindsay & Partners*, 1953–5. A simple cottage chapel with harled walls and slated roof. Birdcage bellcote with ball finial added on the W gable by Lindsay. At the E end the ridge is raised on crowstepped gables and the windows have roll-moulded, chamfered jambs. – Early Christian cross-inscribed STANDING STONE in the vestibule. – Round-headed chancel arch. – Round-arched sedilia and glazed aumbry. – Restored stone FONT, C16(?). – In the GRAVEYARD, several C18 stones; a number of plain marker slabs probably date from the C17.

OLD PARISH CHURCH, Main Road, at the E end of the village. Splendidly romantic ruin in a bosky kirkyard. Perp Gothic by *James Dempster* of Greenock, 1826–7. Bombed in 1941. In 1954 the NE, SE and SW walls were reduced to sill-height around a lawn. Still standing, the NW gable with its crenellated square tower, diagonal buttresses tapering into long tall finials. – The surrounding BURIAL GROUND, its gravestone alleys thick with hydrangea bushes, contains C17, C18 and many C19 stones. – Along the NW margin are several MAUSOLEUM ENCLOSURES. – Two, early C19, have similar castellated SE gables bearing armorial panels below which the doorway is flanked by elliptical wall panels: one contains a table-tomb and headstone to members of the McInnes family, the other records the death of Charles Johnston †1827 in the r. ellipse.

PARISH CHURCH, Station Road. Built as the Free Church by *John Burnet*, 1871–2. Severe, steep-roofed Gothic relieved by the tracery of the E gable window (six quatrefoils in six circles) and a telephone dial rose, added 1878, in the gable of the SW transept. The square entrance tower, which abuts the SE end of the SW wall, has an almost Romanesque starkness. It rises without buttresses in three stages, its solidity emphasized by slit windows, relieved by tall belfry lancets in the topmost stage and reintensified by a stone pyramid spire of funerary gravitas. Vestry added at the NW end of NE wall by *D. Andrew*, 1903. – Church interior renovated, 1899. – Roof carried on oak arch-braced trusses springing from colonnettes with angel capitals. – SW balcony, 1878. – Five BELLS by Glasgow founders, *J. C. Wilson*, dated 1871. – STAINED GLASS. Medallions in the SW window feature Moses, Isaiah, Jeremiah, St Joseph, and the four Evangelists; by *W. & J.J. Keir*, 1878. EMBROIDERED PANELS by *Hannah Frew Paterson*, 1981: an altar triptych; mankind below the Cross with the animal and vegetable worlds and local scenes on each side.

Decorative cast-iron GATES and a single, robust rubble GATEPIER, battered at the base, chamfered from square to octagonal, with a conical cap. Across the street are the blandly inoffensive CHURCH HALLS, 1956.

CARDROSS CREMATORIUM AND CEMETERY, 1.3km. NW of Geilston Halls. Cream harled walls and green copper roofs by *Watson, Salmond & Gray*, 1960. A finial-peaked pyramid over the porte-cochère marks the entrance. Behind, tall clearstorey windows rise under a shallow-pitched chapel roof. Stretching E, a pilastered loggia with winged SCULPTURE by *Hew Lorimer*. Bright airy interior. White marble catafalque in apsidal E end. Four segmental arches open to the S aisle which leads to a small marble-lined Chapel of Remembrance. Light oak panelling to W wall and gallery. Axial link W from vestibule to gardens.

CARDROSS GOLF CLUB, Main Road. 1956. Flat-roofed and asymmetrical, white and airy; Thirties Modernism delayed, but delightful. Three glazed bows look N and W on to the course. Smart, sandstone ashlar, SW entrance added 1994. Plan and section are said to result from the War Damage Commission's demands that the pavilion should maintain the dimensions of the former clubhouse by the local architect *Alexander McTurk*, 1904–5, bombed in 1941.

GEILSTON HALL, at the W end of the village. By *Honeyman & Keppie*, 1889–90. Long low hall with hooded arched doorways in buttressed portals SE and NW, the latter leaning against a battlemented two-stage tower with mullion-and-transom windows. Rural Tudor Gothic reserve, a little affronted by nearby unneighbourly development.

MOORE'S BRIDGE, Main Road. Late C19 reconstruction of a C17 structure. Rubble with red sandstone ashlar dressings. End piers carry two original stones, inset 1922; one with the Montgomery arms and the date 1688, the other bearing the inscription NOT WE BUT GOD above the name of the benefactress Jean Watson whose married name was Moore. Decorative railings.

WAR MEMORIAL, Main Road. Erected 1921. Trapezoidal ashlar block with low flanking walls carrying cast-iron urns.

DESCRIPTION

The modern village links older clachan clusters around Kilmahew (Auchinfroe) Burn in the SE and Geilston Burn to the NW. The ruined tower of the former Parish Church (*see* above) marks the approach from Dumbarton. A few houses on MAIN ROAD recall the kirktoun. Much reduced vestiges of the L-plan CORN MILL, built in 1818, survive at the junction with Carman Road. The old gabled MANSE, 1840–1, by (*David?*) *Rhind*, its Tudor-arched beginnings all but lost in later changes, may retain some C18 fabric. WHITE HOUSE, BURNSIDE COTTAGE and CARDROSS INN, once a farm, are all C18 in origin. BAINFIELD, *c.* 1810, is in similar vernacular vein. Across Moore's Bridge (*see above*), later growth. SHIRA LODGE, mid C19, is small but full of Jacobean swagger; it originally marked the W entry to BLOOMHILL HOUSE, 1837–8, a sprawling, less intensely Jacobean mansion now a residential home reached from Carman Road. AUCHINFROE LODGE, late C19, has a gabled arcaded porch. Arrowhead cast-iron gates, between domed gatepiers with studded ball finials. From these, a drive leads N to AUCHINFROE HOUSE, *c.* 1820, the standard, three-bay, classical model with an added columned and pedimented S porch. Stables ranges (keystone dated 1814) attached NW. ARDENVOHR, 1885, Classical too but grandly Victorian, has a cone-topped, five-light bow and attic windows cutting into a deep cavetto eaves cornice.

Main Road runs on, walled between golf course and trees. On the corner at STATION ROAD the wall rises to support a bracketed slated roof over a 'RURAL SEAT', a sandstone resting (or trysting?) place designed by *Alexander N. Paterson* and gifted by the Scottish Women's Rural Institute, 1932. The Parish Church (*see above*) lies S past VILLAFIELD, 1890, a tenement made to look taller and tougher by its cottagey, brick-and-roughcast neighbour, MARAND, *c.* 1905. In CHURCH AVENUE, feued from 1872, two red sandstone villas, HAWKSDALE and TIGH-NA-DARROCH, *c.* 1880, with complex roofs and bulbous five-windowed bows. Elsewhere there is little to note. Of local authority housing only BARR'S CRESCENT, 1925, early Scots village Modern by *Joseph Weekes*, has a severe modest quality. Among speculative housing, nothing of note.

NW along Main Road, older, plainer properties return. Flatted dwellings: FRUIN and FINLASS in polychromatic sandstone, *c.* 1855; even plainer, BROOMFIELD and LAIGH BARRS, *c.* 1830. Geilston Hall (*see above*), built beside Geilston Burn close to the site of the medieval grain mill of Kilmahew estate, marks the end of the village. ROCKWELL COTTAGE, late C18(?), roughcast with a latticed timber porch, and WOODNEUK, early C19, painted rubble with pilastered dormers, give just a hint of earlier, still humbler, dwellings.

GEILSTON HOUSE, begun 1766, sits apart, approached by a curving drive from the A814. A rather random L-plan accumulation of vernacular forms, unified by their harled walls, crowstepped gables and general lack of pretension. Square DOOCOT, C18, with triangular stone pigeon entrance. Further NW is MOLLANDHU FARM by *Joseph Weekes*, 1946; a white, flat-roofed box with a projecting bow l. of the arched central entrance. BROOK'S ROAD opposite leads to BROOK'S HOUSE, an erect three-bay mansion of *c.* 1785 with a flying stair rising to a central columned SW porch. Close by is MOORPARK HOUSE, an 1864 villa greatly enhanced by ebullient red sandstone extensions in 1892. Bargeboarded half-timbered gables and a battlemented, three-storey SW bastion with a concrete balcony corbelled around the bedroom floor; all in the style of *William Leiper*, perhaps by *Robert Wemyss*. An L-plan COACH-HOUSE, also late C19, survives, as does a crenellated boundary wall with gatepiers topped by orb finials.

DARLEITH HOUSE, off Darleith Road, 2.8km. N. Early C19, though fragments of the fabric may date from the C17. Now an abandoned ruin. A piend-roofed, two-storey-and-basement mansion, the centrepiece of its wide five-bay S front pedimented, but not the portico of coupled Ionic columns. Later E additions only impair any lingering elegance. In the grounds is a derelict DOOCOT, *c.* 1790, a wonderful rubble pile of solid geometries; one cone, two telescoping cylinders, triangular and rectangular prisms.

DRUMHEAD, off Darleith Road, 1.2km. N. Mid C19. Tall attenuated Baronial in square-snecked ochre sandstone with ashlar dressings. L-plan articulated with crowstep gables and cone-topped cylinders that seem to burst from the earth as if driven by some surging subterranean force. High, rocket-like entrance tower set in the SE re-entrant. An earlier T-plan house, probably mid C18, now forms the service wing attached N. Baronial L-plan STABLES, mid C19(?). WALLED GARDEN, C18, to E of main house. Both WEST and EAST LODGES, mid C19, have added porches, each with timber columns.

KILMAHEW CASTLE, 1.4km N of the Old Parish Church. C15 and C17. Ruinous, overgrown tower house, the seat of the Napier family who held lands here from the C13 to the C19. Rubble with ashlar margins. The castle stood five storeys high to a corbelled parapet. Early C19 alterations reduced the height and introduced some pointed-arch windows but the attempt to create a Gothick mansion was abandoned.

ST PETER'S COLLEGE
in Kilmahew estate, 1km. NNE of Old Parish Church

By *Gillespie, Kidd & Coia*, 1959–67. Be sure of a big surprise in these woods, for this is a building of national significance, astonishing in its design and its degradation. Nothing prepares one for the shock of the new grown prematurely old. Banked behind the harled sculpted walls of side chapels and sanctuary, long stepped tiers of repetitive seminary cells rake off into the trees. But the roughcast is spalling, the concrete stained, the windows shattered, the pools dry. In little more than a generation, God, Le Corbusier and Scottish architecture have all been mocked. 'Tell it not in Gath . . .' Here, certainly, the Philistines have triumphed.

The story is brief, at once brilliant and tragic. In 1946 a fire at St Peter's College, Bearsden, the main Roman Catholic seminary in West Scotland, forced the church to transfer its students to Darleith House (q.v.) and Kilmahew House, both large mansions located to the N of Cardross. Recruitment to the priesthood was buoyant and proposals to expand were developed first at Darleith and then at Kilmahew, largely at the stimulation of Father *David McRoberts*, an academic at St Peter's with a particular interest in architecture. McRoberts produced designs for Darleith, 1947, and

Kilmahew, 1953, adopting a collegiate quadrangular plan in each case; neither went ahead. In 1953 the diocesan authorities invited *Jack Coia* of *Gillespie, Kidd & Coia* to become involved with the Kilmahew project. Again progress stalled and it was not until 1959 that the definitive design began to emerge. By this time McRoberts' input was diminishing and the architectural philosophy of the Coia office, now more radically Modern and very much under the influence of Le Corbusier, was being shaped by a cohort of young designers, *Isi Metzstein, Andrew MacMillan* and *John Cowell*.

The final concept, determined in all essentials by 1961, set the new seminary buildings in an L-plan arrangement E and S of the existing mansion. Though later subject to many detail modifications, this configuration remained unaltered throughout a protracted construction period which began in 1962. To the E, the Main Block of the college extended Refectory, Hall and Chapel in an axial N–S alignment with three floors of student bedrooms run-

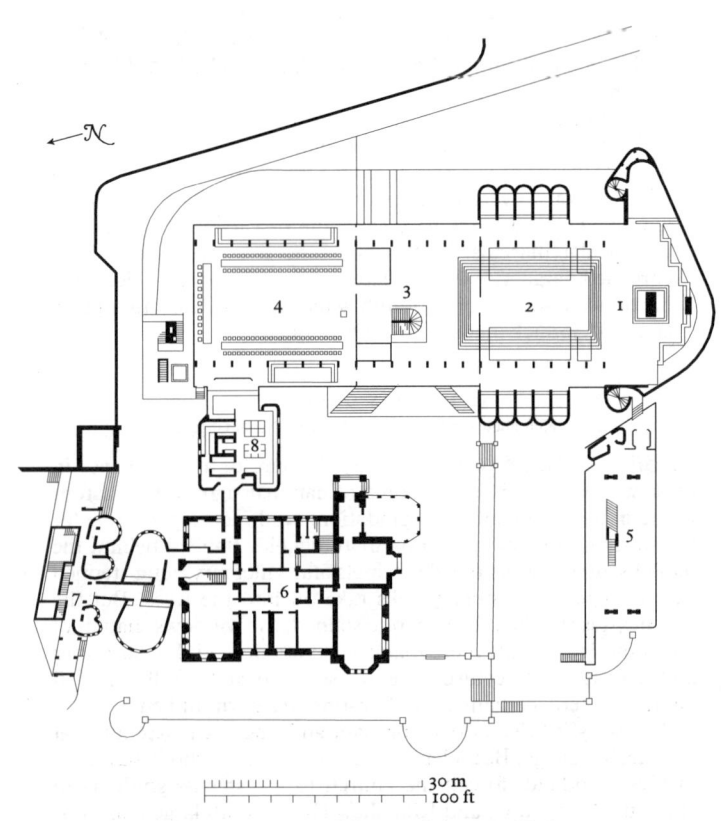

1 Sanctuary
2 Chapel
3 Hall
4 Refectory
5 Library and classroom block
6 Kilmahew House (now demolished)
7 Convent block
8 Kitchen

Cardross, St Peter's College

ning in parallel above in a symmetrical ziggurat section. The free form of a high, top-lit Sanctuary, with Crypt and Sacristy below, was placed at the S end of this block, articulating the composition into the smaller arm of the L, a three-storeyed W wing or Classroom Block. Between old and new was an inner landscaped court. Already adapted for teaching from 1948, the existing KILMAHEW HOUSE, a Scots Baronial pile of 1865–8 by *John Burnet*, was restored to residential use as 'professorial accommodation' and became the administrative focus of the seminary. Its main S and W façades remained untouched, but linkages were established on the N with a small Convent Block and on the E with the college Kitchen. This last closed the N side of the court and connected with the Refectory housed in the N end of the main building.

The building programme was prolonged. Although the inauguration ceremony was held in the autumn of 1966, the interior was not fully fitted out until 1968. All along, the project had received close attention in the popular and professional press. Acclaimed for a design which had brought the hieratic Modernism of Le Corbusier to Scottish architecture, *Gillespie, Kidd & Coia* received an award for the building from the Royal Institute of British Architects in 1967. But, by this time, events in the Roman Catholic world had overtaken the educational and theological ethos of a brief established back in the late 1950s. Among its many radical deliberations the Second Vatican Council, which closed in December 1965, had called for a much more integrated and less sheltered training for priests. Cardross found itself accused of an inappropriate and 'false monasticism'. By 1972 it housed just over fifty student priests, about half the designed capacity. Serious failures in the building fabric exacerbated the financial problems of the archdiocese. By 1979 there were only twenty-one students. One year later the college was closed.

For a brief period (1983–7) the building was used as a Drugs Rehabilitation Centre. But maintenance proved excessive and the church could not afford to continue. Vandalism and decay ensued. Demolition was envisaged. Several differing conversion proposals were advanced. None succeeded. Frustrated by the inflexibility of the building itself, the escalating costs of rehabilitation caused by rapid deterioration in the fabric and services, and by the inhibitions placed on change by a growing recognition that this was one of the most valuable examples of C20 architecture in Scotland (the seminary was A-listed in 1992), attempts to save Cardross have so far failed. Today, the visitor brave or rash or devoted enough to overcome the barriers which preclude entry to the estate will still be stunned. Past the dilapidated SOUTH LODGE (by *Burnet*, 1868), at the end of a long drive, is a magnificent ruin, scarred by neglect, its vast empty spaces echoing with a reproachful silence.

Little or nothing of the strategy which determined the layout of the buildings is at first evident. What emerges from the trees is the E side of the college: the high curving wall of the Sanctuary ugly in neglect, a bank of five equally shabby silo-like side-chapels and a long three-storey block of abandoned balconied bedroom cells stepping back above a once glazed ground floor. Everything is in decay. Roughcast walls are blotched, cracked and peeling. Concrete is stained. Timber rots. Across a shallow moat, long since dried up, a sinister cloistered underpass leads through to the inner courtyard. Here, the L-plan arrangement of the new seminary buildings becomes clear, enclosing the space on the E and S. But there is an enigma, too, for with the demolition of Kilmahew House, necessitated by a fire in 1995, the physical and functional significance of the old in the determination of the new has gone. Yet it is still possible for the imagination, fired by the sculptural immanence of Cardross, to resurrect something of the spiritual and architectural wealth invested here. For that reason, the description that follows is blind to dereliction, concerned instead to try to reveal the creative intentions of the church and her architects.

The MAIN BLOCK of the seminary is forcefully defined by its symmetrical E–W section, a three-storey ziggurat carrying study bedroom cells over the Refectory, Hall and Chapel below. Along the E and W flanks this creates a stepped profile with continuous balconies at each upper level. Bedroom fascias and balconies are clad in brown exposed-aggregate precast-concrete panels, the colour chosen to harmonize with the sandstone of Kilmahew House. Inside, long parallel galleries giving access to the cells overlap each other, heightening the space over the core as they step inwards. At first- and second-floor levels these galleries, fronted by simple pine panelling, can overlook the space below (though timber screening prevents this over the Chapel) but at third-floor level the two ranks of accommodation open from a central corridor. The study cells, 2.5m. wide, determine the structural grid: twenty-three bays of reinforced-concrete framing in which the cross-walls and deep double-cantilevering beams of the upper floors deliver their load to two lines of columns set 15m. apart at ground floor. These columns, positioned close to the glazed W and E walls, define narrow aisles down each side of the building. Between the exposed beams, segmental vaults (of metal lath and white-painted plaster) produce a repetitive scalloped edge along balconies and galleries. At the Hall in the centre of the plan, where the main stair rises from the seminary entrance at the cloister-walk underpass, beams and vaults continue across the building connecting the upper floors. To the N of this circulation bridge is the Refectory, lit on the W, E and stepped N gable by bands of glazing rhythmically subdivided by random mullions. To the S is the Chapel, similarly lit on the W and E. The grey screeded floor of the nave lies six steps below the Hall, aisles and Sanctuary, allowing bench seating to be tiered l. and r. Opening from the W and E aisles, five contiguous bays push out beyond the edges of the building to form apsidal side-chapels hooded like ship's ventilator shafts and secretly lit from above.

A high wall encloses the SANCTUARY, its subtly asymmetrical curve wrapped parenthetically around the S end of the seminary. Six steps lead up from the nave into a double-height space, lit from a gridded ziggurat rooflight half-concealed by a spray of radiating laminated roof beams. A starkly plain altar sits centrally on a square dais three steps high. Behind it, the balconied edge of the floor stops short of the s wall. Stepping back in plan it overlooks a gentle ramp which, descending from the r. of the Sanctuary, follows the white curve of the wall to the Crypt and Sacristy below. At these lower levels, in an austere world of shuttered concrete, coloured light spills from small, deeply set windows on to altars housed in the recesses of the outer wall. Altar tables project from a concrete wall opposite. Behind this is the spacious Sacristy, its N wall forming, as it were, a square bracket in response to the more expansive embrace of the Sanctuary ramp.

From the w end of the Sacristy, a door opens on to a narrow external landing. To the l., a wedge-shaped flight of stairs squeezes s through the end of the curving Sanctuary wall out into the wooded landscape. To the r., a shorter, straighter flight climbs to the cloister walk which, passing around the undercroft below the Chapel where it affords access to the lower levels of the side-chapels, leads to the entrance underpass and up into the inner courtyard. Ahead, cut into the splayed E end of the seminary's w wing, is an entry to the Library.

The three-storey w wing or CLASSROOM BLOCK closes the s side of the seminary courtyard. It is a building dramatic in form and structure. The Library, occupying the lowest floor, acts as a long oblong podium. On the w, where the ground falls away rapidly, heavy rubble walling rises to a ribbon of glazing with random concrete mullions. This windowed band returns on the short E wall, which is indented to provide the entrance already mentioned, and, as if impelled by the curve of the Sanctuary wall, skews SE–NW diagonally across the courtyard in the direction of Kilmahew House. On the N and w sides, the ribbon of mullioned glazing continues, its sill height now at the level of the court. The interior of the Library is lined in timber. At the w and E ends of the space, 18m. apart but within the glazed perimeter, two broad concrete piers support the structure above. A straight-flight stair rises E–w into the Common Room, which can also be reached from a short stair at the NW corner of the courtyard. The walls of the first floor are fully glazed to intensify the contrast between the podium below and the heavy upper storey; a continuous door-height transom emphasizes the horizontal and makes it possible for the glazing to be cut back under the floor above. The concrete piers recur, this time supporting two massive cross-beams, their depth of 1.2m. coincident with the cut-back in the glazing. A two-flight teak stair with angled treads rises w through a timber-lined ceiling into the centre of the Classroom floor above. At this level the SE–NW skew of the E wall of the Library below is repeated and reflected in a NE–SW skew at the w end. The resultant plan, an elongated trapezium, accommodates two classrooms on each side of a triangular central zone which houses the stair. The longitudinal concrete walls of the block, board-marked in herringbone-pattern panels, act as wall-beams supported on the two cross-beams below. The span is thus 18m. but the walls are daringly cantilevered up to 12m. beyond the column lines, the lower booms raked below the stepped seating of the classrooms at each end of the building. The roof structure is a diamond grid of laminated Oregon pine carefully related to the diagonal planning of the classrooms. Light enters through a series of rooflights and glazed screens stretched across the W and E walls.

The destruction of Kilmahew House leaves the remaining elements of the plan in detached or semi-detached limbo. But the relationships can still be sensed. The CONVENT BLOCK lies a short distance N. It is two storeys high, its parallelogram plan set in skewed relationship with the C19 house. A tapering corridor connects old to new between single-storey, free-form rooms, smaller versions of which recur as service spaces below the nuns' cells on the upper floor of the block. The KITCHEN, linked E from Burnet's mansion by a short glazed gap, is a single-storey block, square in plan with rounded corners, its harled walls lit rather arbitrarily with randomly placed windows. A servery zone advances E to make contact with the Refectory at the N end of the Main Block (*see above*).

St Peter's is one of the great buildings of C20 Scotland. It is first a building which celebrates the self-sufficient sanctity of architectural space, a quality which no doubt has much to do with the religious nature of the brief, however contingent upon theological vicissitude this proved to be. But it is also a building which re-established contact with contemporary European architecture in a way lost since the emigration of Charles Rennie Mackintosh. In its international awareness it succeeded, not at all paradoxically, in recapturing something of the fortress-like severity and direct visual vigour of the national tradition. An indebtedness to Le Corbusier is everywhere evident, unambiguous and, indeed, openly acknowledged by the architects. The heavy cellular structure floated over glass, ribbons of window rhythmically punctuated by random mullions, funnelled light falling on side-chapel altars, the clustering of small free-form shapes, the aesthetic of *matières brutes*; all this can be found in the Monastery of La Tourette, near Lyon, 1956–9, in the pilgrimage chapel of Notre-Dame-du-Haut, Ronchamp, 1950–5, and in other works. But it is an insightful indebtedness, rarely mawkish (except perhaps in the perversely quaint window arrangement devised for the Kitchen), and creatively capable of transcending specific allusion, notably in the choice of the ziggurat section which lies at the heart of the Cardross concept or the exciting thrust of the W wing lancing above the tree-tops.

8300

CARNASSERIE CASTLE
2km. N of Kilmartin village

The castle's roofless ruined tower-house, approached from below up the steep W side of the Kilmartin Burn valley, seems strategically poised to command the narrowing routes N to Loch Awe and

Loch Craignish. Closer inspection reveals that the five-storey tower is integrally combined with a three-storey hall-house in an elongated W–E plan. Indeed, despite its fortified appearance, Carnasserie is no product of military exigency but the residence of a cleric, John Carsewell, Bishop of the Isles, who had it built between 1565 and 1572. Carsewell's resources were considerable; enough to build himself a palace and to do so with masons brought from Stirling *au fait* with the latest Renaissance fashion. Although it survives as a floorless shell only, the castle stands almost intact to the wallhead, its C16 form and detail unaltered, save for some late C17 changes to the fenestration of the S wall.

Hall-house and tower-house have a continuous S wall but are distinct in height, the latter rising from a stepped stringcourse level with the hall-house eaves to an almost entablature-like combination of hefty mouldings which wrap a continuous twice-shadowed line around the tower's three corbelled angle turrets and parapets. On the N, the austere rubble face of the tower advances ahead of the hall-house from which a smaller four-storeyed stair tower projects NW. In the re-entrant formed by

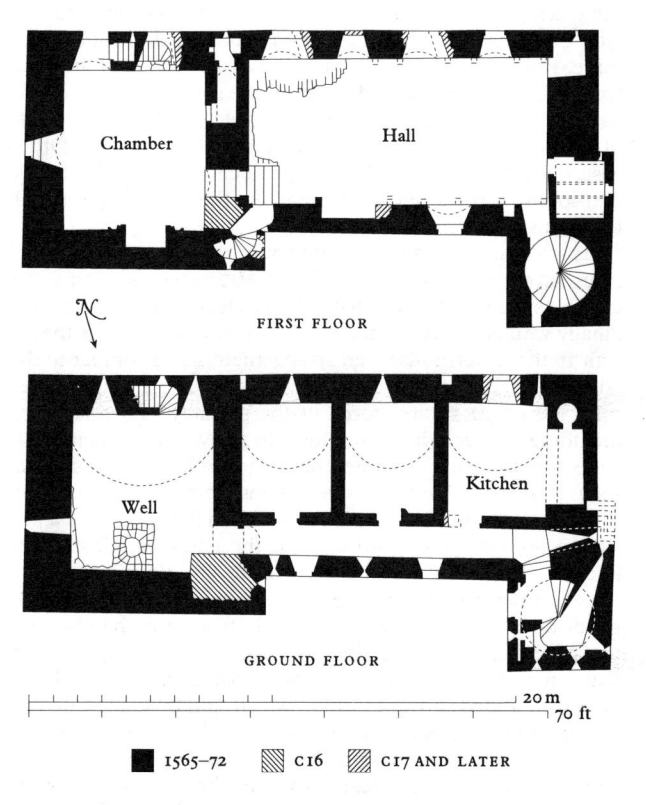

Carnasarie Castle.
Ground- and first-floor plans

this stair is the entrance, a simple doorway with heavy roll-moulded edge, surmounted by a hood-moulded panel bearing the arms of Carsewell's patron, the 5th Earl of Argyll, and the Gaelic motto DIA LE UA NDUIBH[N]E ('God be with O Duibhne') an invocation which the Bishop also used in dedicating his Gaelic translation of the *Book of Common Order* to the head of the Campbell family. Above this is a tall, two-tier, somewhat Mannerist aedicule of superimposed pilasters, its armorial displays missing. It sits within a vertically proportioned panel, framed by a heavy moulding similar to the stair tower stringcourse on which the whole arrangement rests. This stringcourse and a similar one at higher level continue round the tower where, on the w wall, they step up boldly before returning against the gable of the hall-house. Here the junction of stair and gable takes a particularly attractive sculptural form; hanging over a five-step corbel at first-floor level and bevelled back above the upper stringcourse to the curve of a small turnpike rising to the stair tower's caphouse.

Window openings have chamfered surrounds and are checked for shutters. Some attempt at symmetry may have been made in the placing of three high-level s lights to the first-floor hall but later C17 changes to the fenestration make this difficult to determine. Problematical, too, on this s wall, are two half-arch arcs springing from a moulded bracket at eaves level, perhaps the base of some decorative dormer. Three windows are axially placed, one above the other, at the centre of the E wall. Otherwise, openings are random. Numerous defensive 'double-keyhole' gun-loops, vertical and horizontal. At the base of the s wall, three garderobe-chute outlets.

Apart from the vaulted chamber in the tower-house which gives access to the castle's well, the INTERIOR is open to the elements. Ground-floor planning is clear: three rooms, originally vaulted, open off the N corridor which connects the NW stair to the tower-house – an arrangement not dissimilar to that adopted at Kilmartin Castle a few years later. Various architectural FRAGMENTS are stored in the partially vaulted E cellar, including a carved drainage spout. In the w end kitchen a 3m.-wide fireplace recesses into the gable under a reconstructed segmental arch. A circular oven opens from the s ingo and on the N jamb a water inlet has been sculpted in the form of a projecting open-mouthed head. From the entrance, close to the kitchen, the NW newel stair is intact to first floor but ruinous above. A narrow straight flight service stair in the s wall of the tower-house gives access to the single first-floor chamber over the surviving vault. Here the floor has been laid with modern flagstones. In the N wall is a fine chimneypiece framed by a heavily moulded surround within which spindly shafts with caps and intermediate banding flank the hearth and rise through a bipartite overmantel incorporating l. a quatrefoil-in-circle motif and r. a diamond-in-circle. Towards the NW corner of the chamber a vaulted passage leads to a modern platform from which the void of the hall-house can be viewed. Window embrasures, corbel stones for bearing beams and raggles showing the steep pitch of the hall-house roof are clearly seen. The hallside doorway at this platform and the adjacent door to the newel stair in the NW corner of the tower-house both have architrave shafts akin to those of the chimneypiece already described. The great fireplace in the hall, of which only the E jamb remains, shows similar mouldings. In the thickness of the W gable are two small compartments, each with almost identical entresol chambers above, that to N entered from the NW stair, the S accessed by ladder through the joisted ceiling of the room below. Second-floor arrangements are conjectural but the presence of two adjacent garderobe chutes on the S wall and what appear to have been two linked fireplaces on the N indicate the likely position of partitions dividing the hall-house flat into three apartments. Window and fireplace openings in the tower-house suggest a single chamber on second- and third-floor levels. At roof level a partially restored parapet walk can be reached from the NW stair.

While the approach to the castle from the E is a steep climb, land to N, W and S is gentler in profile. Some stony footings, *c.* 35m. NW may be a remnant of Carnasserie (Beg) township, known to have existed here at least until 1825. A walled garden probably lay S, though only its E boundary and a line extending W from the SW corner of the hall-house are marked by rubble walls. Set within the latter, some 23m. W of the castle is a semicircular arched portal with a keystone dated 1681 and inscribed with the initials SDC and LHL, for Sir Duncan Campbell of Auchenbreck and his wife, Lady Henrietta Lindsay. It is possible that it was Sir Duncan who effected the changes to the castle's S front; it was certainly as a result of his support for the rebellious 9th Earl of Argyll that Carnasserie was besieged in 1690.

CAIRN, 700m. NNE of Carnasserie Castle. 20m. diameter cairn, its 3m. height accentuated by modern addition. Intermittent kerbstones.

DUN, Dùn na Nighinn, 600m. ENE of Tibertich above A816. One of the finest examples in Mid Argyll. 15m. by 12m. enclosure constructed on a rock ridge. The wall on the NW has now largely tumbled from the summit area. Elsewhere 3.5m.-thick walling remains, reaching sixteen courses on the S.

FORT, Dùn Chonallaich, 1.5km. NE of Tibertich. Irregularly walled fort on rocky summit, its interpretation confused by recent vandalism and minor structures within the enclosure. But one discovery, a small stone slab incised with a gridded gaming-board, is of a distinctive Early Historic type.

STANDING STONES, 450m. WSW of Carnasserie Castle. Two adjacent stones each *c.* 2.6m. in height.

CARRADALE

Fishing village on the E coast of Kintyre. An attractive setting and sheltered harbour have encouraged holiday growth and with it a personality change. Increasingly more suburban than rural.

KILORAN CHURCH, on s side of B879 immediately E of its junction with the main E coast road from Claonaig to Campbeltown. By *H. E. Clifford*, 1887. Three-bay nave with tapered belfry over N roadside gable and chimney over s. Twinned lancets over pointed-arch gable entrance. No longer in use.

SADDELL PARISH CHURCH, on r. bank of Carradale Water close to Dippen Bridge. Gothic Revival, *c.* 1900; skew-gabled with wheel window and lancets.

AIRDS CASTLE, 400m. s of Carradale Harbour. Scant remains of medieval stone curtain wall encompassing an elongated rocky summit.

CARRADALE HOUSE. By *David Bryce*, 1844. Entrance gable lugged by first-floor bartizans, bedroom gable splay-corbelled from the canted bay of Dining Room below, a Pinkie bartizan: Baronial, softened by traditional harl but emboldened by a vigorously Baroque doorpiece. Despite its irregularly modelled perimeter and plentifully peaked skyline, the main house has a compact square plan, gathering its public rooms around a central stair. More rambling service wing to N destroyed by fire, 1969. Rebuilding in 1970 removed the crowsteps.

CARRADALE PRIMARY SCHOOL. Monopitch classrooms by *Strathclyde Regional Council*, 1980s.

DIPPEN BRIDGE. C18 rubble bridge spanning Carradale Water in a single segmental arch.

SCHOOL AND SCHOOLHOUSE. Red sandstone block with gable-fronted ends. Built for Saddell and Skipness School Board, 1890. Disused.

FORT, Carradale Point. Perched on an elongated rocky promontory, oval fortification, 56m. by 23m., now represented by rubble band with massive lumps of vitrified stone bearing testimony to the ferocity of the destruction by fire.

CARRICK CASTLE

There is more than a castle here, but not much more. The lochside settlement straggles along the w shore of Loch Goil. The timber PIER of 1877, by engineers *Wharrie, Colledge & Brand*, was closed in 1945 but has been replaced by a Ministry of Defence concrete structure built in the 1950s. There are a few respectable late-Victorian dwellings (Groome's 'handsome villas') and more, more recent, undistinguished housing. Of the former, RHUMHOR is rich in whimsical canted bays, while CRAIGARD, towered and Baronial behind massed rhododendrons at the s end of the village, broods darkly; of the latter, DUNROAMIN (*sic*), with its fully glazed first floor, is best.

CARRICK CASTLE CHURCH. By *Honeyman & Keppie*, 1891–2. Gabled hall clad in corrugated iron; re-roofed with profiled metal sheet, 1993. Exposed king-post timbering in the E gable. Painted glass in octagonal w window, by *Fiona Hammill*, 1993: a colourfully naïve burning bush.

CARRICK CASTLE. A large oblong structure of simple prismatic beauty rising from a massive rock base which emerges from deep water. Built in neatly pinned local rubble with extensive use of imported sandstone dressings, Carrick stands sentinel on the old sea and land route from Loch Long up Loch Goil and across Hell's Glen to Loch Fyne and Inveraray. Reportedly once separated from the mainland by a deep ditch, it is now approached from the W across flat, presumably made-up, ground. Entrance is gained, however, from the E through a small barmkin, the ruinous walling of which has been irregularly defined by the rock below and contains a narrow postern gate affording sea access.

The castle probably dates from the late C14, an ascription based partly on stylistic analysis of window arches and mouldings and speculatively related to the emergence of the Campbells as the dominant family in Lochgoilhead parish. By the early C16 it was certainly in the family's hands, held by the Campbells of Ardkinglas acting as hereditary captains. At the time of the Earl of Argyll's rebellion in 1685, however, the castle was burnt out. Its subsequent history is unclear, though 'shortly before 1908', after a century or so of neglect, some clearing and repair work was carried out.

MacGibbon & Ross, who admit to 'little reliable information', speak of a 'fifteenth century keep'. Cruden, critical of the loose use of the description 'keep' but sceptical, too, about dating, observes that Carrick 'combines the elements of both hall and tower'. The plan is certainly elongated, almost a double square, 21.1m. by 11.3m. overall, though chamfered at the NW corner, while the walls rise through three storeys without corbelled interruption to a maximum height of 17m. above ground level. There is evidence of doorways at first-floor level, probably reached by timber forestairs, on each of the long sides of the building. Within the shell all internal arrangements are conjectural. The ground floor provides no indication of subdivision and, although there are vestigial signs of springing stones on W and E walls, vaulting was evidently abandoned in favour of beam and joist construction. A lobby area has been proposed for the N end of the first floor, with the remainder of the plan devoted to the main hall. A high ceiling height, 5m., and remains of what may have been corbel stones at 3m., suggest beams braced by some form of strutting or the insertion of a mezzanine gallery or loft. Sockets in the W and E walls at second-floor level point to a layout with three chambers. Vertical circulation from ground to first floor is unclear: a timber forestair seems likely but there is also foundation evidence of a small newel-stair tower, early C17(?), built in the barmkin towards the N end of the castle's E wall. Above first floor, movement was confined to two straight flight stairs cut into the 2.2m. thickness of this same E wall. Both mural stairs are entered from a single window embrasure: one, running S, reaches the SE corner of the second floor; the other, climbing N, also gives access to second floor but continues to the NE corner of the parapet walk, the battlements of which, flush with the walls below, are peppered with damaged gargoyles.

The wall openings are remarkably varied. Several, including the arches lighting the hall at first-floor level, are two-centred and moulded, some of these with hoods. A number of doors and smaller windows have triangular heads. Windows to the second floor have lintels on the wall face but, like all others, are arched across the wall thickness behind. Surprisingly, the most decorative extant ones are the small trefoil cusped openings in the N and S walls which light a sophisticated arrangement of garderobe-chambers at first- and second-floor levels.

Internal reconstruction by *Ian Begg*, 1988. A joisted first floor rests on existing scarcements. Above the Hall, the second floor is supported on struts angled out from socket holes in the E and W walls. At this level, living quarters are accommodated under a steeply pitched roof springing from the inner parapets of the E and W wallhead walks. A small 'caphouse', its ridge coincident with the new N gable, returns over the stair access at the NE corner.

HILLSIDE. Somewhat the worse for architecturally parsimonious repair, yet incongruously endearing in its Baronial bulk: a tall sandstone tenement of flats and shops facing pier and castle. Built 1877–8, by *Peter Ferguson*, mason in Glasgow, for Lieutenant-General Sir John Douglas of Glenfinart. At the centre of the main E-facing elevation is a crowstepped gable. Tall eaves dormers with scrolled pediments punctuate the second-floor attics to E and N. But the conical roofs of the two-storey bartizans have been lost.

CARSAIG

The 'West End' of Tayvallich (q.v.). Only 800m. separate the inlet of Loch a'Bhealaich on the W side of upper Loch Sween from Carsaig Bay and the Sound of Jura. *En route* some pleasant white-harled cottages, some old, some new. Just before the bay is reached, on the l., is the former manse of North Knapdale Free Church, TIGH NA LINNE, c. 1854, a two-storey, three-bay roughcast house to which canted bays, their roofs linked across the central entrance, have been added. To the r., towards the jetty, a wide-fronted, rubble, gabled HOUSE, asymmetrical in section, its dipping slated roof inset with glazed balcony; by *Diana MacLaurin*, 1983–6.

BURIAL GROUND, at the S end of Carsaig Bay. A serene D-plan plot with many simple gravestones, C18 and C19. The Campbell enclosure contains a MURAL TABLET to Archibald Campbell of Strondour †1719.

DOUNIE, 4.8km. NNE of Carsaig overlooking Sound of Jura. Three-bay gabled house with single-storey wings l. and r. Dated 1771. Much altered.

CARSKIEY

Estate w of Southend at the start of the hill road to Mull of Kintyre Lighthouse.

CARSKIEY HOUSE, Strone Glen. A two-storey harled mansion, 1904–9, in an unaggressively 'Scottish style' by *J. A. Rennison* of Paisley architects *Rennison & Scott*. The commission came through the town's prosperous thread-making Coats family; a home for Kate Coats and her husband James Boyd whose initials are carved in a panel set in the NW wall. A long crowstep-gabled house with wide central projections on each major elevation: to the NW, a forceful canted bay rising to a curvilinear chimneyed gable; to the SE garden front, a segmental bay. The interior layout is simple: a spine corridor plan with public rooms and spaces at the centre including a double-height hall. Straight stair flights flank each side of the hall, linked by a long half-landing opposite the first-floor gallery. Upper floor bedrooms face SE and are served across the corridor by a lavish number of bathrooms. Ancillary service wing to the NE contained by a quadrant wall.

In the garden are two identical octagonal DOOCOTS symmetrically placed in relation to the axis of the main house. Each has a slated pyramid roof with closed eaves beneath which are the entries and a continuous stringcourse perch. That to the E is late C18 or early C19, its companion a later twin. At the entrance to the estate is a harled piend-roofed LODGE which probably dates from the building of the 'modern mansion', *c.* 1880, referred to by Groome, and four round rubble GATEPIERS which may be a remnant of another Carskiey built in the early C19 by Colonel Malcolm McNeil, last to hold a patrimony that stretched back to the early C16.

KEREMENACH FARM, Strone Glen, 2.4km. NW of Carskiey. Elongated single-storey rubble farmhouse typical of working dwellings in early C19 Kintyre townships. Linear arrangement of house, dairy, byre and barn. Derelict.

LEPHENSTRATH BRIDGE, 1.8km. N of Keil Point. Two-span buttressed rubble crossing of the Breakerie Water, C18(?).

LEPHENSTRATH HOUSE, 900m. SSW of Lephenstrath Bridge. C18; plain, five-bay, with a wide two-storey canted bay added, C19, at the centre of the SE front. To the W, a wild single-track road, specially constructed to reach the Mull of Kintyre Lighthouse (*see* below), climbs over the mountain to the Atlantic.

MULL OF KINTYRE LIGHTHOUSE. One of four lighthouses which the Trustees for Northern Lighthouses were empowered to build by an Act of 1786 and the first in Scotland to have a reflector lantern in a purpose-built tower. Sited at the top of a remote 73m.-high cliff, its construction entailed landing men and materials at Carskiey, after which everything had to be transported by the builder, *Peter Stuart* of Campbeltown, using horses, limited to a 50kg. (1cwt) load for the difficult day's journey overland. The writer of the 1845 *Statistical Account* was sufficiently impressed to call it 'the most valuable public building in the parish'. Built 1786–8, in harled rubble to a design by architect *Robert Kay* of Edinburgh working with lighting experts *Thomas Smith* and *Ezekiel Walker*, the domed cylindrical tower, 1788, is encircled by a console-corbelled parapet-walk protected by a diamond square patterned railing in sturdy cast iron. Repairs and alterations possibly by *Robert Stevenson*, c. 1824. Original ancillary buildings *have* been replaced by KEEPER'S HOUSE on NE, 1857, and another HOUSE on SE, 1883, which combine in ungainly flat-roofed grouping. More convincing is the high rubble wall protecting the Keeper's garden which spills downhill to the cliff edge.

BALMAVICAR TOWNSHIP, 1.3km. N of Mull of Kintyre Lighthouse. Much reduced rubble remains of a village already deserted by the last quarter of the C18. Among vestiges of house-byres, outbuildings and enclosures is a small chamber surviving from a horizontal water-mill.

DUN, Borgadale Water, 3.5km. SW of Carskiey House. Small but well preserved with inner and outer wall faces almost entire. Checked entrance access on W.

FORT, Sron Uamha, 1.5km. W of Borgadale Dun. Remote situation at the southernmost end of Kintyre. Precipitous drop of 105m. falls to the shore on SW; protected by three roughly concentric stone walls to landward.

CASTLE STALKER
2km. NW of Appin

The dream redoubt: diamond-hard tower-house dominating the muddied mouth of Loch Laich from its rocky islet site on Eilean an Stalcaire. Lighthouse-like, looking W across Loch Linnhe to the hills of Morvern, it seems to guard the Appin coast. And, indeed, this was its *raison d'être* when, probably about 1540–2, it was built for the Stewarts of Appin at the order, if not at the expense, of James V following his subjugation of the Western Isles. Although the castle passed into Campbell hands in the early C17, when in 1631 its upperworks were reshaped and 'new-roofed' (*NSA*, 1845), it reverted to Stewart ownership in 1686, only to be forfeited a few years later as a result of the family's Jacobite allegiance. Garrisoned during the '45 rebellion and still occupied during the second half of the C18, by the 1840s it was roofless. In 1909, by which time the castle had returned to Stewart hands, repairs ('not amounting to restoration') were carried out, and it was only in 1965 that a serious programme of restoration was begun.

Mud-flats and shallow water suggest the possibility of a causeway, but there is none. Access is by boat from the mainland near Portnacroish across a narrow channel to a sheltered landing on the SE side of the island. A short climb leads to the barmkin, which is now entirely bereft of any evidence of its original enclosing walls except at the W corner of the tower-house where a few footings and part of the rebated jamb of a postern gate can be seen. It seems likely that this doorway was used to reach the castle's only source of drinking water, a small rock-cut pool on the NW side of the island which must have collected rain discharged from parapet drain-spouts. Entrance to the tower, which is oblong in plan and exceptionally well constructed in rubble masonry with quoins and dressings of Morvern sandstone, is through a round-arched SE door worked externally with a continuous quirked edge-roll moulding. This leads, through an inner door with a draw-bar slot, to the largest of three chambers which take up the GROUND FLOOR. In the N corner a turnpike stair rises through all four storeys. A narrow NE window opening positioned close to the E corner formerly lit this chamber but has been blocked by later work to the forestair on the NE gable. Between this window and the turnpike, accessible only from a hatch in the floor above, is a mural pit-prison with a pointed barrel-vault and garderobe. On the partition wall opposite, two doors open to two smaller chambers, lit from narrow openings in the NW gable. All three ground-floor rooms are roofed by a single barrel-vault arched from NW to SE.

While the turnpike stair communicates directly with the level above, the formal approach to the accommodation at FIRST FLOOR is by a door in the NE wall reached by means of an external forestair. At first, a wooden framework, founded upon a late C16 or early C17 stone base built against the centre of the NE wall, incorporated a drawbridge which linked to a timber forestair. But some time in the late C17 or early C18, a lower stone forestair was constructed, and a century later, during the 1909 repairs, this masonry wedge was built up to the threshold of the outer door at first-floor level. This formidably architectonic element is wholly in keeping with the sharp-arrissed bulk of the tower itself, the crisp serrated form of the long, open stair-flight echoing the skyline edge of crowstep gables above. The doorway opening off the platt at the head of the stairs has a jamb moulding somewhat similar to that at the ground-floor entry, though much weathered. Above its pointed-arch head, evidently a rebuilding of an originally semicircular arch, is a heavily framed heraldic panel which bears the now scarcely decipherable royal arms. Within there is one large apartment lit from SW and SE windows, each with splayed embrasures and bench seats, and a smaller opening in the NE wall. At the SW end of the NW wall is a large fireplace opening. Moulded corbel stones along the NW and SE walls support running beams carrying the joisted floor above. In the N corner two doors enter the turnpike, one opening to the flight from below, the other leading up, the two separated by a partition wall supported by tread stones splayed out and in at the newel.

The stair winds clockwise up to SECOND FLOOR where again there is a single chamber. This upper hall has NE and SE windows with bench seats similar to those to the floor below, in the thickness of the NW wall a windowed garderobe equipped with a vent-shaft, and at the centre of the SW wall, under an ashlar relieving arch, a large fireplace which retains a decorative jamb carved in the form of an octagonal column with scalloped capital and base. Once again corbel stones provide support for the floor above. A fireplace set towards the NE end of the SE wall must date from some previous subdivision of this accommodation.

The THIRD FLOOR comprises a gabled garret chamber with parapet walks on all four sides. At the S corner an angle-round corbelled out on four moulded courses; at the N, a small gabled cap-house rises a further storey over the turnpike stair. These arrangements, dating from the Campbell building programme of 1631 but substantially rebuilt in recent times, give to the castle that complex skyline interplay of cubic and conic geometries so much a concomitant aspect of that 'Scottish delight in sheer height' to which Nikolaus Pevsner adverted in his Rede Lectures of 1955. Garret and caphouse are the dominant pitched roofs running SW–NE between crowstepped skew gables and, though lower pitched roofs which ran parallel over the NW and SE parapet walks no longer exist, the punctuation afforded by a few gabled dormers, the intermittent rise and fall at the wallhead, and the bulging drum of the single angle round, accented by its slated cone, maintain a level of aesthetic agitation characteristic of the tower-house tradition at its best. Drain-spouts, gun-loops, pistol-holes, as well as box-machicolations positioned at the eaves directly above the two entrance doorways, all add to the visual stimulation at high level. But perhaps it is the starkly plain walls below, randomly penetrated by only a few windows, which provide that contrast of almost primitive solidity necessary to complement such elevated delights; an architectural polarity no less satisfying than that sensed when, hard and mechanical, the vertical shaft of Castle Stalker first appears out of a wide, flat expanse of mud and sea.

CASTLE SWEEN

10.1km. SW of Achnamara on the rocky E shore of Loch Sween

The ancient stronghold slumbers above sea and turf, ponderously sunk into its rock-gnarled coastal ridge. Crumbling along the skyline, its four fortress walls fall in prismatic masonry curtains scribed to the grass and rock below. The plan is simple: a massive quadrangular enclosure begun by the eponymous chieftain Suibhne at the end of the C12, continued by MacSweens in the early C13, towered at the NW corner a century later by the new Lords of Knapdale, the Stewart Earls of Menteith, and, probably some time in the C15, given a rectangular NE wing by MacNeills or MacMillans then acting as constables for the Lords of the Isles. In 1475, presumably shortly after these last major works had been completed, John, Lord of the Isles, was compelled to forfeit Knapdale and all his mainland possessions. Now a royal castle, Castle Sween passed into the charge of the Earls of Argyll. It ceased to be inhabited from the middle of the C17. Over a century

CASTLE SWEEN

ago MacGibbon and Ross found it 'a remote fortress' all but invisible beneath a luxuriant cloak of ivy. Today's visitor will find the ivy gone; he may be less delighted by the caravan castle-town that has sprung up around the fortress walls. But eight centuries on, Suibhne's castle stands still, stone-solid against time.

The approach from the E dips and then rises again towards the walls. On its elevated site the C12 enclosure occupies an area of ground roughly level except at the SW corner. The plan is not rectangular but takes the form of a distorted parallelogram; walls on the W and E are parallel but connect obliquely on the longer N and S sides. The C12 CURTAIN, upper sections of which have been given a C13 date, varies in thickness from 1.7m. to 2m., increasing at external angles and at the middle of all four sides in broad flat buttresses. The masonry is quartzite rubble, laid to courses with pinnings and bedded in lime mortar. Dressings are in grey sandstone though, since the walls have remarkably few openings and would have been harled, quoining has provided almost the only opportunity for decorative detail. Even the ruinous wallhead which reaches an average height of

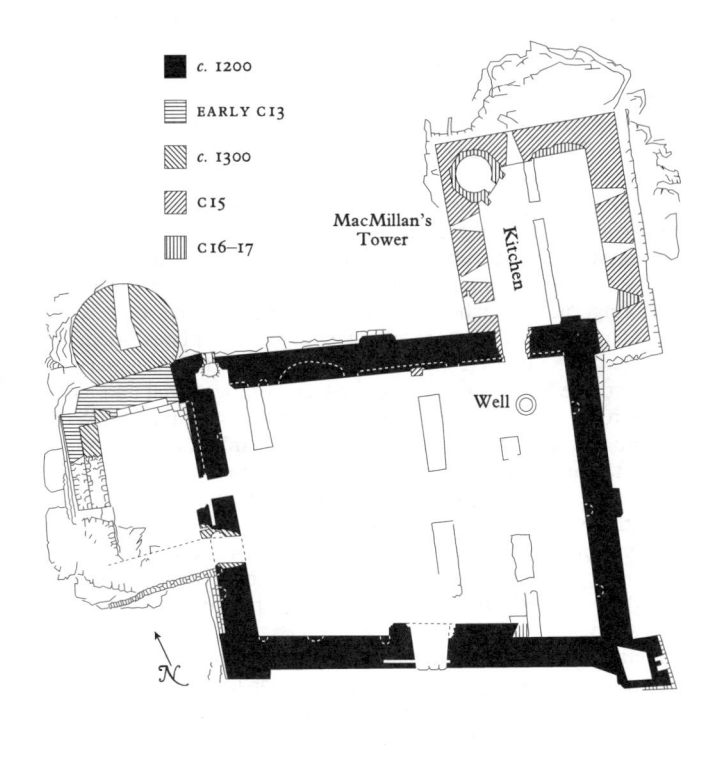

Castle Sween

c. 9m. (and considerably more on the NW where the ground falls away sharply to the shore) is without defensive articulation. A postern gate towards the N end of the W wall is little more than an elongated hole. Only in the placing and detail of the deeply shadowed portal which penetrates the central buttress on the S wall is a real sense of architectural deliberation and elaboration evident. Approached from below, this dark hole, crowned with its semicircular archway of crisply arrissed voussoirs and filling the width of the advancing buttress above, exerts an almost primitive spelaean power. Behind the arch a barrel-vaulted passage leads into the inner court. Immediately r. of this entry a long straight-flight stair, its steps now in a state of utter disintegration, takes advantage of the extra wall thickness provided by the central buttress to return over the portal to the wallhead. Later alterations, evident in the low remains of a short length of wall running N, seem to have enclosed the stair within buildings erected in the E half of the yard; only the first sandstone tread has survived intact, on the wrong side of the stub wall. At the wallhead the stair is enclosed by a short length of walling, C15, carried on the last few treads. The parapet walk itself exists intermittently some 8m. above courtyard level.

The open INNER COURT of the castle reveals no clear picture of the original arrangements. Breaking through the grass are several stretches of rubble footings, indicating the prior existence of internal ranges of building. These are predominantly located on the E side of the yard where, in the NE corner, a rock-cut well, lipped with a schist kerb, can be seen. The footings are of differing periods but, since a C13 date has been suggested for the upper walling of the castle curtain, some inference about internal building can be made. In the upper walling, at a height of *c.* 7m., a marked horizontal chase evidently intended to receive beams or wall-plates is cut on all but one inner face. Additional sockets and chases, particularly those lower down along the E end of the N wall and along the full length of the E wall, complicate speculation. What seems most likely is that while there probably was some building E from early in the C13, this must later have undergone much revision and addition. Whether any building took place on the W side of the courtyard at this early period is unclear. A short stretch of footings at the NW angle does seem related to a corner garderobe in the C12 outer wall and may be associated with a pre-existing structure linking this to courtyard and postern.

A rectangular W WING, attached to part of the outer face of the W curtain wall (where a roof raggle and floor-level chase betray its section) also dates from this second phase of building. A substantial horn of C13 building survives to the NW and, although walls have collapsed on the W and S, it appears that the extent of added accommodation was limited on the S by the position of the castle's W postern. The original gateway probably became a link to the castle yard, while a new postern was cut immediately s of the central buttress in the w wall. Initially only one storey high, the w wing was increased to three in the late C13, or perhaps at the start of the C14. At that time a tall cylindrical tower, incorporating the confined but complex geometries of superimposed mural chambers and garderobes, was built against its N face. Soaring 17.5m. above the craggy shore of the loch and lit only by a few crosslet incisions, it makes an impact out of all proportion to its unprepossessing domestic function. But there is no surviving staircase and, although the sandstone jambs of a blocked doorway at the NW corner of the w wing do incorporate a staircase newel stone and this seems a likely place for a turnpike, the nature of vertical circulation throughout the castle remains unclear.

During the C15, developments occurred both inside and outside the C12 walls. In the courtyard a w range appeared while the E range is thought to have been elaborated to two or three storeys. The resultant plan, leaving a narrow central service yard-cum-light well, could have been similar to that created at Old Castle Lachlan on Loch Fyne, *c*. 1500 (q.v.). But none of this inner building remains; perhaps construction here, unlike the later work in the MacLachlan stronghold, was predominantly in timber. The need for yet more accommodation did, however, occasion masonry work to the N where a second rectangular wing, the so-called MacMillan's Tower, juts out towards the loch. It is reached at ground- and first-floor levels through an opening in the N wall of the C12 *enceinte* close to the NE buttressed corner and doubtless thus connected with the Great Hall and other offices in the internal E range. A ceiling height of 4.5m., vestigial evidence of a wide fireplace opening on the N wall and the presence of a water inlet close to this, all support the suggestion that the whole of the ground floor was given over to kitchens. The scarcements visible along lateral walls and the division of this space by a central axial wall, now standing to a maximum height of 1.5m., indicate a C16 or early C17 intention to insert parallel barrel vaults, but it cannot be determined whether these were ever completed. The circular domed oven in the NW corner was constructed at this time. Unlike the rest of the castle, both lower and upper spaces are relatively well lit by narrow, lintelled lights with sandstone jambs, those at first-floor level on the N and E having lancet heads. All have deeply splayed reveals. Only on the outer faces of the N and S gables has wall thickness been reduced in order to permit a continuous wallhead walk.

QUARRIES at Doide, 1.9km. SSW of Castle Sween. Outcrops of green chlorite schist splitting naturally into large slabs. Used for carved crosses of the late medieval Iona and Oronsay Schools. Quarrying ceased in C19.

DUN, Dùn a'Chaisteil, 900m. S of Castle Sween. On the NW side of a rocky cliff, a circular dun 17m. in dia. has been extended at a later date by the addition of an oval defensive wall to the SW. The resultant kinked enclosure stretches 36m. along the ridge to the SSW where walling is preserved to 2m.

CLACHAIG

A hamlet of detached cottages scattered along Glen Lean between the B836 and the Little Eachaig river 3.5km. W of Holy Loch. Lades cut from the river provided power for the Clyde Powder Works, established here in the mid 1830s. Production ceased in 1876, but from 1891 to 1903 the mills re-opened to manufacture sporting powder. The remains of mills and magazines are still identifiable.

WORKERS' HOUSING, S of the road. Single-storey, white-painted, rubble cottages and terraces, some gabled, some hipped. Most of the houses date from the 1850s when the powder mills were expanded to meet the needs of the Crimean War. Across the road is the former MANAGER'S HOUSE, a five-bay cottage with a gabled porch dated 1863.

GARRACHORAN, 500m. S across the valley. Built 1771. A smart, three-bay, two-storey piended house with a pilastered doorpiece and pedimented eaves. A pointed-arch margin to the central first-floor window pushes up into the pediment.

CLACHAN

A ribbon hamlet along the W shore of Clachan Sound and across the bridge on Seil. Some sense of village focus around the inn, but increasingly suburban rather than rural to the S.

ARDENCAPLE HOUSE, 2km. W. Late C18. Harled, two-storey, laird's house, splendidly set looking SE over a watery landscape. The addition of a flat-roofed porch and some more recent window widening diminish its rude classical restraint. Turnpike stair enclosure projecting at rear under flat-topped conical roof. The original SW wing, connected by a single-storey link, has been raised for dormered first floor, c. 1970(?). The interior is much altered; a pine-and-stucco chimneypiece with a grey marble surround, originally in the first-floor drawing room, survives at ground-floor level. At the start of the curving drive, four rough round GATEPIERS carry topless urns.

ARDFAD CASTLE, 500m. ENE of Ardencaple House. Little can be seen other than a long outcrop of rock rising some 7m. above the surrounding land close to the N shore of the island. Closer inspection reveals the traces of a rubble curtain-wall, best preserved on the NE and E sides. The castle itself, a MacDougall stronghold, appears to have been a hall-house straddling the rocky site from NW to SE with a round tower at the W corner, a layout which suggests a late C16 or early C17 date.

CLACHAN BRIDGE. In context, form and texture, a bridge of the greatest beauty: empirical masonry engineering become transcendent architecture. A single segmental arch thrown 22m. across 'the Atlantic' or, more precisely, Clachan Sound. Overall the rubble structure stretches c. 95m. and rises 8.5m. above water level. Envisaged by *George Langlands* in an estate-plan of

1787, the original design was obtained from *John Stevenson* of Oban in 1790 and built by him in the following year. *Robert Mylne* may also have been consulted; circular recesses in the haunches of the arch and small pyramid-topped markers in the parapets above could be his embellishments.

OLD CLACHAN FARMHOUSE, on mainland 400m. s of Clachan Bridge. Early C19(?). Simple three-plus-two-bay front looking w over Clachan Sound. Extended to double pile on the E.

TIGH-AN-TRUISH INN, on Seil close to Clachan Bridge. C18 core. Two-house roadside inn with two porches, five eaves dormers and two canted bays l. and r. of the S porch.

CLACHAN

Clustering estate village with two churches and a few casually set four-dwelling cottage rows.

KILCALMONELL FREE CHURCH. 1878; probably by *John Burnet*. Italianate gable front unexpectedly daedal, even Oriental, in design. A pagoda-like belfry rises from heavy fretted bargeboards on bracketed eaves. Acroterion-topped porch canopy on twinned consoles over eight-panel double doors. Timberwork by *Denny Brothers*, shipbuilders in Dumbarton. Five lateral bays of round-arched windows sit on a sill-line plinth. Interior now converted to residential use.

KILCALMONELL PARISH CHURCH. Harled and slated oblong kirk built *c.* 1760 to replace an earlier church on the site. Enlarged 1828. Rearrangement, 1879, following seating plan prepared by *Charles Martin* of Campbeltown, introduced a new N entrance with a narrow porch gabled at church eaves height. Later lower extension on the W gable. All openings are squareheaded but two tall S windows frame Gothic bipartite sashes. Interior, refurnished *c.* 1900, has curved gallery on N, W and E, accessed by inside stairs on gables. – Oak pulpit, at centre S wall, backed by a split segmental pediment on consoles on narrow-shafted Roman Doric pilasters. – Art Nouveau STAINED GLASS in tall pulpit-side windows.

The church sits in a walled GRAVEYARD which contains Early Christian, medieval and post-Reformation stones. War Memorial GATEWAY by *Ebenezer James MacRae*, 1921–2. – Early Christian SLAB with carved forms of Latin cross and ring-cross linked on common stem. – Several TAPERED SLABS, C14–C16, portray sword blades, hilts and pommels and carry animal and vegetable imagery. – A later HEADSTONE commemorating Donald McGill †1757, shows a four-horse plough team in profile.

BALINAKILL Farm. C19. Plain two-storey house with porch. Adjacent building, built in rubble with brick lintelling, now converted to dwelling. Charming WALLED GARDEN.

BALINAKILL HOTEL, 500m. E of Balinakill Lodge. Mildly Baronial, two-storey-and-attic country house with many tallwindowed bays, *c.* 1870. An aggrandizement of a smaller pre-existing mansion which was demolished in the 1960s. Built by Sir William Mackinnon, co-founder of the British India Steam Navigation Company. Opulent interior. The lower block to the s, altogether plainer, replaced the earlier house in the 1989–91 restoration by *Tom Grant*.

BALINAKILL LODGE. Coarse little Scottish-style gatehouse, late C19, over-endowed with crowsteps. Low walls and railings fan out in fine quadrant sweeps flanking a four-piered gateway to the estate driveway, now severed by the A83.

BALINAKILL STEADING. Late C19, single-storey-and-loft, U-plan; main front has crowstepped façade gables l. and r. and at the 'gatehouse' centre, where a barrel-vaulted pend penetrates to the inner yard. Round arches continued in windows. Piended dormers to yard, White roughcast with sandstone dressings.

KIRKLAND. Former manse, 1827; by *Edward Stewart* of Campbeltown. Plain gabled Georgian.

RONACHAN HOUSE, 2.3km. WSW of Kilcalmonell Church. Tall, ashlar-fronted mansion, late C19, by 'Mr. *Tregellis* of London', replacing a 'plain white building at the shore' (Smith, 1868). In 1897 it was burnt down but rebuilt and enlarged by the same architect. Copper capping to a corbelled canted bay on w, and to the porch window and ogee pavilion-roofed dormer at the centre of the main façade. Inside, an attractive staircase with timber arcading and a landing neuk. At the entrance to the estate on the A83 is the gabled NORTH LODGE, C19. Square-piered porch in re-entrant of L-plan. Decorative diamond-patterned astragals. 800m. SW is a gable-fronted, courtyard STEADING, C19; attractively asymmetrical by virtue of a conically capped round tower at NW, but crushed by residential conversion.

CAIRN, Corriechrevie, E of A83, 1.7km. SW of Ronachan North Lodge. Largest example in Kintyre, 27.5m. in dia. and 5m. in height.

FORT and DUNS, Dun Skeig, ¼km. NNW of Clachan. At the summit of Dun Skeig, 143m. above West Loch Tarbert is a fort, 113m. by 36.5., encompassed by a much depleted stone wall. At its S end, an oval dun with a vitrified wall. At the N, a smaller, probably later and rather better preserved dun with the remains of a circular wall or large stone blocks and a clearly defined entrance on the NE.

CLACHAN OF GLENDARUEL

A white-walled hamlet lying between the A886 and the E bank of the River Ruel. Across the road from the inn are three three-bay rubble cottages: one, two-storeyed, is dated 1812, but its single-storey neighbours, one of which was the village smiddy, may be earlier.

CAMPBELL BURIAL ENCLOSURE, 3.3km. N. C19. Built at the top of a small but steep tree-shrouded mound. Rubble walls with sandstone coping stones. Corner urns lost. Moulded architraves to a now partially blocked SE entrance. Several mural TABLETS, C19, to Campbells of Glendaruel.

KILMODAN PARISH CHURCH. A piended T-plan kirk, built 1783, strongly symmetrical but modest in scale and almost casually sited in a well-tended grassy graveyard on the w edge of the village. It replaced an earlier elongated medieval church sited a little to the S. The walls are harled with red sandstone quoins and margins. The S front has a central pedimented projection carrying a birdcage belfry with stepped pyramid roof 26 and ball finial. Within the pediment is a blind roundel and, below a sandstone band continuing the line of the eaves-course, two glazed porthole windows cut obliquely through the wall. The plain central doorway is blocked. On each side of this frontispiece, tall round-arched windows with impost-blocks and keystones, and beyond these a double tier of square windows lighting above and below the end galleries within. An armorial panel, set in the harling at the E end of the S wall, is carved with a heraldic shield, the date 1610, and the initials S D C, for one of the church's heritors, Sir Duncan Campbell of Auchenbreck; presumably it records some building programme associated with the earlier church. Entrance through plain doors at the centre of the W and E gables, or to the N aisle through a session-house, C20, added in the NE re-entrant.

The interior is handsome and elegant, yet intimate too. Renovation in 1983 has preserved the late C18 layout and character. At the centre of the S wall the PULPIT, a tall octagonal box reached by five stairs on the r., is possibly original; concealing the original S door, the pilastered back, which carries a pediment block with plain acroteria and urn finial, may be C19. Opposite, in the stem of the T-plan, is the N gallery, supported on end pilasters fluted like those behind the pulpit, a detail appearing again on the single columns under the W and E galleries. All three, which served as lairds' lofts for different Campbell families (Glendaruel (N), Ormidale (W), and Southhall (E)) are reached by corner stairs which begin as stone treads but after a few steps continue in timber. Gallery fronts are panelled below a dentilled cyma recta cornice. The ceiling is flat but pierced at the centre by a tapering octagon rising to a rooflight, a simpler 1980s version of an earlier cupola. – Several commemorative MURAL TABLETS, erected early C20, all plain Neoclassical marble panels. One, with a raised bronze inscription in a lugged and moulded marble frame, recalls three generations of the Maclaurin family, including John Maclaurin †1754, 'the most profound and eloquent Scottish theologian of the 18th century'. – Adjacent N, the MANSE, 1852–3.

A small, harled rubble enclosure, lying a short distance SW of the church, was roofed with a slated pyramid and adapted as a lapidarium in 1970. It antedates the church and may have been built as a MAUSOLEUM by the Campbells of Auchenbreck. Two ball finials lie on the ground flanking the E doorway. – Within are eleven medieval stones, ten of them TAPERED SLABS of Loch Awe school provenance, C14–C15. Several bear the customary sword motifs, plant and animal forms, and interlacing, but there are also two with the carved figures of an armed warrior, one with a praying priest, and one showing a woman with her rosary. – Post-Reformation stones in the walled CHURCHYARD include two with C17 inscriptions and dates. Among a number of C18 HEADSTONES is one commemorating a Greenock cooper, Daniel Black †1778; it bears the relief carving of a shield on which lie dividers and adze and around which is the encircling motto WOOD ROUND WOOD BINDS. Another, marking the grave of a 'taylor', Archibald Weir †1781, and his wife, Janet MacFarlane †1759, carries a Gaelic inscription.

Former ST SOPHIA'S CHAPEL (R.C.), 2.6km. N. By *W. Hunter McNab* of *Leiper & McNab*, 1912; for William Harrison Cripps, who built it for his second wife. Now a dwelling: Chapel Cottage. Small but muscular Gothic chapel in a railed hillside graveyard. Pointed-arch porches N and S, heavy buttressing, arched belfry on W gable, and a half-octagon apsidal E end. Below this last, a lower doorway, set under a block-crocketed ogee arch, gives access to crypt. W gable panel inscription records 'St Sofia / W & S H C / A 1912 D'. – The interior retains its arch-braced timber roof and STAINED GLASS depicting Christ PASTOR BONUS, the Annunciation and two angels playing musical instruments.

BEALACHANDRAIN BRIDGE, 1km. S. Built 1808. Designed by *Thomas Telford* and constructed entirely of rubble masonry by the contractor *James Patterson* to take the Otter Ferry road across the River Ruel. In an overall length of 29m. there are two segmental arches, each spanning 9.9m. and resting on a central pier with rounded, conic-topped cutwaters.

BEALACHANDRAIN FARM, 1.2km. SSW. Archetypal, three-bay, two-storey farmhouse of whitewashed rubble, *c.* 1800. At the rear, enclosing a cobbled court, is a U-plan STEADING, the N range of which abuts the N end of the farmhouse's W wall.

GATEWAY, Glendaruel Park, 2.4km. N. Early C19(?). Crenellated rubble screen in which a wide pointed-arch portal is flanked by similar narrower openings. Blind oculi and 'niches' in spandrel zones.

GLENDARUEL BRIDGE. River Ruel crossing on N edge of Clachan village. C18(?). Two segmental arches with faceted cutwater piers. Rubble with rough slab cope to parapet. Much repaired; steel tie bars.

GLENDARUEL HOUSE, 2.8km. N. The large mansion, 1900–3, which *William Leiper* built in his Kinlochmoidart/Dalmore (q.v.) idiom, necessarily elongated to absorb an earlier house, was burned down in 1970. But roughcast ESTATE BUILDINGS remain, variously converted to support the caravan park which now spreads across the site of the big house. The STABLES, which appear to be a re-modelling by Leiper of earlier, possibly C18, buildings associated with the first Glendaruel House of 1762, have lost their central octagonal doocot turret, but gabled flanking wings survive, defining the limits of a pleasant U-shaped court. Pedimented and piended gables, segmental-arch cart entries and shaped eaves spars add detail charm. Linked to the N are 'The New Model Buildings' of the HOME FARM, 1901–3, in a similar white-walled rural idiom. Derelict WALLED GARDEN. Across the road, also by *Leiper*, the two-storeyed, roughcast WATERMILL, 200m. s, has a frontal turnpike tower with a conical slated roof, a rounded N corner and some hipped-roofed eaves dormers. On the hillside, the LAUNDRY cottage, again by *Leiper*.

GLENDARUEL HOTEL. A simple three-bay inn, early C19(?), elaborated into a black-and-white gabled hotel by *William Leiper*, 1903, with a short N wing and, on the roadside E front, a two-storey, tile-hung canted bay linked to a timber-framed porch. Further extended s, 1990–1, by *J. G. Lindsay Pate Associates* and *Philip Spence Associates*. Downhill to the w are the former STABLES which originally catered for sixteen horses and eight carriages but are now converted to a workshop and dwelling. Comprehensively roughcast and much altered by new openings, they retain their roofline, two segmentally arched doorways and, below the eaves, an armorial device with the feathered motto ICH DIEN.

STEADING, in the village between hotel and church. Symmetrical, one-and-a-half-storey, harled rubble block with gabled end projections, early C19(?). Adapted to semi-detached residential use. At the rear, four broad gableted dormers stand off the eaves.

CLADICH 0921

Scattered hamlet where the B840 dips to cross Cladich River s of its debouch into Loch Awe. Once a weaving village making garters and hose for Highland dress.

CLADICH PARISH CHURCH, 1.9km. NE, near Inistrynich. Undemonstrative 1896 remodelling of the 'paltry' church of 1773, built to replace the medieval kirk on Inishail and already repaired in 1845. Gable-ended oblong with four square-headed windows each side. Blind porthole in the sw gable. Two louvred ventilation peaks in the SE roof slope. Boarded-up and shorn of its 1845 pyramid-topped bellcote, now removed to a nearby garden.

OLD PARISH CHURCH, Inishail, 2.3km. N. Island site with ancient ecclesiastical lineage. The earliest stone church was probably C13, though the existing elongated oblong, surviving as footings and slightly higher w end walls, is of later medieval origin. It was abandoned in 1736. – Within the ruin or in the BURIAL GROUND are a number of tapered SLABS, C14–C16, several identifiable as Loch Awe school, showing men-at-arms, swords, plant scrolls, etc. – There are two carved TOMB-CHEST panels, *c*. 1500–60, and an ALTAR FRONTAL, also C16, with a crucifix flanked by robed figures and, l. and r. beyond these, armed warriors. – A single re-erected CROSS SLAB, 1.64m. high, is Early Christian: on both faces a carved cross emphasized by a raised edge moulding curved around circular bossed recesses in all four armpits.

ACHLIAN, 3.3km. NE. Harled hillside house, standard three bays but with wider than usual solid flanks. Described in 1811 as 'lately built'. Flanking the doorpiece with a cornice on consoles at the centre of the NW front are three-light windows with narrow side-lights. Curved rear projection rising above the first-floor eaves contains a stair.

CLADICH BRIDGE COTTAGES. Two three-bay houses gable-to-gable E of Cladich Bridge. The lower house with gabled eaves dormers is the former Cladich Inn, built 1792.

CLADICH STEADING. Late C19. Open U-court rubble farm, walled and gated to road. Piended W and E wings have continuous ridge ventilation. Farmhouse at E end of rear block.

MONUMENT, 3km. S on the skyline above the A819. By *Colin Sinclair*. Erected by An Comunn Gaidhealach, 1935, as a memorial to the novelist Neil Munro (1863–1930). Tall obelisk cairn of rubble boulders, its profile subtly tapering with entasis. Inset at the top is a carved stone panel like a solid dormer with a pointed-arch pediment; a Celtic book shrine, it bears a cross and the Gaelic words SAR LITREACHAS.

CHAMBERED CAIRN, 500m. NE of Cladich Bridge, uphill from junction of B840 with A819. Oval cairn much reduced with open burial-chamber visible towards NE.

DUN, Tom a'Chaisteil, 1.8km. ENE of Achlian. Well-preserved circular dun, 11m. in dia., sited on a rocky knoll more favoured for all-round observation than defence. Almost entire lowest courses visible on outer face.

CLAONAIG

T-junction hamlet located where the E coast route from Tarbert to Campbeltown meets the road from Skipness. Ferry connection to Arran 800m. SE.

CLAONAIG PARISH CHURCH. Harled skew-gabled oblong, early C19, with three bifurcated pointed-arch windows each side and similar but smaller window in E gable over door. Birdcage bell-cote with ball finial over W gable; ball finial only on E. Lower vestry addition at W. Interior re-cast 1892; E gallery survives, but church no longer in ecclesiastical use.

GLENREASDELL MAINS, 1.9km. NNW of Claonaig Church. White, two-storey, rubble-built, gabled farm approached through two squat gatepiers.

CHAMBERED CAIRN, Glenreasdell Mains. Grass covered mound, *c.* 20m. in dia., with two roofless burial-chambers near centre.

CLYNDER

Hill- and shore-side villas on the W side of Gare Loch. Among the earliest is GARELOCH HOUSE, 1817, symmetrical with an eaves cornice under piended roof. STROUL LODGE, *c.* 1830, is inflated by two-storey bows l. and r. of a blocky porch; crenellated eaves and skews, hood mouldings and a pointed-arch window in the porch add Gothick seasoning. GLENGAIR, *c.* 1830, has mullion-

and-transom windows. More suited to Upper Helensburgh, ARDCHOILLE, 1900–2, by *William Leiper*, is in grandly rambling Arts and Crafts style. At the hamlet of Rahane, N along the coastal road, AIKENSHAW COTTAGES and the quirkily converted, roughcast MILL are early C19 vernacular survivors. AIKENSHAW HOUSE, mid C19, is bargeboarded Gothic.

COLGRAIN

3230

In 1946 the historic estate of Colgrain was sold by auction in twenty-seven lots. Lying mostly in the parish of Cardross, including part of Craigendoran and extending as far W as the West Highland Railway on the E boundary of Helensburgh, the chief attraction of the 2,000-acre sale was the mansion of CAMIS ESKAN, complete with walled garden, home farm, sawmill, gasometer, ice house, doocot and lodges. Nowadays, *Baron Bercott and Associates*' concrete-panelled HERMITAGE ACADEMY, 1966, is more likely to catch the eye than either of the surviving lodges, although the WEST LODGE, probably *David Hamilton*, 1840, is svelte and shallow-roofed, with acorn-fashioned finials.

CAMIS ESKAN. The land belonged for nearly 500 years to the Dennistoun family, who in 1648 built the mansion house now incorporated into the rear of the existing building. A marriage lintel located at ground level on the E façade commemorates the construction. In 1836 ownership passed to Colin Campbell of Breadalbane who in 1840 employed *David Hamilton* to remodel the house. Further substantial alterations were carried out in 1915 by *A. N. Paterson*. The house was used briefly after World War II as a tuberculosis sanatorium and geriatric hospital, and was divided into luxury apartments in 1979.

The principal elevation shows clearly the work of the architects involved. Paterson's remodelling is in large part confined to a two-storey, three-bay symmetrical block incorporating the main entrance. There is a shallow canted bay centre with a balustraded parapet, strapwork quoins and faceted roof. A deep, bowed ashlar portico is advanced at ground level with, on either side, broad single-storey bays with punchy Gibbsian surrounds, cast-iron parapets and flanking stone urns. Above each bay, three windows in a Venetian arrangement. Hamilton's three-bay, three-storey block to outer l. is altogether simpler: symmetrical, harled with ashlar architraves and with an eaves cornice stepped over upper-floor windows. – INTERIOR. Despite subdivision, the building retains evidence of the decorative schemes dating from 1840 and 1915. The main hall has wooden wainscot panelling and Tudor-arched ashlar chimneypieces from the later remodelling. There is some delicate plasterwork in the upper rooms and a fine stair with barley-sugar balusters. – COACH HOUSE. The former service block is located N. Formerly a U-plan court opening E, it is stuccoed with ashlar margins. The main façade has a triangular pedimented archway centre, now partially blocked as part of its conversion to housing. –

HOME FARM. Some distance N of the main house, a group of stone farm buildings unified by a remarkable two-storey arched pend whose gables are surmounted by ashlar stalks and ball finials. – WALLED GARDEN. Late C18 or early C19 rectangular-plan rubble-walled garden s of house. Remains of its boiler mechanism and lean-to glasshouses can be seen. To the E is a two-stage, octagonal-plan roofless DOOCOT, late C18, with a cavetto cornice and round-headed arcaded parapet. Above the doorway is a tall, round-headed window with keystone and impost blocks, allowing light into an interior still complete with stone nesting boxes.

Although the house and farms retain attractively pastoral policies, the land on either side of the A814 into Helensburgh has been extensively developed for housing. DRUMFORK HOUSE, 1748, is the only other building of any real antiquity in the area. Located on what was once the ancient drove road from Loch Lomondside to Drumfork Ferry (from where cattle were shipped to Greenock), it is a two-storey, three-bay rectangular-plan house in harled and painted rubble, with painted ashlar margins and a simple wooden porch. In this form it maintains a dignified silence in its overcrowded surroundings.

COLINTRAIVE

0374

An attenuated village with 'a number of pretty villas' (Groome, 1882) intermittently sited along the E shore of the Kyles of Bute s of Loch Riddon. Ferry crossing to Rhubodach on Bute. The earliest village buildings, which included a smithy, inn and corn-mill, have been demolished. Their existence is recalled by a single rectangular stone (perhaps a lintel) carved with the relief images of a hammer and horseshoe and the date 1808, now built into the s wall of the Community Hall, 1960, 250m. E of the pier.

KILMODAN AND COLINTRAIVE CHURCH, 1.7km. SE of pier. Dated 1840. The white-painted, gabled front stands above its white-painted gatepiers and railings looking SW across the Kyles of Bute. Dressed sandstone highlights the gabled pointed-arch entrance, its flanking lancets and a tall arched belfry made taller by a superimposed obelisk finial. Within, painted pews are gated on each side of a central aisle. Broad, half-octagon, pan-elled pulpit. Above a cornice, a boarded coomb ceiling. Lancet windows, three on each side, have double-hung sashes with Gothic glazing bars. – STAINED GLASS in the two SW lancets commemorates those 'men of Colintraive who fell 1914–18' including the donor, Matthew A. MacFeat. Both St Andrew in blue and a second red-cloaked saint carrying sword and spear are depicted; by *William Meikle & Sons*. – On the NE gable wall, three memorial TABLETS, all in white marble: a rectangular panel, with a pediment-shaped head and corner upstands bearing armorials, to Captain Duncan Campbell †1915; a vertical ellipse in memory of Revd Alexander McGilp, minister until 1931; and a plain plaque again recalling local men who died in the Great War. – Over the entrance door, a more elaborated mural TABLET with a white marble sarcophagus sits against a shaped back panel of grey marble. It honours the church's benefactress, Janet Campbell †1840, the daughter of the Glasgow merchant, Kirkman Finlay, and wife of the local laird, John Campbell of South Hall.

CAOL RUADH, 1.8km. NW of the pier. Late C19(?). Asymmetrical red brick pile edged with sandstone dressings. Canted bays and oriels with mullion and transom windows. Ungainly pretension made worse by flat-roofed, brown brick extensions, 1960s. Terraced lawns fall to the shore and a boarded-up brick boathouse. At the road, red brick GATEPIERS with stone cornices and scrolled ball finials. Now a residential education centre.

FAOILINN. 1908. Harled gabled villa with red-tiled roofs and arcade veranda.

THE OLD MANSE. Built *c.* 1900(?). Hipped-roofed rubble block with Lorimeresque eaves dormers at first floor. Advancing off-centre, a round-cornered crowstep gable with corniced entrance l. and tall landing window r.

SOUTH HALL FARM, 3.8km. SE of pier. Late C18(?). Former Court of Offices of the demolished South Hall House. A bow-fronted screen wall originally linked two gabled wings, though only the W remains. Central round-arch portal also castellated, but higher and surmounted by a bellcote.

STRONE TOWNSHIP, 800m. ESE of South Hall Farm. Depleted drystone remains of a number of small structures lying N–S against the slope of the hillside. Masonry corners both square and round. Abandoned at the end of the C18.

CONNEL

9134

Originally a ferry point for travellers crossing the narrow mouth of Loch Etive. In 1903 a rail bridge carrying the Callander & Oban Railway crossed the Falls of Lora. Ten years later, under threat of a new chain ferry, it was adapted to take motor vehicles too. In 1966 the bridge was converted to road traffic only. On the S side of the loch the village gathers itself around Lustragan Burn where a few buildings reach three storeys. Suburban North Connel has no such focus.

CHURCH AND BURIAL GROUND, Kilmaronaig, 2.25km. E of St Oran's Church. Turf-covered remains of buildings and enclosures which may be ecclesiastical in origin and have been associated with St Ronan or St Cronoc. Dating is uncertain and a C17 secular provenance has also been proposed.

ST ORAN'S CHURCH. Built 1887–8. Gable-ended and cruciform plan, crowned with a square tower over the crossing. Both architectural form and dedication support the belief that the architect, *David Mackintosh* of Oban, drew inspiration from the buildings of Iona (q.v.). Early Gothic tracery to transept and chancel windows. Hooded square tower windows contain four circled quatrefoils. Ironwork finials on the gables. The interior maintains the same square-snecked granite rubble walling. Sandstone is used for window embrasures and the wide pointed arches on which the four walls of the crossing rise to a flat pine-boarded ceiling. Pointed-arch-braced trusses in nave and chancel dip to corbel stones below the wallhead. – The furnishings are unexceptional, but the church is rich in STAINED GLASS. – Sanctuary, three-light s window depicts The Good Samaritan, The Good Shepherd and Jesus blessing the children; circular window below the apex of the arch may illustrate St Oran, a cousin of St Columba, landing on Iona. Tower, s windows: Ruth and St Oran. All *c.* 1925. – Chancel, E side: two pairs of small pointed-arch windows by *Roland Mitton*, 1983, symbolize the four seasons; each design of natural and abstract motifs multi-hued, but given an appropriate colour emphasis (green, orange-red, brown, blue). – Transept windows by *Gordon Webster* with leadwork by *Neil Hutchison*, 1974: w, the Ascension, and, E, the Women of the Bible; both, but particularly the w, predominantly blue. Nave E windows, *c.* 1900, show Christ as King of Kings and Alpha and Omega. W side, closest to the transept, another window by *Gordon Webster*, 1973, St Oran, a gaunt-faced figure in the artist's typical manner; next, again St Oran with Iona Abbey, installed 1935. NW, opposite the entrance porch, the best of all, a powerful evocation of harvest: ripening grain and blue cornflowers under a stunningly hot sun by *Christian Shaw*, 1988.

CONNEL FREE CHURCH. Modest, four-bay, granite-and-sandstone Gothic with E apse vestry, 1893. Pepper-pot vent on ridge. Interior gutted and converted to hall, 1934. Diagonally boarded ceiling.

Former ST MARY THE VIRGIN (Episcopal). 1903. Corrugated-iron shed with half-timber aspirations. Openings have moulded hoods with shaped pelmet facings. Now converted to a shop: The Antiquarium.

ACHALEVEN PRIMARY SCHOOL. Built *c.* 1900. Small, rubble school and schoolhouse. Roll moulded lintels.

ACHNACLOICH (formerly Stonefield), 4km. E. Baronial mansion in rough-faced rubble; dated 1885. By *John Starforth*. Castellated, round-cornered, square entrance tower dominates a wide-spreading s front. Pedimented eaves dormers with thistle and rose finials, Pinkie bartizan at sw corner, canted bays corbelled to crowstepped gables.

CONNEL BRIDGE. Spectacular engineering architecture crossing Loch Etive, 1898–1903; built, originally for road and rail transport, for the Callander & Oban Railway by the Arrol Bridge & Roofing Co. Ltd. Engineers *Sir John Wolfe Barry* and *John Foremans* in collaboration with *H. M. Brunel* and *E. Crutwell*. With a span of 152.5m. this is the second largest cantilevered steel bridge in Britain (after the Forth Road Bridge). Approaches have three round-arch spans in masonry.

DUNFUINARY, 1.2km. E of Connel Bridge, on a rocky knoll above the s shore of Loch Etive. Late C19 Baronial mansion: crow-steps, semicircular pediments to eaves dormers and a cone-roofed NW turret.

FALLS OF LORA HOTEL. Gable-ended and gable-fronted pile, built 1888, in granite and sandstone. Central entrance tower with steep pyramid roof. Two square bays splayed back to canted bays at first floor. Materials, ironwork finials and date of erection all similar to St Oran's Church. Restored after a fire, 1911, by *James G. Falconer* of Oban.

LOCHNELL ARMS HOTEL, North Connel. Three-bay ferry inn, late c18, looking s over Falls of Lora. Many additions, best of which is a glazed-gable 'conservatory' dining room on w, by John Wilson, 1991.

NEW VILLAGE HALL. By *Crerar & Partners*, 1994–5. Wide pitched roof with hipped gables. Lower w wing has half octagon roof over splayed end walls and a stained timber gablet over s entrance.

OSSIAN RETIREMENT HOME, North Connel. Built as a hotel on the site of a war-time communications building and later converted to retirement home by *Crerar & Partners*. Roughcast with cedar-boarded window slots; timber beams cantilever from flat-roofed single-storey lounge.

COULPORT

Used as a military research and training establishment since the 1930s, Coulport is now in large part dominated by the Royal Naval Armaments Depot, established in the mid 1960s in the shadow of the Garelochhead Forest. Two significant buildings were lost to the aluminium anonymity of offices and warehousing. These were COULPORT HOUSE, an Italianate design by *James Boucher* of c. 1860 for engineer, botanist and photographer John Kibble, and Boucher's own Swiss-chalet-style summer residence from the same period. By great good fortune, some years before his death Kibble offered his lovely glass-and-iron conservatory to Glasgow's Botanic Gardens. Towed upriver to its present home in 1872, where it was re-erected in enlarged form (complete with Kibble's collection of classical statues), it escaped the ultimate ignominy of destruction which befell the house and its neighbouring villas.

Former PEATON CHURCH, Rosneath Road, 1870, on the road s out of Coulport, *en route* to Ardpeaton. A corrugated-iron kirk, originally opened for four months every summer to provide holidaymakers with a place of worship. Steeple and bell have been dismantled, and the rose window on the w front sheeted over, but the lancet windows to church and timber porch remain, as does the picturesque former PEATON SCHOOL on the adjoining feu. Closed in 1991.

BARBOUR CEMETERY, Barbour Road. An early c20 graveyard on an elevated site with breathtaking views N and W of Loch Long and Ardentinny. Created for families living on the peninsula who had no right of burial in Rosneath graveyard, the layout is designed as a series of steeply sloping paths – now thick with rhododendron – at the centre of which is a roughly oval plateau on which are the principal monuments. – GATEPIERS. Large drum piers of quartz with ashlar bases and neck rings and rock toppings. – MONUMENTS. A range of Celtic crosses (one with bronze relief) and neo-classical designs. Best are a tall Gothic monument with crocketed detail, a birdcage-like cap and cross-finial to Sir Charles Cayzer (†1900) by *J. and G. Mossman*, and an early C20 classical aedicular monument to William Robertson M.D. (†1906), by the same sculptors. Also notable is a 1930s geometric gravestone and enclosure to the Dunlop family.

Bisecting the Rosneath peninsula is Peaton Road. Past the curved gable end of a roadside barn not far from the shore is the harled and limewashed PEATON HOUSE, early C19. A good, two-storey, three-bay laird's house with piend-roofed slate-hung dormers l. and r. with a tiny triangular attic light between.

COUR

COUR HOUSE, 10km. S of Claonaig overlooking Kilbrannan Sound. Isolated and picturesque, locked into the landscape above the sea, an astonishing country house built for the Nickerson family by *Oliver Hill*, 1921–2. The lingering influence of late C19 Lutyens is unmistakable: the vigorous massing of textured masonry walls, terraces and stair flights spilling into the landscape, the great roof, allusions to Elizabethan forms, perhaps

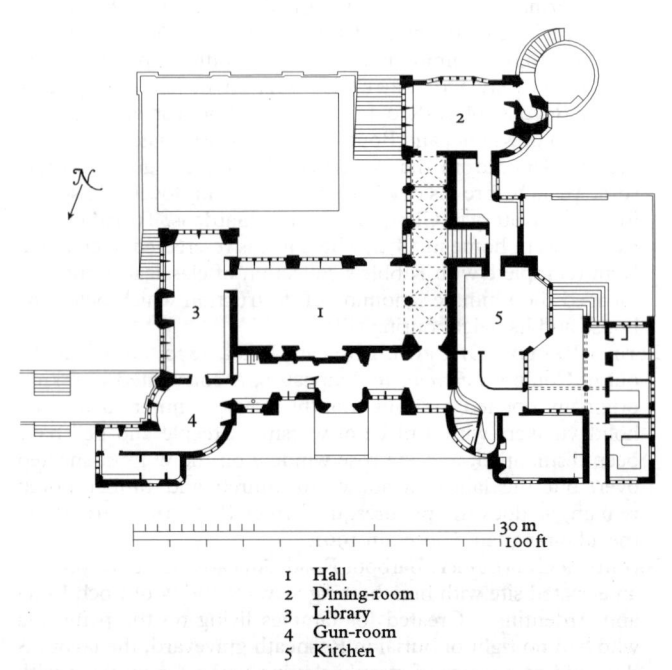

1 Hall
2 Dining-room
3 Library
4 Gun-room
5 Kitchen

Cour House. Plan of the ground floor

the plan. There is a stone-solid Scottishness, too, in chimney-buttressed drums swelling out like bastions at the NW and NE corners of the house, each with its bulging bee-hive of a roof, bell-cast in profile not unlike Lorimer's Dunderave or Ardkinglas (q.v.). Yet the house has a strong horizontality, especially evident in the uninterrupted eaves of the NW entrance elevation, and something 'streamlined in its curving roofs and forms' (Richardson, 1983) which, for all Hill is here so much in thrall to an Arts and Crafts past, points ahead to the Modernism he espoused in the 1930s.

Built of grey-green whin quarried on the site, Cour seems to grow out of the natural landscape. To the NW it is two-storeyed, the deep round-arched reveals of the entrance doorway set midway between those bulbous, ogee-roofed drums which project at each end of the broad façade. Behind the SW drum, beyond which servants' quarters spread out under a lower, dormered roof, the SE wing of the house's L-plan falls a full storey height down the hillside, bayed and glazed like a medieval hall, to terminate in the curving mass of the third corner drum. Overall, the height of the roof ridge remains consistent, exposing vast planes of slating brought not from Argyll but from the Isle of Purbeck. Windows are metal casements set in small arched openings, grouped and sometimes tiered in response to the lighting needs of the plan. In an interior memorable for its generosity of space, floors, doors and solid framed ceilings are of Hereford oak. Nearby is the POWER HOUSE, an external stair curving round its ovoid buttressed plan to the upper floor. Regrettably, its tiled roof, shown as a subtly swelling breast-like dome in Hill's drawings, was never constructed. In the harled PLOUGHMAN'S COTTAGE, Hill repeats the two-light, stone-gabled dormers of the main house.

COVE

The steamship pier at Cove was opened to traffic in 1852, constructed by developers *John McElroy* and *Thomas Forgan* with the express purpose of attracting feuars to the barely populated W side of the Rosneath peninsula. The setting for their speculative venture remains compelling – a gently curving shoreline, washed by the waters of Loch Long, where a narrow quartz and boulder beach is temporarily civilized by the presence of a grassy plain. This gives way to a cliff whose starkness is somewhat softened by greenery and from where commanding views of the Argyll Forests and Arran demanded that the most exclusive of the promontory's marine mansions be located along its length. Indeed, the success of the enterprise can be measured by its architectural quality: the houses that make up the settlement represent a unique collection of mid-C19 villas and grand summer residences, most with their large gardens and ancillary buildings intact. The pier has now gone, but the shore road is scarcely wider than when first laid down in 1848, and the area retains an exclusivity which owes much to the consistent excellence of its domestic architecture.

DESCRIPTION

Forgan and McElroy both employed *Alexander Thomson* to design the first houses. McElroy – a mason and railway contractor, who became the area's first Provost – purchased a sizeable piece of ground on the outskirts of Kilcreggan. The exact extent of Thomson's involvement in the subsequent development is by no means certain: Blackie's *Villa and Cottage Architecture*, published in 1868, confirmed him as author of CRAIG AILEY, but this villa is so uncharacteristic of his later work that it is reasonable to deduce that some of the more unusual of the other houses are his also. Two of these may be KIRKLEA and GLEN EDEN, both close to the BURGH HALL & READING ROOM (see Craigrownie). The first is a slim, two-storey, asymmetrical villa with unconventional entrance front, built mid 1850s. This has an advanced outer l. gable shrouded by steeply pitched two-tier timber bargeboards which terminate in a shallow gablet. There is a square projecting bay with battered base course at ground floor and a cast-iron balcony providing enclosure to a canted, bipartite bedroom window. A bracketed stringcourse above which the balcony projects is returned on to the side walls and used to delineate narrow blind recessed panels. This device recurs on the exotic GLEN EDEN, 1856, a Romanesque whimsy set in woodland garden. The main block is L-shaped with a square, single-storey porch on the re-entrant angle. The shallow roof has segmental-headed canopied bargeboards, supported by sandstone triglyph brackets. The principal façade has a shallow projecting bay with narrow arched windows and a stone bracketed piend-and-platformed slate roof. A small cast-iron window guard gives protection to a first-floor arcade of narrow, round-headed tripartite windows with a whinstone relieving arch arranged above. A grotesque finial which might have confirmed the identity of the architect survives only in fuzzy period photographs. The simple entrance front, however, hints that the designer might have indeed been Thomson. A polygonal-headed door is set into a round-headed opening, the inspiration for which is likely to have been the illustration of a section through a tomb near the Pyramids, published in Fergusson's *Illustrated Handbook of Architecture* (1855). Alongside, lighting the staircase, an oculus with etched glass and, to the basement below, a bipartite round-headed window set into a pointed-arch rusticated surround. The rear wall, harled with bull-faced quoins, features a full-height central bowed bay. – INTERIOR. A surprisingly awkward hall provides access to a series of gracious, richly decorated public rooms and a cantilevered stone stair with cast-iron balusters. Ceiling rosettes are plaster replicas of the terracotta' wreath-like balustrading to the entrance porch. Above the panelled doors, wreath and lyre moulding which is repeated in other houses commissioned by McElroy. – BOUNDARY WALL and

GATEPIERS. The whinstone garden wall along ROSNEATH ROAD is topped with big blocks of local quartz, and is interrupted at the entrance drive by two incredible quartz and ashlar piers, broad with sandstone round-headed niches and pedimented blocking courses with raised flat caps and left-as-found boulder finials. To the S, a cast-iron mile sign is set into the wall.

SOUTH AILEY ROAD leads to the first of the mansions built on high ground. Of *Campbell Douglas*'s 1859 Baronial design for HARTFIELD HOUSE only the gatepiers and boundary walls survive, although these are exceptional. The wall comprises a low plinth of stugged, squared and snecked sandstone, with hefty cast-iron railings completing the gaps between wide stone dies. The piers are Egypto-classical with slender nookshafts in filleted panels at the corners. Three of the four retain their needle obelisk caps. On the other side of the road, the entrance to CRAIGROWNIE CASTLE, *c.* 1854, attributed to *Alexander Thomson*. The Baronial castle core, principally two- and three-storeyed, has been much extended and elongated since initial construction. Sited on ground falling dramatically W, the garden front has additional basement levels whose buttresses are extruded out of the quartz and boulder cliff-face. There are two large, canted, parapeted oriel windows which give depth to this gently receding, thrice-gabled seaward face. Central to the composition is a three-stage tower with narrow blind windows and a deeply crenellated parapet on corbelling. – INTERIOR. Little was left following conversion of the house in 1958 for use as the Stewart Home for the Mentally Handicapped, since which time it has been restored as a family home. – BOUNDARY WALL and GATEPIERS. Beginning at the entrance to the house, moving downhill and terminating some distance along Rosneath Road, a whinstone wall, pierced at regular intervals by quadripartite trabeated openings framed in bull-faced masonry with cast-iron cruciform infills. At the corner with South Ailey Road, a Tudor-arched pedestrian gate is marked by a tall, square, rusticated pier with blind arrowslit and square cap.

Further N on South Ailey Road, the ITALIAN VILLA, now known as CRAIG AILEY, erected *c.* 1852 by John McElroy to designs by *Alexander Thomson*. This diminutive villa in the Lombardic style provided the inspiration for many of the subsequent buildings on the western shore of the peninsula. Two-storeyed with a three-stage tower and single-storey scullery wing NW, the house is raised up on a deep, battered base of masonry set on end. This creates an immediate alliance with the crag on which it sits, anchoring it to its exposed site, an illusion further strengthened by the shallow pitch of the Westmorland slate roofs and the flatness of the pyramidal cap to the belvedere. The entrance porch and tower are located on the re-entrant angle of the L-shaped plan, the door facing SE and thereby downwind. The single-storey porch is piend-roofed with a round-arched arcade of seven narrow lights with colonnette mullions on the SW return. The remainder of the entrance front is relatively conventional, although the tower has a stylized machicolated corbel course and three small horizontal windows below the eaves. On the garden front, however, the drawing-room bow window projects by more than a semicircle on its splayed, striated podium, and with patent rolled plate glass used to maintain the integrity of the curve. Above its projecting, bracketed roof, a single round-arched window lights the principal bedroom. Much of the ornament is missing, fallen victim to extreme exposure. This includes cast-iron finials, terracotta chimney cans, the antefixae on the oriel window, and acroteria on gable ends. Nor is the building quite as illustrated in Blackie's *Villa and Cottage Architecture*, but it is important still for its contribution to the architectural language of the lochside, and its place in the development of the architect's domestic work. – INTERIOR. The layout is economic, as befits a holiday residence. A narrow hall and stair occupy the bottom of the tower with a small, webbed, leaded oculus lighting the upper landing. The belvedere – a former smoking room – is accessed by stepladder. In common with Glen Eden, internal doors are typified by segmental-headed openings and wreath and lyre moulding. – GATEPIERS. The staircase tower is reproduced in miniature as two gateposts to the vehicular entrance: square, rusticated piers with round-headed recessed panels inlaid with quartz pebbles, topped by cubes on stylized corbels with blind quartz squares and low pyramidal caps with ashlar domed finials. The pedestrian entrance l. has a columnar post of quartz chippings with a sandstone fluted neck and domed cap. On either side of the ensemble, a whinstone wall with quartz cope and single oval openings.

Returning to the waterfront and proceeding N, the boundary walling is interrupted first by the portly conch-like gatepiers of CRAIGROWNIE COTTAGE, 1837. Two whipped-cream spirals of ashlar spilling over quartz plinths frame the much recast exterior of a small cottage with quartz pebble-dashed central bay and red rosemary-tiled roof. Next is the pedestrian gateway to the now demolished BARON CLIFF, a broad opening with stepped parapet, flanked by a single pier with narrow blind arched recess and graded ashlar cap. Sharing the pier (if not the same architect), the first of a pair of garden entrances to the CRAG OWLET COTTAGES, the gate hung on a stout stugged ashlar post with conical cap supported on stubby consoles. Crag Owlet, built mid 1850s as a tenement of four flats for Thomas Forgan, was almost certainly designed by *Alexander Thomson*, the composition bearing all the hallmarks of his seaside vocabulary. The building, of two-storey whinstone rubble, is symmetrical about a now-truncated wallhead stack. Flanking this are gabled dormers and most unusual advancing bays l. and r. These are linked at ground level by twin verandas formed under segmental-headed arches with slate canopies, which provide cover to the lower house entrances. Both steeply gabled bays have single-storey scalloped and moulded canted windows, seemingly sculpted out of a deep, battered base course. Behind their cast-iron parapet balustrading with ashlar dies and coping are broad balconies to the segmental-headed windows above. In both gableheads, small, blind tripartite lights complete the Scots-Gothic ensemble. The upper-floor flats are reached through Tudor-arched doors on gambrel-gabled porches which are recessed well to the rear, outer l. and r.

The village shops on BARON'S POINT are dull and unsubtle by comparison, although there is the attraction of a well-preserved K6 telephone kiosk on the road's edge. The idiosyncratic CLAREMONT is next, an exceptionally tall Italianate villa, somewhat arbitrary in its use of decorative architectural features. Even less credible, the frothy confection of the CLEVEDON HOTEL next door is accentuated by the picking out in paint of quoins, bull-faced margins, consoles and hood-moulds. Two-storey over a raised basement, the hotel was built mid C19 as HAZEL CLIFF VILLA, at which time it was linked by a bridge to a handsome (now ruined), square-plan belvedere rising up behind.

COVE CASTLE, 1867, by *James Sellars*. A slender, crowstepped Scots-Baronial tower now without its spectacular two-storey glasshouses. Entered from the N through a small (later) gabled porch. The principal staircase is at once identified by a series of ascending lights whose hood-mould is formed from a roll-moulded stringcourse terminating in a knotted label stop. The roll-moulding pursues a purposeful path on to the westerly, seaward façade. Here the impregnable effect created by squared and snecked yellow sandstone with a few simple openings is unexpectedly relieved at second-floor level by a tall oriel with deeply moulded corbelling and cannon head decoration. There are gunloops and arrowslits, and a fishscale candlesnuffer roof to the NW turret, all executed with the sort of scholarly precision seldom afforded a marine villa.

The location of COVE PIER is marked, not so much by tangible remains of the timber structure (closed in 1946), as by the survival of ASHLEA and ELLERSLIE – twin, gabled houses linked at ground level by a stone veranda, above which are arranged two sets of long six-light windows. A plainer cousin of the Crag Owlet Cottages, this 1850 double villa for some time served as the local hotel because of its proximity to the landing stage. Possibly designed by *Alexander Thomson* for James and Robert Couper, paper manufacturers.

SEYMOUR LODGE by *Alexander Thomson*, 1850. A pretty cottage-orné composition whose principal design elements have been rearranged with varying degrees of success on a series of similar villas in the area. None is better than the prototype, however, although it is without some of the original elaborate decoration. Two storeys, with a single-storey block outer l. and small entrance porch outer r. The steepness of the roof to the broad, projecting gable on the l. of the principal façade is strikingly matched by the adjacent gabled dormer, which has a half-lozenge window and cast-iron trefoil cresting. A wide three-centred arched window admits light from the NW into the first-floor drawing room and provides views to the front. The window opens on to a tiny balcony, formed behind the decorative iron balustrade which crowns the square, corniced window bay to the dining room below. The roof, consistent with the illustrations in *Villa and Cottage Architecture*, is finished in alternating bands of plain and fishscale patterned slates. – INTERIOR. The drawing room has a polygonal, compartmentalized plaster ceiling with floral bosses. The larger ground-floor rooms have leaded, stained-glass upper window panes, possibly added later by *Daniel Cottier*. In the dining room, the space normally occupied by window shutters has been given over to mirrors which, in the words of the architect, give 'an agreeable effect of lightness' and 'reproduces the pleasing external view [of Loch Long] inside the room'. The narrow staircase is generously top-lit by an attractive leaded lay-light.

Next door, FERNDEAN is a large, rambling-plan villa with Tudoresque details, distinguished by what is left of the boundary wall and gatepiers which the publisher Robert Blackie commissioned in 1863. *Alexander Thomson* here designed a simple, stepped sandstone and whin wall with narrow, margined arrow-slits at regular intervals. The main entrance is marked by a massive whinstone drum pier with elongated bell-shaped cap and ashlar finial. Its corresponding pier has been dismantled, but it resembled those flanking the subsidiary entrance – shorter drums with necks and more conventional caps and collars. The gates, red pine with ornamental studs and spikes, are long gone, but are beautifully rendered in *Villa and Cottage Architecture*, where their proportions and construction are described.

A consistently high standard of design was maintained as the feus were developed to the N of the pier, although this is in some part due to the fact that several of the houses are indebted to Seymour Lodge. Examples can be found at BURNCLIFF COTTAGE, STRATHLEE and BIRKEN HILLOCK, all two-storey, three-bay, gabled rectangular-plan villas in the cottage-orné style with Tudoresque details. THE LINN, designed in 1858 by *William Motherwell* and rising in Italianate splendour above the MEIKLE WATERFALL, pays convincing homage to Craig Ailey. The W-facing gable and tower with their broad, bracketed eaves and round-headed windows respond assertively to the elevated site; weight added to the composition by big, bull-faced quoins and dressings. Surrounding the villa, tumbling down the slope as accompaniment to the waterfall, an exotic garden and nursery developed since 1971 by *Dr James Taggart*. Open to the public.

Villas large and small clutter the curve of COVE BAY. GLEN ROWAN and GLEN HOLLY are dainty single-storey-and-attic cottages with demi-barrel canopy porches on slender colonnettes, probably late C19. GRAFTON is medium-sized and a little older. It has a good bow window with ribbed lead roof and a round-headed window at first floor with carved acanthus leaf decoration. This is divided by a centre colonnette from which channelled voussoirs spring. Larger still is CASA BLANCA, two storeys, rambling plan with painted harl and bull-faced margins, and pretty decorative trefoil ends to exposed rafters. WOODSIDE, over-large by virtue of a late C19 remodelling, is none the less interesting for its unusual tower with swept pyramidal roof and tripartite windows under segmental pediments. Together with ARMADALE, an 1863 gabled cottage greatly enlarged by a jolly corner tower, it lies close to the DOWALL BURN. At the foot of this, *Alexander Thomson* completed one of his last commissions in 1874, a simple, single-span bridge terminating in large consoled masonry drums with raised circular caps, carrying the shore road across the water.

KNOCKDERRY CASTLE. By *John Honeyman*, extended by *William Leiper*. Legend locates the dungeons of an ancient Danish or Norwegian fort (dating from the time of the Battle of Largs) below the building. More recent history was made on 15 May 1901, when Andrew Carnegie, a guest at the house, wrote to the then Lord Provost of Glasgow, offering to finance the proposed construction of the city's Branch Libraries. *Alexander Thomson* is credited with having begun the house in 1854, although authorship is far more believably attributed to Honeyman, who certainly extended the original villa in 1869 and 1871, most likely having designed it for John Campbell in 1856. It is magnificently sited on a rocky outcrop, commanding views of Loch Long and, in the distance, the Cumbrae islands. The Scots-Baronial core is an asymmetrical rectangular-plan design, extending to two storeys over a deep basement, and now forms the W wing. There are bartizans, a large battlemented bow on the SW corner, armorial escutcheons and rope-moulded cornices. The building was transformed in 1896 when Leiper more than doubled the accommodation for the Glasgow carpet manufacturer John S. Templeton, adding a tower block to the E and adding to the originally shorter N façade a stepped screen wall to a huge banqueting space. The main entrance is now on the E façade, framed within a round-arched, deeply roll-moulded opening with twin, round-headed, multi-paned lights above and a pediment in which the inscription reads 'As built on rock so be our lives'. On either side of the doorway are monogrammed decorative stone panels, while out of the pediment grows the base corbelling of a two-storey canted oriel, finished in an ashlar battlemented parapet.

Around the head of the tower is a parapet walk. On the N and S sides of the attic storey are crowstepped gables. On the E, there are two very fine dormerheads with broken segmental-headed pediments and triangulated finials. The N façade of the Leiper extension, rising out of a colossal, battered double basement, attempts a less successful marriage of old and new, but impresses through sheer scale. – INTERIOR. Spectacular Leiperian interior in collaboration with *Scott Morton & Co.*, one of the finest of its style in the country. Templeton's hydraulic-powered lift remains intact at the heart of the E tower: the original boiler is still in place in the basement dungeon. The banqueting hall at first floor is a *tour de force* – a wagon roof with stencilled purlins and a painted ceiling of celestial design. There is an elaborate painted processional frieze on oak and pine, arched braces carried on carved pilasters, a panelled dado and a minstrels' gallery at the NW end. A single mosaic tiled bathroom with original fitments survives, as do the Art Nouveau cast-iron fireplaces in the attic bedrooms. In the older part of the building, earlier remodelling by Leiper, including stained-glass panels in one of the bay windows depicting the Battle of Largs, designed by *Sir James Guthrie*, 1887. – GARDEN BALUSTRADE and BIRDBATH. On the S front, a curved, arcaded, ashlar balustrade with an elaborate birdbath placed at the centre of the terrace – a squat column with fruit garlands and cherub heads supporting a broad basin with fluted shell base and acanthus leaf carving.

KNOCKDERRY HOUSE HOTEL, alterations by *William Leiper*, 1897. The original stone-built farmhouse of Knockderry was comprehensively remodelled in the Arts and Crafts style at much the same time as the castle was undergoing enlargement in the Baronial idiom. Added to the W front was a three-stage helm-roofed tower bay, with half-timbered asymmetrical attic storey and with staircase turret to the r. with candlesnuffer roof. To the l. of the tower is a single-storey porch with round-arched doorway and ashlar parapet. To the l. is a long, two-storey frontage with an elegant bowed window supporting a wooden balustraded veranda, on top of which is a further candlesnuffer roof, this time built against a crowstepped gable; on the NW corner, a broad faceted-roofed bay with half-timbering at first-floor level and three dormerheads with bargeboarded gables and coral-shaped decorative finials facing N, NW and W. The multitude of gables and gablets creates an informal, light-hearted composition which contrasts well with the stature of the castle on the clifftop above. – INTERIOR. Much decorative leaded glass in the windows, and an ornate arched timber screen defining the seating area within the ground floor of the bow window. Good chimneypieces and a fine arched inglenook in what is now used as the bar.

Two good lodges appear on the roadside as COULPORT hoves into view. BELLCAIRN LODGE has Egypto-Greek chimneypots and a boundary wall with remarkable cast-iron railings featuring elongated anthemion-like decoration. AUCHENGOWER LODGE has similarly fine railings on a low plinth wall with saddleback coping, and slender gatepiers with gableted cornices and gablet caps. The lodge itself, like so many others in the village, is in some part based on Seymour Lodge, with a slightly advanced ground-floor bay with coped roof and cast-iron brattishing, and a grey slate roof patterned in broad alternating bands of fish-scale and square.

CRAIGENDORAN

A small community on the River Clyde built up around a twin-armed pier which opened in 1882 as a berth for the steamer fleet of the North British Railway Company, whose original intention had been to route a railway along the waterfront of Helensburgh to provide proper coaling facilities for the jetty there. Instead, as a result of local protest, Craigendoran Station was established one mile E of the town. Originally there were through platforms on the Helensburgh line and a bay platform curving down to the pierhead. Now all that remains is the pretty, cubic STATIONMASTER'S HOUSE, designed by *Robert Wemyss* c. 1894 for the West Highland Railway at the end of CRAIGENDORAN AVENUE. The pier was closed in 1972, by which time Gourock and Wemyss Bay had long since become the most convenient railheads in the upper Firth. A seaside flavour is still imparted, however, by the terraced W side of the avenue, 1897, where the single-storey-and-attic marine villas are enlivened with piend and conical-roofed bay and bow windows, attic dormers, patera decoration and simple ironwork.

CRAIGNISH CASTLE

7701

The castle lies 5.5km. SW of Ardfern village towards the end of the Craignish peninsula. Nearby, a few buildings are scattered between Loch Beag and the Bàgh Dùn Mhuilig.

OLD PARISH CHURCH, Kilmarie. Early C13 rubble chapel, oblong in plan, in a rectangular burial enclosure. Repaired in the C19 and consolidated in 1926, the walls stand to eaves height and to the apex of the E gable. SW door with a semicircular arch and late medieval rybats with square arrises. Paired S and E windows have been widened with new outer arches during late C19(?) restoration. The inner arches and splayed ingoes to the S pair are original but those in the sanctuary gable have been renewed. The N window has a new outer arch but its width is unaltered. Aumbries l. and r. of the E windows and immediately E of the S door. The reduced W gable carries a small sandstone finial. In 1974 a roof was erected below eaves level at the W end to protect a collection of funerary stones, around thirty of which can be inspected. – Two Early Christian FRAGMENTS bear incised Latin cross markings. – Numerous tapered SLABS showing floral ornament, swords, etc. of C14–C15 Loch Awe school origin and others, similarly carved, but less specifically attributable, C14–C16. – Cover-slabs and side-slabs of TOMB-CHESTS, C16, probably of Loch Sween provenance, cut with plaiting, floral and animal reliefs.

CRAIGNISH CASTLE. Despite a remote romantic location, embosomed above trees at the head of Loch Beag, Craignish is a clumsy confection concocted by repeated conversions. There are three clearly identifiable parts which, though roughcast overall and packed closely and chronologically S to N, fail to integrate either in massing or scale. First, the broad three-storey tower-house, late C14 or early C15; secondly, the two-bay rump of a four-bay mansion, 1837, commissioned by James Campbell of Jura in austere Elizabethan style to replace an early C18(?) N range; thirdly, a lower, C20 staircase block added at the centre of the new N gable of the truncated 1837 house. The architect of the second phase of building (both *William Burn* and *Joseph*

Gordon Davis, the designer of Kilmory at Lochgilphead, have been suggested) rebuilt the upper walls of the tower-house to create a wide crenellated parapet, raised a battlemented octagonal tower above the entrance bay which he placed at the centre of the main E front between old and new, and aligned and regularized all window openings. The sheer bulk of building imparted some measure of compositional stability. Regrettably, this has been lost. A high hipped roof over the tower-house, reduction in the height of the entrance tower and above all the demolition of so much of the building fabric have achieved only incoherence.

A gabled green ashlar porch, barely advanced from the entrance tower bay above, forms the E entry to the dwelling now occupying what remains of the Elizabethan additions. The interior is unremarkable save for the partial exposure of a C19 queen-post truss at third-floor level. A doorway at the S end of the E wall of the tower-house, probably original but with a C17 surround and restored wrought-iron yett, gives access to a second dwelling formed within the older structure. Though the barrel-vault remains, the plan arrangement at ground level and openings in the 2m–2.5m.-thick walls, including the S doorway, are C20. A partly mural stair opening off the entrance lobby rises through two 90-degree bends to first floor. Here, a dividing partition running W–E and the outer walls on E, S and SW of the tower seem to belong to the C17. Two of the E windows may also date from this period while a small slit in the NW mural chamber survives from earlier work; otherwise all windows at this level and above are C19. Third-floor walls are C17, the parapeting above with its false machicolation and minibartizans being part of the C19 work. Decoration is C20. Both first-floor rooms are oak panelled; a plaster frieze carries foliated ornament based on early C16 tomb-chests at Kilmichael Glassary (q.v.). Other motifs, e.g. on stone chimneypiece, derive from Iona school funerary carving.

The GARDENS, late C18, lie down a grassed bank below the E front. A rampart at the head of the bank has gone and little remains horticulturally. To the SW a long CAUSEWAY extends to a mock battery on Island Trarach.

CRAIGNISH MAINS, 120m. N of Craignish Castle. Square plan courtyard steading opening to the E but originally also entered through a four-centred arch, keystone dated 1810, at the centre of the S front. The latter is now incorporated in the dwelling as a French window. SE façade with three gables with shouldered skews: apex block chimneys l. and r.; central weather vane block above a quatrefoil. Piended byres, stables and barn, ventilated by round-ended cross-loops, survive.

GARTCHARRAN COTTAGES, N side of the road 400m. N of Kilmarie Chapel. Mid C19. Two-storey, four-gabled S front with single-storey gabled porches at the centre and on the W and E gables. Mullioned bipartite windows to ground floor.

DUN, Dùn Mhuilig, 600m. ENE of Craignish Castle. Hilltop dun, 12m. by 9m. internally, wholly destroyed on E and S, discernible as a banking on w and splendidly preserved on the N where, within a thickness exceeding 4m., a 10m.-long intramural gallery can be penetrated. N wall has marked batter. Entrance unclear but possibly in the middle of the w wall.

CRAIGROWNIE

2281

The boundaries of Cove and Kilcreggan, constituted a joint Police Burgh in 1865, included the *quoad sacra* parish of Craigrownie, in the presbytery of Dumbarton and synod of Glasgow and Ayr. Of the six churches built to accommodate the rapid increase in population on the E side of the Rosneath peninsula, Craigrownie Parish Church alone survives. Downhill, on a flat site near BARON'S POINT, the original United Presbyterian Church of Kilcreggan now functions as the church hall.

CRAIGROWNIE PARISH CHURCH, Church Road. The foundation stone was laid on 31 July 1852. A lithograph in the vestry by the original architect, *H. H. MacKinney* of Liverpool, depicts the T-plan Gothic building without the chancel bay, cellar and vestry on the SW gable. The body of the church is rubble-built in whinstone and sandstone with distinctive sliver courses of stonework, and was substantially enlarged by *Honeyman & Keppie* in 1889. The transepts are broadly gabled, asymmetrical and buttressed, that on the SE façade having a perky little lean-to entrance porch with Tudor-arched door. Windows are two- and three-light lancets, the nave punctuated by sawtooth coped buttresses. There is a broad-shouldered, gabled bellcote rising out of the original SW elevation which is now hidden by the chancel. – INTERIOR. The fine open timber truss roof is supported on sandstone corbels. The organ and screen at the NE end of the church are late C19. – STAINED GLASS. Various stained and leaded windows, mostly figurative, including one to John McElroy (1802–76), the principal developer of Cove, who is credited with having assisted in the design of the church. In the NE wall of the porch, a tiny trefoil depiction of a lamb by *Stephen Adam*.

CRAIGROWNIE PARISH CHURCH HALL, Rosneath Road, once the U. P. Church and then Lindowan Church of Scotland, by *Hugh Barclay*, completed in 1869. A massive barn-like cruciform, the building has been stripped of much of its architectural detail and the SW entrance porch is supported on oversized steel posts, yet its weighty demeanour still evokes religious reassurance. Principal façades are gabled, with large Y-traceried pointed-arch windows. On the SW front, two sculpted heads in roundels gaze over the variegated slatework of the porch, on either side of which remain the corbels and pilaster strips which once supported big ornate bargeboards to the gable end. – INTERIOR. Now a large hall with dark dado panelling and much intact stained glass, including two large three-light windows from the Abbey Studio (artist *F. Hase Hayden*) and two 1958 single lights in the NW wall by *Gordon Webster*. – GATEPIERS. Inspired or possibly even designed by *Alexander Thomson*, two pairs of voluptuous irregular gatepiers mark entrance and exit. Masonry-built with exaggerated entasis, completed by stone ogival caps with polished ashlar finials. The outer l. and r. piers are substantially larger and more bulbous, designed to frame big, diagonally braced gates, only one of which has survived.

As COVE is approached, the boundary at the foot of Church Road is marked by the somewhat incongruous BURGH HALL & READING ROOM, formally opened in 1895. The narrow striated stonework acknowledges a local link with its near neighbours, but the red sandstone dressings, hefty Jacobethan detailing and rosemary roof tiles are alien to the area. Two-storey, asymmetrical and L-plan, with a round tower on the re-entrant angle and an elaborate pilastered and pedimented doorpiece to the outer gable. This has a wide arched entrance recess to what is now the local library, the opening framed by fluted arch moulding with alternating banded vermiculated, basket-work and chevron-patterned voussoirs. Above the keystone, an armorial plaque of a mightily-tusked elephant carrying a castle, bearing the legend FORTITUDO ET FIDELITAS.

WAR MEMORIAL. On a bluff overlooking the water, an ashlar Celtic cross *c.* 1920 with Celtic interlacing and pictish details. A delightful zoomorphic design covers the E elevation, whose inscription commemorates those fallen in the Great War, while the W face has a floral interlaced memorial to World War II.

CRAOBH HAVEN

Marina settlement on the NW shore of the Craignish peninsula created in 1983 by building a bouldered causeway and sea wall from Eilean an Dùin and Eilean Buidhe to the mainland. Stimulated by the popularity of west coast sailing and the money that goes with it, Craobh Haven has been deliberately devised by its developers to accommodate holiday demand. The phenomenon of the planned leisure village is familiar enough in more southerly climes but unexpected in these latitudes. Nor is it entirely successful.

The realization of the village plan, conceived and begun in the early 1980s by *Gillespie, Kidd & Coia*, passed quickly into other hands. There are two separate residential developments, placed perhaps 200m. apart. The first consists of a street running SW–NE, on each side of which two-storeyed cottages build up gable-to-gable in casual and ingratiatingly couthy alignment. The effort to be Scottish is clear: harled walls, eaves dormers, crowsteps, forestairs, conically capped roofs. But such contextual intention needs restraint and discrimination. Here there is a variety of form, detail and colour which has more to do with a specious suburban individualism than with the rigorous lime-washed geometries and repetitive simplicities of many West Highland communities. A second L-plan block of two-storey housing, also harled in differing pastel shades, is less aggressively inventive, and all the better for it, though the detailing of lintels and sills is unnecessarily coarse. No attempt seems to have been made to unite these two developments in any way and, beyond the suggestion of a village green down one side of the street and the attention evidently lavished on small individual gardens, no consideration has been given to landscaping.

Another mawkishly Scottish house lies a little s of Craobh Haven village *en route* to the causeway leading to Eilean an Dùin. Roughcast given a bellcast at the first floor; eaves dormers and circular rubble towers capped with finialled pyramid roofs fail to convince.

BUIDHE LODGE. By *Johnston Erdal*, 1987–8. Timber-boarded and timber-framed structure, raised above a rocky knoll on Eileann Buidhe. Verandas in the gables.

LUNGA HOUSE, 1.2km. s of Craobh Haven. An imploding aggregation of gabled blocks of differing dates and heights. The earliest C17 part lies at the centre of the NW front. C18 and C19 additions and alterations baronialized the house with extensive crowstepping in concrete, a few bartizans and a more Gothic SE battlement; architectural and chronological disentanglement is difficult. An C18 ICE-HOUSE, with a barrel vault rising 2.85m., is located 70m. N of the house.

FORT, Eilean an Dùin. Irregular oval plan enclosure, *c.* 53m. by 28m. around a rocky rise at NE end of island now degraded on the N as a result of causeway construction. Walling, 4m. thick, retains some outer faces and shows signs of vitrification.

FORTIFICATION, Dùn an Garbh-sròine, above the A816 1.3km. N of its junction with the Craobh Haven road. An elongated oblong enclosure overlooking the sea from a precipitous summit. The date of construction is unknown. Drystone rubble walls run in straight lengths and return in squared angles. Entrance in NE re-entrant angle. Postern gate embrasure on the NW at head of rock-cut stair. Occupied by the McIver Campbells until the C17.

CRINAN 7893

A canal and fishing village, clambering around a rocky knuckle of North Knapdale pushing out into Loch Crinan. From the E the Crinan Canal bends around the wooded edge of steeply rising ground, past the old crossing point to Crinan Ferry to arrive at its final basin, a unique intimate place of green grass, white walls and black lock-gates. On the W, sheltered by Eilean da Mheinn, is the hamlet of Crinan Harbour, formerly called Port Righ.

KILMAHUMAIG BURIAL GROUND, NE of Bellanoch to Crinan road. Small hillside graveyard assumed to be the site of a medieval chapel, though no remains survive. Ruinous C18 enclosure on the NW.

CRINAN HOTEL. Beheaded Baronial, wide-fronted, mid-Victorian mansion, a long way from the plain gabled inn built by the canal promoters in 1801. Its canted bays are heavily corbelled to bartizaned gables. Burnt out 1899, rebuilt 1900 by Lochgilphead architect *Neil Gillies*. Again destroyed by fire 1917; again rebuilt 1918. Parapet castellations, gables and bartizan peaks have gone and in their place a third-floor roofscape of balconied terraces and *fenêtres en longueur*. This is continued over a high w wing, and on E where more balconies overlook the canal basin. Bulky, agglutinative, but buoyed up by nautical bravura.

Beside the canal basin is the COFFEE SHOP, formerly the Post Office, early C19, a piended white rubble box with four tall buttressed chimney stacks. Across the sea-lock, the white gables of LOCKKEEPERS' COTTAGES, early C19.

FACTORY, Crinan Harbour. Rubble ruins of industrial buildings in which pyroligneous acid was distilled from birchwood. Set up by Poltalloch Estate *c.* 1850. Tall red brick chimneystack with diamond patterning around the summit of the flue.

HARBOUR HOUSE, Crinan Harbour. Late C19. Three-storey rubble tenement with broad chimney stacks on deep-plan gables. Entrances front, at later lean-to porch, and at rear.

DUN, Castle Dounie, 1.7km. SW of Crinan Harbour. Irregular plan enclosure now surrounded by forest. Walling reaches 2.6m. on WSW. Some open recesses on the S and SE inner. N entrance.

CRINAN CANAL

Constructed in order to obviate the long sail around the Mull of Kintyre, the Canal stretches 14.5km. from Ardrishaig on Loch Gilp to Crinan (q.v.). Thirteen inland locks and two sea-locks thus link Clyde traffic on Loch Fyne with the Sound of Jura and the Western Isles. Despite a protracted and costly period of construction, repeated repairs, and its limited width and depth, it is one of only two Scottish canals still in operation.

The project was first seriously proposed (along with a call to link West and East Loch Tarbert) in 1771. The engineer *John Rennie* carried out surveys of 'Tarbit of Cantyre and Loch Gilp' in that year, but it was not until 1785 that the Parliamentary Commissioners, recognizing the benefits likely to accrue to the West Coast trade in timber, slate, kelp, grain and fish, encouraged the formation of a private company to fund the Crinan connection. In 1792 Rennie carried out further surveys exploring alternative routes from Ardrishaig, one terminating at Crinan (or Port Righ, as it was then known) and the other at Duntrune. A year later a development company was formed, largely promoted by the 5th Duke of Argyll and the 4th Earl of Breadalbane, and in 1794 work began. The favoured route was to Crinan with an estimated completion date of 1796. Financing proved difficult. Construction problems were also encountered: on the one hand, cutting through hard whinstone on the S shore of Loch Crinan; on the other, stabilizing peaty soil along the edge of the River Add moss. Rubble masonry collapsed. Poor American oak rotted. Work dragged on until the turn of the century. The Canal opened in July 1801, still in an 'unfinished state'.

Eight years later the project was deemed 'finally complete'. But further flooding ensued, resulting in a re-alignment between Oakfield and Cairnbaan, and in 1813 *Thomas Telford* found things in 'a very imperfect condition'. Between 1816 and 1817 he was supervising the extension of Ardrishaig pier, the substitution of cast-iron bridges for timber, the repair of lock-gates, and various other works carried out by the Aberdeen contractor *John Gibb*. Gibb returned in 1835 to complete numerous 'necessary repairs'. Pier improvements were repeatedly required to accommodate changes in steamship traffic: at Ardrishaig in 1837–8, 1879, 1884, 1905, and at Crinan in 1843 and 1881. In 1906 an enquiry considered proposals put forward by the canal engineer *L. John Groves* and the Glasgow engineering firm *Crouch & Hogg* to cut a ship canal at Crinan, but this, and a parallel proposal to do the same at Tarbert, was rejected.

Throughout the C20 commercial traffic has diminished, despite major renovations, 1930–4, which included the building of new sea-locks in parallel with the originals. Leisure use now sustains the Canal's operation.

CRINAN FERRY

7995

A peaceful place, spellbound in insular enchantment. A handful of buildings served the ferry which until mid C19 carried traffic between Knapdale and Kilmartin.

CRINAN HOUSE. Tacksman's house of *c.* 1710, restored 1976. Harled rubble with no dressings; the skew gables have cavetto skewputts. The NE front was altered by addition of a parapeted forestair and new doorways when the lower floor was adapted as storehouse, *c.* 1800, but small upper windows tucked under the bellcast eaves keep a sense of ordered symmetrical solidity. Garret lit from gables. Original oak roof timbers notched and pegged. The NW outhouse, possibly late C18, now roofless, shows slots for cruck-couple. Adjacent gatepier carries sandstone ball finial.

FERRY HOUSE. Former inn or change-house, originally single-storeyed and thatched, late C18(?). Renovated as dwelling.

FARM STEADING. Early C19 single-storey buildings restored to residential use. Gable with sandstone-dressed vertical ventilation slots and round-arch window in apex.

ICE HOUSE. Built 1833 as a provision for the profitable salmon fishing at Crinan by the Malcolms of Poltalloch whose architect *Joseph G. Davis* was paid for carrying out an inspection of the work. Two chambers cut N–S into rock ridge and barrel-vaulted; filled from high level on the S. Turfed roof.

CUAN

7514

Ferry point on Seil for Luing. A few older dwellings, including a converted church, a handful of newer houses on the bay, and as many cars parked above the ferry ramp. The old rubble pier survives.

CHAPEL and BURIAL GROUND, Ballachuan, 500m. ESE of Kilbrandon and Kilchattan Church. Overgrown footings of small oblong cell aligned NE–SW. Some inner faces of rubble and slate masonry are exposed. A second enclosure to the NE may be a graveyard.

KILBRANDON AND KILCHATTAN PARISH CHURCH, on hillside 1.3km. NNE of Cuan Ferry. Four-bay gabled oblong by *Alexander McIntyre*, 1864–6. Plain or Y-tracery lancets. The apex of the E entrance gable supports a superb belfry in form of ogee-domed octagonal temple. Interior ramped and galleried at the W end. King-post trusses with extended spars and curved bracing spring from corbel stones. – Twin staired PULPIT centred at the E end behind the entrance lobby. – STAINED GLASS by *Douglas Strachan*, 1937–8: three E lancets depict Sea of Galilee scenes from Christ's ministry; NE window, the Resurrection and the road to Emmaus; SE window, Christ in Revelation Glory and the Nativity. All in glowing colour, greatly enhanced against dark, rough rubble masonry exposed by the removal of the original lath-and-strop plaster. – Stone TABLET at E end S wall commemorates Lady Alma Graham of the House of Montrose †1932.

Former OLD PARISH CHURCH. T-plan kirk, built 1735, superseded by the present church in 1864. Converted 1901 to an isolation hospital and later, when the dormers and E extension were added, to residential use (DUNFILLAN). A bruised birdcage belfry survives above the now-windowed W gable.

KILBRANDON HOUSE, 900m. E of Kilbrandon and Kilchattan Church. Gable-ended two-storey manse, built 1827. Rendered rubble S front with dressed margins. The lean-to porch, roof dormers and some gable windows are additions, *c*. 1865.

CULLIPOOL

Originally a slate-workers' village, early C19, serving the quarries on the NW coast of Luing. The usual rubble rows of two-roomed, single-storey WORKERS' COTTAGES, some set in parallel relationship to form short streets. More recent houses stretch S along the shore, extending what is now largely a summer holiday community. There is a small QUAY built for slate shipment in vertically laid masonry.

ST PETER'S CHURCH (Episcopal). Built 1894. Simple, gable-fronted Gothic on hillside site. Now a dwelling.

DUN, Ballycastle, 600m. E of Cullipool road end on the way to Ardinamir. Also known as the North Fort, this oval dun, 32m. by 18.3m., preserves stretches of facing masonry, especially on the SE where ten courses rising 2m. can be seen on the inner face. E entrance shows a check for a door. Traces of a protective E wall screening the entrance point are evident.

DALAVICH

A hamlet on the W side of Loch Awe, 14km. NE of Ford. Since the 1950s, predominantly a Forestry Commission community.

DALAVICH CHURCH. Built *c.* 1771, on the site of an earlier place of worship. A small, gable-ended kirk originally entered through the w gable, with four round-arched windows on the s wall. Random rubble walls and schist slab sills; arched openings have rubble voussoirs and narrow projecting keystones. Painted white. The narrower w addition, now used as a vestry and originally as a schoolroom, may have been added by *William Thomson* in 1831. In 1889 repairs, which included re-roofing, were carried out by *Kenneth Macrae* of Oban, and in 1898 *James Edgar* of Kilmartin rearranged the seating, formed a new entrance door from the window opening at the w end of the s wall and introduced the E gable window. – The church sits in mown grass in a rubble-walled burial enclosure. Among a few C18 graves and weathered headstones, a RECUMBENT SLAB, placed in 1757 and now indistinct, to Dugald and Sara McLerran with an inscription and two ascending souls who appear to be rising heavenwards on angel wings.

CAISTEAL NA NIGHINN RUAIDHE, on an island at the w end of Loch Avich, 5.3km. w of Dalavich on the Kilmelford road. The Gaelic name (Castle of the Red-haired Maiden) is said to recall Bridget, wife of Dugald Campbell of Craignish, †1220, who by this marriage brought the lands of Avich into Campbell possession. Although the first recorded reference to the castle does not occur until the early C15, size and plan form are close enough to those of Fincharn on Loch Awe to suggest a C13 date. But the surviving evidence is minimal and ruinous: a single SE wall, battered on the outer face, stands to three storeys but beyond this there are only rubble remains to confirm a hall-house or tower-house form, its oblong plan paralleling the NE–SW elongation of the narrow island on which it is built. Walling is rubble with sandstone or schist dressings at window sills, quoins and plinth. Besides the few window openings there are signs of a doorway at the NE end of the SE wall, some latrine chutes, and a fireplace at first-floor level. A ruinous intermittent rubble wall appears to indicate some form of barmkin around the castle constricted by the line of the island shore.

DALAVICH SOCIAL CLUB. By *Hird & Brooks*, 1980–1. Attractively landscaped, timber-framed community hall and balcony bar: part of the pine-lined leisure spin-off from forestry enterprise. Profiled metal sheet roof glazed in the gables behind scissors bracing. To the N, carefully laid out among the trees between the road and loch, lie holiday CABINS.

DALMALLY

A leafy village in the Strath of Orchy. Through it the old Oban road, now a loop off the A85, curves and undulates pleasantly. Roofs with dormers at the eaves predominate and there is some notable bargeboarding. To the E is Glenview estate, disappointingly more suburban than rural, and on the other side of the valley, Stronmilchan, running a ribbon of cottages NW along the old military road.

GLENORCHY CHURCH, Clachan an Diseart. White-harled Gothick octagon and tower perched conspicuously on a small river-girt burial hill rising from the strath; 'on an islet in the Orchy', Groome says. The third church to be built on the site. Its design was commissioned by Lord Breadalbane in 1808 from Edinburgh architect *James Elliot*, then engaged on the rebuilding of Taymouth Castle. Constructed 1810–11 under the direction of *Allan Johnstone*, contractor at Taymouth.

The plan is orientated E–W with the tower in the E. Offset buttresses mark where the walls of the octagon meet, while the angle buttresses of the tower duplicate and elongate this vertical stress: all their shafts rise above eaves or parapet to terminate in obelisk finials, those to the tower augmented by additional finials set at the mid-point of each face between plain crenellations. The church is lit by seven large pointed-arch windows, each with chamfered jambs and hood moulding. All are of two lights, with a circle in the arch head. Apart from the W window which retains original timber, this tracery is metal and dates from a major refurbishment by *Kenneth Macrae* of Oban in 1898. The tower rises in four stages defined by narrow stringcourses. At the lowest stage the E entrance door and N and S windows have four-centred arches under square hoods. At the second and fourth stages broader taller windows have been built up, except for those on the E and N at the second stage where the openings retain their original Perpendicular Gothic tracery. Belfry openings blocked but a BELL, dated 1888, mounted on tower roof.

Somewhat surprisingly, under its faceted slated pyramid roof, the church has a flat plastered ceiling, a disappointing sectional response to the octagonal plan but a structural achievement fully appreciated only when the complexities of its construction (cross trussing collar-braced against a central king-post) are viewed from a hatch above the gallery. The massive timbers are said to be 'the last remains of the pine-forest of Glenstrae'. A winding stair which rises on the N side of the stone-flagged vestibule at the base of the tower leads to the U-plan gallery. This has a panelled front and is supported on six cluster-shaft columns also of local pine. – Below the W window, a platform PULPIT, 1898, reached by balustraded stairs l. and r. – Oak communion CHAIR, with elaborately panelled and cusped Gothic back, 1955. – STAINED GLASS is confined to W window: the Good Samaritan and donkey pictured below a number of crocketed Gothic arches, by *W. & J. Kier*, 1889. – All other windows have diamond pattern cathedral glazing with sky blue margins, 1898. – Several wall TABLETS in plain white marble commemorate the Campbells of Glenorchy. In the vestibule, a pointed-arch PANEL dedicated to Colonel Colin Campbell †1866, his wife †1850, and his infant son Arthur †1851 'Aged 2 Years, 4 Months', and bearing the family motto and armorial insignia carved in relief; by Perth sculptor *A. Christie*.

In the hillside BURIAL ENCLOSURE which surrounds the church are several tapered SLABS, Loch Awe school, C14–C15, carved with armed men, floral ornament, interlacing, etc., set within wide borders; among these a smaller slab, evidently the tombstone of a child. – Stylistically different is another tapered SLAB, *c.* 1500–60, divided into four panels containing a foliated cross, a male figure in civil dress, a stag and hound, and an undecipherable image overlaid with a C19 inscription. – Also some recumbent SLABS of late C17 and C18 date.

DALMALLY MANSE, adjacent to church. Built 1804–5 by *John Stevenson* of Oban. Piended house with provincial Palladian aspirations. Venetian windows at the first floor in central gabled projection and l. and r. of the ground-floor entrance. Later oversized gabled porch.

DALMALLY BRIDGE, 150m. NNW of Glenorchy Church. Rubble masonry bridge carrying the B8077 43m. across River Orchy in three segmental arch spans. Built 1780–1, by *Lewis Piccard* (or *Ludovick Picard*?), mason. Cutwater piers with stepped tops. Boulder coped parapets stretch 55m. overall. SSE of the Church a three-arch EMBANKMENT takes the road 63m. over marshy ground; extensive C20 rebuilding but central arch probably contemporary with the bridge.

DALMALLY HOTEL. Originally a three-bay, three-storey inn, built 1781–2 by *Lewis Piccard* (or *Ludovick Picard*?). Described as 'an excellent inn' (*OSA*, 1792), it was soon enlarged by two additional bays to the S and by the addition of a five-bay dormered W wing (1841–4). Further enlarged with mansard bedrooms, a conservatory and a massive hipped-gabled porte-cochère by *Crerar & Partners*, 1995.

Former GLENORCHY ISOLATION HOSPITAL. Corrugated-iron structure by *Speirs & Co.*, 1898. Private dwelling since 1925.

MCINTYRE MONUMENT, Beacon Hill, 2.1km. SW of Dalmally Station. This massive monument of gargantuan granite blocks, variously described as a Druidic or Greek 'temple', commemorates the illiterate Gaelic poet Duncan 'Ban McIntyre †1812 who spent some of his life in the area. By *J. T. Rochead*, 1859–60. Primitive not just in material and texture but in geometry: on a high, ponderously solid, square plinth a circular stylobate of three colossal steps supports a twelve-pier henge open to the elements.

MCLAREN MONUMENT, 2.75km. NW of Glenorchy Church. By *Sydney Mitchell & Wilson*. On a low but conspicuous hilltop site by the old military road NW of Stronmilchan. Tall Celtic cross mounted on a thrice-splayed plinth and three-stepped rubble block base commemorates Duncan McLaren, Lord Provost of Edinburgh, 1851–9, and later MP for the city. The sandstone cross and plinth are beautifully carved with interlacing and knotting and various floral, bird, animal and figural motifs by *William Beveridge*. Bronze relief portrait head in plinth.

RAILWAY STATION. Built *c.* 1877 for the Callander & Oban Railway. Two-storey, crowstep gabled offices with half-width single-storey wing continuing E along N platform. In chunky red sandstone. Steel-framed glazed platform canopy supported on cast-iron columns and bracketed from station buildings. Serrate-edged timber boarding to front and ends of canopy. Abandoned.

THE OLD SCHOOL HOUSE. Two-storey, gable-ended, roughcast schoolhouse with three gablets at first floor. Late C19. Linked r. to a coursed-rubble classroom block with projecting gables, the central gable with a chimney.

WAR MEMORIAL, by Dalmally Bridge. Rubble slab stairs set into the roadside bank climb to a granite boulder monument, c. 1920. On a battered base, a standing stone shaft with Celtic cross in relief.

SHIELINGS, Airidh nan Sileag, in Glen Strae, 7.4km. NE of the McLaren Monument. Early C19(?). Clustered dry-stone remains: the buildings are small, oblong or sub-circular in plan, with most doorways opening downhill SE away from the prevailing wind.

DRUMLEMBLE

Former mining village 6km. W of Campbeltown on the Machrihanish road.

KILKIVAN OLD PARISH CHURCH, 1km. W of Drumlemble. Within the graveyard is an oblong rubble chapel, retaining only its W gable and parts of the N and S walls, the latter largely rebuilt. A pointed-arch doorway survives in the N wall, its ochre sandstone dressings cut with a plain chamfer. Small C18 burial enclosure built against the S wall. At the E end of the church lie eight tapered SLABS. Two are ascribed to Iona school, C14–C15; one bears the effigy of a knight, the other of a cleric. Remainder with usual carvings of swords, animals, foliage ornament, etc., are Kintyre school, C15. In the McWilliam burial-enclosure on the N side of the church is a TOMBSTONE on which are displayed the tools of the flesher's trade.

COTTAGES. Eight single-storey, semi-detached blocks forming miners' row along the B843.

MISSION HALL. Campbeltown polychromy; three lancets in gable. By *Donald McNair* of Campbeltown, 1899.

DUNADD

DUNADD. An imposing rocky outcrop rising to 54m. OD above the l. bank of the River Add on the E marches of the flat marshlands of Mòine Mhór. A natural fortress, its topography has lent itself to defensible settlement from the earliest times, though the surviving vestiges of masonry walling and ramparts date from the period between the C7 and the C9. At this time Dunadd was a centre of considerable political and military significance in the territory of Dál Riata (Dalriada) and a key stronghold in the struggles between Scots and Picts.

The configuration of the built defences develops in a series of fortified enclosures and aprons which spread downhill from summits at the W and N of the massif. The 'Upper Fortress' has three zones. Around the W peak is a pear-shaped masonry girdle, up to 4m. thick and standing to a height of just over 1m.; below this, a smaller sloping shelf of ground, its enclosing wall best preserved on the NE; and beyond this, again NE, a narrow terrace immediately under the N summit. Lying along the SE flank of these upper defences is the 'Plateau Fort' formed by two tiered aprons, each protected by thick rubble walling, still over 1m. high in the NE, which bulges E before returning in a right-angled change of direction to the rock face below the W summit. Through the SE margin of the lower apron, a natural gap in the rock creates a deep passage which formed the fortress's principal portal and may originally have been bridged in some way. From here the ascent begins, passing through the SE wall of the higher apron and climbing up the rocky incline E of the W peak by a path which has now lost its rubble steps to reach the shelf between the two summits. Here some exceptional carvings survive: a small rock-cut basin, a sunken footprint (a recognized feature of inauguration ritual), the incised outline of a wild boar (in fact, a fibre-glass cast laid over the original), and an ogam inscription.

DRIMVORE, 800m. NNW of Dunadd. Two-storey rubble farmhouse, *c.* 1860, with crude dripstone mouldings over the lower windows. Low recessed wings l. and r. are gable-fronted. Dilapidated outbuildings.

DUNADD BRIDGE. River Add crossing in two segmental arches with central cutwater stepped and faceted. Rubble; boulder cope to parapet. Framed tablet on NW parapet dated 1871.

DUNADD FARM. C19. Harled farmhouse built in concrete.

CHAMBERED CAIRN, Baroile, 2.2km. NNE of Dunadd on SE slope of Rhudil Burn valley. Roughly oval cairn, 26m. by 24m., with five upright stones forming façade through the portal stones of which a two-compartment chamber, 3.5m. long, is entered.

DUNBEG

A suburb of local authority housing, by *Argyll County Council*, 1957–61, 4km. NE from Oban.

DUNBEG CHURCH. Built 1981. Small, steeply pitched, gable-ended oblong with low eaves. Burning bush(?) STAINED GLASS in each gable apex.

DUNSTAFFNAGE MAINS FARM, on the N edge of Dunbeg. Late C18(?). Three-bay farmhouse with short, single-storey piended wings. White-painted rubble.

DUNSTAFFNAGE MARINE LABORATORY, at Dunstaffnage Castle entrance. By *Crerar & Partners*, 1962–3. Respectable flat-roofed offices face the bay with six square bays.

DUNDERAVE CASTLE

set behind the rise of a small headland on the NW shore of Loch Fyne,
5.8km. SW from the head of the loch

A late C16 tower-house miraculously both austere and couthy. Archetypally L-plan. The hall and jamb wings enclose a square projection housing a circular turnpike in the E re-entrant; their outer faces hinge on the W tower, a conically-capped drum, four full storeys of superimposed, mostly squarish rooms set within its circular masonry walling. This geometry has its environmental consequences, for while to the W the castle stands hard like a vast cutwater deflecting the winds that blow up the loch, its recessing on the E creates a more sheltered space, entry being gained on the SE side of the turnpike block. To be sure, the protected nature of this approach must have been intended by Sir Alexander MacNaughton or his son John; one or both built the castle in the last years of the C16; they followed a fashionable, tried and tested formula, adopted, too, by Sir Duncan Campbell at the contemporary Barcaldine Castle in Lorn (q.v.). But the intense and surprising intimacy of this inner space is due much more to the restoration by *Robert S. Lorimer* in 1911–12. Not only did Lorimer repair and rehabilitate the then roofless tower-house (though he did not restore its harling) but, with a deftness of touch responsive to landscape and silhouette, he extended the leeward enclosure by building two new lower wings. Placed against the NE gable, a one-and-a-half-storey L-plan block directly mirrors the geometry of the C16 tower to enfold a small square courtyard. Diagonally opposite, a more irregular Z-plan block of similar height: this sits obliquely against the original SE gable with such calculated casualness that the subtle suggestion of concave space it sets up with the SW face of the tower-house and, more especially, its reflective embrace of the courtyard scarcely seem C20 achievements. Thus enclosed, the space seems reassuring, almost snug, save at the E corner where, between low rubble walls, a few steps lead up to the garden. Cobbles, banking up slightly in saucer-like containment around the margins of the yard, emphasize the friendly informality.

So judicious in balance, so consistent in material are the three parts of Lorimer's composition that their differing dates might defy detection. Moreover, all share a common vocabulary of form. The C16 TOWER-HOUSE has high rubble walls penetrated by single-light windows generally in roughly vertical alignment, their sandstone margins rounded on the arris, roll-moulded or cut with hollow chamfers. A few taller windows, set below relieving arches, light the principal first- and second-floor apartments. Numerous gun-loops, many of them C20 insertions. The main NE gable, the NE gable of the stair tower, and the SE gable are all crowstepped, the last being narrowed and raised between two conically-capped corner rounds carried on four courses of corbelling. A larger version of these twin roofs surmounts the circular W tower; all three cones almost imperceptibly bell-cast. Against the W tower a half-gable steps up sharply from the garret eaves on the SW front to an apex chimney, while an equally tall stack rises from the middle of the NW wall. Below the steep stone-slated planes of the roofs, dormers with ashlar pediments interrupt the eaves, most though not all introduced in the 1911–12 restoration.

In the lower, C20 NE WING most of these forms are repeated, including the bellcast cone which caps the two-storey turnpike stair. Hipped roof dormers also appear. Although most windows maintain flush, roll-moulded margins, others sit within new, more boldly worked, projecting surrounds. These variants recur in the more complex SE WING. Though formal and textural affinities with the tower-house predominate, the disposition of space and mass is more inventive here. Facing SW, recessed below the roof which links the tower-house to the crowstepped gabled return of this Z-plan wing, is a columned loggia with a forestair in the SE re-entrant. Floor-to-ceiling glazing set behind the loggia's round rubble piers now encloses this once open space. A vaulted pend, cutting through the return wing, connects the end of the driveway with the inner yard and leads directly to the castle entrance. On the SE, above the round rubble-arched pend opening is a hefty sandstone panel, still uncarved. To the r., elevated on the scarcement of a swollen base of massive loch-washed boulders, a final crowstepped gable corbelled from the round at first-floor level on the S corner. Round the E corner, on the NE front of the wing, the date 1912 and the initials AN, for Lorimer's patron, Sir Andrew Noble of Ardkinglas, beneath a swagged hood moulding surmounted by a thistle.

The MAIN ENTRANCE is particularly interesting. A dog-tooth surround set between two roll-mouldings frames the studded oak door. Above the lintel lies a wide panel or secondary lintel with a two-line text in relief, the words separated by diamond stops: IM AN BEHALD THE END BE NOCHT / VYSER NOR THE HIESTES I HOIP IN GOD. The inscription apparently sets the injunction 'Behold the end: be not wiser than the highest' between the initials of John MacNaughton and his wife Anna MacLean (IM AN) and the MacNaughton family motto 'I hope in God'. Over this panel, a much smaller one dated 1598. Set higher in the wall above a relieving arch, a larger blank tablet framed top and sides by dog-tooth and billet ornament within a roll-moulded outer border of dog-tooth similar to that around the door below. Flanking the door in bold relief are a number of indistinct carved heads: two on the l., one crowned, one wearing what seems to be a ruff; three on the r., the topmost bearded and possibly crowned, the middle one perhaps female with a wide head-dress, the lowest too weathered to interpret. Incorporated into the wall masonry r. of these, a carved figure playing a vertically-held wind instrument. Several of these pieces, including the inscribed lintel, appear to be re-used from an earlier building: stylistic links have been suggested with work at Gylen Castle on Kerrera (q.v.) and Blairquhan House in Ayrshire.

Although the INTERIOR is substantially Lorimer's creation,

the ground and first floors retain their late C16 arrangement, save for the connections contrived with both new wings. At upper levels, however, floors and ceilings, panelling, plasterwork, doors and ironwork all date from 1911–12. Original door openings, chamfered or rounded on the arris, survive, as do some fireplaces with roll-and-hollow or plain roll-moulded surrounds.

There are three apartments on the ground floor, all vaulted and all reached by a short vaulted corridor which runs l. from the NW end of the turnpike stair lobby. To the r. the KITCHEN, its vault groined to permit the intrusion of a large segmentally arched fireplace in the NE gable. When a link was made with the later services wing beyond, this opening was partially built up and a connecting door cut through the gable in the E corner. At the same time windows at the NW and SE ends of the vault were enlarged and an aumbry broken through to the stair to act as a serving hatch. The WELL ROOM, a cellar in the W angle of the plan with a NW mural stair, leads to a vaulted circular chamber at the base of the W tower. In the jamb, a second cellar communicates with the floor above by a newel-stair hollowed out in the E corner, and with the SE wing by a door slapped through the gable.

The TURNPIKE STAIR, which has treads with curved quirks against the newel, has been much restored. Stained glass in most of its windows depicts various heraldic motifs. At first floor the stair opens into a slanting passage leading S to the LOGGIA and N into the so-called HALL OF THE RED BANNERS. This Hall is roughly plastered. The restored ceiling of exposed timbers is carried by beams on corbel-stones, a few of which are original. On the NW wall, within a roll-and-hollow surround, a wide lintelled fireplace, repaired during the C20 alterations. On its l., an aumbry warmed through the fireplace ingo. On the opposite wall, close to the stair door, a triangular-headed recess. Next to this in the E corner, a window embrasure adapted to a curving passageway connecting with the upper floor of the NE wing. In the N corner, a small newel-stair climbs up. Opening from the Hall and reached by the mural stair from the Well Room below, a polygonal chamber in the W tower, with gunloops and small slit-windows. In the S corner, a door opens to the BOUDOIR, generously lit by three SW-facing windows of varying size. Unlike the Hall, this room is panelled and has a plaster ceiling of curving ribs. Robustly moulded timber surrounds and mantel reinforce the enclosure of the roll-and-hollow moulding around the SE fireplace.

At the three upper levels, the single apartments in this SE jamb have similar timber panelling and plaster ceilings by *Sam Wilson*, each with differing decorative motifs. All are entered from the turnpike stair, though only that in the turreted fourth floor communicates directly with the main block where the garret is given over to a single boarded loft. At the stairhead, a wrought-iron balustrade elegantly elaborated in a thistle motif; by *Thomas Hadden*. The main block has been subdivided, providing bedrooms and bathrooms over the Hall. On each floor there is a large SW apartment linked with a squarish room formed in the W tower. At second-floor level this apartment has walls lined with sunk panelling, the ceiling joisted on corbelled runner-beams; at third floor, it has a plain plastered ceiling.

In the NE wing, provision is made for kitchen and servants' quarters. But in building the SE wing, not only did Lorimer create a new and welcoming approach to the castle, drawing the visitor gently in through its sheltering pend from driveway to courtyard, but he gave his patron those all-but-indispensable attributes of cultured country-house living: a loggia with a view, a music room and a library. Compact and cosy, the LIBRARY has a barrel-vaulted ceiling enriched with panelled plasterwork by *Thomas Beattie*. Here, between book-lined walls, below the trailing vines that decorate the ceiling, and before a fire roaring in the pillared hearth, the inclement hours might be lost in reading or reverie. Should the sun shine, then one might step down from the loggia to stroll along the slow curve of a rubble sea-wall battered against the waters of the loch, or rest on stone benching wrapped around a mill-wheel table placed at the SE end of the wall. Perhaps one might choose to sail, crossing from the steps at the entrance to the castle pend to cast off from the rubble SLIPWAY that lies in the lee of the low grassy headland. Or, instead, one might potter in the garden, a pleasantly attenuated space on the other side of the house, stretching NE between hedges and tiered above the slow sweep of the rubble retaining wall that marks the landward side of the castle drive. Here, too, is a small sitting area circled by a battered rubble wall. Should the heat become too much or the rain return, a SUMMER HOUSE offers refuge. Built of massive loch-washed rubble boulders, it surges up out of the driveway wall to wide eaves and a stone-slated pyramid roof like a single gigantic gatepier. All this Lorimer built with that unique sensibility so aware of the hard simplicities of the Scottish tradition and yet so sweetly attuned to subtler English harmonies that soften but do not dull the edge between craft and material, between a house and its setting. All this makes Dunderave a master-work of conservation.

DUNMORE

House, steading and cottages on the W shore of West Loch Tarbert.

KILNAISH BURIAL GROUND, Cill an Aonghais, 1.8km. WSW of Dunmore House on the hillside NW of B8024. The presence of a PILLAR, 1.28m. long and incised with a small cross, Early Christian in date, is said to show the antiquity of the site. MAUSOLEUM, C18: high rubble walls with rusticated quoins, a bold cyma recta moulded course below bevelled coping and ball finials at the gateway and two corners. Within are several memorial mural PANELS, some uninscribed, and a recumbent SLAB with texts, mantling, mottos and the symbols of mortality.

ACHAGLACHGACH HOUSE, 1.6km. NE of Dunmore House. Formerly known as Craig Lodge. Large, almost Baronial, country house, *c.* 1870(?), perhaps by *Peddie & Kinnear*: gables, square and canted bays, and a high conically-capped tower, but no crowstepping.

DUNMORE HOUSE. Tower-house conceit and deceit. At first sight convincingly ancient, but mock machicolation and the excellent condition of the stonework quickly betray a C19 date; perhaps *c.* 1850, perhaps a remodelling of an earlier structure. Now only a burnt-out shell after a fire in 1985. On the W, random rubble offices, which probably incorporate earlier work, are charmingly accented with two dunce-capped tube turrets. Duller parapeted two-storey link to tower, *c.* 1950(?).

DUNMORE COURT, off B8024 close to Dunmore House drive. Former steading, early C19, converted to holiday homes. Three piended blocks around courtyard; white harled with concrete tiles.

DUNMORE SCHOOL, W of Dunmore House. 1855. Closed 1964 and now derelict. Single-storey rubble with porch. Steeply roofed with bargeboarded gables and bellcast eaves. A stone tablet in the gable commemorates Eliza Hope Campbell of Dunmore House.

DUN, Dùn a'Choin Duibh, 800m. WSW of Torinturk. Hilltop enclosure 13m. in diameter. Rubble boulder walls survive to 2m. Entrance from N. From the W a lintelled passageway descends into the wall thickness.

FORT, Dùn Mor, 200m. NNE of Dunmore House. Walled summit, 45m. by 22m., in good preservation.

DUNOON

Despite the ancient origins of its castle, nothing more than a 'Highland clachan' (*NSA*, 1845) existed before the early years of the C19. A ferry crossed the Firth of Clyde to Greenock but the village remained isolated, 'the occasional resort of invalids for the benefit of drinking goat's whey' (Groome, 1882). But when the Lord Provost of Glasgow, James Ewing, built himself a marine villa here in 1822, he set a fashion. Others followed, building their own mansions, piers were constructed and, as steam superseded sail and it became possible to commute to Greenock, Paisley or Glasgow, the Cowal shore began to develop. Dunoon itself stretched behind castle and kirk, linking the West and East Bays. In 1868 it amalgamated with the villages of Kirn and Hunter's Quay (qq.v.) to the N to form a single burgh. By the last decades of the century Glaswegians were arriving in thousands for their annual summer holiday; esplanades were formed, hotels multiplied, boarding houses and tenements appeared until, like Rothesay on Bute, the town counted itself one of the West of Scotland's principal resorts. Away from the shore on rising ground W of the centre, a residential suburb was laid out which, whatever Groome might say about Dunoon's 'charming indifference to town-like regularity' (1882), followed a clear, if slightly cranked, grid-iron plan.

Dunoon

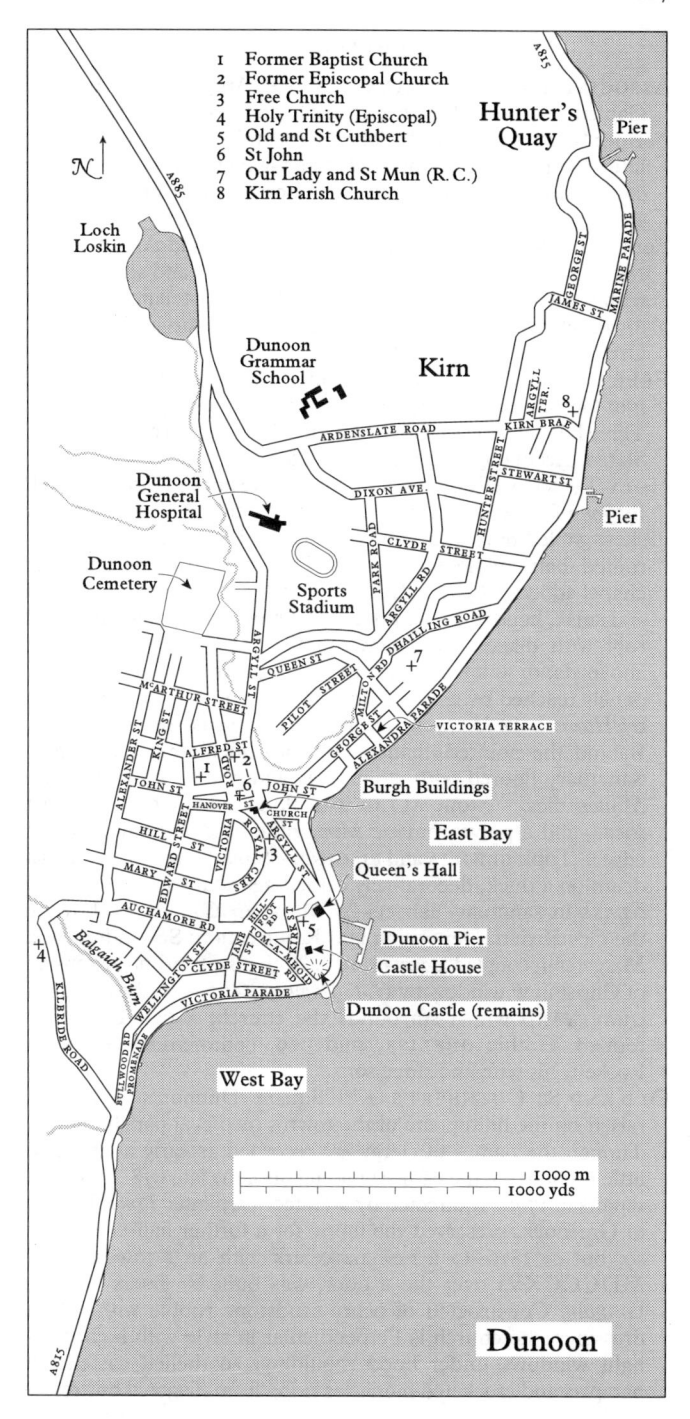

1. Former Baptist Church
2. Former Episcopal Church
3. Free Church
4. Holy Trinity (Episcopal)
5. Old and St Cuthbert
6. St John
7. Our Lady and St Mun (R.C.)
8. Kirn Parish Church

CHURCHES

ASSOCIATED PRESBYTERIAN CHURCH, Argyll Road. Mid C19. Gabled shed with three round-arch windows each side.

Former BAPTIST CHURCH, John Street and Edward Street. 1863. Dull Gothic church and hall. Skew-gables have overlapping coping stones. Four-centred arch doors to John Street. Now in secular use.

Former EPISCOPAL CHURCH, Victoria Road and Alfred Street. 1852. Gabled, three-bay nave with plain lancets and an E window with some Perpendicular ambitions. Small castellated SE belfry tower. W chancel arch and E vestibule screen survive in interior. Used as senior citizens' club.

FREE CHURCH, Argyll Street. Built 1828; gallery added *c.* 1835. Flat Gothic. Bargeboarded gable front set behind a railed wall. Three hooded lancets above a hooded four-centred arch entrance. Slated pyramid on the ridge ventilator.

HOLY TRINITY (Episcopal), on hilltop site above Kilbride Road. By *John Henderson*, 1847–8. Formula Gothic Revival; four-bay, skew-gabled nave and chancel with porches N and S. Pyramid-roofed battlemented SE tower. Low hipped-roofed narthex chapel added W by *Ross & Macbeth*, 1896. Lancet windows, tall and small, hooded by continuous stepping stringcourse. Raftered roof with diagonal bracing; roughly plastered walls painted above dado. – NE corner PULPIT with cusped pointed-arch panels reached by a mural stair from chancel. – ORGAN, 1882, by *Harrison & Harrison*, set in pitch pine case in SE corner. – Behind the pointed chancel-arch, a ribbed timber ceiling. – Sanctuary floored with stone flags and black, red and cream *Minton* tiles. – Stone ALTAR with floral colonnettes, vine leaf frieze, and a polychromatic *Minton* tile base with an alabaster edge. – Triple SEDILIA and PISCINA. – Stone FONT, an octagonal drum on a thick, decoratively carved pedestal base. – STAINED GLASS in sanctuary lancets by *Mayer & Co.*, 1872, showing the Crucifixion, Deposition and Resurrection; SS Andrew and Margaret in coupled lancets S, 1938(?); the Baptism and Ascension of Christ in W window by *G. T. Baguley*, 1872. – In the unwalled GRAVEYARD which surrounds the church, a tapered, cross-topped, Gothic OBELISK, mid C19, commemorates Joseph Lockett, his wife and three sons.

OLD AND ST CUTHBERT'S, Kirk Square. Dunoon's High Kirk, raised on the hilltop site of the town's medieval parish church. Though the names of clergy are recorded as early as the C13, little is known of the earlier building until the late C18. Extensive repairs in 1770–1, directed by architect-carpenter *James Wallace* of Greenock, preserved the fabric for a further half-century or so, but in 1816–17 a new nave kirk with an E tower, dated MDCCCXVI over the E door, was built by *James Gillespie Graham*. Constructed of ochre sandstone rubble with tooled dressings, the church is Perpendicular in style with high, two-light windows under hood mouldings, corbelled castellated parapets and crocketed pinnacles rising from diagonal buttresses at the gables. In 1834, *David Hamilton* extended the nave w in order to accommodate almost 300 more people. The architecture of the earlier church was scrupulously respected, though this deference is no longer apparent since the present w gable, which incorporates a large pointed-arch window, a circular window above and flanking lancets transomed to conceal a floor level, is substantially the result of alterations made in 1909–11 when the orientation was reversed (*see* below). The 1816 tower remained untouched until 1839, when it was raised 2.6m. to receive clock faces; even so, the original castellated parapet and four corner pinnacles were reinstated. A bell was installed at this time and there is a record of gallery alterations being required to provide more seating. By 1909 further expansion was necessary and proposals were prepared by *Andrew Balfour*. The final design reversed the church's traditional liturgical orientation towards the E, creating N and S transepts at the W end. Even so, the architect's claim that he had 'carefully kept in due harmony the new with the old style' proved well justified, for the new gabled transepts, completed in 1911, maintained the tracery, pinnacled buttresses and battlemented parapets of the earlier work. Only the chamfered staircases, introduced in the NW and SW re-entrants to serve transept galleries, seem ill at ease.

Internally, almost everything is the result of Balfour's intervention. The transepts open through two chamfered round-arches carried on tall octagonal columns, the canted fronts of the galleries projecting between. The W end is narrowed by a high pointed-arch opening which creates a chancel and allows space on the N for the rebuilt ORGAN and on the S for a vestry with session house over. A new E gallery rakes across two window bays. Replacing the former flat ceiling is a shallow-pitch, purlined roof carried on trusses with four-centre arch-bracing springing from corbelstones. – Oak CHOIR STALLS set in chancel recess. – Octagonal PULPIT islanded l. also oak. – STAINED GLASS. Chancel window by *Douglas Hamilton*, 1939.

In the walled CHURCHYARD are two late C17 TABLE-TOMBS. Among several C18 tombs and more C19, a marble TABLET in an egg-and-dart sandstone frame set in the E wall of the church tower, commemorating Sir John Campbell †1768, and his wife Anne †1759, and, at the tower's SE angle, a classical marble MONUMENT to James Hunter of Hafton †1834, and members of his family.

ST JOHN'S, Argyll Street, Hanover Street and Victoria Road. French Gothic verticality sharpened in a multitude of aisle-bay gables and a spired steeple. Designed by *Robert A. Bryden* and built, 1876–7, as Dunoon Free Church. An immense achievement of Victorian piety, it replaced the humbler Disruption kirk of 1843 which stood on the same sloping site.

On the N and S sides of the steeply-roofed nave, five transverse roofs end in equally steep gables. Each surmounts a double lancet and cusped circle under a pointed-arch hood-moulding and is separated from its neighbour by a buttress at the valley. From the SE corner, the lowest point on the site, a high belfry tower soars into an octagonal spire clasped by four elongated pinnacles rising from corner buttresses. There is a gabled pointed-arch E entrance with engaged shafts at its base and another uphill on Hanover Street at the W end of the S façade where, beyond the five aisle bays, a higher transverse roof ends in a gable lit by a triple lancet window. In the W gable, a cusped circle set in a ring of circles above five tall lancets. Below, parallel with Victoria Road and fronted by ancillary rooms, lies the main vestibule. Marking its limits N and S are square stair towers roofed with steep slated pyramids. Linked N along Victoria Road is the Hall, completed 1890.

Magnificent INTERIOR arranged for C19 Presbyterian worship: spacious, galleried and dominated by the symmetrically placed table and raised pulpit. Cast-iron columns support the U-plan balcony and rise to high plaster-vaulted ceilings. The nave has a pointed-arch plaster vault with ridge and cross ribs. Gallery bays independently vaulted in ribbed eight-part compartments. At the centre of the railed chancel, approached by stairs l. and r., is a half-octagon, timber PULPIT rising from consoles on foliated shafts. Behind, at higher level, is the three-manual ORGAN, installed by *Bryden* and the manufacturers *Brook & Co.*, 1895, reconstructed 1922 by *Ingram & Co.*, and the CHOIR STALLS, the last row backed by gabled arcading. Above, the organ pipes rise behind thin traceried screens, within a pointed arch which has foliated shafts in the corner returns. – STAINED GLASS in four of the twinned cusped lancets below the galleries. S aisle, World War II memorial windows by *Gordon Webster*, 1948 (male and female figures gathered around an angel who points to the Cross; below, a naval craft in a sea-green sea and a town illuminated by searchlights). – Also S aisle, the Lauder Memorial window, by *Gordon Webster/Stephen Adam Studios*: r., a pilgrim bearing sheaves of corn; l., Motherhood resting a hand on the shoulder of a young knight. The dedication is to Lauder's wife, Ann Vallance †1927 and their son John †1916. – N aisle, the Paterson Memorial window, 1933 (Christ the Good Shepherd and a kneeling knight), by *Webster*(?), and the Stewart window (Martha, Mary and St John), stylistically anachronistic for its date, 1960.

In the church VESTIBULE a five-bay plaster vault with three clearstorey windows, below which segmental arches rest on the fat columns of a three-bay arcade. White marble stair flights rise N and S to the gallery. On the E wall of the inner hall, a Gothic oak WALL PANEL commemorates Robert Macmorran †1908, 'under whose ministry this church was built 1876'. Floor TILES by *Minton & Co.*

OUR LADY AND ST MUN (R.C.). By *James Cameron*, 1929. Eight-bay, skew-gabled nave with short SW chancel and buttressed parapeted NE porch built in random rubble schist without dressings. Pointed-arch window with splayed ingoes in each buttressed bay. Three-tier urn FOUNTAIN in grounds.

CEMETERIES

DUNOON CEMETERY, Alexander Street and Bogleha Road. This extensive walled C19 graveyard lies at the N end of Alexander Street, W of Milton Burn. Regular lawn-lined rows of tombs stripe the gentle slope from W to E. – Two Gothic, gable-wall MEMORIALS, the larger to Catherine Burnley †1866, the smaller to John McCunn †1866; at their centres, a pointed-arch cast-iron panel, cusped and crocketed, framing an inscribed granite tablet. – Helen Fairbairn †1856, and her husband William Wardlaw Smith †1880: on a grey granite plinth, a tall, fluted Corinthian COLUMN, draped with a helical band of ornament, carries an urn. – Fraser family, from 1906: wide, cream-painted HEADSTONE, framed with short paired Ionic pilasters, carrying a flat pediment block; Neoclassical roundel with weeping woman and inscribed inset grey marble panel. – Archibald Robinson, his wife and daughter †1912–15: Ionic aedicule HEADSTONE with sandstone pediment, entablature and columns, bronze capitals with wreath panels between, and a finely lettered, grey granite inscription. – Petrie family HEADSTONE, 1912; granite wall with fasces framing inscription, incut triglyphs and a gorge cornice bridge above. – Caroline Hutcheson †1899, and her husband, Robert McMillan Cooper †1913: on a high plinth, a fluted granite COLUMN with a dove perched on its egg-and-dart capital. – James Hunter of Hafton (1838–76): pink granite Celtic CROSS with fleur-de-lys arms, interlaced ornament and an inscribed shaft.

PUBLIC BUILDINGS

Former BURGH BUILDINGS, Argyll Street. By *Robert A. Bryden*, 1873–4. Knobbly baronial in schist and sandstone. Crowsteps and roll-mouldings in plenty but the high, all-but-symmetrical E façade equivocates between ecclesiastical and castellar: a church-like gable of two tall, lintelled lights and a seven-times-cusped circular window pushes up between gabled, tower-house lugs, corbelled from the round at second floor. Lavish masonry ornament outside but the interior disappoints. Only the ground floor is in use. First-floor hall with E stage and W gallery. – STAINED GLASS by *W. & J.J. Kier* is hidden above a suspended ceiling. – Cast-iron PROVOST'S LAMPS front the Argyll Street entrance.

CASTLE HOUSE, Castle Gardens. In municipal use. Designed by *David Hamilton*, 1822, as a ten-bedroom dwelling for James Ewing, Lord Provost of Glasgow. With Castle Toward (q.v.), it set a fashion for Castellated Gothic which persisted along the Cowal shore throughout the C19. Asymmetrical composition in ashlar sandstone spiked with square corner turrets and one corbelled corner round, crusted with battlemented parapets, and splayed with bays; the whole medievalizing conceit liberally overlined with label mouldings. The three-bay, pointed-arch open porch in the N wing has a rib-vaulted ceiling. So, too, does the main stone staircase which is lit by a tall pointed-arch s window and separated from an inner hall by a later columned screen. At the E boundary, the single-storey LODGE and GATEPIERS are linked by quadrant walls, *c.* 1830, in similar Gothic idiom.

DUNOON CASTLE. A royal castle 'for much, if not all, of the medieval period' (Dunbar, 1998). The site is a prominent one: a rocky rise behind the pier, now part of Castle Gardens, a park landscaped with municipal care where the town noses out into the firth. But, beyond some fragmentary masonry on the summit and indications of scarping and ditching below, there is little to betray the architectural configuration. These meagre traces and a mention of the castle in a C13 document suggest that its plan may have been similar to those 'simple rectangular castles of enclosure' (RCAHMS Inventory, 1992) being constructed along the western seaboard at that time, among them Achadun, Innis Chonnell and Sween (qq.v.). But this is speculation. Only minimal traces of the rubble curtain survive: towards the E corner and at the W, where a modern path capitalizes on what appears to be the original passageway through the outer wall. In the GARDENS, opened 1893, is the HIGHLAND MARY STATUE, 1896, the bronze figure of Burns's love looking across the firth to Kyle. Sculpted by *D. W. Stevenson* and set high on a heavily moulded red sandstone drum.

DUNOON GENERAL HOSPITAL, Bencorrum Brae. 1957–8. Three-storey E–W block with lower entrance wing projecting s. Glazed elevational grids with open balcony recesses. Linked E to the COTTAGE HOSPITAL by *John Burnet, Son & Dick*, 1926; a two-storey building in roughcast and red sandstone with double-height canted bays l. and r. of its central entrance.

DUNOON GRAMMAR SCHOOL, Ardenslate Road. By *Argyll County Council*, 1955 and 1963–4. Greatly extended by *Strathclyde Regional Council*, 1978–84. Vast educational spread dominated by a long four-tier classroom block layered with concrete and glass.

DUNOON LIBRARY, Argyll Street. By *Argyll & Bute District Council*, 1992–3. Low brick block with hip-ended bellcast roof. Continuous eaves glazing punctuated by U-sill windows.

DUNOON PIER. The first wooden jetty, 1835, was replaced by a new pier with offices by *Campbell Douglas*, 1867–8. In 1881 the quay was lengthened to *c.* 130m. Finally, following purchase by the Burgh Council in 1895, the present double-berth pier was built, 1896–8; engineer, *W. R. Copland*. This incorporated the old jetty as a gangway for goods and luggage but added a second for passengers. On the pier between the two, attractively half-timbered WAITING-ROOMS, gabled and bayed with a two-storey octagon set between verandas. At the junction of the new gangway and the s arm of the pier, a pagodalike belfry SIGNAL BOX, now linked to later additions. Both red-tiled buildings brightly restored by *Strathclyde Regional Council*, 1980–1, though the 1937 covered promenade link was removed. Shoreside, at the end of the original passenger approach, is the former TICKET

OFFICE; bowed front and back, it retains its splendid red-tiled conical roofs but, converted to commercial use, has lost the airy slenderness of the columned verandas below. Alterations to the pier, 1972, provide side-loading facilities for the Gourock ferry. A stone-built COAL PIER, *c.* 1900, lies 200m. N.

DUNOON PRIMARY SCHOOL, Hillfoot Street. Tall, two-storey-and-attic, street-front symmetry by Dunoon architect *William Fraser*, succeeded by *Boston, Menzies & Morton*, 1907. Baronial Gothic. Central tower with castellated parapet and rounds; at its buttressed base, a pointed-arch entrance with glazed vesica panels in the doors. Cusped round-arch windows at first floor. Pointed-arch pends penetrate the recessed side wings. The janitor's house has a dipping roof and two-storey corner octagon bay. Gymnasium wing by *Robert Cameron*, 1934. The earlier school, 1876, extended by *William Fraser*, 1899–1901, stood at rear until destroyed by fire, 1958.

KILBRIDE BRIDGE, crossing Balgie Burn *c.* 100m. N of Holy Trinity Church. Early C19. Rubble with red sandstone voussoirs to the segmental arch span.

LAMONT MEMORIAL, Tom-a-Mhoid Road. Grey granite dolmen rising out of a bouldered cairn. By Glasgow sculptors, *Scott & Rae*, 1906. The N face is carved with a ringed and bossed Celtic cross and inset with a bronze scroll commemorating more than two hundred members of the Lamont clan murdered at Dunoon in 1646.

POLICE STATION, Argyll Road. By *Argyll County Council*, 1975–7. White, two-storey shoe-box offices; the first floor slides s to cover the porch. Monopitch service buildings and housing around a courtyard.

Former POLICE STATION, Argyll Street and Argyll Road. Dated 1870. L-plan corner building in slate-and-roughcast Scots vernacular. Turnpike stair with conical roof.

POST OFFICE, Argyll Street and John Street. By *John Breingan*, 1901–2; extended 1911. Classical red sandstone ashlar with wide round-arch windows to both streets.

QUEEN'S HALL, Pier Esplanade. A tired giant now neither respectable nor yet brash enough for its promenade prominence. Glasgow architect *Ninian Johnston* won the commission in competition in 1951. And it shows; not least in the segmental, Festival Hall curve over the glazed second-floor lounge. It was built 1955–8 to a modified design which incorporates a balconied auditorium with stage-house, concert hall, lounges and cafés, with canopied shops along the street. Only the glazed entrance façade, looking s across Castle Gardens, retains some tarnished gaiety.

Former ST MUN'S SCHOOL (R.C.), Edward Street and Alfred Street. 1884. More church than school: gabled single-storey with cusped windows, porch and apex crosses. Now a Community Education Centre.

SHERIFF COURT-HOUSE, George Street. Competition-winner by *John McKissack & Son*, 1899–1900. Two-storey-and-attic street front in whin rubble with plentiful red sandstone dressings.

Dominating the elevation, a pediment-topped gable within which is a large mullion-and-transom window balconied at first floor above the round-arched entrance.

VICTORIA BRIDGE, West Bay. 1878. Steel beams spanning the Balgie Burn carry steel lattice-beam balustrading between castellated Gothic stone piers with blind cross loops. By *Somervail & Co.* of Dalmuir. Circular stone piers mid-stream.

WAR MEMORIAL, Pier Esplanade. Designed by Glasgow architect, *George Barr*, 1922. A flat-topped obelisk set on an open-pedimented base in a raised, railed enclosure. Applied to the face of the obelisk, a grey granite Celtic cross.

DESCRIPTION

Seen from the sea, the town presents itself well. The setting is splendid. Behind the pier, the green hill of Castle Gardens; flagpole on the summit, Highland Mary larger than life on a rocky bluff, and the Gothic Revival skyline of the High Kirk and Castle House (*see* Churches and Public Buildings). N and S, hotels and boarding houses line the shore and hillsides. But seen more closely, streetscape and buildings reveal a faded, often far from prepossessing face. For Dunoon, the prosperous years of steamers, yachts and 'doon the watter' holidays are only a memory.

PIER ESPLANADE provides first impressions. The rehabilitated Pier Buildings (*see* Public Buildings) are again smart, colourful and welcoming, while ARGYLL GARDENS, by *Argyll & Bute District Council*, 1993, a shallow pavement amphitheatre with tiled bell-roofed bandstand, offers *plein air* leisure on the gushet incline between the Esplanade and Argyll Street. But brutal book-ends frame the sea-front: at Castle Gardens, the lustreless bulk of the Queen's Hall (*see* Public Buildings) and, 100m. N, another more squalid exercise in grey, shoebox Modernism, the SWIMMING POOL by *Thomas Smith, Gibb & Pate*, 1967–8. Between the two is the INFORMATION CENTRE, 1994–5, an ochre brick box with a low pyramid roof which fails to conceal the backs behind.

ARGYLL STREET, the town's main shopping street, runs NW from the pier. It begins above Argyll Gardens with the ARGYLL HOTEL, built as a piended three-storey inn, 1837. In 1859 a dormered floor was added and in 1876 the square SE tower appeared, its Ionic porch superseding an earlier streetside Grecian doorway and window redolent (just) of Alexander Thomson. In 1908–9, *David Andrew* added a balconied wing of five round-arched windows in a convex link N to the Esplanade. The NE side of the street at first maintains the hotel's tenement-high scale. No. 78 has carved panels inset over tall first-floor windows. No. 82, the former Union Bank by *Peddie & Kinnear*, 1861, is two-storeyed and dormered but with a gabled centre under which an arched and panelled timber entrance screen recedes between pink granite columns *in antis*. Then, from No. 90 to No. 118, the eaves cornice is consistently lower: two-storey, ashlar buildings, early C19, given over to shops below but retaining their architraved windows to the flats above. An ashlar tenement with similar windows intervenes at Moir Street and at the chamfered corner of Church Street the return to three storeys is confirmed by another, dated 1878 and unconvincingly named DUNOON CROSS. Further on, COMMERCIAL BUILDINGS, 1910, rehabilitated by *G. R. Kennedy*, 1992, carries a wide eaves over corbelled bays, turning the corner into John Street under a porridge-bowl dome.

Shaking off the ill-kempt fringes of Queen's Hall, the SW side of Argyll Street recovers some architectural respect at No. 35, by *David V. Wyllie*, 1894, a big ashlar tenement with canted bays, re-gabled dormers and a run of pedimented windows at first-floor level. CROWN BUILDINGS, by *John Breingan*, 1905, has a hall at first floor lit by coupled round-arched windows set between Roman Doric columns under a portholed parapet. At No. 67, there is an original shopfront, 1858, entered on the gushet with Ferry Brae, and, on the other side of the junction, the slow curve of the CALEDONIAN HOTEL, 1847, a black-and-white convex bend in the street wall, doubly belted with fascia and parapet below six pedimented dormers. Thereafter a tawdry commercialism takes over. The stark gable of the Free Church (*see* Churches above) intervenes, but seems too severe for its main street site. Then, under an overhanging eaves, the MASONIC LODGE, *c.* 1870; below its plain but symmetrical upper floor, suddenly two dignified shops, each with a recessed entry set behind a single Roman Doric column. With a curve in the street line comes an abrupt surge in architectural activity. Hard on the pavement, the craggy Baronial gable of the Burgh Buildings (*see* Public Buildings above); set back on a rising site, the Gothic gable and steeple of St John's Church (*see* Churches); and, confronting each other across John Street through wide, round-arched windows, a regular, red Renaissance Post Office (*see* Public Buildings).

Old Dunoon clusters on the hill behind castle and church. KIRK STREET, aptly named, climbs off Ferry Brae, widens in front of the High Kirk's W gable (*see* Churches) and narrows again in a downhill spill to Tom-a-Mhoid Road. Nos. 2–20, restored by *J. G. Lindsay Pate & Associates* 1986, are two gable-to-gable, three-bay houses, mid C19, plain, painted, but severely attractive. The GLASGOW HOTEL, mid C19, is similar: three-bay but piended, with pilaster banding set widely off its central doorway: it incorporates the former Parish School at the corner of Kirk Brae. BALLOCHYLE HOUSE, again a plain Georgian dwelling, this time with skew gables, is early C19; so, too, No. 44: both are rendered. Opposite the church, a high rubble tenement, Nos. 26–28, *c.* 1860; rehabilitated with broad, gabled dormers by *McGurn, Logan, Duncan & Opfer*, 1986–7. On CASTLE STREET, Nos. 4–8 are three piend-roofed rubble cottages, early C19, probably the oldest houses in the town, though no longer in residential use. Perhaps, however, it is as much the rubble walls, 1835, that mark the boundary of the Castle House grounds and channel the narrow brae down to the W that give this part of town its protective intimacy and charm.

By the 1830s, Ferry Brae, Hillfoot Street and Jane Street connected the East and West Bays behind Castle Hill. A number of early villas survive. Among them on Clyde Street are BEACH HOUSE, dated 1832, a three-bay, gabled dwelling with lower side wings and a pilastered doorway, and GOWAN BRAE, with a single bay and an Ionic porch. On Jane Street, GOWRIE HOUSE has a neat dentilled cornice over its central doorway. From the same period, though only single-storeyed, HAMILTON HOUSE on Wellington Street is distinguished by a pedimented Ionic porch and two tripled chimney stacks.

The WEST BAY Esplanade was opened in 1880. Summer sees no throngs of promenaders now, but seaside memories linger. The slender finial and lacy balcony ironwork of THE YACHTSMAN, a pyramid-roofed Gothic turret-cum-café, seems appropriately light-hearted. Hotels, too, still proliferate along the West Bay shore. MCCOLL'S HOTEL, 1938–9, a radical reconstruction and enlargement of an earlier building by *A. MacGregor Mitchell*, begins the parade in unexpected style; four white storeys of muted Art Deco, rounded on the corners like a 'Thirties sideboard. Then, from MILTON TOWER HOTEL to the WEST END HOTEL, a rippling bay-windowed terrace, late C19, its end pavilions stepping back into steep mansard towers. Round the bay, beyond Victoria Bridge (*see* Public Buildings), the Esplanade was extended, 1923–5. The hotels continue. GLENMORAG HOTEL, C19, is high, wide, but perhaps not handsome. Others are more secluded on the wooded coastal scarp. ABBOT'S BRAE HOTEL, 1843, is calmly balanced by tall canted bays continued into the attic, while ARDFILLAYNE HOTEL, 1835, prefers the romantic irregularities of crowstepped Gothic. Lining the shore on BULLWOOD ROAD is a procession of twelve semi-detached villas, Nos. 3–47, each with its broad, iron-crested, bay window affording a view of the firth.

EAST BAY development began in the 1820s. Some early dwellings survive in poor condition in and around GEORGE STREET. On the front, however, CLYDE COTTAGE, *c.* 1830, maintains its self-respect; plain but neat, the pediment of its Ionic doorway nicely coincident with a moulded eaves course. ALEXANDRA PARADE begins at TIGH-NA-MARA, mid C19, unremarkable but for the attenuated proportions of a broken-pedimented porch. Along the Esplanade, to which major improvements were made in 1900 and 1905, houses and hotels vary in size and style, but there is nothing to make one turn from the sea. VICTORIA TERRACE, mid C19, no more than two houses long, has a certain late Georgian reserve. Less rigorously ordered, CRAGROY sheltered housing by *Argyll & Bute District Council*, 1980s, is, none the less, well disposed and scaled to conceal its bulk. But better things lie N at Kirn and Hunter's Quay (qq.v.).

Away from the shore and the centre of town, a few random discoveries can be made. On ARGYLL ROAD, through a four-centred arch pend, some COACH-HOUSES, *c.* 1840, converted to flats around a cobbled yard, and a memory of Moderne, EDGEMOUNT, *c.* 1935–6, a splay-fronted, bayed-and-balconied cube waiting for a face-lift. Among many two-storey, mid or late C19 dwellings with upper flats reached by curving stairs, FIRTH VIEW on Alexander Street is unique, its two swinging stair-flights enclosed by glazed timber tubes. Nearby is AUCHAMORE HOUSE, *c.* 1830, a three-bay gabled farmhouse with a pilastered doorpiece and some of its piend-roofed rubble outbuildings converted to residential use. On AUCHAMORE ROAD, Victorian villas. AVON BANK has a small but attractive Gothic gate. And in the garden of GLEN LODGE, dated 1864, a splendid Japanese-style summer-house.

DUNSTAFFNAGE CASTLE

on the S shore of Loch Etive, 5km. NE of Oban

8834

The location is of great strategic significance. Situated on a peninsular promontory at the mouth of Loch Etive, the castle casts its gaze W over the Firth of Lorn and E to the Pass of Brander and the route into Central Scotland. With such advantages of prospect and the added benefit of a sheltered anchorage close by, the site could hardly be more propitious for settlement; an impression which the massive, all-but-windowless walls only serve to intensify. Indeed, more than anything else, it is stone that arrests the eye at Dunstaffnage. First, bursting through the neat sward of conservators' grass, the great bulging base of conglomerate rock from which the walls of the fortress rise so dramatically; and secondly, the masonry itself, coursed in split rubble boulders laid on edge, somewhat randomly conspicuous and brought to level with well-bonded pinnings, this varied mural texture bordered by dressings of Ardtornish or Carsaig sandstone.

62

Building of a curtain-wall structure with some form of E gate-house probably began in the second quarter of the C13 at the instigation of Duncan, Lord of Lorn, the founder of Ardchattan Priory (q.v.) on the opposite, N side of Loch Etive. In 1309 the castle fell to the Scottish crown, from whom it passed first into Campbell and then Stewart hands. Restored to the 1st Earl of Argyll in 1469–70, it remained in Campbell care until 1958, when custody was accepted by the state. During this long period several programmes of alteration and reconstruction work were completed, notably to the gatehouse, late C15–C16 and again in the C17, the NW range in the C16 and early C18, and to the parapet walks, which were reconstructed in the early C17. The Campbells remained in residence until 1810 when a fire destroyed the main living quarters in the gatehouse tower. Partial repairs and re-roofing were carried out by the Duke of Argyll in 1903–4, but a proposal of 1908 to restore the entire castle came to nothing. Since the early 1960s repair and consolidation of the masonry have continued under state guardianship.

The plan is an irregular quadrangle enclosed by thick rubble curtains rising to between 6.1m. and 8.2m. above the inner courtyard level and articulated at rounded corners which, more diffident swellings than advancing drums, seem to emphasize

1 Prison
2 Entrance
3 Well

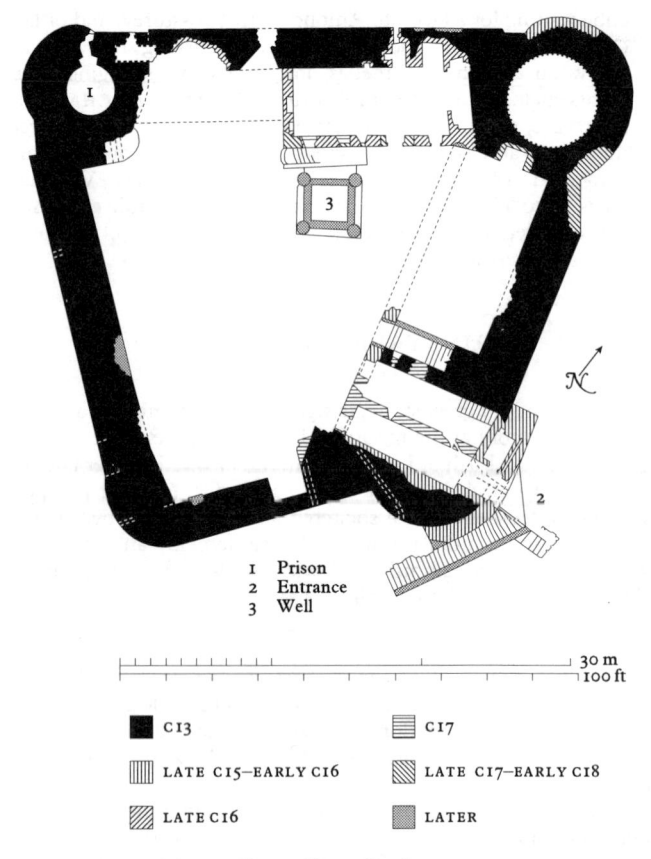

- C13
- LATE C15–EARLY C16
- LATE C16
- C17
- LATE C17–EARLY C18
- LATER

Dunstaffnage Castle

the compact solidity of the castle's mass. Both the N and W corners emerge more strongly as towers, indented slightly from the walls, shallow set-backs marked by quoining in the latter case. Entrance is from the E where the original approach capitalized on a fissure in the rock base. The GATEHOUSE has a bowed frontal structure begun in the late C15 or early C16 which, as a short curved length of walling returning from the SE curtain seems to indicate, superseded an earlier E tower of similar proportions to that at the N corner. Centred in this convex E wall, high above ground level, is a pointed-arch recess within which is a round-arch entrance doorway, reached by a long straight-flight forestair stepping up from the SW against the outer face of the gatehouse masonry. At the door's S jamb a modern timber landing negotiates the crossing from stair-head to threshold formerly achieved by a draw-bridge, the mechanism of which remains unclear. The arched entrance doorway is rebated for double doors and provided with draw-bar recesses. Within, to the r., is a guard chamber with a small aumbry in the N wall, and, ahead, a timber-roofed transe ramped through to the courtyard. This access passageway was originally much wider than at present, as the outline of a large pointed arch built into the harled w wall of the gatehouse shows, but was curtailed in the C17 when a transverse wall was constructed, creating the present narrow transe and a parallel cellar with gunloop supervision and its own window and door to the yard. A blocked door in the N wall indicates that communication with the now-destroyed E range was provided for in the C13 arrangements. C13 stonework may still survive at first-floor level in this N wall but the masonry of the upper floors is generally late C16. Although a small staircase rises in the NE corner of the cellar, this was introduced in the late C17 or early C18. The principal access to the first floor of the gatehouse is at the E end of the N wall. There a door, reached by steps from the yard, opens into a chamber lit by two W windows with chamfered arrises, C17, and a large E window, C17, with a C16 segmentally arched embrasure. N of this embrasure is the door to the small stair from below and, in the N wall immediately E of the entrance doorway, another door which leads into a round conically-capped stair turret corbelled into the corner between the gatehouse and the E curtain wall. The harled walls, turret and crowstepped gable of the gatehouse now rise independently behind the parapet of its lower frontal structure, allowing the wallhead walk to pass between. The second floor is lit by W, E and S windows, the central opening of the S three providing access to the parapet walk. There are C18 fireplaces with moulded stone jambs in the W and E gables and a NE door into the stair turret which may still be partly C13. In the garret, the masonry of the gables, dormers and turret is recent, probably 1903–4, the pediments of the three S dormers being transferred here from the dwelling house built in the NW range in the early C18 (*see* below). Two have ogival heads; one is dated 1725 with the initials AEC for Aeneas (Angus) Campbell, 11th Captain of Dunstaffnage, and DLC for his wife Dame Lillias Campbell, while the other is carved with swags and fruit falling from a scallop-shell. The third, which is triangular, bears the Campbell arms and the words LAUS DEO.

Of the EAST RANGE, virtually nothing survives. Cellarage presumably occupied the ground floor while the hall would have taken up most of the level above. The hall was evidently lit by two double-lancet windows, the blocked form of which can be seen in the E curtain. Both these openings have been successively altered but that to the S, close to the return of the N wall of the gatehouse, still preserves some dog-tooth ornament on the outer jambs and, on the inner side of the wall, a wide pointed-arch embrasure. Socket-holes for roof timbers survive below the level of the parapet-walk. A large fireplace opening was formed on the S side of the N tower, probably *c.* 1740 when the demolition of the E window of Dunstaffnage Chapel (q.v.) made a quantity of good-quality freestone available. Repairs to the N end of the E curtain, resulting in the oblique recess which almost certainly replaced the quoined set-back still to be seen at the W tower, must be contemporary. In both cases dressed stonework from the Chapel has been incorporated in the work. The ruinous NORTH TOWER, its interior filled with rubble debris and inaccessible, presents similar interpretation problems. While it is likely that it accommodated the more private apartments of the castle, the only clues to its use are the trace of a mural staircase rising clockwise from first floor and a ruinous E window at the level above. A garderobe chute projecting from the NW curtain wall a little to the SW may have been related to mural chambers in, or close to, the tower. Excavation, 1987–94, revealed an earlier curtain wall at the base of the tower.

In the NORTH-WEST RANGE, it is the roofless shell of the dwelling house formed in 1725 which survives. Its rubble walls, built against the C13 curtain and occupying the NE half of the gap between the N and W towers, are, in fact, largely those of the castle's C16 KITCHENS. A lintelled doorway, C18, enters the ground floor accommodation from the yard. To the r. is a wide kitchen fireplace, C16, with a salt-box recess in the chimney-breast and a segmental-arch, rebuilt 1971. Two deep recesses are located in the NW wall, both segmentally arched and one with a slop-sink discharge. Light is obtained from the yard, with a window at each end of the SE wall. Two other window openings have been blocked by the C18 forestair. The upper floor appears to have had two apartments, in each of which similar fireplaces, round-arrissed and round-cornered in yellow sandstone, survive; that in the SW gable fully framed, the other at the NE end of the curtain wall retaining only the jambs and a carved fire-back under its relieving arch. To the r. of this fire there is a deep narrow recess with a blocked window opening at high level, while on the l. two small windows with deep splayed embrasures penetrate the curtain. While the middle recess of the three has a lintel below the line of ceiling timber sockets, the two outer recesses rise into what must have been garret space under a lean-to roof. A short distance above their arched heads just below the wallhead are the socket holes which would have received the truss members of a monopitch roof. On the lower SE side of the roof, lighting the upper floor of the house, were three eaves dormers, the pediments from which are now incorporated in the gatehouse garret. Evidence regarding the rest of the range is confined to the NW curtain: an arched splayed aperture, a C16 fireplace insertion, and a blocked double-lancet window.

Access to the C13 WEST TOWER was originally by a forestair to a first-floor doorway close to the SW curtain. This door is now blocked but a modern timber stair allows access to the parapet-walk. Within the tower a ruinous mural stair rises anti-clockwise to the upper levels. At first- and second-floor levels there are two timber-lintelled embrasures for fish-tailed arrow-slits as well as traces of garderobes. At the wallhead, some C16 reconstruction. In the ground-floor core of the tower was a prison reached by trap-door from above.

DUNSTAFFNAGE

The SOUTH-WEST and SOUTH-EAST CURTAINS have several deep embrasures for arrow-slits similar to those in the W tower. For the most part these arrow-slits were superseded in the C17 by gun-loops, though one became a window. Two embrasures at the S corner of the courtyard were also walled off at this time, changes which, coupled with the evidence of unearthed foundations, point to the possibility of a building having existed in this area. During C19 restorations all but one of the embrasure openings were vaulted and arched. This century the parapet-walk has been rebuilt with new paving and the timber access stair already mentioned erected close to where the W tower forestair must originally have ascended to the wallhead. The only other feature in the yard is the rock-cut WELL, now rather grandly elaborated with a modern rubble superstructure of four flat-topped piers linked by bench seating.

DUNSTAFFNAGE CHAPEL, on a slight knoll in woods 150m. WSW of Dunstaffnage Castle. A long roofless rubble chamber, *c.* 20m. by 6m., built in the second quarter of the C13 with a grasp of burgeoning Gothic which has led to its being described as 'worthy in all respects, save that of mere size, to take its place alongside the noblest ecclesiastical monuments in contemporary France or Britain' (Simpson, 1968). Perhaps an exaggerated claim to make for a building which was never vaulted and which, although much still stands to the wallhead, is in ruinous condition; none the less, the quality of the design and carving is exceptional. The coupled windows on the N and S sides of the chancel (windows similar in composition to contemporary work at Killean Church, Kintyre (q.v.)) were chamfered, rebated and carved with dog-tooth ornament on the outside. On the inner face, the deeply splayed openings were framed by nook-shafts linked by semicircular arch-heads with roll-and-fillet mouldings 19 set between deep hollows. For all of this there is now only fragmentary evidence; moreover, only the N windows fully retain their round-arched heads. In the E window all mouldings have been cut down to sill height while the S door to the chancel is now also without dressings. In the nave, which was originally separated from the chancel by a timber screen, there are two opposed single-light windows with splayed ingoes. The S doorway survives in ruinous state; a N door opposite is barely discernible. At all four corners of the building the vestiges of robust edge-roll quoins.

In 1740 a short BURIAL-AISLE was added to the E gable by the Campbells of Dunstaffnage. The rubble walls of this small enclosure, originally harled like those of the Chapel, rise to a cornice coping stone set a little below the Chapel wallhead. There are no windows, only a tall gated gap at the centre of the E wall, framed by elongated Ionic pilasters carrying an entablature and a pediment at coping level. Reliefs of a skull and thigh bone project on each side. Set into the upper third of the gateway is a slate TABLET with an inscription, dated 1930, calling for the prayers of SS Fiacre of Brie, Margaret of Scotland and Louis of France. The aisle is crowded with commemorative stones and sculpture. Amongst the clutter, two inscribed recumbent SLABS: one in memory of Beatrix Campbell †1741; the other, erected in the late C17 for John Campbell †1677, depicting a man and woman holding hands under an arcaded bower. Built into the sill-height centre of the W wall, a large ogival-headed PANEL, probably C18, with an angel holding a trumpet aloft in each hand and the inscription ARISE YE DEAD & COME TO JUDGEMENT.

DUNTRUNE

7995

A promontory castle on the N shore of Loch Crinan. Some associated estate buildings.

DUNTRUNE CASTLE. Conspicuous and formidably picturesque, the castle emerges out of sea-girt basal rock to rise into a skyline of crenellated parapets and crowstep-gabled, slated roofs. The topography and location imply that some fortification existed from earliest times, though the present compact enclosure and dwelling date from C15 and *c.* 1600 respectively. Campbells retained the lands until the lairdship of the Malcolms of Poltalloch began in 1796. At that date the castle underwent major rehabilitation and in 1833–5 *Joseph G. Davis* was responsible for 'repairs and additions', the precise nature of which is unclear. With the completion of Poltalloch House (q.v.) in 1853, Duntrune ceased to be the Malcolms' home. A century later, however, the family returned, restored the castle and continue in residence.

It may be, as MacGibbon and Ross recorded, that 'the house now presents few features of importance' but this external simplicity distinguishes Duntrune as a fine example of C17 Scots domestic architecture. The seaward SE front, three storeys between crowstepped gables, has a calculated mansion-house dignity. Three rake-roofed eaves dormers, flanked by slab-weepers, surmount three tall windows which light the first-floor hall and drawing room; only the smaller ground-floor openings retain an earlier, less regimented character. At the rounded S corner, which is the external angle of the L-plan, the heavily pointed rubble walling curves below the corbelled skew of the SW gable. Shadowed in the craggy base of this angle is the open mouth of a garderobe chute, relic of an earlier tower located at this S corner of the C15 *enceinte*. Older masonry survives here at lower level, determining the somewhat acute alignment of the C17 house's return wing above. This W face, first gable then eaves, repeats the fenestration arrangements of the SE front at first and second floors. At the NW gable, wallhead and roofline drop over ancillary accommodation enclosed by the crenellated sweep of the curtain wall to the N. In the NW face, a single French window opening marks a former sea-gate postern, below which rubble steps lead down to the lochside.

The landward approach from the N crosses a grassy dip that may have had some early defensive significance. Beyond a raised terrace, gaunt masonry screens an inner courtyard but cannot

- C15
- c. 1600
- 1796 AND LATER
- 1954-7

Courtyard

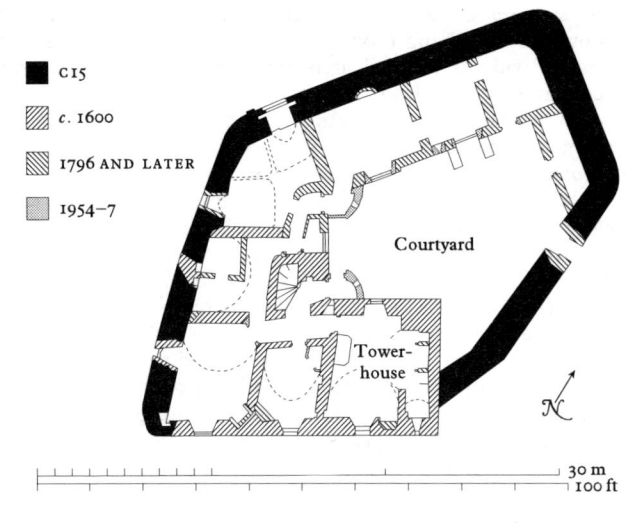

Tower-house

Duntrune Castle

quite conceal the slated roofs and gables of the L-plan house behind. From the l. a blank battlemented forework, late C18, elbows forward to terminate above a rocky excrescence. Behind, on the r., a similar wall from the same period of restoration curves out to enclose the terrace on the NW. Between the two a cranked alleyway leads l. ramping up s to a narrow lintelled gap, again late C18, penetrating the older walling which encloses the castle yard and outbuildings. This 5m.-high, C15 curtain, battlemented probably at the time of the late C18 renovation, follows a polygonal plan, wrapping around the irregular court on the N and engaging with the NE gable of the three-storey house to the s. The curtain gate has an embossed armorial panel, dated 1851, brought by the Malcolms from Poltalloch House. Once through it, the castle is immediately more intimate than intimidating. To the r., a single-storey NE range houses stores below a swept gabled doocot; ahead is the NW kitchen range with bedrooms above: both restored from late C18 shells, 1954–7, as the dated rainwater heads testify. In the W and S corners of the yard are two single-storey curved appendages added in these 1950s changes. The former connects ground-floor apartments in the house proper with the NW range; the latter is an entrance porch leading to the hipped-roofed stair tower in the re-entrant.

All four cellars (now rooms) filling the L-plan of the C17 house around the winding newel-stair in the re-entrant corner are vaulted. So, too, is the dining room located between the house's NW gable and the NW range. The original kitchen, which occupied the full width of the NE cellar, retains a wide gable fireplace, though the segmental arch and piers have been rebuilt. To the r. of this, a vaulted recess with a SE slit window and signs of an early stair which would have served the hall above. In the dining room, the embrasure of the former NW postern with its pointed arch has been retained. First-floor accommodation follows the early C17 arrangements; hall and adjacent drawing room occupy the SE block. In the drawing room, a pine chimneypiece with reeded pilasters, dentilled cornice mantel and white marble surround, late C18.

Near the start of the castle entrance ramp, mounted on a wrought-iron frame is a BELL probably brought here from Kilmartin Church (q.v.) in the C19. A Latin inscription records its casting for the minister by *Robert Maxwell* of Edinburgh in 1712. 150m. N of castle, single-storey rubble estate OUTBUILDINGS and COTTAGES, early C19(?), in two parallel blocks face each other across a court closed by a gated wall on S. Round rubble GATEPIERS carry bronze antlered deer brought from Poltalloch (q.v.). At the entrance to the estate grounds, 250m. NE of castle, sandstone GATEPIERS, C19, also from Poltalloch(?), form broad double-pilastered plinths carrying carved obelisk urns; wrought-iron gates and side railings. WALLED GARDEN, *c.* 1800; redesigned in the late 1950s by *Muriel Malcolm* incorporating architectural salvage from Poltalloch and elsewhere. TEMPIETTO with columns from Burlington House; ironwork by *Peter Campbell*.

DUN, Ardifuir, 1.4 km. NNW of Duntrune Castle. Excellently preserved circular dun, 19m. in internal dia., lying NW of Ardifuir Steading. Drystone walling reaches 3.5m. in thickness and is substantially intact on the inner and outer faces. The battered outer face stands 3m. at the NW. The WSW entrance is rebated for a door and has a massive sill stone. An opening on the S side leads down four steps to a small oval mural chamber. Some 10m. N of the entrance, another opening leads from the inner wall face to a rising flight of intramural stairs.

FORT, 1km. ENE of Duntrune Castle. Oval plan, 45m. by 27m., defined by rubble remains, but now concealed in woods. N and W stretches show heavy vitrification, indicating timber strengthening of the structure. To the NW is a cliff face while on its other sides the fort has been protected by at least one outer wall.

ELLARY

Wooded estate on the craggy NW side of Loch Caolisport reached at the dead-end of the single-track shore road from Achahoish.

BURIAL GROUND, Cladh a'Bhile, 550m. SW of Ellary House. Ancient site enclosed by a rubble wall in the 1870s. Exceptionally rich in cross-marked STONES and SLABS dating from the C7 and C8. One splendidly elaborate example, 2.06m. high, carved with hexafoil and cross motifs set in circles.

ELLARY HOUSE. Scottish-Jacobean house, 1870, by *David Bryce*; moderate in stylistic zest but considerable in size. It spreads N into not just one but two service courts. Following a fire,

Robert S. Lorimer carried out extensive repairs and alterations, 1894–8. These entailed the creation of a crenellated square entrance tower, rising through three floors towards the s end of the w front, and the building of a single-storey billiard room, also crenellated, in the sw re-entrant r. of the entrance vestibule. Within the Bryce shell, which required some reconstruction of the E and s walls, Lorimer rebuilt most of the interior, providing new floors of reinforced concrete, new timber staircases and a new roof. Decorative plasterwork features floral and oak motifs, on occasion breaking out from the confinement of the cornices.

DUN, A'Chrannag, 1km. w of Ellary. An oval dun 16.5m. by 12m. at the highest point of the A'Chrannag ridge. The walling is now indistinct but evidence of vitrification, especially clear on the N, points to timber-laced construction. Outer walls of intermittent rubble spreading to the NE and w may have enclosed further settlement.

DUN, Dùn a'Bhealaich, 600m. WNW of Ellary. A 3m.-thick wall, visible on its outer face, defines a circular enclosure 14m. in diameter.

ELLENABEICH and EASDALE

7417
7317

Once the centre of Nether Lorn's productive slate-quarrying industry, Ellenabeich and Easdale survive as holiday villages on the black w edge of Seil, saved from dereliction blight by the drama of the landscape and, more recently, the respect of conservation repair. From the early C18 the quarries were organized on a commercial basis. At first, work was restricted to above-water-level seams, but at the start of the C19 improvements in pumping arrangements, powered by windmill and steam engines, made deeper operations possible. A depth of 50m. was reached. So immense was the output that Ellenabeich, hitherto an island like Easdale, became linked to Seil by a causeway of quarry waste. In 1881, however, the rock and masonry wall which protected the main quarry at Ellenabeich from the sea was breached, creating what now appears to be a natural tidal basin. Production slumped, several quarry pits on Easdale were also flooded, and by World War I it was all over.

The slate is ubiquitous still: not only in the cottage roofs, garden and allotment enclosures, dry-stone walls, pathways, piers and jetties left by industry but along the black rock-girt margins of a ragged shore-line and, above all, on the scree-drenched cliff-face of Dùn Mór, towering over the villages on the N. A hard dark landscape softened by the green of grass and moss but sharpened by the white-walled rows of slate-workers' housing.

The harbours on each side of Easdale Sound, constructed *c.* 1826, have QUAYS and JETTIES built of vertically laid slate rubble. At Ellenabeich a long wall of this masonry protects a rubble and rock track which curves from the jetty to a T-plan PIER, *c.* 1870, now a barren scaffold of timber and iron carrying a derelict post crane. Conservation work has greatly improved the condition of both harbours; sea-walls, slipways and steps have been repaired, shore banking stabilized and new paving and bollards put in place. In both villages single-storey rows of two-roomed WORKERS' COTTAGES, built for the quarrymen's families in the early C19, are gradually recovering their original 'neat and comfortable appearance' (*NSA*, 1845), many as holiday homes. All are slated with rubble walls harled, roughcast or cement rendered. In Ellenabeich the disposition is tightly ordered: two back-to-back rows, Nos. 1–12 and 13–24, lie roughly E–W facing narrow streets which separate them from small walled gardens on the N and a parallel row of similar dwellings, Nos. 25–32, on the S. This last extends W towards the pierhead in two more cottages, a higher eaves betraying the presence of additional loft space. E lies the two-storeyed OLD INN and, at the entrance to the village, a pleasant enclave of white-harled 1980s(?) houses, plain but respectful. On Easdale, the layout of the same gable-to-gable rows is less geometricized. Here there are no streets, only grass and a few slate tracks, and though the right-angled relationship of houses S of the harbour creates a sense of enclosure, this common space is more white-walled field than prim village green. A single iron LAMP-POST, incongruously cast with the words 'City of Lincoln', scarcely adds civic conviction. More urban, the former DRILL HALL, a square slate-rubble structure with a high pyramid roof. More provocative, looking S over Camas Mór, the fussy head-and-tail form of a HOUSE, 1987–92, by *Julian Wickham*, part pill-box pyramid, part latter-day black-house.

KILBRANDON UNITED FREE CHURCH, Kilbride, 1.5km. ESE of Ellenabeich. 1908–9. Corrugated-iron and timber gabled hall lit by high, three-light windows with segmental arches. Octagonal window in rear gable. Derelict.

AN CALA. Three in-line cottages, C19, converted to a single dwelling, 1930–40. Two-storey painted rubble with swept dormers, late C19(?). Higher, half-octagon SE wing, added early C20, has waney-edge boarding to first floor. Shuttered windows and a pale-blue-and-white colour scheme add to an almost incongruous anglicized intimacy. A 5m.-high brick wall, 1934, shelters the house and protects a lovely 'plantsman's' GARDEN, 1930–40, from the SW winds.

EASDALE PRIMARY SCHOOL. Dated 1877. Symmetrical single-storey rubble, gabled l., r. and centre. Roof spars carried into eaves.

INSHAIG PARK HOTEL. Tall, piend-roofed, three-bay rubble house, mid C19(?). Painted quoins and dressings. Square ground-floor bays l. and r. with pilastered central doorway.

DUN, Dùn Aorain, 460m. W of Dunmore House. On a rocky height above the shore, this sub-oval slate-built dun cannot be easily reached except from the NE. In its thick E wall, now a grass-covered bank, evidence of slate steps leading to a mural cell has been found. Traces of a protective outwork covering the landward approach.

ERISKA

An island at the mouth of Loch Creran, said to be named after the Norse invader, Erik the Red. Until the beginning of the C20 access was by boat or, at low tide, by fording the An Doirlinn channel just over 2km. NNW of Barcaldine Castle.

BRIDGE. Erected *c.* 1900. Single-track carriageway runs between steel lattice-trusses crossing the narrows between Loch Creran and the Lynn of Lorn. Granite abutments and central pier. The bridge, which has finialled railings along the trusses and flanking the N and S approaches, is gated.

ISLE OF ERISKA HOTEL. Immaculate Baronial country house by *Hippolyte Blanc*, 1884. The usual accumulation of canted bays, crowstepped gables, castellated parapets and pedimented eaves dormers, unusually polychromatic in silver-grey Creetown granite and red sandstone ashlar. At the W corner, the composition masses around a four-storey tower with asymmetrical stair turret, corbelled rounds and mock cannon; yet the entrance is not here, nor at the centre of the all-but-symmetrical SW front which looks out across a small balustraded terrace to croquet lawns, but rather under a cable-hooded archway set between the broad buttresses of a NW porch. Oak panelled interior. Late C19 STABLES, built with poured concrete walls, converted to swimmimg pool and leisure facilities by *Crerar & Partners*, 1993–5.

FASLANE

A naval base on Gareloch since the time of James IV. This century, geo-political strategy has increasingly exploited its sheltered deep-water anchorage. Now HM Naval Base *Clyde*; a vast secret city sealed behind barbed wire and closed-circuit television surveillance. Range upon range of buildings line the contours. Implacably bland and repetitive offices, immense sheds and cranes, dedicated to the maintenance of surface and submarine naval power.

FASLANE CHAPEL, in Faslane Cemetery (q.v.). C13 church dedicated to St Michael. Ruined rubble oblong: E gable almost entire; N and S walls stand to *c.* 1.5m. In the gable, two chamfered lancets with deep round-arched inner reveals. Aumbry at the E end of the N wall.

FASLANE CEMETERY, 1.6km. SE of Garelochhead Parish Church. Walled enclosure with C19 and C20 graves. At the entrance, a grey granite OBELISK and group of some thirty similar sandstone HEADSTONES to the men lost in submarine K13 in the Gareloch, January 1917. Also near the gates, a thick barley-sugar pillar MONUMENT to the ironfounder David Davidson †1919, his wife and two children who died in infancy. The column, which has a capital with carved faces at the four cardinal points, supports a block sundial. Tall marble angel MONUMENT on a grey granite base: to James Robertson Watson †1923, Professor of Chemistry at Anderson's College, Glasgow.

FINNART

Deep-sea tanker terminal and oil storage installations, from 1951, on the E shore of Loch Long.

ARDARROCH HOUSE, Arrochar Road. Asymmetrical multi-gabled villa peppered with chimney pots. Built for Glasgow merchant John McVicar by *William Burn*, 1838. Now serves as oil company offices. Main block constructed in rubble with polished sandstone dressings; lower services wing spreading NE. Over the E entrance, consoles support a Baroque broken pediment with a shell-topped escutcheon clasped between its volutes. To the l. of this doorway, a full-height canted bay rises into a gable. To the r., embedded in a re-entrant, a cylindrical stair tower is corbelled to square and gabled. On the W, more canted bays swept on cavetto curves to gables. In 1846–7, *David Bryce* added a conservatory (demolished) on the S side of the house and extended the services wing. He may also have built the EAST LODGE, *c.* 1846, a gabled, asymmetrical T-plan.

FINNART HOUSE, Arrochar Road. By *William Burn*, *c.* 1835. A rambling, two-storey, gabled dwelling set on a terrace with lower kitchen court extending NE. Similar in layout, material and character to Ardarroch House (q.v.) but now abandoned among oil storage tanks. The contemporary FINNART LODGE is also by *Burn* and much more fun. Built in rubble with red sandstone dressings, it retains its picturesque charm: a sturdy roundhouse rising from the stream below to a slated conical roof from which gabled and piended projections emerge.

GLENMALLEN HOUSE, Arrochar Road. Early C19. Symmetrical two-storey, three-bay house with lower wings l. and r. Pilastered doorpiece with cornice. To the W, a five-bay STABLES block.

FORD

Bridgehead village in a pleasant undulating landscape at the SW end of Loch Awe.

FORD CHURCH. 1850, small skew-gabled kirk in heavily pointed rubble. Triple lancet in the S gable; gable belfry above. Plastered interior; roof with collar beams. Brass WAR MEMORIAL with Celtic border. – STAINED GLASS in gable lancets personifies Fides, Caritas and Spes as haloed Pre-Raphaelite females in browns and reds. Temperantia in the E lancet is similar. Above and below all four figures a delightful small pane background of varied flower motifs drawn with childlike charm, 1887.

OLD PARISH CHURCH, Kilneuair, 1.1km. SW of Fincharn Castle. The medieval church of St Columba in Glassary was replaced by Kilmichael Glassary Parish Church by the early C17. Ruinous 5.6m.-wide oblong, its length of 21m., showing changes in masonry, indicates successive phases of building. Chancel walling, later C13; W half of N wall, C14 or C15; S wall early C16. The splayed S ingo of the two-light chancel window is still apparent. Window, aumbry and piscina at the E end of the S wall are also from the earliest period of construction. The location of two doors and a second window in S wall and the existence of another aumbry halfway along the N wall suggest a later nave altar separated from the chancel by a screen. The lintel of the W doorway in the S wall bears the sunk carving of a cross. – Medieval stone FONT with circular basin. – TOMB-CHEST side- and end-panels, C16, in chancel; W end-panel carved with short length of cusped arcading which curves into floral interlacing. – In the churchyard, three carved tapered SLABS, Loch Awe school, C14–C15, one carrying the relief figure of a small man armed with sword and spear.

Close to the SW corner of the church is a roofless Gothick BURIAL ENCLOSURE, late C18(?). At the centre of S lateral wall a blind, sharply pointed arch rises from the ground; on either side two blind 'windows', even more acutely arched. Arched openings similar to these provided in the W and E end walls. Vermiculated rustication with decorative mock Celtic ornament cut in the alternate quoin courses and voussoirs of the large arch.

EDERLINE HOUSE, 1.2km. SSE. The Baronial mansion by *Wardrop & Reid*, 1870, densely packed around a four-storey turreted tower, was demolished in 1966; a craggy mound of masonry survives among the rhododendrons. An older soberer Ederline, late C18(?), built on a T-plan three storeys high, has also gone; in 1983 a gable collapsed, necessitating its demolition. A cobbled COURT OF OFFICES, early C19, remains. BURIAL ENCLOSURE on a wooded peninsula of Loch Ederline, 1727.

FINCHARN CASTLE, on SE Loch Awe shore, 3.2km. ENE of Ford village. Much ruined rubble remains of a small oblong C13 hall-house strongly sited on a rocky promontory. Vestiges of walling stand on the N, NE, and to maximum height of *c.* 6m. on SE. The entrance was through NE end wall where bar-hole and splayed ingo survive. Rock-cut ditch on SW.

FORD HOTEL. Originally Auchinellan Inn, a 'changing house'; latterly almost a tenement. Begun in 1864 with two storeys and a S canted bay, later increased to three storeys with five barge-boarded eaves dormers, and later still, early C20, extended S by two additional bays.

TORRAN BEAG, set above the S end of Loch Awe. Corrugated-iron cottage with a sprocketed veranda, *c.* 1905.

CRANNOGS, Loch Awe. Of twenty confirmed sites in Loch Awe four crannogs are located in the vicinity of Ford. The largest, 37m. by 27m. and 3m. high, lies closest to the village, *c.* 100m. off Ederline boathouse.

STANDING STONE, 50m. E of Torran Farm. Broad stone, 3.3m. high, with grooved lines of an open-armed cross on the NW face and a less distinct cross pecked on the SE.

STANDING STONE, Glennan, 2.75km. SW. Stone with pointed top, 2.2m. high, incorporated into a rubble wall.

STANDING STONE, 270m. SW of Ford Hotel. Straight-sided 3m. stone with flat top.

FRAOCH EILEAN

An island at the N end of Loch Awe, 3.4km. SW of Kilchurn Castle. Pennant called it 'the Hesperides of the Highlands' (1774), recalling the Ossianic legend of Fraoch who came to the island to gather its delicious fruit but was killed by a guardian serpent.

FRAOCH EILEAN CASTLE. Ruinous C13 hall-house erected by Macnaughtons on the authority of Alexander III. Built on the higher NE end of the island and now surrounded and invaded by trees, the rubble walls of its rectangular plan stand to varying height and exhibit little architectural refinement. The building is aligned W–E and it seems probable that it was of two storeys, perhaps with a garret. Two door openings in the E wall suggest the possibility of a N–S transverse wall at ground level, though no masonry evidence survives, while a socket-hole in the W wall indicates that an axial beam supported first-floor joists. From the middle of the E wall a mural stair descends N to an unlit prison at the buttressed NE corner; from this point too a timber stair would have risen W to the hall above – or perhaps to an intervening solar at the E end of the first floor. Towards the W end of the hall's N wall a few stone treads are all that remain of another mural staircase which presumably ascended to a parapet walk.

Having become derelict, the castle was reinhabited by the Campbells of Inverawe early in the C17, the SE corner being adapted as a small three-storeyed house. Later in the century this dwelling was extended to take in the full width of the E end of the old hall-house, the latter's N and S walls being raised as gables. One of these still stands, along with vestiges of the inner wall which separated the new accommodation from a courtyard now adventitiously defined by the ruined walls of the hall-house.

Of the enclosed bailey W of the castle only a short S stretch of walling can be seen. Signs of a circular tower at the island's SW extremity. Minimal remains of a boulder jetty to SE. A drystone irregular oblong on the S shore may be a boat-house.

FURNACE

Former industrial village 11.5km. SW of Inveraray straggling down the W shore of Loch Fyne from its rivermouth origins. In 1754 the Duddon Company of Cumbria obtained a concession on Loch Fyne timber, leased land at the hamlet of Inverleckan, dammed Loch Leacann, cut a lade from the E bank of the Leacann Water and in the following year began to build a charcoal-burning iron furnace some 100m. N of a boulder-built quay on the Loch Fyne shore. Nearby, on slightly higher ground to the E, several rubble sheds (perhaps four) were built to store imported iron-ore and the charcoal obtained from the Argyll woods. For more than half a century the Craleckan Ironworks maintained production and the company contributed greatly to improvements to roads and bridges in the area. In 1788 a proposal for a planned village was drawn up by *George Langlands* but remained on paper. Thereafter, output began to decline, and in 1812 the Argyll Furnace Company ceased operations. The village's industrial activities resumed, however, in 1842 when the Lochfyne Powder Works were established. Once more, a plentiful supply of local charcoal was critical and, since the gunpowder drying process required steam, provision for water-power was again made: Loch Leacann was dammed, the river deepened and more lades cut, this time from the W bank. Building took place over an extensive area but much was destroyed in a catastrophic explosion in 1883, after which production was abandoned. A few ruinous structures survive in overgrown desolation.

CUMLODDEN PARISH CHURCH, on A83, 900m. SW of The Furnace Inn. Bare Gothic, barely Gothic. Built by Lochgilphead mason *David Crow*, to a design by *James Nairn* of Balloch, 1841. Almost classical E gable-pediment opened by a pointed-arch window at its centre. Above this, a spiky birdcage bellcote; below, twinned round-arch openings, originally doors but altered to windows in 1894 when the seating was recast and the S porch added. Plain, flat-ceilinged interior. Retained in the church is the upper part of a freestanding Early Christian CROSS SHAFT, C8 or C9, removed from Killevin Burial Ground, Crarae, in 1992; the stone is carved with a bearded figure, ring and cross, and is holed transversally. – STAINED GLASS in round-arched E windows by *William Meikle & Sons*, 1924. Lean-to hall with parapet; vestry added across W gable by *William Todd* of Lochgilphead, 1911.

CRALECKAN IRONWORKS. Built 1754–5. Dominating the small group of single-storey cottages which lie between it and the river, the massive granite rubble bulk of the tapering furnace-stack, similar to those at Bonawe (*see* Taynuilt) and Duddon but larger, seems more fortification than manufactory. Its battered outer walls reach 7.9m. to the ruinous parapet of what was originally a roofed wallhead walk around the central chimney-stack. N and W walls present a revetted bastion of gaunt stonework. Hidden on E and S, where the roofless blowing-house and re-roofed casting-house still abut, are the wide-splayed reducing openings which housed the bellows nozzle and through which molten metal could be tapped. Deep in these masonry maws is the furnace hearth, above which an inverted cone splays upwards to the base of the conical brick-lined stack and the circular charging mouth. Above this is the flue, bottle-shaped in inner section but stepped three times as its outer profile rises to a bevelled top 11.5m. above ground level. Single-storey gabled CASTING-HOUSE to S, unremarkable. BLOWING-HOUSE, to E, a three-storey, empty shell. A sloping scarcement at second-floor level indicates the ramped line of the bridge-loft floor which rose to the charging mouth from the E gable doorway which in turn was linked by a stone-banked ramp to a terrace in front of the STORAGE SHEDS. Only one of these remains, some distance N; it was much altered and re-roofed, *c.* 1880.

FURNACE PRIMARY SCHOOL. Late C19. Schoolhouse with gabled central projection links r. to wide-gabled classroom block. Roughcast gabled classroom block added at rear by *Argyll County Council*, 1964.

KENMORE VILLAGE, 4.2km. NE on flat ground between two bays on the W shore of Loch Fyne. Small fishing settlement of two parallel cottage rows, 1771–2, separated by village green, planned by surveyor *William Douglas* for the 5th Duke of Argyll. Those single-storey dwellings which remain have been adapted as holiday homes. Some trees from a central NE–SW avenue survive. Quay built against rocks at NE bay. Nearby a tapering obelisk CAIRN of square snecked rubble; by *Colin Sinclair*, 1930. A bronze plaque and relief head, by *Alexander Proudfoot*, commemorates the Gaelic poet Evan MacColl †1898, born in Kenmore ninety years earlier.

POWDERMILLS COTTAGES, at N end of village just off A83. Mid C19, single-storey, workers' row of three three-bay brick houses. The two-bay N extension tries but fails to keep in keeping.

THE FURNACE INN. Gable ended, one-and-a-half-storey inn, C19, in heavily pointed red rubble. An earlier(?), independently symmetrical, hipped-roofed wing advances slightly on the E side.

WAR MEMORIAL. 1921; the design by quarry manager *Francis Nicol*. Tall obelisk of rough-faced local granite blocks. Small arm-pitted cross atop.

GARBHALLT

0295

A few houses in the lovely rural valley of the Strathlachlan River, 8km. SW of Strachur.

CHAPEL and BURIAL GROUND, Kilbride, on a level headland above Loch Fyne, 1.3km. N of Old Castle Lachlan. A rubble enclosure wall, now little more than a turf-covered excrescence, marks a circular, evidently sacred, space. Within, somewhat to the S, are the equally degraded remains of a small oblong chapel dedicated to St Bridget. Both are of Early Christian date. To the E lie the ruins of Kilbride township.

OLD PARISH CHURCH, Kilmorie, on the l. bank of the Strathlachlan River. All that remains is the roofless rubble shell of the MacLachlan burial aisle, late C16. This has two small windows on the N wall, one on the S, and another at high level in the E gable; all are now blocked. A large round-arch doorway opens through the W gable. The height of this gable, its slight projection beyond the N wall of the aisle, and the survival of a concave moulded skewputt at the NE corner, indicate that this is the surviving E wall of the original C15 church. This building was still standing at the end of the C18 when it was replaced by Strathlachlan Church (*see* below) but within a few years it was being quarried and had fallen into ruin.

A few funerary SLABS, C14–C16, lie in the burial aisle. In the BURIAL ENCLOSURE, the tapered shaft of a damaged C15 CROSS has been erected in an octagonal socket-stone with sloping sides. The shaft, 1.97m. high, is lozenge-shaped in plan and is carved on one facet near the base with the image of a pair of shears. The foliated head has lost its upper portion. Tradition asserts that this is a market cross or 'bargain cross' (Drummond, 1881) but it is more probably religious in origin like those at Kilmory Knap (q.v.). Among the graves is a simply mantled TOMBSTONE marking the death of Archibald McKellar †1786, with the socially challenging inscription – IN THE LORD IS OUR TRUST/PRINCES THIS CLAY MOST BE/YOUR BED/IN SPITE OF ALL YOUR POURS/THE RICH THE WISE THE/REVEREND DEAD/MOST LIE AS LOW AS OURS.

STRATHLACHLAN PARISH CHURCH. A high-walled gabled church of harled rubble built off a bouldered plinth, *c.* 1792. Rustic quoins with alternate blocks projecting like tusking stones; a procedure repeated in the surrounds to a blind lancet and quatrefoil at the centre of the SW gable and the pointed-arch window on each side. The NE entrance gable is barge-boarded; the SW skewed and crowned by a crude birdcage belfry with a flat slab roof and ball finials. The roof is late C19: bracketed arch-braced trusses with tie rods. The early C19 NE gallery, supported by two Roman Doric columns, has a panelled front bearing the arms of the MacLachlan of MacLachlan family. Extensive renovation carried out, 1901.

BRIDGE, 1km. SW of Parish Church. A rubble crossing of the Strathlachlan River in two segmental arches, C19(?).

NEW CASTLE LACHLAN, on the r. bank of the Strathlachlan River halfway between Garbhallt and Old Castle Lachlan. When built by Robert MacLachlan, *c.* 1790, it was a three-bay, two-storey-and-basement, L-plan dwelling with a central flying stair rising to the *piano nobile*. Altogether 'a remarkably sensible small house', Cockburn called it in 1840; only a crenellated wallhead provided a modest reminder of the Old Castle which the family had abandoned. But in 1903 all this classical calm was lost when the house was radically baronialized: a tall battle-mented tower with mock cannon and a crowstepped cap-house rose at the centre of the SW front, a balustraded entrance stair swept up in the re-entrant to the r., and from the S corner a two-storey, room-size drum burst out, corbelled below and capped by a slated ogee dome above. Nor was this all, for packed against the NE side of the old house massive extensions in similar idiom reach three and four storeys. Everywhere walls are roughcast and the Baronial detail cut in ashlar dressings: crowsteps, string-courses, roll-mouldings, corbel-courses, window pediments, etc. In the tympana of the two SW attic dormer pediments, there are the wreathed carvings of a galleon and a fish; in the pediment over the central first-floor window in the S drum, the date 1903, the numbers infected with just a hint of Art Nouveau. Towards the rear of the building, dressings and detail diminish, the roughcast carrying across changes of plane in a smoother, more vernacular manner. Like it or not, the trans-formation is ebullient, complex and accomplished; not a sign of C18 order remains, save perhaps in a vestige of quoining which can still be seen at basement level at the NW end of the main façade. NE of the house, the original COURT OF OFFICES, *c.* 1800, does survive, however, though only just: a symmetrical arrangement of four ranges, the SW front entered through an elliptical archway set below a pediment carrying a heavy plain birdcage belfry with a flat pyramid top. Further NE is the desecrated ruinous WALLED GARDEN.

OLD CASTLE LACHLAN
on the E shore of Loch Fyne commanding the entrance to Lachlan Bay

A romantic silhouette emerging from a low promontory knoll. Heaving through the rock, gaunt rubble walls with battered plinths rise out of the loch-edge landscape; turf and trees are pushed aside but ivy, clinging to the stone, seems to have been carried to the wallhead some 13m. above the upswept profile of the ground below. The plan, a deformed rectangle, recalls Castle Sween (q.v.), though it is neither so large nor so early. Here the curtain is C15, perhaps as much as three hundred years later than that at Sween. There is documentary evidence of an earlier MacLachlan stronghold on the site but it is planning rather than dating that establishes the similarity between the two. Within the oblong defined by the early C15 walls are two ranges, NE and SW, separated by a narrow central courtyard. This arrangement, adopted at Castle Sween though no longer surviving there, appears to be C15, although the inner buildings date from *c.* 1500

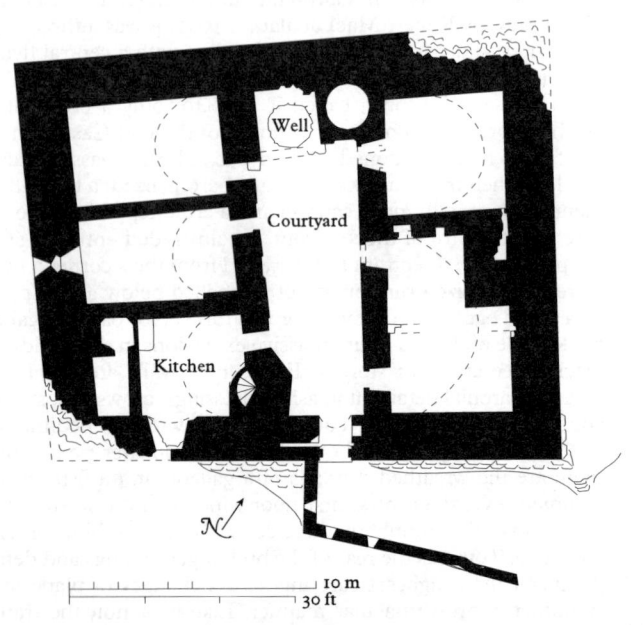

Garbhallt, Old Castle Lachlan.
Ground-floor plan

when extensive remodelling, including the widening of the SW range, took place. Apart from some minor works a century later, the castle has retained this distinctive form (one range of accommodation for the hall, the other given over to the private chambers) and remained inhabited until the last years of the C18 when New Castle Lachlan was built nearby. A hundred years later its condition necessitated stabilization and repairs, resulting in the blocking up of many windows, doors, stairs and fireplaces.

The CURTAIN-WALL, which retains signs of early harling and later refacing, preserves some sandstone quoining, despite the collapse of masonry at the N and S corners during the C19. The wallhead is generally ruinous, though sections of the parapet walk still exist on the NW, NE and SE. Along the NW walk, where a stretch of transverse slabbing and a run of projecting drain-spouts have survived, pronounced crenellation is still evident. Windows are few, square-headed, most with straight embrasures. On all but the NW wall, blocked apertures indicate earlier openings; several sills remain, including one for a two-light opening framed by roll-moulded edges with a dowel-hole cut to receive the central mullion. At the middle of the SE wall is a round-arched doorway, probably early C15 but later given a lintel and infilled below the arch. It is reached by a ramped approach from the NE and protected by a late C16 parapet wall, through which three splayed gun-loops cover the beach below, and gives access to the castle yard. From this protected inner space, never more than 4.2m. wide, doors open l. and r. into the SW and NE ranges. Ahead, against the NW curtain, is a well and above it, carried on a wide segmental arch, a narrow strip of accommodation bridging between the ranges at upper levels. Turnpike stairs, diagonally opposed at the S and N corners of the court, served the public and private apartments above but were blocked during the late C19 repairs.

The SW RANGE is divided on the ground floor into three vaulted compartments, each entered from the yard. The SE cellar is the kitchen; it was lit by a small window in the SE curtain and had a segmental-arched fireplace and an oven in the SW wall. The middle chamber, originally with a window to the courtyard and a connecting door to the kitchen, has a gun-port in the SW wall which is splayed on each side of the mid-wall sockets in which a timber gun-mounting was fixed. The NW cellar is unlit. Occupying the entire first floor is the HALL, which would have been reached by the now-blocked S stair. It has two windows side by side at the NW end of the SW curtain: both have segmental-arched embrasures but one has been blocked and the other, the SE, though it appears to relate to the two-light sill mentioned above and thus belongs to the early C15 building period, has had its daylight opening reduced. On the NE wall, a single chimneypiece jamb carved with triple shafts, moulded bases and capitals, survives, though the 5.8m. fireplace opening has been built up, leaving only the springers of its relieving arch. To the NW of this jamb, a door gave access to a narrow gallery which crossed the end of the courtyard under a lean-to roof to connect with the NE range and its staircase. In the N corner of the hall another door opened into a small chamber behind the gallery. SE of the fireplace a window opens to the courtyard. No floor levels exist above the hall but moulded corbel stones indicate the position of runner-beams at a ceiling height of about 4.5m. The survival of a window ingo at high level in the E corner of the hall suggests that a SE mezzanine gallery, entered from the adjacent turnpike stair, may have been provided, but the collapse of the S angle of the curtain wall makes inference difficult. Above the hall ceiling, window openings and blocked fireplaces indicate further accommodation at third-floor and garret levels.

The arrangement in the NE RANGE is determined by a single cross wall which preserves evidence of fireplace openings at the upper levels. Two vaulted chambers at ground floor are entered and lit from the yard. Within each was an entresol floor, the SE compartment lit from the court through two small elliptical-headed windows, now blocked. Interconnection appears to have existed at the NE end of the cross wall where a mural service stair rose within the C15 curtain, but this, too, has been closed up. At second floor, which survives over the vaults, more formal access was obtained from the staircase at the N corner of the yard. Windows again to the courtyard, but a blocked doorway approximately halfway along the SW wall seems at first oddly located. Moulded corbel stones at this level and similar corbels and drip stones at the level above make it clear, however, that the SE chamber at second floor was reached by an open timber gallery overlooking the courtyard. This room is lit by an early C16 SE window which, though its opening is small, has a larger embrasure with an aumbry in the NE ingo. A similar NE window has been blocked, but a C15 garderobe chamber remains in the E corner of the curtain. Masonry collapse at the N corner of the curtain makes it impossible to determine the window arrangements of the NW apartments. At wallhead height moulded corbel stones gave support to the garret floor and parapet walks.

GARELOCHHEAD

Eponymously located village, blighted by the vast naval installations at nearby Faslane and swamped by indifferent local authority housing spilling down from Feorlinbreck.

PARISH CHURCH, Old School Road. Built 1837–8. Gable-ended hall church, white-harled with sandstone dressings. A S entrance gable advances slightly to carry a Gothic belfry spirelet. To the W and E, four tall narrow windows with cusped Y-tracery. In 1893–5 a semi-octagonal apse and hall were added against the N gable. Restoration by *J. Jeffrey Waddell*, 1935–6. Plain plastered interior with rear gallery. Flat ceiling with bold cornice and three roundels with cast-iron ventilator grilles. Ribbed plaster vault over the apse. – Oak PULPIT l., panelled with complex tracery detail and vine cornice, 1935. – To the r., a simple oak casing houses the ORGAN; by *Casey & Cairney* of Glasgow. – STAINED GLASS. High in the S gable, a burning bush quatrefoil. N window on W side; St Margaret and Dorcas in purples, violets and blues, *c.* 1950. – SW of the church entrance is a Celtic cross MONUMENT, late C19, with heavy interlacing and bosses; to John McDonald of Belmore †1891.

OUR LADY, STAR OF THE SEA (R.C.), Feorlin Way. By *Thomas Cordiner*, 1964. Roughcast flat-roofed box enlivened by a steep dorsal rooflight over the altar and side walls four times skewed to create tall slit windows. The sources of light may be 'hidden' to the congregation within, but the clichés (downmarket Coventry Cathedral) are all too patent. Bare interior. Clearstorey-lit hall abuts NW.

GARELOCHHEAD EDUCATION CENTRE, Old School Road. By *Strathclyde Regional Council*, *c.* 1970. Three-storey, roughcast residential block with ribbon windows and a tile-hung wall. Behind is the former PRIMARY SCHOOL, rough red sandstone with half-timbered gables, by *William Leiper*, 1895.

GARELOCHHEAD STATION. Opened 1894. Standard West Highland Railway island platform, probably by *James Miller*. Brick and timber-framed construction; the original shingle cladding from Switzerland. Wide eaves under bellcast piended roof. Dated 1894, the STATION MASTER'S HOUSE, Station Road, by *Robert Wemyss*, working for *J. J. Burnet*: asymmetrical gabled cottage, harled with bull-faced red sandstone dressings.

GIBSON HALL. Dated 1897; probably by *David Barclay*. Pedimented N gable in rough-faced polychromatic sandstone.

DESCRIPTION

Depressed and decayed at the core, though the Parish Church lifts the spirit briefly. Elsewhere there is little to discover. On STATION ROAD, Nos. 1–8, by *Joseph Weekes*, 1938, form a symmetrical U-plan group, cream-rendered cottages with scalloped corbelling over corner entrances; inventive yet vernacular, an example sadly ignored in the village's plethora of post-war council housing. A few late C18 houses cling to tarnished distinction. Just S of the church, a decoratively hinged and studded timber door set in a crowstepped arched portal lends medieval mystery to LILYBANK, early C19. Round the corner, a scruffy path hugs the shore. Some gabled villas make the most of the view. ELDERBERRY, mid C19, is best: painted rubble with attic bay dormers and lower piended wings on the flanks. Ironwork railings survive at ANCHORAGE where a trefoil-edged canopy shades a veranda between canted bays. Overlooking the B833 on the W side of the loch is TALIESIN WEST, by *Robert McLaren*, 1980, tiered concrete and cedar with jutting balconies, bold but scarcely worthy of its allusion to Frank Lloyd Wright. Further S, between road and shore, three picturesquely gabled villas built in the 1860s: ROCKVILLE (now derelict), CARLOCH and DAHLANDHUI HOTEL. All three flavoured with Gothic detail, especially in their decorative bargeboards. In the hotel garden, a battlemented Gothic gazebo. DUNCHATTAN COTTAGE, mid C19, has a Gothic porch flanked by hooded tripartite windows. Still Gothic, LOCHSIDE, 1857, by *John Honeyman*, with quatrefoil ornament to a central bargeboarded gablet.

GIGHA

Fertile, low, ridge-back island with one N–S road. Social life centres around the Post Office Shop, Church and Hotel at Ardminish close to the ferry jetty on the E coast.

GIGHA OLD PARISH CHURCH (St Catan's Chapel), 1km. S of Ardminish Post Office. Red and yellow sandstone rubble remains of a small rectangular chapel. Probably C13. N wall and E gable still stand, the latter with a tall window, originally a pointed arch but later reconstructed to its present round-headed form. Small pointed-arch, single-light windows at E end of N and S walls. In the walled GRAVEYARD surrounding the church are several SLABS, variously carved with swords, scrolls and animals, the majority C14–C15. One such, in one of three low walled enclosures E of the church, shows the effigy of a West Highland warrior. A recumbent SLAB, C18, carries the arms of the Stephenson family. Illegibly inscribed HEADSTONE, C18, incised with elements of the milling trade. Within a fenced enclosure, 90m. NW, the OGAM STONE, a four-sided pillar stone known as Cnoc na Carraigh, with an ogam inscription on the NW edge; not readily transliterated.

GIGHA AND CARA PARISH CHURCH, Cnocan a Chiuil, Ardminish. By *John Jeffrey Waddell*, 1923–4. Rough-cut Romanesque in very random rubble. Skew gables, single-light round-arched windows, saddle-back open belfry shaft. L-plan arrangement comprises the church with its projecting gabled chancel in an E–W alignment, and the vestry/session house wing to the N. Plain interior: boarded purlined roof on three collar-braced trusses springing from corbelstones, plastered walls over timber dado, semicircular chancel arch and door dressings in stone. Sanctuary raised two steps. – Simple box PULPIT. – STAINED GLASS in seven windows. On the S wall, first from E gable, a strongly coloured window in memory of Revd Kenneth MacLeod; by *William Wilson*, 1958. Second from E gable, pale coloured figure of a saint protected by an angel in a Celtic border, by *Gordon Webster*, 1949. Small purply-blue Martha and Mary windows l. and r. of chancel, also by Webster, 1972. War-memorial window in the E gable depicts the crucified Christ with Mary and John; by *Stephen Adam Studios*, 1924. Medieval FONT basin, cut as irregular octagon from schist block, formerly in Church of St Catan (*see above*).

SCARLETT MAUSOLEUM, immediately S of the Old Parish Church. Enclosure entered through a cast-iron gate in red sandstone Gothic Revival portal, the ashlar coursing of which bleeds off into a rubble wall. To William James Scarlett †1888, and his wife Henrietta Catherine †1885, second generation of the Yorkshire family who were Gigha's lairds from 1865 until 1919.

ACHAMORE HOUSE, 1.3km. SW of Ardminish Post Office. First rebuilding by *John Honeyman*, 1882–4, who greatly altered and extended the original late C18 dwelling. Then, *c.* 1900, rebuilt without a top storey which, along with almost everything else except the billiard room, had been lost in a fire in 1896 (an entry in *Honeyman & Keppie*'s Job Books refers specifically to the provision of fire hydrants, etc.), it became a rambling white-harled house plentifully endowed with bays, bows and crowstepped gables. Classical portico with Baroque pediment. Ogee profile dome to an octagonal belfry rising at the centre of the plan. Oak panelled interior with moulded plaster ceilings. Chimneypieces: two English Gothic stone, C16; four mid C18 pine. – Surrounding the house is a magnificent woodland GARDEN, now luxuriant with azaleas, rhododendrons, rare shrubs and trees planted by Sir James Horlick who lived at Achamore from 1944 until his death in 1972. WALLED GARDEN, late C19. Since 1962 the gardens have been in the care of the National Trust for Scotland.

ACHAMORE LODGE. Gabled cottage built for estate factor; dated 1895. Central cylindrical porch has witch's hat roof.

ACHAMORE FARM, on S edge of wooded estate. Long harled gabled steading, early C19. Forestairs rise to three loft-door gablets on the N, each with moulded skewputts and an apex ball finial. Three segmental-arch openings at ground level. Parallel extension S, dated 1900.

GIGHA HOTEL, Ardminish. Two-storey gabled dwelling, *c.* 1790, with later canted bay dormers. Close-packed, well-scaled rear wings by *Morris & Steedman*, 1977–8; the whole unified with deceptive simplicity by slate and harl.

MANSE, Ardminish. Austere two-storey-and-attic harled house with skew gables and central full-height gabled projection incorporating porch. By 'architects' *John Russel* and *John Dawson*; dated 1816, repaired 1828. Drawing room on the first floor has original moulded chimneypiece and shuttered windows.

WATERMILL, Port an Duin, 1.9km. NNW of Ardminish Post Office. Former oatmeal mill, early C19; rubble walls now roofless and ruinous. Overshot all-iron, 8-spoke millwheel served by cast-iron lade from artificial loch.

CAIRN, Carn Ban, at N end of island 2.5km. NE of Tarbert Farm. Overgrown circular area, *c.* 17m. in dia., reduced at the end of the C18 but still retaining at its centre four cists.

CROSS, 2.7km. N of Ardminish Post Office, E of Tarbert Farm. Badly weathered and damaged schist cross standing 1.83m. high on the site of a former burial ground.

FORT, Dùn Chibhich, 1.2km. NNW of Ardminish Post Office. Crowning the NE end of a ridge, the courses of the fort's wall are preserved to a height of 1.2m. along a curving S edge. Entrance, with threshold, at SE.

STANDING STONE, Carragh an Tarbert, 550m. NE of Tarbert Farm. Immediately E of road, the leaning 'Druids' Stone' stands to a height of 2.34m.

GLEN ARAY

The A819 follows the valley of the River Aray. Formerly the s end of the military road route from Dalmally to Inveraray.

MONUMENT, 10.4km. N of Inveraray. *See* Claddich.

OLD SCHOOLHOUSE, 5.7km. N of Inveraray. 1781. Two-storey rubble ruin, roofless but originally harled under a slated pyramid. s front has a central pointed-arch entrance with a triangular arch above and blind quatrefoils l. and r. at each level. Single-storey E extension, pre 1850. Larger detached schoolroom E, post 1862.

STRONMAGACHAN HOUSE, 500m. WNW of the Old Schoolhouse. 1781. Built as a three-bay, single-storey 'Country Villa' with a central door flanked by narrow blind recesses and round-arch windows. Given gables and eaves dormers in its C19 L-plan transformation. 50m. SW, a two-storey STEADING, early C19, with piended return wings.

GLEN CRERAN

Wooded valley running NE from the head of Loch Creran.

BURIAL GROUND and WELL, on the s side of Beinn Churalain, 500m. N of the A828. Rectangular rubble-walled enclosure with some C18 gravestones. TOMB of Hugh McColl †1794, carved with a musket. No remains of the medieval chapel shown on Roy's mid-C18 map and mentioned in the mid-C19 *New Statistical Account.* – A WELL-HOUSE lies some 300m. E: though of dry-stone construction, its masonry is carefully worked with lintelling and shelving across the well-chamber. Perhaps C16.

Former ELLERIC CHURCH, Fasnacloich, 2.7km. NE of Invercreran Hotel. Small gable-ended, rubble kirk with s porch, built as a mission church, 1887–8, by *David Mackintosh*, architect in Oban. Open-cage, timber belfry with slated pyramid cap and haunches. Converted to dwelling with galleried interior, early 1980s.

Former ST MARY'S CHURCH (Episcopal), 300m. from the A828 on the right bank of the River Creran. Simple Gothic, built 1879; *Revd J. H. Latrobe Bateman* 'devised the fabric'. Compact, nave-and-chancel with parsonage added on the sw gable. Marking the junction is a slated pagoda-roofed timber belfry swept up from the roof pitch. The house has gabled attic dormers and a porch swept down from the roof. Church now adapted to residential use.

CNOC LODGE. Three-storey early C20 tower-house perched above the steep N shore of Loch Creran, 500m. NE of Creagan Viaduct. Built to two storeys in poured concrete walls using aggregate from the loch. A third floor, corbelled out from the wall faces below, was later added. The steep roof, busily crested with hipped-roofed dormers and tall NE chimneystack, achieves an almost Scottish skyline, but screeded walls and metal windows diminish the romantic allusion.

CREAGAN BRIDGE, built 1903 to take the Oban–Ballachulish railway across upper Loch Creran where it narrows at Creagan Ferry. Now disused. Battlemented, rough-faced granite approaches with a single pointed-arch vaulted span on each bank. From these, two steel lattice trusses carried the track over the water, meeting on a central pier constructed in the same rustic masonry.

DRUIMAVUIC (Balliveolan), at the head of Loch Creran just N of the Allt Buidhe. A three-bay, two-storey-and-attic laird's house, built on hefty rubble footings, probably the dwelling which *John Menelaws*, mason in Greenock, contracted to erect in 1768. The short S extension, C19, continues the same wall and roof planes but a jump in ceiling height increases the window sizes on the W front. Picturesque intimate gardens. Two-storey block at rear, late C18(?), with E gable forestair.

FASNACLOICH, 2.2km. NE along the glen road from the A828 junction. 1964. Plain but well-scrubbed Scotstyle house replacing a castellated Gothic mansion of the 1840s, demolished in 1962. Two-storey, conically-roofed SE bow projecting to the lochside; Venetian stair window. To the NE, around a courtyard opening to the SE, lies the splendidly idiosyncratic STEADING, *c*. 1885, partially derelict but preserving its complex multi-hipped roofing and full of endearing Arts and Crafts gaucherie.

GLENURE, on the N bank of the River Ure where Glen Ure narrows before opening W into Glen Creran. A mid-C18 laird's house converted to shooting lodge early in the C20. There are two two-storey, harled rubble buildings: facing NW, the five-bay house, 1740–1, described by the 1975 RCAHMS Inventory as 'the best-preserved example of its class' in Lorn, and, at right angles to this, a SW kitchen block built in 1751 to the design of *Duncan Campbell*, mason in Stirling. C18 window openings have been preserved on the NW façade of the house, though the surrounds are altered, while on the SE side, one small central window on the ground floor, two even smaller at the first-floor level and a wallhead chimney stack are original. Behind the modern porch, the SW jamb of the main entrance retains a wood-lined draw-bar socket. Ahead is a wooden geometric stair curving to first floor where bedrooms l. and r. retain fielded pine panelling to walls and doors. In the kitchen wing, which was at first connected to the dwelling by a short, single-storey, three-bay colonnade, a large segmental-arched fireplace opening and brick-lined oven survive in the NW gable. C20 alterations have effected a gabled, two-storey link between the two C18 blocks.

INVERCRERAN COUNTRY HOUSE HOTEL, 1.2km. NE along the glen road from the A828. By *Charles Cochrane*; built as a private house, 1968–70. Converted to a hotel, 1984. On a steep hillside, two two-storey wings meet obliquely in a conically roofed, central bowed projection, now the hotel dining room. Below this, supported on concrete beams cantilevered out of the rock, a long, convex, SE-facing sweep of bedrooms, its flat roof acting as a terrace to the accommodation above. Some marble floors; painted ceilings executed in Italian Renaissance manner.

INVER BOATHOUSE, on the N shore of Loch Creran, E of Creagan Ferry. From a two-storey, castellated octagon base, built late C19(?) as a boat-house to serve Fasnacloich (q.v.), there now emerges a fully-glazed second floor, roofed by an eight-sided pyramid rising to an octagonal lantern. Residential conversion by *Paul Bradley*, 1992–3, arranges split-level inner space around rubble stove-and-stair core with flue stack rising through lantern. The battlemented terrace overlooking the loch is original.

GLEN FYNE
1810

Valley of the River Fyne running SW into Loch Fyne.

KILMORICH BURIAL GROUND, 200m. NE of Clachan Farm at the head of Loch Fyne. An overgrown hillside graveyard with a few mantled headstones, C18, and a single TAPERED SLAB, C15–C16. The enclosing rubble wall is of C19 date but a slight terraced area at the centre may be the site of the medieval parish church dedicated to St Muireadhach and first recorded in the mid C13. Its post-Reformation successor was built 2.2km. SSW at Cairndow (q.v.) in the early C18.

AALT NA LAIRIGE DAM, in upper Glen Fyne. 1950s. The first pre-stressed concrete dam in Europe, 425m. long and 24m. high.

BRIDGE OF FYNE. Four-arch crossing of the River Fyne, built 1754 by *John Brown*. The three cutwater piers, which are of sandstone ashlar and are bevelled on the front and sides, support slightly projecting rectangular refuges on the carriage-way above. The arches are segmental, polished schist being used for their voussoirs and edge bands. Overall, the bridge stretches 83m. Although here and there repaired, the low parapet retains most of its schist coping stones, lavishly covered in incised markings which, besides initials and dates, include such images as hands, feet, hearts, boats, horseshoes, a hammer, a thistle, a horse, and a capped head.

GLEN KINGLASS
1335

A remote river valley debouching W into Loch Etive.

INVERGHIUSACHAN CHURCH, 2km. NE of the mouth of the River Kinglass. Roofless rubble rectangle, built mid C19 to replace a late C18 building. There are four openings (three windows and a door) in the SE side wall but none in the wall opposite, a blocked window in the SW gable and another doorway in the NE gable; an arrangement reminiscent of Dalavich Church on Loch Awe (q.v.) which is also of identical length.

GLEN KINGLASS IRONWORKS, on the NE bank of the River Kinglass where it is bridged 800m. E of the Loch Etive shore. Amongst a number of ruinous early C18 buildings are the incomplete remains of the FURNACE, a degraded structure of granite boulders, 7.9m. square in plan: some evidence of the splayed openings to the central hearth can still be seen. Between 1721 and 1723 an Irish company entered into contract with local landowners for the supply of timber, and by 1725 smelting had begun. By 1738, however, production had ceased.

GLEN SHIRA

A long narrow valley running NNE from the head of Loch Shira, 2km. NNE of Inveraray (q.v.).

BARN, Elrigbeag, 2.3km. NE of Maam Steading. Built 1797; *John Tavish*, mason. Rectangular five-bay structure of rubble block piers and gables. Timber cladding originally filled the gaps between piers but these were built up in the C19 with crosslet slits provided for ventilation. Clasping buttresses at the corners. Each gable has two tall pointed-arch openings (also infilled, but retaining timber louvres at the heads) with tailed quatrefoils in the apex, perhaps an indication of *Robert Mylne*'s involvement. Central spine of rubble piers divides the interior space, providing support for the upper floor. Some original timbers.

BOAT-HOUSE, on the SW shore of Dubh Loch. Built 1751–2 by local mason *James Potter*. Rubble structure with segmental arch in N gable. Reroofed 1987.

BRIDGE, Kilblaan, 800m. NNE of Maam Steading. 1760–8. Begun by Dumbarton master-mason *John Brown*. Two segmental arches, each *c.* 10.6m. span, crossing the River Shira. Rubble-built with schist ashlar up to springing level. Triangular cutwaters.

DUBH LOCH BRIDGE, at the S end of Dubh Loch. Designed by *Robert Mylne*, 1783; built in random rubble by *John Tavish*, 1785–7. Hooded segmental-arch span of 18.3m. with two voussoir courses in ashlar schist. Granite corbel band under parapets which continue as quadrant-wall approaches. Crosslets inset in face of parapet walls. Rounded abutments become crenellated quarter-round refuges above.

GARRON BRIDGE (Drochaid Gearr-abhainn), at the head of Loch Shira. Designed by *Roger Morris*, *c.* 1747(?); built 1747–9 by a mason named *Christie* under the supervision of *John Adam* and *William Caulfield*, inspector of military roads. Segmental arch spanning 19.6m. with radial-jointed buff sandstone masonry extending from the voussoirs. Rectangular abutments become refuges above. Balustraded parapets incline to meet solid central parapets which, like the abutment piers, have heavy cornices. Ball finials survive on the outer cornices only. Closed to traffic *c.* 1980.

GARRON LODGE, 45m. WNW of Garron Bridge. Built 1783–4. Together with the wall linking E to Garron Bridge, one half of a symmetrical design prepared by *Robert Mylne* in 1777. Short, harled, gabled block set transversely between lower, equally brief, gable-ended wings. In the S gable, a round-arch recess flanked by lintelled lights with circular windows above. Hipped-roofed, N apsidal projection contains stair. W gable has two round-arch recesses filled with door and window; a memory of the arcaded loggias Mylne proposed for the wings. Seven-bay, arcaded SCREEN-WALL, the arches blind except at the centre where, under a raised wallhead with tablet, cornice and stepped pedestal, the opening leads to the lodge-keeper's garden.

MAAM STEADING, 2.7km. NNE of Garron Bridge. A surprising piece of rural geometry, like Maltland Square a testimony to the architectural and agricultural improvements made by the 5th Duke of Argyll to his Inveraray estate. Designed by *Robert Mylne* in the mid 1780s as a circular court with Gothick arcading and towers. Only the N half, a hollow semicircle of double-width sheds with a two-storey barn at the centre of the arc, was completed by *John Tavish*, 1787–90. Its timber Gothic pinnacles and ornament have been lost but the barn preserves its pointed-arch openings, portholes and crenellated parapets peculiarly frozen in a tripartite Palladian front. Though still in use, the buildings have been much altered. 80m. N is MAAM FARMHOUSE, early C19, a harled two-storey dwelling with a central S projection under a catslide roof.

ROB ROY'S HOUSE, 7.8km. NNE of Garron Bridge. C18. Ruined rubble dwelling, doubtfully associated with Robert Campbell alias Rob Roy MacGregor.

SALMON DRAUGHT COTTAGE, 300m. NE of Burial ground at Kilmalieu (*See* under Inveraray). 1799(?). Attractive harled rubble dwelling built into a bank on the Loch Fyne shore. At the lower level, two segmental arches open to fish cellar and former byre.

SHIRA DAM, 11.2km. NNE of Garron Lodge. 1950s. Round-headed, buttress-type concrete structure, 725m. long and 45m. high.

TOWNSHIP, Blairowin, above Dubh Loch, 1.2km. S of Maam Steading. Traces of dwellings, barns, etc. in two groups of turf-covered footings with an overgrown corn-drying kiln between. Abandoned mid C18 when the S end of the glen was enclosed as part of the agricultural improvements carried out by the Argyll Estate. SE is a small round-arched BRIDGE of schist rubble blocks, *c.* 1752.

GLENBARR

An unremarkable church and a short straight street of stepping single-storey cottages, the village lies above Glenbarr Abbey on the N side of the leafy Barr Water valley.

GLENBARR CHURCH Mid C19(?). Roughcast gabled hall with dressed stone margins to pointed-arch windows.

GLENBARR ABBEY (Barr House). An abbey only by romantic assumption. The original Barr House, seat of the Macalisters of Glenbarr, sits at the centre of the N front, immediately E of the present entrance. The three-bay laird's house of mid-C18 date was probably approached from the S but, during the enlargement programme by Colonel Matthew Macalister, *c.* 1815, became a mere wing of a much grander scheme. This added a tall Gothic Revival block containing porch, staircase and public rooms on the W, and extended a short service wing from the E gable of the earlier structure. The new house affected medieval guise – traceried windows, lancets, hood mouldings, crocketed finials rising from corner buttressing and a unifying crenellated parapet – all carried out in a manner pointing to the hand of *James Gillespie Graham*, then at work for the Macalisters at Torrisdale, on the other side of Kintyre. Now styled 'Abbey', Glenbarr continued its transformation in 1844 with coach-house and other offices extended downhill S behind a stepping castellated screen: viewed from the W, the final composition is a splendidly scenographic elaboration of the Gothic conceit. A Gothic GATELODGE, by *John Honeyman*, 1887, was demolished in 1968.

The triple-arched porch, originally open, leads to a Hall with a ribbed plaster vault. Sculpted heads at corbelled springing points. Three wooden panels of blind tracery, possibly medieval. To the r. is the Dining Room, its W windows now without astragals; marble chimneypiece with four-centred arch. To the l., where the C18 house is entered, the scale reduces; dentilled cornice, low timber dado. Staircase has iron banisters in Gothic style. Three tall lancets light the landing from which a narrow passage gives access to the original house.

GLENCREGGAN HOUSE, 1.6km. N of Glenbarr village. Elegant C18 Georgian mansion with platformed piended roof; rebuilt after a fire, *c.* 1905. Five-bay harled front with fine three-bay porch with Ionic pilasters, entablature and arch over door. Mullioned tripartite windows l. and r. Dentilled cornice eaves. Round-pedimented dormers.

BURIAL GROUND, Cladh nam Paitean, between A83 and sea, 2.1km. S of Glenbarr village. Macalister of Glenbarr burial ground dating from C17. Present walled enclosure has a pointed-arch entrance and obelisk pinnacles at the corners and piers. HEADSTONE, 1753, commemorates James McMillan, his wife and son, with the representation of a plough-team and the inscription

> SO LET ME LIVE
> SO LET ME DIE
> THAT I MAY LIVE
> ETERNALLIE

GLENBRANTER

A hamlet 2km. NW of Loch Eck just W of the A815. The eponymous valley climbs SW along the course of the Allt Robuic.

BALLIEMORE FARM. Two-storey, three-bay house with piended roof, *c.* 1800.

BRIDGE, over River Cur. Rubble structure of two segmental arches on cutwater piers. By *William Douglas*, 1744–54.

GLENSHELLISH HOUSE. A symmetrical, two-storey, hipped-roofed farmhouse with single-storey wings curving convexly

l. and r. to form a U-plan cobbled court at the rear. Built in the late 1820s as an estate 'mansion house', the three-bay dwelling affects a rather steep-sided pediment with a blind oculus. Hood mouldings.

LAUDER MEMORIAL, Invernoaden. A rough-faced rubble block, built off a three-stepped base on a grassy knoll above the A815. Red sandstone steps, quoins and flat pyramid top. A bronze pedimented panel with portrait bust and two Art Nouveau angels commemorates John Lauder †1916, in action in France.

GLENDARUEL

A long glaciated valley running N–S through Cowal. From Dunans at the S end of the steep-sided Caol Ghleann, the River Ruel coils along the flat-floored valley on its course to Loch Riddon.

BURIAL GROUND, Dùn an Oir, 500m. SW of Achanelid Farm. A rubble-walled burial enclosure, square in plan, probably early C19. The walls have sandstone copings and corner pedestals from which fluted urns have fallen. SW doorway blocked. There are three MURAL TABLETS, all C18, commemorating various members of the family of the Campbells of Glendaruel.

BRIDGE, Dunans. Dated 1815. Three-arch rubble bridge, 28m. long, carrying a road from the A886 to Dunans House. The central two-centred arch spans 7.85m. over the River Ruel at a height of 13.3m., its narrower, more lancet-like, flanking arches stepping up the gorge on each side. All the openings have impost bands which return on the soffits. Between the arches are octagonal piers topped with shallow domical copes at parapet height. On each side of the bridge, the sandstone parapet rises at the centre to surmount a tablet with the initials JF for John Fletcher of Dunans †1822, and, on the N panel only, the date. Below the S panel is a gargoyle carved in human form, the only one of several drainage spouts over the arch-heads elaborated in this way.

DUNANS HOUSE. A Baronial house of three high storeys, c. 1864–5, by Edinburgh architect *Andrew Kerr*. Rubble with chunky ashlar dressings. Coiled cable moulding over W entrance. Tall eaves dormers on the W and S fronts sit on a continuous stepping corbel course; all have pediments, each monogrammed for a different member of the Fletcher family. Room-sized drum tower at SW corner; corbelled SE bartizan. Third-floor chapel betrayed by its small round-arch windows, three on the E wall and three in a solid canted bay corbelled to N. Lower N wing, screened by castellated wall to W, may contain C18 core. Rubble LODGE, 400m. SW, early C19(?), has Gothic lancets.

FLETCHER MAUSOLEUM, Dunans, hidden on a thickly wooded knoll above the River Ruel. Late C18. Skew-gabled, rubble burial chapel. In the E gable, open tracery in a pointed-arch shouldered against a gated doorway. At the apex, a carved angel and the words MORS JANUA VITAE; over the door, armorial bearings and the motto RECTA PETE. Raftered timber roof with dog-tooth ornament and painted shields. White marble MURAL TABLETS commemorate members of the family, including Alexander Fletcher, 1st of Dunans, †1763.

MOTTE, 500m. S of Achanelid Farm. Flat-topped earthwork rising some 5m. above the W bank of the River Ruel. Traces of two small rectangular structures, possibly late medieval date.

TOWNSHIP, Kildalvan, on the NW side of the valley. Ruined drystone remains of a settlement first recorded at the end of the C15. The community may have grown up around an ancient CHAPEL, the site of which, now no more than turf-covered footings, lies 250m. NE. There are two three-cell buildings, small byres, and two overgrown corn-drying kilns. Abandoned since early C19.

GROGPORT 8044

Village on the E coast of the Kintyre peninsula 10km. N of Carradale.

GROGPORT CHURCH. Small skew-gabled nave, 1897. N gable has dated Jubilee inscription with Celtic cross finial at apex. The E wall, which has had new windows inserted during a recent conversion to residential use, preserves a red sandstone tablet carved with a book (Bible?) set within knotted rope ring.

GROGPORT HOUSE, 1km. uphill S of village. A former manse. Three-bay gabled Georgian preserving 12-pane sashes. Later porch has flat roof with trefoil pattern iron parapet railing.

HELENSBURGH 2982

Named in honour of Lady Helen Sutherland, wife of Sir James Colquhoun, 8th Baronet of Colquhoun and Luss, who in 1752 purchased the lands of Malig (or Milligs) on the N bank of the Clyde. Anticipating the development of a rural community based on textile industries, a notice was placed in the *Glasgow Journal* of 11 January 1776, offering attractive rental terms to 'bonnet-makers, stocking, linen and woollen weavers'. No such settlement materialized, however, although a feuing plan of the district was commissioned from *Charles Ross* of Greenlaw, surveyor to the Luss Estates.

To this attractive planned settlement on the water's edge – a Burgh of Barony from 1802 entitled to weekly markets and four annual fairs – came Henry Bell in the early 1800s. Building for himself the Baths Hotel on the eastern seafront, he became the town's first Provost in 1807. Despite the Admiralty's refusal to support his proposals for steam navigation, he at last succeeded in launching the paddle-steamer *Comet* in 1812, securing for himself a place in history as the first man to develop a practical sea-going steamship in Europe, and for Helensburgh a reputation as a 'regular fashionable sea-bathing place, for merchants and manufacturers of Glasgow and Paisley'. By 1828, despite the inadequacy

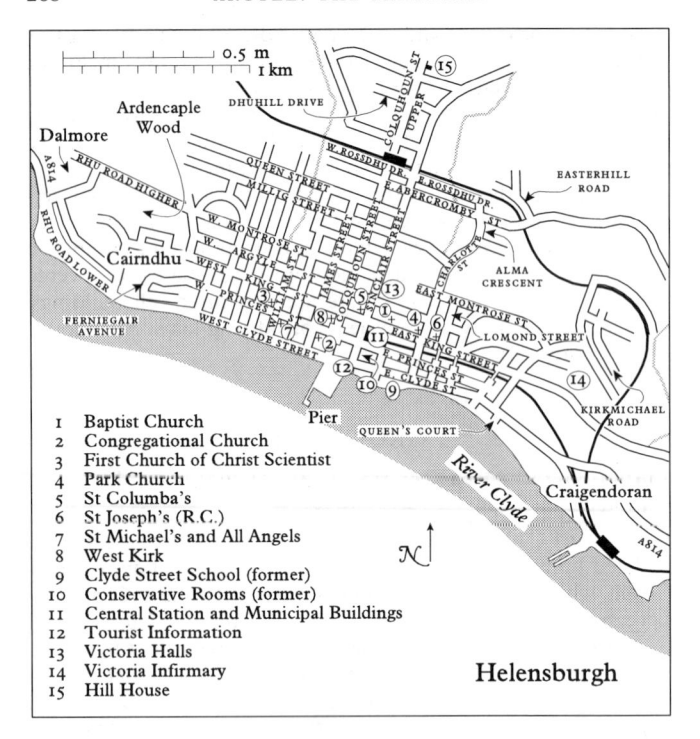

1. Baptist Church
2. Congregational Church
3. First Church of Christ Scientist
4. Park Church
5. St Columba's
6. St Joseph's (R.C.)
7. St Michael's and All Angels
8. West Kirk
9. Clyde Street School (former)
10. Conservative Rooms (former)
11. Central Station and Municipal Buildings
12. Tourist Information
13. Victoria Halls
14. Victoria Infirmary
15. Hill House

of the little pier, there were no fewer than six daily sailings between Glasgow and the fast-growing town.

In 1857 the Glasgow, Dumbarton and Helensburgh Railway reached the outskirts of town, bringing with it a period of expansion which confirmed Helensburgh's status as a popular commuter suburb, and saw the population double to nearly 5,000. Development, spreading N from the shore and commercial centre was confined within a distinctive grid pattern of two-acre plots, with only four houses permitted per plot. In 1860 the Town Council undertook to reinforce the chequerboard rhythm of the street plan by planting rows of flowering trees, creating a veritable 'Victorian Letchworth'. Not that the town was without an industrial base of sorts, having a slaughterhouse, gasworks, steam laundry, distillery and aerated mineral waterworks.

With the opening of the West Highland Railway Line in 1894 and the establishment of a station to serve the upper slopes of the town came the opportunity to develop land where the view was at its most compelling. Here was created an outstanding collection of houses whose like cannot be found in such concentration elsewhere in the country. A predilection among local architects Leiper, Paterson and Wemyss for Shavian detailing provided surprisingly sympathetic company for *M.H. Baillie Scott*'s White House (1899), with *Charles Rennie Mackintosh*'s Hill House (1902) virtually alone in its acknowledgement of a Scots ancestry. In fact, it was only with the onset of municipal housing – begun in 1919 with the construction of a small garden-city development in the grounds of

Ardencaple Castle – that the town showed any real promotion of a national style.

By the 1960s, the pressures of expansion had begun to take their toll on the town, the very popularity of Helensburgh as a commuter suburb has placed demands on the grid-iron which it was ill-designed to accommodate.

Today, tourism still provides an annual boost to the local economy, although reduction in the number of hotels, closure (and subsequent demolition) of the outdoor bathing pool, and the systematic removal of seafront pavilions has left the town with few conventional facilities designed to attract the day tripper. Instead, a heightened awareness of Helensburgh's exceptional turn-of-the-century architecture now attracts a different kind of tourist: the National Trust for Scotland, for instance, welcomes over 40,000 visitors to Hill House on a yearly basis.

Whether increased recognition of Helensburgh's importance as a planned town can prevent further disintegration of the original layout is, however, still uncertain. The qualities of location, accessibility and 'salubrious marine breeze' which first drew settlers to the area may yet prove to be the downfall of a popular town whose boundaries are now blurred and where the threat of further development is ever present.

CHURCHES

BETHESDA EVANGELICAL CHURCH, Colquhoun Street, late C20. Gabled, prefabricated structure in roughcast with few architectural pretensions.

BAPTIST CHURCH, East King Street. An unprepossessing early Gothic design by *D. Abercrombie*, 1886. The chubby SE tower rises through two stages, square and octagonal, with largish louvred lucarnes. W to the rear, etched glazing depicting an allegorical River Jordan is framed at first floor above the vestry entrance. – STAINED GLASS. In the S window set in cusped geometrical tracery, a celebration of the founding of the Zenana Mission in India by parishioner Elizabeth Sale, possibly by *Stephen Adam*, installed later than the church.

CONGREGATIONAL CHURCH, West Princes Street. Occupying the site of the town's first place of worship – the Tabernacle – the 1850 Independent Church has served as a hall since completion of *John Honeyman*'s robust late C13 Gothic extension of 1884. Apart from its graceful timber porch with fishscale slates, the older building lacks the appeal of its replacement. This is set at right angles to the E, entered through a stout gabled porch on the W front. Above the highly decorative pointed-arch doorway, a large vesica enclosing a blank sandstone panel. Clutching the skewputts, sinewy snarling beasts carved by *James Young*. Internally, the nave is separated from the single W aisle by polished Peterhead granite clustered columns with richly finished capitals. Oak PULPIT and CHOIR BENCHES carved by *John Craig*. On the S wall, an early C20 ORGAN in memory of John Ure of Cairndhu (q.v.) is located below a brightly coloured wheel window with decorative surround and STAINED GLASS by

Miller of Glasgow. Below the balcony, in a small enclosed space, a good early C20 window dedicated to Ian Ure.

FIRST CHURCH OF CHRIST SCIENTIST, West Princes Street. Set well back on a level grassy lawn, designed by *Margaret Brodie* in 1956. Diminutive in scale, deriving presence from the variegated freestone to the s entrance front. Period features include a shallow copper-roofed porch, decorative window grilles and subtly curving entrance steps.

PARK CHURCH, Charlotte Street. By *John Honeyman*. Erected as the Park Free Church in 1862, the building assumed its present status as a Church of Scotland in 1928. The twice gabled E front – dominated by a large rose window with quatrefoil tracery – advances from aisle to entrance, culminating in an elegant tower with broach spire and open belfry on the NE angle. At the opposite end, what appears to be a chancel is in fact occupied on the ground floor by the vestry with a hall above. In 1888 *William Leiper* added a canted stair tower on the s front with small pointed-arch windows, at the same time remodelling the interior, 'the roof of the nave and aisles being in dark blue, relieved with gold, red and white flowers, and ornate borders'. Surviving in slightly altered form from this period is the Gothic reredos at the W end. The marble and alabaster PULPIT is from 1888, the octagonal FONT dating from 1904. – STAINED GLASS. Geometrically patterned E rose window, inserted in 1884. The handsome church HALL to the N, designed in 1924 by *G.A. Paterson* of *Stewart & Paterson* and executed with minor alterations by *Henry Mitchell*, was opened in 1930.

ST COLUMBA'S, Sinclair Street. By *William Spence*, 1860. A powerfully Presbyterian entrance front with as centrepiece a three-stage tower, altered by *William Leiper* following storm damage in 1874. Thus the corbels, cusped tracery and pierced parapet which crown the belfry hint better at the graceful interior than do the otherwise severe external features. Tall, transomed, pointed-arch windows N and S, with Y-tracery, allow much light into the barrel-vaulted nave with raking U-plan gallery. To the W a much modified ORGAN all but hiding the only STAINED GLASS, a N-facing floral composition probably by *Mulloch*, 1861. Marble baptismal FONT decorated with large winged angels, 1896. Removed to the courtyard outside, the BELL, cast by *James Duff & Sons* of Greenock, 1861. The original 'Wee Kirk', by *Brown & Carrick*, 1845, sits alongside on West King Street. Stripped of its pulpit and gallery, its serviceable appearance befits its function as church HALL.

ST JOSEPH'S (R.C.), Lomond Street. Stocky in form and feature, *Charles J. Menart*'s 1911 design wears its bull-faced red sandstone well. Cruciform in plan with side aisles and gabled stair towers flanking twin E entrances. Extremely large rose window patterned with Free Style tracery. Below this, a statue of St Joseph is housed in a canopied niche flanked by a foliated frieze. At the base of either stair tower, a tapered bollard with conical cap confirms the building's C20 origins, as do the entrance piers and stylized gates. Inside, plastered walls and blind passage aisles below a broad timber-boarded vaulted roof create a Catholic calm.

ST MICHAEL'S AND ALL ANGELS (Episcopal), William Street, replacing the 1843 Holy Trinity Chapel. *Robert Rowand Anderson*'s early French Gothic church was built for a fast-growing congregation which included among its subscribers Gladstone and the Earl of Glasgow. The building was begun in 1867 but remained without its tower until 1930. Low, heavily buttressed aisles flank a lofty W entrance front whose most arresting feature is a tympanum exquisitely carved in cream Caen stone by *Donaldson & Burns* of Edinburgh, 1915. This depicts Christ and a group of angels, with symbols of the four evangelists, all framed within a deeply chamfered doorcase. Dragon gargoyles, for which the architect prepared special drawings, ponder on the poor choice of stone (an alarmingly soft Dumfriesshire red) from N and S eaves gutters. The interior, reckoned initially to be somewhat plain, has been transformed into the town's finest through the munificence of its members, although the encaustic tiles patterning the deep chancel walls in almost Moorish fashion and the finely structured ogee-arched rood screen erected under Rowand Anderson's direction were never dull. An alabaster and mosaic REREDOS was added in 1872. Artistic licence depicting a Roman centurion with halo takes pride of place at the altar. In 1915 *Arthur Balfour Paul* supervised the installation of an elaborate internal Austrian oak porch, with delicate diaper work by *Scott Morton & Co*. This has now been relocated around the N doorway, being replaced inside the main entrance by an oak and etched glass screen with Celtic patterning by *James Anderson*, 1996. – STAINED GLASS. An impressive collection, begun in about 1876 by *Shrigley & Hunt*'s Noli Me Tangere 2nd from r. on the N wall. *Clayton & Bell*'s formal but outstanding God in Glory and Lord is My Shepherd extreme l. on the S aisle was commissioned around 1889. A pale three-light window in the chancel (Resurrection, Ascension and Pentecost in the centre), a brighter vesica above, and a two-light in the N wall depicting St Michael and St John, all by *Stephen Adam* in 1881, were supervised by the architect. On the N aisle, magnificent perspective in two windows by *Charles Kempe* (Noli Me Tangere, 1888, and St Luke and St Paul, 1893) and on the r. Charity and the Good Samaritan, using yellow in the manner of the *Glasgow School* after *Daniel Cottier*, 1884. On the S, Mary Magdalen washing the feet of Christ, wonderfully rendered by *Kempe*, 1882, a disappointingly loud Annunciation and the Manger by *Barraud & Westlake* (a gift to St Michael's from South African Churchmen), and an 1889 Presentation in the Temple, again by *Clayton & Bell*. Above the entrance, a pretty rose window by *Kempe* and, on either side of this façade, powerful colourful compositions by *Alexander Walker*, on the l. Christ walking on the Water, on the r. Christ and the Little Children. Single storey and basement HALL dedicated in 1912, by *Rowand Anderson & Paul*.

WEST KIRK, Colquhoun Square. The wealth and union of three congregations have ensured the survival of this prominently located building, constructed from stone quarried out of the square on which it stands. Recognizably by *J. W. and J. Hay*, 1853, on a squat and broad-shouldered cruciform plan, the tower on the re-entrant angle of the S transept is muscular in the extreme, although the broach spire does ultimately aspire to delicacy with pinnacles and slender gabled lucarnes, and the flèche is very dainty. Three large windows with curvilinear tracery are no match for *William Leiper*'s spectacular E porch of 1892, erected in honour of Revd Alexander Anderson. This much-crocketed extension is alive with fantastic birds and beasts munching their way around the stepped cornice. Gutted by fire in 1924, the church was restored by a local man, *Robert Wemyss*, to whom the interior owes its present rich appearance. Panelled throughout, the building has a plaster and timber-beamed vaulted roof supported on stylish stone corbels. The chancel walls are picked out in attractive stencilwork restored in 1992. – STAINED GLASS. A wide range of work including an incongruous commemorative piece to John Logie Baird by *Arthur D. Speirs*, 1992. In the apse, three windows depicting the Twelve Apostles, 1926, and in the N chancel wall, a modern two-light by *Gordon Webster*, 1963. A murky Christian Act of Mercy in the N transept is signed *G. MacWhirter Webster* 1931, who in the 1950s designed the two transept dormers: Columba, Giles, Francis and, on the l., the Crucifixion. A good clear memorial on the S wall to the Aitkens of Landsdowne Park, while Praise and Prayer opposite is dated 1926. The large E window, Christ Blessing the Little Children, presented *c.* 1878, is dedicated to the memory of Andrew Bonar Law, sometime Prime Minister who worshipped in the church. Finally, in the original entrance porch, a tiny window coloured in the manner of the *Glasgow School*. To the rear, the SESSION HOUSE by *James Sellars*, 1879.

CEMETERIES

HELENSBURGH CEMETERY, Old Luss Road. Established in 1850 on land adjacent to Kirkmichael Farm, now much desecrated and robbed of its original dignity through over-close proximity to poor municipal housing. An unexceptional GATE-LODGE stands usher at the SE corner, but many of the MONUMENTS are extremely fine. – Among these, a good cast-iron Grecian surround to John and William Carlaw, watercolourists, mounted on the E wall; a finely lettered grey granite tablet to Hugh Kerr †1891, tobacco merchant, erected N of the central path – the pink granite plinth, black Doric columns and scrolled pediment designed by *William Leiper*, the much eroded medallion by *Birnie Rhind*. A stocky single-sided Celtic cross commemorates John Kerr Anderson †1898, featuring an exquisitely carved marble lamb in a roundel, the design again by *Leiper*. Most interesting of all is an innovative collection of red granite CELTIC CROSSES concentrated at the heart of the graveyard, sculpted during the 1880s and 1890s by *Peter Smith* of Glasgow.

PUBLIC BUILDINGS AND MONUMENTS

ARDENCAPLE CASTLE, Ardencaple Wood. Of the building in its most modern manifestation – that is, substantially remodelled by *Dick Peddie & McKay* in 1877 – only the NW Argyll tower and the great retaining wall (said to represent the original shoreline) escaped demolition in 1957. The Clan MacAulay, landowners in the area since mid C13, had abandoned the original castle, whereupon parts of the estate were purchased in *c.* 1752 by Archibald, 3rd Duke of Argyll, at the time occupied in orchestrating the transformation of castle and town at Inveraray. No doubt as a consequence of his family's involvement in this work, *Robert Adam* was commissioned to prepare drawings (dated 1764 and 1772) for Lord Frederick Campbell (son of the 4th Duke, and later Lord Clerk Register of Scotland), for alterations to 'Ardincaple House', creating a U-shaped tower fortalice comprising a palace block with vaulted basement and two jambs projecting N. All but engulfed by subsequent extensions, these first additions nevertheless represented an early development by the architect of his Inveraray castle style. The surviving four-stage tower, constructed further N following a fire in 1828, now serves as a mount for transit lights for vessels navigating the Rhu Narrows. Blind bipartite windows with pointed lights and hoodmoulds decorate three façades, while on the s front can be seen the blocked-off links to the original building. Set high on the massive flank of the retaining wall is the 1578 cartouche formerly located above the E entrance of the house.

The former CLYDE STREET SCHOOL, East Clyde Street. Fetching Scots Revival composition on a splendid seafront site by *A.N. Paterson*, 1903. Side and seaward façades are severe, but the entrance front is friendlier: a two-storey attic gable lit by a large Venetian window with projecting cloakroom bay below, flanked on either side by squared towers with lead-capped ogee roofs finished in pronounced bellcasts and jolly starfish finials. Two low bellcapped teachers' rooms form diminutive octagonal wings on either side. – INTERIOR. Glasgow-style galleried hall arcaded to classroom flanks and with a fine hammerbeam roof. JANITOR'S HOUSE to the W, two-storey with turret stair. To the E the more stylized cookery and laundry rooms. Last used as the Clyde Community Education Centre.

The former RIFLE VOLUNTEERS' HALL, East Princes Street. By *Isaac Dixon*, Windsor Iron Works, Liverpool, 1885. Corrugated-iron hall, one of the largest of its kind in Scotland. Large semicircular window to gabled front and full-length lantern and ridge cresting to roof.

FIRE STATION, South King Street. *Stirling County Architect*, 1976. Three-bay engine shed with two-storey offices and accommodation quarters to E, bound together by a deep corrugated fascia.

The former HELENSBURGH AND GARELOCH CONSERVATIVE CLUB, Sinclair Street. Extraordinarily lush façade by *Honeyman & Keppie*, 1894, marred by a modern shopfront. Originally comprising two ground-floor shops, a top-lit public hall at saloon level, reading and smoking rooms, caretaker's flat and an attic storey with top-lit billiard hall and committee rooms. The club was commended as 'one of the most artistic in Scotland', but is now in the ownership of a clothing chain and used in large part for storage. Above the ground-floor shop there is on the l. a two-storey bay with, at first floor, a three-light stone mullioned and transomed window, the deadlights patterned with Prince of Wales feathers in leaded glass. From the transom, springing out of mask label stops, scroll moulded surrounds terminating in naturalistic foliage rise to encase the attic window. Above this framework a stylized tree bursts forth to disturb briefly the sinuous flow of the parapet. In the centre of the façade, a niche containing a statue of St Andrew is raised up to first-floor transom height. On the right-hand side is an attic bay with foliage carving below sill level knotted around a proud thistle. Most unusual of all, a central piercing of the parapet leaving elongated tracery less medieval than Art Nouveau, certainly less typical of Honeyman & Keppie than of a young *Charles Rennie Mackintosh*, then working for the practice. Such sensuous shaping of the red sandstone – the shallow bays are sculptural rather than functional – renders vulgar the more conventional tenements alongside. Precision carving heightens the impact of the imagery, but the symbolism (if such was intended) defies decipher. – INTERIOR. Both hall and billiard room have attractive braced collar roofs, while there is some good wainscotting and several chimneypieces; in the hall, Glasgow-style moulding to the overmantel. Staircase with odd stylized newel posts.

HELENSBURGH CENTRAL STATION, East Princes Street. Twice relocated, each time closer to the town centre, the present building opened by the North British Railway Company in 1899. Four-platform terminal station, incoming tracks originally sheltered by glazed steel-framed awnings supported on cast-iron columns with foliated lugs and by lengthy perimeter walls, that to East Princes Street an impressive specimen of brick engineering. Booking office and stationmaster's quarters housed behind a four-bay Renaissance frontage, with circulation and ancillary facilities in a U-plan range below arched roof with large glazed ends. Refurbished 1998.

HELENSBURGH GOLF CLUB, East Abercromby Street. Once pretty 1908 clubhouse by *Mitchell & Whitelaw* (six matching villas were built adjacent), altered beyond recognition by 1965 and 1973 additions.

HERMITAGE PARK, Sinclair Street. The grounds of the now demolished Hermitage House presented to the Town Council in 1911 for use as a public park, the name perpetuating the long-held myth that a hermit lived and preached in the area. – MALIG MILL. Scant remains of an ancient meal mill on the edge of Milligs Burn largely comprising three engraved roundels and a grindstone. – WELL. Trabeated enclosure tucked into NE corner containing stone trough. – FLYWHEEL. 2m.-dia. cast-iron flywheel from the paddle-steamer *Comet* and the anvil on which it may have been forged, presented in 1912, centenary year of the vessel's maiden voyage. – PAVILION. Pagoda-style shelter, 1965. – WAR MEMORIAL. Erected on the suggestion of local artist *J. Whitelaw Hamilton* in the walled garden of the park, *A.N. Paterson*'s domed and gilded war memorial, 1923. N of a formal pool, a tall squared plinth on stepped base is surmounted by an arcaded rotunda, ashlar urns framed by alternating arches. Fine cast-iron gates and railings complete the perimeter of this attractive garden of remembrance.

HERMITAGE PRIMARY SCHOOL, East Argyle Street. *Dunbarton County Architect*, 1975. Low, load-bearing brick structure with series of shallow monopitches concentrated around a central hall with exposed pine-finished laminated beams. At the rear, the original primary school, 1924, by the *Education Offices' Master of Works*. – LODGE. On the SW corner, the bonny baronial an incongruous reminder of the 1879 secondary school by *William Spence*, cleared following construction of more modern facilities at Colgrain (q.v.).

JOHN LOGIE BAIRD PRIMARY SCHOOL, Winston Road. Designed in 1967 by *Dunbarton County Council* to accommodate an abrupt expansion of naval housing in the NE of town. No less sprawling than the estate in which it sits, only the concrete-panelled three-storey classroom block achieves some tautness.

The former LIBERAL CLUB ROOMS, Colquhoun Street. Comparisons can be cruel: built for the Helensburgh and Gareloch Liberal Association in the same year as the Conservative Club Rooms on Sinclair Street (q.v.) to provide similar accommodation, but with considerably less imagination exercised by the burgh surveyor *J.R. Wilson*. Three-bay, the entrance tower slightly advanced and capped in a slated peak. An extensively glazed 1995 attic extension has done much to improve its appeal.

LOMOND INFANT SCHOOL, James Street. In 1977 the Larchfield Preparatory School for Boys and St Bride's School for Girls combined to form Lomond School, assuming joint ownership of a sizeable portfolio of properties, the most interesting of which is CLARENDON, originally an unpretentious mid-C19 villa, later a boarding house for St Bride's School. Twice extended by *William Leiper* in a quirky Jacobean style; in 1888 to provide a cloakroom and kitchen bay extension (the former clothed most grandly as an angle tower complete with crenellations, crocketed finials and yobbish gargoyles), in 1891 to add a W wing with big stone mullioned and transomed bays to W and S (the gargoyles making a triumphant second showing). – INTERIOR. Former drawing room with segmental-arched inglenook, coffered ceiling and deep decorated frieze.

LOMOND MIDDLE SCHOOL, former Larchfield Boys' School, Colquhoun Street. Extensive villa of mid C19 in use as school from 1858 until 1998. Venetian window to l. gabled bay; decorative bargeboards to porch.

LOMOND SENIOR SCHOOL, former St Bride's Girls' School, Stafford Street. The original broad red sandstone villa in use as a school since 1895 burned down in 1997, leaving two good extensions to rear; the first in 1901 by *A. N. Paterson* to provide a north-lit assembly hall with three large (now blocked) oculi in gablets to the playground elevation, the second the music room by *Campbell Douglas & Paterson*, 1908. Replacement classrooms built in 1998 by *G. D. Lodge & Partners* attempt to strike a balance between tradition and modernity. – INTERIOR. Sombre yet impressive finishings to hall, which has lofty hammerbeam roof.

MASONIC HALL, West Princes Street. By *J. J. Laird*, 1907. Low-budget symmetrical gabled frontage with disproportionately high apex above ground-floor windows.

MEDICAL CENTRE, East King Street. *Roxby Park and Baird*, 1996. Three sides on pilotis to overcome a split-level site and the need for extensive parking. Built in an area already impoverished architecturally, the blockwork, roughcast and concrete-built development misses the opportunity either to reinforce the town vernacular or radically to update its vocabulary.

MUNICIPAL BUILDINGS, East Princes Street. Replacing the old townhouse – a theatre converted to civic use – *John Honeyman*'s municipal buildings of 1878 dignify an important yet oddly under-stated junction. Scholarly Scots-Baronial with, on the S front, angle tourelles flanking a crowstepped gable around which runs a stepping corbelled stringcourse with rope moulding and, facing W, a large corbelled oriel to the council chamber with nepus gable above. – MEMORIALS. Acting as keystone to the arched entrance, a sculpted head of Henry Bell. Nearby, a plaque set into the S front commemorates John Logie Baird with the inscription 'Audiverunt omnes ipse vidit'. – EXTENSION. Free Scots Revival erected 1906 to designs by *A. N. Paterson*. Two-storey police office linked by staircase bay to older building, with three-storey fire station completing the ensemble. Particularly good entrance with armorial plaque to what were the police headquarters (a cheeky inclusion the stone handcuffs and recumbent cat carved at second-storey stringcourse level). Splendid rear façade, harled with sandstone dressings, a high level drying green and soaring hose-drying stack.

PIER and ESPLANADE, West Clyde Street. Helensburgh's harbour was woefully inadequate for a good part of the C19, the three breakwater walls to which the 1838 town plan made optimistic reference remaining unbuilt. The pier was three times extended before being superseded as the principal steamer berth by the jetty at Craigendoran (q.v.). In the 1880s public subscription enabled the esplanades W of the pier and at the E bay to be built, although the foreshore never amounted to much more than lengths of fenced grass. *McGurn Logan Duncan & Opfer* attempted improvements in 1996, restoring the sea wall and marking the termination of three principal shopping streets at their junction with the waterfront.

POLICE STATION, East King Street, 1972. Largely anonymous, the main block patterned by alternating vertical panels of window and dun-coloured brick wall. Low cell block to the rear with pronounced window grillage.

POST OFFICE, Colquhoun Square. By H.M. Office of Works under W. W. Robertson, 1893. Elaborate L-plan cornerpiece with elongated cupola topping entrance tower. Rich in decoration betraying Beaux Arts influence, including parapet urns, a beautiful cartouche and mask panel above the side entrance and a corbelled ashlar post box centred on the single-storey sorting office wing. – TELEGRAPH EXCHANGE. *W. T. Oldrieve*, 1911. Two-storey-and-attic extension married effortlessly to its neighbour.

REGISTRY OFFICE, West King Street. Pretty little parish council chambers by *Robert Wemyss*, 1890. Two storeys, asymmetrical with broad overhanging eaves and pend on r. leading to rear and semi-glazed stair to first-floor apartment.

RESERVOIR, Sinclair Street. In 1868, some years after his death, Henry Bell's scheme to supply water to Helensburgh from a reservoir in Glen Fruin was realized. Today the town is served by an extended network of three reservoirs with the filter works and tanks located at the N entrance to town, the treatment plant discreet but for a butterfly wing roof providing light at high level. Engineers, *Crouch & Hogg*, 1966.

ST JOSEPH'S R.C. PRIMARY SCHOOL, Havelock Place. *Strathclyde Regional Council*, 1977. Single storey with exaggerated boiler room, the janitor's house a more successful composition with steep monopitch roof and small modernist entrance porch.

SWIMMING POOL, West Clyde Street. *John B. Wingate & Partners*, 1976, superseding the stylish outdoor bathing pool gifted to the town in 1929. Low-slung, the pool itself articulated by a slight sloping of the roof.

(OLD) TEMPLETON LIBRARY, John Street. Drumgarve House, opened as town library in 1950, closed in 1998, converted to private housing 2003. Square-plan villa in pinky sandstone with prominent quoins and protruding central bay. – ASSOCIATED ARTEFACTS. At the road edge, a pair of Victorian ornamental cast-iron lamp standards. Formerly in the grounds, the town's coat-of-arms salvaged from *Robert Wemyss*'s 1898 pierhead arch, demolished 1960s. Relocated to the new library on West King Street, a 1930 John Logie Baird 'Televisor' donated in 1951, and a stunning portrait of the inventor by *Stephen Conroy*.

TOURIST INFORMATION CENTRE, East Clyde Street. Housed in what remains of *Charles Wilson*'s Italianate Established Church of 1846, the nave and hall of which were demolished in 1982. A prominent landmark still, the four-stage clock tower exhibits the same tripartite round-arched louvred openings the architect used to such good effect in his Free Church College towers in Glasgow in 1856. Stocky little entrance porch added by *Robert Wemyss*, 1923.

VICTORIA HALLS, Sinclair Street. *J. & R. S. Ingram* of Kilmarnock, built 1887 by public subscription. Chunky T-plan town hall in Scots-Baronial with French pavilion roof to central bay. Crow-stepped gables l. and r. featuring angle bartizans, those on l. with conical lead caps. Hefty first-floor balcony on great console brackets, Queen Victoria presiding over. – INTERIOR. Unimaginatively renovated 1935 in commemoration of King

George V's Silver Jubilee, erasing all but an Art Nouveau vestibule door from *A. N. Paterson*'s classy 1899 refit.

VICTORIA INFIRMARY, East King Street. Lovely, slightly lop-sided cottage hospital, reassuringly domestic in scale, designed by *William Leiper* in 1893–4 in the manner of a two-storey villa (reception, dispensary, operating room and matron's quarters) with single-storey wings (six-bed male and female wards). Flanking the arched entrance, two bulbous bellcapped octagonal bays in contrasting red and cream sandstone. Matching canted extensions with polygonal roofs added to either ward in 1923 by *W. Hunter McNab*. Now dedicated to care of the elderly.

DESCRIPTION

Town Centre

The grid has at its core the crossing of Sinclair Street and Princes Street, located one block uphill of the waterfront. Here, the principal approach into town from Loch Lomond to the N meets one of the main routes running parallel to the River Clyde. Marking the site are the Municipal Buildings and Central Station (*see* Public Buildings above). Commerce is concentrated S and W of this junction, with the main shopping thoroughfare being the seafront itself on Clyde Street. The buildings here are for the most part uniformly unpretentious, saved from monotony by frequent shifting of scale and by the occasional architectural highlight.

Among the chief landmarks on Sinclair Street is MACKAYS, the former Helensburgh and Gareloch Conservative Club (*see* Public Buildings above), subtle and surreal in an otherwise unexceptional street. Alongside, *Frank Burnet & Boston*'s three-storey-and-attic CARLTON BUILDINGS, designed in 1898 with stabling and kennels behind, is handsome but overlarge. Opposite, at Nos. 33–41, a surprisingly decorative tenement by *John Douglas*, 1878 – symmetrical grey sandstone with recessed canted oriels, paired consoles, swags, roundels and festoons. WH SMITH, occupying the remains of a pretty single-storey-and-attic range built in 1904, is more typical of the townscape.

Where Sinclair Street meets Clyde Street views of the river and Rosneath peninsula unfold. On the opposite bank, the N-facing sprawl of Greenock and Port Glasgow provides almost shocking contrast. The WEST ESPLANADE is briefly double-sided following land reclamation, although the effort is hardly justified by the unexceptional swimming pool (*see* Public Buildings above) or the poorly placed GRANARY RESTAURANT, 1986. Nearby, the Italianate clock tower of the former Parish Church still fulfils a public function as Information Centre (*see* Public Buildings above), but *Alan Berry*'s yellow brick courtyard housing of 1982 is little substitute for the loss of nave and hall. At No. 12 West Clyde Street a former Tontine Inn from *c*. 1830 – the IMPERIAL HOTEL – quoins and stringcoursing picked out in colour. Further W at No. 18, a bold twin bow-fronted Glasgow-style tenement, 1909, by *T. and J. Low*, the corbelled stepped parapets mourning the loss of their original spiky turrets. Then the 1933 stripped Art Deco infill of WOOLWORTHS, survivor from a bygone era when the town drew visitors in real measure. On the corner of COLQUHOUN STREET, the former National Bank of Scotland, built in 1928 by *A.N. Paterson & Stoddart*; near-symmetrical façades with on the s a slightly advanced gabled bay with apex stack and elongated urn finials.

If the PIER (*see* Public Buildings above) lacks presence, the 1996 improvements to the esplanade have at least attempted to acknowledge the axial framework of the town. Signalling the foot of JAMES STREET, the Henry Bell Monument, a powerful pencil obelisk standing sentinel on the water's edge. A 7.5m.-high monolith on squared base in red Aberdeenshire granite with a simple inscription on N face which reads, 'Erected in 1872 to the memory of Henry Bell. The first in Great Britain who was successful in practically applying steam power for the purposes of navigation. Born in the County of Linlithgow in 1766. Died in Helensburgh in 1830'. Its counterpart at the end of JOHN STREET is a viewing platform, and in celebration of WILLIAM STREET a bronze bust of John Logie Baird gazes sightlessly to sea. A copy of one in the National Gallery by *Donald Gilbert*, it was first unveiled in Hermitage Park in 1960 in memory of the inventor of television, who was born in the town in 1888. These aside, there is little to divert attention from the view other than No. 36, stocky Scots-Baronial with an elaborate canted oriel by *William Petrie*, 1876, and Nos. 42–45, a good mid-C19 three-storey tenement with intact Victorian shopfront.

The virtual squares defined by the grid are not large. On James Street, the refined classicism of the CLYDESDALE BANK, 1857, jostles for room between the bulk of the former LA SCALA CINEMA and the ascetic attire of the Congregational Church Hall (*see* Churches above). A faint whiff of cinematic glamour clings bravely to the principal façade of the old picture house. Designed by *Neil C. Duff* in 1913, it is a nine-bay composition, the eaves cornice springing to an arch in the centre. Below, an oriel flanked by oculi pops out at first floor from the projection booth. Otherwise, the rendered façade is relieved only by pilaster strips and long, narrow indents with squared remnants of Art Nouveau glass. The interior largely gutted, the building is no longer in use.

On the junction with WEST PRINCES STREET, a good Arts and Crafts tenement with corner conical cap and big-shouldered gable with stack by *Robert Wemyss*, 1896. Five doors along at the former WAVERLEY PLACE, same architect, same date, but this time asymmetrical variegated red sandstone with two-storey gabled bay to l. and the barest hint of Jacobean in the details.

E on West Princes Street is COLQUHOUN SQUARE, once an unfenced quarry developing by dint of its unstable status into a formal clearing. Post Office (*see* Public Buildings above) and West Kirk (*see* Churches above) combine well as opposing gate-keepers of the space, being joined in this role by a handsome BANK OF SCOTLAND, erected in 1861 in a square-plan classical style for the Union Bank, probably by *John Burnet*. Bringing up the rear, *David Morgan*'s 1982 banking hall with stylish pyramidal roof over an ambitious umbrella structure. The CELTIC CROSS, removed to the NW corner from the centre of the square, where it was the frequent cause of collisions, was gifted by Sir James Colquhoun, 12th Baronet of Luss, in 1903 to mark the burgh centenary. Pinkish granite, carved by *Stewart McGlashen & Sons* of Edinburgh. Sense of enclosure has only recently come to the SW and SE flanks of the square through the completion of *Alan Berry*'s three-storey yellow brick flats and shops, 1986 and 1988, although the vocabulary defies local lineage. E of the square, Nos. 14–28 West Princes Street by *William Tait*, 1878, represents a decent seven-bay tenement with delicately brattished first-floor sill course and diamond wall-head stacks. Alongside, projecting ashlar teeth from the E gable confirm the unfinished status of *W. Hunter McNab*'s punchy Jacobean-style tenement of 1911, impressive nevertheless for the conviction of its sculpted skyline and knobbly finials. From the corner with Sinclair Street, the view N picks up the self-effacing Baptist Church and considerably more assertive Church of St Columba (*see* Churches above), but is otherwise dominated by the bland brickwork of the local superstore.

East Bay

EAST PRINCES STREET is immediately depressing. Industrial archaeologists may delight in the merits of the station wall, gasometer and former Rifle Volunteers' Hall (*see* Public Buildings above), but the railway effectively ostracizes the terraces and tenements grown up in the lower east of town. MAITLAND COURT, completed in 1975 by the Town Council shortly before regionalization, is a sizeable U-plan development in two-tone roughcast with deck access to East Princes Street, designed by *Baxter Clark & Paul* on the site of the old gasworks. At Nos. 7–9 MAITLAND STREET, an early C19 cottage range with bold Gibbsian door surround; further E on EAST CLYDE STREET, the Scots Revival of the former Clyde Community Education Centre (*see* Public Buildings above); and at Nos. 87–91 (N side), a crisp Glasgow-style tenement, 1905, typical of *T. & J. Low* of Greenock. Signalling the start of the EASTBAY ESPLANADE, reclaimed in 1877, LOMOND STREET strikes N. At the junction with East Princes Street, a pretty turnpike stair, all but detached from the rear of Nos. 17–21 and, alongside the railway line, *Babtie*'s robust 1900 DRILL HALL extension, complete with big blind brick oculus. Running parallel, GEORGE STREET is occupied on the lower W side at Nos. 5–11 by a two-storey tenement range with extruded stair towers and handsome doorcases. Further refinement occurs at No. 121 East Clyde Street, where a mid-C19 villa is distinguished by a recessed porch with segmental-arched lintel on purposeful columns.

The land wedged between railway and water's edge retains its narrow depth despite a swing S. The tiny esplanade ventures no further than GLENFINLAS STREET, where *Noad & Wallace*'s stylish single-storey public shelter of 1950 – red brick, tile and big curved glass bay windows – has been demolished. A curious collaboration between working- and middle-class housing persists, the former well represented by the banded sandstone and patera decoration of Nos. 149–151 East Clyde Street – a late C19 three-storey tenement with corner bow – and by the dramatic concave corner of the municipal housing at ADELAIDE STREET and East Princes Street; *Burgh Surveyor*, 1931.

Prominent on the blustery foreshore are four exceptional villas and the 1984 conversion to housing of the Queen's Hotel, built by Henry Bell in the early 1800s as the Helensburgh Baths (or Baths Hotel), now QUEEN'S COURT. The building was strategically located on the stagecoach route which linked Glasgow and Inveraray, being served also by a small stone pier at which P.S. *Comet* called. Originally a square, three-storey castellated block with dentilled cornice, now with the battlemented parapet infilled, E and W wings raised and a large, L-plan brick-built flatted E wing added by *Baxter Clark & Paul* at the time of conversion. A once commodious inn with hot and cold baths, stables and reading room, now largely unrecognizable.

Further along East Clyde Street but best appreciated from the shore, near contemporary CROMALT was built in 1802 and was one-time home to novelist Neil Munro. A graceful, Regency-style villa with single-storey bowed wings E and W and pedimented doorcase to N, incorporating at its core an older farmhouse. The building is flanked on the E by an attractive triple-gabled stables and granary block, matching the house. This is surmounted by a diminutive domed cupola and weathervane.

Next comes ROCKLAND, early *Alexander Thomson*, 1854, breaking away from Romanesque and cottage orné to design a T-plan Greek classical villa, two-storey with long single-storey service wing and matching gatelodge on East Clyde Street (extended by *T.L. Watson*, 1881). Wide overhanging eaves on an uncompromisingly shallow pitch impart breadth and bulk to advanced gabled bays N, S and W. The defensive nature of the N frontage gives way to a first-floor window wall facing S, where five- and seven-light windows with slender ashlar pilaster mullions stretch the length of bedroom bays. Important for its place in the development of the architect's constructional and decorative language, being a departure from the round-arched or seaside villa style, it is at the same time unusual for its clear expression of function, with servants' quarters, scullery and kitchen court immediately identifiable. – INTERIOR. Richly decorated with pilaster flanked panels to entrance hall, around which runs an anthemion and palmette frieze; Egyptian-style doors and surrounds to the dining room, and a bronze balustrade with inverted palmette motif to the dog-leg stair.

Contrast to the apparent severity of Rockland comes in the shape of the 1905 additions and alterations carried out by *William Leiper* at

TIGH-NA-MARA. Doubled in size, harled with sandstone dressings, and draped in red rosemary tiles, it projects a blowsy image, redeemed by a wonderful entrance doorpiece with Moorish overtones – arched opening set in squared surround with rose and thistle carving to the spandrels, little round-headed leaded lights separated by big floreate consoles, and a pierced stone balcony with gargoyle spouts. Across the lintel piece, the inscription 'Fides praestantior auro'. Finally, perilously located atop the sea wall, the Tudor revival L-plan villa, ROCKFORT, 1849, its hoodmoulds, tall polygonal stacks and decorative bargeboards combining effectively. In the grounds, a picturesque roofless folly with pointed-arch openings, reputed to have been used as a resting place for coffins landed by water at a nearby jetty.

East End Park

Between Charlotte Street and Grant Street, ALMA PLACE, its back to the railway, represents one of the town's finest municipal achievements; by *Stewart & Paterson*, 1936. Thirty-five flats in three symmetrical three-storey tenement blocks around twin courtyards. Linked along the main frontage by screen walls with arched gateways, recurring details include stylized stair towers lit by lunettes and Art Deco door surrounds picked out in render on harl. Opposite, the spire of Park Church (*see* Churches above) meets its match in the abrupt gradient of CHARLOTTE STREET, up whose climb can be spotted the outstanding timber and glazed prow of *Tony Vogt*'s BOWHOUSE, 1988 in East Argyle Street. Further E, the 1857 grid pattern is frustrated by the contrary contours of GEORGE STREET, EAST MONTROSE STREET and KING'S CRESCENT, the latter pursuing lazy lines around the triangular EAST END PUBLIC PARK of the same period. Commanding an elevated position where George Street collides with Montrose Street, TOWERVILLE by *John Honeyman*, 1858 – a brooding affair heavy with Tudor Gothic overtones, six-bay with crenellations, decorative bargeboards and a gabled bay at oblique angle to the E, by *Peat & Duncan*, 1888. – INTERIOR. The stained-glass panels to doors, fanlights and windows dating from the 1888 remodelling include a figure of a knight in the vestibule by *Oscar Paterson*. – LODGES. On George Street, 1858, tiny with lancets and a circular crenellated tower. At No. 5 King's Crescent, 1858, matching the house, and at No. 15, 1864, by *John Honeyman*, a pretty cottage with colonnette and roll-moulding to window surrounds and mullions.

A series of good extensions can be found to the mid-C19 houses on East Montrose Street. Best of these are the thin service wing with chinaman-hatted oriel added on the E side of No. 19 by *William Leiper*, 1893, and a big mullioned and transomed drawing-room bay built by the same architect on the l. side of BRAEHOLM in 1887. None of this work is in the half-timbered style with which Leiper shaped his adopted town, but its absence is more than compensated for by REDCOTE, a compact Shavian/Arts and Crafts villa in red tile, timber and stone by *T.L. Watson*,

1881, for Maxwell Hedderwick. Also on this street – at No. 12 – a spectacular T-plan timber-framed conservatory. HENRY BELL STREET leads ultimately to Kirkmichael (q.v.) and the suburban sprawl of the 1960s CHURCHILL ESTATE.

Kirkmichael

The WEST HIGHLAND RAILWAY LINE's route out of Craigendoran (q.v.) effects an eastern boundary to the town, looping w around the lands of Kirkmichael Farm. Here, in 1935, was begun an idealistic garden city development on a skewed grid to designs by *James Stirling, Burgh Surveyor*, who erected three flagship blocks on the curve of KIRKMICHAEL ROAD, two- and three-storey with wallhead dormers, glass block stairhead lights, concrete balconies and Art Deco trimmings. Following World War II, *Stewart & Paterson* completed the development in a series of Scots Art Deco terraces and tenements. On BEN BOUIE DRIVE, chubby angle towers, mansards and niches in brickwork; elsewhere pediments, portholes and diamond lunettes. An architecturally inspired municipal housing scheme, sadly much neglected.

Hermitage Park

Returning over the West Highland Railway Line, EAST ABERCROMBY STREET winds w to ALMA CRESCENT. At the crossing, textbook examples of period excellence. Oldest is HAPLAND, a late C19 villa with swept eaves, a four-light bowed window with shallow conical cap to the s, and an excellent rubble boundary wall with ashlar balustrade. Opposite, built on the foundations of Balvaird, destroyed by fire in 1932, the streamlined GREENPARK, *John S. Boyd*, 1935. Classic '30s/Art Deco home, originally primrose above a blue/brown base, with stuccoed façades, flat roof and metal casements. Powerful horizontality on the s created by a cantilevered curved deck-balcony and veranda, and contrasting verticality to the rear in the tall staircase tower. – INTERIOR. Period walnut and mahogany panelling in hall, wonderful etched glazed panelled door leading to a roof terrace by *Charles Baillie*, whose murals survive hidden in the living room. In the grounds, to EAST ROSSDHU DRIVE, *A. N. Paterson*'s stables and garage with portly cupola, 1910, sensitively refurbished by *Robert Sills*. s are the so-called ENGLISH VILLAS, three charming yet economical Arts and Crafts houses designed by *William Leiper* for John Jack, a local builder. No. 41, 1906, has a red sandstone base and stacks, harled and half-timbered bedroom storey and a lovely pointed-arch entrance; No. 43, 1906, is similar but with weighty bargeboards, gablets in lieu of polygonal roofs and sparing use of stone. No. 45, 1909, is once again L-plan, based on No. 41, and with billiard room addition by *W. Hunter McNab*, 1913. Completing the architectural ensemble, *Stewart & Paterson*'s tribute in Tudor to Lutyens, the 1916 flat-roofed extension to ARDEN, squared and snecked sandstone with a broad window bay with ashlar mullions and leaded lights.

The E spur of ALBERT STREET draws up short at MOORGATE, quirky Scots-Revival by *A. N. Paterson*, 1903. Despite the loss of the domed top to the semicircular bow, authorship is advertised in the form of wallhead dormers, scrolled skewputts, crowsteps, corbels and giveaway thistle tops to soil stacks, but the curious-shaped entrance gable with Venetian window still surprises. CROSSWAYS, a little S where Alma Crescent turns into VICTORIA ROAD, is a more conventional U-plan Arts and Crafts house with largely unaltered interior by *Stewart & Paterson*, 1913. Where Victoria Road meets SINCLAIR STREET, the substantial PRINCE ALBERT TERRACE by *William Tait*, 1879, a N-facing terrace disguised as tenement, the better to block the view from LANDSDOWNE PARK, a large villa (now burned down) built by a warring neighbour. S, in the grounds of Hermitage Park (*see* Public Buildings above), tidy SHELTERED HOUSING complex by *McGurn Logan Duncan & Opfer*, 1991. From the nearby Victoria Halls (*see* Public Buildings above), views N and S are returned in full.

West End

WEST ARGYLE STREET runs straight and true for over a km., defining a line above which density of development decreases and virtually all houses face S. The last of the N-facing plots are occupied here by a massive four-bay tenement with round-arched pediment, *T. & J. Low*, 1903, standing shoulder to shoulder with a pretty cottage range from an earlier date. Opposite, at ROSEMOUNT two delightful Arts and Crafts extensions in tile-hanging and timber; on the r., a full-height canted bay by *William Leiper*, 1895; on the l., a flat bay on stone corbels, *Robert Wemyss*, 1907. James Street intersects, dropping to WEST KING STREET and WAVERLEY COURT – 1982 sheltered housing strong in scale and street frontage by *Baxter Clark & Paul*. Diagonally opposite, the gabled, angled link block of *Stewart & Paterson*'s concrete-faced municipal housing, erected 1953. Past the pinkish façade and lead-capped bays of *Alan Berry*'s library and flats, 1997, JOHN STREET makes a purposeful crossing. S are some good tenements – on the E, two blocks of two-storey-and-attic flats built 1873 and 1877, handed and semi-detached, with buckle quoins and moulded wallhead stacks with fret-patterned pots: on the W, the pink and grey patchwork of No. 27, three-storey with Venetian windows at ground floor, canted oriels on voluptuous consoles and a single pedimented dormer offset by a tall corniced stack. By *Robert Wemyss*, 1896. Turning into West Princes Street, the eye is drawn first to Nos. 73–79, an understated two-storey tenement from 1864, rendered and lined as ashlar with balustraded parapet and blind segmental-arched windows. Next, on the corner with WILLIAM STREET, the buttressed swagger of St Michael's and All Angels (*see* Churches above) squares up to the threat posed by the leering terracotta gargoyles squatting on the villa opposite. The stretch to the foreshore is enlivened by Nos. 5–7, a near-symmetrical composition at whose centre is an unusual C19 sandstone villa with broad pedimented dormer, ogee-headed attic window and fleur-de-lys decoration. Older still is FLOWERBANK, on the corner with West Clyde Street, two-storey-and-attic in an early C19 vernacular with at the rear two curved turnpike towers. Both features repeat with some frequency as Clyde Street assumes the role of the A814 *en route* to Rhu and Rosneath. Neither the COMMODORE HOTEL nor *McDonald Williams*'s retirement home are much in sympathy with their seafront sites, although the latter at least attempts the form of a large villa. Exposure to the elements is reduced up SUTHERLAND STREET, where at Nos. 4 and 6 two late C19 villas stand out by virtue of their elegant cast-iron porch columns with ornate foliate flanges. Inland, an early shore farm at BRANDONGROVE on West Princes Street confirms the whitewashed appeal of the town's origins; while ROSEBANK, on the corner of CAMPBELL STREET, is a good early C19 villa elaborately extended by *William Leiper*, 1891, who added a large oriel with polygonal bellcast roof on hefty bracket supports. The climb N to West King Street provides glimpses of a sweet little terrace at Nos. 72–76 with lacy iron window guards to attic bays, *c.* 1875. Beyond that, a sizeable development by *John Dingwall*, begun in 1875 with the construction in stone of the bow-fronted GLENAN GARDENS on West Argyle Street, and followed by shorter, plainer terraces, 1888–96, on the remaining three streets delineating the plot. NW, GLASGOW STREET displays the single-storey curtain wall of No. 40A by *John McIntyre*. Next met is West Argyle Street, where at No. 32 an interesting attic extrusion by *Robert Wemyss*, 1927, sits astride an early C19 classical villa, and at No. 121 canted and flat bays act as stopends to the entrance loggia of the birthplace of John Logie Baird, site of the first electric lighting in Helensburgh. Uphill, Glasgow Street encounters WEST MONTROSE STREET, direct link to Rhu and the ancient seat of Ardencaple (*see* Public Buildings above). On the SW corner, a delightful Free Style villa by *Robert Wemyss*, 1898, with pedimented Venetian dormers to garden, and a stepping, stone-traceried staircase window facing the street.

William Spence's 1857 revisions to the feuing plan sought to impose great crescents and curves where the grid was not yet established, although only the twin semicircular paths of UPPER and LOWER SUTHERLAND CRESCENT survived his proposals. N on the upper crescent is TERPERSIE, *William Leiper*'s own home, built in 1871 and sharing the 'shy and retiring disposition' of its author. Banded red and cream Arts and Crafts, the garden front is M-gabled with a plain wallhead stack, detail being saved for the pointed-arch doorway and protruding boar's head snout, said to have been acquired from the ruins of Terpersie Castle, Aberdeenshire, allegedly the home of Leiper's forefathers. – INTERIOR. Exceptional woodwork and Aesthetic Movement stained glass in stair window – portraits (possibly medieval) of Lord Darnley and Mary Queen of Scots, and monograms WL and MJ. On the neighbouring feu, the villa known as RHU-ARDEN, built speculatively by *Leiper*, c. 1871, in the Greek Revival style favoured by his friend and contemporary, Thomson, but with a Roman porch and fine hexagonal conservatory on ashlar plinth.

MILLIG STREET is outstanding, bee-line straight from E to W, verge-trimmed and narrow, with on the S great boundary walls with punched-in service entrances, and on the N impenetrable hedges broken only by gateposts hinting at the grandeur of the architecture at the head of the drive. At its W end, four model villas in red stone and harl built by *A. N. Paterson* (one for himself) in 1895. Family features of this Scots ensemble include crowsteps, low attic dormers and corniced canted bays. No. 22 has a fat angle tower, its neighbour a striking split-pediment entrance with canted bedroom window rising from the tympanum. Also by *Paterson*, the 1910 internal alterations to WOODEND at No. 20 for ship owner Sir William Raeburn, including a superb ashlar chimneypiece and overmantel to stair hall. Octagonal conservatory by *William Leiper*, 1901. Recognizable by its distinctive scrolled and shouldered wallhead stack, No. 39 has a studio built for the artist J. Whitelaw Hamilton by his brother-in-law *A. N. Paterson*, 1910. Uphill on SUFFOLK STREET, abrupt gables, gablets and pointed-arch lights give AUCHENTEIL, 1864, a look of perpetual surprise. On the rear façade, a series of corbels which carried guttering to a storage cistern prior to the arrival of piped water to town. Downhill, KINTILLO with, to the rear, a yellow stone staircase bay with jettied gable and leaded lights, 1888, and to the front a tile-hung billiard room and superb timber porch, built 1899 for Andrew Bonar Law, all by *William Leiper*. Back to MILLIG STREET, with yet more by the same architect, namely WESTER MILLIG, a big French-style villa of 1871 with bracketed, bargeboarded gables and bays. Harled and half-timbered, the former stables, 1898, make a pretty separate dwelling. A little E, UPPER JOHN STREET interrupts, the grid pattern momentarily corrupted by its swerve SE. At No. 76, the 1889 transformation by polychromy of GLEN KIN by *William Leiper*, who added a jolly chinaman-hatted drum tower in bands of ochre and umber on the SW corner of the original villa, and a night- and day-nursery bay with elaborate canted corniced oriels E. On the corner, as John Street meets QUEEN STREET, four lovely model villas, built 1909, by *Robert Wemyss* in a sandy-coloured stripped Scots vernacular.

Queen Street is especially grand, being wider than the norm. ARDVUELA and WESTWARD, both late C19, are typical of the genre, one with a particularly fine glazed-in porch with balustraded parapet, the other with a 1900 wrap-around loggia by *A. N. Paterson*. Much shorter, WEST ABERCROMBY STREET runs parallel, terminating at RADERNIE, an unusual 1915 bungalow by *Robert Wemyss* with sculpted stone entrance with cockle keystone. As Colquhoun Street halts at WEST ROSSDHU DRIVE, two once-identical c. 1870 villas salute the view: PYNHANNOT with its Glasgow-style angle tower, added by *Robert Wemyss* in 1902 for the shipping family Sloan, and

MARDEN HOUSE, to which *William Leiper* added a bug-eyed museum extension, also 1902. At the road's end, a spectacular barrel-vaulted conservatory E of MOORLANDS, 1873.

LONGCROFT, West Rossdhu Drive, 1901, *A.N. Paterson*. The architect came close to an expression of a C20 national style in this, his own home, built on a site S of the then recently opened West Highland Railway. A principally S-facing L-plan villa with formal garden and burn W and kitchen garden S, the building exhibits a skilful reworking of C17 Scots Renaissance details in grey harl, freestone and Ballachulish and Aberfoyle slates. The design is at its most convincing around the shaped W gable, which has a punched-in mock doocot, corbelled angle turret to 108 l., massive semi-octagonal tower to r., and corbelled balcony with bombe railing and curved stone stair off-centre. The building functioned as house and studio both. Entered from N through a chubby canted tower on the re-entrant angle, a roughly hexagonal lobby with doors W and S permitted access to one without disturbing the other. But this was at all times a family home: on either side of the main door, the Paterson children's heads are reproduced as label stops at the foot of clustered colonnette shafts. – INTERIOR. Almost open-plan in places, possibly as a result of Paterson's travels to America, where he studied the construction of the domestic architecture of the Eastern States and may have met Charles McKim. The SW-facing drawing room enjoys the best views, and is cleverly separated from the studio – which is on the NW corner – by an inner hall, which by virtue of large connecting doors functions as spillover space to the more formal room. At the same time, the hall opens on to the W balcony, from where a descent to the garden can be had. Dining room and kitchen are separated by a secondary stair, at the top of which were the day and night nurseries. The principal stair is contained within the entrance tower. In the drawing room is a coved ceiling with floreate plasterwork by *Bankart* and, above the fireplace, an elaborately worked embroidery by the architect's wife, *Maggie Hamilton*. An Art Nouveau detailed chimneypiece by *George Walton* survives in the original studio. – STAINED GLASS. By *Guthrie & Wells* in the upper sashes of the drawing-room bay, depicting architecture, music, embroidery and painting.

Upper Helensburgh

Upper Helensburgh has a unique collection of turn-of-the-century villas, including one of *the* great houses of C20 architecture; yet the area is grossly overdeveloped and its integrity much eroded. When building the six EASTERHILL ROAD villas on land adjacent to the Golf Course, 1907–12, *Mitchell & Whitelaw* could scarcely have foreseen that their speculative venture in stylish Scots Renaissance would be all but absorbed in the 1960s by the suburban sprawl of the GLADE ESTATE. *James Miller*'s Swiss-style, shingle-hung STATION on the West Highland Railway Line, 1894, fared no better, being demolished in the 1980s, although *Robert Wemyss*'s contemporary STATIONMASTER'S HOUSE survives on the E side of SINCLAIR STREET, square in plan with deep, bracketed overhanging eaves and a broad-shouldered chimneystack straddling the main entrance. (For houses in MUNRO DRIVE EAST see below.)

With the arrival of the railway, any remaining obstacles to the development of the northernmost slopes of town disappeared. *William Leiper*'s BRANTWOODE established a benchmark for excellence in subsequent house building. It was built in 1895 on MUNRO DRIVE WEST for James Alexander, an oil refiner and admirer of Ruskin. Belying the relative formality of the L-shaped plan is an exterior whose intentional imbalance pays homage to the Old English domestic style popularized by Richard Norman Shaw. Jettied out above a suite of s-facing public rooms – all with large stone-mullioned and transomed bay windows with delicate leaded lights – a tile-hung bedroom floor, marked by mock half-timbered gablets and a fishscale-clad Romeo and Juliet balcony. Buttresses, brackets and banded chimneystacks – shades of red all – combine to add weight and rustic charm. – INTERIOR. Fine period detailing, including inglenook fireplaces in living room and drawing room, the latter retaining its gilded *William Morris* wallpaper to the overmantel. Wainscotting, timber beamed ceilings, and inscribed on the hall chimneypiece, *'In the world a home, in the home my world.'*

STRATHMOYNE, 1899, adjoining to the l., and nearby ROKNEYS, 1898, both by *Robert Wemyss*, are less chunkily confident, although none the less sympathetic to the Shavian ideal. Strathmoyne has a striking entrance gable advanced off-centre, originally sandstone but later partly tile-hung by the architect when adding a billiard room E in 1910. Below a carved ashlar plaque, a tripartite stairhead window, symmetrical around a tall arched light with tracery and pretty floreate stained glass, forms a striking focal point. Rokneys, on the corner of Sinclair Street and MUNRO DRIVE EAST, shows the same concentration around the entrance, this time in the form of a porch on the diagonal in the re-entrant angle, complete with moulded arch supporting a bold decorative panel with mask, date and finial. A tile-hung top floor and unusual fenestration set the house apart from its neighbours, among which the only notable house is *Mitchell & Whitelaw*'s scrolled and harled EASTERHILL, 1903.

To the NW, LENNOX DRIVE WEST remains faithful to the palette of red tile and harl. CLAIRINCH, *H. & D. Barclay*, 1904, is a voluminous example, if a little lumpen. Of greater interest is the 1935 BROOM COTTAGE by *A. Gardner, Gardner & McLean*, an elegant U-plan villa in white painted brickwork with flat-roofed wallhead dormers and two great planes of purply slate descending to the metal-framed windows on either side of the entrance. WHINCROFT, on nearby COLQUHOUN STREET UPPER, is *A. N. Paterson* in surprisingly sombre mood – cream bull-faced sandstone with only a hint of half-timbering, completed in 1915. Uphill is a much jollier mansion (now a drug rehabilitation centre), the capacious RED TOWER, 1898, by

William Leiper, built for James Allan, a provision merchant from Candleriggs. The building is an amalgam of C17 Scots and Shavian Old English. Two-storey-and-attic, it is clothed principally in warm red snecked and stugged rubble with a big circular angle tower with conical roof w, and a massive canted bay with polygonal top E. Between, a Renaissance-style entrance porch, weighty ashlar balcony on consoles and a balustraded parapet behind which an M-gabled half-timbered dormer emerges from a swathe of sea-green slate. – INTERIOR. Spectacularly finished in C17 Scots decorative style: coffered ceilings, inglenook fireplaces, ashlar and marble fire surrounds and much stained and waxed Kauri pine wainscotting. By comparison, its next-door neighbour, TORDARROCH, on the corner of Douglas Drive and Sinclair Street, also *Leiper*, *c.* 1883, while by normal standards an arresting array of red tile and timber with bargeboarded dormers and bays, seems a little restrained.

Returning along Douglas Drive, the view N reveals THE WHITE HOUSE, Colquhoun Street Upper, 1899, *M. H. Baillie Scott*. How remarkable that this Voyseyesque villa designed by an Isle of Man architect should find itself in such harmonious company in a resort on the River Clyde. Even more remarkable, the house plan – where three s-facing sitting rooms flow into one another and are connected by an entrance hall to the rear – had already found favour at Brantwoode (q.v.). But the younger building remains modern in its simplicity, looking forward rather than to a bygone age. It effectively bridges the visual gap in Upper Helensburgh which separates the Old Englishness of local architects and the 'new' Scottishness of Charles Rennie Mackintosh's The Hill House (q.v.). No projecting sills or hoodmoulds here, no skews or copes or bargeboards; rather, flush whitewashed walls, originally quite minimalist, stripped back to shadowless planes. The barest ashlar framework around metal casement windows does little to relieve the severity. Acknowledging the spectacular seaward view, the dining room breaks out suddenly into a semi-octagonal bay wrapping around the w corner of a lop-sided gable. The drawing room, too, has a flat-roofed single-storey bay s and tiny leaded lights snuggling up to either side of the E chimneystack. – INTERIOR. Furnished by client H. S. Paul to designs by *E. A. Walton*. Regrettably, the double-height entrance hall has gone, and with it the gallery, Art Nouveau stencilwork in grey and green, and soaring s window. Remaining, however, many original fittings and fixtures, including inglenook benches and, in the living room, an arched brick chimneypiece with embossed copper hood. – STAINED GLASS. In the living room to the stair screen, and to the dining room bay, curvilinear and stylized floreate inserts by *Baillie Scott* himself. Removed from the house are the entrance gates whose wonderful floreate finials hinted at the internal decorative scheme. Diagonally across DHUHILL DRIVE, however, BRAERIACH, 1908, retains its fine Art Nouveau ironwork and has an attractive two-storey-and-attic service wing with the varied fenestration typical of *Robert Wemyss*. On the adjoining plots to the E, neither

DHUHILL HOUSE nor DHUHILL, both mid C19, is typical of the area. The first is Franco-Italianate, rugged red and grey with a tall w tower and steeply pitched roof. The other is chaste and classical, two-storey with ground-floor tripartite bays supporting and linked by a decorative iron balcony, but most notable for its lozenge-patterned slate roof. The lodge to the former is chubby and charming, 1898 Scots-Baronial in miniature by *William Leiper*.

Uphill, behind a tiny wooded public park (the aptly named WALKERS' REST), two housing sites beautified by their proximity to the leafy gorge of the MILLIGS BURN.

BALLYTRIM is a severe late Arts and Crafts villa built in 1926 by *Stewart & Paterson*. ALBION LODGE (so named after Albion Motors purchased it as a 'hotel' for their employees) is one of a trio of near-identical villas designed in 1883 by *William Leiper*, the others being Aros in Rhu (q.v.) and Ganavan in Oban (q.v.). This lack of uniqueness is disguised by mirroring the plan-form and, in the case of the Helensburgh villa, sheathing the upper storey in red fishscale tiles. A good house, nevertheless, distinguished by the detailing of the pretty engaged canted attic dormer on the s front, the honeycomb and geometric glazing on all sides, and the substantial billiard room and service wing extension added N and E with great reverence by *Stewart & Paterson* in 1910.

On the outskirts of town, where Sinclair Street becomes LUSS ROAD, are the remains of the 1925 filter works, converted to housing; the former Toll House, a three-bay cottage to which the town boundary was extended in 1875; *William Leiper*'s prim and trim ARDLUSS, built in 1900 for the factor of the Luss Estates, and *A. N. Paterson*'s 'House in the Wood' of 1909, the asymmetrical Arts and Crafts DRUM-MILLIG. A powerful crowstepped chimney wall occupies much of the entrance façade where a small, single-storey porch with bellcast roof is located on the re-entrant angle. This leads to a walnut-timbered INTERIOR, where the dramatically coved ceiling in the drawing room recalls the splendours of the architect's own house at Longcroft (q.v.).

KENNEDY DRIVE forges W, passing CUILVONA, 1907, by *Duncan McNaughtan*, an H-plan Arts and Crafts villa with mock half-timbering and a semicircular inglenook centred on the s front and capped in ashlar. COLQUHOUN STREET UPPER intersects, terminating N at MORAR HOUSE, built for Thomas Bishop in 1903 by *William Leiper* and now offices. Similar in plan and choice of materials to Brantwoode (q.v.), the fine balance of the garden front was upset by Leiper himself in 1907 through the addition of a second-floor bedroom level, which creates a top-heavy effect. Neither this nor the modern conservatory E can detract from the exceptional N façade, where the entrance door is framed by a depressed-arched opening with crocketed ogee-arched moulding over. At its apex, a beautiful foliated boss and, on either flank, short columns capped by lurching animals and supported by corbelled figures carved in deep relief. Alongside, a corbelled turret above a squinch sheltering a hanging bell. – INTERIOR. Fine decoration intact with timber wainscot panelling and a balustered timber screen to the dog-leg stair.

LYNTON, further s, is one of *Leiper*'s last Helensburgh houses, the taut plan-form of 1908 expressed in what had become an effortless – if slightly unexciting – amalgam of Arts and Crafts and Shavian Old English. W on DHUHILL DRIVE, three elongated villas compete for attention. *Frank Burnet, Boston & Carruthers*' BRINCLIFFE of 1907 is the largest but easily most dull of the trio, the quality of the surrounding architecture demanding more than a mildly Free Style villa can muster. GRAYCOURT, on the other hand, makes real virtue out of its asymmetry. Designed in 1910 by *A. N. Paterson*, it exhibits trademark lopsided gables and a two-storey octagonal tower with bellcast roof on the SW corner, but rises additionally, if not a little eclectically, to an attic storey on the E side. This is forcibly expressed as a gablehead projecting ambitiously over a canted entrance tower. Deep strip glazing, including a semi-octagonal headed fanlight, frees this level from the floor below, where the central feature is a tall arched recess. At the base of the tower, C17 Renaissance roll-moulded stonework and carved panels commemorating client and construction. Finally, LETHAMHILL, *John Burnet & Son*, 1914, is also an L-plan Arts and Crafts composition, this time heavy and half-timbered.

THE HILL HOUSE

Colquhoun Street Upper, 1902–4, by *Charles Rennie Mackintosh*. Helensburgh's most famous house. The site still represents one of the most desirable feus in town. In 1902 the publisher Walter W. Blackie, attracted to Helensburgh by the sea air and ease of travel to Glasgow, secured a plot of land on the southern outskirts of the Blackhill Plantation (as far N as development had reached). Almost a century later, the views S continue to be unrivalled. The steepness of the site at the top of Colquhoun Street Upper permits panoramic vistas of the Firth of Clyde and the former shipbuilding town of Greenock on the S bank. The house was completed in 1904 (delayed by a strike at the Ballachulish slate quarry) and remained in the ownership of the Blackie family for fifty years. In 1972, the Royal Incorporation of Architects in Scotland purchased it from T. Campbell Lawson, who moved to nearby Shandon (q.v.), and in 1982 it passed into the care of The National Trust for Scotland. It has become one of their most popular visitor attractions in the West of Scotland.

The firm of Blackie and Son was established in 1809. Robert Blackie, younger son of its founder, was in his time a supporter of the work of Alexander Thomson and responsible for the publication of *Villa and Cottage Architecture* in 1868, which illustrated two of Thomson's designs for seaside villas in Cove (q.v.). Charged with responsibility for the art department of the firm, Robert Blackie appointed *Talwin Morris* as artistic director in 1893. It was Morris, designer of a distinctive range of stylized book covers for the publishers, who, nine years later, recommended to Robert Blackie's nephew Walter that he approach Charles Rennie Mackintosh to design his new home in Helensburgh.

The upper slopes of the town were by this stage characterized by houses clothed in red tile and timber, whitewash and sandstone, Arts and Crafts in the main and with Shavian overtones. They gave to the area a peculiarly English flavour, reinforced by the construction of *M. H. Baillie Scott*'s White House (q.v.) in 1899. When Mackintosh first met his new client, it was to hear him dismiss the style which had found favour with his neighbours, musing that grey roughcast and slate might be better materials in which to finish the building. In this, architect and patron were in agreement, as they were over the principle that architectural effect should be achieved through the massing of the parts rather than through superfluous decoration. As a result, the finished product could not have been more different from the surrounding villas: austere where they were frivolous, steeped in Scots ancestry where they had English antecedents, unique where they shared a common vocabulary. Not that Mackintosh could have failed to study The White House, with its purist assembly of flat walls, buttressed chimneystacks and single-storey, flat-roofed bay windows; but his inspiration was of an earlier vintage, found in his study of C17 Scots tower-houses, yet modernized to meet the demands of the new century.

The house is basically L-shaped, the longer wing – which contains the principal accommodation – aligned on an E–W axis. It is two-storeyed but with an attic floor concentrated on the shorter E wing, which housed the kitchen quarters, servants' rooms, nursery and schoolroom. One feature shared with many of the houses downhill of the site was the location of the principal entrance on the side façade, in this case facing W. This maximized the availability of the S wall of the building for windows to library, drawing room and dining room (in a sequence already established at *William Leiper*'s Brantwoode (q.v.) of 1895), and guaranteed a degree of privacy to these spaces. The main stair was located on the N and rear wall.

The W FAÇADE, by virtue of the omission of the billiard room and den intended for the NW corner, is an exceptionally angular composition which, seen from the street, is first framed by the horseshoe-shaped cut-outs of the boundary wall, and then by the clustered uprights of the wrought-iron double gates. The off-centre entrance is deeply recessed within a simple opening framed in yellow sandstone. With the exception of this surround, and the toothy stone jambs of two narrow side lights to the library on the r., the elevation is finished in harl. This serves to accentuate a projecting plane of walling l. of and directly above the entrance, where a flat-fronted cloakroom bay supports a big, half-buttressed chimneystack. In turn, this acts as the l. jamb and apron walling of a small canted window bay which, while highlighting the location of the entrance below, also permitted views to the firth from Walter Blackie's dressing room. The harl on the W and other gables is carried up and over the wallheads. There are no crowsteps, skews or even chimney

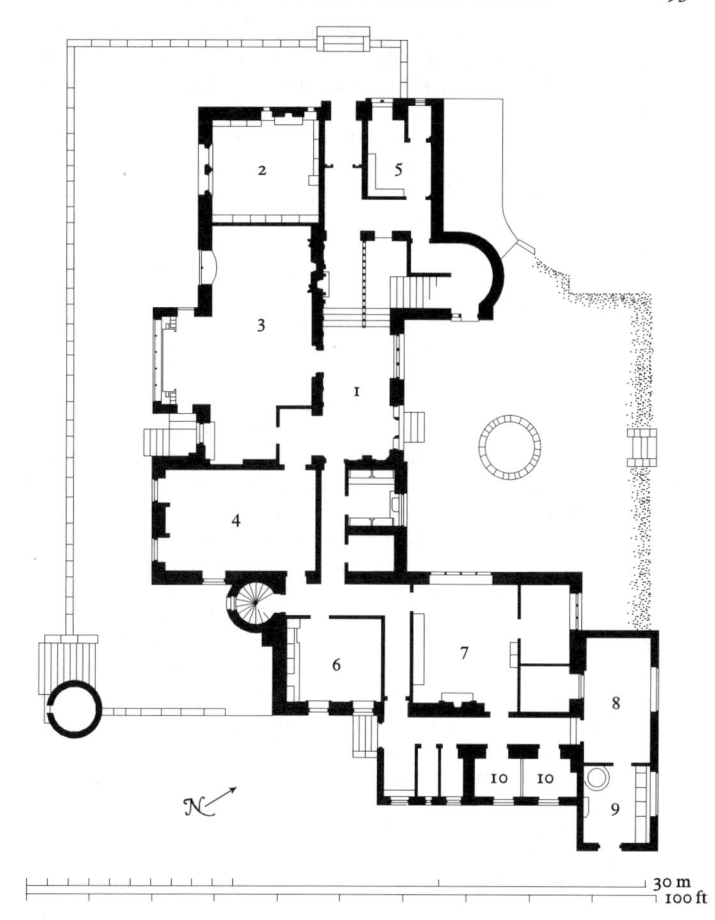

1	Hall	6	Larder
2	Library	7	Kitchen
3	Drawing-room	8	Laundry
4	Dining-room	9	Wash-house
5	Cloaks	10	Coal

Helensburgh, The Hill House

copes. This contrasts with the long elevations, where the steep Ballachulish slate roof has broad overhanging eaves with exposed rafter feet. The GARDEN FRONT, which faces s, is terminated on the r. by an advanced gable at whose ground storey two conventional sash and case windows light the dining room. Further r. is the receding gable of the service and nursery wing and, in the re-entrant angle, a stair tower with simple conical cap. Unlike the dining room, the library and drawing room are identified by their unorthodox fenestration. On the l. the leaded lights of the library window are very deeply recessed, the shade to a room where direct south light would have been undesirable increased by the shallow bow of the master bedroom window above. The squared drawing-room bay projects out to line up with the dining-room gable alongside, the gap between just wide enough to accommodate a short set of steps to the garden. The bay is flat-roofed, with large leaded lights set flush with the outer face: a minimalist modernist element in an elevation otherwise inspired by the Scots vernacular. The stair tower is appropriately robust, only half-emerging from a broad flat-topped chimneystack which braces the recessed gable of the day nursery.

The E GABLE has an informality which responds to the accommodation requirements of a typical service wing. A series of garden stores and rooms ancillary to the kitchen are expressed as a single-storey shed. Rising up behind, a series of projecting and receding planes, which begin on the l. with the three-storey flank of the dining-room bay, dropping to and advancing as a two-storey nursery extension, and projecting again further r. in the form of a blocky squared bay topped by the canted window to the schoolroom. This window, fully glazed and almost skeletal in structure, is a precursor to the architect's 'hen run' on the S front of the Glasgow School of Art of 1898–1907. Also on the E gable, a small concession to the art of decoration appears in the form of a pointed, bud-like gablet carved in sandstone and slightly protruding above parapet level over the l. attic bedroom window.

The most striking feature of the N FAÇADE is the curved walling of the principal staircase tower, which is lit by a series of tall, narrow leaded lights. Although this extruded cylinder has a pitched, slated roof, it is so deeply sunk behind the harl-topped parapet that it disappears when viewed from ground level. The effect is remarkably streamlined and modernist, whereas the little dormerheads which appear only here, on the rear wall, are traditional in origin.

To examine the exterior of the building on an elevation-by-elevation basis does not do it justice. The skilful massing of the parts, the constant shift between recession and projection with the resulting play of light and shade, and the modelling of roofscapes and gables, all combine to produce an exceptionally powerful three-dimensional image. The impenetrability of a C16 or C17 Scottish keep is achieved without compromise on this hilltop site, the inclusion of large areas of finely leaded glass in selected openings serving to underline rather than diminish the solidity.

The Glasgow Style INTERIOR is far lighter in character and more ethereal than the exterior suggests. Mackintosh was employed to prepare a complete decorative scheme for the house, which included furniture design, stencilling, light fittings, wall and floor coverings and ironmongery. The completeness, cohesion and consistency of the concept are outstanding. The entrance lobby opens into a long HALL which virtually doubles in width at the head of a short flight of steps. The eye is drawn from relative gloom to the brightness of a N-lit space. On the l., a screen of slender timber uprights, into which are punched tiny teardrops of pink and purple glass, reveals the main staircase. The lower walls of the hall are subdivided by tall vertical strips of dark-stained pine up to doorhead height, the panelling incorporating an unusual chequered stencilled frieze in subtle shades of blue and grey and, on the E wall, a purpose-built pendulum clock. The theme of squares within rectangles which is established on the walls is carried through to the carpet, doors, occasional chair and silvered pendant lights. The LIBRARY, immediately r., shares the dark formality of the lower hall, the walls lined with oak shelves and cupboards enlivened by little inserts of blue and purple glass. The sobriety of this space, which served as Walter Blackie's study and a reception room, contrasts vividly with the adjoining DRAWING ROOM, into which south light floods through the deep window bay. It was originally intended to incorporate a separate morning room E, but has instead an alcove for music. Opposite, the living space was warmed by an open fire set within a beautiful tessera surround, inset with five droplet-shaped, coloured and mirrored mosaics. The decorative scheme, restored by the National Trust for Scotland, uses the rose as its theme, the walls subdivided vertically by bands of silver with stylized roses arranged between, and even stray painted petals scattered across the ivory background. There are wall lights – also decorated with stained-glass roses – gossamer-thin curtains, a recessed china cabinet defined by the outline of a stylized tree, and a gesso panel designed by *Margaret Macdonald Mackintosh* above the fireplace. The quality of light within the room can be extraordinary, and the transparency of the window alcove – allied with the floral theme picked out on the walls – blurs the boundaries between indoors and out.

The DINING ROOM was largely furnished with items brought by the Blackie family from their home in Dunblane, although Mackintosh did design a handsome fireplace and stained-glass central light. The remainder of the ground floor was taken up with the service quarters, from where a spiral stair on the SE corner gave access to the servants' wing above. The principal stair is altogether grander, lit naturally by three long openings of delicate leaded glass and artificially by a spectacular cubic light fitting made of dark burnished metal and pinky-purple glass. The first-floor hall is relatively plain, but has a pretty, raised alcove (for sewing) with views over the N courtyard. At the W end is Walter Blackie's dressing room and a bathroom, complete with the original Edwardian fittings. But it is the MASTER BEDROOM, painstakingly restored since 1989, which is of principal interest. The room is L-shaped, with the bed located at the narrow end below a barrel-vaulted ceiling, and complete with most of its furnishings, including built-in bedside cabinets lined with dusky-pink glass, white-painted wardrobes with stained-glass panels and extruded decoration, a wash-stand and bowls, an inglenook settle with embroidered covers, two dark ladderback chairs, an Art Nouveau full-length cheval dressing-mirror, a fireplace with steel and tile surround, and a superb pendant light fitting. The layout of the furniture, mostly fitted, was meticulously planned by Mackintosh, but overriding the essentially practical nature of the scheme (a timber-and-glass screen which allowed the sleeping area to be curtained off was never executed) is a sense of prettiness and delicacy created by the extent and elegance of the decoration. For a long period the walls were finished entirely in white. This had the effect of isolating the individual items of furniture and rendering the room far starker than had been intended. Paint scrapes revealed the extensive wall stencilwork which once again adorns the space with a fantastically ornate pattern of trellis and roses.

The EAST WING contains less of note, although there are some good fireplaces and interesting window configurations. An excellent permanent exhibition designed by *Anne Ellis* now occupies the remaining bedrooms. – GARDEN. A slightly elevated terrace wraps around w and s walls. At the SE corner, a miniature version of the circular stair turret has been built as the gardener's hut. To the N is the kitchen garden and, closer to the rear wall of the house, a sheltered courtyard which now houses a kinetic sculpture given by *George Ricky* in 1997. – OUTBUILDINGS. NW of the main house, an attractive U-plan range of buildings, harled and with slate roofs. Extended in 1928 by *Robert Wemyss*. – LAMP STANDARDS. On the roadside, six lamp standards adapted from designs by Mackintosh by *Strathclyde Regional Council* in 1990.

Rhu Road Lower

The growth of the town w, towards Rhu, was for some time limited by the lands of Ardencaple Castle (q.v.). The castle lawn extended to the carriageway along the foreshore at CAIRNDHU POINT, while the castle wood effectively separated town and village. First erosion of the great estate occurred when in 1919 it was determined that land was required for municipal housing. ARDENCAPLE QUADRANT provided much-needed homes for men returning from World War I and gave to architects *Stewart & Paterson* their first opportunity to design a garden village in an economic Scots idiom, with gablets, wallhead dormers and harling enlivening buildings whose individual construction costs were set at under £358. Later, in 1936, a series of small feus were derived from the castle parkland where builders *Charles Murrie of Kirkintilloch* and *Thomas Watson of Largs* erected a succession of villas and bungalows, the best of which is at No. 18 LOCH DRIVE, 1938, where a white cube is given streamlined distinction by the curving corners around which metal-framed windows wrap. FERNIEGAIR ESTATE lying to the E is later, developed in patchy fashion by *Noad & Wallace* in 1958. But there is an outstanding group of five houses in FERNIEGAIR AVENUE completed by project architect *Tom Humphreys* in 1959. The two-storey buildings present stepped profiles to the street; physically linked by garages and garden screens and thematically by grey and white cement render.

CAIRNDHU, Rhu Road Lower, 1871, *William Leiper*. An exceptional château in the manner of François I, Cairndhu was built for John Ure of Glasgow, a grain miller and merchant who became Lord Provost of the city, and whose son became Lord Strathclyde. Virtually square in plan, the house enjoys an uninterrupted view of the Clyde, the windows on the S front large and many as a result. Groups of windows are linked vertically by fluted and banded pilasters, and horizontally by cornicing, balustrading and ball finials aplenty. Thus, the large W tower with French pavilion roof and lantern is visually bound to the principal façade despite the intervention of a circular, flat-topped stair tower. – INTERIOR. The remarkable Aesthetic Movement/ Anglo-Japanese scheme of decoration created in collaboration with *Daniel Cottier*, with whom the architect had completed work on Colearn in Auchterarder only a few years earlier, has survived use as hotel and now nursing home. In the long narrow hall, beyond a barrel-vaulted entrance, there is a timber-beamed ceiling with sunflower motif, a chimneypiece with lion-head corbels and gilded and stencilled overmantel, and a sequence of three rectangular stained-glass windows in which are set stunning decorative figure compositions. In the dining room, wainscotting, more ceiling stencilwork (this time with beams supported on carved ashlar angels) and a good timber chimneypiece with large oval mirror; in the staircase window, three beautiful neo-classical panels representing Truth and Beauty, Love and Audacity, and Knowledge and Prudence; but in the drawing room, the *pièce de résistance*, a jaw-droppingly lovely coved and coffered ceiling on which sunflowers and songbirds are picked out in gold on black. – LODGE. Exquisite miniature of the parent house, although with playful pretensions towards Scots Renaissance. The boundary gateposts comprise quatrefoil clustered columns topped by elongated pyramids balanced on ashlar balls.

DALMORE, Rhu Road Lower, 1873, *William Leiper*. Two-storey-and-attic Baronial mansion entered from the rear and with an impregnable S front worthy of the C16 and C17 Scots castles from which the details are derived. Relief from the powerful planes of unbroken red rubble comes in the form of a two-storey bow window far r., surmounted by a semi-octagonal attic storey with finialled polygonal roof and wallhead dormers on either side with decorated heads. The architect famously reproduced the design, with the addition of a basement storey, ten years later at Kinlochmoidart in the Highlands (see 'Highlands and Islands' in this series). – INTERIOR. Extensively redecorated *c.* 1881 by *W. Scott Morton*. Now flatted. – LODGES. Generously proportioned W lodge at the junction of RHU ROAD HIGHER and LOWER, designed 1893 by *Leiper*. Exposure to the elements has eroded the fine details of the cherub cartouche on the seaward face, but the carved-head label stops representing four ages of man on the W bay are in good order. The 1873 E lodge features a detail similarly derived from Maybole Castle in Ayrshire, this time a beaded, engaged triple horseshoe motif on the S front.

KIDSTON PARK, 1877, 'wee but wondrous bonnie' clings to the curve of Cairndhu Point, from where the Duke of Argyll's barge would depart for Rosneath Castle (q.v.). Here stood the original CAIRNDOW INN, which was demolished and the stones used in the construction of the stables to the nearby ARDENCAPLE HOTEL, Rhu Road Lower, early C19. Used as a posting inn on the road between Glasgow and Inveraray; the architectural allegiance to the latter is clearly evident. A classical, three-storey, three-bay rectangular-plan block is flanked on either side by identical single-storey advanced, open-pedimented pavilions. These have large recessed arched panels with keystones and blind windows. The arches are repeated at ground floor on the principal block, which is completed by a hefty balustraded parapet with urns. Details are picked out in black on white stucco. While completely modernized internally, the building is nevertheless a striking boundary marker at the meeting of Helensburgh and the village of Rhu. On the hillside behind, a classic split-level home clad in western red cedar weatherboarding, by *Law & Dunbar-Nasmith*, 1960.

HUNTER'S QUAY

The name admits the origin. A stone pier built by Robert Hunter of Hafton in 1828 stimulated development. Like its neighbour Kirn, the holiday village soon grew to become a suburb of Dunoon.

HUNTER'S QUAY. The first stone-built quay, 1828, replaced or extended by a T-plan timber pier, by *Thomas Warrin*, 1858. Late C19 rubble slip by engineer *D.J. Stevenson*. Closed in 1964, it re-opened in strengthened and adapted form in 1973 as a ferry link to Gourock.

DESCRIPTION

Most of the esplanade houses on MARINE PARADE are those plain Victorian Gothic villas familiar all along the East Cowal shore: bargeboarded gables and battlemented bays. But there are exceptions. Prominent above the pier, for example, are the arches, balconies, bays and gables of the ROYAL MARINE HOTEL, a stripy, half-timbered Tudor hall by *T.L. Watson*, 1888–9. Built to serve as a yachtsman's palace, the headquarters of the Royal Clyde Yacht Club, the interior has a well stair opening through columned arches at ground- and first-floor level, with painted glass by *J. & W. Guthrie* in a tall mullion-and-transom window. HUNTER'S QUAY HOTEL, almost as grand, is, in fact, aggrandized; a house of *c.* 1870, with a lampshade-roofed tower, extended S and enlarged with mansards to Frenchified Baronial pretension *c.* 1900. Corinthian columns in the hall, a glazed dome above the flying stair and, in the later S lounge, finely carved hardwood doors and console-framed fireplace enriched by textured ceramic tiles flanking a brass grate.

Towered, too, but symmetrical, ROSEMOUNT, late C19, has filigree ironwork cresting on roofs, bays and porch. Some unexpected if unremarkable ashlar tenements lie uphill: MADEIRA PLACE and Nos. 40 and 40A GEORGE STREET, late C19, lined with moulded, floor-level stringcourses. At the top of James Street, BONNIEBLINK, dated 1878, three storeys tall with mock gargoyles at the parapet, tries hard to assume tower-house dignity.

INNELLAN

Development began in the 1840s. A concatenation of diverse villas lining the E Cowal shore from Bullwood to Toward. A high road parallels the coastal strip.

INNELLAN MATHESON CHURCH. Named for the blind preacher and hymn writer, George Matheson (1842–1906), whose sermons once filled the hillside church with Victorian holidaymakers. Built 1853; side aisles(?) added 1890. Nave and aisles present a triple-gabled W front below Wyndham Road; porch added by *John T. Rochead*, 1866–7. Gabled E end and transepts built over vestry undercroft; SE turnpike stair. Sharp lancets grouped in twos and threes. Triple lancets under single pointed-arch hood-moulding in principal gables. Timber steeple removed 1984. – BELL, cast by *John C. Wilson* of Glasgow in 1880, now hangs within a wooden frame at the approach to the church. – Three-bay interior defined by slender cast-iron columns. S gallery. Triple roof of arch-braced trusses made visually complex by diagonal bracing between purlins and interpenetration of transepts. – Heavy stone drum PULPIT carved with circular panels between colonnettes. – Pipe ORGAN installed l. in chancel, 1933. – STAINED GLASS in triple lancets of main gables. Chancel: Christ at the Door, a strongly coloured portrayal of the Holman Hunt painting, by *Stephen Adam*, 1906. W, by *W. & J. J. Kier*, 1879 (Mary meeting Christ in the Garden, with Peter and John in the side lights), lacks such effulgence.

Former WEST CHURCH. Built as the Free Church, 1855; steeple and back gallery added by *John T. Rochead* as a gift, *c.* 1870. Lancet Gothic in grey-green rubble with pink sandstone dressings. Splayed chancel linked NE to halls. Spire removed from SW steeple. Converted to residential use.

INNELLAN PIER. Quay constructed 1850–1; extended by engineers *D. & C. Stevenson*, 1899–1900. As at Toward Lighthouse, a curving walled forecourt, here battlemented with saddleback coping stones, leads to the long timber pier. Closed 1972.

INNELLAN PRIMARY SCHOOL. By *Robert A. Bryden*, 1875–6. Long single-storey classroom block with N gable and one-and-a-half-storey schoolmaster's house S.

KNOCKAMILLIE CASTLE, on the hill above the pier. A Campbell house; C16 or C17. MacGibbon and Ross recorded that 'nothing can now be made out as to the size or strength of the castle' (1892); today there is less. A short length of S-facing wall stands *c.* 7m. A stabilizing stub wall at right angles is relatively recent.

DESCRIPTION

Opposite the pier, a three-storey tenement with a chamfered SE corner, the steep incline of Pier Road and a two-storeyed stretch of shops and flats running s to another tenement give some sense of scale and arrival. Otherwise, the village is a two-tier parade of mid-C19 'marine villas'. Many are shabby. None is remarkable. But a few have redeeming features. On the road N to Dunoon, ROCK BANK has a delicate porch with a fretted edge and retains good ironwork railings and gates. Porches also distinguish DHUNELLAN and AVOCA: one battlemented, the other a bracketed gable. CLUNITER sits back, but sits up too: steeply gabled white Baronial marred by window changes yet held erect by the sharp slated cone on its full-height staircase tube. Further s towards Toward, DUNFEURACH affects an Italianate air with a three-storey tower and round-arched, triple-light windows, while the tall, inverted-W fronts of LABRADOR and JOPPA HOUSE have balconied double-height canted bays under fretted bargeboards. Octagonal corner bays corbel l. and r. from the white gable of UNDERCLIFF. At AUCHNASTRUAN, more fretted bargeboards. At the BRAEMAR HOTEL, finials on the gables. Dingy and drab, but atmospheric, CROSSAIG LODGE boasts a conservatory with a curving glass roof and crested lantern. THE PRIORY is appropriately if naïvely Gothic and has gatepiers topped with what must be the biggest ball finials on the Cowal shore. Breaking the prevailing, somewhat dishevelled, gable-fronted mould, CARRISBROOKE is full of suburban Victorian rectitude; incongruous perhaps but refreshingly respectable. DALRIADA GROVE, too, is different; a pleasant enclave of polychromatic brick housing by *SSHA Architects*, 1987–9, with its own quiet privacy and a perfectly landscaped pollarded tree.

INNIS CHONNELL CASTLE

island fortalice close to SE shore of Loch Awe, 14 km. NE of Ford

Family stronghold built by the Campbells of Loch Awe in C13, its insular security later made it a favourite place of incarceration for the enemies of the Earls of Argyll. Hereditary captains, MacArthurs and later MacLachlans, occupied the castle until the early C18; a century later it was in ruins.

The main structure and middle bailey occupy the entire W half of the rocky island site, separated from the outer bailey to the E by a narrow neck of land where a gatehouse commanded landing-places N and S. The C13 castle, built at the extreme W end of the island on a *c.* 25m. square plan, was probably defensively and structurally stiffened by angle-towers, though only the SE one survives. Entrance was from the middle bailey on the E and within the walls accommodation would have been grouped around a courtyard. Existing inner buildings (four barrel-vaulted cellars ranged along the W wall with the hall above and a rectangular apartment rising through four storeys in the SE)

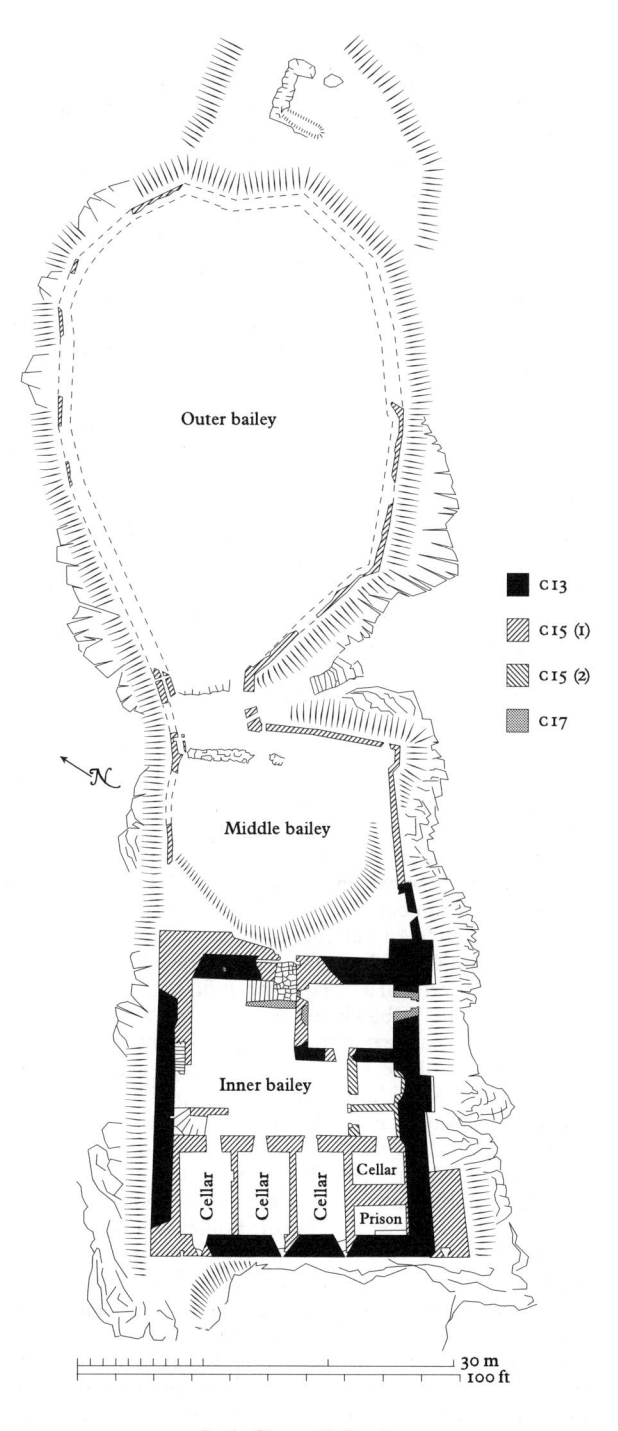

Innis Chonnell Castle

date from the C15 when extensive remodelling was undertaken. At this time the outer walls, which retain signs of harling, were rebuilt to parapet level, NW and NE corners being wholly reconstructed and a new broad SW angle-turret added. Openings in the masonry vary: most are square-headed but there are round arches and some half-hexagonal and 'round-cornered' lintels. The E entrance gate was revised with a lintelled outer opening, a segmental arch through the thickness of the wall and an inner, higher, pointed arch. The level of the threshold, puzzlingly located above middle and inner baileys, necessitated a ramped outer approach and, on the inside, a forestair, originally timber but replaced in stone in the C17, leading down N into the castle yard. Against the thickened inner face of the N curtain a long straight-flight forestair rises E to the partially intact parapet walk. At the NW corner of the inner bailey a third stone forestair ascends against the W range.

From the outer landing of this NW stair, a round-arched doorway opens into a screens area separated from the hall by a stone partition now no more than a low ruined wall. N of the screens, a cramped kitchen space, identifiable by the wide C17 fireplace in the N gable, the segmentally arched opening of which seems to be a modern reconstruction, and a slop-sink below the narrow W window. From the S end of the hall a door gives access to a lobby through which an inner chamber is reached. This private apartment, which retains moulded corbels from a canopied fire, links to a barrel-vaulted oblong space in the SW tower provided with latrine and discharge-chute. It seems likely that this relationship of rooms was repeated on upper levels. The SE block, now a floorless shell, appears to have had a single apartment at each of its four levels. At first floor a S doorway opens into a mural passage which leads E to a stone-flagged chamber in the C13 SE angle-tower and, although now blocked after a brief continuation W, may formerly have connected with the lobby at the S end of the hall. In this zone at the centre of the S wall a three-storey infill was constructed, late C15, between the SE block and W range. Its two small ground-floor apartments are extant but its upper arrangements unclear. Apart from the three forestairs rising from the inner bailey, vertical circulation within the castle is also problematical; timber stairs may well have sufficed, but their location remains a mystery.

Innis Chonnell is now an almost impenetrably overgrown place. Moss and ivy add a romantic patina to the texture of crumbling rubble but, hidden under trees and shrubbery, the configuration of the castle's fortified outer works is difficult to discern. A short length of C13 masonry extends E from the SE angle-tower beyond which C15 walling, nowhere more than 2.5m. high, continues to a vantage point overlooking a stone staircase rising from the S landing before turning N to reach the gatehouse. Enclosure of the middle bailey is thus complete on the S; on the shorter N edge it is intermittent. E is the outer bailey, a roughly oval enclosure limited in extent by the rocky perimeter of the island and now defined by rubble walling only along the SW shore and vestigially on the N. The surviving masonry of the gatehouse, stretching across the nipped neck of the island's hour-glass plan, indicates a low building opening to the courtyards W and E and, below parapet walks, to the loch-landings on the N and S.

CHAPEL, Innis Sèa-Ràmhach, 1km. SSW of Innis Chonnell. Diagonally sited in an approximately square enclosure marked by earth banks, the low rubble walls of an oblong chapel of unknown dedication, C15 or C16(?). Jambs of N door and windows in the N, W and E walls have been rebuilt. Small basin carved in sill of W window. When the loch level is particularly low, access by causeway is possible.

CHAMBERED CAIRN, Ardchonnell, 2km. NE of Innis Chonnell. Stony mound in forestry clearing, *c.* 33m. long tailing from 19m. wide at NE to *c.* 12m. at SW. 3.7m.-long irregular chamber of Clyde type at NE end, with the capstone of the inner portion still *in situ*.

INVERARAY

0908

A town on the W shore of Loch Fyne at the mouth of the River Aray. For centuries the seat of the Campbell Earls and Dukes of Argyll who constructed their castle here in the C15. Well placed for trade by land and sea, the town became a burgh of barony in 1472 and in 1648 a royal burgh. Still small, by the C18 it prospered as an administrative centre for the county and was the focus of much legal activity tied to the local Sheriff Court and the regular circuit visits of the High Court of Justiciary. Herring fishing was the only industry.

In 1743 the 3rd Duke succeeded to the estate, intent on improvements. In fifty years Inveraray was transformed. The old castle, which the Duke's mason reported 'Cannot be Repaired for use Except at near the Expence that would build such ane other', was demolished and replaced (*see* Inveraray Castle). The town, too, was razed. Demolition began in 1758 and was substantially completed in the period 1771–6. Tolbooth, church, schools and the rows of thatched and slated dwellings that had lined an irregular triangle of streets on the r. bank of the river between castle and loch all disappeared. In their place or, rather, a short distance S on the lochside at Gallows Foreland Point, out of sight of the new castle and separated from the estate by the Mall, a long line of beech trees planted in the C17, the planned New Town of Inveraray gradually emerged.

Several proposals contributed to the final street layout. An early plan, ascribed to the 3rd Duke and Lord Milton, 1743, showed two NE–SW streets parallel to the Mall, a short central street at right angles to these and a third street (the present Front Street) running NW back along the loch shore towards the castle grounds. The stress on the central crossing, the idea of *point-de-vue* siting for important buildings and the presence of a 'Great Inn' on Front Street remained significant, though the Duke's commercial plans

304 ARGYLL: THE MAINLAND

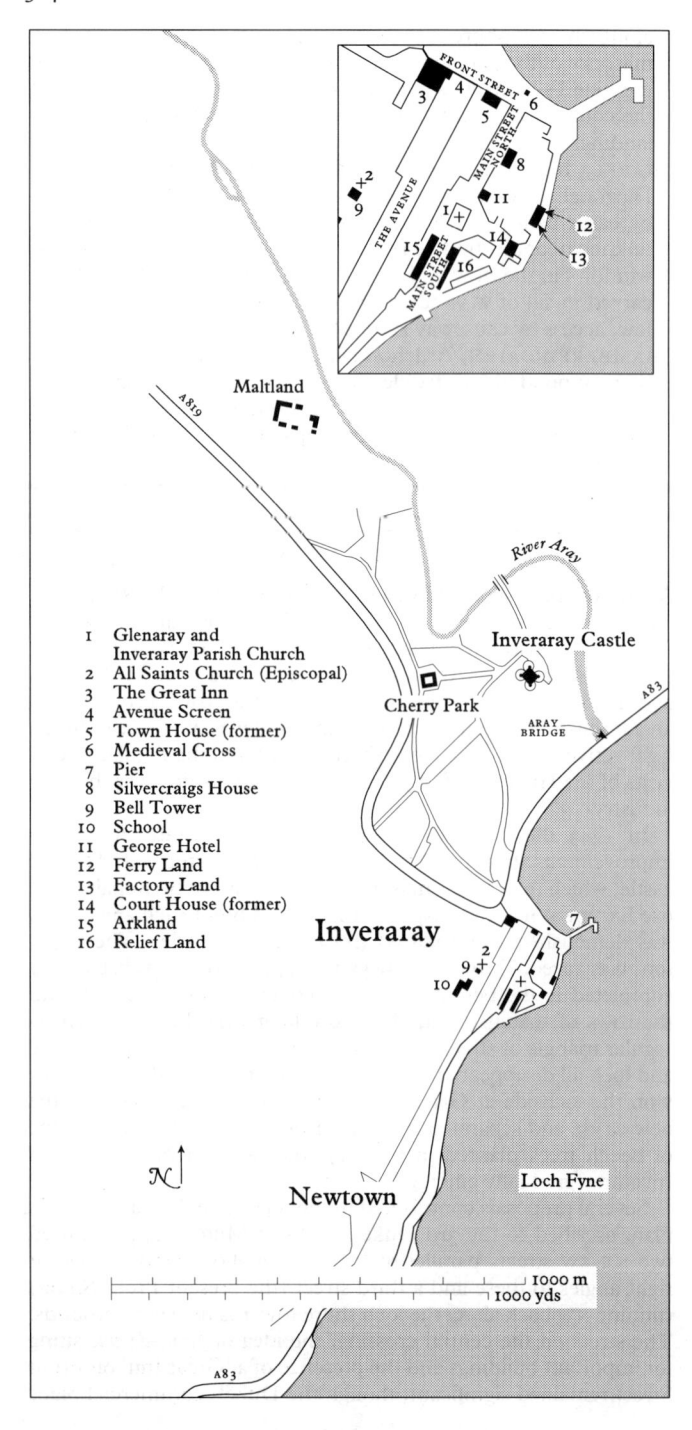

1   Glenaray and
    Inveraray Parish Church
2   All Saints Church (Episcopal)
3   The Great Inn
4   Avenue Screen
5   Town House (former)
6   Medieval Cross
7   Pier
8   Silvercraigs House
9   Bell Tower
10 School
11 George Hotel
12 Ferry Land
13 Factory Land
14 Court House (former)
15 Arkland
16 Relief Land

for granaries, warehouses, a tannery, brewery and stocking manufactory were never realized. More developed drawings by *William Adam*, c. 1747, proposed a half-octagonal sea-wall with bastions enclosing a symmetrical layout which had at its centre a circular 'double church' in an open square. This church survived in *John Adam*'s two plans of 1750, though these abandoned the previous rectilineal grid for oblique ranges of houses which formed a blunted arrow-head layout echoing the shoreline of the headland site (*see* Fernpoint Hotel below). Through the 1750s the town began to find its final form. The plan reverted to a single NE–SW line (Main Street), a short cross-axis creating the central focus, and the coastal frontage looking NE up to Loch Shira (Front Street). A town wall along the line of the Mall was erected by the mason *James Potter*, 1757. By this time The Great Inn and the Town House had been built, the site for the double church determined, a pier was under construction and several private houses were occupied. Buildings were of stone, harled, with slated roofs. Progress was slow. Attempts to establish a textile industry stuttered and failed. Yet, by the end of the C18, Inveraray had, albeit unwittingly, invested instead in architectural assurance. From Thomas Pennant's perceptive travel note of 1776 that 'This place will in time be very magnificent', through the burgeoning tourism of the C19 to the present, no visit to the Highlands has been complete without a sight of Inveraray's bare black-and-white beauty.

CHURCHES

ALL SAINTS' CHURCH (Episcopal), NW of the Town Avenue. By *Wardrop & Anderson*, 1885–6. First Pointed Gothic in pink granite rubble with pink Ayrshire freestone dressings. Nave and chancel under one roof. Six-bay interior roofed with arch-braced trusses springing from corbelstones. Chancel defined above by pointed-arch opening and below by low freestone wall with blind arcading and iron gates. Patterned *Minton*(?) floor tiles in red, black, ochre and gold. – ALTAR of pink Catrine freestone. – Composite oak SETTLE with a back of three ogival panels with blind tracery and finials (two at least from late-medieval bench-ends). – Rough stone bowl FONT, pre-Reformation, from Kilmalieu (*see* below). – Alabaster STOUP on four-column stone pedestal, 1932. – Standing separate from the church, hugely and controversially tall at over 38m., is the Gothic DUKE'S TOWER, 1923–31, by *Hoare & Wheeler*, erected as a memorial to Campbells killed in World War I. Square in plan and built without buttresses in pink granite rubble; dressings and half-octagon engaged stair tower of red Ballochmyle sandstone. Single bifurcated pointed-arch windows superimposed in the lower stages but coupled in the belfry which, like the castellated parapet above, is intaken slightly. Tusking stones indicate an unfulfilled intention to connect the tower with the church. – Ten BELLS, cast by *John Taylor & Sons*, Loughborough, 1920. – Former BELL HOUSE, 1921: slated pyramid with slatted timber-framed walls.

BURIAL GROUND, Kilmalieu, on the NW shore of Loch Fyne, 1.3km. NE. Site of the medieval parish church of Inveraray and graveyard of the town's burgesses. A catalogue prepared in the 1960s records *c.* 540 monuments, over 300 pre-1855. – A few TAPERED SLABS, C13–C16; one, showing a four-ring cross, C13–C14, re-used and dated 1755. – Many TABLE-TOMBS and lying SLABS, late C17 and early C18, bearing armorial shields, emblems of mortality and inscriptions. – Among the former, one to Alexander Brown and his wife Mary Sym †1721, with an added HEADSTONE carved with an angel's winged head, mantled shield, the initials AB and the date 1721. – In a walled enclosure, a MURAL MONUMENT aedicule of fluted Ionic columns carrying a round pediment filled with heraldic shield; to John Campbell of Stonefield †1731. – Another of the same with Corinthian columns and a flaming urn on the pediment; to Colin Campbell of Braiglenmore †1736(?). – To Alexander McNuier †1748, a classical HEADSTONE with fluted pilasters and crossed spades in the pediment. – For the family of James Black, mason, a similarly framed HEADSTONE, 1753, carved with mason's square and dividers. – Plain bevel-edged SLAB in memory of William Douglas †1782, 'late architect in Inveraray'. – The children of John MacNiven, wright, remembered in a mantled HEADSTONE, 1825, with angel head and naïve framing pilasters. – To Thomas Hislop †1785, his wife Martha MacPhun †1815, and their children, a large MURAL MONUMENT with consoles, broken pediment and urn. – MURAL TABLET to John McKellar †1832 inscribed with exquisite penmanship. – In a plot enclosed by cast-iron railings with repetitive anthemion and lily motifs, a grey granite plinth supporting a blocky memorial CROSS to Quintin Montgomerie †1886.

GLENARAY AND INVERARAY PARISH CHURCH, Church Square. Centrepiece of the town designed for the 5th Duke of Argyll by *Robert Mylne*, 1792, and built 1795–1802; re-roofed and steeple

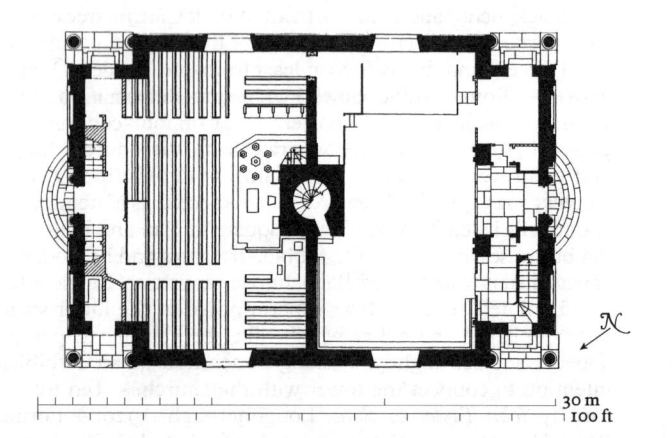

Inveraray Parish Church

rebuilt 1837–8; recast internally 1898–9. A pedimented temple with portico façades to the N and S gables. Conceived as a double church housing Highland (Gaelic-speaking) and Lowland (English-speaking) congregations. The plan is thus symmetrical on both axes, the pulpits in back-to-back relationship against opposite sides of the base of a central steeple tower. The N and S fronts, which combine Arran freestone with panels of harling, are solid, except at each end where, under the full-width pediment, a single Tuscan column, part granite, part sandstone, is released as the façade recesses in an open corner. These columns, which have fluted necks, are echoed in half-columns attached to the lateral walls. The gables are divided into three bays by broad pilaster strips and have tall Venetian windows at the upper level, their surrounds and blind side lights of St Catherines stone. Below, the central entrance is a lintelled opening framed by Tuscan columns in antis. Blind segmental arch windows fill the bays l. and r. Above, in the ashlar tympanum, a circular recess is swagged by a low relief moulding which subtly suggests an inner pediment related to the central bay. In the S opening, a BELL, dated 1724, cast by *Robert Maxwell* at Edinburgh; in the N, a clock. The harled W and E walls are plain with two tall round-arch windows; *Mylne*'s proposals to stress the cross-axis with semicircular porticoes and colonnades, 1800, failed to find favour. At the heart of the plan, the steeple emerged from the roof ridge as a square plinth, became a domed octagonal belfry with engaged columns, before finally rising in an obelisk pinnacle. Demolished in 1941, its (literally) crucial impact on the townscape is lost.

Only the N church remains in use for worship, its twin (much altered 1913) converted to a hall, 1957. From the small lobby, stone stairs rise l. and r. to a gallery carried on cast-iron columns, the side galleries added 1898–9. Four-bay interior with kingpost trusses. False clearstorey arrangement (the outer struts of the trusses linked by open timber screens perforated by cusped lancets and quatrefoils), boarded rafters above and ribbed plaster panels on the ceiling margins, 1898–9. Plain cornice with egg-and-dart frieze. – FURNISHINGS installed 1898. – Terrazzo sanctuary floor edged with green and black marble. – Three-tier-high, seven-bay-wide, timber SCREEN with elaborate Gothic tracery and crested canopy, by *Charles & Edward MacLaren*; screen and elders' stalls l., painted grey. – COMMUNION TABLE with cusped round-arches on fluted colonnettes. – Huge hexagonal PULPIT arched on fluted Corinthian columns with evangelists and angels on the abaci; a copy of the pulpit in the Baptistery at Pisa by *Charles & Edward MacLaren*. – Dwarfed l., stone bowl FONT on column cluster, carved in local bluestone by *Donald MacVicar*. – Brass eagle LECTERN. – Tall, bronze, war memorial MURAL PANEL, 1924, set in hardwood surround, l. of pulpit. – In the gallery, a metal PANEL with intertwined leaf border by *Alexander & Euphemia Ritchie*, Iona; to Victoria Campbell †1910, third daughter of the 8th Duke of Argyll. – Also a white marble TABLET to Lord Walter Campbell †1889.

CROSS, Front Street. Iona school, late C14 or early C15. Erected close to the loch shore on the axis of Main Street, 1839. It formerly served as the old town's market cross and may originally have come from the medieval chapel at Kilmalieu. 1.54m. high with flared arm-pitted cross-head lugged at the top of the tapered shaft. Both faces carved with plant scroll decoration and animal forms. Figural images have been removed, as in the Campbeltown Cross (q.v.). Latin inscription to three generations of 'noble men' in the MacCowan family.

Former FREE CHURCH, Newtown. 1895. Asymmetrical Gothic Revival front in pink granite rubble with red sandstone facings. Gabled pointed-arch entrance l. Now Masonic Hall.

Former UNITED SECESSION CHURCH, Newtown. 1836. Harled curvilinear gable with ball skewputts and central oculus. Two tall segmental arch windows. Now St Malieu Hall.

PUBLIC BUILDINGS

ARAY BRIDGE, 500m. NNE of the town. Designed by *Robert Mylne* in 1773, built 1774–6, to replace *John Adam*'s three-arch, crenellated 'King's Bridge', 1758–60, destroyed by floods 1772, this elegant 180m.-long structure of two segmental arches, each spanning 19.8m., carries the A83 across the River Aray. Surprisingly polychromatic: green schist in the cutwaters and spandrels, buff sandstone for the abutment buttresses, pink sandstone voussoirs and parapets. A 3.3m. dia. void penetrates the central pier above triangular cutwaters. Momentarily poised over this void, the traveller sees ahead the long lacustrine elevation of the 3rd Duke's New Town.

Former COURT HOUSE, Crown Point. Designed by *James Gillespie Graham*, 1813, following a proposal by *Robert Reid*, 1807–8. Built 1816–20 by *William Lumsden* and *James Peddie* of Leith. Now a Visitor Centre. Very much a stage-set façade, the three-storey w elevation fronts the court-room, offices and jail which superseded those of the Town House (*see* below), at the same time providing a grandly symmetrical closure to the town's cross-axial plan. Above the rusticated ground storey, first and second floors are absorbed in a high *piano nobile* of sandstone ashlar. Tuscan pilasters, coupled at the margins of the centre-piece but single in the outer bays, define a classic tripartite composition. At its heart is a large Venetian window distinctly reminiscent of Robert Adam, its Tuscan column mullions carrying a lintel which continues as a moulded stringcourse across the façade. This horizontal stress reverberates in the entablature above (there is no pediment) and in the parapet, which is solid but fluted in the middle and balustraded in the flanks. Barely visible is a shallow hipped roof. Symmetrical plan with a central scale-and-platt stair leading at first floor to Roman Doric screens l. and r. through which access is gained to the semi-circular court-room at the rear. Here, in a central niche recess flanked by Roman Doric columns, a white marble BUST of Lord Colonsay by *Sir John Steell*, 1874, set on a plinth of Peterhead

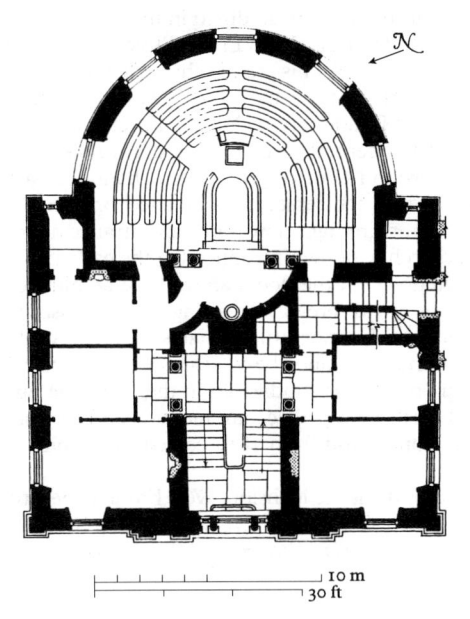

Inveraray Court House

granite. Various harled prison buildings: NE block by *Gillespie Graham*, 1820; SW by *Thomas Brown*, 1843-5. These are starkly plain though dramatized somewhat by the bastion walls which Gillespie Graham's assistant *James Stevenson* had to construct in order to raise the foundations clear of high tide. Partial reconstruction to house Post Office, 1931.

THE GREAT INN, West Front Street. By *John Adam*, 1750; design amended by amateur architect *Harry Barclay* of Colairny. Built by *William Douglas*, mason, and *George Haswell*, wright, 1751-5. Plain, nine-bay, three-storey front to loch, painted white with black dressings. A central segmental arch pend led to the stables court at the rear. The pend was later filled to form an entrance hall. Conservatory vestibule added *c.* 1900. On each side of this, wide blind-arch recesses unite two window bays, a round-headed mock window between creating a broad Venetian arrangement. Semicircular S stair tower and three-storey SW wing with semi-circular bow, both with semi-conical roofs, by *John Tavish*, mason, 1793-4, probably to a design of *Robert Mylne*. At the same time, the original STABLES were altered and a second court added (lean-to stabling demolished, *c.* 1960).

PIER. 30m. jetty designed by *John Adam*, 1759-62; raised in height, 1765, but by 1771 ruinous. Following repair the quay was strengthened by *James Gillespie Graham*, 1805, following plans prepared by *William Johns*, and enlarged, 1809. In 1836 it was again extended, this time by the engineer *Joseph Mitchell* for the Herring Fishery Board. In 1877, to cope with steamer traffic, the masonry structure of granite blocks acquired a timber T-plan extension, further modified in the C20.

Former TOWN HOUSE, East Front Street. Designed by *John Adam*, 1750, as part of his grand scheme for the white N edge of the town. Built 1754-7 by *George Hunter*. Harled, five-bay, three-storey N façade, given Palladian pretension by the slight advance of the central three bays under a holed pediment. A rusticated ground floor of grey-green, channelled ashlar schist emphasizes this centrepiece. Its arcaded openings, built as a loggia with iron gratings, now frame an entrance door and flanking round-arch windows introduced in the early C19. The three central windows on the floors above have architraves. At first-floor level a broad, grey-green stringcourse crosses the façade. Of the original interior little remains: a single vaulted prison cell at ground floor and the W scale-and-platt stair. The first-floor court-room was subdivided in the C19. The building was criticized for its cramped accommodation and very public exposure of prisoners and from 1819 ceased to perform its original function.

WAR MEMORIAL, at the lochside, West Front Street. 1922. High, rough, granite cairn with bronze panels and a bronze statue of a kilted soldier by *Kellock Brown*.

DESCRIPTION

The show piece is FRONT STREET. A white band of building between leaden skies and loch is seen suddenly from the eminence of Aray Bridge. Even on the dreichest of Highland days, its clean, civilized order raises the spirit. In sunlight, its symmetries sparkle, 'the mixture of regularity and irregularity in the buildings' (Dorothy Wordsworth, 1803) teasing and inviting. It begins at the Dalmally Road where a high round-arch SCREEN, by *Robert Mylne*, 1787, crosses the carriageway linking buildings on each side. It is roughcast with blind portholes in the spandrels and lower flanking pedestrian arches. Set obliquely r. are the INVERARAY WOOLLEN MILL, formerly the Smithy, 1772, a three-bay dwelling with gabled eaves dormers and an outside stair on the S gable, and No. 4, 1752, the former Bakehouse; both with late C19 roofs. To the l., beginning the parade, THE GREAT INN (*see* above). Then more arches, a five-bay ARCADE, harled with porthole openings and grey-green stone dressings, by *Robert Mylne*, 1787-8. The outer arches are blocked below impost height, the others railed and gated. The slightly higher central arch, which also advances, marks the axial entry to THE AVENUE, a straight estate walkway more than 1km. long, established in the late C17 and, until 1955-7, lined with beech. Next comes a symmetrical group of three harled gabled houses by *John Adam*, 1755-7. Higher, at the centre, the former TOWN HOUSE (*see* above), now the Tourist Information Centre. Linking it to the arcade, IVY HOUSE; on its E gable, CHAMBERLAIN'S HOUSE: both three-bay, two-storey, with piended attic dormers, a stringcourse at first-floor sill level and porches added later.

INVERARAY: DESCRIPTION

Across Main Street, another three-unit, gabled group. Here the centre is lower, a five-bay, two-storey HOUSE, 1759–60, harled with dressed quoins and surrounds, one of the best in Inveraray, built for the shipmaster Neil Gillies. Flanking this are two lower, three-bay dwellings built as MANSES, 1776, by *Robert Mylne*: that to the r. matches Chamberlain's House; to the l., The Pier Shop, enhanced by a rusticated arched door with segmental fanlight but traduced by widened windows. The Pier itself (*see above*) extends NE from the end of E Front Street. S, round the corner, is THE POACHER, c.1880, harled but with tall gabled dormers, chimneys and parapeted canted bay in decorative ashlar. Built as a Public Reading Room and Coffee-House in memory of Elizabeth, Duchess of Argyll †1878; memorial tablet in curvilinear N gable.

If Front Street intrigues with alternating symmetries, MAIN STREET is unequivocal. Straight and short, its axiality is potent. From the Parish Church (*see above*), islanded halfway along the street, a pedimented portico commands and contains the view. Gabled houses, all but identical, flank the entry from Front Street. Thereafter there is a general consistency of form and scale on both sides of the street. Gable-to-gable dwellings, 1755–80, are three or two storeys to the eaves with attic dormers, shop cornices repeat intermittently, walls are harled white with black-painted margins. Here and there, a Gibbsian detail; notably in the five-bay MACPHERSON'S HOUSE, 1755–6, towards the S end of the W side of the street. Mid-street on the E side, a wide, three-storey tenement, SILVERCRAIGS'S HOUSE, 1773–80, with in-and-out quoins, an elliptical-arch pend and a central chimney gable. Ending the E side is the GEORGE HOTEL. Built 1777–9 by *Robert Mylne* as two large contiguous houses which accommodated the Highland and Lowland congregations until the completion of the Parish Church, the S house became a hotel in the 1820s, the N in 1954. Stepped tripartite windows l. and r. of the N entrance; characteristic Mylne porthole in the S gable. Across the street, the aberrant single-storey APOTHECARY, late C18; one door, one window, wonderful.

On the W of CHURCH SQUARE, the ROYAL BANK, dated 1865, three storeys of square-snecked rubble and ashlar with tripartite windows at first floor and a central chimneyed gable above. Beside it, more tripartites in the three-gabled front of the former GRAMMAR SCHOOL, 1905–7, by *E.J. Sim*. Converted to a Community Hall, 1970. Behind, across The Avenue, is All Saints' Church and, incongruously tall above the trees, the Duke's Tower (*see above*). Axially placed on the E side of the Square, a pink granite bowl FOUNTAIN with a round obelisk stoup; by *J. & G. Mossman*, 1893. BANK OF SCOTLAND, mid C19, single-storey, harled and very domestic with exposed spars at the eaves. Higher and grander, the black-and-white BANK MANAGER'S HOUSE, late C18, dormer storey added late C19; railed steps to a central corniced door with bipartite windows l., r. and above. Closing the axis E, the classical façade of the Court House *see above*). Lanes lead l. and r. N, overlooking the loch, is FACTORY LAND, 1774, a white vernacular range with small window openings. Built by the mason *John Marr*, it provided an upper-floor workroom with dwellings below in what was once the industrial quarter of the town but is now picturesquely residential in an austere Scottish way. Beside it, FERRY LAND, 1777, three-storey, piended, with a rear forestair; erected when the woollen factory moved to Claonairigh (*see* Auchindrain). Both buildings restored by *Ian G. Lindsay*, 1960. Beyond this is FERNPOINT HOTEL, 1752–3, a detached, two-storey, piend-roofed house built at an oblique angle conforming to John Adam's superseded 1750 plan for the town. Timber doorpiece with Doric columns and pediment projects from conically roofed W stair tower. S of the Court House is the snecked rubble front of the former police station, CROWN POINT HOUSE, 1869–71. Then, two more vernacular ranges, obliquely set parallel to the shore: CROMBIE'S LAND, 1822–5, restored by *Ian G. Lindsay*, 1959, a two-storey, flatted range of three-bay dwellings, one of them the birthplace of the novelist Neil Munro (1863–1930), and FISHER ROW, single-storey, rebuilt by *Lindsay* 1962.

MAIN STREET continues S, its brief axis dominated by the portico of what was the Gaelic-speaking half of the town's double kirk. Two white-harled, three-storey tenement ranges, both designed by *Robert Mylne*, impart a severe coherence to the short street. Fifteen windows long at the upper levels, each consists of five three-bay, flatted units. Above the eaves, broad chimneystacks articulate the perspective. At pavement level, five close-entries lead through the blocks to access stairs at the rear. On the E, devoid of stone dressings, RELIEF LAND, built for labourers by the mason *John Brown*, 1775–6. Through the closes, dog-leg-reinforced concrete stairs, constructed during the 1950s renovation by *Lindsay*, give access to the upper flats. On the W is ARKLAND, 1774–5, erected by *John Marr*, mason, marginally less dour by virtue of its black-painted, Dumbarton stone surrounds. At the rear, piend-roofed stair projections. Here, along BACK LANE, are several piended, rubble outhouses, late C18, and ARKLAND II, late C18, a harled house of brutal but compelling simplicity. Beyond Mylne's tenements, Main Street is one-sided, a shore road open to the loch on the E. Still black-and-white, BLACK'S LAND, *c.* 1777 and MACKENZIE'S LAND (formerly McCallum's Land), 1775, drop the scale. A segmental arch links to CROSS HOUSES, 1776–7, restored *c.* 1958, three harled cottages with a deeply coved eaves and hipped dormers added late C19, the row set at right angles to the street. Then comes a long rubble wall bordering The Avenue as the road bends into Newtown.

NEWTON ROW, known variously as Fisherland, Gallowgate and Long Row, dates from 1749 when, as the new Inveraray began to take shape, a few cottages housed the Duke's dispossessed tenants. Still with a sense of suburban detachment, a variety of buildings pack together along the lochside road. Three COTTAGES, mid C19, with eaves dormers and small staircase windows jumping to the eaves. FREE CHURCH SCHOOL, dated 1848 in a steep central gable; symmetrical, piend-roofed extension, dated 1880. Between the former Free and United Secession Churches (*see* above), two harled HOUSES with piended dormers, perhaps late C18. Next, a plain, three-bay, Georgian HOUSE, early C19; and next to it, the tall, ashlar front of THE OLD RECTORY, *c.* 1810, upmarket Georgian with Ionic pilasters, entablature and cornice framing its central doorway. Another COTTAGE, mid C19, like those N of the Free Church School. A former MANSE, *c.* 1810, harled, with a pilastered doorpiece and tall double-hung windows. More COTTAGES, early to late C19. Then, another manse, 1851, now CREAG DHUBH, a gabled rubble villa with projecting eaves and a later gabled and bracketed porch. Diamond-shaped TABLET with bust of Dr Guthrie, sculpted by *William Brodie*, 1874. Finally, LOCH FYNE HOTEL, *c.* 1865, a gable-fronted house in pink granite rubble with sandstone dressings: canted bay, mullion-and-transom lights and a trefoil window in the attic; an attractive but rather suburban intruder by *George Devey*.

INVERARAY CASTLE

700m. N of Inveraray

Glimpsed from the crest of Aray Bridge, the 'grand castle built by the Duke of Argyll' (Richard Pococke, 1760) is instantly apprehended: a solid square pile crenellated with triangle-topped dormers; high battlemented prisms rising behind; four cylinders at the corners peaked with cones. Overall, a Gothick symmetry. Solid geometries precisely peppered with pointed arches. Paradox perhaps, but there is nothing in this C18 intimation of Romanticism that might be deemed medieval, nor even Ruskinian. This is the realization of Batty Langley's *Gothic Architecture, improved by Rules and Proportions*. It is the classical Gothic of *Vanbrugh* who, indeed, had submitted a not dissimilar foursquare proposal for Inveraray, *c.* 1720, only to have it rejected. There may be traces of the Tudor tradition of Michelgrove, Wollaton and Lulworth. There is certainly something of the castellated and turreted polygonal design (also rejected) which the military engineer *Dugal Campbell* submitted, probably in 1744. But whatever the stylistic provenance of the final design which Archibald, 3rd Duke of Argyll, obtained in that same year from his English architect *Roger Morris*, the castellar mansion which was to become the Campbells' splendid new country seat is, on first sight, like nothing so much as a 'vast toy fort' (Lindsay & Cosh, 1973).

Work began in 1745 and continued under the direction of *William Adam* until his death in 1748. *John Adam* then succeeded his father, supervising progress until the death of the 3rd Duke in 1761, by which time the building was architecturally complete. After a decade's inactivity (the so-called Interregnum of the 4th Duke) *William Mylne* was in charge, altering the castle's entrance from the SW to the NE front, 1770–2. There then commenced an association of some thirty years which saw William's brother *Robert Mylne* enhance the castle with its lavish interior decoration and furnishings and the estate with a variety of minor buildings and bridges (*see* below). Alterations contemplated by the 6th Duke elicited plans from *Joseph Bonomi*, 1806, but little was done. Nor were the 8th Duke's proposals to baronialize the castle in the early 1870s pursued, though his architect, *Anthony Salvin*, was responsible for carrying out repairs and adding the dormered attic storey after a fire in 1877. In the 1950s the ubiquitous involvement of *Ian Lindsay & Partners* in and around the town of Inveraray included the renovation of the castle for the 11th Duke. Two decades later the same architects were again engaged in restoration after a second serious fire in 1975.

The new house is positioned some 80m. sw of the Campbells' old castle. This was a four-storey tower-house built by Sir Colin Campbell of Glenorchy probably in the 1450s, converted to an L-plan in the last years of the C16, condemned in 1744 as 'greatly shattered' by the 3rd Duke's mason *William Douglas* and subsequently demolished in 1774–5. The C18 building was aligned sw with a well-established Lime Avenue laid out a century earlier. It sits in a wide fosse or dry ditch whose quatrefoil-like perimeter, completed 1756–8, responds radially to the four corner turrets of the castle plan. Vaulted cellars, grouped in threes and fours, open off the ashlar revetment-wall on the outer side of the ditch; on the SE side the central cellar leads into a vaulted tunnel, intended to provide service access. The kitchen quarters in the basement are also reached from stone stairs which drop to the fosse from the SE terrace l. and r. against the quadrant retaining walls. The main entrances are at ground level, at the centre of the sw and NE fronts, the former designed as the principal entry but now private, the latter catering for public access. Both are approached across two-bay Gothic bridges vaulted on hooded two-centre arches; constructed by *George Hunter*, 1755–6. Parapets, set on an arched corbel-table, follow a cusped trefoil pattern adapted by *Daniel Paterson* from Morris's original design. This survives in its openwork form at the sw bridge, where it is augmented by crocketed obelisk finials carved by *William Templeton*, 1756–8. The parapets of the NE bridge were, however, infilled when the glazed ironwork porch, designed by *Sir Matthew Digby Wyatt*, was erected in 1871. A third bridge, affording a private SE entrance, was created c. 1956, by *Ian G. Lindsay*.

The four elevations of the castle, constructed to the eaves corbel-course in green chlorite-schist from Creggans, are simply but consistently ordered. Plain stringcourses, which wrap around the corner turrets, divide the façades vertically, their spacing indicative of the relative importance of the functions at basement-, ground- and first-floor levels. Hood-moulded, pointed-arch window openings repeat regularly along the seven bays of the NE and sw sides and the five on the NW and SE. Some are blind; some retain their intersecting glazing bars. At each floor their heights vary: those to the service rooms in the basement with projecting sills at impost level; the tall ground-floor windows dropped to the floor-level stringcourse by *Robert Mylne*, 1782–7, in a programme which also introduced delicate, bow-fronted, ironwork balconies and round-headed sashes to many of the windows at the upper levels. Only the entrances have decorative elaboration. The SW door is framed by cluster-shaft pilasters with annulets supporting a crocketed ogival arch terminating in a foliated finial; the NE entry, under the raking glazing of Wyatt's porch, has a lancet surround in a hood-moulded rectangular frame.

At the wallhead, where the masonry changed in 1751 to St Catherines stone, Morris's design set a crenellated parapet on a projecting stringcourse carried by moulded corbels. The corner turrets, which rose a storey higher, were also castellated in this way, though without the stringcourse. The roof, redesigned by *John Adam*, 1751, rose in a mansard profile to the central tower. In the late 1870s the crenellations on the main block were infilled when *Anthony Salvin* added an ashlar attic storey of eaves dormers, square-headed with moulded cornices under steep-sided triangular panels more gable than pediment. New pitched roofs were constructed and the tall slated cones and Jacobean chimneys added over the corner turrets. Salvin's changes made the skyline more lively but reduced the impact of Morris's clearstorey tower. Devised with a tall centre rising over the hall at the heart of the plan and two slightly lower and narrower sections over the staircases on the NW and SE sides of the hall, the tower is provided with crenellated parapets and on all four sides has large pointed-arch windows with intersecting glazing through which light floods into the interior. This core element of the C18 design was, moreover, elevated well above the level of the outer walls and turrets, its tripartite composition evident over the SW and NE entrance fronts. It was clearly intended to supply that hierarchical axial stress otherwise all but lacking in the simple organization of the façades below. That it no longer does so is a loss that may be weighed against the fairy-tale fun gained from Salvin's 12m.-high candle-snuffer corners.

The rectangular PLAN, in its rigorous axial symmetry and internal arrangements, is faintly redolent of Palladian precedent. Indeed, it barely engages with the four corner turrets. The central block is divided into three zones lying NW–SE and further partitioned by a balancing of apartments on each side of the main NE–SW axis. Its core is an Armoury Hall which rises full-height to the clearstorey tower. Two narrower halls, through which the main stairs rise in straight flights, lie parallel to this central space, but separated from it by walls accommodating fireplaces at ground level and pierced by wide round-arch openings at the floor above. These halls, too, are lit from the tower.

In the BASEMENT these flights, which originally rose against the inner flue-bearing walls, were reconstructed by *Joseph Bonomi*, 1806, on the opposite sides of the stair halls. The upper flights

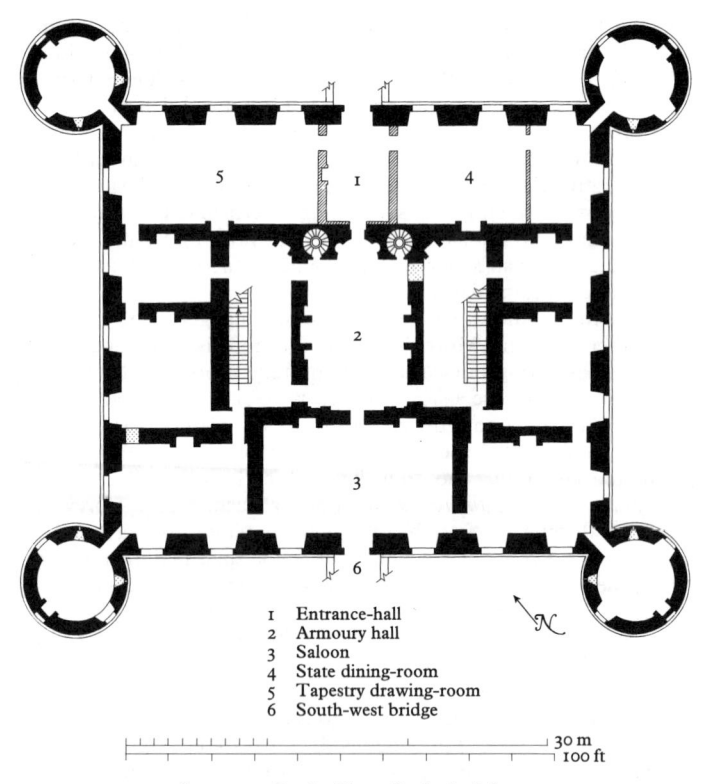

1 Entrance-hall
2 Armoury hall
3 Saloon
4 State dining-room
5 Tapestry drawing-room
6 South-west bridge

Inveraray Castle. Plan of principal floor

of the main staircases remained unaltered as did Morris's two spiral service stairs, tucked symmetrically into the masonry on the NE side of the central wine cellar (now a chart room). The NE zone of the plan is divided into seven apartments, five with fireplaces on the inner wall. The N room and its neighbour in the turret have been adapted as a shop; the others are stores. The original kitchen, at the centre of the SW zone, is little changed: ogival smoke-hoods on each end-wall, segmental-arched recesses on each side of the central round-arch NE doorway, splayed shuttered embrasures to the three SW windows. In the N and W turret rooms, a rusticated stone chimneypiece by Morris. Floors throughout are flagged, the ceilings barrel-vaulted with groin-vaults over doors and windows and in the stair halls.

In the plan which Morris devised for the PRINCIPAL FLOOR, the visitor was led from the SW entrance into a large hall and then into the central top-lit space with its flanking staircases and NE apse beyond which, entered axially, was a gallery extending across the full width of the NE front. In 1771, *William Mylne* reversed this sequence; the gallery was subdivided with a small central entrance hall placed between the tapestry drawing room and state dining room and the original SW entrance hall converted into a saloon or 'summer parlour'. This arrangement survives, with the smaller rooms on the NW and SE providing accommodation for the family.

INTERIOR. The interior design and furnishing are particularly fine throughout, both in the main public apartments which *Robert Mylne* decorated in the 1780s and in the other rooms which retain the *John Adam* work of the 1750s. The small NE ENTRANCE HALL has plain plastered walls with a moulded skirting and chair-rail. Delicate plaster ornament on the arch soffit of the main entrance doorway. Three other eight-panel, two-leaf doors are flanked by pilasters carrying individual moulded cornices but no entablature. Chimneypiece of painted pine and gesso decorated with urns, swags and paterae; inner surround of pink and green Tiree marble. At the base of the deeply coved ceiling, a cavetto cornice corbelled on foliated arches; above, a three-panel ceiling with corner quadrants of Perpendicular tracery and a central roundel with ribbed pendant and diamond-framed quatrefoils in its outer ring. Plasterwork by *John Clayton* using moulds from *John Papworth*, London, under Mylne's direction.

The DINING ROOM, entered l. from the lobby, is two window bays long, the remaining bay given over to a small dressing room linked to the E turret. It is perhaps the most exquisite of Inveraray's interiors with an all-but-symmetrical decorative scheme which displays the full refinement of Mylne's classical ornament. At each end of the room, flanking a large arched mirror, are two eight-panel, two-leaf doorways, those closest to the NE wall opening to the Entrance Hall and Dressing Room respectively, the others blind. All have elaborate consoles carrying cornices and pedestals, tablets set into the friezes, and fluted decoration in the cornices and door panel mouldings. Above the doors are circular panels depicting the pleasures of warmth, food, drink and scent in grisaille relief set in square frames. Almost at the centre of the SW wall is a fireplace, its white marble chimneypiece with fluted frieze, urns on the pilasters and a moulded cornice, obtained by the 5th Duke in London in 1772. Above this, a tall rectangular mirror panel in a decorative plaster frame and, on each side, two equally tall but round-headed plaster panels echoing the window openings opposite. A deep acanthus frieze surrounds the room below a finely dentilled cornice with rosette-in-guilloche motifs. The ceiling, executed by *John Clayton*, 1781–2, is divided into a central square panel, within which concentric circles define zones of ornament (leaf sprays, scrolls, floral garlands, etc.), and two narrow outer panels in which bluebell florets mark out lozenge shapes enclosing wreaths and flowers. Walls and ceiling are painted in pale green and white, the work of (?)*Jean-François Guinand* and *Irrouard le Girardy* with gilding by *Leonard Dupasquier*: a decorative scheme, light and delicate in its classicism, with precise, often tendril-thin, motifs.

The DRAWING ROOM occupies the full length of the former Gallery between the NE Entrance Hall and the N turret. Larger than the Dining Room, it has fewer doors, similar though more richly ornamented. The three NE windows and that in the NW wall have panelled concave reveals behind fluted architraves. At the centre of the SW wall is a white marble chimneypiece brought by the 5th Duke from Bellevue House, Edinburgh, in 1800: it may be by *Robert Adam*; on each jamb, a draped female figure in bold relief extends an arm towards an urn carved on the lintel. Apart from some painted panels by *le Girardy*, 1788 (classical ruins over the doors; floral arabesques in the window ingoes and two narrow strips flanking the portrait of Lady Charlotte Campbell by *Thomas Hoppner* over the fireplace), the walls are devoted to the display of seven large Beauvais tapestries by *Jean Baptiste Huet*, depicting pastoral scenes, commissioned in 1785. These are hung in gilded timber frames below an acanthus frieze rather more floral than that in the Dining Room. This last, the dentilled cornice and the fine plaster ceiling are again the achievement of *John Clayton* working to designs from *Robert Mylne*, 1780–2. Bands of guilloche ornament delineate two narrow panels at each end of a long rectangular area which, from a central octagon enclosing a floral roundel of guilloche-edged scalloped rings, divides into a pattern of halfoctagons filled with semicircular scalloped fan motifs and squares filled with rosettes. Swags of bluebell florets border the ceiling, feathery floral sprays, and much gilt add to the ceiling's sumptuous delicacy. In the N turret, Mylne's 1773 design for the shallow papier-mâché dome has a cooler, more restrained elegance. The saucer ceiling, a scalloped star with peripheral scrolls, is rimmed with a guilloche-band over a cornice of small corbelled arches like that in the Entrance Hall. Sandwiched by two curved classical bookcases is a white marble chimneypiece with decorated pilaster jambs, a lintel with a rose in an oval between swags, and a dentilled cornice.

The central ARMOURY HALL is entered axially from the NE lobby. The lofty symmetrical space rises 22m. to a modern beamed ceiling (originally groin-vaulted) set above the traceried clearstorey of the central tower. This ceiling, which has the arms of different branches of the Campbell family painted in full colour in each of its eight panels, is a 1952 replica of the beamed ceiling constructed after the fire of 1877. On the NE and SW walls below the clearstorey and in the round-arched recesses at first floor and ground floor are sprayed displays of weaponry: halberds and muskets were arranged by *Mylne* in 1784 but reordered, with added fans and quadrants, in 1953. First-floor galleries cantilevered from the NE and SW walls on console corbels designed by *Morris*, 1746, connect the stair halls which lie behind the NW and SE walls. Below the NE gallery is an apsidal recess with a half-dome ceiling patterned in a close-meshed radial grid filled with square foliate motifs. A central roundarched doorway, with consoled cornice following the concave curve of the apse, opens to the entrance lobby between flanking niches. To l. and r. of the recess are low round-arched doors leading to the turnpike service stairs. From the springing-level of the apse arch an egg-and-dart moulding and reeded plaster frieze extend around the room, linking the round-arch architrave of the apse to those over the fireplace recesses in the NW and SE walls and the SW door to the Saloon. Two late C19 chimneypieces with hefty fluted consoles as jambs. On each side of the fireplace recesses are eight-panel doors with moulded architraves and delicately dentilled cornices; only three of the four connect with the stair halls, the door in the E corner having been blocked in the C19. The floor of black marble dates from 1782.

Beyond the Armoury Hall is the SALOON, originally the entrance hall but recast by *Robert Mylne* in the 1780s. While the central SW doorway and adjacent windows have round-headed architraves and sashes, the eight-panel door at the centre of the NE wall has a consoled cornice similar to those in the Drawing Room. It sits between two fireplaces, their late C18 white marble pilastered chimneypieces, decorated with sphinxes, urns and swags under a dentilled cornice, brought back from Rosneath in 1952. Symmetrically placed at each end of the NW and SE walls are low-lintelled doorways with moulded architraves but without cornices, those at the NE ends dummies. Two wooden girandoles, garlanded pendants dropping to lyres, add gilded enrichment to these end walls. A cornice of swags and rosettes borders a plain plaster ceiling.

The remaining smaller rooms on the SE and NW sides of the ground floor are in private use. The fine Rococo plasterwork of the cornices and ceilings in the SE apartments, incorporating floral sprays, leaf-scrolls, fruit, birds, shell motifs, etc., is probably the work of *Thomas Clayton* following *John Adam*'s late 1750s designs. These rooms also have white marble chimneypieces of differing classical pattern, some with variegated marble inlays. In the S turret, four glazed bookcases (originally installed in the E turret, 1795–6), their pilaster-framed Neoclassical design capped by four circular medallions, each with a different figurative scene cast in plaster. The apartments on the opposite side of the plan are less decorative. At the middle of the NW front, the Brown Library, converted from a bedchamber in 1871, has a gallery on three walls with an open metal balustrade busy with Campbell monograms and emblems. Cornice and frieze in the adjacent Green Library are C18 but plain; the arched marble chimneypiece late C19. In the W turret, the curved, white marble chimneypiece was ordered in 1757; under a dentilled cornice, a lintel swagged between urns and garlands and jambs scrolled with rinceau-like ornament frames a plain inner surround of painted schist.

The FIRST FLOOR is wholly given over to bedrooms ranged symmetrically around the upper landings of the stairhalls and the linking balconies which overlook the Armoury Hall. On the NW and SE sides of the central void, large round-arched openings, similar in dimension to the fireplace recesses below, allow light from the clearstorey into the stairhalls. Impost mouldings of egg-and-dart and reeded frieze link these openings to the wide round-arched recess on the SW balcony and the NE apse opposite. Within the apse was a chamber-organ built in a Gothic casing by *Alexander Cumming*, 1757; something of a focal point on the gallery until its destruction in the fire of 1877. The turnpike service stairs l. and r. of the apse originally gave access to the ATTIC FLOOR where accommodation for the servants was provided under low ceilings. *Salvin*'s restoration in the late 1870s increased the number and height of bedrooms. After the 1975 fire a metal truss roof was introduced by *Ian Lindsay & Partners* and the attic space devoted to archive storage and caretaker's flat.

GROUNDS. The earliest landscape arrangements at Inveraray date from the C17, though changes were made in the 1720s and again, in the middle of the C18, by *William Patterson* of Edinburgh who established a vast formal layout. Between 1770 and 1790 the 5th Duke, assisted by *Alexander Nasmyth*, reshaped the estate in picturesque fashion. Today, the principal axis of the castle plan extends SW into the landscape as the central walk of a FORMAL GARDEN. On each side, closest to the house, lie open lawns. Then come two rectangular beds filled with shrubs forming a saltire pattern and two more with flower-beds set within circles, before the path widens between the trees of the last surviving section of the C17 Lime Avenue. The garden design is pre-1870 and supersedes layouts prepared by the surveyor *John Brooks* in the 1820s and the architect *W.A. Nesfield* in 1848. There is a SUNDIAL with a bronze dial, 1843, on an octagonal sandstone pedestal. Marble SCULPTURE includes two draped figures of Emma and Julia Campbell set on a swagged cylindrical plinth, by *Lorenzo Bartolini*, early C19; also a Perseus and Andromeda group by *Michael van der Voort*, 1713. Since the 1950s, two square GATEPIERS in ashlar sandstone, with cornices carrying urns, mark the entrance to the private garden on the SE side of the castle; they date from the C18 and come from Rosneath. In the private garden, an incomplete disc-headed CROSS, Iona school, late C15, removed in the late C19 from the burial ground at Kirkapol, Tiree (q.v.): carving depicts the Crucifixion, St Michael and the dragon, a stag and hounds, a bishop or abbot with his crozier, etc., and much interlace ornament. The earlier socket-stone bears an inscription to Finguine MacKinnon, abbot at Iona in the second half of the C14.

INVERARAY CASTLE ESTATE

BEEHIVE COTTAGE, on SW slope of Dùn na Cuaiche. By *Alexander Nasmyth*, 1801. Harled, single-storey gamekeeper's cottage; now ruinous. Unsophisticated but fundamentally architectural in form; circular in plan with a slated cone roof (originally thatched) rising to a central ashlar chimney ringed to shed rainwater. E doorway enclosed in later curved porch excrescence.

BUSHANG COTTAGE, close to the A83 at the NW end of Loch Shira. Early C19. Single-storey with a central door flanked by latticed windows. Later piended roof with wide eaves overhang.

CAMPBELL MONUMENT, 200m. NNW of the Castle. Erected 1754 by Duncan Campbell of Skipness to commemorate 17 Campbell Covenanters, martyred 1685–8. Originally sited in Church Square, Inveraray, but moved to the castle grounds, 1983. High, two-stage pedestal carrying urn. Incised inscriptions in Latin on opposing faces.

CARLOONAN BRIDGE, 270m. N cf Carloonan Mill. Built in granite rubble, 1755–7, by *William Douglas*, mason; approaches widened by *Robert Mylne*, 1785. Segmental arch, 12.2m. span, of chlorite-schist voussoirs.

CARLOONAN MILL, on the E bank of the River Aray opposite the Fishing Pavilion (q.v.). Probably late C18, though established in the C16. Ruinous L-plan structure of granite rubble but with some chlorite-schist ashlar, mid C18, on the SW wall where the overshot water wheel was located. The lade, paved with schist slabs, runs NW. In the SE gable, a segmental-arch opens to the gear-pit. Above were the loft and, probably, the miller's house with the kiln in the NE leg of the L.

COURT OF OFFICES, Cherry Park, 230m. W of the Castle. Designed by *John Adam*, 1759; partially built 1761; altered and completed by *William Mylne*, 1772. Four single-storey ranges, built in St Catherines grey-green, chlorite-schist ashlar, enclose a courtyard 24.6m. square. At the corners, two-storey, pyramid-roofed pavilions with apex ventilators. A seven-bay E front terminates the avenue axis leading from the Castle in a pedimented elliptical-arch pend entry. End pavilions have decorative Palladian windows set below small horizontal openings in moulded frames. On the S front, where this treatment of the pavilions is repeated, seven elliptical-arch cart-entries, filled with harled walling in the C19. W range converted to dwelling, C19. The buildings now house the Argyll Estate Office and a museum.

DAIRY, Tom-breac, 1.8km. N of the Castle. By *John Adam*, 1752–8. Vestigial walling of the N range of a courtyard plan which had milking sheds W and E and (probably) a crowstepped Gothic S façade. Dismantled *c.* 1880.

DOOCOT, Carloonan. Distant lighthouse-like *point-de-vue*, 1.3km. NW of Frew's Bridge (q.v.). Designed by *Roger Morris*, 1747, and built by *William Douglas*, 1748, under the supervision of *William Adam*. Harled rubble cylinder, 9.3m. to the eaves from which rises a slated cone topped off by a domed cupola pigeon-entry. SE door to lower dome-vaulted chamber; in the lofty circular chamber above, also domed, eleven tiers of nesting boxes. Proposals by *Robert Mylne*, 1776, to transform the building's simple but powerful geometry into a peripteral temple fortunately failed to find favour.

FISHING PAVILION, overlooking Carloonan Falls on the River Aray. Built 1802–3 by *John Tavish*, mason, perhaps to a design by *Alexander Nasmyth*. Hexagonal with a slated pyramid roof, originally thatched. Lintelled recesses on five faces: one doorway, one blind and three framing pointed-arch timber windows with lattice glazing. Chimney on SW face.

FREW'S BRIDGE (Garden Bridge), 250m. NNW of Castle, aligned with the vista to Carloonan Doocot (q.v.). Designed by *John Adam*, 1758; built by the Edinburgh mason *David Frew*, 1759–61. Elegant elliptical arch crosses the Aray in a span of 18.2m. between semicircular abutments which become seated refuges at the carriageway. Blind oculi and ashlar masonry radiating from the voussoirs in the spandrels. Balustraded parapet. Long ramped approaches of coursed granite penetrated by riverbank passages entered through fully developed Roman Doric aedicules; in each passage, two semicircular seated recesses with opposed half-dome vaults.

ICE-HOUSE, 100m. NNW of Cherry Park. 1785–6. Domed brick-vaulted cell clad in a rubble shell. Circular plan (6.5m. overall dia.) with egg-shaped section now filled to the threshold of a short NE entrance passage. The dome, now partially exposed, originally roofed with a slated cone; the walls harled.

MAIN LODGE, at the NW end of Fore Street (*see* Inveraray). Built 1795–6. Three-bay, single-storey symmetrical with a central NE door to the castle drive. Shallow piended roof. NE and SE fronts in tooled ashlar are slightly recessed, framed by eaves course, pilaster quoins and plinth.

MALTLAND SQUARE, 1km. NW of the Castle on the W bank of the Aray. A vast enclosed court which, despite the ruinous and disregarded fabric of its enclosing buildings, evokes the agricultural ambition of the Argyll Estate. The plan emerged gradually, developing on the N side of a WALLED GARDEN built by the mason *James Potter*, 1752–5, which, though overgrown, still has some of its lean-to greenhouses. First came the COACH-HOUSE, a five-bay hipped-roofed building, placed by *John Adam* against the 5.5m.-high N wall of the garden. Its five rebated, elliptical-arch openings are still detectable, though compromised by later residential conversion. It was probably *William Mylne* who completed this S RANGE, 1760–71, with lean-to stables and cottages (most of which have gone) and erected a large rubble HAY BARN directly opposite the coach-house 44m. N. With the width of the court thus determined, *Robert Mylne* then added THE 'GREAT SHADE', 1774–5, a huge harled building over 36m. long, 14m. wide and effectively three storeys high, set at right angles to the W end of the S range. It survives, but in poor condition. On the W and E elevations, between three tiers of windows in the two end bays, five round-headed arches rise to just below eaves height. These openings, filled over doorways with early C19 glazing, repeat through a central spine wall which originally supported the valley of a double roof. In 1780 *Robert Mylne* was designing the RIDING SCHOOL, more or less a mirror-image of The Great Shade, closing the yard 98m. E. It was destroyed by fire in 1817, but re-created by the 8th Duke in the restored form of The Jubilee Hall, 1897. Rubble with sandstone ashlar dressings. Seven high arches, three over doorways, face the courtyard; on the five-bay E front, a pedimented centrepiece projects slightly over three round-headed arches. In 1782 the hay barn, a tall, five-arch structure of rubble, coursed schist and ashlar, was doubled in width to the N. It was dismantled in 1960 and stands to the wallhead, an empty overgrown shell. Lower drying sheds, arcaded to the yard, extended W and E from the barn gables, returning to link with The 'Great Shade' and Riding School; only fragments remain to the NW. As for the court itself, it is chaotic with clutter, untidy and uncared for, its spatial grandeur shamed by neglect.

NORTH CROMALT LODGE, 1.5km. SW of Fore Street, Inveraray. 1801; by *Alexander Nasmyth*(?). Two-storey rectangular dwelling with hipped roof. Semicircular recesses and windows to first floor. Below chimneystacks rising symmetrically from the longer side walls are single-storey lean-to blocks, now altered.

SOUTH CROMALT LODGE, 2km. SW of Fore Street. Late C18 two-storey symmetry, miniaturized and compressed but vigorously architectonic. A harled cube with pyramid roof, apex chimney and tiny windows. Central porch added.

WATCH TOWER, at the summit of Dùn na Cuaiche. Skyline folly designed by *Roger Morris* and built in local granite rubble by *William Douglas*, 1747–8, supervised by *William Adam*. Square in plan and set into an incline; a lower, pointed-arch S door opens into a dark, domed, semicircular chamber while a lintelled N door enters a circular upper room, also domed, lit by S and E lancets. Stepped roof repaired 1989. An encircling earthwork may be related to *John Adam*'s unrealized plans to elaborate the tower into a battlemented hilltop ruin.

WELL HOUSE, Bealach an Fhuarain. On SE slope of Creag Dhubh, 1km. SW of Castle. 1747–8; by *William Adam*(?). Grotto-like, barrel-vaulted chamber built over a rock face through which water percolates into a rough basin. The façade is robustly classical: a semicircular arch with vermiculated voussoirs under a pediment, also vermiculated in alternate blocks along the cornice and angle mouldings.

INVERCHAOLAIN

0975

Lonely parish church and graveyard on a wooded rise above the E shore of Loch Striven 7km. N of Ardyne Point.

INVERCHAOLAIN PARISH CHURCH. Wayside Gothic by Edinburgh architect *Alfred Greig*, 1912. Last in a succession of churches built on this quiet hillside overlooking the loch. A medieval chapel, reputedly dedicated to St Bridget, was followed by a C17 post-Reformation kirk and its 1745 replacement; all of these sited 220m. NNE. In 1812 a piend-roofed, galleried church was erected. Extensive repairs and alterations, 1871 and 1891, but a fire, 1911, necessitated complete reconstruction.

Four-bay, buttressed oblong, skew-gabled W and E, with a gabled S porch and an asymmetrical gabled vestry projecting N. W apex bellcote. Roughcast exterior with sandstone dressings but interior pointed rubble. Arch-braced collar roof trusses on sandstone corbel-stones. – Half-octagon PULPIT with linen-fold panels. – In the N wall, a horizontal RECESS for communion plate, 1925. – Three memorial wall TABLETS, 1912, each white marble with a block pediment and engaged colonnettes at the sides: E gable, to Alexander Lamont †1897 'on the Indian frontier' and the brothers Boyden and John Lamont †1837 and †1850 in Trinidad; w to Colin Campbell Finlay of Castle Toward †1899. – Above the S door from the porch, a stone FRAGMENT, crossed ridges with a finial socket, dated 1723. – STAINED GLASS. E window by *Douglas Strachan*, 1921, depicts St Michael surrounded by an angel host overcoming Satan; reds and yellows over greens and blues, a War Memorial. – By the same artist, w end s wall, a Good Shepherd window.

The church sits in a walled BURIAL ENCLOSURE. A table-tomb with Latin inscription records the passing of the Revd Neil Cameron †1676.- Several C18 headstones; one with a carved adze and dividers set in a shield to Archibald McArthur †1769, and another to Daniel McIntyer †1786, whose work as a gardener is symbolized by spade and rake. – Among many well-preserved inscriptions, a monitory memory of the miller, Duncan Ferguson †1785,

> MY DEBT IS PAID MY GRAVE YOU SEE
> THEREFORE PREPAIR TO FOLLOW ME

Within a railed enclosure, the tall plinth-block TOMB of James Lamont of Knockdow †1829, and his daughter Margaret †1820, from which an urn-finial has fallen. – Similarly protected, an ogee-arched granite HEADSTONE, mid C19, commemorating members of the family of Kirkman Finlay of Castle Toward. – Escaping such Victorian *gravitas*, a roughly shaped HEADSTONE to Major Andrew Coats of Castle Toward †1930, and his wife †1954, carved to show a yacht in full sail.

MANSE. Built below the church with a prospect S to the loch. Two-storey-and-attic, three-bay, skew-gabled house, 1807; a design by *James Laurie*, mason, and *Archibald Brown*, wright, seems to have been preferred to a proposal by *James Gillespie Graham*. Repaired in 1832 and again in 1898 when bay dormers may have been added. Offices, built in 1791 to serve an earlier manse, were repaired and adapted in 1807.

INVERECK

A few houses between the Eachaig and Little Eachaig rivers at the head of Holy Loch.

HOLY LOCH FARM PARK (Dalinlongart Farm), immediately N of the B836 junction with the Dunoon–Strachur road. Mid C19(?). Unremarkable three-bay, two-storey house dignified by being set centrally in the outer E face of the E range of a single-storey court lying behind. Painted rubble; all gables crowstepped.

INVERECK HOUSE. Begun 1876, halted by the City of Glasgow Bank crash in 1878, and finally completed 1886. Polite but unexciting Baronial mansion in rough-faced, square-snecked sandstone, perhaps by Paisley architects *Rennison & Scott*.

Battlemented porte-cochère to s façade. Tall first-floor windows breaking through eaves are capped by shaped pediments. The E garden front recedes at centre under a balustraded first-floor balcony. Three-storey NE tower with double-height canted bay, bartizans and a corbelled parapet. The interior exceeds expectation. An oak entrance screen of fluted pilasters and delicate Grecian detail divides the porch from an outer hall, which in turn is separated from the inner hall by dark marble columns set on socles. Panelled doors and ingoes; consoles along cornice. A grand staircase returns l. and r. to an upper hall bulging back in a half-round gallery over the first flight. Above this, reflecting the curve, is a shallow twelve-part glazed dome with painted glass decoration. Stair balustrading with small timber urns over the newel posts. – In the tall, three-light landing window, STAINED GLASS depicting Minerva flanked by putti placed above the figures of Music, Industry and Painting. Since 1946 a Church of Scotland Eventide Home.

INVERNEILL

8481

On the w shore of Loch Fyne, 4km. s of Ardrishaig. A ruined church and a handful of houses, some along Whitehouse Bay, others close to the Inverneil Burn, barely turn the name into a place.

INVERNEILL CHURCH, on a rocky knoll between the A83 and Loch Fyne. Overgrown roofless ruin standing more or less to wallhead. Built 1775, or perhaps a few years later. It has long been in ruins, superseded by the creation of parishes at Lochgilphead and Ardrishaig in the C19. Its T-plan is formed by a semicircular bow projecting s from a squarish oblong. Rubble walls, here and there still harled, have offset margins of red sandstone. The N, W and E elevations are all three-bay; in each a central doorway sits below a circular window, with round-arched windows on each side. Traces of a corbelled belfry are evident on the E gable. The original interior arrangements are unclear but it seems likely that there were W and S galleries. Alterations carried out in 1817 by *Thomson & Robison* of Lochgilphead included seating and the construction of a separate Session House, axially related to the N.

CAMPBELL MAUSOLEUM, in woods 850m. wsw of Inverneill House. Built 1802 by *John Wilson*, mason. It now commemorates General George Campbell †1882 and Lorne Campbell †1883. Gabled Gothic of coursed rubble with pale red sandstone dressings. A pointed-arch recess on the w frames the entrance doorway; the mason's name is cut in the soffit.

AUCHBRAAD BRIDGE, on the Kilberry road 1.6km. w of its junction with the A83 N of Inverneill. 1846–7. A spectacular segmental arch high-flying over the deep ravine of Inverneil Burn. The span is modest, 10.9m., but the gentle curve and elevated springing above the rocky gorge (now stabilized with battered concrete abutments) give the bridge great sculptural power.

INVERNEILL BRIDGE. Random rubble, single-span crossing of Inverneil Burn, completed 1770. Segmental arch formed from slab voussoirs.

INVERNEILL HOUSE, 300m. W of outflow of Inverneil Burn. This three-storeyed crenellated gabled block of *c*. 1890 affects a cubic tower-house character, with curved corners returned to square at base and parapet. The gabled E façade, symmetrical with square bay at ground level, looks into a walled garden meadow. The outline of a building can be seen which, until 1955, abutted on the S. This earlier structure, 'The Cottage', was a three-bay, two-storey, late C18 or early C19 dwelling terminated by a wider bow-fronted wing with superimposed tripartite windows. Now isolated, the battlemented tower wing nevertheless manages to hold its own, though its single-storey accretions disappoint and its relationship with the garden to the E remains unresolved. In the sitting room is a four-centred arched fireplace in grey marble. A small STONE of tapered schist, C7 or C8, cut in the form of a cross with barred terminals, came to Inverneill from Taynish House in 1929. It may originate from Eilean Mor at the mouth of Loch Sween.

The WALLED GARDEN, 1790, orphaned by the loss of 'The Cottage' or some intended mansion that never was, is a free-formed enclosure with a largely sinuous perimeter defined by high slab-topped rubble walls. Straight E front with a central entrance archway, stretched between two crenellated, cone-roofed drum pavilions. The upper chambers of these summer-houses are each lit by a Venetian window and reached by forestairs. GATEPIERS capped with small urns stand close to the SE pavilion. The garden is uncultivated.

STRONACHULLIN LODGE, 1.6km. S of Inverneill House road-end. By *Robert S. Lorimer*, 1894–6, in his soft Scots style. Harled walls, now heavily ochred, thicken above first-floor level. Red sandstone dressings to the curvilinear eaves dormers and around the unprepossessing entrance where, between rosettes, the lintel bears the date 1896; the arms and motto of Graham Campbell of Shirvan (*see* Castleton House, Port Ann) have been carved in a panel above. Outbuildings to the W, extended and converted in the C20, all but enclose a sheltered inner courtyard. The house and the garden to the E are embosomed among high rhododendron bushes.

INVERUGLAS

A power station on the W shore of Loch Lomond halfway between Tarbet and Ardlui.

CASTLE, Inveruglas Isle. Rubble ruin; the original plan, a parallelogram with drum towers, is scarcely discernible.

CASTLE, Island-I-Vow. Built 1577, by Andrew McFarlane, Laird of Arrocher. Only E and S walls stand.

CRAIGENARDEN VIADUCT, 700m. N of Power Station. 1891; engineers *Formans & McCall*, Glasgow. High-level permanent

way of the West Highland Line. Above the trees, a towering 134
arcade of eight deep, rough-faced whinstone piers carrying segmental arches under a crenellated parapet.

LOCH SLOY POWER STATION. By *Harold O. Tarbolton* for the North of Scotland Hydro-Electric Board, 1946–50. Flat-faced, flat-roofed monumentality cased in precast slabs of Rubislaw and Corrennie granite. Four principal bays, demarcated by broad pilaster strips with tall windows between, rise from an *in-situ* concrete base of four segmental arches bridging the water outfall pouring E into the loch. Lower office wing S. Random whinstone rubble walls along the roadside; ironwork gates N and S set between slab piers. In the hills, 3.5km. WNW, is LOCH SLOY DAM, a concrete wall of fifteen bays with round-arched buttressing, 357m. wide and 56m. high, the first of its kind in Scotland; the design by engineer *James Williamson*, 1936; built from 1946.

KAMES

Village on the W shore of the Kyles of Bute. Much older than its linear neighbours to the N, Auchenlochan and Tighnabruaich, it marks the start of the road across SW Cowal to Portavadie and the ferry crossing Loch Fyne to Tarbert.

KYLES PARISH CHURCH. Built 1898–9 as Kames Free Church. Broad E gable of grey-green rubble and red sandstone dressings. The central portion projects slightly: at its centre, a four-light, cusped, mullion-and-transom window segmentally arched and, below, under another segmental-arch lintel, the splayed reveals of the main entrance doorway. Smaller three-light cusped windows sit l. and r.

FREE PRESBYTERIAN CHURCH. Gabled roughcast shed, 1939. Double lancet astragals effect a pusillanimous symbolism.

PIER. Rump jetty constructed of vertically laid rubble, 1856; lengthened in 1880; closed 1928. Ruined timber pier. Pierhead area unkempt and visually squalid. A second, private pier, the so-called Black Quay, 1839, served the gunpowder works at Millhouse.

DESCRIPTION

More developed and less attenuated in layout than its two neighbouring communities, Kames has little of architectural note. KAMES HOTEL, mid C19, is but a bigger version of the typical Kyles shore villa but it does have an ironwork entrance canopy with slender fluted Ionic columns tapering downwards. Also looking E to Bute are ROCKHOLM, 1900, which has a more elaborate iron porch arched on Corinthian columns, and NETHERTON, 1900, gabled, bayed and dormered in the usual manner but with a black-and-white, half-timbered first floor.

STANDING STONES. Three standing stones at village cross-roads, the largest 2.8m. high.

KEILLS

Now a remote road-end at the SW tip of the Tayvallich peninsula but once a major landing-place on the cattle-drovers' route from Islay, Jura and Colonsay.

KEILLS PARISH CHURCH, on a hillside overlooking the aptly named inlet of Loch na Cille. Dedicated to the Irish saint Abban moccu Corbmaic. After the long single-track drive the C12 church is less romantic than expected: no ruin, but a well-appointed shed; re-roofing in 1978 to house the site's superb group of carved stones has had banal consequences. Keills remained in use as the Parish Church of Knapdale probably until the late C17. It was repaired in the late C19 but remained a roofless ruin until the late C20. The gabled cell, of roughly coursed rubble, measures 10.9m. by 4.8m. internally and lies E–W within a C19 rubble enclosure. N entrance and small N and S windows reconstructed. The small round-arched opening at the centre of the E gable retains its original form. On the internal face, two aumbries symmetrically l. and r. with a third almost at ground level. Excavations in 1977 found an altar base, but the location of the two-step change in floor level created in 1978 has no precise archaeological legitimacy.

What the church itself lacks in medieval evocation its contents amply provide. Over forty stones are displayed: Early Christian SLABS bearing cross and plait motifs, and tapered SLABS of Iona, Kintyre, Loch Sween and Loch Awe provenance, C13–C16. One such stone, Loch Sween school C15, is richly endowed with imagery: sword, comb, shears, mirror, salmon, bird, and a particularly detailed carving of a clarsach. – Outstanding is the magnificent KEILLS CROSS, Iona school C8–C9, 2.25m. high, carved, on the former E face only, from grey-green Loch Sween stone similar to the bluestone of Islay's Kildalton Cross. The shaft is decorated with spiral work, animal forms and key patterning, the crossing with a bird's nest boss around which are four lions with the prophet Daniel below and St Michael(?) above. An uncarved replica stands on the hillside above the church.

CHAPEL, Eilean Mór, 6km. SSW of Keills. Early C13 chapel, like Keills, dedicated to Abban moccu Corbmaic. It measures 9.5m. E–W by 4.2m within the walls, is rubble-built and preserves areas of harling and internal plastering. Some turf roofing survives. The N doorway and S and W windows are blocked but two small arched openings survive in the E gable. In the C14 a barrel vault was constructed over the chancel. It has a small longitudinal chamber in its crown. For what purpose this confined space was contrived is unclear but it was provided with an aumbry and a small opening in the E gable. Over the nave, early C18 alterations have left two small gable windows and a fireplace. – SHAFTS and FRAGMENTS from two freestanding crosses have been removed to the Royal Museum of Scotland, Edinburgh. – SE of the chapel stands a cross SHAFT, C10, the carving on its E face including some strange monsters separated by a panel of very regular key patterning. – In the chapel, a tapered SLAB, Iona school C14–C15, with priest's effigy. – Close to the island's SE shore is a terraced gully with masonry evidence of what was perhaps an early CHAPEL connected, originally by tunnel and now by vertical hole, to a cave retreat. Graffiti crosses in the cave suggest a C7 date.

HARBOUR, Keills Port, on an inlet on W side of promontory. A drovers' quay existed here certainly from the mid C18 and a battered 20m. length of rubble pier incorporating five steps may include part of the early jetty. A new slipway was recommended by engineer *John Sinclair* in 1812 and constructed 1817–20 by contractors *James Campbell* of Jura and *John MacNeill* of Gigha. It follows an L-plan and is built of coursed rubble, the top course set on edge and inclined inwards on the ramp.

LIME-KILN and STOREHOUSE, Port nan Gallan, Danna. Isolated industrial outpost on the limestone 'Island' of Danna. Double kiln, late C18. Two-storeyed, three-bay, skew-gabled storehouse, 1795. It may have been residential with an E forestair to an upper flat; the ground floor, entered through gable doors, has a full-length 5.6m.-span brick segmental vault rising to 3m.

KERRERA

8128

A small undulating island in the Firth of Lorn. Separated from the mainland by the narrow Sound of Kerrera, it affords both shelter and beauty to Oban Bay.

CASHEL, Cladh a'Bhearnaig, on a raised beach at the N end of the island. The site appears as 'an old monastery' on James Dorret's map of 1750 and the 60m.-dia. circle which can still be detected as a turf-covered ring may well have enclosed some medieval religious settlement. A few short stretches of faced rubble walling still survive in this enclosing edge, but the foundations of several small rectangular structures clustered in the SW quadrant are probably later. Only the largest of these buildings, the footings of which straddle the ring in the S, has been identified as of possible medieval origin.

GYLEN CASTLE. Improbably dramatic and romantic in its siting, the tower-house rises narrow and erect above a pinched neck of land towards the end of a rocky promontory at the S of the island. It was completed in 1582 by Duncan MacDougall of MacDougall and Dunollie but abandoned in 1647 after besieging Covenanting forces had successfully demanded its royalist garrison should destroy it by fire. No subsequent changes other than the removal of carved stones for safe keeping to Dunollie House (q.v.) in the C19 and some consolidating work carried out by H.M. Office of Works in 1913.

The accommodation is conventionally arranged in an L-plan of two squares, the dimensions of which (roughly 6m. by 6m. and 4m. by 4m.) are exceedingly small, the three upper floors each

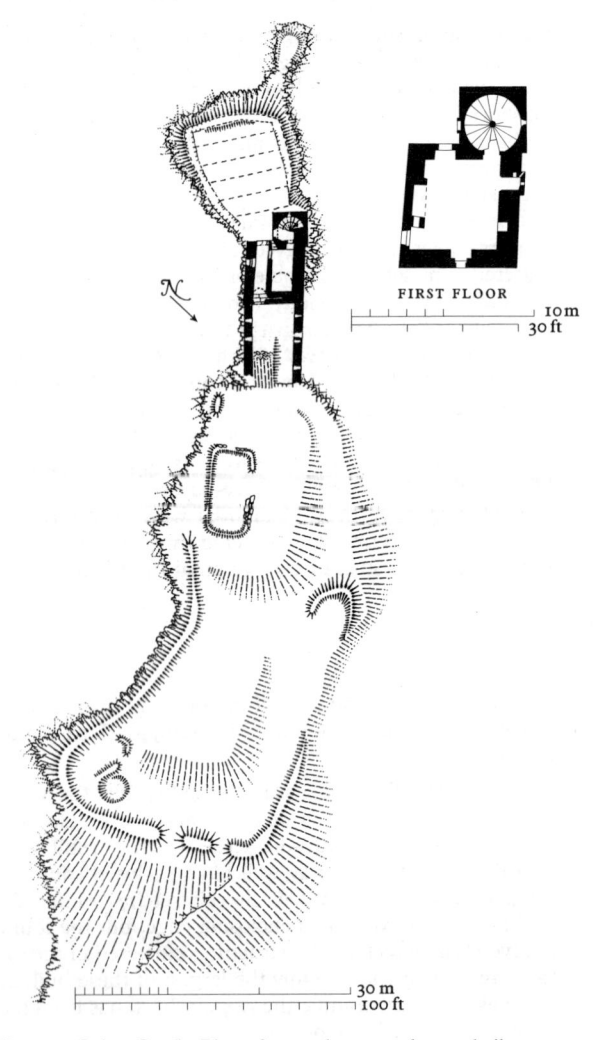

Kerrera, Gylen Castle. Plan of tower-house and outer bailey

with a single room, the square jamb simply enclosing the turnpike stair. The castle's limited width, pushed NE in two parallel forework walls, corresponds to that of the rocky ridge on which it sits. Yet within these constraints, or perhaps because of them, the tower attains remarkable power. Even without the slated planes of the roof and the harling that once coated the walls, both qualities that would intensify the stark geometry, there is a simplicity of form, an elegance of composition, and a balance of mass and detail that is wonderfully and quintessentially Scots.

This is particularly evident on the approach from the NE. Across the elongated outer bailey, now marked by turf-covered banks running along the edges of the ridge, the four storeys of the PRINCIPAL FAÇADE rear up ahead. At first the view is orthogonal but, channelled between the forework walls, it becomes increasingly dramatized by the the advancing impact of the perspective overhead. On the l., through a square-headed doorway wrought all round with a semicircular moulding, a vaulted passage gives access to the ground-floor cellar, also vaulted, and to the turnpike stair at the rear. Beyond, an irregular-shaped piece of land at the end of the promontory, formerly walled, must have served as an inner courtyard or garden. Above the doorway, lighting the first- and second-floor apartments at the middle of the NE wall, are two identical squarish windows, each with a splayed horizontal gun-loop below the sill, and at the wallhead, passing through the cavetto-moulded eaves cornice, two projecting elements which, though no longer intact, provide the high-level, three-dimensional accent and decorative incident characteristic of the best tower-house architecture. The more unusual of these two features is an eaves dormer ORIEL which advances from the wall-face on three triple-coursed corbels set almost directly above the doorway at ground level to provide machicolation defence. In it a single window with chamfered jambs and lintel carved with billet-ornament framed by a roll-moulded surround. Tight to the lintel is a moulding, formed from a series of lozenge shapes, and stopped by a grotesque head. Below the sill, a large, irregularly edged stone bears a problematical inscription, evidently a moral exhortation from Proverbs. Below this, a sculpted female head whose halo of hair folds into the cable moulding which runs above the three corbel supports and returns for a short distance l. and r. across the tower to terminate in figurative bosses. The window almost certainly had a pediment and it is likely that two of the carved stones removed to Dunollie (q.v.), one of which is dated 1582, came from this. What makes this feature intriguing as well as attractive is its rarity; only at Dunderave Castle in Argyll (q.v.) and in SW Scotland can stylistic affinities be found. By contrast, the other skyline form is much more familiar: a fat cylindrical turret at the N corner corbelled on four moulded courses, the upper two of which pass around the corner. There are pistol holes with stepping sills where the round meets the tower, sill and jambs of a single window and a short length of a three-tier chequered cornice, but the turret has lost its upper stonework and conical roof.

On the NW SIDE of the castle, the underbuilding of which drops some way to the rocks below, the masonry plane changes as the wall thickens to accommodate a number of garderobe chutes. A corbelled swelling towards the top of the wall marks the small spiral stair rising from the third floor to a roof space chamber, itself corbelled out from both the NW and SE sides of the main stair tower. This corbelling gives a further emphasis to the upper works, particularly below the crowstepped SW gable, as does the broad chimneystack which emerges from the wider crowstepped gable on the SE. The castle is relatively well lit with lintelled openings on all faces, most with chamfered arrises.

Some vaulted embrasures at first-floor level have collapsed and concrete repairs to lintels were made in 1913. At this level, where the floor rests on the vault below, is the principal surviving feature of the voided interior, a wide fireplace opening, still spanned by a rubble relieving arch and with a rebated salt-box in the NE jamb.

When MacGibbon and Ross recorded Gylen in 1887 they made an enthusiastic plea for its preservation, remarking that 'the walls are almost perfect, the roof only being wanting'. Some repair work was carried out in 1913, and in 1972 *Leslie Grahame MacDougall* exhibited a proposal for restoration at the RSA which he 'believed to be as at the original date'. The castle's claim on 'a little care and attention' (MacGibbon and Ross) continues: consolidation of the fabric by *Martin Hadlington* began in 1993.

HUTCHESON MONUMENT, overlooking Ardantrive Bay. A tall obelisk erected 1883 in memory of David Hutcheson †1880, co-pioneer with David Macbrayne of steamship services to the Western Isles. Conspicuous skyline marker seen from Oban Bay.

FORT, on a rocky hill on the S side of The Little Horse Shoe bay. Irregular oval formed by dry-stone wall following the edge of the summit. Several facing stones visible on SW close to entrance gap.

KILBERRY

A roadside hamlet separated from its kirk by 5km. of single-track road rounding Am Binneag hill on the W coast of South Knapdale N of Loch Stornoway.

BURIAL GROUND, in wooded ground E of Kilberry Castle. Disused since the 1760s. Minimal rubble footings may indicate the vestigial SW corner of Kilberry's medieval parish church of St Berach or Berchan. Some alignment appears to exist with the walls of the adjacent MAUSOLEUM, to local mariner Captain Dugald Campbell of Kilberry, who had seen Mediterranean service with the Royal Navy. The round-pedimented entrance bears the date of his death, 1733, and a relief carving of a seaman's quadrant. In the W wall a full-height mural MONUMENT, framed in fluted pilasters and heavily overmantled, is divided in two panels: the upper elaborately armorial, the lower showing two trumpeting angels. – SW of the mausoleum, standing in its socket-stone, a truncated CROSS, C14–C16, carved with an archiepiscopal figure and helmeted rider on one side and foliage knotting on the other. – Since 1951 most other funerary stones have been gathered in a small shelter near the entrance to the Castle grounds. They include three Early Christian FRAGMENTS, tapered SLABS carved with armed figures, animals, plants and swords, C14–C16, of Kintyre school or Iona school provenance, and a number of roughly rectangular SLABS, C16–C17, more crudely patterned with abstract ornament.

KILBERRY PARISH CHURCH, at Largnahunsion, overlooking the head of Loch Stornoway 600m. SW. Piend-roofed limewashed rubble kirk built in 1821 by *George Johnston* of Dunmore, following plans prepared by *Alexander Grant* of Leith in 1814. The three-bay S front is wide and implacably solid; windows identical at each level, those to the upper storey round-arched and 'blind'. A pediment-shouldered belfry may have risen from the wallhead above the central windows, but the eaves are now uninterrupted. The N wall, of four bays, has the usual two tall round-arched windows flanking the central pulpit. W and E entrances at ground level and by a forestair to the gallery were originally provided but these were built up and superseded by the W porch in 1881 and a new dog-leg stair introduced inside at the W. A ridge belfry was added to the porch in 1888. Seven years later space was partitioned off below the W and E sides of the gallery to create a lobby and vestry. Simple cam-ceiled interior, boarded and plastered. The U-plan gallery, supported on three columns with fluted pilaster casings, is panelled, as is the half-octagon PULPIT.

BURIAL GROUND, 400m. SSW of Kilberry Parish Church on l. bank of Abhainn Learg an Uinnsinn. In use from mid C18. HEADSTONES and SLABS, late C18 and early C19.

CARSE HOUSE, 700m. E of Kilberry Parish Church. An Edinburgh New Town town-house translated to Argyll. Three-bay Georgian, built in 1828 by local builder *George Johnston* for Captain John Campbell of Druimnamucklach. Johnston adopted plans prepared by *J. Shepherd*, architect, in 1816, but introduced a skew-gabled roof and pushed the centre bay forward slightly, giving it an Ionic rather than Doric pillared portico. Rubble with ashlar dressings, quoins, and dated blocking course. Much interior woodwork (architraves, ingoes and chimneypieces) is fluted or reeded. – Castellated Victorian LAUNDRY, located at the rear, on the axis of the main house. – 50m. uphill to N, a ruinous piended COACH-HOUSE elevated above its central archway in a simple pediment.

GORTEN STEADING, on B8024, 200m. E of Carse House entrance. Early C19. U-plan. The main front, in which blind windows alternate with vertical ventilation slots, has piended end pavilions and a pedimented doocot gable over the elliptical central archway.

KILBERRY CASTLE, 600m. NE of Kilberry Bay and 700m. SW of B8024. A tall Baronial mansion, a little spooky in wooded seclusion, it conceals a complex building history. What is clearly visible is clearly C19 though less evidently the result of two distinct phases of construction. Still less to be guessed is the hidden presence of Colin Campbell of Kilberry's late C16 tower-house. But the castle has stood on this spot since *c.* 1595. Refurbished in 1727 for Captain Dugald Campbell, but gutted by fire in 1772, an event which led to estimates for rebuilding being obtained from *Thomas Menelaws*, master builder in Greenock then lately responsible for the design of nearby Ardpatrick House (q.v.). Nothing was done until, in 1843, John Campbell commissioned the Edinburgh architect *Thomas Brown* to prepare plans for the rebuilding of Kilberry 'Because it was the family place!' (Cockburn, 1843). Over the next five years, 1844-9, the castle was re-created in somewhat reserved Baronial style.

A very vertical T-plan house, each of its three crowstepped gables chimneyed at the apex and lugged with slim cone-capped bartizans. Public rooms are accommodated in the main N-S block from which the third wing projects E. At the centre of its gable below two plain superimposed windows is a surprisingly unassertive round-arched entrance approached up a short flight of balustraded stairs. s and E wings closely follow the L-plan alignment of the old tower-house, much of which was removed by blasting. In the NE re-entrant, pushing into the corner, is a large cylindrical stair tower with a slated candle-snuffer roof peaking at chimney-pot height. These arrangements still largely shape the appearance of the castle from the E. On the N and W, further extensions by *Peddie & Kinnear*, carried out in 1873, proved remarkably successful in maintaining the architectural character as well as the texture and masonry detail of earlier construction. A second N-S block, laid alongside the first, produced a double-pile plan and a new, more generously lit W façade with high canted bays corbelled to gables at attic level and pedimented eaves dormers. Running E-W across the N gables of the main house, a lower crowstep gabled wing incorporated new kitchens at ground level and, above, that most necessary element in Victorian country-house living, the billiard room. Next to this, a tall, now barely glazed, conservatory.

In the E gable, above the main entrance, a small pediment-shaped stone bears initials and the date 1497, a C19 reference to the dubious presence of a medieval monastery on this site. Immediately below, carved in a lintel(?) relic, the words 'Plundered and Burnt by Capt. Proby, an English Pirate 1513; rebuilt J(ohn) C(ampbell) 1849'.

KILBERRY FARM, 200m. NNW of the entrance to Kilberry Castle driveway. Built *c.* 1845 and extended 1881. Piend-roofed rubble steading terminated by two-storeyed gabled pavilions each fronted by ridge-high castellated walls.

STANDING STONES, 250m. E of burial ground at Largnahunsion. Two stones set 2.5m. apart and both aligned N-S. The more northerly 2.4m. high, the other 3.2m.

KILBRIDE

A tiny settlement 4km. s of Oban. A few farms and houses are scattered SW along the valley of the Allt Criche to Ardentallen Bay and the N shore of Loch Feochan.

OLD PARISH CHURCH, Kilbride. Roofless rubble rectangle standing barely to the wallhead. As at Kilmore (q.v.), some 3km. E, the building was deliberately contrived as a romantic ruin in

1. Tobermory, Mull, general view of harbour

2. Inveraray, general view looking towards Front Street

3. Slockavullin, Temple Wood, stone circle of the third millennium B.C.

4. Cairnbaan, cup-and-ring markings of the third millennium B.C.

5. Kilmartin, Ballymeanoch, standing stones with cup-and-ring markings of the third millennium B.C.

6. Lismore, Tirefour, broch of late first millennium B.C.

7. Dunadd, fort occupied in the seventh to ninth centuries A.D.

8. Bridgend, Islay, Dun Nosebridge, fort, possibly of mid first millennium A.D.

9. Kildalton Cross, Islay, eighth century

10. Iona Abbey, Iona, with the village in the background and a corner of the Early Christian monastic vallum in the foreground

11. Eileach an Naoimh, Garvellachs, Early Christian beehive cell

12. Iona Abbey, Iona, with St Oran's chapel in the foreground and the island of Mull in the background

13. Iona, St Oran's Chapel, twelfth century

14. Iona Abbey, the east arch of the crossing and the choir from the west

15. Iona Abbey, cloister, early thirteenth century

16. Iona, Nunnery, early thirteenth century

17. Oronsay Priory, Oronsay, fourteenth to fifteenth century

18. Kingarth, Bute, St Blane's Church, twelfth century

19. Dunstaffnage Chapel, thirteenth century

20. Kilmory Knap, chapel, early thirteenth century

21. Skipness, Kilbrannan Chapel, late thirteenth to early fourteenth century

22. Kilfinan, parish church, possibly early thirteenth century, rebuilt 1759, with renovations by John Honeyman, 1881–2

23. Lismore, Cathedral of St Moluag and Parish Church, Clachan, from thirteenth century

24. Bowmore, Islay, Kilarrow Parish Church, 1767

25. Kilchrenan Parish Church, by Donald Campbell, 1771

26. Clachan of Glendaruel, Kilmodan Parish Church, 1783

27. Cairndow, Kilmorich Parish Church, by Andrew McKindley, 1816

28. Tayinloan, Killean Parish Church, A'Chleit, 1787

29. Ardchattan Parish Church, by John Thom, 1836

30. Ardchattan Parish Church, interior

31. Poltalloch, St Columba's Chapel, by Thomas Cundy, 1852–4

32. Poltalloch, St Columba's Chapel, memorial chapel, interior

33. Tarbert, Parish Church, by McKissack and Rowan, 1885–6

34. Campbeltown, Lorne Street Church, by James Boucher of Boucher & Cousland, 1867–8

35. Dunoon, St John's Church, by Robert A. Bryden, 1876–7

36. Portnahaven, Islay, Parish Church, by William Thomson, 1828

37. Taynuilt, Muckairn Parish Church, 1829

38. Dervaig, Mull, Kilmore Parish Church, by Peter MacGregor Chalmers, 1904–5

39. Mount Stuart, Bute, chapel, by R. Rowand Anderson, 1896–1903

40. Lochawe, St Conan's Kirk, by Walter Douglas Campbell, 1881–1930

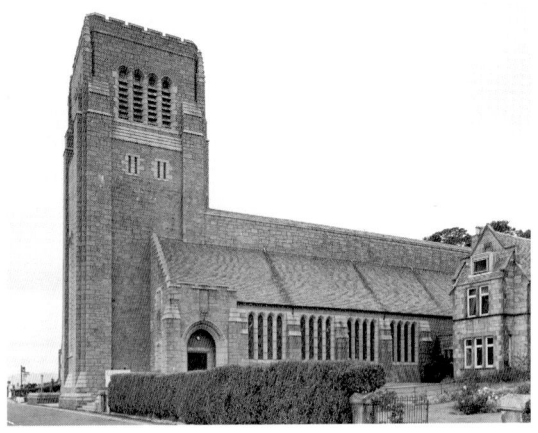

41. Oban, St Columba's Cathedral, by Sir Giles Gilbert Scott, 1930–53

42. Oban, Kilmore and Oban Parish Church, by Leslie Grahame MacDougall, 1954–7

43. Oban, Cathedral Church of St John the Divine, 1863–1968

44. Cardross, St Peter's College, by Gillespie Kidd and Coia, from the east, main block with chapel 1959–67

45. Cardross, St Peter's College, from the north-west, library and teaching block on the right

46. Luss, St MacKessog's Church, hog-backed stone, eleventh century

47. Campbeltown Cross, detail of head, c.1380

48. Kilmory Knap, MacMillan Cross, fifteenth century

49. Rothesay, Bute, St Mary's Chapel, canopy tomb, sixteenth century

50. Oronsay Priory, Oronsay, MacDuffie graveslab, sixteenth century

51. Oronsay Cross, Oronsay, sixteenth century

52. Kilmun Parish Church, Argyll Mausoleum, by James Lowrie, 1795–6

53. Lochgoilhead Parish Church, Campbell of Ardkinglas monument, late sixteenth century

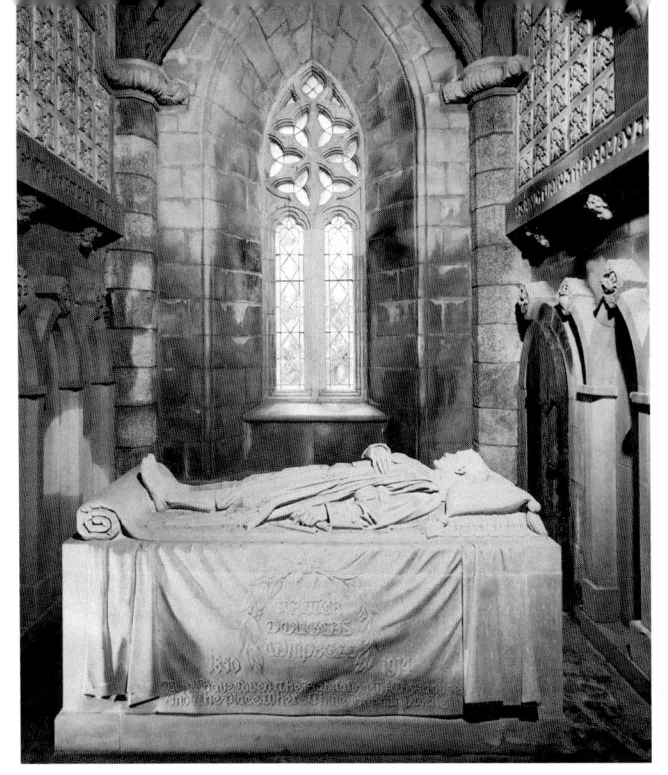

54. Lochawe, St Conan's Kirk, monument to Walter Douglas Campbell (1850–1914)

55. Kilchoman Parish Church, Islay, graveyard monument, 1845

56. Keils, Jura, Campbell monument, late seventeenth century

57. Castle Sween, late twelfth-early thirteenth centuries

58. Castle Sween, fourteenth- and fifteenth-century additions

59. Skipness Castle, late thirteenth or early fourteenth century

60. Duart Castle, Mull, thirteenth century in origin, restored by J.J. Burnet, 1912

61. Lismore, Achadun Castle, thirteenth century

62. Dunstaffnage Castle, thirteenth century, with late fifteenth-early sixteenth-century entrance

63. Kilchurn Castle, mid fifteenth century to 1690–8

64. Rothesay Castle, Bute, twelfth to sixteenth centuries

65. Carrick Castle, late fourteenth century

66. Castle Stalker, mid sixteenth century

67. Kerrera, Gylen Castle, completed 1582

68. Breacachadh Castle, Coll, mid fifteenth century, before restoration; in the background, New Breacachadh Castle, 1750

69. Carnasserie Castle, 1565–72

70. Moy Castle, Mull, early fifteenth century

71. Barcaldine Castle, early seventeenth century, restored by Alexander Buttar, 1896–1911

72. Barcaldine Castle, hall

73. Inveraray, aerial view with street layout and Parish Church

74. Inveraray, Main Street North, 1755–80

75. Inveraray Castle, from south-west, design by Roger Morris, 1745–61

76. Inveraray Castle, dining room, decorated by Robert Mylne, 1780s

77. Inveraray Estate, court of offices, Cherry Park, by John Adam, 1759–61, completed by William Mylne, 1772

78. Inveraray Estate, Maltland Square, the 'Great Shade', by Robert Mylne, 1775

79. Inveraray Estate, Carloonan Doocot, by Roger Morris, 1747–8

80. Inveraray, Glenaray and Inveraray Parish Church, by Robert Mylne, 1792, built 1795–1802

81. Inveraray Courthouse, by James Gillespie Graham, 1813

82. Ardmaddy Castle, 1737

83. Rossdhu House, core probably by Sir James Clerk of Penicuik, 1772–4

84. Strachur, Strachur House, 1780s and later

85. Strachur, Strachur House, entrance hall

86. Glenbarr, Glenbarr Abbey, probably by James Gillespie Graham, c.1815

87. Ardnadam, Hafton House, by David Hamilton, 1816

88. Tarbet, Stuckgowan House, c.1820

89. Minard Castle, by John T. Rochead, 1842–8

90. Minard Castle, entrance hall and staircase

91. Stonefield Castle, by William H. Playfair, 1836–40

92. Kilberry, Kilberry Castle, by Thomas Brown, 1844–9

93. Torosay Castle, Mull, by David Bryce, 1856–8

94. Arden, Auchendennan House, by John Burnet, 1864–6, porte cochère by A. N. Paterson, 1902

95. Helensburgh, Brantwoode, No. 4 Munro Drive West, by William Leiper, 1895

96. Rosneath, Ferry Inn, by Edwin Lutyens, 1896–7

97. Cour, Cour House, by Oliver Hill, 1921–2

98. Ardkinglas House, by Robert Lorimer, 1906–8

99. Dunderave Castle, 1598, restored by Sir Robert Lorimer, 1911–12

100. Dunderave Castle, library

101. Mount Stuart, Bute, by R. Rowand Anderson, 1897–1902

102. Mount Stuart, Bute, grand staircase

103. Helensburgh, The Hill House, by Charles Rennie Mackintosh, 1902–4, garden front

104. Helensburgh, The Hill House, hall

105. Colonsay House, Colonsay, north front, 1722, with nineteenth-century additions

106. Cove, Craig Ailey, Alexander Thomson, 1850

107. Hunter's Quay, Marine Hotel, by T. L. Watson, 1889

108. Helensburgh, Longcroft, by A. N. Paterson, 1901

109. Campbeltown, Town House, by John Douglas, 1758–60

110. Campbeltown, Public Library and Museum, by J. J. Burnet, 1897–9

111. Dunoon, Castle House, by David Hamilton, 1822

112. Rothesay, Bute, Town Hall and County Buildings, by James Dempster, 1832–4

113. Kilmory, Kilmory Castle, extended by J. G. Davies, c.1828–36

114. Oban, Argyll Mansions, by Leiper & McNab, 1905–7

115. Rothesay, Bute, Glenfaulds, c.1880

116. Arrochar, Kirkfield Place, by Joseph Weekes, 1938

117. Oban, Regent Hotel, by James Taylor, 1936

118. Rothesay, Bute, Winter Garden, by Alexander Stephen, 1923–4

119. Rothesay, Bute, Winter Garden, interior

120. Rothesay, Bute, Rothesay Pavilion, by J. & J. A. Carrick, 1936–8

121. Campbeltown, Picture House, by Albert V. Gardner, 1912–13

122. Oban, Social Work Department, by Strathclyde Regional Council, 1988–90

123. Oban, Lorn and Islands District General Hospital by Reiach & Hall, 1992–5

124. Skerryvore Lighthouse, Tiree, Alan Stevenson, 1838–44

125. Taynuilt, Bonawe Ironworks, Blast Furnace, 1753

126. Taynuilt, Bonawe Ironworks, Charcoal Shed and Iron Ore Sheds, mid to late eighteenth century

127. Strachur, Strachur House, Ornamental Bridge, late eighteenth century

128. Inveraray, Aray Bridge, by Robert Mylne, 1773–6

129. Glen Shira, Garron Bridge, design by Roger Morris, *c.*1747, built under the supervision of John Adam and William Caulfield

130. Inveraray Castle estate, Frew's Bridge, by John Adam, 1758

131. Clachan, Clachan Bridge, by John Stevenson, 1790

132. Leargybreck, Corran River Bridge, Jura, by David Wilson, 1809–10

133. Connel, Connel Bridge, by Sir John Wolfe Barry and John Forman, 1898–1903

134. Inveruglas, Craigenarden Viaduct, by Formans & McCall, 1891

135. Kilchiaran, Kilchiaran Steading, Islay, *c.*1826

136. Ellenabeich, Main Street

137. Tiree, vernacular housing

138. Bowmore, Islay, Distillery, photographed in 1981

139. Bowmore, Islay, Distillery, Still House

140. Caol Ila, Islay, Distillery, by G. L. Darge, 1972–4

141. Crinan Canal at Dunardry

1876 when the two congregations united at a new church at Cleigh. The fabric, though altered, is substantially that of the 1706 'meeting house' (Lorn Presbytery Minutes, 1706) erected on the site of the medieval kirk of St Bridget which by the late C17 had already been demolished. The S door, later blocked, doors at lower and upper levels through the W gable, and another in the now degraded E gable are all original, as may be some of the windows. Those with splayed jambs must have been formed during alterations, *c.* 1744, and result from the widening of earlier openings. In this first reworking, the pulpit was probably moved from the S to the N wall. A W gallery, indicated by joist socket holes in the gable, may also date from the mid C18. In 1842–3, the Oban joiner *Peter MacNab* added a N session house and rebuilt the church's upper walls, introducing elliptical arches to the windows.

In the CHURCHYARD, several TAPERED SLABS, Loch Awe school, C14–C15, with the usual imagery of swords, animals and plant forms. – Two SLABS, Iona school, C14–C15; one carved with sword and spiked staff, a motif also appearing on a similar slab on the floor of St Oran's Chapel, Iona (q.v.). – The MACDOUGALL BURIAL-AISLE, a rectangular enclosure, is dated 1786 in the keystone of an elliptical-headed arch in the W gable. Family's armorial panel above. – Beyond the churchyard, 230m. NNE, stands a 3.13m.-high, disc-headed CROSS, dated 1516 in an inscription which records Alexander Campbell of Lerags as the donor. Until 1926 its greenish schist shaft lay broken close to the church. Reassembled, it displays the figure of Christ, arms outstretched into the arms of the cross, and below, the inscription, a rosette of interlace pattern, and a unicorn.

LERAGS HOUSE, 1.8km. SW of Kilbride. Three-bay, piend-roofed house, 1822–3, austere in detail and material. At the centre of the W front is a gabled porch with semicircular fanlight above panelled doors. The sprocketed roof is late C19, matching E extensions.

KILCHENZIE

A few houses on the Campbeltown–Tarbert road where it skirts the N side of Aros Moss.

KILCHENZIE OLD PARISH CHURCH (St Kenneth's Chapel). Elongated rectangular rubble ruin, 22.5m. by 6.7m., comprising two compartments: that to the W, C12; later E chancel, C13. The arrangement is similar to Killean Church, 21km. N on A83. Lying within the church are several tapered SLABS, Kintyre school C15, carved with the familiar imagery of swords, ships, vegetation and beasts; one with full-length knight's effigy. The burial ground which surrounds the church ruin is entered between square gatepiers carrying salvaged(?) urns.

DRUM FARM, 500m. NW of Kilchenzie Church. Two-storey gabled house with three façade gables, each crested with an iron finial. Flanking single-storey wings have open iron-bracketed eaves.

TANGY MILL, 2.6km. NNW of Drum Farm. Three-storey, whinstone structure with kiln extension to the S forming L-plan. Erected *c.* 1820 on the site of an earlier mill. Production ceased in 1961. Cleverly converted to residential use by the Landmark Trust. Cast-iron overshot wheel, 5.44m. dia., on the E gable of the main block, has been retained, as has dressing, drying, hoisting and grinding machinery in the interior adaptation.

FORTS, Largiemore, 1.3km. NNE of Kilchenzie Church. Two forts, one within the other, on a salient above Largiemore Farm. Of the outer, no walling survives; the smaller retains two courses of large facing blocks.

FORT, Ranachan Hill, 1.5km. E of Kilchenzie Church. Small Iron Age fort on summit. Vestiges of three defensive outer walls to E; entrance on NW above steep rocky incline.

STANDING STONES, 1.7km. W of Kilchenzie Church at the N end of Machrihanish Links. In a hollow of the dunes, two stones 1.9m. and 1.4m. high.

0322

KILCHRENAN

A hamlet in hilly country 9km. S of Taynuilt and 1.2km. N of Loch Awe.

PARISH CHURCH. White-walled, skew-gabled oblong built 1771 by *Donald Campbell* of Sonachan. Dimensions and orientation follow those of several medieval churches in Lorn, suggesting the C18 plan may be determined by C13 remains. Repairs carried out 1807 and 1842. Present arrangements, locating pulpit and table in the E end, result from a radical recasting of the interior by *James Edgar*, 1904. The C18 church, liturgically organized about its shorter N–S axis, had galleries on W, S and E, each reached by an external parapeted forestair rising at right angles to the lateral walls. Of these three, two remain. The NE has gone but the NW now serves the single W gallery created in the 1904 longitudinal reorganization, while that located at the middle of the S elevation survives, incongruously rising to a blank wall. This S front with its balanced arrangement of round-arched windows and blind recesses flanking the central forestair retains its characteristic C18 appearance, though the gallery door under its catslide dormer has gone and the original intersecting glazing bars have been replaced by round-arch astragals. W entrance door, gable windows and fragments of medieval dog-tooth ornament incorporated in gable walls, all 1904. C19 E gable birdcage bellcote carrying stepped pyramid and ball finial. N vestry added early C20.

Plain plastered interior with boarded coomb ceiling. – A tall marble MURAL TABLET on S wall commemorates Robert McIntyre, surgeon, †1815, in a long eulogistic inscription. – STAINED GLASS. E window by *Gordon Webster*, 1976 (leadwork by *Neil Hutchison*): at the centre, a crowned Christ mantled in red, a 'playing card' king, dominates a variegated panel of complex figuration and patterning. – In the churchyard, a few broken and tapered SLABS, mostly Loch Awe school, C14–C15. – A later SLAB, *c.* 1500–60, carved with a claymore, scrolls, lion, and griffin, and inscribed with a commemorative dedication and the words 'Collinus, son of Angus, made it', has been set vertically in the E gable of the church. – Built against the E end of the S wall is the Campbell of Sonachan BURIAL ENCLOSURE, 1779, possibly constructed on medieval footings. – In a small railed enclosure, the MCINTYRE MONUMENT, early C19; Neoclassical composition comprising a tall plinth with projecting cornice on which acroteria flank a dumpy pediment-topped obelisk. – Still more Greek, a MONUMENT commemorating Alexander McCalmine of Drissaig †1844, a fluted Doric column carrying cinerary urn; by *D. Smith*.

ARDANAISEIG HOUSE, 5.5km. ENE. A two-storey mansion of stugged granite with greenish sandstone dressings by *William Burn*, 1833–4. Known first as New Inverawe. The house was converted to a hotel, 1979–80. Designed in a modest crow-stepped Jacobean idiom, the house sprawls N to a stable court. W entrance in a panelled architrave frame surmounted by stone tablet crested with strapwork. Facing S from a NW service wing, a three-bay Roman Doric loggia now demeaned by a corrugated-iron roof. The E front, though architecturally dull, enjoys a splendidly contained prospect of Loch Awe across terraced lawns. Laundry, below stables E wing, is groin-vaulted to a central pillar.

HAYFIELD STEADING, 3.8km. ENE. Early C19, built on a symmetrical courtyard plan. SE front with pedimented central archway and piended two-storey end pavilions with Venetian windows at ground floor. Progressive conversion to residential use began 1979. The NW dwelling, in which arched cartshed doors have been fully glazed, is by *John Peace*, 1989. All but inaccessible amid rampant vegetation 200m. SE is the burnt-out shell of HAYFIELD HOUSE, a mid-C18 two-storey-and-basement classical mansion, destroyed by fire *c.* 1912. Pedimented SE front with a central doorpiece with moulded architraves and cornice.

KILCHRENAN INN. Five-bay, eaves-dormered, painted rubble house with off-centre gabled porch. Part may be the public-house built *c.* 1771, otherwise early C19.

TAYCHREGGAN INN, 1.6km. SSE. Ancient drove road inn on N shore of Loch Awe at ferry crossing to Port Sonachan. The oldest part of the present hotel, facing SW down the loch and returning NE in the lee of a rocky rise, looks early C19, though it probably engrosses earlier work. Successive late C20 wings running NW have created a long-tailed U-plan now curtailed by a glazed entrance link forming a sheltered court. Glazed archways open cloister-like into this inner space. In all this a consistent addiction to white walls, slated roofs and rural eaves-dormered scale imparts an admirably modest sophistication.

TIGH-NA-UISGE. Uncompromisingly modern house on lochside by *Morris & Steedman*, 1961. Steel frame construction in box-frame form: plan of four squares stepping back to achieve view and shelter. White rendered lower storey; cedar boarding to external walls, balconies and interior of upper living areas. Alien, now evidently disdained, but a creature of bolder times.

CAIRN, Làrach Bàn, 800m. WSW of Hayfield Steading. Circular cairn, 11.8m. diameter, disturbed by forestry operations. Kerb of large boulders can be seen on the W.

CHAMBERED CAIRN, Auchachenna, 2.25km. SW. 30m.-long cairn rising to 1.7m. at SE where a now rather denuded chamber is located. SW portal stone stands 1.45m.

DUN, Caisteal Suidhe Cheannaidh, 2.1km. NNW. Well-preserved ring dun, c. 12.5m. in dia., built of dry-stone walls almost 5m. thick still coursed on outer and inner faces up to 2m. height. Checked entrance passage at NE. 1890 excavations discovered hearths and animal bones.

FORTIFIED DWELLING, Eilean Tighe Bhàin, Loch Tromlee. Ruined rectangular rubble cell located on 25m.-dia. island 200m. from SE shore of loch. Tiny splayed slit opening with stepped sill survives in W wall.

KILCHURN CASTLE
at NE end of Loch Awe

Kilchurn erupts from the waters of the loch like some heaving creature glaucous with submarine slime. Scaly grey-green walls crumble along its ragged rubble back. Setting and silhouette are spectacular. The rocky site is peninsular but, surrounded by marsh and delimited from the landward approach by a ditch, seems to be an island – indeed may have been in earlier times. The castle began conventionally enough as a tower-house, built mid C15 by Sir Colin Campbell, 1st of Glenorchy, and this still anchors the plan in the E. Later in the same century the 'laich hall' was added on the SW side of the barmkin. By the third quarter of the C16, another Sir Colin, the 6th of Glenorchy, was adding corbelled rounds to the tower in a reconstruction of its top storey. Between 1614 and 1616 the laich hall 'being ruined ... was reedifiet and reparyt' to two storeys and a new SE range built connecting it with the tower. Further extensive repairs were carried out in 1643. Finally, c. 1690-8, the castle was greatly enlarged under the supervision of master mason *Andrew Christie* in a programme of works instigated by John, 1st Earl of Breadalbane, which entailed the building of several cylindrical angle-towers and a four-storeyed L-plan barracks range on the NW. Though garrisoned during the 1745 Jacobite rebellion, by the 1760s the fortress lay unroofed and abandoned.

Entry to the TOWER-HOUSE is at ground level through a NE doorway, the lintel of which, dated 1693, bears armorial insignia, the motto FOLOW ME (*sic*) and the initials EIB and CMC for John, 1st Earl of Breadalbane, and his wife, Countess Mary Campbell. The cellar is barrel-vaulted. Within the 4m. thickness of its SE wall, a small vaulted prison chamber with latrine and a mural stair rising to the first floor. The main stair is, however, the tight W turnpike added in 1691, as its dated lintel shows, to serve all

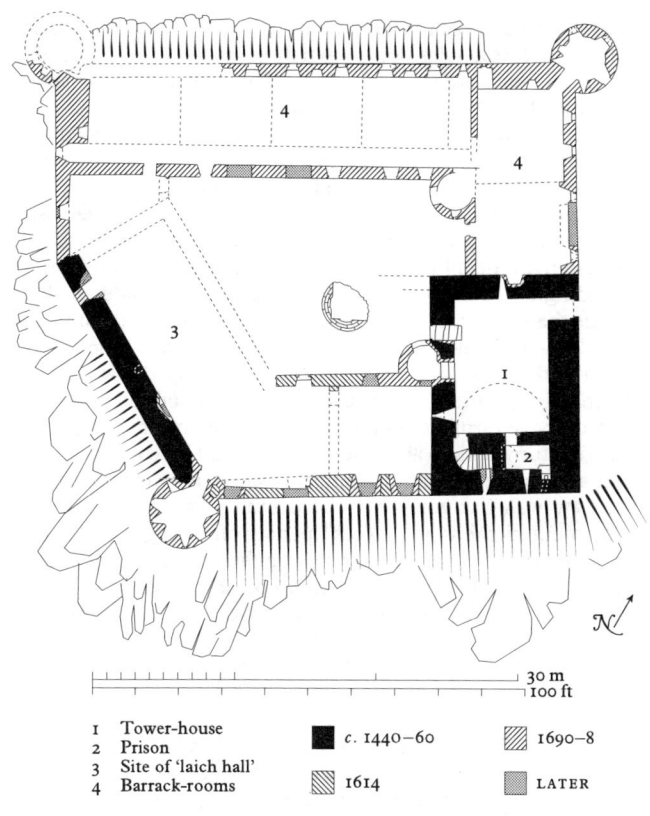

1 Tower-house
2 Prison
3 Site of 'laich hall'
4 Barrack-rooms

■ c. 1440–60

▨ 1614

▨ 1690–8

▨ LATER

Kilchurn Castle

levels in the tower. By this the hall above is reached, though the original access would have been by forestair from the courtyard. The SE wall is again hollowed out, this time for two vaulted spaces which may have been sleeping chambers. Between the two, the mural service stair rises from below while a further small stair, designed to lead to a latrine, now climbs to the timber stairs and platforms introduced to afford the visitor access to the upper levels of the tower-house shell. Splayed window openings in the hall have been reduced and the fireplace, presumably located on the NE wall, hidden by later alterations and patching. Above first floor, moulded corbel stones for joisted upper floors survive. At second-floor level there were probably two apartments for there are two separate mural stairs at the NW and SE corners in addition to the C17 turnpike. A similar subdivision seems likely on the third floor, though the two surviving fireplaces are C16 or C17. At parapet level the bases of three of the late C16 rounds are largely intact, each with four corbel courses, some of which bear masons' marks; the W turret has, however, fallen and lies in the grassed courtyard below. All would have been cone-roofed. From the gabled garret-chamber direct access to each turret and to NE and SW parapet walks was obtained. Pistol holes slope down through the turrets' corbelling and also penetrate the walls above. Parapets have water spouts and may have been linked to bretasches.

Apart from two low-level stretches of the S curtain (C15 on the SW and early C17 on the SE), the ruinous but still substantial COURTYARD BUILDINGS date from the 1690s. The two earlier sections are hinged on the later S angle-tower, a cylinder rising from a massive plinth two storeys to an eaves course with cavetto moulding, a detail repeated in the contemporary upper-storey building and rebuilding of the ranges on each side. At both levels the single room in the tower was well supplied with small windows and gun-loops. Similar but taller towers appeared at each end of the long NW range, though only the N survives. Vertical circulation in this barracks accommodation was provided by the turnpike stair located in the re-entrant where the N range returned SE to abut the tower-house. Once again only the outer masonry is extant, and not wholly so for the W portion of the NW wall has gone, but the planning can be determined. Basement kitchens and stores opening off a long corridor running the entire length of the range on the courtyard side; a large fireplace with a segmental-arched opening survives at the SW gable. At each of the upper levels, four barracks rooms, each with a fireplace and two windows in the outer wall, would have opened from the SE corridor. In the shorter NE range the arrangements were similar: basement kitchens and upper floors subdivided into two barracks rooms lit by NE windows and warmed by fireplaces in the NW and SE walls.

Throughout, openings are square-headed. Those in the tower-house have chamfered margins and many dressings show masons' marks. Gun-loops exhibit circular and elliptical mouths. Three FRAGMENTS in grey-green stone, two from dormer pediments, one with fleur-de-lis finials and the carved initials SDC for Sir Duncan Campbell, 7th of Glenorchy, are preserved, bracketed from the SE wall of the barracks block; they date from the reconstruction of 1614–16. Their museum-like presentation is, of course, a more recent phenomenon, part of that extensive programme of consolidation begun in 1976 which has made it possible to view the castle at close quarters and at all levels. And yet, welcome as this conservation is, Kilchurn's principal appeal does not rest on the quantity or quality of its ornament but rather on the extent to which architecture and landscape together admeasure the sublime.

KILCREGGAN

Until 1848, a scattering of small farms and cottages on a track heading SW out of Rosneath (q.v.). The village takes its name from an ancient chapel whose existence was supported by the discovery in the early C19 of a number of stone coffins at nearby PORTKIL. Its expansion was largely speculative, generated by the creation of a carriage drive around the foot of the peninsula and the opening of a pier in 1850. Served mainly by steamers out of Greenock and Glasgow, Kilcreggan became a fashionable watering place where fresh air and accessibility, combined with panoramic views of the Firth of Clyde and Loch Long, ensured its popularity. The wood-piled pier, replaced in 1897, remains operational, although no longer critical to the survival of the village, now less of an actual resort than settlement. Happily, development has long since slowed to an imperceptible pace, preserving many of the features which first attracted feuars to the area.

DESCRIPTION

ROSNEATH ROAD, the shore route established by the 8th Duke of Argyll, still functions as the principal thoroughfare, driving N through Kilcreggan and the contiguous ribbon resorts of Craigrownie and Cove, before terminating abruptly at RNAD Coulport.

Lending weight to the notion that Kilcreggan has a commercial element, five muscular tenement blocks of shops and flats, 1888–1903, are placed strategically on Rosneath Road opposite the pier. The three-storey frontages of whinstone rubble with slaister harl pointing are distinguished by Jacobethan strapwork, attic gables and hoodmoulds on decorative consoles. Uphill, on DONALDSON'S BRAE, the KILCREGGAN HOTEL, built 1880s and extended W late C19 through the addition of a bulky battlemented tower on whose S and W faces are superimposed two-storey-and-attic gabled bays. – INTERIOR. The original staircase with plate traceried and stained-glass windows complete with figurative panels survived conversion from a private house. The nearby HEATHFIELD, 1887, now the KILCREGGAN CENTRE (WEC), was also built by the same stockbroker family Donaldson. A large rambling-plan house with three-storey canted tower, segmental-headed attic shell pediments to the S, and parapets punctuated by ball finials, the interior preserves some good column-flanked chimneypieces and Glasgow-style window glass.

Returning to the lochside, the diminutive AIDENBURN COTTAGE, mid C19, has an advanced entrance bay gabled behind open geometric bargeboards. Next are DUNVRONAIG and DUNVORLEIGH, originally mirror-image cottage orné villas whose disposition is in large part derived from Alexander Thomson's Seymour Lodge in Cove (q.v.). Hence, both buildings show the outer bay advanced as a two-storey gable with a square projecting window outshot on deep base at ground level, and a tripartite Tudor-arched opening above. Flat-roofed entrance porches with battlemented copings are located in the re-entrant angles. Cloned from the same components are GLENLEA and WINTON, both near Craigrownie, mid C19, the latter with a diaper cornice and decorative wrought-iron balustrade to the parlour bay.

AUCHENDARROCH, mid C19, represents an increase in scale. A two- and three-storey cumbersome Italianate villa, now flatted. Its roof nevertheless aspires to originality, being edged in a curious two-tiered eaves of slate overhanging a ribbed lead canopy. Neighbouring ARDSLOY is dainty by comparison. Probably by *Alexander Thomson*, *c.* 1850. A delightful shallow-roofed two-storey villa, single room wide with a broad bow window on high base facing seaward. This has a dentil cornice and low cast-iron and ashlar balustrade outlining the bedroom balcony. GLENTRAE, further N, is similar but with additions N and S.

As Kilcreggan Bay is left behind, the mouth of the Holy Loch is clearly evident. Raised up to better appreciate the vista, AIDENKYLE has a full-height canted window on deep whinstone battered base to the garden front. In the gablehead, a little lunette window and, linking the entrance front to a piend-roofed glasshouse, an elevated terrace with anthemion and floral motifs making up the cast-iron balustrade. At lower level, contemporaries CLAREMONT, HOLYROOD and LOVEDALE are similar, with seamed lead caps to two-storey window bays and rustic painted quoins.

As the steep incline of SCHOOL ROAD draws near, corniced and urn-topped gatepiers frame the view to BALGAIR. Mid-C19 Italianate two-storey, four-bay harl and ashlar house with squat campanile, the composition carries greatest conviction in the relationship between the pyramid-roofed tower, located on the re-entrant angle, and the outer left-hand gable, which has tripartite round-headed windows and a high decorative cast-iron balcony screen. Homage to Alexander Thomson's Craig Ailey in Cove (q.v.) is paid in the form of a frieze of little square recesses lined up above a dentil cornice bound around the belvedere.

LETHINGTON, to the W, attempts less and subsequently achieves more: an asymmetrical gabled villa in honey sandstone with a broad ground-floor bow window with pilaster mullions outer r. From the top of this springs a bipartite Romanesque-style window framed by an arched opening with tympanum decorated by circle and triangle motifs. Post 1865. Next door, GREENHILL is unremarkable, but boasts a pair of fine early C20 Glasgow-style gates whose languid whorls are infinitely more creative than the severity of the stone piers.

School Road is named for the succession of buildings which have at some time served as the local school. It provides one of the few links between the shore and BARBOUR ROAD, an elevated highway connecting a series of hill farms which extend to Peaton. The COVE & KILCREGGAN COMMUNITY CENTRE, single-storey Gothic with a gabled transept E, round-headed windows and a pretty gabled bellcote with sawtooth copes and a trefoil finial S, was once the Free Church School, endowed in 1859 by Lorne Campbell, chamberlain to the Duke of Argyll. In 1933 the building was extended N in a respectful shallow hipped aesthetic by County Architect *Joseph Weekes*, before being superseded in 1968 by *Ross & Lindsay*'s big folding-roofed classroom blocks. Close by, Kilcreggan's only really significant flirtation with modern architecture, *Scottish Special Housing Association*'s MEIKLE AIDEN housing scheme of 1969. Traditional in style and construction, albeit featuring staggered planforms and split sections, white cement rendered walls, strip glazing, boarded infill panels and neat garden enclosures.

KILDALLOIG

Bay E of The Doirlinn sand spit which separates Davaar Island from the mainland.

DAVAAR HOUSE, opposite Davaar Island. Two-storey-and-attic house to which has been added a projecting gabled wing with two-storey canted bay. Walled garden with ironwork railing remains. C19.

DAVAAR LIGHTHOUSE, on the N side of Davaar Island at the entrance to Campbeltown Loch. Erected 1854. Short circular tower with piended building close to base. Single-storey row of keepers' houses and boundary wall. Limewashed.

KILDALLOIG HOUSE, 700m. s of Davaar House. Built 1926. A wide-fronted harled house with a short gabled wing advancing l. To the r., four hipped-roofed dormers break through the eaves, lined up regularly above a classically elaborated doorpiece and three plain windows. Very much 'after Lorimer', down to the vine clusters on rainwater hopper-heads.

KILFINAN

A roadside hamlet picturesquely gathered along a curve in the B8000 above Kilfinan Burn and 1.5km. E of Kilfinan Bay on the E shore of Loch Fyne.

KILFINAN PARISH CHURCH. Described by the writer of the *New Statistical Account* of 1845 as 'a plain building, long, low, and narrow', the church's elongated form and its clear E–W orientation are almost certainly medieval. A late C12 or early C13 dating seems probable as the proportions are close to churches of that date at Kilkivan and Killean in Kintyre and Kildalton on Islay (qq.v.). The N aisle, the Lamont Aisle, was added in 1633; perhaps a revision of earlier medieval work. By 1690 the church was in serious disrepair and, although refurbishment and reseating restored it to use a few years later, by 1759 it required to be 'almost rebuilt' (*OSA*, 1795). Two-light windows in the s wall, doors at ground- and gallery-level in the w gable, and the obelisk-urn on the E all date from this time. The N aisle was closed at ground level but remained open as a loft gallery above. In 1837 the fat-legged birdcage belfry on the w gable was built. Finally, in 1881–2, *John Honeyman* carried out a further renovation. The church was re-roofed, skews and skewputts introduced on the gables, and the walls harled. Two new N lancets were formed on either side of the N aisle and similar arch heads introduced over the C18 S openings. In the E gable a pointed-arch doorway, Early English in style, became the principal entrance; above it, an eight-cusped circular window with dog-tooth ornament. At the W end the Ardmarnock gallery was eliminated and a vestry and boiler-house created, reducing the overall length of the church. The interior, orientated W towards the PULPIT with its low screen panelled in blind quatrefoils, is disappointingly dull. Only the six open trusses, arch-braced with curved struts, offer some decorative interest.

The LAMONT AISLE has eaves coincident with those of the church. Its gable is crowstepped with the initials S / CL, for Sir Coll Lamont, and the date 16/33 carved on cavetto skewputts. An C18 forestair rises against the gable but the door to the loft, like the opening of the loft into the church, has been blocked. The ground-floor burial vault is entered through a gated doorway, the lintel of which bears the date 16/33 and the initials D / BS for Sir Coll's wife, Dame Barbara Semple. Within are several funerary MONUMENTS. Three SLABS, of Early Christian date, are carved with crosses, one C9 or C10, ringed and overlaid and surrounded by complex interlacing ornament. – A number of TAPERED SLABS, mostly C14–C15 Loch Awe school, bear the usual sword, plaitwork and floral scroll motifs. – The head and three shaft fragments of a free-standing CROSS, C14–C15, 'the only inscribed monument of the Loch Awe school' (RCAHMS Inventory, 1992), are preserved. The cross is carved on both faces with plaitwork, plant stems and nailhead and on one side of the cross head the relief image of a helmeted rider on horseback; it carries a dedication in Latin to Patrick MacNeilage. – A rectangular SLAB, with a winged angel head, crowned lion in a shield, and the customary symbols of mortality, records Jean Urry †1706, in a double-banded marginal inscription. – An elaborate C18 wall MONUMENT lies in pieces: amongst these are a scrolled pediment, a corbelled base, a grotesque circular finial, and a mural tablet commemorating Archibald Lamont of that Ilk †1712.

The walled GRAVEYARD surrounding the church contains many C18 and C19 tombs. Amongst these is a HEADSTONE in memory of Duncan Thomson †1814, with an hourglass and the not quite rhyming reminder: MY GLASS IS RUN / AND YOURS IS RUNNING / BE WISE IN TIME / YOUR DAY IS COMING. – W of the church, above a bend in a tributary stream of the Kilfinan Burn, is a ruined WALLED ENCLOSURE with a pedimented sarcophagus set in the W wall and commemorative inscriptions to three members of the MacFarlane family, all of whom died in the 1820s.

RANKIN BURIAL ENCLOSURE, 100m. S of Kilfinan Church. Beyond neo-Greek gatepiers and anthemion-crested, scrolled ironwork gates, a straight path leads to a rectangular ashlar enclosure, *c.* 1900. Sandstone walls plain from plinth to cornice. Pilastered aedicule in pink marble around gated round-arch opening. Mural tablet.

KILFINAN MANSE, across road from church. High, two-storey-and-garret, symmetrical house, completed 1808. In 1827 a porch was built but the present heavy Victorian doorpiece probably dates from 1849–50 when various repairs were carried out and the rear wing added. Hip-and-gable dormers also probably mid C19.

KILFINAN HOTEL. Four white-painted, rubble houses gable-to-gable along the roadside. All have eaves dormers with open timberwork in bargeboarded gablets. The s house, dated 1760 on gabled porch, preserves a mid-C18 sandstone chimneypiece. Vaulted cellar. The taller N house, probably mid C19, has cornices on grooved consoles over its ground-floor windows and door.

FEARNOCH MILL, 1.1km. NW of Kilfinan Church. A mid-C19, single-storey-and-attic, rubble building which until 1971 preserved its threshing mill. Converted to residential use. Iron overshot wheel retained.

LINDSAIG MILL, 600m. N of Kilfinan Church. Two-storey, L-plan rubble mill converted to dwelling, c. 1965.

DUN, MacEwan's Castle (Caisteal Mhic Eoghainn), on a promontory at the N end of Kilfinan Bay. Oval dun, 22m. by 20m., with a stone wall some 3m. thick. Some facing stones can still be seen intermittently.

STANDING STONE, 400m. s of Fearnoch. An exceptionally broad stone (1.95m. at widest) standing 2.5m. high. The N face is vertical, but the s is hipped below its pointed top.

KILMARTIN

The 'regular plan' (Groome, 1883) on which Kilmartin was rebuilt c. 1835 seems to have resulted in little more than a string of neat one- and two-storey slated rubble cottages which follow the rise and fall of a bend in the A816 12.5km. N of Lochgilphead. All lie on the higher E side of the road, looking W past church and manse to the valley of the Kilmartin Burn below.

KILMARTIN PARISH CHURCH. A well-sited but gawky Gothic church by the London-based architect of Kilmory Castle, *Joseph Gordon Davis*, 1834–5. A predecessor of 1601, possibly an adaptation of an earlier medieval structure, was described as 'incommodious' at the end of the C18 and, despite extensive rebuilding, 1798–1801, was pulled down a generation later. The church sits in a large hillside graveyard falling to W and S. The W tower, seen in splendid relationship with the village from the S, is battlemented and as broad as the tall four-bay nave which rises behind between lower aisles. Openings, including the two entrances, one in each aisle gable, are all four-centred arches; two-light clearstorey windows, quatrefoils in the spandrels. Variations in the roof slope and eaves detailing of nave and aisles, crude parapet crowstepping, and some stepped buttressing gratuitously applied, are ungainly and at odds with this Perpendicular idiom. The interior is better: below the clearstorey windows set high in plastered walls, slender four-bay arcades emphasize the vertical; all the more so since 1899–1900 when *James Edgar* deprived them of their side galleries. The timber-lined lobbies formed at the E end of each aisle and the slightly pitched panelled ceiling belong to these changes of 1900. – The Malcolm of Poltalloch LOFT, carried on two thin metal columns and penetrating into the depth of the tower through a wide pointed-arch, retains its timber front of narrow vertical panelling with cusped triangular heads and grapes-and-vine cornice. – But the original PULPIT has gone. It was centred high in the E under a three-light Perpendicular window and was attenuated in form, not least in a tall-finialled sounding board. Present arrangements in the sanctuary, 1900, are unexceptional.

Several Neoclassical MURAL TABLETS of white marble with grey marble detail or backing, each with a long inscription, commemorate members of the Campbell or Malcolm families. Three on the N wall, each panel carrying armorial insignia between two small urns and 'resting' on guttae feet: to Neil Campbell of Duntroon and Oib †1791, erected 1819, and his sons, Major-General Neil Campbell †1827, 'a sacrifice to the baneful climate of Africa', and General Patrick Campbell †1857. On the S wall are two more, both in the form of pedimented sarcophagi with anthemion finials and claw feet: to Neill Malcolm of Poltalloch †1837, and the infant children of Neill Malcolm the Younger of Poltalloch; both manufactured by *T. Denman* of London. – STAINED GLASS: N aisle, Jesus, the Light of the World, by *A. Ballantine & Son*, c. 1905.

CHURCHYARD. Stepped granite arch WAR MEMORIAL, erected 1921, over the entrance. – Close to the SW angle of the church, a small stone MAUSOLEUM to Bishop Neil Campbell, perhaps in part C16, but now with a glazed roof, it serves as a lapidarium. Over its W door, a stone PANEL inscribed '1627 HEIR LYIS MR / NEIL CAMBEL AND CRISTIANE C ...' – Lying in the yard, another PANEL, decorated with scrolling, records the building of the 1798 church. – But it is the wealth of burial stones, one of the largest collections in the West Highlands, which must command attention. Three Early Christian SLABS show Latin cross outlines while a fourth, late C9 or C10, takes the same form as a freestanding CROSS, 1.55m. in its modern base, carved on both sides with plaiting, knotting and diagonal key patterns. – More than eighty tapered SLABS and CROSS FRAGMENTS, dating from C13 to C16, predominantly the work of Loch Awe school sculptors, are to be found in the churchyard or lapidarium. Numerous SLABS and TABLE-TOMBS, C17 and C18, exhibit a variety of heraldic devices. Two stones, dated 1707 and 1711, are carved with an unexpectedly primitive naïvety. – MACLACHLAN MONUMENT, late C17, to William MacLachlan, 'rector of Kilmartin', his wife, Grisel, and his children. Endearingly unsophisticated: a rubble mural panel framed by rude pilasters and raised at the top to include an armorial shield mantled by a garland of fruit. – Several monuments relate to the family of James Gow †1855, who was largely responsible for supervising agricultural improvements on the Poltalloch estate from *c.* 1796.

To Gow's son James †1837, an OBELISK with raised disc carved with blasted tree and broken column, the work of the Glasgow sculptor *Mossman*.

KILMARTIN CASTLE, on a hillside ridge 300m. NNE of Kilmartin Church. Classic gabled hall-house with circular towers at E and W corners. Probably constructed for Neil Campbell who became rector of Kilmartin in 1574 and Bishop of Argyll in 1580. Ruinous and roofless since the early C19. Its three storeys of rubble walling are intact to eaves, though only the SW gable survives. The simple wallhead cornice is interrupted on the NW wall by the irregular sill line of three former eaves dormers. Openings are random in size and disposition: gun-loops in the angle towers, small double-lintelled voids at ground level and larger windows above, square-headed below rubble relieving arches. Entrance doorway, close to the W stair tower, with chamfered jambs and draw-bar slot. Asymmetrically placed in wall above is a chamfered framed armorial panel, now badly weathered. Under reconstruction, 1997–8.

All three apartments on the ground floor are vaulted. The plan bears some resemblance to nearby Carnasserie Castle (q.v.). The original kitchen, occupying the full width of the NE end, links to a small square-plan room, also vaulted, in the E tower. A spiral service stair, projecting from the NW wall, connects the kitchen with both upper floors. Main vertical circulation is by the turnpike in the W tower. This leads to the hall, beyond which is the customary private chamber. Both rooms were heated by fireplaces, now destroyed, though the relieving arch of the one in the NW wall of the hall remains. A small vaulted space at the S corner of the hall may have been a safe store. The arrangement of the second floor is uncertain.

KILMARTIN HOTEL. Built *c.* 1835; altered and enlarged by *James Edgar* in the 1890s. Plain three-bay with gabled attic dormers. Single-storey wings l. and r., each with door, window and dormer.

KILMARTIN HOUSE, 100m. NNW of Kilmartin Church. A three-bay, two-storey manse, built 1789, the *First Statistical Account* described it as 'a tolerable commodious house'. A proposal to add a two-storey addition, prepared by *John Thom* of Oban in 1822, seems not to have been carried out but in 1863–4 a similar project by *Alexander Fraser* of Slockavullin produced a double-pile plan, the new W block stepping downhill to a third storey. Now a centre for archaeology and landscape interpretation. Adjacent rubble outbuildings cleverly converted on three levels to shop, café, etc. by *Jeremy Walker*, 1994–7; roofing, staircases and conservatory in dowel-nailed green oak construction.

OLD POLTALLOCH, 3.3km. NW of Kilmartin. Now surrounded by afforestation and somewhat remote above the SE shore of Loch Craignish, the ruins of the house and steading date from *c.* 1799. When Neil Malcolm left for Duntrune in 1796, his younger brother George undertook the renewal of the family's older seat, building farm, walled garden and 'a Small neat Mansion House'. Little enough of the HOUSE remains (indeed, it may never have been finished) but what there is indicates a typical tripartite Georgian plan. A single-storey pavilion to the NW is answered by another on the NE. The garden or forecourt lay S. SSE is the STEADING, c. 30m. square, entered on the W through a gabled flat-arch, flanked by partially blind Venetian windows decorating the rubble walls.

CAIRN, Kilmartin Glebe, 180m. NW of Kilmartin Church. Reconstructed cairn, 30m. dia. and 3m. high. Excavations in 1864 found cists containing two food vessels and a jet necklace.

CAIRN, Nether Largie North, 500m. SW of Kilmartin Church. Reinstated cairn, c. 18m. dia. Excavation in 1930 revealed a cist, the capstone of which bore axe-head and cup-ring decoration. *See* also Slockavullin.

CAIRN, Nether Largie Mid, 150m. SSW of Nether Largie North cairn. 30m. dia. cairn excavated in 1929 when two empty cists were uncovered. Some kerbstones on S. *See* also Slockavullin.

KILMELFORD

8413

A village of neat local authority houses on the Oban road 500m. NE of Loch na Cille at the head of Loch Melfort.

KILMELFORD PARISH CHURCH. The church, already rebuilt in the latter half of the C18, was renovated in 1890. Though thoroughly late Victorian, the oblong plan may perpetuate that of the late medieval church of St Maelrubha. Bargeboarded W gable front with eight-spoke wheel window over a chamfered pointed-arch entrance. Birdcage belfry. Plain but tall interior in narrow space; king-post collar trusses between boarded roof spars. The W gallery balcony is reached by an attractive spiral stair with barley-sugar balusters. Bolection moulded dado around sanctuary. – White marble MURAL TABLET with block pediment commemorates Revd Colin Campbell †1887.

CULFAIL HOTEL. High two-storey-and-attic, three-bay, mid-C19 house. The heavily pedimented and consoled doorway sits between tripartite windows. Gabled extension N by *J. Fraser Sim*, c. 1880. Former billiard room has pitch pine panelled interior.

KAMES FARM, 3.4km. WSW. Early C19. Firmly symmetrical three-bay piended farm. Tripartite windows on the ground floor. Hipped-roofed steading ranges lie to W.

GLENMORE, 700m. S. A high, hipped-roofed, rubble house, three bays wide with a central doorway in roll moulded sandstone frame. Mid C19. Reconstruction by *Dick Peddie, Todd and Jamieson*, 1935–6, introduced dormers, raised the S wing to two storeys and added an advancing N wing. Both wings have hipped roofs with eaves dormers. Leadwork to canted bays and rainwater pipes decorated with vine and acorn motifs. Two-storey, U-plan STEADING to S may antedate house. Round-arch entry under central gable.

KAMES BAY, overlooking Loch Melfort from above S shore. By *Henry Paterson*(?). A single-storey, hillside house in roughcast and green-stained timber, begun 1985, its original L-plan was extended NE with an oblique viewing bay at lower level, 1989, and NW, 1994, in a dramatic, two-storeyed, pyramid-roofed octagon, fully glazed around its upper floor.

SCHOOL, 400m. N of Kilmelford Church. 1863–4, by *William*(?) *Menzies*. L-plan with mullion-and-transom window in the gable.

FORTIFIED DWELLING, Loch a'Phearsain, 800m. NE of Kilmelford Church. Small walled island enclosing on N what appear to have been two drystone buildings, that to SW larger, though only 10.7m. by 7m. overall, subdivided by a stub wall and enclosing the other on the N. A still smaller circular structure lies NE close to a walled inlet from the loch. Perhaps late medieval in date; ruinous since the mid C19.

KILMICHAEL GLASSARY 8593

Lengthily named village in River Add valley, 7km. N of Lochgilphead, but not much more than the 'mere church hamlet' Groome described in 1883.

PARISH CHURCH. Dumpy little kirk with a deceptively Romanesque look. The four-bay gabled oblong is distinguished by its plain but forceful W tower, pyramid roofed, tight at the eaves, and shouldered N and S with lean-to roofs pitched in parallel with the church gable skews above. The tower of 1826–8 was built according to plans for a new church by *John & Donald McIsaac*, perhaps with the assistance of *William Thomson*, resident engineer on the Crinan Canal. This 1828 church provided more space than its 'long and narrow' predecessor of the late C17 or early C18, but was itself later considered too large. It was replaced in 1872–3 by a smaller structure. Its designer, a Lochgilphead 'architect' named *Kirkwood*, retained the tower and some of the older fabric. In 1907–8 a minimally projecting gabled chancel with round-arched windows was added by *Peter MacGregor Chalmers*. Boarded coomb ceiling with arch-bracing of trusses exposed. Timber COMMUNION TABLE and octagonal PULPIT with almost Islamic ogee arch motif, 1908. – STAINED GLASS in the chancel; the Crucifixion, 1912.

Numerous noteworthy funerary stones can be found in the well-populated GRAVEYARD. These include an Early Christian tapered SLAB with ringed cross in relief and numerous other tapered SLABS, C14–C15, carved with plant motifs, fret patterning, swords, galleys, animals, and helmeted and armed figures, all of Loch Awe school character. – There are also CROSS FRAGMENTS, C14–C16, and covers and side-slabs from two TOMB-CHESTS, early C16, splendidly carved with inscriptions commemorating members of the MacIver and MacLachlan families. – Amongst post-Reformation monuments are a roughly hewn CRUCIFORM STONE, perhaps C16 or C17, but incised with the name Arch(ibald) McCallum in the early C19, and a TABLE-TOMB, C18(?), bearing a mantled shield, skull and crossed bones in high relief.

MANSE, 170m. s of Church. 1838–40. Built by *David Crow* of Lochgilphead with design advice from *David Hamilton*.

GLASSARY PRIMARY SCHOOL. 1876; by *James Maitland Wardrop*. Gabled classrooms and schoolhouse with wide eaves and heavy purlin projections. Rubble with sandstone dressings.

STANDING STONE, Torbhlaran, 1.1km. NNE of Kilmichael Glassary Parish Church. Close to the road to Ederline stands a flat-topped cup-marked stone, 2.1m. in height.

STANDING STONE, An Car, Leckuary. 2.6km. NE of Kilmichael Glassary Parish Church on the N bank of the River Add. A 3.9m.-high straight-sided stone.

KILMICHAEL OF INVERLUSSA

A clustered bend of buildings set in and above the winding gorge of the Lussa River, 1.2km. s of Achnamara.

CHAPEL and BURIAL GROUND, 400m. NNE of North Knapdale Parish Church. Turf-covered footings of hillside enclosure with evidence of a chapel cell on the W. Nearby, 'The Priest's Well' spring.

NORTH KNAPDALE PARISH CHURCH. Built 1820 to a design by *Alexander McDougall*, architect in Edinburgh. The customary two-storey, five-bay piended box. The s front has a central pedimented projection carrying a pillared bellcote. All five upper 'windows' round-arched but blind. On the N, two tall arched windows at the centre. All of this points to a galleried interior with cross axial focus on a N pulpit. But the E entrance betrays change: inside, a late C19 longitudinal orientation is revealed. Galleries have gone and low lop-sided intrusions forming lobby and vestry disrupt a space now bleak rather than austere. Pine ceiling and dados, 1987–8. – In the churchyard, an Early Christian FRAGMENT carved with a ringed cross, C8 or C9, and some tapered SLABS, C17. – Also several inscribed recumbent SLABS, late C17 and C18.

INVERLUSSA HOUSE, 200m. from E shore of Loch Sween. Former manse, built 1820. Designs submitted to Presbytery included those by *Alexander McDougall* of Edinburgh and by *Donald McDougall*, 'architect from the parish of Craignish'. While the former built the Church, it was the latter who won the manse commission. Shorn of its intended pediment, the plain W façade remains elegant: a white three-bay two-storeyed front rises to a central gable in which is placed a small round-arched window. On each side, low piended wings sit against the main chimneyed gables. In the principal rooms, original joinery includes architraves, skirtings and fielded doors and shutters. In the N ground-floor room, an elliptical timber arch to a window recess. Timber chimneypiece with reeded jambs and lintel in room above. Rear yard surrounded by various OFFICES early, mid and late C19.

BRIDGE, 90m. s of Parish Church. Semicircular arch with radially set rubble voussoirs spanning 6m. across Lussa gorge. Late C18.

KILMORE

A hamlet 1km. NNE of the head of Loch Feochan. Houses lie E of the A816 Oban road along the banks of the River Nell.

KILMORE AND OBAN CHURCH. By *J. Fraser Sim*, 1875–6. Humble, barely Gothic, gable-ended hall. S front in square-snecked rubble, four lancets long. Two lancets and apex quatrefoil in W gable.

OLD PARISH CHURCH, Glen Feochan, 1.2km. ESE. Ruined, elongated oblong, C15 or C16, inscrutably described by the *Statistical Account* of 1794 as 'originally in the form of a cathedral'. Rubble walls, which show signs of harling both outside and in, have quoins and margins of local greenish sandstone. The nave was probably lit by a single off-centre window in the W gable, the chancel by windows in the N, E and S, although repeated slappings and blockings have made original openings difficult to determine. A doorway was located at the middle of the S wall. Following the Reformation, W and E galleries were installed (socket holes for their timbers survive) and the church layout recast with a pulpit on the N wall. The S door and window remained, while a new window W of the doorway may have been opened. New windows and an additional doorway were also formed in the N wall. At some time in the C18, possibly in the 1730s when re-roofing was carried out, a birdcage belfry appeared on the W gable, but this has gone. In 1838, an architect named *Dalzel* rearranged the S wall to create three pointed-arch openings, provided new doorways and forestairs for the galleries at the W and E ends of the N wall, and built a porch/vestry on the E gable where the church's main entrance was now positioned. In 1859 the S door became a window. Finally, in 1876, in a calculated attempt to produce a picturesque ruin, partial demolition reduced the fabric to its present roofless state. Still preserved inside, at the E end of the S wall, is a late medieval TOMB-RECESS framed by a semicircular arch with a deeply cut roll-moulding intermittently carved with rosettes, bosses and short lengths of dog-tooth ornament. It now contains a white marble TABLET in memory of Isabella Campbell of Glenfeochan †1844. In the walled graveyard which surrounds the church, four TAPERED SLABS, Loch Awe school, C14–C15. Inset at the base of the W gable, within framing stones which have leafy branches carved on the sides and an open book in relief on the lintel, is a MURAL MONUMENT commemorating, in a Latin inscription, the Revd James Campbell †1756.

DUNACH, 1.6km. SW of Kilmore above the N shore of Loch Feochan. An older house much remodelled by *William Burn* in 1828. A wide-spreading two-storeyed mansion, its canted bays and dormers jagged with gablet cresting. Burn's SW wing removed in 1980s.

GLENFEOCHAN HOUSE, 1.4km. SSE. By *John Starforth*. Tudor-bethan estate mansion in droved ashlar, built 1875. SE entrance tower, almost baronial, banded with stepping stringcourses, witch's hat roof and smaller attached staircase turret capped by leaded ogee. Beautiful woodland garden and arboretum. WALLED GARDEN lies E.

KILMORE HOUSE. Two-storey-and-basement, piend-roofed house built as a manse in 1828 by *John Thom* of Oban. The aspirations are classical: a tripartite plan with chimneyed transverse walls, a pedimented centre to the wide, three-bay NE front, and a pilastered doorpiece flanked by narrow side-lights. A large segmental bay, which appears to have three windows at all three levels (though some openings are mock) advances at the centre of the SW façade between the transverse walls. In the room behind this curve at ground-floor level and in the neighbouring SE apartment there are two timber fireplace surrounds, early C19. Doors and shutters are panelled. A U-shaped timber stair rises over the NE entrance door to reach a generous landing.

THE OLD SCHOOLHOUSE. One-and-a-half-storey, with central porch and two gabled eaves dormers, 1862.

CAIRNS. A collection of ten cairns is concentrated in the valley of the River Nell from Dalineum Farm in the N to Kilmore House in the S. The best preserved is that which lies 550m. E of Moleigh Farm; 21.3m. in dia., rising 1.4m., it still possesses a few kerb-stones and has an exposed cist at the centre.

CHAMBERED CAIRN, 275m. S of Dalineum farmhouse. Oval cairn, 18m. by 15m., aligned NE–SW. At the centre is a Clyde type chamber, similarly aligned, and behind it, to the SW, a large cist.

KILMORY

Former estate on the E shore of Loch Gilp. From the mid 1970s, when Kilmory Castle became the centre of local government administration, the factories and sheds of light industry have been spreading over the hillside.

BURIAL ENCLOSURE. Until the early years of the C19 the overgrown foundations of the C13 chapel of St Mary could be seen *c.* 150m. from the loch close to a lodge-house, but now only the burial ground remains. There are many late C18 and C19 graves and one earlier scrolled HEADSTONE, in memory of Duncan Campbell †1727, brought here from Minnigaff in Galloway.

CLOCK LODGE, on the A83, 750m. N of the entrance to Kilmory Estate. One of three lodge houses (the others, Red Lodge and Lingerton Lodge, bear no stylistic comparison) probably designed by *J. G. Davis* in the 1830s during his work at Kilmory Castle (q.v.). A symmetrical, two-storey structure of red sandstone rubble with ashlar dressings. Distinguished by a steeply hipped roof peppered with three small, sharply gableted attic dormers front and back and a twelve-paned clock-face dormer towards the top of each roof plane; all of which give the building a Germanic look. A carriageway passes through the centre under round arches with mock portcullises (an arrangement which recurs at Kilmory). Above this, on the W front, is an unfilled corbelled and canopied niche. Eaves gutters discharge down long spout-pipes bracketed from each corner. First floor of fireproof brick arch construction. In the 1950s the lodge ceased to be used as a dwelling and is now derelict.

KILMORY CASTLE. As at Minard Castle, some 12.5km. NE on the W shore of Loch Fyne, Tudor Gothic grandeur disguises more modest C18 beginnings. The architectural character of the earlier house remains obscure; it was enlarged, 1816–20, and at least some of its fabric appears to be incorporated in the S range of the much-enlarged mansion Sir John Orde began to contrive when he purchased the estate from the Campbells of Kilmory in 1828. Orde commissioned the London architect *Joseph Gordon Davis* who, between 1828 and 1836, extended the original house in an L-plan configuration by building a long W wing. The existing range, rubble-built with freestone dressings, must have been remodelled at this time: it is symmetrical, five bays long and three storeys high, has a gabled porch and is gabled at the centre and ends, the outer gables corbelled out slightly at second floor. At the SW corner, old and new are articulated by a massive, three-storeyed octagonal tower lit by superimposed two-light windows on each of its ashlar faces, mullioned-and-transomed on the two lower floors but smaller and blind at second-floor level. The tower is ringed with stringcourses and heavily crowned with corbelled battlements. At the N end of the L-plan is another tower, similar in scale and detail but square in plan. Between the two, set slightly forward between one-bay castellated links, is the house's principal façade. Roughcast with ashlar dressings, it is seven bays wide; in a central projection a five-light window sits above the four-centred arch of a carriageway entry visually protected by a mock portcullis. Both openings, like all the windows in this central range, have hood-moulds.

Around 1860 Sir John Orde initiated further extensions. These were carried out in Tudor style. From the rear of the W range, on the N side of the carriageway which passed through the building, a new E wing was constructed parallel to the older S side of the house. This was terminated by a short return wing orientated N–S which in turn was echoed by a similar E addition across the full width of the S range. On the N and S gables of these end blocks, canted oriels were corbelled at first floor, that projecting from the extended S façade bearing the date 1863. The house now conformed to a U-plan with an inner courtyard open to the E. By the time of Orde's death in 1878 additional service buildings had appeared and the overall disposition ordered by the building of an E screen-wall with a central round-arch portal and gabled corner towers peaked with helm roofs. Above this service entrance the wall stepped up to an ogival gable. To the N of the house a retaining wall takes account of an abrupt change in level but there is space enough for a driveway to pass. This is crossed by two archways, the W castellated, between which it is bridged at first-floor level.

Some time after the sale of the estate in 1949, Kilmory functioned for a spell as a hotel but in 1974 it became the administrative centre of the new local authority. In 1980–2, a four-storey office block was built by *Argyll & Bute District Council* on the higher ground to the N. Uncompromising in form and materials, its two upper storeys sleekly clad in a curtain of bronze anti-sun glass, it sits well in the estate landscape, connecting to the C19 mansion through a glazed link across the existing first-floor bridge. After a fire in 1983 comprehensive refurbishment, which included the conversion of the carriageway entry into a glazed reception hall accessible both from the W and from the E, was undertaken. But despite extensive alterations, several interior features survive. In the original entrance hall, which lies s of the new reception area, there is a floor of Minton tiles, 1837, a bordered Moorish design in black and yellow. Located between this and the inner NE face of the octagonal SW tower is a smaller, top-lit, octagonal space in which an open-well timber stair, carved with grapes and cartouches on the balusters, climbs on a curving outer stringer to the floors above. In the tower itself are some of Kilmory's finest rooms: at basement level a central octagonal pillar radiates plaster ribs; at ground floor, no central column but again a ceiling of radiating plaster ribs; at first floor, the walls are punctuated by Gothic shafts, from the capitals of which spring the moulded ribs of an elaborate plaster vault with a central pendant.

Across the modern car-park to the SE lies the COURT OF OFFICES, c. 1816; remodelled by *J. G. Davis*, c. 1830. Built on a square plan around an inner courtyard with a central circle of cobbles, it is entered on the NW through a gabled four-centre arch flanked by Venetian windows with blind side-panels. Because of the slope of the ground the SW elevation is two-storeyed; it has end gables, nip-stepped on the skews, and arched cart-entries at the lower level. Forestair on SE. – A large diameter HORSE-GANG(?) lies NW, ruinous and overgrown. – Marooned N of the WALLED GARDEN are classical GATEPIERS, dated 1816 (*see above*).

STANDING STONE, Kilmory Castle. At the driveway junction, a 2.03m.-high stone with pointed top.

KILMORY KNAP

Chapel and the ruins of an abandoned township 3.8km. SSW of Castle Sween.

CHAPEL. Early C13 gabled oblong. Documentary evidence from late C13 associates it with St Mary but local tradition prefers dedication to St Maelrubha of Applecross. Bouldered walls, robbed of their sandstone quoins and dressings, stand to a 4m. wallhead. Partial renewal of Gothic ingoes to the SW door; the original weathered base course shows engaged shafts with keel moulding. Sandstone dressings to twin round-arched E windows largely intact. The church was restored in 1934 when the flat glazed roof, kept below the wallhead, was installed to protect over thirty carved stones. Seven tapered or rectangular SLABS, Early Christian, with ringed cross carving. – Numerous tapered SLABS and FRAGMENTS, C14–C16, Iona, Kintyre, Loch Awe and Loch Sween schools, include some with vocational images (cloth worker's shears, smith's anvil, etc.), others with effigies in ecclesiastical or military dress. – A reconstituted CROSS, early C16, richly carved with interlacing on both faces. – The MACMILLAN CROSS, splendidly preserved, stands 2.81m. The W disc-head shows the crucified Christ flanked by smaller figures of Virgin and St John and surrounded by intertwining bands which spread into the upper part of shaft above a large sword. E disc filled with interlaced bands plaited into the top third of the shaft above a deer hunt scene. At the base of this E face an inscription commemorates Alexander MacMillan, keeper of Castle Sween (q.v.) before 1481.

MILL (Stronefield Mill), at Aironn on the W bank of the Abhainn Mhór, 300m. N of Loch Caolisport shore. Built late C18. Roofless, two-storey corn mill, ruinous by 1869; rectangular shell with evidence of a kiln in N corner. Wheel-pit against SE gable. Footings of the miller's house lie adjacent E.

CAIRNS, Ardnaw. 100m. NW of Ardnaw, a 22m.-dia. cairn preserving some massive kerbstones on the S arc. Another, Dun Fuarlit, 19m. dia., 300m. WSW of Ardnaw, with kerbstones on the S.

DUN, Dùn Rostan, 3.2km. NE of Castle Sween. Summit site with cliffs on the NW and SE, now in a forestry plantation. Circular dun, 11m. dia., with well-preserved walling rising to 2.5m. maximum in twenty-two courses. The NE entrance is checked and slotted for a draw-beam on both jambs. Several mural spaces.

FORT, Dùn a'Bhuilg, 500m. S of Chapel. Oval enclosure, 26m. by 18m., defined by overgrown footings more than 3m. thick.

KILMUN

A linear village on the NE shore of Holy Loch. Unlike its neighbours Strone and Blairmore (qq.v.), which extend this coastal strip SE and then N along Loch Long, Kilmun is a settlement of some antiquity, though its modern growth from 'paltry clachan' (*Imperial Gazetteer, c.* 1865) to watering-place begins in 1827 with the building of a quay by marine engineer *David Napier*.

KILMUN PARISH CHURCH (ST MUNN). An ancient site dedicated to the Irish St Munn. A church is recorded in the C13 but the roofless medieval TOWER, standing immediately W of the present building, bears traces of the later C15 collegiate church constructed by Sir Duncan Campbell of Lochawe after he had received papal approval in 1441. The coursed rubble tower, in residential use until the C17, rises through three storeys to a ruinous wallhead. Windows are few and small; at second-floor level, S and W, trefoil-cusped, hollow-chamfered lancets. In the sw corner of the 6m.-square plan is a turnpike stair which originally climbed to an attic garret, the w gable of which still stands. At ground-floor level this sw corner seems to have been rebuilt to a rounded plan and a lintelled s doorway formed, possibly towards the end of the C17. About a century later the door was blocked, entry to the barrel-vaulted ground-floor apartment being gained from the ruinous medieval nave which abutted on the E. Ragged fragments of the nave walls adhere to the tower base, while the diagonal chases cut for the flashings to the church roof can be seen on the E wall.

In 1688 the choir of the C15 church was renovated to serve as the parish kirk and in the 1790s, further repairs were undertaken. But in 1840–1 the old building was demolished and the present CHURCH, designed by Glasgow architect *Thomas Burns*, erected a short distance E of the tower over the medieval foundations. The layout is a T-plan, the stem of the T forming a N aisle. Initially, the pulpit was positioned at the middle of the five-bay S wall with a gabled vestry projecting on the S front. Above this is a square belfry tower of ashlar with cross-traceried parapet and corner finials. Tall lancets, set on a continuous weathered stringcourse, light the interior, except in the gables, where pointed-arch openings over the doorways have Perp timber tracery, and in the NE re-entrant of the T, where the Argyll Mausoleum was accommodated (*see* below).

In 1898–9 *Peter MacGregor Chalmers* radically recast the interior, though the external arrangements remained largely unaltered. The S wall was opened up through a foliated archway to create a sanctuary where the vestry had been, Perpendicular arcades were introduced to separate the central space from W and E wings and the original W gallery reconstructed over the principal W entrance. Walls are plastered with red sandstone dressings. Below the gallery, an open oak screen with cusped Perpendicular tracery defines an area part-vestibule, part-baptistery. Similar tracery fills the spandrels of the four-centred arch-bracing which springs from corbelstones below a flat, four-bay ceiling. – Oak chancel furnishings, designed by *Chalmers*, maintain the same Perpendicular precision. – COMMUNION TABLE with vine cornice and the carved figures of the apostles, Petrus, Paulus, Andreas and Johannes. – REREDOS panelling below sill of S window, octagonal PULPIT to l. and LECTERN to r., all delicately worked with traceried bays divided by slender crocketed finials. – PEWS bear the names of the heritors as determined by a court case in 1904. – Simple cylindrical sandstone FONT under W gallery. – Onyx TABLET in the baptistery area records that the 1899 restoration was paid for by Henry Johnston Younger of Benmore. – Hydraulically powered *Norman & Beard* two-manual ORGAN, 1909. – STAINED GLASS of high quality. In 1895 the artist *Stephen Adam* gifted the Children's Window by the font. There followed a string of commissions for his studio. – Chancel: three superimposed vesicas depict the Magi, the Agony in Gethsemanae and Christ enthroned, 1899. – S wall, W wing: pen and book in hand, St Matthew, 1908, a portrait of George Miller of Invereck House (q.v.). E wing: St John, purple-robed, below Faith, Hope and Charity, 1908. Also Christ the Good Shepherd, 1908. – W wall: amid whorls of olive-green leaves, Dorcas 'full of good works' holds children to her deep blue cloak; one of the last of Adam's works, 1909. – Two years after Adam's death, his successor *Alfred A. Webster* designed the King David window in the W wing, 1912 (the Lion of Judah robed in purple and Prussian blue under a bower of dripping grapes). – Ten years after that the studio was responsible for the War Memorial window, N gable, in which a mailed knight kneels before Christ. – In the adjacent N window, St Munn surrounded by inset scenes from his life, 1924, the designer unknown.

A small hipped-roofed HALL was added in the NW re-entrant in 1909–10. Also by *Chalmers*. In the hall itself ashlar sandstone walls over an oak dado. Coomb-ceiling panelled and boarded in oak above a carved frieze of grapes and vine leaves.

ARGYLL MAUSOLEUM. Until the late C18 Argyll Campbells were buried in a small vault attached to the NE end of the choir of the medieval church. In 1794 this was demolished and a new mausoleum built, 1795–6. It was designed on a square plan by *James Lowrie*, who had three years earlier carried out repairs to the church. Its slated pyramid roof rose above the walls of the old church until, in 1841, Burns's new church tucked the mausoleum into its NE re-entrant. In 1891–3 the slated roof was replaced by the present ribbed metal-covered dome with its twelve small skylights, and the principal N façade, an unscholarly three-bay front of rudely Corinthian pilasters carrying a banded entablature and cornice, was enhanced by a hooded and moulded pointed-arch doorway filling the central bay. Flanking, blind pointed-arch windows with flat Y-tracery may be of similar date. The entrance leads into a short N–S aisle running between 2m.-high arcaded platforms, within which are the coffins of the Dukes and Duchesses of Argyll, their names recorded on marble panels. Ahead, in the S wall, is a tall blind pointed-arch, probably 1795–6, and below this, within a wide arched recess cusped with eight round-headed arches, 1893, are the splendidly carved and remarkably well-preserved mid-C15 effigies of Sir Duncan Campbell and his wife.

The church sits on a grassy knoll above the road in a densely populated BURIAL ENCLOSURE walled in 1818–19. Most graves lie S and E. There are a few TAPERED SLABS, C14–C16, but the wealth of post-Reformation grave markers is exceptional. Some 60 HEADSTONES and TABLE-TOMBS merit mention in the RCAHMS Inventory (1992). – Typical are a small stone with ogee-shaped top, dated 1697 and carved with tailor's scissors and goose; on the rear, an inscription naming 'John McKellor, taylor, 1762'; another, 1758, commemorating Daniel Taylor, ship's carpenter in Greenock, with a panoply of tools carved in relief; and a third, to John McViccar †1764, 'late Gardiner in Killmunn', similarly symbolic with the images of tree, shears, rake, spade and pruning knife. – Two more, each the grave of

Duncan Clark (one a farmer at Inerchapple †1782, the other a farmer at Strachur, †1877) carry the enigmatic family motto, FREE FOR A BLAST. – Collapsing in the SE corner, a small piend-roofed structure, early C19, described in a letter of 1901 as 'the old watch-house at Kilmun'. On the N side of the church, the DOUGLAS OF GLENFINNART MAUSOLEUM, 1888, of Gatelawbridge red sandstone on a chamfered square plan with an eight-faceted stone slab roof; in the pediment over the door, the scrolled family motto, JAMAIS ARRIERE. Domed interior has shelves of polished Arbroath stone. – Two COFFIN COVERS, early C19, lie against the N wall of the C15 tower.

Later GRAVEYARDS lie N, rising in tiers up the steep S-facing slope of Kilmun Hill, and W, reaching to the garden wall of Old Kilmun House. In the former part, among the customary obelisks, urn-topped headstones and crosses, is an open-ringed CELTIC CROSS, richly carved and bossed, marking the graves of David Graham †1923 and his two wives †1901 and †1941.

Former ST ANDREW'S CHURCH. Built as the Free Church, 1843–4, and re-roofed almost immediately, 1845, by *John T. Rochead*. Grey-green rubble with sandstone dressings around round-arch windows. Gable to road has corbelled arched bellcote. No longer in religious use.

KILMUN HALL (Younger Hall). By *Angus Cameron*; 1910. Red-tiled roofs, a rough-faced, red sandstone plinth and white harled walls unify a picturesque composition of half-timbered gable, battlemented tower and conically roofed corner bow. The hall has a five-bay, king-post roof closed at collar height. Leaded glass patterned in swags, shields, and harebells.

KILMUN PIER. Block masonry quay erected by marine engineer *David Napier*, 1827; wooden pier beyond, late C19(?). Closed 1971. Access to pier flanked by single-storey, gabled, pierhead buildings symmetrically splayed to form axial entrance: shop to W, former smithy E.

OLD KILMUN HOUSE. Six-bay, two-storey-and-basement gabled house, probably early C18. Pointed rubble with sandstone quoins and the plainest dressings. Entrance door, third bay from W, with moulded architraves and a pediment positioned below the lintel height of the adjacent windows. These enrichments and others, including a cavetto eaves-course and the crowsteps on the gables, carried out *c.* 1870 when the low-key, Baronial W extension may also have been added.

DESCRIPTION

A single lochside road continues the parade of varied C19 villas that stretches on to Strone and Blairmore. SE of the pier, FERN GROVE is unique; not for its grotto gateway of quartzite rocks nor its diamond-canted two-light bay, for these features recur, but for its timber-strip bargeboards dripping icicle-like to a decorative scroll edge. FINNARTMORE has grown too big, gables and bays adrift in nursing-home inflation. On the other hand, HILLSIDE HOUSE, *c.* 1840, has a piended, three-bay dignity, its well-scaled symmetry stressed by a central porch with a spiky ironwork cornice. Isolated by the shore at Rheumore Point is a small grey granite obelisk rising from a dished plinth of the same material; a MEMORIAL, 1906, to James Duncan of Benmore, sculpted by *Alexander Macfarlane Shannon*. The inscribed bronze panel has gone but the oval bust relief of Duncan remains. NW of the pier, the parade comes to order. Lined up along the road are six three-bay, two-storey houses, the so-called TEA CADDIES, built 1829 by David Napier when he began to develop communications between the Holy Loch and Loch Eck. All are piend-roofed Georgian and none is untainted by modification; WOODBURN VILLA, with its pilastered porch and broad ashlar quoins, seems to be in charge. The discipline does not last but FINNART, mid C19, reiterates some classical symmetry: a Corinthian pilastered doorway between square bays and, above, broad dormers with pediments and a neat cresting of Grecian detail. About 1km. beyond St Munn's Church (*see* above) and Old Kilmun House (*see* above) is the gabled, three-storey bulk of the former CONVALESCENT HOMES, by *Hugh Barclay*, 1873–4; extended by *Ninian McWhannell & Reid*, 1939. Half-timbering, white walls and glass-canopied verandas, all showing their age. Half-timbered too, but anglicized Arts and Crafts in feel, ARDBEG, *c.*1890, sits comfortably amid trees close to the junction with the A815 N to Loch Eck and Loch Fyne.

KILNINVER

T-junction village S of the River Euchar's entry into Loch Feochan.

KILNINVER PARISH CHURCH. Medieval foundation originally located 200m. NE on an exposed hill-top. By the late C18 its condition was wretched; so bad, it was said, that when the wind blew the minister could not be heard. A new building was erected on the present site, 1792–3, after a plan prepared by *John Clark*, mason in Oban. In 1891–2 this was radically reconstructed and reroofed. The gable-ended oblong plan was retained, round-arch windows introduced and a simple traceried triple light provided in the E gable. Contemporary gabled S session-house and timber porch with pointed arch entry concealing the church's off-centre round-arch W entrance door. Plain plastered interior. Panelled rear gallery on two timber columns. – Octagonal panelled box PULPIT, pitch pine. – Below the gallery an alabaster TABLET with decorative border, *c.*1900, erected by W.R. Galbraith, 'for many years Lessee of the Kilninver Shootings', in memory of his wife and younger son.

On the site of the medieval church is an abandoned BURIAL GROUND. Several C18 stones, the earliest 1721.

Former KILNINVER & KILMELFORT FREE CHURCH, 400m NW of Kilninver Parish Church. Built 1862. Four-bay rubble, barely recognizable as a kirk. Coolie-hat roof to simple belfry. Now a dwelling.

KILNINVER LODGE. Mid C19. Originally a shooting lodge for Ardmaddy Castle (q.v.) but later much extended. An abundance of gabled dormers. In the sw gable, a shallow canted bay.

THE OLD POSTHOUSE, 250m. NW of Kilninver Church. Late C19. Tall, three-bay house with central timber porch. To the l., hunched below its door-height eaves and corrugated-iron roof, is a primitive white-painted rubble biggin, early C19(?), battered on the gable.

DAIRY COTTAGE, NW of Old Posthouse. Early C19(?). Another wonderfully white, three-bay archetypal cottage.

DUACHY, 2.3km. SW above B844 looking SE across Loch Seil. Two-storey symmetrical steading linked to gabled wings.

RAREY HOUSE, 1.3km. SE above W bank of River Euchar. Tacksman's house of 1743 originally no more than single-storey-and-attic accommodation but later extended in higher L-plan wing. Slate panel over central door inscribed with date and initials IC, probably for John Campbell of Barcaldine. A small earthwork 120m. NE is thought to be the site of the CASTLE or 'mansion of the ancient and brave McDougalls of Rarey' (*NSA*, 1845), but configuration and date are unclear.

DUN, Dùn Mhic Raonuill. Shoreside dun occupying the roughly oblong summit of a rocky stack some 9m. high, 1.8km. NNW of Kilninver. The dun itself is some 19.8m. by 10.7m. within a substantial wall. Much degraded. Defensive walling in two further arcs on the SW.

FORT, Losgann Larnach, 2.5km. W. Triangular summit of Beinn Mhór protected by precipitous cliffs except on SE where a stone wall gave added defence and a gully afforded access.

STANDING STONES, 300m. W of Duachy Farm. Three stones in NNW–SSE alignment, 2.8m., 1.9m. and 2.2m. high respectively. A fourth stone, originally of similar size, survives as a stump 38m. E of line.

TOWNSHIP, Tigh-cuil, 530m. W of Barnacarry Farm. Roofless ruins standing to eaves height and gable-ended; most buildings date from 1790 when the earlier township was split into more dispersed units. Two principal structures combined byre and dwelling in long rectangular units; their rubble walls retain slots for cruck-framed roofs. Visible signs of rig-cultivation. Abandoned late C19.

KINTRAW

Farm, bridge and prehistoric site at the head of Loch Craignish.

KINTRAW FARM, between the A816 and the loch shore. Early C19 and later. Two-storeyed, three-bay house with seaward SW prospect. Three gabled attic dormers and a central gabled porch. Twin-gabled double pile developed to NE. Single-storey wings.

KINTRAW BRIDGE. C18(?). High rubble arch of slab voussoirs carries the A816 across a deep gorge in a 6m. span. Between tall, gently battered buttresses on the N and S, the bridge's superstructure is marked by a rudely cut, pediment-angled moulding. Barrel-vaulted passage on s.

CAIRNS, 200m. SSE of Kintraw, at the W end of the Bealach Mór through which the road N from Kilmartin passes. Two adjacent cairns, the larger, rebuilt, 15.5m. in diameter, the smaller, to SW, 7.3m. Both have lost almost all their kerbstones. Between the two is a re-erected STANDING STONE, *c.* 4m. high, aligned NNE–SSW.

KIRN

1877

A suburb of Dunoon lying at the N end of the East Bay. Only an abandoned pier suggests some former independent existence.

KIRN PARISH CHURCH, Kirn Brae and Marine Parade. Formerly St Andrew's Church. Superbly sited; solidly architectonic Romanesque Revival by *Peter MacGregor Chalmers*, 1906–7. Built in red sandstone from Corrie on Arran. Located on a sloping gushet site by the esplanade, the traditional W–E alignment permits additional low-level accommodation under an equally traditional E end, formed by a large semicircular chancel and two smaller flanking apses. The extra height dramatizes the mass of these three half-cylinders, each roofed from differing eaves levels with a slated half-cone set against the nave or aisle gable or, in the case of the SE apse, the S transept wall. At the higher side of the site, placed against the S nave wall only a short distance E of the W gable, is a tall, exquisitely simple tower, subtly intaken at each of its four stages, with coupled round-arch belfry openings in the topmost stage and a steep, slated pyramid roof. All windows and doors have single semicircular arches. Only a few, at the base of the tower or in the W gable, have moulded reveals and engaged shafts, their capitals scalloped or carved with foliated or Celtic ornament. Reverence is the prize won by such simplicity and restraint.

The church is entered from beneath the tower at the rear of the nave. Inside, it is red sandstone, square-snecked, with here and there biblical texts carved in the stonework. Arch-braced trusses, the curve of the bracing matching that of the chevron-moulded chancel arch, define the nave's six-and-a-half-bay length. Spherical plaster vault over the chancel. The aisle lies N, screened by five round arches on circular piers; at its E end, through another round arch, the baptistery apse. In the S transept, two arches wide, the choir, its apse cleverly accommodating a stone turnpike stair to the vestry and stores below. Most piers have multi-scalloped capitals, but those near the E end are more decorative, notably the last of the aisle piers in which a serpent, birds and a dog are intertwined with Celtic lacing. The chancel is furnished in oak: SEATING for six elders on each side of the minister's chair rings the apse round a COMMUNION TABLE of three round-arches. – Panelled oak PULPIT carved with various symbols and set on an octagonal, heavily moulded stone base. – Stone FONT in baptistery apse;

an octagonal bowl curved onto a fluted stalk and base. – STAINED GLASS warms and enriches throughout. Chancel: central window, the Crucifixion commemorating the fallen of World War I, with the Resurrection and Ascension in windows l. and r.; all three by the same artist, *c.* 1922. Also, St Andrew, with the high-cheekboned countenance favoured by *Gordon Webster*, 1956. – s wall: close to the choir, a memorial window to Mary Isobel Macfarlane †1988, by *T. Macfarlane*, 1989; a strangely naïve, even sentimental, depiction of a mourning woman among leaves and flowers clasping a pink heart; next to it, a crowned figure holding a lyre, by *Gordon Webster*, 1964, and, in the small porch window under the tower, Christ portrayed by the same artist, 1959, accompanied by the promise that 'The Lord shall preserve thy going out and thy coming in ...' – A boldly variegated composition of Faith, Hope and Charity, surmounted by a red- and green-robed scribe, perhaps Timothy, fills the w gable window. – N wall, w end, a somewhat fuzzy Good Shepherd surrounded by sheep under a cluster of scrapbook angels. – Baptistery apse: below the Star of David, a blue-robed Mary and the infant Christ, by *Webster* again: a memorial to the church's designer.

Former KIRN PARISH CHURCH, Hunter Street. Dated 1858. Built as a Chapel of Ease. E gable front with ill-fitting porch and a buttressed SE belfry without a bell. Abandoned.

Former ST MARGARET'S CHURCH, Hunter Street. Built as the United Presbyterian Church, 1858–9; gallery added, 1865–7. Nave and hall, added 1879, in unimaginative Gothic. Pointed-arch entrance between lancets in bargeboarded W gable. Stair to gallery in plain half-round SW tower, the ungainly rump of a circular steeple. Segmental arch-bracing to church roof trusses. Now in use as a Parish Centre.

KIRN PRIMARY SCHOOL, on Park Road. By a 'Mr *Gibson*', architect, 1880–1; a long, hip-gabled classroom block with a ridge belfry and a schoolhouse W wing. Extended 1936 and further enlarged by ten dreary roughcast classrooms in 1956–8, by *Argyll County Council*.

DESCRIPTION

Kirn's PIER has vanished. A ruinous jetty, 1823, crumbles into the sea; but of the L-plan pier of 1845–6, nothing. The jaunty twin-towered Pier Buildings, designed by *Henry E. Clifford*, 1895, have also gone. Across the road, the QUEEN'S HOTEL, 1905, *Boston, Menzies & Morton*, puts a brave but strained face on things. Outside, *fin-de-siècle* Tudor, dowdy and disfigured, but with a cocky, coolie-hatted corner carried on carved console heads; inside, a pair of glazed doors, patterned with Art Nouveau grids and roses. N of the pier, mid-C19 shops and flats face the firth across the ESPLANADE, 1893. ALEXANDRA PLACE, rubble with stop-chamfered windows and attic bays, reaches three storeys. So, too, does BROUGHALLAN GARDENS, *c.* 1905, an altogether more urbane tenement in red sandstone ashlar accented with finialled semi-cones over full-height bows. FOUNTAIN QUAY, roughcast sheltered housing by *Boys Jarvis Partnership*, 1987, keeps the scale up but compromises with a series of gablet projections from a mock-mansard roof. Behind Kirn Parish Church (*see* above), less distinguished flatted and terraced housing climbs up KIRN BRAE, but the high tenement wall of ARGYLL TERRACE, late C19, sixteen canted bays long, is impressively urban. With its ageing villas and two tired churches (*see* above), HUNTER STREET is decidedly suburban. Idiosyncrasy apart, the street lacks the architecture to match its strong E–W linearity. At its N end, DUNOON HOSTEL, by *The National Building Agency*, 1967–8, two CLASP-built blocks of exposed aggregate concrete panelling with monopitch rooflights. Further w and more peripheral, the KIRN & HUNTER'S QUAY BOWLING CLUB, late C19(?), on Ardenslate Road is a prim, piend-roofed pavilion with a glazed, eight-bay Roman Doric veranda placed perfectly to catch the sun across the green. Next door, No. 16 reiterates the same classical elegance in a pillared semicircular porch.

LISMORE

A narrow island, 15.5km. long, lying between Loch Linnhe and the Lynn of Lorn. Settlement is scattered, though a few houses cluster around the pier at Achnacroish and the church at Clachan. Now dependent largely on sheep-farming and the occasional holidaymaker, life on Lismore can trace an ancient lineage stemming mutually from Gaelic culture and the Celtic church. Unexpectedly, there is, too, an industrial past for, throughout the C19, limestone was quarried and burnt at An Sàilean, Port Kilcheran and Port Ramsay before being shipped to the mainland.

CATHEDRAL OF ST MOLUAG AND PARISH CHURCH, Clachan. The island's principal architectural monument, its white-walled country kirk charm conceals the lingering evidence of grander distinction. Whatever the truth of a traditional association with the C6 Irish saint Moluag, by the early C13, not long after the creation of the diocese of Argyll, Lismore found itself the episcopal centre of the new see. A cathedral church was begun but work proceeded slowly. Not surprisingly in such a relatively remote and impoverished place, realizing such an ambitious project proved difficult. Finance was a recurring concern. In 1411 an appeal to the Pope brought revenue aid for furnishings and repair work. A century later, and not for the first time, there were calls for a move to the mainland. Gradually ecclesiastical polity weakened, and Lismore seems to have sunk into parochial slumber. Roused to renewed life by the Reformation, the church adapted to different liturgical needs. While the cathedral nave fell into ruins, the chancel alone served as a place of worship. But maintenance still proved a problem and in 1679 the building was 'altogether without a roof' (Carmichael, 1948). In 1749, a major reconstruction programme restored the church's fortunes. Since then, repeatedly repaired and altered, it has continued to house the local congregation.

The surviving slated, gable-ended oblong is precisely orientated W–E, at first glance the characteristic mid-C18 Scottish kirk. The walls of its three-bay plan, still buttressed on the S side, are, however, largely those of the late C13 or early C14 choir of the cathedral. Only the W wall is of more recent date, its lower stages associated with a medieval pulpitum, its gable a consequence of C18 changes. Some distance beyond this W gable, excavation has revealed the foundations of the aisleless nave, probably C14, which continued the line of these walls some 20m. to a point which now lies in glebe land beyond the churchyard boundary wall. Here the plan of a square W tower, tusked into the stonework of the nave gable at some late medieval date, has been revealed. Excavations on the N side of the choir close to its E end, prompted by the presence of a blocked medieval doorway and an aumbry recess on the outside face of the wall, suggest that a small chapel may have existed here.

The church owes its present form to three phases of reconstruction and restoration. The first of these, 1749, lowered the choir, truncated the offset buttresses along the S wall and at the angles of the E gable, and blocked the N door. Three round-arched windows were also inserted between the S buttresses, perhaps superseding medieval openings. Certain early features were retained, amongst them the double-splayed plinth (now beneath the graveyard turf) and a hooded round-arched doorway in the S wall. The main entrance was through another round-arched door in the W gable. Above this were two rectangular windows and a birdcage belfry. The internal layout would then have focused on the pulpit at the centre of the S wall with galleries on the W, reached by an internal stair, and on the N and E, reached by a forestair on the E gable. In 1900, following proposals prepared by an unknown architect in 1894, the interior was reorientated towards the W end, a move complemented by the creation of a small castellated E porch which incorporated some of the walling of the C18 forestair, and a lean-to vestry and boiler house attached to the W gable. At the same time the belfry was transferred to the W gable and three round-arched N windows formed to match those opposite. A vertically panelled E gallery, supported by two slender cast-iron columns and reached by an internal NE staircase, and a boarded timber roof on five mock-medieval hammer-beam trusses were installed. – PULPIT. Octagonal pitch-pine box. – STAINED GLASS in the three S windows: Christ in a pale encounter with two fishermen, by *Roland Mitton*, 1987; a bolder red-robed Christ as 'The Good Shepherd' and the female figure of 'Dorcas' with a young boy and child, both erected 1911. – E gallery windows, dedicated to Beatrice Boswall †1926, St Moluag and St Columba, depicted with attractive if anachronistic flavour of Art Nouveau verticality; by *Mary I. Wood*, 1928. – But the church's most precious treasures are those examples of ARCHITECTURAL CARVING which have survived from medieval times and which owe their preserved state to a third phase of refurbishment carried out by *Ian G. Lindsay* in 1956. During this work plaster was removed to uncover the stonework of the N and S doorways and the pulpitum arch in the W gable, and from the three round arches of the sedilia and single-pointed arch of the piscina which are recessed into the S wall. – Three SLABS, Iona school, C14–C15, are kept in the church; two are decorated with tau-headed staves.

In the CHURCHYARD, its limits determined in 1760, are several tapered and parallel-sided SLABS varying in date from C14 to C16. – TOMB-CHEST lid, early C16, particularly fine carving of a claymore; above its quillons a lion and a griffin lose their tails in a wealth of foliage filling the space enclosed by a dog-tooth border. – Built into the E wall are a number of framed, white marble TABLETS including one commemorating James MacGregor of Correctled †1759, and his wife Marjory †1780, the MOTHER OF / 22 CHILDREN TWELVE OF WHOM / ARE INTERRED IN THIS PLACE. – Among many tombs, a crowstepped wall with three round-arched recesses, in two of which are white marble memorial TABLETS, one recording the death of Duncan McColl †1878. – Outside the churchyard, 11m. SE, a CROSS-BASE, perhaps still in its original location.

LISMORE MANSE, Clachan. The oldest part of the double-pile fabric, dating from *c.* 1750, lies at the rear and was built using stones taken from the ruined nave of the nearby Cathedral. The three-bay house seen from the road is the 'large addition' (*NSA*, 1841) carried out by the Oban builder-architect *Andrew Elliot*, 1840–1. Skew gables with moulded skewputts. Gabled eaves dormers and porch, dated 1840.

Former UNITED SECESSION CHURCH, Baligrundle. Built 1845. Harled, gable-ended hall church lit by three tall square-headed windows on each side. Birdcage belfry on NE gable. Vestry added off-centre on NE gable. Single-storey manse in line to SW. The church remained in use until 1970 and now functions as a studio.

ACHADUN CASTLE, 300m. E of Bernera Bay. Under construction at the end of the C13, Achadun was created as the fortified residence of the bishops of Argyll, and so it remained until the early C16 when Bishop Hamilton moved the episcopal seat to Saddell Castle (q.v.). Nearly five subsequent centuries of decay have reduced it to a few stretches of crumbling, cracking masonry.

A largely ruinous curtain-wall barely succeeds in defining a square plan set across a rocky ridge running NE–SW above the sheltered anchorage of Achadun Bay. The SW and SE walls have entirely collapsed but on the NE and NW sides the stonework, originally harled, still stands to an irregular skyline, here and there reaching wallhead height. An entrance, now indeterminately arched, penetrates the NE curtain; there is a draw-bar slot in the NW ingo and opposite this a straight-flight mural stair which led to the parapet-walk. Beyond the doorway lies the cobbled yard, also accessible through the NE wall where a second entrance was reached across some form of bridge latterly supported by a stone-built forework. Filling one side of the castle court was the SE range of accommodation. Little remains of the transverse wall which separated this from the yard, but at ground-floor level a window and doorway do survive at its NE end. The nature of the accommodation at this level is unknown; kitchens and cellarage seem probable but there is no evidence of sub-dividing walls or of vaulting. A fragmentary scarcement, again at the NE end of the inner wall, suggests that the first floor may have been joisted. At this upper level, doubtless the location of the hall, almost nothing remains to determine layout, lighting or construction; the only discernible feature is a slab-lintelled mural passage in the NE gable which, lit by a small window with splayed jambs, evidently led to a garderobe set not far distant from the castle's E corner. Two more garderobe chambers exist at this level, oddly isolated in the NW curtain. They discharge into the re-entrant angle formed by a thickening of the walling, a short distance NE of the entrance forework. They were perhaps reached by some form of gallery linked to a second, probably timber-framed, range of accommodation which rose against the NE wall, as the survival of two small window embrasures indicates.

BACHUIL HOUSE, Clachan. c18. White, two-storey, three-bay house. The drawing room was the island's Baptist Chapel from 1860 until 1890. What is believed to be St Moluag's crozier, the *bachull mór*, is held here by its hereditary keepers, the Livingstone family.

BALNAGOWN MILL. Ruined rubble corn mill centrally situated on the island 1km. NNE of Achnacroish pier.

CAMERON MONUMENT, 800m. NE of Achnacroish pier. Tall granite Celtic cross on stepped base, perched above the Lynn of Lorn. Inscription commemorates Waverley Arthur Cameron of the *Oban Times* †1891.

CASTLE COEFFIN, 800m. WNW of Clachan. Strategically sited by the MacDougalls of Lorn on a raised promontory overlooking Loch Linnhe. Typological analysis has suggested a C13 date, though the earliest documentary mention is in 1469–70. But the unevenness of the topography, the very ruinous condition of the masonry and the encroachment of vegetation make detailed interpretation difficult. The original building, of local rubble with pinnings and beach boulders, appears to have been an oblong hall-house aligned NE–SW and six stands of stonework rising from a higher level can be related to this simple plan. These include the E corner, but the curving N corner, the splayed W face and the irregular fragments of walling forming a bailey at lower level around the castle's E corner all belong to a late medieval reconstruction. The bailey probably had three distinct levels, possibly enclosed or perhaps only defensible platforms; in any event the arrangement was contrived to protect the principal NE entrance to the hall-house. Additional doorways, detectable by draw-slot recesses and dressed ingoes, in the SW and NW walls, the former leading to the end of the promontory, the latter now puzzlingly inaccessible. Signs of window embrasures are all but non-existent. A mural stair evidently rose from ground- to first-floor level in the N corner. But beyond these few vestigial features all is as conjectural as the castle's traditional association with the Norse prince, Caifean.

KILCHERAN HOUSE, 3.5km. SW of Achnacroish. A pleasant grouping of white-walled, slated buildings. The arrangement is linear with two three-bay, two-storey-and-attic houses, the narrow gap between filled by a lower gable-ended building set at right angles. The S house, late C18, came first. In 1803 it became a Roman Catholic seminary, and a decade or so later work was begun to provide more accommodation. Though slightly larger, the N house repeats the pattern of its predecessor, while the single-storey meat in the sandwich, evidently intended as a chapel, has a projecting SE gable with a birdcage belfry, and a slate-roofed canted bay window, evidently later, like the porches protecting the front doors of each house. In 1828 the seminary was transferred to Aquhorthies and then to Blairs; Kilcheran then reverted to residential use, except for a brief period, 1840–5, when a United Secession congregation repaired and occupied the chapel.

LIME-KILNS, Port Kilcheran. Founded by Bishop John Chisholm in 1804, at the same time as the Seminary at Kilcheran was established, the industry seems to have lasted little more than twenty years. Two main structures. One is a harled rubble kiln, almost cubic in dimensions, with crude arch openings on the N and E. The other, rectangular with splayed NE and SE corners, has two barrel-vaulted stores on the W and a double kiln on the E, still accessible above by a ramp from higher ground to the N.

LIME-KILNS and WORKERS' COTTAGES, An Sâilean, on the W coast of the island, 1.6km. W of Achnacroish. Early C19. Two pairs of rubble-built kilns at the base of a 50m.-high limestone cliff. A few quarry-workers' cottages. One free-standing unit, originally of two single-room dwellings, shows evidence of cruck-slots.

LIME-KILNS and WORKERS' COTTAGES, Port Ramsay. The best-preserved example of Lismore's early C19 industrial settlements. A row of nine two-roomed cottages runs SW–NE by the water's edge; re-inhabited as holiday homes, they retain their white-walled, small-windowed charm beneath slated roofs. Similar pairs of dwellings lie separate at the SW and NE ends of the row. The limestone quarries and a pair of rubble kilns lie further NE, while across the bay at the Fennacrochan quarries is another kiln.

LIGHTHOUSE on Eilean Musdile off the SW tip of Lismore. Built 1833 by Inverness contractor, *James Smith*, to the design of engineer, *Robert Stevenson*. White tubular tower and keepers' houses symmetrically arranged around a protected yard, the wall of which bows around the seaward base of the tower. The limewashed, coursed rubble tower, housing a helical stair, rises to a railed parapet walk and lantern 31.4m. above high-water mark. Glazing bars to the sixteen-sided light with cast-iron grips shaped as dolphins. The two houses and flanking byres and privies have flat roofs with beautifully finished leadwork. A substantial rubble BRIDGE, C19, spans the narrow piece of water that divides the island in a single segmental arch. Unmanned since 1965.

THE OLD SCHOOLHOUSE, 750m. NE of Clachan. Mid C19. Symmetrical two-classroom block with schoolmaster's house returning on NE gable to form an L-plan. Built in square-snecked rubble with chamfered dressings. Attractive trefoil window in school porch gable.

6 BROCH (Tirefour Castle), 900m. SE of Clachan. Rightly regarded as 'one of the best preserved prehistoric monuments' (RCAHMS, 1975) in Argyll. Prominently sited on the E side of the island, the broch's ring of masonry, which incorporates some very large boulders, still reaches a height of more than 3m. The internal diameter is 12.2m. and the thickness of the dry-stone walling almost 5m. Facing courses are well preserved on the battered outer circumference but much less well within; nevertheless, a scarcement is detectable at 2.5m. above the original floor level. Stretches of intra-mural gallery roofed with large lintel slabs exist on the NW and E sides of the ring, but elsewhere this probably continuous circuit, like the floor of the central court, has been overlaid with rubble debris. The WSW entrance is clear but shows no sign of door checks, draw-bar slots or guard chamber.

BROCH, An Dùn, Loch Fiart, 5.2km. SW of Achnacroish. Ridge-top rubble remains above the E shore of the loch. The enclosed area is *c.* 13m. in dia. but almost nothing of the original facing work can be seen. On the W, however, there are vestiges of the inner and outer faces and a short stretch of a lintelled mural gallery which supports the identification of this overgrown ruin as a broch.

CAIRN, Barr Mór, 1km. W of Kilcheran House. Small but with an almost complete ring of kerb stones. Reconstructed 1933.

CAIRN, Druim an Uinnsinn, 700m. N of Kilcheran House. Much denuded circular cairn, 13.5m. in dia., in which three cists can be found.

DUN, Dùn Chrùban, 100m. S of Dalnarrow Farm at the S end of the island. A small oval enclosure protected by cliff faces on the N and E and by a dry-stone wall up to 3.6m. thick forming an arc from NW to S. The NW and W stretches of this wall are exceptionally well preserved and stand in a coursed outer face to 3.4m. Vestiges of outer walls survive to the W and S.

DUN, Sean Dùn, 1.2km. SW of Achnacroish. A circular dun, now severely robbed, but strongly sited above cliffs on the S and E. SW entrance protected by outer wall at the base of the knoll, standing to five courses of outer facing stones on the NW.

LOCH RIDDON

A narrow sea-loch running N–S from the mouth of the River Ruel to the Kyles of Bute. Also known as Loch Ruel.

BURIAL ENCLOSURE, 600m. NW of Ormidale House. Mid C19(?). Reconstructed rubble-walled rectangle. Segmental rise on all four walls. Stone balls at corners and at gated opening. Grey granite CROSS. White marble memorial TABLETS in sandstone frames; the oldest commemorate John Campbell of Ormidale †1842, and his widow, Catherine †1843.

CHAPEL, on the hillside, 400m. E above Fearnoch Farm. Rubble walls scarcely 1m. high define the simple rectangular plan of a small chapel of unknown date.

CASTLE, Eilean Dearg. Barely distinguishable rubble remains and sandstone fragments indicate the formerly fortified nature of this small island close to the E shore of the loch. These include a W tower, late C14 or early C15; a NW chapel(?) of uncertain date; and a SE hall range, probably late C15 or early C16. In 1685 the rebellious 9th Earl of Argyll stocked the castle with military supplies and gunpowder, a course of action which, so to say, back-fired when government troops blew up his arsenal.

ORMIDALE HOUSE, W of A8003, 2.5km. S of Clachan of Glendaruel. An asymmetrical accumulation of C19 gables forms the NE front, a trace of the earlier Georgian mansion evident r. C18 rubble OFFICES survive. An obelisk SUNDIAL, 2.8m. high including a plinth and ball finial both probably of modern date, is located in the sunken garden. The shaft is carved with the usual geometrical forms of circles, hearts and crosses, and bears the dates 1719 and 1830. The facets of the central block are cut with circles, triangles and incised dials, which also appear on the obelisk. Simple rubble GATELODGES by *John Honeyman*, 1878–9.

ORMIDALE LODGE (Craig Lodge) on the W shore, 3km. S of Lochead. Mid-C19, L-plan lochside house, originally a hotel, gabled with four storeys and a double-height canted bay to the loch. In the NE re-entrant, a cylindrical stair tower with witch's hat roof. Round-arch door in gabled porch. Single-storey outbuildings with harled flat-roofed dormers wrap around a service yard on the landward side. Close to the house is ORMIDALE PIER, 1856, a robust rubble construction with an inset ramp formed from stepped rubble slabs. This was as far as steamers could come from the Kyles of Bute for, immediately to the N, the depth of the loch reduces quickly to tidal flats around the mouth of the River Ruel.

LOCHAWE

Late C19 railway halt at N end of Loch Awe with station, pier, hotel and church. Little more in the late C20.

ST CONAN'S KIRK. A unique, quirky little church, sited between the Dalmally–Oban road and the N shore of Loch Awe. Built in rough-tooled polygonal and square-snecked Cruachan granite rubble with ochre sandstone dressings to the designs of amateur architect *Walter Douglas Campbell*, brother of the 1st Lord Blythswood. Eclectic Romanesque Revival spiced with Gothic tracery, a Saxon tower and a knobbly, all-but-Baronial ebullience in the detail. Modest in scale though not in architectural ambition, the complex accumulation of gables, apses, buttresses and towers is the result of two phases of building. At first Campbell was content with a small cruciform church, 1881–6, its gabled orthodoxy

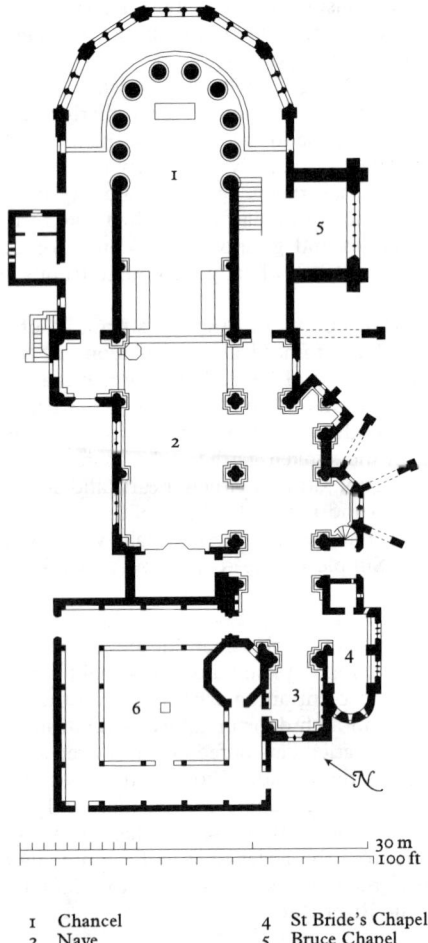

1	Chancel	4	St Bride's Chapel
2	Nave	5	Bruce Chapel
3	St Conval's Chapel	6	Cloister garth

Lochawe, St Conan's Kirk

simply but strongly accented by a parapeted tower over the N porch. Two decades later, however, in 1907, he initiated a programme of aggrandizement which outlasted his death in 1914 and that of his sister, Helen Campbell, who continued her brother's dream until 1927. Building was finally completed only in 1930. This second, extended period of construction elongated the earlier chancel, closing it on the E with a columned semicircular apse wrapped in a five-sided ambulatory, added a cloister garth on the W and opened the original two-bay nave S into a new St Columba's Aisle, much modelled by adherent chapels, buttressing and towers packed together above the loch. The church is thus substantially a C20 creation.

LOCHAWE

The exterior of the 1880s building remains visible in the square N tower, the traceried wheel window in the W gable and in the saddleback form of the nave roof. Originally slated, this roof is now sheeted in lead, while the W gable has lost its crowsteps; both changes part of the prolonged second phase of construction. The tower itself, which continues to mark the main entrance to the church, is largely unaltered: pointed-arch W doorway, narrow pointed-arch N window lighting the porch and, at high level, a small vesica opening on the W; overall, a steeply pitched, still-slated pyramid roof rises from a bellcast eaves to a dolphin-topped ironwork weather-vane. Otherwise, the N wall of the church is C20. W of the tower, two round-arch openings with reticulated Gothic tracery sit below a plain parapet. To the E, a two-storey vestry block projects from the ambulatory wall, its parapet castellated over a corbelled stringcourse. A similar parapet continues around the apsidal E end, each of its five faces generously lit by three close-set, round-arch windows inset with trefoil cusping. Here the lie of the land, banking steeply to the lochside, permitted the creation of a crypt below the chancel; and this extra height coupled with the more complex massing of the S front, designed by *Walter Campbell* but realized only during the period of his sister's superintendence of the work, 1918–27, greatly dramatizes the architectural impact of this side of the church.

Projecting from the S ambulatory, which is known as St Fillan's Aisle, is the Bruce Chapel, a rectangular parapeted box with angle buttresses and a broad, pointed-arch, six-light S window with splendid dagger tracery, a late C15 survival relocated from St Mary's Parish Church, South Leith, but here incorporated 'inside out'. A single flying buttress, aligned with the E wall of the original church's S transept and introduced to resist the downhill thrust of the later much-elaborated structure, locks itself into the terraced landscape between the Bruce Chapel and a small saddleback tower set obliquely against the S wall of the transept. On the SE face of this craggy tower, atop a central buttress and flanked by two round-arch windows similar to those that light the apse, is the figure of St Conan, patron saint of Lorn, sculpted by *Alexander Carrick*. W of this the S wall takes the form of a tall canted bay with elongated gargoyle spouts at the parapet and a partially carved frieze of owl heads. In a dramatic splay of structural support, three half-arch flying buttresses have been thrown out onto the terrace below from diagonal buttresses blunting the arrises of the bay. Next, projecting from the S aisle, come two more towers: the first, small and square, with blind cusped lights on the upper stage below a steep stone pyramid, almost an obelisk; the second, tallest of all, also square but with a plain parapet on corbel courses, a strange replication of the Saxon tower at Monkwearmouth, County Durham, complete with simulated framing members, oddly shaped windows and fern-like patterning of the stonework. Between the two, below a linking balcony, is a jagged-arched Norman doorway with concentric dogtooth and chevron mouldings springing fom scalloped capitals.

The high Saxon tower seems to gather around it all the complexities of the s elevation, resolving their variety in its vertical pull. But it also has a more specific 'little church' relationship to the apsidal form of St Bride's Chapel which, placed against the w end of the s aisle in a reversal of the liturgical orientation of the church proper, abuts it on the w. The two-bay s wall of this chapel rises to a deep ashlar sandstone parapet, twice striped with bold but plain horizontal granite mouldings and corbelled from the rubble below in a portcullis-like fringe of small round arches with trefoil drops. Under its w gable a castellated apse curves against the wall of a second chapel, St Conval's, which like its neighbour also opens into the s or St Columba's Aisle. This smaller, squarer chapel terminates in a w gable lit by a narrow pointed-arch window with stellar tracery. Below the window, a memorial TABLET with the initials of Campbell and his sister and the carved image of the Lorn lymphad or galley. At high level, located around the apse of St Bride's Chapel, are three whimsical gargoyles, representing a dog in pursuit of two hares, the work of *William Bonnington*. Both chapels have saddleback roofs which lie parallel to each other and to those of the s aisle and nave; a unifying horizontality complementary to the vertical thrust of the Saxon tower. All roofs are leaded.

Behind St Conval's Chapel lies the Cloister Garth tucked against the w end of the nave. The plan is square, enclosed by rubble walls which on the outside are plain, save for a run of regularly spaced, strangely carved stones projecting below the parapet cope, each identically shaped with crudely bovine allusion. At the e end of the N wall a pointed-arch portal set below a gable with blind vesica inset and ball finial leads along the e side of the cloister court to reach the s aisle through the deep reveals of a richly carved Norman doorway. In this same re-entrant corner an octagonal tower with small castellated gables on each parapet face blocks the cloister walk return from the w; now an empty shell, it formerly stood detached from the first church building, housing the bellows for its pipe organ. Along the inside face of the outer rubble walls and rising from a low rubble wall dividing the cloister walk from the garth itself, square wooden pillars with block capitals carry hefty oak eaves beams, the timber for these members, and for some of the pitched roof construction which they support over the walkways, coming from the battleships *Caledonia* and *Duke of Wellington*. Blind arcading fills the bays against the outer wall. Most is rough-cut, without ornament; those few bays which are carved are medieval in origin, brought to St Conan's as exemplars from the Church of St Conval, Inchinnan, on the Campbells of Blythswood estate in Renfrewshire. Leaded roofs decoratively worked with coiling grape-laden vines by *Bonnington*.

While the roof timbers over the cloister walks are only lightly stained, those in the church are dark; though the construction is exposed, it remains difficult to discern in the gloom. Over nave and chancel, collar-braced trusses. Over St Columba's Aisle, arch-braced trusses on corbel-stones. Small rooflights, some dormered, intensify the upper darkness.

Chunky granite masonry prevails throughout the interior. The effect is severe but not grim, for light washing through the chancel arcade from the E can often flood the heart of the church with a lustral brightness. Moreover, the use of sandstone for much of the architectural ornament helps mitigate the hard austerity of the walls. Around the chancel apse, ten granite block columns carry high stilted arches in a characteristically Romanesque arrangement. Here the entire upper structure, from multi-scalloped capitals to nailhead frieze at the wallhead, is sandstone. The same material clearly defines the semicircular wall arches which, down each side of the church, measure out the five bays of its overall length; two in the chancel, one at the crossing, and two in the nave. Though their capitals are plain, the arches are variously carved on the extrados with simple, strongly cut Romanesque motifs. Elsewhere, and particularly in St Columba's Aisle to the s, the architecture maintains this somewhat louche addiction to granite mass, relieved by the relative refinement of sandstone mouldings.

In two places the balance of materials tilts. In the Crypt, which is entered by a straight flight of stairs descending from St Fillan's Aisle, everything is granite: a Piranesi-like cavern of grotesquely robust, roughly tooled masonry arching across the darkness under the concrete floor of the apse above. But, in the two chapels which cling to the sw end of St Columba's Aisle, sandstone dominates, defining the stylistic lineaments of a distinct if unsophisticated historicism. St Bride's Chapel, which contains the tomb of the 4th Lord Blythswood, is Early Norman in form and detail, though its low E door is Saxon, appropriately enough as it opens to a small chamber (which Campbell romantically referred to as 'St Bride's Cell') at the base of the church's Saxon tower. St Conval's Chapel, built over the burial vault of Walter and Helen Campbell, is Early Decorated. w window based on the precedent of tracery from the choir-aisle of Iona Abbey, weathered FRAGMENTS of which are set into a recess in St Columba's Aisle. Three cusped king-post trusses on pointed-arch bracing. On the N and S walls, blind pointed-arch arcading below tablet-flower panelling; separating these, on each side of the chapel, inscribed stringcourses supported on winged cherubs:

> THE LORD SPAKE SAYING LET THEM MAKE ME /
> A SANCTUARY THAT I MAY DWELL AMONG THEM

The church's furnishings vary in stylistic provenance and quality. In the apsidal sanctuary, an oak COMMUNION TABLE, far from austere enough for its position. – Four remarkable CHAIRS, their sides carved in sweeping Art Nouveau curves flaring from the mouths of dolphins, may be Venetian in origin. – Dark CHOIR STALLS of Spanish chestnut set against the N and S walls of the chancel; late C19, canopied and crocketed

Gothic with back panels carved to show the gilded arms of local landowning families. – Box PULPIT on squat, spun barley-sugar columns sits in the NE corner of the crossing; probably the 'octagonal reading-desk' described by *The Oban Times* at the opening of the first church in 1883. – At the E end of the nave, a tall timber ORGAN SCREEN by *Walter Campbell*: a lattice of Celtic interlacing, knots and ribbonwork with dado panels depicting attenuated bird-like creatures. – Ironwork SCREENS to all three memorial Chapels, that to St Conval's crested with the patrons' initials, WDC and HDC, flanking a heart. – Commemorative sculpture includes the EFFIGY of King Robert the Bruce in the Bruce Chapel, a larger-than-life-size representation in stained timber with face and hands in alabaster, by *Alexander Carrick*, and the sandstone SARCOPHAGUS in St Conval's Chapel which bears the kilted stone figure of Walter Campbell. – In the St Columba's Aisle, a MEMORIAL to Ian Alastair Campbell †1899, a wall-mounted white marble oval in a dark drapery-laden wreath. – At the crossing, opposite the pulpit, a coroneted, white marble BUST of the young Queen Victoria, by *H. R. H. Princess Louise*(?), perches on a sandstone shaft. – STAINED GLASS. Mostly painted work; death and resurrection themes in pale yellows, greys and reds. – In the N porch, an angel confronting a cloaked figure outside the tomb; opposite, in the S transept, an angelic scribe and the Revelation text 'I heard a voice from heaven saying unto me, Write, ...' – More winged figures, attired in armour, in the three-light McCorquodale window, now in St Fillan's Aisle but originally on the N side of the 1880s building, and in a small window in St Columba's Aisle where green-scaled dragons succumb to St Michael's sword; the latter by *H. R. H. Princess Louise*, 1893, also reset from the original church. Much less fearsome, the pink-cheeked putti filling the petal-like tracery of the W gable rose; sunburst cherubs from a Victorian scrapbook designed and painted by *Helen Campbell*.

Regrettably the landscape setting of the church is in poor repair. The crowstepped, gabled GATE-LODGE survives with its leaded peak-roofed summer-house, but a STONE CIRCLE, contrived to lend a spurious antiquity to the approach, is in disarray. Along the S side of the church, overlooking the loch, much of the stonework of the SUNDIAL TERRACE is dislodged and dangerous. From the Norman portal at the centre of the S Aisle steps drop to a small square area and then to the main terrace which is semicircular in plan. At the centre, the SUNDIAL, a rough granite shaft, 1900, commemorating Caroline Agnes Campbell of Blythswood, with a bronze gnomon inscribed to record its repositioning in 1992. Cut into the seven raised coping stones of the terrace's curving parapet are the words THY / SUN / SHALL / NO / MORE / GO / DOWN. On each side, stairs descend further to ruinous terracing and a long stretch of salvaged sandstone balustrading running W along St Modan's Walk. On a steep knoll NW of the Cloister Garth a tall Celtic CROSS, carved with leafy interlacing on the faces and knotwork around the cross-head bosses, also honours 'the loved memory' of Walter Campbell's mother, Caroline Agnes (1814–97).

CARRAIG THURA. Baronial mansion, by *George P. K. Young*, 1904, now a nursing home. Crowstepping and corbelled corner turrets with witches' hat roofs. The s front overlooking the loch has a wide canted bay corbelled back at the first floor to a two-storey, crowstepped gable.

CRUACHAN POWER STATION, 3.8km. W of St Conan's Kirk. An engineering *tour de force* by *James Williamson & Partners*, 1959–65; the showpiece of the North of Scotland Hydro-Electric Board's Awe Project, which also included power stations at Inverawe and Nant. Hidden in the hills, a 45m.-high buttressed dam with hydraulic gates contains Cruachan Reservoir. Deep in the mountain, the Machine Hall, 91m. long by 23m. wide, a vast cavern roofed at 38m. by a segmental-arch concrete vault. Linked to the Machine Hall by an access tunnel 1.1km. long is the VISITOR CENTRE by *James Shearer & Annand*, long, low, loch-side offices, flat-roofed and a little severe.

LOCH AWE HOTEL. Vast Baronial pile overlooking the loch above its own railway station and pier. In style and purpose very much a railway hotel though built, 1880–1, to a design by *John Young* of Perth for the Earl of Breadalbane. Three storeys of granite rise from terraces, lawns and porches to a jagged skyline of crowstepped gables and dormers. SW corner marked by huge bow-fronted projection corbelled out to support a three-storeyed gable over. In the re-entrant, rising higher still, a conically-capped turret and, at first-floor level across the three bays between SW bow and SE canted bay gable, a stone balcony with cast-iron railings on massive stone brackets. Four-storey NE wing, also granite, also by Young, 1891–3. More compromising, two-storey W wing, crowstepped but roughcast, 1991.

POST OFFICE. Granite rubble house and shop, *c.* 1885, distinguished by unusual hoop bargeboarding to its three gabled eaves dormers.

ST CONAN'S TOWER. Built *c.* 1895. Hillside tower-house in gnarled granite, reaching six storeys to an onion-domed rooftop gazebo.

SCHOOL, 100m. NE of St Conan's Kirk. Built 1892. Two-storey schoolhouse and attached classroom with tripartite window and pepper-pot ridge ventilator. Converted to dwelling.

THE TIGHT LINE. Symmetrical artisan Baronial, *c.* 1881. Crowstepped gables l. and r.; arched openings at rear. Former coach-house, stables and gardeners' accommodation for Loch Awe Hotel. Now a restaurant and pub.

TOWER OF GLENSTRAE. By Edinburgh builder *John Lownie*, 1895–7. Aptly if pretentiously named sub-Baronial house. Dated 1895 in saltire panel on S wall. A turret-tower, at the NE corner, steps down in a half-gable to N staircase window. Interior of sitting room, formerly dining room, added *c.* 1905(?): high timber dado with flat Gothic panelling and Glasgow Style chimneypiece flanked by canted cupboards; rich blue tiling to fire surround. Compact well-stair with pitch-pine balusters and urn-topped newels.

LOCHGAIR

The village lies on both sides of the A83, absorbing the former fishing hamlet of Gallanach clustered around the w shore of Loch Gair. With its oblique interplay of spaces and apparently randomly sited cottages, this older part has the feel of a township. Several rehabilitated rubble structures were, indeed, originally thatched and cruck-roofed. But with well-tended gardens, lawns and trees, the look is now softer, more picturesque than rugged. Some timber buildings, converted to dwellings, once served as net stores.

BURIAL GROUND, Kilbride, close to E shore of Loch Gair. Oval enclosure defined by a C19 mortared rubble wall with N gates. Drystone rubble remains may be the 'chapel of Kilbryde' recorded 1617. Gravemarkers are late C18 or C19. An earlier HEADSTONE, commemorating Iohn Paterson †1722, 'gardinar' at Lochgair, has been carved with the tools of his craft: saw, shears and pruning-hooks(?).

LOCHGAIR CHURCH. Roughcast, three bay, skew-gabled oblong, built 1867. Renovated 1964 and again in 1980 when it was re-roofed. Ceiling at collar height over a starkly plain interior. Half-octagon box pulpit centred S between blind lancets.

ASKNISH HOUSE, 1.1km. NE of Lochgair village. Classical mansion-house, built in the 1780s by Robert Campbell of Asknish, sheriff-depute of Argyll. Elevated on a raised terrace to enjoy the prospect of the loch 250m. S, the principal S FRONT, of squared and coursed rubble blocks alternating with vertical pinnings, is three storeys high and five bays wide with a centre-piece which advances 1m. This tripartite division is marked by four giant pilasters on ashlar bases linked by a continuous string-course at first-floor level. Above Tuscan capitals, an entablature and blocking course define a strong eaves-line across the full unpedimented width of the façade. The roof is hipped with a flat deck, and panelled chimneystacks, coincident with the pilastered margins of the centrepiece, rise from the cross walls of the plan. Entry is at ground level through a central door flanked by side lights, in a frame of Doric pilasters and entablature that is a compressed echo of the façade's overall geometry. Above this, reiterating the tripartite theme in more attenuated form on the taller *piano nobile*, is a Palladian window with fluted Ionic pilasters. Over this in turn, a smaller and more cramped version of the same with a central niche set between its side lights. Plain windows in the outer bays. Windows on the harled W and E elevations are correspondingly plain, with some dummies, while pilaster quoins repeat those on the S. The N front, also harled, has a centrepiece with paired round-arched windows lighting the stair landings above ground- and first-floor levels. A small service court is enclosed by screen walls curving from the angles of the house.

The internal arrangement is similar to that at Barbreck House (q.v.), the main stair and service stair being placed alongside each other at the centre rear of the plan. Here, however,

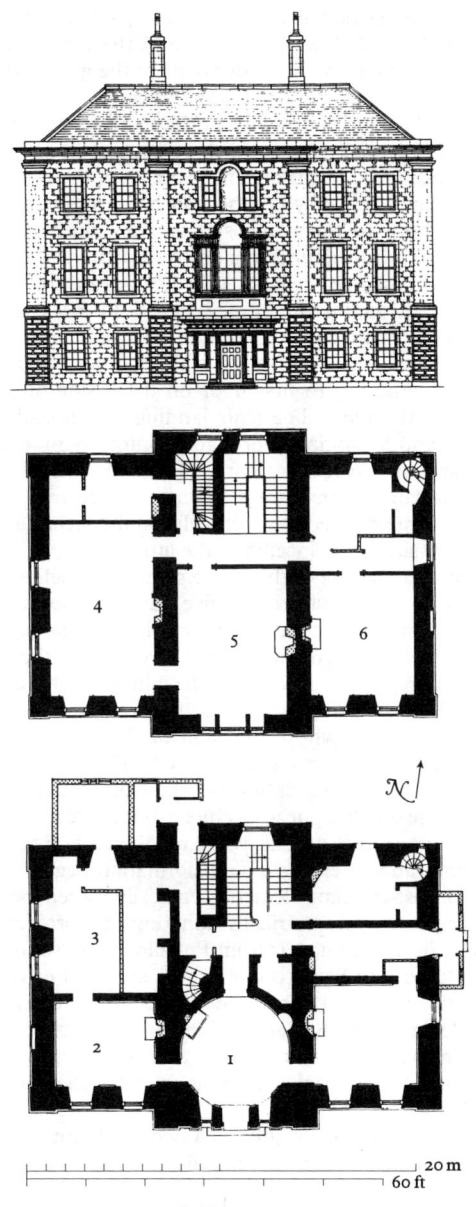

1 Lobby
2 Family dining-room
3 Kitchen
4 Dining-room
5 Drawing-room
6 Bedroom

Lochgair, Asknish House.
South elevation, ground- and first-floor plans

the stairs are reached axially through a spacious circular lobby. Panelled doors, following the curve of the lobby wall, lead l. and r. to rooms in the outer divisions of the ground-floor plan; a round-arched niche located in the NE arc is matched by a fireplace, now blocked, in the NW. The latter has a timber chimneypiece with bluebell swags which re-appear along the cornice and around the delicate concentric circles of the ceiling plasterwork. Beyond the lobby lies the stair hall, from which access is gained l. both to the rising service stair at the rear and to another stair which returns in a downward curve at the centre of the plan to basement cellars. A further private stair, rising in a circular shaft within the stonework of the NE corner of the house, is reached through a room opening r. from the stair hall. The principal scale-and-platt stair ascends axially, unlike Barbreck, returning to first floor on the E side of the central division of the plan. The stair landing and first-floor public rooms W and S (originally probably dining room and drawing room) have more elegantly figured plasterwork with friezes showing tritons, lamps, urns, swags, amorini and portrait medallions. Bedrooms are arranged symmetrically on the second floor, while servants' quarters are located in the attic.

In a field 130m. SE of the house stands an obelisk SUNDIAL, late C17, its shaft divided into five panels on each of its four faces and carved with sunken hemispheres, hearts, and other geometrical shapes. Metal gnomons are set into the S face. On the N, a saltire, the date 1695, and the initials S / D C and L / HL for Sir Duncan Campbell of Auchinbreck and his wife Lady Henrietta Lindsay whose mansion of Kenlochgair antedated Asknish. Four-step circular base, late C19(?).

LOCHGAIR HOTEL. Originating as a small inn built at Gallanach, 1855, by the Lochgilphead architect-builder *David Crow*, the hotel has grown into a smart white roadhouse in a succession of rebuildings and extensions. Transformation began *c.* 1950; the most motorist-catching element a conically-roofed, bow-fronted entrance porch asymmetrically adhering to a projecting gable. Panelling in the public bar from Poltalloch House (q.v.).

LOCHGAIR POWER STATION, E of A83 at N end of village. Tall shed with shallow-pitched roof and unconvincing panels of rubble masonry. By *Ian G. Lindsay*, 1961–2. Incorporated into roughcast gateway walling is a broken arch-head, C13 or C14(?), recovered from a ruinous island settlement in Loch Glashan.

POINT HOUSE, scenically sited at Lochgair Point, 800m. SE of the village. Late C18 or early C19 folly, also known as 'Catherine's Castle', it seems to guard the entry to the loch. Slated pyramid on a two-storey, rendered rubble block, 5.6m. square. Short chimneystacks rising from each corner stress the cubic symmetry, though only the S one has a flue. NE and NW blind pointed-arch recesses at the first floor; similar large NE archway at ground level, NW lean-to. Single-storey 'bothy' to the N adjacent to the boat-landing. Now derelict.

Former SCHOOL. By *Wardrop & Reid*, 1876. Now a dwelling.

LOCHGILPHEAD

The town's location at the head of Loch Gilp, where the routes from Inveraray, Campbeltown and Oban meet, seems an obvious place for settlement, but it was only after late C18 improvements in road communications that development began. By the first years of the C19 two almost contiguous villages had been established. A few houses sprang up along the N shore of the loch on the Oakfield estate of John MacNeill of Gigha while, a little to the E, Peter Campbell of Kilmory set out a smaller hamlet on the edge of his lands. Campbell built Kilmory Quay but could not compete with MacNeill's deep-water pier at the canal town of Ardrishaig on the W shore. Nevertheless, the proximity of the Crinan Canal (q.v.) helped stimulate development, while fishing, too, played a part in the local economy. But it was Lochgilphead's geographical position which ensured its growth and today makes the town the administrative centre for Argyll.

By the mid 1820s the population exceeded 1,000. From 1811 Poltalloch Street and Lochnell Street carried the coastal Inveraray road, separated from the loch by reclaimed land grassed for fairs and other public events. At right angles to Poltalloch Street, Argyll Street became the main thoroughfare. It ran N from its junction with the shore route at Colchester Square, begun in 1822, to terminate in the Parliamentary Church of 1828. Back streets were laid out parallel to Poltalloch and Lochnell Streets, producing, with their associated lanes, two minor grids. Piped water was provided in 1807, street drainage in 1831, and gas street lighting, 1844–6. A woollen mill, dye-house and distillery lay along the Cuilarstich Burn on the N side of town. In 1859 the town became a police burgh and, two years later, population peaked at 1,674. Building continued through the second half of the C19 especially to the NE around Manse Brae and Hospital Road. C20 expansion has been to the NW with much local authority housing redevelopment occurring in the Lochnell Street and Union Street areas.

CHURCHES

BAPTIST CHURCH, Argyll Street. Built 1815. Simple preaching hall of snecked rubble lying along the E side of street. Three rectangular windows W and E. Squat S entrance porch. Late C19 alterations raised wallhead, replaced piends with gable ends and renewed internal furnishings.

CHRIST CHURCH (Episcopal). Behind a high rubble wall church and rectory lie side by side in leafy glebe-land between Bishopton Road and the Badden Burn. A design by *William Butterfield*, then at work on his Collegiate Church of the Holy Spirit, Isle of Cumbrae, for the Honourable George Frederick Boyle, later 6th Earl of Glasgow, proved too expensive for the resident bishop of Argyll and the Isles, and the commission was given to the Edinburgh architect, *John Henderson*. His nave-and-chancel church, 1850–1, in good if orthodox Decorated style, has a shallow N porch and acquired a N chapel housing organ, and vestry

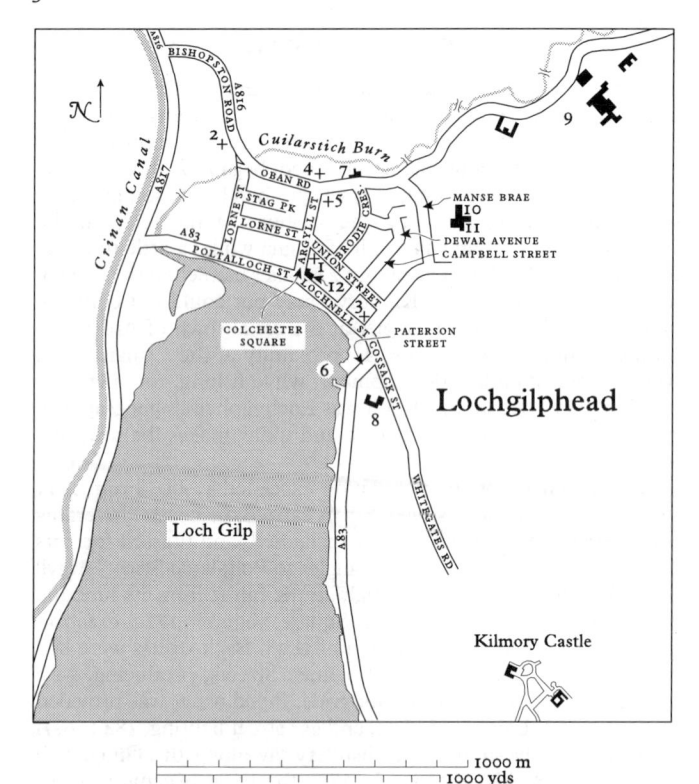

1 Baptist Church
2 Christ Church (Episcopal)
3 Free Church
4 Parish Church
5 St Margaret Church (R.C.)
6 Kilmory Quay
7 Council Engineer's Office
8 Lochgilphead Resource Centre
9 Argyll and Bute Hospital
10 Mid Argyll Sports Centre
11 Lochgilphead High School
12 Council Offices and Post Office

in 1888. Thin gritty render applied to square-snecked rubble masonry. Interior divided by a tall pointed chancel arch. Piscina and triple sedilia on the s wall of chancel. The sanctuary floor is tiled; brick in the choir and nave. The polychromatic stencilled decoration has been overpainted, but some vestiges are exposed. – To the l. of the chancel arch is the hexagonal PULPIT, its inverted pyramid base cantilevered from the wall and from its access stairs. – Octagonal lidded FONT at the back. – ORGAN by *William Hill & Son*, 1888; rebuilt by *Rushworth & Dreaper*, 1960s, and by *Alexander F. Edmonstone*, 1990. – STAINED GLASS in all four chancel windows: triple lights in sanctuary have Christ on a Gothic throne flanked by apostles in niches. – A classical TABLET mounted r. of the chancel arch commemorates Thomas Lloyd of Minard †1905: brown and white mottled marble frame with mosaic inlay in blue, white and gold, depicting infant angels and floral motifs. – Carved wooden TRIPTYCH shows Christ and fishermen.

The chancel arch wall continues s to form the E wall of the large, much gabled RECTORY, this link cleverly incorporating an open traceried belfry. The BELL, by *C. & G. Mears* of London, is hung in a vesica frame; weather vane with copper cockerel. Gate in the wall from Bishopston Road to the rectory garden has traceried arch.

FREE CHURCH, Lochnell Street. 1843–4 three-bay, bare Gothic box, with a finialled rectangular belfry shouldered into the street gable over a bifurcated lancet and a pointed-arch entrance. Plastered interior. The nave separated from aisles by three high, flat arches on columns on socles. The arches are high enough to frame side galleries but only the rear gallery was built. – Stained timber communion-table corral and PULPIT, *c.* 1905, almost Art Nouveau. – The FREE CHURCH SCHOOL, Union Street, is a severe, four-bay, gabled rubble hall, *c.* 1850. Tall, double-light windows.

LOCHGILPHEAD PARISH CHURCH. The most important site in the town, looking s down Argyll Street to Loch Gilp. It was occupied, from 1828, by a Parliamentary Church of standard twin-doored *Telford* and *Thomson* design. From 1884–5 the present Early English church by *John Honeyman* has enjoyed the axial setting. The three-light gabled front asymmetrically partnered on the w by a clock-and-belfry steeple over an arched entrance seems a perverse response to the urban context. But the plan is symmetrical: four-bay nave with two s bays opening w and E through an arcade of pointed arches into a transept. Scissors truss roof. – COMMUNION TABLE by *Honeyman*, 1891. – STAINED GLASS in sanctuary lancets by *Henry Holiday* of London, 1903–4, of highest quality. Complex in design and richly variegated, the three windows portray scenes from Christ's Nativity. The dedication commemorates the family of mason-architect, David Crow, who built much of the town's Colchester Square. W transept N double lancet depicts SS Matthew and Paul; by *Ballantine & Gardiner*, Edinburgh, *c.* 1900. E transept N double lancet, by *Christian Shaw*, 1983, shows l. Christ saving Peter from drowning and r. the Miraculous Draught of Fishes. – The CHURCH HALL, 1911, by *William Todd* lies immediately w. Hard-edged Arts and Crafts. Roughcast with sandstone dressings including saddleback copes on gable skews and skewputts. Wide-eaved vent at ridge.

Former REFORMED PRESBYTERIAN CHURCH, Union Street. Built *c.* 1849. Now converted to flats.

ST MARGARET'S (R.C.), Argyll Street. Village Norman despite its main street site. By *Reginald Fairlie*(?), 1927–9. Skew-gabled T-plan with the apse terminating the stem of the 'T'. Porch with a glazed gable and rubble flanks by *John G. Peace*, 1987. Barrel-vaulted Lady Chapel to r., confessionals l. Plastered interior with braced collar roof. – Stylistically unified STAINED GLASS by *John Hardman Studios*, 1956–8, fills all windows. SS Francis, Pius X, Mungo to l.; John Ogilvie, Ignatius, Patrick on r.

St Columba, Christ and St Margaret of Scotland in the sanctuary apse. In the gable rose, the Nativity. In the garden is an incomplete Hebridean CROSS standing 1.27m; ring markings within the armpits identify it as C10 or C11.

PUBLIC BUILDINGS

ARGYLL & BUTE HOSPITAL, Hospital Road. The bleak, three-storey wings of East House by *David Cousin*, built 1862–4 as the District Asylum for the Insane, stare symmetrically across banked lawns, bringing a dismal order amid the chaos of later *ad hoc* additions and alterations. West House, by *Kinnear & Peddie*, 1881–3, is no less barracks-like: three tall rough rubble storeys, dressed with equally rough red sandstone, stretched to a twelve-bay block. Erected to accommodate 120 'industrial patients', it now stands empty.

ARGYLL & CLYDE HEALTH BOARD STAFF HOME AND OFFICES, Hospital Road. Built as Lochgilphead Combination Poorhouse, 1861, by the local architect-builder *David Crow*. Long two-storey rubble front with advancing gables r., l. and centre.

COMMUNITY EDUCATION CENTRE, Manse Brae. Former Junior School, erected *c.* 1872, extended 1906 and 1912. Gable, hip, and hip-gable roofs over three aggregated blocks.

COUNCIL ENGINEERS' OFFICE, Manse Brae. By *Strathclyde Regional Council*, 1980s. Concrete blocks and hole-in-the-wall windows ranged in regimented repetition below steep roofs.

COUNCIL OFFICES (Dalriada House), Lochnell Street. By *Donald Gillies*. Built 1887 as the Argyll Hotel. Four-gabled, crow-stepped, burgh Baronial ups the street scale to three storeys. Two-storeyed crenellated bays corbelled at the first floor l. and r. Hood mouldings abound.

COURT HOUSE and POLICE STATION, Lochnell Street. By *Thomas Brown*, 1848–9; extended by *Neil Gillies*, 1899. Green rubble street-front returns through a crowstepped W gable to battlemented cylindrical stair tower set in the re-entrant angle. Block porch to stair also battlemented. Consoled entrance.

KILMORY QUAY, Paterson Street. Early C19 L-plan rubble pier approached through shaped, single-slab gatepiers. A pronounced batter on the exposed S face; stair flight in the protected re-entrant angle. Now turf-covered between flat boulder edgings.

LOCHGILPHEAD HIGH SCHOOL, Hospital Road. Flat-roofed brick and glass by *Argyll County Council*, 1964–6.

LOCHGILPHEAD RESOURCE CENTRE, Whitegates Road. By *Strathclyde Regional Council*, 1990–1. A playful grouping of crisp, gabled sheds around a courtyard; continuous glazing below eaves. Portholes, step-silled windows and astragal grids.

MASONIC LODGE, Lochnell Street. Dated 1909. Roughcast street front with an arresting quirkiness that suggests its architect, *William Todd*, knew something of Mackintosh and the Glasgow Style. The canted bay pressed into wall thickness below the central gable may be derivative, but not the bow-fronted dormers swept back into the roof within flat-topped leaded parapets. Set in a splayed recess below the bay, the consoled entrance doorway carries a broken pediment enclosing Masonic insignia.

MID ARGYLL SPORTS CENTRE, Hospital Road. Inevitable rendered boxes on brick base. The cut-back S corner under a cantilevered stair flight is reminiscent of the W gable of Carnasserie Castle.

OAKFIELD BRIDGE, crossing Crinan Canal 150m. S of A83 roundabout W of Lochgilphead. Steel swing bridge constructed, 1871, by *P. & W. MacLellan*, Glasgow. Adjacent is the BRIDGE-KEEPER'S COTTAGE, *c.* 1800, two-storeyed W front with a plain classical doorway to the canal, three-storeyed with segmental arch door to the road.

DESCRIPTION

Argyll Street has the width, incline and prospect appropriate to a main street. It is generously broad, looks up N to a Parish Church *point-de-vue* and opens S through Colchester Square to Loch Gilp. Moreover, it preserves enough architectural consistency to sustain the provincial urban dignity its developers planned. COLCHESTER SQUARE is symmetrical in layout though not quite in building. On the W side, gable to gable, Nos. 5–11, three three-bay, two-storey houses, each with Roman Doric pilastered doorpieces. 1822 is inscribed on the SE roll-skewputt. On the E, THE INSTITUTE and POST OFFICE, 1841, by *David Crow*, an eleven-bay, two-storey-and-attic terrace turning three bays into Lochnell Street: pilastered shopfronts, windows above alternating lugged or consoled surrounds, strong eaves cornice. From the Square, the W side of ARGYLL STREET maintains an early C19 two-storey scale with irregular attic bay dormers. Nos. 7–13 retain decorative ironwork gutter brackets; No. 9 has a blocked door with pilasters and dentilled cornice. Off the lane behind, a rough rubble store with stone forestair on the gable looks early C19. Then, across Lorne Street, corbelling out a conically roofed two-storey masonry bow to mark the corner, the white, three-storeyed, chimneyed bulk of the STAG HOTEL, completed 1938 by *Colin Sinclair*. Eleven hip-dormered hotel bays to the N, Argyll Street reverts to two storeys. Lining a final stretch of pavement, cobble-ramped to the road, Nos. 71–85 comprise five flatted units, the two S tenements dated 1859, the next, 1828. The symmetrical five-bay fifth unit, early C19, has a central pediment-gable, with chimney and oculus, below which the close entry gives access to a turnpike stair at the rear and preserves a neat sunburst fanlight. On the E side of Argyll Street, Nos. 2–4 and 6–8 are three-storey, early C19, the latter now much altered. Then, at Nos. 10–12, come the window arches of a splendidly Victorian painted shopfront and the grave Baptist Church (*see* Churches above). N across Union Street, two-storey continuity. No. 24 is a smart one-bay 'infill' with a segmental arch acoss its glazed shopfront. Nos. 34 and 36 are identical but mirrored, 1844; good doorpieces, bad dormers. Finally, a two-storey-and-attic tenement, *c.* 1860, with a central chimney stack splitting four gabled dormers, two with ball finials.

Hefty quoins mark the two-storey turn W into shoreside POLTALLOCH STREET. A run of low, early to mid-C19 roughcast houses survives, interrupted by two high tenements, by far the better of which is Nos. 2–4, green rubble, late C19, with canted bays corbelled from the first floor l. and r. Then detached villas. THE HOLLIES, late C19, is also of green rubble with heavy sandstone dressings; gabled, bayed and castellated. More Baronial and better cut is the CLYDESDALE BANK, by *William Railton* of Kilmarnock, 1868. Symmetrical and best is ISLAY LODGE, early C19, plain two-storeyed and gabled with short lower wings, only the E preserving its round-arched window.

LOCHNELL STREET, too, is at first open to Loch Gilp. It begins in the erect, busily gabled Baronial of the Council Offices (*see* Public Buildings above) but then relaxes to an older, lower scale. Shops and flats are varied but indifferent mid C19. Nos. 37–41 retain iron eaves brackets similar to those in Argyll Street. From MacBrayne's Lane, building begins on the seaward side with the Police Station and Court (*see* Public Buildings above). No. 14 keeps to two storeys, a neatly asymmetrical two-bay front with small hipped dormer, mid C19, but Nos. 16–20 are three-storeyed local authority tenements in bare-faced 1950s style. Opposite, intensifying the enclosure, Nos. 55–57 and 59–61 repeat this municipal pattern. All three blocks by *Colin Sinclair*. But the older eaves height returns on the N at the white roughcast ARGYLL HOTEL, mid C19, and runs on over a segmentally arched pend until the Free Church (*see* Churches above). On the S, the highlights are the Masonic Lodge (*see* Public Buildings above) and CORONATION MANSIONS, *c.* 1905, a polychromatic tenement with corbelled canted bays parapeted at the roof, a cut-down central chimneystack and a roll-moulded close entry.

Building in UNION STREET, which lies parallel N of Lochnell Street, reflects its later development. Shops and flats at Nos. 3–11 are two-storey but high, late Victorian: No. 9 is dated 1878 over its flat-arched pend. Nos. 32–38, by *Donald Gillies*, in green coursed rubble, have mullioned windows with chamfered ingoes and the date 1886 inscribed in a small eaves pediment. Nos. 40–48 run gable-to-gable, four three-bay houses with pilastered doorpieces; No. 46 dated 1878. Equally robust and similar in detail are two flatted blocks on the S side of LORNE STREET, one dated 1887. But the best domestic architecture in this part of town is at Nos. 43–57 Union Street, a long white terrace of harled cottages by *Ian Lindsay & Partners*, 1963, crisply detailed vernacular with minimal means, plain yet poetic.

Uphill, on MANSE BRAE, are the villas. SPRINGBANK, mid C19, is three-bay, gabled, its eaves rising to two finialled gablets. At the junction with Hospital Road is ERSKINE VILLA, probably by *Donald Gillies*, *c.* 1865, a wide hipped-roofed front with attic bays fringed at the eaves and a good ironwork railing running along its coped rubble wall. The OLD MANSE, built as a single-storey Parliamentary manse in 1828, retains its flanking piended wings but has been transformed, late C19, to two gabled storeys with a rear staircase extension. CRUACH, late C19, has a piended porch with big bracketed eaves; CRAIGDENE, an early C20 roughcast bungalow, with a bell roof and veranda. DRIMPARK, *c.* 1880, unpretentious in green rubble with chamfered sandstone dressings, is tidily symmetrical. In contrast, DUNCRAOBHAN, 1906, designed by *William Todd* for himself, charms with a rambling Arts and Crafts approach not without a flavour of its architect's flirtation with Art Nouveau.

At the E end of Lochnell Street, on the gable of Nos. 1–2 COSSACK STREET, the Inveraray road turns sharply S, the corner marked subtly by two bowed sills. KILMORY GUEST HOUSE, appropriately tall and detached, has an early C19 three-bay elegance marred by later accretion. Fortunately, Nos. 1–7 PATERSON STREET, by *Archibald Paterson, c.* 1815, preserve the four-house wall that formed most of the main street of Kilmory village, while on Whitegates Road are the coursed rubble GATEPIERS, copes swept up into ball finials, through which the drive to Kilmory Castle originally passed.

At Achnabreck, 2km. N of Lochgilphead, is MILLHOUSE, 1992, by *Diana MacLaurin*. Cruciform in plan, the house cleverly bridges Achnahoish Burn in a split-level section. At once convincingly traditional and confidently contemporary.

LOCHGOILHEAD

2001

Still the 'peaceful little place, with ... lovely surroundings of wood and water, mountain and glen' which Groome described in 1884, the village no longer boasts its daily boat connection down Loch Long to the Clyde. Without the steamer, it has become a *cul-de-sac* in Argyll's road system, condemned to some of the dangers of dead-end tourism. Along the E shore of the loch 'a good many villas and pretty cottages' survive, but to the W lies the chalet-spattered landscape of Drimsynie Estate.

LOCHGOILHEAD FREE CHURCH. Converted to church hall, 1952, but now disused. By *Campbell Douglas & Sellars*, 1883. Limited Gothic in heavily pointed rubble with hammered sandstone dressings. Triple lancet set below hooded pointed-arch in the S gable. W porch has slated spirelet belfry rising from ridge.
– STAINED GLASS. N rose window, 1883, by *Adam & Small*.

LOCHGOILHEAD AND KILMORICH PARISH CHURCH. A T-plan kirk, apparently C18 in character, though its ochre rendered rubble walls conceal a more complex provenance. The longitudinal core (that part of the church formed by the E and W aisles) seems substantially derived from the medieval Church of the Three Holy Brethren, first mentioned in a late C14 papal document. The N aisle, forming the stem of the 'T', was added in the C18 and a smaller session house extension opposite this on the S, behind the central pulpit, in 1832. All gables have sandstone skews, that to the session house crowned by an open bellcote of crude character rising from a crenellated base.

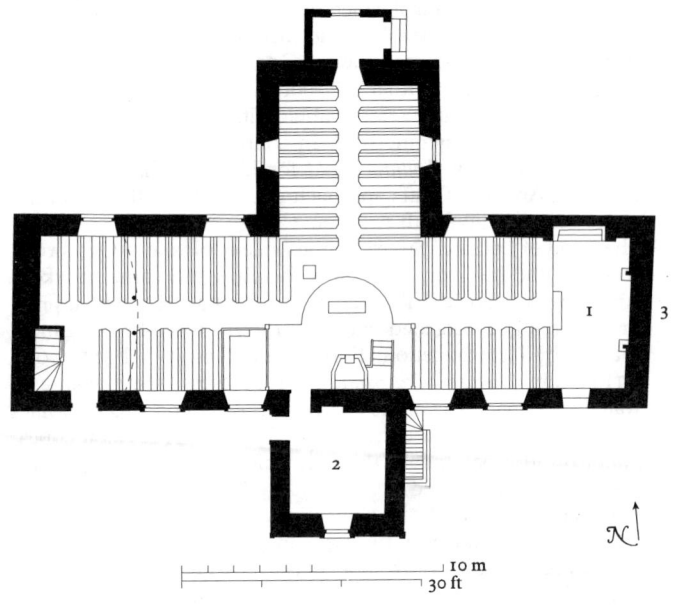

1 Site of medieval chancel
2 Session-house
3 Site of burial-aisle

Lochgoilhead and Kilmorich Parish Church

N porch added by *Campbell Douglas*, 1894–5. An attempt to regularize the positioning of windows has clearly been made, probably in the early C19. All are sash-and-case and most square-headed, though the two tallest flanking the pulpit area are round-arched with Gothick glazing bars. Doors at the W and E ends of the S wall, each with a small window over, indicate the presence of two galleries, only one of which remains.

The interior, largely refurbished by *Ian G. Lindsay* in 1957, retains its C18 layout. In the W aisle is the Drimsynie Loft, early C19, a gently convex panelled gallery carried on two round timber columns. Boarded coomb ceiling, 1888. Pews installed 1895. – A sandstone FONT, carved to receive an inset basin and supported on a modern pedestal, is of unknown origin and date. – The PULPIT, 1791, came to Lochgoilhead from Kiltearn, Ross and Cromarty, in 1955; its dentilled cornice is not dissimilar to that at Kilmorich, Cairndow (q.v.). – The communion table sits on a one-step, semicircular apron at the centre of the church while at the end of the E aisle the floor drops a step to the level of the medieval chancel. Here, defined by a semicircular moulded sandstone arch set within a slight projection of the N wall, is a medieval TOMB RECESS. Above it runs an incomplete cornice moulding overlapped at centre and ends by bulbous corbels, foliated and heraldic, forming the bases for three flat niches, each surmounted by a rib-vaulted Gothic canopy. Armorial bearings on r. corbel identify John Campbell of Ardkinglas, donor of the vanished Lady altar, 1512. The tomb-chest in the recess incorporates two relocated SLABS, probably C16, carved with arcade moulding. – Nearby lies a tapered SLAB, dated 1591, densely incised with an agglomeration of motifs and interlacing. – Placed centrally in the E gable wall, like a massive chimneypiece, is the Campbell of Ardkinglas MONUMENT, late C16; ashlar 'fireplace' wall, marked by crude columnar division, its triangular 'overmantel' zone decoratively encrusted with scrolls and dumpy finials. In the middle of the former is a low blocked doorway which led to the Ardkinglas burial-aisle, removed 1850; centred above, under a small steep pediment, is a carved memorial inscription to Sir James Campbell of Ardkinglas †1592.

The L-plan GRAVEYARD, walled 1802, contains C18 and C19 HEADSTONES amongst which the tombs of Andrew McFarlane, miller, †1801, and John Weir, 'sheepherd', †1803, are carved with appropriate vocational imagery. In the s wall, axially related to the centre line of the church, is a GATEWAY, its iron gates set between circular rubble piers, each of which is crowned by eight flat Art Nouveau iron bands bent inwards in ogee curves and gathered in a skeletal finial.

DRIMSYNIE ESTATE OFFICES, 700m. W of village. Former stables court, early C19. Façade range with piended end pavilions and pedimented central archway. Converted to office and residential use.

DRIMSYNIE HOUSE, 800m. W of village. Blocky, two-storey-and-basement mansion with castellated parapets, built, 1859–60, for the Liverpool merchant Ronald Livingstone by Glasgow architect *James Smith*(?). Roughcast with painted dressings. Square SW entrance tower rises an extra storey; square corner turrets with crossloops. Ground-floor windows are lintelled, others have segmental arches; most are heavily hooded; none has a pointed arch. Spreading SE are the low but hugely emphatic flat roofs of the LEISURE CENTRE, 1970s: swimming pool, skating rink and bowling lanes.

LOCHGOILHEAD BRIDGES. Rubble-built *c.* 1810. At the N end of the village, two segmental arches on a central cutwater pier with splayed top. A second single-arch bridge crosses the River Goil 500m. NNE.

VILLAGE HALL. Slated and roughcast but a decidedly English exercise by *James Salmon & Son*, 1898. Stained half-timbered gables, eaves, bargeboarding and veranda; all windows set forward at the wall face.

DESCRIPTION

LOCHGOILHEAD HOTEL marks the village centre. A three-bay C18 inn, it has acquired two additional bays on the E, some gabled dormers and a glazed porch with ironwork cresting. Looking out to the loch is THE COTTAGE, a harled, gabled L-plan villa, mid C19; here, too, a porch with decorative ironwork ridging. In the garden, an obelisk SUNDIAL, dated 1626.

C19 houses straggle down the E shore to catch the evening sun; the earlier dwellings, *c.* 1840, closest to the village. At GREENBANK, which retains its original glazing bars, gabled dormers break through the eaves. At PRIMROSE BANK, which has a peaked gable over its central entrance, the attic dormers are piended. DAISY BANK is identical but preserves iron finials on the dormer ridges. Spar ends are everywhere evident. Some distance S, ALMA sports a five-bay veranda with filigree ironwork in the spandrels. BURNKNOWE, *c.* 1875, is grander: two Thomsonesque storeys with arched windows, bargeboarded gables and a tall Italianate tower. INVERMAY is plain, a piended mansion, symmetrical with ground-floor Venetian windows, but at WOODLANDS, 2km. S of the Hotel, iron balconies on timber posts enhance an otherwise similar three-bay villa. Almost opposite, spectacularly sited on the W side of the loch, is THE LODGE. Begun in 1863–4, probably by *Boucher & Cousland*, in 1874 it was transformed by *William Leiper* in his 'Swiss-American-Japanese style' (Green, 1996), a charmingly light-timbered pavilion of bracketed balustraded balconies and fringed and fretted gables.

LOCHNELL HOUSE
overlooking Ardmucknish Bay, 2.3km. WNW of Benderloch

An L-plan amalgam of three contiguous but chronologically distinct houses: a SW service wing surviving from a late C17 dwelling, a SE wing which comprises two-thirds of an Early Georgian mansion and, forming a right-angled connection between the two, an overblown castellated pile of 1816–20. Until the late C20 much of this last and largest element lay derelict after fire swept through the property in 1853. Rehabilitation of both the earlier sections of the fabric took place in the late C19.

The service wing, a long, two-storey-and-basement, rubble structure aligned NE–SW, is all that remains of the C17 residence, largely built or re-built by Alexander Campbell, 6th of Lochnell, who succeeded to the estate *c.* 1671. Dating is problematical and parts may be of greater antiquity. Gables have crowsteps and moulded skewputts. Below an ovolo eaves-cornice, windows are widely spaced and farmhouse-plain with dressed sandstone surrounds, regular on the SE, random on the older(?) NW elevation. In the basement, four barrel-vaulted apartments interconnect and it seems likely that these were originally cellars serving kitchens on the ground floor. Sink outlets at each end of the NW wall and the ruinous remains of a bake-oven projecting close to a forestair on the SW gable support this interpretation, though late C19 alterations transformed these entirely domestic arrangements, removing the first floor to create a single spacious interior with a NE gallery. Nothing is known of the rest of the C17 house but, whatever its size and qualities, these were to be superseded when 'ye superfluous part of ye Old house' was put 'in another order' (Johnstone, 1738) by the improvements which Alexander

Campbell's son, Sir Duncan Campbell, 7th of Lochnell, set in train during the first half of the C18.

Between 1737 and 1739 a new self-contained mansion was raised a little to the E of the old house. Building was supervised by the Penicuik wright, *John Johnstone*, and the design, possibly involving the architect *John Baxter* with whom Johnstone was in good relations, followed contemporary fashion: a three-bay, three-storey, hipped-roofed house with a pedimented NE centrepiece and a semi-octagonal SW projection containing 'a staircase and back stair very well contrived' (Pococke, 1747–60). It is still substantially intact; a small residence with an orthodox tripartite plan only one room deep. Yet the principal façade, commanding the approach from the NE, is not short on pretension. Harled walls with grey sandstone dressings and quoins (later superseded by cement rendering and replacement mouldings) are unexceptional, but in the projecting pedimented centre the design affects an unexpected grandeur. The main entrance doorway, set at ground level between lug-moulded windows with heavy keystones, carries a segmental pediment in the marble tympanum of which, almost invisibly cut, are the date 1737 and the initials DC and MC, for Donald Campbell and his second wife, Margaret, daughter of Daniel Campbell of Shawfield. The motto and crest of each family flank this central dated monogram. At first floor, three high round-arched windows with exaggerated keystones mark the *piano nobile* with unequivocal assurance. A continuous moulding connects all three at sill height while at impost level a moulded stringcourse passes uninterrupted across the full width of the façade, separating the rusticated quoins which border the lower portion of the elevation from panelled pilasters rising to the corners of the main pediment above. Second-floor windows are similar to those on the ground floor but lack keystones. Carved in relief in the pediment are the weathered heraldic arms of the Campbells of Lochnell and above, strongly silhouetted on the skyline, three magnificently sculpted urns. There is nothing to compare with all of this on the SW, except perhaps the circular recesses set at mid-height into the wall planes of the staircase block, probably intended to receive busts, which seem to echo the aspirations of the main façade. Otherwise, the raised garden level, some simple fenestration and the late C19(?) insertion of a central doorway to connect with the staircase half-landing make this very much a rear elevation. Yet there is more than this to diminish Georgian grace and balance, for the third phase of building at Lochnell, though it united the rump of the C17 house with its C18 neighbour, could do so only by destroying, or at any rate concealing, the NW third of Sir Duncan's mansion.

This final elaboration, built 1816–20 to the design of *Archibald Elliot*, interposed a high L-plan block of battlemented three- and four-storey accommodation between the NW gable of the Early Georgian house and the NE gable of the older service wing. Rising a storey higher, a half-octagon tower with a corbelled crenellated parapet marked the new N corner, while a staircase projected in the S re-entrant. Seen from the NW, where an abrupt storey-height drop in the ground adds extra drama, the mock-castellar manner works well enough: the high N tower with its engaged stair turret, higher still; a stepping parapeted skyline over asymmetrically disposed windows; the round W tower replete with hood-moulded windows and crosslet loops; the texture of rubble masonry. From the NE, however, inevitable conflicts of scale and style are exposed. In an attempt to fuse new with old, Elliot stretched a battlemented NE rubble wall from the N tower to the pedimented centrepiece of the 1730s mansion, at the same time making a complementary move by introducing into this wall three storeys and three bays of windows similar to those at the centre of the Early Georgian design. Despite maintaining this arrangement of windows around the N tower (and across the NW elevation, where a central round-arch window, dated 1820, opens on to a canted, cantilevered, stone balcony) the composition lacks convincing resolution, not only because of the lop-sided bulk of the new but because the strategy has denied the old its fundamental classical integrity.

In a programme of restoration, 1987–8, Elliot's work was re-roofed, the windows infilled with random rubble and the structure stabilized; in effect, the shell became a five-storey drive-in garage. At the same time the wall fronting the service court on the NW was reduced in height between battlemented octagonal N and W bastions.

The early C18 house remains in residential use, along with some of the accommodation in the N tower. Entry is by the heavily framed doorway at the centre of the NE front. Beyond the Hall, in the half-octagonal projection at the rear, the main geometric stair survives, though its construction and pitch pine balustrading are probably Victorian; the smaller service stair has gone. Opening r. from the Hall is the Dining Room, extended c. 1818–20 to reach the wall of the N tower. Its mid-C18, white marble chimneypiece was brought here later from Castle Gwrych, Denbighshire, as was another decorated with medallion figurines now in the Drawing Room, situated at first floor in the N tower. The principal room at this level, lit by the three arched windows at the centre of the NE façade, has a similarly arched, glazed display cupboard and a three-panel Victorian plaster ceiling with acanthus cornices.

A WALLED GARDEN lies SE on lower ground between the house and lochside. In its E corner, a roofless rustic rubble FOLLY, or 'meditating hut', castellated over pointed-arch openings on a quartz dado. Adjacent to this, close to the loch shore, U-plan STABLE-COURT, early C19, entered from the NE through a segmental archway flanked by coupled blind round-arch recesses; much altered in conversion to residential use. ICE-HOUSE, late C18 or early C19, with an egg-shaped vault, 50m. S of the house. Some 800m. SW, LADY MARGARET'S TOWER enjoys panoramic seaward prospects. A small random rubble structure, square in plan with a turnpike stair at its core rising to a domed square caphouse. It gives access to a viewing gallery with crenellated parapets. Below this corbelled gallery all four wall faces recess under round arches springing from rough impost courses. In the NE recess is the doorway to the stair. Above it, a stone tablet inscribed ERECTED / BY LADY CAMPBELL / ANNO 1754.

LUSS

A conservation village with a timber-framed hammer-head pier on the W shore of Loch Lomond. Where Lord Cockburn found 'dirt and squalid wretchedness' (1838), houses and landscape are today prim and well scrubbed, the visitor charmed by a couthy intimacy almost too self-consciously picturesque.

ST MACKESSOG'S CHURCH. Built in 1875 by the laird, Sir James, 12th Baronet of Colquhoun and Luss. Delightfully located on the N bank of the Luss Water close to the loch. Small yet cruciform in plan with steep gables and a hipped roof over the half-octagonal E end. Windows have Dec plate tracery with hooded quatrefoils in the gables. Gabled W porch with N and S pointed-arch doorways. An open timber belfry sits astride the ridge at the crossing, capped by a steep, subtly bellcast, slated pyramid.

Inside, above seating directed to the crossing rather than the E end, is a splendid roof of Scots pine. Arch-braced trusses, springing from plain corbelstones, carry purlins, spars and boarding but there are free struts and collars, too, creating a dense grid of timbers. In the N arm of the plan is the LAIRD'S LOFT, carried on projecting beams over a leaded glass screen. Opposite, a small, railed chancel set against the shallow S 'transept'. – Half-octagon Gothic PULPIT with winder steps each side. – Oak COMMUNION TABLE with cusped-arches, 1956. – Beside the chancel is the FONT, a stone cube with round bowl, and lying in the E a carved robed EFFIGY, perhaps St Mac Kessog; both medieval and formerly in the Chapel of St Mary at Rossdhu (q.v.). – All windows have STAINED GLASS. – In the E, the pale figures of SS Andrew and James commemorate James, 11th Baronet of Colquhoun and Luss, and Alan John, 13th Baronet, late C19. – In the SE window, a memorial to Sir Iain Colquhoun of Luss, †1948: above a tranquil view of the loch and a wreath unifying elements from the family's armorial bearings, the background deepens into a glorious blue; originally flanked by dense floral panels of geometric design. – All other windows in the church are late C19 memorials to members of the Colquhoun family. – In the porch, a three-lancet design of roses, vines and lilies, 1892. – To the l. of the chancel, a white marble MURAL TABLET incised with a Latin inscription dated 1772, a memory of the previous church of 1771–2. – A similar panel, also dated 1772, has been inset on the outer face of the S gable. – Below this, a tall red sandstone MURAL TABLET, relettered 1876, records the ministries of Duncan M. Gilchrist †1716 and James Robertson †1772. – Still older, high at the NE corner, is the so-called MACFARLANE STONE: a skull between pick and shovel and crossed bones above an illegible inscription above the text AFTER . DEATHE . / REMAINIS . VERTEW . / MEMENTO . MORI . / I . M . 1612.

Gravemarkers fill the CHURCHYARD, the walled enclosure entered through gambrel-roofed, timber-framed LYCHGATES on the N and W. – Near the W porch, a Norse HOG-BACK STONE, C11, with scaly top and arcaded sides. Two broken schist SLABS, one lined with a simple cross motif, stand against the NW corner of the church. – Several TAPERED SLABS, some ridge-backed, some with chamfered edges. – Numerous broader lying SLABS, C17–C19. – Scroll-topped early C19 HEADSTONES: inscribed to Andrew Crawford †1798 and Ann Campbell †1827, both column-framed; to Ludovic Colquhoun †1799, under a deer's head and thistle frieze; to Mary Grant †1819, with thistle sprays and a rose frieze. – Against the E wall of the N 'transept', a pedimented and pilastered HEADSTONE, 1823, records the deaths of Isabella Tait and her infant child. – Husband and father, the Revd Robert Carr, is commemorated alongside on an egg-and-dart-edged white marble ellipse set in a grander aedicule MONUMENT, 1846, with open pediment and buckle-capped pilasters. – Nearby, a cross-topped CAIRN of quartzite rocks to James, 11th Baronet of Colquhoun and Luss, and his four companions drowned in the loch, 1873.

CHAPEL HILL BRIDGE, in Glen Luss, 3.5km. WNW of village. Built 1777 by *William Johns*, according to the inscription. Single-span rubble with a crude label moulding over the voussoirs and a line of rough stones projecting from each outer face *c.* 1m. below the parapet cope. Horned ram's head carved above arch on downstream side.

CULAG FARM BRIDGE, close to the A82, 2.3km. N. Segmental rubble arch, built *c.* 1747 on the military road from Dumbarton to Inveraray.

EDENTAGGART BRIDGE, in Glen Luss, *c.* 200m. past Chapel Hill Bridge. 1777. Another segmental arch in rubble; this time with a very low parapet.

FOOTBRIDGE over the A82 Luss By-pass. 1991. Single-span laminated timber structure; tangentially merged segmental arch and walkway beams.

LOCH LOMOND PARK VISITOR CENTRE. By *Dallmann & Johnstone*, 1993–4. A smart pitched-roof shed, walled in pink sandstone and glazed to the loch under the overhang of the E gable. Pine lined soffits and minimalist steel trusses. Careful landscaping enhances the scene.

WAR MEMORIAL, Pier Road. 1921(?). Elevated in a hedge-sheltered recess, an octagonal stone base and tall, tapering, sword-fronted cross.

DESCRIPTION

Single-storey cottages, old and not so old, predominate. At the W end of PIER ROAD, three with decorative bargeboards and fascias date from the early C19; one with Gothic metal casements in coupled windows. Further E, along both sides of the road, several low-roofed, wide-eaved estate dwellings, built *c.* 1850, in coursed rubble with pink sandstone dressings, play variations on a theme; single and semi-detached. Three painted rubble cottages, late C18 or early C19, face the loch N of the pier; another, with a catslide roof over its central door, lies 150m. S. Off School Road, Dorset pea render seems a perverse choice for GLENBURN COTTAGES, *c.* 1955, a gabled row penetrated by narrow arched pends. On the Old Road, the restored OLD TOLL HOUSE, early C19(?), a long, white, piend-roofed cottage, plain but elegantly symmetrical. Also white, the roughcast COLQUOHOUN ARMS HOTEL, C18 core(?), rising from two storeys, attractively piended at the N end, to a dismally severe three facing S.

MACHARIOCH 7309

A country house E of Southend with its own wood and sandy bay.

MACHARIOCH HOUSE. A rambling two- and three-storeyed gabled house, completely rebuilt and enlarged by *George Devey* for the Marquess of Lorne, 1873–7. Devey achieves his customary picturesque composition, though here with a harder, less English edge: tall chimneys, gabled projections and stone-mullioned bays are familiar but the parapeted four-storey SW tower with its accompanying angle turret seems a concession to northern castellar fashion. The house has been flatted. KENNELS form a square yard. The LODGE is another tower, its creamy harled drum seen for miles around; this time a three-storey buttressed cylinder with conical slated roof, reminiscent of the Tower Lodge which Devey had designed for Dunrobin in Sutherland in the 1850s. GATEPIERS have stone ball finials.

MACHARIOCH MOTTE, 800m. W of Macharioch Farm. A flat-topped conical earthwork with traces of an encircling ditch crossed by a narrow causeway on the SE.

MACHRIHANISH 6320

A village of villas strung out along the Atlantic shore 8.5km. W of Campbeltown and S of Machrihanish Links. Originally a fishing settlement known as Salt Pans, but for more than a century golfing has been its *raison d'être*.

LOSSIT HOUSE, 500m. S of W end of village. Piend-roofed, two-storey ashlar mansion built for the Macneils of Lossit and Ugadale, 1824–30, somewhat overpowered by later enlargement. Pedimented additions, recessed l. and r., broaden the façade, but it is a three-storey central tower, *c.* 1890, by *Sydney Mitchell & Wilson*, which dominates the composition. This rises over a porte-cochère fronted by a Palladian screen complete with port-holed spandrels. In its top storey Venetian windows repeat the Palladian motif. Two-storey, piend-roofed OFFICES, early C19, with pedimented pend entry. WALLED GARDEN.

HIGH LOSSIT, 1.3km. s of w end of village. Gabled rubble farm buildings with some segmental archways.

MACHRIHANISH HOTEL. By *Sydney Mitchell & Wilson*, 1898. Two-storey-and-dormered-attic pile: l. and r. are three-storey canted bays surmounted by half-timbered gables. Lower two-storey wing to w part of earlier hotel(?).

E of Machrihanish Hotel are several white, red-tiled villas, Arts and Crafts in provenance but with a harder northern edge. All are probably the turn-of-the-century work of *H. E. Clifford*. DUNLOSSIT has a central canted bay and two-storey, octagonal bay corners capped by shallow ogee-profile leaded domes. SWALLOWHOLME is more complex with gables, piends, bays and another ogee dome over a stair tower.

WEST TRODIGAL FARM, 1km. E of Machrihanish Hotel. Neatly symmetrical gabled farmhouse, C19, with gabled eaves dormers and single-storey piended wings returning around rear yard.

MELFORT

Small settlement at the head of Loch Melfort now predominantly dedicated to leisure pursuits. Along the shore road which skirts Loch na Cille to reach Fearnach Bay and Melfort are a few attractive new houses, 1980s. Oblique and straight, glazed and solid, the wide w front of MAELSTROMA elaborates the formal potential of the canted bay beneath a deep eaves overhang. COILLE DARAICH, by *Crerar & Partners*, escapes the ordinary with a transverse double monopitch; the second monopitch added by *Diana MacLaurin*, c. 1990. Beyond Melfort Pier, 1km. wsw, lies the hillside hamlet of ARDANSTUR where a number of low rubble cottages survive in neat white conversion.

Former FREE CHURCH, 1.2km. s. Plain two-bay mini-kirk, Mid C19. Cusped lancets l. and r. of gable entrance with quatrefoil over. Front buttresses corbel to support eaves brackets.

MELFORT HOME FARM. Early C19. Erect three-bay, two-storey house with high piended roof and bellcasted eaves. Hipped central porch. Broad chimneystacks on lateral walls. Some eaves-dormered estate cottages at roadside.

MELFORT HOUSE. A strangely anachronistic, two-storeyed mansion by *Leslie Grahame MacDougall*, built 1962–4 on the site of an earlier house. Roughcast and slated. It seems more Cape-colonial Dutch than Scots: garden terraces, white screen walls, ironwork gates and canopies, all evoke a more southern world. The sw front advances axially, bulging out in a balconied bow below the conical sweep of the roof. SE and NW walls swell gently under piends. On the NE, a central hipped-roofed block pushes forward between lower flat-roofed, single-storey flanks. Obsessively symmetrical, it somehow manages to eschew any intimidating self-conceit, perhaps because the approach is casual, the entrance from the SE on the minor axis. The interior is equally paradoxical, far from the brutal stereotype of 1960s architecture: polished oak floors, a staircase of Connemara marble, and, in the sitting room, the more recent installation of a columned chimneypiece in white Italian marble by *Roger Pearson*, 1994.

MELFORT PIER. A small group of timber-clad holiday houses, *c*. 1980(?), carefully related to pier and moorings on Fearnach Bay. The detailing of the waterside edge is carefully considered and the materials, cedar and rubble, work well. A tanned horizontality ties cladding and boarded balconies together while the mass and texture of rubble establishes continuity between quayside walling and the hefty chimneystacks.

MELFORT VILLAGE. Former gunpowder-works established along the valley of the River Oude in 1838 by the owners of the Lorn Furnace (*see* Taynuilt). Water power was obtained by damming the Eas Tarsuinn burn and cutting a mill-lade, which still survives. The lade served four mills in succession, three grinding constituent powders and one an incorporating or mixing mill. A corning-house, press-house, glazing-house, packing-house and dusting-house were located NNE upstream, while storage sheds for sulphur, saltpetre and charcoal were SSW of the line of mills. Although the former brick-built structures have almost all disappeared, the latter, more robustly constructed in rubble, have remained and it is these which have been adapted to form part of the present holiday village. This, too, has been the fate of a third group lying W of the storage sheds; used as a cooperage by the gunpowder-works, they antedate the industrial undertaking and were probably the COURT OF OFFICES for the original Melfort House.

In 1867 an explosion in the magazine destroyed the powder works. Buildings were rebuilt and production resumed, but the invention of dynamite and more automated methods of manufacture accelerated decline. By 1874 the enterprise was no longer viable and the estate was sold. Over a century later rehabilitation began. Between 1983 and 1987, the older rubble buildings forming the U-plan court of offices and those to the E which had served as storage sheds for the works were converted to holiday flats, administrative accommodation and a first-floor restaurant with dormers, timber forestair and balcony. The powder store was transformed into a swimming pool, 1984–5. Some 500m. WNW, symmetrically landscaped within the former WALLED GARDEN, the *David Newman Partnership* have created a semicircular arc of one-and-a-half-storey, pitched-roof COTTAGES, 1987–9. Adjusting to the hillside site, roof ridges step up around the S-facing court to lock on to the transverse gable that marks the centre of the arc.

DEGNISH, 6km. WSW. Severely plain three-bay, two-storey house of harled rubble. Bordered stone panel, probably removed to its off-centre position when a gabled porch was added, records the builder, *Niel* (*sic*) *Campbell*, and the date, 1786.

KILCHOAN HOUSE, 4km. WSW. Bargeboarded, gable-fronted house of mid C19, formerly known as Melfort Cottage. Site of medieval chapel dedicated to St Congan or Comghan.

DUN, Dùn Fadaidh, 750m. WNW of Degnish farmhouse on a

hilltop site overlooking the sea. Irregular plan, roughly 18m. in dia.; the wall is best preserved on the W where it is about 3.4m. thick. E entrance gap.

MILLHOUSE

9570

Cross-roads hamlet 3.3km. SW of Tighnabruaich. In 1839 a gunpowder-works was established and it remained in operation until 1921. Various mills and process-buildings were constructed N and S of the Millhouse–Kames road along the line of the Craignafeoch Burn. A small-gauge railway was laid and trees planted to minimize the effects of possible explosion. Some foundations, earthworks and abandoned rubble shells, with later brick or concrete alterations, survive. 500m. NE, S of the B8000, is the much altered main magazine, c. 1865.

WORKERS' HOUSING. Two semi-detached, single-storey, brick-built cottages, mid C19(?), each with projecting gabled porches l. and r. Adjacent on the W is the MANAGER'S HOUSE, a symmetrical, three-bay dwelling with a central gabled entrance. Above the doorway is a blank circular disc in a square-framed panel, the shorn face of the works clock.

ASCOG CASTLE, 1km. W on the NW shore of Loch Ascog. A Lamont tower-house which may date from the mid C15. It is built of random rubble with some dressings of white and red sandstone. Though ruinous and much engulfed by parasitic vegetation, parts of all but the SE wall still stand, in places to the original wallhead of c. 15m. Evidently the lowest floor was vaulted, for a trace line can be seen on the SW wall above a single, splayed window in an arched embrasure. The NE wall has two vaulted mural chambers, one on each side of a central passage opening to a dog-leg stair which led to first-floor level. Little can be determined of the upper arrangements.

MINARD

9796

Linear village on the W shore of upper Loch Fyne. New house building and lochside bungalows threaten to engulf Minard in suburban anonymity but, along a short narrowed stretch of the A83, school, church, village hall and a few older cottages crowd together to preserve some sense of social and spatial focus.

BURIAL GROUND, Killevin, Crarae, 1.3km. NE of Lochfyneside Church. Modern cemetery enclosing older graveyard on higher ground above Crarae Burn. Though there is now no evidence of the medieval chapel recorded in C19, an incomplete CROSS SHAFT, C8 or C9, now in Cumlodden Church, and a small rudely incised CROSS, removed to Lochfyneside Free Church manse, testify to an Early Christian origin. – The CAMPBELL ENCLOSURE is a rubble-walled oblong, roughly corniced and coped. Cut into the lintel of the S doorway is the date 1727 and below, against the blocked entrance, a grey-green schist memorial panel, 1874, with a dedication to the Campbells of Knockbuy and Kilberry buried here. – Among later gravemarkers is a holed HEADSTONE, cut from a millstone to commemorate John †1831, infant son of Angus Turner, 'millar in Braleckan'.

LOCHFYNESIDE CHURCH. Up-market corrugated-iron shed built 1910 as Lochfyneside United Free Church by *Speirs & Co.* of Glasgow, 'Designers and Erectors of Iron and Wood Buildings'. Painted in pale lemon green with dark green emphases. – Ash PULPIT, 1952, designed by *Ilay M. Campbell.*

LOCHFYNESIDE FREE CHURCH. Roughcast rubble oblong with saddleback skews, *c.* 1848. Hefty apex belfry with bell hanging in pointed arch opening. NE gabled porch. Double lancet lights.

CRARAE LODGE, 1.5km. NE of Lochfyneside Church. First an inn, built in rubble *c.* 1810(?), but later the home of the Campbells of Succoth who enlarged it in the late 1870s. In 1898 much was demolished and the present comfortable if undemonstrative mansion constructed in local granite. SE wing survives from original inn. Some crowstepping. Delightful wild GARDEN in Crarae Glen developed in the C20.

MINARD HALL. Gable-ended L-plan in rust common brick with quoins, surrounds and shallow-arched lintels in ochre brick. Gifted by Thomas Lloyd of Minard, 1899.

MINARD PRIMARY SCHOOL. Conjunction of schoolhouse and classroom block by architect *William Mackenzie*, 1871. Built in square snecked rubble with bargeboarded gables and open eaves. A buttressed chimneystack separates two tripartite windows at the centre of the asymmetrical front.

POST OFFICE BUILDING. Elevated symmetrical block of roughcast one-and-a-half-storey housing, mid C19. A two-storey piended house with steeply gabled projection is linked l. and r. by two three-bay units to gable-fronted wings. The NE return, BEANNAICHTE, has an attractive glazed porch addition, stepping sills towards loch.

CHAMBERED CAIRN, on raised beach in Crarae Gardens, 175m. N of shore. Roughly trapezoidal cairn, *c.* 38m. by *c.* 22m., with a flat ENE front leading to a three-compartment chamber.

MINARD CASTLE
at Tullochgorm, 2km. SSW of Minard

9794

On the face of it, an overblown, lavishly expensive exercise in castellated Gothic. But this medievalizing, carried out between 1842 and 1848 with almost admirably vulgar bravura by *John T. Rochead*, is a front (and a back and sides) to an earlier, more modest and more compact house known as Knockbuy which Archibald Campbell had built for himself in 1784 as part of his estate improvements. This Georgian residence is all but invisible. Its plan, organized along orthodox Palladian-derived lines as nine squares within a square, can be found embedded in the present mansion shrouded by Rochead's Victorian ashlar arras. Its three-storeyed, hipped-roofed external form, crenellated but not pedimented, if the evidence of a pictographic rainwater-head bearing the precocious date 1775 can be relied upon, is more difficult to detect but is still discernible at the higher levels of the SW, NW and NE elevations.

The alterations of the 1840s changed the character and composition of the house, replacing rational order with romantic affectation. But it was boldly done. A wide SE front, big in scale with a mechanical edge to its battlements and turrets, lies along the face of the older building. Centred on the staircase axis of the C18 plan is a tall square tower with a taller turret clasped asymmetrically at its S angle. In front of it, a lower, two-storey porte-cochère with four-centred archways set between square corner turrets. Behind this covered entrance the building extends SW in three storeys to a room-sized rectangular tower with a two-storey SW canted bay and a corbelled SE oriel. To the NE the façade is two-storeyed and quieter in mood. Then, continuing to develop the asymmetrical grouping expected in such Gothicizing caprice, a lower gallery-range runs out further to the NE to end in yet another square turret within which is the chapel. Battlemented towers adhere at the N and W angles of the C18 plan, the latter linked along the SW façade to the S tower by a single-storey arcade of five flat arches under a crenellated parapet. On the skyline another parapet conceals the rooflight over the old stairwell. Overall, a liberal application of label mouldings and mullion-and-transom windows.

Rochead's interiors, particularly those in the public spaces of the SE block, are even more exuberantly Gothic. Plaster vaults, ribbed and bossed, canopy the lower and upper halls, while the heavily panelled ceilings of the stair hall and first-floor drawing room are lavishly modelled with cusped tracery. At the end of the entrance hall a doorway flanked by two windows, all three openings under four-centred arches, leads into the hall of the C18 house and so to the inner, now more domestic, stairwell. But it is to the l., through a stone arcade of three massive strongly moulded four-centred arches, that the visitor is drawn. Above, all the more magnificent after the low flattened vault of the entrance hall, the space soars to the dark ceiling over Rochead's new staircase hall. Ahead, aligned on the axis of the central arch, the first flight of the staircase rises towards the SW, dog-legs r., and returns against the wall of the old house to reach the upper hall where the triple arcade and plastered vaults of the lower entrance hall are repeated. The stair is oak, its balustrade an open-traceried grid of dagger-like motifs. At first-floor level the balustrade closes the gap between the shafted piers of the upper arcade before returning along a gallery which leads to the drawing room in the SW tower. The prevailing Gothic idiom is graceful in the cusped panelling of doors, but crass and grandiloquent in some remarkable chimneypieces.

On the lawn a short distance SE of the house sits a baluster-shafted SUNDIAL, perhaps C18. A WALLED GARDEN, mid C19, lies W. Linked to the main house on the NE, a mid-C20, two-storey block, roughcast with crowstep gables, runs parallel to the

SE gallery wing, creating a long service yard between. Heraldic ironwork GATES, 1980s. 250m. N is the early C19 court of offices, a two-storey, piend-roofed square surrounding a cobbled yard. Converted to residential accommodation, it is known as the STABLE HOUSE. A central segmental-arch pend leads through the S front to the roughcast inner court where a double forestair is axially located on the N range.

MUASDALE 6840

Undistinguished hamlet of caravans, bungalows and a few local authority houses.

OLD BRIDGE. Rubble segmental arch span of 7.8m. over Clachaig Water. Late C18 or early C19.

TIGH NA CHLADAICH. Manse built 1803, to the design of *George Dempster* of Greenock, to serve the churches at A'Chleit (*see* Killean Parish Church, Tayinloan) and Bellochantuy (q.v.). Standard three-bay skew-gabled house, harled and slated. Porch added 1858 by Campbeltown builder *Robert Weir*. Tripartites l. and r. of porch, that to the l. with blind side. Open well stair has stone treads and iron balustrade. Adjoining offices, 1820; decorative cast-iron stall-posts in stable.

STANDING STONE, 230m. N of South Muasdale Farm. 3m.-high stone incorporated into wall.

NEWTON 0498

Secluded lochside hamlet 5.5km. SW of Strachur defined by a short, straight shoreline row of gable-to-gable, rubble COTTAGES, early C19(?), some painted, some roughcast. Behind, catching the view in big attic bays, sits HIGHER MID VILLAGE, an older dwelling raised to modest distinction by *Douglas Abrahams & Partners*, 1989: white walls, a broad conservatory-porch and diagonal timber boarding filling the gables. Here and there, a few rubble STORES with corrugated-iron roofs.

OBAN 8530

The largest town in Lorn and the major settlement on Scotland's Atlantic seaboard. Tumbling around its eponymous bay in the picturesque lee of Kerrera, Oban is the mainland's link to the Western Isles, its prosperity sustained by agriculture, fishing and tourism. Growth is comparatively recent. In the middle of the C18 the place amounted to no more than three fermtouns: Glenshellach, Glencruitten and Soroba. Then, in 1758, the engineer *Daniel Paterson* surveyed the area for the Duke of Argyll and other local landowners, as a result of which the Duke transferred the Custom House from Fort William and started to lease land now forming Shore Street and High Street. Cattle and herring brought some

400 ARGYLL: THE MAINLAND

- Dunollie Castle
1. Cathedral of St John the Divine (Episcopal)
2. Congregational Church
3. Free Presbyterian Church
4. Free High Church
5. Kilmore and Oban Parish Church
6. Oban Baptist Church
7. Oban Parish Church
8. St Columba Cathedral (R.C.)
9. Former St Columba Parish Church

10. Oban Distillery
11. Sheriff Court House
12. District Council Offices
13. Post Office
14. Police Station
15. Unemployment Benefit Office
16. Telephone Exchange

Oban

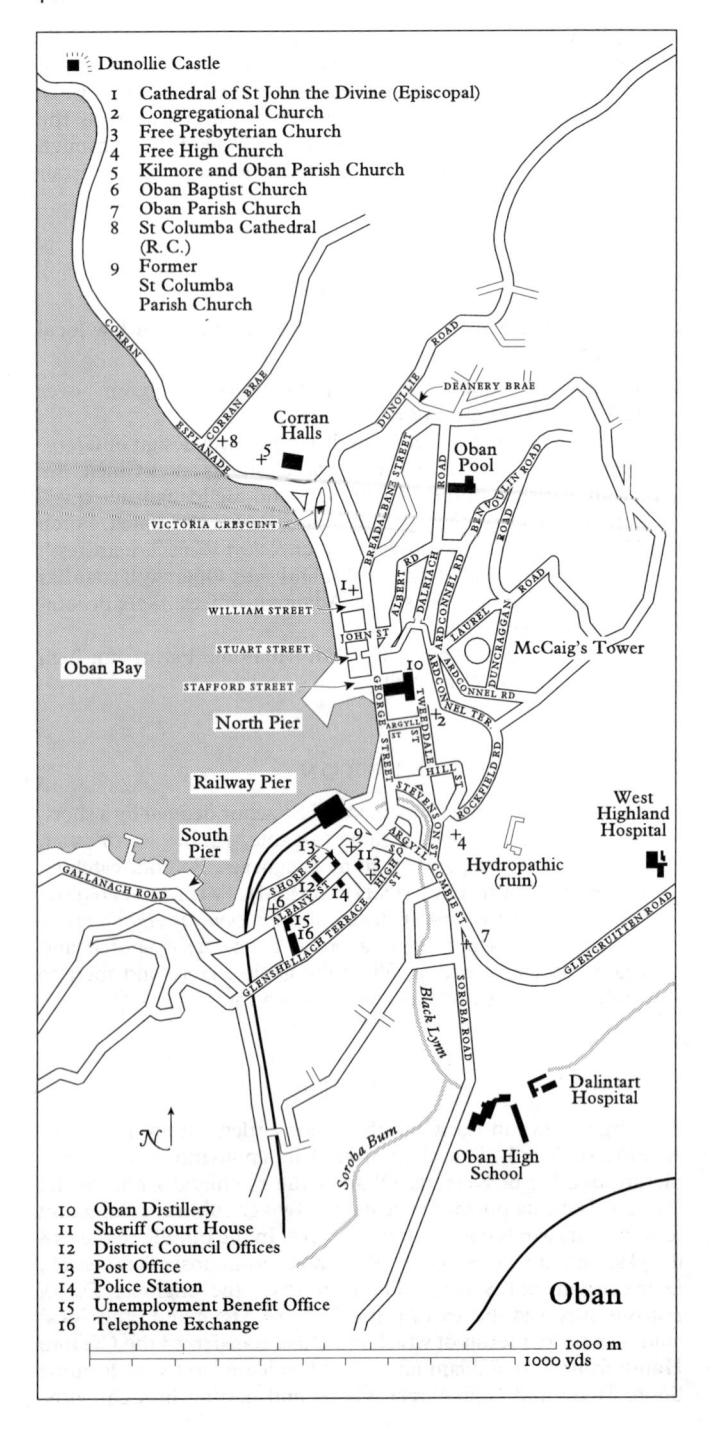

trade to the new village, while Boswell and Johnson's tour in 1773 helped establish that romantic allure which Oban and the Hebrides have continued to exert. In 1791 *George Langlands* produced a proposal for further development N of the Black Lynn. Around the turn of the century, a simple single-block grid was begun, bounded on the shore side by George Street and on the E by Tweeddale Street. Building started and the town grew slowly to this more ordered plan. Then, under the stimulus of the Napoleonic Wars' economic boom in beef, expansion accelerated. George Street, clearly intended to become the town's principal thoroughfare, was extended N while Combie Street went S. Argyll Square, a green space at the centre of town, took more positive urban shape. Shore Street stretched SW as Cawdor Place, 1812, and a year or so later the South Pier was constructed. In 1816 steamboat services connected Oban with Glasgow and in 1819 the two were linked by coach.

By the time Oban finally attained burgh status in 1820 it had acquired a distillery, a tannery, a schoolhouse, and several inns; a property in Tweeddale Street was being converted into a church and work on a hotel was under way. A chapel of ease, two banks, and a carding mill followed within a few years. In 1832, with a population approaching 1,500, Oban became a parliamentary burgh. By mid century the town was prospering, its attractions as a fashionable resort to visit *en route* to the Western Isles reinforced by Queen Victoria's remark that it was 'one of the finest spots we have seen'. It was soon at the centre of a reorganized network of inter-island steamer and puffer transport. From the new pier, built at the end of Stafford Street to cope with the increase in coastal traffic, to the older S quay, development stretched around the bay, articulated N and SW of Argyll Square, in several 'streets of good and commodious houses' (*NSA*, 1845). Meanwhile, on Oban Hill and Pulpit Hill, where plots were being feued and roads laid out, an explosion of villa building was about to begin. In the 1860s and '70s trade and tourism continued to boom; hotels, churches and schools proliferated. The coming of the railway, which in 1880 swept in from the S to a new quayside station between Shore Street and the bay, added a further boost to growth. More hotels appeared, including the abortive Hydropathic on Oban Hill. The esplanade, already constructed in 1860, was now extended N to Corranmore. In 1888 Albany Street was created; it became the town's civic heart as courthouse, police station and municipal offices were built. But while the density, diversity and scale of development increased in the flat, central areas of town, residential expansion continued along the narrow coastal strip to the N and S and up on the hilly periphery of the town, where labyrinthine streets wound around the steep rocky topography, ensuring for the middle-class families who built on the edges and heights some of the finest views imaginable. No prospects pleased more than those framed by the arches of McCaig's Tower, that hollow but hauntingly monumental ring of granite which gives such a memorable skyline to the distant sea-seen prospect of Oban itself. Left unfinished in 1900, it seems at once to crown the town's rise to prosperity and to memorialize the beginning of decline.

As the C20 began, Oban acquired some of its finest sea-front buildings. The population had reached 5,500 and the future looked bright for the 'Charing Cross of the Highlands'. But the rate of growth was already decreasing: whereas in the fifty years from 1851 to 1901 the population increased threefold, the next half-century raised the town's total to little more than 6,000. Today tourists still come; the relationship with the islands remains a vital aspect of the community's *raison d'être*; and the town has grown as post-World War II local authority housing at Corran Brae, Glencruitten and Soroba pushed the boundaries further out into the country. But things are less well-groomed now. In recent years little has been built to compare with the legacy of Victorian or Edwardian fashion.

CHURCHES

CATHEDRAL OF ST JOHN THE DIVINE (Episcopal), George Street. Intermittently constructed from 1863 to 1968. An unprepossessing exterior of disorganized Gothic, muddled together on a corner at the N end of the town's main street. Multi-roofed complexity gives the game away; this is a monument to frustrated ambition, the result of repeatedly unsuccessful attempts to complete a church worthy of the cathedra. Yet within, evidence of this persistence and creative resilience constitutes a unique architecture, a deconstructed, or at any rate aggregated, world of start and stop in stone and steel. Surprisingly, the combination of Gothic masonry and riveted, raking steel shores produces an interior of genuinely contemporary spirituality, a materialization not of perfection but of perfectibility.

The sequence of events is best understood if the plan is read as three adjacent zones, two set gable-end-on to George Street, the third lying laterally to the N. The SE entrance, close to the corner with William Street, is through a pointed-arch doorway in a small E porch. This leads into the gable-end of a five-bay aisle (now effectively a narthex) roofed with arch-braced trusses on corbel stones and lit by simple lancets along the S wall, a three-light traceried W window and a cusped circular E window over the porch. In the SW corner a stair descends to hall accommodation made possible by the slope W across the site towards the esplanade. Aisle and hall date from 1882, added by *Thomson & Turnbull* to the S of the Parish Church of St John, built in 1863–4 by *David Thomson* who had picked up the commission of his recently deceased partner *Charles Wilson*. A SE steeple was proposed but not built. Aisle and church are now visually linked by a fully glazed timber screen, the sliding panels of which slip back to increase the space as required. This removal of the aisle arcade is made possible by a long steel beam introduced in 1968 to carry the trusses which meet under the mutual valley of the two old roofs (*see* below). But if, as can be seen, the support afforded here is ingenious, the structural solution contrived on the N side of the 1864 fabric remains a mystery, for there, apart from a short length of wall returning from the W

Sanctuary, choir, and one bay of nave, 1910

Original church, 1863–4

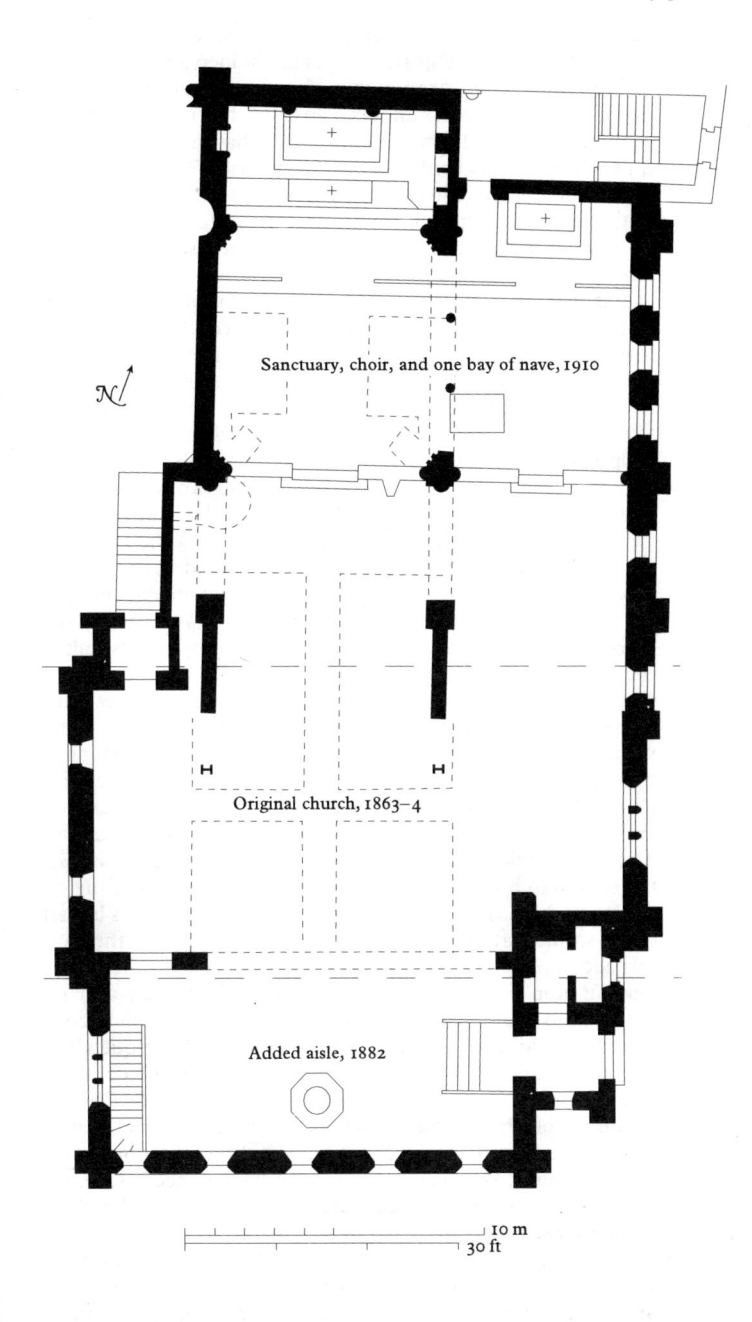

Added aisle, 1882

10 m
30 ft

Oban, Cathedral Church of St John the Divine

gable, all support vanishes as space flows freely N into the third zone of the church. This structural feat, hidden above a boarded ceiling along with, presumably, the diaper patterning which decorated the old roof timbers, is part of that 1968 programme of intervention and consolidation which has given St John's its quite exceptionally fissile but exciting interior. Thus the original church building of 1864 survives as little more than two gables, both exposed as random rubble on the inside face, the W with two lancets and a circular window above, the E with a three-light traceried opening in a pointed arch.

It is the third zone which, literally, raises St John's to cathedral status. As early as 1846, when the first synod of the revived Episcopalian diocese of Argyll and the Isles met in Oban, there were thoughts of a cathedral. More modest aspirations prevailed and the church in George Street was in due course erected. In 1881 the dream revived and *Ross & Mackintosh* prepared a proposal designed along the lines of Iona Abbey. Again, the idea was abandoned, the S aisle being added to the Thomson church in the following year. By the end of the century a New Church Fund had been established and by 1903 the ground to the N of the existing building had been purchased. A competition was held for the design of a new and larger building and in 1908, from five designs submitted, that by *James Chalmers* was chosen. This time work began. In 1910, when the project was halted, the sanctuary, choir, one transept bay to George Street, and one bay of the nave had been built in warm pink St Bees sandstone. Raking steel shores were introduced to counteract the thrust into the nave; incongruous but exciting, they remain buttressing the interior. The style of Chalmers's work is predominantly Norman with cluster piers and moulded semicircular arches springing across choir and nave from scalloped capitals. The scale is bold; at the eaves, the transept gable, which has three tall round-arch windows, reaches a height twice that of the old church to the S. Above this, had it been built, Chalmers's lantern tower would have soared almost as much again. But the work was incomplete and remained unfinished, despite the official inauguration of the church as a cathedral in 1920 and the preparation of a scheme by *Harold O. Tarbolton* in 1928 to complete the building in an asymmetric modern Romanesque idiom that contemplated the raising of a huge tower at the corner of William Street. A 1958 proposal by *Ian G. Lindsay & Partners*, the design of which entailed a lantern tower raised over a central altar, proved no more successful but it did reveal serious structural problems. By 1968, working with the engineers *T. Harley Haddow & Partners*, the same architects had consolidated the foundations, raised the nave floor, created the narthex screen already noted, and introduced a series of rooflights along the S edge of the nave above the new screen. Between 1982 and 1984 *Simpson & Brown* were engaged in a further attempt to complete the cathedral. Their proposal foundered. It had entailed the demolition of everything S of the Chalmers building in order to release valuable development land and thus realize capital.

Instead, in 1987, they began an extensive repair programme, the most significant aspect of which has been the introduction at high level of additional steel framing to reinforce the stability of the crossing. Flooded with light from the glazed roof over the choir, this patent honesty acquires a sanctity which seems (and yet should not seem) paradoxical.

FURNISHINGS are lavish if, like the church itself, disparate in character. – Magnificent canopied Gothic REREDOS of gilded and stained carved oak, 1910, made by *Wylie & Lochhead* to the design of *James Chalmers*: its oil paintings, cleaned in 1989, are by *Norman M. MacDougall*, and depict the Pietà and the Ascension envisaged in a West Highland setting. Below two outer paintings illustrating the Annunciation are sculptures by *Martyn & Co.* of St John and St Columba, the latter resembling Bishop Chinnery-Haldane †1906, who had vigorously promoted the building of the New Church. – ALTAR, 1910, of pink stone with Iona marble retable and inset panels of Greek and Italian marble. – To the r., three SEDILIA inset in sanctuary wall below a single round arch; on the l., a round-arched seat recess. Steps down to choir in green-veined white Iona marble. – Twelve oak CANONS' STALLS, 1910, by *Wylie & Lochhead*, dedicated to Celtic saints, their 'poppy head' ends looking a little like gravemarkers. Drum PULPIT, 1910, of St Bees stone, with an open round-arch arcade in which coupled round-headed arches of varied marbles and Mexican onyx are set. Mounted high in the blocked w transept arch is a bronzed metal SCULPTURE of an eagle, symbol of St John the Evangelist; by *George Wyllie*, 1972. – Brass eagle LECTERN, 1882, by *Jones & Willis*. – In the Lady Chapel, E transept, an ALTAR of golden Siena marble with a table of light green Swedish marble, by *Tarbolton*, consecrated 1939. There is a Della Robbia PANEL of Our Lady above the credence. – Adjacent octagonal PULPIT, 1883, of timber with gilded Gothic motifs and narrow buttress-legs, comes from St Columba's Church, Portree, and may therefore be the work of *Alexander Ross*. Both choir and side-chapel are floored in terrazzo and fronted by flat brass altar railing decorated with vines and cut-out quatrefoils. Iona marble steps. – Timber panelled ORGAN LOFT, 1910, raised on steel supports and triple-arch arcade in lozenge plan bridge between choir and Lady Chapel; organ by *J. Wood & Sons*, 1994. Positioned in the narthex in 1968 is a heavy Gothic FONT, 1882, in onyx and marble; lid, 1928. – STAINED GLASS. Traceried E window, 1864, illustrating episodes in the life of St John the Evangelist, by *William Wailes*. Two round-arch windows on E wall of Chalmers's church depict Christ the Good Shepherd and a kneeling red-cloaked Christ in a dark Gethsemane, *c.* 1910(?). – PAINTED GLASS, 1990, in the two w gable lancets of the 1864 church in a light naïve style by *Sarah Campbell* of Dunstaffnage: Jacob's Dream at Bethel and the Vision of St John the Divine.

CONGREGATIONAL CHURCH, Tweeddale Street. Classical w front in ashlar sandstone, pedimented and pilastered. Dated 1880; vestry added, 1894. Central round-arch entrance door, sitting between pilastered, round-arched windows with vermiculated keystones, opens to a balustraded terrace above street level. Decorative chimneys and six round-headed windows at the sides. Coffered ceiling coved on to corbel stones. Art Deco sunburst glazing above central pulpit, 1938.

FREE PRESBYTERIAN CHURCH, Campbell Street. Built 1895–6. Dull Gothic in grey granite. Small circular window and two plain lancets in High Street gable.

FREE HIGH CHURCH, Rockfield Road. Designed by *David Cousin* after a proposal prepared by a local architect named *McNab* and favoured by the congregation had been rejected by the Marquess of Breadalbane. Dated 1846, though Cousin appears not to have been paid for the plans until 1850. Pugin-derived E.E. in greenish Ardentallen sandstone. A triple-lancet W gable looks down over the town. NW three-stage belfry tower with clasping buttresses: at the base, a hooded pointed-arch entrance; at the summit, a low slated pyramid protected by a battlemented parapet. The five-bay interior has two separate open timber roofs, with arch-braced trusses resting above the capitals on opposite sides of the aisle arcade wall. The layout of pitch pine pews focuses somewhat unexpectedly, but successfully, on the centre of the S wall (in effect a typical Scots Presbyterian T-plan) where the raised PULPIT, 1846, is a Gothic aedicule canopied by a finialled spire, 1861, faceted towards the congregation in two gablets; in each of these, cusped clock-faces measuring the sermon with a minatory immediacy. BELL in tower, 1860, by *John Wilson* of Glasgow.

KILMORE AND OBAN PARISH CHURCH (Christ's Church, Dunollie), Corran Esplanade. By *Leslie Grahame MacDougall*, 1954–7. Funded in part by the legacy of Ann McCaig whose 1901 will had left site and money to build a 'Stately Church'. The result is scarcely 'in the style of a Cathedral' which Miss McCaig envisaged, but the white splay-gabled building with its copper roof and distinctive S tower catches the eye on the prom, even beside its grander neighbour, the Roman Catholic Cathedral of St Columba (q.v.). MacDougall's conception draws on greater things, for the proportions and window placement of the square tower and, above all, the copper-clad columned octagon which sits on top, all come from Ragnar Ostberg's Town Hall in Stockholm, 1909–23. The scale at Oban is diminutive by comparison but the forms are in a provincial way almost as picturesquely successful in their harbour-side setting as those in the Swedish capital are in theirs. Bronze cross on the tower by *Charles Henson & Son*. The interior attempts cathedral allusion with sanctuary arch, clearstorey windows and passage-aisles beyond the main portal frame structure. The seven-step rise to the communion table scarcely seems presbyterian. – Canopied PULPIT boxed in l. corner. – Octagonal biscuit-barrel FONT in timber. – STAINED GLASS in the tall chancel window, by *A. Carrick Whalen*, 1978; the Ascension, the imagery intensified with pieces of strongly-coloured Norman Slab glass. It commemorates the architect, and saves the church interior from its airy blandness.

OBAN BAPTIST CHURCH, Albany Street and Shore Street. Four-bay gabled nave, 1903–4, in grim, grey granite Gothic. Gabled porch with hooded pointed-arch doorway. By *Alexander Shairp*.

OBAN PARISH CHURCH, Soroba Road and Glencruitten Road. Built 1893–4, replacing 1821 Chapel of Ease. Muted Norman Revival by local architect *Alexander Shairp*. Gushet-sited, the gable front, with squat obelisk finials on outer buttresses, looks N up Combie Street. Projecting at the centre, a tall slender steeple almost wholly in ashlar in the taller upper stages and octagonal broached spire. Porches lean-to l. and r., repeating nave roof pitch and obelisk corners. Constructed in Cruachan granite rubble with dressings of Giffnock sandstone. Paved triangular forecourt. The church is six bays deep, each with a single round-arch window set between saw-tooth coped buttresses. Inside, there is a rear gallery with quatrefoil panelling supported on two very slender cast-iron columns; these have no capitals but scalloped abaci, each with four cast cockle shells on the soffit. In the tower's winding stone stair is a stone TABLET, the date A.D. 1821 within a cable-moulded ellipse, a relic from the bell turret of the old Chapel of Ease. The coved ceiling follows the arch bracing of trusses with a flat at truss tie level. Marble FONT, *c.* 1908. – ORGAN console and pipes, l. of sanctuary, by *Ingram & Co.* of Edinburgh. – White marble bowl FONT, *c.* 1910(?). – Large white marble WAR MEMORIAL; flat pedimented block with acroteria. – STAINED GLASS. Three-light memorial window over pulpit by *Herbert Hendrie*, 1930(?). Single round-arch w window by *William Wilson*, 1951, portrays the Nativity, Anointing, Crucifixion and Ascension of Christ.

In the GRAVEYARD behind the church are memorials to the surgeon, J.D. McGrigor †1840: an urn-topped OBELISK on pedimented plinth base by local builder, *D. Smith*; and to Donald Campbell, professor of physics at Anderson's College, Glasgow †1898, a ringed Celtic CROSS, with floral whorls on the shaft and bossed in the arms and centre. Cast-iron grave marker, 1861, with vine leaf ornament.

OBAN UNITED PRESBYTERIAN CHURCH, Dunollie Road. See Description below.

ST COLUMBA'S CATHEDRAL (R.C.), Corran Esplanade. By *Sir Giles Gilbert Scott*, 1930–53; foundation stone laid 1932. Erected by local contractors *D. & J. MacDougall*, glowingly commended by the *Oban Times* as 'among the best builders in Britain'. The cathedral is the decidedly permanent successor to the impermanent prefabricated pro-cathedral clad in corrugated iron, the so-called 'tin cathedral', which had been erected in 1886 and furnished in lavish style by the 3rd Marquess of Bute. Built in snecked, pink Aberdeenshire granite and designed in a controlled Gothic that wants to be, but is not quite, Romanesque (an aborted design of 1913 by the London architect *Alfred W. Johnston* was also in Romanesque style), Scott's unambiguous nave-and-aisles formula is executed in grand scale and fronted by a crenellated SW tower with three tall equal lancets, broad set-back corner buttresses, and an engaged octagonal NW stair turret all soaring above the esplanade. Behind this massive tower (not completed until the post-war phase of building) the plain parapets of the nave run back without a clearstorey. Below, hidden by crowstepped half-gables, sloping slated planes over the aisle roofs overlap the tower to cover lateral vestibules with buttress-flanked, pointed-arch, NW and SE doorways. Lancets in level-headed groups of four light the aisles between buttresses and screen the belfry louvres high in the tower.

The stone-flagged interior is lofty, bare and agreeably austere. Architectural ornament is minimal; almost the only concessions to decorative carving are the simple scalloped capitals and a bold 'modern Gothic' hood-moulding in the form of a flattened ogee arch which appears over lintelled doorways. It is the space not the detail which impresses. Thick, pink Peterhead granite piers carry arcaded walls of rough blue-grey Inverawe granite down the darkened height of the nave. In the gloom above, oak king-post trusses with curving struts support the purlins and spars of the roof, while half-trusses cross the aisles below. At the NE end of each aisle the last bay becomes a chapel, while the king-posts of the nave roof continue for two further bays into the chancel. The chapels are separated by stone screens of eight trefoil-arched slots set below the aisle truss ties from a seventh bay housing the organ chamber on the l. and the sacristy on the r. The sanctuary terminates in a vast expanse of blue-grey snecked granite lit from lancet windows on the N and S. At the opposite end of the church the same material closes the view. There, under the tower, is the baptistery, separated from the nave by a high pointed-arch and bathed in light falling from tall lancets.

The FURNISHINGS make a sharp impact in this stark masonry interior. The dominant element, set within a marble border carrying a zig-zag vine motif, is the high timber REREDOS designed by *Scott* himself and carved by *Donald Gilbert*. Below a finialled canopy are two vertical oak panels, each crowned with intricate Gothic fretwork; one showing the submission of the Pictish king Brude to St Columba, the other the meeting of St Columba and St Kentigern. Between these is a crocketed spire and traceried steeple. – The HIGH ALTAR is of Hornton stone with a top slab of Italian marble. – To the l., in the Lady Chapel, is a plain ALTAR of similar stone and a second REREDOS here depicting the Assumption of Our Lady carved in limewood by *Peter Watts*. – Placed nearby is the BISHOP'S CHAIR, 1982, bearing the symbols associated with St Kentigern and shaped in free idiosyncratic style by *Tim Stead*(?). – On the wall, a Madonna and Child PANEL, possible Early Renaissance Italian in provenance. – Over the Sacred Heart Chapel, r. of High Altar, hangs a BALDACCHINO which seems to take the form of an inverted open book. – STATIONS OF THE CROSS in gilded timber. – In the baptistery, a wide, copper-lidded, saucer FONT of pink granite, by *Charles Gray*.

Former ST COLUMBA'S PARISH CHURCH, Argyll Square. By *J. Fraser Sim*. Dated 1888, completed the following year. Originally Argyll Square Free Church. E.E. Gothic in grey granite rubble with sandstone dressings. E corner steeple cut down to pyramid capped tower, 1977. Gable to Square has three bipartite lancets over a pointed-arch entrance. To the r., the oblique wall of the gallery stair continues down Shore Street under a blind arcade parapet which bears the architect's monogram. Behind the tower the four-bay nave stretches along Albany Street to a traceried transept gable. – In 1929–30 the church was renovated; redecoration design by *Sir D. Y. Cameron* does not, however, survive. Now converted to an Information Centre, the interior has little to commend it. – STAINED GLASS in the SW cogwheel window: St Columba and companion in a small boat. – Gable-ended halls, 1892, by *Alexander Shairp*, return down Campbell Street.

ST COLUMBA'S PARISH CHURCH, George Street. *See* Description below.

CEMETERIES

GRAVEYARD, Oban Parish Church. *See* Churches above.

PENNYFUIR CEMETERY, 2km. NE on the NW side of the A85. A neatly tended spread of C19 and C20 graves ranged around and beyond a central hillock. Among the expected obelisks, Celtic crosses, draped urns and broken columns are a few stones of special note. Most are located around the mound at the centre of the cemetery. – Standing highest is the MONUMENT to the steamer service pioneer David Hutcheson †1880, a mechanically cut ringed Celtic cross in pink granite. – Next to this, a weathered marble HEADSTONE commemorating, amongst others, Neil Macleod Macdonald †1881; a Gothic aedicule within which an airborne angel holds an arm aloft. The lair is bordered by a railed marble kerb with the sculptor's name, *L. A. Malempre* of Kensington, London. – MONUMENT to the Oban painter, Alexander Low Gray †1916, and his wife and family: a grey granite plinth carrying a pensive female figure in white marble. An artist's palette and brushes incised at the plinth base recall the decorative interiors Gray prepared for Oban's hotels and churches. – A powerfully carved Celtic CROSS, bossed but not ringed, marks the grave of John Miller Maxwell †1907, and his wife: pink granite decorated with whorls, plaitwork, floral forms and the words MORS JANUA VITAE. On the sides, a griffon or dragon and the figure of a harpist. By *McGlashen*, Edinburgh. – An asymmetrical white marble HEADSTONE to the family of J. Smith †1912, of Cawdor House, Oban, bears an Art Nouveau angel sculpted by *McDougall*. – A tall plain MONUMENT of polished grey granite given a bold gorge cornice commemorates William Chalmers †1929, and his wife. A short distance SW, a still more Egyptian, grey granite pyramid MONUMENT to Angus Gregorson †1873.

PUBLIC BUILDINGS

Former CHEST HOSPITAL, Laurel Road. Originally Benvoulin House, c. 1880, a large double-pile gabled house with modest castellation. Converted to serve as administrative offices of Argyllshire Sanatorium, 1907, by *Neil Gillies*, who also added unremarkable pavilions, chalets, laundry, etc. Boarded up and abandoned.

CORRAN HALLS, Corran Esplanade. By *Crerar & Partners*, 1963–5; the design preferred to an earlier proposal by *William Kinninmonth*, 1958. Brutally horizontal affront to the front. Twelve-bay, flat-roofed box contains glazed restaurant opening to S terrace; two-storey halls, and first-floor library to N and E.

COUNCIL OFFICES, Albany Street. Oban's Municipal Buildings: two tall storeys and seven pilastered bays by *Alexander Shairp*, 1897–8. Italianate, but complex and mannerist in character with pediments, pulvinated architraves and an out-of-scale Palladian motif at the centre of a busily detailed façade. Dated on the Campbell Street elevation. Two cast-iron lamp standards with fluted and swagged bases. Former council chamber on first floor NE has floral cornice, dado panelling and a pilastered chimney-piece with pedimented overmantel.

DALINTART HOSPITAL, Miller Road. Built as Lorn Combination Poorhouse by *John McKillop*, 1862. Plain two-storey L-plan with dated central gable. Extended in 1896 by *Kenneth Macrae* and in 1912 by *James G. Falconer*. Abandoned.

ESPLANADE. From the early C19 some form of sea-wall retained the W side of George Street from the debouch of the Black Lynn to the North Pier. In 1860–1, the Esplanade proper was formed, taking the sea-front promenade from the North Pier as far N as the Great Western Hotel and Columba Terrace. In 1879, Macfie of Airds built the present crenellated wall along George Street; ten years later he extended the Esplanade S by Shore Street to Pulpit Hill. While this last was soon removed to make way for the Railway Pier (*see* below), further stretches of sea-front road and walkway were constructed at Corran Road, 1894, and Ganavan Road, 1903.

FOUNTAIN, Argyll Square. By *Alexander Shairp*, 1904. An octagonal mercat cross plinth on stepped base supports a central column with block capital and ball finial. Fountain niches in plinth. Commemorates the town's Medical Officer, Robert Barbour McKelvie †1901.

KILBOWIE HOUSE, 1.9km. WSW of South Pier. Built as a private residence, 1888, but subsequently adapted as a hostel for schoolboy pupils from the Islands, before becoming the offices of Strathclyde Regional Council Roads Department in 1991. Baronial mansion in rough red sandstone; L-plan with square stair tower in the S re-entrant. All the usual features: crowstep gables, stepping stringcourses, cable moulding, a bartizan on the E corner and a full-height, conically roofed, N corner bow with battlemented parapet and mock cannon. Open cast-iron spiral escape stair. Large conservatory extending from NE front in poor repair. Battlemented NW terrace, with mock bastions, overlooking the Sound of Kerrera. Despite its vicissitudes, the house retains some fine timber- and plasterwork. In the oak-lined hall, diagonal boarding on panelled walls and coffered ceiling. Doors and window shutters panelled in oak or yellow pine(?). Several carved oak fireplaces with decorative tiles. In the former study, a panelled plaster ceiling; dentilled cornice with consoles. Oak open well stair. Former billiard room on the second floor boarded throughout in pitch pine. On the Gallanach Road are the long low OFFICES, also in red sandstone but without Baronial swagger. Above a pointed-arch coach-pend the gable is carved with quatrefoils and daggers. Triangular vents and doocot in the roof.

LORN AND ISLANDS DISTRICT GENERAL HOSPITAL, Soroba Road, Glenshellach. A suave design of the simplest, unaggressive elegance by *Reiach & Hall*, 1992–5. What appears as a white-rendered, pitched roof block of two storeys stretches out along the valley, concealing deep-plan provision and inner courtyards; above a continuous first-floor sill course, grey panelling set between the windows emphasizes the long horizontal of the eaves. Single-storey Accident and Emergency wing extends E. In the re-entrant, a steel-framed porte-cochère with a glazed pyramid roof. Well landscaped, especially at N where grass banks sweep up to first-floor balconies sheltered by the piended overhang at the roof end.

MCCAIG'S TOWER, Duncraggan Road, Battery Hill. Built 1895–1900. Two tiers of pointed arches, fifty over forty-four, in a Colosseum ring of grey rough-faced Bonawe granite. Entry from NE through a high round arch with flanking pointed arches in battlemented portal. Above the portal keystone is a pink granite TABLET dated 1900 with the inscription JOHN STUART MCCAIG / ART CRITIC / AND PHILOSOPHICAL ESSAYIST / AND BANKER, OBAN. *McCaig*, who designed the ring, intended it to be a family Valhalla, with statues in the arches and a 100-foot (30-m.) tower at the centre, but he died before his dream could be realized. His unfinished Folly, a quiet landscaped enclave which is yet so ubiquitously evident on Oban's skyline, could scarcely be a better memorial.

MASONIC LODGE, Albany Street. Two-storey street front of rough grey granite by Edinburgh architect *John C. Hay*, 1889–90. Three round-arch first-floor windows surmounted by masonic symbols in tympana. Hall decorated in 1893 by *A. L. Gray*; a colourful scheme incorporating masonic iconography including 'All-seeing Eye' set in the keystone of an arch springing from one Doric and one Ionic column painted above chimneypiece.

MATERNITY HOSPITAL, Dalriach Road. Built as Craig Ard Hotel, *c.* 1865. Baronial mansion with crowstep gables, a castellated arched porch and a conically capped SW bow. Roll-moulded ingoes and weathered first-floor stringcourse. Boarded up and abandoned.

NORTH PIER. The earliest plan of Oban, prepared by *R. Stevenson* in 1846, shows that both a South Pier (*see* below) and a North Pier already existed. Improvements to the latter were made in 1855 in order to cope with the increase in coastal traffic stimulated by the new shipping company which G. and J. Burns had set up with David Hutcheson and David MacBrayne a few years earlier. In 1863 the pier was enlarged and improved and again, in the last quarter of the C19, it was extended on the NW where the quayside swept round into the Esplanade. Rebuilding in concrete took place in the 1920s. Symmetrical, single-storey PIER BUILDINGS, erected in brick in 1927 to a design by *David Galloway*, Burgh Surveyor, have a central pend surmounted by a squat square tower and broached metal dome. Piend-roofed wings return to define a landward forecourt.

OBAN HIGH SCHOOL, Soroba Road. By *Alexander Shairp*, 1890. Extended first by Shairp, 1896, and more radically in 1908 by *John A. Carfrae* whose high symmetrical NW front has skew gables at the centre and ends, with intermittent ball finials on linking parapets. 'Belvedere' ridge vent. Vast curtain wall extensions spreading NE by *Argyll County Council*, 1955–7(?).

OBAN POOL (Atlantis Leisure), Dalriach Road. Upgrading of earlier structure by *Crerar & Partners*, 1997–8. Bow-trussed roof over pool-shed with overhanging eaves on splayed struts. Buttressed blockwork walls.

POLICE STATION, 29 Albany Street. Late C19. By *David Mackintosh*, 1881; cell wing by *Alexander Shairp*, 1897. Two-storey terrace in bull-faced grey granite with sandstone dressings. Hooded, round-arched doorways. Fourth house in row of five by *Charles MacIntyre*, 1907.

POST OFFICE, Albany Street. By *W. T. Oldrieve* of *H.M. Office of Works*, 1908–10. C17 Scots in Ballachulish grey granite rubble and Giffnock sandstone ashlar. A crowstepped gable and four tall eaves dormers to the street front. Decorative dressings, such as strapwork, crisp and precise. At the rear, opening to Shore Street, is the later Post Office Garage by *H.M. Office of Works* under *John Wilson Paterson*, built 1934, in a similarly asymmetrical Scottish manner but roughcast with minimal freestone dressings.

RAILWAY PIER. Sea-wall and quay of masonry construction with concrete superstructure built by Callander and Oban Railway Co., 1879–80. At the same time, the railway station was erected: a nine-bay shed of lattice-girder trusses on cast-iron stanchions fronted by entrance hall, offices and a clock-tower in pierhead frame-and-panel construction, lightweight and lighthearted. Quay reconstructed and extended several times during the last quarter of the C19. The trim but hardly comparable replacement RAILWAY STATION, built by *British Rail*, 1987–8, following demolition of the C19 structures, is of ochre brickwork with a stepped boarded fascia and a grid-glazed wall to the ticket office. New PIER BUILDINGS, *c.* 1990, comprise a commercial development of close-packed slated pyramids, some with apex rooflights and most topped off with pagoda vents raffishly reminiscent of the distillery.

ROCKFIELD PRIMARY SCHOOL, Hill Street. The town's first School Board school, completed 1876 by *Alexander MacQueen*; extended 1894 and 1902 by *Alexander Shairp*. High-ceilinged, two-storey classroom blocks packed round an ironwork-crested French tower. A hint of Gothic; commercial rather than ecclesiastical.

SHERIFF COURTHOUSE, Albany Street. Symmetrical Italianate

grandeur by *Ross & Mackintosh*, 1886–8. Parapeted eaves cornice on consoles. Tall *piano nobile* of five round arches, deeply moulded in the ingoes and linked by impost stringcourse. Ground floor of channelled ashlar; central doorway has consoles carrying a balustraded canopy with urns. The interior of the first-floor court-room refurbished *c.* 1990 but the acanthus and egg-and-dart cornice to the coved ceiling survives.

SOCIAL WORK DEPARTMENT, Soroba Road. Imaginatively formed but street-conscious, roughcast offices by *Strathclyde Regional Council*, 1988–90(?). Under a pitched roof, running eaves-on to the pavement, oblique indents exploit the three-dimensional potential of diagonal planning. The idea is most fully developed below the open E and N gables where, supporting the leaded ends of roof purlins, exposed queen-post trusses rest their shaped leaded tie-beams on two, two-storey-high free-standing concrete columns. Projecting at the rear is the single-storey LORN RESOURCE CENTRE, the monopitched L-plan wings of which, repeating and extending the long runs of horizontal glazing of their neighbour, define a pleasant U-plan court open to the S.

SOUTH PIER. Rubble quay built *c.* 1814, to provide for the first steamship services from Glasgow. Slipway to W passes in front of the contemporary PIERMASTER'S HOUSE, a white-washed rubble cottage with a piended roof. Symmetrical three-bay E entrance front. Small round towers at NW and NE corners, each with a slated cone roof and a pointed-arch window viewing the harbour. Respectful C20 addition W and S.

TELEPHONE EXCHANGE, Drimvargie Road. Massive and bleakly symmetrical block in rough-faced sandstone by *H. M. Office of Works* under *John Wilson Paterson*, 1938. Three tall storeys with balustraded eaves. Lintelled ground-floor windows have splayed keystones and Gibbsian surrounds. Built a year earlier by the same architects is the EMPLOYMENT EXCHANGE on the corner with Albany Street, a one-storey-high trial-run in similar intimidating idiom.

WAR MEMORIAL, Corran Esplanade. Monument on bouldered cairn by *James S. Richardson*, 1919–23. Sandstone group of two kilted soldiers carrying a comrade, sculpted by *Alexander Carrick*. Bronze plaques on all four faces list the dead.

Former WEST HIGHLAND COTTAGE HOSPITAL, Glencruitten Road. Two-storey hipped-roofed block in rough-faced Bonawe granite with sandstone dressings; competition-winning design by *G. Woulfe Brenan*, 1895–6. Above the entrance is a dated stone, 1895, and above that, in a scalloped roll-moulded frame, a stone tablet naming the building as THE / WEST HIGHLAND / COTTAGE / HOSPITAL. Alterations made and pavilions added, 1898, 1911, 1934 and 1945. Boarded up and abandoned.

DESCRIPTION

ARGYLL SQUARE still acts as a pivot in Oban's townscape, as it has done since the beginning of the C19. Its architectural qualities are moderate: some respectable Italianate building on the s side, Nos. 17–19, by *Ross & Mackintosh*, 1883–4, the tower-and-gable front of the former St Columba's Church, now the town's INFORMATION CENTRE (*see* Churches), and a corner dome on the five-storey ROYAL HOTEL, probably also by *Ross & Mackintosh*, 1880. But a fussy traffic-island garden and the brutal elevational grid of Boswell House, occupying the High Street corner, demean the scene. Too many streets open off what has become a roundabout. The short length of STATION ROAD leads NW to Railway Quay (*see* Public Buildings) and the bustle of pierhead activity. Three streets, among the earliest in the town, run SW. SHORE STREET begins brightly with the Mannerist vigour and navy blue, ochre and gold paint of the CLARENDON HOTEL, late C19. Then come Nos. 1–7 CAWDOR PLACE, early C19, a continuous two-storey terrace of three-bay houses, one of which, No. 5, has a Greek Doric porch (formerly at No. 4, the centre of the row) of attached columns supporting a block pediment with solid acroteria and minute unscholarly guttae. ALBANY STREET has civic pretensions. On the r., after the buttressed bays and gabled transept and halls of St Columba's Church come the Municipal Buildings and, across a gap-site, the Post Office (for these *see* Public Buildings) and then, in complete textural contrast, CAMERON HOUSE, 1960–2, a flat-topped, flat-fronted office block in red sandstone ashlar with relentlessly repetitive fenestration. At the end of the street, past the Baptist Church (*see* Churches) and across the railway are Nos. 6–14 ALMA CRESCENT, a three-storey, thirteen-bay, rubble wall of tenements, *c.* 1880, with moulded sills and heavy alternating concrete quoins, stepping and curving downhill to Gallanach Road.

DUNGALLAN PARKS lie further on, dignified by the columned loggia of an ashlar SHELTER set between balustraded ramps leading down to the grass and the shore; by the Burgh Surveyor, *David Galloway*, 1933. On the l., Albany Street starts with some good four-storey tenements, late C19, passes the Masonic Lodge and crosses Campbell Street to the Sheriff Court (*see* Public Buildings above). A two-storey, grey granite terrace of five houses, each with a round-hooded, round-arch entrance in sandstone, incorporates the POLICE STATION (*see* Public Buildings above) and reaches almost as far as Drimvargie Road. Finally comes the grey, rough-faced granite of CAWDOR TERRACE, 1903–4, a Baronial tenement with corbelled octagonal corners and some polychromatic fish-scale slating. HIGH STREET, despite its name no more architecturally distinguished than Shore Street, is nevertheless well walled. It begins with OCTAVIA PLACE, an early C19 tenement which reveals a piended canted gable to Argyll Square but conceals a cone-topped rear turnpike. Dull but consistent mid or late C19 tenements follow; only No. 5, with a 1930s shopfront of green and black Vitrolite, brightens the street. Opposite the end of Campbell Street is the former INDUSTRIAL SCHOOL, 1861: walls reharled and crowsteps leaded – Scots vernacular adapting easily to domestic use.

Finally come the white walls of DRIMVARGIE TERRACE, 1993–6, by *Andrew Merrylees Associates*, a fresh-faced linear rise of piend-roofed housing high enough to be seen across the bay.
COMBIE STREET is funnelled from the SE corner of Argyll Square over the Black Lynn burn. It continues the tenement scale; three-storey buildings, dated 1894 and 1898, the latter on a scrolled frontal chimneystack. Hidden in Back Combie Street, a two-storey rubble block, late C18, with rear forestair. Ahead, the axial steeple of Oban Parish Church (*see* Churches above) marks a gushet junction. From an asymmetrical NE gable on Glencruitten Road the white roughcast wall of the CHURCH OF SCOTLAND CENTRE, 1994, by *Crerar & Partners*, negotiates the fall SW across the glebe land behind the churchyard. On SOROBA ROAD, containment disintegrates. Brick housing at DUNMAR COURT by *Crerar & Partners*, 1991–2, connects with the street in a bold convex curve of glazing and four canted bay attic dormers, while the Regional Offices of Strathclyde Social Work Department (*see* Public Buildings above), though highly modelled, still run parallel with the pavement. But the gaps increase. On its elevated site Oban High School (*see* Public Buildings above) stands aloof from the streetscape.

From the E end of Argyll Square two streets, both created in the late C19, curve along the sides of the Black Lynn to meet the S end of George Street. Neither AIRDS CRESCENT nor STEVENSON STREET has much to remark. In the latter, No. 19, the former Free Church Mission Hall, dated 1879, is a high two-storeyed building in robust Victorian Gothic, and Nos. 5–11, a well-ordered, six-bay, mid-C19 tenement of four ashlar storeys with architraved windows and cornices above both first and second floor.

GEORGE STREET is both the longest and straightest of streets, as it is in several of Scotland's principal towns. It is the backbone of Oban's narrow early C19 grid-plan. From the Black Lynn to Stafford Street it looks W over the harbour, except at its S end where a wedge of building separates it from Queen's Park Place and the swing of the promenade SW to Railway Quay. This wedge is taken up by the towered bulk of the CALEDONIAN HOTEL, by *William Menzies*, 1880–1, built as the Station Hotel to serve the new railway terminal. By the end of the century it had been extended N and several times altered by *Alexander Shairp*, who was probably the original designer: the result, an ashlar wall busy with set-backs, canted bays and curvilinear gables and a slated roof equally agitated by pyramid, dome and cone. In the N gushet, decoratively surmounted by finialled ironwork, is a wedge of tall flat-roofed shops defined by stilted segmental arches carried by stout Corinthian columns in pink granite; also by *Shairp*, 1884. In 1907–8 *W. L. Menzies* gave the hotel a new porch, its heavy entablature and balustrading continued over the curving SW wall of an enlarged dining room. On the E side of George Street, things begin well at Nos. 8–16, the former Queen's Hotel, 1891 – four storeys rising in Queen Anne style from a street-level loggia to a seven-gabled eaves. The PALACE

HOTEL, 1905, by *Gardner & Millar*, maintains the height in three-bay, pilastered order, while KING'S ARMS FLATS, formerly the King's Arms Hotel, 1888, by *Peddie & Kinnear*(?), just as high, has a crowstepped asymmetrical gable. Abruptly, eaves and quality drop and the harbour front degenerates. Just as suddenly, it recovers: rising erect and majestic to a wonderfully serrate roofscape, ARGYLL MANSIONS, 1905-7, by *Leiper & McNab*, saves the day. This is one of Scotland's finest tenements. Four storeys of rock-faced pink granite dominated by dressings of red Arran sandstone ripple across a gabled sea-front, splay round a dormered conical corner, and thrust upwards into four soldier-straight chimneystacks marching into Argyll Street. At street level, bulging Roman Doric three-quarter columns, lugged under a full-width cornice crisp with fine dentillation (and lugged again, below, at mezzanine height) mark out a shopfront range altogether worthy of such promenade prominence.

ARGYLL STREET, running E from George Street, keeps an earlier, simpler order on its N side: plain three-storey tenements, mid C19, interrupted at No. 9, a narrow roughcast slot of tiered tripartite bows capped by an equilateral gable, by *Leiper & McNab*, 1906. At the head of the street, not quite commanding the axis, the pedimented front of the Congregational Church (*see* Churches above). Round the corner in TWEEDDALE STREET are more tenements: No. 13, three storeys of grey granite centred on a chimneyed gable dated 1907, and, side by side, Nos. 7-9 and the WOODSIDE HOTEL, *c.* 1800, seven painted rubble bays with two segmentally arched cart entries.

After the excitement of Argyll Mansions, an insipid ordinariness returns to George Street. Only at STAFFORD STREET is a proper urban scale re-established. To the r. lies the dark granite of Oban Distillery (*see* Industrial Buildings) and, at the end of the short street, in the same material, the severe pavilion-like façade of the company's offices. Downhill l., fronting a public space that until the late C19 was known as George Square, three storeys of street wall look S across the harbour with a cool classical reserve. At Nos. 15-19, dated 1883 on the gable return to George Street, tripartite windows are symmetrically disposed at first- and second-floor level. Nos. 5-13 are plainer but wider; two three-bay units in rough grey granite. No. 1, the OBAN HOTEL, early C19, is again symmetrical, presenting a windowed gable to the S with a central Doric doorway, pilastered and pedimented. Pilasters and pediments of a more mannered Edwardian variety ('Queen Anne with Glasgow Style detailing', say Historic Scotland's Lists) enliven the red sandstone façades of the COLUMBA HOTEL, 1902, which sits at the W end of Stafford Street screening the North Pier (*see* Public Buildings). Chimneystacks and corner bows rise high above the eaves, the latter capped by porridge-bowl domes of red tiling. The earlier part of the hotel, 1885, by *J. Fraser Sim*, which extends N defining the approach to the Esplanade, is enhanced by a tall French tower and the black lacework of iron balconies crossing its grey Cruachan granite walls.

GEORGE STREET continues N of Stafford Street, busy with shops. On the W side is the puzzlingly named JOHN SQUARE, 1865; not an open space but a high flat-roofed range of shops, Nos. 97–101, with four identical units grouped under a dentilled cornice, two in their original roll-moulded frames. Nos. 103–105, late C19, rise three storeys to a cable-moulded eaves, turning a gabled Baronial corner down John Street. Then, two ashlar tenements: Nos. 107–117, dated 1897, six bays with another dentilled shop cornice accented over the close entry by a scrolled anthemion motif, and Nos. 119–121, plainer, symmetrical and dated 1894. Across William Street, the rust-painted gables of the Episcopal Cathedral (*see* Churches above) jump erratically along the pavement to ALBANY TERRACE, late C19, where the grid-plan ends in a gently curving tenement wall. On the E side, Nos. 94–100, *c.* 1870(?), two three-bay units wide with arched and cornised bipartite windows in the upper storeys, match the four John Square shops across the street, though here only one retains its roll-moulded framing. A bartizaned corner on John Street leads to canted bays corbelled over the pavement on hefty 'sawn-off' brackets at Nos. 102–112, 1888. In the gabled, red sandstone façade of No. 120, dated 1901, a single canted bay dominates a composition bristling with Mannerist detail below the whorled carving of an Art Nouveau parapet frieze. Finally, comes the former ST COLUMBA'S CHURCH by *David Thomson*, 1874–5; traduced almost beyond recognition by commercial violation, it lost its spire in 1953 but retains a rose window in the E transept gable – stained glass by *W. & J. J. Kier*, 1875, depicting five Old Testament prophets.

At the end of Albany Terrace, roads split. NURSERY LANE climbs uphill into villa-land past a T-plan tenement with quoined gables, 1894, by *William Mackenzie*. BREADALBANE STREET maintains urban dignity, at least as far as BURNBANK TERRACE, *c.* 1880, a long ashlar tenement with windowed chimney gablets, originally built for railway workers and now rehabilitated. DUNOLLIE ROAD is already suburban. Locked in the fork between the two is the former UNITED PRESBYTERIAN CHURCH, by *John McKillop*, 1867–8; adapted as halls and later secularized with uninspired respect, it has lost its short broached spire but keeps some vaguely Art Nouveau glass, 1902, in its lancet windows.

CORRAN ESPLANADE is Oban's fashionable face, a long slow arc of baywatch hotels and boarding houses. Its beginning at the North Pier marks the shoreside edge of the town grid, a legacy still legible in the modest painted rubble of the Oban Hotel (*see* above) and the muted baronial of the ARGYLL HOTEL, early, mid and late C19. But later vogues are quickly in evidence. The REGENT HOTEL, originally the Marine, a 'High Class Temperance House', is first a five-storey front of full-blown Baronial by *Alexander Shairp*, 1890, and then eight cream-rendered storeys of uncompromising, appropriately marine, horizontality. In 1936, after a fire which destroyed Renaissance decoration by *A. L. Gray*, the Glasgow architect *James Taylor* renovated the Marine's interior and built a wide five-storey bedroom extension from which the curved flat-roofed forms of reception and restaurant project seaward, embracing an elevated entrance terrace. Bridge links connect new to old across a narrow lane. Stair towers with corner windows 'oddly reminiscent of those in the Hoover factory, London' (McKean, 1987). Two further floors, added later, above Taylor's nautical metal-railed parapet and *fenêtres en longueur* do nothing to adulterate the 'Thirties ambience; this is a Fred Astaire world of film-set fancy. If only it were white – and its vestigial Art Deco interior more stylishly presented. Next, the OBAN TIMES BUILDINGS, by *J. Fraser Sim*, dated 1883; tall ashlar symmetry with two shop windows, two round-arched entrances and two canted bays rising from first floor to a heavy cornice on console brackets. Tall, too, but plain, calm and somehow sophisticated is ALEXANDRA PLACE, a mid-C19 range of two three-bay tenements with a stringcourse at second-floor sill level and a crudely dentilled cornice. ESPLANADE COURT, by *Crerar & Partners*, 1994, also has the size but neither the style nor the detail for the site, least of all in its absurd ironwork. But the barely concave, symmetrical front of Charles Wilson's GREAT WESTERN HOTEL, 1863–5, extended by *Ross & Mackintosh*, 1884–5, reconstructed by *Dick Peddie McKay & Jamieson*, 1945–6, despite having lost length and balance in its lower, wide-stretching wings, still manages to cling to a classical smartness that is, perversely, more evocative of a Sussex promenade than a West Highland harbour.

At this point, VICTORIA CRESCENT, late C19, four cleverly stepping houses in a never-finished terrace, hints at an expansiveness that might have been. But grass and tarmac intervene as the shoreside road sweeps up to become the A85. The Corran Halls (*see* Public Buildings) blight the scene, as much by isolation as by form, but at Christ's Church (*see* Churches) the Esplanade begins to recover quality and continuity. The ALEXANDRA HOTEL, begun 1871, extended 1898 and 1901 by *James M. Monro* and again in 1928–9 and 1936, by *Alexander McInnes Gardner*, is a wide-fronted agglomeration of canted bays and scrolled and stepped gables with an octagonal pyramid tower l. and an earlier French tower r. Both are dwarfed by that of St Columba's Cathedral (*see* Churches). Thereafter comes a run of late Victorian mansions, most attuned to the needs of C20 tourists, some to architectural disadvantage. The LANCASTER HOTEL affects a half-hearted, half-timbered pose. Both GLENCAIRN and KILCHRENAN HOUSE, 1883, have splendidly scrolled bargeboards, the latter further enhanced by a château tower. Less decorative but with a maritime freshness, the QUEEN'S HOTEL, late C19, relies on broad bows swept into convex gables, portholed in the attics. CORRIEMAR and GLENBURNIE, 1897, have canted bays three storeys high rising into stepped bargeboarded gables. At SEAFORTH it is a filigree cast-iron balcony that catches the eye, and at BARRIEMORE, 1895, last in the line, openwork bargeboards.

MANSIONS

DUNOLLIE HOUSE, 1.8km. NNW of Railway Quay. A plain house of four ranges which surround a central covered area. Built by the MacDougalls to take the place of Dunollie Castle (q.v.). The E range may date in part from the C17; the T-plan N range from 1746–7. The later buildings, forming two tallish, two-storey-and-attic, gabled blocks on the W and S were added c. 1834–5. Three single-storey rubble ranges form U-plan STABLES; part converted to dwelling.

DUNGALLAN HOTEL, Gallanach Road. Sandstone gabled château; two storeys with four-storey tower in re-entrant angle and single-storey-and-attic wings spreading S and E. In 1919 the Edinburgh architect *James S. Richardson* altered the main house including the attic formerly used as a chapel.

GALLANACH, 5km. SW of Railway Quay. Designed 1814 by *William Burn* for Dugald MacDougall, it replaced a much humbler laird's house. MacDougall had first commissioned *James Gillespie Graham* in 1812 but nothing came of this. Burn maintained the castellated Gothic idiom of his predecessor but proposed a grander symmetrical house of two storeys and sunk basement, with a square-turreted frontispiece at the centre of the NW façade, round angle-towers, and bowed towers at the centre of the side elevations. Building proceeded 1814–17 but the house remained unfinished, the rear areas behind the lateral bows being omitted. All openings are four-centred arches, the taller ground-floor windows and entrance door on the NW front being hooded. The rubble masonry and sandstone dressings have been cement rendered. A three-storey block by *Sir J.J. Burnet* was added asymmetrically at the rear E, c. 1903. Challenging in scale, it is at least in similar battlemented mould.

Interior intentions were compromised by the failure to complete the house as planned. A two-storeyed oval saloon at the heart of Burn's design accommodated the main stair while two open-well staircases, originally placed l. and r. of this central space, were abandoned. The stair preserves its swept mahogany handrail and cast-iron balusters. In the dining room and drawing room, each of which has a concave end-wall separating it from the entrance hall and stairwell, original marble chimneypieces survive.

GANAVAN HOUSE, 2.6km. N. By *William Leiper*, 1888; a variation on the Shavian design used at Aros, Rhu (q.v.), a few years earlier. Tiled roofs, half-timbered harled walls and gabled tile-hung bays, hidden in a wild wooded garden above the sea. The house has a faded autumnal charm, intensified by the russet colour of sandstone, tile and paintwork. Lych-gate porch. Atmospheric Arts and Crafts interior.

GLENCRUITTEN HOUSE, 2.3km. E of Railway Quay. Roughcast muted Baronial with a battlemented square entrance tower withdrawn into the NE re-entrant. A marriage stone over the round-arched entrance doorway gives the date, 1897, the initials J S B for the owner, James S. Boutein, and E J E, presumably for his bride. To the E is the crowstepped library wing, again roughcast with red sandstone dressings, added by *Lorimer & Matthew*, 1927–8. The library itself is at first-floor level, a tall elegant room lit by elongated eaves dormers with trefoil pediments and a high canted bay set in the E gable.

HYDROPATHIC. Silhouetted on the skyline above the Free High Church on a site which in May 1881 the chauvinistic *Oban Times* described as 'perhaps the best that could possibly be obtained in the Kingdom', two isolated stands of whin rubble walling (both rising to four storeys, one with a corbelled staircase tube) are all that survive of an ambitious but aborted late Victorian project to erect one of the country's biggest hotels. Stimulated by the coming of the railway, building began in 1881 to a design by the Glasgow architect *J. Ford Mackenzie* which envisaged 137 bedrooms, Turkish baths, hydraulic lifts and a private gasworks. A year later the contractor, *Robert Macalpine*, stopped work. The masonry shell was complete and sarking already on the roofs; but the money had run out. The unfinished building became a quarry. In 1896 an unsuccessful attempt was made to revive the project, but in 1908 the hotel was finally demolished, reduced to two ruinous remnants at opposite ends of the vast structure that had once overlooked the town. Perhaps the presence of concrete rather than ashlar dressings to some of the rubble walling betrays the financial crisis that wrought such a fate.

KILBOWIE HOUSE. *See* Public Buildings above.

THE MANOR HOUSE, Gallanach Road. Late C18, but before 1789. Plain, two-storey, gable-ended block with single-storey-and-attic piended wings which advance l. and r. Unharled walls of coursed whinstone with ashlar dressings. Possibly built as the Duke of Argyll's estate house; used by the National Bank, 1826–30, and latterly as a hotel. Fluted cast-iron lamp standards on each side of entrance door. Hall has three-centred archway with fluted pilasters. Larder (ice house?) and boat-house, both barrel-vaulted, in garden to N.

SOROBA HOUSE HOTEL, Soroba Road. Late C18; largely rebuilt. Three-bay, two-storey gabled house with shallow bows l. and r. on NW front. White walls cement rendered and lined.

VILLAS

By the 1880s, detached houses were beginning to appear on the fringes of town and especially on the heights overlooking the bay. Narrow roads climbed uphill to follow the contours, the villas orientated to enjoy the seaward view W. The Oban Hills Hydropathic Sanatorium Company began to construct a vast hotel (*see* Mansions). Corran Esplanade stretched N along the shore, while on the S side of the bay a leafy suburb sprang up on Pulpit Hill.

ARDCONNEL ROAD. CRAIGVARREN HOUSE, late C19, a white-painted, L-plan villa with French and Tudor Gothic flavouring.

ARDCONNEL TERRACE. Opposite Jacob's Ladder staircase is COLUMBA VILLA, dated 1894; a two-and-a-half-storey muscular mix of gabled bow and bay.

BENVOULIN ROAD. Polychromatic MANDERLEY, late C19,

makes an unusual, somewhat Italianate impression: grey granite, red sandstone ashlar, round-arch windows breaking through the eaves, cast-iron bracketed balconies.

DALRIACH PARK TERRACE. A grey granite run of eight houses in pairs: canted bay gables separated by coupled eaves dormers and entrances.

DRUMMORE ROAD. Now an Eventide Home, EADER GLINN, 1892, by *Alexander Shairp*, is an Italianate L-plan villa in granite and sandstone with a three-storey entrance tower in the re-entrant.

DUNUARAN ROAD. At the start of the climb to Pulpit Hill, MARIDON HOUSE, late C19, a plain gable-ended block with round-arched windows at first floor.

GANAVAN ROAD has provided the views and suburban detachment for more recent house building. Little is remarkable, though CUANRA, 1977, by *Crerar & Partners*, is long, low and elegantly glazed.

HILL STREET. Set into the curving hillside gushet below Rockfield Road, THE MAINS, a mid-C19 conjunction of three-storey house and single-storey cottage stepped up E.

ROCKFIELD ROAD'S E side begins with squeezed semi-dets stepping in plan and section. ROSSLAIRE, ATHOLL VILLA and BLAIR VILLA have attenuated canted bays corbelled back to gables and columned porches under a gabled bedroom overhang.

INDUSTRIAL BUILDINGS

OBAN DISTILLERY, Stafford Street. Two side-by-side, piend-roofed, four-storeyed malt-barns built in rough-faced, square-snecked, grey granite with dressings painted black and pointing white, *c.* 1800. Windows half-shuttered, half-glazed; smaller windows on top storey fully shuttered. Timber floors on cast-iron beams and columns. Extensive warehousing etc., C19, to the S, but the kiln roof by *Charles C. Doig*, 1898, has gone. Closing the E end of Stafford Street is a wide, three-bay, pavilion-roofed OFFICE block, 1894, by *Alexander Shairp*(?). Tripartite window in corbelled square bay at centre. Urns on blocking course over an eaves cornice.

DUN, 455m. W of Gallanach. D-plan enclosed by thick rubble wall. Well-preserved stretches of coursed faces, especially on the E where the wall rises 1.5m. ENE entrance gap. Internal wall revetment on SSW.

FORT, Dùn Ormidale, overlooking Gallanach from N. A large hilltop site at the S end of a long ridge. The entrance was probably from the N which is the least precipitous approach. Little walling survives but the defensible area, some 3 hectares, makes this the largest fort in Lorn.

DUNOLLIE CASTLE
1.75km. N of Oban Pier

Roofless rubble tower perched on a precipitous outcrop of rock overlooking the narrow strait which leads from the Firth of

Lorn into Oban Bay and the Sound of Kerrera. Excavations, 1978, have confirmed three phases of occupation, C7–C9, and it is easy to see why the kings of Northern Dalriada made this their stronghold. Ravaged by time, crag and castle alike struggle to resist the green grasp of parasitic vegetation. The tower, pitted from the pillage of dressed masonry, barely retains its architectural edge; only on its NW face does the quality of its rubble coursing and freestone quoins survive, while moulded ornament amounts to no more than a few chamfered arrises.

The square-plan tower stands back from the cliff face, angled obliquely into the NE corner of a ruinous barmkin wall which itself defines an almost square perimeter to the rock summit. Tower and enclosing wall, which stands to c. 4.6m. on the N and E but is otherwise much reduced, date from the C15, though most of the W curtain is later, probably C16. A restored E gateway has a draw-bar slot; a zig-zag N postern has been sealed. The tower walls rise through four storeys, the lowest with a barrel-vault which shows traces of wicker-centring, an Irish constructional technique found at Castle Tioram, Inverness-shire, but otherwise rare in Scotland. A single chamber evidently occupied each level. At ground level, which is entered through a SW doorway, there are narrow, deeply splayed slot openings in the SW and SE walls (the latter now blocked). A mural stair, to the r. of the SW entrance, rises in the SW and SE walls to first floor, while entrance to this upper level could also be gained through a second SW door, presumably accessible from a now absent forestair. NW and NE windows have arched heads and splayed ingoes, as do those in the SW, SE and NW walls at the level above. At first- and second-floor levels superimposed garderobe chambers have been located towards the SW end of the NW wall. A second mural stair rose in the SW wall, winding into the second-floor hall apartment at the S corner. Nothing remains of the garret, and the encroachment of ivy makes any determination of the parapet arrangements impossible.

Since medieval times the lands of Dunollie have been held by the MacDougalls, though not without forfeiture and subsequent restoration. Set in a ragged recess S of the E entry to the overgrown courtyard is a ringed Celtic CROSS to Alexander James MacDougall †1953, and his wife, Colina Edith †1963. Below are the family arms and, carved in relief within a circle in the plinth, a galley with dragon's head prow and stern.

ORMSARY

Estate stretching along W coast of South Knapdale.

BURIAL GROUND, Miadan Beag, 70m. E of Loch Caolisport shore near Ormsary Estate Office. Mostly C19 headstones with a few older broken gravemarkers. Forming the W wall of an otherwise railed enclosure is an asymmetrical gabled wall with MURAL TABLETS, early and later C19, to the Campbells of Ormsary on the inner face and incorporating a blind double lancet on the outer. Among graves in the N part of the site is one dated 177-(?), commemorating the tragic death of the mason, Alexander Bryce, with the lines WARNING TAKE YE / MORTALS ALL / FROM THIS / MY UNEXPECTED FALL / REMEMBER DEATH IS ALL / MENS DOOM / AND I WAS / CWT OF IN MY BLOOM. In the s, a finely carved sandstone TABLE-TOMB, mid C20, to the laird of Ormsary, the Port Glasgow shipbuilder, Sir James Lithgow †1952, and his wife Gwendolyn †1975.

DRUIMDRISHAIG FARM on estate road accessed off B8024 c. 1.5km. s of crossing of Ormsary Water. Gabled, two-storey-and-attic farmhouse with dormers. Late C18.

DRUIMDRISHAIG STEADING. Early C19. Three rubble buildings with lofts forming U-plan court. Piended roofs gabled at the open ends of the U. Central pavilion pedimented and pended to yard.

ORMSARY HOUSE. Three-bay, two-storey-and-attic core, late C18(?); extended late C19 and baronialized by *Charles S. S. Johnston*(?), 1905. Harled, with ashlar dressings.

OTTER FERRY

9384

A hamlet on the E shore of Loch Fyne from which, N of the mile-long oitir or sandbank jutting out into the loch which gives it its name, a crossing could formerly be made to West Otter or to Lochgilphead.

OTTER FERRY QUAY. In 1773 John Campbell of Otter completed a quay at East Otter for the Commissioners of Supply. This was replaced by the present L-plan rubble quay before the end of the C18. The angled outer arm has a slipway on its sheltered inner side, while the inner arm incorporates steep steps on the NE face. The steamboat PIER, 1900, is 1.6km. NNE; it closed in 1948.

THE OYSTERCATCHER. Black-and-white ferry-house inn, late C18. Its three-bay NW front has a plain pediment with a blind oculus and apex block. Behind a small central porch, C19, a round-arch doorway. First-floor window above is slightly off-centred to the r. A long, single-storey NE wing, probably a boathouse, has gone but its SW equivalent remains. Pine-panelled interior, 1993.

BALLIMORE HOUSE, 1.3km. SSW of Otter Ferry Quay. A 'chaste and elegant mansion' (*NSA*, 1843) in an asymmetrical castellated Gothic by *David Hamilton*, c. 1832, reworked and extended in Baronial style by *William Leiper*, 1898–9. A roughcast NE extension, 1914, probably by Leiper's partner *William Hunter McNab*, maintains a softer Scottishness, almost pusillanimous by proximity. Fortunately, Leiper's Baronial dominates. Yet though its bulk is scarcely endearing and some of its detailing inelegant (a castellated parapet is uncommonly massive and crude), the fusion of corbelled, conically-capped rounds on to the stugged ashlar masonry of the early C19 NW façade is almost imperceptibly done. Moreover, Hamilton's porch, often erroneously referred to as a porte-cochère, survives intact. From the steps beneath its wide, four-centred arch, the distant view NW to Loch Fyne is cleverly framed by trees. This once wonderful GARDEN, 1900–1, is the work of *Thomas Mawson*. In the foreground is a levelled terrace which returns for a considerable distance past the SW side of the house; it is bordered by a low wall regularly accented by obelisk markers. Steps and terraces lead down to lower levels disappearing into the luxuriant undergrowth of a lost garden. A roofless SUMMER-HOUSE with small Diocletian windows sleeps at the SE end of the terrace walk. But all is in decay. Lawns and flower-beds once cropped to the rigour of square and circle lie untended and unkempt. The ordered forms of parterre and topiary have gone. And somewhere SW of the house, hidden in the thickets of neglect that fill the valley of a meandering stream, are the coiling paths that Mawson so carefully contrived to wander among the azaleas and rare rhododendrons and above the sequence of pools and ponds which he and *James Pulham* had devised 'for fish to sport in'.

Some 250m. SE of the house is the COURT OF OFFICES, also by *Hamilton*. Dilapidated and repeatedly subject to alteration, it preserves a tall round-arched birdcage belfry corbelled above the carriage entry. Not only is the bell still in place but the copper-covered belfry dome is itself shaped in the form of an elongated bell. Buried deeper in the estate grounds, 500m. SW uphill, is a deserted but delightful Arts and Crafts dower house, BARNLONGART, *c.* 1899, probably by *William Leiper*. No Baronial bulk here, but rather a soft, roughcast Englishness: abandoned but almost intact, captivating in form and detail from its gabled two-storey bow to its dentilled bargeboards.

CHAMBERED CAIRN, Auchnaha. From its NE concave forecourt, 13.5m. wide, the cairn tails to a maximum length of 23m., but presumably was once much longer. Five façade stones still stand, one to a height of 1.5m., but both the end markers and portal stones have fallen. The chamber, 5m. long, was composed of at least two compartments. Two stone slabs set at right angles to each other appear to define a lateral chamber at the SW end of the cairn. Latin cross incised on SE façade stone.

DUN, Bàrr Iola, 1.8km. SSE of Otter Ferry Quay. Hilltop dun, its oval plan defined by 3m.-thick rubble walling best preserved on the N. Indistinct W entrance.

PENINVER

Hamlet extended along Ardnacross Bay, 7km. N of Campbeltown on the Carradale road.

CHAMBERED CAIRN, Ardnacross, 1.3km. NE of Peninver. Grassy mound, 24.5m. by 17m., with NE burial chamber where excavation has revealed a concave forecourt of dry-stone walling.

CHAMBERED CAIRN, Gort na h-Ulaidhe, Glen Lussa. Located on the N side of the valley, this long tapering cairn, measuring 35m. E–W, is 'the largest and most elaborate in Kintyre'. At the higher and broader E end a concave forecourt has been defined by upright stones; at its centre is the principal chamber, 3.8m. by 1.4m., aligned E–W. Four other chambers lie deeper in the cairn, all of these aligned N–S.

DUN, Kildonan Bay, 4.2km. NNE of Peninver. Well-preserved dun, C1 or early C2, of roughly oval shape on a rocky site close to the shore. Dry-stone walling of inner and outer faces still well preserved, and an unusual 'median face' within thickness of wall. Paved SW entrance. Internal opening on W leads to stairs l. and r. within wall core.

TOWNSHIP, Drumgarve, by Glenlussa Water 800m. SW of Drumgarve Farm. Ruinous remains of byre-dwellings on both sides of stream. Mill and its associated dwelling on r. bank. Signs of rig cultivation to N.

POLTALLOCH 8196

Gently rising parkland estate N of the Crinan Canal and River Add moss.

POLTALLOCH HOUSE, 4.4km. NNE of Bellanoch. Wide-spreading mansion in English Jacobean style by *William Burn*, 1849–53. A first design had been proposed in 1845 but protracted discussions with the clients, the Malcolm family, delayed the project's start. Known first as Calltuin Mór (place of the great hazel trees), the house is beautifully sited below a wooded ridge. Balustraded terraces and lawns with extensive views to the S and E; the work of *W. A. Nesfield* whose on-site involvement as Burn's representative seems to have entailed not only landscaping control but considerable detailed design advice as well. The exterior of the house remains largely intact, its roofless ashlar shell haunting the estate parkland like some gargantuan *gloriette*. It was dismantled in 1957 when the Malcolms moved to Duntrune Castle (q.v.).

Accommodation on two floors was arranged around an inner court open on the N, the main public rooms looking S. W, S and E façades have shaped quoins, continuous string cornicing at first-floor level and a balustraded cornice at the eaves intermittently accented with obelisk finials. Mullion-and-transom windows throughout; those to public apartments on ground floor dropped to low sills. Two-storey flat-roofed bays advance beneath strapwork cresting set ahead of curvilinear gables at each end of S elevation, a feature reiterated on W front and on lower private wing to NW. Projecting at the centre of the asymmetrical E front is a massive entrance block on to which a canted bay has been superimposed over a simple arched entrance flanked by Tuscan columns. Cornices to columns and bay coincide with those at stringcourse and eaves on main façades, but the eaves balustrading solidifies into a base for a high strapwork parapet carrying a central semicircular armorial panel axial with doorway below. In the re-entrant, N of the entrance block, is a decapitated three-storey octagonal clock tower turning the corner to the long S front of the stables wing, at the end of which is a similar two-storey corner. Both are without their original strapwork parapeting and ogee roofs, while the single-storey stables front has lost its dormered skyline and the upper part of a central curvilinear gable. Rear elevations are generally plain but with pedimented gables and dormers. The internal layout is more or less clear but the decorative plasterwork, including strapwork ceilings, timber panelling and stone chimneypieces is lost or dispersed.

ST COLUMBA'S CHAPEL (Episcopal), 200m. E of Poltalloch House. First conceived as the private chapel of the Malcolms of Poltalloch but realized as a church with congregation and incumbent. Built 1852-4 to a design by the London architect, *Thomas Cundy*, after the abandonment of William Burn's 1845 proposal to incorporate a family chapel at the SE corner of his Poltalloch House plan. Straightforward nave-and-chancel arrangement with gabled N porch and memorial chapel set parallel on the S side of chancel. Strict Early English: shafted lancets and plain stepped buttresses. Octagonal stone pyramid raised on W gable apex belfry. The droved ashlar interior has head-stop carvings on label mouldings and foliated capitals to the pointed chancel arch. Oak roof with pointed arch bracing to corbelled collar trusses. Panelled ceiling to chancel decorated with stars on a blue background. Diagonally laid red *Minton* tiles in nave; more tiles in the chancel patterned with quatrefoils and foliated crosses. An oak screen with wrought-iron gates separates chapel from chancel. – In the chapel, wall arcading with MURAL TABLETS to members of the Malcolm family. – Memorial BRASS to Neill Malcolm †1857, 'founder of this church of St Columba'. – Octagonal timber PULPIT with Gothic aedicule panels, set on a stone base. – Lidded octagonal FONT of Purbeck marble, also on stone base. – Three timber CHOIR STALLS, early C16 English, have been adapted as individual seats in the nave. Their origin is unknown but the front standards of the side panels and misericords are carved with idiosyncratic figurative forms. – STAINED GLASS in E and grisaille in all other windows by *William Wailes*. – CORONA by *Hardman & Co*. – Outside the church, fixed in a boulder base, is a cross-marked SLAB, C7–C9, brought here in 1928 from Barnakill Farm but of uncertain provenance. The cross form is deeply cut and has flat terminals; below it is a problematical inscription. – Inset in N porch gable, a rectangular sandstone PANEL of unknown provenance carved with the figure of a bishop in a vesica frame cusped with leaf forms.

BARSLOISNACH STEADING, now Poltalloch Home Farm, 750m. SSW of Poltalloch House. Slate-roofed, single-storey, rubble U-plan, constructed by *John MacCorquodale*, 1860–2, for Neil Malcolm of Poltalloch. The S range, 80m. long, terminates W and E in a two-storey, gabled house with rudimentary dripstones over the lower windows. Central unit, gabled over the pend entry to the court, inappropriately re-roofed. The steading replaced a smaller farm unit erected by the Malcolms as part of the agricultural improvements carried out in Crinan Moss at the end of the C18.

EAST LODGE, 1.3km. ESE of Poltalloch on B8025. By *William Burn*, 1854–5, who also designed the North Lodge (*see* Slockavullin). Much gabled, two-storey rusticated rubble with sandstone quoins, dressings and chimneys. Canted bays. Elaborately scrolled and bracketed bargeboards. Diamond-patterned balustrades lead convexly to obelisk-finialled piers of the estate GATEWAY and continue beyond over the BRIDGE across Kilmartin Burn, to the second set of finialled piers.

CHAMBERED CAIRN, Kilchoan, 500m. W of Poltalloch House. Little of the cairn remains, but a three-compartment, partly covered chamber measures 4.8m. Excavation in 1864 recorded a height of 2.5m. under the capstones but debris has reduced this now to *c.* 1m.

PORT ANN

9086

A handful of local authority and Forestry Commission dwellings on the W side of Loch Fyne.

CASTLETON HOUSE, 3.25km. SW. A pleasant Victorian house, unexceptional but bright, friendly and fresh-faced. The E front, harled with ochre sandstone dressings, looks across a dipping lawn to Loch Fyne. It seems to have grown in stages. At the centre, a two-storey unit, the earliest part of the house, *c.* 1840(?), incorporates a stone tablet dated 1875 carrying the initials J. G. C. for John Graham Campbell of Shirvan. Perhaps it was at this time that the ground-floor windows were widened and the three-storey S wing added. The E gable of the wing is the house's most charming asset: a wide canted bay becomes a balcony to a broad three-part first-floor window, with a superimposed sequence finishing beneath overhanging eaves in three attic lancets, all with diamond lattice glazing. A conservatory leans against the returning S wall. Recessed on the N gable is a parapeted link with a roll-moulded doorway and beyond this a single-storey, pediment-gabled wing which has a blind porthole at its centre above two bipartite windows linked by a broad droved ashlar mullion. Above the entrance is another stone panel bearing the inscription PRO ARIS ET FOCIS with the associated pledge PIGNUS AMORIS and the date 1898. Perhaps this N wing is the work of *Robert S. Lorimer*, then at work on Stronachullin Lodge (q.v.) on the W shore of Loch Fyne.

PORT APPIN

9045

A charming village on the ragged SW coast of Appin. Ferry point for Lismore. A few C18 cottages, now modernized, some C19 villas, and a surprisingly large, early Georgian, country house.

AIRDS HOME FARM, a little N of Airds House. Early C19. Much altered hipped-roofed, rubble ranges with a raised gable projecting at the centre of the principal front.

AIRDS HOTEL. Dormered roadside inn, C19. Elongated by later extensions NE and SW. Original two-bay centre has a pilastered doorpiece with cornice; now fronted by conservatory porch.

AIRDS HOUSE, 500m. SE of the village, sited at the head of Airds Bay with splendid views SW to the Firth of Lorn and Mull. A substantial classical mansion of almost unrelieved stolidity built 1738–9 for Donald Campbell, 5th of Airds. It may derive from Palladio's Villa Emo, perhaps via the S front of Marble Hill House, Twickenham, with the design of which the 9th Earl

Airds House, elevation

of Pembroke and perhaps Colen Campbell were associated a decade or so earlier. Certainly the disposition is eminently correct: a piend-roofed, five-bay block, three storeys high, pedimented at the centre of its main SW façade, extends quadrant arms l. and r. to lower pedimented pavilions. The walls are harled and, besides the grey-green sandstone of the rusticated quoins and plain window margins, only a minimum of architectural or ornamental elaboration enriches the otherwise cold face of provincial classicism. This interest is concentrated at the centre of the three-bay, pedimented frontispiece, which projects slightly. A pilastered entrance doorway carries a deep but plain frieze under a segmental pediment; in its tympanum a shield bearing the date 1738, perhaps a C19 remodelling but probably based on an earlier inscription. Above, at first-floor level, a round-arched window under an open pediment, and above this a heavily keystoned window with lugged architraves. But it is the ashlar pediment with its bold armorial carving set between bull's-eye openings and its three elegant urn finials which supplies a certain measure of superintendent sophistication. All other elevations are exceedingly plain, the NE front scarcely improved by two flat-roofed, square bay projections, added symmetrically l. and r. some time in the latter half of the C19. At the centre of each quadrant is a round-arched door with Gibbsian surround, now adapted as a window, and immediately above, sitting on a corniced coping stone, a ball finial. The pavilions are two storeys to the eaves, their two upper windows square rather than vertical like those to the ground floor. Each gable is chimneyed and pedimented, though only those pediments to the SW have central roundels. Behind the SE pavilion, which originally served as the kitchen, there is a lop-sided excrescence of service accommodation and billiard room added in 1858.

The PLAN of the main block is conventionally tripartite with a semicircular geometrical stair within an oval stair hall at the centre. This produces large single apartments on the outer sides of the two flue-carrying partition walls at both ground and first floors. It also means that windows in the SW frontispiece provide light either to the staircase halls, which at first- and second-floor levels are shaped in segmental reflection of the main stair, or to small awkwardly shaped areas created l. and r. at each of these upper levels in the gaps between the curve of the oval and the façade. On the other hand, by locating a tight turnpike stair within the thickening return of the façade wall at the NW end of the frontispiece, advantage is taken of some of these spaces to provide service to the upper floors. The principal staircase is perhaps the house's most attractive internal feature; its first flight is of stone but, above, its treads, risers and twisted balusters are of oak. A number of panelled doors and shutters survive and in one of the NW second-floor rooms some C18 wall panelling and a bead-moulded stone chimneypiece. C18 timber-and-stucco chimneypieces exist in the ground-floor dining room and first-floor drawing room, the latter brought from Smeaton, East Lothian.

AIRDS LODGE, 1.3km. NE of Airds House. Painted rubble cottage with half-hexagon end and piended roof, late C18 or early C19. Known locally as the 'Threepenny Bit'.

APPIN MANSE, below Airds Hill overlooking Loch Laich. Built c. 1869. Two-storey, three-bay, painted rubble house with single canted bay l. of centre.

DRUIMNEIL HOUSE, 1km. SSE. Victorian villa, 1850, built in square-snecked rubble with ashlar dressings, now painted white. Three-gabled SW front with central canted bay opening to small balustraded terrace, a later addition. The eclectic interior included Jacobean oak panelling believed to have come from Suffolk and an open-well pine staircase, mid C18, of unknown origin. Recent renovation has removed the panelling but the staircase remains. Walled garden. U-plan COACH-HOUSE, 1830, 100m. NNE, has a raised gable centre-piece over segmental-arch cart entry; narrow cobbled court at rear.

OLD FERRY HOUSE. Early C19. Two parallel, painted rubble cottages, bow-fronted to the sea with slated conical roofs; converted to restaurant, the flat-roofed space between the cottages originally used as a boat-house now adapted as a bar. Segmental terrace links bows. SW is the small PIERHOUSE HOTEL, 1993–4, a one-and-a-half-storey block with a slated pyramid roof; three barrel dormers fore and aft seem modelled on two earlier gentler versions of the Ferry House roof.

PORT APPIN PIER. Early C19. Rubble and concrete pier with remains of a wood-piled head.

PORT SONACHAN

Linear hamlet edging Loch Awe between Ardbrecknish House and Sonachan House. Formerly a ferry crossing point: here cattle herded s on the drove road through Glen Nant to Kilchrenan came ashore after crossing the Loch from Taychreggan.

BURIAL ENCLOSURE, Sonachan. E of Sonachan House, between B840 and Loch Awe. Private graveyard of Campbells of Sonachan, walled in 1760. Ball finials and MURAL PANEL, carved with full family arms in relief, have fallen.

CHAPEL and BURIAL GROUND, Creag a'Chaibeil, Ballimeanoch; 5.3km. SW of Port Sonachan Hotel. Minimal remains of oblong chapel(?) in irregular enclosure.

PORT SONACHAN CHURCH. Early C20. Corrugated-iron shed; its religious pretensions indicated by bifurcated sashes in pointed-arch windows. Porch canopy on brackets.

ST JAMES ARDBRECKNISH (Episcopal). 1891. Small nave-and-chancel church with gabled S porch. Rubble with grey granite dressings. Simple lancets. Central buttress to W gable above which is a gabled two-bell belfry. Bells re-hung, 1991. Scissors-raftered roof. – Round-arched, coloured faience TABLET; Mary and Christ child relief in a border of fruit edged with egg-and-dart. – STAINED GLASS includes three-light E window depicting the Crucifixion with Our Lady and St John, 1891.

ARDBRECKNISH HOUSE. A compressed accumulation of slated roofs and crowstepped gables, attractive in incident if ill-at-ease in composition. The oldest element is the SW saddleback tower; wall thickness suggests a medieval origin, although the earliest recorded mention of Ardbrecknish is 1633. Running N from the tower is a solid two-storey, three-bay house with a chimneyed wallhead gable, possibly C17, probably C18. By mid C19, tower and house were being let as a shooting lodge but, following a change of ownership in 1857, a period of expansion and baronialization began. Two phases of later C19 building developed E, though it is difficult to disentangle and date these accretions. The first may have been that begun behind the E gable of the tower; its S front, which now provides the principal entrance to the whole complex, a wider version of the older house, but with roll-moulded ingoes and crowstepped wallhead gable. Behind this wing, creating a double-pile core to the plan, is another, indented in plan and probably of later date. It looks N to the loch across a battlemented terrace and banked rhododendrons. More exuberant in form and detail, it too stretches E, recessing and advancing until it culminates in a tall NE tower, the gabled saddleback summit of which is boldly corbelled from the round at second-floor level. Except in the towers, roofs maintain a common ridge height and are liberally iced with crowstepped skews. On the other hand, while earlier walling has been rendered and painted, later work remains rubble and sandstone, visually a not altogether satisfactory stratagem, though one which does go some way to clarify phasing and hints at the flatted subdivision of the property carried out by *Donald Wilson*, 1979–82.

HILL HOUSE. By *Donald Wilson*, 1990–1. Y-plan set on a rocky knoll exploits level changes, shelter and view. White roughcast with exaggerated quoining. Wings roofed in profiled metal sheeting with S valley plane extended as canopy over angle entrance. The N wing, which is in effect a fully-glazed canted bay incorporating a spacious lounge and gallery studio, opens on to a terrace and enjoys a prospect of Loch Awe.

PORT SONACHAN HOTEL. Six-bay-long, black and white inn, mid C18, its vernacular rigours softened by the later lochside sophistication of a broad-fronted, canted bay rising through two storeys to gabled dormers with windowed cheeks, *c.* 1870. An inn existed here in the C15, though on slightly higher ground to the S where the old road ran. Pyramid-roofed dining room in NW angle, late 1940s. Conservatory entrance foyer and offices added on E and N, 1991. Mid-C18 STABLES BLOCK on S side of road, converted to annexe and bar by *Tom Grant Associates*, 1991.

SONACHAN HOUSE. Built by the Malcolms of Poltalloch following their purchase of the Sonachan Estate in 1850 and enlarged by them in 1875. A battlemented three-storey tower dominates the W front but there is neither Baronial ebullience nor detail. Roughcasting dulls the edge of any delight. A third storey was added to the SW wing *c.* 1900. Converted to flats, 1957.

UPPER SONACHAN HOUSE. Symmetry and simplicity in white roughcast: the familiar three-bay laird's house formula, probably mid C18, dignified by later elaboration. The original house, two-up and two-down with a central stair, may have required rebuilding in the early C19, for Upper Sonachan does not appear on George Langlands's 1801 map of the county. It faced S on to the old road but, at some time during the third quarter of the C19, the plan was recast with an entrance on the opposite side of the house to relate to the new road which followed a more northerly line closer to the lochside. Ground-floor N windows widened to double lights and symmetrical gable-fronted wings added N and S. A stone TABLET, placed below the sill of the round-arched upper window in the E wing gable, displays a swan, heraldic symbol of the Campbells of Sonachan who carried out these alterations. The reversal of the hall staircase and the building of a single-storey S extension probably date from *c.* 1915. In 1965–6, upper floor accommodation was added over this extension, raising the rear elevation to two storeys in a five-bay front with central gablet, and over the hitherto single-storey links E and W in order to connect with the first floor of the outer wings. Another stone TABLET, this time set in the W wing gable, bears the arms of Sir Charles McGrigor as a record of these latest changes.

CHAMBERED CAIRN, 235m. SE of Port Sonachan Hotel. Remains of cairn, 29.5m. by 13m., with disturbed chamber at W end.

PORTAVADIE

A 'ghost town' on the SW coast of Cowal intermittently brought to life by summer ferry traffic across Loch Fyne to Tarbert. In 1974 Portavadie was designated an appropriate deep-water site for the building of concrete platforms for the burgeoning oil industry. Work began a year later on a 'support village' for the 500-strong labour force. It was never occupied.

CHAPEL and BURIAL GROUND, 450m. WSW of Stillaig Farm. Low rubble walls, less than 1m. high and overgrown with turf, mark the position of a small rectangular chapel of unknown date. The D-shaped burial enclosure, also ruinous and indistinct, contains no tombstones, although a single rough cairn may be a gravemarker.

WORKERS' VILLAGE. Built at Pollphail, 1975–7, in the 'national interest', this astonishing complex still scars the landscape, a monumental indictment to bungling in high places. Designed by *Thomas Smith, Gibb & Pate*, the numerous two-storey dormitory units, some linked by access balconies, gather around a central amenity block accommodating restaurant, lounge and recreation rooms. Monopitch roofs covered in profiled metal sheeting, rendered rounded stair towers and walls clad in horizontal timber boarding. Abandoned without ever being occupied, it is absurd, bleak, and sadder than a deserted holiday camp.

CAIRNS, Ascog Bay. Two cairns lie *c.* 1km. S of Stillaig Farm, the larger 17m. in dia. and 1.8m. high. In 1927 a small cist was uncovered at the centre.

STANDING STONES, Cnoc Pollphaill, 660m. NNE of Low Stillaig. Two stones 7.5m. apart. To the N, the taller stone stands 2.9m.; the other has been broken off at 0.65m., the missing shaft used, it is believed, to form a byre lintel at Low Stillaig Farm.

STANDING STONE, Creag Loisgte, 550m. E of Low Stillaig. Pointed top stone, 1.9m. high.

PORTINCAPLE

A scatter of cottages among the trees and rhododendron bushes tumbling to Loch Long halfway between Finnart and Garelochhead. On Feuins Road, close to the A814, DALRIADA, by *Watson & Salmond*, 1909. Despite its name, an Anglo-Indian conceit; a big, white-harled bungalow with casement windows, red-tiled piended roof and a wide segmental dormer over a central entrance porch, semicircular in plan. Down by the shore, INVERALT, by *Eric Sutherland*, 1900; harled Arts and Crafts with a crowstepped gable.

PORTNACROISH

A hamlet in Appin overlooking Castle Stalker where the silted mouth of Loch Laich opens W into Loch Linnhe. Along the SW side of the A828, several old rubble houses group together in a strong stretch of linear townscape. POST COTTAGE, early C19, is piended with painted dressed surrounds; FORGE COTTAGE, early C19, gabled and limewashed; then comes the OLD INN, C18, a three-bay, two-storey rubble structure with rough slate sills, converted to a dwelling in 1984; and, finally, a low rubble barn with ventilation slits.

CHURCH OF THE HOLY CROSS (Episcopal). Architecturally humble, gable-ended, three-bay church built in rude pointed rubble. It was consecrated in 1815, but may have been erected a few years earlier. The S front has three pointed-arch windows, the central opening set in a slightly projecting gable topped with a stone cross finial. A doorway and pointed-arch window originally in each gable-end. It began as a simple oblong, liturgically arranged with the altar 'in the side of the church' (Craven, 1907) below the central S window and galleries at each end. In 1887 the church layout was revised with the altar placed in the E end. Later still, *Donald Marshall* restored the original arrangement centred on the S, installed new cusped timber windows, and reconstructed accommodation on the N to provide a NE vestibule, NW vestry and a N aisle opened up to the older part of the church. The interior is unremarkable but retains its three collar-beam king-post trusses. – Octagonal stone FONT, carved with leaves and flowers, with pitch pine lid. – STAINED GLASS. In the N aisle are three small, late C19 windows: the Nativity, the Annunciation and one depicting children. More attractive are the ice-green margins to the lattice glazing in the other windows.

In the churchyard stands the STALCAIRE MEMORIAL, *c.* 1910, a rough obelisk commemorating the defeat of the Macdougalls by the Stewarts at the Battle of Stalcaire, 1463.

APPIN HOUSE, 2.2km. Nothing remains of the five-bay, early C18 house, built by the Stewarts of Appin as a three-storey (or two-storey-and-attic) classical mansion which may or may not have been pedimented. It was demolished in the 1960s, long since submerged in a remodelling of 1831. There remain some high harled walls which originally enclosed the extensive court of offices and, architecturally more prepossessing, the single-storey, white-painted SE wing added in the recasting of 1831. This wing, symmetrical with a windowed half-octagon projecting at the centre of the SW façade, has a piended roof set behind a balustraded eaves with square turrets at the angles. It now forms the *grande salle* of a modern two-storey residence which, along with a returning range of self-catering apartments, has been contrived by the *David Newman Partnership*, to fill the gap between the early C19 wing and the older walls to the NE. These new buildings, pitch-roofed and straightforwardly detailed with black artificial slates carried down over the wallhead of white, smooth-rendered walls, do not quite succeed in masking a sense of disruption and loss. Only the older harled walls beyond, which now conceal a tennis court, have the scale and crumbling dignity to evoke the past; in particular, the wide, symmetrically organized NE wall, flanked by tall, cross-marked corner towers and marked at the centre by a lower gable-fronted projection, also indented with a recessed cross and two small octagonal openings. – Of the C18 house's pine panelling and plasterwork nothing has been preserved. Two stone fireplaces survive, both framed by a hefty roll-and-hollow moulding interrupted in one case by a carved thistle motif.

APPIN HOME FARM, downhill from Appin House. Early C19, U-plan rubble steading.

RHU

Formed out of land petitioned from Rosneath on the one side and Cardross on the other, the original parish of Row (pronounced 'roo-a') was one of twelve which made up Dunbartonshire. The area was for the most part owned by the ancient family of Lennox, whose seat was at Faslane. It included what would become the villages of Garelochhead and Shandon and the town of Helensburgh, and was given independence in 1648 when MacAulay of Ardencaple (q.v.) undertook to finance the construction of a small church and manse on a triangular outcrop at the mouth of the Gareloch. From the Gaelic 'rudha', meaning promontory, was thus derived the name of both parish and village, the spelling being altered as recently as 1927, by which time it applied only to the village.

During the C18 a cluster of thatched cottages grew up around the kirk and ferry to Rosneath. In 1792 the population was estimated at less than 100, mainly because few trades were practised in the area. Lime and slate were extracted locally in small quantities, but neither quarries nor salmon fisheries added much to the produce of the parish. The only profitable enterprise appears to have been the distillation of illicit whisky: the Duke of Argyll was rumoured to have procured a barrel for George IV from a still based at the mouth of Aldownick Glen.

Completion of a pier on the Clyde in 1835 confirmed the area's attractiveness to summer visitors, and by the mid C19 what had once been a simple shore village began to extend beyond its boundaries. A series of handsome 'marine mansions' – for yachting has to this day continued to account in large part for the area's popularity – were built on the wooded slopes rising gently from the water's edge. Despite predictable overdevelopment, an image survives of these handsome houses, framed by greenery and themselves forming a backdrop to the cottages and parish kirk. This, and the rural charm of the shingle-scattered bay, ensure Rhu's distinctiveness.

CHURCHES

RHU & SHANDON CHURCH, Church Road, 1851, *William Spence*. The second parish kirk, built in 1763, shared its site with its successor for over five years, and the ivy-clad remains of rubble walls and a Gothic window can still be seen in the churchyard. Sir James Colquhoun of Luss, the principal heritor and feudal superior of the parish, co-funded the replacement building with the help of Robert Napier, marine engineer, shipbuilder and parishioner. The church is particularly striking when seen in silhouette; Gothic, cruciform in plan and symmetrical around a two-stage entrance tower with diagonal buttresses. A magnificent pinnacled octagonal lantern with clock crowns this square tower, soaring telescopically above the pretty graveyard. *Honeyman & Keppie* lengthened the nave in 1891, the addition disguised by the use of harl, and by the 1938 vestry. – INTERIOR. The main body of the church has a plasterwork ribbed ceiling springing from slender colonnettes with floral capitals. – STAINED GLASS. A series of windows dedicated to local notaries, including a 1935 nave window by *William Wilson* to R.M. Donaldson of Blairvadach (q.v.), and some contemporary pieces by *Emma Shipton*. Most poignant of all is the memorial window installed in 1925 to the Revd John McLeod Campbell, where *Louis Davis* of Pinner has depicted a procession of saints up the steps of light. The young Campbell had come to Row in 1825, 'bearing gifts of scholarship, culture, and zeal for the Gospel'. Six years later he had been deposed as minister of the parish and of the Church of Scotland on account of preaching 'doctrines contrary to scripture and the Confession of Faith'. This gave rise to what became known as the Row Heresy Case and, although Campbell was in due course vindicated, he chose to spend the remainder of his life travelling the country on horseback, preaching to huge congregations. – CHURCHYARD. In 1850, 'literally packed with bodies, one on top of the other', on account of there being no cemetery in Helensburgh. Many monuments of interest, including a 1709 wall tomb at the S end to the memory of Revd Robert Anderson; a sculpted seated figure of engineer and shipbuilder Henry Bell on an inscribed plinth erected *c.* 1850 by his longtime friend Robert Napier; and a classical white ashlar monument with sculpted angel's head in memory of artist Sir James Guthrie, his wife and son. – SUNDIAL. Presented around 1946, bulbous ashlar base and copper gnomons, dated 1637 and sited immediately SE of the church.

PUBLIC BUILDINGS

RHU COMMUNITY EDUCATION CENTRE, Hall Road, 1905, probably *A.N. Paterson*. A very fine L-shaped Arts and Crafts hall and reading room with Baronial details, the reading room running N–S and united to the E–W hall at the re-entrant angle by a canted porch with battlemented parapet. Pretty in grey harl with ashlar dressings and crowsteps, overhanging timber eaves, trademark thistle-top downpipes and a ventilator flèche with lead spirelet and finial. Stocky drum piers with conical caps terminate the boundary walling.

RHU MARINA LIFEBOAT STATION, Gareloch Road, 1997, *Robert Potter & Partners*. Crisply detailed welcome addition to the waterfront.

RHU POST OFFICE, Gareloch Road, early C20. Incongruous,

twin bow-fronted post office and shop with big mansard roof, notable for a hint of Arts and Crafts detailing on the sw façade in the pronounced taper of the chimneystack.

RHU PRIMARY SCHOOL & LIBRARY, School Road. Replacing the original 1875 schoolhouse. Single and two-storey c. 1970s construction with an exposed concrete frame; buff brick, timber and glazed infills.

WAR MEMORIAL, off Church Road, 1920, *A. N. Paterson & Stoddart*. Granite Celtic Cross with panels of interlacing. Located on village green against s wall of churchyard (q.v.).

DESCRIPTION

Rhu Village

Kirk and village green occupy a prominent position on the bay at the mouth of the Gareloch. Dating from the early development of the foreshore are ROW HOUSE and RHU INN, both early C19, the former once home to the Chairman of the Row Association for Watching the Dead (bodies being apt to disappear from the nearby churchyard). A rectangular-plan house, two-storey and attic, it is linked to the hostelry by a broad gable, outer l. The two-storey, four-bay inn was remodelled early in the C20, the additions including two gently bowed oriels at first floor, scrolled cast-iron window guards and much leaded glass with opaque Art Nouveau stained inserts using Favrille glass patented by *Tiffany* in 1893. CHURCH ROAD contains some good period villas: UPPER CRAIGARD – early C20 with canted bays at ground floor linked by a timber porch canopy – and GREENSIDE – a tiny three-bay cottage in squared rubble – sharing a low boundary wall with arrowhead railings.

On MANSE BRAE, 15–37 BRAEHOUSE, sophisticated Dunbarton County Council housing built 1938 by *Joseph Weekes* is less conventional, but wholly suited to its village location and steeply sloping site. A large U-plan layout providing twelve homes on two floors, the largest flats are accessed by staircase towers with conical caps and arrowslit windows. This device reinforces the changes in level as the building mounts the hill, with the towers also linked to pends into the backcourt area by flat, semicircular canopies. The outer corners of the 'U' are marked by corbels and curves. This is local authority housing of the highest order, economic house plans matched to C17 Scots detailing to produce a modern vernacular style in cement harl, in this instance with 'Thirties overtones. Cited as model housing of its type in the Scottish Housing Advisory Committee Report 'Planning our New Homes' (1942). Following Weekes's retirement, the Council's post-war housing programme continued to include construction of nearby CALDWELL PLACE, designed 1947. The twelve four-apartments flats are this time arranged in a long symmetrical block of three T-shaped units with lop-sided gabled fronts. Recessed bedroom wings link the principal accommodation while also providing pend access to the rear, through pointed-arch openings defined by the architect's trademark: black slate-on-edge.

Nos. 1–10 CUMBERLAND TERRACE, Cumberland Road, *c.* 1870. An attractive whitewashed terrace of ten houses, very rhythmic with advanced end pavilions and massive paired wallhead stacks on the gables. M-gabled timber and slate canopy porches to the smaller houses which have swept-roofed and piended dormers. The terrace was built to accommodate officers serving on board the Clyde training ship HMS *Cumberland*, which had been purchased after the Industrial Schools Act in 1866, and anchored off Rhu. She was a ship-of-line battleship, a three-decker with 70 guns, and could hold 400 boys in training for recruitment in the Royal Navy. In 1889 she perished by fire and was succeeded by HMS *Empress*, one of the last wooden men-of-war, which remained in the bay until 1923.

Rhu Point

In the heyday of the Dumbarton horse and cattle fairs, animals brought from Argyllshire to Rosneath would circumvent the ten-mile trip around the head of the loch by swimming the short stretch of water between the twin promontories at its mouth. Nowadays, the distance is greater owing to removal of the spit at Rosneath to permit increased submarine traffic to the naval base at Faslane. On the 'bleak and unpromising aspect' of this grazing ground Lord John Campbell, Duke of Argyll, built the still picturesque ROW LODGE, early C19, siting it on the tip of the headland. Alongside is the 1849 Italianate mansion ROSSLEA which was rebuilt in 1973 as a hotel while retaining the tower and arched garden frontage.

First sight of the estate of ARDENVOHR is altogether more impressive, although the voluminous hothouses have been dismantled and the slated peak of the entrance tower to the mansion removed. Worse, the Royal Northern & Clyde Yacht Club, whose headquarters the building has been since 1937, have added a flat-roofed SW bar extension in brick. Nevertheless, *Gildard & MacFarlane*'s scholarly Scots-Jacobethan detailing of 1857 is otherwise crisply intact and includes good buckle and star features, rope moulding to the entrance door, strapwork, cannon spouts, ball finials and, to the S terrace, stylized sandstone balustrading and corniced dies with buckle motifs. – INTERIOR. Galleried stair hall with elaborate plasterwork and rooflight. – STABLES. Once exceptional U-plan courtyard range of 1858 replicating the features of the mansion. A slender circular stair tower remains, as do three of the four segmental carriage-arches, but the building is sadly in need of repair. – BASTION. Octagonal tower on the loch shore linked to the stable block by a sandstone balustrade, an intriguing addition to the estate in the late C19, now largely ruinous. – LODGE. The 1858 lodge and boundary wall complete the ensemble where GARELOCH ROAD briefly leaves the water's edge. A big ball finial on wallhead pedestal with banner scroll beneath marks the location of the original entrance, the T-plan lodge having been extended w. More than a match for this oversized detail are the ashlar gatepiers with stacked, shouldered conical caps and balls – their attestation to wealth repeated in only marginally reduced stature along the long shore wall with fleur-de-lis ironwork.

MANSIONS

ARDENCONNEL HOUSE, off Manse Brae, c. 1790, by *David Hamilton*. Ownership of the land on the lochside began to change when Andrew Buchanan, a Glasgow merchant, purchased 2,000 acres from the MacAulays of Ardencaple. At the core of the new estate was Ardenconnel Wood, in many senses still at the heart of modern Rhu. Here was built a handsome harled and ashlar-trimmed mansion, two-storey over basement, symmetrical with three-bay hipped pavilions separated by a Corinthian columnar porch with balustraded parapet. Central to the pavilions were shallow arched-head ashlar recesses bearing single windows with blind side panels. After a destructive fire in 1907, the house was restored and extended N, E and W, preserving the elegant garden front in its new guise as flatted accommodation. – INTERIOR. Good Adam-style chimneypiece in attractive (now common) entrance hall. – STABLES. Former U-plan coach buildings, round-headed carriage arch with keystone, comprehensively modernized.

Vestiges of the original beech-lined approach from the water's edge to Ardenconnel remain, although largely built over by PIER ROAD. Construction of the quay at the foot of this route brought with it a building boom, the slopes of the lochside developed by a series of fingery avenues threading their way upwards to generously proportioned feus. Early among the country houses built were ROWMORE and LAGGARY HOUSE. Dated 1831, in Gothic gabled harl with blonde sandstone margins and Tudor detailing, the former is distinguished by a fine S front with cross finial, ogee-arched entrance with scalloped parapet, and ornate cast-iron balcony on slender fluted posts. To this peaceful setting came Sir James Guthrie in 1915 to paint 'Some Statesmen of the Great War'. Less typical of the village genre, being Italianate and ashlar-built, Laggary House sits now in the centre of parkland developed for modern housing. The house is mid C19, solemn and unexceptional with wide campanile towers SW and NE. Now divided into four flats. GLENARN ROAD terminates at GLENARN, an asymmetrical gabled villa with tall moulded Tudorbethan chimney cans; originally single-storey and attic, now with a large modern lean-to conservatory occupying the site of the demolished SE bay. Built in 1837 by Professor MacGeorge, who with the assistance of Sir William Hooker, Professor of Botany at Glasgow University, laid out the structure of the magnificent woodland garden. This is renowned for its rare rhododendrons, including the largest leaved of the species. House, outbuildings and grounds have been sympathetically restored by *Michael and Sue Thornley*, who open the garden to the public annually.

INVERGARE, Glenarn Road, 1855, by *James Smith*. The architect selected a spectacular site at the head of falling ground for his own home, living there for only three years owing to the scandal created by daughter Madeleine's trial in 1857 for the alleged poisoning by arsenic of her lover. Although the verdict given was Not Proven, the family scarcely had time to enjoy their L-shaped Scots-Baronial mansion, with its copper-clad towers, tourelles and tall, s-facing window bays. Its haughty grandeur unmoved by the controversy, the house was in due course extended to the rear in 1923 and 1933, gaining an octagonal entrance tower with ornate doorpiece and bellcast roof, and billiard room with lead-capped five-light bay, all almost certainly by *A. N. Paterson*. Good cast-iron rinceau balustrade to the s terrace, a matching length to the first-floor balcony now missing. Uphill is ROWALEYN, 1997, *Page & Park Architects*, an unusual two-storey villa built on a small elevated plateau at the foot of a rocky outcrop. Rising and curving from E to W, the s wall comprises a series of cement-rendered masonry planes linked together and topped by recessed glazed panels. Over this fans a zinc monopitch roof whose stained timber spars and soffit are also expressed internally.

A scrubby path leading to TORWOODHILL ROAD passes *James Smith*'s coolly classical CARBETH, *c.* 1855, built as the dower house to Invergare. Two side-lit window bays matching those on the larger house nicely frame the simple s entrance, while supporting a full-length cast-iron balcony on modillion cornice at first floor. Alongside, TORWOOD HOUSE has at its core a pretty harled cottage with attic dormers, more than trebled in size by Scots-Gothic extensions of 1836 and 1845, including a broad, battlemented bay W with paired squat finials at its corners. Likewise, HAZELWOOD HOUSE has been remodelled, this time with late C19 Arts and Crafts additions. The tile-hanging and red sandstone dressings combine more effectively on the roadside face of COACH-HOUSE and STABLE, where a curving harled wall with battlemented parapet, eyelet windows and gabled hoist door draw the eye around to the drum and pyramid gatepiers.

The descent s provides glimpses of mansions young and old: CLIFFTON – harl and honey stone, early C19 Italianate with arcaded loggia W and timber bracketed eaves; AUCHENLEA, 1981, by *Ian Smith*, a triangular villa built in concrete blockwork, expansively glazed with a ship's deck s veranda; and TORWOODHILL HOUSE (now flatted), a two-storey early C19 L-plan perked up by Tudor and Baronial decorative devices such as low-slung pepperpot turrets, hoodmoulds and a candlesnuffer roof on the stair tower.

LAGARIE, Torwoodhill Road, 1901, *A. N. Paterson*. A large, rectangular-plan two-storey and attic Arts and Crafts villa, flatted following a spell as a children's home. Simpler than it at first appears. The asymmetry works best on the approach elevation E, where the original dining room and bedroom above are extruded vertically in the manner of a battlemented keep with stepped, ashlar parapet on roll-moulded corbelling. Rising from within the confines of the parapet (with walkway around) is a half-timbered, gabled attic storey, or caphouse, most likely inspired by Richard Norman Shaw's Cragside, 1870, in Northumberland. At the base of the 'keep', a single-storey bowed cloakroom bay with conical cap, adjoining vestibule, and angled porch with interlacing thistle carving to the bargeboards. Rising out of the vestibule, a tall canted bay facing E, half-timbered on harl, and itself projecting out from the gable of a jerkin-headed library pavilion. A calmer S front, with pavilions r. and l., both with shallow single-storey bows linked by the original schoolroom veranda. – INTERIOR. Queen Anne style chimneypiece in the original entrance hall with a good panelled, depressed-arch buffet recess to the butler's pantry.

On LAGARIE CROFT – the shore field adjacent – is ARMADALE, an early C19 villa elegantly upholding the tradition of the area in cream harl with stone margins and window bays. There is a good E entrance porch with delicate open-work piers in cast iron. The same limited yet effective palette of materials is used at nearby ARTARMAN, c. 1838, which has a lead-capped timber trellis veranda on the S side and Tudor-Gothic finials.

The establishment of a kirk at Row allowed the small community in GLEN FRUIN, some distance NE but still within the parish, to worship in the village. Part of the route used survives as a moorland track known as the HIGHLANDMAN'S ROAD, which now descends into Rhu past the hill farm of TORR, where the last smugglers' still was abandoned c. 1830. Crossing the WEST HIGHLAND RAILWAY line as STATION ROAD, the path no longer extends as far as the church, passing instead two good modern houses on S-facing sites. TIGH GAEL, 1976, by *Fred Walker*, is the younger; a commanding country house with sun terraces at all three levels, the uppermost sunk into a great slate ski-slope of a roof. ORCHARD HOUSE, 1973, by *C. R. Kelly*, is similarly angular, a house and studio built in blue brindle brick in a stripped-to-bare aesthetic which is timeless. Downhill, DUNARD, mid C19, represents a return to painted harl framed by sandstone, the original two-storey cottage much enhanced by a fat drum tower with deep ashlar cornice band, conical roof and elaborate wrought-iron finial, *A. N. Paterson*, early C20.

LINESIDE WALK falls W to AROS ROAD, but not before passing through SMUGGLERS' GLEN, now the site of a large 1970s naval housing estate whose density and unremitting monotony are almost frightening. Relief comes in the form of *William Leiper*'s AROS, completed around 1883. Whinstone-built with red ashlar dressings, half-timbered and tile-hung bays and a broad bargeboarded gable jettied out on scrolled timber consoles. An attractive design which Leiper used in mirror-image at Albion Lodge in Helensburgh (q.v.) and Ganavan at Oban (q.v.). Close by, the L-plan ARDLARICH, of 1937, displays the unexpected lushness of thatch on both house and lych-gate.

A farm and a mill E of the A816, halfway between Cairnbaan and Kilmartin.

KILBRIDE CHAPEL, 2.2km. NE of Rhudle road end. Roofless oblong, 11.1m. by 5.1m. within rubble walling, which stands almost intact on the E gable but is otherwise somewhat reduced. The site, dedicated to St Bridget or Bride, may have been sacred since Early Christian times, for a stone FRAGMENT, carved with a cross and spiral ornament and dated to the C10 or C11, was found in paving at nearby Kilbride Farm (where it is retained). The plan of the chapel points to a C13 date. At the W end of the S wall, a doorway with splayed ingoes and roll-moulded jambs is probably original although its arched head must date from *c.* 1900 when restoration work repointed the masonry and the low rubble enclosure along the S side of the church was constructed. The E end, marked by a rock outcrop coincident with a slight rise in floor level, is lit by small windows, now archless, in the N and S walls and by two tall lancets in the gable. The inner masonry of these lancets is particularly well carried out. There are three aumbries.

RHUDIL MILL, 300m. NE of A816. Late C18 corn mill. The three-bay, three-storey block has lost its millwheel, originally located on the NW gable, but preserves a gableted winch-house in the roof and the two-storey, piended kiln-house built against the SE gable. Cast-iron columns at ground- and first-floor level. In the 1950s the building was used as a grain store and was refloored. Conversion to a dwelling in the 1980s by *Diana MacLaurin* added three new windows in the SE wall of the kiln wing and retained exposed asymmetrical king-post trusses in an attic studio.

BALLYMEANOCH, on A816, 1.25km. E of Poltalloch East Lodge. Mid C19(?); perhaps by *W.A. Nesfield*. Scaled-down North Oxford. Gabled red brick (from the brickworks set up locally, *c.* 1849, to supply material for the partition walls at Poltalloch House) with sandstone dressings; mullion-and-transom windows; pseudo-Tudor chimneystacks. DUNCHRAIGAIG, 500m. N, was similar but has been harled.

CAIRN, 280m. NW of Dunchraigaig across the A816. Boulder cairn of unclear perimeter, *c.* 30m. dia. Three cists found, only two of which are still visible.

HENGE MONUMENT, Ballymeanoch, 150m. SSW of nearby standing stones. Outer banks and inner ditches forming circle, *c.* 40m. dia., with causeway gaps to N and S. Two cists discovered.

STANDING STONES, 500m. NW of Ballymeanoch. Two parallel lines of stones, set 41m. apart, both having their long axes aligned NW–SE. The NE line comprises four closely spaced stones varying in height, SE to NW, from 4.1m. to 2.75m.; two have cupmark decoration. The SW line has only two stones, their plan positions and heights corresponding roughly to the middle stones of the NE row.

ROSNEATH

A village at the mouth of the Gareloch opposite Rhu. Boat-building sheds and council housing dominate the scene. The old kirktoun survives as The Clachan, a row and cluster of cottages close to the church.

ROSNEATH PARISH CHURCH, in the graveyard at The Clachan. Roofless remains of the oblong galleried church erected in 1780 to replace its cruciform C16 predecessor. The single surviving SW gable carries an unusual two-tier birdcage bellcote which may be of earlier date. Wide flat-arched SW doorway. Little of the NW wall is extant but most of the SE wall stands to a broken eaves; enough to incorporate two tall round-arched windows with impost blocks and smaller superimposed lintelled windows close to the gable. The whin and sandstone rubble walls preserve traces of harling. – Two much-weathered SLABS, one with the clearly incised lines of cross and sword, sit in a SE window opening. – On the inner face of the SE wall are several MURAL TABLETS in granite and sandstone; to members of the Campbell and Crum families. – On the outer face of the SW gable, two more MURAL MONUMENTS, c. 1860, inscribed white marble panels in flat-pedimented trapezoidal sandstone frames.

The site is ancient. A church is known to have been granted to Paisley Abbey, 1225–6. The BURIAL ENCLOSURE, too, is long established. A record of 1627 reports the repair of its rubble dykes, while the avenue of yew trees leading to the ruined church may also date from the C17. There are several C18 and early C19 gravemarkers. Among them, a naïvely carved HEADSTONE to Hugh Marquis †1734; an angel head between two skeletal images superimposed on a reclining draped figure holding an hourglass. – OBELISKS include an unusually dumpy example in memory of Revd Dr George Drummond †1818 and his wife Christian (*sic*) Buchanan †1807. – A Celtic CROSS, heavily bossed, with a dove in relief below the crosshead, recalls Revd John McLeod Campbell †1872, cruelly expelled from the ministry for alleged doctrinal deviation in 1831.

ST MODAN'S PARISH CHURCH, The Clachan. Dec Gothic by *David Cousin*. Built 1852–3 as a short buttressed nave and shorter W chancel, more Episcopalian than Presbyterian, the church was enlarged in 1862 when the double-gabled S transept with geometric traceried windows was built and again in 1872 when the matching N transept and vestibule were completed. In 1894–5, *Burnet Son & Campbell* revised the seating arrangements, built a vestry and session house in the SW re-entrant, and refurbished the chancel, creating a new chamber for the existing organ. To honour those who had fallen in the Great War, a tower was proposed in 1918 but failed to materialize. Instead, in 1921, the chancel was altered slightly to accommodate a memorial reredos (*see* below), while *Peter MacGregor Chalmers* supervised extensive repairs. In 1931, *J. Jeffrey Waddell* added a new vestry and converted the session house to a memorial chapel. Throughout these changes, stylistic integrity was maintained.

There is an inner spatial coherence. Dark-stained arch-braced trusses carry purlins and rafters. On each side of the nave a single multi-shaft column supports a plated steel beam (rivet heads exposed) running under the valley of the transepts' M-section roof to the outer walls. The S, N and E gable walls are exposed as slivered rubble; the side walls of the transepts and the W wall are plastered. Each transept has box pews, the floor level set a little above the nave. A chamfered pointed-arch rises high at the stepped entrance to the richly appointed W (liturgical E) end. – Chancel floor in grey and white marble and polychromatic sandstone. – Around the sanctuary, delicately detailed *fin-de-siècle* Gothic wall panelling, carved in oak by *John Craig* of Glasgow, 1895. – Oak COMMUNION TABLE, part gilded and painted red, by *John Taylor & Sons*, Edinburgh, 1896; extended, 1933: complex traceried panels flanking Christ with the communion cup. – Behind the table is a remarkable oak REREDOS depicting the Last Supper; designed and painted by *M. Meredith Williams* and carved in shallow relief by *Thomas Good*, it was installed in 1931, the gift of Princess Louise in memory of her husband, the 9th Duke of Argyll. – Four linked oak SEATS l. and r. – Oak PULPIT, 1896, carved with kneeling angels; a half-octagonal stall set on a marble base. – Octagonal oak FONT on alabaster pillars, 1896. – Brass LECTERN by *Jockel & Son*, Edinburgh, 1896. – Two-manual *Hill & Son* ORGAN, 1875. – In the N transept is the former church BELL; cast by the Dutch founder *Jan Burgerhuis* in 1610, it was replaced in 1907 after three centuries of use.

STAINED GLASS, plentiful and exceptional. – War Memorial W window, 'The Glory of Sacrifice', by *Stephen Adam & Son*, 1921. – In the N transept: W, a naïvely bright three-light window with the crucified Christ at its centre, 1861, originally in the chancel; E, a rather feminine Jesus calls Peter and Andrew in a characteristic composition of metallic blues and turquoise by *Gordon Webster*, 1976. – In the N wall, Jesus walks on water; by *Clayton & Bell*, 1888. – In 1873 the same designers had installed the memorial window in the E gable to the unfortunate Revd Dr John McLeod Campbell (*see* Rosneath Parish Church above); its three lights picture Christ under elaborate Gothic canopies, with the communion elements, in Gethsemane, and in the 'Light of the World' pose popularized by Holman Hunt's painting. – Magnificent S transept windows, wonderfully full of incident, by *Douglas Strachan*: E, in strong purpley blues against a steel-grey background, Christ healing the sick and carrying the Cross, 1915; W, much paler, the cleansing of the temple and Jesus preaching by the shore, 1908. In the Memorial Chapel, a Nativity scene by *Charles E. Stewart*, 1955.

MONUMENTS. Erected to the r. of the chancel arch, the 2.0m.-high ST MODAN STONE, C8 or C9, a weathered sandstone slab, unearthed at the W end of the kirkyard in 1881; carved with low relief crosses on both faces, one showing a spiral motif at the intersection and interlacing on the shaft. – In the S transept, to Revd

Robert Story, a pointed-arch MURAL MONUMENT of Ayrshire stone, by *William Brodie*, 1861; there are two white marble insets, one bearing a carved portrait head, the other (behind a Gothic arcade) the dedication in Gothic script. – Adjacent is a wide illuminated TABLET on which the Ten Commandments and the Lord's Prayer have been drawn and coloured in medieval manner by *W. A. Muirhead* of Edinburgh, 1862; originally in the chancel. – White marble pointed-arch TABLET on the w wall of the N transept; to Gordon Carnachan †1884. – Alongside, two stone PANELS cut with pointed-arch insets of white marble inscribed to James Stewart †1862 and John Campbell †1865. – Below the pulpit, a small stone carved with a Campbell monogram, the family motto, NE OBLIVISCARIS, and the date 1634; presumably a fragment from the C16 Parish Church. – A large BRONZE inlaid in the chancel floor, 1929, a stiffly interlaced Celtic cross, commemorates the Revd Alfred Warr during whose ministry the improvements of 1895 were carried out.

ST GILDA'S (R.C.), Main Road. 1967–8. By *Peter Borthwick* of *Thomas Cordiner, Cunningham & Partners*. A yacht under sail! The roof planes, floated on clearstoreys, soar dramatically, folded and split across the diagonal axis of the plan like mainsail and jib. From a low start cantilevered over the corner entrance, the ridge rakes up to the sanctuary opposite, tilting back so that wedges of light spill on to the altar below. A cruciform mast, first mounted at the high prow-like apex of the roof, has been less hazardously sited on *terra firma*. – Bronze CROSS on a reredos of turquoise glass tiles, by *Jack Mortimer*.

DESCRIPTION

The oldest part of the village, the houses probably no older than early C19, lies immediately N of the graveyard and St Modan's Church (*see* above). A row of single-storey roughcast cottages runs W, turning into a small knot of similar dwellings; this is THE CLACHAN, pleasantly rural in scale but tired and a little tawdry. AVENUE COTTAGE sits separate, gabled with lattice glazing. HEATHER COTTAGE, at the entrance to the graveyard, is white two-storey vernacular. Behind it, EASTER GARTH, the former manse, a two-storey, three-bay house with a pilastered E door. Built in 1838 by *James Dempster* of Greenock. Bay windows and attic bedrooms were added in 1881 by *John Honeyman*. Across the burn, just N of The Clachan, is CLACHAN BRIDGE, 1938, a modest recessing range of dwellings by *Joseph Weekes*, County Architect; piend-roofed with a hint of Baronial. The earliest and by far the best of the village's council housing. The former POLICE STATION, with its bellcast-roofed entrance tower, is also by *Weekes*, 1937.

Between Main Road and the loch, grey ranks of local authority housing. But through the trees at the foot of Ferry Road is FERRY INN, 1896–7, an Arts and Crafts villa by *Edwin Lutyens*, at once stunningly incongruous and splendid. Commissioned by the 9th Duke of Argyll's wife, Princess Louise, who may have been introduced to the architect by Gertrude Jekyll. It was built as additional accommodation for an early C19 hotel, providing a large E wing. Now a private residence. Not yet thirty, Lutyens is still in picturesque mood. The coastal location adds immeasurably to the design's success; seen across the loch, the house's whin rubble basement and ground floor seem bedded into the shore, its white-harled, jettied upper floor, capped by a steeply piended slated roof, shining lighthouse-like above the water. The plan is rectangular, pushing out E to the shingled shore. A s entrance porch, gabled whin with a bellcast roof, advances from the main block, the round-arched doorway placed asymmetrically. To the r. a massive whin and sandstone chimneystack raises three diamond-set chimneys high above the projecting eaves. Windows group horizontally: ashlar dressings and mullions on the lower floors, the original metal sashes set flush at first floor. On the E elevation five small, regularly spaced oriels look out to the Gareloch from the upper bedrooms. The original interiors have been lost, though two round-arched fireplaces survive; pine and beech panelling dates from the 1950s. FERRY INN COTTAGE, also by *Lutyens*, 1896–7, lies E on rising ground. Formerly the W extension of Ferry Inn, it too is now a detached white-harled dwelling. A gabled wing, pinched between two tall wallhead chimneystacks with slated copings, juts E above a driveway.

ROSNEATH CASTLE

an estate SE of the B833 between Rosneath and Kilcreggan

Originally the demesne of the powerful Lennox family, in the late C15 the lands of Rosneath were forfeited and passed by royal gift to the Earl of Argyll. The estate remained in Campbell hands until the C19. An ancient castle may well have existed. Groome (1885) reports that some such structure was 'fitted up' by the Marquess of Argyll, *c.* 1630, 'as a subsidiary residence to the castle of Inveraray', and there is evidence that further improvements were made in 1678 under the supervision of *John Slezer*. The building was a simple L-plan, castellated, with a round corner tower and a turnpike stair in the re-entrant opposite. In 1744 *Roger Morris* proposed additions which would have produced a rectangular plan with towers at all four corners, an evident echo of his contemporary designs for Inveraray Castle (q.v.). Some enlargement resulted (both *William Adam* and *John Adam* were involved) although, when the 3rd Duke finally re-occupied Rosneath in 1757, the L-plan remained intact. *Robert Mylne* visited the castle in 1769 and from 1783 repeatedly advised on further changes. In 1802 a fire swept through the building. A new mansion was immediately envisaged but Mylne's proposals failed to find favour and the opportunity went to the Edinburgh artist and occasional architect, *Alexander Nasmyth*. The commission was short-lived. The Home Farm (*see* below) is his but, while he was able to fix the site of the new castle, he was not to be responsible for its design. Despite the misgivings of the

5th Duke, who had some sympathy for 'poor Mylne', his son, Lord Lorne, looked to London, appointing *Joseph Bonomi* to design a new Rosneath Castle. Largely built between 1803 and 1806, the house was cast in Neoclassical mould with wide façades N and S. Continuous balustraded entablatures emphasized this horizontality, the skyline broken only by a domeless drum rising out of the bowed library at the centre of the S front. To the N, a five-column porte-cochère projected slightly. A three-column portico at each end of the façade repeated the Roman Ionic order used at the centre, though with an unfortunate disregard for the intercolumniation. The interior was never finished. Finally, Bonomi's 'ducal palace' suffered the same fate as its predecessor; damaged and abandoned, in 1947 it went up in flames. In 1961 it was demolished.

BATHWELL, in Dark Wood W of Parkhead (*see* below). Mid or late C18. Overgrown grotto. The rusticated N wall is pedimented; lintelled opening in a round-arched recess with flanking windows. Some similarity to the Well House, Bealach an Fhuarain, Inveraray Castle Estate (q.v.), suggests *William Adam* may have been responsible. *Robert Mylne* is also a possible designer.

PARKHEAD, 500m. N of Rosneath Home Farm. Mid or late C18; perhaps by *Robert Mylne*; reconstructed in the 1970s. Built as estate workers' housing; now a private residence. Two-storey range on a segmental plan forming the NE side of a former walled garden. Buff-coloured walls and gables. A short distance E is the early C19 ICE-HOUSE built for Rosneath Castle (q.v.).

ROSNEATH HOME FARM, 2.1km. SSE of St Modan's Church. By *Alexander Nasmyth*, 1803. Sadly mauled by agricultural impressment indifferent to its romantic conceit. A symmetrical Gothick spread on a canted bay plan. Plenty of hooded pointed arches but none of the lacy tracery shown on early drawings. At the centre, a 30m.-high square ashlar tower with blind elongated arches, bartizans and a trefoil balustrade, but no steeple. Pyramid roofs over octagonal pavilions at the knuckles of the plan. At each end, a castellated circular drum bulges out between two similar but taller towers.

WELL HOUSE, Gallowhill Plantation. Early C19. Small circular structure with brick-lined dome.

ROSSDHU

Ancient demesne of the Colquhoun family on the W shore of Loch Lomond between Arden and Luss. In the late 1980s an international golf course was laid out and Rossdhu House (*see* below) rescued from genteel decay as its clubhouse.

CHAPEL OF ST MARY, 50m. NNW of Rossdhu House. Dedicated 1469; restored to C17 appearance as 'The Private Burial Place of the Colquhoun family', 1996. Simple skew-gabled rubble structure. The slated roof is new and the rebuilt walls heavily pointed. E end originally lit by a lintelled window S and N; the latter now blocked. S doorway at W end. All openings have chamfered dressings. Pigeon holes tiered in the E gable. On the W gable apex, a small chimney linked to the fireplace of what may have been a chaplain's room. Inside, the floor is paved with inscribed burial slabs placed over the vault below.

ROSSDHU CASTLE. C16. Square-plan tower-house now reduced to a single three-storey stand of rubble walling. Home of the Colquhouns until the late C18. At ground level s, a round-arch door with chamfered voussoirs; above this, a ruinous doorway with oblique ingoes. Higher still, puzzlingly superimposed, two sets of roofline raggles. On the N face are several splayed recesses and, below a relieving arch at first floor, the moulded jambs and cracked lintel of a badly repaired fireplace. Structure stabilized 1997.

ROSSDHU HOUSE (Loch Lomond Golf Club). Classical mansion with a portico and lower flanking wings, its compositional elegance enhanced by decorative restraint. The central, two-storey-and-basement core of the house, in pleasant pinkish ashlar, was erected, 1772–4, at the behest of Sir James 23rd of Colquhoun and 25th of Luss. Above the channelled rustication of the basement the windows of the *piano nobile* have lugged architraves and cornices. A Vitruvian scroll stringcourse runs across the façade at first-floor level. There is an eaves cornice with soffit blocks. It seems likely that the design came from *Sir James Clerk* of Penicuik whose protégé *John Baxter* may have supervised the work. There is, however, explicit evidence of payment to 'Mr *Thomas Brown*, Architect at Renfrew, for his attendance' during the construction. For the subsequent enlargement of the house, detectable in the ochre-coloured sandstone of the N and S wings, balustraded parapets and pedimented E portico, no such attribution is possible. Yet these additions, carried out for Sir James 25th of Colquhoun and 27th of Luss, during the second or third decade of the C19, seem to ennoble the sophisticated simplicity of the original design. In the two-storey, four-bay wings, the E windows of the upper floor, though somewhat taller than those of the main block, maintain the same dressings; they are composed in pairs, the two outer windows set between broad plain pilasters under a solid parapet, the inner openings below a balustraded eaves. Similar balustrading, added to the six-bay C18 house, stops at the new pediment which, entirely plain in tympanum and frieze, is carried on paired Tuscan columns, two storeys high, advancing at the *piano nobile* on basement plinths. Between these coupled columns, from a Gibbsian arrangement of doorway and flanking windows under a common cornice, steps spill down to the forecourt.

Restoration, following the creation of the lochside golf course in the 1980s, began in 1991 and continued (with an interruption, 1992–4) until 1997 under the direction of *The William Cowie Partnership*. Foundations were stabilized to halt subsidence, stonework was cleaned and the house extended by adding accommodation N and S of the main block behind the wings. Refurbishment as a world-class clubhouse occasioned substantial recasting of the interiors. At ground level, locker room facilities, club restaurant, bar and service areas have been provided. On the upper floors of the late C18 core there are bedrooms grouped around a cupola-lit central well, those at attic level lit by dormers on the N, W and S faces of a restored piended roof. Interior design by *Wiseman & Gale* of Phoenix, Arizona, and *Amanda Rosa*, Glasgow. Only the public rooms of the *piano nobile* remain intact, though extensive repair and renewal of plasterwork and timber panelling has been necessary.

Entered from the portico, the central HALL has a stone-flagged floor. Door-height timber wall-panelling gridded in squares. On the N wall, a heavily lugged and moulded stone fireplace set between tall fluted pilasters linked by a cornice. Plaster frieze and cornice in a vigorous Doric idiom: sheep heads and paterae alternate in the metopes; soffit blocks co-ordinate with the triglyphs. Well stair of cantilevered stone treads. To the r. is the LIBRARY (formerly the Chinese Drawing Room). On the S wall, interrupting a low dado with dentilled cornice, is a classically framed fireplace in grey-green marble. The frieze is Doric again with wreathed paterae in the metopes, the ceiling patterned in delicate husk garlands and fans. Beyond, in the N wing, is the MAIN DRAWING ROOM, reconstructed after a fire in the early C20, its walls of limed oak with fielded panels, bolection mouldings, lugged architraves, and pulvinated lintels and cornices over the doors. Plain ashlar fireplace with a bold but simply moulded and lugged oak surround under an egg-and-dart strip and mantelshelf cornice. The plaster ceiling, laid on a segmental barrel vault reputedly of *in situ* concrete, is divided into panels by strips of dense grape and vine ornament. The former Library, now the COCKTAIL LOUNGE, lies l. of the entrance hall; a more intimate room with a finely proportioned classical fireplace of white marble inlaid with black and gold panels in the frieze. Plaster ceiling with a central fanned disc, arabesques and swags; cornice toothed with short consoles and a deep frieze of paired scrolls and urns. Cornice and frieze are similar in the adjacent WINE ROOM, though here there are five ceiling discs in line, each decorated with foliate sprays around a central floret. Essentially an ante room, it leads to the DINING ROOM in the S wing. Wide panelled doors open between Tuscan columns into an exotic interior; woodwork stained green, the walls mirrored and papered in green and white stripes. On the W wall, a chimneypiece of black and gold marble with a plain mantelshelf carried on the swollen capitals of three-quarter columns. Doric frieze with paterae and stag heads alternating in the metopes and a cornice with guttae blocks above the triglyphs. On the ceiling, Vitruvian scrolls and vine swags.

CARRIAGE HOUSE (former offices, once known as The Byre). Early C19. Two contiguous, two-storey, piended blocks aligned N–S. Parapeted screen wall S façade: coupled pilasters and entablature framing the fanned voussoirs of a recessed semicircular-arch opening. This is now filled by a blind Diocletian window over a tripartite window. Refurbished for residential use by *The William Cowie Partnership*, 1996–7.

COTTAGES, 1.25km. s. Early C19. U-plan group of three-bay, three-storey mill and two single-storey ranges. Asymmetrical Dairy. Refurbished as residential accommodation by *The William Cowie Partnership*, 1996–8.

ICE-HOUSE, built into the slope behind the Chapel. Late C18. From the N a short lintelled passage leads to a circular chamber, brick-lined and domed.

LAUNDRY(?). Early C19. Roofless and gazebo-like. Symmetrical canted N front in ashlar: central round-arch door in a round-arch recess flanked by coupled round-arch windows in splays. Windowed projections W and E repeat doorway design. Moulded eaves cornice. Rubble S gable with open pediment skews.

NORTH LODGE, 500m. NW. Early C19. The main entry to the estate. Two single-storey buildings flanking the drive present identical piend-roofed, half-octagon fronts to the N approach. Gothic glazing bars to round-arch windows in arched recesses. Impost band. – Two square GATEPIERS with pyramid tops.

ROSS LODGE (Yew Tree Lodge), 1.6km. SSW. Early C19. Symmetrical piend-roofed cottage with a central canted porch projecting on Tuscan columns. – Plain GATEPIERS with pyramid tops; ornamental railings similar to those at the South Lodge (q.v.). Refurbished 1996.

SOUTH LODGE, 2.8km. s. Early C19. Theatrically sited and grandly symmetrical high ashlar archway carrying an entablature which advances over coupled Tuscan columns. A heavy parapet block follows suit and rises in the centre to support the Colquhoun arms in full colour. Ironwork gates, spear-headed to an inverted arch profile, fill the portal. Matching railings, set on low walls, link l. and r. to outlying pavilions. Squat and flat-roofed, these have coupled pilasters flanking mock, round-arched windows; a reverberative echo of the central gateway theme.

WALLED GARDEN, 1km. s. Early C19. High rubble walls (coursed on the inner faces); enclosure almost 100m. square. Small segmental-arch entry from s. Bellcote over W doorway. Ruinous greenhouses along N wall.

SADDELL

7832

A ruinous abbey, a castle and a Georgian house gathered at the foot of Saddell Glen close to the Carradale–Campbeltown road.

SADDELL ABBEY. A good imagination is necessary to evoke a picture of this C12 Cistercian house. The only clues are a few stands of rubble walling and some turf-covered mounds; enough, however, to confirm if not immediately reveal the lines of an aisleless nave and presbytery with transepts N and S and monastic buildings around a cloister court to the s. The writer of the *Statistical Account* of 1794 recorded the church's overall extent as 136 feet 0 inches (41.5m.), but of this length of building only some masonry vestiges of the presbytery at the E end of the nave can now be seen, and even these show signs of relatively recent reconstruction. Some walling from the N transept, C13, also stands. Other than this, part of the s range of claustral building is all that remains visible. This much-depleted structure, undercroft to the Abbey's refectory, doubtless survives because of its continued use as a burial enclosure in post-Reformation times. Almost nothing of detailed architectural interest can be found *in situ* apart from a piece of chevron-and-roll moulding in the E wall of the presbytery. Carved fragments from the Abbey now in Campbeltown Museum have been stylistically related to contemporary Irish Romanesque work. The Abbey itself, founded *c.* 1160 either by Somerled, Lord of Kintyre, or perhaps by his son Reginald, came under the jurisdiction of Mellifont in the diocese of Armagh until the start of the C16 when, much impoverished, it was united with the Argyll bishopric.

In the BURIAL GROUND, exhibited beneath a rather ugly display shelter, are several tapered SLABS, C14–C16. These bear differing carved representations: mailed knights, clerics clad in ecclesiastical vestments, a huntsman, animals mythical and actual, swords, ships, etc. Sculptural provenance: Kintyre, Iona and Loch Awe. – Also on display are two pieces of a once free-standing CROSS, C15, which must originally have stood to a height of 2.6m. – At the W end of the graveyard, in an enclosure surrounded by a low wall with cast-iron railings and urns, is a MURAL MONUMENT commemorating Colonel Donald Campbell of Glensaddell †1784; marble inscription framed on ashlar wall between Roman Doric pilasters which support full entablature and pediment.

SADDELL CASTLE, 7.50m. SE of Saddell Abbey. Oblong plan tower-house of four storeys and crowstep-gabled garret, built 1508–10 by David Hamilton, Bishop of Argyll, following the annexation of Saddell Abbey and the creation of the free barony of Saddell. Fired in the Earl of Sussex's raid on Kintyre in 1558; neither the extent of damage nor repairs is known. In 1650 reconstruction of roof, floors and masonry was begun by William Ralston, who, as one of the plantation lairds then settling in Kintyre, leased the castle from the 1st Marquess of Argyll during the second half of the C17. Several fireplaces date from C18 alterations. Further restoration and internal remodelling by Colonel Macleod Campbell in the late C19 and, more radically, 1975–7, by the Landmark Trust. Plan rearrangement is extensive but the Victorian sitting-room ceiling has been renewed while surviving C18 panelling in a top-floor bedroom set a pattern for several new rooms created within the shell.

The harled rubble exterior is substantially original. Random windows have chamfered arrises. Parapet rests on a single-spaced corbel course with similar course below, staggered to produce a decorative chequer pattern. Corner rounds on triple corbel stones and machicolation slots; a fifth round appears on the W wall beside the gabled caphouse of the turnpike stair.

Offices forming L-plan court on W and S date from C18. NW range built with material quarried from Saddell Abbey. Stretch of C16 barmkin wall incorporated along S range. Additional outbuildings C19 and C20.

SADDELL HOUSE, 400m. NE of Saddell Castle on the l. bank of Saddell Water. Two-storey-and-attic Georgian mansion on sunk basement, erected by Colonel Donald Campbell of Glensaddell, 1774. Harled with bracketed eaves cornice, dressed margins and in-and-out quoins. Roof piended to platform from which rise two ashlar-edged chimneystacks. NW façade conventionally pedimented but with a late C19 Roman Doric porch placed asymmetrically. Semi-octagonal projection at the centre of the SE front merely repeats standard single-light windows on all three faces. *George Langlands*'s drawings of 1784 reveal a more prepossessing house with balustraded eaves, small central cupola and lower flanking pavilions advancing on NW front. Interior remodelled after 1900 fire.

SHORE COTTAGE, 250m. S of Saddell Castle. Symmetrical cruciform conjunction of one- and two-storey gabled blocks. Mid Victorian.

SANDA ISLAND

7204

A small island lying some 4.0km. SE off Southend.

ST NINIAN'S CHAPEL. Ruined late medieval chapel and its 'circumjacent cemetery which appears to have long possessed some superstitious celebrity'. Oblong plan, of which lateral walls still stand, though gables have fallen. Door and single intact window are both square-headed. Primitive altar formed by broken freestone slab on a rectangular rubble base. Within the chapel is a much-weathered upright SLAB, Early Christian in date, carved with a wheel-head cross on its W face. 14m. N of chapel in the walled burial enclosure stands a heavy cross-shaped SLAB, its decorative treatment now indistinguishable.

SANDBANK

1680

On the SW shore of the Holy Loch. Once a place of holiday homes and yachts, the village has grown slovenly from its years of symbiotic dependence on the American Polaris submarine base. A few signs of peace dividend improvement since the last US vessel sailed out in 1992.

CHAPEL and BURIAL GROUND, 600m. NW of Loch Loskin. Between two streams an earth bank defines an irregular enclosure, probably of Iron Age origin, within which are the drystone remains of a small Early Christian cell. At the angles, four ground sockets doubtless associated with the roof timbering. W of the chapel, more than 40 shallow oval graves; crouched or infant interments.

SANDBANK PARISH CHURCH. Dated 1868. The SW gable front has a triple lancet with three trefoil windows aligned below. Small SE gabled porch. In the re-entrant a neat cylindrical tower with a twelve-arch belfry ring and a candle-snuffer slated roof.

SANDBANK PRIMARY SCHOOL, on the A885, at the s end of the village. By *Thomas Smith, Gibb & Pate*, 1976. Crisp and elegant, flat-roofed Modernism faced in Dorset pea render. 1km. NW along the road, the OLD SCHOOL, *c.* 1875, still in use, preserves three lancet windows with Perp glazing bars.

DESCRIPTION

With no obvious centre the village seems to focus on its single tenement, OAKFIELD PLACE, *c.* 1905, red ashlar shops and flats with four canted bays under hooped and bargeboarded gables. Across the road by the loch, BENMORE VIEW, 1902, was formerly a reading room but is now residential; a single house with white roughcast walls, immense lead-cheeked dormers and a bracketed eaves of exceptional depth. But most buildings shoreside are lower, older dwellings. Among them, CLYDE COTTAGES, a four-in-a-row rubble run with droved red sandstone dressings, and the three-bay OAKBANK HOTEL which seems to be sinking into the shore. Beyond, the usual marine villas run NW along the coast road. But there is little to admire. Nor is there anything to evoke the great sailing days of the past. ROBERTSON'S SLIP at the end of the village is now no more than a cleared and levelled site boulder-banked to the water. Down Rankine's Brae are more tired lochside villas. WINDSOR LODGE, *c.* 1860, is best; a steeply gabled Gothic house with pointed-arch doorway, windows and dormer. There is little to relieve a pervasive shabbiness. VULCAN PLACE, 1851, no less untidy than most, attracts by its quirkiness. SOMMERVILLE PLACE, 1869, on the other hand, is rigorous; a rubble terrace with six gabled eaves dormers, its severity lightened by a bowed NW corner.

CHAMBERED CAIRN, 250m. E of Ardnadam Farm. Known locally as Adam's Grave or The Cromlech. Disturbed cairn material piled against a chamber of parallel schist slabs orientated SW–NE. Portal stones mark NE entrance.

SHANDON

There are still traces on the hillside of the 'sean-dun', the old fort and stronghold of the Earls of Lennox from which Shandon derives its name. Little else about the settlement is properly ancient; popular and populated only since the mid C19, the village has become a victim of its own success. Following the widening and re-routing of the A814 in 1969, Shandon has become an overdeveloped (and, in places, overgrown) extension of Rhu, now without the piers, parish kirk and station on the West Highland Railway which supported its autonomy. Even in its heyday, however, it was served by little more than a small sub-Post Office located at the gates to West Shandon (q.v.), while Kirk Brae – site of the Shandon Free Church, and then of the sturdy iron pier at which steamers from the Glasgow & South Western and Caledonian Railway Companies called regularly – represented a modest village core.

The setting is none the less superb; the original houses almost exclusively sw-facing with views across the Gareloch and to Rosneath. Proliferation of the redwood Wellingtonia was encouraged by the Donaldson shipping family, who purchased Blairvadach (q.v.); and an extensive retaining wall, erected as part of the road improvements (alongside which the old shore route survives), has over time been softened by great bouffants of beech and rhododendron. Of the surviving houses (and many have been lost to *cul-de-sac* development), the best are exceptional examples of the marine mansion genre.

DESCRIPTION

ARGYLL AND BUTE COUNCIL OFFICES. Formerly BLAIRVADACH, designed *c.* 1850 by *J. T. Rochead* for Sir James Anderson, Lord Provost of Glasgow from 1848 until 1851. Ebullient rather than elegant, the whole is dominated by a NW corner keep, weighty with machicolations, an ogival domeheaded stair tower and two great bay windows, one a canted oriel corbelled from a chamfered centre shaft, the other two-storey with battered base and elaborate cast-iron window guard. Linking the keep with a tall, seaward-facing wing with flanking pepperpot bartizans is a two-storey section with pedimented dormers topped by floral and thistle finials. The composition is united by a rope-moulded stringcourse, woven into hoodmoulds and threaded around the pendant consoles supporting the impressive entrance porch. – INTERIOR. Jacobean in flavour, with a spectacular entrance hall, panelled and with a carved, arched screen and intricate chimneypiece. – LAUNDRY. Attractive, albeit ruinous, single-storey-and-attic outbuilding with circular stair tower and arrowslit windows.

On the shoreline opposite, the timber-clad observation tower of the BLAIRVADACH OUTDOOR CENTRE punches free of the parent building – a low-slung monopitch affair with a spinal array of pyramidal rooflights which terminates as a broad sunshade over a viewing window. The Celtic WAR MEMORIAL of 1920 by *A. N. Paterson & Stoddart* stands close by on a grassy knoll, a little less assertive and somewhat forlorn since its relocation from the grounds of the parish church. Also on the water's edge, trim in black and white, the many-gabled GULLYBRIDGE HOUSE, a late Victorian fishing lodge now extended for use as a residential nursing home.

CROY appears next, the original urn-capped balustrade rebuilt atop the 1969 retaining wall. Begun in 1834 by *Sinclair* of Caithness, and enlarged *c.* 1865 by a billiard room to the S. A large, rambling-plan Tudor-Gothic villa with ornamental bargeboards and diamond-set chimneystacks on pedestal bases. – LODGE. Separated from the larger building by the approach road to the QUEEN'S POINT housing estate, a pretty Gothic gatehouse with pointed-arch windows.

ARDGARE, a large Italianate mansion, for which *J. J. Burnet* prepared a decorative scheme in 1884, has made way for more mediocre housing, although the campanile tower of the original STABLE BLOCK sustains the original aesthetic. STUCKENDUFF, the dainty single-storey-and-attic dower house dating from c. 1830, survives, as does GARESIDE COTTAGE, the Arts and Crafts gamekeeper's house, built in London brick with corbiestepped chimneystacks and Cumberland green pegged slates covering the roof.

ARDCHAPEL is named after an ancient chapel, the site of which can be found on the hill slopes NE of the West Highland Railway. The house was built in 1854 by *James Smith* as an asymmetrical two-storey villa in sandstone and harl. Subsequent additions of c. 1865 increased the accommodation and upset the gentle balance of the elevated w façade. CHAPELBURN is smaller and cottagey: early C19 with Victorian attic dormers (all three different) and a long trellis veranda facing w.

LETRAULT, from the Gaelic for 'mill', has a core dating from 1855, and includes a two-stage square entrance tower with Jacobethan hoodmoulds and stepped parapet picked out in sandstone on a cream harl background. A lower gabled extension to the l., which bears an armorial plaque dated 1864, is attractively completed by a canted conservatory salvaged from a contemporary villa in Rhu which perished by fire in 1982.

KIRK BRAE lies at the heart of the village, where the former SHANDON FREE CHURCH has been converted into housing. The rubble and whin building was erected in 1844, the congregation having had to meet temporarily in the malt house of a nearby distillery. Beginning as a simple rectangular building by *John Burnet*, it benefited greatly from the addition in 1883 of tower and transepts designed by *William Landless*. In the mean time, school and schoolmaster's house, later the church reading rooms, had been built behind in 1845–6, also to designs by *Burnet*, and the adjoining MANSE erected by *Angus Kennedy* in 1864. Used latterly as Shandon Parish Church, it had its extremely elegant spire truncated as part of a 1985 conversion into four self-contained houses. With the upper stage of the steeple removed and capped as a campanile, and the spirelet dismantled, the broad w front – despite a good gabled porch and lancet windows – appears squat and much diminished.

Uphill, a row of whitewashed gardeners' cottages terminates in the 1977 corner pavilion of BRAIDHURST by *Michael Henderson*. Spreading its wings below projecting eaves is a colourful carved bird whose (spiritual) task is to prevent the roof from blowing off. More conventionally converted, the nearby COACH-HOUSE and STABLES to the demolished BASHLEY retain a good 1880 courtyard arch with pediment and lazy volutes. Older still is nearby LINNBURN, begun in 1836 by Samuel McCall, a Glasgow merchant noted in the 1897 'Annals of Garelochside' as having been 'very particular in the straight line of his avenue ... and the symmetry of his garden'. The house was remodelled in 1884 and is distinguished by the boldness of its Baronial and Jacobethan details from that date, in particular by a series of mannered dormerheads supported on bulky corbels, and by the leisurely arc of the cushion-coped ashlar balustrade which delineates the elevated terrace. LINNBURN COTTAGE, originally the stable block, was skilfully converted by *Jack Notman* for T. Campbell Lawson after he sold Hill House in Helensburgh (q.v.) in 1972. The delightful cobbled courtyard was enclosed by the addition of a library wing, whose recent origins are confirmed by the tall, barrel-headed windows N and W.

As the main road approaches Faslane, three distinctive villas rise above the passage of traffic. First is GLENFEULAN, a ground-hugging classical house in peach harl and yellow sandstone, single-storey over raised basement with a symmetrical entrance block and small flanking pavilions. Added emphasis is given to the central portion by the inclusion of two full-height canted windows and an undemanding pierced parapet on which are balanced a family of fat figurative urns. S is a period conservatory, broad and low with coloured glass in spandrel panels. – STABLES. An effective combination of square-plan wash house and three-bay stables (the doors separated by timber pilasters and columns), the U-plan range of flat-roofed ancillary buildings itself forms a raised terrace, the whole linked together by a further pierced parapet with urns, and a two-stage campanile with oculus on every face.

On the neighbouring feu, the stylish CRAGMHOR, *c.* 1830, crowns a raised plateau whose western slope is formalized by a purposeful balustraded parapet. To the S is a now detached winter garden with a canted bay under broad flat eaves and a pretty Gothic rooflight whose sides and Y-traceried gable are infilled with decorative glass.

SHANDON HOUSE, built in 1849 by *Charles Wilson*, is a huge rambling-plan Scots Baronial mansion clothed in coarse harl with Jacobethan details, the original character greatly diminished by a series of Victorian alterations and additions which include a billiard hall designed in 1883 by *John Honeyman*. Of the entrance elevation, the tall three-stage round tower with basket-arched door and rusticated and moulded surround is original. So too is the elaborate strapwork and owl motif, and gabled outer l. bay with big canted oriel on corbelled base. The SE corner, despite a datestone reading 1800, is later, as are the assorted bay windows on E and W fronts, but the central square-plan tower with serpent finial on weather-vane and the low servants' wing to the rear with square bartizan and strapwork dormerheads are relatively unaltered. The building became a reform school from 1965 until 1986, and was sold to the Ministry of Defence in 1990. At the time of writing it has been uninhabited for some time, wrapped in a great swathe of ivy whose progress across the harl remains unchallenged. – INTERIOR. The principal reception rooms retain compartmentalized ceilings with decorative crocketed plasterwork. The 1849 owl motif is repeated in the form of corbels supporting the arched ribs of the hall ceiling, while what remains of the balustrade to the grand double stair suggests Jacobean-style decoration in carved oak.

Shandon House was unrivalled in scale for barely two years, but its competitor no longer survives. Nearby, Robert Napier, marine engineer, used the proceeds from the manufacture of the famous iron ships of the Cunard fleet to erect the Scots-Jacobethan palace of WEST SHANDON on the water's edge, begun in 1851 to designs by *J. T. Rochead*. The building housed Napier's collection of books, art works and exotic plants, having a picture gallery (with organ), sculpture court, museum and clock tower. Sandstone quarried in Bishopbriggs was transported to the site using the Forth and Clyde Canal, while internal woodwork was executed by craftsmen loaned from the Govan shipyards. Following Napier's death in 1876, the house and grounds found a new lease of life as the Shandon Hydropathic, complete with Russian, Turkish and salt-water swimming baths. Used afterwards as an emergency hospital and then hotel, the building was eventually demolished and the grounds cleared in 1960 as part of the development of the submarine base at Faslane, q.v. Today, only the original garden wall with one extant bartizan and the S LODGE survive, and while the latter is in poor condition it nevertheless represents the great mansion in microcosm, with an elaborately shaped W gable and – above the entrance a quasi-broached (turning into octagonal) turret with lead conical roof and slender finial. A sweet but sad reminder of summer days at the coast.

SHUNA

A small island off the Appin coast NW of Portnacroish.

CASTLE SHUNA, at the S end of the island 1.1km. N of Castle Stalker (q.v.). Oblong tower-house of rubble with schist dressings; late C16 with a turnpike stair tower added on the SE wall some time during the C17. Domestic rather than defensive in character, it is now largely ruined, though the SW and SE walls stand to second floor. The ground floor, still vaulted, was divided into two apartments. The NE kitchen, entered through a door in the SE wall against which the later stair was built, had a large fireplace in the gable but this has completely collapsed. In the thickened W corner of the SW cellar a small spiral stair rises to serve the floor above; it has a corbelled roof. At the upper level, the hall is ruinous, though a segmental-arched fireplace in the SW wall survives. Some adjacent overgrown footings to the SE may be those of a later dwelling and byre built with stones plundered from the castle.

THE FARM. Traditional three-bay, two-storey-and-attic, harled farmhouse. C18.

SKIPNESS

Attenuated village of rubble cottages edging the bay W of the debouch of the Skipness River into Kilbrannan Sound. Now a *cul-de-sac* settlement reached only by a single track road running NE along the rocky shore from Claonaig jetty, its location on the

Clyde estuary made Skipness one of the great lordships of Kintyre in medieval times.

KILBRANNAN CHAPEL (St Brendan's Chapel), close to beach 350m. SE of Skipness Castle. Despite great age (late C13 or early C14 work by masons enlarging Skipness Castle) walls and gables still stand remarkably unreduced by time. Elongated oblong plan, 25.1m. by 8.2m, originally subdivided into nave and chancel by a timber screen. Narrow splayed lancets, but a larger bifurcated light in the E gable. Red Arran sandstone dressings enhance the rubble construction at windows, doors, quoins, stepped plinth mould and skew-stone verges.

In the chapel or its walled GRAVEYARD are three tapered SLABS, Kintyre school, C14–C16, carved with a variety of images. – A fourth tapered SLAB, Loch Awe school, *c.* 1500, shows dragons' heads, a mailed knight, foliage and other beasts, all contained by dog-tooth border. – Abutting the S wall of the chapel are two contiguous BURIAL ENCLOSURES. In that to the E, which is gated, a Tuscan pedimented porch canopies a white marble mural monument commemorating Colin Campbell, Captain of Skipness, †1756. Its neighbour to the W repeats the Tuscan motif as a wall aedicule within which is a further pilastered frame with a scrolled broken pediment but no inscription. – Among many C18 HEADSTONES are those of Angus Mckinnin †1739, carved with a winged angel and four-horse plough-team, and Donald Kaymand, tailor, recalled by goose and scissors, 1727.

ST BRENDAN'S CHURCH, close to bridge over Skipness River. By *Bertram Vaughan Johnson*, 1896–7. Small skew-gabled nave built in coursed rubble with red sandstone dressings. Lancets in gables. Open timber ceiling. – STAINED GLASS with Celtic interlacing designed by *R. C. Graham* of Skipness, 1897, and manufactured by *Powell & Sons*.

SKIPNESS CASTLE. Evidently chosen for its seaward prospects which command the Sounds of Kilbrannan and Bute and the entrance to Loch Fyne, the castle's open location on relatively flat terrain offers no natural defensive advantage. MacGibbon and Ross suggested that a moat and inclined glacis may have afforded some protection, the former draining around the N and S sides of the castle into a nearby stream, but there is little to substantiate this. Yet a surprising amount has survived at Skipness; it retains features not only early and rare but even unique in Scotland.

The present plan is that of a rectangular castle of enclosure. Massive rubble walls, rising from a splayed plinth to *c.* 10m. in places, surround a courtyard which now measures 33m. N–S by 20m. E–W but was originally of lesser dimensions by virtue of the castle's earlier inner structures. W and SE towers project at wall height. A third higher tower, contained within the NE corner, rises 15.7m. to a parapet walk. This arrangement, substantially defined by the late C16, survived abandonment at the end of the C17 and conversion to a farm a century later until in 1898 R. C. Graham of Skipness set preservation in train.

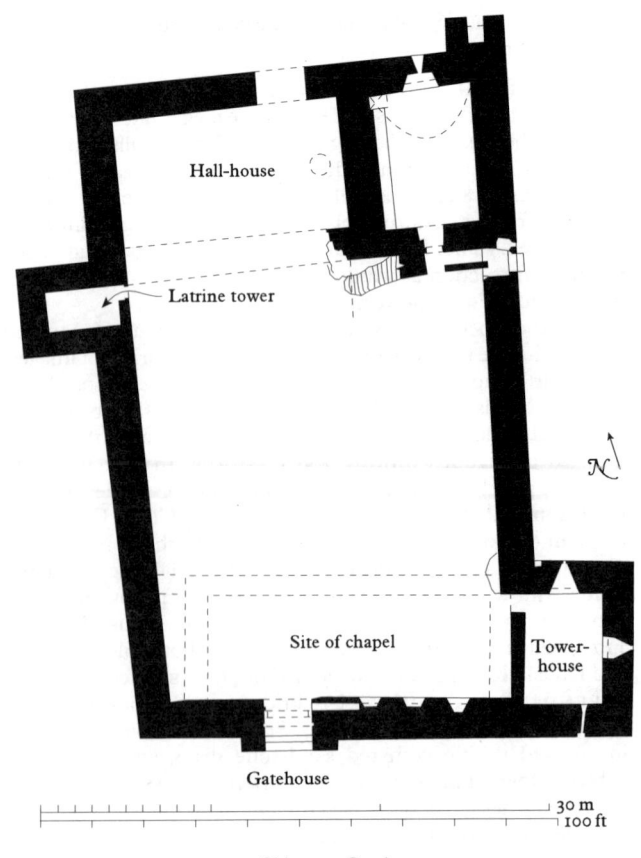

Skipness Castle

While discovery of Christian graves in the SW corner of the courtyard suggests the site's religious significance may be ancient, the castle itself is first recorded in the C13 as a possession of the MacSween family. It may well have been a consequence of Alexander II's pacification of the Isles. This early structure was a simple hall-house aligned E–W, three walls of which now constitute the NW corner of the castle courtyard. Lying parallel, 18m. S, was a chapel, the patronage of which had been granted to the monks of Paisley by Dougald MacSween in a charter of 1261. Of this early church only mural vestiges survive incorporated in the existing S wall. For reasons still unclear, the castle was greatly enlarged and reinforced at the end of the C13 or beginning of the C14, a process which entailed the assimilation of hall and chapel into a new plan determined by the construction of a rectangular masonry curtain over 2m. thick penetrated by an entrance portal on the S. The great walls were defensively strengthened by the W, SE and NE towers and by a battlemented parapet. At this time, too, a new shoreside chapel was erected (*see above*).

For two centuries Skipness was in MacDonald ownership but, following the forfeiture of the Lord of the Isles, it passed to the Crown and then in 1502 to Archibald, 2nd Earl of Argyll. It was Campbells who, in the early C16, raised the NE tower by three storeys and later in the same century reconstructed the upper tower, adding rounds and a parapet walk, and clearing away courtyard buildings in the E range to reveal the new 'tower-house' in its present form.

The castle is entered from the N through a round-arched opening formed during C18 alterations when the building was adapted to serve agricultural purposes. The approach leads into the C13 hall-house, originally free-standing but now embedded in subsequent growth. N, W and E walls are of local schist rubble with red sandstone dressings brought from Arran, a combination continued by later builders. The hall-house, of three unvaulted storeys, retains neither floors nor stairs and has lost its S wall. Windows are round-arched, small in size and few in number. To the r., the W wall of the hall-house merges into the late C13 or early C14 curtain. A three-storey latrine tower, converted to a doocot at the end of the C18, projects W, two pointed-arch doorways giving access at ground and first floor. The latter opening and four others each with wide-arched squared and splayed embrasures to crosslet-loopholes, 'the only systematic display of this type of arrow-slit in Scotland' (Cruden, 1960), indicate the likely prior existence of at least a gallery running along the W side of the courtyard, though arguments have also been made for a more substantial range of buildings.

To the l. of the entrance is the tower-house. This incorporates work from a two-storeyed unvaulted range of buildings, late C13 or early C14, which ran along the E curtain, e.g. the NE latrine tower, again with crosslet-loops, but much is rendered obscure by the changes associated with the early C16 development of the tower-house. At this time the ground-floor apartment at the N of the earlier range was vaulted. Some means of access from the yard to first-floor level must have existed (the present forestair was constructed towards the end of the C16) but a mural staircase, already rising N from first-floor level in a straight flight within the E wall, has been preserved. To serve the new apartments being formed at second- and third-floor levels as the NE corner of the castle was raised, a turnpike stair was inserted into the latrine tower, built in red sandstone ashlar. Its original stone treads have been replaced by timber. The stair ascended to a caphouse, garret and parapet walk at fourth-floor level. The present upper arrangements date from the late C16 when the parapet was pushed forward on a series of individual corbel stones, the four corner rounds continuing this same dentil-like sequence over three corbel courses, and a similar swelling being formed ahead of the tower's S gable where flues from fireplaces constructed at second- and third-floor level rose to a central stack.

Across the courtyard from the hall-house and tower-house all that survives is the s curtain wall with part of the s wall of the original chapel built into its lower courses. Here, too, however, as on the E, a range of late C13 or early C14 buildings existed until their removal at the end of the C18. Towards the w end of the s wall the gatehouse projects slightly; entrance was gained beneath a two-centred arch over which is a vaulted portcullis-chamber. At first floor E, running into the SE tower, would have been the castle's great hall, lit by three deeply embrasured tall narrow openings still to be seen.

SKIPNESS HOUSE, 200m. w of Castle. Spreading Baronial mansion built for Robert Chellas Graham by *John Honeyman*. In 1867 Graham purchased the Campbell of Skipness mansion, a wide-fronted crowstepped gabled house linked to lower piend-roofed wings by quadrant walls, and immediately engaged Honeyman to replace it with a new, more romantically Scottish residence. Building seems to have been delayed, but between 1878 and 1881 there appeared a four-storey bedroom tower-house linked to a two storey wing containing staircase hall, library and drawing room: 'refined and scholarly' is James Macaulay's description, with 'none of the bombast and over-decoration which made much Scots-Baronialism of the late nineteenth century a parody of itself'. In 1969, fire destroyed much of Honeyman's house, including his dominant bartizaned tower. Remodelled, though not restored, 1972. Crowsteps, eaves dormers and a round stair tower with witch's hat roof survive from Victorian work.

SKIPNESS HOUSE LODGE, across bridge at entrance to estate. Late C19 castellar cylinder with a corbelled parapet and tangential chimney tube.

PRIMARY SCHOOL. Dated 1868; by a 'Mr *Ramsay*', though 'entirely planned by Mrs Ramsay' (*Argyllshire Herald*, 1869). One-and-a-half-storey gabled L-plan. Open eaves, bargeboards, and bracketed saddle-back canopy over former entrance (now window).

THE OLD MANSE. Late C19. Single-storey-and-attic; façade gable on massive red sandstone corbels projecting above a canted bay below.

VILLAGE HALL. Former Free Church, 1892. Gabled nave with pointed-arch entrance and low diagonal buttresses.

SLOCKAVULLIN

Hidden, somewhat tumble-down estate village nestling along a stream on the w side of Kilmartin Burn valley.

KILMARTIN PRIMARY SCHOOL, 900m. sw of Kilmartin Church. Built 1835 as the Episcopal School by *Joseph Gordon Davis*; enlarged *c.* 1875. Rubble with red sandstone dressings. Almost symmetrical storey-and-a-half front of two gables with a glass-roofed porch and small central gabled dormer between. Hood mouldings. Small corbelled canted bay in l. façade gable.

NETHER LARGIE FARM, 200m. SW of Kilmartin Primary School. Harled farm, *c.* 1840. Two-storey, three-bay gable-ended house with gable-fronted single-storey wings l. and r. Upper windows altered. The hood-mouldings to ground-floor windows and the ringed cross finial to the central porch are primitive in execution. Steading court behind.

NORTH LODGE, 100m. before road bends l. into village. By *William Burn*. Dated 1855. Mirror version of the East Lodge to Poltalloch Estate (q.v.) complete with gables, bays and ornate bargeboards.

VICTORIA HALL, halfway between Kilmartin School and A816. The Community Centre for Poltalloch Estate; by *James Edgar*, 1897. Wide Arts and Crafts front like a railway station, with half-timbering over three-light mullion-and-transom windows in end gables. Parapeted veranda to central entrance. Harled with red sandstone dressings and red tile ridge and finials. Light metal trusses over assembly hall. Disused.

CHAMBERED CAIRN, Nether Largie South, immediately S of Kilmartin Primary School. Partly grass-covered, irregular oval heap of stones, 34m. by 27m., reconstructed after excavations of 1864. Central chamber of Clyde type, 6.1m. long, is aligned with the NE entrance. Maximum height below the capstones does not exceed 2m. A large secondary cist to the SSW of the chamber is still visible beneath displaced capstone. *See* also Kilmartin.

STANDING STONES, Nether Largie, 250m SE of Temple Wood. Scattered alignment of stones. Two at SW stand 2.75m. and 2.8m. Two at NE, 2.85m. and 2.7m. An intermediate cluster of eight stones is considerably lower, with one exception reaching 2.8m.

STONE CIRCLES, Temple Wood, between Nether Largie and 3 Poltalloch North Lodge. The SW Circle originally comprised twenty-two standing stones (a number on the SE are missing), the spaces between them later filled with interval stones to make a closed ring. This in turn was surrounded by stone banking which covered two small earlier outer cairns. Within the circle is a central cairn. All three cairns had cists but all have been covered. The NE Circle, discovered 1979, is smaller, much vaguer in configuration, and has only one stone upstanding.

SOUTHEND

6908

Established in 1797 by the Duke of Argyll as Newton Argyll, the village lies at the southernmost tip of Kintyre, scattered intermittently along the slow curve of road from Conie Glen to Dunaverty Bay and Keil Point. The settlement is marked at its extremities by two of its three churches.

ST COLUMBA'S CHAPEL, near Keil Point. Despite a geographically plausible association with the missionary saint, there is no mention of Kilcolmkill, as it was first known, until the C14. By the late C17 it lay deserted. Now a roofless, barely gabled ruin, its rubble walls are engulfed in ivy. A long narrow plan results from at least two building periods: E end, of roughly squared pink sandstone, late C13, perhaps replacing an earlier C12 or c13 chapel; the longer w end, which may have had a gallery, is late medieval or post-Reformation. The few single-light windows have deep ingo splays. Double lancet lost when the E gable was rebuilt in recent times.

Recumbent tombstones in the church and graveyard include a number of tapered SLABS dating from c14 to early c16. One, perhaps the earliest, combines the effigy of an armed warrior with carvings of a stag and hounds and a galley with furled sails. Later graves, bearing heraldic escutcheons, commemorate local families; some, like the MacDonalds of Sanda and McNeils of Carskiey, of medieval lineage, others, such as Ralstons and Maxwells, prominent in the Lowland Plantation of c17. Two HEADSTONES depict pursuits that for centuries shaped Kintyre's economy: one, erected in 1805 by farmer James Hall of Pirleyknow, carries the carving of a ploughing team; the other, 1847, raised by Alexander McKenzie, mariner, bears the image of a sailing ship. Some 18m. NW of the Church is a WELL above which, on the rock face, a Latin cross has been cut.

ST COLUMBA'S CHURCH. No longer in use but unmistakably meant for worship. Built 1889–90, by *Robert Hay* of Glasgow on the site of the Lowlanders' Relief Church of 1797–8, its inventively Classical façade, Georgian and rather urban, still sends rhetorical testimony down a hedged axial drive.

SOUTHEND PARISH CHURCH, Machrimore, at E end of village. Erected 1773–4 by *James Stirling*, 'mason and housebuilder', this simple harled and quoined skew-gabled building replaced the earlier Parish Kirk of Kilblaan (St Blaan's Chapel), *c.* 1680, rebuilt 1719, all traces of which have long since been eroded by the Conieglen Water. S elevation symmetrical centred on a high blind porthole flanked by pointed-arch windows and superimposed square-headed lights to the end bays. Later porches, vestry and Sunday School wing, 1973–4, by *William Ramsay*, adhere unattractively. Interior rearranged N–S, 1881. U-plan gallery, on six timber columns, reached by internal stone stairs rising against gables. Most pine PEWS are original as is the PULPIT, though it has been resited. – STAINED GLASS by *Ballantine & Son*, 1910, commemorates the 8th Duke of Argyll and a visit by Queen Victoria; smaller window dedicated to the MacDonalds of Sanda, 1530–1935. Window in S gallery by *Gordon M. Webster*, 1949.

BLASTHILL, 1.5km. E of Mill Park. Three-bay gabled farmhouse symmetry widened by lower single-storeyed wings ending in façade gables. Early c19.

DUNAVERTY CASTLE, on rocky headland between debouch of Conieglen Water and Dunaverty Bay. Recorded in the c8, the castle was rebuilt 1539–42 but dismantled in 1685. Though strongly sited with the sea on three sides, only fragmentary masonry remains, and with it the associations of history: captured by Haakon of Norway in 1263, refuge to Robert the Bruce in 1306, visited by James IV in 1494 and scene of the massacre of 300 royalist troops by the Covenanters under General David Leslie in 1647. A rubble-built burial ENCLOSURE, 1847, is said to contain the bodies of these murdered MacDonalds. Close by are two late C19 BOATHOUSES.

KEIL HOTEL, at w end of village. 1938–9, by *J. Austen Laird*. Bold and once lighthouse-white against the hillside; close to, however, the walls are drab, the Moderne affectation gauche rather than smart. Abandoned.

KEIL HOUSE. By *Campbell Douglas & Sellars*, 1872–5. Erected by J.N. Fleming as 'a most palatial residence, unsurpassed in grandeur and extent by any in the county', it later became home to Keil School. Now, after a fire in 1924, all that survives of this muted version of Shaw's Cragside are a few picturesquely ruined stands of wall, some intact mullioned and transomed windows and a parapeted porte-cochère. By the road, a crowstep gabled LODGE.

MACHRIBEG. 1843. A very formal farm. Pavilion-roofed, two-storey, three-bay steading, with long low symmetrical wings.

MACHRIMORE MILL, Mill Park. Oatmeal mill built 1839. L-plan arrangement similar to Tangy Mill (*see* Kilchenzie); formed by a two-storey oblong skew-gabled block to which a gabled single-storey unit, square in plan, is attached. An overshot cast-iron mill wheel, set against the NE gable, survives with a few timber blades. Disused since 1960.

CHAMBERED CAIRN, 650m. NE of Blasthill Farm. Relatively well preserved and one of the best of its kind in Kintyre; it is 24.5m. long and up to 11m. at the E end where there is a concave forecourt. Portal stones at the centre of the forecourt mark the entrance to a roofless burial chamber. A second chamber, also roofless, at the centre of the cairn is open to the s.

FORT, Cnoc Araich, 1.2km. N of village. On a flat-topped hill immediately N of North Machrimore Farm slight triple rampart and ditch defences can barely be distinguished. Nevertheless, enclosure of 2.5ha. makes this the largest fort in Kintyre.

STANDING STONE, Brunerican, 800m. SE of village. 2.7m.-high red sandstone conglomerate rising out of the sand dunes.

STANDING STONE, Knockstapple, 4.2km. N of village. Large shouldered stone, 3.2m. high.

ST CATHERINES

A few houses spaced along the A815 on the E shore of Loch Fyne. Across the loch sits Inveraray to which a ferry crossed in former times.

ST CATHERINES CHAPEL. On a hillside site overlooking the jetty, low, turf-covered walling, measuring 14.2m. by 5.9m. overall, marks the oblong outline of a C15 chapel. Traces of a cross-wall exist but this bi-cameral plan may be a later development. The building was revealed by early C20 excavation.

ARDNO HOUSE. Built *c.* 1840. Harled three-bay, two-storey, gable-ended farmhouse. Lower hipped wings added late C20. U-plan steading partly rehabilitated.

COTTAGE, at the road-end to Ardchyline Farm. Late C19(?). Tiny three-bay dwelling with corrugated-iron walls and roof and a single chimneyed rubble gable.

PIER. Ruinous stone vestiges of 82m. ferry pier built to the design of *Thomas Telford*, 1818–20.

ST CATHERINES HALL. Erected *c.* 1910. Five-bay, corrugated-iron hall with half-timbering in the gables. Small piended porch. Pepper-pot vent on ridge.

ST CATHERINES HOTEL. A roughcast coaching inn of 1756, two storeys high and three bays wide. Three gableted dormers. Disfigured by a full-width glazed porch.

THISTLE HOUSE. Two-and-a-half-storey, three-bay house, late C19, built in random rubble with sandstone dressings. The central doorpiece is pedimented with a thistle motif carved in the tympanum.

STEWARTON

Road junction hamlet 2.3km. from Campbeltown where the A83 divides W for Machrihanish and S for Southend.

KILLELLAN CHAPEL, 5.5km. S. Nothing more than turf-covered hints of a small medieval chapel.

CAMPBELTOWN AIR TERMINAL, 3.2km. NNW. Crisp skew-gabled farmhouse form; S glazed wall to air strip. Built by *Ministry of Aviation* architects, 1963, after a major reconstruction of the airfield for NATO, 1960–2.

KILCHRIST CASTLE, 2.4km. S on E side of B842. Early C19. Harled free-standing tower with corbelled parapet and round angle-tower.

OATFIELD HOUSE, 2.5km. S on W side of B842. Two-storey harled house with projecting semi-octagonal bay. Late C18 or early C19. Arcuated Gothic fragments, reassembled in a garden grotto, probably came from the nave clearstorey of Dunblane Cathedral at the time of 1893 restorations.

STONEFIELD CASTLE

3km. N of Tarbert on Loch Fyne

Estate mansion in honey-coloured ashlar sandstone built as Barmore House, 1836–40, for John Campbell of Stonefield to replace an earlier house of that name destroyed by fire in 1790. The Campbells, who had purchased the estate in 1746 from the MacAlister family, came from Auchnacloich (or Stonefield) in Lorn and latterly applied the name of their former demesne to Barmore. It became a hotel in 1949.

Liberally gabled and much garnished with crowstepping and strapwork, the two tall storeys and attics have been conceived in that busy but serious Scots idiom which its architect, *William H. Playfair*, seems to have found necessary to adopt in order to win a slice of the lucrative country house market dominated by William Burn. The planning is pure Burn: on the ground floor, drawing room, library and dining room (now the bar) lie in line facing SE, separated by a spine wall from the entrance lobby, hall (or ante room, as Playfair designated it) and main staircase. At right angles, articulated on the pivot of the staircase, a service wing runs NW. This arrangement survives but, since its adaptation as a hotel, additional accommodation has elaborated the planning. Fortunately the complex three-dimensional geometry of Playfair's composition, revealed on the diagonal as the approach drive swings from the S out of the thickly wooded estate, remains unimpaired. Offset l. on the gabled SW front, the roll-moulded entrance doorway is crested by a strapwork pediment incorporating a monogram formed from the letters of Campbell. The door seems to shoulder two corbelled turrets which rise to conical caps taken up to the ridge height of the main roof. Framed near the base of each turret, two biblical inscriptions; above the door's pediment, a third panel dated 1837 and carved with a galley and the boar's head from the Campbell arms. From the longer SE façade two short gabled wings and one central polygonal bay, reroofed with a slated pyramid instead of its original leaded ogee, advance symmetrically on a raised paved terrace. Seen behind and above, the main staircase tower rises over dormer peaks, apex chimneystacks and intersecting ridges to a crenellated parapet with an angle turret on the E also lacking its ogival roof. Making an incongruous impact are two 1970s additions: a large new dining room which locks itself into the E corner formed by the two original wings and a five-bay bedroom extension built on to the converted service wing. There is a price to pay for this aggrandizement but, if the parapeted flat-roofed form and tawdry finish of the bedroom block are enfeebling, particularly on the NE, the simplicity of the fully glazed restaurant walls seems somehow to accentuate the C19 Scots Renaissance detail and Baronial vigour.

Woodwork and plasterwork preserved in the principal public rooms are C17 and C18 in character: bolection-moulded doors and dado panelling, patterned ribbed ceilings. The Library retains its original recessed bookcases, though the oak panelling in the Bar is later. There are several original fireplaces; Drawing Room chimneypiece of brown veined marble, Rococo in style, with a large mirror above. Playfair's drawings for the house are displayed in the staircase and corridors.

The GARDENS are a tribute to the exotic side of Victorian horticulture. Himalayan rhododendrons and azaleas, raised from seed brought to Argyll from Sikkim by Sir Joseph Hooker, grow to gigantic proportions creating attractive wooded walks along the W shore of Loch Fyne. SOUTH GATE LODGE, 3.1km. N of Tarbert, a crowstepped gabled house in stugged ashlar by *Playfair*, c. 1843; enlarged at rear. About 400m. NNE of the estate drive is the U-plan STABLES BLOCK, dated 1839. Crowstepped again with pedimented dormers and segmental arches to coachhouses. Nearby, a four-arched VIADUCT, 1838, also by *Playfair*, carries the drive dramatically across a ravine. Less evidently functional, a ruined rubble TOWER with crenellated parapet; perhaps intended simply as a picturesque folly, c. 1840. In the estate grounds, 700m. N of the Castle lies the CAMPBELL MAUSOLEUM, built 1855 by John Campbell of Stonefield †1857. Gabled Gothic Revival cell with well-buttressed stone slab roof. Above the pointed-arch gable opening are Campbell arms and motto and the date, 1855. On the shore of North Bay is a picturesquely contrived private harbour: rubble JETTY and arched BOATHOUSE.

BARMORE FARM, 200m. S of South Gate Lodge. Scots style, single-storey rubble steading around three sides of yard. Probably by *Playfair*, c. 1840. Converted to holiday homes.

ERINES HOUSE, on the A83, 4.3km. N of entrance to Stonefield Castle estate. Earlier mansion reworked, 1912–14, in knobbly overblown Baronial by *William Todd*, architect in Lochgilphead.

STRACHUR

A village, still known as Clachan, concentrated beside the road rising SE from Loch Fyne to the valley of the River Cur. A few older houses climb up the S side of the old road, but the village seems almost overwhelmed by workshop chaos. More recent growth N and S along the E shore of the loch.

STRACHUR PARISH CHURCH. Elevated slightly within an oval graveyard. Although the fabric, rubble with red sandstone quoins and dressings, is still substantially that of the building erected in 1789, the gabled form and interior layout derive from a major restoration carried out 1902–3 under the direction of the local architect-builder *Archibald Fergusson*. C18 provenance remains clear enough: centred against a rectangular kirk, a pedimented frontispiece carries a short ashlar tower from which rises a birdcage belfry with ogee top and ball finial. The church roof, however, is no longer piended but gable-ended, the two storeys of windows in the end walls have gone and the projecting frontispiece, originally the porch, now houses a vestry. To adjust to a plan recast around a longitudinal axis, the W door is blocked and the church is entered from the E gable through a porch added in 1956. Windows are also altered but remain symmetrically disposed with a circular light and two tall, round-arch openings in each end-wall. Gables have fleur-de-lis finials, a motif echoed in the trefoil tile cresting which runs along the ridge.

Stained timber dominates the interior. Behind a railed sanctuary, the W wall is panelled with a broken pediment on stumpy corbels marking the centre. – To the l., an octagonal oak PULPIT by *John A. Grieve*; cornice, paterae, and round-arch panels. – To the r., an ORGAN by *J. Marr, Wood & Co. Ltd*, rebuilt 1906; its timber casing, decorated with paterae and dentilled stringer, has oil lamps on brackets. – Roof with king-post trusses archbraced to rest on moulded corbelstones. – Only the bow-fronted E GALLERY, supported on two timber Roman Doric columns, survives from the late C18 furnishings. – Non-figurative STAINED GLASS relies on disc motifs of strong colour, boldly variegated in the ring and circle design above the sanctuary.

Eleven TAPERED SLABS, most Loch Awe school, C14–C15, were set into the outside face of the church walls during the 1902–3 restoration. These are variously carved with swords, shears, leaves, interlacing, etc. – In the CHURCHYARD are many later gravemarkers, several delightfully worked. Among these are HEADSTONES commemorating the farmers, John Fearguson †1774 and Dugald Thomson †1785, each bearing armorials on the reverse; also a taller stone of Easdale slate rich in symbols and craft motifs and, between two naïvely cut fluted columns, incised with an inscription recording the deaths of several members of the family of the mason, William Rhind †1829. – The low-walled CAMPBELL ENCLOSURE contains an obelisk inset with a white marble tablet to Janet Campbell of Strachur, †1816, and opposite this, in memory of her grandson, Major Colin Campbell †1824, a broad, three-part sandstone panel cut with wreath and ribbon scrolling, by *A. Clubb* of Glasgow.

STRACHUR HALL (The Old Inn). Two-storey, gable-ended rough-cast inn, built in the late 1790s. Bow-fronted NW projection surmounted by gabled second-floor addition carried on corbel brackets; an uneasy but sculpturally powerful conjunction. Circular window with radial astragals in gable; round-arch window in bow. NE gable cut back, 1804, when the village street was widened. Divided into two flats, late C19. Rubble COACH-HOUSE, across road NW of churchyard, formerly serving the inn; round-arch entry, vertical ventilation slits.

STRACHUR HOUSE. A fine, provincially classical house, hipped-roofed and pedimented, set in wooded grounds W of the village, 250m. E of the Loch Fyne shore. When General John Campbell began to improve his estate of Strachur Park in the early 1770s he first 'formed his garden' (*OSA*, 1792), stocking it plentifully with trees and shrubs. Within a decade work had started on a new house. The mansion, built in rubble, is three storeys high and five bays wide with short lower wings added to the gables, possibly before 1790.

The principal SW FRONT, originally approached from the NW up a drive from the lochside, is painted, with sandstone quoins and dressings. It has a pedimented frontispiece advancing slightly from an otherwise plain elevation. The main architectural elaboration of the façade is focused here. At second-floor level, below an empty tympanum, is a tripartite window, with pilaster mullions supporting an entablature. Below this comes a taller, elegantly proportioned Venetian window. At ground level, the pilastered tripartite theme is maintained by a doorway and side-lights which again carry a full entablature. This vertical continuity is, however, partially masked by a full-width, round-ended porch, early C20, which itself replaced a somewhat more harmonious square-plan version, pilastered and balustraded, that had been added a century earlier. On each side of the central five-bay block, mansarded two-storey wings tuck themselves against the piended gables of the main house. These lower wings, which were at first lit by single windows on the SW front, became two-bay in the early C20, though care was taken to ensure that the alignment and proportions of the new windows co-ordinated with those of the main block. At the same time, new dormered roof accommodation in the wings replaced the original crenellated flat-roofed skyline. A single-storey service wing, also early C20, extends SE.

The dominant element of the NE GARDEN FRONT is a three-storey central bow crested with a crenellated parapet carried on arched corbelling. There is a hint of Robert Adam's Castle Style but the harled walls and the generous fenestration of the drum greatly diminish the allusion. At each level there are three windows lighting the large rooms behind. Those to the *piano nobile* are especially tall while those to the floor below carry their margins to the ground, though only the central opening is in fact a doorway. Flanking the bowed projection, the walls of the main block are plain with a single tier of windows l. and r., apart from a small opening which appears impertinently at second-floor level. This, and the adjacent service-lift tower in the E re-entrant, are both again early C20 intrusions. The lower wings extending NW and SE have, of course, received the mansard addition already mentioned. But here the corbelled crenellated parapets survive. Moreover, the NE windows are all late C18 tripartites; two to each wing, the lower openings later given central arches transforming them into Venetian windows. Though scarcely to be detected visually, the sill and lintel heights in these wings do not correlate across the façade, an anomaly corroborated by internal level changes.

INTERIOR. From the SW porch the original entrance opens into the stair-hall. Immediately l., a scale-and-platt stair of moulded sandstone treads begins its rise to the attic, its iron baluster-rods bulging along returning flights and landings. The ceiling cornice, enlivened with modillions, recurs at the levels above. To the r. is an inner hall opened up to the stair-well during early C20 alterations and screened from it by a pair of coupled timber columns

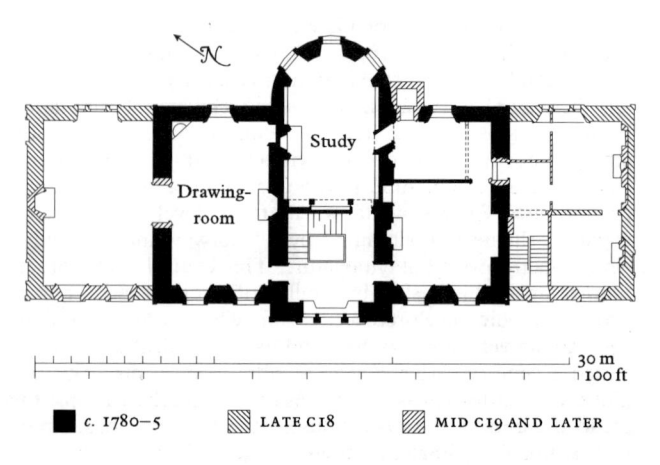

Strachur House

with plaster capitals which appear to support the wide lintel carrying the transverse masonry wall above. In the porch and throughout the entire SW half of the main block the floors are stone-flagged. At the centre of the plan is the DINING ROOM, bow-fronted to the NE and defined by a three-bay screen of timber columns with pilaster responds on the wall opposite. At each side of this screen the shorter bays match those of doors close behind, one opening from the hall, the other false. There is a plaster frieze decorated with swags, paterae and ovals, but the ceiling is plain. A cupboard, doors gridded with Chinese-style glazing bars, recesses in the SE wall. Opposite is a timber-and-gesso chimneypiece with fluted columns. To the SE of the dining room lie the kitchens; to NW, a laundry which has a barrel-vault ceiling.

At the stairhead, a door opens l. from the landing into the STUDY, formerly the drawing room. Like the dining room below, it is bow-ended to the NE and is entered through a three-bay screen placed close to the SW wall. Again, there are two doors, one opening from the hall, its twin merely concealing a cupboard. The mahogany doors, panelled like all the others in the house, are here enriched by moulded architraves and fluted friezes interrupted by three oval medallions. The columns and their respond-pilasters have acanthus capitals. Acanthus ornament appears again, alternating with urns, in the cornice frieze which, as in the dining room, surrounds a plain ceiling. At the centre of the NW wall, a marble chimneypiece, veined in yellow with a white and grey cornice. On the other side of this wall, where there is another fireplace in white and grey marble, is the room now known as the DRAWING ROOM. Entered from the broad SW landing through a door reflected in the access to the bedroom opposite, it leads in turn through double doors at the centre of the NW gable wall to a sitting room in the wing, furnished in the early C20 with wide glazed and pedimented bookcases. At second-floor level, the reflected doors which originally opened on each side of the SW landing have been blocked. Instead, communication to the bedrooms is contrived from corridors running NW and SE through the house to reach the wings. The bedroom occupying the NE bow is centrally entered behind the staircase. Its interior has been concavely shaped around the SW wall to produce a flattened oval plan on the SE wall of which is a sandstone fireplace with a Carron grate.

On the NE side of the house is a FORMAL GARDEN laid out in the early C20. A SUNDIAL in the form of a swollen fluted baluster, with a copper plate bearing the name *Bryson*, Edinburgh, sits on the lawn. Beyond lies the WALLED GARDEN, late C18 or early C19. But it is the architectural enhancements of the estate which are particularly fine. Opening off the A815 is the original WEST GATEWAY, a tall round-arched portal in a flat-topped rubble wall flanked by two lower walls which advance slightly and have similar arches, each blind save for a single square-headed window. Behind the N window is a small lodge, C19; behind the S, no trace of its partner. From here the old drive runs SE to pass in front of the house before crossing an ornamental BRIDGE of the most elegant and sophisticated classical design. Between abutments ennobled by pedimented aedicules that open into riverbank passages with arched recesses for privies, a single arch of rusticated voussoirs spans 4.6m. This has a continuous square-section hood-moulding repeated in half-arches which spring from the aedicules in reverse direction over the banks. Within the resultant spandrels, and in the aedicules and parapet, a pink sandstone ashlar; below the reverse arch mouldings the rubble masonry may have been harled. On the apex of all four pediments and at the centre of each parapet wall, urns sit on pedestals. Stylistic affinities with Robert Mylne's bridge over the Aray (q.v.) and John Adam's Garden Bridge at Inveraray (q.v.) can be found but the author of this delightful design remains unknown. To the SE the drive leads to an impressive COURT OF OFFICES, late C18; four two-storeyed ranges which, as the writer of the *Old Statistical Account* unkindly observed, 'perhaps, exceed the proportion they should bear to the house'. The piended NW range, which is directly approached from the bridge, has an elliptical arch entry set below a pediment on which a tall octagonal timber doocot rises to a leaded ogee dome. The NE stables range has a similar centrepiece without the doocot; forestairs climb against its skew-gables to round-arch loft doors. Nearby, to the W, is a hipped-roofed square out of which rises a pyramid-roofed roughcast core; abandoned but still geometrically intriguing and forceful. A second BRIDGE, 'Betty Jenkins's Bridge', crosses the Eas Dubh 300m. NE of the house. Decidedly rural in character, it has a segmental arch of rubble voussoirs spanning 7.8m. between thickened abutments beyond which rubble parapet walls curve out convexly to reach an overall length of 24m. An uninscribed tablet on each face of the arch and red sandstone rings in the abutments are the only occasions for dressed masonry.

STRACHUR PRIMARY SCHOOL. Schoolmaster's house and gabled classroom block with quasi-Gothic, splay-arch-headed windows, 1912; by *Archibald Fergusson*. Plain, two-storey S addition by *Argyll County Council*, 1956.

MOTTE, 700m. SSW of Balliemeanoch. Rectangular flat-topped mound, 24m. by 20m. and 7m. high. Rectangular building on the summit.

STANDING STONE, 90m. WNW of Strachur House. Fallen stone, originally 3.1m. high, recorded as one of 'two stones of the same appearance' (*OSA*, 1792) said to have been survivors of a 'Druidical Circle' which was largely destroyed for building stone in the late C18.

STRONE

A coastal road and a high road rounding Strone Point into Holy Loch. Like Blairmore (q.v.), the village is a C19 creation, its growth stimulated by the steamer connections across the Firth.

Former ALLIANCE CHURCH (now Highgate Hall). Built c. 1875(?). Five-bay buttressed nave. Gable front to road has had its rose window filled in but retains a vesica in the apex.

STRONE (ST COLUMBA'S) CHURCH. The square battlemented tower with its ashlar spire survives from the first church of 1858–9 but the gabled nave and chancel, the SE transept with its aisle link to the tower, and the Norman entrance at the base of the tower are the work of *Peter MacGregor Chalmers*, 1907–8. In effect, an entirely new church was created using 'old material' from the earlier building to unify the exterior: Corrie sandstone was preferred within. Inevitably this is not Chalmers at his most Romanesque but the rough-faced, snecked rubble masonry and carving of the interior are predictably of good quality. Semicircular arch to chancel. Three-bay arcade to transept and aisle has one circular and one octagonal pier. Lean-to aisle and gabled transept communicate under a leaning arch which carries the separating wall above. Stained arch-braced trusses, with purlins and intermediate framers, spring from corbelstones carved with heads or floral ornament. Shallow timber-lined, barrel-vault over chancel. – Oak, half-octagon PULPIT and chancel FURNISHINGS carved in a slender Decorated idiom with delicate cusping. – Sandstone FONT in transept; a dished drum with octagonal moulded base. – To the l. of the chancel, a hooded marble WAR MEMORIAL, 1921, removed from St Andrew's, Kilmun, at union, 1937. – STAINED GLASS in the chancel window commemorates Hugh Highgate of Blairmore: Christ bearing the Cross, 1909. In the lancet above the font, a blue-cloaked Virgin with a host of rose-pink scrapbook angels around her halo, 1908. Both by *Stephen Adam Jr*. – Moses, Isaiah and Daniel colourfully depicted in superimposed vesica frames in cusped lancet SW of porch, 1924. – Opposite this, in memory of the Revd Alexander MacArthur †1925, a young shepherd carrying a lamb in a pastoral scene set below a 'purple-headed mountain'; *George MacWhirter Webster*, 1933. – Purple dominant again in the triple lancet at the rear of the nave: Christ entering Jerusalem on a donkey, dedicated 1925. HALL behind the church and finialled Gothic GATEPIERS in front survive from 1858–9.

OLD SCHOOL, uphill off the high road. By *R.A. Bryden*, 1875. A wide single-storey rubble building with gable-fronted classrooms at each end, now converted to residential use.

STRONE PIER. 1847 jetty of vertically laid boulders, repaired 1856; now concreted over, the quay leads out to a concrete pier, 1930. Closed 1956.

STRONE PRIMARY SCHOOL, on the high road. By *Argyll County Council*, 1965. Wide, flat-roofed front with shallow butterfly slopes behind.

DUNSELMA, on the hill above Strone Point, a prominent landmark seen from the firth. And deliberately so; for from here the immensely rich Coats family, thread barons in Paisley, enjoyed summer-time sailing on the Clyde. Designed by Paisley architects *Rennison & Scott* in Scots Baronial style, 1885–7, it is a centripetal confusion of jumping stringcourses, rusticated quoins, corbels, and crowstep gables finally resolved in a combination of high square tower, machicolated and battlemented, and a smaller but taller round tower telescoped in diminishing corbel stages at its side. Harled with sandstone dressings. Lodge and boathouse (*see* Description) lie downhill by the shore while 150m. N along the high road are the former stables and servants' quarters; all are in similar Baronial vein.

DESCRIPTION

Little more than a linear parade of varied villas; there is some slight sense of focus at the pier. Expectantly sited, the ARGYLE HOTEL, mid C19, is a symmetrical house with ground-floor bays l. and r. and, at the centre, under a steep gable, a first-floor window with a parenthesis-profile lintel and a cast-iron balcony. BELLEVUE, mid C19, though semi-detached and flatted, is more architecturally ambitious: Gothic symmetry with finialled diagonal buttresses, hood-moulded windows and a pointed-arch double porch. Beside the church (*see* above), is THE BOATHOUSE, *c.* 1886–7, a crowstep-gabled oblong built by *Rennison & Scott* for Dunselma (*see* above). Ashlar parapets along the side walls have ball finials above and a stringcourse below, continuous with the segmentally arched opening in the gabled front, but the design has been sullied by 'domestication'. DUNSELMA LODGE, however, is untarnished by interference; again the work of *Rennison & Scott*, *c.* 1886–7, it retains its Baronial affinities with the house on the hill. A short distance N is STRONE HOUSE, grandly named and appropriately masterful behind a balustraded banking; a tall, rectilineally classical mansion with square bays l. and r., pilastered tripartite windows above, and a central square first-floor bay over a pillared porch. Then CRAIGIELEE, gable-fronted with wide eaves, a pyramid-roofed room on the ridge hinting at the towers to come along the Blairmore shore. NW of the pier, the chain of villas is maintained along the landward side of the road. A few early C19 houses (best is RHUBEG, *c.* 1840(?)), hidden behind high walls, front the shore, separated from the pier by a long, pleasantly curving promenade wall.

STRONTOILLER

A few farms NE of Loch Nell on the hill-and-valley, single-track road through Glen Lonan from Taynuilt to Oban.

CRUCK-FRAMED BYRE, Torr-an-tuirc, 1.7km. SSW. Rubble oblong, late C18 or early C19, five cruck bays long with half crucks forming a piend roof over the end bays. Ruins of township.

CAIRN AND STANDING STONE, 450m. S of Strontoiller farmhouse. A small cairn with twelve surviving kerb-stones, traditionally the grave of the Irish hero Diarmid. 4m.-high granite stone 12m. NW.

STONE CIRCLE, 280m. SSW. 20m.-dia. circle formed by rounded boulders, none more than 1m. high. The only known example in Lorn.

TARBERT

An ancient castle and castle-town strategically sited at the head of East Loch Tarbert to command the routes E–W and N–S across the narrow isthmus of land connecting Knapdale and Kintyre. Although established as a royal burgh by Robert I as early as 1329, it was not until the C18 that the village grew, its 'curious and singularly safe and land-locked natural harbour' (Groome, 1885) proving a crucial asset to the developing herring industry. By the mid C19 Tarbert's topographical advantage had been reinforced by the Parliamentary Commissioners' improvements to its rubble-built quays, while the original settlement had spread downhill to the lochside. Fishing in Loch Fyne and beyond brought local prosperity, and although proposals for the cutting of a canal through to West Loch Tarbert (urged on economic grounds in 1845 and again in 1882) were never realized, the village continued to grow around the harbour, reaching its present-day form before the turn of the century. Fishing still figures in the local economy, though tightly trimmed ranks of halyard-chattering yachts are now a more familiar feature of Tarbert's sheltered anchorage than coastal smack or puffer.

TARBERT CASTLE

Situated on a readily defensible natural plateau some 30m. above the S shore of East Loch Tarbert and reached by lane from Harbour Street. The castle's strategic location, both regional and local, is easily grasped. Much less clear is its built configuration. Two ruinous ivy-covered walls stand, but otherwise the signs of construction, though evident over a considerable area, appear only in undulating turf-covered terrain and occasional rubble outcrops. In fact there are three castles, or at any rate three phases of building.

The building of the first castle at Tarbert may have been the work of the MacDonalds of Islay but it could equally well have been a royal project. Certainly it was King Robert the Bruce who, strengthening his hold on Argyll, ordered the second phase of construction: accounts of 1325–6 confirm masonry work as well as the erection of clay and timber structures. Royal interest continued in the new works carried out for James IV. From the beginning of the C16, guardianship of the castle was vested in the Campbell Earls of Argyll, from whom it passed, *c.* 1750, to the Campbells of Stonefield.

To the SW of the plateau, four sets of low, barely discernible parallel ridges can be seen. These define the four sides of a roughly square plan, 41.5m. by 37.2m. overall, which can reasonably be construed as a courtyard castle of the C13. Gaps in the raised coursing indicate door openings and it seems likely that the fortress was entered from the flatter ground to the NE. In the early C14, this extensive 'outer bailey' area was incorporated into the fortified fabric by the building of a 2m. wall following the rocky lip of the summit. This second development is no more immediately clear than the first, though the defence of the NE perimeter can still be read in two circular towers, each 8.7m. in dia., where

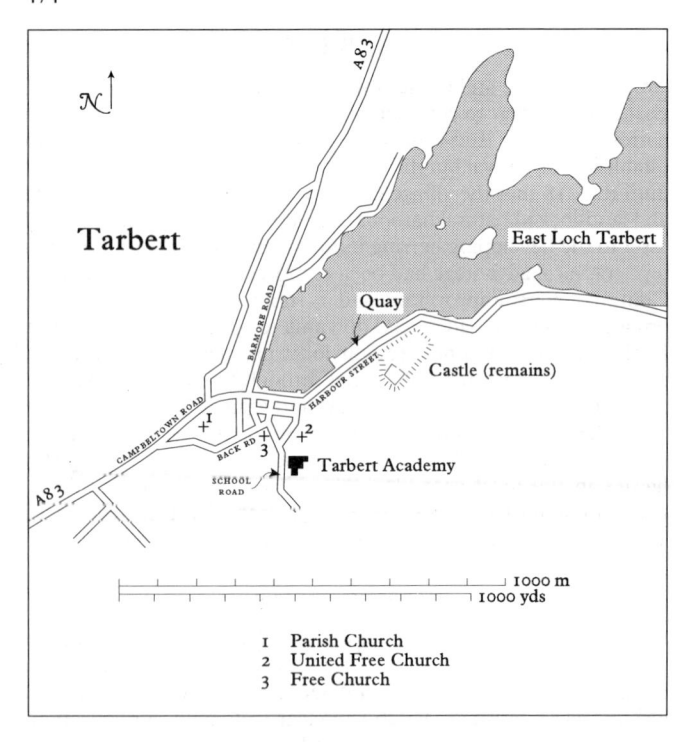

[Map of Tarbert showing:
1 Parish Church
2 United Free Church
3 Free Church]

the original walling survives to a height of over 4m. Finally, in 1494, as part of James IV's campaign in Kintyre, work began on the oblong tower-house which still maintains a precarious elevation from line of the SE curtain. Once again entrance was from the NE, a half-landing lobby leading to mural stairs up to first-floor level and down to a barrel-vaulted basement, now inaccessibly packed with debris. No upper floors exist and the remains of the four-storeyed rubble structure, though stable, cannot be closely approached. The corbelled wallhead is all but invisible beneath its shroud of vegetation. A segmentally arched window embrasure, once with bench seating, can be seen in the NE wall; above that, at the centre of the NW wall, a roll-moulded fireplace; various window openings and gun-loops. Two horizontally mouthed gun-ports flank the shattered entrance to the forework which was added at the base of the tower towards the end of the C16.

CHURCHES

FREE CHURCH, School Road. By Mr *Petrie*, architect in Glasgow, 1894–5. Red sandstone Gothic six-bay nave with lean-to aisles. The N front has a Decorated traceried window rising above the gabled entrance arch. Tall spire demolished in 1946. Triple lancets in the s gable.

PARISH CHURCH, Campbeltown Road. More than a match for the ruinous Castle to the E, Tarbert's church has dominated the village from its hilltop for over two centuries. First in 1775 came a mission chapel, a symmetrical piended hall, later expanded into a T-plan kirk with the addition of a bellcoted gabled wing in 1841–2. Still inadequate to house a growing congregation, this building was demolished and the present church completed, 1885–6, to the design of Glasgow architects *McKissack & Rowan*. As at their almost contemporary commission at Strathbungo, Glasgow, the glory here is a tall tower, stoutly framed by prominent angle buttresses which recede, step by small step, to reach the four finialled corners of a bold crown-and-lantern Scots Gothic spire. At the base is the round-arched 33 entrance, dramatized by a stepped approach and the splayed flanks of the corner buttresses. The nave, which runs SW from the tower, presents a NW twin-gabled façade to the road below. Recessed alongside, a gabled wing containing hall and offices and incorporating, above the lintel of the basement boiler-house door, a stone from the old church elegantly carved with the inscription 'Built 1775. Enlarged 1841'. Windows throughout maintain a round-arched simplicity.

Despite its rear gallery, reached by a stair within the tower, the interior seems surprisingly small. It disappoints, too, in layout and furnishings. A single NW aisle, defined by cast-iron columns with scalloped capitals supporting an arcade of four round arches (two small, two large), appears disturbingly ill proportioned. The arrangement of the reworked sanctuary, three steps up, lacks cohesion. But the roof redeems these weaknesses: arch-braced natural timber trusses with Romanesque motifs painted in colour on the ceiling boarding. – STAINED GLASS. In an arched ashlar panel in the sanctuary gable, two small round-arched lights depict figures representing Prayer, blue-clad and head bowed, and Praise, cloaked in red and carrying a lyre; centred above, in a circular window, Christ stands within a vesica frame flanked by biblical texts. On the NW nave wall, a similar arangement, *c.* 1920, this time with the three openings in line: Faith, holding a staff; Hope, beside an anchor; and, in the central circle, the trinity of Christian virtues completed by, presumably, Charity, a red-winged angel from whom two female figures receive a blessing. – BELL, cast by *Munro Thomson & Co.* of Glasgow, installed in 1886.

TEMPLARS' HALL, Harbour Street. Plain single-storey gabled hall, eaves-on to street, dated 1872. Two doorways, each set between two elongated double-hung windows with segmentally arched astragals in the upper sashes.

UNITED FREE CHURCH, Castle Street. Modest Arts and Crafts gabled nave by *Alexander Cullen* of Hamilton, 1908. Roughcast with open timbered gabled W porch. Belfry shaft attached to E of N gable. Derelict.

BURIAL GROUND, off School Road. Oddly marooned with no obvious ecclesiastical provenance. Some C18 TABLE-TOMBS and SLABS with heraldic and other devices. A 2m.-high-walled

BURIAL ENCLOSURE contains MacAlister graves and a SLAB, probably early C16, carved with claymore and plait.

PUBLIC BUILDINGS

FISH MARKET, Harbour Street. Smart quayside focus for Loch Fyne fishing. 1994. Metal-decked pavilion roof on rendered walls; broadly belted below wide eaves by a recessed blue frieze.

HERITAGE CENTRE, Campbeltown Road. 1995. Low timber-boarded building with glazed gable projecting to s. Architecturally little more than a shed but pleasantly landscaped.

PIER. Steamboats entered the old inner harbour as early as 1815. By 1825 they could tie up at an improved and extended quay but by 1866 a new outer pier had been built. This was rebuilt in 1879 and again in 1958, and serves still when the *Waverley* cruises up Loch Fyne

TARBERT ACADEMY, School Road. Topless three-storey tower and tall classroom block, its four attenuated upper-floor windows pushing through the eaves as gabled dormers. Rubble with proud sandstone dressings. 1893. The clutter of dull classroom extensions, principally by *Argyll County Council*, 1956–9, does nothing to relieve the intimidating severity.

DESCRIPTION

A continuous wall of gable-to-gable shops and housing clasps the water-borne activity at the harbour head of the loch. Scale and quality vary, a few brightly painted walls (blue, salmon pink, turquoise and egg-yolk yellow) make an aggressive impact in an otherwise black-and-white world, but the sense of townscape enclosure is tight. BARMORE ROAD runs down above the W side of the loch into the village: plain, C19, two-storey-and-attic scale, intermittent then continuous; a stretch of five lower and earlier houses sharing the same ridge; and then come three tenements. The first of these, *c.* 1900, asymmetrical with square and canted bays, still has its cast-iron shopfront but was deteriorating rapidly in 1995. LOCHVIEW, 1893, and BANNOCKBURN BUILDINGS, 'Built by Donald Douglass', 1884, are flatter but better, the latter sporting an unusually peaked central gablet.

HARBOUR STREET turns E along the quayside and then NE past yachts and fishing boats, its generally indifferent architecture brightened by a determined, sometimes desperate, jauntiness. Some buildings resist or survive the enthusiasm for optimistic awnings, shutters, balconies and bays. KNAP, *c.* 1890, three shops with flats above in red sandstone, risks a witch-hatted corbelled corner bay at Brunswick Street, but the BANK OF SCOTLAND, *c.* 1860, is stiff and strait-laced. The brashly black-and-white TARBERT HOTEL, early C19 and later, joins wholeheartedly in the waterfront spirit: decorative two-storeyed oriels linked by balustraded balconies over a glazed ironwork porch. CALADH, *c.* 1880, surprises with some ebullient joinery, *c.* 1905, – a consoled fascia with pilastered and pedimented bays above.

Severe and symmetrical, where the street cranks l., TARBERT INFORMATION CENTRE, a symmetrical three-storey tenement of, *c.* 1880, stays sufficiently aloof to preserve its original shopfronts. Thereafter, only the Templars' Hall (*see* Churches above) merits a glance until, opposite the quayside activity around the Fish Market (*see* Public Buildings above), ARDENCORRACH, another late C19 tenement, has a smooth ashlar wall poised above an original chaste and elegant glazed shopfront. Set above the roadway is the wide but naïve three-bay front of the former POLICE STATION, 1872, and, beyond, a run of rubble-built fishermen's stores and flats, mid C19, several with arched harbourside pends, tucking themselves into the hillside below the Castle. There are only a few back-stage discoveries to be made behind this quayside display. BRAESIDE, *c.* 1890, a respectable ashlar-fronted tenement standing tall in Castle Street; some venerable rubble walling in Church Street which may be the vestigial trace of the OLD FREE CHURCH, *c.* 1843–4; two surviving church buildings and a grim school (*see* Churches and Public Buildings above); a bold cyma recta corbel at the splayed corner of School Road and Church Street. In all this there is little to remark; still less in the dreary harled terraces of local authority housing straggling uphill to the S. The leafier W side of the village is more rewarding where the crown spire of the Parish Church (*see* Churches above) marks the road to Campbeltown. And lochside, N along Garvel Road, are BALLOCHMYLE and LOCHFYNE, both mid-C19 rubble cottages with a rough rustic attraction, but much the worse for losing their original mullions. LORNE VILLA, *c.* 1870, is child's drawing Victorian, rubble-plain and piended, with a rudimentary classical doorway, like its single-storey offspring, LORNE COTTAGE.

Tarbert's best houses lie across the Loch, where PIER ROAD curves around the S shore past the ferry slip and out towards Loch Fyne. ROCKFIELD, ROSEMOUNT and QUEENSGATE are all Victorian twin-gabled villas, *c.* 1885, with saw-tooth eaves and bargeboarding, the last two enhanced by lacy fretwork in each gable apex. Rather grander is the ashlar front of the COLUMBA HOTEL, *c.* 1880; three storeys with tripartite windows at the first two l. and r. of a narrow central bay projection which rises from square-piered porch to tall lampshade pyramid. PIER HOUSE, a whitewashed rubble cottage with gabled attic dormers, is earlier, no doubt contemporary with the building of the first outer pier opposite (*see* Public Buildings above). Further on, treasure trove. A single-track road climbing up the Allt a' Bhacain valley reaches SEALLADH MOR and its neighbour, two similar but separately sited dwellings; modern black-houses by *Peter Speakman,* 1974. Roofs, like slated triangular prisms, seem to float over massively thick rubble walls, for the eaves are deliberately recessed. The external effect is both ruggedly contextual and unmistakably C20. The interior is spacious and airy: bedrooms, cosily tented within the dormerless roof, held back in plan to overlook the full-height living area, itself given a panoramic prospect of Loch Fyne through glazing in the gable.

TARBET

Road junction village on the w shore of Loch Lomond. Loch Long and Arrochar (q.v.) lie only 2km. w over a low saddle isthmus.

Former ARROCHAR FREE CHURCH. 1844. Cruciform plan with a broached belfry steeple, low but sharp, in the SE re-entrant. Worship ceased in 1966. Lancets and N rose window survive in conversion to craft shop and restaurant.

BURIAL ENCLOSURE, Ballyhennan, adjacent to the church. A variety of C18 and C19 TABLE-TOMBS carved with the symbols of mortality, trade tools and heraldic insignia. Some TAPERED SLAB fragments. Several mantled HEADSTONES, early C19, with attractively incised inscriptions. Rubble WALL MONUMENT with framed sandstone panel recording the deaths of John Sime of Stuckgowan and his brother George †1790. In a railed enclosure, the Macmurrich of Stuckgowan MURAL MONUMENT, c. 1801: pedimented white marble panel set between two tapered stones. An austerely plain STONE, erected 1994, remembers the men who died working on the West Highland Line, 1890–4.

ARROCHAR & TARBET STATION. 1894. Ascribed to *James Miller* but the design may be by *Robert Wemyss*, then in the employ of *J.J. Burnet*. Island station approached from below, its design conceived 'after the style of Swiss chalets'. Long, gently bellcast, piended roof overhanging both platforms. Waiting room and office spine framed in timber on brick base with scalloped shingle cladding 'brought from Switzerland' (Thomas, 1965). The nearby STATION HOUSE is by *Wemyss*: a slated pyramid on rubble walls with rough red sandstone margins.

STUCKGOWAN HOUSE, 1.7km. SSE. Built c. 1820. 'The most beautiful house on the loch' (Walker & Sinclair, 1992). A bow-fronted, hipped-roofed cottage-villa best described as Regency Gothic. Under overhanging eaves, square label-moulds frame lancet windows grouped in twos and threes. Attic dormers too are lancet lit. S entrance leads to a top-lit inner hall with a charming elliptical gallery. Lower N wing. By the roadside W, the two-storey NORTH LODGE(?), a three-bay, piended house with four-centre arched windows and central door; L-plan offices (former kennels/stables) behind. Across the A82, a second lodge, STUCKGOWAN COTTAGE, c. 1820; single-storey, with a piended roof overhanging hooded four-centre arch openings.

TARBET HOTEL. Centuries-old coaching inn site. The present buildings date from c. 1850, though their sheer bulk, busy with crowstepping, canted bays and towers, is the result of a rambling Baronial transformation in 1878–80. Four-storey E drum tower with a wrap-round ironwork balcony at first floor and a corbelled castellated parapet.

DESCRIPTION

A few older cottages lie N of the hotel. At the head of STILL BRAE is LOCHVIEW, early C19, a plain piend-roofed house, its symmetrical black-and-white front commanding the bend in the A83. An L-plan wing of POST OFFICE and gable-fronted TEA-ROOM creates a small forecourt. W of this is BALLYHENNAN CRESCENT along which are ranged some stone-built dormered cottages constructed, *c.* 1950, for the hydro-electric workers of Loch Sloy (q.v.). S of the village on the A82, EDENDARROCH HOUSE, *c.* 1860, a gabled villa in whinstone rubble with a piend-roofed Italianate tower, and, at ROSSDARROCH, greatly daring, a spirited house of sweeping roofs and panoramic views across the loch, by *Coleman & Ballantine*, 1997–8. Raking eaves and much glass; an excess of zest extended to a detached granny flat gauchely set on an old boathouse.

TAYINLOAN

6945

A small village on the W coast of Kintyre with ferry connection to Gigha.

KILLEAN OLD PARISH CHURCH, on W side of Tarbert–Campbeltown road, 1.5km. S of Tayinloan. Ivy-drenched rubble ruin, roofless except for N aisle. The church nave, aligned W–E, dates from the C12 and retains its lateral walls only. Both gables have gone, the W destroyed by early C19 quarrying, the E when a chancel was added at the beginning of the C13. This chancel has some fine moulding detail to its quoin stones and round-arched windows: the double-light opening in the E gable, 'an unusually handsome composition', having, on the outside, dog-tooth ornament and a stringcourse which steps up to hood both arches and, on the inside, wide-splayed ingoes and foliated capitals. Chancel windows were blocked in mid C19, probably by the MacDonalds of Largie, who at that time carried out restoration work associated with their use of the C15 N aisle for family burials. This aisle, which has a pointed barrel-vault, is accessed from the chancel through a narrowed opening above which is inscribed 'Here Lie The Bones of the House of Largie'. Both the MacDonalds' vault and the church's walled GRAVEYARD contain many interesting stones. – Several tapered SLABS, C14–C16, are carved with swords, foliage, animals, etc. One bears the full-length figure of a mailed knight in high relief, Iona school, C14–C15. – Three later HEADSTONES carry vocational imagery: a carved ship, sextant and compasses in memory of sailor Niell McGill †1712 and his son Rodger †1738; similar subjects commemorating Alexander McKinnon †1788; and a two-horse plough team recalling Donald McKinnon, farmer, †1810.

KILLEAN PARISH CHURCH, A'Chleit, 3.1km. S of Killean Old Parish Church. Harled shoreside kirk, built 1787–91, by contractor *Thomas Cairns*. High piended roof on oblong plan. SE central projection incorporates pilastered and pedimented door-piece, blind arched alcoves and portholes, and is itself pedimented from church eaves height. At the apex, a tall birdcage belfry topped by concave pyramid and ball finial, erected 1879 by *Robert Weir*. Interior has a renewed pulpit at centre NW wall, laird's loft opposite and galleries on SW and NE, carried on timber columns.

Wide goalpost frame introduced to carry later projection of laird's loft. Symmetry now destroyed by the closing off of the NW gallery. Pilastered back-board to pulpit, panelled gallery fronts, and perhaps pews, all original, though reseating and repair work were carried out in 1887 and again in 1945. – Mural FUNERARY MONUMENT in white marble, erected 1818 in memory of Col. Norman MacAlister of Clachaig †1810, governor of Prince Edward Island.

To the NE, completing an L-plan, is KILLEAN SCHOOL, a plain skew-gabled building by *Robert Weir*, dated 1861, with round-arched windows matching those of the church façade.

BALLURE HOUSE, 4km. NNE of Tayinloan. Plain two-storey harled house with piended roof, *c*. 1805. The projecting central bay of the W front is dignified by a chimney-topped ashlar pediment and an arched entrance set within pilasters carrying full entablature. The interior preserves panelled doors, moulded architraves and fireplace surrounds, and decorative plaster cornices and friezes.

GORTINANANE HOUSE, 1.9km. NNE of Tayinloan. Three-bay two-storey harled house. Piended roof. Early C19.

KILLEAN COTTAGES, across road from Killean Old Parish Church. Arts and Crafts whimsy in chunky rubble. Two semi-detached 'Dolls' Houses', probably by *J.J. Burnet c.* 1895 (though *Henry Edward Clifford*, who had links with the Burnets and was active in Kintyre and Glasgow, may have been involved). Asymmetrical façade gables reflected l. and r. of covered veranda, steep tiled roofs, open eaves, corner casements. A third detached building, the Mission Hall, is equally anglicized in detail. Garden Suburb idiom on the Atlantic edge; incongruous but enchanting.

KILLEAN HOME FARM. Wide-fronted rubble steading, late C19, lying parallel to A83. Raised pavilion with pyramid roof over central segmentally arched pend. Piended wings flank the yard behind.

KILLEAN HOUSE. Baronial mansion in warm fawn sandstone built for James Macalister Hall of the British India Steamship Navigation Company. In 1873, shortly after Hall had purchased the estate, work began on the modernization and extension of the original Killean House of *c*. 1840, which stood some 250m. NE of the present house. Plans for this enlargement had been obtained from *John Burnet*. Two years later, however, fire destroyed everything save a billiard room addition, which survives, converted to residential use, and a splendid new timber porch manufactured by shipbuilders *Denny* of Dumbarton. In July 1875, the decision was made to build a second Killean, the architect again *John Burnet*. Work continued into the 1880s and it seems likely that the proposals of Burnet *père* were much revised by his son *John James Burnet*. As late as 1891 *Burnet Son & Campbell* were still involved at Killean, although a drainage drawing of that year does show the perimeter of the house complete except for an extension of the S service wing carried out in 1907.

Baronial, but not exuberantly so. At the NE, a bulbous corner of tall arched windows corbels into a first-floor ring of gabled eaves dormers circling a conical roof. On the w, the familiar transition from canted bay to crowstepped gable, but also a more inventive three-storey parapeted tower with an open balcony on massive console corbels. In the sw re-entrant, at the linkage to the s service wings, a five-storey stair-tower capped by a tall pyramid roof. The interior has a more classical restraint. Apartments are arranged around a central hall over which a square scallop-cornered well opens to the top-lit first floor. Entering from the E, an elliptical Library lies r. Ahead is the Sitting Room; Jacobean chimneypiece over four-centred arch fireplace. To the l., the Dining Room; cornice of wheatsheaf sprays between triglyphs; consoled fireplace. Also l., the dog-leg stair, entered between fluted Ionic pilasters. Doors lug-corniced with pulvinated architraves.

CHAMBERED CAIRN, 155m. NW of Beacharr Farm. An irregular oval mound, c. 21m. by 15m., in which excavation has revealed lengths of dry-stone façade walling running E and W from the burial chamber entrance. The chamber is the longest in Kintyre, 6.25m., and has four in-line compartments. The important group of round-based neolithic vessels found in 1892 is now in Campbeltown Public Library and Museum.

STANDING STONE, 135m. NW of Beacharr Farm and 27.5m. S of the chambered cairn. Tallest in Kintyre at 5.03m. high.

TAYNUILT

0031

A widely spread village, clustering between road and railway 1km. S of Loch Etive but more dispersed towards the loch shore through the hamlet of Brochroy with its surprising legacy of early industrial buildings. A notable but easily overlooked asset is the but-and-ben rubble cottages that survive from the C18 and early C19, no longer thatched but roofed in slate or corrugated metal and adapted in plan and fittings for modern living. Groups exist in Ichrachan township around the junction of the Brochroy road with the A85, at Kirkton, S of Taynuilt Hotel, at the W end of the village and (in poor condition) on the road to Airds Bay.

CHURCH OF THE VISITATION (R.C.), Brochroy. Built 1901–2. Four-bay gabled nave, broad lancets, plain traceried E window. NW saddle-back belfry tower with leaded spirelet rising from ridge. Starkly plain, stepped sanctuary with splayed and canopied plywood 'reredos' concealing the E window; by *John Gallagher*, c. 1955–6. Tall, dull and intimidating presbytery to E, begun as single-storey in 1905; extra storey and attic, 1916–17.

MUCKAIRN PARISH CHURCH. A variant on the standard Telford kirk, built 1828–9 in coursed, mainly Bonawe granite, rubble with buff sandstone dressings. This skew-gabled oblong is aligned W–E, with a step-roofed birdcage belfry over W entrance gable. Large four-centre arch windows. Symmetrical N and S fenestration indicates that the interior was originally galleried with a pulpit at the centre of the S wall. The hipped-roofed vestry on the E gable appears original but may formerly have acted as a second entrance with a stair leading to the laird's loft and small retiring room. Flat-ceilinged interior, orientated to the E in 1887(?), plain. Only a W gallery, supported below its panelled and corniced front on two Roman Doric timber columns, survives. It is reached by a stone stair rising against the gable from the vestibule below. Belfry BELL cast in Edinburgh, 1857. In the church, another BELL, dated 1733, which presumably hung in an earlier building.

The church is recorded as a *re*-building, which may mean that it is built on the footings of an early C18 structure or that it simply replaced the late medieval PARISH CHURCH OF KILESPICKERILL, rubble vestiges of the E end of which stand, drenched in ivy, a few metres S. A tomb-chest recess and small aumbry can be found beneath the vegetation. Two CARVED STONES, probably deriving from this medieval chapel, are incorporated at high level in the S wall of the C19 church: one, possibly a skewputt, has been interpreted as 'a grinning ecclesiastic'; the other is a 'sheila-na-gig' (Gaelic sile-na-gcioc), a fertility fetish figure, perhaps C13. In the churchyard, three TAPERED SLABS, *c.* 1500–60, one delineated with a claymore, its hilt surrounded by animals from the chase. Also some C18 TABLE-TOMBS, one of which, commemorating Alexander Campbell †1751, is carved with a coat-of-arms, inscription, and angels bearing the soul of the deceased heavenwards.

Former MUCKAIRN FREE CHURCH. Built 1860. A NE entrance tower, with a somewhat Italianate pyramid cap roof, fronts a gabled oblong. The tower walls and gable buttresses are both splayed. Converted to church hall, *c.* 1930. Now gawkily adapted to residential use.

BRIDGE, over River Awe, 2.9km. SE. 48m. single segmental arch span in reinforced concrete by *Sir Frank Mears*, 1937–8. Rubble facing seems a mistake for the crown of the arch looks uncomfortably thin.

BRIDGE OF AWE, 3km. SE. Of the three-arched bridge built 1778–9 for the Commissioners of Supply for Argyll under the supervision of *Lewis Piccard* (or *Ludovick Picard*?), mason, only the approaches and the E span of 13.6m. with its cutwater pier remain. By-passed in 1938; flood destruction has left rubble and earth infill exposed in both shorn abutments.

BROCHROY FARM, Brochroy. Unpretentious group of gable-to-gable vernacular dwellings, C19, stepping up the incline like a village street. Prettified in pastel shade renders but unaffected, coherent and genuinely rural in form.

ICHRACHAN HOUSE, 2km. SE. Splendidly sited hilltop house designed by *Robert S. Lorimer*(?), *c.* 1908(?), with unexpectedly heavy-handed, vernacular austerity. Two roughcast storeys with skew gables. Sun terrace on SE. Positioned on the NW forecourt is a stone column SUNDIAL bearing an inscription in Gaelic. Simple, cone-topped rubble GATEPIERS mark the start of a long climbing drive from the Kilchrenan road out of Taynuilt.

INVERAWE HOUSE, 1.9km. ENE, on the r. bank of the River Awe. An impressive surge of white-harled gabled blocks, the chronological aggregation of which remains unclear. Rising at the centre is a high saddleback tower of uncertain date heavily crow-stepped on the N and S gables and lugged with corbelled box turrets which, like the tall windows all-but-symmetrically arranged on the W garden front, are evidently Victorian interventions. A slightly lower but similarly crowstepped gable pushes E to align with the house's other main façade. N and S of the central block, two-storeyed gabled wings plug in, elongating both E and W fronts along driveway and lawn respectively. All seems C19 (some Baronial remodelling by *Charles Wilson* is known to have occurred, 1850–2), with the exception of the N end of the E façade, a three-bay house which must surely be early C18: it retains its central doorway and radial fanlight but lacks the dressed sandstone margins which prevail elsewhere. Too insignificant to serve the completed E façade, its door cedes the limelight to a larger entrance, stone-framed with moulded architraves surmounted by a scrolled panel, placed below the crowstepped gable already mentioned. Beyond this frontispiece there is little or no other decorative stonework but a carved STONE PANEL, said to have come from the fort at Fort William, *c.* 1890, set into the W wall. It bears a repaired and partially re-cut inscription FEAR / GOD / OBEY / THE / KING and is dated [?17]54.

In 1913–14 *Sir Robert S. Lorimer* remodelled the house, especially inside where refurbishment was carried out by *Scott Morton & Co.* But more radical changes were wrought by *Leslie C. Norton*, 1953–4, in a programme of demolition and paring which removed a N wing, eliminated a high chimneyed gable which rose from the W face of the central tower, and, reducing the height of the square corner turrets on this same façade, rebuilt the parapet to its present form.

To the S of the house lies a group of low C19 OUTBUILDINGS arranged casually but agreeably around a walled court. Most are now in residential use, including a delightful conically capped 'dairy'(?). A mellowed mix of slated and moss-covered, corrugated-sheet roofs.

INVERAWE POWER STATION, 700m. NW of Inverawe House. By *Shearer & Annand*; engineers *James Williamson & Partners*. Vast riverside shed walled in pink granite random rubble; part of the Awe hydro-electric developments of 1959–65. High, wide and heavily framed doorway with exaggerated quoining and a flat block pediment in local grey granite.

LONAN HOUSE, 1.4km. SW. Formerly Barguillean House; harled with slate-hung bays, piended slated roof and dormers by *Robert S. Lorimer*, 1906–8. At the centre of the E front two round arches open into a recessed entrance porch. Now subdivided.

MUCKAIRN MANSE. Standard two-storey, T-plan Parliamentary Commissioners' manse by *William Thomson*, 1829. Built in coursed granite blocks which exacerbate the austerity of its three-bay, door-less, symmetrical front.

TAYNUILT HOTEL. A two-storey-and-attic, harled block, seven gabletted dormers long, fronting the Dalmally–Oban road. The original C18 inn lies at the centre. Wide-pedimented Tuscan porch carried on four columns, part of an early C19 enlargement. At the rear, ruinous outbuildings, some roofless, C18 and C19; early C19 rubble COACH-HOUSE, adjacent to the buttressed E gable of the hotel, has a round-arched entrance in its N gable.

TAYNUILT PRIMARY SCHOOL. By *Strathclyde Regional Council*, c. 1990. Two monopitch roofs with olive-painted flanks and fascias on rust pink rendered classroom walls. Red grid-framed windows with stepping sills.

TAYNUILT PUBLIC SCHOOL. Rubble schoolhouse and classroom block, c. 1895, the latter with tripartite windows in the N and S gables. The double-pile W extension, 1912–13, by *G. Woulfe Brenan*, incorporates a sandstone TABLET from the demolished Muckairn School which records in four idiosyncratically split lines that the earlier school was 'Erected by Augusta Mrs / Campbell of Lo / chnell on the 14 / Septr 1834'. Derelict.

TAYNUILT STATION. Timber-framed and boarded, gable-ended station built along the S platform. Below the central S gable, in the small semicircular cresting to the cornice which is bracketed on consoles over the entrance, are a crown, the initials 'C. & O.R.' for Callander and Oban Railway, and the date 1879 in Roman numerals. A glazed platform awning is supported on eight large cast-iron brackets infilled with decorative plant whorls. Serrated fretted boarding decorates the ends of this canopy. Piended, timber-framed SIGNAL BOX, adjacent E.

VILLAGE HALL. By *G. Woulfe Brenan*, 1905. Basic slates-and-roughcast hall struggling for Arts and Crafts credibility with a few dormers and minimal half-timbering in bargeboarded gables.

BONAWE IRONWORKS
at Brochroy

Land close to the shore of Loch Etive between the mouths of the Rivers Nant and Awe is the site of the 'longest-lived of the charcoal blast-furnaces in the Scottish Highlands' (Stell and Hay, 1991). In 1752–3 Richard Ford & Company of Cumbria, later known as the Newland Company, established Bonawe Ironworks, negotiating agreements with local landowners for the supply of wood to provide the charcoal needed for smelting. A kilometre-long lade was cut from the River Awe to provide water power and a jetty built on the loch (*see* below) to receive the iron ore which had to be imported by sea from Furness in Lancashire and Central Scotland. Despite its relatively isolated location, the industry prospered and a community, whose members included both local labour and English immigrants, developed. Workers' housing was built and allotments and grazing rights allocated. Oak bark, a by-product of charcoal production, was exported, as for a time was yarn spun by the workers' wives. A century after its foundation the Lorn Furnace was still in production and a new lease of wood rights was signed. But the drift of the industry to the coal seams proved inexorable: output from the charcoal-burning furnaces fell and by 1876 production at the Lorn Furnace had ceased. Today the furnace and shed buildings at Bonawe are in the care of Historic Scotland. Carefully restored and presented to the public, their monumental quietness, more ecclesiastical than industrial, cannot capture the productive energy that must have gripped Taynuilt for more than a hundred years.

The principal building, both industrially and architecturally, is the BLAST FURNACE, 1753. It is centrally located and constructed where a marked change in the natural section of the ground

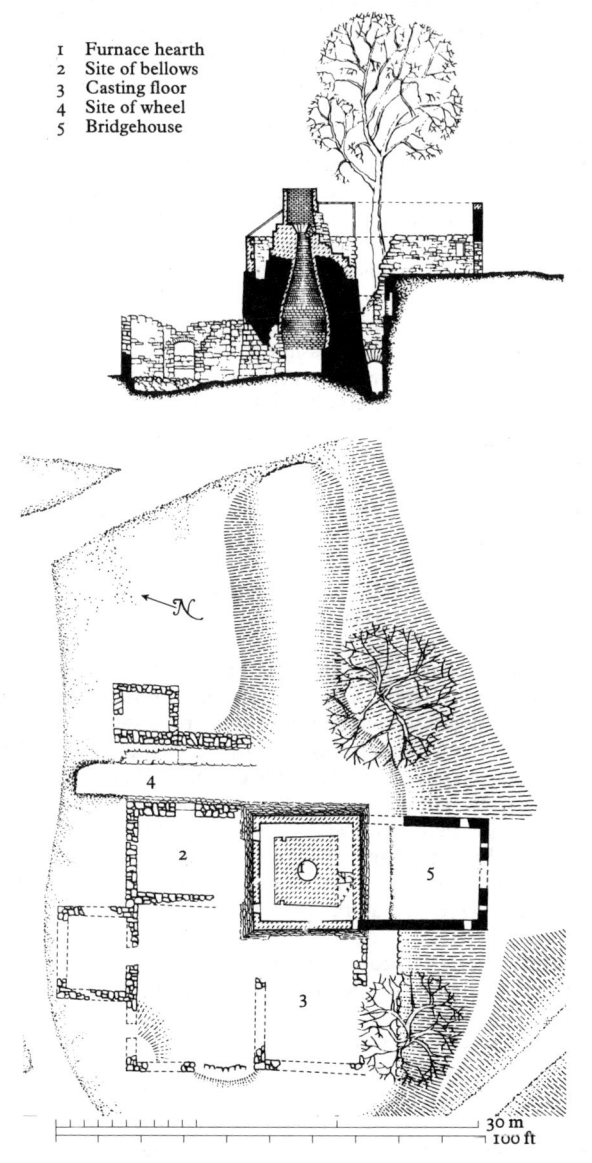

1 Furnace hearth
2 Site of bellows
3 Casting floor
4 Site of wheel
5 Bridgehouse

Taynuilt, Bonawe Ironworks. Plan and section of the blast furnace

facilitated loading through the bridgehouse at the upper level and driving the waterwheel, which powered the blowing apparatus, at low level. The furnace plan is square, its mortared granite rubble bulk battered to a height of 6.4m. above which reconstruction in the second quarter of the C19 raised the walls vertically to an 8.9m. wallhead. Here, beneath a piended slated roof leaning against the chimneystack and continuous with the roof over the bridgehouse to the S, an internal walkway was provided around the reconstructed furnace-tunnel. It is lit by small lintelled openings in the N and W (and possibly originally also in the E) walls; also in the W and E walls are smaller steam vent openings. At the lower level, large, deeply splayed recesses permitted the input of the blast from the N and the withdrawal of slag on the W, though the buildings housing these operations are now reduced to little more than a few ruinous walls. In each case, three cast-iron lintels, separated by red sandstone lining, span the reducing openings; some bear the cast inscription BUNAW. F. 1753. The furnace hearth within is square but, on corner lintels of curved cast iron, transforms to a circular base for the familiar inverted cone above. This terminates, at the base of the chimney, in a splayed loading mouth accessible from firebrick steps added in the bridgehouse during C19 reconstruction. The bridgehouse, its E and W walls continuous with those of the furnace, spans the gap created between the retaining wall, which stabilizes natural and made-up ground at the higher level, and the S wall of the furnace. This sectional arrangement was used to contrive a narrow low-level chamber which probably accommodated the founder. Its floor does not survive but there is a window in the W wall and a fireplace opening in the retaining wall.

Ranged conveniently but informally to the S of the furnace are the CHARCOAL SHEDS and ORE SHED. All are rubble-built and are set into bankings to permit high-level loading. Two buildings constructed for charcoal storage exist. The E is older, probably mid to late C18, a wide pitched roof structure built of coursed rubble diminishing in thickness by offsets. Its N elevation had three arched accesses (E arch now replaced by lintel) springing from one such offset course. The W sheds, late C18 and C19, lack the symmetrical simplicity of their earlier neighbour. The iron-ore shed, located immediately NE of the older charcoal shed, has three compartments, mid to late C18, and a fourth, on the E, slightly later. The roof is pitched, the N slope extended to create a covered unloading gallery supported on timber posts. Masonry, roof timbers and slating of all these buildings have been restored, slating and carpentry detailing following the Lakeland practice adopted by the immigrant craftsmen in the C18. Trusses are of collar and tie-beam form, except in the E charcoal shed, where king-posts are used.

WORKERS' HOUSING, Brochroy. The oldest example is a cottage row, c. 1755, some 100m. SE of the sheds described above. There were eight houses, each no more than a ground-floor room and an attic loft reached by a ladder stair opening off the entrance lobby. Behind the row is a piend-roofed byre, late C18, which retains some cruck and blade timbers. Built 100m. N of the furnace in an E–W alignment is a two-storey flatted tenement, late C18. To the W end of this, forming a right-angle turn N, was added a larger two-storey dwelling, traditionally believed to have been the overseer's residence. Finally, in the early C19, a further tenement row with forestair access to the upper flats was attached to the N gable of this house, completing an L-plan block of accommodation. These buildings, much altered, remain in residential use, though part of the earliest wing is undergoing considerable reconstruction in 1995.

BONAWE HOUSE, Brochroy. Mid-C18 house built by the partner-manager of the Bonawe Ironworks. It has a five-bay, three-storeyed, symmetrical N front with a splendid timber doorpiece of fluted pilasters, Doric entablature, and pediment. Ground-floor windows l. and r. have been replaced by canted bays, *c.* 1900(?). Nevertheless, the N façade retains a provincial Georgian solidity intensified by an extra high wallhead. W wing begun as single-storey, with broad canted bay added to N, *c.* 1900(?) and later raised to two. Offices, C18 and early C19, arranged in a shallow arc plan to the S. Converted and subdivided into separate dwellings, *c.* 1980. In the garden, a small cluster-shaft SUNDIAL.

KELLY'S QUAY. A long, turf-topped, rubble finger jutting out into Airds Bay. Built for Bonawe Ironworks, late C18, it saw the import of iron ore and the dispatch of pig-iron, bark, kelp and salmon. The asymmetrically broadened pierhead has stairs in the re-entrant angles at each side; degraded masonry stabilized with concrete, *c.* 1962.

DUN, Dùn Chathach, 4.75km. NW. On steep ground 50m. above the shore of Loch Etive, a circular dun, 18.3m. in external dia. Visible outer walling with some facing stones of massive size. Several gaps prevent identification of the entrance.

STANDING STONE, in an elevated position N of Taynuilt Primary School. One of a number of 'pillar stones' said to have lain in a field near Airds Bay, this 3.43m.-high stone was removed, 'not in the best possible taste', as the writer of the *New Statistical Account* wrote in 1845, to its present site in 1805 and there raised by the Lorn Furnace workmen as a monument to honour Lord Nelson. Brief inscription on the N face.

TAYVALLICH

A beautiful, almost secret place discovered through the woods of upper Loch Sween. Encircling the sheltered inner basin of Loch a'Bhealaich, the village looks on all sides towards the water. The yachts have brought life, but also a ring of indifferent holiday cottages now outnumbering the few surviving old rubble cottages. From the N caravans advance ominously.

TAYVALLICH CHURCH. A preaching house, established here before the middle of the C18, was successively rebuilt 1752–5, enlarged 1820 and finally replaced by a new church by *George Johnston* in 1827. In 1893–4, this was superseded by the present building by *James Edgar*. Roughcast with dressings of pink sandstone; a plain five-bay gabled box lit by lancets. Above the porch on the SW gable, a timber canopy to the bell. Piended vestry added 1931.

SCOTNISH LODGE, 2km. NE of Tayvallich. Harled shooting lodge by *Albert E. King & Co.*, 1912–14. Mullion-and-transom windows. High pitched roofs, gabled and piended, spiked with chimneystacks.

TAYNISH HOUSE, 4.5km. SSW of Tayvallich at the end of the Taynish peninsula. Two-storey, harled and slated house impressing by mass rather than architectural detail. Unusually it is not gabled but terminates in the SW and NE in full-bodied bows, their conical roofs continuous with that of the main block. At the core is a five-bay laird's house built by the MacNeill family in the early C18. The SE front retains some small original windows and has two entrance doors. The bows came later, added by Sir Archibald Campbell of Inverneill after he had purchased the estate in 1780. Changes wrought by Campbell may well have removed some C17 work. John Leyden, visiting the house in 1800, records that Taynish had 'lost all its ancient appendages by the present possessor preferring convenience to barbarous grandeur'. In the early C19, a further slightly wider bow, accommodating kitchens at the lower level, was attached to the cheek of the NE bow. This buttock plan, capped by half-cone roofs, produced a powerful, bastion-like front to the NE. At the rear, two much narrower bowed additions, *c.* 1920s, protrude to the NW, the smaller applied on to a cylindrical C18 stair-tower. Following a fire in 1955 the interior was extensively reworked and, apart from the panelled shutters of the former Dining Room in the SW bow, no C18 features remain.

The WALLED GARDEN probably dates from late C18. The Gothick DAIRY, 100m. SE of the house, is early C19. It is a two-storeyed harled octagon subdivided at some later date into a gun-room with bedrooms above. The roof is a slated pyramid and the windows pointed-arch openings with intersecting astragals. Linked with the adjacent steading is a large five-bay piended BARN, also probably early C19, conceived along the lines of an C18 kirk. It incorporates a dovecote and has a winding timber stair. Near the shore, a small round SUMMERHOUSE similar in style to the dairy and a PIGGERY with arched pens.

TAYNISH MILL, 2.1km. NNE of Taynish House close to NW shore of Loch Sween. Overgrown ruins of corn-mill, early C19, once powered by a culverted mill-lade from Lochan Taynish.

TAYVALLICH PRIMARY SCHOOL. Completed 1874. School-master's house and classroom block in white-painted rubble. Gabled with oversailing roofs revealing spar and purlin ends.

GALLACHOILLE FARM, 4km. NE of Tayvallich. Late C19. Three-gable rubble front with a central entrance gable projecting. Outbuildings to NE gabled and pended at centre.

ARICHONAN TOWNSHIP, 5.5km. NNE of Tayvallich. Some C18 work may survive but most rubble remains are C19. In 1800 there were four tenants, each having a cruck-roofed dwelling, barn and bothy. By mid C19 the community had gone. On NW edge, a roofless winnowing barn with opposed doors, triangular vent holes and a lintel dated 1833.

DUN and SETTLEMENT, Dùn Mhuirich, on NW shore of the Linne Mhuirich, roughly halfway between Tayvallich and Keills. Sub-oval dun, 15.5m. by 12m., situated on a defensible elongated ridge falling 25m. to the loch. Walling survives best on the S and SW where an entrance is protected by a hornwork. Outer walling encloses an area of level ground below the summit. At the lochside is a 60m. length of bouldered wharf and three rudimentary jetties; these coastal constructions are probably contemporary with a number of small rectangular structures later located within the dun.

ISLAND DWELLING, Eilean na Circe, in the Caol Scotnish arm of Loch Sween, 3km. NE of Tayvallich. Rocky island with ruinous drystone walling, late medieval(?), around the summit. Within the enclosure are the drystone remains of a rectangular structure, C17 or C18. Cruck slots in the masonry.

STANDING STONE, Barnashalg, 1.4m. SW of Tayvallich. 3.5m.-high leaning stone. Some cupmarks.

STANDING STONE, Upper Fernoch, 1.7m. SW of Tayvallich. Straight-sided stone, 2.5m., but now leaning SE.

TIGHNABRUAICH

The northernmost of three linear villages straggling picturesquely along the W shore of the Kyles of Bute (the others are Auchenlochan and Kames, qq.v.). It owes its mid-C19 origins as 'a recent watering place' (Groome, 1885) to the steamer connection with Greenock which brought Glasgow's businessmen and their families to enjoy the summer. The houses they built still line the shore and the wooded slopes above.

Former TIGHNABRUAICH PARISH CHURCH. Built as Tighnabruaich Free Church, 1863, by *Boucher & Cousland*. Gabled rubble front with a tall steeply-pitched gabled belfry rising from the apex, the bell hung in an open Norman arch. Round-arch windows with engaged shafts l. and r. over a central Norman doorway with concave ingoes, engaged shafts and scalloped capitals. – STAINED GLASS by *Ballantine & Son*.

PIER. Timber and cast iron; built 1843 by the Castle Steamship Company, rebuilt 1884–5, and still in occasional use. The original pierhead building, *c.* 1857, housed a shop and dwelling but, *c.* 1905, was much altered and extended to provide a first-floor restaurant and tea-room. Slated mansard with wide hipped dormer to S and half-octagon roof over a canted bay N dormer. A timber balustraded balcony looks to the Kyles. White roughcast walls. Now a dwelling.

TIGHNABRUAICH HOUSE, above the shore road. A grand residence set high amid banking lawns patrolled by peacocks. By *William Leiper*, 1895; it follows his 'second Arts and Crafts style' (Hume, 1995), that very English Shavian idiom successively explored in several of his late C19 Helensburgh houses. There are gables and bays, mullion-and-transom windows with leaded glass in the upper lights, red brick chimneystacks, even a veranda, but the absence of tile- or slate-hanging, not much half-timbering and a combination of rough-faced local whin and red Corrie sandstone admit none of the subtleties of Shaw: this is Arts and Crafts with a hard edge. The layout is a reversed L with the three public rooms facing SSE and the kitchen quarters returning NNW. In the grounds, a petrol-driven gas plant installed to provide gas lighting is still in working order. From ENE, a pointed-arch porch leads into a long hall panelled in Kauri pine to door lintel height. Library, Drawing Room and Dining Room lie l.; all have Kauri pine panelling, exposed timber beam-and-joist ceilings with painted stone corbels, and stone fireplaces with four-centred-arch openings and ceramic tile surrounds, green, white and turquoise respectively. Pitch-pine well stair r. in re-entrant angle of plan. At the upper landing, two timber-arched bays, one balustraded as a short gallery.

DESCRIPTION

The village centre is marked by a short length of double-sided street. On the E, a slow, two-storey curve of shops and flats, c. 1860, backing on to the Kyles shore; W, above a grassy bank, the black-and-white cubic bulk of TIGHNABRUAICH HOTEL, 1867, with a double-height canted bay and, over the central entrance, an arched canopy with consoles. Beyond this is the Parish Church (*see* above) and then, scattered along the shore to enjoy the view across the narrows to Bute, a succession of C19 villas. As at Dunoon, dormered and gabled fronts find favour. THE GROVE, 1876, has lost its porch but has good ironwork, including sill fringing, bracketed at first floor. Arcaded iron railings enhance OAKFIELD, late C19. THE SQUARE is older than it looks; probably 1840s, but converted to a sprawling U-plan bungalow in the 1920s and later deadened by heavy concrete tiling. Uphill is Tighnabruaich House (*see* above). The gabled front of CREAGANDARAICH, c. 1855, sports a trefoil window over the door. DUNMAR, c. 1855, has a quatrefoil and a Gothic parapet to its canted bay. Whorl-fretted bargeboards and cast-iron finials enliven the gables of WELLPARK HOUSE, 1864. Stone strapwork and more ironwork filigree over the ground-floor windows at EDEN KERRY, 1857. The CHALET HOTEL, 1857, perched higher on the hillside, looks Tyrolean (it was originally known as Swiss Cottage), an aberrant concoction, balconied and bayed below wide shallow-pitched roofs. Further N, no less odd, ARGYLL VILLA, 1868, a squat rubble fort with castellated round towers at all four corners. Then come four similar houses, 1868–9, with round-arch canopied entrances; at RHUBAAN LODGE, a timber summer-house with stained glass. Hidden by trees is SHERBROOKE, 1878, a Victorian variation on a Georgian theme; hipped-roofed symmetry with a pilastered porch and tall tripartite windows l. and r. Finally, STRONCARRAIG, c. 1880, a symmetrical classical house, the upper windows arched, the lower lintelled with cornices and consoles.

TOBERONOCHY

A village of rubble WORKERS' COTTAGES on the E coast of Luing, built for slate quarrymen in the early C19. The single-storey rows, generally three or four gable-to-gable, relate in a pleasant but casual arrangement that seems to defer to neither geometry nor orientation. Most houses have been rehabilitated as holiday homes, some painted, some roughcast; phased refurbishment by *Kinghorn Mee*, 1988–92. A small QUAY of vertically set rubble masonry survives.

OLD PARISH CHURCH and BURIAL ENCLOSURE, Kilchattan, 500m. NW. Roofless ruin of rubble masonry with extensive pinnings. A ragged gap in the N wall suggests this might have been the doorway. The church is narrow and, although the disappearance of the E wall makes it difficult to determine its length, its plan bears some similarity to Killean in Kintyre (q.v.). A C12 date is thus possible. Several stones on the outer faces of the N, W and S walls bear the incised outlines of crosses, geometrical figures and West Highland galleys, probably cut in late medieval times. Laid flat within the church are a number of slate funerary SLABS, C18, including some with primitively executed inscriptions.

The graveyard has many interesting stones. Most notable and most verbose are those commemorating Alexander Campbell †1829. Incorporated into the W enclosure wall, where they are set into both the outer and inner faces below a gablet rise in the cope, are two round-headed PANELS with long inscriptions full of biblical references and the assertion that it will be 'marvelous [*sic*] to most that I digged my grave before I died'. In front of the inner panel is a TABLE-TOMB which records Campbell's Covenanting adherence 'to the whole work of the second reformation in Scotland between year 1638 and 1649'. – Another TABLE-TOMB, bearing the family coat-of-arms, records the deaths of Hugh McDougall †1785, and his brother, John †1809. – A slate HEADSTONE with Gaelic and English verses and a variety of small emblems and figures carved randomly in a rounded pediment to Archibald McArthur †1826. – Quite different in design is a framed sandstone TABLET in the W wall: horizontal rather than vertical and carved with flourishing curves more suited to penmanship than funerary sculpture. It marks the grave of 'Duncan Campbell, Late Merchant in Glasgow' †1818.

ARDLARACH, 1km. W of the Old Parish Church at Kilchattan. Three-bay, two-storey, 'improved farmhouse'; a slate panel inset on S front between two upper windows records 'BUILT BY / PATRICK MCDOUGALL / 1787'. An E wing, early C19, continues the line of the S front two more bays of larger-sized windows and extends N to form L-plan. S porches added later.

KILCHATTAN FARM, 400m. NW. Designed by *Hugh Birrell*, Largo, 1853–5, and later described by Groome as 'a remarkably fine suite of dwellings and offices'. Long rubble range containing cottages, hay house, implement house, etc., with lofted corn barn projecting at centre. Other ranges accommodated stables, cart shed, joiner's shop, byre, piggeries, sheep pens.

TORRISDALE CASTLE
3km. s of Carradale

At the core of the existing winged mansion is the original castellated house built for General Keith Macalister by *James Gillespie Graham* in 1815. This house, though higher than the later wings added symmetrically to the N and S, was a relatively modest residence. It closely followed a compositional formula established by Graham at Culdees Castle, Perthshire, 1810, and further refined in a contemporary commission at Edmonstone, Lanarkshire. Graham's approach entailed the Gothic Revival transformation of a typical C18 country house plan which, while it maintained the balanced order of classical tripartition (albeit caparisoned with the trappings of medievalism), did not forbear to intrude some formal gesture of perverse romantic sensibility. At Culdees, this was a tower raised asymmetrically above one corner of the house as a large drum; at Edmonstone and Torrisdale it became octagonal, smaller on plan, but still successful in its picturesquely disturbing intent.

Viewed from the W, Graham's Torrisdale appears as a two-storeyed ashlar mansion with narrow square-plan corner towers and a raised centre. A heavy, almost brutal, corbelled and battlemented parapet conceals a piended roof around which diagonal chimneystacks rank in military precision. Windows are hooded, with Gothic tracery in square-headed openings (*see* Glenbarr Abbey) with the exception of a large four-centred arch lighting the staircase landing and hall at the centre of the façade. Beneath this window a single-storey porch projects, its arched entrance guarded by two round turret sentries. The porch is, in fact, a bridge concealing a sunken basement which is exposed on the opposite side of the building by the change in ground level. On this E façade the deliberate lop-sidedness of Graham's composition is clear as the crenellated parapet steps up to the NE corner tower.

At the beginning of the C20, *H. E. Clifford* added a N wing, c. 1904(?), and a S wing, c. 1910(?), 'in accordance', James Macaulay has written, 'with Gillespie Graham's original intentions' (1975). Certainly, use of the same Wigtownshire sandstone was maintained and, in every external detail, the architectural language of the original house perpetuated. For example, a barely discernible but crucial increase in the breadth of his own end towers shows just how subtle and effective Clifford's sympathy for his predecessor's work could be.

Graham's interiors were evidently given less respect. The main staircase has an open Gothic balustrade, while the Dining Room, l. of Hall, retains his curved doors, panelled in Perpendicular Gothic, and a four-centred chimneypiece in black marble. Clifford, however, seems to have made alterations to the Hall, creating a wide opening r. between Ionic pilasters into the panelled Library. From here a Gothic sliding door opens to the Drawing Room in the S wing: lined walls with fluted Ionic pilasters at all windows and a ribbed plaster ceiling with flowered panels. In the N wing, a Billiard Room: walls panelled to door height, timber beamed ceiling, raised floor at end wall fireplace with turret alcoves on each side. – STAINED GLASS introduced by Clifford: Edwardian Art Nouveau motifs in several glazed doors; stair window carries images of six Scottish kings.

BRIDGES. Two single-span rubble bridges over Lephincorrach Burn; one pointed arch, one segmental, early C19.

BRIDGE, over Torrisdale Water at Gate Lodge. Two segmental arches. Inscribed 'AMA / 1840' on outer sides.

GATEHOUSE and STABLES (The Arch), 100m. SW of Torrisdale Castle. Pointed archway surmounted, on a pronounced corbel course, by a high attic held between open rounds. Macalister coat-of-arms carved in attic panel; blind cruciform loops in rounds. Castellated gabled stables around three sides of square.

SOUTH GATE LODGE, on Carradale to Campbeltown road. Harled Gothic Lodge beside gateway to estate, linked by screen walls to bridge. Ashlar porch has a crenellated parapet. Late C19.

TORRISDALE SQUARE. Castellated rubble steading, *c.* 1850, with small piend-roofed entrance tower containing a doocot. U-plan around yard.

TORSA

Uninhabited isle off the NE coast of Luing.

CAISTEAL NAN CON. Overgrown remnants of a late medieval, oblong tower-house, possibly C15. The plan of the tower and barmkin is elongated SW–NE over the entire length of a rocky ridge close to the NE shore of the island. In the preserved masonry of a round tower at the NE corner of the barmkin, the discharge chute of a garderobe can be seen; otherwise the ruin is without architectural detail.

TOWARD

Settlement at the S end of the Cowal peninsula scattered along the coastal strip between Toward Point and Toward Quay.

TOWARD CHURCH. Three-bay gabled Gothic tightly enclosed by a low rubble wall railed and gated at the front, with two cast-iron light standards. Built as a Chapel of Ease, 1839. Skew-gabled S front with corbelled bellcote at apex and projecting porch with stepped skews. Side walls have hooded, double-hung windows with Perpendicular glazing bars. Chancel arch extension formed in N gable, 1935, by *Jeffrey Waddell & Young*. Stonework exposed inside. – PULPIT by *Thomas W. Wilson*. – STAINED GLASS. Central W window by *Heaton, Butler & Bayne*, *c.* 1900 (Death of St Columba). – Adjacent E is a corrugated-iron-clad, timber-framed, gabled HALL, *c.* 1905, formerly the United Free Church at Tayvallich but moved here in 1950.

CASTLE TOWARD, 600m. SW of Toward Quay. By *David Hamilton*, 1820–1. A 'marine villa' in picturesque castellated Gothic for the

Glasgow merchant and former Lord Provost, Kirkman Finlay; one of three such mansions which appeared more or less contemporaneously on the Cowal shore, the others being Castle House at Dunoon and Hafton House, Ardnadam (qq.v.). A century later, Finlay's house was absorbed as the E wing of a much larger residence, 1920–4, contrived in similar, almost indistinguishable style by *F. W. Deas* for Major Andrew Coats, a member of the immensely rich threadmaking family of Paisley. After a period of wartime service as 'H.M.S. *Brontosaurus*', the house was adapted, 1947–9, as a residential school.

The Hamilton house is asymmetrical, in ashlar sandstone rising to two and three storeys. At the E end of the s front, a battlemented and turreted porte-cochère leads into a vast entrance hall. Above this rises a square tower, turreted at the corners and lit by a hooded pointed-arch window with tripartite tracery. On the E façade, under a single hood-moulding, are two shields inscribed with the initials KF / JS and the date A.D. 1820. Another crenellated tower projects NE, this time circular with a tall, mullion-and-transom window of three round arches lighting the main landing of a spacious imperial staircase, the upper flights of which follow the curving plan of the drum. On the N, elevated above crenellations and groups of octagonal chimneystacks, is a high machicolated tower, splayed to an octagonal plan at third-floor level. The principal s façade originally extended three bays w from the entrance tower to another, square tower, again machicolated and battlemented, beyond which was a single lower bay, turreted at the corners. In the 1920s, however, this W wing was greatly extended to include a ballroom, several public rooms and many bedrooms, a T-plan arrangement of additional accommodation terminating in a near-symmetrical w elevation where a T-plan staircase rose to a loggia of three four-centre arches set between two more square towers. In effect, a 'multiplicity of towers' (Macaulay, 1975) now existed but, though the C20 works are remarkably sympathetic in stylistic idiom, the introduction of bay windows, attic bedrooms behind the parapets and some alterations to fenestration give the aggrandizement game away.

Of the early C19 interior, plaster rib-vaulting on slender clustered wall-shafts survives in the SE porch, hall and staircase, and there are Perpendicular-traceried windows and doors. But the decorative work is almost all C20: Gothic-Jacobean in the Ballroom and W Hall, Adamesque in the SW room, and Louis XVI in the Drawing Room.

On the A815, opposite Toward Quay, is the COURT OF OFFICES, 1820–1, a long two-storey wall of accommodation executed in the same castellated Gothic manner. The entrance passes through a four-centre archway in a square battlemented tower, turreted at the corners, the SE turret rising higher than the others. Some work dates from the 1920s.

OLD AUCHAVOULIN HOUSE, at the NE corner of the walled garden at Castle Toward (q.v.). No more than a two-storey length of windowed walling remains of this early or mid-C18 dwelling. Random rubble masonry with dressings of local red sandstone. Vestigial evidence of original vaulted ground-floor apartments but the vaulted w cellar is early C19, the tracery infill of its segmental-arch entrance early C20.

KNOCKDOW HOUSE, 3.2m. NNW of Toward Castle. A broad-fronted, two-storey dwelling which, despite repeated alterations and extensions made by the Lamont family, whose estate mansion it has been from the mid C18 until 1949, has managed to retain its dignity; cool and provincially chaste on the s, more outspokenly classical on the E. Easy-to-see C18 core of five bays, pre-1765, by the Greenock mason *John Menelaws*, later responsible for the very similar Ardpatrick House (q.v.). By *c*. 1820, bow-fronted, single-storey wings had appeared and in 1849–50 the principal s façade was further widened w by the gable of a two-storey addition, terminating in a round NW tower. At first roofed with a slated cone, later battlemented and the witch's hat removed, probably by *David Thomson*, 1867. As if to counteract this asymmetrical aberration, in 1884 the hipped-roofed ends of the C18 house were removed, chimneyed gables built and new hip ends constructed which extended the main roof over w and E wings, now raised an extra storey to the original eaves height. Finally, *George Mackie Watson* built the E wing, 1919–21, creating a new entrance to the house complete with porte-cochère. Later minor alterations and extensions by *R. Nelson Macnab*, 1927–35.

The two façades differ considerably. The s front, rendered and painted in grey and white, is flat, save for the slight swelling of the bowed wings, and decoratively undemonstrative; the cornices, pediments, window surrounds and dormers of the five-bay core are 1884 additions and, like the plain tripartite ground- and first-floor windows in the wings, simply serve to stiffen the symmetrical calm. The E front, also symmetrical, is much more self-consciously a façade. Two-storey canted bays at each end, a central entrance projection crowned at eaves level with a segmental pediment, and a linked porte-cochère of round-arches set between banded pilasters bearing open pediments; the whole composition carried out in a strongly cut rusticated Renaissance idiom drawn from Watson's mentor, Robert Rowand Anderson.

The interior has been much altered, especially by Watson who removed the stair tower at the rear of the C18 block to give access to a central galleried hall. This inner space is two-storeyed, overlooked at first-floor level by four delightful little balconies which push through Ionic columned screens. Above is a glazed dome. High quality hardwoods from the Lamont estate in Trinidad in the hall, in the entrance and staircase of the E wing and in the panelled library Watson created in the gabled w wing. In the SE room of the C18 block is a pine and gesso fireplace, *c*. 1800, with anthemion frieze and putti. N of the central hall are the service quarters, extensively recast in the 1920s.

Some 80m. N, the former COURT OF OFFICES. The s range, probably C18, contained stables, barn and loft. By mid C19, w and E ranges, linked to the s one by archways, had been connected with a N range, pre-1817, to enclose a courtyard.

TOLLARD HOUSE (The Tower). Late Victorian mansion with high first floor and higher SW corner block, almost a tower, gabled on three sides with a three-storey, square bay rising under the S gable.

TOWARD POINT LIGHTHOUSE, at the SE end of the Cowal peninsula. Built 1812 by the Cumbrae Lighthouse Trust to provide a bearing for Clyde shipping passing N between the Cumbrae and Cloch lights. Tapering cylindrical tower of limewashed droved ashlar. Narrow lancets, some blind. The stair spirals around a hollow circular newel which originally housed weights for the clockwork mechanism of the revolving light. Below the lantern a projecting course and iron brackets support a cast-iron balcony. Originally the diameter of the tower reduced at this point, the balcony being carried on the wallhead, but some time after 1867 the present arrangement was contrived, raising the height of the tower to 19m. above high-water level. The glazed lantern-room, now an electric light, has a metal dome.

Rectangular, single-storey PRINCIPAL KEEPER'S HOUSE, late C19, axially linked N. It replaced the original circular dwelling which, before 1867, embraced the tower eccentrically, touching it tangentially on the S face (raggles for flashings on the W and E sides of the tower can still be seen). Hipped roof, tall octagonal chimneys with moulded copings rising from the piend peaks. To the W, an ASSISTANT KEEPER'S HOUSE. A short distance NE lies HAZEL COTTAGE, mid C19(?), similar in form with hood-moulded windows. All are of droved ashlar, painted white. Also white, but brick, is FOGHORN HOUSE, late C19, a small detached structure built off the rocky foreshore SE of the tower. Its round-arch windows, lattice glazing and dumpy, tower-nave-and-porch symmetry mark it as a chapel: in fact, before its conversion to a dwelling, it housed the foghorn mechanism. Nearby, on the E shore, was the wooden PIER, 1863; only the walled forecourt, curving symmetrically to a pillared gateway, remains.

TOWARD PRIMARY SCHOOL. Dated 1875; by *R.A. Bryden*. Gabled classroom with tall bipartite window and a moulded corbel-stone at the NW corner. Two-storey, three-bay, gabled schoolhouse linked l.

TOWARD QUAY, opposite the gates of Castle Toward (q.v.). Built *c.* 1821. Battered rubble wall on curve with jetty on lee side.

TOWARD SAILING CLUB. Built *c.* 1973. Tan and cream profiled metal (added *c.* 1986), altogether more industrial than nautical. Glazed commodore's eyrie peaks S through roof.

TOWARD CASTLE
500m. SE of Castle Toward

Through the trees, some 200m. across a raised beach, a single stand of rubble wall rears up from a steep motte-like rise, in fact a natural salient of rock. This is the S wall of an otherwise tumbledown tower-house built by the Lamonts, *c.* 1470. Sacked and partially dismantled by the Campbells in 1646, it has remained ruinous, a continuing reluctance to restore motivated perhaps by respect for the Lamont men massacred after the castle's surrender.

The s wall of the TOWER rises through three storeys to a corbelled wallhead. Its W edge is ragged and incomplete but the SE angle is intact, returning N a short distance before it, too, falls in sudden disarray. Two s windows, one lighting what was probably a garderobe recess at first floor, the other opening to a segmentally arched second-floor embrasure, enjoy the view across the Firth to Bute and Cumbrae. Both were altered *c.* 1600 but have all but lost their moulded jambs. Dressed chamfered margins survive on two smaller ground-floor windows and around the round-arched E entrance door, now isolated at first-floor level with no sign of a forestair. Of the interior, little remains; indeed, there is no sense of enclosure for the E, N and W walls have collapsed, much of the rubble falling inwards over the vaults that covered the two ground-floor chambers, making access to this lowest level difficult and dangerous. From the larger of the two vaulted apartments a round-arrissed doorway in the tower's E wall gives on to what may have been a mural stair. A rebated N opening probably gave access to a now-vanished newel-stair, though MacGibbon and Ross suggest that 'It is just possible that this door led into a wing' (1892). The smaller W room, vaulted E–W like its neighbour, was two-storeyed with a joisted floor over a deeper basement. It retains signs of a mural stair in the NW corner. Few clues as to the layout of the upper levels, though a small masonry haunch in the s wall provides proof that the first-floor hall must also have been vaulted, this time in a N–S direction.

Beyond the debris spilling over the lower vestiges of the N wall of the tower-house is the barmkin, an elongated grassy enclosure, *c.* 1600. It is bounded on the W by a long rubble wall running N from the W face of the tower, and on the opposite side by the E RANGE. Set in a slightly oblique relationship with the otherwise rectilineal geometry of the castle yard, this roofless, single-storey, rubble block is a gabled oblong of three apartments, each with ruinous window or door openings, a number of aumbry recesses, and a fireplace. In the s apartment (the kitchen) the fireplace is defined by a wide segmental-arch added parallel to the gable in the early C17 and reconstructed 1972–4. At the opposite end, in the N chamber, the fireplace is original but smaller, with an edge-roll moulding. Between the two, in the hall, the largest of the three spaces, the chimney-breast of a 3m.-wide fireplace projects through the E wall; there are pistol-loops in the ingoes, roll-mouldings on the jambs and a stone scarcement along the back of the recess, but neither lintel nor relieving arch survives.

Some 22m. N, the N RANGE closes the barmkin. It also dates from the beginning of the C17. At its centre, a gatehouse passage, formerly barrel-vaulted but now roofless. Only at its N end, behind the projecting ashlar of the entrance gateway, is there some indication of this construction in the rubble rear-arch formed in the thickness of the wall. The gate itself has a weathered dignity, unexpectedly impressive. Round-arched with a double roll-and-hollow surround and a triple arc of billet moulding under a cable hood, it is lugged l. and r. with three corbel-courses, each double-rolled, under a cavetto cornice. Between gate and W wall is a chamber which probably served as a bake-house or brew-house, roofless and largely unwalled to the S. What lay E of the gate is unclear but there is evidence of a newel-stair at the S end of the E wall of the passageway, pointing to the existence of an attic or garret.

WHITEHOUSE

No more than a brief line of houses along one side of the old west Kintyre road, Whitehouse won its wedge-shaped village green with the realignment of the A83. Some pleasant vernacular cottages.

GARTNAGRENACH FARM, 2.2km. SW of Whitehouse. Two-storey-and-attic gabled dwelling with a conically roofed semicircular tower in front, late C18. Three connected dormers, each gabled, added at the rear later. – 45m. S of the house is a STANDING STONE to which is affixed a SUNDIAL head of late C17 or C18 date.

GLENREASDELL HOUSE, 800m. SE of Whitehouse. Wide-fronted, two-storey harled house; a crude aggregation of ill-fitting bits; part C19, part *c.* 1905. Now flatted.

CILLE BHRIDE, 1.7km. NE of Whitehouse on the slopes of Cnoc na Caorach. Two small enclosures: one of sub-rectangular, round-cornered plan visible in scant rubble wall remains – perhaps a chapel of medieval date; the other, its rubble walls intact, the former burial plot of the Campbells of Stonefield. Surviving memorial stones in the latter suggest a date of *c.* 1790.

ARGYLL: THE ISLES

COLL
(see map p. 501)

A low-lying island NW of Mull, linked to Oban by car-ferry. A moon landscape of weathered rock outcrops in the NE; sandy bays, dunes and machair in the SW. Overpopulation in the 1840s (almost 1,500) led to wholesale emigration. Today fewer than 200 people live on the island.

ACHA
1854

House, school and mill half-way between Arinagour and Crossapol Bay.

ACHA HOUSE. C19. Two-storey-and-attic, harled, gable-ended house with later lower extensions r.

ACHA MILL. C19. L-plan rubble structure. Converted to a dwelling with an arched rubble entrance bridge across the lade.

ARINAGOUR
2257

The island's only village and harbour, founded by Alexander MacLean of Coll at the beginning of the C19. Some good gable-to-gable rows: MAIN STREET, c. 1814, harled or painted rubble cottages on boulder footings. The ISLE OF COLL HOTEL, looking s on to Loch Eatharna, is a double-gabled C19 house, extended in the 1880s and again in 1968; inside, some original timber-lined walls.

PARISH CHURCH. 1907. Lancet Gothic in gneiss rubble. Four buttressed bays; on the E gable, a square tower, crenellated with corner finials. The interior is plain save for a most unusual timber roof. Above collar height the trusses are divided vertically into five cusped openings; below, they are supported tangentially by arch-bracing springing from corbels. In the coomb ceiling of each bay, above a four-centred wall arch, diagonal timber ribs bend upwards from the corbels to meet at the collar, creating vaulted zones the double-curved panels of which are lined, herringbone pattern, with pitch pine boarding. This triumph of joinery is a wholly unexpected delight.

FREE CHURCH. 1884. Skew-gabled with four pointed-arch windows each side. Simple bellcote on E gable.

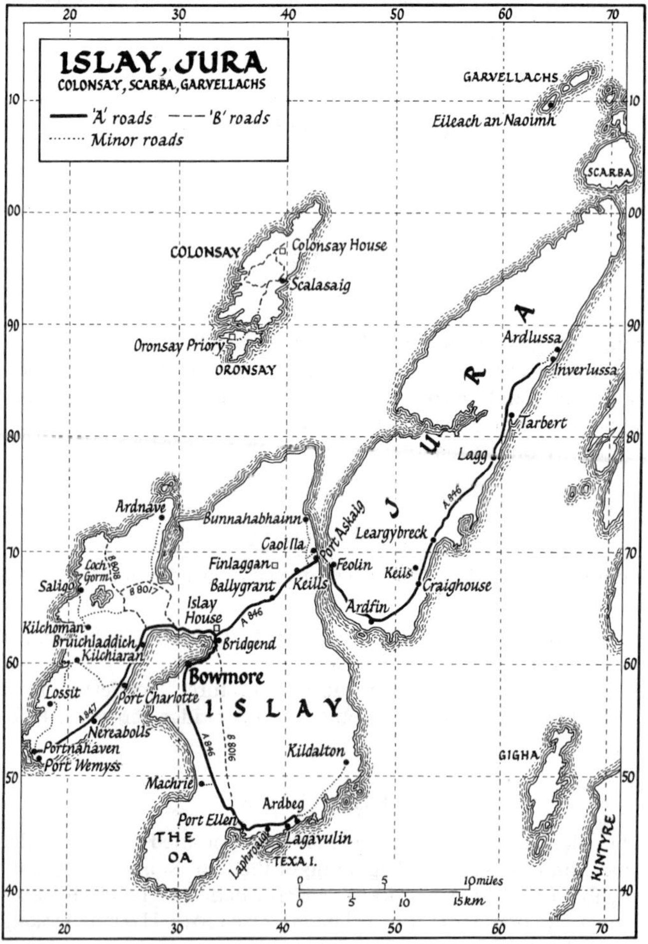

ISLAY, JURA
COLONSAY, SCARBA, GARVELLACHS
'A' roads
'B' roads
Minor roads
GARVELLACHS
Eileach an Naoimh
SCARBA
COLONSAY
Colonsay House
Scalasaig
Oronsay Priory
ORONSAY
J U R A
Ardlussa
Inverlussa
Tarbert
Lagg
A 846
Leargybreck
Keils
Craighouse
Feolin
Ardfin
Port Askaig
Ardnave
Bunnahabhainn
Caol Ila
Finlaggan
Ballygrant
Keills
Loch Gorm
B 8018
B 8017
Saligo
Kilchoman
Bruichladdich
Kilchiaran
Islay House
Bridgend
Bowmore
I S L A Y
Lossit
Port Charlotte
A 847
Nereabolls
Portnahaven
Port Wemyss
A 846
B 8016
Kildalton
Machrie
Ardbeg
Port Ellen
Lagavulin
Laphroaig
TEXA I.
THE OA
GIGHA
KINTYRE
10 miles
15 km

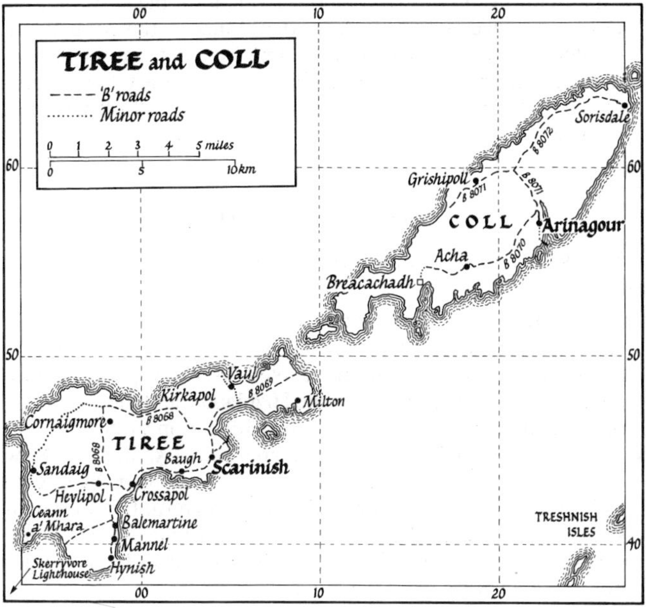
TIREE and COLL
'B' roads
Minor roads
0 1 2 3 4 5 miles
0 5 10 km
00
10
20
60
50
40
Sorisdale
B 8072
Grishipoll
B 8071
COLL
Arinagour
Acha
B 8070
Breacachadh
Vaul
B 8069
Kirkapol
Milton
Cornaigmore
B 8068
TIREE
Baugh
Scarinish
Sandaig
Heylipol
Crossapol
Ceann a' Mhara
Balemartine
Mannel
Hynish
Skerryvore Lighthouse
TRESHNISH ISLES

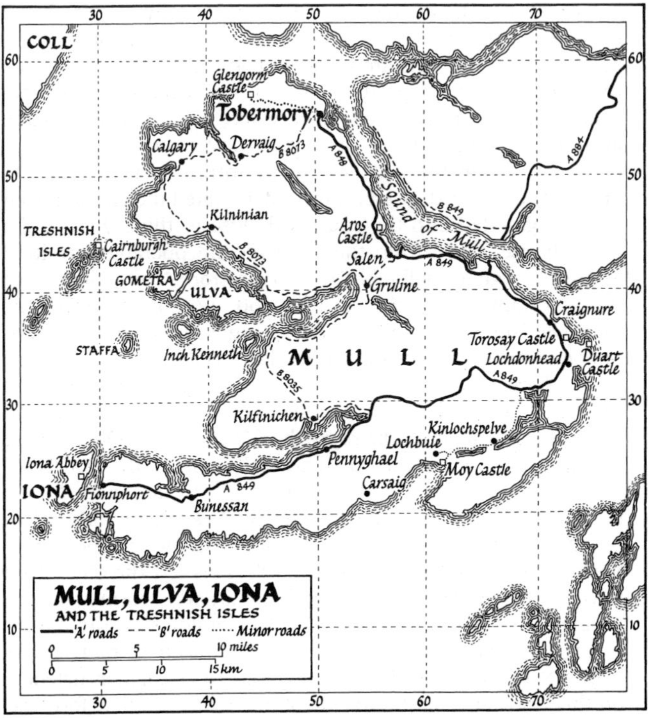
COLL
30
40
50
60
70
Glengorm Castle
Tobermory
Calgary
Dervaig
B 8073
A 848
A 884
Sound of Mull
B 849
Kilninian
TRESHNISH ISLES
Cairnburgh Castle
Aros Castle
Salen
A 849
GOMETRA
ULVA
Gruline
Craignure
STAFFA
Inch Kenneth
MULL
Torosay Castle
Lochdonhead
Duart Castle
B 8035
A849
Kilfinichen
Kinlochspelve
Lochbuie
Iona Abbey
Pennyghael
Moy Castle
IONA
Fionnphort
A 849
Carsaig
Bunessan
MULL, ULVA, IONA
AND THE TRESHNISH ISLES
'A' roads
'B' roads
Minor roads
0 5 10 miles
0 5 10 15 km

PIERS. Below Main Street, the OLD PIER, a rubble jetty, built by 1843, reconstructed 1997. A short distance s, the MID PIER, *c.* 1968, rubble and concrete with steps both sides and a protective wall seaward. 1km. s of the village is the NEW PIER, completed 1987, but extended to provide roll-on roll-off facilities, 1991–2.

BREACACHADH

Two castles and two dune-flanked bays at the sw end of the island.

CROSSAPOL GRAVEYARD, 100m. SE of Crossapol House. Walled enclosure subsiding to the shore below. Among the gravemarkers, an OBELISK set on a plinth: to Neil McLean †1848 'whose memory is savoury throughout the Highlands' and 'his eminently pious, and prudent wife', Catherine McKinnon †1882.

MACLEAN BURIAL GROUND, Crossapol Bay, 1.5km. sw of New Breacachadh Castle. Erected *c.* 1835 by Alexander MacLean, 15th of Coll. Almost square enclosure of high rubble walls with sandstone dressings. Angle buttress turrets frame the castellated wall of the N façade in which blind pointed arches flank a larger pointed-arch entrance. Despoiled interior.

BREACACHADH CASTLE. Tower-house cluster plastered with sandy harl like a heavily iced cake plated on the machair at the head of Loch Breacachadh. Though repeatedly modified, the elements of the rude castle contrived by the MacLeans of Coll between 1430 and 1450 are still identifiable. A four-storey oblong tower-house with a garret chamber set behind the parapet walk. Creating a protected inner space, a curtain wall swung around the s side of the castle from sw corner to NE. And, bulging SE from the wall, a roughly formed drum tower. As originally conceived, two entrances penetrated the curtain: from the E, a gate led into the courtyard close to the E door of the tower-house, while from the sw a second opening permitted access through a small lobby to a single-storey hall built against the s curtain and to the yard beyond. Within the tower the plan was simple: on each level a single chamber with peripheral mural chambers and garderobes. As at Moy Castle, Mull (q.v.), there were no fireplaces. A straight-flight stair rose within the s wall. Towards the end of the C16, as the castle recovered twice from siege and seizure by the MacLeans of Duart, these arrangements were altered. The wall around the courtyard was heightened, with machicolation protection added over the entrances and the level of the yard raised by an infill of boulders and sand. As a result, a new entrance to the tower-house was needed at first-floor level. This led directly into a lower hall from which a turnpike stair, now formed in the SE angle, rose to the parapet-walk. More building occurred early in the C17 when the construction of an artillery battery was begun N of the tower-house. Intended to strengthen defences on this vulnerable landward side of the castle, the new fortification also enclosed late C15 kitchens which, located outside the walls (perhaps to take advantage of spring water), must hitherto have depended upon some form of earth and timber structure for protection. Work on the battery remained unfinished though the tower-house itself was again altered, the parapet and garret being raised and a small SE turret added over the turnpike stair. In the late C17 the single-storey hall built against the S curtain was transformed into a three-storey dwelling-house, the crow-stepped gables of which now appear above the parapets of the outer wall.

With the construction of New Breacachadh (q.v.) in 1750, the old castle was all but abandoned. Some buildings remained occupied; alterations and repairs to the old kitchens were carried out in the C18 and C19. The tower-house was still roofed in 1843. Minor work on the fabric took place 1930–8. In 1961, however, a full programme of restoration was begun under *Ian G. Lindsay*. The rehabilitation of the castle as a residence was continued by *Richard Avery* and completed in 1993.

CROSSAPOL HOUSE, above the W shore of Crossapol Bay. C18. Harled, skew-gabled dwelling with rubble outbuildings.

NEW BREACACHADH CASTLE, 140m. NW of Breacachadh Castle. Built 1750 by Hector MacLean, 13th of Coll; a plain three-storey, hipped-roofed mansion linked S to lower flanking wings by quadrant wings with blind Venetian windows. Harled with sandstone dressings. Visiting in 1773, Dr Johnson found this 'new-built gentleman's house ... a mere tradesman's box'. A fourth storey was added, *c.* 1860, and both the main block and wings remodelled at the eaves with a crenellated parapet and corner bartizans. N porch, late C19; S porch, 1936. To the SW, the two-storey STEADING, late C18 or early C19, has a symmetrical NE front crenellated at the centre and ends, the former carrying a small pyramid-roofed bellcote. A screen wall continues l. to terminate in a fourth crenellated bay. WALLED GARDEN, mid C19, 700m. NE of main house.

GRISHIPOLL

1959

A few houses on the NW side of the island between Arnabost and Ballyhaugh.

GRISHIPOLL HOUSE, 3.7km. NW of Arinagour. Mid C18. Built by Hugh MacLean, 14th of Coll. Now a roofless gable-ended ruin. Harled rubble walls with widely spaced openings. E door has a draw-bar slot; the window above was formerly a door reached by a forestair.

PROJECT TRUST HEBRIDEAN CENTRE, Ballyhaugh. Slate and harl simplicity. Two-storey C19(?) dwelling extended by *Richard Avery*; completed 1992. Additions comprise parallel single-storey wings, double-banked against the gables of the old house and enclosing a paved forecourt. Two of the four wings have half-octagonal ends, two are gabled.

SORISDALE

An all-but-abandoned settlement at the NE end of the island. The remnants of a TOWNSHIP survive. A few rubble cottages, probably early C19: one with a corrugated-iron roof, one with a collapsed thatched roof, and a roofless byre with floor channel. A single small rubble structure retains its stone-loaded thatch.

CHURCH, Killunaig, 2.2km. NE of Arnabost, on the road to Sorisdale. Late medieval remains of the church of St Findoca of Coll. Turf-covered rubble walling sunk in the sand. A few recumbent SLABS, C17 and C18; most illegible.

COLONSAY

A small island lying W of Jura. Car-ferry connection to Oban, Islay and Kennacraig on W Loch Tarbert. Thanks to low numbers and the sympathetic attitude of the MacNeil lairds, the population escaped the clearances of the C19. Today there are fewer than 100 permanent residents.

BAPTIST CHURCH, Kilchattan. Built 1879. Harled, skew-gabled hall with four lintelled windows each side. Gabled SW porch and NE vestry.

BURIAL GROUND, Balaruminmore, 2.8km. SSW of Scalasaig Pier. Semicircular enclosure defined by a low bank. Foundations of small oblong building. Beside this, a railed enclosure in which are two broken, cross-marked STONES, Early Christian.

CHAPEL (Teampull a'Ghlinne), Garvard. C14(?). Ruined oblong, c. 10m. by 6m., built off a plinth in random rubble. W and E gables(?) have gone but the N wall, which incorporates a slit window at its E end, and the W end of the S wall, within which is a lintelled doorway, stand to a 2m. wallhead. Aumbry in NW corner. Some burial cairns(?) lie S.

CHAPEL and BURIAL GROUND (Cill Chaitrìona), Balnahard, at the N end of the island. Overgrown footings of round-cornered rubble cell dedicated to St Catherine of Alexandria. Reputedly the site of a C13 convent. Some RECUMBENT SLABS and a much-worn CRUCIFORM STONE.

OLD PARISH CHURCH, Kilchattan. Late C14. Ruined chapel of St Catán, c. 10m. by 6m., built of rubble boulders and pinnings. N, E and part of the S walls survive to just over 2m. A splayed window may have existed at the centre of the E gable(?); below its inner sill are two aumbries. In the walled BURIAL GROUND, many fragmentary gravemarkers; C19 and C20 headstones.

PARISH CHURCH, Scalasaig. Solid Presbyterian geometry built on a grassy rubble-walled platform, 1801–4; by *Michael Carmichael*. Cement-rendered, piend-roofed kirk lit by two tall round-arch windows E and W and a single lintelled window N and S. Plain porches attached N and S are the remnants of forestairs to former lofts (S forestair removed, 1922). The pedimented E centrepiece carried a tall birdcage belfry with BELL. Below the pediment, a blind oculus above the conical roof of a projecting semicircular vestry. Plain recast interior with diagonally boarded, panelled cam-ceiling. Half-octagon PULPIT centred E in railed podium. Hinged on the rail, a pewter baptismal BASIN.

COLONSAY HOTEL, Scalasaig. Built *c.* 1750; extended S, probably by *Michael Carmichael*, *c.* 1804; and N, *c.* 1890. White-harled, gabled inn. Behind is a detached A-frame chalet block with timber-boarded gables and W-facing terraces separated by cross walls; by *John Fox*, Edinburgh, 1987.

COLONSAY HOUSE (formerly Kiloran House), Kiloran, 2.6km. N of Scalasaig. Begun in the early C18 (1722 is incised under the NW eaves cornice) after the McNeill family had acquired the island estate from the Duke of Argyll. The compact core, harled with plain margins, is readily identified at the centre of the N front; a two-storey, three-bay block with steeply hipped roof; the first classical mansion in Argyll. The hipped dormers, N and S, and the gabled N porch with its Palladian window, date from the first half of the C19 when extensive additions were built. More significantly, this programme of deliberately symmetrical aggrandizement included, on the N, quadrant wings and piended pavilions with opposed, mostly blind, Palladian windows and, on the S, the elongation of the façade, achieved by attaching bow-fronted, single-storey rooms (each having a large Palladian window with intersecting glazing bars) to the W and E gables. Linear service accommodation extended E from the NE pavilion and the SE bow-fronted room, the latter range raised to two storeys and an attic, *c.* 1910, when more offices and shingle-roofed STABLES were added E by the new laird, the 1st Lord Strathcona. The C18 interior has been much altered. Splendid lawns enhance the house's provincial dignity, especially on the N. Exceptional tropical GARDENS. SUNDIAL with moulded pedestal dated 1803; bronze gnomon and plate by *Adie & Son*, Edinburgh. HOME FARM, mid C18(?), with estate workers' HOUSES by *Basil Spence*, *c.* 1935. Also in the grounds, brought from a medieval chapel site at Riasg Buidhe, a CRUCIFORM SLAB, C7 or C8, carved with a fish-tailed cross which has spiral scrolls in the arms and a bearded head at the top.

FORTIFICATION, on an island in Loch an Sgoltaire, 3.2km. N of Scalasaig. Constructed early C17, at the same time as Loch Gorm Castle, Islay (q.v.). Pentagonal *enceinte* with corner bastions reduced to *c.* 1.25m. high. Round-arched N gateway set between drum-bastions. Evident reconstruction. E walling at water's edge. Beyond the curtain on the N, W and S, a masonry kerb marks the shoreline. Inner *enceinte*, *c.* 15m. by 14m. overall, also has angle bastions and stands to 2m. Round-arch N gate and crenellated parapet, probably early C19. Within the inner walls is a piend-roofed SUMMER-HOUSE with a rounded pediment over the N entrance, also C19.

HARBOUR, Scalasaig. Constructed *c.* 1850. Long L-plan pier with curved re-entrant and stair flight of finely jointed masonry, wide landing slip and breakwater of rounded section; designed by Board of Fisheries engineer *Joseph Mitchell*. Pier reconstructed 1965. Long, roll-on, roll-off pier extension in steel and reinforced concrete, 1988.

LORD COLONSAY MONUMENT, on the hilltop overlooking Scalasaig from the S. In memory of Duncan McNeill, 6th of Colonsay (1793–1874). Designed and erected 1879 by *S. McGlashan & Sons*, Edinburgh. Tall obelisk constructed of four pink, Mull granite blocks on a plinth with block pediments and stepped base. It replaced an earlier version destroyed by lightning.

MACHRINS FARM, 2.8km. W of Scalasaig Pier. Early C19 or perhaps earlier. Two-storey, gabled, T-plan farmhouse. U-plan steading with octagonal horse-gang.

MILL, Kiloran, 2.3km. NNW of Scalasaig Pier. C19. Rubble-built, two-storey, L-plan of which only the longer NW arm survives, reconstructed as a dwelling, 1994, with the iron wheel still on the SW gable.

WAR MEMORIAL, Scalasaig. Erected *c.* 1920. Grey granite Celtic cross with interlacing ornament. A mock scroll carved in the boulder base records the names of the fallen.

CAIRN and STANDING STONES, Buaile Riabhach, Scalasaig, 200m. N of Colonsay Hotel. Small D-shaped cairn incorporating two stones in its kerb; one 2.3m. high, the other 1.15m. but leaning.

DUN, Dùnan nan Nighean, 2.2km. NE of Colonsay House. Small D-shaped enclosure on a rocky knoll. E wall very well preserved to four courses. E entrance with three lintel stones over 1.25m.-high opening. Annexe enclosure E.

FORT, Dùn Cholla, 600m. SE of Teampull a'Ghlinne. Rocky site with cliffs on S and W. NE drystone wall reaches 6m. thick with four courses of well-laid outer facing stones to 1.25m. high. NE entrance passage has been reduced in width.

FORT, Dùn Eibhinn, 700m. WNW of Colonsay Hotel. Prominent summit enclosure with drystone remains of inner and outer defences.

FORT, Dùn Gallain, 1.8km. W of Machrins. Oval ring, *c.* 30m. by 20m., with wall preserved on E and S to five courses.

STANDING STONE, 60m. W of Scalasaig farmhouse. Irregularly shaped stone, 2m. high with 2m. base.

STANDING STONES, 'Fingal's Limpet Hammers', Drumclach, 70m. NE of Lower Kilchattan farm. Two stones, 3.1m. and 2.6m. high.

TOWNSHIP, Riasg Buidhe, 2km. NE of Colonsay Hotel. Ruined range of eight dwellings, barns, etc.; the remains of a small C19 fishing community abandoned 1918. No secure evidence survives of a medieval chapel 35m. S, but an Early Christian CRUCIFORM SLAB was removed from the site to Colonsay House in 1870.

GARVELLACHS

A deserted archipelago midway between Jura and Mull. There are four main islands strung out SW–NE; all have steep cliffs falling to the sea along the NW shore. Three (Garbh Eileach, Dùn Chonaill and Eileach an Naoimh) retain evidence of early habitation.

MONASTIC SETTLEMENT, Eileach an Naoimh. Scattered remains of a pre-Norse Early Christian religious community. The island has long been associated with St Brendan 'the Navigator' of Clonfert who may have founded a monastery here *c.* 542; Groome (1883) suggests St Columba re-established the settlement in 560. Most of the small ruinous buildings which survive are gathered in a hollow on the island's summit, but a few are more dispersed. There is a T-shaped boat-landing on the SE shore. From here a gully, crossed successively by three defensive walls, climbs N to the main group. Immediately beyond the opening in the third wall is an underground CELL with two chambers, its use unknown. The outer polygonal chamber, which is roofless, is entered from a flagged path and steps; the small inner chamber, 1.4m. in dia., has a flat ceiling, a sloping floor and an aumbry in the W wall. 5m. N is a roofless CHAPEL, C11 or C12, an oblong cell *c.* 8.5m. by 5.3m. overall. Constructed in clay-mortared masonry with turf-topped flagstone walls standing to *c.* 2.5m. The W doorway is headless. In the E gable, a small lintelled window, to the r. of which internally is a flagstone shelf. The chapel houses a much-worn TAPERED SLAB, C14–C15, carved with a sword and interlace ornament. A short distance SW of the chapel and contiguous with the third wall crossing the gully is the so-called MONASTERY. This comprises a small rectangular ruin aligned NW–SE constructed of flagstone walls, partially rebuilt on the SW and NE, almost 2m. high. Probably a dwelling, it may be medieval in origin (perhaps a priest's house) but association with a C17 or C18 farm is more likely. A small room added to the SE gable and a NE wing forming an L-plan appear to confirm this later date. A curving SE drystone wall, 1859, defines a sheepfold. S of the 'monastery' is what is thought to be a medieval CHURCH. With the exception of a short stretch of its coursed rubble NW wall, only footings remain to define an oblong 10.3m. by 6.4m. overall. An annexe adjoining the NE gable may have been a sacristy or a post-Reformation burial aisle. 30m. SW of the church is a flat, roughly square BURIAL GROUND. It contains four small stone platforms which may mark graves and a sandstone SLAB, Early Christian, incised with a plain cross with expanded terminals. Situated on the E side of the gully is an oblong BARN, late C18 or early C19. In the side walls, which stand to a maximum height of *c.* 1.8m., there are cruck-slots and opposed doorways for winnowing.

40m. N, a drystone KILN, of similar date, preserves its NW gable and, surrounding the platform which houses the kiln's conical bowl, a curved SE wall built into the slope.

The remains of a number of other buildings and enclosures lie somewhat separate from the above group. Of these, two are of considerable antiquity. A double BEEHIVE CELL, Early Christian in date, sits on sloping ground close to the shore 130m. NE of the boat-landing. It has two circular chambers, 4.1m. and 4.8m. in dia., built of thin sandstone slabs forming a figure-of-eight plan. Each space has its own entrance on the S and there is a connecting passage between the two. The larger outer chamber, set at the lower level, is roofless with walling substantially rebuilt in the C18 or C19. The inner cell preserves half of its corbelled dome which has an offset on the outer face suggesting that it may have been turf-covered. Some of the masonry has been consolidated by the *Office of Works* in 1937. 65m. SW of the burial ground on the summit is a small circular enclosure, also Early Christian, defined by a ring of flat kerb-stones and known as EITHNE'S GRAVE, the reputed burial place of St Columba's mother. On one of two upright slabs at the NE edge an equal-armed cross has been cut.

CASTLE, Dùn Chonaill. Strategically located on the sea passage between the Hebrides and Lorn and Mull, the castle may date from the mid C13 though it is first mentioned as a royal strong-hold granted by David II to John I, Lord of the Isles, in 1343. The island is strangely symmetrical in its topography: a 60m.-high, cliff-ringed mass connected to much lower NE and SW knolls by isthmus links formed between deep sea-inlets. The 'great castle of Dunquhonle', as John of Fordun described it in the late C14, occupied the central, flat-topped summit with outer defensive arrangements NE and SW. Scant evidence survives, though it is clear that a curtain wall enclosure of flaggy rubble reinforced the natural strength of the site. Within this perimeter the remains of ten small sub-rectangular buildings are barely discernible. The approach to the fortress climbs through three gateway defences from the boat-landing in the SE inlet at the NE end of the island. Across this inlet are five more small buildings, round-cornered rubble cells.

CRUCK-FRAMED HOUSE, Garbh Eileach. Late C18 or early C19. Clay-mortared rubble house and adjoining barn or byre, roofless and ruinous. Recesses for three cruck-couples in the NW and SE walls of the house. Corn-drying kiln 70m. W, excavated 1972. Rubble walling stands to the height of the kiln-bowl platform.

IONA

An island lying off the W tip of the Ross of Mull, to which it is connected by the ferry to Fionnphort (*see* Mull). Blessed with white sands and turquoise seas and sanctified by its association with St Columba who brought Christianity from Ireland in the C6, it was and is a place of pilgrimage. The village, created by Argyll Estates on the E side of the island in the first decade of the C19, stretches NNE from the jetty, a single-sided street of closely packed, pink granite houses, most now with gabled eaves dormers.

IONA ABBEY
500m. N of the jetty

Restored medieval church and claustral buildings; small by European standards but 'by far the largest and most elaborate ecclesiastical monument of the West Highland area' (RCAHMS Inventory, 1982). Begun by the Benedictines who, supplanting the more ancient Columban monastic community, established themselves here at the start of the C13, building their Abbey on the site of the earlier church. Physical evidence of the Celtic foundation is minimal. Archaeological excavation and field surveys, particularly those carried out in the second half of the C20, have, however, revealed the extent of the monastery vallum. Remains of this substantial ditch with its inner and outer ramparts are visible NNW of the Abbey beyond Burnside Cottage and to the W at Cnoc nan Càrnan. The significant location of three C8 high crosses (*see* below), the survival of a small Early Christian oratory known as 'St Columba's Shrine' absorbed into later restoration (*see* below), and the excavated evidence of several timber buildings, provide some clues as to the configuration of the Columban settlement. But interpretation remains difficult.

The Benedictine church of *c.* 1200 appears to have been cruciform in plan, the N and S transepts arranged with coupled chapels recessed in the E wall. A small detached chapel (now known as the Michael Chapel) standing some 20m. N of the choir may antedate the church or may have been constructed for worship while major building operations continued. Early in the C13 the church was extended E with choir-aisles N and S and an undercroft below. Meanwhile, the cloister ranges (unconventionally developed N of the nave in order to take advantage of a nearby stream) were under construction, the refectory being completed in the last quarter of the C13. A vast extension of the S transept with a three-bay vaulted E aisle was also begun and though this seems to have been quickly aborted it anticipated further changes. By the middle of the C15 the entire S side of the church had been demolished; choir and nave were widened and a new S choir-aisle added. The W end of the older N choir-aisle was removed and the remainder adapted as

c. 1200

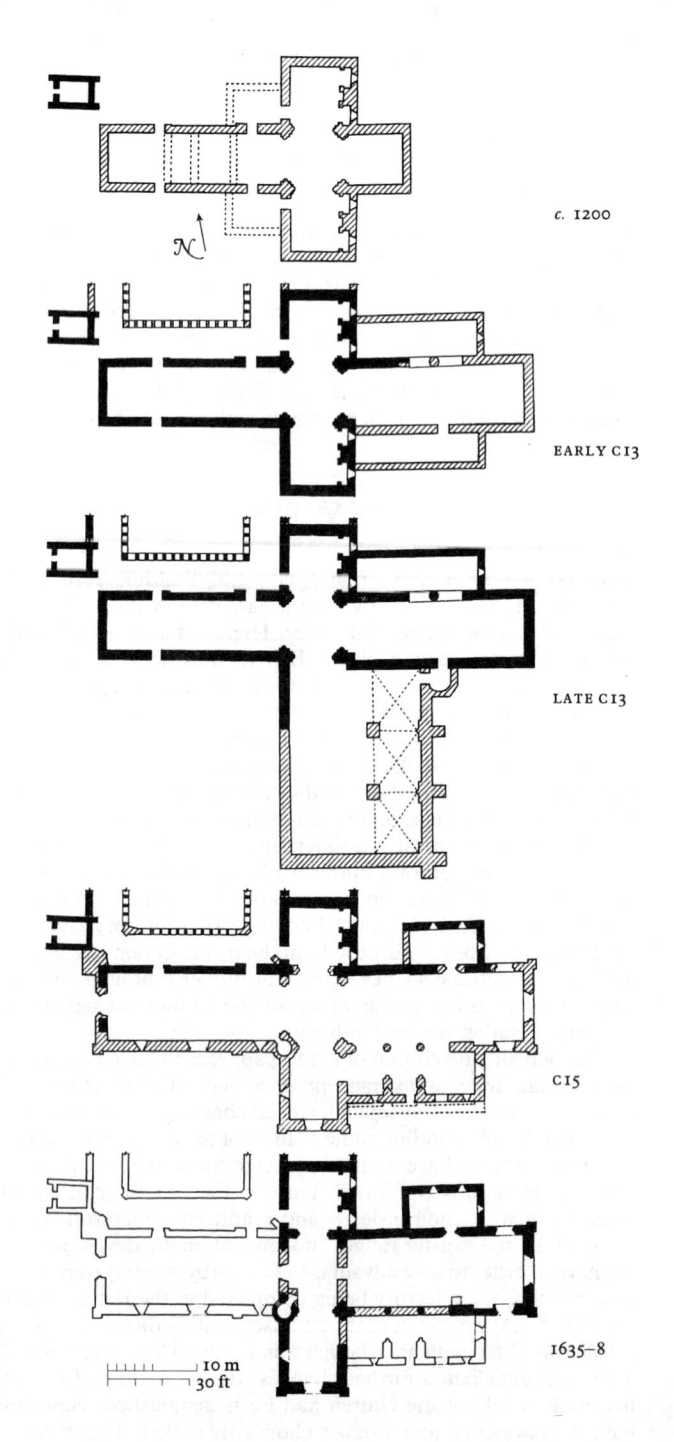

EARLY C13

LATE C13

C15

1635–8

10 m
30 ft

Iona Abbey. Development plans

IONA ABBEY 511

a two-level sacristy. At the W end of the nave a door was formed and the floor level raised to its threshold. A small NW angle-tower closed the re-entrant between the W front and 'St Columba's Shrine'. Behind this junction, crossing the cloister walk diagonally in an intervention repeated at each of its four corners, a round arch and pier replaced the clustered shaft angles built in the C13. Work on the E range of the cloister, where the chapter house was rebuilt, may have extended into the early C16.

Abandoned after the Reformation, the Abbey was briefly conscripted to episcopalian use in 1635 when a royal warrant authorized the Bishop of the Isles to carry out repairs. Only the E end came into use, the crossing and S aisle being blocked with masonry torn from the nave walls. In the 1640s an attempt to make a parish church of the Abbey proved no more favourable to the fabric and the buildings soon succumbed to decay. Antiquarian interest continued, however, and by the latter decades of the C18 Iona's ruins figured prominently in the itinerary of romantic tourism, their attraction doubtless heightened by the collapse of the N transept gable and parts of the E range. A century later, efforts were made to halt disintegration when, between 1874 and 1876, *Robert Rowand Anderson* consolidated the structure for the 8th Duke of Argyll. In 1899 the Duke passed ownership to a body of trustees who engaged *Thomas Ross* and *John Honeyman* to restore the choir, crossing and transepts, 1902–4. In 1908–10, *Peter MacGregor Chalmers* rebuilt the nave. But despite this enthusiastic conservation, a use for the buildings remained elusive; only with the emergence of the Iona Community in 1938 did the Abbey's future become secure. Work recommenced in 1939 under *Ian G. Lindsay* who, developing proposals prepared by *Reginald Fairlie* in 1931, began the reconstruction of the monastic buildings. By 1965 the restoration was largely complete.

Set apart from the village across the Reilig Odhráin (q.v.) and Liana Mhor, the restored Abbey's relationship with the landscape is at first disconcertingly sanitized. The low, rubble-wall perimeter of the precinct may be too precise, the grassed curtilage too smart, the junction of masonry and ground too abrupt and clinical, the planar clarity of roofs and walls perhaps too adroitly crafted to convince. So carefully has rehabilitation been effected, particularly in the latter-day use of the same quarries on Iona and Mull which provided the Torridonian flagstone, pink granite and schist slates for the C15 enlargement of the Abbey, that antiquity seems compromised. It takes a little time to dispel the romantic dream. For this is no ruin merely arrested in its decay to charm or intrigue the tourist but a working church restored to worship and religious study, brought back to the island, however improbable as it may seem, by C20 faith.

DESCRIPTION

The oldest part of the Abbey is the small cell known, with no archaeological credibility, as ST COLUMBA'S SHRINE. Substantially rebuilt and roofed, its restoration was completed by *Lindsay* in 1962. A diminutive round-arched doorway, shadowed by a replica of St John's Cross (*see* below), opens only a few metres to the l. of the main W entrance to the church. Flanking the door, vestigial *antae* dressed with sandstone (short projections of the lateral walls characteristic of early Irish churches) indicate a C9 or C10 date. Originally freestanding, it was later incorporated against the tower raised in the C15 at the NW corner of the nave. This latter structure, a quoinstone of which is carved with a consecration cross, survives in part, its curtailed height only a little higher than the line of a stringcourse dividing the lower medieval masonry of the W front of the NAVE from later restoration by *Chalmers*. The main door, a hooded pointed-arch with three roll-and-hollow orders on the jambs, is C15 work, as is the SW clasping buttress. But above, the fine five-light window, a splendid concatenation of trefoil-headed windows in round-arched embrasures for which St Machar's Cathedral in Aberdeen may have provided inspiration, the boldly horizontal wallhead advancing on its corbelcourse, and the steep gable behind are all by Chalmers. On the S wall, below the restored return of the corbelled wallhead, the fusion of C20 and late C15 rubble is all but invisible. Four buttresses with widely splayed plinths define the original structural bays. The inner pair are splayed back into the wall a short distance above the plinth: over one, Chalmers built up around a narrow hooded lancet; above the other, he completed a three-light traceried window, also hooded, similar to the C15 window on the N side of the presbytery. The N wall, wholly rebuilt from footings, repeats the corbelled wallhead and incorporates four, more regularly spaced, round-arched, clearstorey windows with deeply splayed inner embrasures. Three are trefoil-headed lights; the fourth, closest to the crossing, a plain two-light opening.

The S TRANSEPT is solidly C15. Wallhead parapets carried on corbelcourses recur, but only on the W and E walls, giving the S gable a slightly lugged look. Half-height buttresses, similar to those of the nave, clasp the corners of the gable. The three-light S window, set in a hooded, pointed-arch opening, has restored tracery, 1875, based on the C15 window on the S side of the presbytery. Below the sill, a stunted buttress, rising like its neighbours from a widely splayed plinth. The N TRANSEPT is equally solid, embedded between the church and the monastic buildings which flank the E side of the cloister. But some of the stonework is older. For though the N gable, which had fallen in the late C18, was substantially rebuilt in 1904, much of the lower masonry, especially below the round-arched windows in the E wall, is of early C13 date. Moreover, both E and W walls retain overhanging eaves, unlike the parapeted C15 treatment seen elsewhere in the church.

The CHOIR, largely rebuilt in the second half of the C15, seems to reflect the nave. The lengths are almost identical. The same corbelled parapets mark the N and S wallheads. The same splay-based buttresses grip the angles of the E gable or are weathered back below the sills of the presbytery windows. Clearstorey windows are again small. Unlike the aisleless nave, however, the choir must assimilate lower lean-to accommodation on both the N and S. N is the sacristy, the truncated remains of the early C13 aisle, as raggles in the tower re-entrant betray. At the NE angle, a triple-roll quoin. In the E wall, an unusual triangular-headed window over a narrower lintelled opening. The C15 S aisle, much restored in 1904, extends E from the S transept. Tracery from the original E window is now at St Conan's Church, Lochawe (q.v.), replaced under the original stilted pointed-arch hood-moulding by a six-spoked wheel of trefoils over two cusped lower lights. Both sacristy and S aisle stop short of the main E gable, an astute decision which not only permits the presbytery to be lit by three tall, hooded, pointed-arch windows each with fine flamboyant tracery, partly restored in 1874–5 by *Anderson*, but also allows the emergent choir to assert its architectural affinities with the nave.

This balanced prismatic clarity is reinforced over the crossing where the oblique roof planes of nave, choir and transepts abut the flat faces of the late C15 square TOWER. Just above the ridge of nave and choir, a roll-moulded stringcourse crosses each side. At the angles, triple-roll quoinstones rise to the familiar corbelled wallhead. Centred above the ridges are four hooded, lintelled openings to the bell-chamber. Three, approximately square, are elaborately traceried: the E filled with a grid of ogival quatrefoils, the W with a regular pattern of circled quatrefoils, the S with a circle of cusped daggers rotated around a small hexagonal centre. On the N, the opening is narrower: Y-tracery in a pointed arch with blind spandrels. Above these belfry grids a number of smaller openings give access to a doocot. At the top of the tower the wallhead coping-stone, laid in 1904 when the parapet-walks were renewed, is as relentlessly horizontal as those over the parapets fronting the gutters below. Restoration of the tower's saddle-back roof was long delayed. Despite Ian Lindsay's 1946 recommendation that it 'would undoubtedly add to the dignity of the tower', it took fifty years more before the caphouse was finally reconstructed by *John Renshaw*, 1996, with the S gable finial cross by *Graciela Ainsworth*. The tower BELL, cast in 1931 by *John Taylor & Co.*, Loughborough.

INTERIOR. Through the W door a timber-framed lobby with Perp tracery opens l. and r. into the reconstructed nave. Everything (with the exception of a few stretches of low-level masonry) is the work of *Chalmers*, 1910. In the NW corner, a stair ascends to a small barrel-vaulted chamber. The paved floor of the nave is at first C20 but soon drops five steps to C15 polygonal flagging. At this lower level, at each end of the N wall, round-arched doorways lead to the cloister walk. The walls are bare rubble save for dressed stone around the openings. A timber ceiling, boarded above the ties, conceals the roof construction, though twelve bays of hefty curved struts drop below to corbelstones. Below the C15 tower, a high pointed arch with two broad chamfers opens into the crossing. This is repeated over the opening to the S transept while on the N and E sides of the crossing the arch-heads have filleted-roll-and-hollow mouldings. Over the N arch the dressed stone profile of the C13 church's crossing arch survives; evidently the lower narrower opening was formed in the C15 to counteract settlement. It appears that this rebuilding of the crossing, coincident with the widening of nave and choir to the S, entailed the construction of the N and E arches before those on the S and W. This sequence is suggested not only by the differing arch-head mouldings but also by the detail below, for though all four arches rest on cluster piers of nook-shafts, the capitals and bases of those on the N and E are wrought in greater detail. Besides the familiar leaf and plant-scroll ornament, these carvings depict a wonderful variety of composite beasts and figural sequences; biblical allusions dominate but some compositions suggest genre scenes. On the capital of the W respond of the N arch, the Temptation of Adam and Eve. On the S respond of the E arch, an inscription in Lombardic letters, †DONALDUS O [BROL/CHAN F] ECIT HOC OPUS, records the name of the C15 master-mason, *Donald O Brolchán*.

As the floor level drops one, then two, steps from nave into crossing, the paving changes to smooth regular sandstone. To the l., two steps up, is the N transept, partially screened by a simple timber partition, 1956. On its E wall, surviving from the church of *c.* 1200, a much-weathered arcade of three round arches: a central niche, in which a sandstone figure once stood, flanked by two wider arches on nook-shafts opening into chapels within the thickness of the wall, each with its own small, round-headed window. At the S end of the W wall, a round-headed C15 door with a continuous roll-and-hollow moulding in jambs and arch, opens to the cloister. To its r., a stone stairway, 1954, located in the likely position of the medieval night stair, rises into the E range. In the rebuilt N gable is the rose window inserted by *Honeyman*, 1904–5, blocked on the outside by later reconstruction. Vestigial shafts in the NW and NE angles, the former destroyed in 1875, seem to indicate a C13 intention to vault the transept, especially as the height of their capitals coincides with those of the earlier crossing arch (*see* above), but this was never accomplished and the present roof is of timber. No such ambitions were entertained in the C15 S transept. Here the rough rubble walls support a modern, three-bay, trussed roof with arch braces springing from corbelstones. In the E wall, a boldly moulded semicircular archway set on dissimilar jambs (the S bearing a consecration cross) leads into the S choir aisle.

If it is possible to sense the religious interdependence of austerity and certainty in the stark simplicities of nave and transepts, then the inner complexities of the choir seem to bespeak a less solid, less rudely assured faith; the architecture is enigmatic, it betrays both conviction and equivocation, there is at once more sophistication and more doubt. This is particularly evident in the N wall where disturbing solid-to-void relationships result from successive phases of reconstruction. The oldest masonry, *c.* 1200, is at the W end: *c.* 4m. high, its extent is marked by the line of the original floor level 400m. above the present floor and, more clearly, by an abruptly terminated stringcourse. Above this, rising to the clearstorey sills but dipping below the three-light window at the E end, the wall is C13, while its completion to the wallhead dates from the C15. At the centre of the wall, a short length of scarcement indicates the level of the presbytery after the choir was extended E and raised over an undercroft in the early C13. This explains much: the elevation of the arcade, left at its present otherwise puzzling height when the choir floor was lowered during the extensive C15 rebuilding; the lower, cusp-headed doorway intruding into the arcade, a C15 conversion of an earlier opening, doubtless associated with the undercroft, to link the choir with the sacristy created in the curtailment of the N choir-aisle; and, to the r. of the arcade, the partial survival of a stepping stringcourse which must have risen over a former window in the N wall. The C13 arcade, blocked when the sacristy was formed, was opened and restored in 1904. Its two two-centred arches have two orders of keeled edge-rolls with flanking dog-tooth ornament repeated on the soffit, all much renewed. The central column is circular, the capital carved with broad leaves, the abacus octagonal. The lower door, roundheaded with inner cusping, has shafted jambs bearing capitals of foliated ornament. In the sacristy, E of this doorway, a damaged piscina. Above the arcade, the three clearstorey windows, all with deeply splayed reveals, are positioned within the spandrel zones, an aspect of design which, like the stepping stringcourse, can also be found in the Nunnery (q.v.).

This same relationship recurs on the S wall, though the S arcade has three (not two) bays and, being part of the changes made in the second half of the C15, opens directly into the choir. The roll-and-hollow moulded arches, more pointed than those of the N arcade, spring from heavy circular columns whose capitals are ringed with a variety of carved foliated ornament, fabulous animals and birds, and figural scenes which include John the Baptist, the Virgin and Child enthroned among angels, and the Crucifixion. Behind the capitals leans a 'primitive system of internal arches' (RCAHMS Inventory, 1982) buttressing the wall above the arcade to a degree which scarcely seems

Iona Abbey, capitals of south choir arcade

justified. These crude half-arches, which have boldly chamfered sandstone voussoirs, carry rubble walls up to the lean-to roof. At the E end of the aisle, below the window, a piscina bowl carved with oak leaves indicates the location of a medieval altar.

After a single step down from the crossing to the choir, three widely spaced steps up punctuate the approach to the sanctuary. The sills of the three tall presbytery windows are linked by a moulded stringcourse which jumps to abacus height at the S arcade. On the S wall it is interrupted by the sedilia; three hooded, pointed-arch recesses linked over a continuous bench seat, each with inner ogee cusping, the centre arch carried on foliated bell-capitals on carved corbelled brackets (W restored, C20). To the l., a canopied piscina, much degraded. Paving-slabs, thought by Honeyman to be C17 when relaid in the sanctuary, may well be medieval; W of the sacristy door they are C20. The seven-bay roof, by *Ross*, 1902, is carried on modern corbelstones by arch-braced trusses which have cusped gaps separating seven vertical struts above the main ties; following Anderson's consolidation of the fabric in the late C19, this re-roofing of the choir began the modern restoration of the Abbey.

FURNISHINGS by *Peter MacGregor Chalmers*, installed c. 1910. – COMMUNION TABLE of Iona marble; vertical panels of cusped arches with delicately traceried heads. – Oak CHOIR STALLS ranked l. and r. – At the crossing, oak LECTERN and CHAIR carved with Gothic detail, linenfold, vines and figural forms. – At the W end of the nave, a hefty sandstone FONT carried on a white marble pedestal and four green marble colonnettes; convex outer surfaces of the massive bowl decoratively carved. – A bronze SCREEN at the S transept incorporates the arms and motto of the Dukes of Argyll (*see* Monuments below).

STAINED GLASS. Surprisingly spare. In the N clearstorey, SS Columba, Bride and Patrick by *Douglas Strachan*, 1939. – St Columba again in the S window of the N transept, by *William Wilson*, 1965. Window in the S gable of the caphouse by *Patrick Ross Smith*, 1997.

MONUMENTS. Lying on the S side of the presbytery, a headless EFFIGY in Carsaig sandstone; carved in full Eucharistic vestments, it is probably Dominic, Abbot of Iona, 1421–*c.* 1425. – Opposite, on the N, a similar EFFIGY, identified by its incised inscription in Lombardic capitals as John MacKinnon, Abbot of Iona, 1467–*c.* 1498. Set on a base-slab raised on four supporting lions (one original), it was restored by *John Honeyman*, 1904. – Laid at the centre of the presbytery floor is a matrix-slab of Tournai marble from which a monumental BRASS showing the outline of a man in armour has been removed. Stylistically similar to Flemish brasses, it can be dated to the second half of the C14 and probably depicts a MacLean of Duart. – In the choir floor, a worn and damaged SLAB showing a man wearing a bascinet set above a pattern of intertwined plant stems emanating from the tails and legs of two opposed animals; Loch Awe school, C14–C15. – In the S transept, behind a bronze screen (*see above*), the white Carrara marble EFFIGIES of the 8th Duke of Argyll †1900 and his third wife, Ina, †1925. Both figures by *Sir George Frampton*; the Duke, who is buried at Kilmun (q.v.), carved 1908 (installed 1912), the Duchess later.

CONVENTUAL BUILDINGS. The restoration of the Abbey's monastic buildings, which lay in ruins until World War II, is almost entirely the achievement of *Ian G. Lindsay*. Fragments of the CLOISTER arcading were identified during Anderson's consolidation in 1875–6 and again when Honeyman undertook restoration in 1904, but it was not until 1921 that the *Office of Works* re-used this original material in rebuilding two arches at the N end of the W arcade. In 1959 Lindsay reconstructed the whole cloister, basing his design on the accumulated knowledge of the early C13 arcading. On a low plinth wall on double bases, coupled octagonal shafts with a pronounced entasis and plain capitals carry two-centre arches strongly moulded on the inner side. Original fragments incorporated show that the capitals were variously carved with leaf ornament and the mouldings on the arcading separated by bands of dog-tooth. At the corners, Lindsay retained the solid piers introduced in the late C15 to carry diagonal arches across the cloister walk, even though there was evidence to show that a lighter four-column cluster had been adopted in the C13. The lean-to roof is stiffened by diagonal struts and collars. – A BELL, named Anna, bearing a Flemish inscription which records that it was cast by *Peter van den Ghein* in 1540, hangs at the N end of the W wall. – At the centre of the garth is a bronze SCULPTURE, 'The Descent of the Spirit', by the Lithuanian *Jacques Lipchitz*, 1959.

Lindsay's reconstruction had begun in 1938 with the E RANGE which ran N, continuing the width of the N transept. The C13 W wall then stood to the wallhead, the E wall was reduced to a few courses or less, while two transverse C15 walls, which projected beyond the E wall in very roughly parallel alignment to house the gabled chapter house, though in disrepair were sufficiently intact to guide the course of restoration. At ground level the range accommodates a small chamber with fireplace, a late C15 or early C16 conversion of the original slype passage adjacent to the N gable of the N transept, the vestibule of the CHAPTER HOUSE, and a room to the N of this. Above is the DORMITORY, 1953–4, and, over the chapter house, a library with timber-panelled walls and a segmental ceiling, 1938–40. The vestibule is entered from the cloister walk through a hooded, round-headed doorway, C15, with roll-and-hollow moulded jambs run directly into the arch-head. The threshold lies below the cloister floor but four steps above the inner level. A double archway, springing from corbels on the side walls to a central column, separates the vestibule from the chapter house. Filleted-roll-and-hollow mouldings in the arches with rows of dog-tooth. Varied leaf ornament on the capital and corbels. In the chapter house, which is rectangular in plan, four round-headed bench-seat recesses in the N and S walls. Pointed-arch E window with Y-tracery. Segmental barrel-vault.

The N RANGE, restored 1942–9, comprises an undercroft, now serving as a shop, and, above, the refectory. In the buttressed N wall, late C13, lancets and Y-tracery windows renewed by *Anderson*, 1875, and a small gabled projection at the E end marking the position of the reader's pulpit. The S wall, C13, must at first have been no more than a screen to the cloister. At the W end of this wall, the shop is entered tightly through the abutment of the diagonal arch added in the C15 when the dimensions of the cloister were increased. Adjacent is a small late C13 doorway, blocked, but originally leading to a timber stair which rose to the upper floor. Access is now by the former stone stair to the dormitory entered at the NE corner of the cloister. The REFECTORY is a large space with a semicircular timber-boarded ceiling, below which three roof ties are exposed. At the W end, a small gallery has been inserted over a timber screen fronting the servery area. At the E end of the N wall is the reader's pulpit, lit by a lancet and reached by mural steps.

The W RANGE, completed to Lindsay's design in 1965, has no medieval legitimacy as a restoration. Foundations, exposed 1874–5, have not been securely identified and were in any case not extensive. Nevertheless, this two-storey-and-attic, skew-gabled, rubble-built block effectively closes the W side of the claustral group and, through a round-arch W doorway, marks the entry to the Abbey's living quarters and cloister. It houses administrative offices, kitchens and residential accommodation.

To the N of the E range is what was the REREDORTER, restored 1942–4, the Abbey's latrine-block, located here at the closest point to the stream whose existence had determined the siting of the monastic buildings N of the church. The original C13 drainage channel can be seen. A narrow link connects with the N gable of the E range. Together these buildings now serve as the caretaker's house, 1950. Over a door at the N end of the E wall, a TABLET records this restoration and honours Revd Donald Macleod whose fund-raising efforts 'rescued the Abbey from ruin' in 1905. Nearby is a second stone TABLET carved with a flying bird, the word SANCTUARY, the date 1956, and initials MRC. The ABBOT'S HOUSE, C13(?), which connects to the S end of the W wall of the reredorter, had its own garderobe arrangements on the N wall and probably housed a hall at the upper level; it was restored as a laundry and residential accommodation in 1956–7.

A short distance E of the N end of the E range is the freestanding, skew-gabled MICHAEL CHAPEL, late C12 or early C13. The name dates from the 1959–61 restoration, but a C16 reference to a St Michael burial-aisle on Iona may validate the dedication. Interestingly, the chapel is, unlike the church, orientated to the E. What Anderson's consolidation of the rubble walling had begun in 1875, Lindsay completed. Round-headed N door widened by removal of innermost roll-moulded jamb. Boarded ceiling follows an elliptical section. Plastered walls and boarded dado. Stone-flagged floor rises one step at E end. In the E gable, a pointed-arch window with Y-tracery: l., a timber-lined aumbry;

r., a lamp-bracket corbel. Bench seating with individual divisions along N and S walls. At the W end, a plain timber PULPIT with panelled back and sounding board.

Some 13m. N of the Michael Chapel and parallel to it is the Abbey's putative INFIRMARY, a long rubble building with tifted gables. Until its restoration, 1964, the walls stood little more than 0.5m. Only the threshold of the S door is medieval. Lintelled windows with chamfered rybats. Collar-roof, part attic. The building now serves as the Abbey's Museum and houses a vast collection of architectural fragments and carved stones brought here from the Reilig Odhráin, Nunnery, St Oran's Chapel and Abbey. Incised crosses, relief crosses, ringed crosses, cross-slabs, cross-bases, cruciform stones, shrine-posts, grave-slabs, etc., are exhibited. – Pride of place is given to the C8 St John Cross (*see* High Crosses below), the surviving parts of which have been re-assembled on a special frame structure since 1990. – Fragments of the St Oran Cross and St Matthew Cross (*see* below) also on display. – There are ten funerary EFFIGIES. Most are of men in armour carved in high relief, Iona school, C14–C15. – One with an inscription to Gilbride MacKinnon. – Another recording the name of the mason, *Mael-Sechlainn O Cuinn*. – Less deeply cut and more bookish in design, a partial slab depicting Anna MacLean, prioress of the Nunnery, †1543; Oronsay school, C16. – Numerous TAPERED SLABS carved with the usual plant scrolls, plaitwork, swords, galleys, etc. – One, Iona school, C14–C15, is carved with intertwined stems and leaves, a West Highland galley and, at the top, a foliated cross recalling that on the back of the late C14 Campbeltown Cross (q.v.). – On a second, similar in provenance, a man on horseback rides over a casket containing a kneeling woman superimposed on the familiar sword motif. – On a third, in which a galley sits on four small animals resting on a sea of scrollwork, a Latin inscription to Colum, a chief of the MacLeods of Lewis; Iona school, early C16. – Another, not tapered but again Iona school, early C16, is divided into four foliated crosses bordering which is an inscription to John, Hugo, Patrick and 'another Hugo' [Campbell], all priors at Iona. – From the S choir-aisle of the Abbey, a reconstructed stone with two canopied armour-clad figures over a galley and foliated cross, inscribed to John MacIan †*c.* 1518; Oronsay school, 1500–9.

CLADH AN DISIRT (Burial Ground of the Hermitage), 400m. NE of the Abbey. Barely discernible footings of a small rectangular chapel, possibly C12. Close to the SW corner are two granite 'gateposts' marking what must have been the entrance to some kind of enclosure.

HIGH CROSSES

In all, the remains of fourteen freestanding crosses and eight cross-bases, both solid and composite, are known from the Early Christian period (most housed in the Abbey Museum). Evidently the production of these sacred objects continued at Iona from the c8 until the c10, and perhaps even later. Three crosses from the second half of the c8 survive in whole or in part. Though each differs in design, they share certain stylistic qualities, notably a predilection for 'bird's nest' bossing and granulation derived from Hiberno-Saxon jewellery and manuscript arts and tentatively identified as the work of a group of itinerant Pictish stone-carvers. Of a fourth, decidedly Irish in character and dated to the c9 or early c10, there are but fragmentary remains. All are associated with the island's early monastery. Their designations to SS Oran, John, Martin and Matthew are traditional but by no means sure; it is possible that any one 'could originally have been set up in honour of St Columba or St Adomnán, and there are also cross-bases lacking their crosses, which might have been similarly dedicated' (Ritchie, 1997).

MACLEAN'S CROSS. Monolithic freestanding cross, 3.15m., 40m. SSE of the Parish Church. Medieval in date, not Early Christian, stylistic affinity with the MacMillan Cross at Kilmory Knap (q.v.) indicating a late c15, Iona school, provenance. Disc-headed with short lateral arms, carved on both faces with intertwined stems and plaitwork. A crucifed Christ emerges in relief in the W disc.

ST JOHN'S CROSS. Mid to late c8. A post-tensioned concrete replica stands 11.6m. NW of the Abbey's W door; artistic supervision by *John Laurie*, engineer *John R. Scott*. It sits in a masonry box-base, still largely original. Raised in 1970 to replace the original which, already patched together with concrete in 1927 and twice blown down in the 1950s, has, since 1990, been imaginatively re-assembled in the Abbey Museum. Standing 5.3m. with an arm span of 2.2m., stability has always been a problem. At an early date, in an effort to counteract this weakness, the cross's mortice-and-tenon construction was adapted to incorporate four curved stones forming an open ring around the armpitted centre. A surviving fragment is mica-schist from the Ross of Mull, unlike the shaft and arms which are of a greenish chlorite-schist probably from Loch Sween. Reduced to several broken pieces but splendidly displayed, the cross exhibits a rich texture of 'bird's nest' bossing, spirals and diaper patterning. At the centre, E face, is a single large boss surrounded by a border of smaller nodules; on the W face, circled by a band of interlacing, a round recess intended to receive a bronze(?) inset.

see fig. p. 27

ST MARTIN'S CROSS. Mid to late c8. Best preserved but least ambitious in dimension. Carved from a single piece of grey Argyll epidiorite. Located on a solid base of Ross of Mull granite in its original position 21m. W of the SW corner of the Abbey nave, it stands 4.3m. with a span of 1.19m. Slots cut in the peculiarly short side-arms may have held metal panels broadening the horizontal dimension, 'though the limited projection of the side-arms is a common feature of Irish crosses' (RCAHMS Inventory, 1982). Ringed and armpitted, the cross is carved with boss and serpent motifs, though without the delicacy of

see fig. p. 27

detail seen in those dedicated to St Oran and St John. Four large bosses surround a particularly bulbous one at the centre of the E face. On the W face, the carving is predominantly figural: within a ring at the centre, the Virgin and Child and four very small angels; on the arms, lion-like animals; on the upper shaft, four Old Testament dramas and, at its base, traces of an inscription, now illegible.

ST MATTHEW'S CROSS. C9 or early C10. Superimposed scenes similar to those on the St Martin Cross evidently appeared on this later monolithic shaft. A few broken pieces are now in the Abbey Museum. Severe weathering has affected the Colonsay(?) sandstone and only one group on the E face, The Temptation of Adam and Eve, can be recognized. Fragmentary evidence suggests that this was a ringed cross, at least 2.7m. high, set into the socket of its solid granite base.

ST ORAN'S CROSS. Mid to late C8. Fragments housed in St Oran's Chapel (q.v.) in the C19, and more recently in St Ronan's Church, are now in the Abbey (*see* Infirmary above); enough to show that it was constructed in three pieces of Ross of Mull mica-schist. The transom, 1.99m. wide, is mortised to receive the tenoned shaft and upper arm. There is no ring around the cross but curved armpits are formed. At these constrictions, small panels of figural carving can be distinguished, especially on the face which preserves the better decorative evidence. At the top of the shaft is a tightly packed group depicting the Virgin and Child flanked by angels, though above this the treatment at the centre of the transom is indistinct. In the shaft and arms, a texture of varied bossing laced with C-spirals at the extremities.

NUNNERY

Well-tended remains of church and conventual buildings established as an Augustinian foundation *c.* 1200: one of the best-preserved medieval nunneries in the British Isles. Unlike the Abbey (q.v.), the layout is conventional with the cloister garth lying on the SW side of the church. Constructed in very varied rubble masonry, the ruins are considerable and much survives from the original building period. The church nave and chancel, the N aisle with its chapel, and the E range in which the chapter house was located, all date from the early C13. S and W claustral ranges were reconstructed at the end of the C15 when accommodation was increased and the cloister enlarged. Abandoned following the religious reforms of the C16, the buildings became ruinous. By the late C18 what remained was largely what stands today. In 1822–3 part of the chancel vault fell; ten years later it collapsed completely. Repairs and consolidation were carried out under *Robert Rowand Anderson*, 1874–5, and in 1917 *Peter MacGregor Chalmers* envisaged a major restoration, though the resultant works were limited to the N chapel, sacristy and cloister garden.

The CHURCH has a simple rectilinear plan of orthodox orientation. The nave opens N through three round-arch bays into a

- EARLY C13
- c. 1500
- C19 AND LATER

Aisle

Nave

Cloister

Chapter-house

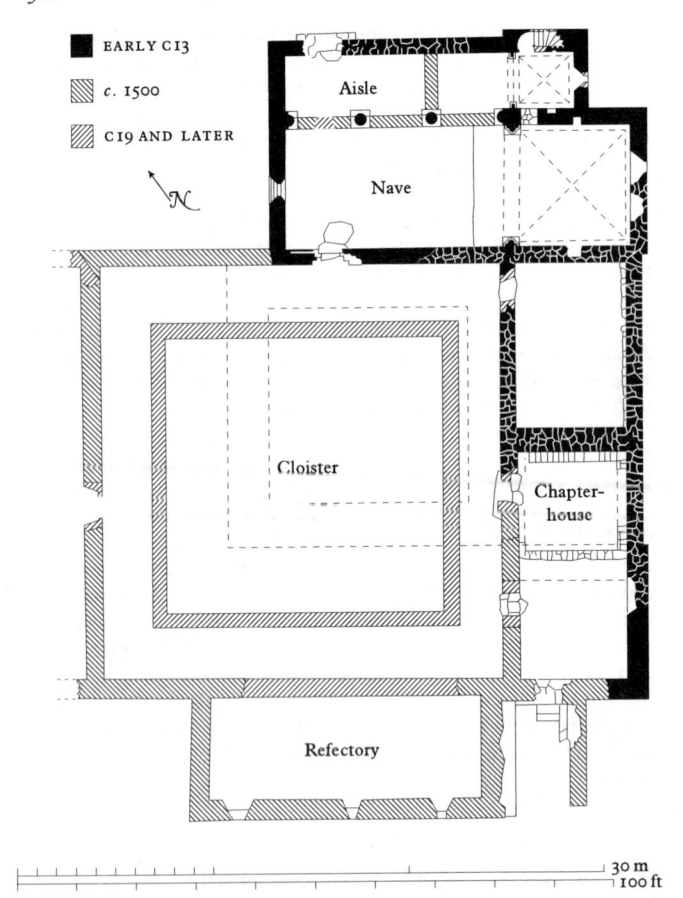

Refectory

Iona Nunnery

narrower parallel aisle. Nave and N aisle maintain their width E into chancel and chapel, both of which were originally roofed by square quadripartite ribbed vaults, though only the chapel vault, which supports an upper chamber, survives. The W gable to nave and aisle is entire, reaching a height of 11.6m. to the apex. It has two superimposed single-light, round-arched windows: the lower and larger with splayed ingoes inside and outside, the latter rebated and moulded on arch-head, jambs and sill with two bands of hollow chamfer; the upper and smaller, also rebated outside, deeply splayed to the inside face only. A hood-moulding over the lower window crosses the gable as a stringcourse, returning to the N and S walls, where it evidently acted as a weather-table over the lean-to roofs of the N aisle and N cloister walk. On the inner face, on each side of the upper gable window, are wide lintelled recesses which may have accommodated timbering associated with a late medieval belfry structure.

Over the lower window, the outer hood-moulding is reflected, this time descending l. and r. in a series of steps to the height of the capitals of the N arcade (*see* Iona Abbey, N choir-wall and transept). These capitals, carved with animal forms over the circular W and E responds and scalloped over the piers, carry abaci which share the moulded profile of the stepping string-course. The arches have a broad inner roll with chamfered bands. The arcade, however, is walled up, blocked by rubble masonry in the late medieval period. Some of this infill has been removed, but not in the W arch where socket-holes betray the former existence of a gallery, and there is evidence of a doorway which would have connected with the main entrance to the church on the N side of the N aisle. Above the arcade, the N wall of the nave rises to the wallhead. Two round-arch clearstorey windows, similar to that in the upper W gable, are centred on the piers (a relationship seen at Brechin Cathedral and Crail Parish Church, both C13, and perhaps more significantly to be found in several C12 and C13 Irish churches).

Except at its W and E ends, the N wall of the aisle has been reduced to a few courses above ground level. Little remains of the N doorway. There are footings of a cross-wall, late C15 or early C16. Opening E into a square chapel is a semicircular arch, its outer order springing from weathered imposts, the inner, with dog-tooth ornament, from thin, quatrefoil plan responds (N respond C20). The quirk-roll ribs of a quadripartite vault rise from corner imposts. In the E wall, a window with splayed ingoes, triangular-headed behind the wall-rib of the vault. Aumbry in the S wall, piscina in the N. A mural staircase in the N wall is substantially the work of 1923 restoration, as are the walls, gable and skews of the upper chamber.

Similar but larger and grander, the chancel retains little sense of sanctuary. Its vault has gone (*see* above) and with it the high pointed-arch which faced the nave. The N wall still stands, retaining angle shafts, capitals and springing ribs in the NW and NE corners, but returns S only as far as the N jamb of the first of two tall round-arch windows which originally lit the church from the E. Altar footings. In the S wall, a piscina and aumbry with moulded surround. In the N wall a smaller aumbry and a flat-arched doorway. A few pavement slabs, the sandstone quarried at Inch Kenneth or Gribun on Mull.

For most of its length, only the lower courses of the S wall of chancel and nave exist. At the W end, part of the jamb of a doorway into the N cloister walk survives, enough to indicate an opening rather tall and narrow in proportion with circular nook-shafts. On the inner face of this short return of walling are several carved corbelstones inserted to support the W gallery (*see* above).

Abutting the low E end of the S wall is the E range of the CONVENTUAL BUILDINGS. This comprised the E cloister walk off which opened three rooms; the middle room was the chapter house, set at a slightly lower level, with a peripheral sandstone bench. Only footings survive. Above this range would have

been the nuns' dormitory. A thickening of the E wall towards its
S end seems to suggest a gabled return W, marking the extent of
the C13 nunnery. Work carried out at the end of the C15 increased
accommodation by enlarging the square plan of the cloister
garth on the S and W. This change is particularly evident in the
Ross of Mull granite-block gables and S wall of the S range which
housed the refectory. There are three windows, each with splayed
ingoes, in the S wall; above the weathered hood-moulding of the
middle opening, an indistinct carving, possibly a *sheila-na-gig*.
Of the W range only a short length of the E wall survives. Nor
does anything remain of the cloister itself beyond a few fragments now kept in the Nunnery Museum (*see* St Ronan's
Church below) and Abbey Museum. From these it is possible
to determine that the arcade reconstructed in the late C15 took
the form of ogee-headed arches on coupled colonnettes of
circular and octagonal plan.

OTHER BUILDINGS

PARISH CHURCH. 1828. Parliamentary kirk designed and built
in Ross of Mull pink granite with sandstone dressings; by
William Thomson to the approval of *Thomas Telford*. The standard
T-plan wing is missing and the W lateral wall has no windows. E
front is twin-doored. Bellcote on S gable. The interior, plastered
above a boarded dado, was reorientated to the S, 1938–9, a pine
screen panelled with four-centre arches erected at the N end to
create vestibule and vestry. – Plain oak furnishings include a
bowl FONT with barley-sugar pedestal; in memory of William
Noble Darling †1949. – The original tall PULPIT with its panelled
back and sounding board was removed to the Highland Folk
Museum, Kingussie. – Adjacent S is the former MANSE (now a
Heritage Centre), 1828, the standard symmetrical single-storey
model by *Thomson* raised a storey at the centre by *Neil & Hurd*,
1934.

Former FREE CHURCH. 1845. Gabled with lancets N and S and
an E apex bellcote. Worship ceased in 1923. Smothered in dry
dash render and awkwardly enlarged, the building is in residential use. Rubble wall enclosure. Located 600m. N, the former
Free Church manse, 1847, had by the 1880s been absorbed in
the growth of St Columba Hotel.

REILIG ODHRAIN. Rubble-walled burial-ground, *c.* 45m. square,
enclosing St Oran's Chapel (q.v.). The site is ancient, dedicated
to St Oran (Odhráin), possibly a cousin of St Columba (though
recent research has suggested a second Oran, perhaps linked to
the 'false bishops' evicted by St Columba). Here are buried 'the
best men of all the Isles' from Early Christian times to the present.
Many remarkable gravemarkers and effigies have been removed
to the Abbey Museum (q.v.) but some weathered TAPERED
SLABS remain. One such, a child's tombstone, C12–C13, bears a
Latin cross in outline; another, C14–C15, a foliated cross. Several
full-size stones, C14–C16, Iona school, carry the usual plant
scroll and sword ornamentation. In 1859 the 8th Duke of Argyll

attempted to bring some order to the scatter of stones which littered the graveyard. Two parallel rows of the more significant tombstones were gathered together in railed enclosures, still extant, known as 'the ridge of the chiefs' and 'the ridge of the Kings', the latter associated with the C12 burial place of kings of Scotland, Ireland and Norway. A little to the NE of St Oran's Chapel is the grave of the C20 politician, John Smith †1994, a large ovoid SLAB of sandstone, simply inscribed.

ST COLUMBA'S CHAPEL and BISHOP'S HOUSE. By *Alexander Ross*, Inverness; 1893–4; extended 1977 and 1986–7. Near-symmetrical, one-and-a-half-storey linear block, C19 work in granite rubble. Hipped attic dormers flank central w and E gables, the latter projecting slightly. In a pointed-arch niche in the E gable, a statue of St Columba, 1893, by *Andrew Davidson* of Inverness. Traceried pointed-arched window in w gable. Below this the entrance opens to a lobby separated by a cusp-arched screen from the chapel at the centre of the plan. On each side and above is residential accommodation, the upper rooms linked over the lobby by a gallery. The four-bay chapel has a boarded purlined roof on simple arch-braced trusses rising from corbel-stones set in square-snecked granite walls. N and S lintelled windows with twinned timber lancets light the sanctuary.

ST MARY'S CHAPEL, 60m. SSE of Abbey. Probably C13. Rubble vestiges of the N and S walls of a single-cell, rather elongated structure, *c.* 17.5m. by 6.5m.

ST ORAN'S CHAPEL, 80m. SW of the Abbey. C12. A skew-gabled rubble cell, 10.4m. by 6.2m. overall, similar in its simple form to contemporary Irish churches. Uncompromisingly architectural and of starkly ascetic Romanesque beauty, it is located on the N edge of the Reilig Odhráin (q.v.), Iona's historic burial ground. Perhaps founded as a mortuary chapel by Somerled, Lord of Argyll, †1164, or his son Reginald †1207(?); certainly the burial place of the MacDonald Lords of the Isles until the forfeiture. Much decayed by the end of the C17, the chapel continued to be used for burials. Partially repaired in 1855–6, the fabric was consolidated by the *Office of Works*, 1921–6, when the paved floor was relaid. Fully restored by *Ian G. Lindsay*, 1957.

The building is entered through the w doorway, a small but powerfully conceived symmetrically set round-arch opening. Engaged columns with cubical bases and capitals carry a strongly modelled archway: inner order of bold chevrons, outer ring of sixteen much-weathered chamfered voussoirs, each carved with animal or human heads, and a semicircular hood-moulding with protuberant pellets in a hollow chamfer. At the l. of the door is a recess formed for a lamp or holy water stoup. The w gable is otherwise plain, as is the E, the skews given a coping of thin pinning stones, restored in 1957. Inside, the floor is of sandstone paving inset with seven graveslabs and a brass commemorative plaque. White plastered walls. Lighting the E end, two small opposed windows: N, round-headed; S, trefoil-headed, a late medieval alteration. Block altar with sandstone top, 1957, set on medieval footing. Three-bay roof with two heavy, scissors-and-tie trusses. In the s wall, a wide, late C15 tomb-recess framed by an inner trefoil arch behind an outer ogival arch and hood-moulding. Horned beasts and leaf sprays fill the spandrels of the inner arch which has a 'green man' motif at the apex. Above this, in the outer order, a mitred head, and, swept up from the apex of the hood-moulding, a panel bearing the figure of the crucified Christ. Carved lions, not identical, mark the springing points W and E; below the former, a weathered water-stoup; above the latter, what appears to be the beginning of another hood-moulding, perhaps intended for a second tomb. It remains unclear for whom this tomb was intended; both MacDonalds and MacKinnons have been suggested.

ST RONAN'S CHURCH, on the N edge of the Nunnery precinct. Iona's medieval parish church, erected c. 1200 on the site of a still smaller church, possibly C8, and an earlier burial ground. Ruinous by the C19, it was consolidated by *R. Rowand Anderson*, 1874–5, and later, 1922–3, adapted as the Nunnery Museum, a glazed roof being set below the wallhead. In 1992–4, *John Renshaw* installed a new glazed roof of flattened W section carried independently of the walls on Douglas fir posts and laminated beams. The plan is oblong, 13.1m. by 6.3m. overall, the original random rubble walls surviving on the N and S and E gable. The masonry of the W gable and W end of the N wall dates from C19 and C20 restoration. The E end is lit by small N and s windows, each with splayed ingoes, the latter original with a triangular-headed embrasure. In the E gable, an even smaller round-arched opening. Below this are altar footings.

The church houses a collection of funerary monuments. SLAB fragment, late C8 or C9, carved with a ringed cross with rounded armpits; formerly part of the paving in front of 'St Columba's Shrine' (q.v.). Several TAPERED SLABS, in whole or part, Iona school, C14–C15, most with bevelled edges and plant scroll ornament. One, early C16, with plain moulded margins, an oak-leaf cluster, foliated cross and an inverted black-letter inscription in Latin ('Here lie Finnguala and Mariota MacInolly, sometime nuns of Iona'). Another, similar in date, in two pieces with traces of dog-tooth and chevron ornament, plant scrolls, a small figure in a niche and a casket. Among those outside the church: to the N, a small, hip-ended, sandstone GRAVE-COVER, from a child's tomb, C12–C13, and an irregular SLAB with the incised outline of a ringed cross, perhaps earlier; also a FRAGMENT from a tapered slab, C14–C16, carved with a pair of shears, now serving as paving at the Nunnery church's s door.

TIGH AN EASBUIG (The Bishop's House), 30m. N of the Abbey buildings. Early C17(?). A single, ruinous wall survives; the gabled dividing wall of a two-chamber dwelling associated with the restoration of the Abbey as the Cathedral of the Isles in the 1630s. Evidence of outer E and W gables, and the N and S walls which connected them, emerge from the turf. Level with the lintel of the door in the partition wall are two corbels indicating an upper floor on the E side of the wall; to the W was 'a large Hall open to the Roof' (W. Sacheverell, 1702).

MACLEOD CENTRE, 200m. WNW of the Abbey. 1984–9. Competition-winner by *Feilden Clegg Design*. T-plan hostel with a two-storey N wing housing sleeping and study accommodation and a double-height, single-storey community arm pushing S. The modesty of roughcast gables and slated roofs a little compromised by changes of material and self-conscious design, particularly on the N: 'more Voysey than vernacular' (Rattray, 1990). Galleried Entrance Hall and lofty Community Room, with a stained, cross-timbered ceiling, form an attractive axial sequence.

FORT, Dùn Cùl Bhuirg, 2.25km. W of the Abbey, looking S over 'The Bay at the Back of the Ocean' (Camas Cùil an t-Saimh). Rocky summit close to the Atlantic coast naturally protected on W and NW with some traces of walling on the S. C20 excavations suggest an Iron Age dating.

DHU HEARTACH LIGHTHOUSE, 23.5km. SW of Iona. By *David & Thomas Stevenson*, 1867–72. Remote storm-swept granite tower, 44.25m. high, constructed under the harshest conditions. Thomas's son, Robert Louis Stevenson, described the location as 'an ugly reef ... one oval nodule of black-trap, sparsely bedabbled with an inconspicuous fungus, and alive in every crevice with a dingy insect between a slater and a bug'. In 1890 the stack was painted with a 10m. red band to distinguish it from 'nearby' Skerryvore Lighthouse (q.v.). Unmanned since 1971.

ISLAY

(see map p. 500)

The southernmost of the Hebridean islands, reached by car ferry from Kennacraig on W Loch Tarbert. For the most part the landscape is undulating rather than hilly. There is good farming land, but also large stretches of peat bog, the latter a source of fuel and flavour for the thriving whisky industry. The island is rich in archaeological evidence. Settled by the Irish in the C3, it became part of the Scots kingdom of Dalriada, fell to the Norsemen in the C9, and in 1150 was absorbed into the island domain of Somerled, King of Argyll and founder of the Clan Donald. Ruins of the MacDonalds' stronghold survive at Loch Finlaggan from where, until the end of the C15, the medieval Lords of the Isles held sway over much of the western seaboard. These remains are important, varied and plentiful but barely three-dimensional. More visible are the white-walled model villages founded by the Campbell lairds in the C18 and C19. Campbell philanthropy revived the island's fortunes to such an extent that by 1841 the population had risen to well over 15,000. Today, tourism, farming and whisky production support about one-fifth of that number.

ARDBEG

Distillery hamlet, 5.25km. E of Port Ellen. The A846 ends at the distillery pier, though a road continues NE to Kildalton.

ARDBEG DISTILLERY. Built 1815; repaired and extended after a fire, 1887; recommissioned and restored, 1997–8. Dispersed white-washed buildings which, though constructed with 'no pretensions to taste and elegance, nevertheless ... look picturesque and are substantially built' (Barnard, 1887). Amongst the group are two three-storey-and-attic malt barns with two pyramid-roofed kilns, c. 1850. Disused wooden pier.

ARDNAVE

Peninsula in NW Islay lying between Atlantic-lashed cliffs and the sand-flats of Loch Gruinart.

CHAPEL and BURIAL GROUND, Nave Island. Gabled roofless remains of a small rubble chapel, located within a barely discernible ovoid enclosure close to the island's SE shore. Architectural features such as a two-light round-arched window and shelf-topped aumbry suggest an early C13 date. The enclosure may be earlier, perhaps associated with monastic settlement, a possibility enhanced by the discovery of an C8 CROSS fragment similar to that at Kilnave (*see* below). During the C19 a lean-to structure was erected along the chapel's S wall while kelp-burners built a brick furnace and an 8.5m. chimney at its NE corner. To the N, traces of several smaller buildings probably associated with agrarian activities in the C18 or early C19. No gravemarkers survive.

KILNAVE CHAPEL and BURIAL GROUND (Cill Naoimh) 1.6km. S of Ardnave House. Oblong chapel, c. 1400(?), roofless but otherwise preserved. Generally thin rubble masonry. Small segmental-arched door in E gable has long draw-bar socket. Round-arched window in E and S walls. In the churchyard is a TAPERED SLAB, C16, shaped with pointed head and carved with the familiar foliage-flanked sword. Also the KILNAVE CROSS with fragmentary base slabs: a ringless cross with semicircular armpits, probably C8, it must once have stood to c. 3m. E face carving only – whorled panels, rectangular and circular, set on a key pattern background within plain margins, now much weathered.

ARDNAVE HOUSE. Harled, two-storey house, probably late C18, with a central full-height bow-fronted S projection. Strongly sculptural composition symmetrically stressed by tall stacks clasping the half-cone roof of this projection and restressed by the chimneyed skew-gables of the main block behind. Rear wing; forestair access to first floor indicates possible flatting. Built for tacksman, Duncan Campbell.

ARDNAVE STEADING. Long SE front screens offices: high harled wall of three blind Gothic arch recesses surmounted by rudely crenellated parapet and flanked by lower stable-blocks. Late C18.

CRAIGENS FARMHOUSE, at head of Loch Gruinart, 4.5km. N of Uiskentuie on Bridgend–Bruichladdich road. Early C19 gabled farm. Steading buildings include dwelling with forestair to upper-storey barn. Gateway has four piers with ball finials.

BALLYGRANT

Halfway hamlet between Port Askaig and Bridgend.

KILMENY OLD PARISH CHURCH, through trees from present Kilmeny Parish Church, 400m. SW. Late medieval. A section of the W wall, partly rebuilt, and a short stretch of overgrown footings along the S are all that survive. Semicircular W arch with dressed voussoirs. In the walled graveyard are four worn and damaged TAPERED SLABS, C14–C16. Other slabs and headstones are of post-Reformation date.

KILMENY PARISH CHURCH, 800m. SW of Ballygrant village. Symmetrically massed skew-gabled kirk of limewashed rubble with red sandstone dressings. The present T-plan form results from three phases of building. In 1828–9, the then existing church, late C18(?), was remodelled by Walter F. Campbell of Islay. The two tall Venetian window groups on the NW wall may be part of these improvements and may be related to the late C18, three-light Palladian windows in the staircases of Islay House (q.v.). Campbell may have added the birdcage belfry on the SW gable, though in 1843 an identical bellcote, with stepped pyramid, was provided on Kilchoman Free Church, Port Charlotte (q.v.). During the second half of the C19, a central gabled porch was added, its tall round-arched window matching the Venetians and smaller lights in the main gables but with roll-moulded jambs and hood-moulding similar to the square-headed NE entrance. Interior rearrangement, also late C19, placed panelled PULPIT with balustraded stair at the NE end and timber-columned gallery at SW.

EMERACONART COTTAGE, 2.6km. SW of Ballygrant on Bridgend road. Early C19, single-storey-and-attic, harled dwelling. Skew-gabled with three gabled dormers.

KNOCKLEAROCH FARMHOUSE, 1.4km. S of Ballygrant village. Early C19. Harled, two-storey, gabled L-plan house with round-arched doorway. Rubble steading with loft.

MANSE, Kilmeny, 185m. SW of Kilmeny Parish Church. Two-storey former Parliamentary manse built 1828 by Aberdeen contractors *John Gibb* and *William Minto*. The design by *Thomas Telford*, a modification of original standard proposal by his assistant *Joseph Mitchell*, is plain in the extreme: a harled skew-gabled house of three widely spaced windows.

MILL. Three-storey rubble block with two-storey wing containing an iron overshot wheel, 4.27m. dia., which originally drove two pairs of 1.37m. stones. No longer in use.

BROCH, Dùn Bhoraraig, 2.2km ESE of Ballygrant village. The

only broch on Islay, situated on a high summit surrounded by steep slopes and ditching. Rubble-obscured remains enclose a court 13.7m in dia. Entrance on ESE. Evidence of mural chambers. Much robbed since Pennant's visit in 1772 when the walls stood to a height of 4.3m.

CRANNOG, 'Ellan Charrin', Loch Ballygrant. Northernmost of three small islands is boulder-built around a central natural-rock outcrop. Overgrown drystone remains of seven roughly rectangular single-cell buildings, probably C16 in origin, the largest of which measures 13m. by 7m.

CRANNOG, Eilean Mhic Iain, Loch Lossit. Man-made island near NE shore, ringed by a massive perimeter wall of transported rubble boulders. Overlying this is an inner wall within which are three ruinous rectangular buildings probably dating from C17 or C18. There is no causeway, but an inlet for boat landing is evident on N.

FORT, Dùn Guaidhre, 900m. s of Kilmeny Parish Church. From the summit of a ridge, steep and rock-faced on SE, three ramparts and two ditches spill downhill on N, W and S.

BOWMORE

Planned village on the E shore of Loch Indaal. Developed, 1768, by Daniel Campbell II of Shawfield and Islay as a consequence of estate improvements around Islay House which had entailed the razing of the old settlement of Kilarrow. Bowmore grew, assimilating estate workers, fishermen and weavers. In 1779 a distillery was established. By the 1790s there were around 500 recorded residents living in houses constructed in stone and lime, with slated roofs and chimneys in the gables; half a century later, the population had reached a peak of more than 1,200. Despite subsequent decline, Bowmore remains Islay's administrative and commercial centre.

Campbell's plan is a simple grid, its principal artery, Main Street, rising S for 300m. from pier to Parish Church (*see* below). The layout recalls his eponymous grandfather's building of the Shawfield Mansion on the axis of Glasgow's Stockwellgait some fifty-six years before; only here it is the laird's kirk, not his home, which dominates the scene. Crossing Main Street are two parallel streets, each extending E and W, while a third, closest to the Church, runs E only. Narrow N–S lanes close the grid on E and W.

CHURCHES

BOWMORE FREE CHURCH, High Street. Gothic Revival four-bay nave by *Duncan Macfarlane*, 1859–60. Simple lancets, but circular window in s gable patterned with cusped tracery and quatrefoils. Disused.

ISLAY BAPTIST CHURCH, Jamieson Street. Two-storey, harled rubble house with skew-gables, mid C19(?). Three superimposed windows to street; door at l. may have lost wooden pediment.

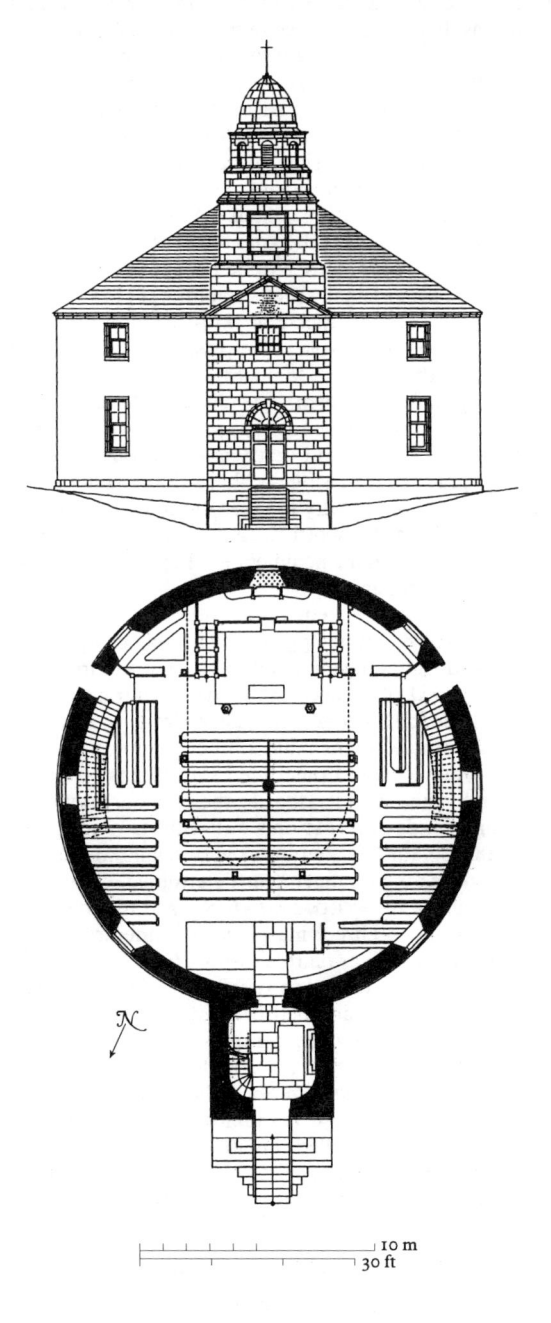

Islay, Kilarrow Parish Church, Bowmore.
Plan and elevation

KILARROW & KILMENY FREE CHURCH, Shore Street. 1844. Roughcast hall church, eaves-on to street, three lancet windows long; central shouldered gable with an apex belfry. Closed 1979.

KILARROW PARISH CHURCH. Powerfully architectonic in conception and resolutely urban in its rural setting, Bowmore's round kirk is quite without native precedent. Built 1767 by *Thomas Spalding* to a design said to have been provided by the laird, Daniel Campbell, out of the cultural spoils of a recent Grand Tour (a tradition which no doubt accounts for the repeated suggestion that the architect was French). Much more probable is the view that Campbell adapted a discarded design of *John Adam*'s, originally prepared, in 1758, for a round church at Inveraray. The geometry is simple, white-harled cylinder, slated cone, and square-plan stumpy stone tower, yet this intense presence at the head of Main Street seems to have distilled the very spirit of Calvinism. The church, 18.2m. in dia., is two-storeyed, lit by coupled windows, square over oblong. The frontal tower contains porch and vestry and is pedimented at church eaves height, before rising in short diminishing stages from square to octagonal belfry to steep stone cupola, all somewhat 'in the tradition of Scottish civic architecture' (RCAHMS Inventory, 1984). In the pediment is a Latin inscription recording Campbell's patronage.

Somewhat unexpectedly, the interior is dominated by a central mast-like timber pillar which, above a plaster ceiling, supports an eight-spoke radial king-post structure. 1828 alterations added a U-plan gallery which has a central convex swelling to define the laird's loft. The gallery front is panelled with a dentilled cornice. Eight plain timber columns on socles give support while enclosed pine-lined stair flights on both sides of the church, each with its door to the outside, provide access. – Wide ship's bridge PULPIT on S wall with stairs advancing l. and r. – In 1877–8 further alterations and repairs were effected and the present seating arrangements determined. Other furnishings are generally C20. – COMMUNION TABLE carved with Dec timber tracery. – Three fine pieces of funerary sculpture: an obelisk-topped white marble MONUMENT with a kneeling Neoclassical figure carved in relief, by *J. Marshall*, 1819, commemorates Walter Campbell of Shawfield and Islay †1816; a TOMB-CHEST in an ogee canopy, in memory of Margaret Susan Campbell †1822; and a double-lidded black marble sarcophagus, by *D. Hamilton & Son*, Glasgow, recalling both Lady Ellinor Campbell, whose name and date of death, 1832, are inscribed within a scrolled wreath, and that of her husband, Walter Frederick Campbell †1855. Graveyard, originally walled in 1775, contains more recent headstones.

PUBLIC BUILDINGS

BOWMORE HALL, Jamieson Street. Tall but plain single-storey block, 1889. Segmental lintels to windows; four to lateral wall, two in Main Street gable.

Bowmore Primary School, Flora Street. By *Strathclyde Regional Council*, 1980–1. Monopitch classrooms with splayed corners. Excessively high flat-roofed Hall.

Islay High School, Flora Street. Bowmore School by *William Railton*, 1876, later incorporated into Bowmore Secondary School by *Argyll County Council*, 1964. In 1985–6, Strathclyde Regional Council architects added a hipped-roofed games hall, administrative accommodation and eight new classrooms. Rising above and behind a roof pediment, glazed with Po-Mo Palladian allusion, is a pyramid roof with a distillery-derived, pagoda vent and bellcote in which the school's original bell has been re-hung; a clever skyline termination on the axis of School Street.

Old Town Hall, Main Street. Detached, three-bay, piend-roofed 'house'; late C18. Upper rooms, once used as sheriff court, have taller windows. Crudely pilastered entrance with round arch band over solid tympanum within which the added words 'Islay R.A. Chapter' curve over a Star of David. Now used as Masonic Lodge.

Pier. Work on Bowmore's jetty was recorded in 1750 but it was 1793 before Walter Campbell completed a rubble block pier at the foot of Main Street. Present concrete pier, C20.

DESCRIPTION

Main Street is the village spine, precisely as broad as the white drum of Kilarrow Church (*see* Churches above) at the brow of the brae. On the E side, by the Pier (*see* Public Buildings above), it starts with two low gabled rubble stores, mid-C18 survivors, each with its forestair to an upper dwelling. The Harbour Inn, mid C19, is more erect: three bays wide and as many storeys with attic dormers and street-level bipartite windows emphasizing the vertical. Then comes a short single-storey-and-attic run with more gabled dormers and a flat-roofed corner catastrophe at Shore Street. Beyond, a series of three-bay, two-storey houses, early to late C19, several altered at ground floor. Ileach, with its quaintly crude doorpiece and buckle-ended strapwork hood-mouldings, marks one side of the junction with Jamieson Street, the gable of Bowmore Hall (*see* Public Buildings above) the other. The Old Town Hall (*see* Public Buildings above) follows. Next, a good three-bay rubble house, mid C19. But the straight street front and gable-to-gable consistency are inexplicably abandoned in local authority houses near the church. On the W side of the street, continuity is broken by the open square on School Street corner where new housing, flats and the Royal Bank seem almost too self-consciously 'Scottish' for the Georgian townscape. Uphill to the S, less ambitious infill housing succeeds better, while N, between School Street and the pier, an older mix remains. A Victorian gable with hood-moulded windows and central door, 1840(?); an in-and-out quoined front, dated 1871, abused below but intact above; and, finally, four three-bay houses, late C19, the last of which, The Inns, has a pre-1900 flat-roofed two-storey porch.

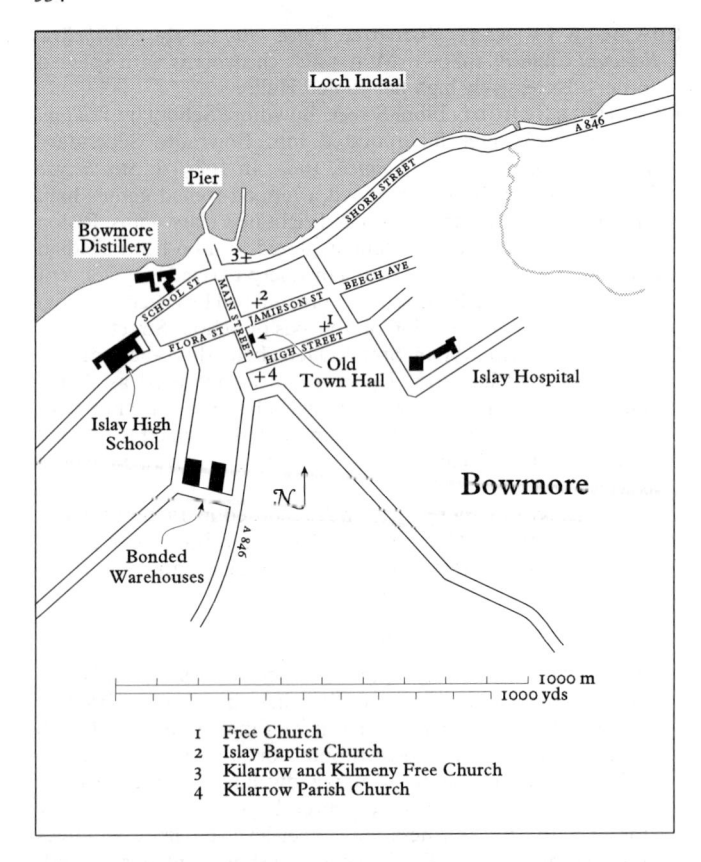

Map key:
1 Free Church
2 Islay Baptist Church
3 Kilarrow and Kilmeny Free Church
4 Kilarrow Parish Church

Two buildings dominate the skyline to the w: Bowmore School (*see* Public Buildings above) with its pyramidal belfry and the baroque silhouette of BOWMORE DISTILLERY, founded 1779. Rising out of Loch Indaal to mass around a courtyard are C19 warehousing and maltings, twin kilns, pagoda-roofed and golden-peaked, and a RECEPTION CENTRE, 1974, by *McKay & Forrester*.

SHORE STREET is a hard-edged urban corridor bending the village grid E along the loch shore. Two-storey houses, mid to late C19, pack gable-to-gable, maintaining a strong street wall and eaves line. The scale drops on the N side at KILMORICH, early C19, but rises again on the s at the BANK OF SCOTLAND, formerly the Police Station, 1895, by *James Quinton*, tall and skew-gabled with superimposed bipartite windows l. and r. Taller still is the MARINE HOTEL, dated 1898, gabled and bayed and perched high on the E edge of town to win a view across Loch Indaal. Along the Bridgend road is KILARROW HOUSE, late C19, a deep-plan mansion in coursed rubble and sandstone, copiously endowed with bargeboarded gables bracketed and cross-treed.

Uphill, the remaining streets of the Bowmore grid are lined with single- and two-storey eaves-on housing but without the enclosure of Shore Street. JAMIESON STREET is broad but domestic, though BOWMORE HOTEL, 1912, asserts itself with a façade gable and some unexpected floral Gothic ironwork. FLORA STREET, equally wide, is uncompromisingly severe. On HIGH STREET, an abandoned church (*see* Churches above) and a few stiffly symmetrical late C19 houses, the best of which is HIGHFIELD, 1894.

BRIDGEND

Unexpectedly picturesque and sylvan riverside village at the heart of Islay. Three island routes converge here: from the S, crossing the River Sorn, the road from Port Ellen and Bowmore; from the W, round the head of Loch Indaal, the road from the Rinns; and from the NE the ferry link from Port Askaig.

KILARROW BURIAL GROUND, 200m. N in the grounds of Islay House. No evidence lingers of the medieval parish church of St Maelrubha, late C13(?), though it survived into the late C18. There are, however, many interesting graves. Eighteen TAPERED SLABS – Nine Iona school, C14–C15, some bearing carving of crosses, foliated ornament, etc., others effigies of priests or warriors. – Two Oronsay school, early C16, both with claymores set in plant scrolls, one having its upper panel filled with a foliated flower-head cross, the other of unusual irregular shape. – One Loch Awe school, C14–C15, with upper and lower panels framed in nail-head ornament, the former enclosing plaited patterning, the latter a sword. – Several other slabs; among them one showing a female figure in cusped niche, C14–C16, and another, medieval in origin but altered to receive a C17 marginal inscription, are specially notable. – Later graves, marked by RECUMBENT SLABS, include many from the C18 and one bearing the date 1674. – Following the erection of a new Parish Church at Bowmore, graveyard walls were built, coped and provided with globe-topped GATEPIERS some time during the 1770s.

ST COLUMBA'S CHURCH (Episcopal), 500m. S in burial enclosure. Built 1888 to a design by Campbeltown priest, Canon *C. T. Wakeham*. Roughcast skew-gabled church with steep red-tiled roof. Basic Gothic. Refurbished 1962–3 when porch and organ chamber were added on the S. Boarded interior walls and ingoes. Hefty timber chancel beam carries cross. Pews from abandoned church on The Oa. – STAINED GLASS in E sanctuary lancet by *George G. Kirk* depicts Kildalton Cross.

CAMPBELL MONUMENT, 700m. S on summit of Cnoc na Dal. Grey granite obelisk on a square pedestal set in railed enclosure. Raised 1887 by An Comunn Ileach to commemorate the antiquary John Francis Campbell, †1885, son of Walter Frederick Campbell of Islay and author of *Popular Tales of the West Highlands* (1860–2). Sculptor *D. Haggart* of Glasgow. Inscriptions in Gaelic and English. High relief portrait panel of Campbell in bronze from a model by *Marion Ferguson*, London. Replacement monument erected after 1911 storm had blown down the original.

DAILL HOUSE, 2.7km. E. Two-storey, harled, gabled house with projecting façade gable and several gabled wings at rear, *c.* 1800(?). Porch and polygonal chimneys in dressed stone.

EALLABUS HOUSE, 800m. N. Wide, upmarket interpretation of traditional laird's house built for the Islay Estate factor, late C18. Three-storey, double-gabled, harled dwelling with sandstone dressings and eaves blocking course. At the centre of the symmetrical S front is a dumpy pilastered porch set below a high tripartite window with moulded architraves and cornice. Two-storey canted bays, executed in ashlar like the porch and presumably added in the mid C19, rise l. and r., the upper lights taller to match the central tripartite. At second-floor level, bipartite windows mark the three bays of the façade.

EAST LODGE, Islay House, 2.6km. NE. *See* Islay House.

NEWTON HOUSE, 900m. E. Early C19. Harled single-storey-and-attic house with piended roof.

NEWTON SCHOOL and SCHOOLHOUSE, 1km. NE. Dated 1878. By *J. Russell Walker*. Gabled front of coursed rubble with sandstone dressings. Schoolhouse at l. rises to two-storey gable with bold cavetto skewputts and a hefty stringcourse at first floor.

WOOLLEN MILL, Redhouses, 2.0km. NE. Rubble mill on the River Sorn's E bank. Erected 1883. L-plan formed by two-storey-and-attic gabled block with single-storey wing projecting S. Main building floored at first and second levels by joists on main beams carried on two rows of timber posts. Machines, some now unique in Britain, belt-driven by water-power. Located in a low wing alongside the S wall of the main block is the iron water-wheel, installed 1928 to replace a wooden undershot wheel, 3.66m. dia. Nearby are rubble ruins of a CARDING MILL, late C18 or early C19.

DESCRIPTION

Bound up with the village's origin and integral to its charm is the SORN BRIDGE, 1860, which spans the river in two segmental arches. The view W is delightful, the river channelled between parallel banks and white-walled buildings. To the r., a harled VETERINARY SURGERY, formerly the National Commercial Bank, two gables deep with a columned porch to the road on the N; dated 1838, but incorporating a later C19 SE wing. Beyond, former STABLES, piended single-storey with two piended eaves dormers. Across the river, the long low rubble wall of some early C19 HOUSING and a BARN with forestair. To the S of this row, the POST OFFICE SHOP, later C19, opening to a forecourt. Opposite, BRIDGEND HOTEL, a Victorian inn, *c.* 1850, with open-timbered eaves and gables; S additions have gabled eaves dormers, *c.* 1880(?). 400m. S, Islay Estates Office occupies CEANNLOCH HOUSE, a tall but plain, late C19 piended house.

FORT, Dun Nosebridge, 4.2km. SE. Seen from the NW, this isolated ridge has a distinctly tiered appeareance. On the summit are the tumbled remains of a wall enclosing a sub-rectangular area, 25m. by 15m. Below this, two, and in places three, successive ramparts can be discerned ringing the W side of the hill.

BRUICHLADDICH

A linear scatter along the NW shore of Loch Indaal which, shortly after the building of the distillery in the 1880s, was described as 'quite an aspiring and tastefully built village' (Barnard, 1887).

BRUICHLADDICH DISTILLERY. Built 1881, with later alterations. White, two- and three-storeyed buildings arranged in a courtyard plan. Flat-topped pyramid roofs create pavilion ends to a twelve-bay malt-barn range along the shore road. This and the still-house range constructed in precast concrete blockwork. Warehouses on N and E, the latter with a segmental roof. Vent-topped pyramid roof over kiln in courtyard.

FORELAND HOUSE, 3.8km. N of Bruichladdich Pier on B8018. Harled, late Georgian mansion built *c*. 1820 by Captain Walter Campbell not long after he had bought the Sunderland Estate from his father, Walter Campbell of Islay. Although the principal N façade follows the traditional three-bay formula, it is both unusually wide and oddly compressed on the upper storey where the lintels of smaller square windows coincide with the eaves course. Narrow columned doorpiece with a plain entablature and pediment. Interior layout, which may be a later remodelling, places the stair in the E end rather than at the centre of the plan; a spine corridor gives access to public rooms. Reeded architraves and ingoes to doors; the curved door to the drawing room sits in a semicircular recess. Upper corridor has a segmental barrel-vaulted ceiling.

Abutting the W gable is a lower L-plan kitchen wing: probably a reworking of an earlier house. On the E gable is a gable-fronted addition, mid C19, and behind this a polygonal-ended stone conservatory of later date. The former coach-house, harled with a blind arcade and pedimented centre, is located beside the W approach off Kilchoman road. WALLED GARDEN to NW.

GORTAN SCHOOL and SCHOOLHOUSE, on coast road 400m. S of B8018 junction. Built 1878; enlarged 1883. Rubble with ashlar dressings. Central façade gable has tripartite window and blind oculus.

LOCH GORM HOUSE, 1km. N of Bruichladdich Pier. Two-storey house in square-snecked rubble with gabled front. 1910.

PIER. C19 rubble pier with wood-piled extension; reconstructed in 1950s and still in use.

TILEWORKS, 400m. NE of Foreland House. Early C19. Rubble masonry remains of engine house and kiln associated with drain tile manufactory. Two lines of 3m.-high battered piers are all that survive of the ten-bay drying-shed.

WAR MEMORIAL, 800m. SSW. By *Scott & Rae*, Glasgow; 1921.

Rough-faced, grey granite obelisk to the 'men of Kilchoman Parish'. Castellated at the top under apex cross.

STANDING STONE, Uiskentuie, 2km. E of B8018 road-end. 3m.-high stone prominently erect on roadside terrace at the N end of Loch Indaal.

STANDING STONE, Gartacharra, 1.2km. W of Bruichladdich Distillery. Located in a field W of farm; 2.7m.-high stone with shouldered top.

DUN, Dùn na h-Uamha, 1.3km. NW of Gartacharra Farm. On a rocky rise, a small enclosure within walls originally *c*. 3m. thick. Battered outer face of drystone wall, completely preserved, reaches 2.4m. on narrower NNW side. Entrance on broader SE flank.

BUNNAHABHAINN

Distillery settlement, 4.2km. N of Port Askaig on the Sound of Islay, the proprietorial grip on which is immediately evident in vast warehouses and local authority housing dominating the upper village.

BUNNAHABHAINN DISTILLERY. 1880–3. Miscellaneous pierside buildings and two- and three-storey piended warehouses, now heavily rendered, line up along the shore. This incongruously industrial 'street' incorporates a rock-faced portal, dated 1881 above its elliptical archway. At the end of the street, three white skew-gabled cottages, mid C19, struggle to retain rural credibility.

RUVAAL LIGHTHOUSE, 6.2km. N of Bunnahabhainn at the entrance to the Sound of Islay. Designed by engineers *David Stevenson* and *Thomas Stevenson* and built by contractor *A. MacDonald* for the Northern Lighthouse Board, 1857–9. Low rubble walls define a generous oblong precinct. The circular tower, 5.8m. dia., constructed in brick with sandstone dressings and originally limewashed, rises 36m. to the lantern. Adjacent SW, two contiguous gabled brick buildings provided a store and dwelling units for two keepers. SUNDIAL, by *Adie & Son*, Edinburgh, located at SE of enclosure, has a fluted pedestal and engraved brass dial.

SHIELINGS, Margadale, 2km. NW of Bunnahabhainn. Group of some twenty-five shieling shelters on upland pasture scattered 200m. along l. bank of Margadale River. Huts are of rounded oblong or roughly circular shape, the majority of single-cell plan but six with two rooms; rubble remains stand less than 1m. high.

CAOL ILA

Spick-and-span whisky village on Sound of Islay shore, 500m. N of Port Askaig but accessible only from A846 1km. W. The road descends past three parallel two-storey terrace rows. Hillside landscaped in neatly trimmed grassy banks. Below lies the modern distillery, all but invisible – except from the sea.

CAOL ILA DISTILLERY. Founded 1846, extended and upgraded 1879, but substantially rebuilt and much enlarged with a vast still house, designed, 1972–4, by *G. L. Darge*, with full-height glazing E towards the Sound of Islay. Stretching along the quayside is a brick-built, three-storey-and-attic warehouse, late C19. Pilastered along twenty-bay front, with timber floors designed to provide through ventilation, it is the last traditional-style warehouse built on Islay.

HEATHERHOUSE, 700m. W of Caol Ila. Neat gable-to-gable row of single-storey rubble cottages, early C19(?), formerly thatched.

FINLAGGAN

Loch Finlaggan, 2km. NNW of Ballygrant off the Port Askaig–Bridgend road.

Architecturally disappointing but archaeologically and historically of great importance, the remains of this densely planned and much-overgrown complex of buildings on two islands at the NE end of Loch Finlaggan belie their significance. From this settlement, the administrative focus of 'a powerful chiefdom or incipient state' (Caldwell & Ewart, 1993), the MacDonald Lords of the Isles exercised their domination of the western seaboard until the forfeiture of the Lordship at the end of C15.

Eilean Mór is the larger of the two isles. Its role in MacDonald hegemony is retrospectively described in a document of 1549: 'Into this Ile of Finlagan the Lords of the Iles, quhen thai callit thame selfis Kings of the Iles, had wont to remain oft in this Ile forsaid to thair counsell: for thai had the Ile well biggit in palace-wark according to thair auld fassoun, quhairin thai had ane fair chapell.' The island is accessible across marshy ground at the N end of the loch. Excavation suggests that in medieval times its perimeter was protected by a wooden palisade constructed on a stone base, with intermittent projecting towers. There is evidence, too, of a bouldered causeway. While the N and NW of the island appear to have been given over to rig cultivation, turf-covered remains of perhaps as many as twenty small buildings cluster along the E and S shores. Among them, two somewhat more substantial stands of rubble walling survive. On the E, situated within what is likely to have been a burial enclosure, is KILFINLAGGAN CHAPEL, 10.1m. by 6.1m. overall, its walls reaching a maximum height of *c.* 3.0m. The ruins are probably C14, though they may have been raised on the site of an earlier structure, for the chapel is dedicated to St Finlagan, the reputed contemporary of St Columba, who later gave his name to the whole settlement. At the narrowing SW end of the island is a group of much less well-preserved buildings, the largest of which, 16.5m. by 7m., appears to have been a HALL, C14 with C15 modifications, which included a fireplace and sprung timber floor. Between this and the tip of the island are vestiges of three smaller buildings which, by virtue of their secure location, have been tentatively identified as residential quarters.

From Eilean Mór a second stone causeway, 2m. wide, ran SW to connect with Eilean na Comhairle. Traces of boulder paving can be found at the NE and in the middle of the 50m. crossing, although not at the SW where a bridge may have completed the crossing. This smaller, almost circular, island appears to be an artificial construction: a crannog, reinforced with man-made masonry banking on the W, S and E. The C16 source already referred to speaks of 'ane uther Ile sumquhat les, fair and round, quhairin thai had thair Counsellhouse biggit' but, although the island's Gaelic name, 'Council Isle', perpetuates this tradition, archaeological proof has proved elusive. Recent excavations do, however, reveal an exciting sequence with the collapsed stonework of an Iron Age dun or broch forming much of the island on which later structures were built at two distinct periods, a small stone-walled castle, C13 (probably dismantled in the C14), and finally the traces of three C15 buildings presumed to relate to the Lordship, including the residence of the Lords of the Isles and what may be the vestiges of the Council Chamber.

Excavation at Finlaggan continues and interpretative revision can be anticipated. Most of the surviving remains are late medieval and post-date the Lordship period. During the C16 there was a substantial township on Eilean Mór; the HOUSE of roughly square plan, 7.3m. by 6.4m., both gables relatively intact with small window openings and an aumbry, is from this period or may even be of C17 date. In what is presumed to be a BURIAL GROUND adjacent to the Chapel is a stone CROSS on a plinth, its head of Iona school provenance, C14–C15. Several West Highland TAPERED SLABS, C14–C16, are laid out between the Chapel and the loch; outstanding is one carved with the relief image of a mailed figure and galley and bearing a Latin inscription which may commemorate Donald McIllaspy, who held land here in 1541. On the hillside NW of the SW end of Loch Finlaggan are the ruins of two adjacent TOWNSHIPS, West Sean-ghairt and East Sean-ghairt; in both, barns, byres and dwellings cluster around an open yard.

ISLAY HOUSE
in wooded grounds 450m. NW of Bridgend

A surprisingly substantial residence begun as Kilarrow House in 1677 and repeatedly enlarged until the early C20. Despite these successive phases of alteration and extension intended to regularize its bulk into some kind of symmetrical grandeur, it has retained the vernacular character of a vastly inflated farmhouse. That such evident cultural pretension should be given so distinctly rural an interpretation may have something to do with Islay's relative remoteness; whatever the reason, the mismatch between scale and style is patent. Yet the mansion does not deserve to be dismissed, as it was by one critic visiting the island, as that 'large uncouth structure' (Mitchell, 1827). For there is both a bold simplicity and a charm, at once innocent and subtle, pervading the elevational patterning of its limewashed windowed walls and gables, a discernible disorder within order which somehow manages to humanize the great white mass of the building.

The earliest structure is an L-plan dwelling of 1677 built for Sir Hugh Campbell of Cawdor but subsequently absorbed as the core and wing of a larger U-plan house which from 1726 the family of Daniel Campbell of Shawfield contrived as their Islay seat. This mansion is three storeys high with additional attic accommodation in the gabled wings. The house faces sw: its three-bay centre, window openings enlarged in the c19, flanked on the same wall plane by twin-chimneyed, crowstepped gables. Each of these gables adopts the same pattern of fenestration, though that to the r., the late c17 wing, retains its original, widely spaced, small openings, while those on the l. are larger. This N wing, which is dated 1731 on a moulded skewputt on the w angle, is contemporaneous with a corridor link which connects it to the earlier wing across the rear of the central core. On the NW and SE sides of the building, where the eaves line drops to just above second-floor level, staircase towers were added in the second half of the c18, perhaps c. 1760. These are of half-octagon form, rise through three storeys and are flat-roofed, that to the NW retaining its balustraded parapet. The stairs, which climb within an inner circular plan, are lit by two Palladian windows on the NW and SE faces and by landing lights to the sw. At ground floor these sw windows were originally doors, but this arrangement has been superseded by a doorway, early c19, formed in the SE wall immediately sw of the adjacent stair tower. Constructed in red sandstone and defined by fluted pilasters surmounted by an architrave (also fluted between paterae) and cornice, this doorpiece encloses an elegant entrance with side lights and a radial fanlight under a segmental arch, the house's single external feature of real architectural sophistication.

Linked to the main block of the house are two wings of ancillary accommodation: to the N, single-storey buildings, c18, and, spreading E, a larger development added by *W. H. Playfair*, 1841–5, to replace earlier offices. This service wing of single- and two-storey buildings, carried out in a Scots Baronial idiom with a jagged skyline of pedimented dormers and crowstepped gables, was itself subsequently remodelled along its sw edge in order to provide a new dining room, servants' hall, bedrooms and a nursery. Between 1909 and 1911, *Detmar Blow* raised the sw front to a consistent two-storeys-and-attic height, terminating it in a crowstepped, twin-chimneyed gable, similar to those higher gables marking the ends of the principal façade. By this reverberation of motif and an admirable restraint which attempted no more than the repetition of identical window openings in a plain harled wall, Blow ensured that his intervention harmonized with the white simplicity of earlier work.

In the interior, several fireplaces have become the focus of architectural attention. Installed in the dining room in the SE range, c. 1910, in veined marble, is a somewhat severe chimneypiece with lugged surround, pulvinated architrave and cornice; in the library, at the NW end of the main block, another of the same; and, in the first-floor drawing room, a timber surround of more ornamental classical character with fluted Composite columns and delicately carved decorative frieze and cornice. In the late C18 staircase wells, cantilevered moulded stone treads ascend in a graceful helix, interrupted only by floor-level landings, the soffits of which are decorated with radial consoles.

The estate contains a number of buildings of interest. The HOME FARM, which is extensive and lies some 90m. E of Islay House, has a long, harled, two-storeyed SW range, late C18, through which a segmental-arched pend, surmounted by a pediment and stone clock-turret, gives access to a large inner yard. This is bordered by agricultural and service structures of various sizes and dates, including the farm-manager's house which sits behind a screen wall on the NW side. Kennels at NE by *W. H. Playfair*. The GARDENER'S HOUSE, early C19, is a straightforward gable-ended cottage and has been much altered. Gatepiers, harled like the cottage, carry ball finials, though these appear to be of C20 date. Close by, raised over a gun battery site, is the EAST TOWER, *c.* 1775, a fanciful octagonal structure of coursed rubble rising over 11m. Towards the top of the tower is a corbelled stringcourse and above that three corbel courses support a crenellated parapet. Four-level interior (its circular plan within an octagon recalling the staircase towers at Islay House) is lit by slit openings; turnpike stair lost. Above the doorway, a two-part decorative lintel, carved in relief with Rococo scrolling, bears the monograms D C, for Daniel Campbell, and G R, for Georgius Rex(?). To the NE, 2.6km. along the A846, is the EAST LODGE, by *W. H. Playfair*, built in 1845 in a crowstepped, stugged ashlar Scots style similar to that adopted by the architect for his extensions at the main house. On the A847, 700m. NW of the Gardener's House, is the white roughcast FORESTER'S HOUSE (or Bluehouse), early C19, a two-storey, three-bay dwelling with single-storey, gable-ended wings l. and r. Three porches; the central a half-octagon with slated faceted roof, a round-arch doorway and side lancets. Urns sit on gatepiers ahead of the porch and at the ends of the roadside rubble wall. Restored by *David Taylor*, 1997–8. 800m. further W is the blocky WEST TOWER, probably late C18, a crudely crenellated folly on a square plan, 5.2m. high, with blind pointed-arches and oculi recessed into its rubble wall-faces.

KEILLS

4168

Founded 1829: a village of green verges, a farm, some local authority housing and a few older cottages. 1.6km. WSW of Port Askaig.

KEILLS CHAPEL and BURIAL GROUND (Cill Chaluim Chille). Small sunken sacred space within ruined random rubble walls which survive to *c.* 3.0m. on N but are otherwise much reduced.

Though dedicated to St Columba, the chapel is of late medieval date. In the graveyard, in addition to C18 and C19 headstones, is a TAPERED SLAB, Iona school, C14–C15, carrying the image of a ship with its sail furled, below which is a sword set in interlaced vegetable ornament.

MULREESH CHAPEL and BURIAL GROUND (Cill Eileagain), 1.6km. NW of Keills. Turf-covered indication of cell. STONE FRAGMENT found here and now in the Museum of Islay Life, Port Charlotte, bears an incised rope-looped cross; possibly from some form of gravemarker, C10.

CROSS, 300m. ENE of Keills Chapel. Shaft only, standing in original(?) socket-stone. Plant scrolls and dragons' heads; Iona school, C14–C15.

KILCHIARAN 2060

Narrow valley of the Abhainn na Braghad falling W to Kilchiaran Bay on the wild Atlantic coast of Islay. Notable farm, ancient chapel and abandoned slate fields.

KILCHIARAN CHAPEL and BURIAL GROUND. Roofless oblong ruin with single standing E gable. High quality rubble masonry with slate pinnings flatters to deceive, for the N, W and S walls were 'restored' to their present irregular profile in 1972–3. Two door openings, three reconstructed steps to the chancel, and a rubble altar block are based on the evidence of 1972 excavations. The E gable, with its three aumbries, one with triangular arch, is original but of indeterminate late medieval date. A low-walled enclosure E of this gable is probably C18. At the W end is a damaged, drum-shaped basin FONT, quartered by four carved ribs; medieval but mounted on a modern base. In the nave and chancel are some TAPERED SLABS, C14–C16, including one with the carved effigy of a priest set in a cusped ogival niche. The burial enclosure around the church has been reduced by modern road construction on the SE and by erosion to the stream on the NW.

KILCHIARAN FARM. Two-storeyed, piend-roofed house, *c.* 1826, facing SW down the valley across steading and chapel to the sea. Central doorpiece with cornice.

KILCHIARAN STEADING. Lying below Kilchiaran Farm, some 130m. WSW, a splendidly symmetrical model steading, *c.* 1826, of a size and architectural sophistication wholly unexpected in such a remote setting. Two long ranges of parallel hip-ended rubble buildings orientated approximately W–E contain a cobbled yard *c.* 48m. by *c.* 12m. At the centre of the N range, between cart-sheds and byre, is a barn with a threshing-mill projecting N. Low breastshot iron water-wheel, 4.8m. dia., originally powered from the mill pond; stone-lined lade with tail-race. In the S range are stables beside which a modern Dutch barn has been built and a milking parlour formed by unfortunate C20 alterations. Between, access is gained S to a large D-shaped cattle court divided into three equal sectors by radiating walls. Around its semicircular perimeter runs a continuous wall of pitched roof rubble building which once had four timber-lintelled openings to each sector of the yard. Though much altered and degraded, the strong geometry and texture of this exceptional building still make a powerful impact on the landscape.

STANDING STONE, S side of Gleann Droighneach, 1km. SSE of Kilchiaran Farm. Tapering stone 2.7m. high.

STANDING STONE, 1.8km. E of Kilchiaran Farm. Straight-sided stone rising 2.7m.

DUN, Dùn Chroisprig, 1.5km. N of Kilchiaran Farm. Circular walling and outworks set on a steep-sided rocky outcrop from cliffs rising abruptly to the SE. The dun is 12.0m. in dia. with drystone walling preserved to five courses on N. Evidence of mural galleries.

KILCHOMAN

An ancient religious settlement above Machir Bay on Islay's W coast.

KILCHOMAN OLD PARISH CHURCH and BURIAL GROUND. Records of the medieval church date from C14 but the foundation goes back to Early Christian times. There are no remains of early buildings. The present church, 1825–7, is a harled gabled block lit originally by four bays of superimposed pointed-arch windows W and E. Gothic astragals survive in some sashes. Three-stage tower projecting from the N gable has angle buttressing rising to a battlemented parapet. Interior galleried on U-plan. Broad, panelled PULPIT with corniced back-boarding designed by *William Railton* of Kilmarnock, 1889. Church closed 1977.

Two Early Christian CROSS-SLABS, each *c.* 1m. in exposed height, were formerly to be found in the vicinity of the church: one, carved with a plain incised Latin cross, is now in the Museum of Islay Life, Port Charlotte; the other, disc-headed with a ringed cross in relief, stands 330m. SW of church. KILCHOMAN CROSS, Iona school, C14–C15, 2.57m. high in its original socket-stone, stands S of church's S gable: disc-headed with tapered shaft. Its E face is beautifully carved with a central Crucifixion scene below which, in a cusped niche, are two figures (probably the donors, Thomas and Patrick Beaton), a Latin inscription, plant whorls, a horse and rider in another cusped niche and, at the base, a panel of interlaced knotting. On the W face geometrical patterning predominates. A second free-standing CROSS, Iona school, C14–C15, similar in shape but smaller (1.77m.) and broken; now in the National Museum of Scotland, Edinburgh. It bears the figure of the crucified Christ in the cross-head but is otherwise generally carved with plant-stem and leaf relief.

BURIAL GROUND, walled 1778, is exceptionally rich in medieval and post-Reformation stones. Numerous TAPERED SLABS, Iona school, C14–C15, carved with swords, plant scrolls, etc. (two with effigies of priests); several recut for later inscriptions. Among more recent graves is a small HEADSTONE, dated 1845, which bears the representation of a lighthouse tower, commemorating the death of a member of the family of James Scott, assistant keeper of the Rinns of Islay Lighthouse from 1842 to 1847.

KILCHOMAN HOUSE. Three-bay, piended house, 1825–6, formerly Kilchoman Parish Manse. The central entrance bay has been given a shallow projection and is surmounted by a plain pediment and apex chimneystack. Doorway has glazed semicircular fanlight over an impost band extending l. and r. Internal staircase scale-and-platt with cast-iron balustrade. Rear wings. Walled garden to SW. Holiday accommodation in former stables block.

KILDALTON

A wooded estate on the SE coast of Islay, some 8 km. ENE of Port Ellen.

KILDALTON OLD PARISH CHURCH, 4.2km. NE of Kildalton Castle road end. Walls and gables of this late C12 or early C13 church still stand, rubble boulders brought to courses with pinnings and dressed with Kintyre sandstone quoins and margins, most of which have been replaced with concrete or North of England sandstone during repair work in 1925 or 1973–4. The oblong plan was probably divided into nave and sanctuary by a timber screen, for the E end of the building is lit by pairs of small round-arched windows in the N and S walls and by two lancets in the E gable, while the remaining two-thirds of the plan is illuminated from a single opening in the W gable. Doorways with draw-bar slots are located in the N and S walls. All openings have splayed ingoes with round-arched embrasures, their dressings robbed or unsatisfactorily replaced. The vestiges of a canopied piscina can be seen at the E end of the S wall and there is an aumbry in the sanctuary gable, the respective heights of these two features indicating that the present ground level is more than 0.5m above the original. The church remained in use until the end of the C17.

The outstanding monument is the Kildalton Cross (*see below*) but, within the church shell and in the GRAVEYARD, which is enclosed by a wall of C19 date, are many TAPERED SLABS, most C14–C15. Notable are an Iona school slab, C14, carved at the top with a foliated saltire cross, the shaft of which separates the image of a sword from a dragon-headed coil of trefoil-leaved scrolls and two Loch Sween school slabs, C14–C15, each showing a sword surmounted by a diagonal cross set within complicated interlaced ornament. Though worn, a RECTANGULAR SLAB, Oronsay school, *c.* 1500–60, still conveys the beauty and delicacy of its decorative scheme: two men in armour stand in crocketed canopied niches above a foliated cross and galley in full sail. There are a number of slabs of post-Reformation date, many now illegible. Pedimented trapezoidal PANEL to Annabella Gillies †1831, and her husband, Neil McNeill of Ardnacross †1848. Mantled sandstone HEADSTONE with an elliptical marble inset commemorates Colina Hay McDougall †1887.

KILDALTON CROSS, in the churchyard of Kildalton Old Parish Church. Powerfully proportioned and richly ornamented ringed cross, 2.65m. high by 1.32m. across the arms, carved from a single piece of grey-green epidiorite. Created for what must surely have been a monastic settlement, this is the outstanding example of a free-standing Early Christian cross in Scotland. Like the Iona crosses of St Oran, St John and St Martin (qq.v.), it probably dates from the second half of the C8 but, as the RCAHMS Inventory of 1984 notes, 'whereas it resembles St Martin's Cross ... in having figure scenes on one face, the delicacy of its carving and the proportions of the cross-head, with its wide armpits, are closer to those of St John's Cross'. The E face has a shaft carved with spirals and roundels, above which the Virgin and Child sit between two angels. The cross itself has a central boss formed from coiled serpents and lizards within a cable-moulded ring and, in the arms, biblical scenes: l., Cain slaying Abel; r, Abraham sacrificing Isaac; and, in the upper arm, David killing a lion, surmounted by two more angels. In the W face, coiled serpents, bosses, etc., decorate the shaft while lions, plaitwork and large gnarled bosses feature in the arms above. The cross is bedded into a damaged socket-stone now set into a double-stepped plinth. NE across the track from the Church is the so-called KILDALTON SMALL CROSS, a disc-headed cross, Iona school, C14–C15, bedded into a small cairn: it stands 1.94m. and is decorated in the centre and tapered arms of the cross-head with interlaced circling and knotting.

ARDTALLA FARM, 7.6km. NE of Kildalton House. Early C19. Harled, skew-gabled farmhouse with attached steading forming three sides of courtyard. Steading with lofts in gabled and piended roofs.

KILDALTON CASTLE. Sprawling estate mansion, in stugged ashlar with dressed facings, replete with crowstepped gables and dormers but lacking Brycean vigour and flair. James Ramsay, who purchased the Kildalton lands 'as far as McArthur's Head' (Ramsay, 1969) in the 1850s, tried hard to get it right. A proposal prepared in 1863 by the Kilmarnock architect *James Ingram* betrays the new laird's predilection for Scots Baronial. But the use of excessively steep crowstepped gables and attenuated organ-pipe bartizans failed to find favour. A second, still Baronial, design, was obtained from *John Burnet* in 1867. This was more ambitious in composition and more convincing in detail and, although in its original form it too remained on the drawing board, seems to have formed the basis of the castle which Ramsay finally built three years later. Burnet's plan and massing remained essentially unaltered, but a battlemented round-arched porch was abandoned while in the obligatory high-rise tower-and-turret, which had survived since Ingram's scheme, two castellated square-plan forms coalesced in a rather simpler conjoined arrangement than that envisaged by either previous proposal.

At the entrance to the estate is a Hansel and Gretel lodge, QUARTZ COTTAGE, late C19, with red-tiled roof, diamond lattice glazing and an L-plan veranda in the re-entrant. Built in rough random rubble with tusking stones on every corner. A high garden wall, also in random rubble, locally gathered, makes a curving approach screening the entrance. 200m. w, an exposed king-post truss, carried ahead of another rubble gable, distinguishes CLOUDS COTTAGE, late C19. Nearby, unusual sunburst astragals pattern the sashes of TIGH NA CROITEAN, two linked, gable-fronted cottages made into one.

MCARTHUR'S HEAD LIGHTHOUSE. 1861; by *D. & T. Stevenson*. Short white drum with chevron-glazed light. Clifftop plot enclosed by sinuous harled walls.

DÙN, An Dùn, Mullach Bàn, 1km. NE of Old Kildalton Church. Situated on a ridge from which steep flanks fall 21m. on NW and SE. Entrance from S. Outer face preserved to five courses. An additional protective outwork crosses ridge on NE side.

FORT, Dùn Beag, above Loch Càrn a'Mhaoil, 2.7km. WSW of Kintour. Irregular drystone wall carried round the summit and shoulder of a rocky ridge except on the NE. Well-preserved outer faces, especially the NW, where ten poorly constructed courses survive. W entrance.

FORT, Dùn nan Gall, 5.2km. N of Old Kildalton Church. Steep-sided promontory fort protected by three lines of rubble walling defending the area from landward attack. The outer wall preserves masonry faces on both sides and has a NW entrance gap; the second wall exists over a short stretch only and appears unfinished; the innermost line, which does cross the narrow peninsula, is of tumbled rubble but shows signs of vitrification.

HUT CIRCLES, 1km. WNW of Kintour. Stony bank traces of four house foundations in line NNE-SSW, the largest 8m. in diameter.

LAGAVULIN

Whisky-making hamlet 4km. E of Port Ellen. Distillery buildings cluster haphazardly between road and sea.

Former KILDALTON PARISH CHURCH, 500m. WSW. Nave and chancel Gothic built in grey-green square-snecked rubble, 1910–11, a gift by Captain Iain Ramsay in memory of his mother Lucy, wife of John Ramsay of Kildalton. Gabled SE transept and SW porch. Bifurcated lancets. Heavy birdcage belfry on SW gable. Slated roofs with tile ridge. Closed in 1972 and subsequently converted to residential use. Galleried interior.

DUNIVAIG CASTLE, on the E shore of Lagavulin Bay, 300m. SSE of the distillery. A case has been made for an ancient or Norse origin for this coastal stronghold. Certainly some of the masonry curtain at the promontory summit is late C14, though most of what survives is a castle constructed in the C16 but reduced by siege and eroded by time to such an extent that it seems almost to have reverted to the rock. An irregular heptagonal rubble wall, evidently between 2m. and 3m. thick but now barely emerging above the natural ground level, encloses an outer court-yard crossing the full width of the craggy promontory on which the castle is sited. The landward gateway can be detected in the

N curtain, set centrally between projecting angle-turret foundations at the NW and NE corners. Ranged within the yard, gable-on to the N wall, are the turf-covered traces of four small buildings which presumably served as kitchens, stores, etc. Two gun-loop embrasures in the W wall are still lintelled. A blocked gateway at the W angle led at one time to the shore below but the castle's main sea-gate survives as a ruinous gap in the SW curtain. Towards the middle of the S wall a vaulted opening leads into a small triangular courtyard wedged between the outer barmkin and the elevated extremity of the headland. At the S corner of this inner space a draw-bridge must have crossed the gap between masonry abutments constructed against the natural rock that rises from the loch, for beyond the gap a staircase continues to climb to the summit of the promontory. Here the natural perimeter of the rock has been reinforced by masonry curtains on top of which a rectangular tower- or hall-house block has been raised, an arrangement that has necessitated corbelling of the upper structure at the SW corner and massive battered underbuilding at the SE. Of the summit block only the SE wall and vestigial returns on the SW and NE remain in a ruinous two-storey stand. A garderobe chamber and some window embrasures are evident and at first-floor level the crumbling recess of the hall fireplace.

LAGAVULIN DISTILLERY. Originally two distilleries, founded 1816 and 1817, but by 1837 only one. Long, gable-ended, three-storey malt-barn runs along S side of road; brick-built, segmental-arched openings and a two-flight cantilevered open stair on the S wall. Two pagoda-roof kilns. Tall, red-brick chimneystack. Warehouses to E. Pier. Set in the gable of the filling-store is a splayed slate TOMBSTONE commemorating Angus Johnson †1820.

CAIRN and STANDING STONE, 650m. WNW of distillery. Grass-covered cairn, *c.* 5m. in diameter, from which a stone rises 1m.

STANDING STONES, 900m. NW of distillery. Large stone, 3.5m. high, built into rubble wall. Nearby, a fallen stone, comparably massive, measures 3.65m.

LAPHROAIG

Clustered distillery complex 2.3km. E of Port Ellen.

LAPHROAIG DISTILLERY. Founded 1820. Early plans of 1840 and 1854 reveal little more than a single line of slate-roofed rubble buildings with adjacent byres and dwelling. By 1900 the nucleated grouping of granary, malt barn, kiln and distillery had been augmented by long parallel warehouses to the W. Rapid expansion occurred in the early C20, and by the 1920s the distillery had become a densely packed mass of gabled and piended buildings with two pyramid-roofed kilns and a three-storey malt barn and loft. Further gabled warehousing was built to the E in the late 1920s and early 1930s.

CHAMBERED CAIRN, Ballynaughton, 1.2km. NNE of distillery

entry. Overgrown, irregularly disposed cairn material. Roofless chamber entered from NE has four compartments with overlapping side-slabs characteristic of Clyde type cairns.

STANDING STONE, Druim nam Madagàn, 750m. NW of distillery entry. Leaning stone with pointed top. 2m. high.

STANDING STONES, Achnancarranan, 750m. NNE of distillery entry. N–S line of three stones: N stone tapers to height of 2.7m.; centre stone, 3m. long, has fallen; S stone, leaning W, is 2.85m. high.

LOSSIT

Farm lying above a beautiful sandy bay on the W coast of the Rhinns peninsula.

DUN, on N side Lossit Bay 1.2km. from Lossit Farm. 8m. dia. within walling *c*. 3m. thick. Some outer face stones are still in position but there is much slippage to the sea. A N outer wall protected the more vulnerable approach.

DUN, Port Froige, 900m. NW of Cladville Farm. Fortified promontory with stretches of outer face stonework surviving along E, especially N of the entrance where thirteen courses reach 3.1m. over a dip in the terrain.

STONE CIRCLE, Cultoon, 1.3km. NE of Lossit Farm. Moorland circle (in fact an ellipse) 40.7m. by 35.1m., with three standing and twelve prone stones. Holes dug for stones exist and are now marked by concrete fill, but excavations suggest that the site was abandoned before most were raised in position.

MACHRIE

A links golf course, hotel and holiday chalets lying between the A846 Port Ellen–Bowmore road and the dunes of Laggan Bay.

MACHRIE HOTEL. The core is a one-and-a-half-storey, gable-ended house with a central frontal gable, C19. Flat-roofed porch and bay-window, respectively r. and l. of this gable, do little to enhance the composition. Returning W on either side are added wings of accommodation, only slightly lower in scale: that to the S, seven eaves-dormer bays long; to the N, a piended single-storey block, forming one side of a U-plan yard with nondescript outbuildings on the W and N. A short distance S of the hotel, lined up in oblique echelon, are several white-rendered chalets with slated monopitches, by *McKay & Forrester*, 1970s(?).

STANDING STONE, Carragh Bhàn, 900m. SE of Kintra. A broad squarish slab, 2.2m. wide, standing 2.2m.

NEREABOLLS

A few dwellings halfway between Port Charlotte and Portnahaven. Once a medieval township.

CHAPEL and BURIAL GROUND, close to shore on the r. bank of Abhuinn Ardnish. Little more than foundation mounds survive of this dependent chapel of Kilchoman. Oblong plan with the suggestion of a raised floor in the E end. C15 or earlier; perhaps dedicated to St Columba. Within the chapel are five TAPERED SLABS, Iona school, C14–C15; four carved with sword images and one with the figure of a priest. Two more can be found in the nearby burial ground. Head and lower shaft of a freestanding CROSS, also Iona school, C14–C15, bearing carvings of crucified Christ, mitred abbot in niche and usual foliated ornament, are now in the Museum of Islay Life, Port Charlotte, but were probably erected here by the MacKays of the Rinns. A second, smaller chapel is barely detectable 300m. NE of Nereabolls Farm.

CHAPEL and BURIAL GROUND, 2.1km. SW of Nereabolls Farm on the S bank of Abhainn Gleann na Gaoith near the shore. Ruined rubble wall remains of a small chapel. The E end turf-covered rise may indicate an altar base. Two stone FRAGMENTS, carved with ringed cross motifs, in burial ground surrounding chapel.

PORT ASKAIG

Harbour-ringing handful of white, gabled buildings gathered together at the foot of a steep wooded gully on the W shore of the Sound of Islay. In 1788 Lord Mountstuart recorded 'a small harbour called Port Ascog' with 'a pier and an exceeding good ferry house of white stone slated'. For centuries the crossing point to Jura, Port Askaig provides Islay with ferry links to Colonsay and to Kennacraig on the mainland.

KILSLEVAN CHAPEL, on moor 2km. SW of Port Askaig. Small drystone chapel; encircling rubble wall. No gravemarkers.

DUNLOSSIT HOUSE. Robust Scots Baronial mansion in rough-faced ochre sandstone with red sandstone dressings. Built 1865, but rebuilt 1909 after a fire. Crowstep gables and pedimented eaves dormers. Bartizans abound. Mullion-and-transom square bays to all public rooms on ground floor. The long SE elevation, rising on a splayed plinth from falling lawns, spreads S beyond a tall, conically capped stair drum through a rubble tower into a lower services wing; disturbed and disturbing, it builds a powerful aggregative grandeur. Glazed Arts and Crafts timber porch added ahead of the battlemented NW entrance. Interiors by Edinburgh decorators *Scott Morton & Co*. Walled HOME FARM lies up drive to S. Crowstepped LODGE to N, halfway up brae from Port Askaig.

PORT ASKAIG HOTEL. Latter-day aggrandizement of ancient drovers' inn, said to date from the C16. Two, formerly detached, two-storey, skew-gabled houses, early C19, somewhat clumsily linked by taller, late Victorian wing set gable-on to harbour. Much unfortunate agitation in window and porch design but white walls and green lawns trim with welcome.

DESCRIPTION

White walls embrace a pierhead apron, heightening the activity that erupts with every ferry. To the S, below Dunlossit woods, the Hotel (*see above*) sits on a green carpet running down to rocks and rubble-walled harbour. Across a tarmac stage, beneath fern-drenched cliffs, more white walls, mostly early C19: POST OFFICE and PIERMASTER'S OFFICE, gable-to-gable, and detached piended STOREHOUSE cast a two-storey curtain round the action.

PORT CHARLOTTE

Trimmest and least changed of Islay's planned villages. Situated on the W shore of Loch Indaal on the road from Bridgend to Portnahaven, which had been completed in 1806 following a survey by *George Langlands* of Campbeltown. It was founded, 1828, as an agricultural and distillery settlement, by Walter Frederick Campbell of Islay and named for his mother, Lady Charlotte Campbell. In 1929 Lochindaal Distillery closed but Port Charlotte has survived as a holiday village.

ST KIARAN'S CHURCH, 1.5km. NNE. By *P. MacGregor Chalmers*, 1897. Snecked rough rubble Romanesque with red sandstone dressings. Skew-gabled nave with gabled transept and E porch. Slated roof, conical over half-round chancel. Gabled arch belfry on N gable. Interior plastered from dado lining to boarded ceiling on collar-braced trusses. Semicircular sandstone arch opens to a raised apsidal chancel. Transept closed off. All windows round-arched with sandstone embrasures. – STAINED GLASS. Two small windows in the apse celebrate the communion elements: to l., Christ with chalice in autumnal brown and red; to r., Christ with loaves, brown and green.

Former KILCHOMAN FREE CHURCH (now the MUSEUM OF ISLAY LIFE). Built 'forthwith' in 1843 when the Kilchoman minister 'came out' at the Disruption. Harled box with pyramid-topped birdcage belfry similar to that at Kilmeny (q.v.). Gabled porch to SE gable. Disused from 1927. Converted to a museum, 1977. Large collection of archaeological finds, farming and fishing implements, documents, memorabilia, etc.

BRAIBRUICH STEADING, 100m. N of St Kiaran's Church. Almost symmetrical arrangement of gabled rubble buildings around yard. Abandoned.

KILCHOMAN MANSE, 600m. NNE of village. White skew-gabled dwelling, built 1847 as the Free Church manse, still smart and elegant in its walled garden. Central segmental-arched entrance with Gothick astragals in the fanlight.

LOCHINDAAL DISTILLERY. Established by 1829. C19 buildings on W side of road now disused; those on E converted (*see* Youth Hostel and Field Centre below). Three bays of a single-storey bonded warehouse survive as stores. Uphill W, another warehouse still stands. Closed 1929.

LOCH INDAAL LIGHTHOUSE, 700m. N. Round tower built 1869; engineers *D. & T. Stevenson*. Two-storey keepers' dwelling in brick.

OCTOMORE FARM, 500m. NW. Early C19. Rubble ranges around a courtyard; some buildings in use as distillery until mid C19.

PIER. Jetty constructed *c*. 1845; restored and improved, 1955.

PORT CHARLOTTE PRIMARY SCHOOL, immediately N of old school. By *Strathclyde Regional Council*, 1976(?).

PORT CHARLOTTE SCHOOL (now Village Hall), at head of School Street (Sraid na Sgoile). Dated 1830. Pedimented gable front with apex belfry and porch. Projecting gabled wing to r., *c*. 1880; low two-storeyed piended S wing. Considerably altered to serve as Hall.

YOUTH HOSTEL and FIELD CENTRE. Neat and modest conversion of two-storey bonded warehouse, 1991–2.

DESCRIPTION

The road from Bruichladdich passes the Museum of Islay Life (*see* Former Kilchoman Free Church above) on a grassy knoll to r., bends l. bridging the leafy course of the Abhuinn Gearach, to enter the village between the white walls of Lochindaal Distillery (*see* above). Immediately, the pattern of three-bay gable-to-gable houses, built early C19 'with two stories and a loft, on the scale of the manses of the clergy', is established. To the r., MAIN STREET NORTH (Bruthach Dubh), a shallow crescent of nine such dwellings, looks E across the road to Loch Indaal. Taking advantage of a shoreside fall in level, PORT CHARLOTTE HOTEL, later C19, rises three storeys, bulky but suitably plain. MAIN STREET (Sraid Ard) restores the two-storey townscape on both sides. Houses on the E sit one floor down with doors to a path below road level – save one, entered from a first-floor bridge. On SCHOOL STREET (Sràid na Sgoile), SADDLER'S BRAE (Sràid na Laimrig), and SHORE STREET (Sràid a'Chladaich), more of the same early C19 terraced rows, alike in form and scale but varied in finish and detail.

CHAMBERED CAIRN, 800m. SW between Portnahaven road and shore. Irregularly shaped chambered cairn, *c*. 22m. broad and now about the same in length though originally much longer. NNE chamber had four compartments, two of which are still defined by slab stones. Excavation discovered twin stretches of drystone walling on each side of the entrance, the outer forming the N edge of the cairn.

PORT ELLEN

A planned village of gable-to-gable houses ranged around the sheltered bay of Loch Leodamais. Founded 1821 by Walter Frederick Campbell, who named it Port Ellinor in honour of his wife. Like Port Charlotte (q.v.), many of its white, harled houses were built 'with two stories and a loft, on the scale of the manses of the clergy, and consequently look down on the lowly habitations of the farmers' (Lord Teignmouth, 1836). Although the herring fishing did not bring instant success, the settlement prospered as a small port serving the nearby distilleries.

CHURCHES

BAPTIST CHURCH, Lennox Street. Dated 1910. Painted ashlar gable front with hooded tripartite window. Crude birdcage bellcote.

KILDALTON UNITED FREE CHURCH, Frederick Crescent. Built 1911. Later known as St Columba's; now used as hall. Angle-buttressed gable to bay has four-centred entrance arch in wide but shallow ashlar reveal. Above this are three lancets under a pointed-arch hood and in the ashlar apex three small blind lancets.

ST JOHN'S PARISH CHURCH, Frederick Crescent. Built in random rubble, 1897–8, to a design by *Sydney Mitchell* adapted from the Romanesque church at Leulinghen-Bernes, near Boulogne. Restored 1987–8 under the direction of engineer *James Campbell Johnston*. The church faces w, a gabled sanctuary fronting a strangely hunched and hipped belfry from which rises a slated octagonal spire. Behind is a four-bay nave with low eaves and a lean-to timber entrance porch on the rear E gable. In the interior the ceiling follows the line of cranked trusses springing from below the wallhead. Pointed-arches, in grey-green stone similar to external dressings, open below the belfry to define chancel and sanctuary. – STAINED GLASS. In the w window, Christ the Good Shepherd, in memory of the Revd James Mackinnon, minister 1894–1938. – In the E gable lancets, in memory of Iain Ramsay of Kildalton †1942; to NE, two missionary saints in a boat, red-sailed yawls, and fishermen mending nets; to SE, a haymaking scene over a pensive shepherd-boy and stone carvers: both windows by the same artist.

PUBLIC BUILDINGS

PIER. The earliest quay, 1826, built in mass rubble with an inset stair, was improved in 1832, extended with a timber and iron steamship pier in 1847, and again enlarged and improved in 1881. A century later, 1981, the present concrete structure was constructed to provide roll-on roll-off facilities for the ferry connection with Kennacraig on West Loch Tarbert.

PORT ELLEN PRIMARY SCHOOL, Lennox Street. By *Strathclyde Regional Council*, 1975. Single-storey, roughcast classroom block flat-roofed with set-back fascias. High central water tank in red profiled cladding. Raised hall block at rear.

RAMSAY HALL, Charlotte Street. Somewhat church-like community hall erected in memory of John Ramsay of Kildalton. By *Sydney Mitchell & Wilson*, 1901–2. Dorset pea render with sandstone dressings and red-tiled roofs. SW gable front has a central three-light, two-tier, mullion-and-transom window which is pedimented with a thistle in the tympanum. To r., a square entrance tower rises to an undulating parapet and pyramid roof; coat-of-arms on parapet carries motto NUNQUAM SINE SPE. Pilastered and pedimented door with inscribed entablature. Five-bay hall has mullion-and-transom windows under 'transept' gables. Ridge ventilator with leaded ogee cap and weather-vane. Hall ceiling formed by cranked and collared trusses rising from corbel stones. Proscenium stage. Refurbishment and extension on NE gable, by *Thomas Smith, Gibb & Pate*, 1978–80.

WAR MEMORIAL, on a rocky knoll at the pierhead. Erected *c.* 1921. A kilted soldier stands, head bowed, on a stepped plinth; in grey granite.

INDUSTRIAL BUILDINGS

PORT ELLEN DISTILLERY. Begun as a malt mill in 1825, the distillery was established in 1827 and extended in 1887. A range of ten hipped-roofed, single-storey warehouses, built between 1846 and 1907, lines up as a white-painted rubble wall along the road to The Oa. There are three pagoda-topped malt-kilns, the largest roofed in red corrugated metal. Partial rebuilding, 1967. Along the A846, clad in blue profiled sheet, malting plant buildings, erected 1973, reach 30m. in height. Closed 1983.

DESCRIPTION

Townscape anchors at the ferry terminal. The pierhead space itself is open, indeterminate and untidy but intermittently alive. Two houses, gable-ended and gable-fronted, both dated 1894, make a tentative introduction to the town's two-storeyed streets, a beginning made immediately more emphatic in a short straight terrace of crowstepped gables, 1899. Then, passing over a pend that leads to a service yard with outbuildings preserving a forestair access, comes the ISLAY HOTEL, 1888, two storeys of square-snecked rough-faced rubble with attic bay dormers; disused and drab but a vital pivot into Port Ellen's two principal streets. CHARLOTTE STREET (Sràid Theàrlaig), running NNW, is an austerely ordered corridor of gable-to-gable, three-bay houses, early C19, each frontage identical in plot width. Save for a few gabled eaves dormers and a gap site at No. 22, both sides sustain a consistent eaves line. Almost all houses are roughcast with stone dressings. Decorative detail is all but absent; only No. 6 has a plain pilastered doorpiece. At the end of the street, raising the scale and the eaves line, is the WHITE HART HOTEL, late C19. Two tall side-by-side black-and-white blocks look W towards Kilnaughton Bay: the first and earlier, three-bay and three storeys with two ball-finialled gabled dormers; the second, four-bay and three storeys, but with the same eaves line and more gabled dormers. Both have Mannerist doorpieces with pilasters and consoles, that to the r. having a broken pediment clasping a small flower-filled urn in the gap. A short distance beyond the hotel, but far enough for its change in colour and texture not to matter unduly, lies the Ramsay Hall (*see* Public Buildings above) and, at the gushet junction of the roads to Bowmore and The Oa, Port Ellen Distillery (*see* Industrial Buildings above), its immense bulk also fortuitously peripheral. Opposite the Islay Hotel, FREDERICK CRESCENT (Corran Fhreadaraig) begins its sweep around the bay at the POST OFFICE, 1894. Two buildings lie on the shore side; one is the POLICE STATION, late C19, a tall, skew-gabled, two-storey mansion in coursed grey-green stone with a central pilastered doorpiece. Otherwise the seaward prospect is unimpaired. Like Charlotte Street the Crescent's houses are built gable-to-gable. But the eaves line jumps erratically and there have been some unfortunate intrusions and changes. Both the ARDVIEW INN, which has a roughly formed roll-moulded eaves, and its earlier three-bay neighbour to the E maintain modest C19 scale and detail. The Inn has gabled eaves dormers, a form which features repeatedly in succeeding wider-fronted flatted houses, bearing late C19 or early C20 dates. Beyond the United Free Church (*see* Churches above) is its former manse, No. 79, 1847–8, a high, skew-gabled, symmetrical house in painted ashlar with a fine doorpiece of fluted pilasters, consoles and cornice. Nos. 80–85 revert to a lower, still irregular, eaves line; No. 83, dated 1894, reintroducing gabled eaves dormers. Across Lennox Street, where a corner shop door has a cornice carried by flattened consoles on pilasters, the upper windows of Nos. 101–109 are all gabled. But beyond St John's Church (*see* Churches above), as the Crescent's arc turns S and then SW, most houses are single-storey – notably the three-bay cottages, early C19, which step smartly along Fisher Row. Finally, almost directly S across the bay from the end of Charlotte Street, come TEXA HOUSE and No. 145, both early C19; plain two-storey, three-bay dwellings, the former with a simple pilastered doorway.

Two other streets form part of the original layout. SCHOOL STREET (Sràid na Sgoile), a right-angled link from the pierhead to Charlotte Street, preserves a five-house gable-to-gable row at Nos. 31–35, early C19. LENNOX STREET (Sràid Leamhna), which is the uphill urban start to the A846 running NE from Frederick Crescent, lacks coherence: on the NW side the familiar three-bay pattern survives, but only just; on the SE, there is no such continuity, though the Baptist Church (*see* Churches above) and LILLEVILLE, dated 1888, a symmetrical house with finialled front gables, add some slight interest.

STANDING STONE, 1km. NE of Port Ellen pier, immediately E of road leading to Kilbride farmhouse. Schist stone, 4.3m. high, dagger-like in side elevation

PORT WEMYSS

Planned village above rocky shore opposite Orsay island. Only 300m. SE of Portnahaven, yet a distinct community. Founded by Walter Frederick Campbell of Islay, 1833, as 'Wemysshaven', taking its name from Campbell's father-in-law, Francis, 8th Earl of Wemyss and March. The street layout follows a D-plan; could this be in memory of 'Great Daniel', the Glasgow tobacco lord, Daniel Campbell, Laird of Islay, 1726–53? The settlement is entirely residential, the original houses being single-storey-and-loft set gable-to-gable along the streets.

PORTNAHAVEN

1652

Sheltered creek flanked by white cottages on Islay's Atlantic edge. Begun as a fishing settlement fostered by Walter Campbell, following his purchase of the Sunderland estate in 1788, but more purposefully developed by his son, Captain Walter Campbell of Foreland and Sunderland, in the 1820s. In place of earlier 'miserable hovels, many of which were merely holes in the bank', rows of three-bay single-storey-and-loft dwellings were built 'on a new plan' (RCAHMS Inventory, 1984) stepping gable-to-gable up the slopes around the bay. On higher ground came a Parliamentary Church and, later, some two-storey houses. After a long decline Portnahaven has revived as a holiday-home village.

CHAPEL and BURIAL GROUND, Orsay Island. Possibly C14. Small rubble chapel at the N end of the island. W gable and N and S walls survive but E gable demolished to permit rubble extension, late C18 or early C19. Two small lancets directly opposed towards E end of lateral walls; door at W end S wall: all three openings with slab voussoir arches. Surrounding burial enclosure of irregular plan; wall dates from the C19 building of the lighthouse (*see* below) but follows ancient line. In extreme N corner, a medieval MORTUARY CHAPEL, 'Hugh MacKay's Grave' (Tung Mhic Aoidh na Ranna); a small rubble structure roofed with slab-lintels and boulders comparable to similar Irish examples. Fragments of an Early Christian CROSS-SLAB, showing Greek crosslet in the lower r. quarter of ring-headed cross, are now in the Museum of Islay Life, Port Charlotte.

PORTNAHAVEN FREE CHURCH, E of branch road to Port Wemyss. Built to gabled T-plan as Free Church School, 1849. Arched belfry at apex of projecting central gable. Small square-headed windows in pairs. In 1875, converted to Church after sanctioning of charge. Taller, two-storeyed gabled MANSE built alongside, 1892. Church repaired, 1893.

PORTNAHAVEN PARISH CHURCH, Campbell Place. Behind its walled lawn, a pristine prim *Telford* Parliamentary kirk to standard double-doored T-plan by *William Thomson*. Built 1828 by Aberdeen contractors *John Gibb* and *William Minto*. Harled rubble with sandstone dressings. Obelisk-topped birdcage belfry on W gable. S windows have been re-glazed with three narrow mullions. N, W and E galleries, added pre-1831, have quarter-round links. – PULPIT has balustraded stairs each side and a pedimented and pilastered back-board.

BROOKFIELD, 250m. E of Parish Church. Built 1828 as Parliamentary Manse to standard two-storey Telford formula by *John*

Gibb and *William Minto*. Two-floor canted bay added to r. of central entrance. Porch and high two-storey T wing at rear also additions.

HOUSE, at NW end of Queen Street. Three-bay, two-storey late C19 house with gabled eaves dormers and canted bays to ground floor l. and r. Plain pilastered doorpiece. Decorative ironwork railings incorporating thistle motif to garden wall and above bays.

PORTNAHAVEN PRIMARY SCHOOL, E of branch road to Port Wemyss. Symmetrical T-plan classroom block in rubble with in-and-out ashlar dressings; dated 1878. By *William Railton* of Kilmarnock. Convex conically roofed entrances in re-entrants below eaves line. Adjacent three-bay gabled SCHOOLHOUSE also by Railton; similar in design but with segmental lintels to first-floor windows.

RINNS OF ISLAY LIGHTHOUSE, Orsay. Built 1824–5 by *John Gibb* of Aberdeen to a design by *Robert Stevenson*. Battered tower of rubble masonry with sandstone dressings, 6.15m. dia. at base, rises through five stages to a corniced balcony and lantern, 45.7m. above high-water level. Balcony railing and lantern framework are original but lens mechanism dates from 1896, modernized 1978. On the approach axis from NE is a semicircular single-storey flat-roofed store, the basement of which has a radial barrel vault. Behind the tower to SW is a courtyard; l. and r., keepers' houses, flat-roofed with coupled octagonal chimneystacks. Present living accommodation and machine room in detached block to E, *c.* 1900. Fluted SUNDIAL with brass dial by *Adie & Son*, Edinburgh.

SALIGO

A few houses above the dunes of Saligo Bay in NW Islay.

LOCH GORM CASTLE, on small island 350m. from SE shore. Scant rubble remains, C16 or C17, indicate an almost square plan fortified by circular bastions at the corners. Within the curtain are three closely related ruined structures; the largest, orientated NW–SE like the outer walls, retains several cruckslots. Never a substantial fortress and now scarcely visible, the castle retains a somehow awesome aura, perhaps a legacy of its role in the MacDonald–MacLean feuding of late C16–early C17 as much as the grim consequence of its bleak, remote location.

DUN, Dùn nan Nighean, 2.7km. N of Saligo. Remains of drystone wall cast around the landward end and flanks of a rocky promontory with 25m. cliff falls to sea. Some stretches of walling survive, the best preserved being a ten-course height of 1.6m. on NE. Unusual wall configuration on SE may suggest an entrance with a 'gatehouse'.

FORT, Dùn Bheòlain, 2.6km. N of Saligo. Described as the 'largest promontory fort on Islay' (RCAHMS Inventory, 1984), the defences comprise two lines of stone walling sealing off a massive, naturally stepped headland between precipitous cliffs. Outer and inner walls can be traced, the latter defining the more defensible higher ground.

FORT and SETTLEMENT, Beinn a' Chaisteal, 4.8km. N of Saligo. A substantial wall with a few outer and inner facing stones visible cuts off the promontory. The most remarkable features are several small circular structures above steep cliffs on the E side of Allt nam Ba' inlet. One such 'hut', ovoid in plan, has a corbelled slab roof. Evidence of rubble walls sealing off rocky promontories, presumably protection from landward attack. Dating unknown, but settlement may be related to seafowling.

HUT CIRCLES, An Sithean, on both sides of B8017, 1km. E of Loch Gorm. Eight hut circles, varying in dia. between c. 5m. and c. 9m., spread over a wide area. Evidence of early field systems.

STANDING STONES, Ballinaby, 1.2km. NE of Saligo. In 1772, Thomas Pennant reported three; two remain. The larger, 200m. WNW of Ballinaby farmhouse, tapers to a height of 4.9m., while the smaller, 220m. NNE of its neighbour, reaches only 2m.

TEXA

Island off the S coast of Islay separated from Laphroaig by the Caolas an Eilein strait.

CHAPEL and BURIAL GROUND, 60m. from N shore. Small, single-cell, rubble-built oblong, possibly of C14 origin. The chapel stands to wallhead height and both gables survive. Ruinous S door preserves a draw-bar slot and some sandstone dressings; evidence of window slots towards E end of N and S walls. Signs of rig cultivation and turf-covered footings of several buildings to the S indicate the existence of a small farming community, though only the banking enclosing the chapel appears to be of early date. A square enclosure close to the W gable may be a C19 addition. Medieval funerary FRAGMENTS found in the area have been removed to the Royal Museums of Scotland.

THE OA

A hilly rock-girt peninsula at the S end of Islay.

CHAPEL and BURIAL GROUND, Kilnaughton, 1.9km. W of Port Ellen. Late medieval oblong cell dedicated to St Nechtan; roofless, ruined, rubble walls stand almost full height but are partially engulfed by accumulated soil and sand, particularly along the S side. Blocked doorways at W end of N and S walls where adjacent socket holes suggest the existence of a gallery at some time. Evidence of small splayed window openings towards E end of both lateral walls and in E gable. Sanctuary has L-shaped aumbry at SE corner and stone shelves across NE angle. In decay by end of C18. There are three TAPERED SLABS, Iona school, in the chapel, one showing a full-length armed warrior in relief. Two other incomplete SLABS, C14–C16, found here are now in the Museum of Islay Life, Port Charlotte (q.v.). A number of other SLABS bearing C17 and C18 dates are in the busy burial ground. The rubble walls of two burial enclosures, C18 or C19, abut the E end of the chapel's N wall. In the graveyard wall is an inscribed TABLET recording that the lairs were enclosed by public subscription in 1852.

THE OA PARISH CHURCH, Risabus. Roofless shell of T-plan *Telford* Parliamentary church erected by Aberdeen builders *John Gibb* and *William Minto*, 1828–9, to standard two-door design by Crinan Canal surveyor *William Thomson*. The church had four-centred arches to the S doors and tall lattice windows; identical to that at Portnahaven (q.v.). It was damaged by fire in 1915 and finally closed in 1930. A pyramid belfry survives over the W gable, but with only one finial remaining. Memorial TABLET to ministers, 1829–1930, on inside wall.

PORT ELLEN LIGHTHOUSE, sited on the promontory of Carraig Fhada, 1.6km. SW of Port Ellen. Built 1832 as a memorial to Lady Ellinor Campbell, wife of Walter Frederick Campbell. Three-storey square tower to which is attached a slightly lower square stair stack forming L-plan. Both elements have a blocky corbel-cornice and parapet. Openings of varied architectural lineage: several round-arched windows, Y-traceried S oriel, shouldered lintel over door in N re-entrant, main W entrance below hooded four-centred arch. – Commemorative marble TABLET above W door; inscription in verse.

AMERICAN WAR MEMORIAL, Mull of Oa. Isolated clifftop monument perched above the sea. Built in memory of American soldiers and sailors who perished when the transport ships *Tuscania* and *Otranto* were wrecked off Islay in 1918. The huge circular cairn, built in splendidly textured green and ochre random rubble and nearing 10m. in height, is the design of architect *Robert Walker*. Below the conical summit are two rings of lighter stone with square recesses revealing the rubble core. Below this, an octagonal tablet, dated 1918, incorporates the American star and Scottish thistle. At the base of the cairn, fronting steps rising from the landward side, are two superimposed bronze PLAQUES set in heavily moulded ashlar frames: the lower and larger, which appears as if it were a doorway to the interior of the masonry, bears commemorative record to the tragedy; the upper, beneath a rubble relieving arch, is cast with the form of a winged eagle carrying a wreath.

FORTIFICATION, Dùn Athad, 2km. SE of Mull of Oa Monument. Headland summit from which cliffs fall to the sea some 105m. below. The landward approach narrows to a 2m. neck. Such natural advantages must have encouraged settlement from prehistoric times but the forework structure, with its frontal plane of facing-stones running E–W across the jutting promontory and returned S a short distance along each shore, probably dates from the C16 or early C17. Within the degraded rubble mass of the forework are signs of intramural cells and to the S turf-bank evidence of two small buildings or enclosures.

TOWNSHIP, Lurabus. A scattering of ruinous, rubble-built dwellings, enclosures, etc., 1.7km. SSW of Kilnaughton Chapel. The much-altered buildings, all of which date from the early C19, show signs of earlier cruck roofing and there are mural aumbries, stone-shelved cupboards and fireplaces. Evidence of rig cultivation.

TOWNSHIP, Tockmal, 2.5km. SW of Kintra. Deserted settlement surviving as a linear WNW–ESE arrangement of narrow rubble buildings now roofless and evidently much reconstructed. Besides dwellings and byres, smaller remains appear to be those of a water-powered mill and a corn-drying kiln. 100m. NW, the turf-covered rubble walls of a small chapel, possibly C15, can be detected; the township ruins are, however, no older than the early C19.

JURA

(see map p. 500)

A long mountainous island across the Sound of Jura from Knapdale. To the S, a short ferry-crossing connects with Islay; to the N, the dangerous waters of Corryvreckan and the uninhabited island of Scarba. Wild and fiercely beautiful, the Paps of Jura reach 785m., dominating the skyline for miles around. The landscape is one of rock and bog, with settlement confined to the more sheltered E coast. Crofting died with the evictions of the C19, and today there are fewer than 200 residents scattered along the island's single road.

ARDFIN

4863

Jura Estate's most fertile farming land, at the S end of the island.

CLAIG CASTLE, on Am Fraoch Eilean. Strategically located to command the Sounds of Islay and Jura, Claig sits on a cliff-edged island summit 20m. above the sea. Ground-floor walls survive to define a tower-house plan. These walls, 2.4m. thick, are of coursed rubble blocks rising from a battered plinth; fragmentary evidence of sandstone dressings and quoins. N entrance leads to a mural lobby from which an L-plan stair rose in the SE corner to upper accommodation now impossible to determine. The ground plan is divided into two compartments lit from narrow openings in the NE and SW walls. The castle, used as a fortress and prison by the MacDonald Lords of the Isles, cannot be securely dated but a C15 date has been suggested. Claims have been made for a C12 origin. When Pennant visited the island in 1772 it was already 'a ruined tower'.

JURA HOUSE. Seat of the Campbells of Jura. Vigorously erect if scarcely refined mock ashlar pile, 1878–83, by *Alexander Ross*. Piended gables and bay windows drawn up around a three-storey balustraded tower. Campbell arms and motto and an inscription JC/MC 1881 on the E wall record patron and date of building. The present house replaced an earlier Ardfin House to which *William Burn* had added offices and coach-house in 1838. In the WALLED GARDEN is a SUNDIAL with moulded square top and a metal plate inscribed 'Calendared for Ardfin in Jura 1812'.

STANDING STONE, 2.5km. WNW of Jura House and 800m. N of farmhouse, Camas an Staca, 'The Harbour of the Stone Pillar'. The finest standing stone on Jura, reaching 3.6m. in height.

STANDING STONES, 2.2km. E of Jura House and 650m. SSE of house of Strone. 3m.-high pointed pillar with its fallen neighbour, 2.65m. long.

STANDING STONES, 300m. NE of Sannaig farmhouse. Three in a row. Only the middle stone still stands, 2.2m. high; to NNE, a fallen stone, 2.6m. long; SSW, a vestigial stump.

ARDLUSSA

6487

An estate towards the N end of Jura, in the ownership of the MacNeills of Colonsay from 1737 until mid C19.

ARDLUSSA HOUSE. The four-gabled, two-storeyed façade, *c.* 1843, looks NE down a grassy meadow to Ardlussa Bay. This entrance wing, which contains the principal public rooms, is the latest part of the house, closing off the court of an earlier U-plan dwelling, itself an aggregation of lower gabled wings. Canted bays on NE and SE fronts. Approach from SW passes through the home farm; early C19 buildings with some blind lancets. A rough road continues past Ardlussa Bay with its early C19 rubble SLIPWAY and on to Lealt and Barnhill.

CROSSMAN BRIDGE, over Lussa River. Crudely battlemented rubble bridge with an inscription recording its construction in 1912 by Alexander Crossman, who, as laird of Ardlussa from *c.* 1902 until 1919–20, greatly improved the estate's roads and fishing. Four cone-capped piers of washed gravel boulders may be of later date.

AN CARN TOWNSHIP, 6.5km. NE of Ardlussa House. 200m. from the shore of the Sound of Jura are the drystone ruins of six small oblong dwellings and storage buildings with associated evidence of enclosures and rig cultivation. 80m. W is a corn-drying kiln, its drystone bowl 5.6m. in dia. An Carn was recorded by Pont, *c.* 1590, as 'Karn', but by the early C19 the township had been abandoned. Several rock surfaces around the buildings bear expanses of prehistoric cupmarkings.

CRAIGHOUSE

5267

The only village on the island; focused on distillery, hotel and piers S of Mill Burn, but strung out N along the coastal road.

JURA PARISH CHURCH, 700m. N of Jura Distillery. Harled skew-gabled kirk, originally with neither seating nor belfry, erected to supersede an earlier place of worship at Keils. Although the heritors decided to build in 1766 and there is a record of Archibald Campbell of Jura providing funds a year later, work was not completed until 1777. Four round-arched windows in the E wall; the second from l. formerly an entrance. In 1842, the church was galleried at the N(?) and altered to a T-plan to accommodate vestry and laird's loft for Colin Campbell of Jura; a conversion which prompted the writer of the *Statistical Account* to speak of 'such an air of comfort and elegance, as is surpassed by no other in the islands of Argyll' (1843). Seating, forestairs and possibly gabled belfry, all date from this time. Further alteration and renovation, 1922, entailed building the S entrance porch, removing the N gallery and forestair, renovation of the roof and recasting the seating to its present longitudinal arrangement. Coomb-ceiling with open scissors trusses. – STAINED GLASS. In the tall round-arch chancel window, Jesus surrounded by children, 'Erected in humble gratitude for the lads who returned safely', 1946. Various commemorative plaques including a plain travertine TABLET on the S wall 'To the Glory of God / and to the memory of / The Campbells of Jura 1666–1938', erected 1954.

CAIGENHOUSE. Slow curve of C19 gable-to-gable rubble cottages, once known as 'Mariners' Row'. FRISCO dates from 1870s; LORNE COTTAGE and MULINDRY are weavers' cottages, *c.* 1840; LAC-NA-BRUICH inserted into the row *c.* 1875.

JURA DISTILLERY. Founded in 1810, out of production by 1875, but revitalized and largely rebuilt, 1884. Single-storey gabled office and laboratory by the roadside may be early C19 cottages, but the buttressed roughcast cooperage and some higher buildings behind date from late C19 recovery. Tall, three-storey, piend-roofed manager's house with corbelled bay at second floor, 'more like a castle than a distillery'. Extended 1961–3 by *William Delmé-Evans*; bonded warehouse, 1971–2; enlarged from two stills to four, 1978.

JURA HOTEL. Two-storey, four-bay, gabled hotel, *c.* 1834, which may incorporate vestiges of the earlier drove-road Craighouse Inn. Attic dormers and lower wings l. and r. probably late C19. Various window changes and bedroom wing curving to SE, 1958–60, fail to add quality. A piend-roofed octagon bar marks the NW corner with more success.

JURA STORES, Small Isles Harbour. Early C19 grouping. Gabled rubble shop with gabled E porch. The adjacent two-storey house with skews and skewputts also has a gabled porch facing the harbour; former forestair replaced by tall piended projection to road.

MILL, across stream from Jura Distillery. Dark, skew-gabled slated block, *c.* 1775. Disused.

NEW PIER. Long concrete and steel pier, built 1952 to replace wooden distillery pier of 1880s, but now little used.

OLD PIER, Small Isles Harbour. Built 1812–14 to a design by road surveyor *John Sinclair* working under the direction of *Thomas Telford* and Commissioners for Highland Roads and

Bridges. Curving L-plan constructed in rubble blocks with landing steps on the inner face and a later flight on the outer side of the sea-wall. Rubble slipway from shore quayside.

STANDING STONES, Carragh a'Ghlinne, 1.5km. WSW of Jura Hotel. Four-stone group now engulfed by forestry plantation; only one, 2.4m. high, remains upright. Two fallen stones are of identical length but a third measures 2.9m.

FEOLIN

Nothing but the modern slip and pierhead shelter for the short ferry connection to Port Askaig on Islay. Feolin marked the start of Jura's Parliamentary road, built 1805–12 by the Commissioners for Highland Roads and Bridges to improve the old drovers' way NE along the Sound of Jura to the next ferry crossing at Lagg.

FEOLIN JETTY. Like that at Lagg, this rubble block jetty was constructed, 1809–10, to serve the cattle-droving route from the islands to the mainland. Designed by *James Hollinsworth* of Crinan, modifying 1806 proposal by *David Wilson*. The jetty is round-ended with symmetrical slipways each side.

INVERLUSSA

A few cottages at the head of Lussa Bay. Built for slate quarriers towards the end of C19, but now holiday homes.

KILLCHIANAIG BURIAL GROUND, on l. bank of Lussa River. No traces remain of medieval chapel. Some C18 slabs and headstones of local slate.

KEILS

Ruinous and conscripted indiscriminately to *ad hoc* modern usage, Keils nevertheless surprisingly preserves all the elements of a West Highland crofting village. The settlement lies some 400m. W of Jura's coastal road at the N end of Craighouse.

KILLEARNADALE BURIAL GROUND (Cill Earnadail), 500m. N of Keils village. No remains of the medieval chapel of St Earnadail are to be found. Fragmentary stone footings on both banks of Abhainn a' Mhinisteir probably indicate a former township. Rubble-walled GRAVEYARD extended S on battered base. In the burial ground are several TAPERED SLABS, C14–C15, carved with swords, plaitwork, plant-scrolls, etc., including one with the representation of scissors – in memory of a tailor(?). Maintaining this vocational custom is a much later slate HEADSTONE to Alexander McIsaac †1811, bearing the square and dividers of the carpenter's craft. Another gravestone commemorates Mary MacCrain †1856, aged 128.

CAMPBELL MAUSOLEUM, on the E side of the graveyard. By *William Burn*, dated 1838. Gothic Revival saddle-back roofed, barrel-vaulted cell with broad angle-buttressing at each corner. Spear-headed cast-iron railings project from moulded segmental arch entry. RECUMBENT SLABS and MURAL TABLETS from C17, C18 and C19, some, carved with splendid armorial achievements, are dedicated to the memory of members of the Campbell of Jura family.

KEILS VILLAGE. Cluster of rough rubble gabled dwellings, byres, stores and a pigsty, early to mid C19. Some thatched roofs survive, as do examples of pine cruck-couple trusses, notably in the byre-dwelling W of a yard marked by several cobbled haystack-bases.

LAGG

Township cluster of cottages on the NW side of the valley which runs NE into Lagg Bay. Until 1814, when the 'New Road' was extended NE to connect with the Loch Tarbert crossing to Colonsay, Lagg marked the end of the Jura drove road. This earlier track to the old pier and slipway (*see* below) still runs along the SE side of the bay.

FARMHOUSE, at head of bay where the 'New Road' begins. Former drovers' inn, early C19; severe two-storey, three-bay gabled house. Adjacent rubble barn has segmental-arch opening.

HARBOUR. At the end of the drovers' road bringing cattle from Jura, Colonsay and Islay for transportation to Keills in Knapdale is a rubble block SLIPWAY, 3.5m. wide, running in a slow curve between rubble parapet walls. Nearby is a PIER of similar construction, 35m. long by 4m. wide, which sweeps elegantly into Lagg Bay; to seaward, the pier wall is battered, while on the sheltered face a flight of built-in steps bends with the concave curve of the jetty. Following a design prepared in 1806 by Lochgilphead surveyor *David Wilson* but later revised by *James Hollinsworth*, engineer at Crinan, work on the harbour was begun in 1809 by Archibald Campbell of Jura and completed in the following year.

LEARGYBRECK

No more than an isolated derelict church at the W end of the bay of Loch na Mile.

JURA FREE CHURCH. Abandoned three-bay rubble shell. S gable with thin gabled bellcote and, below, a panel dated 1866. Rubble arched lancets retain double-hung sashes with Gothick astragals. Interior, entered through N gabled porch, formerly timber lined to dado and coomb ceiling.

CORRAN RIVER BRIDGE, 1km. NNE of Leargybreck. Powerful 32m.-long three-span rubble-built crossing carrying the Jura road N in 1809–10. Segmental arches, central span 7.3m., spring from stumpy cutwater piers. Designed by *David Wilson* of Lochgilphead and built by Lochgilphead masons *William Morrison* and *Peter McEwan* working for Archibald Campbell of Jura.

FOREST LODGE, 2.2km. SSW of Corran Bridge. Multi-hipped and chimneyed house and offices by *Alexander Ross*, 1874–6.

LIGHTHOUSES, on E shore of Lowlandman's Bay. Lighthouse-keepers' accommodation, built 1861, two narrow gables deep. Radical 1992 alterations included a new roof, one crowstepped gable deep with three attic gables athwart.

HUT CIRCLE, Cul a Bhaile, to r. of road 800m. NNE of Corran Bridge. Within the peat-obscured remains of an irregular drystone wall enclosure, a circular dwelling measuring 7.5m. in dia. has been excavated, revealing three phases of building.

TARBERT 6182

A few dwellings around Tarbert Bay which opens S to the Sound of Jura. 1.2km. W, all but bisecting the island, are the headwaters of Loch Tarbert.

ST COLUMBA'S CHAPEL and BURIAL GROUND (Cill Chaluim Chille), 130m. N of Tarbert Bay. Turf-covered vestiges of a small oblong chapel within a C19 rubble-walled enclosure. Entrance gap on S. Beside the W wall of the graveyard is a STANDING STONE, almost 2m. high, possibly of prehistoric date; both faces, however, now bear Latin crosses, the E face better preserved, with a raised square boss at its centre. HEADSTONES, legible and illegible, have been realigned in recent times; earliest inscription 1809.

STANDING STONE, 290m. WNW of St Columba's Chapel. A large stone, 2.5m. tall, readily seen just E of road.

MULL

(see map p. 501)

Largest of the Argyll islands and the most varied in topography. The NE shores are relatively sheltered, separated from the mainland by the narrow Sound of Mull. A chain of castles guards the marches of Mull and Morvern along the channel, always the safe sea-route to the outer islands. Car ferries call at Craignure, some *en route* from Oban to Coll, Tiree and the Outer Hebrides. Mull's only town, Tobermory, lies in the lee of Calve Island near the N end of the Sound. On the N and W lie open seas, the coastline deeply indented by Loch Tuath, Loch na Keal and Loch Scridain. Behind spectacular coastline cliffs Ben More rises 966m. at the mountainous heart of the island. To the S, the Firth of Lorn widens against the Ross of Mull peninsula, a long ragged-ended finger pointing W to Iona.

AROS CASTLE
2km. NNW of Salen

C13 coastal stronghold strategically twinned with Ardtornish Castle (*see* 'The Buildings of Scotland, *Highland and Islands*') visible across the Sound of Mull to the SE of Loch Aline. Sited some 15m. above the sea, Aros commands the central stretch of the Sound and, across the estuary of the River Aros below, the short route through Salen to the west of the island. This critical location ensured its importance as the principal point of contact between Mull and the mainland until the foundation of Tobermory in the late C18.

As with Ardtornish, what remains builds to a bold and dramatic skyline but is architecturally much reduced. At the NW edge of a craggy promontory are the ruins of an oblong hall-house, 25.3m. by 12.5m., constructed of roughly coursed basalt rubble with semi-dressed quoining. The walls, in places as much as 3m. thick, rise to a maximum of 10m. on the seaward N and E sides but otherwise, apart from a single stand on the W, barely survive. A single pointed-arch window to the sea shows signs of Y tracery. A few square-headed slit windows are apparent on this E wall. Two doorways, one blocked, the other ruinous, are also discernible; these probably opened into the bailey, the limits of which can be confirmed by vestiges of a curtain wall on the W and S. Entry to the bailey was probably gained across the ditch from the W. Below the E wall is a stone jetty which must have provided access to the castle from the sea. Interior full of debris and overgrown; joist-sockets and wallhead suggest that the accommodation rose two storeys to a parapet walk and attic chamber.

Built by the MacDougall lords of Lorn but soon in the possession of the Lords of the Isles, Aros has passed through the hands not only of MacDonalds but MacLeans and Campbells too, a violent history which, as Thomas Kirke observed in 1679, 'has cost already much blood'. By the start of the C18, however, Aros was derelict.

CHAPEL, Cill an Ailein, 1.8km. WNW of Aros Castle. Low wall remnants of a medieval chapel, discernible within a C19 walled enclosure now surrounded by C20 forestry plantation. Tapering SLAB carved with plaited cross, ring knots and sword; Iona school, C14–C15. Part SLAB, now a headstone, shows casket, shears and deer forms; C14–C16. A later HEADSTONE has relief of high-heeled shoe and cobbler's hammer; to shoemaker Donald McAlam †1742, and his wife Marie McLean.

AROS BRIDGE. Hump-backed segmental-arch bridge over River Aros, 12.2m. span, built in random rubble with rough copings. Constructed *c.* 1790.

AROS MAINS. Gabled two-storey roughcast farmhouse, long and plain. Piended porch. Mid C19(?).

BROCH, Ardnacross, 4.9km. NNW of Aros Castle. Little more than a stony mound remains, but enough to indicate a circular enclosure, 10.7m in dia., surrounded by a wall 4m. thick.

CAIRNS. 600m. WSW of Ardnacross farm, three kerb cairns; 5.5m.,

4.6m. and 3m. in dia. respectively. NW and SE of these cairns, three STANDING STONES were formerly in a linear setting; only one is still upright, 2.4m. high. 260m. NNW of Ardnacross Broch, a large CAIRN, 17.5m. in dia., rises 1.8m.

BUNESSAN 3821

Like Tobermory and Creich, Bunessan's beginnings were linked to the 5th Duke of Argyll's plans to establish a number of fishing centres on Mull at the end of the C18. The fishing failed but, unlike the more exposed and still more remote site at Creich, 8km. further W along the Ross of Mull, the sheltered bay at the SE head of Loch na Lathaich favoured Bunessan. Today the village is a sad, rather untidy place, only redeemed by its location. At Ardtun, 1.5km. NE, a scatter of small rubble cottages, early C19, some ruinous, some with corrugated-iron roofing, a few renovated.

BAPTIST CHURCH. 1891. Perfunctory gabled Gothic in coursed granite. Concrete columned porch at W end of S wall. Timber lined interior.

KILVICKEON OLD PARISH CHURCH, beyond Loch Assapol, 4km. SE of Bunessan. C13 oblong chapel, retaining its lateral walls only. Evidence of harling and thatching, the latter indicated by a series of pegging holes along the N wallhead. Within the walls is a tapered SLAB, showing a foliated cross, plant scrolls, a fluted column and animal carving, *c.* 1500–60. The BURIAL GROUND contains several post-Reformation graves. Three TABLE-TOMBS: two with armorial bearings commemorating members of the MacLean family, one early C18, the other dated 1755; a third carrying twinned the shields of the Camerons and Campbells, early C18.

PARISH CHURCH. 1804. Simple hall kirk, buttressed and gabled; built by local mason *James Morrison*. Apex bellcote. Boarded ceiling with wide coombs. Repaired 1828 and 1857. Interior recast, probably in 1908 by *Kenneth Macrae* of Oban, though the E gallery, which has a panelled front and is supported on two chamfered timber pillars, may be original.

ASSAPOL HOUSE, 1.3km. ESE. Harled three-bay manse, early C19. A second, shallower, three-bay unit added as SW front, mid C19.

BUNESSAN PRIMARY SCHOOL, 1km. E of village. 1869. Granite rubble L-plan, gabled Gothic with sprocketed eaves. Symmetrical W front has double lancets in end gablets.

MILL. Early C19(?). Roofless rubble ruin. T-plan with remains of wheel race on SE gable.

WAR MEMORIAL, 100m. NW of school. Erected *c.* 1920. Craggy cairn, *c.* 6m. high, topped by grey granite Celtic cross.

CALGARY 3751

Wide sandy bay looking W to Coll. From the small C19 rubble jetty evicted tenant families left for Canada, taking with them the name of their township to a new life in Alberta.

BURIAL GROUND (Cladh Mhuire). Walled, roughly rectangular enclosure situated at foot of wooded slopes which rise some distance back from beach. The graveyard is ancient, its Gaelic name indicating a dedication to the Virgin Mary. Two Early Christian GRAVEMARKERS, each incised with Latin crosses, survive as headstones. Other C18 recumbent SLABS and HEADSTONES.

CALGARY HOUSE. Looking w from the woods above Calgary Bay, this small but boldly castellated Gothic mansion, 1823, built of coursed basalt rubble with ashlar sandstone dressings, was known as Calgary Castle until the mid C20. Erected by Captain Allan McAskill of Skye, who had purchased land in Mornish in 1817. The design may be the work of *James Gillespie Graham*. Its symmetrical tripartite composition, two battlemented storeys tall over a sunk basement, is stressed by bartizans lugged to the raised central bay and by full-height octagonal turrets at the corners, an emphasis repeated on the single-storey flying porch. A short lower wing, similarly treated with battlement and corner turret, extends N. The plan of the original house is compact, only one large room deep, with a curving staircase placed centrally in the rear projection. Late C19 additions extend the accommodation E. Principal windows are Gothic: those to central first-floor apartment, rear stair and E wing set in Perp arches; those l. and r. of the main façade, though square-headed, medievalized by Tudor drip-moulds and lanceted or traceried sashes. A shallow-pitched piended roof with platform rises behind crenellated parapets, its diamond-plan chimneys laterally placed.

FRACHADIL HOUSE, 1.2km. E of Calgary House by B8073. Former manse, 1720. Three-bay, two-storey-and-attic, with chimneyed gables. Later extensions. Limewashed rendered finish.

DUN, Dùn Mhadaidh, 1.2km. NE of Frachadil House. On a summit above rocky inclines. Roughly circular plan with some masonry faces preserved. Exceptionally narrow SE entrance.

INIVEA TOWNSHIP, 1km. NW of Calgary House on S-facing slopes above the bay. Low-walled remains of over twenty dwellings, barns and enclosures, the houses well built of basalt blocks with pinnings. Pont's late C16 map records a settlement, but by early C19 the land had been cleared.

STANDING STONE, 8.5km. WNW of Dervaig, 230m. E of Cillchriosd. Strongly rectilineal stone, 2.6m. high.

CARSAIG

A few estate properties on the S shore of Brolass where the road from Pennyghael across Glen Leidle falls through woods to the sea.

CARSAIG HOME FARM. Early C19 crowstepped steading and cottage linked to Carsaig House by a wall.

CARSAIG HOUSE. A three-bay gabled laird's house, c. 1800, with double piend-roofed wings flanking open court at rear. Built as Pennycross House by the MacLeans of Pennycross.

INNIMORE LODGE. Much-chimneyed, gable-fronted house with battlemented tower; by *David Thomson*, 1877.

PIER. By engineer *Joseph Mitchell* for the British Fisheries Commission, 1850. Broad jetty of large square-cut stones now crumbling into sea. Close by are two single-storey fishermen's stores; one piended, the other gabled with a large armorial panel built into its S gable wall (carved motto VIRTUE MINE HONOUR) brought from Innimore Lodge.

CRAIGNURE

A small village clustering around the old jetty, 1853, on the S side of Craignure Bay. Since the completion of the car ferry pier, 1964, growth has been accelerated by tourism.

CRAIGNURE (TOROSAY) CHURCH. White roughcast kirk, aligned E–W. Built 1783 but repaired 1828, 1832, 1869, 1887 and later. Slated roof has open eaves and verges. Birdcage bellcote over E gable; lower vestry at W. Windows, attractively varied in size, set in segmental-arch openings. N gabled porch. Mirrored forestairs on the S wall provide access to galleries through matching gabled porches.

BAYVIEW HOTEL. Former manse, 1831. Skew-gabled, two-storey-and-basement harled house. Three-bay front with corniced doorway.

CRAIGNURE INN. White C18 inn; two storeys, but low scale. Lower flanking wings emphasize the symmetry of a simple three-bay front.

DERVAIG

A beautiful one-street village of white rubble cottages close to the head of Loch Cuan; a planned community of twenty-six paired houses founded by Alexander MacLean of Coll, 1799. Across a rubble bridge over a burn, short gabled terraces flank the approach. A two-storey gabled house, C19, good in long-shot but poor in close-up, terminates the straight street vista.

KILCOLMKILL PARISH CHURCH, 600m. SE of Dervaig. Stone fragments on the hillside above the village. The walled CHURCHYARD contains a medieval SLAB, Iona school, C14 or C15, carved with sword, plant scrolls and shears, and a number of recumbent post-Reformation SLABS, mainly C18, bearing various armorial panels.

KILMORE PARISH CHURCH. By *Peter MacGregor Chalmers*, 1904–5. Small but powerfully architectonic ochre roughcast kirk rising from a rocky gorse-flowered knoll above the haughlands of the River Bellart. Gabled nave, semicircular E apse and, at the W end, a tapering conically capped round tower evoke Irish Romanesque. Chalmers repeated the simple but remarkably beautiful towered formula in the small memorial kirk he built on Canna (*see Highland and Islands* volume in this series). The church replaces an earlier mid-C18 building of 1754 which itself superseded the medieval Parish Church of Kilcolmkill in Quinish. – CROSS, C14–C15, decorated with beaded interlacing.

BELLACHROY HOTEL. Above the burn at the entrance to the village, a C19 two-storey gabled rubble inn, spreading around rear yard.

DERVAIG PRIMARY SCHOOL, E of Parish Church. Built *c.* 1880. T-plan schoolhouse and classroom with triple windows, round-arched in S gable. Monopitch wing added, 1976, by *Strathclyde Regional Council*.

DERVAIG READING ROOM. Dated 1898; typical single-storey street front cottage now serving as Community Hall.

QUINISH HOUSE, 2.9km. NW of Dervaig village. Plain three-bay dwelling of *c.* 1810, possibly absorbing an earlier house; later extended on both gables. Canted bay wing to r.

STANDING STONES. Three groups, each aligned NNW to SSE: (1) 1.2km. N in forest clearing, four stones (one prone) varying from 2.1m. to 2.45m. in height; (2) 850m. E in clearing, four stones (two upright) all *c.* 2.5m. in length; (3) 850m. ESE, three stones (and a fourth removed to form gatepost in nearby wall), all smaller.

DUART CASTLE
3.5km. SE of Craignure

Like the superstructure of some lithic dreadnought, Duart sits high in the water at the entrance to the Sound of Mull. From this SE corner of the island, it commands the sea-ways, the first in a succession of fortresses which march with the shores of the Sound. And across the Firth of Lorn, Achadun, Dunstaffnage and Dunollie (qq.v.) are all within sight. Erected by the MacDougalls of Lorn in the C13, Duart passed to the Macdonald Lords of the Isles in 1354 and from them to the MacLeans before the end of the C14. Successive alterations and enlargements were made by the MacLeans, who held the castle until, weakened by resistance to Cromwell's troops, the family lost its estates and was obliged to cede Duart to the Campbells of Argyll in 1674. Extensive repairs were then carried out, but by 1748 the Board of Ordnance was reporting the roof 'quite ruinous'. Little was done and the fabric continued to deteriorate until in 1911 the MacLeans resumed ownership and effected a major restoration.

The castle's original C13 disposition, an *enceinte* almost square in plan and comparable in its rugged simplicity to a number of early W coast strongholds such as Castle Sween (q.v.), has been elaborated over the centuries into a more sophisticated courtyard arrangement, surrounded on three of its four sides by later building. First, towards the end of the C14, came a tower-house. Built

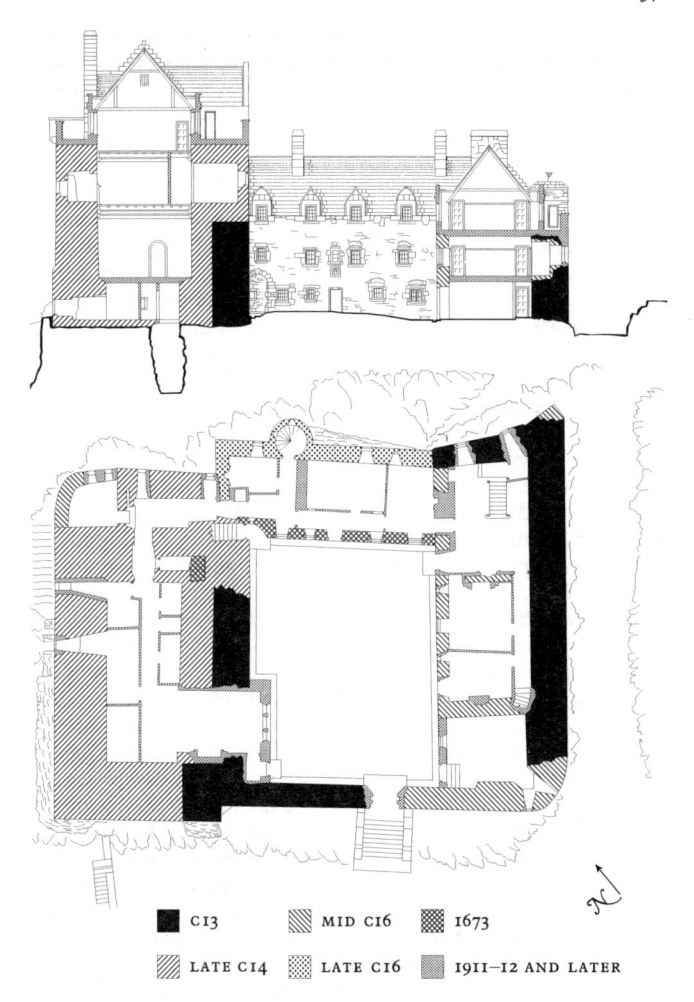

Mull, Duart Castle, ground-floor plan and section

against the NW curtain, which ran parallel with the main axis of its rectangular plan, the four-storey tower was raised above the cliffs on a vestigial area of land hitherto rejected as too confined and difficult. Next, in the middle of the C16, a lower range was erected against the inner face of the SE curtain wall. At the same time the *enceinte* was repaired at its E and S corners, the latter work extended along the SW wall to incorporate a new gatehouse. The tower-house, too, was remodelled: at the N corner an earlier postern was enclosed at ground level within what may have served as a small prison, and at the upper storeys angle rounds were added. Some time before 1600 the NE range (perhaps a rework-ing of earlier accommodation) was inserted. By 1673 this was under reconstruction to provide three storeys of domestic accommodation: most of the outer NE wall, including its projecting turn-pike stair, remained unchanged but the courtyard wall was completely rebuilt with eaves dormers at second-floor level. Thereafter, only intermittently garrisoned, Duart fell into decay until the restoration of 1911–12 by the Glasgow practice of *J.J. Burnet*.

The castle is entered through the SW curtain where a pointed-arch doorway, 1911–12, marks the position of the former gate-house, shown in an C18 drawing as a high crowstep-gabled projection. The chamfered arris at the head of the outer arch is probably C13. Distinctions between the C13 masonry l. and the repaired mid-C16 wall r. are masked by C20 facework around the entrance and at the wallhead. Still clear, however, are a small slit window and an oval-mouthed gun-loop formed in the C16 masonry of the curved S corner.

Diagonally across the courtyard in the N corner, a round-arched recess opens to a mural staircase which leads to the first-floor hall of the late C14 TOWER-HOUSE. In the yard's W corner another doorway, incorporated into a two-storey windowed bay of 1911–12 projecting from the SE wall, affords access to the ground floor. The tower-house walls, constructed of local basalt and granite blocks brought to rough courses with pinnings, are generally between 3.7m. and 4m. thick, but on this SE side where they absorb the C13 curtain they reach 4.9m. Most of the window openings, the parapet walls and crowstep-gabled cap-house, the glazed lean-to ante-chamber to the first-floor hall and an adjacent gabled room, both of which sit against the NE wall of the tower above the C14 postern and mid-C16 prison(?), are all the work of *Burnet*. So, too, are the interior arrangements throughout. At ground floor, an ancient rock-cut well survives but the original ceiling vault has gone, removed in the C17 or perhaps before. The first-floor hall is entered from the NE where, at the head of the mural stair rising from the courtyard, Burnet has created an ante-chamber under an open lean-to timber roof. This Sea Room, as it is known, links the hall to the NE range; it is a delightfully airy lobby, generously glazed to take advantage of the magnificent prospect over the Sound of Mull and Loch Linnhe. In the hall itself, ceiling beams on moulded corbels (most renewed) support the joisted floor above. The wide NW fireplace is of stone, a carved armorial panel set at the centre in a broad voussoir gap between inner and outer framing mouldings. In the S corner is the bay-window projection already mentioned. In the E corner, a cupboard; it once led to a narrow stair, now blocked, which descended to the ground floor. To the r., on the SE wall, a turnpike-stair, originally protected by a draw-bar, rises to the second floor. Here, two mural passages meet in the S corner of the SE wall, before opening to the wallhead walk over the SW curtain. A third passage, in the E corner of the SE wall, connects to a tight turnpike which twists to parapet level under a small gabled projection from the pitched roof of the caphouse. At this level, the entire construction, including the wallhead parapets and N and W rounds, is of C20 date.

The SE curtain, the most vulnerable to attack from the land, is 2.6m. thick, the thickest stretch of the C13 *enceinte*, and was originally without windows. When the SE RANGE was built in the mid C16, four openings were formed at first-floor level to light the new accommodation. At ground floor, there were four barrel-vaulted cellars, each lit by a small round-headed window and entered through round-arched doors in the new NW wall. The upper floor, a single apartment known as 'the old hall' by the time the castle passed into Campbell hands towards the end of the C17, was reached by a forestair from the courtyard. In 1911–12 Burnet reconstructed the C16 walls, adding new partitions and floors and a gable-ended, pitched-roof attic storey with ashlar-gabled eaves dormers on the SE and NW sides. From a return flight staircase which he constructed at the NE end of the range a landing permits access through the C13 walls to a small turnpike stair. Corbelled from the E corner in the middle of the C16, this in turn leads to the wallhead walk which passes in front of Burnet's dormers above the SE curtain.

The outer walls of the NE RANGE, where there is no parapet walk, date from the late C16. Wallhead repairs and re-roofing, including the conical roof over the projecting turnpike, were carried out in the early C20. Most of the few small windows at lower levels and the four eaves dormers were also introduced then. At the same time the inner courtyard wall was carefully restored, largely maintaining the elevational arrangement established by the reconstruction of 1673. While doorways at each end of this wall were converted to windows, the central door with its flanking windows was retained. The lintel of this door is carved with the letters S / A M and the date 1673 in memory of Sir Allan MacLean's rebuilding. Above this in a moulded frame is an armorial panel bearing the much-eroded shield of the MacLeans. Above this, a narrow window has been blocked, the first floor being lit by two restored lintelled windows on each side. At second-floor level Burnet again set four ashlar dormers into the eaves, aligning their height exactly with those on the adjacent SE range.

LIGHTHOUSE, Duart Point. 1899–1900. A low, cliff-edge tower in condensed Baronial, designed by *William Leiper* as a memorial to the Victorian romantic novelist, William Black.

FIONNPHORT

Ferry point for Iona at the W end of the Ross of Mull.

ST ERNAN'S, Creich, 1.5km. E on the N shore of Loch Poit na h-I. 1899. Small mission kirk in square snecked pink granite. Plain lancets. Apex bellcote on S gable.

THE COLUMBA CENTRE. By *John Renshaw*, 1996–7. White-walled, U-plan interpretative centre with low-pitched turf roof. Café/shop lit by glazed drum at the NW corner.

GLENGORM CASTLE

6.8km. WNW of Tobermory

Seen against Atlantic skies, the serrate outline of this isolated Victorian pile merges imperceptibly with the jagged silhouette of the pine wood to the S. Close to, the mansion has a starker presence, snecked rubble walls rising abruptly from grassy terracing to the W. Known first as the House of Sorn, it was built, 1858–60, for James Forsyth of Quinish following his acquisition and clearance of the lands of Mishnish in 1856. *Peddie & Kinnear* enlist all the Baronial forms of their contemporary work at Cockburn Street, Edinburgh, though with less relaxed ease. There is, of course, a general asymmetry in the arrangement of the parts and a corresponding willingness to respond freely in elevation to the internal needs of the plan. A high square tower with offset conically capped stair tube rises above the E entrance. Bulbous bows bulge from the NW and SE corners. Lower two-storey offices spread S. Yet the W front, which affords the first-floor public rooms a magnificent prospect of the sea, is, for all the Baronial vigour of two projecting gables (crowstepped, bartizan lugged, and nipped by splay and corbel into tall canted bays), relentlessly symmetrical. Alterations to the hall and staircase by *Charles S. S. Johnston*, 1911.

DUN ARA CASTLE, 8km. WNW of Tobermory. Ancient fortress on rocky Mishnish coastline. Traces of a stone curtain-wall which followed the irregular perimeter of the rocky summit survive. Within, footings of four buildings are discernible; most clearly those of an oblong Hall with rounded corners which suggest some form of piended roofing. Nearby are the scattered remains of several drystone buildings, cultivation-strips and an artificial harbour and jetty: evidence of a dependent township. Dun Ara has been held by the MacKinnons from C14 but may have more distant Iron Age origins.

DUN, An Sean Dun, 1.2km. SW of Glengorm Castle. Described as 'one of the best preserved duns on Mull', the construction of large masonry blocks – some as much as 1m. long – follows a circular plan. Entrance on ESE.

STANDING STONES, prominently located on ridge W of Glengorm Castle. Three stones stand to a height of just over 2m., though two have been re-erected this century.

GOMETRA

Island off the W coast of Ulva to which it is linked by a causeway over the narrow tidal channel of Am Bru. Now uninhabited.

BURIAL GROUND, Bail' a' Chlaidh, Gometra. Earliest headstone dated 1792. Railed enclosure with grave of Donald Lamont †1805, 'late merchant in Ulva'.

GOMETRA HOUSE. C18. Two-storey-and-garret, gabled dwelling of limewashed rubble.

GRULINE

A handful of estate buildings lying in woods along the course of the River Ba between Loch Ba and Loch na Keal.

ST COLUMBA'S CHURCH (Episcopal). Five-bay gabled nave in walled graveyard plot; by *Alexander Ross*, 1874. Simple lancets. Gabled W porch has REVERENCE MY SANCTUARY incised over arched doorway. Varnished pine interior stepping up to small chancel with tiled floor. – Oak LECTERN, CHAIR and DESK by *Tarbolton & Ochterlony*, 1937, incorporate designs by local carver *Mary Melles* of Gruline, who is remembered in a MEMORIAL TABLET. – STAINED GLASS. Gable window to sanctuary and two small W windows to chancel have abstracts by *Bronwen Gordon*, 1982.

GRULINE HOUSE. Built as Glenforsa House, 1861–5, by *Peddie & Kinnear*. Coursed rubble Baronial with crowstepped gables and a round angle tower. Alterations made 1897–8 by *Kinnear & Peddie*, and again, 1902, by *Peddie & Washington Browne*. A wooden corridor connects with Old Gruline House to SE (*see below*).

KILLIECHRONAN HOUSE. Brightly painted rubble house, *c*. 1840 but enlarged later. Symmetrical, with bargeboarded dormers to upper floor and canted bays on each side of central entrance. Nearby courtyard farm steading now converted to holiday homes.

KNOCK BRIDGE. 700m. SW of Gruline House. A hump-backed random rubble bridge crossing the River Ba in a single segmental arch; probably C18.

KNOCK HOUSE. Immediately W of the Ba crossing, a white C18 mansion looking NE across the fields. The original piend-roofed dwelling is not large, only two storeys high but swollen by full-height convex bays flanking a central piended porch. Later Victorian buildings added in an L-plan to the SE raise the ridge line by an extra dormered storey.

KNOCK BURIAL GROUND. A walled enclosure on raised ground 350m. WNW of Knock House. The oldest HEADSTONE, with a winged angel's head cut in relief, commemorates Florans Moreson †1745.

MACQUARIE MAUSOLEUM, Gruline Estate. Set at the centre of a rubble-walled circle of green sward is a small oblong Gothic blockhouse tomb, gabled and buttressed. White marble and pink granite insets in the end walls are carved with commemorative inscriptions to Major General Lachlan Macquarie of Jarvisfield, †1824, Governor of New South Wales 1810–21, 'The Father of Australia'.

OLD GRULINE HOUSE. Archetypally plain three-bay house dating from the late C18. Gabled with verges; symmetrical W front. Original interior panelling and fittings now in Macquarie University, New South Wales, recalling that Macquarie had owned Gruline (which he renamed Jarvisfield after his first wife, Jane Jarvis) from 1804. The preserved oak lining from the ground-floor parlour dates from the time of Macquarie's return to Mull,

1824, as does a lower one-room wing added to the S gable. E extensions are *c.* 1826 and later.

STANDING STONES. One, 600m. WNW of Gruline House, a straight-sided stone standing 2.3m.; the other, 270m. further to the NW, 2.45m. and tapered. Two indistinct CAIRNS nearby.

INCH KENNETH

Small rock-girt island lying off the Gribun coastline at the entry to Loch na Keal.

INCH KENNETH CHAPEL, on the E side of the island close to a sandy landing-place. Parish church built in the C13, used only as burial place from the late C16 and roofless by the time of Johnson and Boswell's visit to the island in 1773. Oblong plan orientated E–W. Lateral walls stand to eaves height except for the W part of the S wall. Gables much reduced, that to the E reinforced by weathered corner buttresses erected late C16 or early C17. Remains of N doorway indicate triple order jambs rising to a pointed arch. A few simple lancet windows. Altar base, rude aumbries, lamp-basin block. Within the chapel are eight TAPERED SLABS carved with the customary sword, ship, animal and vegetable imagery and including one bearing the effigy of a cleric with crozier; most identified as Iona school, C14–C16. – To the SW is a ring-headed CROSS, early C16, its shaft ornamented with chevron pattern margins. – Several post-Reformation stones are of interest, particularly those in the burial enclosure dedicated to the MacLeans of Brolas, *viz.* C17 SLAB with figure of armed man, C18 HEADSTONE carrying the heraldic honours of the Macpherson and MacLean of Duart families, and another bearing MacLean arms commemorating Donald MacLean of Brolas †1725.

INCH KENNETH HOUSE. Built *c.* 1837 as a 'new mansion' to replace an C18 house. Set on fire, 1882, and then rebuilt in the first years of the C20; a harled, three-storey house with a flat roof to collect rainwater. Extensive remodelling in 1934–5 created a conspicuous four-storey pile with crenellated battlements.

KILFINICHEN

A scatter of isolated buildings along the N shore of Loch Scridain. Some sense of village cluster around the kirk at the S end of Gleann Seilisdeir.

KILFINICHEN OLD PARISH CHURCH, 600m. SE of Kilfinichen Parish Church. Small chapel of uncertain medieval date; only its grass-covered base courses can be seen. – Lower section of a CROSS, C14–C15 Iona school, formerly in the GRAVEYARD, is now in Tobermory Museum. – MacLean MONUMENT, C18, in the form of a freestanding gable, with inset armorial panel and ball finials at wallhead and apex; similar to that at Pennygown Chapel on E coast. – Some C18 HEADSTONES.

Former KILFINICHEN PARISH CHURCH. Erected 1804; repaired 1828. A simple gabled oblong with lower gabled SW extension. Bird-cage NW bellcote. Pointed-arch windows in the side walls have Y tracery; gable windows square-headed. Now prettified into a dwelling, bargeboards and shutters have been added and rubble joints raked out.

KILLIEMORE HOUSE, 150m. NE of Kilfinichen Old Parish Church. Formerly known as Kilfinichen House. Plain two-storey-and-garret late C18 gabled house, five bays wide, later extended by one bay on each side and given a piended roof. Two attic dormers to the S are also piended. Random rubble with dressed surrounds.

STEADING, 200m. ESE of Killiemore House. High two-storey rubble farm with symmetrical piended wings forming a U-plan open to the S.

TAVOOL HOUSE, 6.5km. W. Two-storey three-bay tacksman's house, with gabled eaves dormers, C18(?). C19 gabled enlargements W are higher and wider, but preserve black and white simplicity. Now a youth hostel.

TIRORAN HOUSE, 2.0km. W. White, late Victorian, gabled house with canted bay. Some older buildings around the yard.

DUN, 400m. S of Killiemore House on the tidal isle of Eilean na h-Ordaig. 18m. dia. within walls of varying thickness. Entrances on NNW and SE, the latter checked for a door.

DUN, Dùn Bhuirg, 1.9km. SW of Tavool House. Set on cliff edge 15m. above N shore of Loch Scridain. Squashed oval plan within drystone walling. Entrance on E. Mural chamber entered at NE leads to the remains of a stair flight which must originally have risen to wallhead. Within the dun is a memorial to a drowned girl, 1896.

KILNINIAN

A scattering of houses along the N side of Loch Tuath.

KILNINIAN PARISH CHURCH. Mention in a rental document of 1561 makes it clear that, prior to the Reformation, the revenues of 'Keilnoening' accrued to the abbot of Iona. Later, minister and parish were repeatedly beset by clan warfare between MacLeans and Campbells. The present kirk, 1755, a simple gabled building, roughcast and slated, is orientated E–W on what is likely to be the site of the earlier medieval building. Dated lintel over S entrance door; above this, an arched window, furthest W of three round-headed openings in S wall. Over the W gable is a ball finial bellcote with four square-plan stumpy swollen columns framing a bell, recast 1891. Interior refurnished and perhaps rearranged. W gallery, early C19, is reached by a forestair at the gable. At the E end is a long but plain communion table of similar date.

In the CHURCHYARD are several walled burial ENCLOSURES, particularly along the W boundary where a series steps up the slope from the gate to the W gable. – TABLE-TOMBS, mid C18, record the passing of members of the MacLean family. – HEAD-STONE, dated 1739, recalling Anaball Campbell, 'releck' of Alexander McCalman, Minister of Lismore and Appin; it carries the crest and shield of the Campbells of Dunstaffnage. – In the N vestry extension are seven medieval SLABS, none over 2m., their decorative treatment indicating Iona school provenance, C14–C16.

TORLOISK HOUSE, 1.3km. E of Kilninian Church. Still detectable behind Baronial disguise is the tall three-storeyed bulk of the SW-facing five-bay skew-gabled house which Lachlan MacLean of Torloisk built 'some time before 1784'. Described then as 'a commodious habitation in the modern style', it grew larger still, acquiring a kitchen wing to the NW in 1811–12. In 1863–4 *MacGregor & Miller* added a pyramid-roofed half-octagon bay covering two bays of the principal façade and a high crowstep gabled transverse wing on the E, the latter embellished with a Baronial turret, 1879. A stone balcony, carried on cantilevered consoles, crosses the three unhidden bays of the old house at *piano nobile* level.

BROCH, Dùn nan Gall, 5.2km. SE of Kilninian Church. Although built on a promontory jutting NW into Loch Tuath, the site is relatively vulnerable. Walls survive to ten courses on the N inner face. The E entrance is checked and provided with a recess for a draw-beam. An internal opening on the S leads to a mural staircase. There are several other internal openings.

DUN, Dùn Aisgain, 2km. W of Kilninian Church. Galleried dun on a low rocky summit; circular in plan with exceptionally well-preserved walls. The NW outer wall stands twelve courses (2.75m.) and has a pronounced batter. W entrance, below which are indistinct stone outworks.

KINLOCHSPELVE

Church, manse and farm on a narrow neck of land between Loch Uisg and Loch Spelve.

KINLOCHSPELVE CHURCH, Barachandroman, 3.9km. E of Lochbuie House. Lonely Parliamentary kirk in rubble walled enclosure. Designed and built by *William Thomson*, 1828, to standard *Telford* T-plan. Y-tracery windows under four-centred arches in the N and S gables and in the walls of the projecting E aisle; all have lattice glazing. Porch added against S gable. Bellcote to N. Interior recast, 1902–3(?).

CRAIGBEN (Creach Bheinn), 400m. W of Kinlochspelve Church. Baronial lodge, *c.* 1885, vigorous in texture and form: crowsteps, tall transom-and-mullion stair window, and a two-storey conically capped bartizan in re-entrant angle. The building incorporates fabric from the C19 Kinlochspelve Parochial School.

KINLOCHSPELVE MANSE, Barachandroman. Severe, three-bay, two-storeyed Telford manse looking W down Loch Uisg. Also by *William Thomson*, 1828.

LOCHBUIE

6124

Well-wooded estate settlement occupying the short isthmus separating Loch Buie from Loch Uisg. A little to the W, where the road from Strathcoil and Loch Spelve ends, is a scatter of generally single-storey cottages.

ST KENNETH'S CHAPEL (Caibeal Mheamhair), Laggan, 1.5km. SE of Moy Castle. Late medieval church, consecrated 1500 but largely rebuilt in 1864 as a mausoleum for the MacLeans of Lochbuie. Roof, E gable and the blocking of three narrow windows in the N, W and S walls all date from this restoration. Renovated 1972. In the interior a Gothic Revival screen seals off the E end. – The basin of a late medieval FONT of Carsaig sandstone survives, as do a number of carved SLABS and TABLE-TOMBS of C17, C18 and C19 date.

ST KILDA'S CHURCH (Episcopal), 400m. W of Lochbuie House. Simple Gothic, 1876. In the porch is an Early Christian stone with carving of ring-headed cross.

CORONATION MONUMENT, 850m. W of Lochbuie House. Rubble pyramid on a triangular plan bearing an inscription on a tablet: 'Erected by Lochbuie and his Highlanders'. It commemorates the coronation of King Edward VII and Queen Alexandra, 1902.

LOCHBUIE HOUSE. Completed 1793 by clan chief Murdoch MacLean. Tall, three-storey-and-attic, skew-gabled mansion; 'spacious and handsome', if somewhat gaunt. It follows a familiar Georgian model. Five bays wide with a pediment over the central three. To l. and r. are low two-storey flanking wings with piended projections. The distyle porch is later. The NW wing, *c.* 1910, also two-storeyed but this time high, terminates the wide-spread SW façade in a bow-fronted, pedimented gable. In the interior a wrought-iron YETT from Moy Castle can be seen.

MAUSOLEUM, An Caibeal, 200m. NW of Lochbuie House. Gabled oblong, 5.7m. by 4.3m., now roofed with corrugated iron. Entrance with moulded architraves set asymmetrically in the S gable. To the l. of this doorway a carved stone panel bears the arms and motto of the MacLeans of Lochbuie. Raised 1777 in anticipatory memory of John, 17th of Lochbuie, the builder of Old Lochbuie House, and his family.

OLD LOCHBUIE HOUSE. Shell of 1752 laird's house absorbed into the outbuildings of Lochbuie House. Described by Boswell, on his tour with Dr. Johnson in 1773, as 'a poor house, though of two storeys indeed'.

LOCHDONHEAD

7333

A concatenation of single-storey dwellings strung out in an arc around the N end of Loch Don.

KILLEAN PARISH CHURCH, N shore of channel connecting Loch Spelve to Firth of Lorn, 5.4km. S of Lochdonhead School. Grass-covered traces of an oblong medieval chapel set within its burial ground. Probably abandoned in the C17. In the CHURCHYARD, part of a late medieval SLAB, now a headstone, with foliated cross, Iona school, C14–C15, and a trefoil-cusped window head FRAGMENT, early C16.

TOROSAY FREE CHURCH, in a small burial ground. 1852, renovated 1898. Gabled with birdcage belfry.

AUCHNACRAIG BRIDGE, at S end of hamlet. Single segmental arch span, 10.7m., constructed in rubble with slab voussoirs. Part of the 5th Duke of Argyll's 1790 roadworks connecting Aros to Grass Point.

GRASS POINT FERRYHOUSE. Two-storey gabled drovers' inn; standard three-bay pattern with gabled porch. Single-storey wings and outbuildings including re-roofed byre. Possibly C18; restored 1946–8.

GRASS POINT JETTY, 3.2km. SE of Lochdonhead School. Early C19 structure of large open-jointed stones built for the Kerrera–Oban ferry.

LOCHDONHEAD SCHOOL. Harled, T-plan, double classroom block, c. 1845. Two-storey schoolmaster's house added, 1878, by *James R. Youngson* of Oban. House extended N, c. 1928, when original forestair access was removed. Monopitch classroom linked N, 1977, by *Strathclyde Regional Council*.

CAIRN, Port Donain, 4.2km. S of Lochdonhead School. Well-preserved kerb cairn on gently rising ground at the head of Port Donain Bay. W kerb-stones survive. Close to the SE edge of the cairn is a 4.1m. slab, which may be a fallen standing stone.

CHAMBERED CAIRN, Port Donain, 4.4km. S of Lochdonhead School. Cairn measuring 32m. by 11m., with a ruined chamber at the NE and cist at SW. The portal stones of the chamber survive.

MOY CASTLE
90m. S of Lochbuie House

Stronghold of the MacLeans who acquired Lochbuie estate from the Lords of the Isles in the late C14. Roofless early C15 tower-house rising from a battered base with broad corner buttressing set on a low outcrop of rock at the head of Loch Buie. The plan is square, with the barely discernible evidence of a barmkin, roughly elliptical in shape, tailing off to E. Rubble walls are of beach boulders and schist, still harled in places but extensively overgrown by creeper. They rise some 14m. through three storeys and garret to the remains of two later caphouses. Windows, most with chamfered flush surrounds, are few, their margins wrought in greenish Carsaig sandstone. Detailing is generally crude in random slit openings, but more precise in two NW lancets and a number of square-headed windows which light later upper apartments.

These upperworks, carried out by John MacLean or his son Hector in the late C16 or early C17, effected some modest architectural elaboration. The parapet, not corbelled but flush with the main wall plane, retains a ruinous embattled profile, part original, part the irregular remnants of later remodelling as window openings or infilled crenellation. A series of rubble and slate spouts throws water from what must originally have been an open walk on all four sides of the tower. Corbelled rounds at the N and E corners, each turret windowed, corniced at eaves, but unroofed. A raked pistol-loop in the N round covers the approach to the castle entrance below. Caphouses at the S and W corners; the NW gable of the latter crowstepped with twinned chimneys on a stack carried on a double course of corbel stones and stepped in elevation over a small square window formed from an earlier crenelle.

The tower is entered at ground level from the barmkin on the NE. Behind the door was a wrought-iron yett (now in Lochbuie House) secured by timber draw-bar. To the l. of the vaulted entrance lobby a mural stair of rough stone treads rises in two flights, dog-legging r. past a vaulted entresol chamber at which level another external door, its pointed-arch opening now blocked, seems to have provided access to the barmkin wall-walk. At first floor the stair-head landing leads r. to hall. Ahead, in the tower's S corner, a turnpike stair gives access to the upper apartments.

The main chambers at ground and first floors are barrel-vaulted but in opposed directions. Narrow related entresols, possibly bedrooms, are vaulted in parallel. The lower entresol extrados rises above the level of the first-floor hall along its NE side, perhaps coinciding with a former dais. In the floor of an L-plan garderobe in the W corner is a hatch to a mural pit-prison. The second-floor chamber is entered from the turnpike lobby through a pointed-arch doorway, dating from the original C15 work. NW of this entrance passage was another garderobe connecting to a latrine-chute in the W corner of the tower but, during changes in the late C16 or early C17, this was opened up to form a wide-arched fireplace for the main room at this level. This room is now roofless but five opposed pairs of corbel stones indicate support for the beams which carried a joisted ceiling. Slit windows throughout: all set in deep splayed embrasures, segmentally vaulted; those in the SW and SE walls of the first-floor hall with stone benches. Interestingly, as first built, the tower had no mural fireplaces or flues, a feature shared with Breacachadh Castle, Coll (q.v.), and Kisimul Castle, Barra (see *Highland and Islands*).

Complex changes have occurred at the uppermost level of the tower. At first, a C15 parapet walk on all four sides of gabled garret; later, in the C16 or C17, this walk was restricted by caphouses at the W and S corners. Only ruinous vestiges survive.

On the loch shore, 36m. S of tower, are two rows of large boulders marking a former BOAT-LANDING. An arc of similar stones crossing the river mouth may indicate an artificial anchorage or fish-trap.

STONE CIRCLE, 400m. N of Moy Castle. A 12.3m. ring of nine stones, eight of which are *in situ*. Most slabs are of granite, set with their flat faces directed inwards. The largest stands 2m.

There are a few outlying stones, the most notable of which, 3m. high, lies 38m. SW of the circle.

PENNYGHAEL

A handful of houses between the Leidle River and the Carsaig road lined along the landward side of the Loch Scridain route W to Bunessan and Iona.

CROSS (Crois an Ollaimh) on shoreside of A849, 800m. W of junction with Carsaig road. Rough-cut Latin cross, now standing 1.28m. but probably originally higher, carved on its W face with initials GMB and [D] MB separated by the date 1582. Commemorates members of the Beaton family, who from medieval times were famed locally as physicians.

BRIDGES. 1835–6. Three single-arch rubble bridges carrying the A849 across streams at Pennyghael, Torrans and Beach.

KINLOCH HOTEL, 3.0km. NE. Early C19; three-bay gabled inn. Gabled attic and two-storey canted bay r. added later.

PENNYCROSS SCHOOL. 1872. Combined school and schoolhouse, the latter gabled to road. Square snecked pink granite. An unremarkable work of *R. Rowand Anderson*, carried out, one suspects, *en passant* to more important restoration commissions on Iona.

PENNYGHAEL LODGE, 500m. S of A849. Originally a small C18 laird's house. First extended, 1816–19, on instructions sent from Canada by John McGillivray, founder of the North West Co., but enlarged in the 1920s to its present wide but dull front, gabled at the centre with advancing piended end pavilions. Abandoned.

ROSSAL FARM, 3.5km. NE. Three-bay, two-storey gabled house, early C19(?), its symmetry stressed by a central attic dormer, gabled porch and set-back wings l. and r. Crisply restored in the 1980s.

SALEN

A T-junction village, 2km. SE of Aros Castle, developed early in the C19 by Major-General Lachlan Macquarie of Jarvisfield at a location halfway up the Sound of Mull which, being only 3.5km. NE of the head of Loch na Keal, was within easy reach of Macquarie's estate and the island's west coast settlements. Some single-storey cottages cluster pleasantly around the debouch of the Allt na Searmoin. In the centre, CRAIG HOTEL, early C19, a tall, three-bay, two-storey-and-attic, gabled house shorn of its skews and dressed surrounds. Across the street, a better example of the same, THE COFFEE POT, retains a central consoled and corniced doorway. 500m. N, the village PIER, 1904, decays in squalid dereliction.

PENNYGOWN CHAPEL, 3.5km. E. Ruined remains of an early C13 chapel; possibly abandoned by the C16, it had certainly fallen

out of use by 1787 when a map of Torosay parish described it as
'an old kirk'. Oblong in plan, orientated E–W. Basalt rubble
walls stand to wallhead, the gables having been reduced. Three
narrow windows with splayed ingoes: two opposed at the E ends
of side walls and a third in the W gable; all with chamfered round-
arched heads cut in monolithic outer lintels. Partly preserved
semicircular arch over the W door in the N wall. E aumbry
recess; two corbelled brackets above for lights or images. Paired
corbels at W ends of lateral walls may have helped support a late
medieval gallery.

Erected within the church is part of a CROSS, *c.* 1500–60,
1.3m. high by 0.38m. wide, carved on the front with crucifix,
plant scroll, griffin and sailing galley and, on the rear, in high
relief, the Virgin and Child. In the GRAVEYARD are two C17
SLABS bearing full-length figures, male and female; two more
SLABS, C18, with shields and inscriptions; and a number of
TABLE-TOMBS, C18, several of which commemorate members
of the MacLean family. – MacLeans, too, are honoured in the
armorial panel and inscription of a large sandstone tablet, 1763,
set at the centre of a free-standing gable MONUMENT, rudely
dignified by its contrast with the texture of the rubble wall and
further enhanced by sandstone finials set at apex and wallheads.

Former SALEN FREE CHURCH. Unaisled Gothic nave by *John
C. Hay*, 1882–3; now crassly converted to residential use.

SALEN PARISH CHURCH. Dated 1899; by *William Mackenzie*. A
low nave with N and S gabled transepts. Buttressed gabled porch
overlaps N transept. Built in rough-faced grey granite rubble
with ochre sandstone dressings. Cusped windows and plain plate
tracery. Arch-braced truss and rafter roof. Pews removed and
interior recast with raised chancel in the W end; masonry exposed.
– Octagonal pitch-pine PULPIT, with tracery panelling, raised
on squat pedestal.

SALEN MANSE. Two-storey Parliamentary manse by *William
Thomson*, 1828; additions 1902.

SALEN PARLIAMENTARY SCHOOL. Built *c.* 1850. Additions by
Alexander Ross of Inverness, 1875–6. Altered by *Donald Cattenach*
of Tobermory, 1910.

SALEN PRIMARY SCHOOL. Community school, determinedly
horizontal beneath rust-tiled shallow pitch roofs. By *Strathclyde
Regional Council*, 1984.

CALLACHALLY FARMHOUSE, 2.1km. E. Three-bay, two-storeyed,
harled farm with skew gables. C18(?). Derelict.

PENNYGOWN FARMHOUSE, 2.8km. E. C18. Harled, two-storey,
gabled L-plan.

TOBERMORY

Founded in 1787 by 'The British Society for Extending the
Fisheries and Improving the Sea Coast of the Kingdom', Tobermory
was a natural choice for settlement. Its W coast location and
protected bay could not have seemed more practical, nor its

sheltered, steeply banked, wooded setting more congenial. As William Sacheverell wrote in 1702, 'Italy itself, with all the assistance of art, can hardly afford anything more beautiful and diverting.' In spring 1788 the Society's Governor, John, 5th Duke of Argyll, started to feu his land from the Baliscate Burn at Ledaig around the bay as far as the estate boundary at the Mishnish Burn. Building began on the narrow coastal strip under the direction of the Society's agent, James Maxwell. Masonry breastwork stabilized the shoreline. By 1790 a Public Storehouse, Officers' Lodging and Custom House had been erected in U-plan formation on the harbour front, the Lodging and Custom House designed by *Robert Mylne* as matching pavilion-roofed buildings on either side of an open court. To the NE of this central group, across a track which wound uphill, a New Inn, also by Mylne, was begun. To the SW, edging the bay, a line of neat two-storey houses had, by 1796, created 'a very good parade ... all slated and white'.

Meanwhile, to a master plan which *James Maxwell* had prepared in 1790, a new upper town was also taking shape where the lie of the land levelled out above the abrupt natural rise ringing the harbour. The plan was straightforward: two streets, Breadalbane Street and Argyll Terrace, the latter open to the prospect of the bay, were laid out parallel to the shoreline below. Halfway along their length a third street crossed at right angles. Plots in this simple grid were 24m. (80 ft) deep by 9m. or 18m. (30 ft or 60 ft) wide, the houses one or two storeys in height with slated or thatched roofs. Though the thatching has gone, the same scale and pattern remain today.

As a fishing station Tobermory failed to meet expectations. It did, however, prosper as a trading post, stimulated by the opening of the Crinan Canal in 1801 and later by the completion of the Caledonian Canal. A proper jetty was extended from the Breast Wall in 1814 and a few years later the first steamer arrived. But it was tourism which ensured the town's future, first Mendelssohn and, later, Queen Victoria signalling the romantic attraction of the Hebrides. Over the three decades from 1820 to 1850 the northern edge of the bay developed to its present form, a succession of eaves-dormered, gable-fronted properties reaching two, three and even four storeys in height. Less constrained by topography, the upper town has continued to grow somewhat haphazardly beyond Maxwell's original grid.

CHURCHES

Former BAPTIST CHAPEL, Main Street. Simple four-bay gabled hall in dark rubble. Some surviving Gothick astragals in pointed-arch windows. Walled lawn to shoreside. Built 1862, since 1964 it has functioned as Lodge Tobermory St Mary's No. 1310.

Former FREE CHURCH, Main Street. Nave-and-aisles Gothic in rough rubble by *John C. Hay*, 1877–8. Facing the harbour, a central gable with eight-spoked wheel window above gabled porch arch; to l., an octagonal stair turret with octagonal pyramid

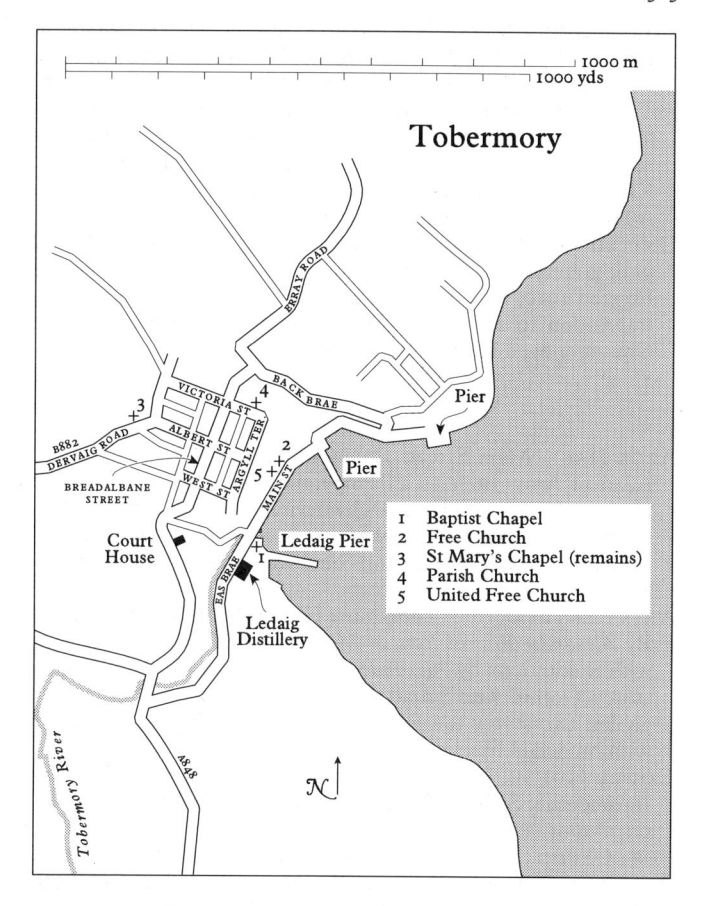

[Map of Tobermory with legend:
1 Baptist Chapel
2 Free Church
3 St Mary's Chapel (remains)
4 Parish Church
5 United Free Church]

roof; to r., a taller belfry steeple with pinnacled broach spire. Converted to 'The Gallery' craft shop in 1964. The church has lost its sanctuary furnishings but retains some stencilling on plaster. Gallery, at rear, now dangerous. – STAINED GLASS in the E gable erected in memory of Bryce Allan of Aros, 1878.

The church's set-back from an otherwise continuous street wall repeats the recessed location of the Storehouse built on this site, *c.* 1790, by the British Fisheries Society.

ST MARY'S CHAPEL, 400m. w of Tobermory harbour. Vestigial remains of uncertain medieval date. – Located within the visible line of the chapel walls is a medieval SLAB carved with two female figures, foliated cross, scrolls and a partially decipherable inscription, Iona school, *c.* 1500–60. – Two other part SLABS, C16. – Later GRAVESTONES commemorate British Fisheries Society settlers. – The site of Mary's Well (Tobar Mhoire), which gave its name to the town, is said to lie 80m. s of the chapel, but is now marked by a granite CROSS, 1902, to the E.

TOBERMORY PARISH CHURCH, Victoria Street. Victorian Gothic, 1895–7, by *John Robertson* of Inverness; a five-bay nave with pinnacled square w tower and adjacent gabled porch. Tobermory's first place of worship, demolished 1895, was also located on this upper edge of the town. It was a *Telford* Parliamentary Church, built 1827–8 for the parish of Kilninian and Kilmore to a standard twin-doored design by *William Thomson*. A Hall, erected in 1890, still survives.

UNITED FREE CHURCH, Main Street. Rough-faced Ross of Mull pink granite fails to invigorate a pusillanimous pointed idiom. Erected 1910; amalgamation with the Parish Church led to its translation to a knitwear factory in 1953. In 1964 the Free Church moved back from next door.

PUBLIC BUILDINGS

AROS HALL, Main Street. Dated 1898. The gift of Alexander Allan of Aros. Built as a Temperance Institute, 1882; rebuilt 1898, and renovated 1974. Dully devised gabled block with pink granite dressings. The site was first occupied by *Robert Mylne*'s Lodging for Comptroller and Surveyor of the British Fisheries Society.

ARTS CENTRE (former Tobermory High School), Argyll Terrace. By *Alexander Ross* of *Ross & Mackintosh* of Inverness, 1875–6, with N additions by *Alexander Shairp* of Oban, *c.* 1897. Single-storey Gothic with broad lancets and blind roundels in the gables; two-storey tower with half-octagon hip. Tall chimneys with broached bases.

COURT HOUSE, Upper Town. 1861–2, by *Peddie & Kinnear*. Intimidating Scottish Baronial blockhouse bleakly symmetrical on all four façades.

POST OFFICE, Main Street. Undistinguished, indeed unattractive, two-storey piended building. Yet this is the original Custom House erected to the design of *Robert Mylne*, 1789–90. Much altered inside and out.

SEA WALL and PIER, Main Street. The original 200m.-long breastwork of 1788–91 which supports the reclaimed land forming part of Main Street can still be seen; retaining wall of massive drystone blocks built by *Hugh* and *John Stevenson* of Oban. Projecting *c.* 90m. SE from NE end of this shoreline reinforcement, the Pier, completed 1814 by *Thomas Telford*, is of similar masonry construction, though stone joints have later been lime mortared. Parapet wall along the Pier's NE side.

TOWN CLOCK, Main Street. 1905, by *Charles Whymper*. Centrally located at pierhead. A tapering granite shaft on stepped plinth supports a corbelled lead-faced cube with clock dial on all four faces. Pyramid roof capping. Endowed by pioneer traveller Isabella Bird in memory of her sister Henrietta 'on a pattern similar to one in Huntingdon her native place', i.e. at the village of Houghton, where Whymper's tower had risen through the centre of a thatched shelter.

DESCRIPTION

The EAST BRAE road from the S falls steeply through the green glen of the Tobermory River to open suddenly on the bay. To the r. are the DISTILLERY, begun 1822, rebuilt 1878 and 'extensively reconstructed' 1970–2, the former Baptist Chapel (*see* above) and Ledaig Pier, 1822; 1835–44. On the l., cut into the hillside, is the distillery's BONDED WAREHOUSE, late C18 or early C19, a seven-bay, four-storey rubble building converted to housing by *Kinghorn Mee*, 1992–3. Facing the sea, MAIN STREET splashes colour round the bay: olive, blue, brick red, black, grey and lemon – Mediterranean rather than Hebridean; controversial perhaps, but with appropriately gaudy nautical zest. A two-storey row, *c.* 1795, at the SW end of the street, retains something of the 'slated and white' scale and character of the first settlement. Towards the Pier, where church spires (*see* above) add a later vertical accent, this has been lost. But at the Post Office (*see* above) and CO-OP BUILDING it returns, the former preserving a piend roof of the original Custom House, the latter a porthole window from the New Inn. BLACK'S LAND and BROWN'S LAND, both early C19, rise to three storeys with attics and façade gables. Original shopfronts survive. Then comes the CLYDESDALE BANK by *John C. Hay*, *c.* 1880, cranking the street E in hefty Baronial, its conically capped corner bartizan like the barrel of some swollen urban hinge. Two storeys next, though with dormered and gabled attics, until at the MISHNISH HOTEL and its neighbours, PORTMORE BUILDINGS and ROYAL BUILDINGS, higher scale is restored. Three four-bay units; attic dormers and one façade gable, a central pilastered and pedimented doorway, more shopfronts: all of this mid C19.

Main Street terminates at Tobermory's deep water PIER, opened 1864, rebuilt 1985. Crude but daring white, 'Thirties Moderne FERRY TERMINAL, 1936; flat roof, corner windows, full-frontal cantilevered balcony. A short stiff climb leads to the WESTERN ISLES HOTEL, 1882–3, by *John C. Hay*, a vast dreary pile of blue whinstone rubble overburdening the brae. Built for the proprietor of the Mishnish Estate, Frederick William Caldwell, who had earlier commissioned the pier below, it captured much of the late Victorian tourist trade. Beside its bulk the neat gable-to-gable dwellings of the upper town belong to another, more diminutive, world. But it is an ordered world, through which runs BREADALBANE STREET, broad and tree-lined, with almost boulevard grandeur. At its N end, MANSEFIELD, 1827–8, by *William Thomson*, the former Telford manse, and SPRINGBANK, 1824, a chunky gabled villa with arched doorway. At the S, GLEN IOSAL, 1980s, a pleasantly grouped enclave of sheltered housing.

ERRAY HOUSE, 1km. N of Tobermory. Two-storey gabled rubble house, early C18. Symmetrical five-bay S front: small windows, narrowed on first floor. NE wing, late C18.

LINNDHU HOUSE, 2.5km. SE of Tobermory. Late C19. Spreading painted rubble house with bargeboarded gables and overhanging eaves rising in gablet peaks over first-floor windows. Tall pointed-arch stair window.

TOROSAY CASTLE
1.8km. SE of Craignure

More mansion than castle, the house is nevertheless a robust affair; bulbous Baronial in square-snecked stone, by *David Bryce*, 1856–8. First known as Duart House, it was commissioned by Colonel Campbell of Possil, whose family acquired the estate from their kinsman the Duke of Argyll at the start of the C19. A farm and walled garden, *c.* 1780, were retained but the existing mansion, Achnacroish House, was demolished to make way for Bryce's replacement, a much grander residence of two tall storeys raised on basement offices. The plan follows one of the three standard solutions adopted by the architect for his many Victorian country houses: Fiddes and Rowan categorize it as 'Plan Type A', an arrangement placing the main entrance in the N under a high square tower with a corbelled castellated parapet, service quarters to the E, and the main public rooms aligned along the S elevation. Though essentially tripartite in layout (dining room, library and drawing room), this S front deliberately disguises its inherent symmetry. Gables push forward on each side of a rather plain centre which has a three-light window below and a pedimented two-light above. Flanking the l. gable, bold corner bows, corbelled out at the floor level of the *piano nobile* and again, more subtly, at first floor, rise through two storeys (three-light windows below, single openings above). They terminate in finialled, fish-scale-slated cones; nipped between them, the narrowed crowstepped gable squeezes upwards. To the r. is a double-height canted bay abruptly corbelled to a crowstep gable above the eaves. To the r. of this, a corbelled corner bartizan with a third finialled cone. Further E, beyond a lower service wing, two dumpy drum towers flanking the courtyard repeat the conical roof theme.

Between 1897 and 1906, three GARDEN TERRACES, each defined by a balustraded retaining wall, were created on the sloping ground S of the house. This tiered treatment of the landscape, which greatly enhances the setting of the house, is attributed to *Robert S. Lorimer*, though much of the credit for planning and execution belongs to the then owner of Torosay, *Walter Murray Guthrie*. From the centre of the uppermost level, Castle Terrace, stone stair-flights descend l. and r. on a wide segmental arch forming a sheltered seating recess. This looks out across Fountain Terrace, an expanse of lawn at the centre of which is a small circular pool with a pedestal bowl fountain. In the SW and SE corners are two small square towers built in greenish snecked rubble with castellated ashlar parapets and slated pyramid roofs; they serve as summer-houses with doocots at the upper levels.

From these pavilions, balustraded stair-flights facing each other at opposite ends of a long buttressed retaining wall fall to Lion Terrace where two marble lions lie like somnambulant guard-dogs above the banked lawn. To the w of the terraces is the STATUE WALK, its passage down the slope from the house punctuated by a series of nineteen Venetian sculptured figures, in the style of *Antonio Bonazzo* (1698–1765), brought from Milan. Each sits on a plinth between herbaceous planting. This avenue leads to the C18 WALLED GARDEN where a colonnaded pergola runs r. to a domed Tempietto. Entered E from Lion Terrace is an intimate rockery and a JAPANESE GARDEN created in the early 1980s.

ULVA

Island on the w side of Mull lying between Loch Tuath and Loch na Keal. From its w coast a short bridge crosses a narrow channel to the smaller island of Gometra.

BURIAL GROUND, Cill Mhic Eòghainn, 4.7km. w of Ulva House. C19 rubble-walled enclosure within which are many unmarked gravestones. The earliest dated stone, recorded in the RCAHMS Inventory of 1980, commemorates John McGuarie †1765. Small rubble rectangle entered E with slate HEADSTONE of Hector McQuarie, erected 1791.

PARISH CHURCH. Parliamentary kirk by *William Thomson*, 1827–8, harled with stone dressings. Standard T-plan built without galleries; now entered through the sw stem of the T. The principal NE elevation had two tall four-centre arch windows flanked by doors, but alterations, *c.* 1950, replaced one of the two doors with a window when a community hall was formed and only the SE end retained for worship. At the same time a small boiler-house and chimneystack were built symmetrically between the principal NE windows. Birdcage bellcote with obelisk finials on SE gable. Unremarkable within, save for a splendid, two-tier, pine PULPIT with hexagonal canopy, moulded panels and fluted Roman Doric pilasters. Now positioned in the s corner, it is a rare survivor of what must have been the standard preaching box installed in Telford's Highland churches. Close to the church is the island's WAR MEMORIAL, a small rubble pyramid capped by a ball finial. Nearby, the piend-roofed, single-storey MANSE, 1828.

ULVA FERRY HOUSE. Early C19. Former inn; rubble dwelling with three gabled dormers.

ULVA HOUSE. Two-storey, harled mansion with a steeply pitched piended roof; built by *Leslie Grahame MacDougall* in the 1950s in emulation of its early C19 forerunner, fragments from which are decoratively incorporated. Symmetrical T-plan, the piended NE entrance block projecting centrally between flat-roofed wings which fill the re-entrants. Round-arch entrance with sunburst fanlight. Wide, five-bay SW front with central gable feature carrying urns at the apex and skews.

ORONSAY

A small island at the S end of Colonsay (q.v.) to which it is connected across The Strand at low tide.

ORONSAY PRIORY. Christian worship undoubtedly came early to Oronsay and both St Columba and St Oran are tentatively linked with a C6 monastic foundation on the island. The ruinous but surprisingly substantial buildings which still stand are, however, those of an Augustinian community founded by John I, Lord of the Isles, in the second decade of the C14. Building seems to have progressed intermittently through the C14 and C15, with further work completed before the Reformation. In 1561 the office of Prior was replaced by that of Commendator, but by the third decade of the C17 the buildings were in ruins. Degradation continued until repairs were begun in late Victorian times; in the

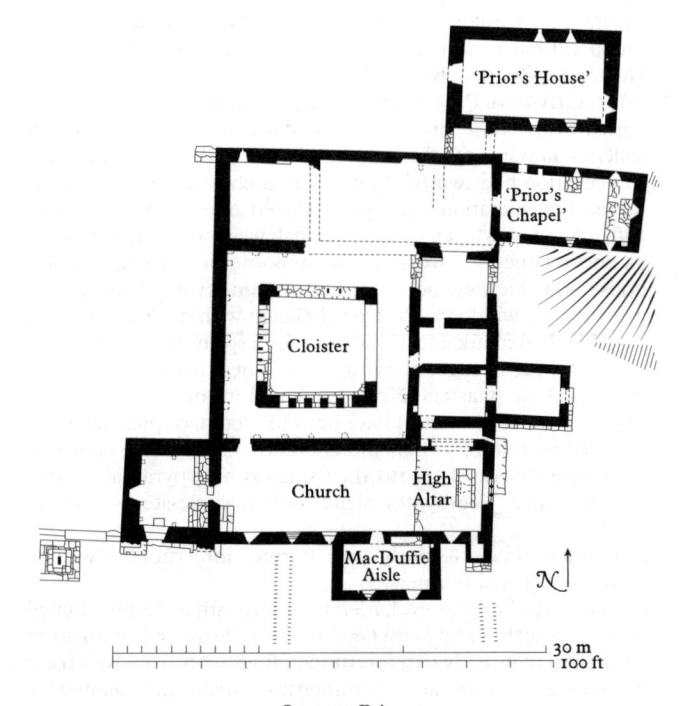

Oronsay Priory

1880s the architect *William Galloway* supervised the restoration of the church's E gable and the W cloister arcade. Further general repairs by the *Office of Works* in 1927 included the roofing of the 'Prior's House'.

Insular remoteness has not prevented the Priory's setting becoming compromised by the proximity of Oronsay Farm and Oronsay House. A C19 rubble wall enclosing the burial ground to the S defies encroachment, but on the W and N the farm buildings press close. Nor do the gabled ruins have the Atlantic sky entirely to themselves. Yet the place preserves its dignity, enhanced perhaps by the atavistic necessity of reaching it only at low tide. The layout, small in scale, is conventionally claustral: ranges on the N, E and S sides of a cloister court forming an oblong group from which a number of smaller appendages project. Walls are constructed in lime-mortared slaty rubble with slab pinnings. There is evidence of harling and plasterwork but little dressed stone.

The E RANGE is the oldest part of the group, built in the second quarter of the C14. Ruinous W and E walls rise S to the wallhead to reach a height of 7.2m. at the apex of the surviving S gable. The N gable, doubled in thickness in the later C14, collapsed in 1883. It is clear that this was a two-storey structure with a dorter above and chapter house and warming house below, separated by a cross-wall. In the late C18, a second cross-wall, built closer to the S gable, defined the burial place of the McNeills of Colonsay. This was later extended in the mid C19 when the McNeill Aisle, an oblong cell with a pointed-arch doorway and armorial panel in its E gable, was attached to the E wall.

The N RANGE may originally have housed a chapel, linked in an L-plan relationship with the E range. Most of the walling, which stands two storeys high at the W and E ends, is of C14 date, though a central stretch of the N wall has been reconstructed in the late C18. Evidence of a fireplace towards the W end of this wall and a high-level aumbry with a square laver and drain at its E end suggest kitchens below and, perhaps, a refectory above. Some slit windows with splayed embrasures survive. Close to the E end of the N wall, vestigial evidence of a short passageway links N with the W gable of the early C14 'PRIOR'S HOUSE'. This is now an independent gabled building but must originally have been connected with the N range and probably served as a reredorter, for there are no fireplaces to support residential use. Wall scarcements in the gables and the position of several slit windows, all repaired or altered, indicate an upper floor. In the S wall, spanning a blocked-up opening, there is an unusual flat slab of chlorite-schist with a grotesque mask carved at its centre. The building is known to have been re-roofed some time after 1772, and in 1927 was extensively repaired to house the site's remarkable collection of funerary monuments.

The so-called 'PRIOR'S CHAPEL', mid C14, is angled E from

the E end of the N range. It is linked to it by a pointed-archway of slab voussoirs, blocked but for a simple lintelled door-opening. Another door, located higher in this same gable, indicates that a gallery or loft must have connected with accommodation on the upper floor of the N and probably the E ranges. At the opposite E end of the chapel the sanctuary has been extended or rebuilt in the early C16. Here the side walls and gable have been heightened and stabilized in more recent times. There are opposed slit windows at the middle and at the E ends of the N and S walls. A stone kerb crosses the sanctuary in front of what was a stone altar. In the SE corner, an aumbry and a fragment of a piscina. Halfway along the N wall, what may be the base for a pulpit.

The mid-C14 CLOISTER is still defined in the corners by all four of its heavy L-plan rubble piers, although only two of the arcades still stand, and only one of these, the five round-headed arches of the S arcade, is original. In the early C16 the N, W and E arcades were rebuilt with gable-headed openings, but by the late C18 the N side had crumbled and a century later a survey of 1880–1 found only the S arcade extant. The W side was again reconstructed, 1883, now as seven triangular arches formed by inclined slabs set on slab capitals into which were morticed monolithic slab piers rising from a low masonry plinth. At the centre of this arcade two of the earlier piers were re-used; they bear decorative black-letter inscriptions which ascribe the early C16 work to the Irish mason-sculptor *Mael-Sechlainn O Cuinn*, working under the direction of Canon Celestinus. No further work was undertaken on the cloister in the late C19 and it remains incomplete and roofless with only corbelstones and water-tabling, most evident on the S and W walls, to indicate the height of the lean-to roofs.

The Priory CHURCH, which can be entered through a doorway at the SW corner of the cloister walk, forms the S range: an aisle-less nave and choir of late C14 or early C15 date extending from the W end of the cloister to the E wall of the E range. The stonework of the side walls, altered and rebuilt in several places, stands consolidated at a 5m.-high wallhead. The E gable, much restored, is intact and rises to 9m. at the apex. At its centre is a three-light pointed-arch window inserted in the late C15. Within its chamfered and rebated surround, plain Y-tracery. A broad buttress with dressed quoins and two bevelled drip-course stones continues the slope of the gable's S skew. To the W of this is the lean-to MacDuffie Aisle, late C15, its consolidated skews falling from the S wallhead. A square annexe, also late C15, probably intended as the base of a tower, has been added against the W gable. Its walls, which are thicker than those of the church and retain some slab-corbels for an upper floor, have been levelled at 4m. high. At the SW corner some ragged masonry and a returning drip-mould set on two ashlar courses indicate a large buttress. At the SE corner, overlapping the W gable of the church, more rough rubble, a drip-course and a splayed plinth betray a second. Under a thin schist hood-mould is the pointed-arch s doorway beyond which, through a door in the church gable (possibly a late C15 adaptation of an earlier window), the nave can be entered.

Within the nave the fenestration of the s wall appears random and is difficult to interpret. Openings at upper and lower levels at the w end suggest that a gallery may have existed. A narrow opening with a rounded monolithic head carved with trefoil cusping, splayed embrasures and a segmental inner arch appears to be original. A lintelled door opens into the MacDuffie Aisle, and above this two inclined chlorite-schist slabs form a triangular arch over an upper doorway which, now blocked, afforded access to the lean-to roofspace. The aisle is lit by two small windows in its s wall; there is an aumbry in the E wall and a tomb-recess set into the church wall under a semicircular arch of thin voussoirs. A stone kerb marks the sanctuary area at the E end of the church. The altar, a slab-topped *mensa* of sandstone blocks within which is a splayed aumbry, sits in front of the E window; it is probably of late C15 date but has been re-assembled. A large L-shaped aumbry penetrates the SE buttress. On the N side of the sanctuary, a high pointed arch, late C15, with plain sandstone voussoirs, bevelled schistose capitals and chamfered responds opens into a shallow recess which may have served as a sacristy.

ORONSAY CROSS, freestanding, 4m. w of the w wall of the Priory church 'tower'. Iona school, late C15. Tapering disc-headed cross, 3.67m. high, set in its original socket-stone on a three-step rubble base. On the w face, carved in high relief, a crucified Christ hangs from the disc-head against a background of interlace ornament. Below are five floral roundels and at the base of the shaft, between two fabulous beasts and a panel of knotted plaitwork, a Latin inscription which records that 'This is the cross of Colinus, son of Cristinus MacDuffie'. There are more roundels on the E face of the shaft and in the disc-head an eight-leaved foliated motif. Incised in the socket-stone are the rays of a worn dial and a second Latin inscription naming the sculptor, *Mael-Sechlainn O Cuinn* (*see* above).

COMPOSITE CROSS, freestanding, 6m. E of 'Prior's House'. A small cross-head, Oronsay school, *c.* 1500–60, joined to the fragment of a cross-shaft, Iona school, C14–C15, and raised on a circular rubble base some time before 1870. The head, 0.34m. in dia., is carved on one side with the bearded robed figure of St John the Evangelist set in a niche. The shaft, 0.79m. high, has intertwined plant decoration, also only on one face.

FUNERARY MONUMENTS. Numerous gravemarkers, eroded and illegible, lie in rough rows in the walled burial enclosure s of the church. A collection of over thirty memorial stones and crosses has been gathered in the 'Prior's House'. – There are twenty TAPERED SLABS. Ten are Iona school, C14–C15, carved with swords, plant scrolls, etc. – They include one decorated with a diaper pattern of intertwined plants commemorating Canon Celestinus (*see* above). – Another, Loch Sween school, C15, bears a sword with a round pommel asymmetrically surrounded by birds, hounds, a deer, a horse(?), and an otter with a salmon. – Seven slabs, Oronsay school, *c*. 1500–60, are elaborately carved with swords, animals, plants and galleys. – Outstanding, with wonderfully natural stags and hounds clustered around the hilt of a claymore, is one bearing a Latin dedication to the clan chief Murchardus MacDuffie of Colonsay †1539. Ten other slabs carry EFFIGIES. – Two are carved in high relief with figures of men in armour, Iona school, C14–C15. – The remainder are Oronsay school, *c*. 1500–60, and include one with a particularly finely detailed figure of Sir Donald MacDuffie, Conventual Prior of Oronsay, †155-, and another, similarly elaborate in its treatment, depicting Canon Bricius MacMhuirich in a voluminous monastic cape with angels at his pillow. – Also housed here are three small CROSS FRAGMENTS.

ORONSAY HOUSE, 25m. SW of Priory. Built 1772. Skew-gabled, two-storey-and-attic tacksman's house. Several rubble byres and an octagonal barn with a slated pyramid roof.

FORT, Dùn Dòmhuill, 450m. ENE of Oronsay House. A rocky W–E ridge on the flanks of Beinn Oronsay, the elongated enclosure barely marked by a low mound.

SCARBA

Uninhabited mountain island separated from the N of Jura by the treacherous Gulf of Corryvreckan.

CHAPEL, Cille Mhoire an Caibel. C14(?). Single-cell rectangle, *c*. 10m. by 5.5m., dedicated to 'the Blessed Virgin'. Overgrown rubble walls stand *c*. 1.5m. high in places. In the burial ground, disused from the mid C19, the earliest grave is the TABLE-TOMB of Margaret MacLean †1741.

TIREE

The outermost of Argyll's islands, lying immediately SW of Coll and, like it, linked to Oban by car-ferry. Spectacular stretches of strand repeatedly interrupt an otherwise rocky shore. At once the sunniest and the windiest place in Britain. The land is flat (Ben Hynish in the S only 141m. high) and fertile. Arable farming and cattle grazing sustained a population of almost 4,500 in 1830 but, by the end of the century, though forced evictions were resisted by the islanders, this had been halved. Crofting has, however, survived and there is now a thriving community of more than 700.

BALEMARTINE

Linear village between road and shore, 2km. N of Hynish Pier.
BAPTIST CHURCH. Built *c*. 1856. Roughcast gabled hall, with a mini-bellcote identical to that at Baugh (q.v.).
BURIAL GROUND, Soroby. Walled enclosure containing many C19 and C20 gravemarkers. Among the former, four stones commemorate the families of craftsmen who worked on Skerryvore Lighthouse (q.v.). Two armorial TABLE-TOMBS with illegible inscriptions, C18. Several TAPERED SLABS, Iona school, C14–early C16. The RCAHMS Inventory, 1980, notes a broken CROSS-SHAFT bearing the figure of St Michael separated from those of Death and a cloaked woman by a Latin dedication to Anna, Prioress of Iona, †1543. Also recorded, a stumpy Early Christian CROSS-SLAB with cable moulded borders; the cross head ringed on one side and bossed on the other. Many graves are indicated by small weathered stones, some of these architectural fragments from the church which stood here from the C13(?) until the early C19.
STANDING STONE, Balinoe, 1.45km. NW of Soroby burial ground. Massive stone, broad at the base but tapering to a height of 3.6m.

BAUGH

A handful of houses on the B8065 between Scarinish and Crossapol.
BAPTIST CHURCH. Built *c*. 1856. Gabled roughcast with only a mini-bellcote to hint at religion.
MONUMENT. Pink granite obelisk on socle on concrete cairn base. Five-pointed star incised near the apex. Erected in memory of the island's long-serving Medical Officer, Dr Alexander Buchanan †1911.
DUN, Dùn Ibrig, 600m. N. Rubble remains on a low knoll rising from former marshland. Oval plan with ESE entrance. Short intramural gallery NNE.

CEANN A' MHARA

Rocky headland at the SW tip of the island, reached from Balephuil across the sands of Tràigh Bhì.
ST PATRICK'S CHAPEL. Set behind a large rock outcrop above the shore, the remains of an oblong cell, the last vestige of an Early Christian cashel or monastery. Part of the E gable and turf-covered footings define a rectangle, 8.08m. by 3.4m. internally. An altar-base survives. Within the chapel are two boulders incised with Latin crosses; outside the walls, close to the ruin's SE corner, another stone similarly marked.
FORT, Dùn nan Gall, 800m. NNW of St Patrick's Chapel. On the summit of a coastal promontory protected S by a 30m. drop and N by steep rocky slopes. Narrow, 8m.-wide, ESE approach with vestiges of drystone walling standing to 5 courses in one stretch.

CORNAIGMORE

Diffuse township on the N shore W of Balephetrish Bay.

CHAPEL, Kenovay. Medieval. Turf-covered footings of a small structure, oblong with rounded corners. A few overgrown grave-markers.

CHURCH. 1899. Four-bay, gabled kirk in pointed coursed rubble. Lancet windows. W bellcote with bell. Now residential.

MILL. Mid C19. Roofless gabled oblong. Segmental-arch opening at centre of E wall has rubble voussoirs. Iron wheel with some timber paddle blades embedded against N gable. High-level lade runs W.

CROSSAPOL

Hamlet on the S shore at the W end of Tràigh Bhàigh. Immediately N is The Reef, site of Tiree Airport, its flat machair-land still littered with wartime detritus.

ISLAND HOUSE, 1.15km. W, on a man-made peninsula in Loch an Eilein. Isolated, two-storey, gabled dwelling, harled and without architectural pretension. Sited over the ruins of a castle which had been reached 'by a made road and drawbridge' (OSA, c. 1794), the house was built, 1746–8, by the 3rd Duke of Argyll for his factor. Originally an elongated rectangle with a S stair turret, it acquired two S gabled projections in the C19. Single-storey L-plan offices, 1769, adjoin the W gable.

TIREE AIRPORT, 1.1km. N. Early 1990s. Single-storey pavilion, square in plan with a low pyramid roof in red profiled metal. In the interior, pine trusses radiate from a central steel column. Adjacent Fire Station, gabled shed in cream profiled sheet; balconied Control Tower in red.

HEYLIPOL

Some houses and a church on the B8065 between Crossapol and Barrapol.

HEYLIPOL CHURCH. By *William Mackenzie*; 1901–2. Isolated cross-roads kirk built to a cruciform plan in rough-faced local granite with ashlar dressings. Said to emulate Iona Abbey, its gabled Gothic tucks a three-stage, parapeted, belfry tower in the NW re-entrant. Lancets and plate tracery. – PULPIT with Celtic interlace ornament carved by local craftsmen, 1906.

HYNISH

A few dwellings and a monument to C19 engineering at the extreme SE tip of the island.

HARBOUR AND LIGHTHOUSE ESTABLISHMENT. The most architecturally substantial group of buildings on the island: constructed 1837–43, under the direction of engineer *Alan Stevenson*, to support the lighthouse on Skerryvore (q.v.). PIER and tidal DOCK built of massive granite blocks quarried at North Bay in the Ross of Mull. Both have walls stepped to the quayside and are battered and stepped to the sea. Walls at the dock entrance slotted for boom-gates. A sluicing system, fed from a reservoir some distance W, cleared the dock of silting sand. Gabled ancillary range S of the pier has been adapted as hostel accommodation with shuttered timber doors and windows: TAIGH ALAN STEVENSON, 1988–9, by Oban architect *John Wilson*.

To the W, LOWER SQUARE, a U-plan court in coursed granite rubble: single-storey service buildings N and W, with a short S range of two two-storey workers' dwellings, the larger with a curving forestair to the upper flat. Also provided were 'working sheds, coal and boat-houses, smithies, etc.' (*NSA*, 1843) and a walled garden for vegetables. These have been conserved by *A. R. P. Lorimer & Associates*, 1995–8. On higher ground W, the cylindrical SIGNAL-TOWER built in coursed local rubble on a granite plinth to a height of 9.3m. Below the parapet, a hefty corbel course and, below this, two stretches of iron-framed windows giving a view E to the harbour and S to Skerryvore. Now a museum. Adjacent is a terrace range of LIGHTKEEPERS' HOUSES, coupled and tripled chimneystacks rising from flat roofs. Four four-apartment dwellings; faced in granite to the E, rubble with granite dressings to the W. Under restoration for The Hebridean Trust by *A. R. P. Lorimer & Associates*.

DUN, Dùn Hiader, 400m. SE of W Hynish farm. Oval enclosure on a craggy promontory protected by cliffs which reach 14.5m. on the SE. Stretches of outer facing stones to 1m. height. NE entrance gap. Outer walling thickens to 4.3m. at landward approach.

FORT, Dùn na Cleite, 1.4km. SW of Hynish. Headland summit with cliffs to S. The rocky site provides natural defence completed by intermittent drystone walls, the facing stones best preserved on the NW.

KIRKAPOL 0407

Four churches (two ruinous, one converted) and a hotel looking SE across Traigh Mhór to Gott Bay.

OLD CHAPEL, *c.* 80m. N of Old Parish Church. Late C14(?). Simple oblong plan, 7.1m. by 3.4m. within the rubble walls which stand as gables W and E and to the wallhead N. The S wall is ruinous but retains a narrow round-arch door at its W end. Two small windows N and S lit the altar area; the former largely survives.

OLD PARISH CHURCH, 400m. N of Kirkapol Church. Late C14(?). Gabled rubble ruin, its skewed rectangular plan 11.3m. by 5.2m. within the walls. Collapsed masonry(?) has created a large opening in the E gable. In the W gable under slab voussoirs, a round-arch door with draw-bar slot has been blocked. Two small S windows, also round-arched with splayed ingoes and sliver voussoirs. Evidence of plastering.

BURIAL GROUND (Cladh Beg), adjacent to the Old Parish Church. Rubble-walled enclosure with many stub gravemarkers. The RCAHMS Inventory (1980) identifies a few TAPERED SLABS, C14–C16. A broken CROSS-SHAFT with scroll ornament, Iona school, C14–early C16.

CEMETERY (Cladh Odhráin), 44m. SE of the Old Parish Church. A large graveyard busy with C19 and C20 headstones. Two TABLE-TOMBS: one, to Farquhar Fraser, Dean of the Isles, †1680, with a long Latin inscription above floral ornament; the other, with armorial carving and the emblems of mortality, to John Campbell of Lochnell and his wife, probably early C18.

KIRKAPOL CHURCH. 1843–4, by architect-contractor *Peter MacNab*. Built to supersede the church erected at Scarinish in 1776. Piended box of roughly coursed rubble with a pedimented SE projection carrying a gableted belfry with stumpy obelisk. Four-centre arch windows. Curved gallery on three sides on cast-iron columns. Pitch pine, superficially Gothic, preaching-box PULPIT, 1893, at the centre of the NW wall. Oak COMMUNION TABLE, almost domestic in scale, with fold-up ends and traceried base, formerly 'IN THE KIRK OF THE CROWN OF SCOTLAND, LONDON'; gifted 1925. Splendid ogee-backed MINISTER'S CHAIR, convincingly carved in Decorated Gothic. White marble MURAL TABLET with scrolled top, erected 1915; to Revd Hector Mackinnon, †1913. Horizontal copper PANEL bordered with Celtic interlacing and depicting the Lorn galley l. and r.; to Victoria Campbell †1910, daughter of the 8th Duke of Argyll; by *Alexander & Euphemia Ritchie*, Iona.

Former FREE CHURCH (Kirkapol Guest House). Built 1880. Four-bay gabled kirk with simple lancets. Now residential.

MANNAL

A trim hamlet of white-walled, black-roofed cottages, 1km. S of Balemartine.

MILTON

A few dwellings and a small harbour at the E end of the island.

BROCH, Dùn Mór a' Chaolais. On a low hill, much disturbed by cultivation. Drystone traces marking the SW side of the circular plan suggest an internal diameter of 12m. Some evidence of mural chambers.

SANDAIG

Township on the W coast.

CHAPEL, Kilkenneth, 1.7km. N. Late C14(?). Rubble ruin banked with sand in a hollow in the dunes. Oblong plan of which the E gable, most of the N and S walls and half of the lower W gable still stand. Evidence of W door.

SANDAIG MUSEUM (The Terrace). Three thatched buildings in line (house, byre and barn), originally part of a longer terrace of traditional island dwellings, restored by *John Wilson Associates* for The Hebridean Trust. Nowhere is Tiree's singular and specific vernacular architecture better exemplified. Shelter from wind and rain dictates all. Dating is difficult but, as the *Statistical Account* of *c.* 1794 confirms, the construction method is centuries old. Thick, double-skin drystone walls with a wide cavity, packed with sand to act as a drain, form a rugged blockhouse base. Windows and doors are set deep within the wall thickness. Painted with limewash from burnt sea-shells, the leeward-facing fronts of the buildings gleam white. Rough timbers rise from the inner wallhead to form a hip-ended roof of primitive trusses, purlins and spars over each of the three buildings, the slope to the rear or windward side slightly steeper; all of this a restoration in imported oak. Turfs, fixed with wooden pegs, cover the roof under sheaves of marram grass thatch held down with stone-weighted ropes.

There are other similar rubble cottages, some thatched, some with tarred and felted timber upper storeys, at Balevullin and Kilmoluaig to the N. At Barrapol, 1.5km. ESE, DROVERS, another small but delightful indigenous dwelling.

DUN, Dùn Boraige Móire, 4.5km. N, at the SW end of Balevullin Bay. Drystone walls between 4m. and 5m. thick define an oval enclosure on a rocky summit above the shore. Outer facing stones survive but at best to three courses only.

DUN, Dùn Boraige Bige, 250m. E of Dùn Boraige Móire. Circle of rubble debris on a relatively unprotected promontory site. Some outer facing stones S.

SCARINISH

Developed as a fishing village by the 5th Duke of Argyll, mid C18, this was the island's first harbour. An open scatter of dwellings which exhibit the range of island types: rubble blockhouses with thatch roofs or tarred tent-like upper storeys; heavily pointed, rubble-walled houses with eaves dormers, the pointing white-painted to produce a strident spotted texture; corrugated-iron structures; more recent roughcast kit-houses.

GOTT BAY PIER. The original steamboat pier by *G. Woulfe Brenan*, Oban, 1908–14. Reconstructed in the early 1950s and later converted to roll-on roll-off car-ferry quay.

SCARINISH PIER. Built *c.* 1835. L-plan quay of drystone rubble.

WAR MEMORIAL, beside the road to Gott Bay Pier. 1920. Designed by *C. Sinclair*. Celtic cross on tapered, rough-faced granite shaft.

DUN, Dùn Heanish, 1.5km. SSW of Scarinish Pier. On a low promontory, a small circle of overgrown footings with outerwork rings evident.

SKERRYVORE LIGHTHOUSE
on reef rock, 20km. wsw of Tiree

Built 1838–44 to the design of engineer *Alan Stevenson*. A 42m.-high tower, 12.8m. in dia. at its solid masonry base but tapering to the lantern in a slow hyperbolic curve. A bold cavetto carries the balcony below the lantern. With the exception of the lowest four courses, which are of gneiss quarried at Hynish on Tiree, the structure is granite ashlar from North Bay, Ross of Mull. From the entrance level, 7.9m. above the rock base, the tower rises through nine storeys of superimposed circular chambers, with shallow-vaulted ceilings at varying heights, to the lantern room. An open cast-iron walk surrounding the lantern has brackets with hand-grips sinuously shaped as dolphins. Part of the iron gangway built across the rocks to the s boat-landing now connects with a helicopter platform. The interior was re-equipped in the mid 1950s, the mechanical oil lamp of 1842 being preserved in the Royal Scottish Museum, Edinburgh.

VAUL

Township on N coast, 1.5km. NNE of Kirkapol.

BROCH, Dùn Mòr Vaul. On a rocky hillock above the shore, 350m. NW of the road-end. Excavation, 1962–4, found evidence for settlement in the late C6 B.C. or early C5 B.C. The broch itself probably dates from C2 A.D. Set on the summit around a natural hollow, the drystone walls define a circle 9.2m. internal diameter and are well preserved (to eight courses NNE). ESE entrance with bar-holes; from the passage a lintelled door leads N to a subcircular chamber. All-round mural gallery entered from S and NNW, the latter accessing a staircase of which ten steps survive. Signs of irregular outer defensive ring.

DUN, Dùn Beag, 250m. N. On a seashore knoll, turf-covered oval with W entrance evident as gap. A few facing stones.

TRESHNISH ISLES

(see map p. 501)

CAIRNBURGH CASTLE

Scattered enclosures and defensive walling on Cairn na Burgh More and Cairn na Burgh Beg, two small uninhabited islands at the NE end of the Treshnish Isles chain, 4km. sw of Treshnish Point on the W coast of Mull. Remnants of the castle survive on both islands. A MacLean stronghold, it has been called 'the ultimate natural fortress' (Whyte, 1991).

Though relatively remote and without safe anchorage, the location had a strategic attraction which, certainly from the C13, led

CAIRNBURGH CASTLE

those who wished to control the Inner Hebrides sea route to fortify and garrison the islands. Most building appears to have occurred on the larger of the two islands, Cairn na Burgh More, but the natural forms of the smaller island, which lies immediately NE across a narrow tidal race, have also been considerably reinforced by rubble construction, doubtless to ensure the safe approach to difficult landing places in the channel.

CAIRN NA BURGH MORE. A deep W–E gully divides the island into a narrow elevated N plateau and a larger area to the S. The S area reaches a height of 34m. above sea level and is protected on the NW, W and SW sides by high cliffs and from S to NNE by steep rock faces falling to a shelving beach. Defensive construction is concentrated along the E side where stretches of random rubble curtain-walling, C16 or C17, some of it lime mortared, some drystone, augment the impregnability of the cliffs. At a break in this natural barrier, S of an indentation in the cliff face, a ruinous stone stairway rises SSW to an entrance gate. The doorway, originally lintelled with a flat-arch, leads to a passageway, part of which has been roofed. At the summit, a little to the S, the ruins of a small rectangular building, perhaps associated with a second, postern-gate approach, which would have begun its climb from a point 40m. S of the main stairway. Along the gully to the N, traces of rubble curtain construction indicate that the defensive walls returned at two points across the gully, enclosing an area which may have been cultivated and which afforded a protected link between the two raised parts of the island. On the W the connecting wall stands 4m. high on a splayed base, while that on the E shows evidence of a small half-tower structure. W and E of this protected natural bridge there are signs of outer walls at lower level.

All surviving structures are roofless and ruinous. Close to the S side of the walled link to the N end of the island is the CHAPEL, possibly C15, a small rectangular rubble building set E–W. Walls and gables, though degraded, still stand. In the N wall, a door and window; both have splayed ingoes and probably had dressings of Carsaig sandstone. Some 30m. S is the BARRACK building, C16–C17, also rectangular but longer and orientated SW–NE. It has a larger and a smaller room, separated by a rubble partition, with fireplace openings to each. Window and door openings survive in the side walls and there is evidence of a loft also lit along the side walls. Cruck slots indicate that the building was hipped-roofed. Both chapel and barrack have roughly formed rubble enclosures attached on the S and NW respectively. A small rubble structure of irregular oblong plan, E of the barrack and linked to the E curtain wall close to the castle entrance, is described as a Guard House on a Board of Ordnance plan of 1741. S of the barrack is a still smaller cell of sub-rectangular form identified on the same plan as a 'House for fireing'.

CAIRN NA BURGH BEG. This smaller island has a rock summit, the Upper Bailey, almost as high as its neighbour and surrounded by sheer cliffs on all but the SW side. Scarcely distinguishable overgrown footings of two small oblong buildings, one a guard-house, within this protected area. Signs of rock-cut steps descending through a rubble breastwork curtain along the more vulnerable perimeter of the summit. Below, in the lower, SW part of the island, lies a second enclosure, roughly defined by the turf-covered remains of drystone rubble walls, and approached from a small inlet landing on the NW shore.

BUTE

(see map p. 604)

An elongated island in the Firth of Clyde clasped in the N by the stubby peninsula fingers of Cowal. Inhabited for over 6,000 years, the land is fertile and well farmed except in the hillier N. For more than eight centuries the Stuarts, hereditary Stewards to the Scottish crown from 1157, have held lands on Bute, and today the island is still very much their demesne. Mount Stuart, more palace than country house, testifies to the family's wealth and prestige. But Bute has its proletarian side too. In the late C19 and through the first half of the C20, frequent steamer links with the mainland brought working-class families from the shipyards, steelworks and mills in the industrial heartlands of central Scotland, turning Rothesay into the Clyde's most popular holiday resort. By the 1930s the island's population exceeded 12,000 and though this has dropped to little more than 7,000, tourism is still the mainstay of the island's economy.

ASCOG

Coastal suburb S of Craigmore.

ASCOG PARISH CHURCH, 1.9km. S of Craigmore Pier. Begun as a Chapel of Ease, 1842–3, but opened as a Free Church. By *David Hamilton* or perhaps his son, *James Hamilton*. Four-bay gabled block with round-arched windows under overhanging eaves. In the SW gable, a blind Venetian window above a hipped-roofed porch with an open aedicule feature set over the central entrance. Axial Italianate belfry tower rises in three stages against the NE gable. – Timber panelled PULPIT with round-arched pilastered screen behind on SW wall. – Decorative plaster ceiling patterned by groins with painted bosses. Armorial shields set in cornice.

DESCRIPTION

The road S bends slowly round the bay to Ascog Point. MILLBURN HOUSE, *c.* 1870, has a Gothic look with fretted bargeboards and four-centred arched attic windows. ASCOGBANK, by *David Hamilton*, *c.* 1833, is cubic and classical: a small but tall *piano nobile* boxed by coupled Ionic pilasters. Despite its name, MEIKLE ASCOG is a humbler affair: symmetrical, three-bay, with a tripartite centre at first floor; by the engineer *Robert Thom*, *c.* 1840. Past the church (*see* above) the segmental arch of

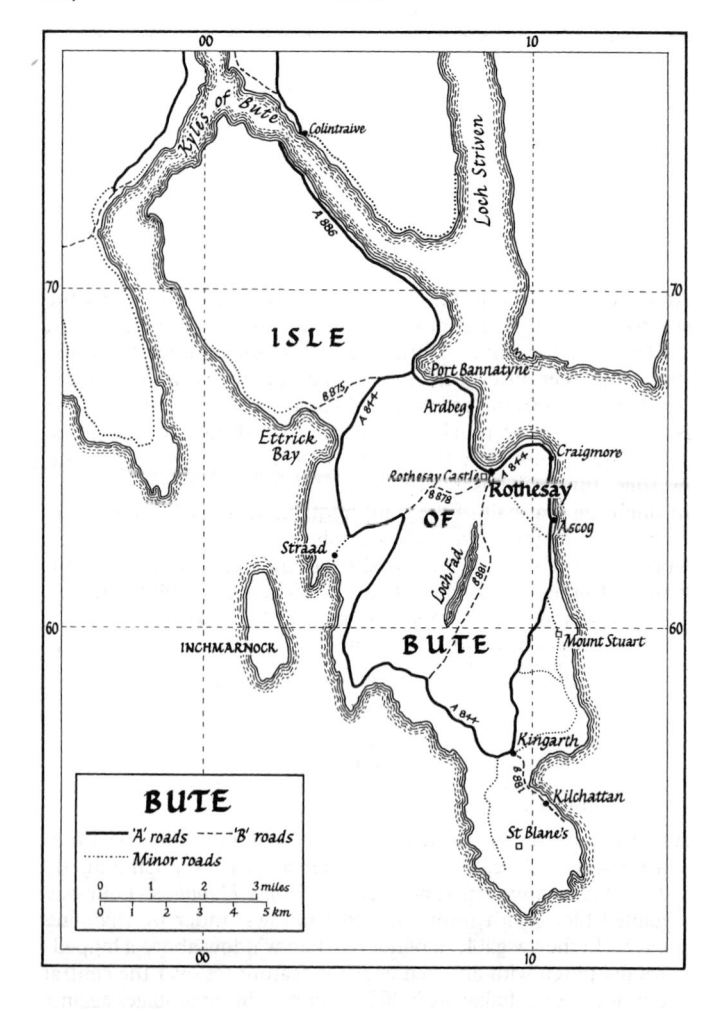

a turreted Baronial GATEWAY, *c.* 1870, marks one of the entries to what was Ascog Estate, until the early C18 an appanage of the Bute family of Mount Stuart (q.v.). Dated 1678, the principal residence of the Stewarts of Ascog, ASCOG HOUSE, is a two-storey, T-plan dwelling with crowstepped skews; Victorian additions have been removed, late C20, but an Edwardian stair-tower survives in detached whimsy. An L-plan gate-house by *James Hamilton*, PINK LODGE, *c.* 1842, also remains with its consoled door and lying-pane glazing, while GATEPIERS and boundary walls may be by *David Hamilton*, *c.* 1833. ASCOG HALL is fairy-tale Baronial, harled with fishscale-slated angle turrets. Begun *c.* 1844, it was altered for Alexander Bannatyne Stewart by *John Honeyman* in 1862. During the 1870s *Edward La Trobe Bateman* landscaped the garden and it was probably he who created the kidney-plan FERNERY, a glass-roofed grotto full of luxuriant growth (restored 1995–6). Then come BALMORY HOUSE, dated 1861, and SOUTHPARK, late C19: two broad piend-roofed ashlar blocks, the former bulging with a pilaster-mullioned, two-storey bow ringed with a balcony bracelet of fine ironwork. Some distance S across Ascog Bridge is THE HERMITAGE, late C19, an asymmetrical house, harled and half-timbered, much addicted to that fashion for Old English forms so favoured at nearby Kerrycroy (q.v.).

KILCHATTAN

A shoreline village in the parish of Kingarth (q.v.).

KINGARTH AND KILCHATTAN BAY CHURCH. Built 1894–5. Dull gable-fronted Gothic in square-snecked red sandstone. Stiff, eight-leaf wheel window, louvres in the apex, vesicas in the flanks and an eccentric open-gable belfry.

QUAY. Early C19 dog-leg jetty in red sandstone rubble. Cast-iron bollards. Much repaired.

DESCRIPTION. A single street. Some plain two-storey houses with pilastered doorways, 1870s, a tenement or two, and the heavily quoined ST BLANE'S HOTEL, dated 1881, symmetrically accented by a French-roofed tower.

KINGARTH

A parish at the S end of Bute. *See* also Kilchattan Bay.

ST BLANE'S CHURCH, 3km. S of Kingarth Hotel, in a valley opening SE towards the Firth above Garroch Head. An ancient ruin sitting in a spellbound garth hidden in the hills. It is a mysterious atmospheric place where Christian worship may have begun as early as the C6; Groome (1883) calls it the Vale of St Blane, a name that might be an aural pun imbued with the fancy that architecture and landscape seem simultaneously to conceal and yet reveal an intense and immanent spirituality. The religious settlement, possibly originally monastic, is marked by low walls running through the trees above the sloping hollow. Within this sheltered dip is a second walled zone, evidently raised, elongated N–S but irregular in outline, in which the chapel lies W–E separating the N end of the enclosure from a larger area to the S with upper and lower graveyards. The site reflects the concerned conservation of the 3rd Marquess of Bute who initiated restoration in 1875. Some twenty years later Bute's architect, *Robert Weir Schulz*, carried out a detailed survey before rebuilding the enclosure walls and stabilizing the fabric of the chapel, work which he effected with scrupulous care, inserting slivers of slate between old and rebuilt masonry.

The C12 CHAPEL has a two-chambered plan orientated W–E. The longer nave, entered towards the W end of the S wall, stands only a few ashlar courses high except for its intact E gable which is penetrated by a Romanesque chancel-arch carved with chevron mouldings and dog-tooth in the springers. The N and s walls of the shorter narrower chancel are of rubble, suggesting some rebuilding or extension, C13(?); they are low in the W but rise to wallhead height at the surviving E gable. There is a single lancet window in the N wall. During the C14 or C15 two higher lancets with deeply splayed ingoes and sills were formed in the E gable and it was probably at this time that the nave was extended W. Within the church itself and in the GRAVEYARDS are many lying SLABS of C12 and C13 date. Immediately s of the chancel-arch gable, a short flight of steps drops into a ditch-like passageway which divides the upper graveyard (said to be for men) and leads to the lower (for women). Close to the W wall of the latter are the vestigial courses of a small rectangular cell. Further W, outside the church enclosure, more overgrown footings, including those of massive thickness belonging to a circular structure known as the DEVIL'S CAULDRON, may be the cellular remains of the early monastic settlement.

KINGARTH CEMETERY, where the road s to Garrochty and St Blane's (qq.v.) leaves the A844. A wall PLAQUE records that this was the site of the former Kingarth Parish Church or Mid Kirk, 1680, destroyed by a storm, c. 1795, and of its replacement, *William Burn*'s church of 1826, demolished after the storm of 1968. The rubble-walled enclosure contains C18 and C19 gravemarkers. Tall HEADSTONE with a wreathed sheaf of corn and draped urn above the cornice; to Robert Mackay †1872, tenant of Kilchattan Mill. To the Stewart family, an aedicule HEADSTONE with inverted torches on the pilasters and a scrolled cornice dated 1877. MURAL PANEL with tapered fluted pilasters, hooded with leaves (the dentilled cornice fallen); to Anne Stirling †1833 and her child John †1832. Plain HEADSTONE naïvely inscribed to Robart Carsuel (*sic*) †1763.

THE GARROCHTY, 800m. s of St Blane's Church. 1898–1901. A gable-fronted villa, its ground-floor canted bays linked by a roof peaked above a columned veranda porch.

DESCRIPTION

A handful of houses at the junction of the B881 with the A844 forms the hamlet of Kingarth. The OLD SCHOOL, 1893, a gabled T-plan with tall paired classroom windows, is now Kingarth Trekking Centre. A piend-roofed playground shelter survives. Adjacent, the OLD SCHOOL HOUSE, c. 1835, a two-storey, three-bay dwelling with a piended roof and a turnpike stair at the rear. There are a few cottages built in the decorative polychromatic brick which was produced locally from 1849; LANGALCHORAD COTTAGES dated 1873. On Bruchag Road, THE MANSE, c. 1769, repaired 1833; a plain, skew-gabled, classical house with canted bay wing added r. 1890.

FORT, Dunagoil, on a rocky massif overlooking the Sound of Bute, 900m. NW of The Garrochty. Remains of an Iron Age timber-laced fortification. The defensive wall of timber and stone, enclosing an area 90m. by 23m., is vitrified in part. Excavations in a cave below the fort, carried out 1915, 1919 and 1925, uncovered evidence of habitation from Neolithic times. On a lower shoulder, c. 400m. N, is Little Dunagoil, evidently an outpost of the fort. Traces of a rampart topping a steep slope on the seaward side. Excavations, 1958–62, revealed that the site had been occupied from the Late Bronze Age until the C13.

STANDING STONES, 600m. s of Kingarth Cemetery. Three impressive monoliths; survivors from a group of seven.

MOUNT STUART

5.5km. SSE of Rothesay

The seat of the Stuart Marquesses of Bute, descendants of King Robert II, hereditary sheriffs of Bute and hereditary keepers of Rothesay Castle (q.v.) for some six centuries. Lodged first in the Castle (q.v.) and later relatively modestly on the burgh's High Street, in the early years of the C18 they embarked on a costly scheme for a grand residence located on Bute's E coast, S of Rothesay. Plans for this first Mount Stuart House were commissioned by the 2nd Earl from *Alexander McGill* in 1716, and in 1718 work began. The design, which took some four years to realize, was competently classical if plain: a seven-by-five-bay hipped-roofed block with attached staircase towers N and S. The W entrance front, two storeys over a basement, developed lower flanking wings around a walled and gated forecourt. On the E, three full storeys overlooked formal gardens. Both harled façades were pedimented over the three central bays but, apart from arched windows lighting the main floor on the E, two superimposed porthole windows at each end of the W front and some rusticated quoining, the treatment was severe.

In 1768 refurbishment seems to have been envisaged. The interior was fitted out with several marble chimneypieces supplied by the Adam family and in the following year *James Craig*, fresh from his success in planning Edinburgh's New Town, carried out a survey which prompted proposals for internal rearrangement and may have given *John Adam* the information he needed to prepare the revised design for Mount Stuart included in an abortive attempt to publish *Vitruvius Scoticus*. Despite such plans it appears little was accomplished. Half a century or so later, excavations along the E side of the house created a new entrance level and in 1874 the 3rd Marquess added a columnar loggia with balustraded entablature across this façade. Then, in 1877, a major fire changed everything.

With the central block of the C18 house a burnt-out shell, the 3rd Marquess turned to *Robert Rowand Anderson* for ideas. A few years earlier Bute had collaborated with Anderson in an attempt to prevent demolitions at Paisley Abbey and had found the Edinburgh architect sympathetic. Proposals for a house on an adjacent site were quickly rejected. Restoration and enlargement were then considered but, by the end of 1878, it had been decided that a new structure ('a splendid palace', wrote the Marquess in a letter to his wife) should be inserted between the undamaged N and S wings of McGill's mansion. The plan, 1879–80, is simple, 'a square within a square' (Stamp, 1995). A tartan grid, a-b-a-b-a, defines the structure and controls the disposition of the principal rooms and staircases around the perimeter; at the centre, a three-storey-high hall, three arcaded bays square, is separated from this accommodation by vaulted circulation routes at the *piano nobile* and floor above (levels which Anderson's drawings refer to as ground and first floor). The layout at second-floor level is similar, though here the lines of circulation are contained within the outer bands of the grid, a move made to bring clearstorey light to the central hall.

EXTERIOR. The geometrical strength of Anderson's plan of 1879–80 is echoed in the planar power of the building's mass: four flat walls of red Corsehill sandstone ashlar rising from a basement plinth through the two principal storeys. Linked by sill-height stringcourses, hooded, pointed-arch windows, varying in size but generally bipartite and traceried, penetrate the solidity of the façades. Above, like a shadowed frieze, a recessed gallery built in brick and timber (completed on the W, 1899) wraps itself around the second floor under the sprocketed canopy of a steeply pitched roof peppered with dormers. The inspiration is Continental secular Gothic: the flat wall planes punctured by pointed arches, Italian or French in derivation; the eaves gallery, certainly French (Anderson had drawn this idea and others from houses at Cordes and Figeac illustrated in his *Examples of the Municipal, Commercial and Street Architecture of France and Italy from the 12th to the 15th Century* published in 1868); the high roof spiked with dormers and chimneys, perhaps German.

For all its Gothic eclecticism, there is an inner rigour in Anderson's Victorian evocation of medievalism, his cubical, hollow-square 'palace', built 1880–5, symmetrically 'clenched between ... white-harled sober Classical wings which survive from the original C18 house' (Gow, 1995). But it is an order accommodated to the contingencies of internal planning, creatively infracted by elevational variations and successively offset by external accretion. Fenestration on the E front, which looks across lawns to the Firth, is indeed symmetrical, with balconies at the centre and a canted oriel chamber corbelled at first floor from a single buttress on each flank. But the elevation stretches S in a wing housing libraries and swimming pool, constructed 1905, and is continued N, from 1896, as the E side of the family's astonishing apsidal CHAPEL, with its high octagonal lantern and spire derived from La Seo Cathedral in Zaragoza; additions which, consistent in material and style, leave the wide garden façade pleasantly asymmetrical. At the middle of the S elevation, a broad projection buttressed by cone-roofed turnpike turrets marks the main staircase well and second-floor billiard room. Here, again, the axiality of the core is thwarted, a high, pitched-roof tower with a parapeted balcony placed off-centre towards the W end of the façade tilting the balance of the composition l. Damaged in a storm, the tower was partially cut down in the mid 1890s. So, too, on the W, a tall, three-light, pointed-arch window, triple-tiered through the two principal floors, emphasizes the main entrance at the N end of the façade. In the middle tier the three cusped openings are filled with heraldic mosaics bearing the arms of the Crichton, Stuart of Bute and Windsor families. A Gothic porte-cochère, added in 1894, intensifies the asymmetry. Far to the r., McGill's S wing disappears behind a kitchen court, the gabled red sandstone walls of which, gridded with mullion-and-transom windows, push forward ahead of the main W façade. His N wing, despite a late request in 1908 that Anderson prepare proposals for its replacement, remains untouched.

That Anderson should still be consulted three decades after his first commission is a measure of the extent to which his work found favour and of the undiminished commitment of the Bute family to the building of Mount Stuart. Even after the death of the 3rd Marquess in 1900, his widow continued to complete many of the interiors. The very prolongation of the work, the alterations and additions, the involvement of many talented artists and craftsmen, seem peculiarly appropriate to the medievalizing intent of client and architect. Yet the house was a most modern residence. Fireproof construction was used over the basement with poured concrete arching between iron beams. Piped hot water provided central heating. Electric lighting, the first domestic installation in Scotland, was introduced from 1883 by the engineer *William H. Massey*, though this was rewired and improved in the late 1890s. In 1887 came the telephone. Even the Gothic swimming pool was heated; another first. Impressive as such innovations are, however, it is the sumptuous interiors at Mount Stuart which take the breath away.

INTERIOR. The house is entered from the Carriage Porch at the N end of the W front. A flight of stairs at the centre of the Entrance Hall rises to the *piano nobile* under a ribbed vault. On the S wall of the upper landing is a fireplace and opposite this a door leading into the first-floor corridor of McGill's N wing, at the end of which is a small room refashioned as a chapel by *William Burges*, 1873. Ahead, filling the central zone on the N side of the plan, is the Outer Hall. On the E wall, a tall Gothic chimneypiece. To the r., the inner space of the GREAT HALL, a majestic atrium seen through the pointed arches of the ambulatory arcade that encloses the core. This arcade, three bays on each side framing the 'square within a square', defines circulation but also acts as a screen or threshold space between the Outer Hall and the Great Hall and between the Great Hall and the Grand Staircase opposite on the S. The ceiling of the ambulatory is timber-beamed, its primary members resting on moulded corbelstones high in the spandrels of the arcade. Polished oak flooring continues into the Hall, interrupted by inlaid marble panels marking the column-line grid. ORGAN by *H. H. Hess* of Gouda, 1781.

In the Hall itself, which took some twenty years to finish, the architecture is richly caparisoned in marble supplied and fitted by the London firm of *Farmer & Brindley*. The ground-floor arches, elegant in profile and moulding, are of pale grey Sicilian marble, their thick columns of striated Cipollino. White marble capitals carved by *Thomas Nicholls* in sprays of foliated ornament, each different under an impost block of Emperor's Red. At the corners, hefty piers clad in Pavonazetta marble are inset with thin ringed shafts of Cipollino. Above a spandrel zone faced in 'pink-flushed' alabaster, the first floor opens as a high arcaded gallery to the Hall. A band of fossil-rich Frosterly marble marks the floor level under bronze grilles copied, at Lord Bute's suggestion, from the railings round Charlemagne's tomb in Aachen and cast for Anderson by *R. Laidlaw & Son*, 1897. The three pointed arches of the ground-floor arcade are repeated on the upper floor but each bay is now divided by a slender double-shaft column carrying marble-sheathed tracery, the main columnar supports and corner piers becoming clustered shafts with scalloped capitals. Variegated marbles, alternating shaft to shaft – Pavonazetta, Cipollino, Emperor's Red and Dove – stress this thinning of the structural elements still further while the placing of white Carrara marble statuary, erected in 1901 on the impost blocks of shafts set proud of the main columns and corners, increases the vertical thrust of the space. Over each figure is an intricately worked Gothic canopy from which ribs rise between the bifurcated pointed-arch windows of the clearstorey tower into a blue stellar vault painted by *Charles Campbell* and scattered with silvered stars to represent the constellations. In the twelve clearstorey windows, STAINED GLASS depicting the signs of the Zodiac, designed by *Horatio Walter Lonsdale* and executed by *William Worral* of *Saunders & Co*.

The DINING ROOM lies on the W side of the Great Hall. Fitted out by *William Frame*, who had already worked for the 3rd Marquess under William Burges at Cardiff Castle, its interior, like several others in the house, was shipped N from the Bute Workshops at Cardiff in the late 1880s. A doorway at the W end of the N ambulatory leads into an ante-chamber from which a wide timber archway set in a lintelled frame opens into the room itself. Fringed by scalloped cusping on the intrados with open trefoils in the spandrels, this arch motif repeats in the embrasures of the three W windows. Walls are panelled in timber; to a dado frieze on the N, E and S, but full height on the W to a frieze of squirrels scurrying among oak leaves and acorns. Wood carving by *Thomas Nicholls*. The ceiling, too, is timber, heavily ribbed with exposed beams and joists. Fitted on the E wall, a five-bay Gothic sideboard by *Frame*. Two white marble chimneypieces, saved from McGill's Mount Stuart, are of mid-C18 date.

On the E side of the house, enjoying views to the Firth, is the stately apartment that Anderson designated the GREAT DRAWING ROOM. It is five bays long, the two outer bays separated from the central space by columnar screens. To this arrangement, doubtless derived from Robert Adam, Anderson gives a Gothic cast: each screen combining three marble-clad pointed arches in a-b-a relationship, the wider opening gracefully cusped.

Perversely, the high marble chimneypiece, 1896, which Anderson designed at the centre of the W wall, is in Renaissance style, vastly ornate, with a depressed arch over the fireplace, deep entablature overmantel and an upper frame of clustered pilasters rising to a cornice that arches over an C18 Adam-style pier glass overpainted with flowers. Above is a heavily beamed ceiling, its painted panels, 1899, displaying the heraldic shields of the 2nd Earl of Bute's descendants against a background of polished mica. Two giltwood tables with marble tops by *William Kent*; from Chiswick House. Two more, with Roman mosaic and marble tops, from Luton Park; attributed to *Robert Adam*.

Approached through the ambulatory on the S side of the Hall, the GRAND STAIRCASE rises in three flights to reach the first-floor gallery, the middle flight pushing out from the S wall of the house between turnpike turrets at the landing corners. In the well, a single marble column with ringed shafts supports a vaulted concrete ceiling finished in plaster between ribs of Sicilian marble. Steps of Carrara marble. Balustrading with colonnettes in variegated marbles. The walls, intended to be faced in alabaster and green Cipollino marble, remain plaster, though the spandrels of the wall arches contain paintings of the Creation by *H. W. Lonsdale*.

The arcaded GALLERY at first floor is vaulted, the eight panels of each bay painted with intertwined foliated scrolls. Off the E passageway are the three principal bedrooms, fitted out by *Frame* in the late 1880s with yellow pine wainscotting and ceilings; carving by *Nicholls*. In the central FAMILY BEDROOM, a deep frieze by *Lonsdale* depicts fifteen scenes from the life of St Margaret; painted in London and erected by 1888. N and S are LADY BUTE'S BEDROOM and LORD BUTE'S BEDROOM, identical in size, each with a canted E bay window with a groined walnut ceiling and marble Gothic arcading parallel to the window. Lord Bute's Bedroom, now the HOROSCOPE ROOM, has an astrological ceiling with outer panels of exotic plants and birds and, at the centre, within a three-dimensional frieze of miniature castles, the planets positioned at the time of the 3rd Marquess's birth. An arcuated frieze with Zodiac signs in the spandrels spills on to the walls. Conceived by *Charles Campbell*, this wonderful conceit was restored in 1992 by *Tom Errington*, who completed the solar system by adding Pluto. Linked S is a teak-framed Conservatory, originally designed by Anderson as an Observatory but converted to its present use in the early 1990s. More bedrooms and bathrooms lie along the N and W sides of the Gallery. On the floor above are the family's private apartments sandwiched between an inner corridor, lit from above the first-floor gallery, and an outer veranda or eaves gallery. The veranda walls of red Suffolk brick are stiffened by framing of Baltic oak; its sprocketed roof, completed 1899, carried on granite columns with bases, balustrades and intermittent pillars of Corsehill stone. In the upper attic, servants' rooms.

Of all Mount Stuart's lavish interiors, the CHAPEL is the most stunning. Bathed in white light tinged with a warm roseate glow falling from the red and russet glass of the lantern lancets, it seems almost to evoke that time, beloved of Le Corbusier, *'quand les cathédrales étaient blanches'*. But not quite. For the whiteness of walls, pillars, arches and vaults is not the simple austerity of whitewashed stone humanized by texture and blemish but the polish of Carrara marble lining every surface with an immaculate perfection. Work on the crypt began in 1896. Seven years later the lantern was complete. The plan is cruciform with a short S end entered from the Great Hall, shallow transepts W and E and an apsidal N sanctuary. The space is generously lit by tall windows with Dec tracery repeated as marble-sheathed screens at the inner wall face. This same white marble, by *Farmer & Brindley*, lines walls, cluster-shaft piers with foliate capitals, arches, vaults and ribs. In the lantern, which is carried on pointed arches at the corners of the crossing, eight triple lancets. Above this, a ribbed vault and octagonal cupola. Saints in the lantern painted in the 1990s by *Tom Errington*. Cosmati work floor in wonderfully patterned geometries of coloured marble and mosaic. – Bronze ALTAR, designed by *Anderson* in 1911 but not cast in Edinburgh until the 1920s; reliefs and silver-gilt figures of Scottish saints by *Louis Deuchars*. – The ORGAN by *Lewis & Co.* of London; designed by *Anderson*, 1903, its gently bowed Gothic screen carved with intricate work of scrolls and vines.

THE GARDENS. Begun by the 2nd Earl of Bute 'spreading his groves all around', 1717. By the middle of the C18 more than 300 acres had been planted. In 1823 the WEE GARDEN was laid out around Racers Burn S of the house. An obelisk SUNDIAL, C17, sits amid the lawns. Upstream W, a picturesque area of pools and bridges is the work of *Thomas H. Mawson*, also responsible for the ROCK GARDEN, 1893–1901, though this was remodelled after the Second World War. At the KITCHEN GARDEN, redesigned by *Rosemary Verey*, 1991, a single stretch of wall from the former WALLED GARDEN survives, strengthened by facing brick buttresses; two round-arched openings have been formed. Nearby is the PAVILION, an octagonal conservatory with a raised octagonal cupola pyramidally roofed and added aluminium finials and weathervane; from the Glasgow Garden Festival, 1988.

THE COLUMN, 100m. NE of Mount Stuart House. Late C18. Erected in the grounds of Luton Hoo Park (whence it was brought to Bute) by the 3rd Earl of Bute and dedicated to Augusta, mother of George III. Tall Tuscan column on a square pedestal bearing the inscription DUM MEMOR IPSE MEI / DUM SPIRITUS HOS REGIT ARTUS ([You will remain in my memory] so long as I am conscious and my spirit controls my limbs). A toga-clad figure stands on the abacus of the capital.

At Kerrycroy (*see* below), the NORTH LODGE, by *William Burn*, c. 1820, has a Tudor-Gothic porch. The SOUTH LODGE, early C19(?), is a Tudor-Gothic L-plan cottage still with its original lying-pane glazing. 1.7km. SSW is the altogether different SCOULAG LODGE: a compact implosion, both Baronial and vernacular, white-walled with three variegated heraldic shields (Stuart, Crichton and Windsor); by *Robert Weir Schulz*, 1896–8.

SHORE CHAPEL, 1.1km. N of Mount Stuart House at Scoulag Point. Built 1727–30 by master mason *James Gillmor* as Kingarth Parish Church; possibly to the design of *Alexander McGill*. Known as Scoulag Church from the late C18, in 1881 it was converted to a Roman Catholic school by the 3rd Marquess of Bute. In 1901 *Robert Weir Schulz* created the present mortuary chapel. The building remains nonetheless essentially Presbyterian: a hipped-roofed T-plan with pedimented gables W and E, and a N wing against which a forestair rises to the laird's loft. Walls are roughcast with rusticated quoins and dressings of red sandstone. W and E pediments support identical belfries, each topped by bell-profile caps and ball finials. The principal S elevation is symmetrical: at the centre, two low lintelled doorways flanked l. and r. by two round-arched windows divided by hefty Y-tracery stone mullions. The interior is in disrepair. Ceiling and walls are plastered save for a boarded dado. The original floor is of flag-stones over which a timber floor has been constructed, except in the N wing. Here, the laird's loft, installed by the wrights *Robert Dreghorn* and *John Taylor*, 1729–30, survives, its panelled front intact above stone vaulting, arches and columns introduced by *Schulz* around the white marble SARCOPHAGI 'sinks' which house the coffins of the 3rd Marquess, John Patrick Crichton-Stuart (1847–1900), and his wife Gwendolyn (1852–1932). Freestanding at the W end is a tall aedicule REREDOS, classically ordered in variegated marbles and alabaster. At the centre of the S wall, the hexagonal PULPIT, possibly early C19; panelled, with fluted Corinthian columns and a high sounding board, also hexagonal, with a dentilled cornice. In front of the Chapel is a graveyard lawn with several lying SLABS and a single Celtic CROSS marking the graves of members of the Crichton-Stuart family. 250m. W is the BEEHIVE WELL, mid C19, a small red rubble dome with decorative wrought-iron N gate.

KERRYCROY VILLAGE. From 1803. Pretty estate hamlet laid out to the approval of the 2nd Marquess's wife in a single segmental curve at the N gates of Mount Stuart House. At the centre, a two-storey, three-bay, harled house with a red tile roof and hood-moulded windows. Simple and severe, it has served as inn and school, and is now flatted. N and S are two six-bay cottages, each comprising two dwellings with slated roofs, hood-mouldings over coupled casements and timber-boarded porches. Inserted later, *c.* 1890(?), between each pair of cottages, a semi-detached Old English house, harled with red sandstone dressings below a half-timbered upper floor. All look W across a village green to Kerrycroy Bay and the early C19 QUAY, a red sandstone rubble jetty with outer parapet and inner steps.

PORT BANNATYNE

A village, formerly known as Kamesburgh, laid out in two parallel streets along the S shore of Kames Bay. Tenements appeared in the holiday boom days of 1890–1900.

KILMICHAEL CHAPEL, on the w arm of the Kyles of Bute, 5.8km. NW of the A844 road-end. Oblong cell with walls standing to *c*. 2m. Altar slab and W aumbry. Indistinct garth wall.

ST COLMAC, ST BRUOC, ST NINIAN. By *William F. McGibbon*, 1885–6. Aisled nave with a circular plate-traceried window in the NE gable and a 33m.-high square entrance tower, recessed l., enlivened by finials and stepping parapets but otherwise of solid, almost Romanesque, dignity.

ST COLMAC'S CHURCH, 1.9km. W of the Old Quay. By *James Dempster* of Greenock, 1835–6; endowed by John, 2nd Marquess of Bute. Simple skew-gabled kirk in coursed rubble with sandstone dressings. Abandoned and roofless. Three tall Y-tracery windows N and S. Square ashlar tower inset in E gable; upper parapeted belfry stage intaken behind corner finials. STAINED GLASS survives in the W gable: the Resurrection and Ascension by *William Meikle & Son*, 1896.

KAMES CASTLE, 'in a low fertile dingle' (Groome, 1883) 900m. WNW of the Old Quay. Five-storey, harled tower-house built for the Bannatynes of Kames in the C16, though perhaps of C14 origin. The original vertical circulation is unclear; the NE jamb with its scale-and-platt stair may have replaced an earlier wheel stair or may be part of more extensive late C18 alterations. In the later C19 *David Bryce* reworked the corbelled crenellated parapet and crowstep-gabled caphouse, adding the small ogee-roofed tower over the link to the staircase wing. In 1911–12, *A. M. Mackinlay* created a courtyard relationship between the tower and its attached steading and new ranges of single-storey, whinstone COTTAGES with crowstepped skews. All are now in holiday-home use. Single-storey, gabled, L-plan LODGE; stop-chamfered ashlar GATEPIERS and rubble walls with crenellated parapets: later C19. Rectangular WALLED GARDEN, late C18, with lean-to greenhouse.

OLD QUAY, Marine Road. Constructed 1801; repaired 1962. Ramped rubble angled to W.

PIER. Built 1857. Derelict since 1937.

WESTER KAMES TOWER, 1.3km. NW of the Old Quay. Conjectural reconstruction of a much degraded, late C17, Z-plan tower-house, by *Robert Weir Schulz*, 1897–1900, for the 3rd Marquess of Bute. Persuasively Scots, four-storey, crowstep-gabled tower with a corner drum corbelled to the square at eaves height and a re-entrant stair turret. Windows have roll-moulded jambs. A subtly intruded brick line distinguishes the old (little more than 4m. high when Schulz surveyed it in 1895) from the new.

DESCRIPTION

Along the shore, Nos. 37–69 MARINE ROAD, two-storey terraced housing, mid C19; most with strip quoins, some with door-pieces, Nos. 64–65 with unusual bowed dormers. CASTLE STREET runs parallel behind, more enclosed and urban. Nos. 1–19 pack closely together, four flat-faced, mid-C19 blocks reached by stair flights rising from the pavement. Opposite, four storeys of canted bays: BUCKINGHAM TERRACE, c. 1900. Rehabilitated terrace housing at Nos. 29–39, C19, with neat doors and dormers by *John Wilson Associates*, 1986–7, and at Nos. 41–43, a flatted terrace of fishermen's cottages, c. 1800, with decoratively balustraded rear stairs. In VICTORIA PLACE, several flatted terraces, c. 1875, planned in the manner of Edinburgh's Colonies, have good pilastered doors and exterior stairs. Continuing SE, HIGH ROAD cuts the corner across Ardbeg Point. A few houses date from c. 1840: Nos. 22–24 (formerly Point House) has a pilastered doorpiece with a good fanlight; FIRCLIFF (No. 42) adds an armorial panel in the doorway pediment and has balustraded aprons to windows l. and r. ETTRICK BANK (Nos. 44–46) is standard two-storey, three-bay with decorative cast-iron balustrading to an outside stair l. On SHORE ROAD some mid or late C19 villas share recurring features: flanking single-storey pavilions at Nos. 2–4, at APPIN HOUSE (Nos. 26–27) and ARDGOWAN HOUSE (Nos. 28–30); fretted king-post gableheads at the last and at No. 6.

CAIRN, Glenvoiden, 500m. E of Kilmichael Chapel. Several chambers of a monument of at least three structural phases. Unearthed pottery vessels and flints now in Bute Museum, Rothesay (q.v.).

STANDING STONE (Kilmachalmaig Cross), 800m. W of St Colmac's Church. Disc-headed cross carved on the face of a broken-topped, obelisk-like stone. The arms of the cross are hammer-headed, the stem cut as two incised lines.

STONE CIRCLE, 1.1km. WSW of St Colmac's Church. Standing in a ring of trees.

ROTHESAY

The main settlement on Bute. A sheltered anchorage at the head of a N-facing bay gave it an early strategic importance, its C13 castle was repeatedly involved in what has been called 'the winning of the west for Scotland' (Tabraham, 1997). It became a royal burgh in 1401. In 1750 linen manufacture was introduced. Ten years later, herring fishing boomed. Then cotton production, begun in 1779, brought the town a measure of industrial prosperity. But it was its success first as a 'watering place' and later, in the C19 and early C20, as the Clyde coast holiday mecca of Glasgow's workers that led to the building of the villas and tenements that stretch along the shore from Ardbeg in the W to Craigmore in the E. A faded elegance lingers along these esplanades, picturesquely elongated between the sea and the island's low hills.

CHURCHES

ARDBEG BAPTIST CHURCH, Ardbeg Road. Built as an Independent Chapel in 1836. In 1882–4 a gallery (now blocked) was introduced and a new Gothic gable front with an eight-leaf wheel window added. Hall and vestry by *G.M. McLintock*, 1923.

BRIDGEND CHURCH, Bridge Street/Bridgend Street. By *Andrew M. Mackinlay*, 1908–9. Red sandstone Gothic gable flirting with Art Nouveau in the tracery and stained glass. Eccentrically bracketed belfry with ogee dome. Playful eight-column ridge ventilator. Interior preserves arch-braced roof, pointed-arch arcading and cast-iron columns. Worship discontinued. Linked l. is a row of shops with church hall above; also by *Mackinlay*.

CRAIGMORE ST BRENDAN'S CHURCH, Mount Stuart Road. Perp Gothic tower retained from the church, 1888–9, designed in competition by Edinburgh architect *David A. Crombie*. Behind it, plain but incongruous, the mock stone front of a low-pitched hall added by *Margaret Brodie*, 1974.

CRAIGMORE UNITED FREE CHURCH, Crichton Road. Chunky Gothic steeple in rough-faced rubble with red Corrie sandstone dressings; all that survives of *John Hutchison*'s church of 1888–9.

Former FREE CHURCH, Chapelhill Road. 1860. Symmetrical ashlar NE front with central belfry steeple shouldered over doors l. and r. Gable behind with quatrefoils flanking the steeple.

HIGH KIRK, High Street. In 1796 the Greenock wrights *Fleming & Ferguson* constructed what was then the third church on this edge-of-town site, a piend-roofed roughcast box arranged with galleries E and W and the pulpit at the middle of the S wall set between tall round-arched windows flanked by superimposed lintelled lights. The design, which included a clock tower (unbuilt), came from *Adam Russell*, architect in Leith. The vestry wing, lit by a three-light window under a pedimented gable, was added N, 1905–6, when the interior was recast with the pulpit in the W by local architect *John Russell Thomson*. Once again an intended tower remained unbuilt. In 1907, the E entrance wing, with its narrow pedimented front and four-light, pilaster-mullion windows under the eaves of the C18 church, was part of extensive refurbishment by *Honeyman, Keppie & Mackintosh*. Their interior is spacious but reserved. Flat plaster ceiling with two floral roses and eight plainer ventilator roses. Cast-iron columns with Ionic capitals support a U-plan gallery which is reached by parallel stair flights rising in the E vestibule. Pitch pine dado to sill height. – At the centre of the W wall, a half-octagon oak PULPIT on an arched base; panels with scroll ornament. – STAINED GLASS concentrated in the W. Above the pulpit, the risen Christ, at the centre of radiating blues, appears to the three Marys; by *Stephen Adam Studios*, 1917. To the l., superimposed memorials to the fallen of World War I, the upper showing a purple-robed Christ over a dark battlefield with cannon, tank and ruined church. To the r., above, the young Jesus in the temple. These three and a tall S window, busy with depictions of women variously at work, all installed by 1922, probably also by *Stephen Adam*. The memorial to World War II, r. of the pulpit below the N gallery, is bright and colourful, though without the lustrous depth of its neighbours; by *D. Hamilton*, c. 1947.

Adjacent SE is ST MARY'S CHAPEL, the rubble remains of

the choir of the C16 parish church. In the E gable, a large pointed-arch window bereft of its three-light intersecting tracery. Single pointed-arch lights at E end of N and S walls. Pointed-arch door at W end N wall. Steep slated roof with glazed W gable added for protection, 1997. Inside, in the E wall, an aumbry and, nearby S, a piscina. On the S wall is a wide MONUMENT, probably C16, defined by a strongly moulded ogee arch set between thin buttresses. In the recess, a knight in plate armour, one of the Stewarts of Bute; below, the base is panelled with quatrefoils. At the centre of the N wall, a second MONUMENT, also C16(?), with a canopied round-arched recess in which lie the effigies of a lady and child. – NE is the small skew-gabled SESSION HOUSE, rubble with traces of harling; probably C18. – Behind the church is the BUTE MAUSOLEUM, a gabled cell in weathered red sandstone, an C18 hybrid of Gothic tracery, Baroque pediments and Neoclassical obelisk finials.

A large BURIAL GROUND surrounds the church. – Numerous lying SLABS, TABLE-TOMBS, and mantled HEADSTONES, C18–C19. – Against the Session House, a pointed-arch SCULPTED PANEL, C19(?), showing an infant baptism scene in high relief; also a pedimented Doric HEADSTONE with triglyph and urn frieze, to Robert Thom of Ascog †1847. – Along a low retaining wall N of the church, several MURAL TABLETS: an urn-topped, pedimented aedicule with inverted torches on the pilasters, to the Brown family, 1844; two similar aedicules with white marble insets, to R. McKirdy †1846 and Janet Bannatyne †1836; another with its marble panel framed by lugged architraves, to Archibald Moore †1835; and a three-part panel heavily corniced, to Robert Orkney †1856. – Across the path, a wide pedimented aedicule, to Archibald MacVicar †1857. – On a grey granite base nearby, a pink granite sarcophagus MONUMENT carrying a bronze figure, bearded, capped and robed; the tomb of James Duncan †1874. – In the lower graveyard W, many decorative C19 and C20 gravemarkers. – Contrasting in simplicity, two grey granite, urn-topped COLUMNS: to James Gillies †1873 and Henry Ormsby †1890. – To the S, among the usual C19 and C20 obelisks, Celtic crosses, etc., a few eyecatchers. To Charlotte Pender McKenzie †1892, a tall extravagantly Gothic MONUMENT with pink granite corner colonnettes. – Debased Doric MONUMENT in grey granite with pink insets; to the Maddever family, c. 1900. – Two white marble aedicule HEADSTONES surmounted by an angel with raised r. arm: one to the Ferrier family, from 1906; the other, to William Gardiner †1931 and his wife Catherine †1949.

ST ANDREW'S (R.C.), Columshill Street. By *Reginald Fairlie*, 1923–5. Bulky, almost Byzantine mass built in concrete blocks faced with crushed red sandstone. Long nave-and-aisles plan continues S into the chancel with flanking chapels E and W. Gaunt and intimidating exterior relieved by severely cut round-arched windows, single in the aisle walls, smaller and tripled in the clearstorey. In the N gable, two doors lead to separate vestibules. From the W lobby a stair rises to the gallery which crosses the first bay of the nave supported on two timber-cased columns with carved splayed dosserets above the capitals. s of the gallery the nave is six bays long with round-arched arcades opening between piers to the aisles. At the clearstorey sill, the inner wall face recesses slightly. Above is a robust roof of kingpost trusses with exposed purlins and rafters. A wide semicircular arch defines the entrance to the chancel which is raised but visually linked to the continuing aisles through two low arcaded bays, the third and final bay of the plan screened to allow an ambulatory below the high s gable and thus complete an uninterrupted processional way around the church. Opening through gated iron screens E and W of the aisles flanking the sanctuary are two chapels dedicated to the Sacred Heart and Our Lady. From the s end of the E aisle a door leads to a hallway linking to the sacristy and PRIEST'S HOUSE, the rooms of which open off an inner cloister court.

Contemporary FURNISHINGS. – In the baptistery a stone, capstan-like FONT. – Half-octagon oak PULPIT, l. of chancel arch. – Oak REREDOS screen with massive posts and deeply cut chevron ornament. – In the gallery, a small pipe ORGAN by *The Positive Organ Co. (1922) Ltd*, London. – STAINED GLASS. N gable: a naïve interpretation of Christ's baptism by *F. D. Tritschler*. High in the s gable, glowing red and blue, SS Blane, Andrew and Columba.

ST PAUL'S (Episcopal), Victoria Street/Deanhood Place. Four-bay gabled Gothic, 1854; choir added s, 1893. Low belfry spire at NW corner. – STAINED GLASS. Four windows by *Norman N. MacDougall*, 1906–7: St Margaret of Scotland, the Vision of St John, St Gabriel, and the Transfiguration. Two-light window showing St Columba preaching, by *James Powell & Sons*.

TRINITY PARISH CHURCH, Castle Street. 1843–5; built as the Free Church by *Archibald Simpson* of Aberdeen and severe enough in design that it might have been built in granite. Bare, square N belfry tower in droved ashlar with angle buttresses terminating in finials at the base of a slender spire. This streetside steeple splays back symmetrically against the church gable. At its base a pointed-arch doorway leads into a tight vestibule; ahead, a central stair returns l. and r. to balcony landings from which winding flights continue upwards, swinging back over the oblique entrance passage-ways below. The plan is rectangular, the floor ramped. The N gallery, supported on three cast-iron columns, extends through a round-arch recess into the tower. Hammer-beam roof, enhanced with Gothic detail, installed in 1907. Arcuated dado panelling rises to the sills of the four tall Y-traceried windows W and E. In the s gable, a triple lancet. – Wide, three-seater Gothic PULPIT, with bowed centre, centrally placed between stair flights, 1907. – Traceried oak organ-pipe screens l. and r.; *Brindley & Foster* ORGAN, 1904, no longer in use. – STAINED GLASS. s gable, 1914–18 War Memorial, by *Oscar Paterson*; a colourful panoply of warriors and saints traversed by a rainbow arc. E window, 1939–45 War Memorial; grim and pallid by *Gordon Webster*, 1948. Rich and warm by contrast, in the w window opposite, Christ stills the waters; in memory of Provost David Munn.

Former UNITED FREE CHURCH, High Street. By *Duncan Dewar*, 1911. Gabled front in bull-faced sandstone. Neither classical nor Gothic; only the façade text, ENTER HIS COURTS WITH THANKSGIVING, makes it clear this is (or, rather, was) a place of worship. Square tower r. with bellcast pyramid roof.

WEST PARISH CHURCH, Argyle Street. By *Charles Wilson*, 1845–6. All that matters is the NE front set back from the street on higher ground: a symmetrical Romanesque gatehouse, from the centre of which, above a round-arched entrance held between parapeted flanks, soars a more Gothic steeple, buttresses, finials and spire attenuated heavenwards. *The Builder* praised Wilson's 'advancement in aesthetic feeling and constructive skill' (1863). Norman interior with fine arch-braced roof trusses. Disused since 1978.

PUBLIC BUILDINGS

BEATTIE COURT, Battery Place. Built as the Royal Aquarium, the first public aquarium in Scotland, 1875–7, by local architect-engineer *John Russell Thomson*. Low ashlar palazzo raised on a rusticated basement. Five-bay pavilion with attic storey and a central pedimented porch with Corinthian columns reached up a circular flight of steps. Recessed wings with balustraded eaves. Basement tanks held 100,000 gallons of sea water and 40,000 gallons of fresh. Converted to swimming baths by *Thomas Beveridge*, 1938. Now residential.

BUTE ESTATE OFFICE, High Street. C17; dated 1681 on the skew. Once the town-house of the Butes; harled T-plan with three-storey crowstep-gabled stair-tower jutting w from the streetface. Continuous stone corbel course at second-floor level. Inside, some C18 panelling; ornate chimneypiece with stylized figures and foliate decoration.

BUTE MUSEUM, Stuart Street. By *A. M. Mackinlay*, 1925–6. Symmetrical with a Venetian window at first floor over a pedimented entrance. Hip-ended single-storey wings l. and r.

CRAIGMORE PIER. The original iron pier of 1877, which had a long arched structure with decorative spandrels, was closed in 1939 and demolished a year later. Stone stump survives.

DUNCAN HALLS, East Princes Street. Competition-winning design by *James Hamilton & Son*, 1876–9, which entailed the raising of an existing three-storey building to five storeys. The remodelled ashlar street-front is symmetrical, the windows arranged 1-1-3-1-1 in a wide five-bay façade; segmental pediments at first floor, consoled cornices above, and at third-floor level a rhythmic march of columns flanking the openings under a deep eaves entablature. Behind a complex balustraded screen of heavily pedimented dormers, three frenchified roof towers emerge against the skyline. A central porch originally crossed the pavement. At the rear, two turnpike stairs; but the halls themselves, converted to form a cinema in 1935, have gone.

ESPLANADE. Following the creation of Victoria Street on land reclaimed in 1840, the town made further encroachment on the sea w of the Harbour (q.v.), 1869–72; engineer *A. Duncan*. Ornamental gardens and walks laid out.

HARBOUR. The earliest or OLD QUAY, which extended the line of the Watergate before curving E, was constructed 1752–81. From 1785–90, a NEW QUAY was built N from High Street; it too turned E, leaving an access gap between it and its predecessor. In 1822 reconstruction to accommodate steam vessels extended the New Quay E, absorbing part of the old pier and necessitating the creation of a new entry to the inner basin. A drawbridge was built between the two quays in 1833. In 1839–40 a slip and building dock were formed w of the New Quay while reclamation work moved the shoreline N (*see* Esplanade). A stone breastwork (later the Albert Pier) appeared off East Princes Street, 1863–5. In 1898–9 the main N pier was broadened and extended E and w by *John Russell Thomson*. Since then the main change to this long convex alignment has been the introduction of a roll-on roll-off ramp in 1977. The earliest waiting accommodation on the pier was of timber construction but in 1884–5 this was replaced by a brick structure conspicuously accented by a clock tower with Baronial finials. Augmented by more waiting space designed by *Andrew M. Mackinlay*, 1904, these buildings survived two proposals for improvement, aborted by war in 1914 and 1939, until they were destroyed by fire in 1962. An 'airport-style terminal' was opened in 1968 but in 1992 this too was superseded. The present PIER BUILDINGS, by *Strathclyde Regional Council*, red-tiled, piend-roofed, the ridge gaily topped with pagoda ventilators and a two-tier central clock-tower crested with a gold cockerel weather-vane, make a spirited effort to find the necessary nautical panache. Restored PIERHEAD TOILETS, 1899, in polychromatic glazed brickwork (with yet more splendid ceramic delights inside). Extending N from Victoria Street, the CABBIES' REST, by Burgh Engineer *Alexander Stephen*, 1930, an eleven-bay, cast-iron shelter carrying light metal trusses under a piended glazed roof. Former WEIGH HOUSE, late C19; neat glazed brick cell, piend-roofed with cast-iron brattishing.

MARKET CROSS, High Street/Stuart Street. C20. On a seven-step octagonal base, a simple square-section sandstone cross incised with the figure of Christ crucified.

POST OFFICE, Bishop Street. 1895–7. Two high storeys in good ashlar with an attic centrepiece, pedimented and scrolled, dated 1896. Rich, Renaissance detail. The order and ornament of the façade maintained in 1908 wing r.

Former REGAL CINEMA, Argyle Street. Aggressive symmetry by *Alexander Cattanach*, 1937–8. Verticals squeezed by horizontals: a high finned front widens its faience cladding l. and r. under brick-banded flanks.

REGISTRAR'S OFFICE, Mount Pleasant Road. Built mid C19 as Eaglesham Lodge but converted to offices, 1939. Gabled Tudor Gothic with fleur-de-lis finials.

Former RITZ CINEMA, High Street. By *Alexander Cattanach*, 1937. Symmetrical, banded and finned but crassly traduced.

ROTHESAY ACADEMY, Westland Road. By *Harvie & Scott*, 1956–9. Jutting from the hillside, three storeys of curtain-walled classrooms on *pilotis*; the long arm of an L-plan. Low accommodation fills the re-entrant with verandas looking NE across the bay. Two cusped arches incorporated as a memory of the school's Gothic Revival predecessor, by *John Russell Thomson*, 1869–70. Uphill, a long two-storey block in reconstituted stone with a raised, vaguely Art Deco centre; by *Andrew M. Mackinlay*, 1936–8.

ROTHESAY HEALTH CENTRE, High Street. By *Baron Bercott & Associates*, 1974. Neat monopitches in brick and roughcast.

ROTHESAY PAVILION, Argyle Street. 1936–8. By *J. & J. A. Carrick*; won in a competition limited to architects practising in Scotland. Uncompromisingly Moderne and stylish, the continuously glazed, bow-fronted cantilever of the first-floor buffet, matched by a curving slab cantilevered over the open roof terrace above, captures something of the boldness of Mendelsohn & Chermayeff's only just completed Bexhill Pavilion. Behind this daring bulge is the high wall of the auditorium faced with artificial stone and fronted by bands of horizontal metal glazing. The structure is a reinforced concrete frame with steel columns supporting the cantilevers. Inside, the chunky geometrical ornament of an Art Deco picture house. 120

Former SCHOOL, Bishop Street. 1798. Hip-ended schoolroom built in rubble with dressed margins. Lintelled window in round-arched recess. Linked r. is the two-storey schoolmaster's house, with similar arched recesses over ground-floor windows and door. Now used by Rothesay Christian Fellowship.

SCHOOL, Union Street, 1901. High symmetrical street front of three gables with mullion-and-transom windows.

THOMSON MEMORIAL FOUNTAIN, Ardbeg Road/Marine Place. 1867.

TOWN HALL AND COUNTY BUILDINGS, Castle Street. A castellated Gothic fort by *James Dempster* of Greenock, 1832–4. Built in olive-brown ashlar lightened by ochre sandstone dressings. The principal elevation is symmetrical: a central square tower, heavily machicolated under a high parapet; flanking this, two bays of triple-lancet, first-floor windows in shallow recesses framed by pilaster buttresses and parapet; at the ends, narrow angle turrets. A double forestair originally rose to the main entrance placed centrally in the tower, the lower floor being given over to prison cells, but in 1883 the jail was closed and the present crenellated three-lancet oriel corbelled at first floor over a new street-level entrance. Rear extensions in 1865–7 (courtyard block with vaulted cells) and 1888–9 produced an E-plan arrangement with short castellated returns down High Street and Watergate. Oval staircase at the rear of the tower, probably 1880s. Tower CLOCK by *Arnold Dent & Co.*, London, 1834; Bell cast by *Stephen Miller & Co.*, Glasgow, 1834. 112

VICTORIA HOSPITAL, High Street. Barely Gothic by *John Russell*

Thomson, 1897; symmetrical with canted bays in gabled wings. Martin wing, 1927, barely keeps in keeping. Maternity department by *Walker, Hardie & Smith*, 1937–8.

WAR MEMORIAL, Esplanade Gardens. Competition-winning design by *Charles E. Tweedie*, 1921–2. Grey Aberdeen granite pedestal carrying a bronze angel by *C. d'O. Pilkington Jackson*.

WINTER GARDEN, The Esplanade. Prefabricated in Glasgow at the Saracen Foundry of *Walter MacFarlane & Co.* and erected, 1923–4, under the direction of Rothesay's Burgh Engineer, *Alexander Stephen*. An octagonal Victorian bandstand was absorbed into the design. Domed circular hall with a bowed s entrance loggia flanked by pagoda-roofed square towers. Shoreside, between piended pavilions, a similar roof rises over the former bandstand. Sixteen steel portal ribs support the dome radially (two carried by N proscenium arch). From cast-iron Doric columns, engaged between glazed panel walls, decorative iron brackets cantilever a glazed awning over an outer ambulatory. Above, around the clearstorey edge of the dome, is a balustraded walkway with cast-iron lamp standards. Ironwork ornament includes scrolls, finials and Art Nouveau motifs. Described by Historic Scotland as 'one of the most important pieces of work from the renowned Saracen foundry surviving in Scotland' (1998), this is perhaps the most valuable C20 building in Argyll & Bute.

DESCRIPTION

Seen from the steamer, Rothesay flatters to deceive. On each side of the bay villas and terraces line the shore below gentle wooded slopes. Gradually the scale rises as tenements and hotels pack together behind the esplanade. Seaside civility; 'a pretty little town', Queen Victoria called it. Then, from the pier (*see* Public Buildings above), some disappointments: disused buildings, gap-sites, a certain shabbiness. At the centre, GUILDFORD SQUARE, well paved, offers urban space with a glimpse of the Castle (*see* Public Buildings above) but little more. To the r., VICTORIA STREET, mid C19, unified in scale, detail and colour but a little dowdy. A Thomsonesque shopfront at Nos. 13–15. Matching curved corners turn into Tower Street at Nos. 37 and 39, mid C19. The VICTORIA HOTEL, mid C19, made grandly French by the addition of a dormered mansard with lacy ironwork cresting, 1879. To the l., the fading dignity of the front continues in ALBERT PLACE. Consoles, a dentilled eaves and a pilastered porch at the former ROYAL HOTEL, *c.* 1850. In BISHOP STREET, opposite the façade-conscious Post Office (*see* Public Buildings above), a few older cottages, late C18 and early C19, with in-and-out quoins and a heavy eaves moulding. To the l., SERPENTINE ROAD climbs in repetitive zig-zags overlooked by CASTLE BUILDINGS, mid C19, three and four storeys of windowed tenement walls advancing and receding uphill with splendid urban bravura. Round the corner in MOUNT PLEASANT ROAD, more good tenements with pilastered close entries and a

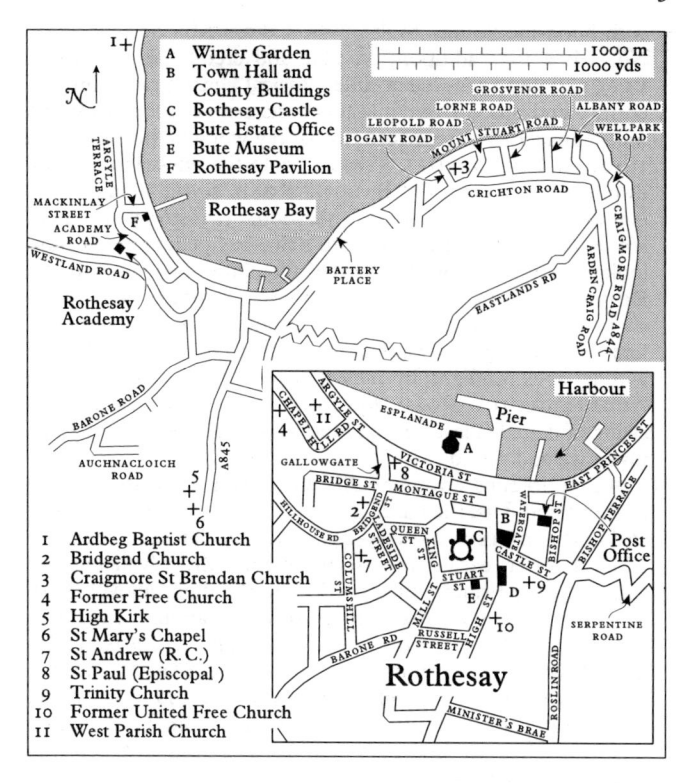

```
A  Winter Garden
B  Town Hall and
   County Buildings
C  Rothesay Castle
D  Bute Estate Office
E  Bute Museum
F  Rothesay Pavilion

 1  Ardbeg Baptist Church
 2  Bridgend Church
 3  Craigmore St Brendan Church
 4  Former Free Church
 5  High Kirk
 6  St Mary's Chapel
 7  St Andrew (R.C.)
 8  St Paul (Episcopal)
 9  Trinity Church
10  Former United Free Church
11  West Parish Church
```

short smart classical terrace, Nos. 30, 32 and 34, *c.* 1840(?), united by a fine eaves cornice. At the centre of town, CASTLE STREET maintains a sense of civic enclosure: the spire of Trinity Church (*see* Churches above) in the E, the tower of the Sheriff Court (*see* Public Buildings above) in the w. Nos. 8–24, early C19, preserve the eaves line; at No. 22, tripartite windows l. and r. Nos. 7–9 repeat this theme, adding pedimented cornices, an Ionic porch and a third storey raised at the centre to a pediment with an obelisk apex. Behind Victoria Street, shops animate both sides of MONTAGUE STREET. Lighting and paving are good but there are no buildings of quality and too many gaps. The TSB BANK, by *Roxby, Park & Baird*, 1979, is smart but overimaginatively vernacular for its town-centre corner. Curved corners, *c.* 1820, again flank the entry to Tower Street. At Nos. 97–99, fins and chevrons in red ashlar above Woolworth's windows; by *D.C. Donaldson*, London, 1938. In GALLOWGATE, returning to the shore, some of the old two-storey streetscape survives, though barely; on the corner with Bridge Street, a painted date, 1780.

Rothesay's mill-town quarter lies w and s of the castle along the banks of the Water of Fad. Much has been carefully rehabilitated. On JOHN STREET, Nos. 1–4, a cottage row, roughcast with hood-mouldings, built by the Cotton Mill Society, 1805. No. 5 is a 1935 addition, credible and creditable. COLBECK PLACE, dated 1772, has a rude classical charm; two-storeyed, cornice and fluted Doric pilasters at its central door: perhaps a mill-manager's house. More two-storey workers' housing, mid 1840s, in COLUMSHILL STREET (note the one-window-wide dwelling at No. 30). Off BARONE ROAD, textile manufacture continues at BUTE FABRICS, a very long, two-storey-and-attic, white-harled mill, early C19, with a five-bay pedimented centre looking w across a walled garden forecourt. Beyond is BUTE BUSINESS PARK: new industry housed in offices and workshops in striped brickwork, the main building lit by continuous first-floor glazing under a shallow pyramid roof of profiled metal with an apex rooflight; by *John Wilson* of Oban, 1995–8. Along AUCHNACLOICH ROAD, looking s across The Meadows, a string of flatted villas, *c.* 1903; rough-and-ready Arts and Crafts, inventive and varied.

HIGH STREET runs s from the Pier. On the r. is the Castle; on the l., shops and flats, the hard castellated wall of the Sheriff Court and CASTLE VIEW, Nos. 45–49, a late C19 Baronial tenement. Then a softer, earlier streetscape: behind the advancing C17 gable of Bute Estate Office (*see* Public Buildings above), Nos. 61–67, *c.* 1820, a long low cottage row with an inset sink in its roughcast wall. Across the street, the MERCAT CROSS and a gabled, whin rubble house, No. 3 STUART STREET, *c.* 1820, flatted 1937, with a turnpike stair at the rear and a datestone, 1626–1826, above its doorway. Baronial again in RUSSELL STREET, Nos. 14–26, 1877 and 1901–2, ashlar tenements enlivened by strapwork ornament, barley-sugar downpipes and a jagged second-floor storey of thistle-topped crowstepped gables. Across the street, Nos. 17–21, *c.* 1840, a two-storey terrace retaining decorative ironwork stairs at the rear. BOURTREE PLACE, another tenement, *c.* 1895, is plainer but for some whimsical ornithological carving below bowed oriels. MANSEFIELD PLACE, *c.* 1900, ripples with canted bays carried up into a mansard attic. Round the corner in MINISTER'S BRAE, stone gives way to brick and timber: five dwellings in a Tudor terrace, *c.* 1905 (each arboreally denominated: ASHLEA, ROWANLEA, etc.), with slated canted bays, bracketed porch canopies, red brick and half-timbered gables, the higher central gable pushed forward on a bold cavetto. Next door, MARIONSLEA, *c.* 1900, in similar style. Both by local builder *William Hunter*. Back on High Street urban enclosure evaporates. A driveway, marked by gatepiers with large ball finials, leads uphill to FOLEY HOUSE, late C18, a harled, piend-roofed mansion with a pedimented front and gables, urns on the eaves and a pedimented doorpiece with fluted Ionic pilasters. On the r., playing fields open on to The Meadows. At Nos. 177–179, a last rude tenement, *c.* 1860. Finally, in almost rural isolation, the High Kirk and the last vestiges of its predecessor, the medieval parish church of St Mary (*see* Churches above).

From Esplanade Gardens ARGYLE STREET marches with the

shore, a coastal ribbon of tenements and terraces running N to Ardbeg. At first the scale is four-storey. Nos. 7–10 have architraves and consoles around first- and second-floor windows and a central chimneystack dated 1882. Canted bays flank Nos. 17–20, 1902, appearing again past the West Church (*see* Churches above) at No. 27 where the skyline crinkles with decorative ironwork. More of the same in the barley-sugar columns and foliated ornament of the porch at GRAND MARINE COURT, *c.* 1880, a red sandstone hotel now flatted. At ARGYLE PLACE the scale drops to two-storey: three-bay houses, early C19, with consoled doorways and decorative fanlights; Ionic pilasters at the door of No. 11. Then three-storey three-bay at No. 14, *c.* 1840(?). And at No. 23, ARGYLE MANSIONS, *c.* 1900, the full four-storey tenement in red ashlar with flanking bays and sill-height stringcourses. Uphill, winning the view, are ARGYLE TERRACE, a quiet, one-sided street of dormered cottages, *c.* 1820, some with forestairs, and ACADEMY TERRACE, *c.* 1905, blazered in black-and-white half-timbering. Higher still, on Westland Road, IVYBANK, *c.* 1800, a regular Georgian villa with Gothick glazing, and the battlemented tower of CHAPELHILL VILLA, once the tiny Museum of the local Archaeological & Physical Society, 1873. Along the shore ARDBEG ROAD runs on to Port Bannatyne (q.v.). At WOODSIDE, *c.* 1875, a full-height, five-light bow with cast-iron mullions. Flavoured with Tudor Gothic, TIGH-NA-MARA, *c.* 1875, sits back from the street line. Not so TOWARD VIEW, 1910, a late twin-chimneyed tenement hard on the pavement.

Across the bay, the same concatenation of tenements, terraces and marine villas lasts longer. EAST PRINCES STREET begins with urban vigour. First, ALBERT MANSIONS, 1908; four banded, bay-fronted storeys of red ashlar with an Art Nouveau interior in the GOLFER'S BAR. Then Duncan Halls (*see* Public Buildings above), taller, grander and altogether more architecturally sophisticated. Next, taller still, LADY MARY MANSIONS, *c.* 1905, and BUTE MANSIONS, 1906; two red, five-storey tenements, bay-windowed but austere. Abruptly, the eaves line drops. Earlier houses appear. Nos. 37–38, 39–42, *c.* 1840, and Nos. 43–44, dated 1843, pack gable-to-gable, most with pilastered doorways. The same motif repeats intermittently along BATTERY PLACE where, at Nos. 5, 7 and 13, mid C19, entrances are further enhanced by Tuscan columns. No. 11 introduces a two-storey bow window with cast-iron colonnette mullions, late C19, an idea boldly developed at GLENDALE (No. 20), late C19, where the bow has an extra storey carrying a mini-broch turret crowned with an ironwork cage. The skyline jumps at Nos. 17–17A, another red tenement, dated 1914, five storeys high with a broken pediment over each close entry; by *G. M. McLintock*. No. 21, mid C19, reverts to earlier scale and reserve, but BATTERY LODGE is aberrant; built in 1827 it was Tudorized in 1910. Then, Nos. 31–32, *c.* 1910; four red flatted storeys, four full-height canted bays. After Beattie Court (*see* Public Buildings above), a gap in the building line reveals the GLENBURN

HOTEL, an imposing, even intimidating palace set high on the terraced hillside to dominate the bay. Designed by *James Hamilton* as Scotland's first hydropathic hotel in 1843; it was later destroyed by fire but rebuilt almost immediately, 1892–4, by *John M. Crawford*, in towered four-storeyed symmetry, classical in detail with arched loggias, verandas and flanking wings. An axial palm-fringed staircase climbs from the road below. Back on the shore, the last of the tenements, GLENFAULDS, *c.* 1880; a windowed wall, bowed and bayed, with stilted lintels and arches carried on cast-iron mullions.

At MOUNT STUART ROAD, the coastal suburb of Craigmore begins. A nine-dwelling terrace at Nos. 19–27, by *John Orkney*, 1868; symmetrical, with a quatrefoil under its central gable and vestiges of arch-braced fretted bargeboards. Then, three series of marine villas, all semi-detached but designed in symmetrical groups of five, five and three: ELYSIUM TERRACE, by *John Orkney*, 1875; ROYAL TERRACE, by *John Duncan*, 1877; ALBANY TERRACE, also by *Duncan*, 1882. Low pitched gables, decorative bargeboards, pilaster mullions on bow and bay windows, and anthemion ornament details, all suggest familiarity with the work of Alexander 'Greek' Thomson. Above this parade, the houses on CRICHTON ROAD have a similar though less lithic quality. At Nos. 1–2 and 3–4, Gothicized Palladian windows; at No. 7, a wide eaves and fret-gabled dormers added to an earlier mid-C19 house; Nos. 10–34 almost rural with bracketed eaves, fretted bargeboarding and balconies: all built between 1875 and 1885; several, if not all, by *John Duncan*.

CRAIGMORE ROAD follows the coast s. A low concrete dome ringed by a battlemented wall, a SEWAGE TREATMENT CHAMBER, *c.* 1930, marks the change of direction at Bogany Point. Detached sandstone villas line the sea-front. Decorative ironwork is much in evidence: brattishing over the bays at No. 7, late C19; a parapet at GLENCRAIG (No. 15), *c.* 1880; veranda pilasters at MADRAS HOUSE (No. 16), *c.* 1853. CRAIGMORE HOUSE (No. 22) affects Jacobean detail; CRAIGEND HOUSE (No. 23) is Italianate with a Regency veranda in cast iron: both dwellings, mid C19, have painted harl walls. At No. 24, late C19, half-timbered Tudor over red sandstone with bracketed eaves and balcony. Then ORCADIA, Nos. 25–30, another terrace of Thomsonesque villas with round-arched bows and more decorative iron; Nos. 27 and 28, dated 1860, carry the monogram JO (*John Orkney?*). MONTFORD HOUSE, *c.* 1850, reverts to plain classical symmetry but maintains the coastal predilection for a balustraded ironwork balcony. At Millburn Bridge, Craigmore becomes Ascog (q.v.).

Uphill on ARDENCRAIG ROAD are Craigmore's grandest houses. Though only single-storey and harled, ARDENCRAIG HOUSE, mid C19, is a 'large and exceedingly handsome mansion, built after a plan modernised from the French' (*The Buteman*, 1876) with a pedimented Doric doorpiece set between multi-paned sidelights. ROCKHILL CASTLE, 1880s and 1891, is larger still and busier, full of late Victorian eclectic complexity: bays, bows, an arcaded arbour and an engaged octagonal tower, the interior equally rich with timber panelling, intricate cornices and stained glass. But the best is TOR HOUSE, 1855, its shallow-pitched roofs, decorative bargeboards and pilaster-mullioned windows instantly recognizable as the work of *Alexander Thomson*. It is not large, but tense and tightly towered and the first of Thomson's lintelled picturesque villas; everything from L-plan composition to key-patterned gatepiers in disciplined place, *sui generis*, at once inventive and strict.

WOODEND HOUSE, 3.4km. SSW of Rothesay Pier. 1824. Built by the actor Edmund Kean as a retreat from the opprobrium that followed his defeat in a court case brought by his mistress's husband. An archetypal, two-storey, three-bay, piend-roofed classical house with twenty-four-pane, double-hung sash windows, a columned porch with cornice and block pediment and single-storey wings recessing l. and r., its simple charm is hidden in a sylvan setting through which a view is channelled to the still waters of Loch Fad. Contemporary whitewashed COACH-HOUSE with pointed-arch entrance and cruciform gunloops. Gothic GATELODGE, piend-roofed with overhanging eaves. Four corniced GATEPIERS, each carrying a carved bust: Massinger, Shakespeare, Kean himself, and Garrick.

ROTHESAY CASTLE
in the centre of town

Massive curtain-wall shell set on a flat-topped mound rising in well-groomed grassy banks from a picturesque moat. The plan is circular, unique in Scotland, with four added round towers and a later N forework. Origins are obscure, but the castle was probably built by one of the hereditary Stewards of Scotland, who held Bute from around the end of the C12, or perhaps by the king himself. Records confirm that the castle fell to the Norsemen in 1230, was retaken by the Scots, succumbed briefly to a second siege, before being recaptured by Alexander III after the Battle of Largs in 1263. By the end of the C13 it was probably in English hands, the ebb and flow of possession continuing through the Wars of Independence. With the accession of the house of Stewart to the Scottish throne in 1371 the castle became a favoured royal residence. Robert II, who spent much of his time there, conferred the hereditary sheriffship of Bute on one of his natural sons, John, whose descendants also became captains of Rothesay Castle and, in course of time, Earls and Marquesses of Bute. During the C15 and early C16 it played an important role in the monarchy's struggle to subdue the Western Isles. In 1544 the Earl of Lennox seized Rothesay for the English. A century later the castle was first a royalist redoubt and then invested by Cromwellian troops, who dismantled the fabric before leaving in 1659. What remained was further reduced during the Earl of Argyll's rebellion in 1685. Abandoned and ruinous, disintegration was halted only in 1816–17, when the 2nd Marquess of Bute, having cleared the castle of 'the accumulated rubbish of ages – consisting, to a large amount, of beef and mutton bones' (*Parliamentary Gazette*, 1851), carried out some minor works. Not until the 1870s, however, was its future as a historic monument secured, the 3rd Marquess obtaining detailed survey assessments, both locally and from the London architect *William Burges*, which were to be the basis of an extensive programme of stabilization and repair principally carried out 1872–9 but not fully completed until the end of the century. In 1961 the Bute family gifted the castle to the state.

The untowered circular curtain or *enceinte* dates from the very earliest years of the C13. It is constructed of squarish ashlar blocks, the original height discernible l. and r. of the forework in crenellations and putlog holes left untouched when the walls were later raised (*see* below) in whinstone rubble. The four equidistant towers, added to the curtain in the last quarter of the C13, rose above the original wallhead. Only one, the NW or PIGEON TOWER, so called by virtue of nesting-box grids built into the upper levels, survives in any bulk, though all four preserve their splayed bases which have spade-shaped arrow-slits, unique in Scotland, cut from the chamfered course at the top of the splay. The curtain wall, too, has a battered masonry plinth; but this, though earlier than the towers, appears to have been an addition, replacing an earth bank originally integral with the construction of the wall and so blocking the W postern gate. The original N gatehouse, built out slightly from the enclosing wall and now embedded in the later forework, retains portcullis slots and a squared and chamfered impost, 'not likely to have been hewn after about 1220' (Cruden, 1960), from which springs a tall pointed-arch. At some time in the late C15 or early C16 the walls were heightened, reaching *c.* 10m., and the projecting rubble FOREWORK was begun, *c.* 1512, extending the entrance passage-way, increasing the guard-house accommodation and incorporating a hall at first floor as part of new royal lodgings. Rectangular in plan with a gabled W latrine tower, it rises through different phases of masonry construction evident on the N and W to a now much reduced corbelled parapet. On the N, above the entrance, is a vertical panel carved with the royal coat-of-arms. Until the late C19 the hall lay open to the elements; its roof and the E wall, built in undisguised red sandstone ashlar, 'a most painful contrast to the old structure' (*Architectural Review*, 1900), are part of the 3rd Marquess's improvements undertaken by *J. R. Thomson*, 1900–1.

The N entrance is approached across the moat by a modern timber bridge, the supporting posts of which are said to be located where burned wooden stumps were discovered during late C19 work on the site. A tunnel-like vaulted corridor leads through the forework to the pointed-arch of the C13 gatehouse built against a wide rounded-arch in the curtain wall. Immediately before the gatehouse arch, a postern opens r. Opposite this, past the porter's lodge and guard room is a small stair up to the HALL. This is much restored, the E wall with four lintelled windows and the beamed and joisted ceiling of late C19 date. At the N end of the W wall is a wide fireplace recess with a segmental-arch lintel. From an ante-room opening s, passages lead W and E through the curtain wall: originally wallhead links to the NW and NE towers, these have been immured by the later increase in the wall height. Slight evidence of groined and ribbed vaulting at a higher level suggests that there may have been an oratory on the second floor of the forework. An open stair leads down into the courtyard.

Within the *enceinte* the foundations of several small buildings can be traced. There is a well in the NW sector. Door openings lead into each tower. Projecting W from the centre of the E wall, where a staircase ascends to the wallhead, is the CHAPEL of St Michael the Archangel, early C16(?), a roofless, two-storey, rubble structure with two pointed-arch windows with a central mullion and branching tracery at the E end of the N and S walls, an E gable, but largely open to the W. In the S wall, E of the E window, a piscina; at the W end, a round-arch doorway once approached by an outside stair.

STRAAD

0462

A few houses on the W side of the island close to the head of St Ninian's Bay.

CRUIKSLAND CHAPEL, 300m. W of Ardroscadale Farm. Footings visible on the shore.

ST MARY'S CHAPEL, near Kilmory Farm. Scrub-hidden remains located in a walled enclosure.

ST NINIAN'S CHAPEL, on a narrow peninsula on the W side of St Ninian's Bay. A roofless rubble rectangle, possibly of Early Christian date, aligned N–S with a ruinous cross wall and small chamber added to the N gable. W and E walls stand to the wallhead. No arched openings. Almost all of the S gable has fallen. In the N wall, a lintelled aumbry. Excavations, 1952–4, uncovered an altar with a relic-holder cavity, unique in Scotland.

KILMORY CASTLE, near Meikle Kilmory Farm. Scant remains.

STEWART HALL, 1.5km. NE of Straad hamlet. 1760. Two-storey, pink harled house, symmetrical and classical, with heavily rusticated quoins, jambs and keystones; built here to enjoy better views than its predecessor at nearby Kilwhinleck. The principal five-bay SW façade, grouped 2-1-2, has a projecting centre with an urn-capped pediment and a robust Palladian motif with fluted columns. Lower wings; the W extended 1975 to link with a grand ten-sided conservatory.

CAIRN, Scalpsie Bay, S of the A844. Still a substantial mass of stone. Bronze Age burial cist discovered in excavation.

GLOSSARY

Numbers and letters refer to the illustrations (by John Sambrook) on pp. 642–9.

ABACUS: flat slab forming the top of a capital (3a).

ACANTHUS: classical formalized leaf ornament (3b).

ACCUMULATOR TOWER: see Hydraulic power.

ACHIEVEMENT: a complete display of armorial bearings (i.e. coat of arms, crest, supporters and motto).

ACROTERION: plinth for a statue or ornament on the apex or ends of a pediment; more usually, both the plinth and what stands on it (4a).

ADDORSED: descriptive of two figures placed back to back.

AEDICULE (*lit.* little building): architectural surround, consisting usually of two columns or pilasters supporting a pediment.

AFFRONTED: descriptive of two figures placed face to face.

AGGREGATE: see Concrete, Harling.

AISLE: subsidiary space alongside the body of a building, separated from it by columns, piers or posts. Also (Scots) projecting wing of a church, often for special use, e.g. by a guild or by a landed family whose burial place it may contain.

AMBULATORY (*lit.* walkway): aisle around the sanctuary (q.v.).

ANGLE ROLL: roll moulding in the angle between two planes (1a).

ANSE DE PANIER: see Arch.

ANTAE: simplified pilasters (4a), usually applied to the ends of the enclosing walls of a portico (q.v.) *in antis*.

ANTEFIXAE: ornaments projecting at regular intervals above a Greek cornice, originally to conceal the ends of roof tiles (4a).

ANTHEMION: classical ornament like a honeysuckle flower (4b).

APRON: panel below a window or wall monument or tablet.

APSE: semicircular or polygonal end of an apartment, especially of a chancel or chapel. In classical architecture sometimes called an *exedra*.

ARABESQUE: non-figurative surface decoration consisting of flowing lines, foliage scrolls etc., based on geometrical patterns. Cf. Grotesque.

ARCADE: series of arches supported by piers or columns. *Blind arcade* or *arcading*: the same applied to the wall surface. *Wall arcade*: in medieval churches, a blind arcade forming a dado below windows. Also a covered shopping street.

ARCH: Shapes *see* 5c. *Basket arch* or *anse de panier* (basket handle): three-centred and depressed, or with a flat centre. *Nodding*: ogee arch curving forward from the wall face. *Parabolic*: shaped like a chain suspended from two level points, but inverted.

Special purposes. *Chancel*: dividing chancel from nave or crossing. *Crossing*: spanning piers at a crossing (q.v.). *Relieving* or *discharging*: incorporated in a wall to relieve superimposed weight (5c). *Skew*: spanning responds not diametrically opposed. *Strainer*: inserted in an opening to resist inward pressure. *Transverse*: spanning a main axis (e.g. of a vaulted space). *See also* Jack arch, Overarch, Triumphal arch.

ARCHITRAVE: formalized lintel, the lowest member of the classical entablature (3a). Also the moulded frame of a door or window (often borrowing the profile of a classical architrave). For *lugged* and *shouldered* architraves *see* 4b.

ARCUATED: dependent structurally on the arch principle. Cf. Trabeated.

GLOSSARY

ARK: chest or cupboard housing the tables of Jewish law in a synagogue.

ARRIS: sharp edge where two surfaces meet at an angle (3a).

ASHLAR: masonry of large blocks wrought to even faces and square edges (6d). *Broached ashlar* (Scots): scored with parallel lines made by a narrow-pointed chisel (broach). *Droved ashlar*: similar but with lines made by a broad chisel.

ASTRAGAL: classical moulding of semicircular section (3f). Also (Scots) glazing-bar between window panes.

ASTYLAR: with no columns or similar vertical features.

ATLANTES: *see* Caryatids.

ATRIUM (plural: atria): inner court of a Roman or C20 house; in a multi-storey building, a toplit covered court rising through all storeys. Also an open court in front of a church.

ATTACHED COLUMN: *see* Engaged column.

ATTIC: small top storey within a roof. Also the storey above the main entablature of a classical façade.

AUMBRY: recess or cupboard, especially one in a church, to hold sacred vessels used for the Mass.

BAILEY: *see* Motte-and-bailey.

BALANCE BEAM: *see* Canals.

BALDACCHINO: freestanding canopy, originally fabric, over an altar. Cf. Ciborium.

BALLFLOWER: globular flower of three petals enclosing a ball (1a). Typical of the Decorated style.

BALUSTER: pillar or pedestal of bellied form. *Balusters*: vertical supports of this or any other form, for a handrail or coping, the whole being called a *balustrade* (6c). *Blind balustrade*: the same applied to the wall surface.

BARBICAN: outwork defending the entrance to a castle.

BARGEBOARDS (corruption of 'vergeboards'): boards, often carved or fretted, fixed beneath the eaves of a gable to cover and protect the rafters.

BARMKIN (Scots): wall enclosing courtyard attached to a tower house.

BARONY: *see* Burgh.

BAROQUE: style originating in Rome c.1600 and current in England c.1680–1720, characterized by dramatic massing and silhouette and the use of the giant order.

BARROW: burial mound.

BARTIZAN: corbelled turret, square or round, frequently at an angle (8a).

BASCULE: hinged part of a lifting (or bascule) bridge.

BASE: moulded foot of a column or pilaster. For *Attic* base *see* 3b. For *Elided* base *see* Elided.

BASEMENT: lowest, subordinate storey; hence the lowest part of a classical elevation, below the piano nobile (q.v.).

BASILICA: a Roman public hall; hence an aisled building with a clerestory.

BASTION: one of a series of defensive semicircular or polygonal projections from the main wall of a fortress or city.

BATTER: intentional inward inclination of a wall face.

BATTLEMENT: defensive parapet, composed of *merlons* (solid) and *crenelles* (embrasures) through which archers could shoot (8a); sometimes called *crenellation*. Also used decoratively.

BAY: division of an elevation or interior space as defined by regular vertical features such as arches, columns, windows etc.

BAY LEAF: classical ornament of overlapping bay leaves (3f).

BAY WINDOW: window of one or more storeys projecting from the face of a building. *Canted*: with a straight front and angled sides. *Bow window*: curved. *Oriel*: rests on corbels or brackets and starts above ground level; also the bay window at the dais end of a medieval great hall.

BEAD-AND-REEL: *see* Enrichments.

BEAKHEAD: Norman ornament with a row of beaked bird or beast heads usually biting into a roll moulding (1a).

BEE-BOLL: wall recess to contain a beehive.

BELFRY: chamber or stage in a tower where bells are hung. Also belltower in a general sense.

BELL CAPITAL: *see* 1b.

BELLCAST: *see* Roof.

BELLCOTE: bell-turret set on a roof or gable. *Birdcage bellcote*: framed structure, usually of stone.

BERM: level area separating a ditch from a bank on a hillfort or barrow.

BILLET: Norman ornament of small half-cylindrical or rectangular blocks (1a).

BIVALLATE: of a hillfort: defended by two concentric banks and ditches.

BLIND: see Arcade, Baluster, Portico.

BLOCK CAPITAL: see 1a.

BLOCKED: columns etc. interrupted by regular projecting blocks (*blocking*), as on a Gibbs surround (4b).

BLOCKING COURSE: course of stones, or equivalent, on top of a cornice and crowning the wall.

BÖD: see Bü.

BOLECTION MOULDING: covering the joint between two different planes (6b).

BOND: the pattern of long sides (*stretchers*) and short ends (*headers*) produced on the face of a wall by laying bricks in a particular way (6e).

BOSS: knob or projection, e.g. at the intersection of ribs in a vault (2c).

BOW WINDOW: see Bay window.

BOX FRAME: timber-framed construction in which vertical and horizontal wall members support the roof. Also concrete construction where the loads are taken on cross walls; also called *cross-wall construction*.

BRACE: subsidiary member of a structural frame, curved or straight. *Bracing* is often arranged decoratively, e.g. quatrefoil, herringbone. See also Roofs.

BRATTISHING: ornamental crest, usually formed of leaves, Tudor flowers or miniature battlements.

BRESSUMER (*lit.* breast-beam): big horizontal beam supporting the wall above, especially in a jettied building.

BRETASCHE (*lit.* battlement): defensive wooden gallery on a wall.

BRICK: see Bond, Cogging, Engineering, Gauged, Tumbling.

BRIDGE: *Bowstring*: with arches rising above the roadway which is suspended from them. *Clapper*: one long stone forms the roadway. *Roving*: see Canal. *Suspension*: roadway suspended from cables or chains slung between towers or pylons. *Stay-suspension* or *stay-cantilever*: supported by diagonal stays from towers or pylons. See also Bascule.

BRISES-SOLEIL: projecting fins or canopies which deflect direct sunlight from windows.

BROACH: see Spire and 1c.

BROCH (Scots): circular tower-like structure, open in the middle, the double wall of dry-stone masonry linked by slabs forming internal galleries at varying levels; found in W and N Scotland and mostly dating from between 100 B.C. and A.D. 100.

BÜ or BÖD (Scots, esp. Shetland; *lit.* booth): combined house and store.

BUCRANIUM: ox skull used decoratively in classical friezes.

BULLSEYE WINDOW: small oval window, set horizontally (cf. Oculus). Also called *oeil de boeuf*.

BURGH: formally constituted town with trading privileges. *Royal Burghs*: monopolized foreign trade till the C17 and paid duty to the Crown. *Burghs of Barony*: founded by secular or ecclesiastical barons to whom they paid duty on their local trade. *Police Burghs*: instituted after 1850 for the administration of new centres of population and abolished in 1975. They controlled planning, building etc.

BUT-AND-BEN (Scots, *lit.* outer and inner rooms): two-room cottage.

BUTTRESS: vertical member projecting from a wall to stabilize it or to resist the lateral thrust of an arch, roof or vault (1c, 2c). A *flying buttress* transmits the thrust to a heavy abutment by means of an arch or half-arch (1c).

CABLE or ROPE MOULDING: originally Norman, like twisted strands of a rope.

CAMES: see Quarries.

CAMPANILE: freestanding bell-tower.

CANALS: *Flash lock*: removable weir or similar device through which boats pass on a flush of water. Predecessor of the *pound lock*: chamber with gates at each end allowing boats to float from one level to another. *Tidal gates*: single pair of lock gates allowing vessels to pass when the tide makes a level. *Balance beam*: beam projecting horizontally for opening and closing lock gates. *Roving bridge*: carrying a towing path from one bank to the other.

CANDLE-SNUFFER ROOF: conical roof of a turret (8a).

CANNON SPOUT: see 8a.

CANTILEVER: horizontal projection (e.g. step, canopy) supported by a downward force behind the fulcrum.

CAPHOUSE (Scots): small chamber at the head of a turnpike stair, opening onto the parapet walk (8a). Also a chamber rising from within the parapet walk.

CAPITAL: head or crowning feature of a column or pilaster; for classical types *see* 3a; for medieval types *see* 1b.

CARREL: compartment designed for individual work or study, e.g. in a library.

CARTOUCHE: classical tablet with ornate frame (4b).

CARYATIDS: female figures supporting an entablature; their male counterparts are *Atlantes* (*lit.* Atlas figures).

CASEMATE: vaulted chamber, with embrasures for defence, within a castle wall or projecting from it.

CASEMENT: side-hinged window. Also a concave Gothic moulding framing a window.

CASTELLATED: with battlements (q.v.).

CAST IRON: iron containing at least 2.2 per cent of carbon, strong in compression but brittle in tension; cast in a mould to required shape, e.g. for columns or repetitive ornaments. *Wrought iron* is a purer form of iron, with no more than 0.3 per cent of carbon, ductile and strong in tension, forged and rolled into e.g. bars, joists, boiler plates; *mild steel* is its modern equivalent, similar but stronger.

CATSLIDE: see 7.

CAVETTO: concave classical moulding of quarter-round section (3f).

CELURE or CEILURE: enriched area of roof above rood or altar.

CEMENT: see Concrete.

CENOTAPH (*lit.* empty tomb): funerary monument which is not a burying place.

CENTRING: wooden support for the building of an arch or vault, removed after completion.

CHAMBERED TOMB: Neolithic burial mound with a stone-built chamber and entrance passage covered by an earthen barrow or stone cairn.

CHAMFER (*lit.* corner-break): surface formed by cutting off a square edge or corner. For types of chamfers and *chamfer stops see* 6a. *See also* Double chamfer.

CHANCEL: E end of the church containing the sanctuary; often used to include the choir.

CHANTRY CHAPEL: often attached to or within a church, endowed for the celebration of Masses principally for the soul of the founder.

CHECK (Scots): rebate.

CHERRY-CAULKING or CHERRY-COCKING (Scots): decorative masonry technique using lines of tiny stones (*pins* or *pinning*) in the mortar joints.

CHEVET (*lit.* head): French term for chancel with ambulatory and radiating chapels.

CHEVRON: V-shape used in series or double series (later) on a Norman moulding (1a). Also (especially when on a single plane) called *zigzag*.

CHOIR: the part of a church E of the nave, intended for the stalls of choir monks, choristers and clergy.

CIBORIUM: a fixed canopy over an altar, usually vaulted and supported on four columns; cf. Baldacchino.

CINQUEFOIL: see Foil.

CIST: stone-lined or slab-built grave.

CLACHAN (Scots): a hamlet or small village; also, a village inn.

CLADDING: external covering or skin applied to a structure, especially a framed one.

CLEARSTOREY: uppermost storey of the nave of a church, pierced by windows. Also high-level windows in secular buildings.

CLOSE (Scots): courtyard or passage giving access to a number of buildings.

CLOSER: a brick cut to complete a bond (6e).

CLUSTER BLOCK: *see* Multi-storey.

COADE STONE: ceramic artificial stone made in Lambeth 1769–c.1840 by Eleanor Coade (†1821) and her associates.

COB: walling material of clay mixed with straw.

COFFERING: arrangement of sunken panels (coffers), square or polygonal, decorating a ceiling, vault or arch.

GLOSSARY

COGGING: a decorative course of bricks laid diagonally (6e). Cf. Dentilation.

COLLAR: *see* Roofs and 7.

COLLEGIATE CHURCH: endowed for the support of a college of priests, especially for the saying of masses for the soul(s) of the founder(s).

COLONNADE: range of columns supporting an entablature. Cf. Arcade.

COLONNETTE: small column or shaft.

COLOSSAL ORDER: *see* Giant order.

COLUMBARIUM: shelved, niched structure to house multiple burials.

COLUMN: a classical, upright structural member of round section with a shaft, a capital and usually a base (3a, 4a).

COLUMN FIGURE: carved figure attached to a medieval column or shaft, usually flanking a doorway.

COMMENDATOR: receives the revenues of an abbey *in commendam* ('in trust') when the position of abbot is vacant.

COMMUNION TABLE: table used in Protestant churches for the celebration of Holy Communion.

COMPOSITE: *see* Orders.

COMPOUND PIER: grouped shafts (q.v.), or a solid core surrounded by shafts.

CONCRETE: composition of *cement* (calcined lime and clay), *aggregate* (small stones or rock chippings), sand and water. It can be poured into *formwork* or *shuttering* (temporary frame of timber or metal) on site (*in-situ* concrete), or *pre-cast* as components before construction. *Reinforced*: incorporating steel rods to take the tensile force. *Prestressed*: with tensioned steel rods. Finishes include the impression of boards left by formwork (*board-marked* or *shuttered*), and texturing with steel brushes (*brushed*) or hammers (*hammer-dressed*). See also Shell.

CONDUCTOR (Scots): down-pipe for rainwater; *see also* Rhone.

CONSOLE: bracket of curved outline (4b).

COPING: protective course of masonry or brickwork capping a wall (6d).

COOMB or COMB CEILING (Scots): with sloping sides corresponding to the roof pitch up to a flat centre.

CORBEL: projecting block supporting something above. *Corbel course*: continuous course of projecting stones or bricks fulfilling the same function. *Corbel table*: series of corbels to carry a parapet or a wall-plate or wall-post (7). *Corbelling*: brick or masonry courses built out beyond one another to support a chimney-stack, window etc. For *continuous* and *chequer-set* corbelling see 8a.

CORINTHIAN: *see* Orders and 3d.

CORNICE: flat-topped ledge with moulded underside, projecting along the top of a building or feature, especially as the highest member of the classical entablature (3a). Also the decorative moulding in the angle between wall and ceiling.

CORPS-DE-LOGIS: the main building(s) as distinct from the wings or pavilions.

COTTAGE ORNÉ: an artfully rustic small house associated with the Picturesque movement.

COUNTERSCARP BANK: low bank on the downhill or outer side of a hillfort ditch.

COUR D'HONNEUR: formal entrance court before a house in the French manner, usually with flanking wings and a screen wall or gates.

COURSE: continuous layer of stones etc. in a wall (6e).

COVE: a broad concave moulding, e.g. to mask the eaves of a roof. *Coved ceiling*: with a pronounced cove joining the walls to a flat central panel smaller than the whole area of the ceiling.

CRADLE ROOF: *see* Wagon roof.

CREDENCE: shelved niche or table, usually beside a piscina (q.v.), for the sacramental elements and vessels.

CRENELLATION: parapet with crenelles (*see* Battlement).

CRINKLE-CRANKLE WALL: garden wall undulating in a series of serpentine curves.

CROCKETS: leafy hooks. *Crocketing* decorates the edges of Gothic features, such as pinnacles, canopies etc. *Crocket capital*: *see* 1b.

CROSSING: central space at the junction of the nave, chancel and transepts. *Crossing tower*: above a crossing.

CROSS-WINDOW: with one mullion and one transom (qq.v.).

CROWN-POST: *see* Roofs and 7.

CROWSTEPS: squared stones set like steps, especially on a crowstepped gable (7, 8a).

CRUCKS (*lit.* crooked): pairs of inclined timbers (*blades*), usually curved, set at bay-lengths; they support the roof timbers and, in timber buildings, also support the walls. *Base*: blades rise from ground level to a tie-or collar-beam which supports the roof timbers. *Full*: blades rise from ground level to the apex of the roof, serving as the main members of a roof truss. *Jointed*: blades formed from more than one timber; the lower member may act as a wall-post; it is usually elbowed at wall-plate level and jointed just above. *Middle*: blades rise from halfway up the walls to a tie-or collar-beam. *Raised*: blades rise from halfway up the walls to the apex. *Upper*: blades supported on a tie-beam and rising to the apex.

CRYPT: underground or half-underground area, usually below the E end of a church. *Ring crypt*: corridor crypt surrounding the apse of an early medieval church, often associated with chambers for relics. Cf. Undercroft.

CUPOLA (*lit.* dome): especially a small dome on a circular or polygonal base crowning a larger dome, roof or turret. Also (Scots) small dome or skylight as an internal feature, especially over a stairwell.

CURSUS: a long avenue defined by two parallel earthen banks with ditches outside.

CURTAIN WALL: a connecting wall between the towers of a castle. Also a non-load-bearing external wall applied to a C20 framed structure.

CUSP: *see* Tracery and 2b.

CYCLOPEAN MASONRY: large irregular polygonal stones, smooth and finely jointed.

CYMA RECTA and CYMA REVERSA: classical mouldings with double curves (3f). Cf. Ogee.

DADO: the finishing (often with panelling) of the lower part of a wall in a classical interior; in origin a formalized continuous pedestal. *Dado rail*: the moulding along the top of the dado.

DAGGER: *see* Tracery and 2b.

DEC (DECORATED): English Gothic architecture *c.* 1290 to *c.* 1350. The name is derived from the type of window tracery (q.v.) used during the period.

DEMI- or HALF-COLUMNS: engaged columns (q.v.) half of whose circumference projects from the wall.

DENTIL: small square block used in series in classical cornices (3c). *Dentilation* is produced by the projection of alternating headers along cornices or string-courses.

DIAPER: repetitive surface decoration of lozenges or squares flat or in relief. Achieved in brickwork with bricks of two colours.

DIOCLETIAN or THERMAL WINDOW: semicircular with two mullions, as used in the Baths of Diocletian, Rome (4b).

DISTYLE: having two columns (4a).

DOGTOOTH: E.E. ornament, consisting of a series of small pyramids formed by four stylized canine teeth meeting at a point (1a).

DOOCOT (Scots): dovecot. When freestanding, usually *Lectern* (rectangular with single-pitch roof) or *Beehive* (circular, diminishing towards the top).

DORIC: *see* Orders and 3a, 3b.

DORMER: window projecting from the slope of a roof (7). *Dormer head*: gable above a dormer, often formed as a pediment (8a).

DOUBLE CHAMFER: a chamfer applied to each of two recessed arches (1a).

DOUBLE PILE: *see* Pile.

DRAGON BEAM: *see* Jetty.

DRESSINGS: the stone or brickwork worked to a finished face about an angle, opening or other feature.

DRIPSTONE: moulded stone projecting from a wall to protect the lower parts from water. Cf. Hoodmould, Weathering.

DRUM: circular or polygonal stage supporting a dome or cupola. Also one of the stones forming the shaft of a column (3a).

DRY-STONE: stone construction without mortar.

GLOSSARY

DUN (Scots): small stone-walled fort.

DUTCH or FLEMISH GABLE: *see* 7.

EASTER SEPULCHRE: tomb-chest, usually within or against the N wall of a chancel, used in Holy Week ceremonies for reservation (entombment) of the sacrament after the mass of Maundy Thursday.

EAVES: overhanging edge of a roof; hence *eaves cornice* in this position.

ECHINUS: ovolo moulding (q.v.) below the abacus of a Greek Doric capital (3a).

EDGE RAIL: *see* Railways.

EDGE-ROLL: moulding of semicircular section or more at the edge of an opening.

E.E. (EARLY ENGLISH): English Gothic architecture c. 1190–1250.

EGG-AND-DART: *see* Enrichments and 3f.

ELEVATION: any face of a building or side of a room. In a drawing, the same or any part of it, represented in two dimensions.

ELIDED: used to describe a compound feature, e.g. an entablature, with some parts omitted. Also, parts of, e.g., a base or capital, combined to form a larger one.

EMBATTLED: with battlements.

EMBRASURE: splayed opening in a wall or battlement (q.v.).

ENCAUSTIC TILES: earthenware tiles fired with a pattern and glaze.

EN DELIT: stone laid against the bed.

ENFILADE: reception rooms in a formal series, usually with all doorways on axis.

ENGAGED or ATTACHED COLUMN: one that partly merges into a wall or pier.

ENGINEERING BRICKS: dense bricks, originally used mostly for railway viaducts etc.

ENRICHMENTS: the carved decoration of certain classical mouldings, e.g. the ovolo with *egg-and-dart*, the cyma reversa with *waterleaf*, the astragal with *bead-and-reel* (3f).

ENTABLATURE: in classical architecture, collective name for the three horizontal members (architrave, frieze and cornice) carried by a wall or a column (3a).

ENTASIS: very slight convex deviation from a straight line, used to prevent an optical illusion of concavity.

ENTRESOL: mezzanine floor subdividing what is constructionally a single storey, e.g. a vault.

EPITAPH: inscription on a tomb or monument.

EXEDRA: *see* Apse.

EXTRADOS: outer curved face of an arch or vault.

EYECATCHER: decorative building terminating a vista.

FASCIA: plain horizontal band, e.g. in an architrave (3c, 3d) or on a shopfront.

FENESTRATION: the arrangement of windows in a façade.

FERETORY: site of the chief shrine of a church, behind the high altar.

FESTOON: ornamental garland, suspended from both ends. Cf. Swag.

FEU (Scots): land granted, e.g. by sale, by the *feudal superior* to the *vassal* or *feuar*, on conditions that usually include the annual payment of a fixed sum of *feu duty*. Any subsequent proprietor of the land becomes the feuar and is subject to the same obligations.

FIBREGLASS (or glass-reinforced polyester (GRP)): synthetic resin reinforced with glass fibre. GRC: glass-reinforced concrete.

FIELD: *see* Panelling and 6b.

FILLET: a narrow flat band running down a medieval shaft or along a roll moulding (1a). It separates larger curved mouldings in classical cornices, fluting or bases (3c).

FLAMBOYANT: the latest phase of French Gothic architecture, with flowing tracery.

FLASH LOCK: *see* Canals.

FLATTED: divided into apartments. Also with a colloquial (Scots) meaning: 'He stays on the first flat' means that he lives on the first floor.

FLÈCHE or SPIRELET (*lit.* arrow): slender spire on the centre of a roof.

FLEURON: medieval carved flower or leaf, often rectilinear (1a).

FLUSHWORK: knapped flint used with dressed stone to form patterns.

FLUTING: series of concave grooves (flutes), their common edges sharp (arris) or blunt (fillet) (3).

FOIL (*lit.* leaf): lobe formed by the cusping of a circular or other shape in tracery (2b). *Trefoil* (three), *quatrefoil* (four), *cinquefoil* (five) and *multifoil* express the number of lobes in a shape.

FOLIATE: decorated with leaves.

FORE-BUILDING: structure protecting an entrance.

FORESTAIR: external stair, usually unenclosed.

FORMWORK: see Concrete.

FRAMED BUILDING: where the structure is carried by a framework - e.g. of steel, reinforced concrete, timber - instead of by load-bearing walls.

FREESTONE: stone that is cut, or can be cut, in all directions.

FRESCO; *al fresco*: painting on wet plaster. *Fresco secco*: painting on dry plaster.

FRIEZE: the middle member of the classical entablature, sometimes ornamented (3a). *Pulvinated frieze* (*lit.* cushioned): of bold convex profile (3c). Also a horizontal band of ornament.

FRONTISPIECE: in C16 and C17 buildings the central feature of doorway and windows above linked in one composition.

GABLE: peaked external wall at end of double-pitch roof. For types *see* 7. Also (Scots): whole end wall of whatever shape. *Pedimental gable*: treated like a pediment.

GADROONING: classical ribbed ornament like inverted fluting that flows into a lobed edge.

GAIT or GATE (Scots): street, usually with a prefix indicating use, direction or destination.

GALILEE: chapel or vestibule usually at the W end of a church enclosing the main portal(s).

GALLERY: a long room or passage; an upper storey above the aisle of a church, looking through arches to the nave; a balcony or mezzanine overlooking the main interior space of a building; or an external walkway.

GALLETING: small stones set in a mortar course.

GAMBREL ROOF: see 7.

GARDEROBE: medieval privy.

GARGOYLE: projecting water spout, often carved into human or animal shape. For cannon spout *see* 8.

GAUGED or RUBBED BRICKWORK: soft brick sawn roughly, then rubbed to a precise (gauged) surface. Mostly used for door or window openings (5c).

GAZEBO (jocular Latin, 'I shall gaze'): ornamental lookout tower or raised summer house.

GEOMETRIC: English Gothic architecture *c.* 1250–1310. *See also* Tracery. For another meaning, *see* Stairs.

GIANT or COLOSSAL ORDER: classical order (q.v.) whose height is that of two or more storeys of the building to which it is applied.

GIBBS SURROUND: C18 treatment of an opening (4b), seen particularly in the work of James Gibbs (1682–1754).

GIRDER: a large beam. *Box*: of hollow-box section. *Bowed*: with its top rising in a curve. *Plate*: of I-section, made from iron or steel plates. *Lattice*: with braced framework.

GLACIS: artificial slope extending out and downwards from the parapet of a fort.

GLAZING-BARS: wooden or sometimes metal bars separating and supporting window panes.

GLAZING GROOVE: groove in a window surround into which the glass is fitted.

GNOMON: vane or indicator casting a shadow onto a sundial.

GRAFFITI: see Sgraffito.

GRANGE: farm owned and run by a religious order.

GRC: see Fibreglass.

GRISAILLE: monochrome painting on walls or glass.

GROIN: sharp edge at the meeting of two cells of a cross-vault; *see* Vault and 2b.

GROTESQUE (*lit.* grotto-esque): wall decoration adopted from Roman examples in the Renaissance. Its foliage scrolls incorporate figurative elements. Cf. Arabesque.

GROTTO: artificial cavern.

GRP: see Fibreglass.

GUILLOCHE: classical ornament of interlaced bands (4b).

GUNLOOP: opening for a firearm (8a).

GUSHET (Scots): a triangular or wedge-shaped piece of land or the corner building on such a site.

GUTTAE: stylized drops (3b).

GLOSSARY

HALF-TIMBERING: archaic term for timber-framing (q.v.). Sometimes used for non-structural decorative timberwork.

HALL CHURCH: medieval church with nave and aisles of approximately equal height. Also (Scots C20) building for use as both hall and church, the double function usually intended to be temporary until a separate church is built.

HAMMERBEAM: see Roofs and 7.

HARLING (Scots, *lit.* hurling): wet dash, i.e. a form of roughcasting in which the mixture of aggregate and binding material (e.g. lime) is dashed onto a wall.

HEADER: see Bond and 6e.

HEADSTOP: stop (q.v.) carved with a head (5b).

HELM ROOF: see 1c.

HENGE: ritual earthwork with a surrounding ditch and outer bank.

HERM (*lit.* the god Hermes): male head or bust on a pedestal.

HERRINGBONE WORK: see 6e (for brick bond). Cf. Pitched masonry.

HEXASTYLE: see Portico.

HILLFORT: Iron Age earthwork enclosed by a ditch and bank system.

HIPPED ROOF: see 7.

HOODMOULD: projecting moulding above an arch or lintel to throw off water (2b, 5b). When horizontal often called a *label*. For label stop *see* Stop.

HORIZONTAL GLAZING: with panes of horizontal proportions.

HORSEMILL: circular or polygonal farm building with a central shaft turned by a horse to drive agricultural machinery.

HUNGRY-JOINTED: see Pointing.

HUSK GARLAND: festoon of stylized nutshells (4b).

HYDRAULIC POWER: use of water under high pressure to work machinery. *Accumulator tower*: houses a hydraulic accumulator which accommodates fluctuations in the flow through hydraulic mains.

HYPOCAUST (*lit.* underburning): Roman underfloor heating system.

IMPOST: horizontal moulding at the springing of an arch (5c).

IMPOST BLOCK: block between abacus and capital (1b).

IN ANTIS: see Antae, Portico and 4a.

INDENT: shape chiselled out of a stone to receive a brass. Also, in restoration, new stone inserted as a patch.

INDUSTRIALIZED or SYSTEM BUILDING: system of manufactured units assembled on site.

INGLENOOK (*lit.* fire-corner): recess for a hearth with provision for seating.

INGO (Scots): the reveal of a door or window opening where the stone is at right angles to the wall.

INTERCOLUMNATION: interval between columns.

INTERLACE: decoration in relief simulating woven or entwined stems or bands.

INTRADOS: see Soffit.

IONIC: see Orders and 3c.

JACK ARCH: shallow segmental vault springing from beams, used for fireproof floors, bridge decks etc.

JAMB (*lit.* leg): one of the vertical sides of an opening. Also (Scots) wing or extension adjoining one side of a rectangular plan making it into an L-, T- or Z-plan.

JETTY: the projection of an upper storey beyond the storey below. In a stone building this is achieved by corbelling. In a timber-framed building it is made by the beams and joists of the lower storey oversailing the wall; on their outer ends is placed the sill of the walling for the storey above.

JOGGLE: the joining of two stones to prevent them slipping by a notch in one and a projection in the other.

KEEL MOULDING: moulding used from the late C12, in section like the keel of a ship (1a).

KEEP: principal tower of a castle.

KENTISH CUSP: see Tracery.

KEY PATTERN: see 4b.

KEYSTONE: central stone in an arch or vault (4b, 5c).

KINGPOST: see Roofs and 7.

KNEELER: horizontal projecting stone at the base of each side of a gable to support the inclined coping stones (7).

LABEL: see Hoodmould and 5b.

LABEL STOP: see Stop and 5b.

GLOSSARY

LACED BRICKWORK: vertical strips of brickwork, often in a contrasting colour, linking openings on different floors.

LACING COURSE: horizontal reinforcement in timber or brick to walls of flint, cobble etc.

LADE (Scots): channel formed to bring water to a mill; mill-race.

LADY CHAPEL: dedicated to the Virgin Mary (Our Lady).

LAIGH or LAICH (Scots): low.

LAIR (Scots): a burial space reserved in a graveyard

LAIRD (Scots): landowner.

LANCET: slender single-light, pointed-arched window (2a).

LANTERN: circular or polygonal windowed turret crowning a roof or a dome. Also the windowed stage of a crossing tower lighting the church interior.

LANTERN CROSS: churchyard cross with lantern-shaped top.

LAVATORIUM: in a religious house, a washing place adjacent to the refectory.

LEAN-TO: *see* Roofs.

LESENE (*lit.* a mean thing): pilaster without base or capital. Also called *pilaster strip*.

LIERNe: *see* Vault and 2c.

LIGHT: compartment of a window defined by the mullions.

LINENFOLD: Tudor panelling carved with simulations of folded linen.

LINTEL: horizontal beam or stone bridging an opening.

LOFT: gallery in a church. *Organ loft*: in which the organ, or sometimes only the console (keyboard), is placed. *Laird's loft, Trades loft* etc. (Scots): reserved for an individual or special group. *See also* Rood (loft).

LOGGIA: gallery, usually arcaded or colonnaded along one side; sometimes freestanding.

LONG-AND-SHORT WORK: quoins consisting of stones placed with the long side alternately upright and horizontal, especially in Saxon building.

LOUVRE: roof opening, often protected by a raised timber structure, to allow the smoke from a central hearth to escape. *Louvres*: overlapping boards to allow ventilation but keep the rain out.

LOWSIDE WINDOW: set lower than the others in a chancel side wall, usually towards its W end.

L-PLAN: *see* Tower house and 8b.

LUCARNE (*lit.* dormer): small gabled opening in a roof or spire.

LUCKENBOOTH (Scots): lock-up booth or shop.

LUGGED ARCHITRAVE: *see* 4b.

LUNETTE: semicircular window or blind panel.

LYCHGATE (*lit.* corpse-gate): roofed gateway entrance to a churchyard for the reception of a coffin.

LYNCHET: long terraced strip of soil on the downward side of prehistoric and medieval fields, accumulated because of continual ploughing along the contours.

MACHICOLATIONS (*lit.* mashing devices): series of openings between the corbels that support a projecting parapet through which missiles can be dropped (8a). Used decoratively in post-medieval buildings.

MAINS (Scots): home farm on an estate.

MANOMETER or STANDPIPE TOWER: containing a column of water to regulate pressure in water mains.

MANSARD: *see* 7.

MANSE: house of a minister of religion, especially in Scotland.

MARGINS (Scots): dressed stones at the edges of an opening. 'Back-set margins' (RCAHMS) are actually set forward from a rubble wall to act as a stop for harling (q.v.). Also called *rybats*.

MARRIAGE LINTEL (Scots): door or window lintel carved with the initials of the owner and his wife and the date of building work, only coincidentally of their marriage.

MATHEMATICAL TILES: facing tiles with the appearance of brick, most often applied to timber-framed walls.

MAUSOLEUM: monumental building or chamber usually intended for the burial of members of one family.

MEGALITHIC: the use of large stones, singly or together.

MEGALITHIC TOMB: massive stonebuilt Neolithic burial chamber covered by an earth or stone mound.

MERCAT (Scots): market. The *Mercat Cross* of a Scottish burgh

GLOSSARY

was the focus of market activity and local ceremonial. Most examples are post-Reformation with heraldic or other finials (not crosses).

MERLON: *see* Battlement.

MESOLITHIC: Middle Stone Age, in Britain *c.* 5000 to *c.* 3500 B.C.

METOPES: spaces between the triglyphs in a Doric frieze (3b).

MEZZANINE: low storey between two higher ones or within the height of a high one, not extending over its whole area.

MILD STEEL: *see* Cast iron.

MISERICORD (*lit.* mercy): shelf on a carved bracket placed on the underside of a hinged choir stall seat to support an occupant when standing.

MIXER-COURTS: forecourts to groups of houses shared by vehicles and pedestrians.

MODILLIONS: small consoles (q.v.) along the underside of a Corinthian or Composite cornice (3d). Often used along an eaves cornice.

MODULE: a predetermined standard size for co-ordinating the dimensions of components of a building.

MORT-SAFE (Scots): device to secure corpse(s): either an iron frame over a grave or a building where bodies were kept during decomposition.

MOTTE-AND-BAILEY: C11 and C12 type of castle consisting of an earthen mound (motte) topped by a wooden tower within or adjoining a bailey, an enclosure defended by a ditch and palisade, and also, sometimes, by an inner bank.

MOUCHETTE: *see* Tracery and 2b.

MOULDING: shaped ornamental strip of continuous section; *see* Cavetto, Cyma, Ovolo, Roll.

MULLION: vertical member between window lights (2b).

MULTI-STOREY: five or more storeys. Multi-storey flats may form a *cluster block*, with individual blocks of flats grouped round a service core; a *point block*, with flats fanning out from a service core; or a *slab block*, with flats approached by corridors or galleries from service cores at intervals or towers at the ends (plan also used for offices, hotels etc.). *Tower block* is a generic term for a high multi-storey building.

MULTIVALLATE: of a hillfort: defended by three or more concentric banks and ditches.

MUNTIN: *see* Panelling and 6b.

MUTULE: square block under the corona of a Doric cornice.

NAILHEAD: E.E. ornament consisting of small pyramids regularly repeated (1a).

NARTHEX: enclosed vestibule or covered porch at the main entrance to a church.

NAVE: the body of a church w of the crossing or chancel, often flanked by aisles (q.v.).

NEOLITHIC: New Stone Age in Britain, *c.* 3500 B.C. until the Bronze Age.

NEWEL: central or corner post of a staircase (6c). For Newel stair *see* Stairs.

NIGHT STAIR: stair by which religious entered the transept of their church from their dormitory to celebrate night offices.

NOGGING: *see* Timber-framing.

NOOK-SHAFT: shaft set in the angle of a wall or opening (1a).

NORMAN: *see* Romanesque.

NOSING: projection of the tread of a step (6c). *Bottle nosing*: half round in section.

NUTMEG: medieval ornament with a chain of tiny triangles placed obliquely.

OCULUS: circular opening.

OEIL DE BOEUF: *see* Bullseye window.

OGEE: double curve, bending first one way and then the other, as in an *ogee* or *ogival arch* (5c). Cf. Cyma recta and Cyma reversa.

OPUS SECTILE: decorative mosaic-like facing.

OPUS SIGNINUM: composition flooring of Roman origin.

ORATORY: a private chapel in a church or a house. Also a church of the Oratorian Order.

ORDER: one of a series of recessed arches and jambs forming a splayed medieval opening, e.g. a doorway or arcade arch (1a).

ORDERS: the formalized versions of the post-and-lintel system in classical architecture. The main orders are *Doric*, *Ionic* and *Corinthian*. They are Greek in origin

642

GLOSSARY

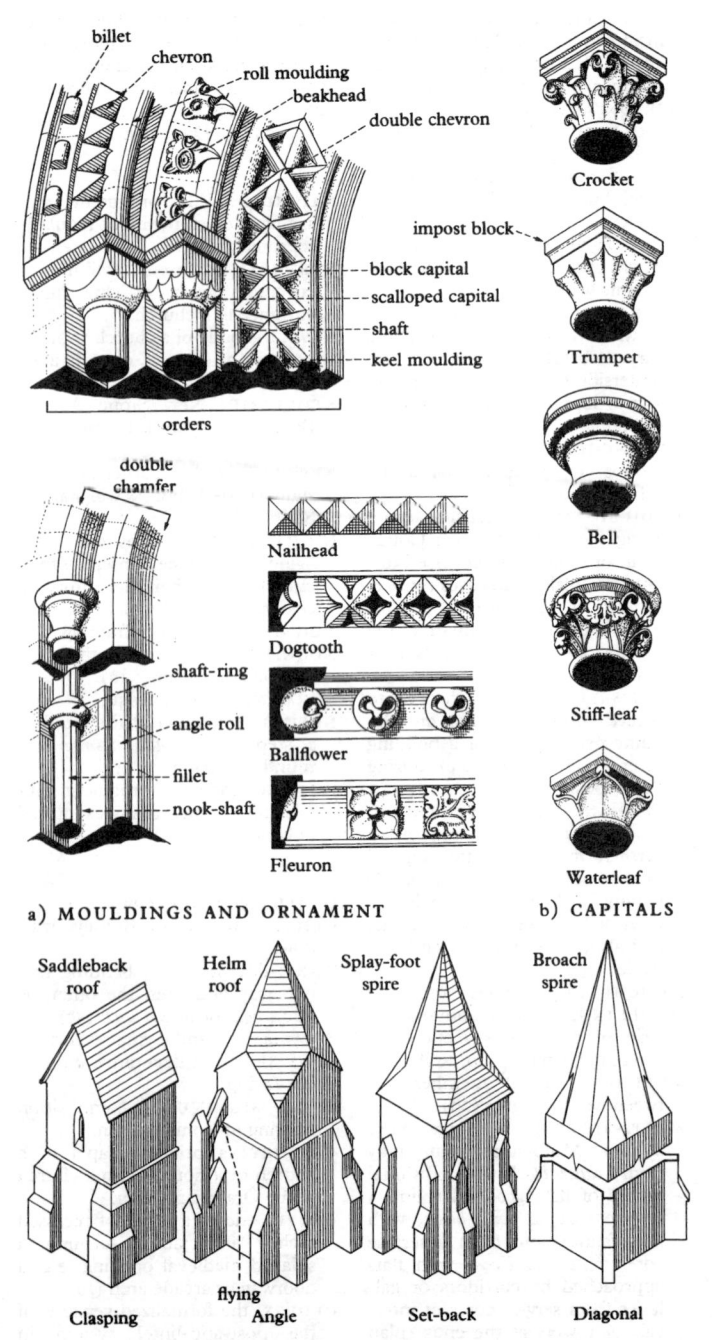

a) MOULDINGS AND ORNAMENT

b) CAPITALS

c) BUTTRESSES, ROOFS AND SPIRES

FIGURE 1: MEDIEVAL

GLOSSARY 643

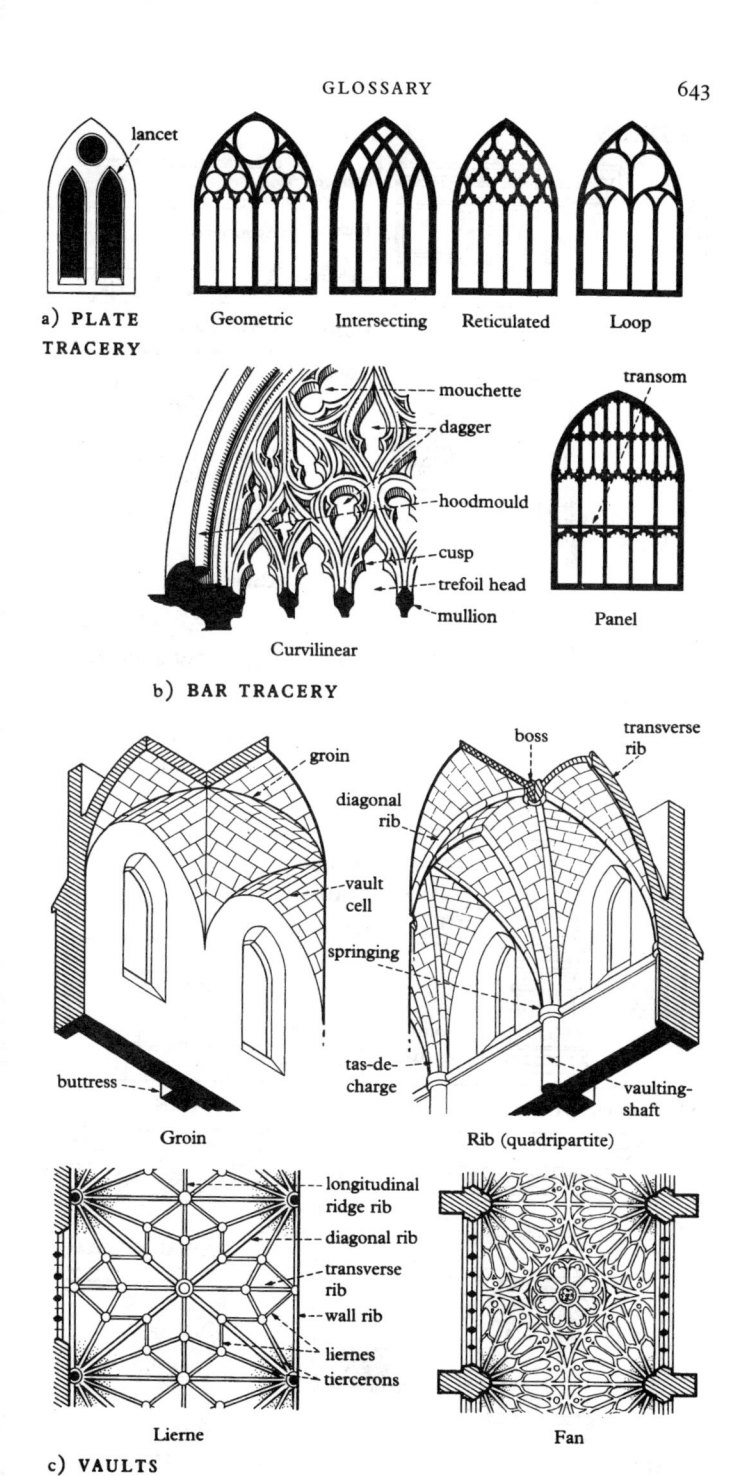

a) **PLATE TRACERY**

- lancet
- Geometric
- Intersecting
- Reticulated
- Loop

b) **BAR TRACERY**

Curvilinear
- mouchette
- dagger
- hoodmould
- cusp
- trefoil head
- mullion

Panel
- transom

c) **VAULTS**

Groin
- groin
- diagonal rib
- vault cell
- springing
- buttress

Rib (quadripartite)
- boss
- transverse rib
- tas-de-charge
- vaulting-shaft

Lierne
- longitudinal ridge rib
- diagonal rib
- transverse rib
- wall rib
- liernes
- tiercerons

Fan

FIGURE 2: MEDIEVAL

644

GLOSSARY

ORDERS

a) GREEK DORIC

b) ROMAN DORIC

c) IONIC

d) CORINTHIAN

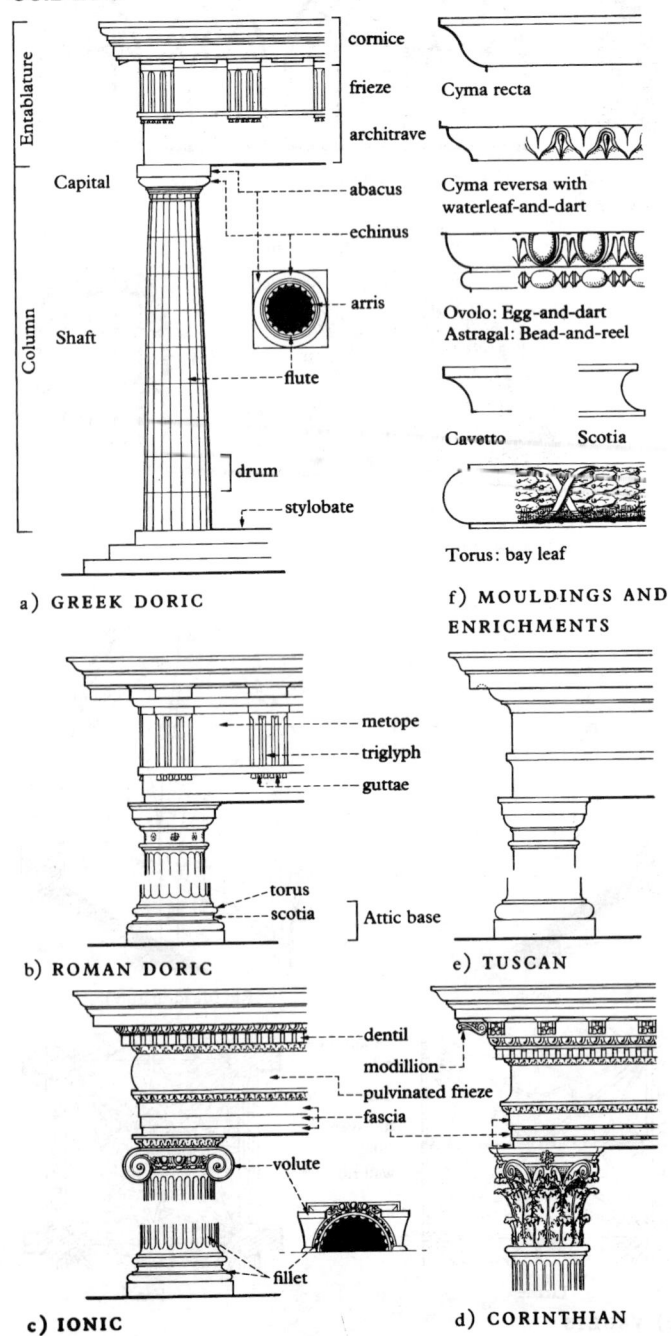

e) TUSCAN

f) MOULDINGS AND ENRICHMENTS

FIGURE 3: CLASSICAL

GLOSSARY 645

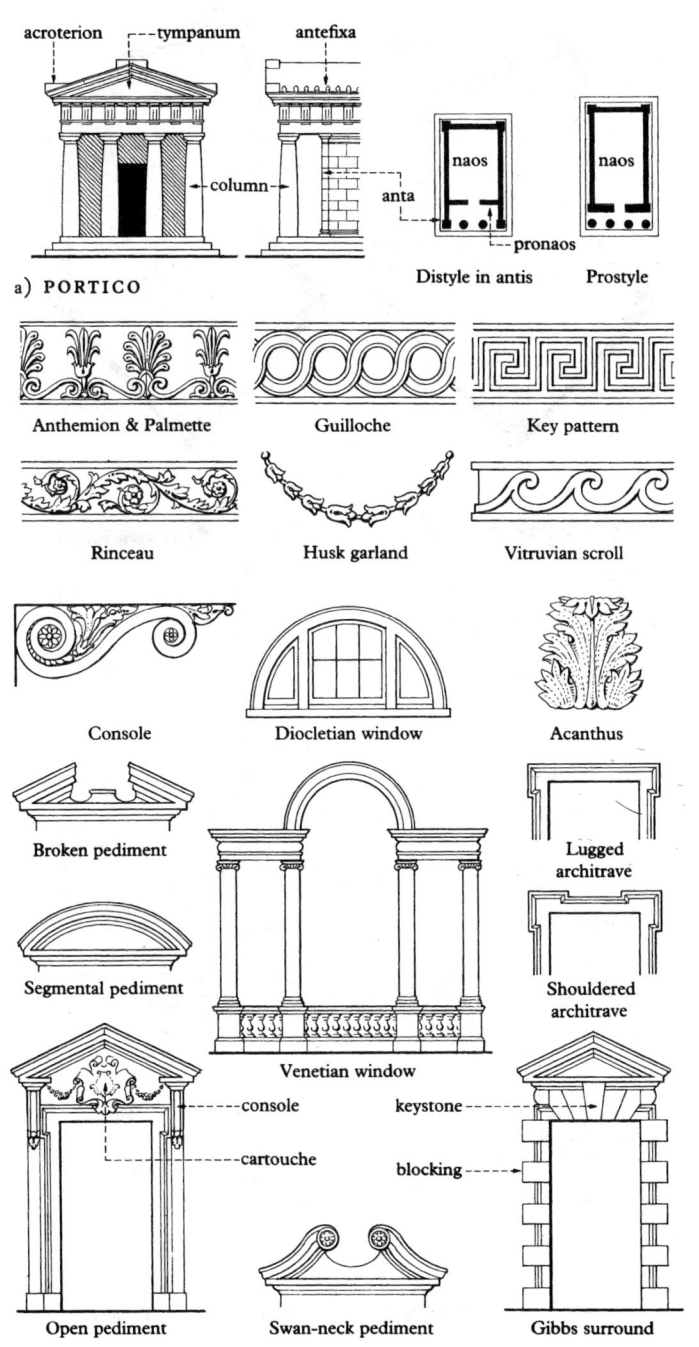

a) PORTICO

- acroterion
- tympanum
- antefixa
- column
- anta
- naos
- pronaos
- Distyle in antis
- Prostyle

Anthemion & Palmette

Guilloche

Key pattern

Rinceau

Husk garland

Vitruvian scroll

Console

Diocletian window

Acanthus

Broken pediment

Segmental pediment

Lugged architrave

Shouldered architrave

Venetian window

Open pediment
- console
- cartouche

Swan-neck pediment

Gibbs surround
- keystone
- blocking

b) ORNAMENTS AND FEATURES

FIGURE 4: CLASSICAL

a) DOMES

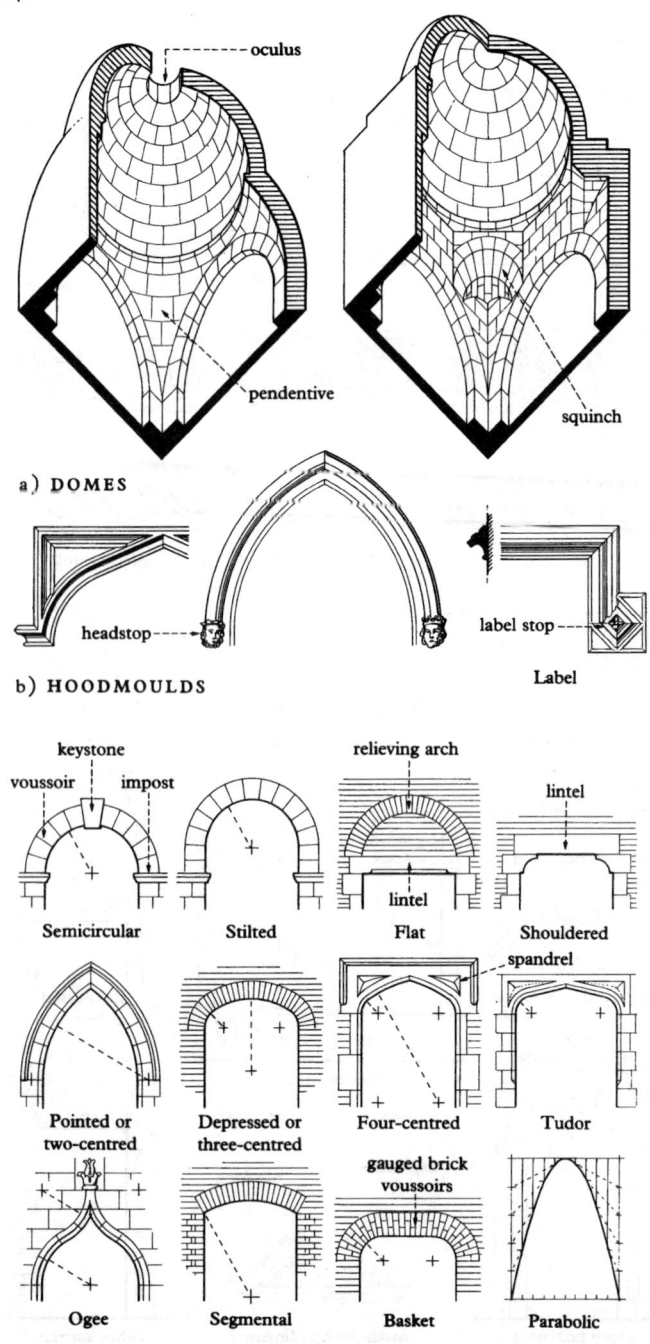

- oculus
- pendentive
- squinch

b) HOODMOULDS

- headstop
- label stop
- Label

c) ARCHES

- Semicircular (voussoir, keystone, impost)
- Stilted
- Flat (relieving arch, lintel)
- Shouldered (lintel)
- Pointed or two-centred
- Depressed or three-centred
- Four-centred (spandrel)
- Tudor
- Ogee
- Segmental
- Basket (gauged brick voussoirs)
- Parabolic

FIGURE 5: CONSTRUCTION

GLOSSARY 647

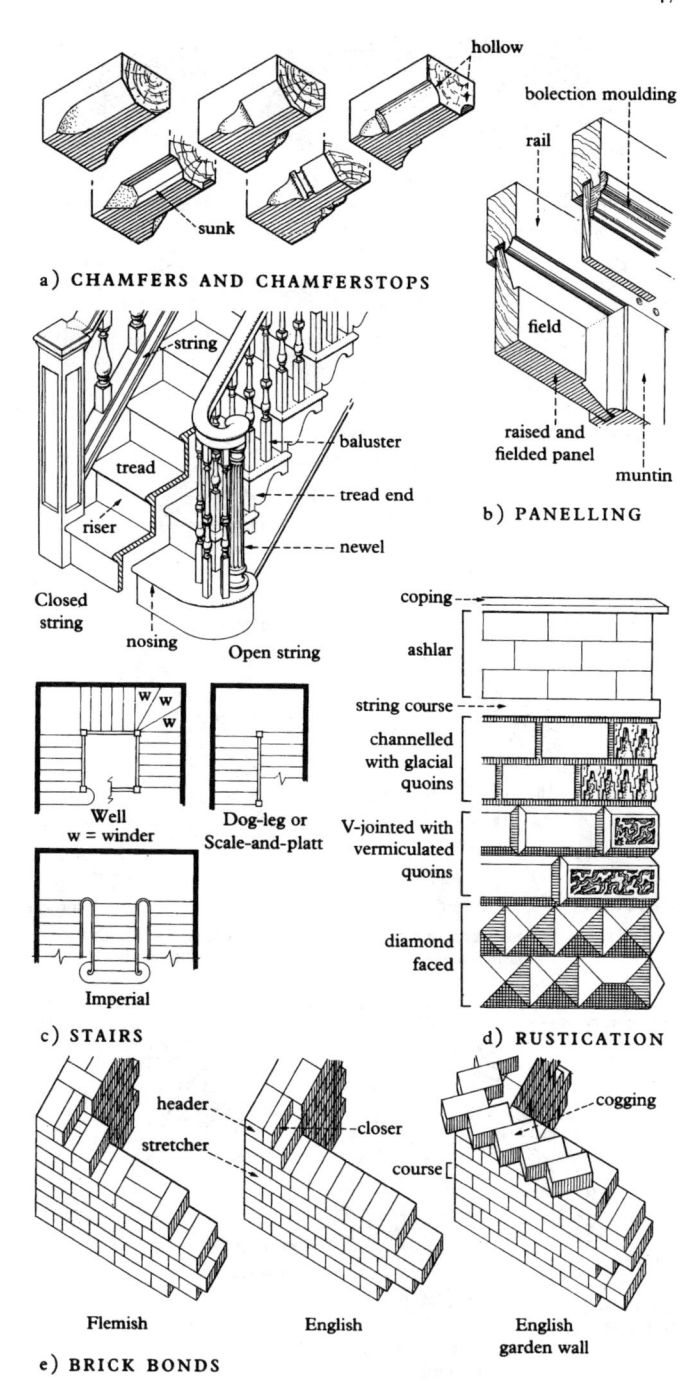

a) CHAMFERS AND CHAMFERSTOPS

b) PANELLING

c) STAIRS

d) RUSTICATION

e) BRICK BONDS

FIGURE 6: CONSTRUCTION

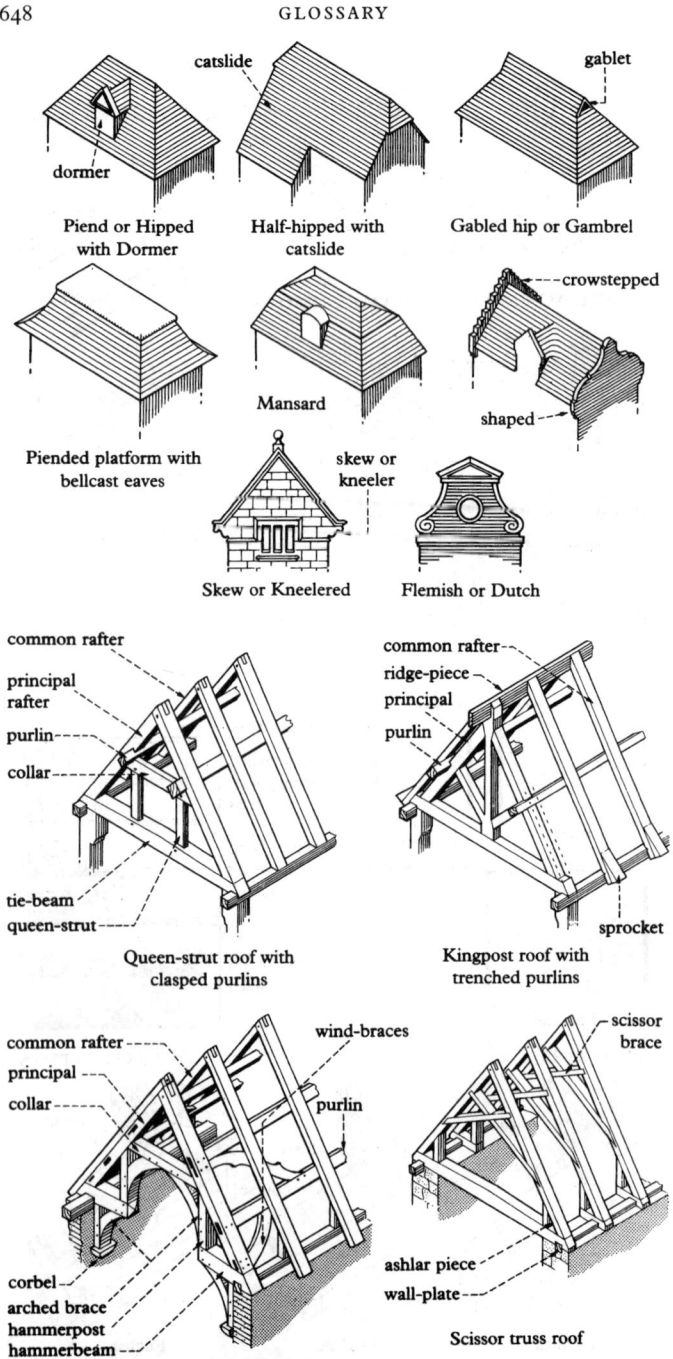

FIGURE 7: ROOFS AND GABLES

GLOSSARY 649

FIGURE 8: THE TOWER HOUSE

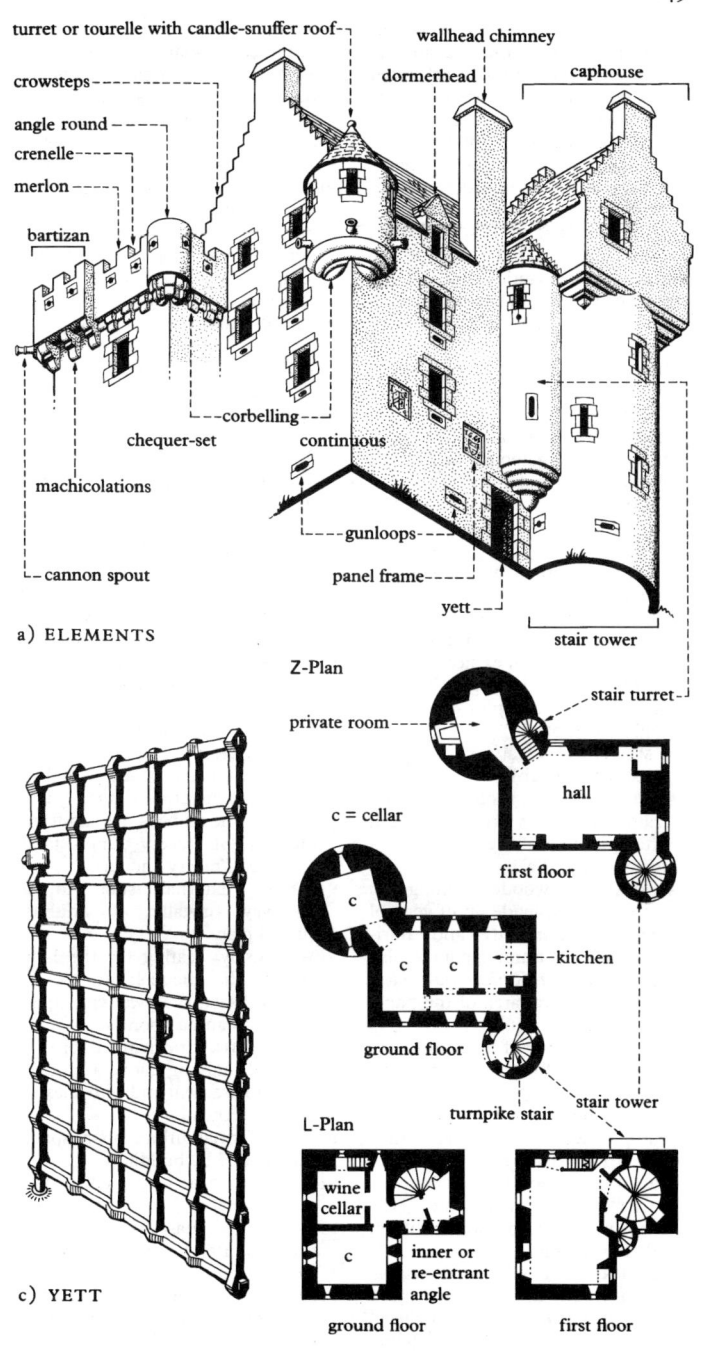

a) ELEMENTS

- turret or tourelle with candle-snuffer roof
- crowsteps
- angle round
- crenelle
- merlon
- bartizan
- chequer-set
- machicolations
- cannon spout
- corbelling
- continuous
- gunloops
- panel frame
- yett
- wallhead chimney
- dormerhead
- caphouse
- stair tower

b) FORMS

Z-Plan
- stair turret
- private room
- hall
- first floor
- c = cellar
- kitchen
- ground floor
- turnpike stair
- stair tower

L-Plan
- wine cellar
- c
- inner or re-entrant angle
- ground floor
- first floor

c) YETT

but occur in Roman versions. *Tuscan* is a simple version of Roman Doric. Though each order has its own conventions (3), there are many minor variations. The *Composite* capital combines Ionic volutes with Corinthian foliage. *Superimposed orders*: orders on successive levels, usually in the upward sequence of Tuscan, Doric, Ionic, Corinthian, Composite.

ORIEL: *see* Bay window.

OVERARCH: framing a wall which has an opening, e.g. a window or door.

OVERDOOR: painting or relief above an internal door. Also called a *sopraporta*.

OVERTHROW: decorative fixed arch between two gatepiers or above a wrought-iron gate.

OVOLO: wide convex moulding (3f).

PALIMPSEST: of a brass: where a metal plate has been reused by engraving on the back; of a wall painting: where one overlaps and partly obscures an earlier one.

PALLADIAN: following the examples and principles of Andrea Palladio (1508–80).

PALMETTE: classical ornament like a palm shoot (4b).

PANEL FRAME: moulded stone frame round an armorial panel, often placed over the entrance to a tower house (8a).

PANELLING: wooden lining to interior walls, made up of vertical members (*muntins*) and horizontals (*rails*) framing panels: also called *wainscot*. *Raised-and-fielded*: with the central area of the panel (*field*) raised up (6b).

PANTILE: roof tile of S section.

PARAPET: wall for protection at any sudden drop, e.g. at the wallhead of a castle where it protects the *parapet walk* or wall-walk. Also used to conceal a roof.

PARCLOSE: *see* Screen.

PARGETING (*lit.* plastering): exterior plaster decoration, either in relief or incised.

PARLOUR: in a religious house, a room where the religious could talk to visitors; in a medieval house, the semi-private living room below the solar (q.v.).

PARTERRE: level space in a garden laid out with low, formal beds.

PATERA (*lit.* plate): round or oval ornament in shallow relief.

PAVILION: ornamental building for occasional use; or projecting subdivision of a larger building, often at an angle or terminating a wing.

PEBBLEDASHING: *see* Rendering.

PEDESTAL: a tall block carrying a classical order, statue, vase etc.

PEDIMENT: a formalized gable derived from that of a classical temple; also used over doors, windows etc. For variations *see* 4b.

PEEL (*lit.* palisade): stone tower, e.g. near the Scottish-English border.

PEND (Scots): open-ended ground-level passage through a building.

PENDENTIVE: spandrel between adjacent arches, supporting a drum, dome or vault and consequently formed as part of a hemisphere (5a).

PENTHOUSE: subsidiary structure with a lean-to roof. Also a separately roofed structure on top of a C20 multi-storey block.

PEPPERPOT TURRET: bartizan with conical or pyramidal roof.

PERIPTERAL: *see* Peristyle.

PERISTYLE: a colonnade all round the exterior of a classical building, as in a temple which is then said to be *peripteral*.

PERP (PERPENDICULAR): English Gothic architecture c. 1335–50 to c. 1530. The name is derived from the upright tracery panels then used (*see* Tracery and 2a).

PERRON: external stair to a doorway, usually of double-curved plan.

PEW: loosely, seating for the laity outside the chancel; strictly, an enclosed seat. *Box pew*: with equal high sides and a door.

PIANO NOBILE: principal floor of a classical building above a ground floor or basement and with a lesser storey overhead.

PIAZZA: formal urban open space surrounded by buildings.

PIEND AND PIENDED PLATFORM ROOF: *see* 7.

PIER: large masonry or brick support, often for an arch. *See also* Compound pier.

PILASTER: flat representation of a classical column in shallow relief. *Pilastrade*: series of pilasters, equivalent to a colonnade.

PILE: row of rooms. *Double pile*: two rows thick.

GLOSSARY

PILLAR: freestanding upright member of any section, not conforming to one of the orders (q.v.).

PILLAR PISCINA: *see* Piscina.

PILOTIS: C20 French term for pillars or stilts that support a building above an open ground floor.

PINS OR PINNINGS (Scots): *see* Cherry-caulking.

PISCINA: basin for washing Mass vessels, provided with a drain; set in or against wall to S of an altar or freestanding (*pillar piscina*).

PITCHED MASONRY: laid on the diagonal, often alternately with opposing courses (*pitched and counterpitched* or herringbone).

PIT PRISON: sunk chamber with access from above through a hatch.

PLATE RAIL: *see* Railways.

PLATEWAY: *see* Railways.

PLATT (Scots): platform, doorstep or landing. *Scale-and-platt stair*: *see* Stairs and 6c.

PLEASANCE (Scots): close or walled garden.

PLINTH: projecting courses at the foot of a wall or column, generally chamfered or moulded at the top.

PODIUM: a continuous raised platform supporting a building; or a large block of two or three storeys beneath a multi-storey block of smaller area.

POINT BLOCK: *see* Multi-storey.

POINTING: exposed mortar jointing of masonry or brickwork. Types include *flush*, *recessed* and *tuck* (with a narrow channel filled with finer, whiter mortar). *Bag-rubbed*: flush at the edges and gently recessed in the middle. *Ribbon*: joints formed with a trowel so that they stand out. *Hungry-jointed*: either with no pointing or deeply recessed to show the outline of each stone.

POPPYHEAD: carved ornament of leaves and flowers as a finial for a bench end or stall.

PORTAL FRAME: C20 frame comprising two uprights rigidly connected to a beam or pair of rafters.

PORTCULLIS: gate constructed to rise and fall in vertical gooves at the entry to a castle.

PORTE COCHÈRE: porch large enough to admit wheeled vehicles.

PORTICO: a porch with the roof and frequently a pediment supported by a row of columns (4a). A portico *in antis* has columns on the same plane as the front of the building. A *prostyle* porch has columns standing free. Porticoes are described by the number of front columns, e.g. tetrastyle (four), hexastyle (six). The space within the temple is the *naos*, that within the portico the *pronaos*. *Blind portico*: the front features of a portico applied to a wall.

PORTICUS (plural: porticūs): subsidiary cell opening from the main body of a pre-Conquest church.

POST: upright support in a structure.

POSTERN: small gateway at the back of a building or to the side of a larger entrance door or gate.

POTENCE (Scots): rotating ladder for access to doocot nesting boxes.

POUND LOCK: *see* Canals.

PREDELLA: in an altarpiece, the horizontal strip below the main representation, often used for subsidiary representations.

PRESBYTERY: the part of a church lying E of the choir where the main altar is placed. Also a priest's residence.

PRESS (Scots): cupboard.

PRINCIPAL: *see* Roofs and 7.

PRONAOS: *see* Portico and 4a.

PROSTYLE: *see* Portico and 4a.

PULPIT: raised and enclosed platform for the preaching of sermons. *Three-decker*: with reading desk below and clerk's desk below that. *Two-decker*: as above, minus the clerk's desk.

PULPITUM: stone screen in a major church dividing choir from nave.

PULVINATED: *see* Frieze and 3c.

PURLIN: *see* Roofs and 7.

PUTHOLES OR PUTLOG HOLES: in wall to receive putlogs, the horizontal timbers which support scaffolding boards; not always filled after construction is complete.

PUTTO (plural: putti): small naked boy.

QUARRIES: square (or diamond) panes of glass supported by lead strips (*cames*); square floor-slabs or tiles.

QUATREFOIL: *see* Foil.

QUEEN-STRUT: *see* Roofs and 7.

QUILLONS: the arms forming the cross-guard of a sword.

QUIRK: sharp groove to one side of a convex medieval moulding.

QUOINS: dressed stones at the angles of a building (6d).

RADBURN SYSTEM: pedestrian and vehicle segregation in residential developments, based on that used at Radburn, New Jersey, U.S.A., by Wright and Stein, 1928–30.

RADIATING CHAPELS: projecting radially from an ambulatory or an apse (see Chevet).

RAFTER: see Roofs and 7.

RAGGLE: groove cut in masonry, especially to receive the edge of a roof-covering.

RAIL: see Panelling and 6b.

RAILWAYS: *Edge rail*: on which flanged wheels can run. *Plate rail*: L-section rail for plain unflanged wheels. *Plateway*: early railway using plate rails.

RAISED AND FIELDED: see Panelling and 6b.

RAKE: slope or pitch.

RAMPART: defensive outer wall of stone or earth. *Rampart walk*: path along the inner face.

RATCOURSE: projecting string-course on a doocot to deter rats from climbing to the flight holes.

REBATE: rectangular section cut out of a masonry edge to receive a shutter, door, window etc.

REBUS: a heraldic pun, e.g. a fiery cock for Cockburn.

REEDING: series of convex mouldings, the reverse of fluting (q.v.). Cf. Gadrooning.

RENDERING: the covering of outside walls with a uniform surface or skin for protection from the weather. *Lime-washing*: thin layer of lime plaster. *Pebble-dashing*: where aggregate is thrown at the wet plastered wall for a textured effect. *Roughcast*: plaster mixed with a coarse aggregate such as gravel. *Stucco*: fine lime plaster worked to a smooth surface. *Cement rendering*: a cheaper substitute for stucco, usually with a grainy texture.

REPOUSSÉ: relief designs in metalwork, formed by beating it from the back.

REREDORTER (*lit*. behind the dormitory): latrines in a medieval religious house.

REREDOS: painted and/or sculptured screen behind and above an altar. Cf. Retable.

RESPOND: half-pier or half-column bonded into a wall and carrying one end of an arch. It usually terminates an arcade.

RETABLE: painted or carved panel standing on or at the back of an altar, usually attached to it.

RETROCHOIR: in a major church, the area between the high altar and E chapel.

REVEAL: the plane of a jamb, between the wall and the frame of a door or window.

RHONE (Scots): gutter along the eaves for rainwater: *see also* Conductor.

RIB-VAULT: see Vault and 2c.

RIG (Scots): a strip of ploughed land raised in the middle and sloped to a furrow on each side; early cultivation method (runrig) usually surrounded by untilled grazing land.

RINCEAU: classical ornament of leafy scrolls (4b).

RISER: vertical face of a step (6c).

ROCK-FACED: masonry cleft to produce a rugged appearance.

ROCOCO: style current between c. 1720 and c. 1760, characterized by a serpentine line and playful, scrolled decoration.

ROLL MOULDING: medieval moulding of part-circular section (1a).

ROMANESQUE: style current in the C11 and C12. In England often called Norman. *See also* Saxo-Norman.

ROOD: crucifix flanked by representations of the Virgin and St John, usually over the entry into the chancel, painted on the wall, on a beam (*rood beam*) or on top of a *rood screen* or pulpitum (q.v.) which often had a walkway (*rood loft*) along the top, reached by a *rood stair* in the side wall. *Hanging rood*: cross or crucifix suspended from roof.

ROOFS: For the main external shapes (hipped, gambrel etc.) *see* 7. *Helm* and *Saddleback*: *see* 1c. *Lean-to*: single sloping roof built against a vertical wall; also applied to the part of the building beneath. *Bellcast*: sloping roof slightly swept out over the eaves.
Construction. *See* 7.
Single-framed roof: with no main trusses. The rafters may be fixed

GLOSSARY

to the wall-plate or ridge, or longitudinal timbers may be absent altogether.
Double-framed roof: with longitudinal members, such as purlins, and usually divided into bays by principals and principal rafters. Other types are named after their main structural components, e.g. *hammerbeam*, *crown-post* (*see* Elements below and 7).
Elements. See 7.
Ashlar piece: a short vertical timber connecting an inner wall-plate or timber pad to a rafter.
Braces: subsidiary timbers set diagonally to strengthen the frame. *Arched braces*: curved pair forming an arch, connecting wall or post below with a tie- or collar-beam above. *Passing braces*: long straight braces passing across other members of the truss. *Scissor braces*: pair crossing diagonally between pairs of rafters or principals. *Wind-braces*: short, usually curved braces connecting side purlins with principals; sometimes decorated with cusping.
Collar or *collar-beam*: horizontal transverse timber connecting a pair of rafter or cruck blades (q.v.), set between apex and the wall-plate.
Crown-post: a vertical timber set centrally on a tie-beam and supporting a collar purlin braced to it longitudinally. In an open truss lateral braces may rise to the collar-beam; in a closed truss they may descend to the tie-beam.
Hammerbeams: horizontal brackets projecting at wall-plate level like an interrupted tie-beam; the inner ends carry *hammerposts*, vertical timbers which support a purlin and are braced to a collar-beam above.
Kingpost: vertical timber set centrally on a tie-or collar-beam, rising to the apex of the roof to support a ridge piece (cf. Strut).
Plate: longitudinal timber set square to the ground. *Wall-plate*: along the top of a wall to receive the ends of rafters; cf. Purlin.
Principals: pair of inclined lateral timbers of a truss. Usually they support side purlins and mark the main bay divisions.
Purlin: horizontal longitudinal timber. *Collar purlin* or *crown plate*: central timber which carries collar-beams and is supported by crown-posts. *Side purlins*: pairs of timbers placed some way up the slope of the roof, which carry common rafters. *Butt* or *tenoned purlins* are tenoned into either side of the principals. *Through purlins* pass through or past the principal; they include *clasped purlins*, which rest on queenposts or are carried in the angle between principals and collar, and *trenched purlins* trenched into the backs of principals.
Queen-strut: paired vertical, or near-vertical, timbers placed symmetrically on a tie-beam to support side purlins.
Rafters: inclined lateral timbers supporting the roof covering. *Common rafters*: regularly spaced uniform rafters placed along the length of a roof or between principals. *Principal rafters*: rafters which also act as principals.
Ridge, *ridge piece*: horizontal longitudinal timber at the apex supporting the ends of the rafters.
Sprocket: short timber placed on the back and at the foot of a rafter to form projecting eaves.
Strut: vertical or oblique timber between two members of a truss, not directly supporting longitudinal timbers.
Tie-beam: main horizontal transverse timber which carries the feet of the principals at wall level.
Truss: rigid framework of timbers at bay intervals, carrying the longitudinal roof timbers which support the common rafters. *Closed truss*: with the spaces between the timbers filled, to form an internal partition.
See also Cruck, Wagon roof.

ROPE MOULDING: *see* Cable moulding.
ROSE WINDOW: circular window with tracery radiating from the centre. Cf. Wheel window.
ROTUNDA: building or room circular in plan.
ROUGHCAST: *see* Rendering.
ROUND (Scots): bartizan, usually roofless.
ROVING BRIDGE: *see* Canals.
RUBBED BRICKWORK: *see* Gauged brickwork.
RUBBLE: masonry whose stones are wholly or partly in a rough state. *Coursed*: coursed stones with rough faces. *Random*: uncoursed

stones in a random pattern. *Snecked*: with courses broken by smaller stones (snecks).

RUSTICATION: see 6d. Exaggerated treatment of masonry to give an effect of strength. The joints are usually recessed by V-section chamfering or square-section channelling (*channelled rustication*). *Banded rustication* has only the horizontal joints emphasized. The faces may be flat, but can be *diamond-faced*, like shallow pyramids, *vermiculated*, with a stylized texture like worm-casts, and *glacial* (frost-work), like icicles or stalactites.

RYBATS (Scots): see Margins.

SACRAMENT HOUSE: safe cupboard in a side wall of the chancel of a church and not directly associated with an altar, for reservation of the sacrament.

SACRISTY: room in a church for sacred vessels and vestments.

SADDLEBACK ROOF: see 1c.

SALTIRE CROSS: with diagonal limbs.

SANCTUARY: part of church at E end containing high altar. Cf. Presbytery.

SANGHA: residence of Buddhist monks or nuns.

SARCOPHAGUS: coffin of stone or other durable material.

SARKING (Scots): boards laid on the rafters to support the roof covering.

SAXO-NORMAN: transitional Romanesque style combining Anglo-Saxon and Norman features, current *c.* 1060–1100.

SCAGLIOLA: composition imitating marble.

SCALE-AND-PLATT (*lit.* stair and landing): see Stair and 6c.

SCALLOPED CAPITAL: see 1a.

SCARCEMENT: extra thickness of the lower part of a wall, e.g. to carry a floor.

SCARP: artificial cutting away of the ground to form a steep slope.

SCOTIA: a hollow classical moulding, especially between tori (q.v.) on a column base (3b, 3f).

SCREEN: in a medieval church, usually at the entry to the chancel; see Rood (screen) and Pulpitum. A *parclose screen* separates a chapel from the rest of the church.

SCREENS or SCREENS PASSAGE: screened-off entrance passage between great hall and service rooms or between the hall of a tower house and the stair.

SCRIBE (Scots): to cut and mark timber against an irregular stone or plaster surface.

SCUNTION (Scots): reveal.

SECTION: two-dimensional representation of a building, moulding etc., revealed by cutting across it.

SEDILIA (singular: sedile): seats for clergy (usually for a priest, deacon and sub-deacon) on the S side of the chancel.

SEPTUM: dwarf wall between the nave and choir.

SESSION HOUSE (Scots): a room or separate building for meetings of the minister and elders who form a kirk session. Also a shelter by the church or churchyard entrance for an elder collecting for poor relief, built at expense of kirk session.

SET-OFF: see Weathering.

SGRAFFITO: decoration scratched, often in plaster, to reveal a pattern in another colour beneath. *Graffiti*: scratched drawing or writing.

SHAFT: vertical member of round or polygonal section (1a, 3a). *Shaft-ring*: at the junction of shafts set *en délit* (q.v.) or attached to a pier or wall (1a).

SHEILA-NA-GIG: female fertility figure, usually with legs apart.

SHELL: thin, self-supporting roofing membrane of timber or concrete.

SHEUGH (Scots): a trench or open drain; a street gutter.

SHOULDERED ARCH: see 5a.

SHOULDERED ARCHITRAVE: see 4b.

SHUTTERING: see Concrete.

SILL: horizontal member at the bottom of a window-or door-frame; or at the base of a timber-framed wall into which posts and studs are tenoned.

SKEW (Scots): sloping or shaped stones finishing a gable upstanding from the roof. *Skewputt*: bracket at the bottom end of a skew. See 7.

SLAB BLOCK: see Multi-storey.

SLATE-HANGING: covering of overlapping slates on a wall. *Tile-hanging* is similar.

SLYPE: covered way or passage leading E from the cloisters between transept and chapter house.

GLOSSARY

SNECKED: see Rubble.

SOFFIT (*lit.* ceiling): underside of an arch (also called *intrados*), lintel etc. *Soffit roll*: medieval roll moulding on a soffit.

SOLAR: private upper chamber in a medieval house, accessible from the high end of the great hall.

SOPRAPORTA: see Overdoor.

SOUNDING-BOARD: see Tester.

SOUTERRAIN: underground stone-lined passage and chamber.

SPANDRELS: roughly triangular spaces between an arch and its containing rectangle, or between adjacent arches (5c). Also non-structural panels under the windows in a curtain-walled building.

SPERE: a fixed structure screening the lower end of the great hall from the screens passage. *Spere-truss*: roof truss incorporated in the spere.

SPIRE: tall pyramidal or conical feature crowning a tower or turret. *Broach*: starting from a square base, then carried into an octagonal section by means of triangular faces; *splayed-foot*: a variation of the broach form, found principally in the south-east of England, in which the four cardinal faces are splayed out near their base, to cover the corners, while oblique (or intermediate) faces taper away to a point (1c). *Needle spire*: thin spire rising from the centre of a tower roof, well inside the parapet: when of timber and lead often called a *spike*.

SPIRELET: see Flèche.

SPLAY: of an opening when it is wider on one face of a wall than the other.

SPRING OR SPRINGING: level at which an arch or vault rises from its supports. *Springers*: the first stones of an arch or vaulting-rib above the spring (2c).

SQUINCH: arch or series of arches thrown across an interior angle of a square or rectangular structure to support a circular or polygonal superstructure, especially a dome or spire (5a).

SQUINT: an aperture in a wall or through a pier, usually to allow a view of an altar.

STAIRS: see 6c. *Dog-leg stair* or (Scots) *Scale-and-platt stair*: parallel flights rising alternately in opposite directions, without an open well. *Flying stair*: cantilevered from the walls of a stairwell, without newels; sometimes called a *geometric* stair when the inner edge describes a curve. *Turnpike* or *newel stair*: ascending round a central supporting newel (8b); also called a *spiral stair* or *vice* when in a circular shaft, a *winder* when in a rectangular compartment. (Winder also applies to the steps on the turn.) *Well stair*: with flights round a square open well framed by newel posts. See also Perron.

STAIR TOWER: full-height projection from a main block (especially of a tower house) containing the principal stair from the ground floor (8a).

STAIR TURRET: turret corbelled out from above ground level and containing a stair from one of the upper floors of a building, especially a tower house (8a).

STALL: fixed seat in the choir or chancel for the clergy or choir (cf. Pew). Usually with arm rests, and often framed together.

STANCHION: upright structural member, of iron, steel or reinforced concrete.

STANDPIPE TOWER: see Manometer.

STEADING (Scots): farm building or buildings; generally used for the principal group of buildings on a farm.

STEAM ENGINES: *Atmospheric*: worked by the vacuum created when low-pressure steam is condensed in the cylinder, as developed by Thomas Newcomen. *Beam engine*: with a large pivoted beam moved in an oscillating fashion by the piston. It may drive a flywheel or be *non-rotative*. *Watt* and *Cornish*: single-cylinder; *compound*: two cylinders; *triple expansion*: three cylinders.

STEEPLE: tower together with a spire, lantern or belfry.

STIFFLEAF: type of E.E. foliage decoration. *Stiffleaf capital*: see 1b.

STOP: plain or decorated terminal to mouldings or chamfers, or at the end of hoodmoulds and labels (*label stop*), or stringcourses (5b, 6a); see also Headstop.

STOUP: vessel for holy water, usually near a door.

STRAINER: *see* Arch.

STRAPWORK: decoration like interlaced leather straps, late C16 and C17 in origin.

STRETCHER: *see* Bond and 6e.

STRING: *see* 6c. Sloping member holding the ends of the treads and risers of a staircase. *Closed string*: a broad string covering the ends of the treads and risers. *Open string*: cut into the shape of the treads and risers.

STRINGCOURSE: horizontal course or moulding projecting from the surface of a wall (6d).

STUCCO: decorative plasterwork. *See also* Rendering.

STUDS: subsidiary vertical timbers of a timber-framed wall or partition.

STUGGED (Scots): of masonry hacked or picked as a key for rendering; used as a surface finish in the C19.

STUPA: Buddhist shrine, circular in plan.

STYLOBATE: top of the solid platform on which a colonnade stands (3a).

SUSPENSION BRIDGE: *see* Bridge.

SWAG: like a festoon (q.v.), but representing cloth.

SYSTEM BUILDING: *see* Industrialized building.

TABERNACLE: safe cupboard above an altar to contain the reserved sacrament or a relic; or architectural frame for an image or statue.

TABLE STONE or TABLE TOMB: memorial slab raised on freestanding legs.

TAS-DE-CHARGE: the lower courses of a vault or arch which are laid horizontally (2c).

TENEMENT: holding of land, but also applied to a purpose-built flatted block.

TERM: pedestal or pilaster tapering downward, usually with the upper part of a human figure growing out of it.

TERRACOTTA: moulded and fired clay ornament or cladding.

TERREPLEIN: in a fort the level surface of a rampart behind a parapet for mounting guns.

TESSELLATED PAVEMENT: mosaic flooring, particularly Roman, made of *tesserae*, i.e. cubes of glass, stone or brick.

TESTER: flat canopy over a tomb or pulpit, where it is also called a *sounding-board*.

TESTER TOMB: tomb-chest with effigies beneath a tester, either freestanding (tester with four or more columns), or attached to a wall (*half-tester*) with columns on one side only.

TETRASTYLE: *see* Portico.

THERMAL WINDOW: *see* Diocletian window.

THREE-DECKER PULPIT: *see* Pulpit.

TIDAL GATES: *see* Canals.

TIE-BEAM: *see* Roofs and 7.

TIERCERON: *see* Vault and 2c.

TIFTING (Scots): mortar bed for verge slates laid over gable skew.

TILE-HANGING: *see* Slate-hanging.

TIMBER-FRAMING: method of construction where the structural frame is built of interlocking timbers. The spaces are filled with non-structural material, e.g. *infill* of wattle and daub, lath and plaster, brickwork (known as *nogging*) etc., and may be covered by plaster, weatherboarding (q.v.) or tiles.

TOLBOOTH (Scots; *lit.* tax booth): burgh council building containing council chamber and prison.

TOMB-CHEST: chest-shaped tomb, usually of stone. Cf. Table tomb, Tester tomb.

TORUS (plural: tori): large convex moulding, usually used on a column base (3b, 3f).

TOUCH: soft black marble quarried near Tournai.

TOURELLE: turret corbelled out from the wall (8a).

TOWER BLOCK: *see* Multi-storey.

TOWER HOUSE (Scots): for elements and forms *see* 8a, 8b. Compact fortified house with the main hall raised above the ground and at least one more storey above it. A medieval Scots type continuing well into the C17 in its modified forms: *L-plan* with a jamb at one corner; *Z-plan* with a jamb at each diagonally opposite corner.

TRABEATED: dependent structurally on the use of the post and lintel. Cf. Arcuated.

TRACERY: openwork pattern of masonry or timber in the upper part of an opening. *Blind* tracery is tracery applied to a solid wall.

Plate tracery, introduced c. 1200, is the earliest form, in which shapes are cut through solid masonry (2a).

Bar tracery was introduced into England *c*. 1250. The pattern is formed by intersecting moulded ribwork continued from the mullions. It was especially elaborate during the Decorated period (q.v.). Tracery shapes can include circles, *daggers* (elongated ogee-ended lozenges), *mouchettes* (like daggers but with curved sides) and upright rectangular *panels*. They often have *cusps*, projecting points defining lobes or *foils* (q.v.) within the main shape: *Kentish* or *split-cusps* are forked.

Types of bar tracery (*see* 2b) include *geometric(al)*: *c*. 1250–1310, chiefly circles, often foiled; *Y-tracery*: *c*. 1300, with mullions branching into a Y-shape; *intersecting*: *c*. 1300, formed by interlocking mullions; *reticulated*: early C14, net-like pattern of ogee-ended lozenges; *curvilinear*: C14, with uninterrupted flowing curves; *loop*: *c*. 1500–45, with large uncusped loop-like forms; *panel*: Perp, with straight-sided panels, often cusped at the top and bottom.

TRANSE (Scots): passage.

TRANSEPT: transverse portion of a cruciform church.

TRANSITIONAL: generally used for the phase between Romanesque and Early English (*c*. 1175–*c*. 1200).

TRANSOM: horizontal member separating window lights (2b).

TREAD: horizontal part of a step. The *tread end* may be carved on a staircase (6c).

TREFOIL: *see* Foil.

TRIFORIUM: middle storey of a church treated as an arcaded wall passage or blind arcade, its height corresponding to that of the aisle roof.

TRIGLYPHS (*lit*. three-grooved tablets): stylized beam-ends in the Doric frieze, with metopes between (3b).

TRIUMPHAL ARCH: influential type of Imperial Roman monument.

TROPHY: sculptured or painted group of arms or armour.

TRUMEAU: central stone mullion supporting the tympanum of a wide doorway. *Trumeau figure*: carved figure attached to it (cf. Column figure).

TRUMPET CAPITAL: *see* 1b.

TRUSS: braced framework, spanning between supports. *See also* Roofs.

TUMBLING or TUMBLING-IN: courses of brickwork laid at right angles to a slope, e.g. of a gable, forming triangles by tapering into horizontal courses.

TURNPIKE: *see* Stairs.

TUSCAN: *see* Orders and 3e.

TUSKING STONES (Scots): projecting end stones for bonding with an adjoining wall.

TWO-DECKER PULPIT: *see* Pulpit.

TYMPANUM: the surface between a lintel and the arch above it or within a pediment (4a).

UNDERCROFT: usually describes the vaulted room(s) beneath the main room(s) of a medieval house. Cf. Crypt.

UNIVALLATE: of a hillfort: defended by a single bank and ditch.

VAULT: arched stone roof (sometimes imitated in timber or plaster). For types *see* 2c.

Tunnel or *barrel vault*: continuous semicircular or pointed arch, often of rubble masonry.

Groin vault: tunnel vaults intersecting at right angles. *Groins* are the curved lines of the intersections.

Rib vault: masonry framework of intersecting arches (ribs) supporting *vault cells*, used in Gothic architecture. *Wall rib* or *wall arch*: between wall and vault cell. *Transverse rib*: spans between two walls to divide a vault into bays. *Quadripartite* rib vault: each bay has two pairs of diagonal ribs dividing the vault into four triangular cells. *Sexpartite* rib vault: most often used over paired bays, has an extra pair of ribs springing from between the bays. More elaborate vaults may include *ridge-ribs* along the crown of a vault or bisecting the bays; *tiercerons*: extra decorative ribs springing from the corners of a bay; and *liernes*: short decorative ribs in the crown of a vault, not linked to any springing point. A *stellar* or *star* vault has liernes in star formation.

Fan vault: form of barrel vault used in the Perp period, made up of halved concave masonry cones decorated with blind tracery.

VAULTING-SHAFT: shaft leading up to the spring or springing (q.v.) of a vault (2c).

VENETIAN or SERLIAN WINDOW: derived from Serlio (4b). The motif is used for other openings.

VERMICULATION: *see* Rustication and 6d.

VESICA: oval with pointed ends.

VICE: *see* Stair.

VILLA: originally a Roman country house or farm. The term was revived in England in the C18 under the influence of Palladio and used especially for smaller, compact country houses. In the later C19 it was debased to describe any suburban house.

VITRIFIED: bricks or tiles fired to a darkened glassy surface. *Vitrified fort*: built of timber-laced masonry, the timber having later been set on fire with consequent vitrification of the stonework.

VITRUVIAN SCROLL: classical running ornament of curly waves (4b).

VOLUTES: spiral scrolls. They occur on Ionic capitals (3c). *Angle volute*: pair of volutes, turned outwards to meet at the corner of a capital.

VOUSSOIRS: wedge-shaped stones forming an arch (5c).

WAGON ROOF: with the appearance of the inside of a wagon tilt; often ceiled. Also called *cradle roof*.

WAINSCOT: *see* Panelling.

WALLED GARDEN: in C18 and C19 Scotland, combined vegetable and flower garden, sometimes well away from the house.

WALLHEAD: straight top of a wall. *Wallhead chimney*: chimney rising from a wallhead (8a). *Wallhead gable*: gable rising from a wallhead.

WALL MONUMENT: attached to the wall and often standing on the floor. *Wall tablets* are smaller with the inscription as the major element.

WALL-PLATE: *see* Roofs and 7.

WALL-WALK: *see* Parapet.

WARMING ROOM: room in a religious house where a fire burned for comfort.

WATERHOLDING BASE: early Gothic base with upper and lower mouldings separated by a deep hollow.

WATERLEAF: *see* Enrichments and 3f.

WATERLEAF CAPITAL: Late Romanesque and Transitional type of capital (1b).

WATER WHEELS: described by the way water is fed on to the wheel. *Breastshot*: mid-height, falling and passing beneath. *Overshot*: over the top. *Pitchback*: on the top but falling backwards. *Undershot*: turned by the momentum of the water passing beneath. In a *water turbine*, water is fed under pressure through a vaned wheel within a casing.

WEALDEN HOUSE: type of medieval timber-framed house with a central open hall flanked by bays of two storeys, roofed in line; the end bays are jettied to the front, but the eaves are continuous.

WEATHERBOARDING: wall cladding of overlapping horizontal boards.

WEATHERING: or SET-OFF: inclined, projecting surface to keep water away from the wall below.

WEEPERS: figures in niches along the sides of some medieval tombs. Also called *mourners*.

WHEEL HOUSE: Late Iron Age circular stone dwelling; inside, partition walls radiating from the central hearth like wheel spokes.

WHEEL WINDOW: circular, with radiating shafts like spokes. Cf. Rose window.

WROUGHT IRON: *see* Cast iron.

WYND (Scots): subsidiary street or lane, often running into a main street or gait (q.v.).

YETT (Scots, *lit.* gate): hinged openwork gate at a main doorway, made of iron bars alternately penetrating and penetrated (8c).

Z-PLAN: *see* Tower house and 8b.

INDEX OF ARTISTS

Abercrombie, D. 269
Abrahams (Douglas) & Partners 399
Adam, John (1721–92), 58, 64, 66, 74, 79, 80, 86, 263, 305, 308, 309, 310, 313, 315, 317, 319, 321, 322, 323, 445, 532, 607, Pls. 77, 130
Adam, Robert (1728–92), 115, 273, 318, 611
Adam, Stephen (glass-stainer, 1848–1910), 42, 211, 269, 271, 299, 356, 616
Adam, Stephen Jr (glass-stainer, 1873–1960), 471
see also Adam & Son
Adam, William (1689–1748), 79, 305, 313, 321, 323, 445, 446
Adam & Small (glass-stainers, 1870–86), 385
Adam (Stephen) & Son (glass-stainers: Stephen Adam, q.v.; Stephen Adam Jr, q.v.), 41–2, 131, 443
Adam (Stephen) Studios (glass-stainers: Stephen Adam, q.v.; Stephen Adam Jr, q.v.; Alfred a Webster, q.v.), 230, 258, 616
Adie & Son (dial makers), 505, 538, 557
Ainsworth, Graciela (sculptor), 513
Alexander, Robert (mason), 133
Anderson, James 271
Anderson, Sir Robert Rowand (1834–1921), 38, 39, 41, 62, 64, 83, 271, 511, 513, 518, 521, 526, 582, 607–12, Pls. 39, 101, 102
Anderson (Rowand) & Paul (1904–36: Sir Robert Rowand Anderson, q.v.; Arthur Forman Balfour Paul, q.v.), 271
Andrew, D. 166
Andrew, David 234
Argyll & Bute Council 132

Argyll & Bute District Council 144, 232, 234, 236, 354
Argyll County Council 157, 221, 232, 233, 252, 362, 382, 412, 470, 471, 476, 533
Avery, Richard 503
Babtie 280
Baguley, G.T. (glass-stainer), 228
Baillie, Charles (glass-stainer), 283
Baird, Mr 145, 146
Baird, John I (1798–1859), 154
Baird, John II (1816–93), 145, 146
Baldie, Robert (*fl.* 1862–89), 122, 148
Balfour, Andrew (1863–1948), 229
Ballantine & Gardiner (glass-stainers: 1892–1905: Alexander Ballantine, d. 1906), 381
Ballantine (A.) & Son (glass-stainers: 1905–18: Alexander Ballantine, d. 1906; James Ballantine II, q.v.), 131, 346
Ballantine (James) & Son (glass-stainers, 1860–92: James Ballantine, 1808–77; Alexander Ballantine, d. 1906), 462, 489
Ballantine James II (glass-stainer, 1878–1940), 131
Bankart, George Percy (plasterer, 1886–1929), 287
Barclay, David, (1846–1927), 257
Barclay, H. & D. (Hugh Barclay, q.v.; David Barclay, q.v.), 288
Barclay, Harry 309
Barclay, Hugh (1828–92), 211, 359
Baron Bercott & Associates 195, 621
Barr, George 234
Barry, Sir John Wolfe (engineer), 73, 198, Pl. 133
Bartolini, Lorenzo (sculptor), 320

INDEX OF ARTISTS

Bateman, Edward La Trobe (landscape architect), 604
Bateman, Revd J. H. Latrobe 260
Baxter, John (d. *c.* 1770), 389, 447
Baxter, Clark & Paul 90, 132, 280, 281, 284
Beattie, Thomas (plasterer, *c.* 1961–1933), 117, 225
Begg, Ian (b. 1925), 180
Berry, Alan 85, 278, 280, 284
Beveridge, William (sculptor), 219
Binning, A. M. 115
Birrell, Hugh (1794–1873), 491
Blanc, Hippolyte J. (1844–1917), 37, 62, 143, 247
Blow, Detmar (1867–1939), 541
Bonazzo, Antonio (sculptor, 1698–1765), 589
Bone, Phyllis M. (sculptor, 1896–1972), 146
Bonnington, William 372
Bonomi, Joseph (1739–1808), 58, 314, 315, 446
Borthwick, Peter 444
Boston, Menzies & Morton 233, 362
Boucher, James (*c.* 1932–1906/7), 37, 90, 132, 156, 199, Pl. 34
Boucher & Cousland (James Boucher, q.v.; James Cousland, *c.* 1833–66; Henry Higgins, d. 1922), 37, 156, 388, 489, Pl. 34
Boyd, John S. 283
Boys, John 150
Boys Jarvis Partnership (John Philip Boys; Geoffrey Jarvis), 363
Bradley, Paul 262
Breingan, John 84, 233, 235
Brenan, G. Woulfe 143, 413, 484, 599
Brindley & Foster (organ builders), 156, 618
British Rail 412
Broad & Hughes 129
Brodie, Margaret 270, 616
Brodie, William (sculptor), 313, 444
Brook & Co. 230
Brook (Joseph) & Co. (organ builders), 157, 230
Brooks, John (surveyor), 320
Brown, Archibald (wright), 324
Brown, John (mason, d. 1773), 262, 263
Brown, John (mason, possibly son of above, *fl.* 1770–80), 262, 263

Brown, Thomas (*fl.* 1837–68), 60, 309, 334, 382, 447, Pl. 92
Brown, Thomas, 447
Brown, W. Kellock (sculptor, 1856–1934), 310
Brown & Carrick 270
Brunel, H. M. (engineer), 198
Bryce, David (1803–76), 61, 122, 130, 178, 244, 248, 588, 614, Pl. 93
Bryden, Robert A. (1841–1906), 37, 81, 83, 229–30, 231, 299, 471, 496, Pl. 35
Bryson (of Edinburgh) 469
Burgerhuis, Jan (bell-founder), 443
Burges, William (1827–81), 609, 628
Burgh Architect (Helensburgh) *see* Stirling, James
Burgh Surveyor (Helensburgh) 281
Burn, William (1789–1870), 44, 58, 60, 61, 67, 115, 129, 209, 248, 337, 351, 419, 425, 427, 461, 561, 564, 606, 612
Burnet, John (1814–1901), 37, 61, 85, 111, 112, 156, 164, 166, 171, 189, 280, 454, 480, 546, Pl. 94
Burnet, Sir John James (1857–1938), 61, 84, 89, 158, 159, 163, 165, 257, 419, 453, 478, 480, 572–3, Pls. 60, 110
Burnet (Frank), Bell & Partners (Frank R. Burnet, 1848–1923; James Bell; James Rennie, 1929–99), 148
Burnet (Frank) & Boston (Frank R. Burnet, q.v.; William J. Boston, 1861–1937; John Nisbet), 89, 163, 278
Burnet (Frank), Boston & Carruthers (Frank R. Burnet, q.v.; William Boston, q.v.; James Carruthers, b. 1872), 291
Burnet (John) & Son (John Burnet, q.v.; Sir John James Burnet, q.v.), 291
Burnet, Son & Campbell (John Burnet, q.v.; Sir John James Burnet, q.v.; John A. Campbell, 1859–1909), 120, 442, 480
Burnet (John), Son & Dick (John Burnet, q.v.; Sir John James Burnet, q.v.; Norman Aitken Dick, 1883–1948), 232

INDEX OF ARTISTS

Burnet, Tait & Lorne (Sir John James Burnet, q.v.; Thomas Smith Tait, 1882–1954), 165
Burns, Thomas 33, 356
Buttar, Alexander 140, Pl. 71
Butterfield, William (1814–1900), 38, 157, 379
Cairns, Thomas 479
Caldwell, Frederick William 587
Cameron, Angus 358
Cameron, Sir D. Y. (painter, 1865–1945), 409
Cameron, James 230
Cameron, Robert 233
Campbell, Charles (painter), 610, 611
Campbell, Colen (1676–1729), 115
Campbell, Donald 336, Pl. 25
Campbell, Dugal (military engineer, d. 1757), 55, 313
Campbell, Duncan (mason), 261
Campbell, Helen (d. 1927), 374
Campbell, Ilay M. 397
Campbell, James 329
Campbell, Niel (mason), 395
Campbell, Sarah 42, 405
Campbell, Walter Douglas (d. 1914), 36, 369–74, Pl. 40
Carfrae, John A. (1868–1947), 412
Carmichael, Michael 504, 505
Carrick, Alexander (sculptor, 1882–1966), 371, 374, 413
Carrick, J. & J. A. 621, Pl. 120
Carrick, James (1880–1940), 86
Carsewell, Ronald 154
Casey & Cairney (organ builders), 257
Cattanach, Alexander 85, 620, 621
Cattenach, Donald 583
Caulfield, Edward (Major) 148
Caulfield, (Major) William (d. 1767), 68, 148, 263
Chalmers, James (d. 1928), 41, 404, 405
Chalmers, Peter MacGregor (1859–1922), 36, 41, 349, 356–7, 361, 442, 471, 511, 512, 513, 516, 521, 551, 569–70, Pl. 38
Christie (mason), 263
Christie, A. (sculptor), 218
Christie, Andrew (mason), 338
Clark, John (mason), 359
Clayton, John (plasterer, *fl.* 1780s), 317, 318
Clayton, Thomas (plasterer, *fl.* 1710–60), 319
Clayton & Bell (glass-stainers; John Richard Clayton, 1827–1913; Alfred Bell, 1832–95; John Clement Bell, 1860–1944; Reginald Otto Bell, 1864–1950; Michael Charles Farrar Bell, b. 1911), 41–2, 271, 443
Clerk, Sir James, of Penicuik (1676–1755), 447, Pl. 83
Clifford, Henry Edward (1852–1932), 90, 155, 156, 157, 158, 162, 164, 165, 178, 362, 394, 480, 492
Clubb, A. (sculptor), 467
Cochrane, Charles 261
Coia, Jack (1898–1981), 170
Coleman & Ballantine 63, 479
Conroy, Stephen (painter), 277
Copland, W. R. (engineer), 232
Cordiner, Thomas (d. 1965), 257
Cordiner (Thomas), Cunningham & Partners (Thomas Cordiner, q.v.), 444
Cottier, Daniel (glass-stainer, 1839–91), 206, 271, 297
Cousin, David (1808–78), 35, 37, 60, 81, 84, 159, 382, 406, 442
Cowell, John 170
Cowie (William) Partnership, The 447, 448, 449
Craig, James (1744–95), 607
Craig, John (woodcarver), 269, 443
Crawford, John M. (b. 1854), 626
Crerar & Partners 199, 219, 221, 247, 394, 410, 412, 415, 418, 421
Crombie, David A. 616
Crouch & Hogg (engineers), 215, 277
Crow, David 251, 350, 378, 382, 383
Crutwell, E. (engineer), 198
Cullen, Alexander (d. 1911), 37, 475
Cumming, Alexander (clock-maker and organ builder, *c.* 1732–1814), 320
Cundy, Thomas (1790–1867), 38, 426, Pls. 31, 32
Dallmann & Johnstone 84, 392
Dalzel 351
Darge, G. L. 539, Pl. 140
Davidson, Andrew (sculptor, d. 1925), 525

INDEX OF ARTISTS

Davidson, D. & A. 129
Davis, Joseph Gordon 35, 59, 83, 209–10, 215, 242, 345, 352, 353–4, 460, Pl. 113
Davis, Louis (glass-stainer, 1861–1941), 42, 435
Dawson, John (wright), 259
Deas, F.W. (*c.* 1871–1951), 494
Delmé-Evans, William 562
Dempster, George 154, 399
Dempster, James 35, 81, 166, 444, 614, 621, Pl. 112
Denman, T. (sculptor), 346
Denny Brothers 189
Dent (Arnold) & Co. (clockmakers), 621
Deuchars, Louis (sculptor, 1871–1927), 612
Devey, George (1820–86), 313, 393
Dewar, Duncan 619
Dingwall, John 285
Dixon, Isaac (builder), 273
Doig, Charles C. 421
Donaldson, D.C. 623
Donaldson & Burns (sculptors; William Donaldson, b. 1882; Robert Burns, 1869–1941), 271
Douglas, Campbell (1828–1910), 160, 203, 232, 386
Douglas, John (d. 1778), 160, Pl. 109
Douglas, John 278
Douglas, W.T. (engineer), 164
Douglas, William (mason, d. 1782), 78, 252, 265, 309, 314, 321, 323
Douglas (Campbell) & Paterson 276
Douglas (Campbell) & Sellars (Campbell Douglas, q.v.; James Sellars, q.v.), 385, 463
Douglas (Campbell) & Stevenson (Campbell Douglas, q.v.; John James Stevenson, 1831–1908), 37, 162
Dreghorn, Robert (wright), 613
Drummond, John (mason), 141
Duff, James (mason), 107
Duff, Neil C. (d. 1924), 85, 279
Duff (James) & Sons (bell-founders), 270
Dunbarton County Architect 275
Dunbarton County Council 275
Duncan, A. (engineer), 620
Duncan, John 90, 626
Dupasquier, Leonard (gilder), 317

Edgar, James 217, 336, 346, 347, 461, 488
Edmonstone, Alexander F. 380
Education Offices' Master of Works 275
Elliot, Andrew 365
Elliot, Archibald (1761–1823), 58, 389
Elliot, James (1770–1810), 218
Ellis, Anne 296
Errington, Tom 611, 612
Fairlie, Reginald (1883–1952), 39, 381, 511, 617
Falconer, James G. 199, 410
Falconer, Lake 143
Farmer & Brindley (decorators), 610, 612
Feilden Clegg Design 527
Ferguson, Marion (sculptor), 536
Ferguson, Peter (mason), 180
Fergusson, Archibald 466, 470
Fleming, Peter 79, 267
Fleming & Ferguson 616
Forgan, Thomas 201
Formans, Charles (engineer), 73
Formans, John (engineer), 73, 198
Formans & McCall (engineers), 72, 326, Pl. 134
Fox, John 505
Frame, William (1848–1906), 610, 611
Frampton, Sir George (sculptor, 1860–1928), 517
Fraser, Alexander 347
Fraser, William 233
Frew, David (mason), 322
Fry, Roger 117
Gallagher, John 481
Galloway, David (surveyor), 412, 414
Galloway, William (*c.* 1832–97), 591
Gardner, Albert V. (*fl.* 1900–35), 85, 158, Pl. 121
Gardner, Alexander McInnes 418
Gardner, John (engineer), 142
Gardner, R. 132
Gardner (A.), Gardner & McLean 288
Gardner & Millar 416
Gauld, David (glass-stainer, 1867–1936), 131
Gibb, John 215, 529, 556–7, 559
Gibson, Mr 362
Gilbert, Donald (woodcarver), 279, 408

INDEX OF ARTISTS

Gildard & MacFarlane 437
Gillespie, Kidd & Coia (J. Gaff Gillespie, 1870–1926; William A. Kidd, d. 1928; Jack Coia, q.v.), 39, 131, 165, 169–71, 212, Pl. 44
Gillies, Donald (mason), 382, 384
Gillies, Neil 213, 382
Gillmor, James (mason), 613
Glasgow School 271, 272
Good, Thomas (woodcarver), 443
Gordon, Bronwen (glass-stainer), 575
Gordon, John 147
Graham, James Gillespie (1776–1855), 35, 58–9, 60, 64, 66, 81, 106, 122, 141, 228, 265, 308–9, 324, 419, 492, 568, Pls. 81, 86
Graham, R. C. 457
Grant, Alexander 333
Grant, Tom 190
Grant (Tom) Associates 431
Gray, A. L. (decorator), 411, 417
Gray, Charles 408
Greig, Alfred 323
Grieve, John A. 466
Groves, L. John (engineer), 129, 215
Guest (Douglas) Associates 135
Guinand, Jean-François (d.? 1787), 317
Guthrie, J. & W. (glass-stainers), 298
Guthrie, Sir James (1859–1930), 208
Guthrie, Walter Murray (1870–1911), 588
Guthrie & Wells (glass-stainers), 287
Hadden, Thomas 224
Haddow (T. Harley) & Partners (engineers), 404
Hadlington, Martin 332
Haggart, D. (sculptor), 535
Hamilton, D. (glass-stainer), 616
Hamilton, David (1768–1843), 36, 59, 64, 125, 163, 195, 229, 231, 350, 423, 424, 438, 493–4, 603, 604, Pls. 87, 111
Hamilton, Douglas (glass-stainer), 229, 616
Hamilton, J. Whitelaw 286
Hamilton, James (c. 1807–62; son of David), 64, 125, 603, 604, 626
Hamilton, Maggie (embroiderer), 287
Hamilton (D.) & Son (marble masons), 532
Hamilton (James) & Son 619
Hammill, Fiona (glass-stainer), 178
Hardman & Co. (glass-stainers; John Hardman Powell, 1828–95), 426
Hardman (John) Studios (glass-stainers; John Tarleton Hardman d. 1959), 42, 381
Harrison & Harrison (organ builders; *fl. c.* 1885–1959), 154, 228
Harvie & Scott 83, 621
Haswell, George (wright; ?1726–84), 154
Hay, J. W. and J. 35, 272
Hay, John C. 411, 583, 584, 587
Hay, Robert 462
Hayden, F. Hase 211
Heaton, Butler & Bayne 493
Henderson, John (1804–62), 38, 228, 379
Henderson, Michael 454
Hendrie, Herbert (glass-stainer; 1887–1946), 407
Henson, Charles 406
Hess, H. H. (organ builders), 609
Hill, Oliver (1887–1968), 63, 200, Pl. 97
Hill (William) & Son (organ builders), 132, 380, 443
Hird & Brooks 217
H.M. Office of Works 84, 277, 412, 413
Hoare & Wheeler 305
Holiday, Henry (glass-stainer; 1839–1927), 42, 381
Hollinsworth, James (engineer), 563, 564
Honeyman, John (1831–1914), 34, 37, 61–2, 81, 83, 127, 157, 207, 258, 259, 265, 269, 270, 276, 282, 343, 369, 381, 444, 455, 460, 511, 514, 516, 604, Pl. 22
Honeyman & Keppie (John M. Honeyman, q.v.; John Keppie, 1862–1905), 82, 167, 178, 211, 259, 273, 435
Honeyman, Keppie & Mackintosh (John M. Honeyman, q.v.; John Keppie, *see* Honeyman & Keppie; Charles Rennie Mackintosh, q.v.), 616

INDEX OF ARTISTS

Hoppner, Thomas (painter), 318
Huet, Jean Baptiste 318
Humphreys, Tom 296
Hunter, George (mason; d. ?1787), 310, 314
Hunter, Stephen 142
Hunter, William 624
Hutchison, John 616
Hutchison, Neil 198, 336
Ingram, J. & R.S. 82, 277
Ingram, James 546
Ingram & Co. 230, 407
Jackson, C. d'O. Pilkington (sculptor; 1887–1973), 622
Jamieson, John 156
Jockel & Son 443
Johns, William 309, 392
Johnson, Bertram Vaughan 457
Johnston, Alfred W. 407
Johnston, Charles S.S. (1850–*c.* 1924), 423, 574
Johnston, George 333, 487
Johnston, James Campbell 553
Johnston, Ninian 86, 233
Johnston Erdal 213
Johnstone, Allan 218
Johnstone, John 389
Jones & Willis (church decorators), 405
Kay, Robert (1740–1818), 182
Kelly, C.R. 440
Kempe, Charles (glass-stainer and decorator; 1834–1907), 42, 271
Kennedy, Angus 454
Kennedy, G.R. 235
Kent, William (?1685–1748), 611
Kerr, Andrew (d. 1887), 266
Kier, W. & J.J. (glass-stainers; *fl.* 1865–90), 156, 167, 218, 231, 299, 417
King (Albert E.) & Co. 488
Kinghorn Mee 135, 141, 491, 587
Kinnear & Peddie (*see* Peddie & Kinnear), 382, 575
Kinninmonth, William (b. 1904), 410
Kirk, George G. 535
Kirkwood (of Lochgilphead) 349
Laidlaw (R.) & Son 610
Laird, J. Austen (*fl.* 1910–40), 87, 463
Laird, J.J. 276
Landless, William 454
Lane, Bremner & Garnett 131

Langlands, George (land surveyor, *fl.* 1780–1800), 77, 78, 188, 251, 401, 451, 551
Langlands (George) & Son 153
Laurie, James (mason), 324
Laurie, John 520
Law & Dunbar-Nasmith (Graham Cowper Law; Sir James Duncan Dunbar-Nasmith), 298
le Girardy, Irrouard (painter, *fl.* 1784–98), 317, 318
Leiper, William (1839–1916), 61, 62, 65, 84, 90, 168, 192–3, 195, 207–8, 257, 270, 272, 275, 278, 281, 282, 283, 284, 285, 286, 287, 288, 289, 290, 291, 292, 296, 297, 388, 419, 423, 424, 440, 489, 573, Pl. 95
Leiper & McNab (William Leiper, q.v.; William Hunter McNab, q.v.), 85, 89, 192, 416, Pl. 114
see also McNab, William Hunter
Lewis & Co. (organ builders), 612
Lindsay, Ian G. (1906–66), 150, 312, 314, 364, 378, 503, 511, 517, 518, 525
Lindsay (Ian G.) & Partners (Ian Gordon Lindsay, q.v.; et al.), 89, 110, 166, 314, 320, 384, 404
Lipchitz, Jacques (sculptor, b. 1891), 517
Lonsdale, Horatio Walter 610, 611
Lorimer, Hew (sculptor, b. 1907), 167
Lorimer, Sir Robert Stodart (1864–1929), 63, 65, 66, 103, 114–18, 146, 151, 222–5, 245, 326, 427, 482, 483, 588, Pls. 98–100
Lorimer, Robin 146
Lorimer (A.R.P.) & Associates 597
Lorimer & Matthew (Sir Robert Stodart Lorimer, q.v.; John Fraser Matthew, 1875–1955), 420
Louise, H.R.H. Princess (sculptor, 1848–1939), 374
Low, T. & J. 279, 280, 284
Lownie, John 375
Lowrie, James 45, 357, Pl. 52
Lumsden, William 308
Lutyens, Sir Edwin (1869–1944), 87, 444–5, Pl. 96
Macalpine, Robert 420

INDEX OF ARTISTS

McCaig (of Oban) 411
McConville, Douglas 276
MacCorquodale, John 426
MacDonald, A. 538
McDougall (sculptor), 409
MacDougall, D. & J. 407
McDougall, Alexander 350
McDougall, David 114
McDougall, Donald 350
MacDougall, Leslie Grahame (a.k.a. Leslie Grahame Thomson, 1896–1974), 36, 63, 332, 394, 406, 589, Pl. 42
MacDougall, Norman M. (glass-stainer, *fl.* 1874–*c.* 1927), 405, 618
McElroy, John 201
McEwan, Peter (mason), 565
Macfarlane, Duncan 530
Macfarlane, T. 362
MacFarlane (Walter) & Co. (founders), 622
McGibbon, William F. (1856–1923), 614
McGill, Alexander (d. 1734), 33, 607–9, 613
McGlashan (Stewart) & Sons (sculptor of Edinburgh), 280, 409, 506
MacGregor & Miller 578
McGurn, Logan, Duncan & Opfer 235, 276, 284
McIntyre, Alexander 216
MacIntyre, Charles 412
Macintyre, Donald 104
McIntyre, John 107, 285
McIsaac, John & Donald 349
McKay & Forrester 534, 549
Mackenzie, J. Ford 420
Mackenzie, William 397, 417, 583, 596
McKillop, John 410, 417
McKindley, Andrew 150, Pl. 27
Mackinlay, Andrew M. 614, 616, 619, 620, 621
MacKinney, H. H. 211
Mackintosh, Charles Rennie (1868–1928), 62, 65, 66, 91, 268, 274, 291–6, Pls. 103, 104
Mackintosh, David 35, 197, 260, 412
Mackintosh, Margaret Macdonald (1864–1933), 295
McKissack, John (*c.* 1844–1915), 81

McKissack (John) & Son (John McKissack, q.v.; James McKissack, 1875–1940), 233
McKissack & Rowan (John McKissack, q.v.; William Gardner Rowan, 1845–1924), 36, 475, Pl. 33
McLaren, Robert 257
MacLaren, Charles & Edward 307
MacLaurin, Diana 180, 385, 394, 441
MacLellan, P. & W. (smiths), 383
McLintock, G. M. 616, 625
MacMillan, Andrew (b. 1928), 170
McNab (of Oban) 406
MacNab, Peter 335, 598
Macnab, R. Nelson 495
McNab, William Hunter (*fl.* 1889–1937), 39, 85, 192, 278, 280, 283, 423
see also Leiper & McNab
McNair, Donald 220
McNaughtan, Duncan (1845–1912), 290
MacNeill, John 329
MacQueen, Alexander 412
MacRae, Ebenezer James (1881–1951), 189
Macrae, Kenneth 217, 218, 410, 567
McRoberts, David 169
McTurk, Alexander 167
MacVicar, Donald 307
McWhannell (Ninian) & Reid (Ninian McWhannell, 1860–1939), 359
Malcolm, Muriel 244
Malempre, L. A. (sculptor), 409
Marr, John (mason), 312
Marr (J.), Wood & Co. Ltd (organ builders), 466
Marshall, Donald 433
Marshall, J. (sculptor), 532
Martin, Charles 156, 157, 189
Martyn & Co. (sculptors), 405
Massey, William H. (engineer), 609
Mawson, Thomas H. (landscape architect, 1861–1933), 66, 424, 612, 66, 424, 612
Maxwell, James 74, 78, 584
Maxwell, Robert 244, 307
Mayer & Co. (glass-stainers), 228
Mears, C. & G. 381
Mears, Sir Frank (1880–1953), 482

INDEX OF ARTISTS

Meikle (William) & Sons (glass-stainers), 132, 196, 251, 614
Melles, Mary (woodcarver), 575
Menart, Charles J. 39, 270
Menelaws, John (mason), 127, 261, 495
Menelaws, Thomas (mason), 127, 333
Menzies, W.L. 415
Menzies, William 415
Meredith, Williams, M. (sculptor), 443
Merrylees (Andrew) Associates 90, 415
Metzstein, Isi (b. 1928), 170
Meyer (of Munich) 143
Miller (of Glasgow, glass-stainer), 270
Miller, James (1860–1947), 73, 148, 257, 287, 478
Miller (Stephen) & Co. (bell-founders), 621
Ministry of Aviation 464
Minto, William 529, 556, 557, 559
Minton 228, 305, 426
Minton & Co. 230
Mitchell, A. MacGregor 236
Mitchell, Henry 270
Mitchell, Joseph (engineer, 1803–83), 309, 506, 529, 569
Mitchell, Sydney (1856–1930), 162, 553
Mitchell & Whitelaw 274, 287, 288
Mitchell (Sydney) & Wilson (Arthur George Sydney Mitchell, q.v.; George Wilson, b. 1845), 82, 87, 219, 393, 394, 553
Mitton, Roland (glass-stainer), 42, 198, 364
Monro, James M. (*fl.* 1872–1912), 163, 418
Montgomery-Smith & Partners (engineers), 158
Moodie, John (mason), 133
Morgan, David 280
Morris, Roger (1695–1749), 55, 58, 68, 263, 313–18, 321, 323, 445, Pls. 75, 79, 129
Morris, Talwin (graphic designer, 1865–1911), 291
Morris, William (designer, 1834–96), 288
Morris & Steedman (James Shepherd Morris, b. 1931; Robert Russell Steeman, b. 1929), 63, 259, 337–8
Morrison, James (mason), 567
Morrison, William (mason), 565
Mortimer, Jack (sculptor), 444
Morton, W. Scott (decorator), 297
Mossman (sculptor, Glasgow), 47, 347
Mossman, J. & G. (sculptors: John Mossman, 1817–90; George Mossman, 1823–63), 156, 311
Motherwell, William 206
Muirhead, W.A. 444
Mulloch (glass-stainer), 270
Murrie of Kirkintilloch, Charles 296
Mylne, Robert (1733–1811), 34, 63–4, 66, 74, 79, 84, 88, 93, 189, 263, 264, 306–12, 314, 315, 317, 318, 319, 321, 322, 445, 446, 584, 586, Pls. 74, 76, 78, 80, 128
Mylne, William (1734–90), 313, 316, 321, 322, Pl. 77
Nairn, James 251
Napier, David (marine engineer, 1790–1869), 355, 358
Napier, Thomas (mason), 118
Nasmyth, Alexander (1758–1840), 58, 76, 320, 321, 323, 445, 446
National Building Agency 363
Neil & Hurd 524
Nesfield, W.E. (1835–88), 66, 320, 425, 441
Newman (David) Partnership 395, 433
Niblett (of Gloucester) 157
Nicholls, Thomas (carver), 610, 611
Nicol, Francis 252
Noad & Wallace 281, 296
Norman & Beard (organ builders), 356
Norton, Leslie C. 483
Notman, Jack 455
O Brolchán, Donald (mason), 514
O Cuinn, Mael-Sechlainn (mason), 519, 592, 593
Office of Works 84, 508, 517, 525, 591
see also H.M. Office of Works
Oldrieve, W.T. (1853–1922), 84, 277, 412
Orkney, John 626

INDEX OF ARTISTS

Page & Park Architects (David Page; Brian Park), 130, 439
Papworth, John (plasterer, 1750–99), 317
Pate (J.G. Lindsay) & Associates 193, 235
Paterson, Alexander N. (1862–1947), 65, 81, 82, 83, 87, 90, 111, 131, 132, 160, 168, 195, 273, 275, 276, 278, 283, 284, 286, 287, 288, 291, 435, 439, 440, Pls. 94, 108
Paterson, Archibald 385
Paterson, Daniel 314, 399
Paterson, G.A. (1876–1934) *see also* Stewart & Paterson, 270
Paterson, Hannah Frew (embroiderer), 167
Paterson, Henry 348
Paterson, John Wilson (1887–1970), 412, 413
Paterson, Oscar (glass-stainer, b. *c.* 1862), 164
Paterson (A.N.) & Stoddart 279, 436, 453
Patterson, James 192
Patterson, William 320
Paul, Arthur Balfour (1875–1938) *see also* Anderson (Rowand) & Paul, 271
Peace, John 337
Peace, John G. 381
Pearson, Roger 395
Peat & Duncan 282
Peddie, James 308
Peddie & Kinnear (John Dick Peddie, 1824–91; Charles George Hood Kinnear, 1830–94), 61, 81, 226, 234, 334, 416, 574, 575
Peddie (Dick) & McKay (John More Dick Peddie, 1853–1921; John Ross McKay, 1884–1961), 273
Peddie (Dick) McKay & Jamieson 418
Peddie (Dick), Todd and Jamieson 348
Peddie & Washington Browne (John More Dick Peddie, q.v.; Sir George Washington Browne, 1853–1939), 575
Petrie, Mr 474
Petrie, William 279
Picard, Ludovick 482

Piccard, Lewis 219, 482
Piccard, Ludovick 219
Playfair, James (1755–94), 115
Playfair, William Henry (1790–1857), 60, 464–6, 541, 542, Pl. 91
Positive Organ Co. (1922) Ltd, The (organ builders), 618
Potter, James (mason, *fl.* 1750–60), 263, 305, 322
Potter (Robert) & Partners 435
Powell & Sons (glass-stainers: James Powell d. 1840; Arthur Powell; James Cotton Powell; Nathaniel Powell), 457
Powell (James) & Sons 618 *see also* Powell & Sons
Property Services Agency Architects 146
Proudfoot, Alexander (sculptor), 252
Pulham, James (garden designer), 424
Quinton, James 534
Railton, William (1820–1902), 84, 384, 533, 544, 557
Ramsay, Mr 460
Ramsay, William 462
Reiach & Hall 84, 411, Pl. 123
Reid, Robert (1775–1856), 308
Renfrew County Council 113
Rennie, John (engineer), 74, 214
Rennison, J.A. 181
Rennison & Scott 62, 181, 324, 471, 472
Renshaw, John 513, 526, 573
Rhind, Birnie (sculptor, 1853–1933), 272
Rhind, David (1808–83), 167
Richardson, James S. 413, 419
Ricky, George 296
Ritchie, Alexander & Euphemia 307, 598
Robertson, John (*fl.* 1880–98), 586
Robertson, W.W. (1845–1907), 84, 277
Rochead, John T. (1814–78), 47, 59, 61, 64, 219, 299, 358, 397–8, 453, 456, Pls. 89–90
Rosa, Amanda 448
Ross, Alexander (1834–1925), 38, 104, 405, 525, 560, 565, 575, 583, 586
Ross, Charles (surveyor, 1722–1806), 79, 267

INDEX OF ARTISTS

Ross, Thomas (1839–1930), 511, 516
Ross & Lindsay 342
Ross & Macbeth (1887–1907:
  Alexander Ross, q.v.; Robert J.
  Macbeth, d. 1912), 228
Ross & Mackintosh (Alexander
  Ross, q.v.; David Mackintosh,
  d. 1891), 81, 87, 404, 413, 414,
  418, 586
Rowatt, Alexander 164
Roxby, Park & Baird 85, 276, 623
Rushworth & Dreaper (organ
  builders), 380
Russel, John 259
Russell, Adam 616
Salmon (James) & Son (James
  Salmon, 1805–88; William
  Forrest Salmon, 1843–1911;
  James Salmon Jr, 1873–1924), 387
Salvin, Anthony (1799–1881), 314,
  315, 320
Saunders & Co. (glass-stainers),
  610
Schulz, Robert Weir (1861–1951),
  67, 605, 612, 613, 614
Scott, Sir Giles Gilbert (1880–1960),
  39, 41, 407–8, Pl. 41
Scott, John R. (engineer), 520
Scott, M.H. Baillie (1865–1945),
  91, 268, 289, 292
Scott Morton & Co. (decorators),
  117, 207, 271, 483, 550
Scott & Rae (sculptors), 233, 537
Scott, Wilson, Kirkpatrick & Co.
  (engineers), 158
Scottish Special Housing
  Association 343
Sellars, James (1843–88), 61, 205,
  272
Shairp, Alexander (d. 1906), 82,
  407, 409, 410, 412, 415, 417, 421,
  586
Shannon, Alexander Macfarlane
  (sculptor, 1850–1915), 359
Shaw, Christian (glass-stainer), 42,
  198, 381
Shearer (James) & Annand (James
  Shearer, 1881–1962) 375, 483,
  375, 483
Shepherd, J. 333
Shipton, Emma (glass-stainer), 435
Shrigley & Hunt (glass-stainers:
  Arthur William Hunt, 1849–1917),
  271

Sills, Robert 283
Sim, E.J. 311
Sim, J. Fraser 87, 348, 351, 408,
  416, 418
Simpson, Archibald (1790–1847),
  36, 618
Simpson & Brown (James Walter
  Thorburn Simpson, b. 1944;
  Andrew Stewart Brown, b. 1945),
  404
Sinclair (of Caithness) 453
Sinclair, C. 599
Sinclair, Colin (c. 1879–1957), 194,
  252, 383, 384
Sinclair, John (engineer), 74, 329,
  562
Slezer, John (d. 1714), 445
Smith, D. 337, 407
Smith, Ian 439
Smith, James (1808–63), 367, 387,
  439, 454
Smith, Patrick Ross (glass-stainer),
  516
Smith, Peter (sculptor), 272
Smith, Thomas 76, 182
Smith (Thomas), Gibb & Pate 83,
  234, 432, 452, 554
Somervail & Co. 234
Spalding, Thomas 532
Speakman, Peter 477
Speirs, Arthur D. (glass-stainer),
  272
Speirs & Co. 148, 219, 397
Spence, Sir Basil (1907–76), 505
Spence, William (1806–83), 130,
  268, 270, 275, 285, 434
Spence (Philip) Associates 193
SSHA Architects 300
Starforth, John (1823–98), 198, 351
Stead, Tim (woodcarver), 408
Steel, James 160
Steele & Balfour (Henry Bell
  Wesley Steele, c. 1852–1902;
  Andrew Balfour, q.v.), 113
Steell, Sir John (sculptor, 1804–91),
  308
Stephen, Alexander (engineer), 620,
  622, Pl. 118
Stephen & Maxwell 148
Steuart, George (c. 1730–1806), 93
Stevenson, Alan (1807–65), 76,
  600, Pl. 124
Stevenson, D. & C. (engineers),
  299

INDEX OF ARTISTS

Stevenson, D. & T. (David Stevenson, q.v.; Thomas Stevenson, 1818–87), 547, 552
Stevenson, D.J. (engineer), 298
Stevenson, D.W. (sculptor, 1842–1904), 232
Stevenson, David (1815–85), 538
Stevenson, David & Thomas (David Stevenson, q.v.; Thomas Stevenson, q.v.), 76, 527
Stevenson, Hugh (mason), 586
Stevenson, James 309
Stevenson, John (mason), 189, 219, 586, Pl. 131
Stevenson, Robert (1772–1850), 76, 182, 367, 411, 557
Stevenson, Thomas (1818–87), 538
Stewart, Charles E. (glass-stainer), 443
Stewart & Paterson (John Stewart, c. 1869–1954; George Andrew Paterson, q.v.; 1876–1934; David Hally), 89, 270, 282, 283, 284, 290, 296
Stirling, James (C18) (mason), 462
Stirling, James (C20, Burgh Architect, Helensburgh) 283
Stirling County Architect 273
Storry & Smith (engineers), 159
Strachan, Douglas (glass-stainer, 1875–1950), 41–2, 216, 324, 443, 516
Strain, John (engineer), 71
Strathclyde Regional Council 128, 144, 178, 232, 257, 277, 296, 382, 413, 484, 533, 552, 553, 580, 583, 620, Pl. 122
Stuart, Peter 181
Sutherland, Eric (1870–1940), 432
Taggart, Dr James 206
Tait, William 280, 284
Tarbolton, Harold O. (1869–1947), 327, 404, 405
Tarbolton & Ochterlony (Harold Ogle Tarbolton, q.v.; Sir Matthew Montgomerie Ochterlony, 1880–1946), 575
Tavish, John (*fl.* 1780–1805), 263, 264, 309, 321
Taylor, David 542
Taylor, James (b. 1890), 417–18, Pl. 117
Taylor, John (wright), 613

Taylor (John) & Co. (bell-founders), 513
Taylor (James) Partnership 146
Taylor (John) & Sons (*see* Taylor (John) & Co), 305, 443
Telford, Thomas (engineer, 1757–1834), 34, 69, 74, 129, 192, 214, 381, 464, 524, 529, 556, 559, 562, 578, 586
Templeton, William (stone-carver), 314
Thom, John 106, 347, 352, Pl. 29
Thom, Robert (engineer, 1775–1847), 603
Thomson, Alexander (1817–75), 62, 90, 202, 203, 204, 205, 206, 207, 211, 281, 342, 627, Pl. 106
Thomson, David (*c.* 1830–1910), 61, 66, 145, 146, 402, 417, 495, 569
Thomson, John Russell 83, 616, 620, 621–2, 628
Thomson, William 34, 217, 349, 381, 483, 524, 556, 559, 578, 583, 586, 587, 589, Pl. 36
Thomson (Munro) & Co. (bell-founders), 475
Thomson & Robison 325
Thomson (James) & Sons 89, 160, 164
Thomson & Turnbull 402
Thornley, Michael and Sue 439
Thornley, Sue 130
Tiffany 436
Todd, William 82, 129, 251, 381, 382, 385, 466
Townsend, John 160
Tregellis, Mr (of London) 190
Tritschler, F.D. (glass-stainer), 618
Tweedie, Charles E. 622
van den Ghein, Peter (bellfounder), 517
van der Voort, Michael (sculptor), 320
Vanbrugh, Sir John (1664–1726), 55, 313
Verey, Rosemary 612
Vogt, Tony 282
Waddell, John Jeffrey (1876–1941), 36, 256, 258, 442
Waddell (Jeffrey) & Young (John Jeffrey Waddell, q.v.), 493

INDEX OF ARTISTS

Wailes, William (glass-stainer, 1808–81), 405, 426
Wakeham, C.T. 157, 535
Walker, Ezekiel 182
Walker, Fred 440
Walker, J. Russell 536
Walker, Jeremy 347
Walker, Robert 559
Walker, Ronald 157
Walker, Hardie & Smith 622
Wallace, James 228
Walton, E.A. (painter, 1960–1922), 289
Walton, George (1867–1933), 287
Wardrop, James Maitland (1824–82), 83, 350
Wardrop & Anderson (1886–98: Hew Montgomerie Wardrop, 1856–87; Sir Robert Rowand Anderson, q.v.), 38, 305
Wardrop & Reid (James Maitland Wardrop, q.v.; Charles Reid, 1828–83), 249, 378
Warrin, Thomas 298
Watson, George Mackie (1859–1948), 495
Watson, T.L. (c. 1850–1920), 87, 89, 90, 161, 162, 163, 281, 282, 298, Pl. 107
Watson & Salmond (John Watson, b. 1901), 432
Watson, Salmond & Gray (John Watson, q.v.), 167
Watson of Largs, Thomas 296
Watt, James (engineer, 1736–1819), 73
Watt, Robert 154
Watts, Peter 408
Webster, Alfred A. (glass-stainer, d. 1914; see also Adam (Stephen Studios), 357
Webster, George MacWhirter 272, 471
Webster, Gordon (glass-stainer, b. 1908), 41–2, 198, 211, 230, 258, 272, 336, 362, 443, 618
Webster, Gordon M. 462
Weekes, Joseph 81, 89, 91, 132, 168, 257, 342, 436, 444, Pl. 116
Weir, James 162
Weir, Robert 399, 479, 480
Weir (Robert) & Son 161
Wemyss, Robert 89, 90, 148, 169, 209, 257, 272, 277, 279, 284, 285, 286, 288, 289, 296, 478
Whalen, A. Carrick (glass-stainer), 406
Wharrie, Colledge & Brand (engineers), 178
Whymper, Charles 586
Wickham, Julian 63, 246
Williams, M. Meredith, 443
see Meredith Williams, M
Williams, McDonald 285
Williamson, James (engineer), 97, 327
Williamson (James) & Partners (engineers), 375, 483
Wilson, Charles (1810–63), 36, 60, 61, 86, 109, 110, 145, 277, 402, 418, 455, 483, 619
Wilson, David 70, 563, 564–5, Pl. 132
Wilson, Donald 63, 431
Wilson, J.R. 275
Wilson, John (C19) 325
Wilson, John (C20) (mason), 199, 597, 624
Wilson, John C. (bell-founders), 166, 299, 406
Wilson, Sam (plasterer), 117, 224
Wilson, Thomas W. 493
Wilson, William (glass-stainer, 1905–72), 258, 407, 435, 516
Wilson (John) Associates 158, 599, 615
Wingate (John B.) & Partners 277
Wiseman & Gale 448
Wood, Mary I. (glass-stainer), 364
Wood (J.) & Sons (organ-builders), 405
Worral, William 610
Wyatt, Sir Matthew Digby (1805–86), 314
Wylie, James 157
Wylie & Lochhead (decorators and cabinetmakers), 405
Wyllie, David V. 235
Wyllie, George 405
Wylson, James (b. 1811), 157
Young, George P.K. 375
Young, James 269
Young, John 375
Youngson, James R. 580

INDEX OF PLACES

Principal references are in **bold** type; demolished buildings are shown in *italic*. For guidance about the arrangement of the gazetteer, see p. xiii.

Acha (Coll) 94, **499**
Achadh-Chaorann *see* Ardpatrick
Achadun Castle *see* Lismore
Achafolla **99**
Achahoish **99–103**
Achallader *see* Bridge of Orchy
Achamore House *see* Gigha
A'Chleit *see* Tayinloan
Achlian *see* Cladich
Achnaba (Loch Etive) *see* Ardchattan
Achnaba (Mid Argyll) *see* Port Ann
Achnabreck *see* Cairnbaan; Lochgilphead
Achnacree 18
Achnacreebeag 18
Achnacroish *see* Lismore; Torosay Castle (Mull)
Achnamara **103–4**
Airds Bay *see* Taynuilt
Airds House *see* Port Appin
Aldochlay **104**
An Sàilean *see* Lismore
Appin 72, 84, **104–6**
  Kinlochlaich House 59, **105–6**
  see also Castle Stalker
Appin House *see* Portnacroish
Aray Bridge *see* Inveraray (public buildings)
Ardanaiseig House *see* Kilchrenan
Ardanstur *see* Melfort
Ardarroch House *see* Finnart
Ardbeg (Bute) *see* Rothesay (Bute)
Ardbeg (Islay) 95, **528**
Ardbrecknish *see* Port Sonachan
Ardchattan **106–7**
  Achnaba **106**, **107**
  Ardchattan Church 35, 39, 40, **106**, Pls. 29, 30
  Ardchattan House *see* Ardchattan Priory
  Ardchattan Point 57, **107**

Ardchattan Priory 11, 15, 26, 29, 31, 32, 33, 43, 45, 46, **107–11**
Ardchattan House 60, 109, **110–11**
Arden 61, **111–12**
Auchendennan 61, **111–12**, Pl. 94
Ardencaple *see* Helensburgh (public buildings)
Ardentinny 70, 86, **113**
Ardfern 33, 39, 40, 57, **113–14**
  see also Craignish Castle
Ardfin (Jura) **560–1**
Ardkinglas House 12, 63, 65, 66, **114–18**, Pl. 98
Ardlamont **118–20**
  Ardlamont House 56, 59, 66, **118–20**
Ardlarach *see* Toberonochy
Ardlui 68, **120**
Ardlussa (Jura) **561**
Ardmaddy Castle 11, 13, 54, 60, 64, 66, **120–3**, Pl. 82
Ardmarnock 19, **123–4**
  Ardmarnock House 56–7, 59, **123–4**
Ardminish *see* Gigha
Ardmore **124–5**
  Keppoch House 56, **124–5**
Ardnadam **125–6**
  Hafton House (Orchard Park) 59, 64, 66, **125–6**, Pl. 87
Ardnave (Islay) **528–9**
  Kilnave Chapel and Cross 24, 30, **528**
  Nave Island 24, **528**
Ardoch **126–7**
Ardpatrick **127–8**
  Ardpatrick House 57, **127–8**
Ardrishaig 11, 72, **128–30**, 214–15, 379
  churches 35, 37, **128**
  public buildings 74, 82, 83, **128–9**

INDEX OF PLACES

Arduaine 5, 66, **130**
Arichonan *see* Tayvallich
Arinagour (Coll) 76, 94, **499–502**
　Parish Church 10, **499**
Aros Castle (Mull) 11, 12, 15, 50, 51, 70, **566–7**
Arrochar 35, 71, 72, 73, 87, 89, **130–2**
　housing 89, 90, **132**, Pl. 116
　see also Tarbet
Ascog (Bute) 36, **603–5**
　Ascog Hall 66, **604–5**
Ascog Castle (Cowal) *see* Millhouse
Asknish House *see* Lochgair
Auchendennan *see* Arden
Auchenlochan **132–3**
　see also Tighnabruaich
Auchindrain 70, 78, 91, **133–5**
　Claonairigh 57, 95, **133**, 312
Balemartine (Tiree) 37, **595**
Ballimore House *see* Otter Ferry
Ballinaby (Islay) *see* Saligo (Islay)
Ballygrant (Islay) 94, **529–30**
　Kilmeny **529**, 551
Ballymeanoch *see* Rhudil
Balmavicar *see* Carskiey
Balvicar 13, 78, 94, **135**
Barbreck **135–8**
　Barbreck House 56, 58, 64, 66, 93, **135–8**, 377–8
　Turnalt House 56, **138**
Barcaldine **139–42**
　Barcaldine Castle 52, **139–40**, 222, Pls. 71, 72
　Barcaldine House 58, 139, **141**
Barmore House *see* Stonefield Castle
Barsloisnach *see* Poltalloch
Baugh (Tiree) 37, **595**
Beacharr Farm *see* Tayinloan
Bealachandrain Farm *see* Clachan of Glendaruel
Bellanoch 37, **142**
Bellochantuy **142–3**, 399
Belnahua 13, 96
Benderloch 21, 37, 82, 83, **143–4**
　see also Barcaldine
Benmore House 5, 61, 66, **144–6**
Blairmore 90, **146–7**
Blairvadach *see* Shandon
Bonawe *see* Taynuilt
Bowmore (Islay) 58, 78, 79, 86, **530–5**

　churches 33, 37, 45, 46, 47, 79, **530–2**, 535, Pl. 24
　Distillery 95, **534**, Pls. 138, 139
　Kilarrow 33, 45, 46, 47, 79, 530, **531–2**, Pl. 24
　public buildings 80–1, 83, **532–3**
Breacachadh (Coll) 44, **502–3**
　Breacachadh Castle 51, 53, **502–3**, 581, Pl. 68
　New Breacachadh Castle 56, **503**, Pl. 68
Bridge of Awe *see* Taynuilt
Bridge of Orchy 73, **147–9**
　Achallader Castle 2, **147–8**
　Inveroran Hotel 86, **148**
Bridgend (Islay) 47, 70, 83, **535–7**
　Dun Nosebridge **537**, Pl. 8
　Kilarrow Burial Ground 46, **535**
　Redhouses Mill 95, **536**
　see also Islay House
Bridgend (nr Kilmichael Glassary) 69, **149**
Brochroy *see* Taynuilt
Bruichladdich (Islay) 83, **537–8**
Bunessan (Mull) 35, 70, 78, **567**
　Creich 78, **567**
　Kilvickeon Old Parish Church 30, **567**
Bunnahabhainn (Islay) 92, 95, **538**
　Ruvaal Lighthouse 76, **538**
Bute 13, 14, 16, 17, 70, 95, **603–29**
　see also under place-names
Butter Bridge *see* Cairndow
Caibeal Mheamhair (Mull) *see* Lochbuie (Mull)
Cairnbaan 18, **149**
　Achnabreck 18, **149**, Pl. 4
Cairnburgh Castle (Treshnish Isles) 49, **600–2**
Cairndow 86, **150–1**
　Butter Bridge 68, **150**
　Kilmorich Parish Church 33, 35, 40, **150**, 262, 386, Pl. 27
Caisteal na Nighinn Ruaidhe *see* Dalavich
Calgary (Mull) 59, **567–8**
Campbeltown 13, 14, 53, 69, 72, 77, **151–65**
　castles: House of Lochhead (C17) *151*, *154*; Island Muller (C13/14) *165*; Kilkerran (C15) 51, *165*
　churches 34, **153–7**; Castlehill Church 33, 34, 77, **153–4**; Highland Parish Church 34,

77, **154–5**; Kilchousland Old Parish Church 46, **155**; Kilkerran Old Parish Church and Cemetery 45, 46, 138, **155–6**; *Lochend Kirk 37, 162*; Lorne Street Church 37, 154, **156**, 162, Pl. 34; *Old Gaelic Church of 1642 32*, 153, *154*, **155**; Old Lowland Church (Highland Parish Church Halls) 33, 153, **155**; St Kiaran **157**; St Kieran 38–9, **157**
Cross *see* public buildings *below*
Dalintober 74, 77, 89, 151, 153, **154**, **158**, **159**, 164
distilleries *see* industrial buildings *below*
houses *see* streets and houses *below*
industrial buildings 95, 153, **160–1**
Kilkerran *see* castles *and* churches *above*
Limecraigs House 54, **164**
public buildings 83, 84, **157–60**; Argyll & Bute Council Offices (Poorhouse) 83–4, **157**; Cross 31, 151, **158**, 163, 519, Pl. 47; Picture House 85, **158–9**, Pl. 121; piers and quays 74, 75, 151, **158**, **159**; Public Library and Museum 84, **159**, Pl. 110; *Tolbooth* 151, **160**; Town House 81, 158, **160**, Pl. 109; War Memorial 47, **160**
streets and houses 54, 65, 77–8, 89, 90, 151–3, **161–5**; Barochan Place 89, **163**; Craigdhu Mansions 89, **163**; High Askomil Walk 65, **164–5**; Kirk Street 88, 153, **163**; Low Askomil Walk 65, 90, **165**; Main Street 89, 151, **162–3**; Parliament Place 89, **164**; Pensioners' Row 89, **163**; Royal Avenue Mansions 89, **163**; Springfield House 89, **164**
White Hart Hotel 87, **162–3**
Caol Ila (Islay) **538–9**
Distillery 95, **539**, Pl. 140
Cara **165–6**
Cardross 89, **166–74**
churches 35, 37, 44, **166–7**
Geilston Halls 82, **167**, 168
Kilmahew 25, **169**

St Peter's College 39, **169–74**, Pls. 44, 45
see also Colgrain
Carloonan *see* Inveraray Castle Estate
Carnasserie Castle 10, 52, **174–7**, 347, Pl. 69
Carradale 21, 61, 83, **177–8**
Carrick Castle 51, 89, **178–80**, Pl. 65
Carsaig (nr Tayvallich) **180**
see also Tayvallich
Carsaig (Mull) 10, 11, **568–9**
Carskiey 62, 92, **181–2**
Balmavicar 92, 94, **182**
Mull of Kintyre Lighthouse 76, **181–2**
Castle Coeffin *see* Lismore
Castle Shuna *see* Shuna (Appin)
Castle Stalker 13, 52, **182–4**, Pl. 66
Castle Sween 10, 48, 49, 50, **184–7**, 254, Pls. 57, 58
Doide 9, 10, **187**
see also Kilmory Knap
Castle Toward *see* Toward
Castleton House *see* Port Ann
Ceanloch-Kilkerran *see* Campbeltown
Ceann a' Mhara (Tiree) 24, **595**
Clachaig 96, **188**
Clachan (Kintyre) 46, **189–90**
Clachan (Lismore) *see* Lismore
Clachan (Loch Fyne) *see* Glen Fyne
Clachan (Seil) 86, **188–9**
Clachan Bridge **188–9**, Pl. 131
Dun Skeig 21, **190**
Clachan of Glendaruel **190–3**
Bealachandrain Farm 93, **192**
Kilmodan Parish Church 33, 39–40, 44, **191–2**, Pl. 26
Cladh a'Bhile *see* Ellary
Cladh nam Paitean *see* Glenbarr
Cladich 47, 68, **193–4**
Achlian 57, **193–4**
Inishail 30, **193**
Claonaig **194**
Claonairigh *see* Auchindrain
Clunary (Claonairigh) *see* Auchindrain
Clyde Submarine Base *see* Faslane
Clynder 62, **194–5**
Colgrain **195–6**
Colintraive 70, **196–7**

INDEX OF PLACES

Coll 8, 23, **499–504**
  Parish Church *see* Arinagour
  see also Acha; Arinagour;
    Breacachadh; Grishipoll;
    Sorisdale
Colonsay 17, 23, 70, 76, 86, 94,
  500, **504–6**
  churches 33, 37, **504–5**
  Colonsay House 54, **505**, Pl. 105
  Loch an Sgoltaire 52–3, **505**
  Riasg Buidhe 25, 505, **506**
Connel 35, 42, 71, 72, **197–9**
  Connel Bridge 12, 73, **198**, Pl. 133
  North Connel 18, 86, **199**
Cornaigmore (Tiree) **596**
Coulport 76, 90, **199–200**
Cour **200–1**
  Cour House 63, **200–1**, Pl. 97
Cove 90, **201–8**, 211
  Burgh Hall & Reading Room *see*
    Craigrownie
  Cove Castle 61, **205**
  Craig Ailey 62, 202, **203–4**, 206,
    342, Pl. 106
  Craigrownie Castle 62, **203**
  Knockderry Castle 61, **207–8**
  Seymour Lodge 62, **205–6**, 208,
    341
  see also Craigrownie; Kilcreggan
Craigendoran 71, 72, 73, **208–9**
  see also Colgrain
Craighouse (Jura) 74, 86, 95, **561–3**
  Jura Parish Church 33, **561–2**
Craigmore (Bute) *see* Rothesay
  (Bute)
Craignish Castle 51, 60, 93, **209–11**
  Kilmarie Old Parish Church 30,
    31, 32, **209**
Craignish Parish Church *see*
  Ardfern
Craignure (Mull) 76, **569**
Craigrownie **211–12**, 341
  Burgh Hall and Reading Room
    82, **212**
  Craigrownie Castle *see* Cove
Craleckan *see* Furnace
Craobh Haven **212–13**
  Eilean an Dùin **213**
Crarae *see* Minard
Creagan Bridge *see* Glen Creran
Creich (Mull) *see* Bunessan (Mull)
Crinan 78, **213–14**, 215
  Crinan Harbour (Port Righ) 213,
    214

Crinan Canal 72, 73–4, 75, 128,
  142, 149, 213, **214–15**, 379,
  383, Pl. 141
Crinan Ferry 213, **215**
  Crinan House 57, **215**
Crossapol (Coll) *see* Breacachadh
Crossapol (Tiree) **596**
  Island House 57, **596**
Cruachan Power Station *see*
  Lochawe
Cuan 57, **215–16**
  Kilbrandon and Kilchattan
    churches 33, 42, **216**
Cullipool 78, 96, **216**
Cultoon (Islay) *see* Lossit (Islay)
Cumlodden *see* Furnace
Dalavich **216–17**, 262
  Caisteal na Nighinn Ruaidhe 50,
    217
Dalintober *see* Campbeltown
Dalmally 7, 47, 57, 68, 71, 72, 86,
  217–20
  Glenorchy Church 33, 35, **218–19**
  railway station 73, **219–20**
Danna *see* Keills
Davaar *see* Kildalloig
Degnish *see* Melfort
Dervaig (Mull) 19, **569–70**
  Kilmore Parish Church 36,
    569–70, Pl. 38
Dòid Mhàiri (Islay) 27
Doide *see* Castle Sween
Drumgarve *see* Peninver
Drumlemble 96, **220**
  Kilkivan Old Parish Church 158,
    220, 343
Duart Castle (Mull) 11, 15, 49, 50,
  53, **570–3**, Pl. 60
Dun Ara (Mull) *see* Glengorm
  Castle (Mull)
Dùn Chonaill *see* Garvellachs
Dùn Mòr Vaul (Tiree) *see* Vaull
  (Tiree)
Dùn na Cuaiche *see* Inveraray
  Castle Estate
Dun Skeig *see* Clachan (Seil)
Dunadd 22, 25, **220–1**, Pl. 7
Dunagoil (Bute) *see* Kingarth
  (Bute)
Dunans *see* Glendaruel
Dunaverty Castle *see* Southend
Dunbeg 93, **221**
Dunderave Castle 52, 63, 65,
  222–5, 331, Pls. 99, 100

INDEX OF PLACES

Dunivaig Castle *see* Lagavulin (Islay)
Dunmore **225–6**
  Kilnaish 44, **225**
Dunollie *see* Oban
Dunoon 72, 74, 80, 85, 86, 87, **226–37**
  cemetery 45, **231**
  churches **228–30**; Holy Trinity 38, 41, **228**; Old and St Cuthbert's (Parish Church) 35, 59, **228–9**; St John's 37, 40, 42, **229–30**, Pl. 35
  Dunoon Castle *see* public buildings *below*
  houses and mansions *see* streets *below*
  public buildings 83, 84, **231–4**; Burgh Buildings 81, **231**; Castle House 59, 64, 80, 226, **231–2**, Pl. 111; Dunoon Castle 48, 226, **232**; Dunoon General Hospital 84, **232**; Dunoon Grammar School 83, **232**; Dunoon Pier 75, 76, **232–3**, 234; Lamont Memorial 47, **233**; police stations 81, **233**; Post Office 84, **233**; Queen's Hall 86, **233**; Sheriff Court-House 81, **233–4**
  streets, houses and mansions 89, 91, 226, **231–2**, **234–7**
Dunstaffnage Castle 49, 53, 221, **237–42**, Pl. 62
  Dunstaffnage Chapel 29, 30, 239, **241–2**, Pl. 19
Dunstaffnage Mains Farm *see* Dunbeg
Duntrune 52, 214, **242–4**
Easdale *see* Ellenabeich and Easdale
Eileach an Naoimh *see* Garvellachs
Eilean an Dùin *see* Craobh Haven
Eilean Mór *see* Finlaggan (Islay); Keills
Eilean Musdile lighthouse *see* Lismore
Ellary 61, 63, **244–5**
  Cladh a'Bhile 24, 25, 31, **244**
Ellenabeich and Easdale 13, 63, 75, 78, 96, **245–6**, Pl. 136
Eriska 62, 87, **247**
Faslane 30, 47, 72, 76, 96–7, **247**, 434
Feolin (Jura) 70, 74, **563**

Fincharn Castle *see* Ford
Finlaggan (Islay) 96, 527, **539–40**
  Eilean Mór 50, **539–40**
Finnart 60, **248**
Fionnphort (Mull) **573**
Ford 44, 70, **248–9**
  Fincharn Castle 50, **249**
Fraoch Eilean 11, 50, 51, 53, **250**
Furnace 12, **250–2**
  Craleckan Ironworks 78, 96, **250–1**
  Cumlodden Parish Church **251**, 396
  Kenmore Village 78, **252**
Gallanach (nr Lochgair) *see* Lochgair
Gallanach (nr Oban) *see* Oban (mansions)
Garbh Eileach *see* Garvellachs
Garbhallt **252–6**
  Kilbride 24, **252**
  New Castle Lachlan 56, 62, **253–4**
  Old Castle Lachlan 50, 187, **254–6**
  Strathlachlan Parish Church 35, **253**
Garelochhead 39, 73, 89, **256–8**
Garron Bridge *see* Glen Shira
Garvellachs (Garvellach Isles) 49, 92, 500, **507–8**
  Dùn Chonaill Castle 49, **508**
  Eileach an Naoimh 24, **507–8**, Pl. 11
Gigha 25, 29, 36, 57, 94, **258–9**
  Achamore House 61–2, 66, **259**
Glen Aray 58, 68, 82, 93, **260**
Glen Creran **260–2**
  Creagan Bridge 73, **261**
  Glenure 57, 64, **261**
Glen Feochan *see* Kilmore
Glen Fyne 150, **262**
  see also Cairndow
Glen Kinglas 68, 96, **262–3**
  see also Cairndow
Glen Luss *see* Luss; Peninver
Glen Shira 93, **263–4**
  Garron Bridge 68, **263**, Pl. 129
  Maam Steading 93, **264**
Glenbarr 46, 58–9, 64, 155, **264–5**, Pl. 86
Glenbranter **265–6**
  Glenshellish House 56, **265–6**
Glencruitten 399
  see also Oban

INDEX OF PLACES

Glendaruel 39, 44, 70, **266–7**
  Dunans 44, **266–7**
  see also Clachan of Glendaruel
Glengorm Castle (Mull) 61, **574**
  Dun Ara Castle 49, **574**
Glenorchy Church *see* Dalmally
Glenshellach 399
  see also Oban
Glenshellish House *see* Glenbranter
Glenure *see* Glen Creran
Glenvoiden (Bute) *see* Port Bannatyne (Bute)
Gometra (Mull) **574**
Gott Bay (Tiree) *see* Scarinish (Tiree)
Grishipoll (Coll) 57, **503**
Grogport **267**
Gruline (Mull) 38, 44, **575–6**
  Old Gruline House 57, **575–6**
Gylen Castle *see* Kerrera
Hafton House *see* Ardnadam
Hayfield *see* Kilchrenan
Helensburgh 65, 77, 79, 85, **267–98**
  Ardencaple Castle *see* public buildings *below*
  cemetery **272**
  churches 37, **269–72**, 277; *Old Parish/Established Church* 36, **277**; Park Church 37, **270**; St Joseph 39, **270–1**; St Michael and All Angels 38, 41–2, **271**; West Kirk 35, 36, **271–2**
  Hill House, The *see* streets and houses *below*
  houses *see* streets and houses *below*
  public buildings and monuments 71, 81–2, 83, **273–8**, 279, 280; Ardencaple Castle 268, **273**, 296, 434; Clyde Street School 83, **273**; Fire Station 82, **273**; La Scala Cinema 85, **279**; Municipal Buildings 81, **276**; Pier 74–5, 268, **276**, 281; police stations 82, **276**; Post Office 84, **277**; railway stations 71, 73, 268, **274**, *287–8*; Victoria Halls 81–2, **277–8**; Victoria Infirmary 84, **278**
  Queen's (Baths) Hotel 87, 267, **281**
  streets and houses 62, 65, 85, 86, 89, 90–1, 267–9, *274*, 275, **278–98**; Albion Lodge **290**, 440; Alma Place 89, **282**; Brantwoode (Munro Drive West) 65, 90, **288**, 290, Pl. 95; Cairndhu 90, **296–7**; Colquhoun Square 85, **279–80**; Dalmore 90, 192, **297**; The Hill House 13, 62, 65, 66, 91, 268, 269, **291–6**, 455, Pls. 103, 104; John Street 89, **279**, 284; Kirkmichael 272, **283**; Longcroft 65, 90, **287**, 290, Pl. 108; West Princes Street 85, 89, **279–80**, **284–5**; The White House 91, 268, **289**, 292
  Upper Helensburgh 62, **287–91**
Heylipol (Tiree) **596**
Holy Loch 125, 324
Hunter's Quay 75, 80, **298–9**
  Royal Marine Hotel 87, **298**, Pl. 107
  see also Dunoon
Hynish (Tiree) 75, **596–7**
Inch Kenneth (Mull) 30, 46, **576**
Inishail *see* Cladich
Innellan 75, 83, **299–300**
Innis Chonnell Castle 48–9, **300–3**
Inveraray 11, 12, 53, 58, 68, 69, 70, 72, 74, 76, 78–9, **303–13**, Pls. 2, 73
  Castle and Castle Estate *see separate entries*
  churches **305–8**, 311; All Saints' Church and Duke's Tower 12, 30, 38, 41, 43, **305–6**; cross (Front Street) 31, **308**; Glenaray and Inveraray Parish Church 12, 34, 79, **306–8**, Pl. 80; Kilmalieu 43, 45, 305, **306**
  cross *see* churches *above*
  George Hotel 86, **311**, Pl. 74
  houses *see* streets and houses *below*
  public buildings 12, 74, 303, 305, **308–10**, 311, 312; Aray Bridge **308**, 470, Pl. 128; Court House 79, 81, **308–9**, Pl. 81; The Great Inn 86, 305, **309**; pier 76, 305, **309–10**; post office 84, **312**; schools 83, **311**, 313; Town House 80, 81, 305, 308, **310**
  streets and houses 88, 303–5, **310–13**; Arkland 84, 88, **312**; Chamberlain's House 88, **310**;

Church Square 85, **311**, 321;
Factory Land 95, **312**; Fore
Street **322**; Front Street 88,
305, **310–11**; MacPherson's
House 88, 311; Main Street
North and South 88, 305,
311–12, Pl. 74; Relief Land 88,
312; Silvercraigs House 88, **311**
see also Glen Shira
Inveraray Castle 10–11, 51, 52,
54–5, 58, 63–4, 67, 303,
313–23, Pls. 75, 76
see also Inveraray Castle Estate
Inveraray Castle Estate 10–11, 55,
58, 65, 72, 93, 94, 314, **320–3**,
446
   Carloonan Mill and Doocot 94,
321, Pl. 79
   Court of Offices (Cherry Park)
10, 66, **321**, Pl. 77
   Dùn na Cuaiche Watch Tower
58, **323**
   Frew's (Garden) Bridge **322**, 323,
470, Pl. 130
   Maltland Square 93, **322–3**,
Pl. 78
   South Cromalt Lodge 67, **323**
Inverchaolain 35, 42, 46, 57,
323–4
Invereck **324–5**
Inverlussa (Jura) **563**
Inverneill 44, 69, **325–6**
   Stronachullin Lodge 63, **326**
Inveroran *see* Bridge of Orchy
Inveruglas 72, **326–7**
   Craigenarden Viaduct 72, **326–7**,
Pl. 134
   Loch Sloy Power Station 97, **327**,
479
Iona 8, 11, 13, 15, 22, 40, 501,
509–27
   high crosses 26–7, 30, **519–21**,
546
   Iona Abbey 10, 15, 22, 23, 25,
26–7, 28–9, 31, 32, 95, **509–27**,
Pls. 10, 12; abbey church 29,
32, 41, 42, 373, **509–17**, 523,
Pl. 14; conventual buildings
29, **517–19**, Pl. 15; St
Columba's Shrine 29, 509,
511–12, 526
   Nunnery 28, 515, **521–4**, 526,
Pl. 16
   Parish Church 34, **524**

Reilig Odhráin 511, **524–5**
Rubha na Carraig Géire 95–6
St Oran's Chapel 28, 29, 31,
525–6, Pls. 12, 13
St Ronan's Church 24, 29, **526**
Island House (Tiree) *see* Crossapol
(Tiree)
Island Macaskin 96
Islay 8, 16, 17, 19, 23, 24, 27, 31,
70, 75, 78, 88, 94, 96, 500,
527–60
   Islay House *see separate entry*
   see also place-names
Islay House (Islay) 53, 54, 60, 529,
530, **540–2**
Jura 9, 16, 23, 70, 94, 500, **560–5**
   Jura Free Church *see* Leargybreck
(Jura)
   Jura Parish Church *see*
Craighouse (Jura)
   see also place-names
Kames **327**
Kames Castle (Bute) *see* Port
Bannatyne (Bute)
Kamesburgh (Bute) *see* Port
Bannatyne (Bute)
Keills (Islay) **542–3**
Keills (Knapdale) 70, 74, **328–9**
   Danna 96, **329**
   Eilean Mór 30, 31, 326, **328–9**
   Keills Cross *see* Parish Church
below
   Parish Church and crosses 24,
26, 29, 30, 31, **328–9**
Keils (Jura) 44, 92, 562, **563–4**,
Pl. 56
Kenmore Village *see* Furnace
Kennacraig 76
Kerrera 24, 47, **329–32**
   Gylen Castle 11, 52, 53, 223,
329–32, Pl. 67
Kerrycroy (Bute) *see* Mount Stuart
(Bute)
Kilarrow (Islay) *see* Bowmore
(Islay); Bridgend (Islay)
Kilberry 31, 33, 43, **332–4**
   Carse House 56, **333**
   Kilberry Castle 60, 61, **333–4**,
Pl. 92
Kilbrandon and Kilchattan Church
see Cuan
Kilbrandon Old Parish Church *see*
Balvicar
Kilbrannan Chapel *see* Skipness

Kilbride (Loch Fyne) *see* Garbhallt
Kilbride (nr Oban) 43, **334–5**
Kilbride Chapel *see* Rhudil
Kilbride Church *see* Ardlamont
Kilchattan (Bute) 19, 89, **605**
Kilchattan (Luing) *see* Achafolla; Toberonochy
Kilchenzie 94, **335–6**, 463
Kilcheran *see* Lismore
Kilchiaran (Islay) 30, 93, **543–4**, Pl. 135
Kilchoman (Islay) 31, 35, 46, **544–5**, Pl. 55
see also Port Charlotte
Kilchousland *see* Campbeltown
Kilchrenan **336–8**
  Ardanaiseig House 60, 65, 87, **337**
  Hayfield 66, **337**
  Parish Church 33, 43, 47, **336–7**, Pl. 25
  Taychreggan Inn 86, **337**
  Tigh-na-Uisge 63, **337–8**
Kilchurn Castle 7, 11, 15, 51, 53, **338–40**, Pl. 63
Kilcreggan 83, 202, **340–3**
Kildalloig **343**
Kildalton (Islay) 77, **545–7**
  Kildalton Castle 61, **546**
  Kildalton Cross 26, 30, 328, **546**, Pl. 9
  Kildalton Old Parish Church 30, **545**
  Kildalton Parish Church *see* Lagavulin
  Kildalton U.F. Church *see* Port Ellen
Kilfinan 57, 94, **343–5**, Pl. 22
  Parish Church 26, 33, 40, 43, 44, 45, **343–5**, Pl. 22
Kilfinichen (Mull) 82, **576–7**
Kilkerran *see* Campbeltown
Kilkivan *see* Drumlemble
Killean *see* Tayinloan
Killevin *see* Minard
Kilmahew *see* Cardross
Kilmalieu *see* Inveraray
Kilmarie *see* Craignish Castle
Kilmartin 17, 19, 93, **345–8**
  Kilmartin Castle 52, 176, **347**
  Kilmartin House 18, 57, **347**
  Kilmartin Parish Church 31, 32, 35, 40, 43, 45, 46, 47, 93, 244, **345–7**

Nether Largie 17, 19, **348**
Old Poltalloch **347–8**
see also Slockavullin
Kilmelford **348–9**
Kilmeny (Islay) *see* Ballygrant (Islay)
Kilmichael Glassary 18, 31, 32, 83, 210, 248, **349–50**
see also Bridgend
Kilmichael of Inverlussa 33, 57, **350**
Kilmodan and Colintraive Church *see* Colintraive
Kilmodan Parish Church *see* Clachan of Glendaruel
Kilmore **351–2**
  Glenfeochan House 66, **351–2**
  Kilmore House 57, **352**
  Old Parish Church 11, **351**
Kilmore Parish Church (Mull) *see* Dervaig (Mull)
Kilmorich *see* Cairndow; Glen Fyne
Kilmory **352–4**
  Castle 59, 94, 352, **353–4**, 385, Pl. 113
  see also Lochgilphead
Kilmory Knap **354–5**
  chapel and crosses 10, 29, 30, 31, **354–5**, Pls. 20, 48
Kilmory Oib 24
Kilmory Quay *see* Lochgilphead (public buildings)
Kilmun 75, 77, 82, 90, **355–9**, 471
  Kilmun Parish Church 30, 31, 33, 41, 42, 45, 46, **355–8**, Pl. 52
  Old Kilmun House 57, **358**
Kilnaish *see* Dunmore
Kilnave (Islay) *see* Ardnave (Islay)
Kilneuair *see* Ford
Kilninian (Mull) 33, **577–8**, 586
Kilninver 94, **359–60**
Kilvickeon (Mull) *see* Bunessan (Mull)
Kingarth (Bute) 82, **605–7**
  Dunagoil fort 21, **606–7**
  Kingarth Parish Church (former) *see* Mount Stuart (Bute; Shore Chapel)
  St Blane's Church 23, 25, 27, 30, **605–6**, Pl. 18
  see also Kilchattan (Bute)
Kinlochlaich House *see* Appin
Kinlochspelve (Mull) 34, **578**
Kintraw 19, **360–1**
Kirkapol (Tiree) 46, 320, **597–8**

INDEX OF PLACES

Kirn 36, 41, 42, 75, 80, 83, 89, **361–3**
see also Dunoon
Knockderry *see* Cove
Kyles of Bute *see* Kames
Lagavulin (Islay) 95, **547–8**
  Dunivaig Castle 48, 53, **547–8**
Lagg (Jura) 70, 74, **564**
Laphroaig (Islay) 95, **548–9**
Leargybreck (Jura) **564–5**
  Corran River Bridge 70, **564–5**, Pl. 132
  Jura Free Church 37, **564**
Lismore 12, 94, 96, **363–8**
  Achadun Castle 49, **365–6**, Pl. 61
  Achnacroish 363
  An Sàilean 96, 363, **367**
  Bachuil House 23, **366**
  Castle Coeffin 50, **366–7**
  Cathedral of St Moluag and Parish Church (Clachan) 23, 29, **363–5**, Pl. 23
  Eilean Musdile lighthouse 76, **367**
  Kilcheran House 38, **367**
  Port Kilcheran 96, 363, **367**
  Port Ramsay 78, 96, 363, **367**
  Tirefour 20, **368**, Pl. 6
Loch an Sgoltaire (Colonsay) *see* Colonsay
Loch Awe Hotel *see* Lochawe
Loch Creran *see* Glen Creran
Loch Gorm Castle (Islay) *see* Saligo (Islay)
Loch Riddon (Loch Ruel) **368–9**
Loch Ruel *see* Loch Riddon
Loch Sloy *see* Inveruglas
Lochawe 7, 72, **369–75**
  Cruachan Power Station 97, **375**
  Loch Awe Hotel 87, **375**
  St Conan's Kirk 12, 36, **369–74**, 513, Pls. 40, 54
Lochbuie (Mull) 19, 47, **579**
  Lochbuie House 56, **579**
  St Kenneth's Chapel (Caibeal Mheamhair) 30, **579**
Lochdonhead (Mull) **579–80**
Lochgair 83, **376–8**
  Asknish House 55, 64, **376–8**
  Gallanach 376, 378
Lochgilphead 11, 19, 58, 69, **379–85**
  Achnabreck **385**
  churches 34, 36, 37, 38, 41, 42, 79, **379–82**

Oakfield 379, **383**
public buildings 82, 83, 84, 86, 379, **382–3**
streets 79, 85, 88, 89, 379, **383–5**
Lochgoilhead 25, 82, 90, **385–8**
  Lochgoilhead and Kilmorich Parish Church 31–2, 33, 39–40, 43, **385–7**, Pl. 53
  The Lodge 90, **388**
Lochhead *see* Campbeltown
Lochnell House 53, 54, 58, **388–91**
Lossit (Islay) **549**
  Cultoon stone circle 19, **549**
Luing 13, 30, 96
  see also Achafolla; Cullipool; Toberonochy
Lurabus (Islay) *see* The Oa (Islay)
Luss 13, 84, **391–3**
  St MacKessog's Church 25, 27, 35, 45, 131, **391–2**, Pl. 46
Macharioch **393**
Machrie (Islay) **549**
Machrihanish 87, 90, 93, **393–4**
Machrimore *see* Southend
Mannal (Tiree) **598**
Mannel *see* Mannal
Melfort 77, 96, **394–6**
  Degnish 57, **395**
  Melfort House 63, **394–5**
Millhouse 96, **396**
  Ascog Castle 51, **396**
Milton (Tiree) **598**
Minard **396–7**
  Crarae Lodge 5, 66, **397**
  Killevin Burial Ground, Crarae 44, 251, **396–7**
  Minard Castle 55, 59, 64, **397–9**, Pls. 89, 90
Mount Stuart (Bute) 39, 46, 62, 64, 65, 66, 67, **607–13**, Pls. 101–2
  chapel 39, 41, 608, **611–12**, Pl. 39
  Kerrycroy 67, 78, 605, 612, **613**
  Scoulag Lodge 67, **612–13**
  Shore Chapel (former Kingarth Parish Church) 33, 35, 40, **613**
Moy Castle (Mull) 51, 579, **580–2**, Pl. 70
Muasdale 57, **399**
Muckairn *see* Taynuilt
Mull 8, 11, 12, 17, 23, 24, 31, 75, 80, 501, **565–89**
  see also place-names
Mull of Kintyre Lighthouse *see* Carskiey

Mulreesh (Islay) 96
Nave Island (Islay) see Ardnave (Islay)
Nereabolls (Islay) **549–50**
Nether Largie see Kilmartin; Slockavullin
New Castle Lachlan see Garbhallt
Newton 78, **399**
North Connel see Connel
Oa, The see The Oa (Islay)
Oakfield see Lochgilphead
Oban 8, 11, 12, 13, 17, 22, 68, 71, 77, 79–80, 86, **399–422**
  Argyll Mansions (tenement) 9, 13, 15, 85, 89, **416**, Pl. 114
  cemeteries **409**
  churches 37, 401, **402–9**, **417**; Cathedral of St John the Divine (former parish church) 11, 12, 36, 38, 41, 42, **402–5**, Pl. 43; Congregational Church 37, **405–6**; Free High Church 11, 37, 40, **406**; Kilmore and Oban Parish Church (Christ's Church) 36, **406**, Pl. 42; Oban Parish Church 12, 15, **407**; St Columba's Cathedral 12, 13, 39, 41, **407–8**, Pl. 41
  Columba Hotel 12
  Dunollie Castle 22, 51, 419, **421–2**
  Dunollie House see mansions below
  hotels 86–7, 401, 411, **414–16**, **418**, **419**; Columba Hotel 12, 87, **416**; Hydropathic see mansions below; Regent (Marine) Hotel 87, **417–18**, Pl. 117
  Hydropathic see mansions below
  industrial buildings 95, 401, **421**
  local authority housing (Corran Brae, Glencruitten, Soroba) 402
  mansions 12, 62, **410–11**, **419–20**; Dunollie House 329, 331, **419**; Gallanach 58, **419**; Ganavan House 62, 90, **419**; Hydropathic 401, **420**; Manor House 57, **420**
  public buildings 83, 84, 401, **409–13**; Corran Halls 84, 86, **410**, 418; Council Offices (Municipal Buildings) 82, **410**; Lorn and Islands District General Hospital 84, **411**, Pl. 123; McCaig's Tower 401, **411**; piers 71, 75, 76, 79, 401, 410, **411–12**, **413**; police station 81, **412**; Post Office 84, **412**; Sheriff Courthouse 81, 82, **412–13**; Social Work Department **413**, Pl. 122; stations 71, 73, 401, **412**
  streets 79–80, 399–401, **413–18**, **420–1**; Albany Street 80, **414**; Argyll Square 71, 401, **413–14**; Cawdor Place 88, 401, **414**; Combie Street 401, **415**; Drimvargie Terrace 90, **415**; George Street 71, 80, 88, 401, **415–17**; High Street 399, **414**; John Square 84–5, **417**; Shore Street 71, 80, 399, 401, **414**; Stafford Street 80, 401, **416**; Tweeddale Street 80, 401, **416**
  villas 401, **420–1**
Old Castle Lachlan see Garbhallt
Old Gruline House see Gruline
Old Kilarrow (Islay) see Bridgend (Islay)
Ormsary **422–3**
Oronsay 17, 23, 500, **590–4**
  crosses 31, **593**, Pl. 51
  Priory 29, 30, 31, 32, 42, 43, **590–4**, Pls. 17, 50
Orsay see Islay
Otter Ferry **423–4**
  Ballimore House 59, 65, 66, **423–4**
Peninver **424–5**
  Drumgarve 92, 94, **425**
Pennyghael (Mull) 83, 93, **582**
Pennygown Chapel (Mull) see Salen (Mull)
Poltalloch 25, **425–7**
  Barsloisnach Steading 93, **426**
  Old Poltalloch see Kilmartin
  Poltalloch House and Lodges 60, 66, 94, 243, 378, **425–6**, **427**, **461**
  St Columba's Chapel 38, 41, **426**, Pls. 31, 32
Port Ann 92, **427**
  Castleton House 326, **427**
Port Appin **427–9**
  Airds House 54, **428–9**
Port Askaig (Islay) 70, 76, 86, **550–1**

INDEX OF PLACES

Port Bannatyne (Bute) 89, **613–15**
  Glenvoiden 17, 18, **615**
  Kames Castle 52, **614**
  St Colmac's Church 35, **614**
Port Charlotte (Islay) 36, 78, 82, 529, **551–2**
Port Ellen (Islay) 78, **552–5**
  Port Ellen Lighthouse *see* The Oa
  public buildings 76, 82, **553–4**
Port Kilcheran *see* Lismore
Port Ramsay *see* Lismore
Port Righ *see* Crinan
Port Sonachan 38, 86, **430–1**
  Ardbrecknish House **430–1**
  Hill House 63, **431**
  Sonachan House 430, **431**
  Upper Sonachan House 57, **431**
Port Wemyss (Islay) 78, **555–6**
Portavadie 96, **432**
Portincaple **432**
Portnacroish 38, **432–4**
  Appin House 54, 64, **433–4**
Portnahaven (Islay) 70, 78, 83, **556–7**
  Orsay **556–7**
  Parish Church 34, 39, **556**, Pl. 36
  Rinns of Islay Lighthouse 76, **557**
Redhouses (Islay) *see* Bridgend (Islay)
Rhu 73, 82, 89, **434–40**
  Aros 290, 419, **440**
  churches 35, 42, **434–5**
Rhudil 94, **441**
  Ballymeanoch 19, **441**, Pl. 5
  Kilbride Chapel 30, **441**
Ri Cruin 19
Riasg Buidhe *see* Colonsay
Rinns of Islay Lighthouse (Islay) *see* Portnahaven (Islay)
Rosneath 81, 89, 93, **442–5**
  churches 35, 39, 41, 45, **442–4**
  Ferry Inn 87, **444–5**, Pl. 96
Rosneath Castle 58, **445–6**
Rossdarroch *see* Tarbet
Rossdhu 391, **446–9**
  Rossdhu House 56, 65, 67, 87, **447**, Pl. 83
Rothesay (Bute) 27, 58, 77, 80, 85, 86, **615–29**
  Ardbeg 37, **615–16**
  churches **615–19**; High Kirk 33, 45, 47, **616–17**; St Andrew's 39, **617–18**; St Mary's Chapel 31, **616–17**, Pl. 49; Trinity Church 36–7, 40, **618–19**; United Free Church (former) 37, **619**; West Parish Church 36, **619**
  Craigmore 65, 90, **616**, **619**, **626–7**
  public buildings 82, 84, 86, **619–22**, 625; Bute Estate Office (Bute town-house) 88, **619**; cinemas 85, **620**; Duncan Halls 82, **619**; Harbour and pier buildings 74, 75, 76, **620**; Rothesay Pavilion 86, **621**, Pl. 120; schools 82, 83, **621**; Town Hall and County Buildings 81, **621**, Pl. 112; Winter Garden 86, **622**, Pls. 118, 119
  Rothesay Castle 14, 48, 49, 607, **627–9**, Pl. 64
  streets and houses 88–9, 90, **622–7**; Foley House 56, **624**; Glenfaulds 89, **626**, Pl. 115; Tor House 62, 90, **627**
  textile mills 95, **623–4**
Ruvaal Lighthouse (Islay) *see* Bunnahabhainn (Islay)
Saddell **449–51**
  Saddell Abbey 28, 29, 32, 45, **449–50**
  Saddell Castle 51, **450**
Salen (Mull) **582–3**
  Pennygown Chapel 9, 11, 15, 576, **582–3**
Saligo (Islay) **557–8**
  Ballinaby standing stones 23, **558**
  Loch Gorm Castle 53, 92, 505, **557**
Salt Pans *see* Machrihanish
Sanda Island **451**
Sandaig (Tiree) 94, **598–9**
Sandbank 83, **451–2**
Scalasaig *see* Colonsay
Scarba **594**
Scarinish (Tiree) 598, **599**
  Gott Bay Pier 76, **599**
Seil 12, 13, 96
  see also Balvicar; Clachan (Seil); Cuan; Ellenabeich and Easdale
Shandon 73, **452–6**
  Blairvadach 61, **453**
  Shandon House 61, **455**
Shuna (Appin) 52, **456**
Shuna (Luing) xiii
Skerryvore Lighthouse (Tiree) 13, 75, 76, **600**, Pl. 124
  see also Hynish (Tiree)

INDEX OF PLACES

Skipness **456–60**
  Kilbrannan Chapel 29, 30, 43, 45, 46, **457**, Pl. 21
  Skipness Castle 10, 11, 50, 51, **457–60**, Pl. 59
  Skipness House 61, **460**
Slockavullin 82, 83, 93, **460–1**
  Nether Largie 18, 19, **461**
  Temple Wood stone circle 19, **461**, Pl. 3
  see also Kilmartin
Sonachan House *see* Port Sonachan
Sorisdale (Coll) **504**
Soroba 399
  see also Oban
Southend 87, 93, 94, **461–3**
  churches 30, 33, 35, 39–40, **461–2**
  Dunaverty Castle 53, **462–3**
  Machrimore 462, **463**
  St Blaan's Chapel (Kilblaan) 462
St Blane's Chapel (Bute) *see* Kingarth (Bute)
St Catherines 10, 72, 74, 86, **463–4**
St Ninian's Chapel (Bute) *see* Straad (Bute)
St Peter's College *see* Cardross
Stewarton **464**
Stonefield Castle 60, 66, 87, **464–6**, Pl. 91
Straad (Bute) **629**
  St Ninian's Chapel 24, **629**
  Stewart Hall 57, **629**
Strachur **466–70**
  Strachur House 55–6, 64, 66, 93, **467–70**, Pls. 84, 85, 127
  Strachur Parish Church 33, 44, 46, **466–7**
Strathlachlan *see* Garbhallt
Strone 36, 83, **470–2**
Stronmilchan 68, 217, 219
Strontoiller 19, 92, **472**
Sween *see* Castle Sween
Tarbert (Kintyre) 58, 69, 73, 77, 88, 89, 215, **473–7**
  churches 36, 37, **474–6**, Pl. 33
  public buildings 74, 75, 83, 84, **476**
  Tarbert Castle 48, 51, **473–4**
Tarbert (Jura) **565**
Tarbet 68, 71, 73, **478–9**
  Rossdarroch 63, **479**
  Stuckgowan House **478**, Pl. 88
  see also Arrochar

Taychreggan Inn *see* Kilchrenan
Tayinloan **479–81**
  Beacharra/Beacharr Farm 18, **481**
  Killean House 61, **480–1**
  Killean Old Parish Church 30, 46, **479**
  Killean Parish Church (A'Chleit) 33, 39, 40, 241, 343, 399, **479–80**, Pl. 28
Taynish House *see* Tayvallich
Taynuilt 68, 71, 83, 86, **481–7**
  Airds Bay 481, **487**
  Bonawe Ironworks (Lorn Furnace) 12, 15, 57, 75, 78, 96, 395, **484–7**, Pls. 125, 126
  Bridge of Awe 68, **482**
  Brochroy 94, 481, **482**; *see also* Bonawe Ironworks *above*
  cottages 94, **481**, **486–7**
  Ichrachan House 63, **482**
  Inverawe House 61, 63, **482–3**
  Muckairn Parish Church **481–2**, Pl. 37
Tayvallich **487–9**, 493
  Arichonan 92, **488**
  Taynish House 57, 326, **488**
Temple Wood *see* Slockavullin
Texa **558**
The Oa (Islay) 34, 47, 535, **558–60**
  Lurabus 92, **560**
  Port Ellen Lighthouse 76, **559**
  Tockmal 92, **560**
Tighnabruaich 37, 62, 90, **489–90**
  see also Auchenlochan
Tiree 8, 11, 23, 31, 92, 94, 501, **594–600**, Pl. 137
  Hough circles 19
  Kenvara 24
  see also place-names
Tirefour *see* Lismore
Tobermory (Mull) 57, 58, 78, 85, 86, 87, 88, 95, **583–8**, Pl. 1
  churches 34, 37, **584–6**
  public buildings 74, 81, 84, 584, **586**
Toberonochy 47, 78, 94, **491**
  Ardlarach 57, **491**
  Old Parish Church (Kilchattan) 30, 47, **491**
Tockmal (Islay) *see* The Oa (Islay)
Torosay Castle (Mull) 61, 66, **588–9**, Pl. 93
Torrisdale Castle 58, 64, **492–3**
Torsa **493**

Toward 75, 83, **493–8**
   Castle Toward 59, 64, 66, **493–4**
   Toward Castle *see separate entry*
   Toward Point Lighthouse 76, **496**
Toward Castle 50, 51, **496–8**
Treshnish Isles 49, **600–2**
Turnalt House *see* Barbreck
Ulva 34, 40, 94, 501, **589–90**
   Ulva House 63, **589–90**
Vaul (Tiree) **600**
   Dùn Mòr Vaul 20, **600**
Whistlefield 73
Whitehouse **498**